Margaret Hodg

D1764898

31 st July, 2015

THE BUILDINGS OF SCOTLAND

FOUNDING EDITORS:
NIKOLAUS PEVSNER & COLIN McWILLIAM

AYRSHIRE AND ARRAN

ROB CLOSE AND ANNE RICHES

PEVSNER ARCHITECTURAL GUIDES

The Buildings of Scotland was founded by
Sir Nikolaus Pevsner (1902–83) and
Colin McWilliam (1928–89) as a companion series
to *The Buildings of England*. Between 1978 and
2001 it was published by Penguin Books.

For a considerable period the National Trust for Scotland
carried the financial responsibility for management and finance
of the research programme needed to sustain the first editions
of guides in the Buildings of Scotland series. Between 1991 and
2012 that role was taken over by the Buildings of Scotland
Trust, sponsored by Historic Scotland (on behalf of Scottish
Ministers), The National Trust for Scotland and the Royal
Commission on the Ancient and Historical Monuments of
Scotland. During its lifetime the Trust received the support of
many individuals, charitable trusts and foundations, companies
and local authorities. Without that support it would not have
been possible to look forward to the completion of the series.
From 2012 funding will be administered through the
Paul Mellon Centre for Studies in British Art.

Special thanks are due to the following donors:

H.M. The Queen and H.R.H. The Prince of Wales.

Aberbrothock Charitable Trust, Binks Trust, Dulverton Trust,
Esmée Fairbairn Charitable Trust, Marc Fitch Fund,
Gordon Fraser Charitable Trust, Gargunnock Estate Trust,
A. S. and Miss M. I. Henderson Trust,
Historic Scotland, Imlay Foundation Inc., Sir Peter Leslie,
Leverhulme Trust, Macrobert Trusts,
Colin McWilliam Memorial Fund,
Nancie Massey Charitable Trust, Merchants House of Glasgow,
National Trust for Scotland, Radcliffe Trust,
Joseph Rank Benevolent Trust,
Royal Bank of Scotland plc, Russell Trust, Turtleton Trust,
Walter Scott, VisitScotland, James Wood Bequest Fund

and
AYRSHIRE ENTERPRISE
ARP LORIMER
MACTAGGART & MICKEL
and
THE PILGRIM TRUST

for their grants towards this volume

and

The Paul Mellon Centre for Studies in British Art
for a grant towards the cost of illustrations

Ayrshire and Arran

BY

ROB CLOSE AND ANNE RICHES

WITH CONTRIBUTIONS FROM

RICHARD FAWCETT

STRATFORD HALLIDAY

AND

JUDITH LAWSON

THE BUILDINGS OF SCOTLAND

YALE UNIVERSITY PRESS
NEW HAVEN AND LONDON

YALE UNIVERSITY PRESS
NEW HAVEN AND LONDON
302 Temple Street, New Haven CT 06511
47 Bedford Square, London WC1B 3DP
www.pevsner.co.uk
www.yalebooks.co.uk
www.yalebooks.com

Published by Yale University Press 2012
2 4 6 8 10 9 7 5 3 1

ISBN 978 0 300 14170 2

Printed in China
through World Print
Set in Monotype Plantin

DEDICATION

J. H. B.
1926–2004
"Loyal"

ACCESS TO BUILDINGS

Many of the buildings described in this book are public places, and in some obvious cases their interiors (at least the public sections of them) can be seen without formality. But it must be emphasized that the mention of buildings or lands does not imply any rights of public access to them, or the existence of any arrangements for visiting them.

Some churches are open within regular hours, and it is usually possible to see the interiors of others by arrangement with the minister or church officer. Particulars of admission to Ancient Monuments and other buildings in the care of Scottish Ministers (free to the Friends of Historic Scotland) are available from Historic Scotland, Longmore House, Salisbury Place, Edinburgh EH9 ISH or its website, www.historic-scotland.gov.uk. Details of access to properties of the National Trust for Scotland are available from the Trust's head office at Hermiston Quay, 5 Cultins Road, Edinburgh, EH11 4DF or via its website, www.nts.org.uk. Admission is free to members, on whose subscriptions and donations the Trust's work depends.

Scotland's Gardens Scheme, 42a Castle Street, Edinburgh EH2 3BN, provides a list of gardens open to visitors, also available on the National Gardens Scheme website, www.gardensofscotland. org. Scotland's Churches Scheme, Dunedin, Holehouse Road, Eaglesham, Glasgow G76 0JF, has a searchable database (www.sacredscotland.org.uk) of churches in Scotland including details of opening arrangements and publishes a series of regional guides. *Hudson's Historic Houses, Castles and Gardens Open to the Public*, published annually, includes many private houses open to visitors.

Local Tourist Offices can advise the visitor on what properties in each area are open to the public and will usually give helpful directions as to how to get to them.

CONTENTS

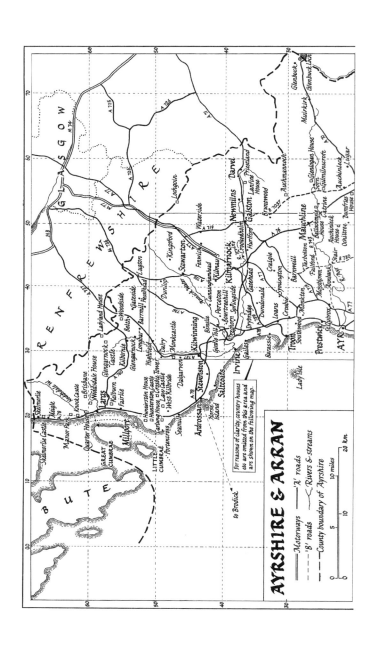

AYRSHIRE & ARRAN

For reasons of clarity, country houses etc are omitted from this area and are shown on the following map.

Motorways
'A' roads
'B' roads
Rivers & streams
County boundary of Ayrshire

0   5   10 miles
0   10   20 km.

to Brodick

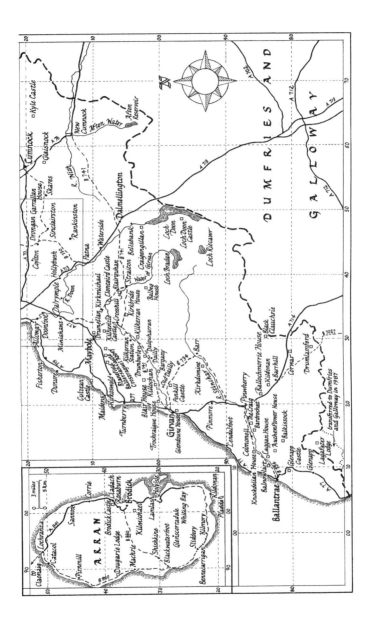

N

R. Nith

Cumnock
Kyle Castle
Geismock
New Cumnock
Afton Water
Afton Reservoir

Carsphairn
Dalmellington

D U M F R I E S
A N D
G A L L O W A Y

Fisherton
Allinvay
Dumain Hill
Cultzean Castle
Maidens
Turnberry
Maybole
Minishant
Dalrymple
Holybush
Coylton
Drongan
Garrallan House
Sinclairston
Rankinston
Waterside
Patna
R. Doon

Maybole
Kirkmichael
Crosshill
Dalquharran
Kilkerran
Dailly
Dalvennan
Drumbuie
Barr
Kirkdominie
Straiton
Blairquhan
Water of Girvan
Loch Bradan
Loch Doon
Loch Doon Castle
Loch Riecawr

Girvan
Pinmore
Lendalfoot
Pinwherry
Colmonell
Ballantrae
Knockdolian House
Balnowlart
Laggan House
Auchenflower House
Balkissock
Glenapp Castle
Glenapp
Lagafater Lodge

Barrhill
Kildonan
Pinmacher
Corwar
Drumlamford

transferred to Dumfries and Galloway in 1987

ARRAN
Lochranza
Catacol
Pirnmill
Machrie
Dugarie Lodge
Corrie
Brodick Castle
Rosaburn
Brodick
Kilmichael
Lamlash
Holy Isle
Shiskine
Blackwaterfoot
Gleniscorradale
Sliddery
Kilmory
Bennecarrigan
Whiting Bay
Kildonan
Pladda I.

3 miles
5 Km.

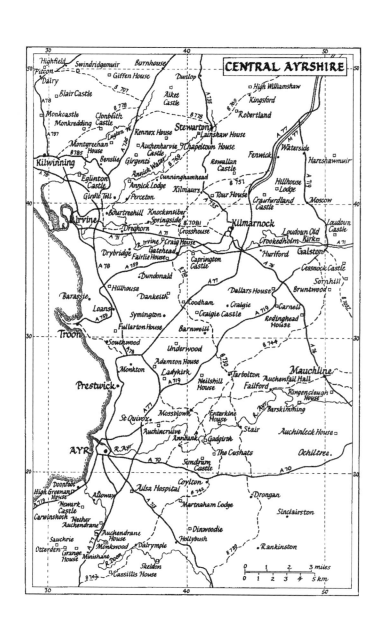

MAP REFERENCES

The numbers printed in italic type in the margin against the place names in the gazetteer indicate the position of the place in question on the area map (pages viii–ix), which are divided into sections by the 10-kilometre reference lines of the National Grid. The reference given here omits the two initial letters (formerly numbers), which in a full grid reference refer to the 100-kilometre squares into which the county is divided. The first two numbers indicate the western boundary, and the last two the southern boundary, of the 10-kilometre square in which the place is situated. For example, Alloway reference 3010 will be found in the 10-kilometre square bounded by grid lines 30 (on the *west*) and 40, and 10 (on the *south*) and 20; Woodside, reference 3050 in the square bounded by grid lines 30 (on the *west*) and 40, and 50 (on the *south*) and 60.

LIST OF TEXT FIGURES AND MAPS

FOREWORD

Ayrshire and Arran is the twelfth volume of *The Buildings of Scotland* series, a project whose own history now covers almost forty years. It was the idea of Sir Nikolaus Pevsner, whose own ground-breaking *The Buildings of England* series was reaching its final volumes, and who wished to see similar series inaugurated for the other constituent parts of the British Isles. For Scotland, Pevsner entrusted the work of overseeing the project to the late Colin McWilliam, and Colin was the author of the first volume (*Lothian*, 1979) and a co-author of the second (*Edinburgh*, 1984). He envisaged a series in which each region of the country was covered by authors who understood their areas, had a respect for scholarship, and were not bound by their own prejudices and antiquarian interests, but were able to accommodate a catholicity of taste, and could defer to others in the treatment of those corners of the wide architectural canon with which they were least sympathetic. Although this approach may upset some building owners, eager to pass on family or local traditions, we hope new information and interpretation will stimulate interest in Ayrshire and Arran's wealth of buildings. McWilliam's influence on architectural history in Scotland has been deep and long-lasting, and we hope, as previous authors have done, that the series achieves something of what he wished for it.

While this series is a full brother to the other series, it has an individuality which arises partly from McWilliam's own belief in what the series should attempt to do, and partly from Scotland's own distinct, and separate, history. This is most obviously seen in the treatment of churches which are, in the English series, arranged in denominational order, beginning with the Church of England. For Scotland, a purely alphabetical order (by present name or, usually, original name if disused or secularized) has been adopted, so neatly sidestepping the vexed, and vexing, issue of ecclesiological history in Scotland. John Gifford, in his fore-word to *Perth & Kinross*, refers to McWilliam's 'acceptance of the value of buildings of all periods, the pleasure he found in those too easily dismissed as second- or third-rate and his delight in the quirky and even the ugly'. These values and ideals we share: as in a play, the stars can shine only when the supporting cast performs well, though for reasons of space, the unremittingly 'ugly' are rarely to be found in the pages that follow.

Until this year the series was managed and overseen, initially for Penguin Books and from 2001 for Yale University Press, by the Buildings of Scotland Trust (BoST), and it was through the Trust that one of us (Anne Riches, who had already been a

co-author of *Glasgow*, 1990) was approached in the late 1990s to
co-author a volume planned to cover the three counties of southern Strathclyde (Ayrshire, Lanarkshire and Renfrewshire), and
invited the other (Rob Close), with his extensive archival knowledge of Ayrshire, to take on the role of co-author. Revision of
the volume boundaries meant that Ayrshire (together with those
parts of the island county of Bute which have transport, and since
1975 administrative, links with Ayrshire) would be treated as a
single volume. The BoST was also responsible for funding a
programme of research established by McWilliam, and undertaken by a number of researchers, most notably John Gifford as
the Head of the Research Unit, who diligently extracted all
Scottish references from the leading architectural and building
journals (*The Builder*, *Building News*, *The Architect*, etc.), and
building references from the minutes of heritors and kirk sessions
and other sources. Their work has been invaluable in the preparation of this volume and along with all the research notes for
the published volumes in this series is deposited permanently
in the National Monuments Record of Scotland for public
consultation.

The division of labour between the co-authors has been largely
along subject lines, with Anne Riches taking responsibility for the
castles, mansions and other country houses, while Rob Close has
been mainly responsible for the buildings of the county's burghs,
towns and villages. There has, of course, been overlap and constant co-operation along the way, especially on Arran, where the
bulk of the visits were carried out jointly. Some entries have been,
as is usual, farmed out: the archaeology has been entrusted to
Stratford Halliday, and a number of important early ecclesiastical
monuments, e.g. the abbeys of Crossraguel and Kilwinning, and
the parish church of Kilbirnie, to Richard Fawcett. Both have
contributed to previous volumes in the series. We are grateful to
them for their contributions to the introductory essays and to
Judith Lawson for her description of the geology and building
stones of Ayrshire and Arran.

Our own researches, over many years, have been conducted
in a variety of libraries, museums and other institutions. In
Edinburgh these include most importantly not only the unrivalled holdings of the Royal Commission on the Ancient and
Historical Monuments of Scotland, where particular thanks are
owed to Diane Watters and Simon Green, but also Historic
Scotland and particularly Deborah Mays and the listing team,
the National Archives of Scotland, and the National Library of
Scotland. The RIBA Library and the Soane Museum in London
have provided valuable information. In Ayrshire, much time has
been spent in the libraries and planning offices of the three local
authorities (East, North and South Ayrshire), and their predecessors before 1996, and in the peripatetic offices of Ayrshire
Archives. Amongst past and present staff of these irreplaceable
but under-funded resources, special mention must be made of
Sheena Andrew, Tom Barclay, Elaine Docherty, Anne Geddes,
Caroline Kennedy, Marion Lynch, Jill McColl, Pamela McIntyre,

Sheena Taylor, Sheila West, and the county's succession of archi-
vists: Robin Urquhart, Kevin Wilbraham and Christine Ewing.

Our greatest debt is, of course, to the owners, occupiers and
custodians of the hundreds of buildings described in the pages that
follow, all of which (with a very few entries marked with brackets
where for whatever reason a personal visit was not possible) have
been visited by one or both of us. They are too numerous to name
and thank individually, but almost without exception, they have
been generous in allowing access, giving us freedom to explore and
in providing kind hospitality. They have answered questions,
shared their own knowledge and sought out their own records,
plans and other useful material. One of the great pleasures of
writing and researching this book has been the enjoyment, love
and appreciation of their properties they have displayed, and we
thank them wholeheartedly. Special thanks are owed to James
Brown, June Bishop, Caroline Borwick, Robert and Katrina Clow,
Rose-Ann Cuninghame, William Cuninghame, Robert Ferguson,
Sir Charles Fergusson, Mark Gibson, Dame Pauline Hunter of
Hunterston, Sandra Liquorish, Charlotte Rostek, the Sasse family,
Richard Vernon, Thomas Hill and David Watts. It is only fair to
reiterate that the mention herein of buildings or lands does not
imply any rights of public access to them, or the existence of any
arrangements for visiting them.

We have received much help and encouragement from a wide
cross-section of people with an interest in either Ayrshire, or
buildings, or both. We have both benefited from long association
with the late James Hunter Blair of Blairquhan, whose knowledge
of the county and its houses and families was unrivalled, and
whose death has left a large vacuum in Ayrshire's cultural life.
This volume is dedicated to him, and we hope he would have
found it worthy of the county. On Arran we have been helped
enormously by Grace Small, Colin Cowley and the enthusiastic
staff of the Isle of Arran Museum, Lady Jean Fforde, Ken Thor-
burn and Lavinia Gibbs. Patrick Lorimer has, according to James
Boswell of Auchinleck, the 'best address book in Ayrshire', and
made it available to us, always remaining a constant and cheerful
source of encouragement and information as well as reading the
text for omissions; Norman Maclean and John Hart arranged for
us to enter the hallowed portals of the county's golf club houses,
while Sheriffs David Smith and Colin Miller eased our passage
through the county's sheriff court houses. Stuart Wilson and John
Sharp in Kilmarnock and the Irvine Valley, and Rosalind Smith
elsewhere in the county negotiated mazy roads and a distracted
passenger with equal equanimity. Bernard Aspinwall provided
many answers anent Roman Catholic churches, and many others
helped in a myriad variety of small ways: Kathryn Valentine,
Linda Fairlie, Stanley Sarsfield, Tom and Audrey Gardner, Bruce
Morgan, Gordon Craig, Gordon Smith, David McClure,
Maureen Irish, Janet Kleboe, James Miller, Peter Drummond,
Andrew Easton, Ian McGill, John Gerrard, Tom Addyman,
Ronald Alexander, Carol Findlay and Christine McWilliam, for
her patient encouragement.

The book would not have been possible without the work of
previous authors and scholars to build upon: a bibliography too
long to include here. But some sources cannot be denied. These
include MacGibbon & Ross's magisterial *Castellated and Domestic
Architecture of Scotland*, and *The Ecclesiastical Architecture of
Scotland* (3 vols, 1896–7) have been consistently useful sources,
as has, for C18 and C19 buildings, the late Sir Howard Colvin's
A Biographical Dictionary of British Architects (4th edn, 2008) and,
for Victorian and C20 buildings, David M. Walker's on-line
Dictionary of Scottish Architects (www.scottisharchitects.org.uk).
Local publications of invaluable assistance have been the volumes
produced by the Ayrshire & Wigtonshire Archaeological Society
and the Ayrshire Archaeological and Natural History Society,
and Mike Davis's *Castles and Mansions of Ayrshire* (1981). Our
debt to Mike is large, and our thanks to him truly sincere and
heartfelt.

At Yale University Press our editor has been Charles O'Brien,
whose limitless patience and good humour we have sorely tried.
Co-ordination of the text through production has been undertaken by Catherine Bankhurst, the picture research by Louisa
Lee, Sophie Sheldrake and Phoebe Lowndes. Bernard Dod has
copyedited the text, Charlotte Chapman has undertaken final
proofreading and Judith Wardman the indexing. The photographs
have mostly been provided by the RCAHMS, and many have
been taken especially for this volume. Picture selection was aided
by Elaine Lee and Clare Sorensen, and the new photographs
taken by Jim Mackie. At the Buildings of Scotland Trust, we have
relied on the support of Ian Riches, especially in the fiscal field,
David Connolly and Peter Burman.

We each have our personal thanks. Without the tutelage and
encouragement of David Walker, Anne Riches would not have
had the confidence or understanding to embark on this volume.
Much is owed too to John Gifford, Kitty Cruft, Ian Gow, John
Hume, Deborah Mays and Geoffrey Stell whose unfailingly high
standards have been an inspiration and whose wisdom has been
enormously appreciated. Rob Close's first steps into the field of
architectural history were aided by the late Frank Dunbar, a
kindly old-school architect, and encouraged by Michael Hitchon,
and the Kyle and Carrick Civic Society. Subsequent help and
support came from Frank Arneil Walker, at the University of
Strathclyde, and Charles McKean, then at the Royal Incorpora-
tion of Architects in Scotland.

Despite the help of innumerable people there are bound to be
mistakes which are ours alone. We would be grateful to anyone
who takes the trouble to tell us about them, or has additional
information.

Our final thanks, though, must be to our partners, Charlie and
Joy, both of whom are probably more pleased to see the book in
print than we are.

INTRODUCTION

The historic county of Ayrshire covers an area of approximately 2,900 square kilometres, ranks seventh by size among Scottish counties, and is the largest county to lie wholly s of the Highland Line. In terms of population, presently estimated at 370,000 (of which Arran contributes a resident winter population of 5,000), only the counties with the country's four major cities are greater in number. But this population is not evenly distributed, and the county has, especially in the s and NW, large tracts of thinly inhabited moor and commercial forest.

Ayrshire is traditionally divided into three 'provinces' – Carrick, bounded on the N by the River Doon, Cunninghame, bounded on the s by the River Irvine, and Kyle, which lies between these rivers. To these are added, for this volume, those parts of the county of Bute – Arran* and the Cumbraes – which have been administered as part of Ayrshire since 1975. One result of this is that, in geophysical terms, this volume covers areas within all three of the traditional divisions of Scotland – the Highlands, the Central Lowlands and the Southern Uplands.

This variety informs, and carries through to, the human interaction with the geology and landscape, with which this introduction begins.

TOPOGRAPHY, GEOLOGY AND BUILDING STONES

BY JUDITH LAWSON

Ayrshire and Arran boast a great variety of ages and types of rocks, their different characteristics helping to give the area its scenic diversity. This scenery ranges from the highest point, the granite of Arran's Goat Fell (874 m.) to the low rolling hills of central Ayrshire; from the basaltic moors in the N of the county to the rounded hills of the s. Crossing the area are two of the major faults of Scotland, the Highland Boundary Fault (which runs from Stonehaven in Aberdeenshire to Kintyre in Argyll) and the Southern Boundary Fault, running from Siccar Point on the E coast to Girvan on the w. These separate the Highlands in the

---

*Arran has its own introduction, p. 681.

N and the Southern Uplands in the S. In between is the Midland
Valley, a down-faulted area of generally younger rocks. On Arran
can be found some of the oldest as well as the youngest rocks of
the region.

The Highland Boundary crosses the northern part of Arran.
To its N are PRECAMBRIAN (Cambrian?) rocks of the upper part
of the Dalradian Supergroup around 600 million years old. These

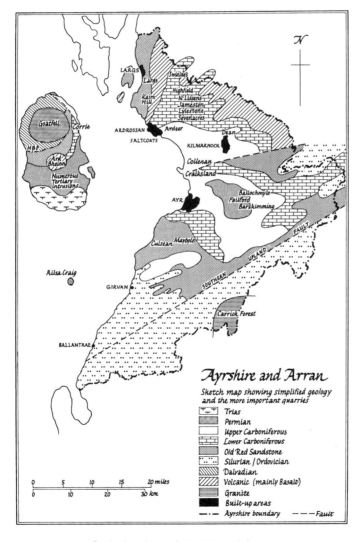

Geological Map of Ayrshire and Arran

rocks were originally sediments such as shales and coarse sands deposited in an ocean, called Iapetus, which separated the land masses of Scotland and England. Earth movements with subduction zones, where oceanic crustal plates slide under the continental plates, gradually reduced the width of this ocean until it disappeared completely by the end of the Silurian period. During the Grampian Orogeny (around 500 million years ago) the sediments were compressed, folded and slightly metamorphosed into schists and schistose grits. It is these rocks which form the relatively low-lying NW coastal area of Arran.

S of the Southern Boundary Fault are thick shales and grits of ORDOVICIAN AND SILURIAN age. They were deposited on the floor of the same ocean, are thousands of metres thick and relatively uniform in hardness, and form the typical Southern Upland scenery of rounded hills rising to a few hundred metres. The final stage of the movements which formed these hills was the intrusion of large granite masses. The granite, a coarsely crystalline rock of quartz, feldspar and mica, solidified far beneath the roots of the mountain chain and is now exposed because of the erosion of the overlying sediments. It is fairly resistant to erosion and forms the high ground of Carrick Forest near the S border of Ayrshire. Round the intrusions is a ring of thermally metamorphosed rocks which are often very hard and resistant to erosion.

Between Girvan and Ballantrae lies one of the most interesting and complex geological areas of the British Isles, of Ordovician and Silurian age. As the movement of plates at the edge of the Iapetus Ocean continued, some of the deep ocean floor was scraped up, and near Ballantrae can be seen the deep-water shales and pillow lavas typically formed under water. Other faulted fragments include shallow, near-shore limestones full of fossils and also deeper water turbidites.

By the beginning of the DEVONIAN/OLD RED SANDSTONE times (about 380 million years ago) Scotland had become a continent with high mountains. The two faults now played an important part with the formation of the Midland Valley between them. The climate was arid with seasonal rains. Rivers eroded the higher ground and spread over the Valley. On the Largs foreshore are exposed some of the typical red sandstones and conglomerates laid down in these seasonal rivers. Higher in the sequence wind-blown sands, now sandstones, were formed in a somewhat drier climate. Such sandstones are found on the hills above Largs.

Above the Old Red Sandstone are the thick rocks of the CARBONIFEROUS. By now erosion had lowered the land, the climate had become wetter and numerous types of plant had evolved. The land was covered by dense tropical forests and crossed by large meandering rivers. As some of these forests were killed off and buried under sediments, the vegetation was compressed and altered to coal while the original soils became the 'seat earths' often found beneath the coals. The commonest sediment is usually shale but sandstone may be locally common. At times during the Carboniferous period there was volcanic activity with the production of mainly basaltic lavas and their associated feeder necks. One such volcanic plug can been seen at Loudoun Hill (Priestland). The main outpourings of lavas form the high ground along the NE border of Ayrshire with Irish Law above Largs, Fenwick Muir and the higher ground towards Darvel. The lava flows are more or less horizontal and weather into a typical trap scenery where the more resistant flow cores form small cliffs separated by softer layers which form terraces. This scenery is well seen above Largs. The Heads of Ayr, S of Ayr, is also volcanic in origin, and here the sea has eroded through an old volcano so that tuffs and agglomerates, formed by explosive activity, and lavas are well seen on the foreshore.

At the end of the Carboniferous there were again major earth movements that formed the broad folds of the Midland Valley. The Carboniferous sediments are preserved in the downwarping of a broad E–W syncline. In the UPPERMOST CARBONIFEROUS times (about 300 million years ago) the climate became much drier. In the Permian 400 m. of wind-blown desert sandstones were deposited, their bright red colour (produced by the oxidization of iron minerals) in contrast to the mainly white or grey sandstones of the Carboniferous. The greatest thickness occurs in the centre of the Ayrshire syncline between Mauchline and Trabboch, and the rock is well exposed in the spectacular gorge of the River Ayr near Howford Bridge. A very similar stone from roughly the same horizon is found on Arran, at Corrie. Younger, MESOZOIC sediments of Triassic age outcrop extensively in the S of Arran where they can be well seen along the island's coast. They are pink or red sandstones with occasional beds of conglomerate and shale. The finer layers sometimes show fossil suncracks, and these sediments are thought to have been formed in shallow water in rivers and lakes which sometimes dried out. In general these are soft rocks which form the lower ground. Some thicker sandstone beds have been quarried locally, for example at Lamlash, for building stone. The Triassic beds dip away to the S and no younger beds are seen *in situ*.

In the Early TERTIARY ERA, some 65 million years ago, there was considerable volcanic activity along a N–S line through the Inner Hebrides. On Arran a volcano was situated at Ard Bheinn S of the String Road from Brodick to the W coast. This must once have been a large cone. Towards the end of its active life the caldera subsided, bringing down some of the surface rocks. These have been preserved as small outcrops and indicate that there had been a cover of the younger Mesozoic sediments, including the Chalk limestone. It is however some other aspects of the Tertiary igneous activity which give the most spectacular scenery on Arran. Nearly half the island is formed of Tertiary igneous rocks. These include massive more or less horizontal dolerite or quartz porphyry sills such as those at Drumadoon, Bennane Head and Holy Isle. The columnar jointing formed as the molten rock cools is particularly spectacular at Drumadoon. Along the S coast are numerous vertical doleritic dykes. Their total thickness is over 1 km. and represents a considerable stretching of the earth's crust. On Great Cumbrae too dykes are well seen along the coast. However, the most spectacular scenery on Arran occurs in the N where Goat Fell rises to 874 m. This is formed of a granite which intruded into, and pushed up, the older rocks before it solidified. It must have cooled well below the surface. It is crossed by many dykes which have eroded to give the jagged appearance, for example, at the 'Witches Step'. A large plug of microgranite, also of this age, forms Ailsa Craig.

The scenery throughout Ayrshire and Arran has been much modified by GLACIATION. All of the area was covered by ice, at times many hundreds of metres thick. Most came from the Highlands, with smaller glaciers originating in the Southern Uplands. On Arran, around Goat Fell, are the typical broad U-shaped valleys of Glen Sannox and Glen Rosa, formed as the ice eroded the former river valleys. There are also arêtes and pyramidal peaks like Cir Mhor. Some higher areas like the lava hills of north Ayrshire have been scraped clean by the ice and may show striations where the ice gouged grooves in the underlying rock. Towards the end of the glaciation deposits of the material carried by the ice formed a thick layer, well seen in central Ayrshire. These sediments, typically a mixture of sizes and often referred to as BOULDER CLAY, are often moulded into the low elongated hills known as drumlins. The weight of the ice on the land also depressed it, causing sea level to rise relatively. After the glaciers melted the land rose again and together with the changes in the sea level, coastlines occurred at several different heights. The most noticeable effect of this is the presence round the coastlines of Ayrshire and the islands of a raised beach about 8 m. above present sea level. The most recent sediments are the blown sands found around Ayr and Troon – ideal material for the justly famous links courses.

Building stones

The Old Red Sandstone, Carboniferous, Permian and Triassic rocks all contain SANDSTONES of variable thickness and quality. Sandstone is relatively easy to cut into convenient shapes and sizes in the quarry or surface outcrop. It usually hardens on exposure to air and comes in a variety of colours. As with all building stone the main problem is that it is bulky and heavy to transport. Before the advent of the railways, water was the only convenient and cheap means of transport. Ayrshire does not have canals or navigable rivers so only a few quarries, notably at Corrie on Arran and Ardeer near Stevenston, were able to make use of this means of transport. Ardeer quarry was described in 1845 as being 'the most valuable quarry of white freestone . . . in the west of Scotland . . . much used at home and still more in request in Dublin and Belfast'. During the great industrial expansion of the C19 many towns developed local quarries in the sandstones which occurred throughout the area. Largs had a quarry just to the S in what are now the grounds of the Kelburn estate, while Dean Quarry supplied Kilmarnock. Ayr had its own town quarry on the S bank of the River Ayr, near the present railway bridge. This CREAM SANDSTONE can be seen in many of the older buildings and was used for the Auld Brig where there is a record of the stone being brought down the river in lighters. At Ballochmyle, the railway viaduct, once one of the largest single-span bridges in the world, is built of this stone, quarried at Mauchline. In Kilbirnie the iron works and thread mills were also built of local stone. In many cases these older quarries have been filled in and built over so that there is now no trace.

Often the small quarries were not of good quality so with the growth of the railways in the C19 new, larger quarries with thicker deposits of better-quality stone were opened, or enlarged. Often they had their own direct rail link. The Clark Memorial Church in Largs, built in 1892, is of good-quality RED SANDSTONE from Locharbriggs and Corsehill in Dumfriesshire. Several large quarries were opened between Beith and Kilwinning including Lylestone, Jameston and Sevenacres.

By far the most important quarries in Ayrshire were those opened in the red sandstones of the Permian. These thick sandstones, virtually free of pebbles, were an ideal building material. They are easy to cut and carve. They are very porous and thus have a good frost resistance. They had been used locally for many years, but the quarries were greatly expanded towards the end of the C19 as many of the old quarries had become exhausted and transportation improved. The stones were exported worldwide, some as far as Burma. In Ayrshire the greatest thickness occurs between Mauchline and Trabboch. The huge quarry at Ballochmyle employed over 200 men in the 1890s while Barskimming had over 100. Many of the quarries closed during the First World War when the men went to the trenches. The quarry at Ballochmyle has been completely filled and there is no trace visible now. A quarry at a similar horizon at Corrie on Arran employed eighty men until it closed in 1907. Stone from here was used in Kinloch Castle on Rum and for Brodick Castle. After the First World War fashions had changed and natural stone became less popular. Many quarries never reopened.

Larger buildings were also built of sandstone. Culzean Castle was built at several different periods. The medieval part used Carboniferous stone quarried from the nearby cliffs. This was of excellent quality and has weathered well. When the castle was extended in the C18, however, stone was quarried at Blanefield about 3 km. away and became severely eroded by the exposed, salt-laden site, requiring repairs using Springwell stone from the NE of England, which does not match the original particularly well. Some Victorian additions came from a quarry near Maybole.

Igneous rocks are in general much tougher to extract and cut to shape. They have been used locally on a small scale. Dolerite and basalt are mainly used for roadstone and setts, or for field boundaries. GRANITE is an attractive-looking stone but again has only been used locally, except where it has been imported from elsewhere in Scotland. The best-known rock is the microgranite which came from Ailsa Craig. This was used for setts and kerbstones but famously this was quarried and taken to Mauch-line to be cut and polished into curling stones.

Metamorphic rocks have only a small outcrop in the area. Small quantities of SLATE were used locally in Lochranza in Arran. Most roofing slates would have come, by sea, from the W coast, from the Slate Islands or from Ballachulish. Most were imported via Ayr Harbour.

There are also many instances of local BRICKS made from the shales which were discarded from the coal mines in the waste tips. The glacial till often has too many pebbles in it to allow it to be used as they may cause the bricks to shatter during firing, but where water has winnowed it, separating the clay from the pebbles, good quality brick clays may be found. Unfortunately these deposits, scattered along the rivers and the coast, are very local. Such brick pits and works generally had a short life. The aluminium-rich fossil soils beneath the coal were also mined for use in the manufacture of fire-resistant bricks and linings. The Ayrshire Bauxitic Clay was a particularly valuable seam.

PREHISTORIC AND ROMAN ARCHAEOLOGY

BY STRATFORD HALLIDAY

The archaeology of Ayrshire and Arran is as rich as its scenery, but it is an uneven veneer, changing in pattern and character from place to place. Just as Goat Fell dominates Arran and pro-vides the focal point for the view westwards from the crescent of the Ayrshire coast, so the clusters of Neolithic chambered tombs and Bronze Age stone circles on the island dominate the early archaeology. Arran's Iron Age record is paltry by comparison, and yet the mainland produces a wide range of settlements of different sorts, from the ubiquitous stone-walled forts and duns of the western seaboard to timber-built enclosures and houses, in some cases the evidence little more than a smudge on an aerial photograph, in others the timbers themselves – crannogs – preserved waterlogged in bogs and lochs.

The individual monuments preserve a myriad of details relat-ing to life and architecture from thousands of years ago, in the case of crannogs including organic objects that are so fragile that it is unreasonable even to expect such evidence to survive, but the unevenness of the record poses a question: to what extent can the history of settlement throughout Ayrshire and Arran be extrapolated from one area to another? The underlying problem concerns the visibility, or indeed invisibility, of archaeological monuments and whether they are a true guide to the areas that were preferred for settlement at different periods of the past. To take the example of Early Neolithic chambered tombs, built by the first farming communities in the early 4th millennium B.C., these are principally concentrated on Arran, with a handful in the southern part of Ayrshire forming part of another cluster in western Galloway. In central and northern Ayrshire there are but three. Are we really to believe that this is a true reflection of Neolithic settlement, in which the richest land in the Ayrshire lowlands was apparently shunned in favour of what are today impoverished soils on the hills and moors? Fortunately there are other sources of evidence to demonstrate that this was not the case. Neolithic polished stone axes, for example, are found throughout the lowlands, and pollen data extracted from lochs and mosses confirm the arrival of Neolithic communities, generally heralded by a decline in the values for elm and followed in short order by the first appearance of cereals. There is no doubt that the lowlands were extensively colonized from the Neolithic onwards.

When the pattern of monuments and artefacts is examined in closer detail, the evident disparity between the distribution of tombs and other Neolithic evidence becomes more explicable. The tombs are mainly situated in moorland, or at least towards the margins of the improved land. In essence they represent a pattern of survival in the places where the landscape has been least disturbed since. The artefacts, on the other hand, are only found where the ground has been laid bare, usually by ploughing over the last 200 years. In other words the very factors that are responsible for removing archaeological monuments are also those that lead to the discovery of artefacts, which in the days of horse-drawn ploughs were more than likely to be harvested by the ploughman.

Ayrshire is by no means unique in this respect, but there are a number of factors that make the situation here particularly acute. The reorganization of the landscape that came with the Improvements of the C18 and C19 was so radical that all but a handful of the monuments that had stood from time immemorial in the lowlands were levelled. And the transformation did not stop there, because all the old farming townships, many of them rooted in the medieval settlement pattern, were swept away, so much so that visible remains of medieval settlements are as scarce here as their Neolithic predecessors. In so far as any pre-Improvement settlements remain visible, they are situated in the margins, where beyond the boundaries of the improved fields occasional farmsteads are encountered, often amidst swathes of rig-and-furrow. Particularly good examples can be found in southern Ayrshire, and yet even here many of them are probably early improved farms. Thus the late medieval buildings on Donald's Isle in Loch Doon are remarkable survivals, preserved by dint of their isolation on a small island.

The Improvements in Ayrshire were no more radical than elsewhere, but with the emphasis on pasture and grazing, the opportunities for discovering hidden archaeological remains in the lowlands are severely restricted. The soils, climate and crops of Ayrshire and Arran simply do not respond to aerial photography, which is the principal tool for discovering monuments in the lowlands. This is not to say that there are no cropmarks in Ayrshire, for there are several revealing unusually fine levels of detail, but by and large this is not a major source of evidence. As a result Ayrshire forms an almost impenetrable buffer between the rash of cropmarkings recorded on freely draining soils in south-eastern Scotland, and the more limited range of stone-built monuments that characterize the Atlantic seaboard. These latter certainly give a misleading impression of the overall character of Iron Age settlement in Ayrshire, and more than likely throughout Arran and Argyll too. The discovery by excavation of a ditched earthwork beneath a long cist cemetery at Montfode, Ardrossan, serves to underline the point in Ayrshire, while a souterrain uncovered at Brodick does the same for Arran.

The Mesolithic and the first settlers (10,000–4000 B.C.)

The first evidence of human settlement in Ayrshire and Arran is for groups of hunters and gatherers, who almost certainly roamed throughout the district and were evidently able to cross the Firth of Clyde to and from Arran, which is shown by the discovery of tools made of Arran pitchstone on the mainland. These coastal waters also offered a wide range of marine resources to exploit, particularly for shellfish, though the only shell midden known is one discovered in the late C19 at Cannon Hill, Ardrossan. In the hinterland scatters of flint and chert tools and discarded waste flakes trace their presence, but excavation near Girvan in 2007 revealed a significant concentration of lithic material and possible examples of the small buildings founded on set posts that have been discovered in Mesolithic camps elsewhere.

The Neolithic and Bronze Age (4000–800 B.C.)

With the arrival of farming in the Neolithic, people are assumed to have adopted a more sedentary lifestyle. Although, as noted above, traces of their settlements in Ayrshire are few and far between, at Dreghorn, excavation in 2003–4 has not only revealed eight groups of pits containing Neolithic pottery, but also what seem to be the posts of a rectangular timber building measuring 23.5 m. in length by 5 m. in breadth. Here, as in many other cases, some of the pottery has been deliberately arranged in the fills of pits, implying that some kind of ritual had been played out, but the inclusion of domestic debris shows that settlement was often close at hand. More detailed publication of this exciting discovery is eagerly awaited.

Alongside the shift from hunter-gathering to farming, for the first time major architectural MONUMENTS were constructed out of timber and stone. In some places the people decorated stone surfaces with CUP-AND-RING MARKINGS. At Ballochmyle, Mauchline, and Blackshaw, West Kilbride, there are spectacular decorated outcrops that rank with the finest recorded anywhere in Scotland.

As has already been hinted, most of the known monuments are on Arran, where there are no fewer than twenty-one Neolithic CAIRNS (i.e. burial tombs), as compared with only seven or eight in the rest of Ayrshire. Even on Arran, where the ground is less heavily improved, many of the cairns have been severely robbed, and in some cases there is little more than a few slabs of an internal chamber remaining. The presence of a chamber, as distinct from a small stone-built cist, is a key characteristic of these Neolithic cairns, which are typically longer than they are broad. In some a stone kerb can be seen defining the outline of the mound, its footprint either rectangular or trapezoidal, tapering away from a forecourt fronting an axial chamber that is divided transversely by what are known as septal slabs to form a series of conjoined compartments. Amongst the Arran CHAMBERED CAIRNS, Carn Ban (Kilmory) is one of the best preserved, though little of its chamber is now visible. It has a deep semicircular forecourt, and excavation in the early C20 revealed that its chamber has four compartments. Others of this plan, comprising from two to five compartments, recur throughout the counties bordering the Clyde estuary and are appropriately enough known as Clyde-type chambers. More often than not they are found shorn of their superstructures and reduced to the basal slabs of the compartments, as can be seen at East Bennan and Torrylin, Kilmory. Excavation nearby at Monamore, Kilbride, has revealed that the basal deposits of the forecourt date from the beginning of the 4th millennium B.C. Excavations elsewhere in Scotland suggest that multiple chambers, set both axially and transversely in the cairns, are probably evidence that many of these monuments were built in several stages. In Clyde tombs, the first chambers in such sequences seem to have been relatively simple single-compartment structures, and typological studies have been advanced to suggest a development to the multiple compartments found at Carn Ban or East Bennan, though there is little direct evidence to corroborate this linear approach to their evolution.

Arran contains so many chambered tombs that it has figured in several studies analysing their distribution in terms of the territories that the communities that built them may have occupied. By comparison the Ayrshire mainland is almost bereft, with a single Clyde-type chamber at Haylie, Largs, in the N of the county. The cairn here, a large mound known as Margaret's Law, was robbed in 1772 and it is not known if it was originally circular or long. A sub-group of Early Neolithic LONG CAIRNS, characterized by relatively simple multiple transverse chambers, include two from the N of the county: Loanfoot cairn, near Priestland, and the Cuff Hill cairn, near Gateside.

A type of chambered cairn known from the uplands of southern Ayrshire, Wigtownshire and The Stewartry is the so-called Bargrennan Group. In these a small rectangular or wedge-shaped chamber is approached by a relatively long passage, and almost without exception they are encased within ROUND CAIRNS. Good examples in Ayrshire can be seen at Balmalloch, Barrhill, and Cave Cairn, Ballantrae. Always regarded as a late development of chambered tomb architecture, recent work is beginning to suggest that these chambered round cairns may date from the Bronze Age rather than the Neolithic, exposing the frailties of classification based on supposed architectural traits of the chambers alone.

While the main weight of the evidence for Neolithic settlement is represented by these stone tombs, there can be little doubt that there were also other contemporary TIMBER AND EARTHEN MONUMENTS scattered through the lowlands of Ayrshire. Amongst the cropmarks, for example, at Drybridge, Dundonald, the ditches of a cursus – a long narrow enclosure possibly for ceremonial processions – have been photographed on a terrace above the banks of the River Irvine. Some 50 m. broad and at least 220 m. long, these linear monuments are relatively common in some parts of Scotland, and it can only be a matter of time before others are discovered in the region. In this case, the cursus passes midway between two circular enclosures about 20 m. across internally, one of which has a broad entrance causeway and is almost certainly a later type of Neolithic ceremonial enclosure known as a henge. The only other example of a henge noted in Ayrshire is at Lindston, Dalrymple, and though heavily ploughed down is still visible as an earthwork measuring about 38 m. in diameter within a broad ditch with an external bank. On excavation, such enclosures are often found to contain internal rings of timbers of the type that have been found at Machrie on Arran (*see* below).

In most places these ceremonial monuments have become isolated spots in the landscape. Machrie Moor, however, provides some insight into how from the first such monuments sat within what were otherwise domestic landscapes. Excavation of two of the remarkable group of stone circles on the moor also uncovered several earlier pits containing Neolithic pottery, and these lie little over 500 m. from the remains of a chambered tomb, one of three on this part of the moor. And here, rather than isolated monuments, the tombs and the later stone circles jostle in a relatively confined topographical niche that is also occupied by extensive traces of hut circles, banks and small cairns, most of them sealed beneath a mantle of later blanket peat. In some senses, Machrie represents a lost landscape that must once have existed extensively in Ayrshire but is now perhaps signalled only by lone standing stones or burial cairns. Hut circles and field systems are found in southern Ayrshire, occasionally with burial cairns in close attendance, but nowhere is there such a spectacular array of monuments as can be seen on Machrie Moor.

Machrie gives many insights into Neolithic and Bronze Age monumental architecture and the way in which this spiritual dimension of daily life took place within a domestic landscape. It also provides a chronological insight into how this developed through time. Neolithic chambered tombs are usually thought of as primarily burial places, though the chambers and the forecourts also formed arenas for ceremonies involving both the living and the dead. In contrast the timber and stone circles seem to have been erected principally as CEREMONIAL MONUMENTS, the timber rings dating from the Late Neolithic, between 3000 B.C. and 2500 B.C., and their immediate stone successors

4

probably after 2000 B.C., though others on the moor are perhaps a little earlier. Despite this shift of emphasis, burials in stone cists were interred at the centre of several of Machrie's other circles, accompanied by ornately decorated food vessels. And yet, for all Machrie evidently having this important and persistent role in spiritual life, and possibly a place from which the midsummer sunrise was observed, it was also a place for the living, witnessed by the fields interleaved between the timber and stone monuments, an intimacy that is equally suggested by the HUT CIRCLES scattered round about. Typically between 7 m. and 10 m. in internal diameter, but occasionally up to 14 m., these ring-banks buried beneath the peat belie their scale; with a conical thatched roof resting on a ring of internal posts and rising to a point 10 m. or more above the floor, these were substantial buildings and in their own way as monumental as the stone circles. Excavations on Tormore, a little SW of Machrie, uncovered one that had been rebuilt on no fewer than six occasions during the 2nd millennium B.C. before finally being abandoned at about 1000 B.C.. The occupation was by no means continuous, but the Machrie circles lay at the core of a vibrant agricultural landscape grazed and cultivated by people living round about.

The Iron Age (800 B.C.–A.D. 200)

With the abandonment of many moorland hut circles that seems to have taken place on Arran and elsewhere at about 1000 B.C., and the progressive encroachment of blanket peat across these same areas during the 1st millennium B.C., places like Machrie ceased to be foci of settlement. This general pattern probably holds on the mainland where hut circles are known from at least eight locations in the S of the county, including two at High Altercannoch, Colmonell, standing within a large enclosure. In the N of the county a single hut circle excavated at Martin Glen, Largs, and others in Renfrewshire, suggest there are more to be found here too. On Arran, however, settlement for the next 2,000 years is represented by little more than a handful of small STONE-WALLED FORTS, perched on hilltops or coastal promontories. Undatable in themselves, they are usually assumed to be of Iron Age date, in the sense of a long Iron Age spanning the Roman intervention and the early medieval period. One, An Cnap at Sannox, on the north-eastern flank of the island, has been burnt and pieces of vitrified stone are scattered along the line of its wall. This has no chronological or cultural significance, but is merely a clue to the way the wall was constructed, with a frame of timberwork throughout its core. Other forts on the island may have been constructed in this way, but they were not apparently burnt. On the Ayrshire mainland, there are another five examples – Portencross (West Kilbride), The Knock (Largs), Kildoon (Maybole), Kemp Law (Dundonald) and Dundonald Castle – but again it is more than likely that this was a common constructional technique in the thirty or so forts that are scattered throughout the Ayrshire landscape.

The role of these forts is very difficult to gauge, but in Ayrshire the thin cropmark record has revealed a range of other types of settlement. Cereal crops on freely draining substrates, particularly in the S of the region around Girvan, have produced details of a succession of timber-built settlements at Enoch, for example, where an enclosure with twin palisade trenches can be seen on the photographs intersecting another enclosure fronted by a ditch, together with the wall-trenches and post-rings of several large ROUND-HOUSES; a similar array of structures has also been photographed at Garphar in the valley of the River Stinchar. Near Prestwick, a small ditched enclosure containing a single round-house has been recorded, together with another palisaded enclosure nearby. Apart from these pockets of detail, invariably on gravel terraces in the lower reaches of the main rivers, only a thin scatter of forts and ditched settlement enclosures have come to light in the hinterland. Nevertheless, commercially led projects are filling in some of the gaps, uncovering several unenclosed timber round-houses near Girvan in the S of the region and a sequence of palisaded enclosures on Loudoun Hill in the NE. It was this that also led to the discovery of a souterrain at Brodick, Arran.

These settlements are almost certainly of Iron Age date, but the lack of excavation makes it impossible to place any of them with greater chronological precision. The forts are probably high-status centres and are clearly the key to understanding the settlement pattern of this period of a millennium. The earlier may even belong to the Late Bronze Age, the most likely candidates being the two that stand out simply by their size. One is Harpercroft, Dundonald, where the outer of two ramparts takes in an area of over 6 ha. The other is the fort of about 8 ha. at Drumadoon, Arran. Unfortunately excavation at Harpercroft, and its smaller neighbour on Wardlaw Hill, failed to recover any evidence of their date. The same is true of Dundonald Castle, where excavation led to the discovery of an earlier vitrified rampart. Evidently the hill had been used since at least the Bronze Age, but in the absence of radiocarbon dates it is impossible to pin down the periods of major occupation and construction. A Roman melon bead perhaps points to one, and early medieval imports to another, while the destruction of the vitrified rampart was dated by thermoluminescence to about A.D. 1000; this latter technique, though tantalizing in its possible implications, has not proved conclusively reliable when applied to vitrified ramparts. Possible Roman coarse pottery and a CI A.D. triskele-decorated fob were discovered in a small fort at Seamill, and a dragonesque brooch, fragments of Roman glass and a piece of Samian ware were recovered from another on Castlehill, Dalry; this latter, now destroyed, may also have been used during the early medieval period.

While it is impossible to reconstruct the pre-Roman Iron Age settlement pattern, a wide range of settlements were occupied during the time that Roman goods were finding their way into Scotland. In addition to the forts that have been mentioned,

several of the smaller fortifications known as duns were occupied
in the Roman Iron Age, as were a number of crannogs, while at
Girvan two small unenclosed timber round-houses were dated to
this period, perhaps representing a more typical settlement of the
rural population. The discovery of the souterrain at Brodick,
which is at least Late Iron Age in date, and several cropmark
examples, make the stone-lined passage found in the C19 at
Ardeer (Stevenston) and re-excavated in 1973, appear a little less
isolated from the main concentration of these structures and
adds yet another type.

Most of the DUNS are circular and measure some 10 m. to
15 m. in diameter within a wall from 3.5 m. to 5 m. in thickness.
Rather than an open fort enclosing other free-standing structures, modern research tends to suggest that they were roofed
over; in effect they are in themselves round-houses, albeit that
the thickness of the wall, which may have stood 4 m. or more
high externally, would have presented a formidable obstacle akin
to that of a small tower house in later periods. They usually
occupy knolls or promontories, and are a typical settlement form
of the Atlantic seaboard. Particularly good examples can be seen
on Arran on Kingscross Point, emptied out at the beginning
of the C20 to reveal the uneven rocky interior, and on Torr a'
Chaisteil, Corriecravie, NW of Sliddery. Several of those on the
mainland also have outworks, again signalling their defensive
character, though also perhaps a measure of display to project
the status of their occupants; at Howmoor, Maybole, for example,
a heavily robbed dun is encircled by a ditch with an external
rampart set at the foot of the knoll. Similarly the dun at Aitnock,
Dalry, was defended by two walls and an outer ditch. Excavations
here at the turn of the C19 showed the interior was about 9 m.
in internal diameter; the stratigraphy was evidently complicated,
but from a paved surface came several sherds of Roman coarse
pottery and Samian ware. Presumably also of this date is the
robbed structure on the crest of the hill at Craigie, though with
its massive facing stones and possible mural chamber, this is
usually identified as the remains of a broch.

The appearance of Roman finds in duns is usually interpreted
as evidence that these were the seats of élite members of contemporary society. By the same token, CRANNOGS (artificial
island settlements) seem to have fulfilled similar roles. Often
inaccessible and overgrown, these are difficult structures to envis-
age today, often appearing as little more than a stony island,
occasionally with the traces of waterlogged timberwork visible
around their margins, but in Ayrshire a remarkable series of
investigations were carried out in the late C19 – Ashgrove Loch,
Lochlee, Lochspouts, Kilbirnie Loch and Buiston. Often little
more than dredging operations, these produced a rich harvest of
Roman and early medieval artefacts although, with the notable
exception of Buiston, the structural records are often incoherent.
Fortunately, the re-excavation of Buiston, N of Kilmaurs, in
1989–90 has revealed its complex history of construction in some
detail. The initial construction took place in the C1 or C2 A.D.,

but most of the evidence, comprising two successive round-houses and a series of perhaps six enclosures, dates from a very short span from the late C6 to the mid C7. One of the most striking aspects of the perimeter was a timber-framed rampart built with squared and jointed timbers in A.D. 608, which included a raised walkway made up of layers of horizontal logs laid radially within the frame; this insight into the architecture of some palisades would have been utterly lost on dry land. As so often, however, it is the wealth of finds that tends to make crannogs such spectacular settlements. Not only do they produce high-quality Roman and early medieval artefacts that imply their social status, but also the stuff of everyday life, measured in a range of wooden tools, pieces of rope, leather and textile.

The Roman invasion and after

There is little doubt that Ayrshire was garrisoned by the Roman army, both in the wake of Agricola's conquest of southern Scotland about A.D. 79 and the relatively brief reoccupation that took place in A.D. 140, when the frontier was re-established on the Forth–Clyde isthmus. Ayrshire formed the western flank of this new addition to the province, with a long and vulnerable coast looking westwards across the Firth of Clyde to potentially hostile unconquered territory. As with other periods of history, however, the character of the Ayrshire countryside militates against the discovery of many Roman installations. Excavations in a fort near Loudoun Hill, which has been entirely quarried away now, revealed a complex Flavian occupation, while near Girvan two temporary encampments constructed by the army on campaign probably also date from this period. Loudoun Hill lies on the line of a road running westwards and making, it is thought, for another fort and a harbour on the coast at the mouth of the River Irvine; perhaps lying beneath the old burgh, no trace of it has yet been discovered. Communications up and down the coast demand the presence of other garrisons, the camps at Girvan perhaps indicating the position of another.

Loudoun Hill was also occupied in the Antonine period and similar arguments can be advanced for the presence of coastal garrisons, the more so because a chain of small outposts seems to have been placed to command the firth and extend the surveillance system from the western terminal of the Antonine Wall round to the Ayrshire coast. Only two of these outposts are known, but one, at Outerwards, lies near Largs.

While the presence of the Roman army was but fleeting, most of southern Scotland lay within their orbit, and certainly felt their influence. So much is clear from the circulation of Roman goods beyond the frontier, presumably pedalled by traders anticipating the profits to be made in new markets. If this is the case, they were destined to disappointment, and whereas C1 and C2 finds are relatively common, C3 and C4 material is much scarcer. Indeed, there is potentially a more sinister presence lying in the background of this simple observation, for throughout southern

and eastern Scotland there is evidence of a fundamental disloca-
tion in the settlement pattern by the end of the C2. It is tempting
to correlate this with the trouble that is known to have broken
out on the frontier in the late C2, culminating in the campaigns
of the Emperor Severus into the north about A.D. 209. The settlement record in Ayrshire has little to offer in this respect and as
we have seen most types of Iron Age settlement also produce
evidence of early medieval use. At Buiston, however, this is clearly
the result of reoccupation after a break of over four centuries,
and this pattern may well be the case elsewhere. By and large,
early medieval settlements like Buiston produce imported goods
and as such represent relatively wealthy members of society. Of
the greater mass of the population we have little trace, unless
some of these lie buried in the long cist cemetery recently discovered at Montfode, Ardrossan.

MEDIEVAL CHURCHES

Ayrshire is situated between Strathclyde to the N and Galloway
to the S, each of which is of the greatest importance for our
understanding of the EARLY CHRISTIAN CHURCH;* it might
therefore have been expected that Ayrshire would itself have
offered fertile ground for the study of that period. But in fact
there is relatively little evidence for Early Christian activity in this
area, whether in the form of physical remains, documentary
evidence or of place names. Of the few known artefacts, at Cairn
Farm, New Cumnock, two fragments with interlace decoration
have been found that may have formed part of the shaft and one
of the arms of a single cross. From the same parish, in the vicinity
of Mansfield House, has come a fragment of a cross-slab with
interlace decoration. One further find that might be mentioned
is a stone of uncertain function found at Chapel House Farm,
Fairlie (now in Fairlie Parish Church) on which is carved a low-
relief band decorated with a recumbent human figure and two
beasts. Beyond these, there is little more to report than a cross
that is incised on the walls of the King's Cave on Arran, the
authenticity of which is by no means beyond question.

The most significant MONASTIC REMAINS in Ayrshire are
7 associated with the older orders of monks. Kilwinning has the
fragments of a Tironensian abbey that was probably founded by
Richard de Morville at an unknown date around the third quarter
of the C12. The gable wall of the S transept and outer wall of the
S aisle, together with parts of the E and W claustral ranges, stand
alongside the parish church of c. 1774 and the bell-tower of 1815
that were built within the footprint of the monastic church. There
are considerably more extensive remains at the Cluniac abbey of
5, 6 Crossraguel. This was built with endowments granted to Paisley
Abbey by Duncan, Earl of Carrick, in the early C13, as a basis

* The description of the early Church and medieval religious houses has been
written by Richard Fawcett.

for establishing a new community, but which Paisley was only persuaded to use for the intended purpose in about 1270. Much of the shell of the small church survives to the wall-head, together with substantial parts of the conventual buildings and abbatial residence. Also associated with a house of one of the older orders is a handsome tower house that was built as a country residence for the Cistercian abbots of Melrose (Borders) on that abbey's grange at Mauchline. Melrose had extensive and highly profitable land-holdings in Ayrshire, and heraldry on the fine quadripartite vault over the hall indicates this residence was built in the time of Abbot Andrew Hunter (1444–65).

For the newer orders, the only foundations were for a house of Gilbertine canons and nuns at Dalmilling, Ayr, and for a community of Trinitarians at Fail, but nothing remains above ground of either. The former, which was evidently a project of the Stewart family in the first quarter of the c13, was probably never effective, and the endowments appear to have passed to Paisley Abbey. Fail was a foundation of the Stewarts of Kyle around the 1330s. There were at least three friaries within the area, of which nothing now survives. Ayr had a Dominican friary founded by Alexander II in about 1242, and an Observant Franciscan friary that was probably founded by James IV in the 1480s or 1490s. At Irvine there was a Carmelite friary established by one of the Fullartons of Fullarton in about 1290. Although they were not religious houses in the strictest sense of the term, mention may be made here of a number of colleges and hospitals that were founded in the area. The most important of these is the college at Maybole, which is 9 probably the oldest surviving example in Scotland of the type of late medieval college of priests whose principal function was to offer prayers for the salvation of its founder, his family and other named beneficiaries. It started life as a chapel endowed in 1371

Crossraguel Abbey.
Engraving, c. 1762

by John Kennedy of Dunure, within the parish churchyard, and it was formally established as a college in 1382. Although it remained a small foundation, never having more than about five priests attached to it, it still stands as an almost complete shell. There was also a college at Kilmaurs, which was founded in about 1413 by William Cunningham of Kilmaurs. It was probably housed within the parish church, but nothing of its fabric is known to have survived the rebuilding of the church in 1888. Hospitals are recorded as having existed at Ayr (where there was more than one), Kingcase (Prestwick) and Fail, the last of those being attached to the community of Trinitarians there. Hospitals at Ayr and Kingcase are known to have been provided for lepers, though the functions of hospitals could change in the course of their history. Nothing now remains of any of them.

The division of the county into PARISHES, which probably began in the late C12, was largely completed by the end of the C13. Parishes, which had defined boundaries, were generally served by a single priest, whose living was provided, in part at least, by the teinds levied on the agricultural produce within the parish. Most parishes were appropriated to monasteries or chapels who appointed the priest, and took a share of the teinds. The pattern of parishes established then has, mostly, endured into the C21. Of the original parishes, two (Perceton and Barnweill) have been suppressed, and two (Prestwick and Monkton) merged. New parishes were created in the C17 as the population of the uplands in the S and E of the county increased: Barr, New Cumnock, Sorn, Muirkirk, Fenwick.

Of the medieval PARISH CHURCHES, none survives intact. The vast majority would have been rectangular, with gabled ends, and subdivided into a nave and smaller chancel. They were almost inevitably orientated W–E, with the chancel at the E end. Nowhere does the level of decoration, nor the aspirations to high architectural quality, match those seen elsewhere in more settled parts of Scotland, nor do these churches, so far as they can be reconstructed archaeologically or architecturally, exhibit the more complex floor plans, with semicircular apses, etc., again seen elsewhere. Of those that remain in use, Lochranza and Symington (despite the later wing) most closely resemble the original form; Symington, too, exhibits the highest architectural quality, especially in the well-known round-arched three-light E window. Others also remain in use, e.g. Kilbirnie, but the original structure is now part of a larger building, the palimpsest on which subsequent generations have writ large. Many others remain in a ruinous, or semi-ruinous, condition. Some are small and almost without feature, e.g. Perceton, while others are much larger, if again simply detailed, e.g. Kirkoswald, Old Dailly and Auchinleck, enlarged in 1641–3. The middling majority include Prestwick Old Church, Barnweill (both on prominent raised mounds), the chapels of Crosbie and Alloway, rebuilt as late as 1653, Loudoun Old Kirk, Coylton, Lamlash and Monkton.

The grandest of these churches were probably in the burghs, e.g. St John's Tower, Ayr (the original parish church, first recorded

Alloway, Auld Kirk.
Engraving, 1789

in 1233), where the fragmentary remains include the springings for a vaulted ceiling, and a circular window in the E gable. Here, too, an E tower was added c. 1400, but such advance is not matched elsewhere. Several churches appears to have been rebuilt, or at least partially so, or extended in the later Middle Ages. Kilbirnie was extensively rebuilt in 1470, while a s aisle was added at Straiton, 1510. This is now attached to the later church, but other aisles of the C16 now stand alone: Beith Auld Kirk and the Kennedy Aisle at Ballantrae. At Straiton is also the only medieval monument in the county: for John Kennedy †1501. The toll of church FURNISHINGS associated with the Reformation of the mid C16 was perhaps at its most vigorous in Ayrshire. The altars, the foci of worship, have vanished, though in some instances, e.g. Alloway, Prestwick, the location can be surmised.

POST-REFORMATION CHURCHES

In 1560 the parliament broke connections with the Pope in Rome, and set in train the subsequent century-long debate in Scotland about the form of worship, and the governance of the Church, principally the replacement of an Episcopal system with a Presbyterian one, where control began with the session courts of the individual parishes, and percolated upwards through presbyteries. John Knox, whose wife was from Ochiltree, preached in

Maybole, and his vision of a Calvinist, preaching-led religion
gained great favour in the county.

Reformation to the Disruption

Post-Reformation worship required an entirely different layout
within the church. The focus was on the minister, and his preaching, and it was important that he was brought into the middle of
the church, and the heart of the congregation. In existing
churches, the altar was usually replaced by a pulpit, placed
against one of the long walls, often the S. If necessary, galleries
could be inserted in the gables, as at St Quivox (1595), but the
preferred method of enlarging a rectangular church was to build
a wing, or 'aisle', outwards from the centre of one flank, giving
the familiar T-plan. This additional aisle was often for the chief
landowner, e.g. the Cunninghame Aisle of 1597 at Kilbirnie.
Elsewhere it takes the form of a gallery above a family burial
vault (for which *see* also p. 24). Inside and out, the Skelmorlie
Aisle at Largs (1636–8) surpasses all for scale and ambition; it
has a coursed ashlar and slate exterior, with strapwork details
and heraldic and date panels inset. The interior contains one of
the best painted ceilings in Scotland, by *J. S. Stalker*, and dated
1638. The wooden barrel vault has a painted framework mimicking three panelled bays separated by ribs. In its Italianate character, the painter's work resembles Pitcairn (Perth & Kinross):
the depictions interweave religious scenes, cartouches with biblical texts, depictions of the seasons, including identifiably local
scenes, heraldic achievements and much else. Other C17 examples of more modest character include the Glencairn Aisle,
Kilmaurs (1600), Monkton, Loudoun Old Kirk (1622) and the
Crawford Aisle at Kilbirnie (1642). The Brisbane Aisle, Largs
Old Churchyard, of 1634 is designed to be free-standing. It pre-
figures the type of independent burial enclosure of which a good
example is the McCubbin enclosure at Colmonell, late C17, with
rustic columns and signed by *John Dicon* of Ayr.

    Of this period are several important MONUMENTS, beginning
with the Kennedy Monument at Ballantrae (1604), displaying a
delightful artisan reaction to Renaissance motifs, mixed with
medieval details, and the similar Cunninghame Monument,
Kilmaurs, 1600 by *David Scougal*. These can be contrasted with
the Montgomerie Monument of 1639 in the Skelmorlie Aisle,
Largs, which is wholly Renaissance in conception, taking the
form of a highly and complexly decorated Corinthian triumphal
arch, a conceit adopted from Maximilian Colt's monument to
Queen Elizabeth at Westminster Abbey. A final memorial in
similar style is Hans Hamilton's tomb at Dunlop, built by Lord
Clandeboye in 1641, and it is again a warring mix of medieval
and Renaissance details, with the figures kneeling on a sarcophagus, within a curtain-like arch, and all enclosed within an ashlar
crowstepped structure.

    In the early C17, especially in the reign of Charles I, opposition
to the reimposition of bishops and the expulsion of ministers

Kilmaurs, Glencairn Monument.
Etching by Robert Bryden, 1912

opposed to Episcopal governance, took armed form, culminating in the Covenant Wars, and the Bishops' War. Cromwell's Commonwealth brought a cautious peace, but the reigns of Charles II and James VII & II saw further action, and the simmering anger was finally quelled by the ascent to the throne in 1689/90 of the strongly Protestant William of Orange. Despite the uncertainty which surrounded the future of the Church nationally, there are a number of NEW CHURCHES from the mid to late C17. These were almost exclusively T-plan, and, in most cases on new sites (e.g. Dunlop, Fenwick, Kilmaurs, New Cumnock, Stewarton and Sorn). The largest and most noteworthy is Ayr Auld Kirk (1653–6), with wings for the three divisions of the town's bourgeoisie: magistrates, merchants and sailors.

Two new churches of the early to mid C18 anticipate later developments in church building: Old High, Kilmarnock, of 1732–40, and the parish church for Ardrossan (now North Ayrshire Heritage Centre, Saltcoats), 1744 (but rebuilt in 1773–4 by *John Swan*) are broadly oblong forerunners of the gabled preaching box that characterizes late C18 and early C19 churches. They are at opposite ends of the decorative spectrum. The assured Old High, a response to Kilmarnock's rapid, industrially led growth, is bold, accomplished, with classical details clustered on its E gable, which culminates in a spire. The influence is clearly James Gibbs's St-Martin-in-the-Fields, London, 1722–6, and finds a closer comparison in St Andrew's Parish Church, Glasgow (1739, Allan Dreghorn). The type reoccurs at Irvine, 1772–3 by *David Muir*.

Ayrshire's increasing population, the settled political and economic situation and the neglect of the county's churches for some
centuries led to a flurry of activity in the late C18 and early C19.
Amongst those churches adhering to the T-plan form are
Colmonell (1772), Kilwinning (*c.* 1774 by *John Swan*), Dailly and
Craigie (both 1776). As before, churches continued to be augmented, as at St Quivox (*c.* 1767) and Symington, by the addition
of aisles. St Quivox is particularly complex. It appears to have
initially received a new 'aisle' parallel to the existing church, to
which a conventional T-wing was then added. This may be related
to the sale of the parish's principal estate, Auchincruive, in 1764.
Features of St Quivox, such as the super-arches, suggest the hand
of *Robert Adam*, who is also linked with the rebuilding of Kirkoswald, 1777. There the T-plan is less pronounced, with the
laird's loft in a shallow projection from the front of the main,
classically detailed elevation. More austere are Kirkmichael, of
1787 by *Hugh Cairncross*, Adam's clerk-of-works at Culzean,
Kilmory (Arran) of 1785 (improved in 1881), and Ochiltree, of
1789. The only departure from normal practice is Dreghorn,
1780, where the laird and probable architect, *Archibald Montgomerie*, created an octagonal church, a type reprised on his estate at
Eaglesham (Renfrewshire) in 1788. An interesting experimentation can be seen at Catrine, 1792, again claimed, without
evidence, for Adam, which freely mixes classical motifs with very
Early Gothick windows.

In the early C19, a rectangular form increasingly becomes the
norm, although this is usually the consequence of filling out the
angles of T-plan churches with internal gallery stairs, e.g. Maybole
(1807–9) Galston (1807–10), Ayr New Church (1807–10) and
Beith High Church (1806–10). Kilmarnock Laigh Kirk, by *Robert
Johnstone*, 1802–3, is a large example, its many exits and stair-
towers an explicable over-reaction to the disaster of 1801. Of a
different mien entirely is Muirkirk, of 1812 by *William Stark*.
Inside, the focus on the (liturgical) E end, with its window, pulpit
and communion table, heralds a significantly early example in
the Presbyterian Church of a renewed emphasis on liturgy. Large
preaching boxes are also common among the churches of the
other Presbyterian denominations⋆ that seceded from the established church in the C18 but which in consequence of their shared
manner of worship erected buildings very similar in style and
planning. Examples are the former Morrison Church, Wallacetown, Ayr, built in 1770 for a Burgher congregation, the former
Relief Church, Irvine (now Emanuel Christian Centre) of
1773, the former Relief Church, Ayr, of 1816, Ayr Free Church

---

⋆ The main Secession churches in the late C18 were the Burghers and Anti-
Burghers, both of which split again into groups known as the Old Light and New
Light groups. In 1820 the New Light congregations, Burgher and Anti-Burgher,
came together to form the United Secession Church. This, in 1847, united with the
Relief Church, itself a late C18 secession, to form the United Presbyterian (U.P.)
Church. Other factions within the Anti-Burghers and Burghers either rejoined the
Church of Scotland, or continued as the United Original Secession Church.

(Wallacetown, Ayr), built for a Reformed Presbyterian congregation in 1832, and the Erskine Church, Kilwinning, of 1838.

By the end of the C18 the port towns of Ayr, Irvine and Girvan all had substantial Irish* populations, and many also moved onward to towns and villages, such as Dalry and Kilmarnock, where employment, particularly in industry, was to be found. Their first churches predate the Catholic Relief Act of 1829, and are often large, in a bristly uncomplicated un-archaeological Gothic, with a nave-and-aisles form suitable to Catholic liturgy. The first, and perhaps the best, is *James Dempster*'s castellated Dec St Margaret's, Ayr (now St Margaret's Cathedral) of 1825–7, a calculated statement of intent and permanence, and a similar air pervades other buildings from this initial phase, e.g. St Palladius, Dalry, of 1851, probably by *Robert Snodgrass Sen.*, with church, hall and school on a visually important site SE of the town centre, and St Joseph's, Kilmarnock, of 1846–7 by *McIlroy* of Glasgow, on an elevated site N of the town centre.

The classical style continues into the Early Victorian Presbyterian churches, e.g. John Knox Church, Stewarton (1841) and St Andrew, Kilmarnock (1841), a masterly Greek Revival design by *James Ingram*. From *c.* 1820, however, the GOTHIC REVIVAL gains momentum. An early, or possibly very late, example of the style is Ballantrae, of 1819, with pointed lancets and Y-tracery. The eyes of heritors, ministers, architects (who are becoming an increasingly recognized profession) and builders are cast backwards, to the churches of the pre-Reformation period. They struggle to make sense of the historical evidence, and to adapt it to C19 requirements. This is seen at Stevenston, 1832, by *Thomas Garven*, where a regulation galleried preaching box is encased in a simplified Gothic carapace. The biggest church of this period, St Andrew's and St Marnock's, Kilmarnock, of 1836 by *James Ingram*, achieves a successful synthesis of Gothic and classical motifs. It belongs with a series of churches, all in a simplified Gothic, which are, or may be, by Ingram. They begin with the Gothicizing of Sorn in 1826, when the present windows were inserted, and the new church of Mauchline, 1829, whose tower is similar to that at New Cumnock, of 1833. The group concludes with Fullarton, Irvine, 1837, and Auchinleck, 1835–9.

A spikier TUDOR GOTHIC is adopted by *David Bryce* for Coylton, 1829–32, and Monkton and Prestwick (now New Life Centre, Prestwick), 1837; both have projecting towers and a decorative reliance on finials. In similar vein are Dunlop, a thorough rebuilding of 1835, the former West Church, Maybole, of 1836–40 by *G. M. Kemp*, Dalmellington, of 1846 by *Patrick Wilson*, and the unattributed Cumbrae, of 1837. Showing greater regard for archaeological Gothic correctness, the frontispiece of *John Kay*'s Wallacetown Parish Church, Ayr, of 1834, is

25

---

*Irish and Catholic are, of course, not synonymous. The economic background to emigration applied equally to the Presbyterian Irish. There was also the Moravian Union Church, which through its settlement in Gracehill, Ulster, became influential in Ayr and Irvine.

copied from the Great Gate of St Augustine's Abbey, Canterbury (1300–9).

INTERIORS for churches built or reconstructed between the C17 and early C19 were generally simple, plain and seemly. Early,
18   and glorious, exceptions to this are Ayr, Auld Kirk (1653–6) and the Crawford Loft at Kilbirnie (*c.* 1705). Old High, Kilmarnock
20   (1732–40), has a fantastically ornate and crowded plastered interior with a coffered ceiling, while Irvine, 1772–4, has a fine wooden gallery front, the decoration neatly graded to match the relative importance of the men behind. These galleries were probably seated from the outset, but the enclosures reserved for the council and the trades have comfortable chairs, not pews.

Many churches from this period had LAIRD'S LOFTS, especially in the country parishes. It was not considered essential by the lairds that these should be penitential. Sublime examples might include, again, the Crawford Loft at Kilbirnie, which had a retiring room and small kitchen behind; Kirkoswald, 1777, where the Kennedys of Culzean also had a retiring room; Kilwinning, for the Montgomeries of Eglinton; and St Quivox, where the Auchincruive Aisle is at half-gallery height, with the family vault beneath. A similar arrangement, on a lesser scale, is found at Craigie, 1776.

Late Georgian and Regency churches differ little from the C18:
25   a few retain good PULPITS, e.g. the delightful one of *c.* 1819 at Ballantrae, the trefoil-planned one, with sounding-board, at Stevenston, 1832, and that at New Cumnock, 1833, with its curvaceous panelled dark oak front and octagonal pineapple-finialled sounding-board. MODEL SHIPS often feature in churches with maritime connections, e.g. Ayr and Ardrossan (now at St Cuthbert, Saltcoats). MONUMENTS are an infrequent adornment in the C18 and early C19. In Ayrshire the earliest appears to be that inscribed to Rev. Hugh Thomson †1731, at Kilmaurs Parish Church.

The Disruption to 1900

The biggest schism in the Presbyterian church occurred in 1843 with the 'Disruption', when a large proportion of the ministers and congregations of the Church of Scotland left, in an orchestrated mass walk-out from the General Assembly in Edinburgh, to form the FREE CHURCH OF SCOTLAND.* The first Free Churches were, almost invariably, cheaply constructed and simply detailed Gothic (e.g. the former churches at Kirkoswald and Monkton) or an unarchaeological Romanesque as at the former Ayr Free Church (1845).

---

*This affected almost every parish in Scotland, with each, no matter how small, ultimately served by an established church and a Free Church. The Free Church merged with the United Presbyterian Church in 1900 to form the United Free Church, which was in turn reunited with the Church of Scotland in 1929, but on both occasions a rump of congregations did not participate in the reunion.

The EPISCOPALIAN CHURCH, hitherto of minor significance in Ayrshire, became very active in the second half of the C19 under the influence of George Boyle, 6th Earl of Glasgow. Inspired by the Oxford Movement in the 1840s, he conceived of developing a collegiate Episcopal community and, with the ideals of Scottish island monastic communities such as Iona in mind, decided to build one on Great Cumbrae, which was part of his estate, for which he commissioned *William Butterfield* (1849–51), whom Boyle had previously engaged for the Episcopalian cathedral in Perth. Episcopal churches of a more restrained character followed at Kilmarnock (1857), Girvan (1859), Ardrossan (1874–5) and Largs (1876). The design of these was partly informed by the Ecclesiological Movement that began in England, advocating planning for worship that gave equal emphasis to preaching and the sacrament. Churches were to be broadly cruciform, with transepts, and a short (liturgical E) chancel containing a communion table, with, at the angles of the junction with the nave, a pulpit to one side and a font to the other.

26, 27

The Ecclesiologists disapproved of galleries and lofts, sanctioning only a w gallery; also disavowed was over-reliance on decoration. Such precepts also suited well the SCOTTISH PRESBYTERIAN CHURCHES. Three of their churches stand out in the period between 1850 and 1870. Of exceptional interest, and national importance, is the former Trinity Church, Irvine, of 1863 by *F. T. Pilkington*, in a robust polychrome Ruskinian Gothic, and on a prominent site, with the motifs gathered together in the architect's inimitable style. The Old Parish Church, Cumnock, is of 1863–6 by *J. M. Wardrop*, as a carefully wrought Dec wrapping applied to what is essentially a preaching box, and making well-controlled use of the cramped town centre site. Trinity, Dalry, is of 1857 by *Robert Snodgrass*, and is Perp, which was an increasingly acceptable template, with a nave-and-aisles frontispiece which is echoed in the galleried interior. The focus is at the liturgical E end, and from hereon the retreat from the preaching box becomes increasingly pronounced in Presbyterian churches. New Trinity, Saltcoats, of 1864–6 by *William Stewart*, shares with Pilkington's work the polychrome Venetian influences, and though it does not have his verve, does make its own statement in the townscape, while *James Ingram*'s 1860 Winton Place Church, Kilmarnock, for James Morison's original Evangelical Union congregation, adopts an E.E. style, and *Campbell Douglas*'s Alloway Church, of 1857–8, displays Dec features, with some idiosyncratic details, especially in the imaginative window tracery.

28

30

There was a quietus in church building during the 1870s, with two major works, one at either end of the decade, and a few smaller constructions. St Margaret's, Dalry, is of 1870–3 by *David Thomson*, a cruciform church in late C13 Gothic style with a powerful E tower. Thomson won the commission on the strength of his church at Eastwood (Renfrewshire), and produced a design of sublime quality, showing fine understanding of the motifs. In 1877–9 *J. & R. S. Ingram*, for whom *R. S. Ingram* was now the principal designer, built the E.E. former Grange Parish Church,

Kilmarnock. Again cruciform with a tower, and a short nave and an intricate internal layout (both occasioned by the tight site and the tensions, never far away in many of these late C19 churches, of marrying the Gothic shell to the functional requirements). This is easily the best of the younger Ingram's churches; his earlier (former) Hurlford Parish Church, Crookedholm, of 1875, also E.E., is less compelling. Better churches of the 1870s include *David Thomson*'s former Coats Memorial Church, Minishant, of 1877, in an unconstrained Early French Gothic, the idiosyncratic former Fairlie Free Church, of 1879 by *William MacChlery*, with circular upper windows, and the unattributed Our Lady & St Cuthbert (R.C.), Maybole, of 1876–8, straightforward Gothic given tremendous character by the series of identifiable carved head corbels inside and out. Fiscal prudence informs others, such as *Harry Blair*'s T-plan E.E. former Barony Church, West Kilbride (1873), *James Salmon & Son*'s Prestwick North and Monkton (1874) and *Allan Stevenson*'s Barr Parish Church (1878), both simplified Gothic. *James I. McDerment* added smart gabled dormers to the Auld Kirk of Ayr in 1877.

The first half of the 1880s was characterized by an increasing rate of new churches, some of which were to provide congregations in expanding areas of population, while others were replacements or enlargements of earlier structures. Churches in the former category included two in the rapidly expanding village of West Kilbride (St Bride's, of 1881 by *James Ritchie*, and Overton, of 1883 by *Hippolyte J. Blanc,* both based on French Gothic, with very different results: St Bride's is expansive, while Overton, on an enclosed site, has a taut, steadfast feel, and a stumpy tower), Crosshouse Parish Church, of 1881 by *Bruce & Sturrock*, Prestwick South of 1882–4 by *James A. Morris*, St James, Newton (Ayr), by *John Murdoch* and Trinity, Beith, by *Robert Baldie*, both of 1883. Reconstructions included *Baldie & Tennant*'s Dec Free Church, Darvel, of 1883. The best church of this period, *W. G. Rowan*'s Girvan North of 1883, a commanding E.E. structure on an equally commanding site, falls somewhere between: a church for an established congregation on a new site. Of red sandstone, like so many of these late C19 churches, and cruciform with a s w tower and short transepts. A little later in 1894–5 *J. J. Stevenson*'s neatly enlarged Fairlie Parish Church.

A similar combination of expansion and renewal characterizes the late 1880s. The three most interesting and innovative Presbyterian churches of this period are all on the island of Arran: *H. & D. Barclay*'s Lamlash Parish Church of 1886 (replacing a 1773 preaching box) and two churches by *J. J. Burnet*: Corrie, 1886–7, composed of nave and chancel, and Shiskine, 1888–90, with nave and aisle, chancel and w gallery. The Free Gothic treatment at Lamlash evinces a growing certainty among architects in the handling of Gothic motifs; Burnet also shows a willingness to take risks with the artistic material, courageously mixing Romanesque and Late Gothic elements to produce something original. Of the two, Shiskine is more assured and well-composed, while Corrie is hampered by a cramped and sloping site beneath cliffs. At Shiskine, especially, many of the elements, such as the stumpy pyramidal tower, which Burnet used for many of his churches, appear for the first time. Very different is *A. J. Grahame*'s St John's, Largs, 1886, a substantial Romanesque rebuilding of a Free Church of 1844. This is studied and well-applied Romanesque, with none of the gaucherie associated with the Neo-Romanesque of forty to fifty years earlier.

Of the OTHER DENOMINATIONS an obvious highlight is Holy Trinity (Episcopal), Ayr, begun in 1886 by *J. L. Pearson* to replace Bryce's earlier church, and completed in 1898–1900, to his father's designs, by *F. L. Pearson*. It is an austere, ambitious exercise in C13 French Gothic, Pearson's best work in Scotland. Perhaps the two best churches of the decade, however, were both erected for the Roman Catholic Church: St John, Cumnock, of 1878–80 by *William Burges*, and St Sophia, Galston, of 1884–6 by *Robert Rowand Anderson*, with *Robert Weir Schultz*. Both owe their appearance to the enthusiasms, interest and patronage of John, 3rd Marquess of Bute, who converted to Catholicism on his 21st birthday, and who had prior associations with both architects: Burges at Cardiff Castle and Castell Coch, Anderson at Mount Stuart, Bute (Argyll & Bute). Burges's church at Cumnock is Early Dec, and is derived from his earlier (1873–4) church at Murston (Kent); it was completed after his death by *J. F. Bentley* and *N. J. Westlake*. The chief glories of St John's are internal, where the decorative scheme was developed by Bentley and Westlake, and extended in 1898–9 by *Robert Weir Schultz*; in contrast Anderson's interiors at Galston are severely plain, but externally this is one of the most unusual and dramatic churches in Ayrshire, a brick, scaled-down version of Hagia Sofia, Istanbul, adapted for Catholic worship. The ritual and mysticism of Byzantine worship appealed to Bute, and he had previously attempted to have a church in this style built at Troon. The Marquess also involved himself practically and financially in many other projects of conservation and restoration, e.g. Loudoun Old Kirk and St John's Tower, Ayr.

Largs dominates the final decade of the C19, for two of the many excellent churches that characterize this period are there; *T. G. Abercrombie*'s Clark Memorial Church of 1890–2, and *Steele & Balfour*'s St Columba's, of 1890–3. Both are E.E., but of a high-powered red sandstone wealth-driven kind; each has a soaring tower and spire, and together they form the defining elements of the town when seen from the sea. They are characterized by a freedom to move away from the restraints of pure archaeological replication, and by the use of decorative elements which are influenced by contemporary movements elsewhere in the art world, particularly the growing awareness of Arts and Crafts, and the flowing imagery associated with such design. Many of the other churches of this period are similarly freed from the shackles of the past, and show a way forward, e.g. *James Hamilton*'s surprisingly good former Free Church, Lamlash, E.E. of 1891–2, *Hippolyte J. Blanc*'s large Dec Troon Old Parish Church, of 1894, based on his slightly earlier Cluny Parish

Church, Edinburgh, and, on a lesser scale, Skelmorlie and Wemyss Bay Parish Church of 1895 by *John Honeyman*, in the C13 style he had used previously for the restoration of Brechin Cathedral. The century closes well with *Duncan Menzies's* flamboyant Dec Cumnock, Trinity, of 1896–9.

1900–1914

In 1900 the United Presbyterian and Free Churches merged, bringing to a close a long chapter of growth and expansion for Scotland's Presbyterian churches. The years before the First World War nevertheless were productive and benefit from a liberation of styles in architecture generally *c.* 1900. This can be seen in some works for other denominations, e.g. Girvan Methodist Church, 1902, by *Watson & Salmond*, the Evangelical Union Congregational Church, Ardrossan, by *T. P. Marwick*, 1903, and the former Salvation Army Citadel in Ayr (1905–6 by *Arthur Hamilton*). Among the best of the rest are two of *Peter Macgregor Chalmers's* austerely mannered *Rundbogenstil* designs: St Nicholas, Prestwick, 1904–8, and St Cuthbert, Saltcoats, 1908. It is to be regretted that the talented architects who flourished in Kilmarnock in the early C20 had few opportunities to design churches. The one major commission that fell to them was given to *Thomas Smellie* for the Henderson Church, Kilmarnock, 1906–7. This is a freely interpreted Arts and Crafts-influenced Gothic exercise with a particularly well-judged tower. Also Arts and Crafts, with some deft detailing, is the former Arthur Memorial Church, New Cumnock, of 1912 by *W. Beddoes Rees* of Cardiff, better known as a chapel architect. *H. E. Clifford's* Portland Parish Church, Troon, of 1912–14 is also in a freely interpreted Gothic, with an especially well-mastered interior. Troon also boasts two high points of the Late Gothic Revival in Our Lady of the Assumption (R.C.), an early design by *Reginald Fairlie*, 1909–11, displaying a skilled handling of C13 Scots Gothic motifs, with a crown spire and an apse modelled on the Church of the Holy Rood (Stirling), and St Ninian (Episcopal) of 1912–13 by *James A. Morris*. This assured essay in his preferred Arts and Crafts idiom, stated simply externally and animated internally by careful attention to the fittings and decoration, is a neat and accessible thesis of Morris's art. Two interesting churches on Arran also adopt an Arts and Crafts Gothic: Whiting Bay and Kildonan Parish Church, of 1910 by *John Russell Thomson*, and the less adventurous Brodick Parish Church, also of 1910, by *D. & J. R. McMillan.*★ Minor changes and alterations of this period include the reordering of Dailly Parish Church, 1913–15 by *Macgregor Chalmers*, *James Wylie's* decorative painting at Stevenston High Kirk 1916, the fanciful façade added to St Columba, Kilbirnie, by *John McClelland* in 1902–3, the Edwardian Baroque chancel at Galston Parish Church, of 1913, by

---

★ Brodick's church hall is a 'tin tabernacle' of *c.* 1900, relocated in 1954. There is one other corrugated-iron church still in use, at Pirnmill.

Gabriel Steel and, most tellingly, *Charles S. S. Johnston*'s external and internal work at Kilbirnie Auld Kirk, 1903–5. Pleasingly suitable outside, but inside a riot of well-carved woodwork, e.g. the roof and gallery fronts, which take their inspiration from, and provide a truly wonderful foil to, the earlier timberwork.

A survey of CHURCH INTERIORS AND FURNISHINGS for the mid C19 to the early C20 should start with St Andrew's & St Marnock's, Kilmarnock (*James Ingram*, 1836), with its astonishingly spacious vestibule, and steeply raked galleries, with Gothic fretwork, pitched ribbed ceiling and Gothic pulpit and communion rail, arranged in a proto-Ecclesiological manner, and ought to have continued with Trinity, Irvine, but the interiors of Pilkington's church have been destroyed. *William Stewart*'s New Trinity, Saltcoats, 1864–6, retains an impressive, compact Gothic interior, with complex fretwork gallery fronts supported on wooden corbels, and more fretwork in the roof trusses, while the best 1870s interior is that of Holy Trinity (Episcopal), Kilmarnock, which has a stunningly elaborate decorative scheme in *George Gilbert Scott*'s chancel of 1876, planned by him and executed by *Powell & Sons* and *Burlison & Grylls*. Another individually conceived and complex interior is that of the former Grange Parish Church, Kilmarnock, of 1877–9 by *R. S. Ingram*, an inspired solution to a cramped site, with a semicircular gallery and pews in semicircles and a richly decorative ribbed and studded ceiling, and undoubtedly influenced by *F. T. Pilkington*'s Barclay Church, Edinburgh (1864). The frenzied High Gothic organ case of 1874–5 at Hurlford Parish Church, Crookedholm, may be by *James Ingram*; it is brightly coloured, with much incised and fretwork decoration; High Gothic, too, *Robin* of Paisley's 1873 claw-footed marble font at Irvine Parish Church, while the Caen stone pulpit and font at St Andrew (Episcopal), Ardrossan are of 1874–5, carved by *Charles Grassby*.

The glory of *W. G. Rowan*'s North Parish Church, Girvan, 1883 is the panelled and painted deep blue star-studded ceiling, with marginal friezes representing earth, sea and the seabed. Fairlie, as reconstructed by *J. J. Stevenson* in 1894–5, has a wonderful timber ceiling, its centre like an up-ended keel. There is nothing simple about the decoration of *J. J. Burnet*'s two Arran churches. Corrie has scissor trusses, an enjoyable excess of well-crafted timber in the aisle and aisle arcade, a stencilled chancel ceiling, and cartwheel-like light fittings, while Shiskine again has scissor trusses and a fine timber arcade, but also a panelled pulpit and imaginative Elders' benches.

Attractive interiors from the 1890s include *T. G. Abercrombie*'s Clark Memorial Church, Largs, of 1890–2, and *Steele & Balfour*'s St Columba's, also Largs, of 1890–3. Abercrombie's interior is particularly superb, and makes highly effective use of the space: broadly Ecclesiological, with one transept and a w gallery. The windows are set high, between a tall panelled dado and a hammerbeam angel roof; in the chancel cusped panelling and a baldacchino. St Columba's is no less impressive, but more conventional, with arcades of clustered columns and a barrel-vaulted roof; there is also a finely carved octagonal oak pulpit by *Miles S. Gibson*. At the other end of the county, *Robert Lorimer* remodelled Colmonell Parish Church in 1899, with a particular weight on the quality and appropriateness of the furnishings and decoration, while *Kinross & Tarbolton*'s 1899–1901 restoration of Straiton Parish Church throws all the emphasis onto the luxurious collarbeam roof and gallery fronts. Elsewhere, *Pearson*'s Holy Trinity (Episcopal), Ayr, has high-quality woodwork, plentiful stained glass, and furnishings designed by the architect, such as the filigree Gothic chancel screen, executed by *White & Son*, and the richly detailed Bath stone pulpit, of 1892, carved by *Nathaniel Hitch*, while *Hippolyte J. Blanc*'s Old Parish Church, Troon, 1894, has a rear gallery, a panelled barrel-vaulted roof, and diapered plaster decoration, all motifs he had previously used at Cluny Church, Edinburgh. At Skelmorlie and Wemyss Bay Parish Church (1895, *John Honeyman*) concentration is on the chancel, with a fine-looking panelled Gothic reredos, communion table and other furnishings designed by *W. G. Rowan* and executed by *John Crawford*. Finally, *Duncan Menzies*'s Trinity Church, Cumnock, of 1896–9, has a single gallery, a collar-beam roof and a pretty Gothic communion rail.

STAINED GLASS is a feature of churches from the mid C19 onwards, prompted by a softening in Presbyterian attitudes to decoration and ornament. Early examples of patterned glass include one kaleidoscopic window of 1858 at Alloway Parish Church, windows with floral borders at St Columba's, Stewarton (1870), and the windows installed at St Andrew's and St Marnock's, Kilmarnock, in 1885–6. Brightly coloured, highly patterned glass from Bavaria was much favoured, see e.g. at St Margaret's, Dalry, 1873. Figurative glass of this period also came from Germany, from where early British designers naturally took their inspiration. Among the earliest were *John Hardman & Co.*, of Birmingham, who executed the brightly coloured, Bavarian-influenced series of saints at the Cathedral of the Isles, Millport, *c.* 1849–51. By the 1860s figurative glass was appearing in churches throughout Ayrshire. The work of *James Ballantine*, of Edinburgh, one of the native pioneers of the glass revival, was also initially Germanic in style, e.g. his two windows at Ayr Auld Kirk, (*c.* 1861, 1863). His firm developed their own competent, if not innovative, style over several decades, as can be seen in schemes for North Parish Church, Girvan, 1890, and Trinity Church, Cumnock, 1906.

Of great significance for Ayrshire, however, was its proximity to Glasgow, which quickly established itself as a leading British centre of glass expertise and design. One early designer, much influenced by his time with Morris & Co. in London in 1861, was *Daniel Cottier*, who opened a studio in Glasgow in 1865. Of this date is his window for Trinity Church, Irvine, but it is no longer *in situ*, and he is now represented by the posthumous window by his firm at St Columba's, Largs, of 1892. Cottier's pupil, *Stephen Adam*, is the figure of greatest importance, producing many windows, almost invariably richly decorated and deeply hued, e.g. the Baird window of 1877 at Alloway Parish Church, with its characteristic Japanese and pre-Raphaelite influences. His firm was especially active in Scotland from the early 1880s: there are windows of 1890 and 1893 at Kilwinning Parish Church, of 1906 in St Columba's Church Hall, Kilbirnie, and one of 1909, with Glasgow Style roses, at Skelmorlie and Wemyss Bay Parish Church. Later windows by the firm, equally good, include the war memorial at Riccarton Parish Church, 1919, and a stunning Te Deum at the New Life Christian Fellowship, Prestwick, of 1925–6. Adam's contemporaries were *W. & J. J. Kier*, who had Ayrshire connections. Two excellent full decorative glazing schemes by the firm are at Irvine Parish Church (1861–1909) and at Old High Kirk, Kilmarnock (1868–72), while good single windows include one of 1877 in Trinity Church Mission Hall, Dalry. One of the larger firms was *J. & W. Guthrie* (*Guthrie & Wells* from 1899 until the 1960s), whose work is predominantly of interest for the Arts and Crafts designers they engaged, e.g. *Harrington Mann* (St Andrew's, Ardrossan, 1894) and *R. Anning Bell* (St Margaret's, Dalry). Bell, Head of Design at the Glasgow School of Art from 1911, also executed windows for Lamlash Parish Church (1909), Barony St John, Ardrossan (1919) and undated windows at Skelmorlie and Wemyss Bay Parish Church. Another late C19 firm widely represented are *William Meikle & Sons*, responsible for the Crucifixion (1892) in Clark Memorial Church, Largs, a comprehensive scheme for Laigh Kirk, Kilmarnock (1904–6), and many other good single windows, e.g. at Crosshouse (1911), Lamlash (1913) and Tarbolton (1920). Scottish designers with their own particular styles include the rather sentimental *Oscar Paterson*. His works in Ayrshire are generally relatively late, e.g. the war memorial window at Galston Parish Church, 1920.

33

Some of the best late C19 and early C20 work is by major English artists, e.g. *Christopher Whall*, who contributed to the outstanding scheme at Clark Memorial Church, Largs, 1890–2, one of the finest collections of Glasgow-made glass of its date. His work, which can be very intimate, yet carry a strong narrative, is also at Kirkmichael Parish Church (1905), Patna Parish Church (1909) and Alloway Parish Church (1922). Whall's most gifted pupil was *Louis Davis*, whose sweeping mobile style is seen at Colmonell Parish Church (1903, 1910). Other, major, English artists of this period are also well represented in Ayrshire. Windows by *Morris & Co.* occur at Troon Old Parish Church (1903, 1904), Fairlie Parish Church (1918) and Skelmorlie and Wemyss Bay Church (also 1918), but their best work in Ayrshire is the chancel window (1906) in Dundonald Parish Church. Of the prolific London commercial firms of the previous generation, there is work by *James Powell & Sons* in various churches, e.g. Dunlop Parish Church (1884) and Holy Trinity, Kilmarnock (1875–6, as part of *G. G. Scott*'s decorative scheme) and by *Clayton & Bell* at Alloway Parish Church, 1891, and Holy Trinity, Ayr, 1899.

The second half of the C19 also ushered in a wider range of stylistic treatments for MONUMENTS, though classical designs

still predominate. Interesting examples include Makdougall
Brisbane, †1860, in St Columba, Largs, with his profile against
a background of astronomical paraphernalia, and the highly
detailed monument to Surgeon-Major Stewart, †1873, in Kilmory
Parish Church. The monument to John Spiers, now in the Auld
Kirk, Beith, is a typically idiosyncratic Gothic design by *F. T.
Pilkington*, *c.* 1888. In the early C20 metal, usually brass, memorials, often nothing more than an inscription and a decorative
border, become more frequent and are associated with the Arts
and Crafts artists, e.g. the bronze bust by *Robert Bryden* of Henry
Fairlie, †1911, in Kirkmichael Parish Church; the stone monu-
ment itself by *James A. Morris*. Also Rev. George Scott, 1908, by
the *Bromsgrove Guild* at the former Wallacetown Parish Church,
Ayr, with the minister's full beard flowing over the border, and
John Findlay-Hamilton, †1918, at Craigie Parish Church, and
Robert S. Lorimer's First World War memorial in St Columba's,
Largs. By Lorimer, too, the carved memorial to Lady Glasgow,
1927, in Fairlie Parish Church.

Churches since 1918

Only one church from the INTERWAR period requires individual
39 comment: St Peter in Chains, Ardrossan, an unabashedly up-to-
date design of 1938 by *Jack Coia* and *T. Warnett Kennedy* of
Gillespie, Kidd & Coia, displaying the strong influence of Scandinavian brick architecture, in particular Sweden. Although no
other new works can compare, a small number of churches have
good FURNISHINGS of the period, including the pulpit at Kirkmichael Parish Church, planned as a war memorial by *James A.
Morris*, with decorative panels designed by *Hugh R. Wallace* and
carved by *Alexander Carrick*. The organ case at Livingstone
Church, Stevenston, is also finely carved, though originally
designed for a church in Glasgow. Some refurnishings were the
consequence of destruction of interiors by fire, e.g. the woodwork
supplied by Beith's cabinet-works for the rebuilding of Trinity
Parish Church by *Fryers & Penman* in 1924–6. Dalmellington
Parish Church was reconstructed internally in 1937–8 by *Leslie
Grahame-Thomson*, with a glazed partition beneath the gallery
and a canvas and oak reredos. Fire also led to conscientious
17 restoration of Fenwick Parish Church by *Gabriel Steel*, 1929, with
a suave undemonstrative interior. In 1951–3, again after a fire,
Steel restored the much larger St Margaret's, Dalry, once more
with panache, and once again with beautifully detailed woodwork
sourced from the Garnock valley cabinet-works.

The POST-WAR Church Extension Scheme produced several
economical churches in simplified style, e.g. Shortlees, Kilmarnock, of 1949–51 by *Alexander Dunlop* or The Schaw Kirk,
Drongan, of 1954–6 by *William Cowie & Torry*. The latter firm
did something similarly straightforward but on a larger scale for
the Good Shepherd R.C. Cathedral at Ayr in 1951–7 (mostly
dem.). More interesting Roman Catholic churches are the barrel-
roofed St Michael, Bellfield (Kilmarnock), 1950–3 by *Reginald*

Fairlie & Partners, like a big brick Nissen hut, *Robert Rennie*'s Our Lady of Perpetual Succour, Millport, of 1956–8, which is a synthesis of Scandinavian and Festival of Britain influences, and two churches by *Charles W. Gray*: the octagonal St Barbara, Dalmellington (1959–61, dem.), and Our Lady of Mount Carmel, Kilmarnock (1961–3), whose hexagonal baptistery contains one of the best C20 rooms in Ayrshire. Other notable designs for the Catholics are Our Lady Star of the Sea, Largs (1962 by *A. R. Conlon*), its steep A-frame structure an abstraction of a sailing boat, *James B. G. Houston*'s St John, Stevenston, of 1962–3, an inverted V with the roofs continued as heavy timber buttresses, and St Paul, Ayr, of 1964–7 by *William Cowie & Torry*, an attentively conceived white octagon.

Late 1960s and early 1970s churches are in a tougher idiom, e.g. the former Howard St Andrew's, Kilmarnock, of 1969–71 by *Allan MacPherson* (of *Alexander Dunlop & Partners*), and especially *James Hay & Steel's* impenetrable St Kentigern, Kilmarnock (1969–72) and Relief Parish Church, Bourtreehill, of 1976–8, which have almost identical internal layouts. The latter is arranged as a pair with *Douglas Niven & Gerard Connolly*'s bold St John Ogilvie (R.C., 1977–9), an octagon of concrete blocks containing an eyecatching sunken interior under a complex timber roof. Late C20 churches provide some interesting alternatives: Girdle Toll Church, Girdle Toll in Irvine New Town, of 1989–90 by *John Hepburn Associates*, moves towards a vernacular-derived style with the octagonal church dropped into the court-yard of an early C19 farm, which was converted to form halls and manse. The trend towards multi-purpose spaces for worship and other uses is typified by the circular Mansefield Trinity Church, Kilwinning, of 1998–2000 by *James F. Stephen Architects*.

Of individual items of FURNISHING there is a brass communion cross by *Benno Schotz*, 1957, at Henderson Parish Church, Kilmarnock, the daring hexagonal pulpit of 1959 at Brodick Parish Church by *William Scott and Archibald Hamilton*, and two wrought-iron abstract sculptures of the 1960s at Galston Parish Church. The reordering of almost all Roman Catholic churches as a response to the new liturgy introduced by the Second Vatican Council led to much renewal of furnishings. Amongst the most interesting are several series of Stations of the Cross, e.g. the tiled ones at St John's, Stevenston, of 1962–3, the polished brass series, of 1984, at St Quivox, Prestwick, and the glass series, of *c.* 2000, by *Susan Bradbury* for St Margaret's Cathedral, Ayr. Striking crucifixes include two metallic ones, at St Brendan's, Saltcoats, of *c.* 1964–5, where Christ's agony is well caught, and at St Joseph's, Kilmarnock, an abstract interpretation of *c.* 1970. Also noteworthy are the egg-like Creetown granite font and other fittings, of *c.* 1963, at St Mary's, Irvine. In some instances, the opportunity was taken to reorientate the church, as e.g. at St Mary's, Saltcoats (1972–3) and St Winin's, Kilwinning (both by *Sam Gilchrist*), with the altar moved from the chancel to one of the long walls. At St Matthew's, Kilmarnock, of 1974–7, the mosaic of the Evangelists by *Alan Potter* is of especial interest.

Mid-C20 STAINED GLASS in Scotland is dominated by *Douglas Strachan* and *Gordon Webster*. Both are represented in Ayrshire. Windows in Strachan's dramatic and masterly executed style are found at e.g. Darvel Parish Church (1923), St Columba's Parish Church, Largs (1919–25), and in abundance at Symington Parish church (1919–42). Glass by Webster is plentiful, though there is no diminution in quality: his windows often feature etiolated, angular figures and a palette strongly emphasizing the blue. Good examples can be found at High Church, Beith (a fine collection, dating from between 1942 and 1962), Kilwinning Parish Church (1951), and Dalmellington Parish Church (1958–9). Contemporaries whose work can match that of Strachan and Webster include *James Wright* (Fisherton Parish Church, 1933), *William Wilson* (St Cuthbert's, Saltcoats, 1947) and *Douglas Hamilton* (New Trinity Church, Saltcoats, 1951; Brodick Parish Church, 1961). Late C20 glass moves away from the naturalistic towards a more abstract, more allegorical approach, and this is especially well seen in the windows of the French artist *Gabriel Loire*, frequently found in Catholic churches of the period, e.g. St John's, Stevenston, and Our Lady of Mount Carmel, Kilmarnock, both of 1962. Homegrown artists of the same period include *Sadie McLellan*, whose powerful and expressive windows can be found at the Auld Kirk of Ayr (1960) and Straiton Parish Church (1977), *John Blyth* (St Andrew's Parish Church, Ayr, 1975; Irvine Parish Church, 1975) and *A. C. Whalen*, whose window in the Old Laigh Kirk, Kilmarnock, is a masterpiece of finely executed detail. The last years of the C20 and the first of the C21 are dominated by *Paul Lucky* and *Susan Bradbury*, partners in the *Stained Glass Design Partnership*, Kilmaurs, whose swirling, often vortical, naturalistic glass, with its seeded glass and frequent use of clear lenses, is found in many churches.

GRAVEYARDS, MAUSOLEA AND MONUMENTS

Church monuments and aisles which doubled as burial vaults have been described above. The majority of memorials are found in the GRAVEYARDS. These were enclosed by a simple stone wall; occasionally a more elaborate entrance was provided, such as the lychgates at the Auld Kirk of Ayr (1656), or Kirkmichael (*c.* 1700). In the early C19 body-snatchers, well paid by anatomists, threatened the sanctity of burial. The MORT SAFES preserved in the lychgate at Ayr were one solution: a lockable iron cage for the coffin.* In other parishes night guards were posted, and these were sometimes allowed a modicum of luxury, e.g. in the hexagonal SENTRY BOXES of 1828 at Fenwick Parish Church.

Graveyards began to be closed to new burials from the mid C19. The first of the purpose-built CEMETERIES were laid out in the 1850s, e.g. Maybole Cemetery, by *Reid*, followed by a rush in the 1860s (Ayr, Girvan, Beith, Irvine, Dalry), reaching the

*Others are displayed at Alloway Auld Kirk.

apotheosis with *Alexander Adamson*'s Kilmarnock Cemetery of
1874–5, with its confident Baronial gatehouse, and promoted as
much as a place of resort for walking and exercise as a burial
ground. This duality also informs many late C19 cemeteries, e.g.
Kilwinning (1870, laid out by *Rae*, the Eglinton estate gardener)
and Largs (*c.* 1886), with its abundant planting and unsurpassed
views of the Clyde. Notable enhancements to churchyards in the
late C19 and early C20 include the lamp of 1893–5 at Skelmorlie
and Wemyss Bay Parish Church, almost certainly by *Charles
Rennie Mackintosh*. More interesting is the full-scale remodelling
of Girvan Old Churchyard in 1907–8 by *James A. Morris*, with
new boundary walls and a disproportionately large triumphal
arch entrance. More suitably scaled is his English-influenced
lychgate at St Ninian's, Troon, 1913, while Lochranza has a
curiously complex memorial lychgate of 1931.

The earliest MAUSOLEA include the Boswell Mausoleum,
Auchinleck, of 1754, built alongside the (then) parish church, and
the larger Fergusson of Kilkerran Mausoleum at Dailly (probably
late C18). Both are plain but the well-tooled ashlar work of the
latter may suggest the involvement of *James Adam*. Of the same
period, but not in a churchyard, is the stylish Macrae's Monument, Monkton, of 1748–50 by *John Swan*, artisan classical
perhaps, but of a high order. Early C19 mausolea are more varied,
e.g. Greek Revival for the MacAdams of Craigengillan in the Old
Churchyard, Dalmellington, the battlemented Gothick Crawford
Mausoleum (1807) in the Old Kirkyard, Millport, Great
Cumbrae, and the correct Doric design for the Campbells of   22
Craigie by *W. H. Playfair*, 1822, at St Quivox.

The first dateable MONUMENTS AND GRAVESTONES date
from the very last years of the C16. These are simple dated wall
plaques at Irvine Parish Church, embedded within the churchyard's boundary wall. An inscribed table tomb in the Old Churchyard, Maybole, is dated 1618. The gravestone at Kirkoswald Old
Church depicting Adam and Eve is thought to be mid-C17, and
like so many of the headstones in the county up to the early C19,
is characterized by deep, robust, artisan but heartfelt carving. A
wide range of subjects can be found, though commonest are
symbols of mortality, such as the skull and crossed bones or the
cheerfully animated skeleton at Kirkoswald, of *c.* 1692, or an
hourglass. Trade symbols are also frequently incorporated, e.g.
mill-wheels, shears and plough teams (Straiton, *c.* 1700, and
Dalrymple, *c.* 1725). Biblical subjects are less common, though
the Adam and Eve motif is popular, e.g. at St Quivox, and pre-   23
sumably symbolizes heavenly reunion. Angels, for instance the
many late C18 ones with encircling wings at Irvine, and ships,
especially in the seaward parishes, are also commonly found. The
carving is often childlike, as at Fenwick (James Brown, 1691),
Dalry (Alexander Boyd, *c.* 1712) or Muirkirk, on the 'wildcat'
stone of *c.* 1755. Late C18 examples include the lively symbols of
death on the Mckilsock gravestone, Colmonell, of *c.* 1758, the
doll-like Kirkton Jean, with her book and woolsack, at Kirkoswald Old Church, and the startled John Turner (Irvine, *c.* 1786)

borne aloft by angels. It is outwith the scope of this introduction, or the gazetteer entries, to do full justice to this rich heritage.

INSCRIBED STONES begin to appear from the late C17, e.g. one of c. †1691 at the Old Churchyard, Girvan, with a floriated frame, and there are many neatly and attractively lettered stones in graveyards throughout the county, with good examples at, e.g., Alloway Auld Kirk. Many late C17 and early C18 gravestones commemorate COVENANT MARTYRS, and these poignant memorials often combine strong carving with heartstopping tales of cruelty and retribution in the 'Killing Times'. The finest examples are at Fenwick Parish Church.

Classical monuments and gravestones begin to appear in the mid C18. Among the best of the early ones is that of Quintin Craufurd, †1747, at Kilwinning, with Corinthian columns, and an astonishing basal frieze of skulls and bones. The mid C19 is characterized by two large, idiosyncratic monuments. The first is the statue of the Chartist Dr John Taylor, of 1858 by *James Shanks*, in Wallacetown Burial Ground, and the other is *F. T. Pilkington*'s unique Greek monument, of 1869, to Simson, the rediscoverer of Euclidean geometry, in the centre of the otherwise dull West Kilbride Cemetery. Two good late C19 monuments are to be found at Muirkirk Cemetery. The memorial to the ironmaster John Hunter, †1886, takes the form of a large classical triptych, while the Covenanters Monument of 1887 is an obelisk with well-executed panels on the plinth. The design was by *Thomas Lyon*, and the execution by *Matthew Muir*. An obelisk, but in Gothic style, was the chosen style for another memorial to a Covenant hero: *R. S. Ingram*'s 1891–2 memorial to Alexander Peden in the Old Churchyard, Cumnock. While Ingram's antiquarian choice was doubtless influenced by the subject, it seems far removed from *Herbert McNair*'s gravestone for the family plot at Largs Cemetery, of c. 1900, with its Mackintosh-influenced lettering and sinuous shape. Aesthetically rewarding stones from the C20 include the attractive chest tomb of c. 1920 of the Ralston-Patricks in Beith Cemetery, the war graves and associated Cross of Remembrance (more commonly found in overseas war cemeteries) of c. 1920 at Dunure Cemetery, and the memorial to Roy Dingley, †1993, in Millport Cemetery, a columnar monument with encircling steel inscriptions.

For secular monuments and war memorials *see* Burgh, Town and Village Buildings, pp. 64.

CASTLES AND TOWER HOUSES

The understanding of castles and tower houses is still in its infancy in Ayrshire; a few thorough archaeological assessments stand to show how much remains to be explained.

In the C11 the historic county of Ayrshire was three separate districts. Cuninghame and Kyle, in the northern half, were part of the kingdom of Strathclyde, Carrick in the s was under the influence of the turbulent Lordship of Galloway. In the second quarter of the C12 David I began the process of feudalization: Strathclyde was broken up and brought into the kingdom of Alba or Scotia and a complete overhaul of the ruling institutions carried out, with many Anglo-Normans placed in positions of power. The southern Strathclyde lands were divided between the King (Southern Kyle or Kyle Regis), Walter Fitz Alan, created Steward of the Kingdom (Northern Kyle or Kyle Stewart), whose family took the name Stewart, and Hugh de Moreville (Cuninghame). Carrick, a substantial area lying s of the River Doon, was awarded *c.* 1185 to Duncan, who became the 1st Earl, as compensation when his cousin Roland was granted control of Galloway. About 1196 Roland Lord of Galloway inherited the de Moreville lands of Cuninghame. The extent of the territories along the western seaboard controlled by the cousins led to the founding of a royal castle at Ayr (now vanished) in 1197 and the establishment of the royal burgh by William I. About 1271 Robert Bruce, descended from an Anglo-Norman family with extensive land-holdings in England and Annandale, became by marriage the 4th Earl of Carrick with Turnberry Castle, perched on the cliff edge, as his base. He was father of Robert I, reputedly born there. Fragmentary remains of enclosure walls and a keep on the Norman model survive.

One impact of the apportionment of land was the appointing of vassals or knights who had to do service for the feudal superior and were required to erect MOTTE AND BAILEY CASTLES. Timber towers were constructed either on existing rock outcrops or man-made mounds and all set within a bailey. A few of these mounds survive: one at the eastern end of Dalmellington built by Thomas Colville, who had received the territory from the 1st Earl of Carrick to guard against incursions from Galloway. Another survives at Tarbolton established by Gilbert fitz Richer under the lordship of the Stewarts of Dundonald on a promontory to the N of the village. At Motte of Montfode, close to Ardrossan, there were two outer ditches, possibly part of the bailey defence.

During the C13, with the western seaboard under Scottish control, the feudal system imposed by the crown began to make its mark. The connections between the holders of lordships with landownership in England provided a fruitful understanding of Norman defensive buildings which, combined with home-grown initiatives, brought about a variety of new castle types. Loch 40 Doon Castle was constructed in the later C13 on an island site as part of the defence against raids from Galloway. It comprises uniquely an eleven-sided strong curtain wall, its form dictated by the topography, enclosing the site in a manner adopted along the western seaboard at Mingary and Castle Tioram (Highland). The ashlar masonry, despite being moved and re-erected when Loch Doon became a reservoir, is particularly sophisticated, rising progressively toward the entrance, the facework exhibiting a technical mannerism in the checked or rebated joints. A feature of these high-walled enclosures is their formidable strength and lack of openings; here the entrance arrangements of a main gateway

with clear evidence of its defensive nature and a small postern
gate are the only breaches. At Dundonald the Stewarts took the
ancient fortified hilltop site and *c.* 1280 put down a marker of
their power and ambition by creating a large curtain-walled
courtyard castle with twin-towered gatehouses, one facing
towards the hinterland, the other W to the Firth of Clyde. This
is similar to the Edwardian castles at Rhuddlan and Beaumaris,
the gatehouse structure also comparable to that at Caelaverock
(Dumfries and Galloway). A courtyard castle with two unequal
towers at the E entrance and an outer defensive ditch existed at
Brodick (Arran) in the C13 and evidence there is still embedded
in the fabric. Dundonald suffered during the Wars of Independence and it was the Stewart monarch Robert II who rebuilt it
c. 1371, transforming the western gatehouse into a formidable
tower – comparable in height with Threave (Dumfries and
Galloway) and Borthwick (Lothian) – and separated from the
entrance. The tower was transformed to give a more commodious
residence, detached from the gatehouse which protected a smaller
courtyard enclosure. The internal arrangements of the tower
reflect the royal usage although the upper floor, now lost, would
have completed the picture with royal chambers. The large
vaulted hall above a lower vaulted storage area has unusual mural
vents to channel the smoke from the braziers. John Dunbar suggests this hall, at entrance level, may have provided for public
and ceremonial functions and the daily needs of a royal house-
hold. In the King's Hall above, originally with a pointed barrel
vault, the survival of corbelled springers carrying decorative ribs
imitated, as pointed out by Richard Fawcett, the sophisticated
quadripartite vaulting found in ecclesiastical buildings. Much of
the C14 courtyard walls survive at their lower level and recent
excavation suggests that among the buildings in the enclosure
was a chapel. Associated with Dundonald is Portencross, of early
C14 date and used by Robert II and Robert III en route to
Dundonald. Its atypical plan of hall range and wing in line is
probably the result of the tight promontory site, but the unusual
provision of two stairways and two kitchens was to accommodate
the needs of royal parties. On a smaller scale than Portencross
but earlier is the first part of Rowallan, a modest tower originally
with no entrance at ground level but a mural stair linking it to
the first floor.

Before 1296 and the start of thirty years of the Wars of Independence there was a period of relative calm which coincides
with the appearance of HALL HOUSES. Because most were later
subsumed into fortified towers or castles it is unknown how many
existed. Stewart Cruden identified Craigie Castle as a two-storey
hall house of the late C12 or early C13. Now fortified by nettles
of monumental size it is nevertheless still possible to identify the
walls of the plain hall-form and to see where its battlements,
lacking any form of corbelling, have been incorporated into the
walls of the C15 hall above. This C15 rib-vaulted hall uses the
wall-walk of its predecessor on which to set its sculptured corbels
and decorative ribs. Lochranza on Arran also appears to have

begun as a hall house, its only defence being from the wall-walk, and Old Dalquharran probably started in a similar way. Such halls would have been enclosed by walls with a gatehouse and service buildings inside. Various fragmentary enclosures and ditches remain at Craigie.

The C14 saw families such as the Boyds, Boyles, Craufords, Cuninghames, Kennedys, Montgomeries, Mures and Wallaces granted territorial charters and firmly settled in the county. Their landed ambitions, sometimes satisfied through advantageous marriages, from this time on can be charted in the buildings they have left behind, testament to restless and acquisitive times. River valleys were the foci for buildings and settlements, a pattern continued into the C19. The sites selected for the family stronghold are frequently on or close to steep bluffs overlooking rivers and the buildings, in the form of imposing KEEPS, are very plain in appearance with massive walls capped with parapets and wall-walks, their thick walls with mural closets and stairs. Frequently the ground floor, used for storage, was vaulted and unlit; above was a vaulted hall with small windows placed for function not symmetry. The walls of later examples became increasingly honeycombed with mural chambers. The Wallaces of Sundrum built a tower in the 1370s high over the Water of Coyle. Although sandwiched between later additions, it still retains a straight mural stair within the N wall. Not far to the s is Cassillis, probably built by John Kennedy in the late C14, on an equally imposing site overlooking the River Doon; the entrance was at first-floor level and a straight mural stair gave access to the upper hall. A newel stair, now replaced, linked the upper floors in the thickness of the NE angle. It appears that the parapet had embryo bartizans or angle rounds, a feature developed in the C15, and here much altered in the C17. At Dean, Kilmarnock, a large, austerely plain keep with no corbelling to the wall-walk, built by the Boyds in the late C14, expresses the status of the family. The first-floor entrance, now altered, is at hall level with an internal stair to the ground level and a newel stair to the upper floors. The tall vaulted hall has a stone bench around the walls and window embrasures with seats, a minstrels' gallery, and within the wall thickness a guard chamber and access to the pit dungeon. Off the second-floor solar, provision was made for a chapel. The earliest part of Cessnock is C15 but probably based on and incorporating earlier fabric to give the keep-like tower built high on a bluff; it has a newel stair within the NE angle and, like Dean, a windowless vaulted ground floor with a double-height vaulted space above, a feature also of the C15 tower at Loudoun but here with an entresol, as at Portencross. These C14 and C15 towers, like Dundonald, had courtyards or enclosures to house the kitchen, ancillary accommodation and often a hall, commonly of timber construction and providing protection for the tower. All are now altered but can still be appreciated in the re-created Dean Castle; in the ruinous Glengarnock Castle (late C15 or early C16), perched precipitously above the River Garnock, where there are remains of a stone-vaulted kitchen inside the enclosure and angle towers

43

protecting the entrance; on a small scale at Carleton Castle (late C14 or early C15), overlooking the Firth of Clyde; and at Terringzean Castle, near Cumnock (*c.* 1400) where archaeological evidence indicates the form of its enclosure.

Ayrshire in the late C15 and C16 has been likened to the American Wild West with frequent feuding within local families and amongst their neighbours; the Kennedys in Carrick, besides kidnapping and roasting Gilbert Stewart, the Abbot of Crossraguel at Dunure, were not averse to murder, the slaughter of Gilbert Kennedy of Bargany by the Earl of Cassillis in 1601 one of the worst atrocities. The constant jostling for status was one reason for the explosion of TOWER HOUSE building from the later C15 to the early C17. Families were also growing increasingly wealthy as a result of the break-up of monastic estates as well as from the granting of feu-holdings by the crown, providing greater security of tenure. Political stability also enabled landowners to invest in buildings.

These towers became the nuclei of landowners' property and were often upgrades of earlier sturdy buildings. Like their predecessors, newly built towers were generally placed on prominent coastal sites: the fragmentary remains of Greenan Castle (late C16) command striking views of the Firth of Clyde, for example, as do the C16 castles at Skelmorlie and Fairlie and the tower on Ailsa Craig. Many others occupy strategic positions in the numerous river valleys which traverse the county from E to W such as Sorn, begun early in the C15 on the River Ayr, Craigneil (C15), Knockdolian (C16), and Pinwherry (late C16) beside the River Stinchar. A few are in towns, such as the Montgomeries' Seagate Castle, Irvine, built *c.* 1562 on an earlier site, the Lockharts' Barr
47 Castle (*c.* 1500) at Galston, the Campbells' Newmilns Tower (*c.* 1525) and Mauchline Castle which was built for the Abbot of Melrose *c.* 1446. This has a finely rib-vaulted hall, a consequence of its ecclesiastical connections. By 1600 in Maybole the Earls of Cassillis and the Kennedys of Blairquhan each had a tower acting as their town house and placed at opposing ends of the main thoroughfare. The Earl of Cassillis made it abundantly clear that he was not only powerful but in the forefront of fashionable decoration by introducing elaborate dormerheads, scrolled details on the straight skews instead of the conventional crowsteps, decorated chimneyheads and the extravagantly detailed oriel window in the upper room of the jamb, illustrated by Billings and beloved of C19 architects working in the Baronial style. For all of these families status and power were as important as defence, expressed in the elaborate and showy use of rope mouldings and other decorative details at Seagate, Irvine. The
53 same highly decorative motifs also existed at Blairquhan Castle (dem.), fragments from which can still be seen in the service court of the C19 house. These details, together with the elaborate armorial panels at Blair, Killochan and Rowallan, underline the importance placed in ancient origins and flamboyance.

Security still played a modest role in the building of C15 and C16 tower houses, essentially to give protection against local violence. This was recognized by the Crown, which granted licences to build fortified residences from 1424. In 1535 a statute ordained that each man possessed of lands valued at £100 'inland or upon the bordouris' was to build a barmkin or enclosure 'for the ressett and defens of him, his tennentis and their gudis, in trublous tyme, with ane toure in the samyn gif he thinkis it expedient'. This may have increased the rate of tower construction, for there had been little such building for the previous quarter-century, partly because of the huge losses of manpower and fortunes after the devastating Battle of Flodden in 1513.

From the early C15 machicolations began to appear, providing greater means of defence than, for instance, the projecting, machicolated box with open slits high above the door at Lochranza (and mimicked at Killochan in the late C16 where it is unlikely that it was used in earnest). Artillery resulted in the need for gunloops, replacing arrowslits. Most frequently found are the horizontal type seen in the windowless ground floors of Craufurdland (c. 1400) and Law (c. 1460). At Old Dalquharran, late C15, the keyhole type was employed, and at Rowallan in the C16 the double-ended keyhole type occurs. Generally, however, the shothole became the most common form, particularly to protect entrances.

COMPACT TOWERS, compressing the functions of the castles of enclosure into one vertical building with a barmkin, were favoured by the growing lairdly class as well as the aristocracy. Until the later years of the C15 the rectangular plan was almost universal, usually with three or four storeys and a garret, a corbelled parapet at the wall-head and wall-walk, open angle rounds or bartizans and a caphouse. The common building material was local rubble, often harled and sometimes with ashlar dressings. Knockdolian is an early C16 example with a corbelled parapet on three sides and the remains of a caphouse. To increase the size of this walk the parapet wall was corbelled, sometimes with a continuous corbel table as at Craufurdland or Law, encircling open bartizans. Increasingly the parapet was supported on individual corbels which became ever more elaborate, tiered on the palace range at Dean Castle c. 1460 or stylishly chequered at Fairlie, Little Cumbrae, Sorn and Barr. The most sophisticated, and clearly indicating status, are found at Old Dalquharran Castle where the corbel table is formed of diminutive ogee-headed arches linking the tiered corbels. This dates from c. 1540 for Sir Hew Kennedy, recently returned from France where he may have come by the idea. Inside, the quality of the aumbry on the s wall of the first-floor hall with a cusped frame and floret carving, details derived from medieval ecclesiastical woodwork, gives a tantalizing glimpse of sumptuousness which must have made Old Dalquharran stand out from the simpler towers. By the late C16 open parapet walks were covered in to create a wall-head gallery, still recognizable at Killochan where a gallery formerly linked a small bartizan to a large, circular chamber tower with its own stair. Galleries were eventually incorporated into the garret but the candle-snuffer roofed turrets remained, often used as closets or small chambers as at Kilhenzie or Skelmorlie Castles. About 1600 the parapet had generally been supplanted by simple eaves, downplaying the need for serious defence. This is clearly the case at Maybole Castle.

The heart of the INTERIOR plan was the first-floor hall, with a large fireplace, often stone seats in the window embrasures and aumbries for storage and display. Chambers were in the upper floors. The ground floors occasionally included a kitchen, as at Barr, but more frequently this function was relegated to a building in the courtyard. An interesting group of rectangular towers in the NW of the county show a real improvement in domestic arrangements: Little Cumbrae (1534–7); Law (mid-C15); Fairlie and Skelmorlie (both c. 1500) all have a bay at the end of the hall screened for a kitchen. In most cases the kitchen is reached from the newel stair at the entrance end of the hall although at Little Cumbrae it was necessary to enter the hall first. On a grander scale this plan appears c. 1450 at Comlongan (Dumfries and Galloway) but there is no immediately obvious connection. Unusually at Little Cumbrae there are two licences to build: the first in 1534 refers to a mansion with hall, chamber, kitchen, barn, byre and other offices, and only in 1537 was permission given to build a tower. Richard Fawcett suggests that closer study of towers, their ancillary buildings, including halls outside the tower, their use and interaction as well as terminology, would add significantly to the understanding of the wider domestic and cultural disposition of towers and surrounding buildings.

The most popular solution for IMPROVING DOMESTIC ARRANGEMENTS in the C16 was the adoption of an L-plan with the jamb frequently used for a larger newel stair; often only to the first floor, the upper floors reached by a stair turret canted out in the re-entrant angle as at Pinwherry of the late C16. At Baltersan, and altogether more sophisticated, the stair rises to the second floor before continuing in a corbelled turret to the upper chambers, the top one in the jamb with a small oriel window, a precursor of the oriel at Maybole Castle. The unusually well-lit hall, with windows placed symmetrically on either side of the large chimney-breast, is the principal apartment but more chambers in the upper floors appear to have specific functions and the detailing, including sliding shutters and incised carving around the aumbries, is smart; there is a small barrel-vaulted compartment, possibly a charter room. An unexplained square opening with deeply splayed reveals in the w wall is found again at Killochan (another Kennedy house) and at the Castle of Park (Dumfries and Galloway). At early C16 Thomaston the jamb has an arch at ground level originally leading into a barmkin, whose shadowy existence can be detected, and the stair in the re-entrant angle serves all floors. Early examples of scale-and-platt stairs appear at Killochan and also at Kirkhill in Colmonell, providing a more gracious and fashionable approach to the principal floor. The C17 embellishments at Cassillis, in the Baronial style celebrating the family's ancient lineage, comprised a new jamb with a dramatic, full-height stair cleverly devised around an open newel replacing an earlier stair in the thickness of the wall. The mural stair in the w wall may have acquired its geometrical and figurative wall painting at this date. The upper storey was rebuilt without a parapet and with carved decoration to the dormers, decoration found more modestly at Penkill (C16). These dormer-heads replace crenellations to increase the emphasis on the upper storey and the syncopation of the roof-line, all part of the display of power and status.

A less common solution to restricted space was ENLARGE-MENT. Development of buildings around a courtyard provided lodgings where the horizontal disposition could provide more usable space. At Dean Castle the need for greater segregation of activities within the tower resulted in the building of a hall and chamber range in the courtyard to the s of the tower. This was probably done *c.* 1460 for the 1st Lord Boyd during his short period of royal favour; influenced by royal works at Linlithgow, Boyd used masons from Roslin Chapel (both Lothian). The first-floor hall with a kitchen and offices below was linked to a five-storey chamber tower and given a new entrance and stair-tower. Meticulously restored in the early C20 by *Ingram & Brown* and *James S. Richardson* for Lord Howard de Walden, the castle provides an excellent impression of the arrangement of a tower and the development of buildings in the courtyard. At Cessnock, like Dean, a hall and chamber block was added in the C16 but transformed by extensive C17 alterations and additions including the two stair-towers with pedimented doorcases, to improve the communication. In the E range is a boarded and painted ceiling – a rare survival in the county of C17 interior decoration. By 1500 there was a range on the s side of the courtyard at Rowallan which was by *c.* 1540 a hall and chamber but much more domestic in scale than Dean. It was linked to the earlier tower block in the 1560s by the picturesque double-towered frontispiece including a gatehouse at the head of a flight of steps with armorial panels over the gate, a potent expression of aristocratic symbolism. Some enlargements continued within the vertical format. At Kelburn in the late C16, the original tower was almost doubled in size and became Z-plan with the addition of two unequal, opposing drums, one housing a larger stair, the other to provide further small chambers. Existing towers at Newark and Brodick were also enlarged in the C17.

With the SEVENTEENTH CENTURY came an increasing need for more space and privacy. Auchans, re-created in 1638 around an earlier L-plan tower, illustrates the trend to horizontality and regularly placed windows and dormers with dormerheads breaking into the roof. Here a solution to the internal circulation was resolved by creating a tall stair-turret in the re-entrant angle, its importance originally proclaimed by finely carved Renaissance details in the doorpiece, panel above and the crowning balustrade. On a more modest scale Stair House straddles the divide between the old and the new; here a taller, L-plan tower, probably late C16, was cut down in the early C17 when a three-storey gabled range with regular windows in neatly moulded frames was added, but still with a vaulted ground floor and a chamber tower. At Old Place of Kilbirnie expansion in the C17 created specifically designated rooms, including a drawing room and private room made to communicate with the hall in the earlier tower. A later C17 wing and a new entrance and stair-tower were added at Old Dalquharran to give more domestic accommodation. The buildings make up two sides of a courtyard entered through a fine classically detailed gateway.

New building in the C17 also continued the tower house tradition but made use of Renaissance decoration to give a degree of grandeur, as seen at Maybole Castle. Clonbeith, a small estate created out of the lands of Kilwinning Abbey, illustrates, even in its ruined form, an advance on earlier towers. It is a simple rectangular block with near-symmetrical openings and a door, once dated 1607 on a broken-pedimented doorpiece, close to the centre of the long elevation, above which was a smartly corbelled oriel window, but inside the arrangements were less radical with a vaulted ground floor and a straight stair on the end wall leading to the first floor with a newel rising to the upper levels. At Monk Castle built around 1600, formerly belonging to Kilwinning Abbey, a T-plan tower was built, with the newel stair in the wing and a vaulted ground floor with a keyhole gunloop to protect the door; its regularity, the size of the windows and the simply crowstepped gabled roof show the increased emphasis on domestic comfort and confidence in very modest defence. The T-plan is found again in fragmentary form at Brunstoun Castle of the early C17 and Crosbie Tower, which bears the date 1676 with Renaissance detail in the pilastered doorpiece. Sornhill of the 1660s or earlier, the best surviving C17 laird's house, looks back to the L-plan tower house with a stair-tower in the re-entrant angle but espouses the horizontal on the main long elevation with windows in neat roll-moulded arrises symmetrically arranged. This compact house had a large arched chimney for the ground-floor kitchen, and in the rooms above fireplace lintels with carved initals and decoration.

The religious upheavals of the C17 were particularly disrupting in Ayrshire and there was little new building on a grand scale. But in 1668 Blair Castle had a substantial three-storey addition to the tower block to provide better domestic arrangements and circulation. It gave the castle its strongly C17 character with symmetrically placed windows in simple moulded frames and wonderfully carved dormerheads. A new stair-tower was attached to the earlier one to provide a better entrance, display the armorial panels, symbols of dynastic antiquity, and importantly to house a spacious newel stair.

The solid nature of towers means that they have regularly been incorporated into C18 and C19 mansion houses either in the rear quarters or cleverly integrated with symmetrical façades. Further study of these hidden structures is needed.

COUNTRY HOUSES AND ESTATES

It has already been shown how tower houses were adapted and enlarged in the C16 and C17 to provide better accommodation and circulation and to express through Renaissance decorative enrichment the status of their owner. At Bargany *c.* 1681–96, however, the Kennedys took a different approach, demolishing the old courtyard house near the river and espousing the new CLASSICAL fashion in the design of its replacement. A U-plan was adopted, providing a symmetrical five-bay garden frontage, two shallow wings on the entrance front, now much altered, and a roughly symmetrical arrangement of rooms. It is the pattern established on a grander scale in the entrance range at Caroline Park (Edinburgh) (1693–6), and more modestly at Gallery House (Dundee and Angus) (*c.* 1680).

Also at the forefront of changing fashion is the extension of Kelburn Castle, begun *c.* 1690 for David Boyle, an influential statesman who became 1st Earl of Glasgow. The bold, twin-gabled centrepiece giving height and presence to a domestically scaled range was complete by 1700, but the whole wing was not finished until 1722. The impressive well stair and the great dining room (now the drawing room), with its panelling, giant Corinthian pilasters with their capitals shadowed in the cove above the cornice and plaster frieze, show Boyle expressing his status and his commitment to the Union. The smartly panelled interiors, particularly in the tower, surely influenced the new classically detailed panelling in the chamber range at Rowallan, inherited by Dame Jean Mure, David Boyle's second wife. 51

Patrons with horizons beyond the county were crucial to architectural changes in the EIGHTEENTH CENTURY. At Kilkerran an old tower was incorporated into a new H-plan classical house *c.* 1729 for Sir James Fergusson, a judge in Edinburgh. If he employed an architect there is no record, but *James Smith* may have been involved on the evidence of its central pediment (now lost) having been raised above the eaves, a motif associated with Smith. The same feature appears also at Craigie House, Ayr, built *c.* 1730, and the swept eaves at both houses again suggest Smith's hand. The NEO-PALLADIAN type of plan with a *corps de logis*, quadrants and pavilions, is seen first at Craigie, and appeared again *c.* 1745, at Fullarton House (dem.), which had a steeply raked pediment drawn from the Smith school but incorporating Gibbsian details characteristic of *William Adam*, and in a much simpler form at Annick Lodge (*c.* 1750). But the most important example of the type is Dumfries House, commissioned after 1748 from *John* and *Robert Adam* by the 5th Earl of Dumfries. Dumfries House owes much to the publications of Gibbs and Ware. Apart from the crisply cut armorial carving in the pediment, the house relies for its impact on its flawless proportions and immaculate masonry. Inside there is a spine corridor with stairs at either end, two public rooms flanking the wall to the S and the family apartments to the N. Plasterwork, some with touches of Rococo, is probably by *John Robertson*, who may also have worked for a close neighbour, James Boswell, Lord Auchinleck, who was consulted on the design of Dumfries House. Auchinleck House (1755–62) is however a quintessential rural villa and it appears that the idiosyncratic design was Boswell's own (though aspects 62 56, 57, 58 55 of it show a debt to Dumfries House and also William Adam's style). However, its Ionic-pilastered temple frontispiece, the elaborately carved pediment and straight flight of steps to the front door give a nod to Dumfries House; the balustrade and urns look back to William Adam; and the arched windows to the first-floor Library, comparable to similar upper windows at Fullarton, and the composition of the house and pavilions in a straight line perhaps owe a debt to John Douglas's Finlaystone House, Renfrewshire. *John Adam* designed the dramatic red sandstone Ballochmyle House, complete in 1760, for Allan Whitefoord who was also consulted over Dumfries House. It is not difficult to see how ideas were disseminated through social contacts.

The first half of the C18 produced few SMALLER LAIRDS' HOUSES. Auchmannoch of 1724 demonstrates a tendency to regularity if not symmetry, but more traditional is the division between the living and the service ends evident in the elevation and the position of the bolection-moulded door with a scrolled frame above. Of simple astylar boxes Monkwood is the best example. A classical symmetry is clear in the elevations at Drumburle, from the mid C18. Its big piend roof comes from the Smith–McGill school, but the surprising feature of a *piano nobile* and, inside, the remarkable giant Doric pilaster, correctly executed, masking the newel at the first floor, draw on designs for larger houses such as nearby Kilkerran.

From the 1750s new wealth from trade, particularly overseas ventures, and from the law saw a sudden burst in construction of handsome classically detailed houses; Richard Oswald, a London merchant involved in the triangular trade, purchased Auchincruive in 1764 with at least a shell of a house designed by *John* and *Robert Adam* for James Murray of Broughton. Oswald sought modifications from the brothers and the house still retains good Adam interiors despite much alteration. A simpler example is Grange House, *c.* 1760, a plain classical box with the principal floor above a raised basement and a Roman Doric-columned doorpiece. Robert Hamilton, whose money came from Jamaican sugar plantations, built Rozelle (Alloway), a straightforward Neo-Palladian house (complete 1760). From the 1760s there is an increasing use of pediments – often over advanced central bays – on front elevations with the projection of curved or canted bays on garden elevation and sometimes the sides, most elements seen originally at Dumfries House and serving to give larger and more stylish rooms to classical boxes. Examples are: Skeldon (*c.* 1760), which has pedimented main elevations, both since modified, and canted bays added to the sides in the late C18, Perceton and Dallars (both *c.* 1770), the latter also with a pedimented entrance front. Hugh Hamilton, again with Jamaican funds, purchased the Belleisle property, close to his uncle's Rozelle, and built a mansion, completed in 1794, with a big, balustraded canted bay on the garden front. Hillhouse, built *c.* 1790 for John McKerrell, whose wealth came from Paisley silk weaving, has advanced pedimented bays to front and back, the latter open with an arched window rising into it; Pitcon, *c.* 1787, is similar but omits the raised basement. At Old Auchenfail Hall, built in 1786 for William Cooper, a Glasgow tobacco merchant, the pediment dominates the front elevation which originally had an entrance in the principal floor reached by steps; Underwood, 1785, has a pediment at the front and a bowed projection at the rear, very like that added to Craigie House, Ayr, in the 1780s.

The outstanding LATER EIGHTEENTH-CENTURY mansion in the county is Culzean where the 10th Earl of Cassillis, after much tinkering over the generations with the tower house and surrounding buildings, employed *Robert Adam* in 1776 to transform this jumble into a coherent appearance. The result is the masterpiece of Adam's CASTLE STYLE, approached through a picturesque ruined gateway and along a curving viaduct, with views of the turreted and crenellated castle perched romantically on the cliff top. It skilfully incorporated the old tower into the large E-facing rectangular range and linking it to the great drum tower facing the Firth of Clyde by the most theatrical of staircase compartments, an oval temple turned inside out with an arcade at ground level and colonnaded galleries giving access at the *piano nobile* to the drum Saloon on the w and the *enfilade* of state rooms on the e. Adam designed all the interior detail but only in the long drawing room, with Jacobean-style decoration in the plaster ceiling, was there a nod to the style of the exterior; elsewhere classical detail prevails with Adam's familiar low-relief plaster ceilings incorporating painted scenes on canvas. Adam used the castle style for Dalquharran (1782–90), which he designed for his niece Jean and her husband Thomas Kennedy of Dunure. Work was supervised, as at Culzean, by *Hugh Cairncross*.* Another ambitious adventure in this style is the now ruinous Loudoun Castle of 1804–11 by *Archibald* and *James Elliot*, incorporating its C15 keep into a huge castellated and turreted picturesque creation. This is one of four substantial mansions conceived during the period of the French Revolution and the Napoleonic Wars, which boosted agricultural profits and stimulated general estate improvements. Among the others is Eglinton Castle, built 1796–1802 for the Earl of Eglinton by *John Paterson*, who managed the Adam practice until 1791, with a hefty, symmetrical, castellated central block looking more to Inveraray than to the picturesque quality of Robert Adam's designs; Paterson's essays in the classical style were far more successful, and contemporaneously for the same client he executed Montgomerie House (1798–1804) at Tarbolton, the most important NEOCLASSICAL house in the county and its greatest loss. Glendoune House (1792–1800) is also by Paterson but, by contrast, is a neat three-bay villa with a projecting centre and bowed central bay at the rear following the mode popular in smaller houses (*see* above).

In the EARLY NINETEENTH CENTURY there are a number of neat villas such as Monkcastle (1802–5), Robertland (*c.* 1813) and

*After 1795, when work from the Adams ceased, Cairncross worked alone and may be responsible for some of the unattributed Georgian boxes in the county after that date (e.g. Wheatfield House, Ayr).

65 Swindridgemuir (*c.* 1815), that use giant angle pilasters or
pilastered bays and columned or pilastered doorpieces. The
64 influential design here may have been Fairlie House of 1781–7
by *David Henderson*, for Alexander Fairlie, an important
agricultural improver; it is a distinguished astylar composition,
but the use of broad angle pilasters is more readily associated
with *David Hamilton*, who is known to have designed Ladyland
House in this style in 1817–21, and may have had a hand in
Montgreenan House (1810–17), which bears the hallmarks of his
interpretation of Greek Revival style, planned with an oval lobby,
a central top-lit galleried staircase and elegant public rooms
overlooking terraced gardens. More severe in the new square
82 style is Coodham (*c.* 1826, possibly by *Smirke*), using Greek
Doric columns for the porch and a big bowed bay on the garden
front comparable to Montgreenan.

Symmetry was retained even in more PICTURESQUE houses,
66 such as St John's Cottage, near Maybole, a delightful villa of
c. 1820, its design taken from Richard Elsam's *Essay on Rural
Architecture* (published *c.* 1803), or the crenellated additions to
Cloncaird in 1819 by Robert Wallace and the Gothic embellish-
72 ments of Caprington Castle in 1829 by *Patrick Wilson*. But from
the 1820s, symmetry was sidelined, beginning with the new house
71 of Blairquhan by William Burn for the Hunter Blairs. In the
TUDOR GOTHIC style, it is an asymmetrical composition defined
by gables and turrets with a tower over the soaring central,
galleried hall and boasting Burn's skilful domestic planning.
Burn's assistant was *David Bryce*, who was paid for the Tudor
addition to Belleisle, Alloway, in 1830–1; Bryce provided a very
similar design for Cassillis in 1830–2 for the 2nd Marquis of Ailsa.
Burn and Bryce used a relaxed Scots Jacobean manner at Carnell
(1843), with pedimented dormerheads and square corbelled
angle turrets, a foretaste of the Scottish Baronial style. The Burn
model was used by *David Rhind* at Knockdolian (1843), a
compact gabled house with service quarters. Tudor detail is
found again at Tour House in its 1841 recasting in the manner
of *David Hamilton*, who was responsible for Dunlop House
73 1831–4, a prodigious NEO-JACOBEAN house awash with gables,
strapwork and diminutive domed turrets, taking its cue from the
C17 Glasgow College; a style carried on inside with dramatic
geometric panelled plaster ceilings. CASTELLATED GOTHIC of
a kind favoured by James Gillespie Graham was employed at
Craufurdland, 1830–4, to provide a theatrical frontispiece linking
the tower and the C17 range (which has in the Kings's Room a
fine plaster ceiling, the only example in the county). In the 1850s
75 Tudor detailing became more academic, seen in the self-
confident Knock Castle, 1851–3 by *J. T. Rochead*, the interior
decoration echoing the exterior.

The advent of the SCOTTISH BARONIAL style in the 1840s,
which David Bryce did much to popularize, aided by R. W.
Billings's magisterial volumes on *The Baronial and Ecclesiastical
Antiquities of Scotland* (1845–52), introduced a profound change
in the appreciation of ancient Scottish architecture and the

opportunities it afforded for contemporary building. Regional variations gave way to a relatively consistent national style often used to extend old towers in order to provide larger and lighter rooms for entertaining. *James Gillespie Graham* adopted the Baronial style for the large addition at Brodick Castle, 1844–6, 74 where its scale and bulk were the perfect foil to the old tower and the C17 extension, respecting but not imitating them. Drawing on detail from the earlier tower, *David Bryce* added an enormous range to Sorn Castle, 1845, continuing the chequered corbelling and parapet. On a smaller scale *David Cousin* added to Newark Castle in 1848–9, using Jacobean strapwork window heads, balconies and little angle turrets, complemented inside with Jacobean-style plasterwork in the drawing room combined with an exuberant Louis XV-style chimneypiece. As late as 1870–6 Bryce used the style in a severely pared-down manner at Glenapp Castle, a completely new build. 78

If deception was not an aim of Baronial architecture, romance surely was. In his restoration of Penkill Castle in 1857 Spencer 77 Boyd created an extraordinary fantasy embodying an imagined medieval culture, fulfilling both his antiquarian obsession and the spirit of the Pre-Raphaelites, the latter most sensationally in *William Bell Scott*'s staircase frescoes illustrating 'The King's 80 Quaire'. Several other houses are also remarkable for their C19 INTERIORS. The fashion for French-inspired design is first seen in the new drawing room at Bargany created for the Duchesse de Coigny in the 1860s in Louis XV taste with elegant plaster panels decorating the walls. At Auchendrane in the 1880s a delightful boudoir is decked out in a frothy Louis XVI manner. But most memorable is the Parisian chic interior inserted into 81 Craigengillan, a previously straightforward laird's house, by *Maison Jansen* of Paris. Prepared materials in a mix of Louis XV/XVI styles, for almost all the ground-floor rooms and the stair, were despatched from Paris and installation completed shortly before 1906. The Adam revival begins early in Ayrshire with *Wardrop & Reid*'s additions to Culzean in 1877 and the creation of a new dining room in sympathetic style. The Aesthetic Movement also influenced a number of interesting interiors. At Moorpark House, Kilbirnie, a villa of *c.* 1860, which had a major re-fit internally in the 1890s, the Gold Room is unexpectedly opulent, elaborately panelled with plenty of geometric plasterwork on the ceiling decorated with gilded and stencilled intertwined curves, flowers, fishes and leaves. Another notable example, of 1898–1902, is at Doonholm, Alloway, where a significant remodelling of the interior is probably by *A. N. Paterson*, with much Jacobean and Renaissance detail. At Sorn Castle *H. E. Clifford* introduced a fine Edwardian interior, with excellent woodwork. An unusually theatrical and ornate interior was put into Cloncaird *c.* 1905, in a thoroughly eclectic manner. But the most sympathetic and stylish additions and decorations are at Dumfries House by 56 *Robert Weir Schultz* for the 3rd Marquess of Bute, 1894–1908, where the wings and quadrants were dramatically enlarged to provide new suites of rooms including a room to house the

Gobelins tapestries, and a chapel (converted to a library and dining room in 1935).

Towards the end of the C19 and well into the next century the Arts and Crafts Movement was the biggest influence on the design and construction of new houses or additions and interior alterations to existing houses. Much was owed to Glasgow's thriving and inventive architectural practices and the wealth of their clients derived from commercial enterprise, coupled with ready access to the county via the railways. Black Clauchrie, built as a sporting lodge by *J. K. Hunter* (1898–1901) combines vernacular crowsteps and gables with a Renaissance-detailed doorcase into a bold asymmetrical composition. More refined are High Greenan also by Hunter (1910) and Blanefield (1913–19), by *James Miller*, characterized by large sweeping slate roofs in varying heights. The contemporary Kildonan by Miller (1914–23) is the last great country house in the county, events making it outmoded by the time it was complete. Arts and Crafts style at its quirkiest is seen at Noddsdale begun by Miller and given (1920) a thoroughgoing dressing of English-derived timber framing, jettying and elaborate chimneystacks recalling Norman Shaw's Cragside, by the talented local firm of *Fryers & Penman*. The rebuilding of Carlung by *J. Austen Laird*, 1932, looks back to C17 English manor houses.

Two houses by *Robert S. Lorimer* display his particular interpretation of Scots architecture of the C16 and C17. Rowallan, 1901–5, planned to be twice the size and still large, cleverly incorporates towers, turrets, dormerheads and crowsteps while decorative treatment is mainly saved for the very complete interior. His much smaller-scale extension to Bardrochat, 1906–8, sits comfortably into the hillside in pleasingly vernacular manner.

Tower house reconstructions are a feature of the later C20. At Aiket C18 attempts to give a tower house as near a symmetrical appearance as possible were reversed 1976–9 when a thoughtful re-creation, by *Robert and Katrina Clow*, created one of the most evocative impressions of a small tower house. At mid-C15 Law Castle Dr Anthony Phillips, *c.* 1990, with the help of *Ian Begg*, meticulously conserved the fabric, added a new roof and re-created a low caphouse turret. The more ruinous C16 Dunduff Castle received similar treatment.

Estate buildings

The country house required a variety of service buildings. LODGES often reflect in a modest way the design of the main house, but there is more architectural pretension at the W gates of Caprington Castle, which have two diminutive classical buildings, probably late C18, with pedimented tripartite windows breaking into the pedimented gables and linked to pairs of gatepiers and decorative cast-iron gates. There was a similar grouping at Culzean, the Cat Gates, of which gatepiers survive in the form of triumphal arches bearing *Coade* stone lionesses. The

Stockiehill and West Gate lodges to Dumfries House of *c*. 1810–15, with Palladian windows in the gables facing the road, show a greater practicality with their L-plans providing more accommodation. Two crenellated lodges were built *c*. 1820 at Lainshaw; at Sorn Castle *H. E. Clifford* took up the Scots Baronial detailing of *Bryce*'s work for his 1910 miniature fort-style gatehouse with a bold archway.

COACHHOUSES AND STABLES, frequently with a dressy front screening a simple courtyard behind, were a necessity. At Barskimming the stables (1774) serving the late C18 house have a conspicuous central tower with a domed cupola over the arched entrance; there is a grander and larger version of 1802, still in use, at Craigengillan with the tower tiered like a church steeple. The late C18 stables block at Blair Castle is essentially classical but with crenellations and quatrefoils while Fullarton by *Robert Adam* (1790) is in his Castle Style. In 1806 *David Hamilton* designed the classical pilastered and pedimented frontispiece for the stable court at Sorn Castle.

All country house estates included a set of buildings associated with the supply of food. WALLED GARDENS were *de rigueur*. Those surviving, although often out of use, mostly date from the later C18 but have their origin in the garden enclosures and orchards which surrounded tower houses in the C17; the most extensive examples are at Culzean, begun in 1782 and enlarged several times in the C19 when glasshouses were added. Other examples include Auchincruive (1773–4), with parts of the glasshouse range incorporating material of that date, Blairquhan (1820s), Carnell (1843) and Swindridgemuir (early C19 incorporating C18 material). DOOCOTS to provide protein are less numerous in this pastoral county than in arable areas, but there are two important beehive doocots: one at Dunure Castle (C15/16), the   42
other at Crossraguel (C16); lectern-type cotes are at Dumfries House (1671, serving the earlier house) and Eglinton Country Park (C18); at Treesbank is an octagonal brick-built example of 1771. ICE HOUSES, usually egg- or bottle-shaped, needed to extend food life and enable special types of cuisine, occur frequently, late C18 at Brodick, well-preserved at Blairquhan *c*. 1823, two at Culzean, one set into the later C18 viaduct, the second early C19. KENNELS for the hunting dogs usually associated with keepers' cottages are numerous, of the 1820s at Blairquhan, at Brodick mid-C19 using Tudor detail. GAME LARDERS are found on estates with a sporting tradition, e.g. Annick Lodge, of *c*. 1800, in a small pavilion with Gothic detailing; Dougarie Lodge, Arran,   70
is of the mid-C19 polygonal type created from tree trunks in the rustic manner.

The C19 saw frequent additions to estates. The fashion for keeping ornamental birds and rare animals is reflected in *Robert Lugar*'s *cottage orné* and aviary at Culzean *c*. 1815 and the Pagoda   69
c. 1815 with housing for animals and birds. The early C19 saw a real interest in sea bathing, and the Round House on the shore below Culzean Castle was provided for a changing room, close to the hot and cold Plunge Bath.

Landscaping

Around 1700 William Abercrummie records that most dwellings in Carrick had gardens for produce and orchards, and the same would have been the case in Kyle and Cunningham. Eglinton Castle (dem.) had gardens, orchards and parks in the early C17, and pleasure grounds by the C18. The *allées* E of Dumfries House, restored by the 3rd and 4th Marquesses, are part of *William Adam*'s involvement in the earlier C18; in the mid C18 a number of wooded mounds to the S of the house were created, as features of extensive views, the Avenue Bridge of 1760–1 serving the more picturesque layout with its introduction of clumps of trees. The Gothic Temple Lodge, completed in 1768 and never used as a lodge, was part of the more romantically planned landscape. The Culzean landscape is given its informal character by the use of castle-style buildings, particularly in the vicinity of the castle itself, and by the early C19 buildings around the Swan Pond, a romantic impression encouraged by curving walks through natural woodland. *c.* 1823 *William Sawrey Gilpin* modified George Robertson's 1774 work at Bargany, creating a large lake, laying out new approaches and setting the scene for extensive dramatic tree and rhododendron planting still visible today. At Eglinton, the C18 pleasure grounds were extended in the early C19 to provide the backdrop for the famed Tournament of 1839, one of the first manifestations of the Romantic phase of the Gothic Revival. The Tournament was a reaction to the absence of cere-
68 mony at Queen Victoria's coronation and the surviving Tournament Bridge provides a taste of its medieval splendour. At Brodick the walled enclosure was greatly enhanced by the discoveries of the C19 plant hunters, their new species enabling the introduction of dramatic planting in the 1840s to produce a highland garden that matched its setting. The mid-C19 Bavarian Summer House, a highly rustic creation, slotted seamlessly into this setting. The craggy setting of Craigengillan is reflected in the substantial rock garden by the fashionable *Pulham & Son*, 1909–10.

COMMUNICATIONS AND TRANSPORT

Roads and bridges

The reappearance after the Roman withdrawal of ROADS suitable for wheeled traffic probably took place in Ayrshire in the C13, perhaps even the late C12, as the power of the nascent Scottish state spread into the SW, and communication would have been required between Edinburgh, Ayr and, particularly from the late C13, with Ireland. Although a myth, the Ayrshire cannibal Sawney Bean (whose cave is still pointed out to visitors N of Ballantrae) is a humanization (or demonization) of the perils of the road S beyond Ayr to Galloway and Ireland. Other roads would have connected Ayrshire with Glasgow, probably following the valley of the Garnock N through Beith and Kilbirnie, and Irvine with Edinburgh, along the River Irvine, broadly following the line now

suggested for the Roman road from Loudoun Hill. There would
have been few roads on Arran until the late C18.

The earliest MEDIEVAL BRIDGES were wooden, as at Ayr, but
were gradually replaced by stone bridges, such as the Auld Brig,   86
Ayr, which may have existed as early as 1491, and the steeply
pitched single-arch Auld Brig o' Doon, Alloway, traditionally C15,   87
but in appearance C17. Both have survived because of their associations with Burns, the bridge at Alloway having provided the
scene of Tam o' Shanter's narrow escape from the witches. A
bridge at Irvine is recorded in 1533, though the street name
Bridgegate is found in 1506, and repaired in 1578; in the early
C17 Pont could record that at Irvine the river 'is over passed by
faire stone Bridge'. Other early to mid-C18 bridges are across the
Ayr at Sorn (the steeply pitched Old Bridge), Riccarton Bridge,
Kilmarnock, across the Irvine, traditionally dated 1723 (though
its present appearance is due to reconstruction in 1806) and Stair
Bridge, Stair, again across the Ayr, dated 1745.

Although legislation in the C17 had been designed to improve
roads, e.g. an Act of 1617 stipulating the width of roads between
market towns, and requiring their upkeep by inhabitants of parishes along their route, and an Act of 1669 introducing statutory
road labour and taxation for road purposes, little effectual was
achieved. John Campbell, 4th Earl of Loudoun, began to make
roads on his Ayrshire estates in 1733, but in 1768 Montgomerie
of Coilsfield could still say that in Ayrshire 'most, if not all of the
great roads leading through it [are] next to impassable for six
months of the year'. The C18 saw two great boosts to road building: military and commercial. The Jacobite uprisings of 1715 and
1745-6 had alerted the state to the necessity of moving troops
around the country expeditiously, while the changes wrought in
agricultural and industrial capacity and output required improved
communication between the producer and the market. TURN-
PIKE ROADS, for which travellers were charged, had been known
in England since the mid C17. The Ayr Road Act of 1767 authorized twenty-four turnpikes, mainly in the N of the county. A
second act, of 1774, extended the network into Carrick; the
combined result is a pattern of roads that remains recognizable
today. Responsibility lay with the Turnpike Trustees, among
whom, from 1787 to 1798, was *John Loudon McAdam*, whose
initial experiments with road surfaces had been made at Sauchrie, the estate he acquired upon his return from the United States
in 1783. Although tradition has it otherwise, he left in Ayrshire
'no road that could be considered to represent his early work,
nor any indication that he had . . . yet formulated his prescrip-
tion for a robust road surface'.*

Hand-in-hand with the turnpikes came a flurry of LATE C18
AND EARLY C19 BRIDGES, often of a more ornate form than the
earlier crossings. One such was *Alexander Stevens*'s ill-fated classically garbed original New Bridge, Ayr, of 1786-9 (dem. 1877),
chosen by the Town Council in preference to *Robert Adam*'s

*D. McClure, Tolls and Tacksmen, *AANHS* (1994).

design of 1785. Other substantial examples include the two-arched late C18 Garnock Bridge, Kilwinning, widened in 1857, *John Herbertson*'s Irvine Bridge of 1825–7 (dem. 1973) and *Laughlen*'s three-arched Galston Bridge of 1838–9. Smaller bridges of the period include the pleasingly decorative Drumgirnan Bridge, Kilkerran, of 1799 by *John Rutherford*. Although on a public road, this last example had been conceived as part of the parkland setting of Kilkerran (for other estate bridges *see* p. 52). The major late C19 road bridge in the county is the present New Bridge, Ayr, of 1877–9 by *George M. Cunningham* of *Blyth & Cunningham* of Edinburgh. It is a five-arch flat-spanned bridge designed to exude strength and stability. A little later are two interesting footbridges: Turner's Bridge, Ayr, of 1899–1900 by *John Eaglesham*, a slender iron bridge on stone piers, and the suspension bridge at Stair, also *c.* 1900, associated with the adjacent hone stone works.

A charming early C20 adornment of roads in Carrick were cast-iron FINGERPOSTS. The best-preserved is probably that at Kilkerran Station. New roads included by-passes for Ayr and Kilmarnock, a new road layout for Irvine New Town, and a motorway from Glasgow, across Fenwick Moor, designed from 2002 by *Balfour Beatty*, and opened in 2005. At Howford, where the Mauchline to Cumnock road crosses the Ayr, the replacement of a notorious bottleneck also produced the period's best bridge: the concrete Ballochmyle Bridge of 1959–62 by *F. A. Macdonald & Partners*, carried high above the river on two graceful arch ribs. C21 bridges include The Bridge of Scottish Invention, Irvine, 2000 by *Bennett Associates*, linking the former Big Idea, a millennium project, with Irvine Beach Park. With its retractable central section, and steel superstructure celebrating Scottish inventors, it is a remarkable artistic and engineering *tour de force*.

Harbours and lighthouses

The coast has several HARBOURS. The shelter provided by the river mouths at Ayr, Girvan and Irvine was an important, crucial factor in the establishment of settlements at these points in the early medieval period, while Lamlash, on Arran, enjoyed the protection offered by Holy Isle. Originally ships and boats would have been pulled up onto the sand and mud flats, where shipbuilding and other trades would have been carried on. Ayr was, and remains, the pre-eminent port. Embanking and lining the riverside with quays began in the C17, though little that is pre-C18 now remains. A similar process took place at Irvine, but here the original harbour site, at the foot of Seagate, quickly proved inaccessible to larger vessels; a new harbour was formed nearer the sea, and much of what survives is C19. Girvan's harbour is the least developed of the three, and it is possible to imagine how it must have looked originally. At Saltcoats, where the bay afforded some shelter for boats exporting salt and coal from the locality, improvements were made in 1686–1700 by *Robert Cunninghame*, who built an L-shaped rubble pier. This was extended in 1805, by which time the rush to profit from the export of Ayrshire coal was on in earnest. For this purpose, the Duke of Portland first promoted a harbour at Troon in 1806 (built 1808–19, the engineer *William Jessop*) linked by railway (*see* below) to the Duke's mines at Kilmarnock. At the same time *Thomas Telford*, in 1805, prepared plans for the Earl of Eglinton to construct a monumental harbour at Ardrossan, which was to be connected to Glasgow by canal. Troon was rebuilt in the later C19 and Ardrossan extended with further dock basins in 1886–92 by *John Strain*, who had previously completed the Slip Dock at Ayr; *Thomas Meik* designed the earlier Wet Dock at Ayr in 1873–8. Buildings associated with harbours include the former harbourmaster's house of *c.* 1805 at Saltcoats and *Martin Boyd*'s Automatic Tide Marker of 1906 at Irvine.

The small, partially rock-cut harbour at Dunure was engineered by *Charles Abercrombie*, and built in 1810–11. A PIER, of which a fragment remains, was built at Largs in 1834, while the small harbour at Millport had been begun *c.* 1750 in connection with the island's role as a station for a Revenue anti-smuggling cutter; it was reconstructed in 1797, with a pier added in 1883. Steamer piers, now all demolished, graced a number of Arran villages, including Lamlash (1885, by *Thomas D. Weir*; the offices, with a squat tower, survive), Lochranza (1888), Whiting Bay (1899) and Brodick, where a pier reconstructed in 1993 now provides the island's link with the mainland. Lamlash became an important station for the Navy in the C18, and continued in such a role through the First World War – the village's Community Centre is a corrugated-iron former Admiralty canteen of 1914 by *Speirs & Co.* – and the entire Firth of Clyde played an important part in the planning of, and training for, the Second World War.*

Shipping, and harbours, require LIGHTHOUSES, and there are a number in the Firth of Clyde. The Old Lighthouse, Little Cumbrae, was erected in 1756–7 by *James Wyatt*, and was a stone tower which carried a coal-fired beacon, while similar beacon towers were erected *c.* 1772 on Lady Isle, and in 1811 on Horse Island. Early conventional lighthouses include Pladda Lighthouse, of 1790 by *Thomas Smith*, with an auxiliary light added in 1800 by *Robert Stevenson*, who also designed the New Lighthouse, Little Cumbrae, of 1793. *D. & T. Stevenson* built Turnberry Lighthouse in 1871–3, Holy Isle (Inner) Lighthouse in 1877 and Ailsa Craig Lighthouse in as late, surprisingly, as 1883–6. At Skelmorlie two MEASURED MILE MARKERS of 1866 were used by Robert Napier & Son, shipbuilders, for speed tests and sea trials.

Railways and aviation

Horse-drawn WAGGONWAYS, carrying coal from the pits to the coast, had existed in the county in the late C18. One radiated out

---

* The interwar Hollywood Hotel, Greenock Road, Largs (dem.), was requisitioned by the War Office in 1941. In 1943, as HMS *Warren*, it hosted a conference at which the nature of the reinvasion of the European Continent was agreed upon.

from Ayr harbour to pits in Newton-upon-Ayr and St Quivox, traces of which can be seen in the line of Waggon Road, Newton, and, in the form of cuttings and bridge piers, near Auchincruive. Other systems existed in the Saltcoats and Stevenston area. In 1806 the Duke of Portland initiated the county's first RAILWAY, linking his coal pits in the Kilmarnock area with his new harbour at Troon (*see* above) and also planned by *William Jessop*. It had a number of engineering problems to solve, including crossing Shewalton Moss, and spanning the Irvine at Gatehead, where a 95 four-arched stone viaduct was thrown across the river, now regarded as the oldest of its kind in the world. A similar enterprise was undertaken in 1827 with the authorization of the Ardrossan & Johnstone Railway, which superseded the Earl of Eglinton's abortive plans for a canal between his harbour and Glasgow. Passenger services between Ardrossan and Dirrans, near Kilwinning, began in 1834. In 1837 the Glasgow, Paisley, Kilmarnock & Ayr Railway was commenced, with a line from Ayr to Glasgow, via Irvine and Dalry, where it was joined by a branch from Kilmarnock, and also incorporating a junction at Kilwinning with the existing line to Ardrossan. The line opened in stages between 1839 (in time to convey passengers to Irvine for the Eglinton Tournament) and 1840, when through running began. The line to Kilmarnock was opened in 1843. The company merged with the Glasgow Dumfries & Carlisle Railway in 1850 to form the Glasgow & South-Western Railway (GSWR), and thereafter the system expanded rapidly, reaching Dalmellington and Maybole in 1856, Girvan in 1860, West Kilbride in 1878 and Largs in 1885. A direct line to Kilmarnock, via Stewarton, was opened in 1873. The system reached its fullest extent in the years around 1900, with Darvel added to the network in 1896 and Catrine in 1903, and the line onward from Darvel to Strathaven (Lanarkshire) in 1905.

John Miller, of *Grainger & Miller*, was engineer to the GSWR and its predecessors. He was succeeded in 1856 by *William Johnstone*, who held the position until 1874 and was succeeded in turn by *Andrew Galloway*, who retired in 1885. The line between Ayr and Glasgow necessitated two VIADUCTS, one across the Garnock at Kilwinning, and the Queen's Bridge, across the Irvine, 2 km. N of Irvine Station. The line from Kilmarnock to Dumfries, however, made much fuller use of Miller's ability, for, as well as a tunnel at Mauchline, it involved the twenty-three-arched Kilmarnock Viaduct, which strides across the town and the river, the Bank Viaduct at Cumnock, and the matchless seven-arch Ballochmyle Viaduct, built in 1846–8. The 56-m.-wide central span was, when built, the largest masonry railway arch in the world. Nothing on the subsequent lines quite compares with these early structures, though the line S from Girvan, built between 1872 and 1876, and engineered by *John Miller Jun.*, required several viaducts along the Stinchar valley.

Early RAILWAY STATIONS are modelled on traditional dwelling houses, e.g. Glengarnock (*c.* 1840) and Waterside by Patna, built by *Young & Co.* of Glasgow in 1857–8. As the railways evolved, the station's function and form changed. Kilwinning was rebuilt in 1862–3, Maybole in 1879–80, and Saltcoats in 1894, while the stations of the major burghs reflected the aggregated self-assurance of town and company. Kilmarnock Station was rebuilt in a confident Castellated Gothic in 1873–7, following the opening of the direct line to Glasgow, while Ayr Station was reconstructed in 1883–6 by *Andrew Galloway* in a lavish textbook French Renaissance, and incorporated a grandly scaled and decorated hotel, evidence of the social changes wrought by the railways in the C19. Of special interest are the stations by *James Miller* for the GSWR in his early easy Arts and Crafts style: Troon (*c.* 1890–2, the biggest and best), West Kilbride and Prestwick Town (both *c.* 1900). Although his *tour de force* is at Wemyss Bay, just over the border in Renfrewshire, the zenith of Miller's association with the GSWR is the fabulously scaled Turnberry Hotel, 117 built in 1904–6 as a hotel for golfers (earlier than Gleneagles) and connected to the outside world by a light railway which also carried Ayrshire's early potatoes to market. Some stations were rebuilt during the C20, e.g. Largs, of 1935–6 in a simplified Modern style, of which little now remains, and Girvan, 1948–9, which demonstrates how the curved corners and strong horizontality of the 1930s reappeared between the Second World War and the Festival of Britain. The latest station is at Prestwick International Airport: by *Holford Associates*, 1994, with a striking silhouette caused by encasing the stairwells in tight-fitting red blockwork.

The sandy coastal plains and broad beaches of Ayrshire suited pioneers of AVIATION. Of particular interest were Turnberry Point and the lands between Prestwick and Monkton. Both were used for military purposes in the First World War, while Loch Doon was the locus of a school of aerial gunnery. Turnberry and Prestwick were again used by the RAF during the Second World War, with Prestwick's peripheral position and fog-free record making it an ideal centre for air links with the United States. At Turnberry is the former control tower, now converted to a house. After the war the commercial side of Prestwick aerodrome was expanded, and between 1954 and 1964 it was rebuilt by *Joseph L. Gleave*. The buildings survive, but the interiors are now to an anodyne inter- and multinational standard.

INDUSTRIAL BUILDINGS

Many early industries were particular to one or two sites, or became associated with particular place. One such in Ayrshire was the SALT INDUSTRY, which was obviously restricted to coastal locations. There are the remains of an C18 salt-panning works at the Cock of Arran, N of Lochranza, but little survives in Saltcoats, which takes its name (first recorded in 1548) from the industry. The most telling remains are the two late C18 Salt 91 Pan houses in Maryborough Road, Prestwick, which have vaulted brick ground floors and residential accommodation above.

Ayrshire's best-known industry has been COAL MINING. The earliest industrial-scale mining of coal was at or near the surface, particularly on the estates of Kilwinning Abbey, and elsewhere in the Garnock valley. Such mines would usually have been in the form of bell pits, which were progressively worked outward from a central shaft until they collapsed. This remained the usual method of mining into the early C18, and was also used at mines of that period, in the E of the county, around Muirkirk, where the dimpled land-forms caused by bell-pit collapse can still be identified.

From the early C18 the pumping engine, developed by Newcomen, prevented flooding in deeper mines and this, coupled with other new technologies, enabled the industry to spread throughout the central part of the county, where coal was found at increasing depths. The major monument of this period is the ruined engine house at Auchenharvie Park, Saltcoats, built in 1719 to house the second Newcomen engine in Scotland, and which pumped water from the collieries of Cunninghame of Auchenharvie. Further expansion continued to take place throughout the late C18 and the C19, transforming formerly rural centres such as Auchinleck and Ochiltree into communities of mine workers; the mid to late C19 also saw the withdrawal of the coal industry from areas such as the Garnock valley, where the coal had been worked out. Although much of Ayrshire's coal was consumed in its houses and factories, a considerable proportion was exported to Ireland, and this is reflected in the building or reconfiguration of the county's ports, e.g. Ayr, Ardrossan and Troon, for this purpose.

C20 mining was largely an industry of consolidation and technical advance. The introduction of electricity enabled greater subterranean areas to be worked from a single shaft, so that men and machinery were increasingly centralized at a few pits, and by the late C20, these were mostly confined to central Ayrshire, e.g. Glenburn (Prestwick), Auchincruive (at Mossblown), Highhouse and Barony (Auchinleck), Kames (Muirkirk) and Knockshinnoch (New Cumnock). Of these little remains: at Mossblown, the former pit-head baths, smartly converted into a house, and at Highhouse the engine house of c. 1896, with a steel head-frame of c. 1968. To the NE of Dalmellington, the mammiform spoil heap of the Pennyvenie Colliery is an unmistakable element in the landscape, but the pre-eminent feature from this period is the iconic welded steel A-frame from the Barony Colliery, of 1945, now pressed into service as a memorial to an industry and its men. Brave plans for late C20 expansion came to naught: Killoch colliery, W of Ochiltree, was sunk from 1952, but was beset by geological problems, and while *Egon Riss*'s pit-head buildings (1952–9) remain, they have been shorn of their winding-gear towers and much other detail. From the late C20, coal extraction in the county has been solely by open-cast methods, which rapidly transform huge swathes of countryside, but require little, and leave less, in the way of built structures.

Ironstone was found, and exploited, in many parts of the county, often in association with, or close to, coal mines. As a

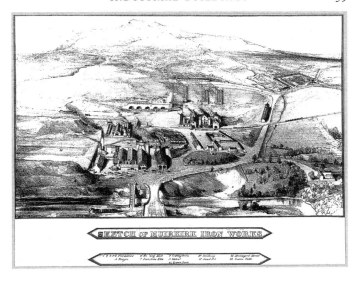

Muirkirk Ironworks.
Sketch, *c.* 1840

consequence IRON WORKS appeared widely from the late C18.
The earliest were in E Ayrshire: the remains of a small mid-C18
foundry can be found on the banks of the Ayr at Tarereoch, w of
Muirkirk, and larger works were in operation in Muirkirk and
Glenbuck by 1800. Others followed throughout the C19, e.g. at
Glengarnock, Hurlford (where the works came to specialize in
propellers), Lugar and Waterside by Patna. All have closed; the
site of the immense works at Glengarnock, which produced both
iron and steel until 1986, is now unrecognizable. The most complete and significant site, though surprisingly little-known, is the
former Dalmellington Iron Company works at Waterside, which
began in 1847, and converted to brickmaking in the C20. The
wonderful Italianate engine house, dated 1847, survives, as do
elements of the furnace bank, two late C19 brick chimneys, and
the C20 brick kilns.

The TEXTILE INDUSTRY started in the home, with handloom
weaving. C18 weavers' cottages are a significant aspect of many
villages, such as Crosshill, and the restored examples at Cathcartston, Dalmellington, give a flavour of the internal conditions,
with the loom at one end and the living quarters at the other.
The first industry in Ayrshire to profit from mechanization and
the development of factory-based production was the COTTON
INDUSTRY. The mill at Catrine, founded in 1787 by the entre-
preneur David Dale and Claud Alexander of Ballochmyle, was
amongst the earliest erected in Scotland. Dale had previously
been involved at New Lanark, and he and Alexander built a
village for their workers, with a brewery and other facilities. There

were also cotton mills in Ayr (founded in the late C18), Irvine, and Kilmarnock, which had a large number of shawl-printing works, while others continued to be built throughout the C19, such as Joseph Hood & Co.'s 1867 Greenholm Power Loom factory, Newmilns. There was an equivalent change in the manufacture of WOOLLEN GOODS, associated with which are the early C19 mill at Waterside by Fenwick, the Bridgend Mills, Dalry, of 1873, for Thomas Biggart & Co. (dem.) or William Templeton's 1824 blanket mill at Skeldon, Hollybush near Dalrymple. There was also increasing specialization: as well as shawl printing, Kilmarnock also developed an extensive CARPET INDUSTRY, though there is little architectural evidence of it, and THREAD MANUFACTURE became a particular speciality of the upper Garncok valley. In Kilbirnie, especially, this skill mutated into the manufacture of NET AND TWINE, particularly for the fishing industry. The major mills were the Dennyholm Mills, founded by W. & J. Knox in 1845 (dem. 1969); in 1864 they also acquired and converted the Stoneyholm cotton mill for this purpose. Stoneyholm is now the most impressive C19 mill complex surviving in Ayrshire. LACE was handmade by the weavers of the Irvine valley until 1876 when a local weavers' agent, Alexander Morton, founded a mill in Darvel, using machinery from Nottingham. The industry flourished, and by the Second World War, there were twenty or so mills in Darvel and Newmilns. The few survivors are early C20, mostly in Newmilns, and many are in alternative uses. The mills at Greenholm, Newmilns, create an urban industrial ambience not now to be found elsewhere in the county.

In the burghs, restrictions ensured that new enterprises of the C18 and C19, as well as noxious industries, tended to be built outwith their boundaries: at Ayr N of the river in Newton and Wallacetown, and also within the Citadel, and at Irvine, across the river in Fullarton. Trade restrictions were looser in Kilmarnock, which enabled it to respond better to the industrial changes of the late C18. As well as the carpets and shawls previously mentioned, the town had cotton and woollen mills, two industrially sized breweries, an important bonnet-making industry, which it shared with Stewarton, and other industrial buildings associated with its rural hinterland, such as GRAIN AND SEED STORES, of which one impressive example founded in 1850 remains in St Marnock Street, and whisky bonds, such as *Gabriel Andrew*'s impressive range in Strand Street, of 1879.

Kilmarnock also developed a significant ENGINEERING INDUSTRY, most notably in the spheres of water engineering and railway locomotives. In 1855 Thomas Kennedy began to manufacture his patented water meter, and ten years later founded the Glenfield Company to produce machines for the meter works. The companies merged in the late C19 as *Glenfield & Kennedy Ltd*, becoming the world's foremost water engineers, providing everything from the familiar lion-headed drinking fountains to valves for major dams. The company closed in the late C20, and its extensive site comprehensively cleared. Andrew Barclay first began to build railway locomotives in Kilmarnock in 1847, when the first section of his Caledonian Works was begun. He flourished, and was joined by competitors, while the works of the Glasgow & South-Western Railway were at nearby Hurlford. Much reduced, the industry continues, in modern premises, while Barclay's original, and much extended, engineering complex, with his private observatory on the roof, has been converted for residential use.

The towns of the Garnock valley, especially Beith, developed an important FURNITURE INDUSTRY from the mid C19. The factories themselves have been lost, but at Auchengree, Longbar, is a foundry founded c. 1823 by Andrew Kerr, and rebuilt c. 1878, by which time it was specializing in wood-turning machines for the Beith factories. In Maybole, neither the shoe industry nor Alexander Jack's agricultural implement works have left an architectural legacy, though the presence of these industries here, one using a by-product (leather) of the dairy industry, and the other servicing the farming community, illustrates some of the complexities of the urban–rural relationship. Mention should be made of Andrew Kay & Co., of Mauchline, who have been making CURLING STONES, originally from Ailsa Craig granite, since the C19, initially in the old mill at Haugh, and since 1912 in the plain early C19 Victoria Works, built to manufacture Mauchline Ware snuff boxes. The Water of Ayr & Tam o' Shanter Hone Stone Works at Stair is another important survival.

C20 industrial buildings, although larger and often obtrusive in the landscape, lack much architectural distinction. Easily the best is the building at Prestwick Airport which began life as the Palace of Engineering at the 1938 Empire Exhibition, Glasgow, and was brought to Prestwick in 1940 for wartime aircraft production. Another relic of the Empire Exhibition, the South African Pavilion, survives at the large Nobel Explosives (later ICI) site at Stevenston, founded by Alfred Nobel in the late C19. For the second half of the C20 one should note the flexible INDUSTRIAL UNITS designed by *Irvine Development Corporation* from the late 1970s (e.g. South Newmoor, Irvine), which with their simple harled shells, timber fascias and strong graphics, established a style that became the norm for similar developments throughout the country. *David Hutchison & Associates'* Isle of Arran Distillery, Lochranza, of 1996–7, reinterprets the traditional form in a clean, uncomplicated way.

The development of coal GAS owed much to an Ayrshireman, William Murdoch of Lugar, and the first successful experiments with gas lighting were carried out in the late C18 at Muirkirk. Many urban gas works were in operation by the 1830s, e.g. Ayr (1826), Beith and Stewarton (both 1832). The mid-C19 gas house at Culzean Castle has been restored, as a memorial to Murdoch, and conveys something of the character of a C19 gas works. ELECTRICITY works were established in the larger towns in the earlier part of the C20 (at Ayr and Kilmarnock in conjunction with the introduction of publicly owned tram systems). Neo-Georgian offices of the Kilmarnock Electricity Board remain, as do a few examples of the Ayrshire Electricity Authority's brick junction houses (e.g. in Monkton, and in Main Street, Prestwick). The county's two present nuclear power stations, Hunterston 'A' (1953–64 by *Howard V. Lobb & Partners*, closed 1989) and Hunterston 'B' (1967–76 by *Robert Matthew, Johnson-Marshall & Partners*) have come to the end of their useful life. A third power station is presently proposed for the Hunterston peninsula. There are a number of major RESERVOIRS in the county; the most rewarding is Afton Reservoir, New Cumnock, of 1935–9 by *William Reid*, decked out, with merited civic pride, in muscular Baronial.

RURAL AND AGRICULTURAL BUILDINGS

The source of much of Ayrshire's wealth has always been the land. The climate is temperate, with rain to encourage the growth of grass. This lends itself to DAIRY FARMING, and this is the industry (for such it now is) with which Ayrshire is most closely associated. The Ayrshire breed is Scotland's premier breed of dairy cow, with a worldwide reputation, while Dunlop cheese and Ayrshire bacon (from whey-fed pigs) built their own national fame on the back of this industry.

The contemporary agricultural landscape, with its large fields, bounded by hedges and stone walls, and sheltering belts of woodland plantation, is largely a product of the late C18 and early C19, when landlords, factors and estate managers pioneered the enclosure of land and restructuring of the farming industry.

Evidence of the PRE-ENCLOSURE landscape is rare. Arran, where the geomorphology is different, and where the late C18 changes were predicated on the creation of large sheep farms, provides the best examples, such as High Corrie (Corrie) and Thunderguy, with largely single-storey cottages scattered in a seemingly random pattern. On the mainland, the best example is perhaps the scatter of cottages associated with Auchmannoch House, perhaps early C18 in origin, though the layout of some farms betrays their origins in a pre-enclosure fermtoun. Some farmhouses also survive from this period, such as the single-storey C17 Baidland Manor (Dalry), and the crowstepped two-bay Drumbuie (Barrmill), dated to 1736. The latter was originally thatched, as was commonplace throughout the county, often using heather thatch.

AGRICULTURAL IMPROVEMENT came to Ayrshire in the late C18, encouraged by the major landowners but also by visionary men such as Bruce Campbell of Sornbeg, and Alexander Fairlie of Fairlie, who improved their own estates, and acted as factors for others. Enterprising farmers from elsewhere, such as Essex-born John Bulley (†1803), employed at Culzean from 1775, were engaged as estate managers, and did much to improve stock breeding and arable techniques.

The NEW STEADINGS associated with improvement were usually stone-built, increasingly commonly roofed in slate (imported from Easdale and Ballachulish as a return cargo for the ships exporting Ayrshire coal thither). A standard pattern evolved of a central farmhouse, with projecting wings (one a byre, the other a barn and other storage). All three elements tended to be single-storey, though some farmhouses must have been two-storey from the beginning. Increasing prosperity was usually reflected in the mid C19 by rebuilding the farmhouse: Skeoch (Mauchline) is a typical example. The longhouse, which had been the standard pre-enclosure pattern, survived in the rugged, less productive areas of the county, and remained the pattern in these areas. One example is Lochgoin, rebuilt in 1858, while the long-abandoned Cairniebottom, E of Muirkirk, of c. 1835, has been the subject of recent archaeological investigation.*

Although most steadings remained firmly in the vernacular tradition, many estates evolved a distinct architectural style. The Cassillis and Culzean estate of the Kennedys is one such, and their early C19 castellated farms are found frequently, e.g. West Enoch (Maybole) or Dunure Mill. On the farms that were farmed 'in-hand', the architecture could be more formal, especially as these were often close to the main house and within the policies. The foremost example is the Home Farm at Culzean, of 1788–9 by *Robert Adam*, as much architectural conceit as functional steading, and the template for the smaller estate buildings, within and without the policies. Others include Gibbsyard (Auchin-cruive) of c. 1760, and Fairlie Mains (Fairlie House, 1812), both with towers over arched openings, similar to stables such as Fullarton or Craigengillan (*see* above). At Dougarie Lodge, Arran, a Hamilton property, the home farm of c. 1850 is a roman-ticized courtyard of towers and mock-ruins.

The late C19 was a period of agricultural experimentation, though largely in stock and crop improvement, rather than in building design. At Myremill, near Drumellan, in the 1850s Prim-rose Kennedy 'sacrificed a large portion of his fortune' (*Ayrshire Post*, 17 July 1890) on ultimately impractical schemes, including the piping of sewage throughout the farm. More palatably, the Duke of Portland established a model farm at Balgreen (Hollybush) in 1883 (by *R. S. Ingram*), but arranged it on very traditional lines, with an internal courtyard.

In the C20 farming has been subject to increasing mechaniza-tion, and consolidation of holdings. The results, architecturally, are unrewarding if understandable. Those farms still in produc-tion need larger sheds, and the farmhouses have suffered from misguided improvement, while others, out of agricultural use, have become 'courtyard' housing developments, with, mostly, equally depressing results. As a result, few farms appear in this gazetteer, though many retain, in part, their essential C19 core, and dominate the architectural experience in rural Ayrshire. Munnoch (Dalry), converted in 2007–9 by *Frank Hirst*, is of note, though largely for the bravura of the new components.

---

*R. Murray and B. Walker, 'Cairniebottom, East Ayrshire: case study of a nineteenth-century smallholding', *Vernacular Building* 34, 2010–11.

Many quasi-industrial endeavours were deeply integrated into the rural economy. Since medieval times, most tenant farmers were obliged to have their corn ground at a GRAIN MILL belonging to the local landowner. Surviving examples range in size from Sea Mill, Seamill, to a series of large mills, mostly rebuilt in the late C19 (mills are notoriously prone to fires), such as Alloway and Dutch Mills, Alloway, Bridge Mill, Girvan, and Dalgarven Mill, where much of the original structures associated with post-fire rebuilding in 1869 can be seen. The dairy industry is evidenced by a number of CREAMERIES and margarine factories, most notably at Mauchline, and at Torrylin, Lagg. The quarrying and processing of lime for agricultural purposes was also important; the quarries were often small-scale, but a large quarry at Craighead, Dailly, is associated with a substantial C19 processing plant, while earlier, probably early C19 LIMEKILNS exist throughout the county, e.g. at Dunure.

In the C18, and until the late C19, the parish MANSE would have been the most imposing house in most villages. Kirkland, Dunlop, was in existence by 1566. It is a scaled-down L-plan rubble-built house with defensive and ecclesiastical details. By the mid C17 the heritors were expected to supply a manse, and glebe, appropriate to the parish. In those turbulent times little was immediately done, though the earlier part of the former manse at Kilmory is of 1701–3, and was initially thatched. Progress had to wait for the more settled late C18, with the result that many manses resonate in style with contemporary mansions. Of these classical C18 manses, the grandest is Traboyack, Straiton, recast in 1795, and incorporating a remarkable mid-C18 interior. Others include Dunlop (1781), Fenwick (1783), Stevenston (1787), and a series by the Kilmaurs builder-architect *John Swan*: Kilmaurs (1779–81), Dundonald (Glenfoot House, 1783–4), Symington (Symington House, 1785–6). The manses built in the first years of the C19 are mostly in Carrick, but remain in the classical tradition: Dailly (1802–3) and Stair (1805–7) are both by *James Rutherford*, while Barr (Barskaig House, 1803–5) is by *Robert McCord* and the austere Craigie (House of Craigie, 1807–8) is unattributed. Somewhat grander are the next generation, e.g. the pleasing Girvan (1818, by *Alexander Jardine*), the substantial manse at Colmonell (1820–2), Kilbride Manse, Lamlash (1827) and the late, Adamesque Tarbolton (*James Paton*, 1836). Hereafter, manses can barely be distinguished from the growing number of country and suburban villas in an increasing variety of styles, e.g. the Burnian Kirkmichael (Gemilston), also begun in 1836.

BURGH, TOWN AND VILLAGE BUILDINGS

Settlements before 1750

Formally chartered BURGHS were first created in Scotland in the C12, though none in Ayrshire is earlier than the first years of the C13. Royal burghs, which answered directly to the monarch, had a monopoly of foreign trade. Domestic commerce could only be

carried on in royal burghs, and in burghs of barony. They had
the right to hold markets, and to exact taxes and dues, while their
citizens (burgesses) alone could trade within the burgh. Ayr was
made a Royal burgh (St John's Town on Ayr) in 1205 by William
the Lion, and Irvine, which had been erected as a Burgh of
Barony in the mid C13, became a Royal burgh in 1372. Burghs
established in Ayrshire before the end of the C16 were Newton-
upon-Ayr, probably in the mid C14, Newmilns (1491), Cumnock
(1509), Mauchline (1510), Maybole (1516), Saltcoats (1528) and
Kilmarnock (1592). In most cases these were existing parochial
settlements, suitably spaced to provide a pattern of market towns
serving the whole county. All flourished, though other burghs
erected during this century failed to establish themselves, e.g.
Auchinleck (1507), Kilmaurs (1527) and Ballantrae (1541). The
creation of burghs, not all of which were successful, continued
in the C17 and early C18. Of these Largs (1625) and Girvan (1668)
are the most important, and demonstrate the spread of urban
values into the remoter parts of the county. Many burghs often
attracted a smaller, unincorporated extra-mural settlement (e.g.
Newton-upon-Ayr), where non-burgesses could trade, and where
proscribed activities, both legal and illegal, could be pursued.
MERCAT CROSSES were often the symbol of burgh authority.
Most of Ayrshire's rather unassuming surviving examples date
from the late C18; the best is at Cumnock (1778) but it is merely
a plain shaft and finial on a series of steps.

The earliest URBAN DOMESTIC BUILDING is Loudoun Hall,   88
Ayr, built perhaps in the late C15 for a wealthy merchant burgess,
and extended after 1534 by the Campbells of Loudoun, hereditary sheriffs of Ayr. It is one of the oldest surviving town houses
in Scotland, first documented in 1517, and symbolizes both mer-
cantile and temporal power. Seagate Castle was rebuilt c. 1562
on an ancient defensive site, but is also a town house, its form
dictated by earlier buildings, and an example of a palace-fronted
house at the cusp between defensive and domestic requirements.
Equally important are two former town houses at either end of
the main street of Maybole, where the Carrick gentry gathered
in winter to 'divert themselves in converse together in their owne
houses' (Abercrummie). That of the Kennedys of Blairquhan is
C16 and now forms the core of the Town Hall, while Maybole
Castle, for the Kennedys of Cassillis, is early C17. As discussed
above (p. 40), they are still firmly in the tower house tradition.
Lady Cathcart's House, Ayr, is also probably C17, but was
refronted in the C18; evidence for a C17 origin is offered by the
vaulted ground-floor room in the rear wing.

Among other C17 building the harled octagonal Powder House,
at Irvine, ascribed to 1642, was built to comply with an order
from James VI that royal burghs should maintain 'pouther magazines', and also associated with conflict is the Cromwellian
Citadel at Ayr, of which much of the external wall survives, built   98
from 1652, in a style mirroring similar structures elsewhere, but
on an unusually grand scale. It was an elongated hexagon, with
bastions at the angles to provide flanking fire.

Urban HOUSING of the early C18 includes the vernacular Nos. 71–73 High Street, Ayr, which retain a gabled front to the street, the common form before the late C18. In Irvine, Nos. 57–59 High Street, with its curvy gable, is probably mid-C18, while the Buffs Tavern in Kilwinning is dated 1714, but looks early C19. The central streets of Beith retain a number of mid-C18 buildings, and convey something of the urban character of that period, as do the restored Glasgow Vennel and Hill Street, both in Irvine. They are late C18 but belong in spirit to the earlier part of the century.

Outside the burghs, most of the population would have lived in small nucleated and largely self-sufficient FERMTOUNS or KIRKTOUNS clustered around the parish churches, of which Sorn remains as an example. Well-preserved examples of early to mid-C18 vernacular domestic buildings in the villages are fairly rare, however, and those that do survive are usually due to their association with Robert Burns and include the thatched cottage built at Alloway by his father in 1757.

Settlements 1750–1837

NEW SETTLEMENTS appeared between 1750 and 1837. Some, such as Catrine (1792), were driven by industrial innovation; here the grid-plan village erected in association with the new mill (*see* Industrial Buildings, above) perfectly demonstrates the Late Georgian desire for rationality. A similar underlying principle informs the weaving village of Darvel, laid out either side of one long E–W main street. Crosshill was established as a village, again for weavers, in the early C19. The houses which flanked the roads here, especially in the long single-sided Dalhowan Street, and in Darvel, were single-storey cottages, invariably originally thatched – the earliest known date from Darvel is 1762 – and differ little from the cottages of the early C18. At Catrine the houses were two-storey, urban in feel, as they were in Millport, another new settlement, where feuing associated with the development of the harbour began in 1780. Two other major new settlements were also associated with new ports (*see* above, p. 55): Ardrossan was laid out by *Peter Nicholson* in 1806–7 for Lord Eglinton on a grid pattern which spreads N and E from the new harbour, while at Troon, where a new settlement began to develop in the late C18 as a sea-bathing resort, further development followed the construction of the Duke of Portland's new port from 1810.

Many of the county's existing towns also experienced PLANNED SUBURBAN DEVELOPMENTS. At Kilmarnock, from the 1790s, the Town Improvement Commissioners laid out, with *Robert Johnstone*, several streets over the irregular medieval pattern and expanded the town to the S. At Ayr in the same period plans for an urban square with flanking terraces were put forward by *John Robertson*: construction of Wellington Square began *c.* 1800. The lands to its N, S and E were developed over the first half of the C19 with terraces of correct Late Georgian rectitude. N of the river, the unincorporated suburb of Wallacetown grew along broadly grid-plan lines, while the burgh of Newton-upon-Ayr developed a grid-plan suburb on land N of the harbour. Similarly styled, well-bred, if small, suburban expansion also took place at Stewarton, where Avenue Street was laid out *c.* 1779–82, Beith (Eglinton Street, *c.* 1810, its architecture vernacular) and at Maybole, where Cassillis Street (*c.* 1808) forms a new, polite straight route between the town and its new parish church. At Mauchline a formal Georgian grid was laid in 1819–20, again on top of an existing irregular street pattern, while Girvan expanded rapidly in the early C19. There elements of the grid-plan are clearly visible, with gradually converging long N–S streets. The houses are mainly single-storey, plain, vernacular, and with the separate ambience of a north-eastern Scottish 'sea town'.

Neither the Girvan cottages, nor the similar contemporary cottages found in Darvel or Newmilns (where the arrow-straight Brown Street was built from 1806), would look out of place in any of the many REBUILT AND REDEVELOPED VILLAGES of this period, such as Dundonald, Dunlop, Fenwick, Kilmaurs, Ochiltree, where the cottages climb the steep hill in spectacular fashion, and Straiton. The row of SHOPS, with houses above, in Lainshaw Street, Stewarton, with their delightfully astylar façades featuring scallops, are probably early C19, and are, behind that unique and quirky façade, essentially vernacular in construction and form.

The growing sophistication and maturity of Ayrshire's Georgian towns is marked by the increasing number of PUBLIC BUILDINGS erected. A sweet little Tolbooth was erected in Newmilns in 1739, and the Town House, Kilmaurs, may be of similar date. It gained a tower in 1799–1800, while Newton Steeple, Ayr, is of 1795 by *John Neill*. These are all essentially vernacular, as is the steeple at Girvan (1825–7), and *Peter King*'s first phase of Saltcoats Town Hall (1825–6). More ambitious are the pedimented pure classicism of the Town House, Beith, of 1817 by *William Dobie*, and *Thomas Hamilton*'s Tudor-Gothic Wallace Tower, Ayr, of 1831–4, but the two major buildings built in Ayr between 1817 and 1832 are of much higher quality. *Robert Wallace*'s County Buildings and Sheriff Courthouse (1817–22) uses its Grecian style to demonstrate the might and power of the law and of the local county administration. *Thomas Hamilton*'s Ayr Town Hall (1827–32), on a prominent site at the heart of the burgh, also uses Greek classicism to convey gravitas but it has been interpreted with inventive relish, especially in the fine soaring spire which acts as a landmark and advertisement for the burgh for miles around.

SCHOOLS of this period differ little from the houses. Rare early examples include the remarkable crowstepped Clandeboye School (now Church Hall), Dunlop, built in 1641, and one at Dreghorn (now Session House) of 1774. Purpose-built schools become more widespread in the early C19, and are often eleemosynary in nature. Easily the best, and on a surprisingly grand scale, is Sorn Primary School (1849–50), with its cherry-cocked ashlar, Venetian windows and wooden clock tower.

DOMESTIC BUILDINGS of the period are found in, and often characterize, every Ayrshire settlement. Many detached houses

90

100

97, *p. 68*

89

Ayr, Town Hall Spire.
Lithograph, 1829

in the villages echo the form and style of the larger mansions. Late C18 examples include Daisybank, Tarbolton, classical in the style of James Paterson, Ayrbank House, Catrine, formally expressed with flanking wings, the restrained Wheatfield House, Ayr, which may be by *Hugh Cairncross*, the mixed classical-traditional garb of Kirktonhall, West Kilbride, which hides an earlier structure, and the attractively enhanced pure classicism of Greenfield House, Alloway. Elsewhere, new houses had to fit into an existing streetscape, though in some cases they help to define or redefine it, e.g. *Alexander Stevens*'s Nos. 1–3 New Bridge Street, Ayr, of *c.* 1788. Much of the fabric of the main town streets was renewed during the early years of the C19, e.g. Polwarth Street, Galston, largely rebuilt *c.* 1800 in a vernacular style with wall-head pediments, Main Street, Kilbirnie or the remarkably uniform Hamilton Street, Saltcoats (*c.* 1835). South Harbour Street, Ayr, was rebuilt at much the same time in a more developed, almost classical idiom, which evolved into the Georgian shops with houses above that form a particularly attractive feature of Ayr's main streets. Individual houses of the early C19 range from the politely correct, such as Bath Villa, Ardrossan, of 1807–9 by *James Cleland*, through the classical in many guises and numberless quantities, such as the pedimented Dolphin House, Midton Road, Ayr (*c.* 1809), Gargowan (now the Ayrshire Hospice), Racecourse Road, Ayr (*c.* 1813), with its matching detached coach and garden houses, and Seafield, Lamlash, (*c.* 1820), to the *cottage orné*, e.g. Templand Cottage, Dalry (1828) and Midton Cottage, Ayr (1834–5). Knockbuckle, Beith, is a well-detailed Tudor Gothic house of *c.* 1820. Tudor Gothic too, but on a zestful grander scale, is The Garrison, Millport (*c.* 1819–20).

In the late C18, Ayrshire and Arran became increasingly popular as tourist destinations, which coincided with the development of SPORTS. Competitive ARCHERY was established, especially at Irvine and at Kilwinning, where a papingo, or model parrot, was shot at annually, the prize a silver trophy. The papingo was placed high on one of the towers of Kilwinning Abbey, and the need to maintain a target was perhaps one of the major reasons for the construction of *David Hamilton*'s replacement tower in 1815, after the original had fallen. GOLF in a clubbable form, i.e. with regular events and ancillary social activities, was at Girvan by the mid C18. HORSE RACING at Ayr had taken place on the sands, as it had also at Irvine and Newton-upon-Ayr, but a new racecourse was laid out to the S of the town in 1770, with a viewhouse added in 1787 (dem.), and the annual autumn Western Meeting, with the race for the Ayr Gold Cup (first run in 1804) its chief attraction, quickly became a highlight of the national social calendar.

The coasts of Ayrshire and Arran were well placed to benefit from the late C18 enthusiasm for the curative effects of SEA BATHING. During this period Barassie (often called New Kilmarnock or Kilmarnock-on-Sea) and Troon grew as wealthy townsmen built summer residences there, conveniently sited for sea bathing, and benefited considerably from the construction of the Kilmarnock & Troon Railway in the early C19. The potential for sea bathing was also recognized at Ardrossan, and a hotel (1806–7 by *Peter Nicholson*, now dem.) and a public bath house (1807–9 by *James Cleland*) were included in Nicholson's plans for the new town to accompany Eglinton's new port. Public bath houses were also built at Largs (1816, now Brisbane Centre) and

Ayr (1839–40 by *David Bryce*), with hot sea-water and vapour baths.

ROBERT BURNS died in 1796 after, be it noted, sea bathing recommended by his physician. His fame was already assured, but it quickly became *de rigueur* for those who could, and wished to, to make pilgrimages to places associated with the poet and his poetry, such as his father's cottage in Alloway, and this was accentuated by the construction of *Thomas Hamilton*'s sumptuous Burns Monument at Alloway, designed in 1817 and built in 1820–3. It is Greek, loosely based on the Choragic Monument of Lysicrates, and imbued with symbols reflecting Burns's life. It is *sui generis*, and established Hamilton as an architect. It was quickly followed by the Burns Monument Hotel (now Brig o' Doon Hotel), *c*. 1829.

Victorian and Edwardian

The communities of Ayrshire continued to grow through the second half of the C19. Some new settlements emerged, particularly in association with mining development, e.g. Rankinston from 1864, Lugar from 1866, and Annbank and Mossblown from *c*. 1880. At first these were almost exclusively of miners' row dwellings; sanitation was poor, the roads unmade, and communication difficult. Many such villages have disappeared, almost without trace, especially from the Irvine–Dalry area, where mining was exhausted by the mid C19, from the hills above Cumnock and Auchinleck, and from the Doon Valley.

Elsewhere, more salubrious developments were taking place. The matchless John Finnie Street in Kilmarnock was planned in 1861 for the Town Improvement Commissioners by *William Railton* and *Robert Blackwood*, and constructed in 1863–4, improving communications between the station and its SW suburbs. Similar thinking had been evident in Ayr. Miller Road (laid out 1852–3) ran between the town's station and primary residential area. This area, to the S of the town, expanded rapidly in the late C19. Troon, too, grew rapidly after 1879, to the S of the mid-C19 grid-pattern town, and the expansion of other coastal settlements can often be linked directly to the arrival of the railway, e.g. Girvan (1860), Skelmorlie (1865, Wemyss Bay Station), West Kilbride (1878) and Largs (1885).

Victorian and Edwardian PUBLIC BUILDINGS are often of a greater level of sophistication and increasing specialism. Most burghs sought a TOWN HALL commensurate with their own self-opinion. Among the grandest is *James Ingram*'s Italianate Town House, Irvine, of 1859–61, with a disproportionately tall tower, surely meant to rival Ayr's. The proud Free Renaissance Town Hall, Cumnock (1883–5, *R. S. Ingram*), speaks eloquently of civic worth and solidity, as do the Scots Baronial extension to the Town Hall, Maybole (*Ingram*, 1887–8), and *W. H. Howie & H. D. Walton*'s 1891–2 vividly decorative addition to Saltcoats Town Hall. Two halls in the Irvine valley were designed by

English architects. The Morton Hall, Newmilns (1896–7, *Arthur Harrison*, Birmingham) is strongly influenced by the Tudor buildings of the English midlands, while the Italianate Darvel Town Hall (1904–5 by *T. H. Smith* of London) could be an inner London town hall. The establishment of a sheriff court at Kilmarnock in 1850 was celebrated by the erection of a joyously exuberant Greek Revival Sheriff Court House (*William Railton*, 1850–2; now Procurators Fiscal's Offices), and the town gloried further in its increasing wealth and status with the grandiose Italianate Corn Exchange, now Palace Theatre, of 1862–3 by *James Ingram*.

109

The size, scale and sophistication of SCHOOLS changed considerably during this period. Mid-C19 examples include the Jacobethan Bradshaw Nursery School, Saltcoats (1858, *Thomas Wallace*) and the gem-like Mair's Free School (now Nursery School), Darvel, of 1863–4 by *William Railton*; the former Lady Flora's Institute, Newmilns, of 1873–7 by *F. T. Pilkington*, is, by his standards, strikingly low-key. By that date, however, the Education (Scotland) Act of 1872 had established School Boards in each parish with powers to build elementary schools. Thus from the mid 1870s BOARD SCHOOLS began to appear. Templates were provided by the Scotch Education Department. A single-storey H-plan was very popular. Particularly fine and largely unspoilt is Cumbrae Primary School, Millport, of 1875–6 by *Alexander Watt*. Others which adopt the same pattern, and interpret it in varying ways, include the former school, now Community Centre, at Crosshill (1881), with its station-like veranda, and Winton Primary School, Ardrossan, of 1897–8 by *John Armour Jun.*, given an Arts and Crafts twist. The former Fairlie Primary School (1887 by *J. J. Stevenson*) is planned to maximize use of a constricted and steeply sloping site, and has some thoughtful detailing. *A. C. Thomson* produced a number of carefully considered smaller schools, e.g. Ochiltree (1909). Towards the end of the C19, and into the C20, larger schools appeared, e.g. *R. S. Ingram*'s Free Renaissance initial phase of Troon Primary School, 1897–1900, Darvel Primary School of 1901–4 (*Henry Higgins Jun.*, Neo-Jacobean), and Hurlford Primary School of 1902–5 (*Gabriel Andrew*, in an inventive Free Renaissance). There was an increased demand for secondary schools and facilities for technical education. Ayr Academy was rebuilt by *Clarke & Bell* in classical style in 1878–80, and consummately extended and remodelled 1910–3, by *James A. Morris*. Kilmarnock Academy was built by *R. S. Ingram* in 1896–9 in Queen Anne style on a prominent site while Irvine Royal Academy was rebuilt in 1899–1902 by *John Armour* in a swagger classical manner. Kilmarnock's first Technical College was erected in 1907–9 by *Gabriel Andrew* in flamboyant Edwardian classical style.

103

111

The educational needs of the adult population were not neglected, provision often associated with recreational facilities. Typically, the working-class male (the target market) would be offered a reading room, stocked with newspapers and a selected diet of approved books, and rooms where he could play cards or snooker or billiards. Initially these PUBLIC HALLS AND INSTITUTES were funded by local landowners, for instance in the series of Brown's Institutes in the Irvine valley (e.g. Darvel, 1872, with a door lintel promising 'Conversations'), or by a major local employer, such as the Eglinton Iron Co. (e.g. Nethermains, Kilwinning, 1899–1900). The Scots Renaissance-style McKechnie Institute, Girvan (1887–8), is on a grand scale and a *tour de force* of High Victorian design. Here is no self-doubt; nor is there in *R. S. Ingram*'s Baronial Baird Institute, Cumnock, of 1889–91. The highly individual Free Renaissance façade of Mother Lodge, Kilwinning, of 1892–3 by *J. B. Wilson*, is a dramatic expression of the craft's influence. The temple, at the rear, is a textbook display of Masonic symbolism.

Of the LIBRARIES provided by public authorities after the Free Libraries Act, the first of note is the Carnegie Library, Ayr, by *Campbell Douglas & Morrison*, of 1890–3, with a richly decorative frontispiece. The Dick Institute, Kilmarnock (*R. S. Ingram*, 1897–1901; rebuilt after a fire, 1909–11), architecturally one of the finest libraries in Scotland, is a massively scaled Edwardian classical conception, with a fifteen-bay pavilion front beneath a statue of Minerva and a central dome, which lights the magnificent galleried entrance hall.

The 1890s also saw the erection of the first VILLAGE HALLS in the county. Architecturally the most distinguished include those at Fairlie (1892 by *J. J. Stevenson*), Gateside (1897) and the bulky Baronial A. M. Brown Institute at Catrine, of 1897–8 and the Kames Institute, Muirkirk (1902–4), both with a heavy corner tower which betrays the hand of *R. S. Ingram*. Two outstanding and thoughtful examples are *J. J. Burnet*'s Brodick Village Hall, Arran, of 1894–5, and *A. N. Paterson*'s West Kilbride Institute of 1898–1900. The halls of the early C20, such as *A. C. Thomson*'s Claud Hamilton Memorial Hall, Coylton (1909), are almost invariably dressed in a simple harled Arts and Crafts style; of them the most interesting is *Thomas A. Jack*'s McCandlish Hall, Straiton, of 1912, so reminiscent of a colonial bungalow.

Changes to poor law legislation in the 1840s encouraged the provision of POORHOUSES. The Kyle Union Poorhouse, now Holmston House, Ayr, of 1857–60, was designed by *W. L. Moffat*, a specialist in the field, in a fresh attractive Jacobethan style. The changes to the Poor Law also encouraged locally funded and managed ASYLUMS. The Glengall Lunatic Asylum, now Ailsa Hospital, Ayr, was built in 1865–9 to plans of *Charles Edward*, of *Edward & Robertson*, again specialists in a narrowly defined field. It is a large structure with a central administrative block, and wards at right angles; changes in perceptions, and treatments, of the mentally ill are seen in subsequent buildings on the site, such as the detached pavilions of the later C19, and the satisfying New Hospital (1903–6 by *J. B. Wilson*). The first general HOSPITAL was *William Railton*'s large Kilmarnock Infirmary, of 1867–8, in a Greek style influenced by Alexander Thomson (dem.). It was joined later in the C19 by the Renaissance Ayr County Hospital

(1880–3 by *John Murdoch*, also dem.)). Elsewhere, a convalescent home built at Maidens in 1886 is little more than a typical villa of the period, as is the Lady Margaret Hospital, Millport, of 1899–1901, by *Fryers & Penman*.

PUBLIC MONUMENTS form an important part of the Victorian and Edwardian streetscape. They can be solely celebratory, like the High Victorian complexity of *William Bone*'s 1896 memorial to Dr Marshall, in the Howard Park, Kilmarnock, or they can have a secondary function, e.g. *Adam Mitchell*'s granite Biggart Fountain, Dalry, of 1876. More often they take the form of a STATUE, and a survey of the county's statuary must begin with the monuments to Burns erected in the county's three main towns. Kilmarnock led the way, with *R. S. Ingram*'s Baronial skyrocket of a monument, with a statue by *W. Grant Stevenson*, which survived the wretched arson attack of 2004, and now stands watch over the anodyne C21 Burns Monument Centre. Ayr's statue of Burns, by *George A. Lawson*, of 1889–91, has the poet gazing towards Alloway, while at Irvine (1896), where he is quite marooned on the town's Moor, *James Pittendreigh Macgillivray* also shows him gazing into the distance. At Mauchline the Burns National Memorial Tower was erected in 1896–8 to an unscholarly Baronial design by *William Fraser* of Glasgow. Earlier statues include Sir James Shaw, Kilmarnock (*James Fillans*, 1848), *Matthew Noble*'s gunmetal statue of General James Smith Neill (1859), the 13th Earl of Eglinton (1865), also by *Noble* (both in Ayr), Lord Justice Boyle (*John Steell*, 1861–7) in Irvine, and the one that best captures the personality of the subject, the kilted, thoughtful 11th Duke of Hamilton, outside the Primary School, Brodick (1868), from the studio of Baron *Marochetti*. Early C20 statues, both in Ayr, are *Thomas Brock*'s Royal Scots Fusiliers Memorial (1900–2) and *W. Goscombe John*'s statue of Sir James Fergusson (1908–10).

The C19 saw an increasing number of exclusively commercial buildings. Quickest to build in styles that suggested competence, integrity and permanence were the BANKS. The first purpose-built bank in Ayrshire is the former Ayrshire Bank, in New Bridge Street, Ayr, of 1830–2 by *Thomas Hamilton*. From *c.* 1850 are *William Railton*'s late classical former Union Bank in Bank Street, Kilmarnock, while *Robert Paton*'s palazzo for the same bank in High Street, Ayr, is of 1858, and would have towered powerfully over its neighbours. For the Royal Bank of Scotland, *Peddie & Kinnear* produced a series of sturdy edifices, mostly with their tell-tale monogram, beginning with Girvan in 1856. Other banks in Ayrshire are also by architects from Edinburgh, e.g. *David Rhind*, who designed for the Commercial Bank in Sandgate, Ayr (1862–3) and Girvan (*c.* 1870), or *David MacGibbon*, who designed the National Bank (now Royal Bank) in Girvan, of 1863–4.

In Ayr, properties combining commercial and residential use continued the style of *c.* 1800 into the 1830s. The first evidence of a change, and the change is also one of scale, comes in 1841–4, with Winton Buildings, built on the site of the original Tolbooth

and market. It is still classical, but the emphasis has shifted
subtly: these are SHOPS, with lettable flats or offices above, not
a shop below the proprietor's house. The MacNeille Buildings,
Newmarket Street, Ayr, of 1868–9 by *James I. McDerment*,
advance the pattern, but for an unrivalled display of late C19
mixed commercial buildings we must look to Kilmarnock, and
particularly to John Finnie Street. Although laid out in 1864, it
was only in the 1870s that the building stances on either side
began to be taken up; the range and quality of the buildings, all
of Mauchline red sandstone and by the town's major architects,
is remarkable. Aided by the directness of the street, and its slight
slope, the townscape is unequalled in provincial Scotland, and
stands comparison with contemporary work in the nation's cities.

The county's other towns have little to compare with this. The
central part of the High Street, Ayr, was widened in the 1880s
– but most of the new buildings are unadventurous, with only
John Baird's Baronial No. 86, of 1883–6, *James A. Morris*'s
Norman Shaw-inspired No. 146 and *Henry V. Eaglesham*'s remarkable mix of the Jacobethan and the Flemish at Nos. 148–156, of
1892–3, demanding our attention. The latter is the first of a series
of increasingly assured designs by this talented architect, which
make his early death to be the more regretted. His former pub
at No. 61 High Street, Ayr, is of 1893–4, and again mixes Flemish
and Jacobethan motifs, while Nos. 17–23 Burns Statue Square
(1894) are an effectively scaled Free Renaissance exercise, but
his masterpiece is Wellington Chambers, of 1904–7, in a modern
classical style, with a solidity and horizontality strongly influenced by American architecture. *James A. Morris* and *J. K.
Hunter*, erstwhile partners, both created their best commercial
buildings for Ayr's Burns Statue Square area: Hunter's D'Auray
Buildings of 1896–7, at the junction of Alloway Street and
Dalblair Road, is an inventive design, and turns the corner with
panache, while Morris's Nos. 1–7 Burns Statue Square (1901–2),
frontage of the Drill Hall, is a typically studied design, mixing
Renaissance and Baronial motifs. Two of Kilmarnock's leading
architects of *c.* 1900 produced a number of attractive commercial
buildings for the town in their own distinctive Arts and Crafts
style, including Nos. 57–65 King Street (1901–2 by *Thomas
Smellie*) and No. 37 Bank Street (*c.* 1905 by *Gabriel Andrew*).
Andrew also designed substantial premises for local Co-operative
Societies, e.g. Westgate House, Newmilns (1898–1900), his most
dramatic work making full use of the narrow triangular site and
showing the influence of Glasgow's architects.

TERRACED HOUSING is less common during this period,
although it continued to be built, especially in Ayr, into the 1860s.
Some, such as Barns Terrace (1857–60), were a continuation of
early C19 norms, but others, such as those on the W side of
Queens Terrace, of 1844–51, above a sunken basement, have a
relaxed vernacular style. The last great terrace, Eglinton Terrace,
was conceived in 1861 by *Clarke & Bell* as the centrepiece of their
development of Ayr's Citadel, but was not completed until the

1890s, a potent demonstration of how public taste had shifted toward the DETACHED OR SEMI-DETACHED HOUSE. Numerous examples, in varied styles, are found in the major burghs: e.g. in London Road and Dundonald Road, Kilmarnock; Racecourse Road, Ayr; and Kilwinning Road, Irvine; and other important series can be found in South Crescent Road, Ardrossan, where they demonstrate an eclectic and unrepeated range of styles, and also in The Avenue and Newton Kennedy (where they are accompanied by a unique rear garden wall constructed largely of river stones) in Girvan, and in smaller numbers in almost every community. VILLAS in a classical style, often attractively interpreted, include Hillside, Beith, of *c.* 1840, Monument Cottage, Alloway, with its rock-faced dressings, of 1868–9 by *James I. McDerment*, or Glenrosa, Newmilns, of *c.* 1885. Elsewhere the form used may be Italianate, e.g. at Inverdon, Ayr, of 1846–7 by *Clarke & Bell*, or Baronial, as at Seatower, Ayr, of 1872 by *David MacGibbon*, or the tidy Victoria Villa, Beith, of 1874, or Gothic fantasy, as at Edendarroch, Ayr, of 1882 and possibly by *Hippolyte J. Blanc*.

There is a greater sensitivity in the villas of the late 1880s and subsequently, as a reaction to some of the excesses of the previous years. Many houses of this period are in a recognizably Arts and Crafts idiom, often using the palette of that style to temper designs whose roots remain classical, Italianate or Baronial. The best house of this period is, undoubtedly, *James A. Morris*'s Savoy Croft, Ayr, built for himself in 1897–9, in which, externally and internally, he allows full expression to his own artistic theories, and there are other houses by him in a similar manner, e.g. Savoy Park Hotel (from 1885) and Wellsbourne (1894), both Ayr, or Glenburn, Prestwick (1894–6). *H. E. Clifford* worked in a similar idiom, e.g. at Redcliff, Troon (1893) or Cragston, Stewarton (1902), as did *Thomas A. Jack* whose houses in Maybole (*c.* 1912) are strongly influenced by Mackintosh, *J. K. Hunter*, e.g. at Stonegarth, Prestwick, of 1907–8, and *J. R. Johnstone*, e.g. Welbeck House, Troon, of 1910–12. A more luxurious style, though still recognizably Arts and Crafts, was preferred by *William Leiper*, whose Piersland Lodge, Troon, of 1898–9, with its richly detailed exterior and interior, is one of his greater works, while *A. N. Paterson*'s Hapland, Mauchline, of *c.* 1905, is an understated gem.

In a class of its own is the unusual development of villa mansions at Southwood, near Troon, by the Portland estate (1890–14). They are by some of the most popular Glasgow architects of the day including *H. E. Clifford* and *John A. Campbell*, as well as *James Scott Hay* of Kilmarnock and the prolific Largs architects *Fryers & Penman*. Grey Gables, the most interesting house, its origins rooted in the English Arts and Crafts movement, was built for the Glasgow publisher William Collins but its architect remains stubbornly unidentified.

TOURISM, already established in the C18 and early C19 by the attractions of sea, sport (especially horse racing, and the increasingly codified game of golf) and the county's Burnsian heritage

113, 114

116

was intensified in the middle years of the C19 by the introduction of regular and consistent steamer services on the Firth of Clyde, and the introduction and expansion of the railway service. With the steamer provision, places such as Skelmorlie, Largs and Fairlie could now be reached conveniently from Glasgow, as could the coasts of Arran, e.g. at Lochranza or Lamlash. MARINE VILLAS began to appear along these coasts, e.g. Beach House, Skelmorlie (1844), the Tudor Gothic Priory Lodge, Largs, of 1829–30 by *David & James Hamilton*, or Ashcraig, Meigle, of *c.* 1840. The particular appeal of Arran led to an interesting and possibly unique solution, thought out by the estate's island factors. The agricultural and village tenants were allowed to build small, often wooden, houses on their properties, generally to the rear of the main house, to which they would remove in the summer, giving themselves the opportunity to rent or lease the main house to mainland visitors. These SUMMER HOUSES are, generally, of little architectural value, but can be found in many of the island's villages. The best, most architecturally refined, examples are the boarded row of 1892–5 behind Hamilton Terrace, Lamlash, by *J. J. Burnet*, long thin sheds running back into the hillside.

The second half of the C19 saw an increasing number of buildings designed specially for sections of this increasing tourist trade. A number of HYDROPATHIC ESTABLISHMENTS and convalescent homes were built, especially in the N of the county. The best-known 'hydros' were at Skelmorlie (begun in 1868; dem.) and Seamill, begun in 1879, while the Paisley Co-operative Society convalescent home (now Community Centre) at West Kilbride was begun in 1885, and the Co-operative Seaside Home (now Seamill Training Centre), Seamill, in 1895–6 by *James Davidson*. A few large purpose-built hotels followed, e.g. the Station Hotel, Ayr (1883–6), Turnberry Hotel (1904–6) (both discussed above) and Marine Highland Hotel, Troon, of 1894–7 by *James Salmon Jun.* and *J. Gaff Gillespie*.

The Burns shrines were equally busy in providing buildings to woo their visitors, especially at Alloway, where Burns' Cottage had been acquired by the Trustees of the Burns Monument in 1881, but remained in use as the low public house which so dismayed Keats until 1900, when *Allan Stevenson*'s peculiarly inappropriately styled museum building was erected alongside.

The majority of the coastal GOLF COURSES were created in the C19, and their clubhouses reflect both this, and their wealth and importance. The finest is the Royal Troon Golf Club, founded in 1878. The comfortable Late Victorian Renaissance clubhouse was begun by *H. E. Clifford* in 1885–6. Old Prestwick, where the first Open was played in 1860, was founded in 1851, and the original, villa-like clubhouse built in 1866–7. It was substantially enlarged in 1893–4 by *James A. Morris & Hunter*. BOWLING clubhouses are often simple, unadorned structures, but two of note are that of Portland Bowling Club, Kilmarnock, founded in 1860, where the original pavilion, with its octagonal tower, is a rare survival, and Girvan Bowling Club, where the clubhouse, of 1959–60 by *T. K. Irving*, is a striking contrast to the general conservatism of the genre: its first-floor semicircular fronted committee room is supported on thin pilotis. For the non-golfing, non-bowling visitor to the seaside, many towns built broad ESPLANADES, which allowed the benefits of sea air and exercise, without the problems of sand and water. Such esplanades were built at, e.g., Ayr, Troon (begun by *J. & H. V. Eaglesham*, 1899–1900) and Largs, and were often accompanied with shelters and seats, such as the chunky stone seats at Largs.

The county's best PUBLIC PARKS are in Kilmarnock: the Howard Park, laid out in 1891–3 by *C. & W. Mitchell & Langharne*, and the larger Kay Park, first gifted to the town in 1879, and extended in 1884, when it was remodelled by *Charles Reid*. With its changing levels, broad avenues and boating lake, this is a model urban park. Elsewhere, the most interesting is Dalry Public Park (*James Johnstone*, 1892–3) which has likenesses of the donor on its elaborate gatepiers.

The First World War to the present

Almost every village and town has its own WAR MEMORIAL. The scale of the First World War, and its unparalleled death toll, required a major reconsideration of how the dead were to be honoured. The design of the monuments varies. The most elaborate include *J. K. Hunter*'s cenotaph-like Ayr War Memorial of 1920–4, *James Miller*'s Kilmarnock War Memorial of 1926–7 and *Balfour Paul*'s Irvine War Memorial of 1921, while bold figures in bronze adorn those at Troon (of 1923–4 by *Walter Gilbert*), Kilmaurs (1920–1) and Dalry (1927), both by *Kellock Brown*, and others display virtuoso stone carving, e.g. Largs (1921, again by *Kellock Brown*), Ardrossan (1922–3, begun by *Peter Macgregor Chalmers*), Crosshill (1920–1 by *Hugh R. Wallace*) and Saltcoats (1922). *James A. Morris* contributed a number; his best are those of Alloway (1919–20) and Girvan (1921–2). Others of note include the startlingly red Mauchline war memorial, by *A. C. Thomson* (1926–7), *James Houston*'s triumphal arch at Kilbirnie (1922) and *J. J. Burnet*'s solid cenotaph at New Cumnock (1919–21). *Robert Lorimer*, too, provided war memorials, e.g. at Colmonell (1920–2) and Galston (1922), but the highlight of his memorial work is the excellent roadside Alexander Morton Memorial of 1926–7 at Gowanbank, Darvel, stone and bronze with superb carving by *C. d' O. Pilkington Jackson*.

The foci of URBAN PLANNING in the C20 were improved general sanitation and increased domestic comfort. The best-known of the various theories of urban reconstruction proposed in the years around 1900 was the Garden City, developed by Ebenezer Howard, with the architects Raymond Unwin and Barry Parker, and its smaller counterpart, the low-density Garden Suburb. At Barassie in 1911 *James Chalmers* proposed a Garden Suburb, but plans were curtailed by the First World War, and only a few houses built. Garden City, Kilbirnie, however, was laid out for the Local Government Board of Scotland in 1916–17 by *J. Walker Smith*, providing accommodation for steelworkers. It has a central spine road, paralleled by subsidiary roads, flanked by harled and slated houses, usually in pairs or short terraces. The influence of the English garden cities and villages is clear. The influence is also apparent in EARLY COUNCIL HOUSING. The late C19 and early C20 saw the collapse of the private rented housing market, and in 1917 the Royal Commission on the Housing of the Industrial Population of Scotland, Rural and Urban reported the stark reality of the situation, presaging the Housing and Town Planning (Scotland) Act of 1919. In Ayrshire, the Commission and the Act had been pre-empted by Cumnock Burgh Council, who in 1913–15 built twelve houses, Urbana Terrace (now Nos. 2–24 John Baird Street) to plans by *John Arthur*, and had embarked on a second scheme, for thirty-six houses by *William Cowie*, before the close of 1919. Each burgh was responsible for its own schemes, while the county council was the responsible body in the landward area. These first council houses were relatively generously funded, and often have minor architectural ornamentation lacking from subsequent projects. A notable example is Henrietta Street, Girvan, of 1919–21 by *Thomas Taylor*, of *Hutton & Taylor*, with twenty houses laid out on spacious Garden City principles. Ayr Burgh Council's first development was at George's Avenue, 1919–22, by *J. K. Hunter*; in Kilmarnock *James Scott Hay* designed houses in Holehouse Road, built 1920–2.*

Further Acts of 1923 and especially that of 1924, introduced by the minority Labour administration, allowed true progress but tightened the financial belt. Schemes under these Acts tend to have fewer folderols, though the first council houses in Prestwick, in Waterloo Road (1926–7), by the burgh's surveyor, *Francis Pritty*, have some attractive details. The county authority reacted more slowly, and though many of the larger settlements under its control, such as Stevenston, Kilbirnie or Mauchline, faced the same problems as the burghs, the first County Council schemes were small-scale and designed to tackle problems of rural housing. The most interesting development of the 1930s is Troon Burgh Council's Muirhead estate (1937–9), designed by *John A. W. Grant*, with 400 houses in a spacious Garden Suburb layout.

After 1945 the need was for quantity rather than quality, and many houses were built quickly using non-traditional methods, e.g. the experimental flat-roofed pre-fabricated cottages at Waterside by Fenwick, built in 1942–3 in Gyproc by *Sam Bunton*. More widespread were the iconic 'prefabs', of which some remain in

---

* This section deals with the Ayrshire mainland. Council housing on the islands before 1975 was the responsibility of Millport Burgh Council and Bute County Council. Both provided a relatively small number of houses; the post-war houses found at various places on Arran, e.g. at Kilmory, and Montrose Terrace, Whiting Bay, are distinguished by deep roofs, flanked by gabled outer bays, and arranged as either pairs or longer terraces.

Vicarlands, Maybole, and the 'Swedish timber houses', which are found throughout the county, e.g. in a well-considered scheme at The Glebe, Dreghorn. *Robert G. Lindsay* (County Architect 1940–63) developed a type of house with a reinforced concrete frame, of which the prototype was built at Dalrymple in 1945, and widely used subsequently.

The Scottish Special Housing Association (SSHA) was formed in 1947 to build houses in key areas, but its work is not well represented in Ayrshire; the NW part of New Farm Loch, Kilmarnock, is a typical estate from *c.* 1970. Little of the great quantity of council houses erected during the decades after the war requires individual comment, though they provide the dominant architectural feature of several villages and smaller towns, especially those administered by the County Council, e.g. Kilbirnie, Muirkirk or New Cumnock. The two latter, along with Auchinleck, Bellsbank and Patna, grew substantially as the remote communities of miners' rows were replaced with houses in accessible, nucleated settlements. Drongan, almost wholly comprising post-war county council housing, was to have been part of a larger new town, linked to new coal pits at Killoch (Ochiltree) and S of the village.

Industrial wealth supported some of the county's C20 PRIVATE HOUSING, e.g. the Free Renaissance splendour of Westlands, Newmilns, of 1927 by *Gabriel Steel*, but such properties are largely confined to the coastal towns and resorts. Communities which grew noticeably during the interwar period through private developments include the seaside towns such as Largs, West Kilbride-Seamill, Troon and Prestwick, but the traditional hipped bungalow also delineates large parts of other places, e.g. the S and E suburbs of Ayr, or those of N Saltcoats and Stevenston. Among individual, architect-designed houses, the strikingly modern is best represented by Hillhome, Portencross, while the English suburban brick tradition is attractively reinterpreted by *James Carrick* in a number of houses in Greenfield Avenue, Alloway, of between 1933 and 1938. Others of note include two in timber, the boathouse-like Pine House, Fairlie, of *c.* 1925, and Greyholme, Rosaburn, of 1938 by *William J. Gibson*, while Doonbank Cottage, Doonfoot, of *c.* 1934 by *Alexander Mair*, is a thatched cottage in the English tradition, and Western House, within the confines of Ayr Racecourse, luxuriant Arts and Crafts of 1923–4 by *Harold O. Tarbolton*. Worthwhile individual houses of the late C20 are scarce. They include two in Fisherton with drum towers and circular bays, of the 1950s, *Clunie Rowell*'s rustic brick house in Station Road, Prestwick (1959–60), *Francis B. Dunbar*'s stepped terrace in Burness Avenue, Alloway (1960), Port Murray, Maidens, of 1961–3 by *Peter Womersley*, resembling a large glazed shoe-box placed precariously on the rocky shore, and *Norman McLean*'s house in Racecourse View, Ayr (1965), which effectively transfers Corbusian severity to a suburban setting.

The period after 1945 was also one of considerable URBAN RENEWAL, assisted by the introduction of legislation which

121

allowed local authorities to clear large areas for reconstruction. In Kilmarnock much predominantly mid-C19 mixed development was cleared to the SE of the town centre and replaced by, largely, flatted blocks of local authority housing, while much of the centre of Galston was acquired and redeveloped by the town's burgh council in the late 1960s, acting with *Stewart Hume* of *Hay Steel MacFarlane & Partners* to produce a thoughtfully considered residential area to the W of the town's parish church. Developments such as Hume's, where the deck-access flats were demolished in 2009, have not always well withstood the changed social criteria and reduced maintenance of the late C20 and early C21. In Ayr in the 1960s, the Town Council commissioned plans for the redevelopment of Wallacetown from *J. C. Holmes* and *A. A. Wood*, of the *Holmes Wishart Planning Group*, and the proposals, which included three high-rise blocks alongside the river, and low-rise housing arranged around traffic-free courtyards, were implemented from the late 1960s by *Cowie & Torry*. Cumnock Burgh Council had, in the late 1950s, appointed *Robert Matthew*, of *Robert Matthew, Johnson-Marshall & Partners (RMJM)*, to mastermind ambitious development plans for the whole burgh; the plans were much lauded in the professional press, but their radicalism was, perhaps, too much for the council, and the proposals were scaled back. The most lasting result of the collaboration is some adventurous local authority housing, notably Barshare, which was planned by *Matthew* in 1957, and built 1959–66. It is an early example of an estate with vehicle–pedestrian separation, wide paths and a variety of housing designs. Its use of vernacular forms and materials also proved influential. The redevelopment of Kilmarnock Town Centre, from 1969, has less theorizing behind it: only Foregate, of 1972–4 by *Percy Johnson-Marshall & Partners*, a rare example of co-operation between local traders, shows any interest in anything other than maximizing the commercial footprint.

The most interesting developments of the 1960s and 1970s were made at Irvine New Town by the Irvine Development Corporation (I.D.C.), established in 1966. Irvine rapidly proved to be one of the most imaginative and innovative of the Scottish New Towns. The I.D.C. built upon earlier work by Irvine Burgh Council, which had acquired a disused munitions factory to the SW of the town in the 1950s and developed it as an industrial estate, while also promoting the burgh as an overspill settlement for Glasgow. The Irvine New Town plan, initially prepared by *Wilson & Womersley*, 1965–7, was revised in 1968–71, with the assistance of the Irvine Development Corporation staff, under *David Gosling*, Chief Architect. The plan envisaged new residential areas, especially to the E and S of Irvine, and W of Kilwinning, linked to one another, and to the commercial and industrial areas, mostly to the SW and SE, by a series of 'community routes' that, it was believed, would help to achieve the sense of unity among the town's people which was felt to be lacking in earlier New Towns. In the town centre the Corporation replaced much C19 mixed development with a dramatic new shopping centre: a

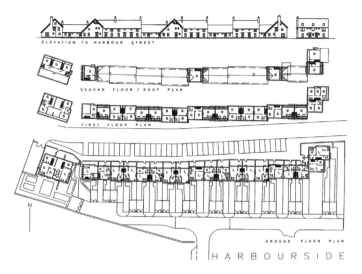

Irvine Development Corporation, Harbour Street.
Elevation and Plan, 1995

bold statement which attempts to integrate old and new. *I.D.C.*'s
housing ranges from traffic-segregated estates such as Pennyburn
(Kilwinning) through starkly vernacular neighbourhoods such as
Bourtreehill, to more strongly, and imaginatively, detailed developments such as Harbourside (Irvine), and also encompasses
urban infill, e.g. in High Street, Irvine, and in Kilwinning, and
special needs housing (Red Cross House, Irvine). If there is a
solemnity to some of it, especially from the late 1980s, all is
marked by a regard for the importance of graphic and other
details (e.g. Gigha Terrace, Bourtreehill), and much of it is joyful
and playful, such as the 'Bookends' in Montgomerie Street,   124
Irvine, and the astonishing pastiche of centuries of Scottish architecture in Linthouse Vennel, Irvine. Joyful, too, much of the
housing built since the 1990s for the newly created Housing
Associations, beginning with *Wren Rutherford*'s prow-like St
Cuthbert's Place, Maybole, of 1998–9, and continuing through
Earl Rise, Dundonald (*Wren Rutherford Austin-Smith:Lord*, 2001–
2), Douneburn Crescent, Girvan (*Robert Potter & Partners*,
2005–6) and George Place, Doonfoot (*Roan Rutherford Austin-
Smith:Lord*, 2005–7).

Fewer PUBLIC BUILDINGS were built in the C20 than previ-
ously. The most noteworthy from the interwar period is *Alexander
Mair*'s massive and highly impressive County Buildings, Ayr, of
1929–35, which extends the early C19 Sheriff Court House. The
Neo-Georgian exterior, which takes its cue from the Court
House, encloses an equally fine interior. Also bold Neo-Georgian

is *James Miller*'s Town Hall, Troon, of 1930–2, while the Town Hall, Galston, of 1925–7 by *James Hay & Steel*, employs a late Scots Baronial template. Other public buildings of this period of interest include *James Miller*'s boat-like Richmond Hall, Kirkoswald (1923–5), *Robert Lorimer*'s Alloway Public Hall (1929–30, a reconstruction of the village school, with excellent plasterwork carving by *C. d'O. Pilkington Jackson*) and the Art Deco Community Education Centre, Galston, of 1937 by *Hay & Steel*. From the end of the C20, two public libraries stand out: that at Dalmellington is well-considered Neo-vernacular of *c.* 1986, while that at West Kilbride, of 1995–6, although also recognizably in a Neo-vernacular tradition, claims its tight triangular site with a full-height window which floods the library with light. The C21 fashion for AREA CENTRES, with a number of community functions under one roof, has produced some interesting dramatic buildings such as Drongan Area Centre, of 2001–3, by *Wren Rutherford Austin-Smith:Lord*, and the North West Kilmarnock Area Centre, Kilmarnock, of 2005–7 by *Austin-Smith:Lord*.

The interwar years witnessed the erection of many SECONDARY SCHOOLS, of which the most important architecturally is Marr College, Troon, of 1925–35 by *John Arthur*, classical and conceived on a substantial scale. *William Cowie* adopted a modern style for his Girvan High School (now Girvan Primary School), begun in 1939, but not completed until 1953–5. The many schools built by *Ayr County Council* in the 1950s and 1960s are largely uninspiring. Some of the PRIMARY SCHOOLS have thoughtful layouts, for instance the butterfly plan of Bellfield Primary School, Kilmarnock (1962–4), while the interest of others is in the use of non-traditional materials, such as the aluminium aircraft panels used at Bellsbank Primary School (1952–5), while Auchenharvie Academy, Stevenston (1969–71), is notable for its utter lack of compromise. The best school of the period is undoubtedly Whiting Bay Primary School, of 1963–7 by *George Horspool* of *Baron Bercott & Associates*, for Bute County Council, a perceptively scaled and arresting design, attentive to the needs of teachers and children.

Recent schools, both secondary and primary, have been budgetarily tight and architecturally timid, though they are often on a substantial scale, incorporating a secondary school, a primary school and community facilities, e.g. at Grange Campus, Kilmarnock, of 2005–8 by *SMC Parr Architects* for East Ayrshire Council. A frequent design element is a big drum tower, often the hinge about which the individual elements hang, but well used by *Ryder HKS* at Kyle Academy, Ayr, to form a free-standing lecture theatre, 2005–7. In a class of their own are the recent primary schools designed in-house by *North Ayrshire Council Technical Services*, such as Lawthorn, Girdle Toll (2000–1, *David Wadsworth*, architect), Mayfield, Saltcoats (2003–4, *Irene Farish*, architect) and Dalry (2006–8, *David Watts*, *Irene Farish* and *Peter Togneri*, architects), which incorporates 'imbedded intelligence', by which concepts and ideas are projected through the design of the fabric of the building, a theory developed by *Bruce McLean*, who worked with the design team to produce this remarkable school. At Colmonell (2009–10, *ARPL Architects*) innovations have concentrated on sustainable building.

New buildings for FURTHER AND HIGHER EDUCATION include the West of Scotland Agricultural College, which moved to Auchincruive in the 1930s with ascetic Neo-Georgian buildings by *Alexander Mair*. Nearby, the Hannah Dairy Research Institute, St Quivox, which specialized in dairy research, was designed by *A. G. Ingham*, of the Department of Agriculture for Scotland, in a Lorimerian Scots vernacular, and a similar style is adopted for the hall of residence (Wilson Hall) at Auchincruive, of 1950–6 by *D. S. MacPhail*. Noteworthy are the National Water Sports Training Centre, Millport, a Nordic-inspired wooden complex of 1974–6 by *Frank Burnet, Bell & Partners* (*James Rennie* and *Robert D. McPhail*, project architects), the addition to Ayr College, 2000–1, and the Kilwinning campus of James Watt College, 1998–2000, both these latter by *Boswell, Mitchell & Johnston*. The latest building is for the University of the West of Scotland, Ayr, by *RMJM* (2009–11).

HOSPITALS built in the interwar period include the Scots Renaissance Davidson Memorial Hospital, Girvan, of 1919–22 by *John Watson*, of *Watson, Salmond & Gray*, and the simplified English Arts and Crafts of the Arran War Memorial Hospital, Lamlash, of 1920–2 by *Archibald Cook*. They are very differently styled, but both are good examples of small local hospitals of the period, while Ayrshire Central Hospital, Irvine, of 1935–41 by *William Reid*, is an equally fine example of a larger general hospital which, with its flat roofs and semicircular stair-towers, is one of Ayrshire's best 1930s buildings, though of its original three main blocks, one has been demolished and another is presently (2012) disused. The unsung Neo-vernacular of the Central Clinic, Kilmarnock, of 1971–4 and Crosshouse Hospital (*Boissevain & Osmond*, 1973–82) have self-belief; the hospital has a striking horizontality, compromised by the subsequent replacement of the flat roof with a pitched one.

The mid-C20 produced little PUBLIC SCULPTURE, with *Benno Schotz*'s bust of James Keir Hardie, outside the Town Hall, Cumnock, of 1929, *Pilkington Jackson*'s 1960 R.S.F. Memorial, Ayr, and *David Gilbert*'s extraordinary Duncan Thomson Memorial Seat (1964), now at the Arran Heritage Museum, Rosaburn, the highlights. The spell was broken by Irvine Development Corporation, particularly through its New Town Artists-in-Residence Scheme: many were sculptors, e.g. *Mary Bourne*, and their work, often small-scale, can be found throughout the Irvine area, and culminates in the sinuous red sandstone dragon, which doubles as a beach shelter, on the shore at Irvine, of 1987 by *Anthony Vogt* and *Roy Fitzsimmons*. From the 1990s public sculpture again became an accepted element in townscape improvement and regeneration, e.g. *Malcolm Robertson*'s Remembrance,

1995, in the High Street, Ayr, or in Kilmarnock, where the classically inspired statue of Robert Burns with John Wilson, his first printer, and the laconic Johnnie Walker, both of 1995–6 by *Sandy Stoddart*, are accompanied by jovial street furniture.

First and foremost among the BANKS from this period is the ostentatious Neoclassical rotunda built by *W. J. Walker Todd* for the Royal Bank of Scotland at Kilmarnock Cross in 1937–9, but equally rewarding are the free Venetian former National Bank in Dockhead Street, Saltcoats, of 1931–2 by *A. Balfour & Stewart*, and the former Glasgow Savings Bank of 1935–7 by *Eric A. Sutherland* in High Street, Ayr. The period is marked by a rash of good POST OFFICES by *H. M. Office of Works* e.g. Prestwick (1927–8), Troon (1928–32) and Stevenston (1938–9). The briskly Modernist Post Office and Telephone Exchange at Brodick (1946–7) is the highlight of the first austere post-war years.

Many new types of building for LEISURE AND ENTERTAINMENT are a feature of the C20 burghs and villages. The first DEPARTMENT STORE in Ayrshire, recognizable as such, had been Hourstons in Ayr, built by *Allan Stevenson* in 1894–5, and extended by him in 1909–10 in a freer style, which is echoed in Kilmarnock's main department store, Lauder's Emporium, of 1923 by *Frederick Sage & Co.*

THEATRES had been erected in Ayrshire from the early years of the C19, e.g. the Theatre Royal, Ayr (now the Baptist Church Centre) of 1815–16, but it was only later in the C19 that they became widespread. The Gaiety Theatre, Ayr, with its amazing Rococo interior, was built in 1902–3 by *J. McHardy Young*. In Kilmarnock, the Kings Theatre, designed by *Alexander Cullen* (1903–4), was subsequently converted to a CINEMA. Although some purpose-built cinemas had been built before the First World War, none of those built in Ayrshire survive. The years of greatest cinema construction were the 1920s and 1930s. Every town had at least one and they were also found in some of the smaller settlements; amongst the best of those that remain are the former Green's Playhouse (now Mecca Bingo), Ayr, of 1930–1 by *John Fairweather*, *A. V. Gardner*'s Orient Cinema, Ayr (1931–2), *Alister MacDonald*'s Broadway Cinema, Prestwick (1934–5), and the stylized streamlined Radio City, Kilbirnie (*James Houston*, 1937–8), now beautifully restored.

There were numerous new attractions for visitors to the coastal towns also. In 1910–11 Ayr Town Council built the idiosyncratic Pavilion, by *J. K. Hunter*, designed to offer entertainments, though it suffered from competition with the theatres and cinemas of the town. More commercially successful was the Barrfields Pavilion, Largs (1930, *William Barclay*). To cater for the strollers on the esplanades, CAFÉS appeared, many run by Scots-Italians. Of these the best-known is Nardini's, at Largs, first opened in 1920, and rebuilt as the present 'super-café' in 1934–5 by *C. Davidson & Son* of Paisley. For the Nardinis' rivals, the Castelvecchis, *James Houston* designed the prow-like The Moorings, Largs, in 1935–6 (dem.).

Open-air SWIMMING POOLS were built at Troon (1931, dem.) and Prestwick (1929–31 by *William Cowie*, closed in 1972, now dem.), which when opened was the largest swimming pool in Scotland, and became the venue for the nationally famous annual bathing beauty competition. The swimming baths at Kilmarnock, of 1939–40 by *Alexander Dunlop* (dem. 1987) featured a wave machine gifted by *Glenfield & Kennedy Ltd*, the town's world-famous hydraulic engineers.

Elsewhere the freedom offered by the car encouraged people to build HOLIDAY HUTS in suitable places, e.g. particularly on the Carrick coast S of Lendalfoot, where they still abound in varied and distinctive splendour. SPORTING FACILITIES continued to improve and expand. Ayr Racecourse moved to a new site in 1903–7 designed by *W. C. & A. S. Manning*, and the earliest surviving stand, also by the Mannings, is of 1913–14. The grandstand at the Dam Park Stadium, Ayr, of 1961–3 by *Maurice Hickey*, is a finely judged exercise in cantilevered concrete, while the Sports Pavilion, Cumnock, of 1965–7, is a stylish result of the collaboration between Cumnock Burgh Council and *RMJM*. Multi-functional LEISURE CENTRES are now a standard part of the urban landscape, but the Magnum Centre, Irvine, of 1971–7 by *I.D.C.*, was a pioneer in the field, with an indoor football pitch, swimming pool, ice rink and much more all under one roof. The swimming baths at Ayr, of 1969–72 by *Cowie Torry & Partners*, were extended to form the Citadel Leisure Centre in 1994–6, while the Galleon Centre, Kilmarnock, is of 1986–7 by *Crichton Lang, Willis & Galloway*. Enhancement of the tourist attractions at Alloway began with *Frank Perry*'s Tam o' Shanter Experience (1975–6, now demolished) with a shop, restaurant and improved interpretation. The same elements shape its replacement, *Simpson & Brown*'s Robert Burns Birthplace Museum (2008–10) for the National Trust for Scotland.

A few individual late C20 buildings, slotted into the existing townscape, have their own particular merits, such as the veterinary surgery in Mauchline, of 1963–4, by *Park & McGill*, attractively of its period, or *Gratton McLean & Partners*' thoughtfully detailed Royal Bank of Scotland, Sandgate, Ayr, of 1970–3, and the *I.D.C.* infill at Nos. 83–85 High Street, Irvine, of 1982–6.

By the date of the latter, there existed an increased understanding of the urban environment, and regard for the organic development of burgh and village cores. Where redevelopment has taken place, it is often behind retained façades, as at the Kyle Centre, Ayr (1985, *Sheppard Robson*). A holistic approach to whole settlements has become increasingly popular in the early C21, beginning with *Page & Park*'s successful involvement at Newmilns (from 1999) and *Robert Potter & Partners*' work at Beith from 2005, both funded by Townscape Heritage Schemes; these attempts to reinvigorate moribund settlements blend sensitive restoration with, where appropriate, modern infill. As this volume goes to press (2012), similar schemes are being prepared for the towns of Irvine Bay, for Kilmarnock's John Finnie Street, for Ayr's New Bridge Street, all with a variety of architectural practices working to agreed master plans, and perhaps most excitingly at Cumnock, where the first fruits of the town's proximity to Dumfries House are being realized and confirm the continued evolution and growth of Ayrshire's rich architectural legacy.

GAZETTEER

AYRSHIRE

(including Ailsa Craig, Great Cumbrae, Horse Island,
Lady Isle and Little Cumbrae)

ADAMTON HOUSE

3020

2.5 km. E of Monkton

Now a hotel. 1885 by *Clarke & Bell*, for the iron and coal master J. G. A. Baird. Full-blown Victorian Jacobean, in randomly coursed red sandstone, set on a huge balustraded platform. Two storeys with projecting bays, shaped, corbelled and pinnacled gables to the attic, and tall, clustered chimneystacks including one of industrial proportions on the entrance front. Bulky *porte cochère* with flat Tudor arches, mock angle turrets and crenellations. In the basement walls, approximately 1.2 m. thick, may belong to the tower mentioned (1543) in the Register of Great Seal. Single storey former billiard room (NE) in a sympathetic style, added *c.* 1900 by *J. H. Craigie*, Clarke & Bell's principal assistant.

Altered inside, but still with much panelling in the hall and other rooms, one with a smart grey-veined marble chimneypiece with low columned overmantel. In the centre of the house a vast, oak imperial stair with squared balusters and a curved balustrade forming a balcony over the central flight. Very substantial additions of 1987–9 by *Dunlop & Paige*.

– LODGES. Touches of Jacobean.

AFTON LODGE *see* MOSSBLOWN

AIKET CASTLE

3040

2.25 km. WSW of Dunlop

A harled tower house, carefully re-created in 1976–9 by Katrina and Robert Clow (with the help of, amongst others, *Geoffrey Jarvis* and *Gavin Walker*) from the ruins left by a fire in 1957 of an ungainly Georgianized (*c.* 1743) tower.

Set on a rocky promontory above the River Glazert and surrounded by gardens, except on the N side where there is a
barmkin (remnants of which also survive on the W towards the
river). Three and four storeys, the taller block (E) containing
the earliest parts, probably later C15. After Cuninghame of
Aiket was assassinated in 1586 for his part in the murder of the
3rd Earl of Eglinton, the tower was largely destroyed but rebuilt
with the addition of the lower W range. Sometime after this the
main entrance was moved from the S to the N front, probably
when the barmkin was created. After the fire C16 walls survived
to second floor in the E range but during the reconstruction
were cut down and the upper parts rebuilt in brick. The top
floor, re-created in a C17 manner, has two plainly pedimented
wall-head dormers: the E one carved with the initials AC and
JK 1479, the other RC KC 1976. Above and to the r. of the
door is a tiny window which lit a small stair, probably late C16,
linking the first-floor hall to the vaulted ground-floor chambers.
The doorway has a bold C17 bolection moulding and a simple
pediment, possibly C18; above the door and in the second storey
at the E, diminutive shot-holes. The lower late C16 W range was
re-created as found except for the addition of a NW angle turret
with conical roof, whose former existence was assumed from
the evidence of former corbel stones.

On the S front of the four-storey tower, three corbels projecting above the ground floor allowed the re-creation of the stair-
turret which had formerly provided access from the first floor to
the attic. The entrance now has an exaggerated ogee lintel,
modelled on a lintel at Badenheath Castle (Lanarkshire), a house
with an almost identical plan. Also added were the two pedimented wall-head dormers, the W one slightly projecting with a
corbelled stone apron below the window, a simplified version of
a detail at Amisfield (Dumfries and Galloway) or the high
window over the entrance of Lochranza Castle, Arran (q.v.).

Inside, the ground floors of both blocks had been vaulted but
only two vaults were intact in 1976. These have been repaired
and reinstated. In the E range (approx. 9.1 m. by 6.1 m.), the
two vaults run N–S, the western one now forming the entrance
hall; in the W block the vault is E–W. To the l. of the S entrance
are remnants of a newel stair, probably disused since the C17
when the wide curving stair to the r. of the N door was constructed. Off the hall to the r., the kitchen with a large arched
hearth with a window on the much rebuilt W gable. This again
is probably C17 and is a smaller version of the C16 arched fireplace whose dimensions were revealed during reconstruction
(it appears to have included the surviving bake oven). The
curved stone stair to the r. of the N door was reconstructed to
the first floor leading to the study on the r. with a small closet.
In the Hall on the l. columned jambs for a fireplace, probably
late C15, with reconstructed lintel. Roll-moulded arched window
recesses were carefully rebuilt and elsewhere chimneypieces
reinstated. The outcome is a thoughtful interpretation of a late
C16 tower sensitively adapted to C20 living.

On the E side of the barmkin is a low cottage range of 1743, given a low-key renovation scheme to provide some of the services not easily accommodated within the castle.

CORN MILL, with lade to S, C18 and C19 L-plan. Renovated and modernized 2003–4.

AILSA CRAIG
16.5 km. W of Girvan

A mighty volcanic plug rising majestically from the Firth of   1
Clyde. Originally part of the lands of the Earls of Carrick, it passed in 1404 into the ownership of Crossraguel Abbey and subsequently to the Kennedys (marquises of Ailsa) of Cassillis and Culzean. The island's granite – ailsite – became commercially valuable, especially for the manufacture of curling stones (*see* Mauchline). The quarries are now silent, the lighthouse auto-mated, and the bulk of the island reserved for its bird colonies.

The remains of a strongly built early C16 TOWER HOUSE cling limpet-like to a ledge on the S side. Its position and character resemble Kildonan (Arran, p. 701). It has a rectangular plan, relatively thin walls and appears to have had a courtyard to its N. E doorway reached from now fragmentary exterior steps. There are two vaulted floors with a vaulted cellar set in the slope of the rock and a ruinous upper floor. A straight flight of stairs turning to a turnpike at the SE corner leads to the main floor where the vaults of the two chambers run at right angles to that of the floor below. Large fireplace and adjoining oven in one room; the adjoining small room over the entrance, only accessed from the turnpike, doubled as a guardroom and store. Traces of recesses at the angles of the fragmentary upper storey suggest that there may have been angle turrets.

LIGHTHOUSE. 1883–6 by *D. & T. Stevenson* for the Commis-sioners of Northern Lights, a surprisingly late date to light such a major and unforgiving obstacle. Circular tower, 11 m. high, harled, with a terminal granite band, from which the lantern rises. Contemporary KEEPERS' HOUSES and other ancillary buildings, including remains of the GAS WORKS, designed and equipped by *James Keith*, which powered the mammoth FOG SIGNALS. Wooden PIER rebuilt in 1922 by *G. M. Holmes Douglas*, principally for the shipment of granite. It was connected to the main quarry face by a narrow-gauge tramway.

ALLOWAY   *3010*

It is impossible to talk of Alloway without reference to Robert Burns, who was born here in 1759, and the village is now defined by the buildings associated with him. This was an old settlement, and a pre-Reformation parochial centre, but by the C18 still little more than a few houses dependent on Ayr. The lands of Alloway belonged to Ayr Town Council, and their sale in 1754 led to the creation of many small estates, still largely extant.

The Burns connection, together with the impetus of these estates, led to a revival of Alloway's fortunes in the C19, marked by the erection of a new church and the re-establishment of parochial status. In the C20 it has become a focus for substantial residential growth.

ALLOWAY AULD KIRK, Alloway. Traditionally dated to 1516, with a rebuilding of 1653, but clearly medieval in origin. Out of regular use by the mid C18, and ruinous by 1790, when it was sketched for Francis Grose, who included it in his *Antiquities* at the suggestion of Burns (who penned *Tam o' Shanter* in return). Extensive conservation work by *ARPL Architects*, 2008. Rubble-built, rectangular, the walls still standing to their full height, with E and W gables, the former with a double lancet and arched bellcote. An arched entrance on both S and N walls, the other openings rectangular. Divided internally to form two burial aisles. The church sits within a small kirkyard; in the SW corner the square MAUSOLEUM of General John Hughes of Mount Charles †1832, its four sides identical, with Greek Doric columns distyle *in antis*.

HEADSTONES mostly C18 and C19, many with deeply incised lettering (e.g. John McLure in Nethertoun of Allouay, †1753), or richly carved imagery, such as that to a smith near the NE corner, with an hourglass, skull, cross-bones and a representation of a smith shoeing a horse. The headstone erected by Burns for his parents, William †1784, and Agnes, †1820, had, by 1838, already 'crumbled away or been carried off piecemeal by rapacious relic-hunters'. Its plain replacement has the epitaph composed for his father on the back.

ALLOWAY PARISH CHURCH, Alloway. Gothic, of an idiosyncratic bent. 1857–9 by *Campbell Douglas*, originally of four bays with a S porch and N transept, simple lancets, low stepped buttresses and stepped skews. S transept of 1876 by *Douglas & Sellars*, with matching detail, and extended W and E in 1889–90 by *J. MacVicar Anderson* (chancel, S session house), reusing the two big Dec windows in the W and E gables, that at the W with seven low cusped lights beneath a triangular spheroid with a central hexagon, from which pairs of cusped lights radiate between quatrefoils. E window more conventional, of six lights, with three big quatrefoils in the head. On the W gable an elaborate muscular bellcote.

STAINED GLASS. A rich and varied collection. – W window, kaleidoscopic decorative glass by *W. & J. J. Kier*, 1858. – Nave S wall, from the E, Resurrection by *Douglas Hamilton*, 1958; Four Seasons by *Susan Bradbury*, 1996, rising from winter at the bottom through the cycle of seasons to return to winter at the top; Robert Burns, also by *Bradbury*, 1996, with a river's movement well captured in lenses and seeded glass. – Nave N wall, also from the E, Suffer Little Children by *Christopher Webb*, 1942, very conventional; Moses, a powerful figure by *James A.*

Crombie, executed by the *Abbey Studio*, 1959; David, by *Gordon Webster*, 1962, the blues well to the fore; memorial to Mary Cubie, *Susan Bradbury*, *c.* 2001, with effective use of lenses in a vision of child-like pastoralism. – s transept w wall, Noah by the *City Glass Co. Ltd*, 1968; in the s wall, the three-light Nativity, a memorial to James Baird, by *Stephen Adam*, 1877, a fine example of his richly decorative style, with Japanese and Pre-Raphaelite influences; in the E wall, a contrasting, more intimate Nativity, of 1922 by *Christopher Whall*, executed by *Guthrie & Wells*. – N transept w wall, Jesus in the Temple by *Douglas Hamilton*, 1955, and though Christ may bear a resemblance to Fotherington-Thomas, the bewilderment of his parents, in the upper panel, is well caught; N wall, Jesus Preaching by *W. & J. J. Kier*, 1881, in memory of William Dixon, of the Glasgow iron works ('Dixon's Blazes'); E wall, Flight into Egypt, by *Mayer & Co.*, 1890. – The six-light chancel window is by *Clayton & Bell*, 1891, while the trefoils in the side walls are by *Gordon Webster* (N, 1958, s, 1969).

PRIMARY SCHOOL, Doonholm Road. 2005–8 by *Ryder HKS* for South Ayrshire Council. L-plan with sheet-metal finishes to walls and roofs, some of the panels finished in cheerful pastels. One gable-ended block has a long central atrium, with classrooms on either side. A further wing, similarly finished, for community facilities such as a library.

DESCRIPTION

The main monuments of the village cleave close to the main street (also called ALLOWAY) between Burns' Cottage and the New Bridge of Doon. BURNS' COTTAGE is a thatched single storey. The s end is the dwelling, of clay beneath whitewashed harl, erected in 1757 by William Burns and consisted of a living room (l.) and byre (r.). Flagged floors, plastered walls and open timber roofs: the s room has a fireplace facing a bed recess. Doubled in length in the late C18 to create a new N byre and barn, the former byre then converted for living. The addition is at a slight angle and of painted stone. The barn has a flagged floor, the byre cobbles and wooden stalls. Museum (now Education Centre) of 1899–1900 by *Allan Stevenson*, who also restored the house and byre. All were restored in 2008–10 by *Simpson & Brown*, with a new entrance to the s.

Opposite the cottage, Nos. 21–31, of 1903–4 by *J. K. Hunter*, a terrace of six two-storey cottages, rather surprisingly in an English-influenced Arts and Crafts style. They have paired porches with columns (some now infilled), and prominent rainwater goods. To the s of these is ALLOWAY PUBLIC HALL, the former school of 1848–9 by *Clarke & Bell*, thoroughly remodelled in 1929–30 by *Robert S. Lorimer*. Single-storey, stone built, with a steeply pitched roof and crowstepped gables. Four bays to the street, the windows with ashlar lintels, incised with ogee heads and central roses; in the centre the WAR MEMORIAL of 1919–20 by *James A. Morris*, sculpted by *James*

A. Young of Glasgow. Scots Renaissance: the bronze panels framed by panelled stone pilasters supporting semicircular stone heads meticulously carved with the royal crests of Scotland, England and Ireland. To the rear, a lower parallel wing, also crowstepped, and linking entrance block. The w range contains a handsome barrel-vaulted panelled HALL with plasterwork by *C. d'O. Pilkington Jackson* including two well-realized tympana, The Deil's awa wi' the Exciseman, and The Jolly Beggars. The former SCHOOLMASTER'S HOUSE, of 1849, in the style of William Burn, with a feast of gables of varying size, the bigger ones stepped, faces DOONHOLM ROAD to the E. Next to it the former MANSE, of 1863, perhaps by *Campbell Douglas* (*see* Parish Church, above): two storey, L-plan, but undemonstrative. Opposite is GREENFIELD HOUSE, a neat plastered classical gabled box of *c.* 1800, but rebuilt here *c.* 1854, with painted dressings and raised quoins. Central doorpiece with fluted Doric columns and a triglyph and metope entablature, the metope decoration of a non-classical bent, with rosettes and a thistle.

Further s, on the w side of Alloway is GREENFIELD AVENUE with, on its s side, a fine run of large villas built 1933–8 by *James Carrick*, some of the best of that date in the county, and including his own house, MARTINS (No. 5). They are in a broadly English traditional style, and while no two are alike, there are some unifying motifs, particularly the narrow, rust-red rustic bricks. Many lighten this with white harl, and others have stone dressings. The houses stand in large, well-wooded grounds.

The other group of significant buildings lie close to the Auld Kirk and Parish Church. E of the Parish Church, off Murdoch's Lone, is the refreshingly modern ROBERT BURNS BIRTH-PLACE MUSEUM, of 2008–10 by *Simpson & Brown* for the National Trust for Scotland, with parabolic sedum roofs, plentiful glazing, and walls of stone and timber. SCULPTURES in the grounds, including two by *Kenny Hunter*: To a Mouse, 2010, and Liberty Regain'd, 2011. s of the Auld Kirk, DOON-BRAE, a spreading faintly Arts and Crafts largely early C20 house, built around a cottage villa of *c.* 1830. Opposite is MONUMENT COTTAGE, built for the keeper of the Burns Monument (*see* below) in 1868–9 by *James I. McDerment*, with rock-faced dressings and rustic chimney-heads, and an echo of the monument's Grecian theme with a central pedimented doorpiece with fluted Corinthian columns and a frieze with wreath decoration. Attractive railings. On the approach to the Old Bridge, the BRIG O' DOON HOTEL of *c.* 1829 but with substantial additions of 1903–4 by *Allan Stevenson* (see the oriel in the N elevation), 1924–5 by *William Cowie* and 1949 by *John E. Murray*. Thoroughly restored in 1997. Its gardens, with their paths, lawns and mature trees, have always been an attraction.

Towering above cottage and hotel is the dizzying and lavish
99   BURNS MONUMENT, a version of the Choragic Monument

of Lysicrates, by *Thomas Hamilton*, 1817 (built 1820–3 by *John Connell*). It had been planned as early as 1814, when Alexander Boswell proposed a subscription. Won in competition, this was the design that established Hamilton as an architect and would be reprised in his monument to the poet at Edinburgh (1830). His interpretation is loose, taking the form of an open temple and built on an exaggerated scale, raised on a massive triangular ashlar base and with nine Corinthian columns 9.1 m. high, their design derived from the Temple of Jupiter Stator, Rome. The upper parts are more faithful, with a wreathed entablature, a full circle of antefixae and finial of an elaborate gilded copper tripod, supported by dolphins. Inside the base is a domed, top-lit chamber with Greek key and a frieze of bucrania. In a niche, framed by fluted columns, a bust of Burns by *John Steell*, 1885, presented by John Keppie. Of the railings which surrounded the monument there survive six circular piers, with heads supported by gryphons. The garden setting is especially attractive and includes the rustic hexagonal STATUE HOUSE, built in 1830 for statues of Souter Johnnie and Tam o' Shanter, carved by *James Thom c.* 1820.* The building now also houses a further statue by Thom: Nance Tinnock.

s is the AULD BRIG O' DOON, scene of Tam's hair's-breadth escape from the witches, and among the best of the county's bridges, in a dramatic and picturesque situation. It is a tall, narrow, single segmental arch, with dressed voussoirs, and low stone parapets extended on either side as wing walls. Traditionally stated to be C15, but more probably C17. Threatened with demolition in 1812, but saved by its connections with Burns, and twice restored, in 1831–2 after 'having become dilapidated by mischievous persons' and in 1929 by *J. Wilson Paterson*, with the present cobbled surface. The NEW BRIDGE of 1812–16 is of coursed rubble with dressed voussoirs. Downstream a castellated four-arch BRIDGE may be seen. Of 1906, it carried the Maidens & Dunure Light Railway.

BURNESS AVENUE, 0.8 km. NE. A terrace of six two-storey houses, of 1960 by *Francis B. Dunbar*. Each at an angle to the road, and set back in turn; of rustic brick, with prominent timber facings, and shallowly pitched roofs.

MANSIONS

CAMBUSDOON, 0.4 km. NW. The porch only of the Jacobethan mansion of 1853–4 by *David Bryce* for James Baird (dem. 1976). Rather jolly Jacobethan LODGE, also by *Bryce*, in Greenfield Avenue.

---

* Thom, a monumental mason, was 'discovered' by David Auld, a keen Burnsian, who admired his bust of Burns. He commissioned statues of Tam o' Shanter and Souter Johnnie, probably the pair now at Kirkoswald (q.v.). Following their success, Thom produced a second pair, and these were exhibited throughout Britain, as far afield as London, before Auld brought them back to this specially created home. At least ten other pairs were also made before Thom emigrated to America.

BELLEISLE HOUSE, 1 km. N. Now a hotel. Originally a plain
classical house completed in 1794 for Hew Hamilton of
Pinmore, whose brother Robert had built Rozelle (*see* below)
– both were built on the proceeds of West Indian estates and
named after plantations. It is now as recast and extended in
1830–1 in a restrained Scots Jacobean manner by *David Bryce*,
while in William Burn's office, for Colonel Alexander West
Hamilton, with a substantial range of 1900 by *James Davidson*
of Airdrie for the Coats family.

Straggling N (entrance) front, the W half of 1830–1 in pinkish
squared rubble with polished dressings. Entrance in a full-
height, narrow, projecting, crowstepped gabled bay at the head
of a short flight of steps. Its extravagantly detailed pedimented
doorpiece is closely related to Bryce's 1830–2 doorpiece at
Cassillis (q.v.). The asymmetrical composition with crowstepped gables and slender turrets with candle-snuffer roofs is
a reminder of Burn's Milton Lockhart (Lanarkshire, 1829). On
the S front the form of the C18 house can still be discerned: three
bays and two storeys over a raised basement (horrible late C20
sun-lounge) and with a big canted bay in the centre, still with
sash and case windows. Davidson's E extension is Jacobean too
but less refined, in a creamier sandstone.

In the HALL a passion for Robert Burns is revealed, with
dramatic wooden and plaster decorations by *Davidson* illustrating his works over the entrance door, in the pilaster plinths
and culminating in the mind-blowing confection of a white
marble chimneypiece, of putti jostling with cornucopia-hug-
ging maidens, the tale of Tam o' Shanter above and festoons of
thistles. Screen between the hall and stair of paired pilasters and
satyr consoles supporting a frieze with a hunting scene. The
STAIR, with open strapwork balustrade, is probably in the position of the C18 stair but has been turned around with a balcony
that opens onto a wide landing extending into the canted bay
of the S front. This area has been decorated with more pilasters
celebrating Burns. The DINING ROOM, off the hall, is the most
complete room of 1830–1. Elegant geometric patterned plaster
ceiling, the sections divided by guilloche-moulded bands and
with modillions in the central oval. In the former DRAWING
ROOM another 1830s Jacobean ceiling and chimneypiece, 1900
detail inspired by the Louis XVI music room at Versailles, e.g.
full-height *boiseries* with musical instruments, and a tall overmantel mirror with luscious floral swags. Double doors set in a
theatrical frame open to the BOUDOIR (Fountenbleau Dining
Room), modelled on Marie Antoinette's boudoir. In the E
extension, a curious room decorated in the Moorish style of the
Aesthetic Movement, perhaps formerly a billiard room. The
elaborate timber chimneypiece has a segmental arch and
columns with pomegranate capitals, a tiled hearth recess, and
above a latticed concave cornice a screen in front of a now
decayed tapestry, reminiscent of the Moorish extravaganza at
Neilshill (q.v.). – STABLES, *c.* 1829. Decayed. – Huge GLASS-
HOUSE rebuilt 1955. – LODGE. Neo-Jacobean, probably 1829.

ROZELLE HOUSE, I km. NE of Belleisle. Robert Hamilton of
  Bourtreehill acquired the property in 1754 and built this small
  Palladian mansion in 1760. Five-bay main block of two storeys
  over a basement and quadrants linking to low two-storey pavilions (cf. John Adam's design for Ballochmyle, q.v.). The main
  entrance front retains much of its C18 character but in 1831
  Archibald Hamilton of Carcluie commissioned *David Bryce* to
  enlarge and update the house. He added the porch, lowered
  the windows in the principal floor and extended the E pavilion.
  The major alterations are to the rear, which has a T-plan addition that has three neatly pedimented gables, rusticated quoins,
  four tall ridge stacks and a cast-iron balcony, originally with
  steps to the garden.
    Completely remodelled inside by Bryce. High-quality wood-
  work and big marble chimneypieces in the principal rooms,
  only the cornices remaining from the 1760s. In the stair balustrade Bryce's familiar scrolled and bursting-leaf uprights
  alternating with simpler balusters.
    The house was given to Ayr Town Council in 1968 and the
  E pavilion and part of the stable court behind converted in
  1972 for the MACLAURIN ART GALLERY, a stylish, low-key
  work by *Cowie Torry & Partners*. Addition with three arched
  windows echoing coachhouse arches. – SCULPTURES. The
  Tragic Sacrifice of Christ by *Ronald Rae*, 1978–9. Granite.
DOONHOLM, 0.8 km. SE. Set in well-wooded policies at the top
  of a steep bank which slopes down to the River Doon. Built
  for Dr William Fergusson *c.* 1760 as a straightforward two-
  storey house, with basement and attic, three bays wide with
  long-and-short quoins, a cill band at second floor and gable-
  end stacks. Overlaid *c.* 1820 by a smart five-bay front with
  pilasters for John Hunter, Fergusson's son-in-law. Big bows on
  the returns and a substantial pilastered porch with steps to the
  garden. In 1898 J. Kennedy commissioned the grandiose
  entrance on the NE gable of the original house from *Campbell
  Douglas & Sellars* (probably by *A. N. Paterson* who had recently
  joined the firm). Edwardian Baroque, with Tuscan columns of
  red sandstone, large oak-panelled door with a delightful external latch including a child nestling in the Baroque swirls of the
  handle. A bow-ended billiard room has been demolished. The
  rear elevation is a restoration of 1980 by *Ronald Alexander*,
  following the removal of a mid-C19 wing. Faithful to the Georgian original in its details, except for the Venetian window and
  basement door.
    Interior primarily of 1898–1902, white marble steps to raised
  ground floor with contemporary embossed paper on the walls;
  Jacobean motifs in plasterwork, chimneypieces and overmantels but the staircase mid-C19. Barrel-vaulted plaster ceiling in
  the dining room with an elaborate light pendant. Handsome
  Edwardian Renaissance chimneypiece in the drawing room.

BRAE OF AUCHENDRANE, 2.6 km. S. Late C18 farmhouse. Above
  the door a sundial flanked by figures reputed to be Adam and

Eve from a house at Millheugh, Larkhall. There is also a stone
owl perched on the N end of the main façade. Charmingly
detailed low S wing of *c.* 1921 for Colin Thomson, an Ayrshire
cattle breeder, probably by *J. K. Hunter*, or his assistant *James
Carrick*. The drawing-room chimneypiece illustrates the
nursery rhyme 'Hey Diddle Diddle', an allusion to Thomson's
business.

NETHER AUCHENDRANE. *See* p. 551
NEWARK. *See* p. 554

ALMONT *see* PINWHERRY

4020   ANNBANK

Former mining village, rebuilt after 1931 (*William Reid*, Ayr
County Architect), with its main street along a ridge in a loop
of the Ayr, with stunning views towards Arran, and wooded
braes on almost all sides. Church and school are at Mossblown
(q.v.).
       MEMORIAL. James Brown, MP, †1929, unveiled 1954.
Clumsy Gothic arch over a flaming urn, in Creetown granite.

ENTERKINE HOUSE. *See* p. 317.

3040   ANNICK LODGE
                          5 km. NE of Irvine

62   Set in an Arcadian landscape with the Water of Annick close to
     its rear and an open parkland prospect to the S enclosed by
     mature shelter belts. Named by Alexander Montgomerie, a
     nephew of the 12th Earl of Eglinton who acquired the property
     c. 1790 and remodelled the house at that time.

The elegant S front has a simple Palladian character. Five bays
     wide and two storeys but no basement, with a piended slate
     roof swept at the eaves; harled with rusticated quoins and a
     central bay slightly advanced with rusticated pilaster-strips
     supporting a steep pediment with terminal urns. The Corin-
     thian-columned and pedimented doorcase is late C18 but the
     window above with eared architrave is earlier. Shallow quad-
     rant screens with ball finials and rusticated openings link to
     simple low rectangular pavilions, each with a blind niche at the
     centre. It has always been accepted that the house took on this
     appearance *c.* 1790 but it seems more likely that this is the
     house known to have been built for John Snodgrass in 1747. It
     was described as 'near an ancient manor-house', and embed-
     ded into the rubble-built rear are two straight joints that provide
     evidence of an earlier building, possibly of the C16 or early C17
     (inside, at ground floor, a stone barrel vault remains with
     0.9-m. thick walls). A further straight joint to the E suggests

the existence of a low gabled wing, altered when a stair compartment was added *c.* 1700. So Montgomerie appears only to
have forged these earlier buildings into an uneasy symmetry
and added the bow onto the W elevation of the front range.

The rubble E elevation incorporates an early C18 range,
raised probably *c.* 1790, and is attached to a N range of low
service buildings including kennels. Another service range
adjoins the W elevation. At the rear, a retaining wall to the river
has small square pavilions at either end with Gothic windows,
the E one fitted out as a game larder. To the W a delicate cast-
iron BRIDGE with intersecting Gothic arches.

Inside, handsome late C18 staircase with alternating twisted
and plain classical balusters and a twisted newel. In the staircase window, late C19 coloured glass emblems associated with
the Montgomeries. The house was extensively and expensively
redecorated at the end of the C19, almost certainly by a
Glasgow firm. In the hall a curious, mannered early C18-style
stone chimneypiece with beaten metal panels and a cut-out
pattern to the ash tray. The SITTING ROOM (late C18 dining
room) chimneypiece with paired Doric columns and a central
panel with a chariot also looks late C19. The alcove was probably created in the late C18 when the original chimneypiece
was removed. The DRAWING ROOM on the first floor also has
an elaborate late C19 chimneypiece and overmantel, with
Adamesque details and mirrors, and *W. A.S. Benson* light fittings. In the principal BEDROOM, a coved ceiling retaining its
mid-C18 egg-and-dart cornice. In the rear of the house a
number of early C18 chimneypieces and alcoves for box beds.

CONSERVATORY. Late C19. Square turning to an octagon,
its upper section an iron and glass lantern. In the E pavilion
the late C19 BILLIARD ROOM. Intricate timbered roof supported on corbels and with arcading around the top light.
Arcaded overmantel. To the E extensive stables, with some fittings, and Home Farm. Square rusticated gate piers with fine
urn finials.

ARDEER *see* STEVENSTON

ARDMILLAN CASTLE *see* GIRVAN

ARDROSSAN   2040

Now best known as a commercial and passenger port, but an
ancient parish, with a church and castle on the rocky headland
around which the town unfolds. In the C17 a new parish centre
developed in the E around the harbour at Saltcoats (q.v.), but the
focus shifted back to Ardrossan in the early C19, when the 12th
Earl of Eglinton set about making it the new port of Glasgow.
A harbour was built, and streets set out to a rigid grid-plan
devised by *Peter Nicholson*. A canal link to Glasgow, which would
avoid the long, tortuous and tidal route up the Clyde, never fully
materialized; only the section from Glasgow (Port Eglinton, no

less) to Johnstone was ever built, before it was swept away in the
tide of railway-mania. The town and harbour prospered, however,
and were linked by railway to Glasgow from 1840, and for a while
in the mid C19 became a fashionable sea-bathing resort, as
attested by the unique group of villas in South Crescent Road.
The harbour was enlarged and modernized in the late C19, and
developed a considerable coal trade, but declined in the C20.
In Glasgow Street and Princes Street, and in South Crescent
Road, Nicholson's and Eglinton's vision lives on, but the town
feels too big for its people.

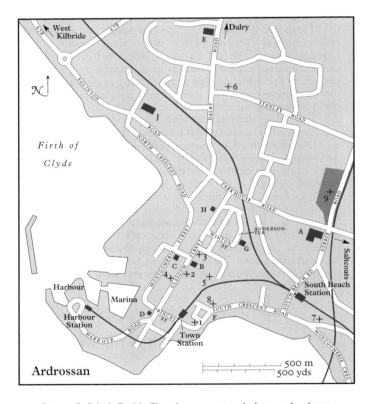

Ardrossan

1	Barony St John's Parish Church	A	Ardrossan Academy
2	Christian Brethren Hall	B	Ardrossan Civic Centre
3	Church of the Nazarene	C	Ardrossan Fire Station
4	Evangelical Union Congregational Church	D	Former Police Station
5	Old Kirk	E	St Peter's Primary School
6	Park Parish Church	F	War Memorial
7	St Andrew (Episcopal)	G	Winton Primary School
8	St Peter in Chains (R.C.)	H	James Moffat Centre
9	Ardrossan Cemetery	J	Seafield School

CHURCHES AND CEMETERY

BARONY ST JOHN'S PARISH CHURCH, Arran Place. Spiky
Gothic of 1844 by *Black & Salmon* of Glasgow. Extended and
the roof raised in 1888–9 by *James Ritchie* of Glasgow. Remarkable polished stone front consisting of a projecting gabled
centre, its clasping buttresses topped by pinnacles, a square
clock tower also with corner pinnacles and a recessed, octagonal
spire with ship weathervane. Galleried interior. The ceiling is
plastered and panelled, ribbed and wagon-headed along the
length of the centre, and is the result of Ritchie's alterations.
– Large ORGAN CASE and PULPIT, both of 1889, with panels
of blind tracery of ogee arches, quatrefoils and open trefoils.
– STAINED GLASS. Mostly *c.* 1889, by *W. & J. J. Kier*, betraying
the continuing German influence in their work: the best Suffer
Little Children, S wall, W window. – N wall, E, a doleful Good
Shepherd by *William Meikle & Sons*, 1897. – In the vestibule a
back-lit war memorial window of 1919 designed by *Anning Bell*,
executed by *Guthrie & Wells*, from St John's Church (dem. 1991).
    CHURCH HALL, to the l., 1886–7, also probably by *Ritchie*.
Low E porch, and big circular window, its centre a Star of
David.

CHRISTIAN BRETHREN HALL, Glasgow Street. Former school
of 1846.

CHURCH OF THE NAZARENE, Glasgow Street. 1857–8 by *Thomas
Wallace*. Tudor Gothic front of three bays with pilasters rising
through the battlemented parapet to form octagonal pinnacles
with onion caps. Plain plastered interior with a rear gallery,
and a flat panelled ceiling with a very large wheel rosette. To
the rear, a simple three-bay red sandstone hall, 1874–5, also by
Wallace.

EVANGELICAL UNION CONGREGATIONAL CHURCH, Glasgow
Street. 1903 by *T. P. Marwick* of Edinburgh. All the interest is
in the main front of rock-faced sandstone. Battlemented octagonal towers project l. and r. of the pointed central doorway and
the wide five-light window above. Foliated vesica in the oddly
shouldered gable. Side and rear elevations harled. Panelled
plaster barrel-vaulted ceiling and a rear gallery. – PULPIT with
crocketed gable, set between two dominating ORGAN CASES
by the *SCWS Cabinet Works*, Beith, 1962. – Contemporary
Gothic LIGHT FITTINGS. – STAINED GLASS of 1903: in the S
wall with appley greens; in the window above the pulpit a
vibrant I Bring You Good Tidings.

OLD KIRK, Castlehill. Very fragmentary remains of the church
first mentioned in 1226. It was destroyed by a storm in 1695.
Oblong plan, 19.5 m by 7.9 m. A few scattered and dumb
gravestones. The site is not enclosed, the indifference almost
palpable.

PARK PARISH CHURCH, Stanley Road. 1958–9 by *James Houston
& Son* of Kilbirnie. Brick with a steeply pitched tiled roof, and
harled gable. Brick offices to the r., and harled low-pitched hall
to the l. Inside, a boarded wooden ceiling, formed into bays
by steel beams which continue to the ground. Plaster Greek

CROSS behind the altar, with symbols of the Evangelists between the arms.

ST ANDREW (Episcopal), South Crescent Road. 1874–5 by *David Thomson* of Glasgow. E.E. Nave, lower chancel and shallow transepts, in pink sandstone. Lancet windows, three-light E and transept windows, and a W porch with a round window above, composed of three quatrefoils and three small circular lights. Complex kingpost nave roof, the chancel a boarded vault. – REREDOS, timber with cusped tracery and paintings of saints by *William Hole*. – Caen stone PULPIT and FONT, both carved by *Charles Grassby*, the pulpit designed by Thomson. – STAINED

33   GLASS. Nave, S wall, an excellent Crucifixion by *Harrington Mann*, executed by *Guthrie & Wells*, 1894. The lower panel, with an angel gathering flowers, especially charming and poignant. – N wall, an unusual etiolated St Cuthbert by *L. C. Evetts*, 1960, and the Maries at the Tomb, a neatly composed design by *Clayton & Bell*, 1913. Also by *Clayton & Bell* the earlier chancel windows: three-light E window, Ascension, 1905, and the animated two-light S window, Healing the Blind Man and Raising Lazarus, 1912.

Behind the church a pretty HALL in red sandstone, 1905 by *John Armour Jun.* of Irvine, with some Arts and Crafts details. To the l. of the church the former RECTORY, 1886–8 by *John Armour Sen.* Its porch has moulded reveals and a stilted pointed arched head.

39   ST PETER IN CHAINS (R.C.), South Crescent Road. By *Gillespie, Kidd & Coia*, of Glasgow, 1938 (job architects *Jack Coia* with *T. Warnett Kennedy*). Easily the best interwar church in Ayrshire: here the young Coia was able to put his ideas into practice, looking beyond the British Isles for his inspiration, to create an enduring design in a Scandinavian idiom. The top of the flat-headed tower with its octagonal copper lantern is evidently influenced by Stockholm Town Hall. Walls of multi-hued Accrington Nori bricks in the gabled nave with low aisles to either side. S elevation unrelieved brick apart from the pointed entrance, with a big decorative panel above by *Alexander Archibald*, the foreman bricklayer, its patterning reminiscent of an American Indian head-dress with a stone exclamation mark; similar E doorway. Six-bay aisles, with a clearstorey above; both with horizontal steel-framed windows. The interior is bright, but does not match the innovative exterior. Plaster walls and coved ceiling supported on sturdy brick pillars, and a rear organ gallery. – Marble ALTAR under a skied baldacchino.

Respectful HALLS to the rear, 1963–4, and 1997–8 by *McMillan & Cronin*, and contemporary PRESBYTERY, with wide eaves, rebuilt 2005–6 after a fire.

ARDROSSAN CEMETERY, Sorbie Road. The N section was opened in 1856. Contemporary single-storey LODGE with bargeboards. Extended 1899 by *Allan Gilfillan*. The harled and half-timbered two-storey lodge probably of that date. Close to the main gates, two marble MONUMENTS to Alexander Cumming †1912, and his sons, all monumental masons in

Ardrossan: prominently signed *Cumming*, and clearly placed to ensure maximum advertisement.

PUBLIC BUILDINGS

ARDROSSAN ACADEMY, Sorbie Road. Two main buildings, one of 1930–3 by *William Reid*, County Architect. Symmetrical, classical, brick, with a single-storey seven-bay stone-faced central block, projected forward, and pavilion outer bays. Of courtyard plan, as is its considerably duller largely three-storey neighbour (1970–1, *Ayr County Council Architects Dept*). Playing fields opposite have attractive stone and bronze GATES, erected as a war memorial in 1954.

ARDROSSAN CIVIC CENTRE, Glasgow Street. The heart is a two-storey Tudor Gothic house (Castle Craig) of 1853. Its wings have crowstepped gables and first-rate barley-sugar chimney cans. Converted for Ardrossan Town Council in 1948 with big harled extensions of 1972–4 by *Robert Rennie & Watson*: to the r. offices; to the l., the single-storey ARDROSSAN INDOOR BOWLING CLUB, with a long oversailing window facing Glasgow Street. Gothick GATEPIERS and, in the grounds, a quirky SUNDIAL, four sides of geometrical shapes, dated 1795, inscribed RW KIRKHALL OWNER on one face, RW KIRKHALL ARCHITECT on another, for *Robert Weir* of Kirkhall.

ARDROSSAN FIRE STATION, Barr Street. 1933–4 by *Black & Shapley*. Large, plain, harled and tiled, with brick details, a barracks to accommodate both the engine and its crew. 1960s dark grey brick engine house behind.

Former POLICE STATION, Harbour Street. 1888–9 by *John Murdoch* of Ayr. Symmetrical red sandstone Scots Baronial, with crowstepped gables to either end, that to the r. corbelled out above a door with thin rope moulding and a battlemented head. A battlemented parapet links the gables. Crowstepped stacks on the side elevations, that to the l. corbelled out.

ST PETER'S PRIMARY SCHOOL, South Isle Road. 1994–5 by *Strathclyde Regional Council*. Two big monopitched teaching blocks, asymmetrically butted together with prominent roofs running down to low walls of windows: this prominence accentuated by the low-lying position of the school.

WAR MEMORIAL, South Crescent Road. 1922–3 by *P. Macgregor Chalmers*, completed after his death by *J. J. Waddell* & *T. P. W. Young*. One of Ayrshire's best war memorials. An inspired and capably executed design, the imagery unusual, but characteristic of Chalmers's thoughtful architecture. Well-proportioned granite Celtic cross, rising from a rectangular base. On the shaft three finely executed carved panels representing religion (St Columba), war (Robert Bruce and Admiral Wood) and peace (Livingstone, Watt and Burns).

WINTON PRIMARY SCHOOL, Anderson Terrace. 1897–9 by *John Armour Jun.* of Irvine. Single storey in grey sandstone with Arts and Crafts details. Symmetrical s elevation, its projecting end bays with Dutch gables and ball finials. The shallower and

lower central bay has a similar gable and a decorative date
panel (*Alexander Cumming*, sculptor). Asymmetrical w elevation with round-arched entrance with keystone and shallow
swan-neck pediment. Pedimented gable wing to the l., and set
back to the l. of this, a congruent brick addition of *c.* 2001.

ARDROSSAN HARBOUR

The brainchild of Hugh Montgomerie, 12th Earl of Eglinton,
who succeeded to the title in 1796. Plans were drawn up by
Thomas Telford, Parliamentary approval was obtained in 1805, and
work began in 1806. Although the first dock was brought into
use in 1810 work continued until 1815; the resident engineer was
David Henry. Of Telford's designs and the 'massive masonry
constructed under [Henry's] sole superintendence' all that
remains is the long SEA WALL at the Winton Dock (car ferry
terminal), probably of 1812–13, with a mid-C19 LIGHTHOUSE at
the seaward end. Further work to complete Telford's plans was
carried out in 1839–45, but these docks have now been infilled.
The harbour was acquired from the Montgomeries by the
Ardrossan Harbour Co. in 1866; in 1886–92 they built the stone-
lined EGLINTON DOCK and EGLINTON TIDAL BASIN to deal
with the increasing traffic in coal exports, and growing passenger
traffic. The engineer was *John Strain*. The BREAKWATER between
Ardrossan and Horse Island also dates from this period. Of buildings, in contradistinction to engineering, little requires comment.
The former POWER HOUSE, 1892, converted to restaurant 2007,
is tall, gabled and single-storey and originally held three boilers,
with an Italianate brick tower designed to house a hydraulic ram.
Harbour CONTROL TOWER, 1963–4, tall, with a cantilevered top
storey, brightly painted, 'a modification of a Swedish design'.
More recent the ARDROSSAN HARBOUR PUMPING STATION,
1993 by *Strathclyde Regional Council DARS*, two big brick sheds
with tall red sandstone base courses and porthole windows. Brick
boundary walls with nautically themed terracotta panels and
swooping hull-like metal detailing.

DESCRIPTION

Peter Nicholson's plans of 1806–7 for the Earl's new town envisaged a strict grid pattern, with long and short axes. The long axis
is today represented by Glasgow Street, and Harbour Street.
Princes Street forms the short axis. The two main streets lie to
the w and s of the Castle Hill, which effectively created a boundary for the town. Nicholson's streets are broad. The original
houses survive only occasionally: most of the town appears to
have been rebuilt in the third quarter of the C19.

GLASGOW STREET runs arrow-straight NE from its junction with
   Princes Street. On the l., as far as the E.U. Congregational
   Church (*see* churches, above), late C20 redevelopment, e.g.
   Nos. 53–67 of 1986 for Cunninghame Housing Association,

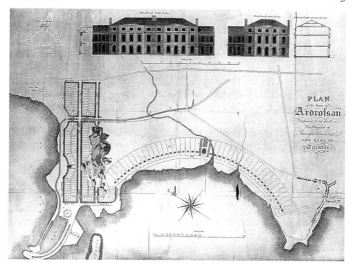

Ardrossan, New Town.
Plan drawn by Peter Nicholson

brick and gently curving with semicircular projections over the
entrances. On the r., Nos. 1–20, mid-C19, an eleven-bay two-
storey block, mostly rendered, with prettily bargeboarded
dormers and wide pilasters at one end and centrally. Earlier
C19 simply harled two-storey houses in PRINCES PLACE. In
Glasgow Street, a long run, Nos. 22–68, of, again mid-C19,
two-storey houses, mostly harled with smooth stone dressings,
enclosed circular rear stairs and the occasional pilastered doorpiece. Renovated in the late C20 for the Three Towns Housing
Association, as was much of Glasgow Street; the standardiza-
tion of doors and windows restoring some unity.

On the l., CURRIE COURT, 1980–2, a sheltered housing
block for Cunninghame District Council. Harled, and unex-
ceptionally detailed, but with an intricate footprint which, seen
from Castlehill, invokes (knowingly?) the symbol of the SNP.
On the r. No. 82, the former POST OFFICE, 1929–30 by *H.M.
Office of Works*, is single-storey red sandstone with a central
Roman Doric entrance and flanking Gibbsian windows.
Further out, Kilmahew Court (1997) and James Moffat Centre
(2005) both by *McMillan & Cronin*.

PRINCES STREET, the shorter axis of *Nicholson*'s plan, runs W–E.
On the l., three two-storey blocks, early C19 in date, one with
a wall-head chimneystack, one with canted dormers, a pilastered doorway and wide pilasters, and one, crudely harled, with
moulded upper-floor windows. Blocks such as these must have
been the norm in early C19 Ardrossan, being replaced from the
middle of the century when the town's fortunes began to rise.

The classical embellishment of the former LYRIC CINEMA exemplifies this change: a paired entrance and flanking windows, all with pilasters. Upper-floor windows with moulded architraves, aprons and heads with bracketed scrolled keystones. Two early C19 blocks beyond, both with wide pilasters with fluted heads. The s side begins with the two-storey former TOWN HALL of 1858–9 by *William Railton*. Red Locharbriggs sandstone, four bays to Princes Street. The main entrance in the three-bay Harbour Street elevation, recessed in a rusticated cavetto-moulded reveal. Curving pilastered corner bay, with a clock in a moulded frame above the parapet. Nos. 46–70 are a long and remarkably unified run of mid-C19 properties, with many surviving ground-floor pilasters; it begins as grey sandstone, with windows with dressed margins, and then changes to pink sandstone, with windows in architraves.

On the l. No. 93, a former bank of 1856 by *Thomas Wallace*. Wide end pilasters and a slightly advanced central bay. Closing the vista along Princes Street is BATH VILLA, all that remains of the Baths built 1807–9 on a tontine scheme projected by the Earl of Eglinton; the plans were provided by *James Cleland* of Glasgow. This attractive and commanding square of dark grey stone was the 'commodious lodging' attached to the Baths. Red sandstone dressings, wide eaves, a tall hipped roof and a prominent central stack. Restored in 1989 by *E. C. Riach* for the Three Towns Housing Association.

HARBOUR STREET runs SW, continuing the line of Glasgow Street, between the return elevations of the Old Town Hall and Nos. 10–12 PRINCES STREET, a three-bay two-storey villa of 1839, with wide corner pilasters. Big central porch on this elevation; on the front elevation a Roman Doric porch and a shallow central pediment. On the r. the surviving boundary WALLS of the Eglinton Arms. The hotel, which faced Princes Street, was of 1806–7 by *Nicholson*, and these red sandstone walls, with irregularly spaced piers and pairs of narrow lancets, must be contemporary.

As well as the Baths (*see* above) the Earls of Eglinton also built a summer establishment for themselves – the Pavilion – long vanished, whose site is occupied by St Peter in Chains (*see* Churches, above). Houses of mid-C19 date in ARRAN PLACE seem to have been conceived as 'guest houses' from the start. They form an attractive terrace, mostly two-storeyed and largely of painted stone or plaster. Some are perhaps as early as 1827. SOUTH CRESCENT ROAD is also a remarkable survival, providing a flavour of mid-C19 seaside living unequalled in Scotland: the houses (now subdivided or in other use) are mostly detached, mostly two-storey, in spacious grounds arranged around the curve of the bay, with a broad open space (enlarged in 1921 by the Town Council who built the sea wall) between them and the sea. Most have ancillary stables and much of the rubbly wall enclosing the rears of the feus survives. No two are identical and their architects remain unknown. No. 2, 1809, is harled with dressed margins, canted bays to l.

and r., hipped roof; No. 3, also 1809, ashlar, hipped roof, porch
(now infilled) on Roman Doric columns; No. 4, 1821, hipped
and harled, with a pilastered porch and wide angle pilasters;
the brown ashlar No. 5, 1823, has a pedimented fluted Roman
Doric, semicircular ground-floor bays, panelled angle pilasters,
a balustrade and a pedimented attic window with four pilasters; No. 6, 1846, is red sandstone, with a hipped roof and a
Roman Doric porch. To its rear, a striking reinterpretation,
c. 2002, of the chauffeur's house, boldly glazed living accommodation above a double garage. No. 7, SOUTH BEACH
HOUSE is of 1846. Porch with fluted Roman Doric columns
and pediment in slightly projected central bay; No. 8, 1855, red
sandstone, with canted bays to l. and r., a hipped roof and end
stacks: moving towards the conventional, which cannot be said
of Nos. 9–10, the oddest and most gaunt, 1856, three storeys
and six bays of almost unrelieved grey harl. No. 12 was built
by *Peter King* of Saltcoats, 1835–6. Double gabled block, the
rear block shorter; grey-harled with end stacks and diagonally
placed cans: 'for many years it stood alone among the whins'.
Finally, No. 14, c. 1860, the most confidently ornate, with bow
windows with colonnettes on the front and side elevations, a
Corinthian porch, and other slightly projected bays on front
and side elevations.

CASTLE HILL offers views across the town, the harbour and the
sea beyond, and scanty evidence that it was the original *ard
rossan*. Most obvious are the remains of ARDROSSAN CASTLE.
The Montgomeries acquired the lands of Ardrossan by marriage in 1396, and such details as survive suggest a C15 date.
It appears to have been a square courtyard castle, with a
vaulted kitchen to the SW, and a NE main tower. This retains
a few corbels of the parapet and the jambs of a second-floor
fireplace. The kitchen vault has two loop windows on the S.
The castle is said to have been destroyed by Commonwealth
forces (its strategic position on the Firth makes this likely) and
the stone redeployed in the construction of the Citadel at Ayr.
To the N of the castle, the Old Kirk (*see* above). SW of the castle,
an OBELISK, c. 1848, erected to the memory of Dr Alexander
MacFadzean, with a well-worn carved stone LION at its foot.

SEAFIELD SCHOOL, Eglinton Road. A country house of c. 1820,
considerably enlarged and Baronialized by *Thomas Gildard* in
1858. He is better known for his writings, especially on 'Greek'
Thomson, though Seafield is far removed from the Thom
sonian aesthetic. Asymmetric front elevation, with crowstepped
outer bays, that to the r. with a corbelled turret in the re-
entrant, while a much taller full-height turret rises to the l.
above the entrance, with its doorway with roll-moulded dressings. The whole front rich in crowstepped gables, decorative
wall-head gables, boldly carved coats of arms, crests and other
decoration, mostly of Jacobean inspiration, and these extend
to the return elevations. To the rear a tall French tower, added
in 1880–1, lies directly above the half-landing of the main stair,

which is the only important Gildard interior to survive conversion to institutional use in 1936. The stair hall has a highly decorative plaster ceiling and cornice, and attractive wooden balusters and newels. To the l. of the house a big STABLE range, probably from *c.* 1858, with more crowstepped gables and Jacobean decoration. Low stone boundary wall with good drum GATEPIERS with bellcast caps and ball finials. The wall, gatepiers, stables and house are all finished in a deep pink paint, unifying yet detracting from this important house.

ABBOTSFORD, NW of Seafield School, *c.* 1900, a crowstepped rock-faced sandstone villa, with a corbelled oriel to the l. Massive round-headed porch, with a pedimented two-light window, with curious pilasters; round-headed windows beneath the oriel.

GLENFOOT HOUSE, 3 km. NW. Three-bay two-storey late C19 villa, with a canted bay to the r. Dentilled cornice and pilastered doorpiece with dentilled head. Of *c.* 1900 the lower gabled bay to l., with its stone twin-arch entrance, and oriel above.

MONTFODE CASTLE, 2 km. N. Probably late C16; the possession of the Montfodes of Montfode. Apparently a Z-plan castle; what survived destruction in 1833 is a fragment of wall attached to a round entrance tower. Doorway with a moulded stone surround. In the adjacent fields, brick and concrete BUNKERS testify to the importance of the Firth of Clyde in the Second World War.

ASSLOSS *see* KILMARNOCK

AUCHANS *see* DUNDONALD

AUCHENDRANE
1 km. NE of Minishant

3010

A rambling two-storey house perched above the River Doon. Towered, in the Baronial manner. Built in 1856 on the site of the tower house celebrated by Sir Walter Scott in the 'Auchindrane Tragedy'. Extended in 1881 for Sir Peter Coats, possibly by *D. Thomson & Turnbull* (cf. Minishant church) and in 1907.

The mid-C19 house, at the centre of the (W) entrance front, comprises three crowstepped gabled bays, the outer with apex stacks, mimicking Kelburn (q.v.), the central recessed bay probably housing the original door. The outer gables are mirrored in the E front which is three storeys high because of the fall in the land, and appear again on the S elevation of the service wing. The aggressively Baronial additions of 1881 include the curiously turreted entrance tower, for most of its height detached from the house, its form but not its detachment surely modelled on the turret of the Crossraguel Abbey gatehouse (q.v.). Its little candle-snuffer roofed turret is reproduced more boldly at the NE angle of the garden front, where

it is lashed into the building by hefty corbelling which continues below the crenellated parapet of the adjoining large canted
bay, designed to achieve river views. Service wing badly
damaged by fire and rebuilt in 1919, possibly by *J. K. Hunter*.
   The interior is mainly 1880s with much panelling and a
strongly French influence in the drawing room and delicious
boudoir including much Rococo detailed plasterwork with
delicate swags and scrolls.

AUCHENFLOWER
1080

4 km. E of Ballantrae

A rambling house in Scottish vernacular vein with plenty of
crowsteps and gable-head stacks. All the ranges are harled
with contrasting ashlar dressings. Built *c.* 1860 for James
McIlwraith, it is a traditional two-storey three-bay farmhouse
with a lower rear wing, possibly an older cottage. Linked to
this rear wing, three further ranges of one, one-and-a-half and
two storeys form a small E courtyard. Sympathetic taller wing
added for Reginald Hughes Onslow by *James Miller* in 1900
(*see* also Balkissock), its upper-floor windows breaking through
the wall-head under gablets and with finials at the gables.

AUCHENHARVIE CASTLE
3040

5 km. NW of Kilmaurs

Ruinous C15 tower house, principal residence of the Cunninghames of Auchenharvie until the C18. A small example of the
group of Ayrshire tower houses that includes Law (West
Kilbride) and Little Cumbrae Castle (q.v.). Rectangular plan,
the ground floor with a semicircular vault, the first-floor hall
also vaulted, according to MacGibbon & Ross. Traces of a NW
wheel-stair. The walls had continuous corbel courses, bartizans
and a parapet. The craggy position is the result of quarrying.

AUCHINCRUIVE
3020

1.5 km. SE of St Quivox

The house, now called Oswald Hall, and estate were purchased
in 1927 by John M. Hannah and donated to the West of Scotland
Agricultural College (until 2011 the Ayr campus of the SAC).
   James Murray of Broughton purchased the Auchincruive
estate, including an existing house, from the Estate Commissioners of the 9th Lord Cathcart in 1758. Plans had been commissioned from the *Adam* brothers to build a new mansion on a
picturesque site above the Ayr and undated drawings for the
principal elevations of 'Auchincrew House' depict a simple,
modified Palladian-style villa, a *corps de logis* with lateral links
to low pedimented pavilions. But only a partial shell existed

Auchincruive House. Principal elevation.
Engraving, before 1764

when Richard Oswald, a London wholesale merchant trading in
America and Africa, a slave-trader and the owner of a Jamaican
plantation, purchased the estate in 1764. Oswald supervised and
simplified much of the work, purchasing materials from abroad
(chimney tiles and wainscotting from Rotterdam; timber from
Germany and Norway) and all the time corresponding with *John*
and *James Adam*. John visited the site early in 1766 and in that
year Oswald commissioned James for designs for ceilings and
chimneypieces in the drawing room, dining room and hall. But
in May 1767 Oswald's agent wrote to him saying 'The whole work
in your New House goes on very slowly and in short I have no
pleasure in looking at what is done & a doing. . . . The ornaments
that are made look in general very heavy and are not clean done',
spurring him to employ *William Crouch*, a master carpenter from
London. The exterior was complete by the end of the year, the
rest by 1771. The house 'built more for convenience than mag-
nificence' was 'handsome though not pompous'. Oswald again
improved the mansion from 1803 until his death in 1809 and in
1811–12 George Oswald continued to enlarge the house.

Numerous uncoordinated additions and alterations to both
wings have destroyed any hope of symmetry or the recognizable articulation proposed by the Adams. On the entrance (sw)
front, the house is two storeys over a raised basement. Built in
soft creamy sandstone with the roughly dressed squared
masonry contrasting with neatly polished dressings but originally smartly rendered (or at least from 1807 and now unfortunately removed). The principal part is seven bays with the
central three slightly recessed and outer bays defined by pilaster-strips and band courses at ground- and first-floor levels.
These were originally designed to have elegant overarched
Venetian windows with single square windows above (cf. Carn-
salloch House, Dumfries and Galloway) but built with a
monotonous repetition of the plain central windows. Pilastered
porch with mahogany-framed fanlit doors, 1806 by *Balfour
Balsillie*. Five-bay side elevations, clearly visible on the NW
elevation, with two big stacks on the cross walls flanking the
central bay.

The s wing began as a single-storey-and-basement, three-bay link to the former kitchen range, but raised to the full height 1808–12; the principal stair was reconstructed to serve it, at a stroke reducing the impact of the *corps de logis*. The lower service bays beyond were substantially altered *c*. 1840 when the return s elevation was given its smart articulated façade with paired angle pilasters, a recessed centre bay and tall first-floor windows. The N wing was probably built or recast *c*. 1845 and has an advanced pedimented pavilion extending through to the garden front, beyond the narrow three-bay linking block, paying lip service to the Adams' design. Adjoining the pavilion another lower extension with a canted bay to the garden. The N range, like the lower and later parts of the s extension, is faced with a bland cement render. The centrepiece to the garden front is a big full-height, canted bay, a pattern used in later Adam houses (e.g. Kirkdale, Dumfries and Galloway). Windows enlarged mid C19 when the big flanking canted windows were inserted into the basement and ground floors. Steps descend from the *piano nobile* to the garden with a curious small, cusped archway below.

Inside, the Entrance Hall and Dining Room have survived with their late C18 decorative schemes largely unaltered. The large formal ENTRANCE HALL has a bold Doric pilastered doorpiece, a deep metope frieze of rosettes with triglyphs and a dentilled cornice. The ceiling is made up of geometric compartments and naturalistic ornament derived from contemporary work at Osterley Park (London). The outer bands of swags and honeysuckle with a central oval wreathed thyrsus, look to Shardeloes (Bucks., 1759–63). The ensemble is completed with carved details to the shutters, dado, architraves and doors, all backward-looking with raised and fielded panels and lugs. White marble chimneypiece with swags and an attenuated urn with big egg-and-dart cornice, boldly wrought to Oswald's brief and probably by local craftsmen. From the hall a door leads from the NE corner into the MUSIC ROOM, formerly the drawing room. Decorated in a Frenchy Rococo manner in the late C19; frothy central ceiling rose with birds and dainty sprigs and scrolly leaf patterned band on the ceiling flat. The walls have elaborate panelled details with floral urns, repeated in the angles of the ceiling, some with instruments set against delicate latticed backgrounds, others with mirrors in the Louis XVI manner, a popular fashion in the county. This is the most sumptuously decorated room from skirting and dado to cornice and ceiling. Lugged and corniced doorcases with much use of egg-and-dart, modillion and rosette cornice C18. The tall white marble chimneypiece is probably one imported from Leghorn, Italy, for Oswald but with the late C19 addition of cherubs supporting an oval mirror.

The DINING ROOM, w of the Music Room, has presumably James Adam's decorative scheme, the symmetry of the ceiling plasterwork disrupted by the big added canted window. The central vine-swagged circle has flowered roundels and husks extending diagonally to the corners, all more adventurous than the Hall. On the wall opposite the chimneypiece three deep buffet alcoves with panelled cupboards below the dado. Large Ionic-pilastered, delicately veined white marble chimneypiece with swags of pears, probably locally carved in mid C19. The MORNING ROOM leads from the Music Room to the E, simple detail with carved skirting and dado rail, lugged, pedimented doorcases, a modillion cornice and smart white marble chimneypiece, with anthemion frieze. Off the Entrance Hall to the SE the OFFICE (formerly Richard Oswald's sitting room), simply detailed and with a charming white marble chimneypiece with the central panel depicting a child warming its hands in front of a brazier and a small puppy tugging its skirts.

The STAIR HALL dates from 1811 when the stair was enlarged and remade in order to provide a link to the adjoining wing. The mason was *William Gibson*, the carpenter *John Paterson* and decorative plasterwork by *John Anderson*. All very competent but lacking a guiding hand. It has an unusually long straight flight to the half-landing flanked by massive paired Ionic pilasters, framing the landing arch to the addition, and rises to a handsome pedimented doorcase with a rope-moulded archway. This screen symmetrical on the stair elevation but not to the passage behind. The balusters – delicatedly scrolled wrought-iron alternating with plain, paired rod balusters – are unusually widely spaced (*see* Skeldon). Elegant geometric ceiling with a central circle, semicircles and triangular decorated panels. On the first floor through the arch, a spine passage leads to the LIBRARY occupying the room above the Music Room and also with a canted bay. The bookcases, with a lozenge glazing pattern, retain much of their original blown glass. A further arch toward the W end of the passage partially conceals a delicate geometrically glazed panel screening the service stair.

The E addition, originally to provide extra bedrooms, was fitted out in the earlier C19 with plenty of reeded architraves and anthemion-detailed, grey-veined marble chimneypieces. The inserted stairwell provides access to the upper floor, E of the main stair. It copies the detail of the earlier stair and the square cupola above again retains the C18 style.

Below the house to the SE a dramatic HANGING GARDEN beside the river path, *c.* 1830, a tall revetment-like, terraced sandstone wall in three stages with semicircular buttresses, steep steps to the first terrace. Spearhead and urn cast-iron railings provide a barrier on the viewing platform at the level of the house drive. – BRIDGE. Late C18. Three arches, with a large central opening, big, boat-shaped cutwaters, bowed pedestrian retreats and ashlar copings. – WALLED GARDENS. 1773–4; in two sections with a curved dividing wall. Much modified but the surviving structures may incorporate some early glasshouses.

LODGES. Built 1806–7 by *James Paterson*, mason. Single-storey piend-roofed lodges with doors set into a pilastered arched centrepiece. Also by Paterson, an ICE HOUSE of 1808. Single-chambered, rectangular plan.

TEA HOUSE or Oswald's Temple, 1 km. NW of the house. By   60 *Robert Adam*, 1778. One of the few surviving parts of Oswald's designed landscape and the outstanding piece of architecture on the estate. More than any other building it symbolizes Oswald as a gentleman of respectability. Described as 'a hybrid style of various origins', it is based on Theodoric's C6 mausoleum at Ravenna but with Renaissance details incorporated. Built in sandstone ashlar and composed of two concentric drums, one above the other with a conical roof and ball finial. Lower drum (servants' room and kitchen) supported by four clasping towers with four arches between; twelve tall relieving arches, four glazed, circle the Tea House in the upper drum – a motif which recurs in the apsed kitchen at Culzean Castle (1779, q.v.). Tooled paterae in each arched head. Machicolated and crenellated wall-head. At ground level, a passage circles the servants' room and kitchen, equipped with sophisticated heating and serving apparatus. Spiral stair to the tea room above, which has its own fireplace.

GIBBSYARD, 0.8 km. W of the mansion. Very substantial stable court, begun *c.* 1760, altered 1838. Dominated by bold, square-plan, two-stage doocot tower over the entrance pend, capped with big quadripartite domed roof with square cupola and weathervane. Set into elegant symmetrical frontage with low ranges to either side. Tower restored in 1930–1 for the agricultural college and courtyard much rebuilt, see the Lorimeresque dormer window heads. Technically advanced dairy and cattle management ranges added at the same time set an international standard. The buildings for the West of Scotland Agricultural College are mostly by *Alexander Mair*, 1929–31, in brick and harl (APIARY, classically detailed DAIRY SCHOOL and DAIRY RESEARCH BUILDING, with extension by *Cowie Torry & Partners*). WILSON HALL (student accommodation). By *D. S. MacPhail*, 1950–6. Striking in its harled simplicity with sparing use of C17 Scots-style curvilinear gables and a variety of gableted windows. Butterfly-plan. Pilastered, segmental-headed entrance in shallow advance, curvilinear gabled central bay on NW elevation and surmounted by a balcony.

AUCHINLECK   5020

A name which resonates, owing to its associations with the Boswells, especially James Boswell who lived at Auchinleck House (*see* below). Until the mid C18, little more than a small kirktoun, known as Keithstoun, clustered around the church; it had been made a Burgh of Barony in 1507, but this did not prosper. In the late C18 the village was improved, and increased in size throughout the C19, as coal and iron mining and processing industries expanded. New estates (e.g. Backrogerton) were built in the C20 to replace outlying villages of miners' rows, such as Common and Darnconner. In the late C20, and early C21, Auchinleck's fortunes have continued to shadow those of the coal industry.

CHURCHES AND PUBLIC BUILDINGS

AUCHINLECK AULD KIRK, s of the Parish Church, is pre-Reformation, but enlarged to its present size in 1641–3. Simple N entrance and windows with square heads. Crowstepped gables. The mannered ogee-headed open bellcote on the E gable was authorized in 1722, but appears not to have been built until 1747. Restored as a museum (now closed) in 1971–8 to plans of *Robert S. Wallace* of Troon, with a simple slated roof, and an exposed stone interior. Attached to the N elevation the BOSWELL MAUSOLEUM, built in 1754 for Lord Auchinleck. Four-square, of ashlar, with a hipped flagged roof, and a central finial urn. Long-and-short quoins, and similar treatment to the sole entrance. On the N wall a stone armorial, quartering Boswell with Cunninghame, added *c.* 1845.

Large and varied CHURCHYARD. The older W part crowded with many C18 and C19 headstones, mostly well weathered. WAR MEMORIAL of 1921–2 by *James A. Morris*. Sandstone obelisk with a small Celtic cross, supported on a circular panelled plinth, alternate panels filled with bronze inscription panels.

AUCHINLECK PARISH CHURCH, Church Hill. T-plan Gothic of 1835–9 by *James Jamieson** of Catrine. Gabled red ashlar, with a pointed W main entrance, and tall lancets, usually with stone Y-tracery. The partly gabled addition to the s wing was added by *R. S. Ingram* in 1891 as was the dumpy two-stage N tower, with its corner chamfered and corbelled to give the pinched-waist look characteristic of many of his towers (cf. Kames Institute, Muirkirk and the A. M. Brown Institute, Catrine (qq.v)). Almost fussily detailed when contrasted with the austerity elsewhere; it has pointed bell-openings, pierced foliated balustrades and a castellated parapet. Ingram's chancel, of 1896–7, is sympathetic to Jamieson's work: the two-light N window is reused. Gothic three-light E window. The galleried interior dates from restoration by *J. & J. A. Carrick* after a fire in 1938. Plaster walls and coved ceiling; stone chancel arch and complex panelled, hipped and coved wooden chancel ceiling. – PEWS from Darnconner (1897 by *Ingram*). – STAINED GLASS. Chancel N window a fine, characteristically blue Solomon and Moses by *Gordon Webster*, 1947. Chancel E, Charity, also by *Webster*, 1947, and less successful, perhaps because he was attempting to reprise the 1897 window by *Stephen Adam* lost in the fire.

OUR LADY OF LOURDES & ST PATRICK (R.C.), Sorn Road. A U-plan group about a central open space. The church, of 1963–4 by *Charles W. Gray* of Edinburgh, is gabled with a brick

---

* Plans had been commissioned from *James Ingram* in 1831, and *William Kay* of Ayr in 1835, the latter rejected in favour of Jamieson.

front, stepped round-headed windows, and harled sides and porch. It lacks the aesthetic charge of his Our Lady of Mount Carmel, Kilmarnock (q.v.), being too respectful of *Alexander Dunlop*'s brick hall of 1939–40 to its l.

AUCHINLECK ACADEMY, Sorn Road. 1966–71 by *Clark Fyfe*, Ayr County Architect. Five-storey main block, with alternating bands of brick and glass, the harled ground floor set back behind pilotis. To the l. of this a hulking windowless concrete lecture theatre, rearing up from its brick base. To the l. again the concrete panelled sports hall. The three are linked at first floor by a broad glazed corridor.

AUCHINLECK PRIMARY SCHOOL, Arran Drive. 1998–2000 by *Barr Technical Services*. Brick, and startlingly plain.

INDOOR BOWLING STADIUM, Well Road. 1978–80 by *Rennie, Watson & Starling*. Large and powerful asymmetrically gabled, steel-framed, brick-faced hall, with a steel roof. Recessed entrance to the r., the bowling green itself lit by five tall, narrow windows, the articulation of the façade increased by having three of these in the shorter side of the gable. Such a purpose as this could so easily be provided, and so often is, within an unthinking and unfeeling shell; this is the antithesis, it has true quality and imagination and still looks fresh.

DESCRIPTION

In MAIN STREET, the BOSWELL ARMS, single storey, ashlar, with a central gable with a thistle finial. The circular corner tower with a conical turret, added by *Robert Ewen* of Glasgow, 1902, is the first of a series of Glasgow-style corner towers which act as staging posts along the village's gap-toothed and much abused Main Street. This was developed from 1756 by the Boswells, replacing the settlement at the church. No. 57, set back from the street line, is late C18, of thinly bedded large ashlar, with a central entrance with cavetto reveals and broad end pilasters. Further out SHILOH TERRACE, dated 1905, single-storey red sandstone cottages terminating in the final turret, this one octagonal, panelled above the windows, and with a slated conical roof.

Former BARONY COLLIERY, 2.5 km. W. First sunk between 1906 and 1912 for William Baird & Co., and closed in 1989. One of the first Scottish collieries to be dependent on electricity as a source of power and, with shafts of 626 m., one of the deepest. Of the colliery buildings only the landmark HEAD-FRAME for No. 3 shaft (sunk 1945) survives: a stark, sculptural structure with four legs of welded steel, forming a giant A, topped by the pulley wheels.

Former HIGHHOUSE COLLIERY, 0.2 km. NW. Now an industrial estate. Sunk for William Baird & Co. in 1894, and closed in 1983, at which time it was one of the oldest mines in Scotland in continuous operation. ENGINE HOUSE of *c.* 1896: its HEAD-FRAME an open steel structure of *c.* 1968, replacing the previous wooden superstructure.

126

AUCHINLECK HOUSE
4.75 km. W

55   The quintessential mid-C18 rural villa, set confidently at the heart
of its estate. Built 1755–62 for Alexander Boswell, Lord Auchinleck, and little altered. Carefully conserved in 1986–2001 by
James Simpson of *Simpson & Brown* for the Scottish Historic
Buildings Trust, and the Landmark Trust (now the owner).
Authorship remains tantalizingly unsolved. Was it Boswell
himself, in consultation with his Edinburgh circle or his Ayrshire
neighbours (the 5th Earl of Dumfries was employing John Adam
to build Dumfries House in the 1750s) or his Dumfriesshire
friends? The whole planning and decorative treatment of the
house suggest that it is the conception of the patron with the help
of an architecturally minded builder, a highly skilled plumber and
competent wrights. The Edinburgh wright *John Johnston*, who
was employed at Auchinleck, may have been just this man. He
had worked at Duff House and Haddo House with the master-
mason John Baxter the Elder, and through him came into the
circle of Sir John Clerk of Penicuik, author of the *The Country
Seat* and the inspiration for the rural villa in Scotland. The
elegant, classical style and plan look back to William Adam (cf.
Mavisbank, Lothian).

Built in mellow grey sandstone, rectangular plan with slightly
projecting pedimented central bays to front and rear. On the
E FRONT the pediment crowns a giant Ionic pilastered frontispiece and is filled with deeply undercut sculpture emblematic
of a cultured mind. To the Duchess of Northumberland
writing in 1760, however, 'the Pediment is terribly loaded with

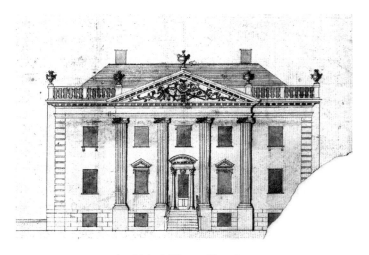

Auchinleck House. Elevation.
Engraving, mid C18

Ornaments of Trumpets and Maces and the Deuce knows what.' This form is distinctly old-fashioned but reflected the patron's undoubted knowledge of the classical world. In the frieze below a quotation from Horace is carved 'Quod petis hic est: Est Ulubris, animus si te non deficit aequus' ('Whatever you see is here, in this remote place, if only you can keep a steady disposition'). A small rectangular window is uncomfortably punched through the centre (a similar motif existed at Fullarton House (q.v.) of 1745). The pediment is defined by urns at its apex and at the outer angles; further dumpier urns crown the angles of the balustrade which encircles the house. Bold straight flight of steps (originally with iron railings, the stone balustrade is one of the few later alterations) to the front door, itself disguised as a window, with double-panel leaves below a putative sill level. The doorway and two flanking windows on the principal floor have pediments, the curved one over the door cramped below the first-floor window. In contrast to the busy central bays, the outer bays are severely plain with one window to each floor and channelled pilaster-strips, unusually set slightly in from the outer angles.

Symmetry dictates the SIDE ELEVATIONS with three windows in each of the upper floors, the upper of which have curious aprons placed above them, perhaps to disguise the fact that the simplified cornice has no frieze. The rather cumbersome arrangement of the front door may account for the later, surprisingly grand pedimented porch on the S courtyard elevation at lower ground level, giving access to the spine corridor in the basement and the foot of the lower flight of the main stair. On the N side the central window in the ground floor is blind to accommodate inside a buffet recess in the dining room.

The REAR ELEVATION is again dominated by the pedimented centre, but the effect is entirely different from the entrance front with rusticated quoins only, an oculus in the tympanum, and four windows below the pediment with the round-headed first-floor windows lighting the library emphasized. This arrangement existed also at Fullarton House (q.v.).

Slightly later straight walls conceal the service areas N and S and link the house to four PAVILIONS, proposed in 1765 but not added until 1773–4 and in a contrasting red sandstone. Each has pilasters and pediments but also large Baroque terminals like birdcage bellcotes with an open arcaded first stage, big scrolls supporting the smaller second stage with oculi and classical urns as finials. These terminals are a response to the Rev. William Temple who in 1767 begged 'not to make the wings to the house little band boxes'. The composition also appears to conflate the designs for the terminal piers and lodges which existed at Fullarton House (q.v.). James Boswell, the diarist, recorded that the pavilions were whitened in 1775 when perhaps the whole house was limewashed.

The regular elevations do not reflect a conventional plan form inside, which was divided into public and private rooms

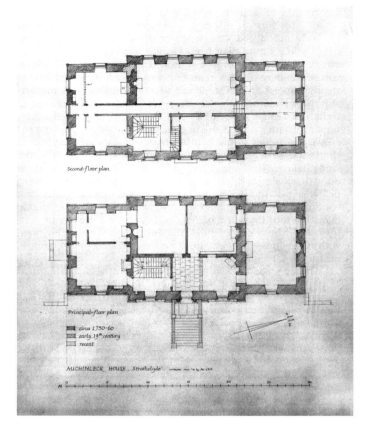

Second-floor plan

Principal-floor plan

circa 1750-60
early 19ᵗʰ century
recent

AUCHINLECK HOUSE, Strathclyde

Auchinleck House.
Plan

on two floors, tailored to Lord Auchinleck's needs for entertainment and perhaps influencing the comparable plan for
Caldwell House (Renfrewshire), 1773. On the principal floor
the entrance hall, ante-room (r.) and stair (l.) fill the three
central bays with two parlours behind, opening from the hall
and facing W with the large library above. Filling the N end is
a large dining room; here and in the library guests could gather
for conversation. Apart from the stair compartment, the S end
of the house on the ground floor was devoted to Auchinleck's
private apartments comprising a sequence of bedchamber,
dressing room with a closet and morning room or study. The
DINING ROOM is the only room with sophisticated plasterwork. Elaborate modillion cornice and ceiling with a delicate
Rococo scheme on an Arcadian theme with the Boswell hooded
falcon, the motto 'vraye foy' and a mailed fist holding a sword

with the motto 'Je pense plus' inset. The chimneypiece was removed in the C19, its replacement modelled on a John Adam design for Hawkhill Villa (1757), dem. Edinburgh for a Session Court Judge, Lord Alemoor. Buffet alcove framed with panelled pilasters, and with elegantly shaped shelves and a drop-leaf serving table. In the semi-dome a garland of oak leaves and acorns and on the wall above delectable Rococo decoration. Concealed behind a shutter is a basin or pissoir, one of a number in the house, that were supplied by rainwater tanks in the attic, part of a remarkably advanced system of running water, which also served the closets with waste pipes for soiled water.

From the Dining Room, guests progressed to the PARLOUR (sensitively altered to form a kitchen), which has the best of the surviving chimneypieces, and then back into the hall. The STUDY, entered through a squint door beside the stair, is the only room fully panelled with cupboards inset – all rather old-fashioned. The chimney-breast is flanked by arched headed panels, and the chimneypiece has a carved bolection-moulded frieze and central plaque with a floral swag, above it a lugged panel. The STAIR HALL with a well stair rising to a narrow gallery, all with simple bombé-section cast-iron balusters. Papier mâché Rococo ceiling decoration with a lantern suspended from an unlikely and impotent-looking hooded hawk, re-created during the restoration. All the other floors have a N–S spine corridor. On the first floor the LIBRARY, whose coved ceiling with a deep modillion cornice rises into the attic. Chimneypieces on the N and S walls. Its early C19 bookcases have been replaced.

STABLES, S of the house. A simple well-proportioned court of three mid- to late C18 ranges. At the rear a C19 DOOCOT raised on a tall base of open arches.

DR JOHNSON'S SUMMERHOUSE, N of the house. A semi-domed grotto carved out of the rocky cliff beside the Dippol Burn, c. 1760. Arched entrance and windows. Dr Johnson visited in 1773 at the end of his Hebridean journey. Lower down the burn, also in the rock, an ovoid ICE HOUSE.

NORTH DRIVE BRIDGE, over the Dippol Burn 1830.

OLD PLACE OF AUCHINLECK, 1 km. W. Ruins of a C17 laird's house, L-plan, in a courtyard enclosure. Even more fragmentary, the earlier CASTLE on a bluff above the junction of the Dippol Burn and Lugar Water. Upstream on the Lugar, WALLACE'S CAVE, probably later C18 with Gothic arched window and vaulted ceiling.

AUCHMANNOCH

5030

4.3 km. NNW of Sorn

A delightful laird's house inclining to symmetry, above Auchmannoch Burn on the edge of moorland. Built for John Campbell and his wife Jean Mitchell, and dated 1724 on a very worn lintel with their initials. Two storeys and an attic. Off-centre

door in roll-moulded architrave with bolection-moulded frieze
and cornice; panel above with emblems set into a later frame
with scrolled top. Two roll-moulded windows in each floor to
the r., one to the l. Crowstepped gables, with primitive masks
to the skewputts. Very steep roof, almost certainly originally
thatched (see the thacking stanes in the rebuilt stacks). Tiny
attic windows on the sw gable. Low, L-plan, and later, service
range to the NE.

Uphill to the N are three low detached ranges, in a rough
U-plan, giving the appearance of an unimproved farm. At the
highest point is a simple three-bay, limewashed cottage, with
lintel dated 1794 and the initials of Arthur Campbell and
Margaret Schaw. It probably incorporates an earlier dwelling.

AYR

INTRODUCTION

The mouth of the River Ayr forms one of the few sheltered har- [2] bours on the coast of the Firth of Clyde, and was recognized as such from an early period; it may have been known to, and used by, the Roman forces during their occupation of the zone between Hadrian's Wall and the Antonine Wall. Concrete evidence of a settlement at the site begins, however, in the late C12, by which time SW Scotland was coming under the settled control of the kings of Scotland. The system of feudal control was extended into the area initially by David I (1124–53), and consolidated by William the Lion (1165–1214), who established a royal castle in Ayr in 1197. This was on a prominent hill to the S of the river mouth, whence it could control both the harbour and coastal approaches, and landward approaches from S and E. Nothing of the castle can now be seen, but the site must have been close to modern Montgomerie Terrace, and was later overlain by the C17 Citadel (*see* below).

A small settlement would have grown up in association with the castle, and a church, too, first recorded in 1233 (*see* St John's Tower, below). It is conjectured that this original settlement

broadly followed the line of modern Sandgate; it became the
basis for the Royal Burgh created by William in 1205, with extensive trading and fiscal powers. It is conjectured, too, that the
town's unusual plan, with two main streets meeting at right
angles, may date from this period, as a street running broadly
parallel with the river, as High Street does, may have been less
at risk from persistent sand blown from the coastal dunes. Both
streets were lined with tenement plots, usually long and narrow,
and on the N side of High Street, stretching back to the river.
The original harbour would have been close to the junction of
the two roads, with an adjacent ford (on the site of the present
New Bridge). A subsidiary unincorporated settlement, Newton-upon-Ayr, grew up on the opposite bank. The river was later
bridged, upstream from the ford, perhaps as early as the mid C13,
with a wooden bridge.

As an important royal administrative centre, and a regionally
important market with foreign trading rights, the small town
grew steadily, so that by the end of the C15, the burgage plots
had been built up as far as the present junction of High Street
and Alloway Street, the wooden bridge had been rebuilt in stone,
on the same site, and the town's transpontine twin had continued
to grow, and had, indeed, received its own charter of incorpora-
tion in the C14.* Loudoun Hall, one of the earliest surviving town
houses in Scotland, is first recorded in 1517, but is probably of
c. 1500; when built it would have been at the heart of the town,
lying as it does between the Cross and the then wharves on the
S bank of the river. A Dominican friary had been founded in
the town in 1230, and a Franciscan friary in 1472. A Tolbooth,
in the High Street, is first mentioned in 1427, but was superseded
by another, on a new site in Sandgate, in 1575. Otherwise the
structure of the town changed little during the C16 and early C17,
though the friaries were suppressed during the Reformation; in
1634 it could be described as 'a dainty pleasant-seated town, most
inhabiting in which are merchants trading into and bred in
France'. Major change came with the Commonwealth, which
controlled Scotland through a series of powerful citadels, one of
which was built at Ayr in 1652–4 by *Hans Ewing Tessin*. The site
chosen was that on which the castle had stood, and the parish
church still stood; it still possessed the same strategic values as
it had in the C12. The church was commandeered, and a new
church built on the site of the Franciscan friary: it is one of the
very few churches built anywhere during the Commonwealth.

Following the Restoration, the Citadel was demilitarized, and
was subsequently created a Burgh of Barony (Montgomeriestoun), for the Montgomeries of Eglinton, and became, like
Newton-upon-Ayr, a haven for trades which were not permitted
within the Royal Burgh. By the mid C18, the whole area within
the burgh boundaries was built up, while new streets, such as
Newmarket Street (1767), were laid out to create new frontages.
The last quarter of the C18 and the first half of the C19 saw major

---

*Newton-upon-Ayr's subsequent development is discussed below (p. 161).

expansion of the town to the S and W, with the creation of a substantial suburb of broad, straight streets, stylish squares, and grand houses, usually in terraces. The first of these was Barns Street, begun in the late C18, followed by Wellington Square, laid out from 1799, and followed by further developments both to the S of Wellington Square, and to the N, on land which had previously been the town's public washing green. The same period saw some major new public buildings, beginning with *Alexander Stevens*'s New Bridge (1788), and continuing to include *Robert Wallace*'s Sheriff Courthouse and County Buildings of 1817–22, and *Thomas Hamilton*'s Town Hall of 1827–32, which was sited prominently at the junction of the two main streets, with a proud and mighty steeple unrivalled in Scotland: a signal of civic pride and expectation. The Jail (dem.), built behind the Court House, and the Town Hall rendered the Sandgate Tolbooth redundant, and as it also impeded access to the town from the New Bridge, it was removed in 1826, while the earlier Tolbooth in the High Street, known as the Laigh House, had been removed *c.* 1800. Many of the buildings facing the main streets were refaced at the same time, so that attractive three-storey Georgian shops with houses above form the dominant image in many parts of them, e.g. in Sandgate to the S of the Town Hall, and in High Street, to its E, while Winton Buildings, of 1844–6, which fills much of the former market place at the dog-leg turn in High Street, was the last major building in the town to be designed in this Late Georgian manner. The same period also saw the establishment of facilities such as Assembly Rooms (dem.) and a Theatre (1815–16, now Baptist Church Centre), which reflect the town's growing importance as a resort for the gentry of the county, seen also in the establishment of formal horse-racing festivals from the late C18.

The railway to Glasgow was fully opened in 1840, and Ayr became increasingly popular through the late C19 for summer and permanent houses for Glasgow merchants and returned Indian nabobs. To accommodate this much new housing was built to the S of the town, in and off Racecourse and Midton Roads; Miller Road, which links these, was constructed in 1852–3 to improve communications between this area and the station, rebuilt to the SE of the town in 1856–7. Although some terraces continued to be built, e.g. in Park Circus, the emphasis was now on detached and semi-detached villas, and the area remains a largely unspoilt example of a wealthy Late Victorian suburb, with villas in a variety of styles, from the simple classical to the highest Scots Baronial. The Citadel, acquired by John Miller in 1854, was also developed for housing, to a plan by *Clarke & Bell*, with one magnificent terrace and a variety of villas. More modest housing spread to the E and SE, while the poorest housing, together with almost all the town's industrial buildings, were to the N of the river, in Newton and Wallacetown. Public work projects of the period included the Poorhouse (1857–60 by *W. L. Moffat*, now Holmston House), the second New Bridge (1877–9 by *George Cunningham*), and the construction of major additions to Ayr's

harbour, including a wet dock of 1873–8 by *Thomas Meik* on the
Newton bank. Much of the High Street was reconstructed during
the late C19, allowing it to be straightened and widened, while
commercial properties spread into Alloway Street and Burns
Statue Street. Many of these buildings are by *James A. Morris*,
Ayr's nationally important Arts and Crafts architect, whose work
can be seen in the High Street and in Burns Statue Square, or
by *H. V. Eaglesham*, whose buildings are often in a Free Flemish
style but whose masterpiece is the American-influenced Wellington Chambers, Fort Street, of 1904–7. Morris also designed
houses, such as his own house, Savoy Croft, in Savoy Park, and
the Savoy Park hotel, Racecourse Road.

    The C20 was a period of continued, sometimes accelerated
residential growth, and the town's outer suburbs now extend as
far as Alloway and Doonfoot to the s, and merge seamlessly into
Prestwick to the N. The interwar housing is characterized by
hipped-roofed bungalows, and the late C20, and C21, developments by estates created by local and national mass builders.
Architecturally more rewarding are some of the facilities provided for the town's many tourists, such as *J. K. Hunter*'s rather
jolly Pavilion (1910–11), and some good cinemas, especially the
Green's Playhouse, Boswell Park (now Mecca Bingo), of 1930–1
by *John Fairweather*. Some comprehensive redevelopment has
been carried out s of the river in the late C20, especially in the
Mill Street area, but Ayr's medieval street pattern and layout have
remained intact, though very few of the burgage plots can still
be traced. Many have been lost to developments such as the
reconstruction of much of High Street w of its junction with
Carrick Street, or the Kyle Centre of 1984–6. Modern interventions into the main streets have been few: one bank in Sandgate
is deserving of notice, and forms one end of a block which has
at its other corner Lady Cathcart's House, restored by *Simpson
& Brown* in 1991–6.

    Early C21 Ayr, with a population of *c.* 47,000, remains the
largest town in the county, and an important social, administrative
and commercial centre, and while much of the commerce is now
carried out at soulless and architecturally barren suburban sheds,
as debate continues about how best to revitalize the lower part of
the High Street, and the properties which flank the New Bridge,
the town still has much to offer the architectural historian.

CHURCHES

AULD KIRK OF AYR, Kirkport. Gothic survival of 1653–6 by
Theophilius Rankine. An important, and large, example of a
church built during the Commonwealth period, erected after
St John's had been requisitioned by the Commonwealth forces
and enclosed within their Citadel (*see* p. 146). The site had
previously been occupied by a Dominican friary. Originally a
T-plan, rubble-built (harling removed in 1873), with slate roofs,
but a Greek cross plan since sympathetic extension of the
vestry in 1932 by *Charles J. McNair*. Broad, low main entrance

113, 114 (margin)

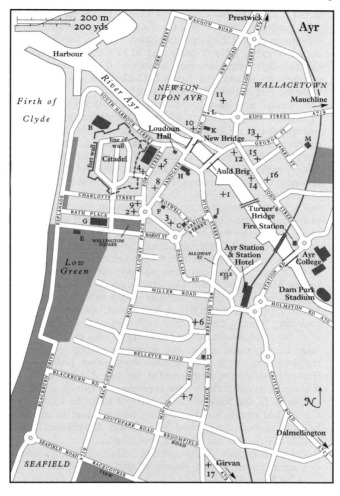

1   Auld Kirk of Ayr
2   Baptist Church Centre
3   Holy Trinity (Episcopal)
4   Former New Church
5   Former Relief Church
6   St Andrew
7   St Columba
8   Former Sandgate Church
9   Former Wesleyan Methodist
    Church
10 Former Darlington Place
    U.P. Church
11 Newton Wallacetown
    Church
12 Free Church
13 Former Morrison
    Congregational Church
14 Riverside Evangelical
    Church

15 St Margaret's Cathedral (R.C.)
16 Former Wallacetown Parish
    Church
17 St Leonard's

A   Ayr Academy
B   Citadel Leisure Centre
C   Gaiety Theatre
D   Grammar Primary School
E   Pavilion
F   Former Playhouse Cinema
G   Sheriff Courthouse and
    County Buildings
H   Town Hall
J   Wallace Tower
K   Carnegie Public Library
L   Newton Steeple
M   Wallacetown Nursery School

in the N gable, below a two-light window; and pairs of windows with pointed arches, l. and r., of a type recurring on the other elevations, where the upper tier lights a gallery which is entered at the W gable. The N gable and its side elevations also have tall two-light windows with Y-tracery. The attractive gabled dormers are of 1877, by *James I. McDerment*, who was responsible for restoration after a fire in 1871.

18   Spacious, and busy, INTERIOR dominated by a *tour de force* of original timber fittings, of an ornamental artisan classicism unexpected in a Commonwealth church in the heart of Covenanter country. A broad segmental arch on cushion corbels distinguishes the N arm. Within the N arm the MERCHANTS' LOFT, with a panelled front: an arcade divided by fluted pilasters with Corinthian heads. The loft is supported on three pairs of neatly turned columns. The SAILORS' LOFT, in the E arm, has a similarly detailed front, but rests on four columns with pronounced entasis, while, in the W arm, the TRADES' LOFT has a more elaborate front: its arcades have colonnettes with freely interpreted Corinthian heads, while the arches have pendants. It, too, is supported on four columns, more slender than those to the Sailors' Loft, but without the virtuosity of those in the Merchants' Loft. The craftsman may have been *John Hunter*, who made the equally remarkable double-decker PULPIT of 1654–6: it has a bow front, panelled back and sounding boards, carried on scrolly consoles. Containing this is an outer enclosure, also bow-fronted, with geometric panelling. In the same spirit, the boarded ceiling with exposed trusses of the 1870s. Simple dark wood pews; pale wood and frosted glass vestibules inserted at the rear of the W and E arms, a glazed screen in the N arm creating a vestibule at the main entrance. In the Sailors' Loft, on the N wall, the LONGUEVAL CROSS, of rough wood and zinc, first erected on the battlefields in 1916, and relocated here in 1931. Suspended from the roof, a MODEL of the ship *Arethusa*, 1802.

STAINED GLASS. An interesting collection, contrasting late C19 conventions with a variety of C20 approaches. – S wall, 1878 by *James Ballantine & Son*: St John and the Annunciation (l.); Christ sowing, and women reaping (r.). – W arm, S: *Roland Mitton*'s 1986 Boys' Brigade window; w: Suffer Little Children, 1927, an early *Gordon Webster* design for *Stephen Adam Studios*; N: a dramatic Burning Bush by *Crear McCartney*, 1988. – In the Trades' Loft, two more *Ballantine* windows (David and Solomon, 1861; Jesus and Lazarus, 1863) and an unidentified Christ and St John, of after 1886. – N arm: Ayr and the Holy Land (W), by *Christian Shaw*, 2001, from a sketch by *Claire Howat*; Women's Guild window (E) with expressive faces and heavy leadwork by *Sadie McLellan*, 1960. – E arm: Baptism (E) by *William Wilson*, 1953; Faith, Hope and Charity (S), recherché work of 1909 by *Ballantine & Gardiner*. – In the Sailors' Loft two German-inspired windows by *James Ballantine & Son*, both of 1863; between them Be Of Good Cheer, by *Crear McCartney*, 1990, with his usual verve.

The number of MONUMENTS in this presbyterian setting is striking. – John Fergusson †1791, with an urn and weeping woman. – Robert Gairdner †1795, an oval tablet 'suddenly called . . . from a world of frail and fleeting pleasure'. – First World War memorial, 1922, by *Charles J. McNair*. – At the angle between the Trades' and Merchants' Lofts, a bronze STATU-ETTE of Robert Burns, arms folded, by *George A. Lawson*, 1891, presented to the church in 1931, when *James Vallance* prepared its supporting corbel.

The generous irregularly shaped CHURCHYARD is open to the river to the E. – LYCHGATE, dated 1656, with a round-headed arch, screen-fronted on the outer face, an open timber roof, and a cobbled pavement. Narrow stone benches along the sides, beneath the iron MORT SAFES of 1816. Very few grand MONUMENTS. – Rev. William Adair †1684: the minister kneels in prayer beneath a dentilled pediment broken by a huge coat of arms; Corinthian columns and scroll brackets to either side. Restored by *James A. Morris* in 1909. – James Smith and others (SE) †1666, Covenanting martyrs. Erected in 1814 by the Incorporated Trades of Ayr.

CHURCH HALLS, 1966–8 by *Stevenson & Ferguson*. – FONT, 1891, by *James A. Morris*, executed by *John Reid & Son*, cabinetmakers, Ayr. Expressive, freely treated Arts and Crafts. Designed for the New Church (*see* below).

BAPTIST CHURCH CENTRE, Fort Street. The former Theatre Royal of 1815–16, converted in 1886–7. The theatre was refronted in 1862–3 when it was then 'only occasionally hired by some company of strolling votaries of Thespis, or, not much better, an itinerant MP vending his damaged political wares to lieges more remarkable for gullibility than gumption'. Plastered, of five bays, with a central pediment and the outer upper bays flanked by pilasters with plain pinnacles; round-headed windows with sills and keystones. The projecting lower storey is by *CRGP*, 2000. Rubble sides, with four square-headed windows high on the N wall; the S wall blind. Hipped slated roofs.

HALLS of 1962–3 by *Robert B. Rankin* wrapped around the W and S elevations. Spacious interior, altered in 2000, with a gallery at the E end, with a concave centre, and a platform at the W end. Plaster walls and flat ceiling, with a simple cornice. – STAINED GLASS. Five windows from Glenapp Castle (q.v.) installed in 1929: the Four Seasons and, centrally, The Taming of Merlin. Pre-Raphaelite style, attributed to *Robert Henderson*. In the vestibule (of 2000), a portrait MEDALLION of pastor John Horne by *Robert Bryden*, 1934; it was formerly affixed to the pulpit.

CATHCART STREET HALL, Cathcart Street. *See* former Relief Church.

HOLY TRINITY (Episcopal), Fullarton Street. N end (chancel) of 1886–8 by *J. L. Pearson*, as an addition to a 'chaste and beautiful' church of 1837–9 by *David Bryce*, working for *William Burn*. The rest completed by *F. L. Pearson*, to his father's designs, in 1898–1900. It is Pearson senior's finest work in Scotland. The style is C13 French Gothic, in pale brown sandstone, and conceived on an ambitious scale, and very austere, with mostly single lancets. Gabled nave and chancel of uniform height, with flanking chapel and vestries. SW tower rising higher with clasping buttresses, with alternate blind lancets in the second stage. The 56-m. spire proposed was abandoned; the crenellated, concrete, final stage and pyramidal roof are of 1962–4 by *Pinckney & Gott* of London. The entrance a recessed and vaulted porch behind a two-bay screen, each bay further halved by pointed arches on simple columns; they are separated by a low stepped and gabled buttress.

The darkly numinous interior is a delight: here Pearson's ambition is revealed in the quality of the masonry and joinery (the builders in 1898–1900 were *Cowlin & Son* of Bristol), and the outstanding fittings and stained glass. Walls of exposed stone, beneath an open kingpost roof. The nave arcades of four bays, carried on quatrefoil piers, with single attached shafts rising higher to support the transverse arches which, in turn, support the roofs; arched, too, the baptistery beneath the tower. Similarly detailed chancel arch, and also the arch to the NE 'morning' chapel, known as St John's Chapel. Chapel and chancel separated by a further four-bay arcade; in the final arch sedilia and a piscina. The chancel roof was rebuilt, after a fire, by *J. & J. A. Carrick*, 1936. – Exquisite metalwork SCREENS separate nave from chancel, aisle from chapel. The CHANCEL SCREEN is particularly fine, filigree Gothic, culminating in a flourish of finials, designed by *Pearson* and executed by *White & Son* of London; the CHAPEL SCREEN is more restrained, with exuberant decoration limited to the upper band. – PULPIT of 1892, again by Pearson, and executed by *Nathaniel Hitch*. Of Bath stone, its semicircular front is divided into deeply recessed panels which hold sharply carved figures of Jesus, John the Baptist, St Paul and, as smaller figures in tiered panels, the apostles. – ALTAR of 1891, again by Pearson, with a pillared front and richly carved, some of the stone brought from St John's Tower (*see* p. 147). – Remarkable wooden triptych REREDOS by *F. L. Pearson*, 1903, carved by *Hitch*, painted by *Clayton & Bell* and assembled by *Luscombe & Son*, of London. 4.25 m. wide when fully open, carved in the highest of high relief. The central panel, the Adoration of the Magi, is flanked by two lower panels, with Gabriel in one, Mary the other, depicting the Annunciation; these three panels have elaborate cornices and finely detailed traceried canopies. The outer panels have simpler canopies, and the whole stands on a panelled and traceried gilt base. – FONT by *C. d'O. Pilkington Jackson*, 1951. – Simple PEWS; good dark wood CHOIR STALLS with panelled fronts, book stands raised on metal brackets and fleur-de-lis bench ends.

STAINED GLASS. An excellent collection, but in the high windows, robbed of some of its impact and immediacy. – The chancel N windows (Crucifixion and Resurrection) are by

Clayton & Bell, 1899; W wall, SS Peter and Paul, SS Matthew and Mark, three similar pairs in the E wall, all probably by *James Powell & Sons*, Matthew, Mark, Luke and John certainly so, and installed in 1896. – In St John's Chapel, the gable window illustrates the spread of Christianity in Scotland, and those in the E wall, episodes in the development of the episcopal church in the country. A bright and well-composed set, on an unusual theme, by *A. O. Hemming & Co.* of London, 1889, as a memorial to Bishop William Wilson, who is seen in the rightmost light, with labourers building the original church and school on this site. – In the E aisle, *A. O. Hemming*'s 1903 St Stephen (l.) is being vigorously stoned in the lower panel; St Mark (r.), of 1918 *C. E. Kempe & Co.*, is more conventional. – N rose window, the Virgin Mary and angels, 1901. – W aisle, from the S, St James, probably by *Hemming*, and the Royal Scots Fusiliers memorial by *Mayer & Co.* of Munich, 1894. – High up in the baptistery, Moses and Joshua, by *Clayton & Bell*, 1902.

To the W, the CHURCH HALL; the former school of 1861 by *John Murdoch*, converted by *James Scott Hay*, 1928.

Former NEW CHURCH, Fort Street. Now a dance studio. 1807–10 by *David Hamilton*, extended by *J. & H. V. Eaglesham* in 1901 and converted 1984 by *J. & J. A. Carrick*. 'New', as it was built to relieve pressure on the Auld Kirk. An elegant painted stone pedimented classical E front of five bays, separated by broad pilasters; the three central bays each have an arched doorway and window above, both with architraves. Recessed panels in the narrower outer bays, and tall stair windows on the return elevations. Four bays behind, with two tiers of segmentally headed windows. Spacious vestibule. As built the church had a panel-fronted gallery on three sides, supported on decorative pillars, and linked by more to the choice shallow-panelled plaster ceiling. A chancel was added by the Eagleshams, separated by a classical grey stone screen, with trumpeting angels in the spandrels of the main arch. Much of this has survived the Carricks' careful conversion: a new floor was introduced at gallery height, the chancel arch largely infilled, and walls built shy of the ground-floor columns to produce a large ground-floor studio, a smaller studio in the upper part of the chancel, and an 'arena' in the gallery, which retains its pews. Broad linking passages beneath the gallery, the skilfully done underside of which is now accentuated. STAINED GLASS. Decorative glass of 1880 by *W. & J. J. Kier.* – S wall, an angular Feeding the Five Thousand, by *Clokey*, 1960. – N wall, Ruth, an eyecatching design by *T. S. Halliday*, for *Guthrie & Wells*, 1928. – To its E, a damaged window of 1933 by *Herbert Hendrie.* – Good original railings and also a handsome classical GATEWAY, with a segmental archway, flat-headed openings to either side, and iron gates: a war memorial of 1929 by *William Cowie*, originally at the Relief Church.

Former RELIEF CHURCH, Cathcart Street. Built in 1816, roughly contemporary with the new street, for a congregation founded in 1814. A surprisingly grand, if simply detailed, rubble-built preaching box. Five bays to the street, the central bays slightly projected beneath a pediment with a circular window. Entrance with flanking sidelights, Doric columns, triglyph frieze and pediment; other windows segmentally headed. Octagonal windows in the pedimented w and e gables. Now residential; the halls to the e (CATHCART STREET HALLS) remain in ecclesiastical use. 1936. Gabled brick harled hall behind a severe stone screen façade with recessed panel decoration in the head. Single-storey flanking entrance bay.

ST ANDREW, Park Circus. The Free Church of 1892–3, by *J. B. Wilson* for the suburb being developed on the Bellevue estate (*see* p. 158). Dec, in Ballochmyle red rock-faced sandstone, with a soaring NW tower and spire (45 m. high) with lucarnes and crocketts, forming a prominent landmark, and a big seven-light window with panel tracery; three pairs of cusped lights in square heads below. In the head of the gable, blind tracery. To the r. of the main gable, a low octagonal tower, its uppermost stage a cusped panelled band, below a slated pyramidal roof. Side elevations of aisle, clearstorey and gabled transept, in the same plane; the windows echo the w front, the upper windows of four lights. Lower gabled chancel beyond the e gable, with a three-light window.

The warm, light INTERIOR of nave, aisles and transepts has plaster walls, a low boarded dado, and a coved plaster ceiling, divided by simple tie-beams on slender corbels, and cusped braces. Full-height arcades on clustered columns; galleries on three sides, with cusped panelled fronts, the side galleries divided by, and brought forward of, the arcade; the effect rather like two sets of theatre boxes. Pointed chancel arch on triple columns, the void almost entirely filled by the dark wood pulpit and chancel screen, and the organ.

– STAINED GLASS. In the lower windows only, and mostly late C20; in the three lights under the gallery anonymous glass of after 1983, the bright imagery of Ladybird Books. – s wall, three windows by *John Blyth*, 1971–5, one, a Good Samaritan, particularly well realized. – N wall, three windows with much clear background glass, a contrast to Blyth's full-colouring windows. From the E, firstly, Whither Thou Goest, I Will Follow, of after 2001, the serpents up the sides an inspired touch; then, Jacob, of 1989, and finally, a seamstress and a plough team, of 1991, photographically realistic. These two latter windows are by *CWS Design*, of Lisburn. WAR MEMOR-IAL, s wall, 1921 by *Robert Bryden* in bronze; marble surround by *Galbraith & Winton*.

Gabled HALL of 1897 by *William McClelland* set back to the r., and further brick halls of 1962–4 by *Stevenson & Ferguson* to the rear.

ST COLUMBA, Midton Road. 1897–1902, by *J. B. Wilson* as a United Presbyterian church, i.e. later than his St Andrew, nearby, and with similar details, but Perp, freely treated, in red Ballochmyle stone. NW tower with a lively bell-stage, with gargoyles under a pointed roof, aisles and SW transept. Big Perp windows to the gable and flanks, those on the sides with hoodmoulds linking over shallow buttresses. Gabled hall across the S gable, and an additional suite of halls of 1965, by *William Cowie & Torry*.

Airy INTERIOR of nave and aisles. Pointed arcades on squat columns; the chancel arch also pointed on clustered responds with decorative heads. Deep rear gallery and an open timber coved roof, with tie-beams, open cusped decorative work, and a boarded ceiling. Panelled gallery front, with cusped openings below the rail. – STAINED GLASS. In the chancel, Suffer Little Children by *Alexander Walker*, 1912–13, executed by *McCulloch & Co*. – W wall, from the S, the first and fourth lights represent The Creation, realistic pastoral scenes of 2002, linked by either end of a rainbow, by *Moira Parker*; the second light St Columba, of 1997 by *Susan Bradbury*: the Bible-carrying boyish saint stands in a swirling bubbling sea of blue; the third light St Andrew, of 1971, perhaps by *John Blyth*. – E wall, from the S, firstly, an unsigned holy warrior, a war memorial of 1948; secondly, a Resurrection of 2002 by *Roland Mitton*, pictorial, in the manner of the late C20, rather than the allegorical approach which often characterizes contemporary glass; and thirdly, a Good Shepherd of 1945 by *Guthrie & Wells*. In the fourth window, Nativity, of 2004, again by *Mitton*; in the fifth window an anonymous C19 Faith, and in the final window, The New Jerusalem, by *Moira Parker*, 2005, the 800th anniversary of the creation of Ayr as a Royal Burgh; the two bridges and the mouse recall Burns. – WAR MEMORIAL, between the NE windows, a bronze plaque in a stone frame, with ogival head and crocketed finials, by *J. K. Hunter*, executed by *Holmes & Jackson*, 1921 – Also the WAR MEMORIAL from the former New Church (*see* above), of 1922, marble, with a bronze medallion bust of the minister, who died on active service.

Former SANDGATE CHURCH, Sandgate. Now a pub. 1844–5 by *William Gale* in grey ashlar, for Ayr Free Church. 'Somebody's idea of a Romanesque church' (Colin McWilliam). Nave, recessed flanking aisles and clearstorey. The E front has a tall triple window with ringed shafts and chevron moulding above an arched doorway with arcaded moulding, all within a shallow recess with a corbelled arcade. Five-light clearstorey windows. Shallow buttresses. At the rear, facing Fort Street to the W, and with its own identity is the former MISSION HALL of 1878–9 by *Allan Stevenson*. It too is Neo-Norman, but with more conviction. Three-light window above a projecting porch with its own gable; round-headed entrance with simple columns and one order of rectilinear decoration.

Former WESLEYAN METHODIST CHURCH, Fort Street. Now offices. 1813, by *Reid*. A two-storey gabled preaching box, the ends of painted stone, the side walls, where visible, plastered. Closed by 1916, and in 1970 extended by *William T. Davie* with a single-storey apron wrapped around the N and E elevations.

PUBLIC BUILDINGS AND MONUMENTS

AYR ACADEMY, Fort Street. An impressive late classical design
of 1878–80 by *Clarke & Bell*, replacing *John Robertson*'s school
of 1800, much extended and altered in 1895, 1906–7 and
1911–13, on each occasion by *James A. Morris*, a former pupil.
The central part is two-storey, in Ravenscraig ashlar, with an
advanced and raised three-bay pedimented centre, with Corinthian pilasters to the upper floor, and flanking pavilion wings
with advanced fronts, and channelled pilasters at the angles.
All the windows have plain reveals, except the upper floor of
the pavilions with consoled cornices. Above the central windows
busts of Wilkie, Burns and Watt (art, literature, science) in
roundels, by *James Young* of Glasgow. Set back to the S is the
addition of 1895, very respectful of the earlier work, and
reusing, in a more restrained manner, many of the details, but
with four storeys, and smaller undemonstrative windows.
Morris's ART WING, added at the N end in 1906–7, is masterly.
L-plan, creating a courtyard between it and the main block. It
is executed in the same stone, and, on this side at least, equally
respectful. But on the N front, best seen from across the river,
glass replaces stone in a more avowedly C20 idiom, with buttresses between four enormous studio windows at first floor,
which merge into glazed roofs. Inside, the master's room,
above the smaller of the two studios, has access to a viewing
gallery within the larger studio, a delightful touch. In 1911–13
Morris redesigned much of the late C19 interior, creating a new
central full-height ASSEMBLY HALL, with a railed gallery
around all four sides, panelled and plastered walls, prize boards
and plaster ceiling. Subsequent extensions and alterations
include the big plastered rear addition of 1936–8 by *William
Reid*, County Architect. He also created the first-floor MEMO-
RIAL HALL in 1940. Simple caretaker's LODGE, by *Clarke &
Bell*, 1878–80.

AYR STATION AND STATION HOTEL, Smith Street. 1883–6 by
Andrew Galloway, replacing an earlier station of 1856–7.
Extravagantly scaled French Renaissance in red sandstone,
with two wings for hotel (S) and station offices (N). Inside, the
hotel stair has elaborate cast-iron balusters, and the public
rooms on the first floor have marble fireplaces and wooden
and beaten copper panels. Within the station, GSWR WAR
MEMORIAL, of 1922 by *Robert S. Lorimer*, a prodigious
Dalbeattie granite tablet with bronze panels (from St Enoch
Station, Glasgow, re-erected 1966).

BUS STATION, Sandgate and Fullarton Street. 1924 by *James Hay
& Steel*. Long and symmetrical, single-storey, the outer bays
gabled with pilaster-strips, the others with round-headed
windows. The original vehicle entrances, under raised parapets, altered to match the others in 1949 by *H. S. McNair*.

CITADEL LEISURE CENTRE, South Beach Road. Swimming
pool of 1969–72 by *Cowie Torry & Partners* (*Ian McGill*, project
architect), extended 1994–6 by *Kyle & Carrick District Council*.

The original pool is four-square, faced in dark brick, with generous glazing on the W and N elevations, and the roof expressed at the eaves as a series of projecting pentagonal pyramids. Covered walkway to W and N with zigzag arches. The addition, E, is in pale brick and harl, and has the FOUNDATION STONE of 1970 re-set. Concrete and coloured glass, lovingly done, by *Francis B. Dunbar*.

Former COUNTY POLICE HEADQUARTERS, Charlotte Street. Now local authority offices. 1858 by *James I. McDerment*, but given its rather featureless appearance in 1920 by *J. K. Hunter* and converted to present use in 1975–6 by *Robert B. Rankin & Partners*. H-plan, plastered, with gabled wings, and a gabled porch. Substantial additions to the rear.

GAIETY THEATRE, Carrick Street. 1902–3 by *J. McHardy Young*, rebuilt after a fire, 1903–4 by *Alexander Cullen* of Hamilton, and refronted 1938 by *H. S. McNair* (of *McNair & Douglas*) in Art Deco style. The result of all this three storeys, with a projecting centre with a stepped head, in faience and plaster. To the l. is an addition of 1995 by *Kyle & Carrick District Council*. The glory is the original Rococo-style auditorium, one of the best of its date in Scotland. Two tiers of horseshoe galleries, and flanking bowed boxes (the upper ones under arches), all with decorative plasterwork – cartouches, figures, diapering, the boxes framed by pilasters and swags.

GRAMMAR PRIMARY SCHOOL, Midton Road. A single-storey building of 1867–8 by *James I. McDerment*, thoroughly recast and enlarged to two storeys in 1908–9 by *J. K. Hunter*. Edwardian classical. Stone-faced and symmetrical front, with two shouldered gabled bays, each with full-height Ionic pilasters, channelled ground floor and quoins. Above the main entrance a typically Hunterian open segmental head.

Former LADY JANE HAMILTON SCHOOL, Charlotte Street. Now residential. 1840–3 by *Robert Paton* as an infants' school. A well-composed, three-bay, two-storey building with a projecting central bay, with a stepped gable; stepped also the flanking half-dormers and end gables.

LOUDOUN HALL, Boat Vennel. *See* Descriptions.

PAVILION, Pavilion Road. Won in competition in 1904 by *J. K. Hunter*, but built to a reduced scheme in 1910–11. Designed as a beach theatre, and given a suitably light-hearted exterior. Its most prominent feature the campanile-inspired square towers with pyramidal tiled roofs at each corner, rising above projecting bays with swept gables. Otherwise a harled, slated and gabled hall rising above subsidiary, mostly single-storey ranges, but two-storey and gently curved to the E. The auditorium has an arched and ribbed roof, carried on pillars, and balconies with bulbous fronts.

Former PLAYHOUSE CINEMA, Boswell Park. Now Mecca Bingo. 1930–1 by *John Fairweather* for the Glasgow cinema magnate George Green and, when completed, the second largest cinema in Scotland. A free interpretation of classical motifs. Raised central section, with giant plaster triglyphs and flanking ornament; the entrance beneath in a projecting doorpiece, with three tall lights below the entablature, and a rayed semicircular window above it. The galleried interior survives.

Former POST OFFICE, Sandgate. 1892–3 by *Walter W. Robertson*, of *H. M. Office of Works*. Thoughtful and carefully controlled Scots Baronial in red sandstone. Crowstepped projecting central bay and a conical roofed entrance tower. Nice decoration, e.g. a curved broken pediment and panelled shield over the three-light window in the gable, and the small pedimented light above the entrance.

SHERIFF COURTHOUSE AND COUNTY BUILDINGS, Wellington Square. Of two principal phases. The first part, which provides the set piece at the w end of Wellington Square, is of 1817–22 by *Robert Wallace* of London, an early commission for this architect and perhaps explained by family connections in the county. He was appointed instead of *David Hamilton*, who had prepared plans in 1814. The main elevation is built of ashlar Garscube sandstone, is of two storeys and eleven bays wide, with the ends slightly projecting. Prostyle Ionic portico in the centre and, rising above the balustraded attic, a dome with a lantern. Behind the portico a second porch – distyle *in antis*. First-floor windows with cornices on consoles, the ground-floor openings round-arched with corresponding blind niches in the outer bays. Set back to either side, lower pavilions added s by *John Murdoch* (1863–5) and N by *M. Wardrop* (probably 1874). These create a link with the extensive, assured and well-mannered addition of 1929–35 by *Alexander Mair* for Ayr County Council, which has its main front to the w. Blaxter stone, with twenty-nine-bay side elevations, and a seventeen-bay w entrance front, and planned around a spacious inner courtyard, the details a restrained rehearsal of Wallace's. The w elevation has a channelled ground floor, and a central pedimented centrepiece with channelled pilasters, Ionic columns and the county arms and thistle swags in the pediment. First-floor windows have balconies. Advanced pavilions on the long elevations, again with balconies; similarly treated the central bays, with pends beneath; on the s elevation a slate-hung attic storey, set back from the roof-line.

The grandiose early CI9 INTERIORS of the Court House remain largely complete, though this section of the building has undergone a thorough rearrangement since 1999. The important rooms all on the first floor, reached by a central stone-walled STAIRCASE (the ROUNDEL) under the coffered dome, with a circular stair rising within a ground-floor peristyle of eight Doric columns; doors and windows with consoles, niches; the newel terminated by a large gilded tripod. To the s the original rectangular courtroom (now COURT NO. 1), with Ionic columns along the sides, pilasters at the ends and original armorial stained glass in a lunette at w end; to the N the original County Hall (now COURT NO. 2), with paired pilasters at the w end, flanking arch; E end with richly decorated frieze, three niches in the side walls with decorative aprons. In both courts identical elaborately decorated door frames with consoles and almost Celtic decoration; each court, too, has a central raised clearstorey. Much original plasterwork in other rooms, such as the ADVOCATES' LIBRARY, to the N, with a panelled ceiling and clearstorey, and the former Robing Room, now the ATRIUM, where old and new come forcibly together. Equally spectacular the C20 interiors of the County Buildings: stepped VESTIBULE leading to spacious ENTRANCE HALL, with tiled floor, panelled wooden walls, and two stone stairs with gryphon-ended banisters. Stair windows with painted panels depicting the arms of the county's many constituent burghs. Equally spacious first-floor panelled corridors, with consoled doorpieces. The present COUNTY HALL occupies the bulk of the first-floor W front.

Within the grassed area at the seaward end, the ROYAL SCOTS FUSILIERS MEMORIAL. Bronze statue by *C. d'O. Pilkington Jackson*, 1960; *J. & J. A. Carrick*, architects. Neatly delineated soldier in fatigues, including camouflaged helmet, on a granite plinth, with a low screen wall behind. Also the STEVEN MEMORIAL FOUNTAIN. A bravura cast-iron design of 1892 by *Steven Bros & Co. (Milton Ironworks)*, of Glasgow and London, and given to Ayr by one of the partners, Hugh Steven. Circular pool, from which rises a square pedestal with angle shafts supporting the first basin. Above this a smaller basin, supported by dolphins and putti rowing on turtles. Finally, the smallest basin and a finial with an otter catching a fish.

TOWN HALL, New Bridge Street and High Street. 1827–32 by   97
Thomas Hamilton (Archibald Johnston of Glasgow, mason), the commission his reward for his generosity to the Burns Monument at Alloway (q.v.); extended 1878–81 by *James Sellars* of *Campbell Douglas & Sellars*. Asymmetrical. The style of the principal elevations to the street is Grecian, with a *piano nobile* of round-arched windows, but what one remembers is the outstanding 69-m. tower, a feat of inventive detail, unrivalled in Scotland, which starts conventionally enough, before above the roof level transforming into something altogether more elaborate and Roman before culminating in a slender spire. The channelled first stage projects forward of the frontage, with a large doorpiece in a simple pedimented architrave, while the second and third stages are framed by giant pilasters and a frieze of triglyph-like consoles, with a round-arched window to the second stage, and decorative roundels at the third, which rises above the flanking bays. The audaciously decorated fourth stage is octagonal, with coupled Doric columns on the angles; it has a boldly swagged base and is guarded at the corners by four fearsome gryphons bearing torches. Corinthian columns, also in pairs, and amphorae on pedestals at the angles for the final stage, and entablature-carrying volutes, from which the slim obelisk-like spire soars away to the weathervane.

The building itself has, l. and r. of the tower, three flanking bays, with ground-floor shops, a *piano nobile* with round-headed

windows, flat pilasters and a balustraded parapet. To the r., a
wing projects forward under a pediment. To High Street, the
façade has been extended from three bays to eleven, with a
barely advanced central five bays. These, at first floor, have an
Ionic colonnade with round-headed windows behind, and a
hipped upper floor with windows recessed behind a pilastrade
and iron balustrades.

The INTERIOR was largely rebuilt after a fire by *J. K. Hunter*
in 1901. Of Hamilton's interiors, the original Assembly Room
(now Council Chambers), with its coffered ceiling and paired
wooden Corinthian pillars, survives, but it was heightened by
Sellars as part of alterations to make the building suitable for
Council use. The broad flight of stairs and the three-light
window (glass by *W. & J. J. Kier*) in the Council Chambers
also date from these changes. The galleried Town Hall itself is
Hunter at his most flamboyant.

WALLACE TOWER, High Street. The highlight of the High
Street into which it thrusts. A square Tudor Gothic four-stage
clock tower and memorial folly of 1831–4 by *Thomas Hamilton*
(*John Parker*, mason), a rival to the steeple of his contemporary
Town Hall. It replaced an earlier tower, which had formed part
of the town house of the Cathcarts of Carbieston. The first
stage has a pronounced batter and four-centred arches, opened
once the street was widened in the late C19 leaving the tower
to mark the former street line; the second stage has tall three-
light windows on three sides, and on the fourth (w) face, a
canopied niche containing a statue of William Wallace by *James
Thom*. Angle buttresses carry up to crenellated turrets around
the octagonal top stage with quatrefoil bell-openings and crenellated parapet.

Adjoining are the WALLACE TOWER HALLS, Tudorbethan
of 1886–7 by *John Mercer*; two-storey, with gabled Y-tracery
windows to Mill Street, and a gable to the l. bay to High Street.
This rises behind a parapet with pointed merlons, a detail borrowed from Hamilton.

HARBOUR

Originally, boats would have been pulled up onto the banks on
either side of the river, but increasingly wharfs, quays and piers
were constructed. Until the C19, most of the development was
on the Ayr (S) side, while the Newton (N) side was largely given
over to shipbuilding. Major expansion took place in the late
C19, particularly on the N side, and this is now the heart of the
functional modern harbour. The late C20 saw a retreat from
the S side, which is now largely given over to aesthetically
unexciting housing, while on the N side, development consists
of large industrial sheds. Stone-built QUAYS, C18 in origin,
but much rebuilt in the C19, can be seen on either side, e.g.
in NORTH HARBOUR STREET, opposite York Street. Elsewhere, on the S side, the stone-lined former SLIP DOCK, now
drained, of 1880–2 by *John Strain*; on the N side, a circular

LIGHTHOUSE of 1842–3, with a machicolated parapet and an attached cottage of 1863–4, and the WET DOCK of 1873–8 by *Thomas Meik* of Sunderland, again stone-lined.

RIVER CROSSINGS

Described upstream from the river mouth.

Former HARBOUR BRANCH RAILWAY BRIDGE. Only the piers remain of the cast-iron girder bridge of 1898–9 by *William Melville*, which carried the railway to the s harbour, and was demolished in 1978.

NEW BRIDGE. Between New Bridge Street and the Main Street of Newton. 1877–9 by *George M. Cunningham* of *Blyth & Cunningham* of Edinburgh. The contractors were *W. & T. Adam* of Callander. Flat, of five segmental arches, with round-headed cutwaters and pilaster strips at the spandrels. It is of rubble sandstone, with dressed arch-rings, and a granite parapet, with quatrefoil piercings, supported on the outer sides on continuous granite corbel tables. A decorative cast-iron lamp standard rises above the parapet at each pier. On the site of one of the main fords across the river and in place of the original New Bridge, of 1786–9 by Alexander Stevens, which was found to be unsafe and taken down in 1877. It was apostrophized as 'you'll be a shapeless cairn' by the Auld Brig in Burns's poem 'The Twa Brigs', the truth of this assertion cementing the poet's reputation as an architectural critic for all time.* *p. 136*

AULD BRIG. One of the finest medieval bridges in Scotland, and now reserved for pedestrians. The present structure was in existence by 1525, if not earlier, and probably succeeded an earlier timber structure. Four segmental arches, with large triangular cutwaters, built of coursed rubble, with dressed voussoirs with a moulded inner ring. It rises seamlessly into tall parapets which flank the setted pavement. The pressures exerted have caused the s arch to spring up slightly. The N end fell in 1753 and was repaired; at this end it broadens out, with a flanking wall to the W, and the footings of a guardhouse exposed to the E. Cast-iron lamps rise from the parapet above each cutwater; they date from the restoration of 1907–10 by *William S. Wilson*, engineer, Glasgow, and *James A. Morris*, who orchestrated a campaign to save it, after the Town Council began to plan for its replacement. Burns was invoked, and the bridge saved. 86

TURNER'S BRIDGE. 1899–1900 by *John Eaglesham*. Provided by Andrew M. Turner, whose Mill Street brewery stood close to the s end. Three-arched openwork steel structure, resting

---

*Much more could be said about the first New Bridge. Although plans had been obtained from *Robert Adam* and rejected on cost, there is no reason to suspect Stevens had sight of these, as is often inferred. He was a perfectly competent bridge designer and architect, as Nos. 1–3 New Bridge Street, and other bridges, attest. The failure of the first New Bridge has not been fully examined; the structure was probably fatally weakened by the widening carried out in 1845.

Ayr, view from the New Bridge.
Engraving, *c.* 1840.

on red sandstone piers, with fancifully decorative cast-iron
parapets.

RAILWAY VIADUCT. Built in 1856, but rebuilt *c.* 1878 for the
Glasgow & South-Western Railway. A four-arched masonry
bridge, with dressed voussoirs and round-headed cutwaters.
Plain parapets, that to the W obscured by the CAGE WALK, a
metal pedestrian path cantilevered out on brackets, and probably contemporary with the rebuilding.

VICTORIA BRIDGE. A three-arch flat-span steel girder bridge
resting on stone and concrete cutwaters, of 1960–1 by *F. A.
Macdonald & Partners*, with *Charles Eddie*, Burgh Surveyor.

DESCRIPTIONS

The first description covers the town centre, the heart of the old
burgh, the plan of which is still predominantly medieval, with the
two principal streets, Sandgate and High Street running N–S from
the river, and an outer ring of streets denoting the original burgh
boundary.

1. The centre

The best approach to the heart of the old burgh is the New
Bridge (for which *see* p. 135) across the Ayr at the E end of the
harbour. W of the bridge along the waterside one can see the
remaining buildings of SOUTH HARBOUR STREET. This
important, if presently desperately neglected, part of the Ayr
streetscape starts with a series of late C18 and C19 façades,
including the three-storey Nos. 1–5, with a pedimented Doric
doorpiece, and tripartite windows. This has been altered at
some stage during the C19, and was originally two-storey, with
Venetian windows, and probably late C18 in origin. This series
ends with the early C19 Nos. 9–13, a former inn, whose main
façade faces W, with a balustraded single-storey apron projection, added in 1833, while beyond Fort Street, the early C19
Nos. 23–25 has a single-storey rear wing with a curved end.
Straight ahead is NEW BRIDGE STREET, the introduction to
the town centre, which succeeded Water Vennel, a narrow lane
that ascended from the river side. The new street, wide and

spacious, is contemporary with the first New Bridge of 1786–9 by *Alexander Stevens*; he was also the architect of Nos. 1–3 (E side), which to the river has a pair of handsome full-height bows. This imaginative and thoughtful foil to the bridge has three storeys over a tall basement, round-headed ground-floor windows and a jerkin-headed gable behind a quatrefoil parapet. The street elevation has a pilastered early C19 shopfront, decorative first-floor window friezes, and an eaves cornice that continues into its simple late C18 neighbour, and this group finishes with another late C18 block, the five-bay Nos. 13–17, with a central key-blocked entrance. Opposite, rounding the corner from South Harbour Street, are the four-storey Nos. 2–4, of 1834 by *John Kay*, an equally effective foil for the bridge, with three-light windows in the curved bay, that at first floor with a bracketed cornice. Nos. 6–10, of *c.* 1825, are in a similar idiom, with C19 pilastered shopfronts and a rounded bay to Boat Vennel.

BOAT VENNEL, its form evidence of the medieval street pattern, is dominated by the remarkable survival of LOUDOUN HALL, an early C16 gabled stone-built merchant's house, which was saved from demolition by the intervention of the Marquess of Bute in 1937 and restored 1946–56 by *Neil & Hurd*. The house, one of Ayr's finest buildings and one of the oldest surviving town houses in Scotland, is first referred to in 1517 as 'the house of James Tayt, burgess of Ayr', but was possibly built for his father Thomas (†1512). It is an L-plan, the principal part of three storeys, the N wing of two and very probably added *c.* 1534 after the house was purchased by Hew Campbell of Loudoun. Gable stacks, and many small windows, irregularly placed; larger windows on the longer elevation with, below, two doors, with flanking windows, to the vaults. Relieving arches above both doors, and a large off-centre relieving arch above. The details of the wing similar, with a gabled W dormer. Correctly, but far-sightedly, no attempt was made by the restorers to re-create lost details: the original stair may have been in a re-entrant tower, but had been lost, so the present stairwell was inserted in the wing and concealed by timber cladding (the stair itself replaced by *Patrick Lorimer*, of *ARP Lorimer & Associates* in 1997–8*). To its r., a new entrance is similarly simple, and on the front of the earlier house are jettied wooden galleries. Inside the wing a small entrance hall. At first floor, the full length of the original house is given over to a spacious 12.1-m.-long hall, with plastered walls and a panelled ceiling. Fireplace in the E wall, and an ogee-headed stone aumbry to the l. of the door. A stone stair in the S wall leads to one of the three ground-floor vaults. The courtyard was re-landscaped in 1995–7 by *Reaich & Hall* (*Neil Gillespie*,

88

---

* *Hurd*'s stair had only served the first floor. It was made of oak which had originally formed part of the Marquis of Ailsa's yacht *Marquessa*, had been reused to form a staircase at Culzean Castle, and removed from the castle to make room for the lift to the Eisenhower National Guest Flat.

project architect) and the artist *Gordon Young*, who designed
the wooden seat, chain-like bollards, bronze model and vary-
ingly punctured sandstone N wall. The lucent coloured glass S
wall is by *Louice Lusby Taylor*.

NEW BRIDGE STREET continues with some of the best early
C19 townscape in Ayr, including *Thomas Hamilton*'s superlative
Town Hall on the E side (*see* Public Buildings), and a constantly rewarding group opposite, beginning with No. 12, with
another quadrant corner and windows in architraves, and continuing with a coherent run of similar three-storey fronts, of
three bays, slightly varied in height and width but with one
agreeable template. They conclude with the stately former
Ayrshire Bank, also by *Hamilton*, 1830–2, in grey ashlar, with
a channelled ground floor and a five-bay fluted Ionic colonnade between paired antae at the first floor, with tall windows
and aprons behind, and podia and set-back pedimented attic
with lunette above. Next S is the narrow and setted ACADEMY
STREET, with a single rubble-built six-house terrace of *c.* 1776
on the N side, with a regular cornice line, and broad agreement
in the form, but varied in their details. Below the terrace lie a
remarkable series of WINE CELLARS, indicative of Ayr's important trade with France. Three parallel brick-lined vaults
running the length of the terrace, with brick dividers between
the bins, which are identified by lead numbers. They are dated
to *c.* 1760–76 and remain in daily use.

SANDGATE continues New Bridge Street S, but is much
earlier; this was one of the main streets of the C13 burgh and
undoubtedly much that is medieval is concealed by Georgian
refrontings. But much is also new work of *c.* 1830, especially
on the E side where the street was widened to provide a proper
setting for the Town Hall, which continues to dominate the

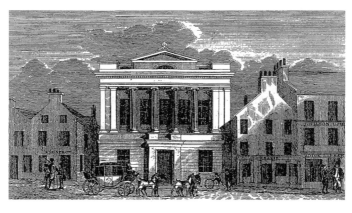

Ayr, Ayrshire Bank.
Engraving, 1832

streetscape, especially in views N, where the slight rise and fall, and imperceptible bend of the road, come into full play. The street's character derives from the interplay between the simpler buildings of the early C19, and the more elaborate buildings of the mid and late C19, many of which are, or were, banks, with suitable gravitas. Several of the houses in that first stretch on the E, as far as Newmarket Street, are simple Late Georgian classical, similar to those in New Bridge Street, often with decorative friezes and, as in New Bridge Street, variations on the same agreeable template. One, No. 3, with its Ionic shopfront, was built by *Thomas King* in 1828–30 as the Ayr Arms Inn. No. 15 is respectful Neo-Georgian infill, of 1929–30 by *Thomas O'Beirne*, while Nos. 27–29 are brasher, late C19 red ashlar, busily ornamented. At the junction with Newmarket Street, No. 37 is late C18 of fashionable character; one bay to Sandgate, and three, the outer ones slightly advanced, on the return, each with a first-floor Roman Doric pilastered Venetian window in a recessed super-arch. The inspiration is Adam; could this be by *Hugh Cairncross*?

The opposite side of the street S of Academy Street is less cohesive, of mixed heights and styles from late C18 to early C20, including the narrow early C19 No. 14, the first floor of which is almost wholly taken up by a tall pedimented and consoled three-light window.

CATHCART STREET, running W, was laid out, or widened, in 1807. Some typically attractive three-storey classically detailed houses in a terrace (Nos. 8–20) along the S side, facing the former Relief Church (*see* Churches, above). Nos. 5–7 E of the church, with pedimented wall-head gable and one cavetto-revealed entrance, are probably late C18. At the S corner with Sandgate, LADY CATHCART'S HOUSE, a tall two-bay, four-storey vernacular town house, probably C17, but refronted in the C18 and now with a yellow limewash. Narrow two-bay gabled side elevation, and lower rear wing with a gable stack and simple dormers. Restored in 1991–6 by *Simpson & Brown* for the Scottish Historic Buildings Trust; the front dormer-heads of this date. Surviving interiors include a vaulted ground-floor room in the rear wing. Sandgate continues with the former BANK OF SCOTLAND of 1876–7 by *Alexander Petrie*, Scots Baronial with three crowstepped gables and a central entrance beneath a solid consoled balcony, and the ROYAL BANK OF SCOTLAND, 1970–3, by *Gratton McLean & Partners*, uncompromisingly Modernist but with a very heavy corbel table, forming a continuous head to the upper band of windows, clearly influenced by its Baronial neighbour. At the corner with St John Street, the former COMMERCIAL BANK, of 1862–3 by *David Rhind*. A tall parapeted three-storey three-bay Renaissance palazzo, with a four-bay return elevation; off-centre Roman Doric doorpiece, prominent rusticated angle pilasters, and round-arched pilastered first-floor windows with carved head keystones. Hereafter the W side of the street is smaller-scale, mostly two-storey, and interrupted midway along by the former Sandgate Church (*see* Churches, above), which stands back from the street. Close to it is No. 56, of 1894 by *H. V. Eaglesham*, red sandstone, with a mansard roof and a pilastered four-light window beneath a carved cornice. Crossing to the E side, at the S corner with Boswell Park, a grandiose commercial block in the Burnet-Baroque manner, of 1909–11 by *J. R. Johnstone*. Heavy central entrance, with an open pediment, Doric columns, a freely interpreted Gibbsian surround, and a caduceus carved in the tympanum. Almost restrained by contrast is the corner circular tower with domed head and heavily swagged drum. To the N, the C19 former Post Office (*see* Public Buildings, above), and the former Ayr County Club (QUEENS COURT CENTRE), of 1872–3 by *John Murdoch*. Scots Baronial, with a crowstepped gable to the street, and a corbelled and crowstepped dormer gable on the N elevation, which also has a graceful cast-iron veranda to the entrance court. A lower rubble-built wing belongs with a complex of C18 stable and other ancillary accommodation, restored and converted by *ARP Lorimer Architects*, 1975–80. The S junction with Newmarket Street is marked by the former Royal Bank of Scotland (now QUEENS COURT HOUSE), of 1856–8 by *Peddie & Kinnear*, a five-bay three-storey palazzo with shell tympana to the entrances in the outer bays, round-headed windows under consoled heads, and much ornament, especially in the friezes and spandrels.

NEWMARKET STREET, running dog-legged E between Sandgate and High Street, was cut through in 1767 but little that is obviously C18 remains. What one remembers are the C19 and C20 contributions, e.g. the gravitas of the two-storey nine-bay late classical MACNEILLE BUILDINGS of 1868–9 by *James I. McDerment*, with its elaborately detailed doorpiece, which has a keystone of John Knox and decorative double consoles, with heads (Bruce and Wallace) in the upper halves, while the lower halves have dainty small head pendants, and the black Vitrolite shopfront of 1948 by *H. S. McNair* at Nos. 6–10. This is at the junction with the narrow HOPE STREET, which runs N–S parallel with High Street. The buildings on its E side, mostly with their principal fronts facing High Street, have been built up, from the C18, on the site of the old market place. One, however, has frontages only to Hope and Newmarket Streets: No. 4 Newmarket Street, a well-kept three-storey town house of the late C18, built for one sept of the Kennedys, with a three-bay gabled entrance front to the street and a longer elevation, of five bays, to Hope Street.

Now HIGH STREET, which for its first section between New Bridge Street and Old Bridge Street (N side) runs parallel to the river, but at Hope Street turns S. A busy, in both senses, street, which obtains much of its character from its lazy sinuous nature, with buildings such as the Town Hall or Wallace Tower coming into, or passing out of view. Initially the frontages marked individual burgage plots, often with closes and back properties, but most of these have been lost to larger-scale C20

developments, though some still remain, especially in association with the groups of early C19 houses. Predictably, shopfronts are largely modern and corporate; some earlier ones are
mentioned below. Much of the STREET FURNITURE dates
from 1995, under a scheme by *Donald Carruthers*, Strathclyde
Regional Council Engineer, and *Parr Partnership*. In the first
section, on the S side E of the Town Hall, Nos. 13–21, more of
the good Georgian townscape seen in New Bridge Street: three
three-storey blocks of *c.* 1811–25 linked by a continuous roof-
line and cornice, one (of 1811) with an original consoled shopfront. Opposite, the four-storey Nos. 8–10 are late C18, with
decorative friezes to the windows. But, then, bigger interwar
commercial frontages predominate: the former WOOL-
WORTH'S (1935 by *W. L. Swinnerton*, with faience work supplied by *Shaws*); former BURTON'S (1936, a typical simplified
classical design by their usual architect, *Harry Wilson*) and
former MARKS & SPENCER (1934–5 by *James M. Monro &
Son*). Much more characterful are the two skilfully detailed red
sandstone buildings before the junction with Old Bridge Street,
both of 1879–80 in Renaissance styles: the first by *Allan Stevenson*; its larger neighbour by *John Mercer* as the Ayr Coffee
House.

The street now turns towards the S, and also widens noticeably to create the FISH CROSS, an informal open space once
the town's fish market, presided over by a SCULPTURE, Remembrance, of 1995, by *Malcolm Robertson*: a fisherman holds a
fish as if in supplication. On the E, mostly late C20, e.g. the
brick bulk of *Monro & Partners*' 1972–4 MARKS & SPENCER.
On the W, the curving late C19 red sandstone SCOTTISH
TRANSIT TRUST CHAMBERS, and a plastered four-storey
house of 1777, with a tall wall-head gabled stack, and stone
dressings. Early C19 three-storey blocks flank Hope Street,
before the impressive three storeys and gabled attic of No. 57
swiftly narrow the perspective. This is late C18, built on the site
of the original market, and has a paired Roman Doric doorway
to the r. It is a house of some importance, deserving further
investigation. The street now narrows again; the buildings on
the W were also built on the site of the market and Tolbooth,
demolished in the early C19, and form an eclectic and interesting group. No. 61 is a Flemish Renaissance former pub of
1893–4 by the inventive *H. V. Eaglesham*, with a snaking balustraded balcony and blind tympanum with cherubs in the spandrels, while the single-storey former GLASGOW SAVINGS BANK
is of 1935–7 by *Eric A. Sutherland*: black Aberdeen granite
Tuscan columns supporting an almost painfully plain stone
pediment. The harled vernacular Nos. 71–73 is probably mid-
C18, its gabled front a reminder that this was once the norm,
and altered, *c.* 1900, when two canted small-paned bays were
added at first-floor level. No. 75 is asymmetrical light brown
Scots Baronial of 1886–7 by *Allan Stevenson*: three storeys of
lively articulation on two elevations, all crowsteps, crenellations, corbelling and strapwork. At the angle with Newmarket

Street, a splayed corner is corbelled out to a diagonally set
turret, gabled with many small pinnacles, with, in a niche to
its l., a STATUE of William Wallace, with targe and sword, by
William Reid, of 1810, from the previous building on the site.
Beyond Newmarket Street, the three-storey painted ashlar
WINTON BUILDINGS brings a large dash of mid-C19 sobriety,
and forms one of the most prominent buildings in the street:
of 1841–4, by *John Parker*, mason,* in a restrained classical
manner, with rounded angles, first-floor cornices and a balustraded and panelled parapet. s of this another section of the
old market place, in front of another consistent sequence of
early C19 streetscape (Nos. 85–103, five buildings in the same
satisfying manner first seen in New Bridge Street; the smartest,
the southmost, with panelled end blocks to the window architraves, and second-floor guttae, had been 'recently rebuilt' in
1834). In the rather cramped open space, a SCULPTURE, Poet
and Scholar, by *Doug Cocker*, 1995. To the s, the BANK OF
SCOTLAND, grand seven-bay grey freestone Georgian Revival
of 1901–2 by *Peddie & Washington Browne*, with a channelled
ground floor and a huge cartouche of the burgh arms in the
pediment. At the N junction with Carrick Street the red sandstone Nos. 155–157 of *c.* 1874, simply detailed with thin pilasters and balustraded parapet, and a return elevation, with two
blind bays, to Carrick Street. In CARRICK STREET, some
mid-C19 houses and one, probably late C18, cottage, now
steeply slated, but probably originally thatched.

The E side of High Street between Marks & Spencer and
the Wallace Tower is predominantly late C19 and to a larger
scale, e.g. the narrow Neo-Baronial No. 86, of 1883 by *John
Baird* of Glasgow, of grey coursed rubble, and BHS, also of
1883, by *John Mercer*: Italian Renaissance style, not quite symmetrical, of 4:1:3:1 bays, the single bays with Venetian
windows and dormers with pediments. At the N junction with
Kirkport, the Italianate Nos. 112–114 of 1862 by *Andrew
Hunter*, mason, and *William Alexander*, joiner, and corresponding to the s, the Renaissance-style No. 116 of 1905 by *J. K.
Hunter*. KIRKPORT itself is a short, narrow, setted street
running up to the Auld Kirk's lychgate (*see* Churches, above)
with a nice, if modest, C18 and early C19 ensemble of houses,
restored by *Robert Allan & Partners* in 1972. The former
UNION BANK of 1858, by *Robert Paton*, is a symmetrical three-
storey six-bay palazzo with first-floor windows with pediments,
pulvinated friezes with laurel decoration and panelled aprons.
Ground floor refaced by *F. Durward* in 1963, but largely following the original design with Doric porches in the outer bays.
The bank originally towered over the buildings to its s, but
they were rebuilt following road widening in 1885, as the position of the Wallace Tower shows to the s. The best and most

---

*Parker was certainly the builder. Neither he, nor anyone else, is specifically
mentioned as architect, even though the buildings were recognized as a 'great
embellishment' to the town (*Ayr Advertiser*, 1844).

interesting of this group is also the smallest: No. 146 (EARLY LEARNING CENTRE), 1886 by *James A. Morris & Hunter*, in a free Italian Renaissance style which owes much to Norman Shaw. Three tight bays, surmounted by a swagger broken segmental pediment and segmentally headed aedicule. The rusticated first floor has windows under similar pediments, with pulvinated friezes and linking cornice. To its r., Nos. 148–156 are another effective design by *H. V. Eaglesham*, 1892–3, an unusual but successful mix of Jacobean and Flemish motifs including stepped and scrolled gables, one with an aedicule and balcony, the other with a porthole. A pend leads into NILE COURT, which has *Eaglesham*'s awesomely large MASONIC HALL (1895–6) on its N side, and a good harled Neovernacular housing development (BLACKFRIARS COURT, *c.* 1999) at its E end.

Beyond the Wallace Tower High Street curves lazily, before bifurcating to form Kyle Street and Alloway Street. Mostly late C19 and C20 on the E, which lacks any sense of cohesion, with only the TAM O' SHANTER of particular interest. Thatched and harled pub, rebuilt in 1808, but clearly earlier in spirit, i.e. wide windows with painted margins, and pilastered central doorpiece. Above this a painted panel and a late C19 cast-iron lantern. The W side is much more consistent, two storeys rising to later commercial buildings of three and four storeys, such as Nos. 213–217 of 1909, by *Murdoch & Lockhart* (in pale ashlar) and Nos. 219–225 of 1894–5 by *William Kerr*, with lunettes in pierced gables. They also provide an effective screen for the massive KYLE CENTRE, of *c.* 1985 by *Sheppard Robson*, with *Cowie Torry & Partners*, which extends over a large area to the rear. Its entrance is stone-faced with a stepped gable. High Street concludes with an early C20 Baroque flourish in red sandstone: *J. & H. V. Eaglesham*'s former Plough Inn, with giant Doric pilasters ending in shields at the entablature blocks, and No. 239 by *William Cowie*, with pilaster-strips ending in cartouches. Both are of 1904 and must have been conceived together.

KYLE STREET linked the town with its eastern hinterland, until it was severed by the railway. Rebuilt and widened in 1891, with many buildings of that period, but also the brash AYR CENTRAL shopping mall of 2005–7 by *iLo Design*, which has an open precinct running in a dog-leg from here to Smith Street. Mostly glass, with stone fascias and exposed metalwork. ALLOWAY STREET is the S continuation of High Street. It gained its ascendancy over Kyle Street in the mid C19, as Kyle Street was truncated and the S suburbs grew. Mostly, especially on the E side, two-storey mid-C19 buildings, usually painted or plastered, with some first-floor windows in frames, and one group (Nos. 25–31) with bracketed door cornices. On the same side, the mannered CLYDESDALE BANK of 1985–6 by *Cowie Torry & Partners* injects some variety: its solid red sandstone first floor punctuated by projecting cage-like windows. The street's W side is busier, more varied, and later. It begins with

the boldly announced former POPULAR SUPPLY STORE of
1924–5 by *James K. Hunter*, then HOURSTON'S Department
Store of 1894–5 and 1909–10, both phases in red sandstone
and both by *Allan Stevenson*. The later part (r.) the more
assured, and with a touch of bravado – Ionic pilaster-strips,
bracketed first-floor iron balconies and decorative lead panels,
including a sundial, to the central canted oriel. Beyond, a row
of late C19 single-storey shops, with a screen façade topped by
a balustrade said to have been reused from the first New
Bridge, is dwarfed by the ARRAN MALL, with lumpen concrete
offices above, 1962–5 by *Ian Burke, Martin & Partners*; the mall
prettified *c.* 1995 by *ARP Lorimer & Partners*. At the corner
with Dalblair Road, D'AURAY BUILDINGS, inventive Free
Baroque of 1896–7 by *James K. Hunter*, one of his major commercial buildings. The three-bay balustraded quadrant is
flanked by raised bays with prominent aedicular second-floor
windows topped by key-blocked ovals. The outer bays are
recessed and canted, and have gabled overarches, while a
further overarch fronts a squat eaves-height tower on the
Dalblair Road elevation.

    Alloway Street opens out into Killoch Place, which with
Beresford Terrace (s) forms the w side of BURNS STATUE
SQUARE. This is an inchoate triangular open space, too much
given over to traffic and parking. It developed from the mid
C19 on what had previously been unenclosed land used for
cattle and other markets. The eponymous statue, dwarfed by
trees, fails to give the square focus, and allows the Royal Scots
Fusiliers' memorial to its E to steal the thunder, but together
they form the square's highlights. Bronze STATUE of Robert
Burns, 1889–91 by *George A. Lawson*, on a tall square well-
composed granite pedestal by *James A. Morris & Hunter*, with
a pulvinated frieze, intermixing foliage with scrolls bearing
place names associated with Burns. Lawson's poet stands,
facing s (towards Alloway), pensive and introspective, a likeable and engaging representation. The carving of the pedestal
was modelled by *David McGill* of London and carved by
Arthur Taylor of Aberdeen. Later bronze relief panels on each
face: Tam's Ride (1894), the witch's sark a cutty sark indeed;
a quiet Cottar's Saturday Night (1893), both by *Lawson*, and
a boisterous revelling Jolly Beggars (1894) by McGill. In a very
different style, a rather mawkish Burns Leaving Highland
Mary, 1895 by *George E. Bissell* of Poughkeepsie, New York. To
the w, facing towards the station, is the ROYAL SCOTS FUSIL-
IERS MEMORIAL, 1900–2 by *Thomas Brock*, on another
Kemnay granite pedestal; this by *Arthur Taylor*. The thoughtfully modelled bronze soldier stands hatless, holding a rifle
with bayonet fixed, his other fist clenched, his 'set lips telling
of the determination to face danger, death or whatever might
befall'.

    On the NE side of the square, as it funnels out from Alloway
Street, a group of three tall red sandstone commercial blocks:
Nos. 1–7, 1901–2 by *James A. Morris* in restrained Edwardian

Free Style, with an oriel window rising into a crenellated D-plan tower;* Nos. 9–15, 1899–1900 by *J. & H.V. Eaglesham* (*William Cowie*, job architect), Renaissance, with the tall centre of its steeped roof-line topped by a panelled stack breaking through the cornice; Nos. 17–23, of 1894 by *H. V. Eaglesham*, with a striking second-floor balustrade and bracketed balcony, and a deep plain parapet with banded stacks. Well detailed, and effectively scaled. The s side of the square has the hideously ill-scaled BURNS HOUSE, 1972–4 by *Gavin Paterson & Son* of Glasgow, and the ODEON CINEMA of 1937–8 by *Andrew Mather*, now rather drably harled. In KILLOCH PLACE, the former BRITISH LINEN BANK of 1936 by *Thomson Sandilands & Macleod*. Stone-faced, of two storeys above the modern shopfronts, with a curving corner bay ending in a flat conic tower, with flat double corbel-like decoration. The windows in tall recesses, with further recessed panels between. A subdued but successful variation on the grandly classical manner brought to West of Scotland banks by *James Miller*. On the opposite corner of Miller Road, the former ROYAL BANK OF SCOTLAND, of 1970–1 by *Robert Allan & Partners*. A remark-ably unspoilt period piece, and a good foil for the earlier bank. Ground floor with vertical glazing; upper floors of rough-finished concrete, with projecting rectangular two-storey windows with panel aprons.

The last streets to be described mark the original burgh bound-ary and are described clockwise from SMITH STREET. At the junction with Kyle Street, the red sandstone No. 67, dated 1883, by *James A. Morris* as a bonded store. A curved corner, flanked by two hipped bays, of differing height, breaking through the eaves. Opposite, the richly detailed former RAILWAY TAVERN, 1891, for the Musselburgh brewer, Young's, turns the corner with a curved bay that rises into a drum with cartouche panels and a broad-eaved ogee-headed and finialled dome. The architect deserves to be known. DAL-BLAIR ROAD, w of Burns Statue Square, begins with a con-tinuous wall of well-articulated and neatly detailed red sandstone tenements of *c*. 1900, very probably all by *Allan Stevenson*; an earlier terrace (Nos. 17–25) of *c*. 1880 by the same architect, with crisp paired consoled doorheads. But much else has been lost, and the ugly seven-storey MERCURE HOTEL, of 1969–70 by *Leach, Rhodes & Walker* of Manchester, now domi-nates the junction with Carrick Street, overshadowing *William Cowie*'s No. 2, of 1904, with his usual austere detailing and a generously lit studio in the r. bay.

FULLARTON STREET runs w from here to Sandgate and Fort Street; it too has been extensively cleared, leaving *Pear-son*'s Holy Trinity (*see* Churches, above) isolated on the N side, but better preserved on the s side, where a row of early to mid-C19 two-storey houses, of varying height, such as Nos.

---

* Built for the Royal Scots Fusiliers, whose Drill Hall, also by *Morris*, later a notable dance hall, lies behind, roofless and fire damaged.

18–20, with a pretty fanlight over one entrance, abuts the unmissable red sandstone presence of *H. V. Eaglesham*'s WELLINGTON CHAMBERS of 1904–7. Four-storey, with two nine-bay façades, (that to Fort Street in three planes), and a square tower at the angle rising a further storey. His best work, in a modern classical idiom, and strongly influenced by American urban architecture. The channelled and banded stonework gives it a gripping horizontality.

Finally FORT STREET, N to the riverside. Opposite Wellington Chambers the well-mannered grey brick MEWS HOUSE, of 1966 by *Robert Allan & Partners*, of its date but a tactful intervention on a prominent site, the Baptist Church Centre (*see* Churches, above) and Nos. 47–49, of 1824 by *Thomas King*, a plastered four-bay pair with a central entrance with big consoles, and a pedimented wall-head gable. Also by *King*, on the E side, the seven-bay Nos. 50–52, of 1825, gabled and plastered, with two asymmetrically positioned doorpieces with deep consoles; the rear of the former Sandgate Church (*see* Churches, above); and a three-storey red sandstone terrace of the 1890s, with a leaded octagonal corner turret, banded stacks and triangular pedimented heads to the first-floor windows. The N half is of 1895 by *William Kerr*, the plainer S half of 1893 by *Allan Stevenson & Kerr*. At the N end of the street, on the E, the ashlar double-bow front of THE OLD CUSTOM HOUSE, of *c.* 1810; opposite are the former New Church and Ayr Academy (*see* Churches and Public Buildings, above), the erection of the church and the school's predecessor the catalyst for the transformation of the original back boundary lane into the present broad street.

2. *West of the centre: Citadel of Ayr and Wellington Square*

Ayr's royal castle, established *c.* 1197, stood outwith the burgh on the low sandy hillocks S of the river mouth, overlooking both river and the sea (to the W) close to the parish church (*see* St John's Tower, below). From 1652 the site was occupied by the Cromwellian CITADEL, designed by *Hans Ewing Tessin*, gradually demolished after 1660, of which some walls survive. This was an elongated hexagon, mirroring similar Commonwealth establishments, though on a more than usually ambitious scale. The longest sides faced W and E, the latter with the main landward entrance, of which a fragment, in the form of a moulded segmental head in a short stretch of wall can be seen in Citadel Lane, and at the angles four-sided bastions giving flanking protection to the walls. These, where they survive, are of large blocks of stone, and up to 4.5 m. high, with a pronounced batter on the outward elevation. The Earl of Eglinton acquired the demilitarized Citadel in 1663, and raised it into a burgh of barony, Montgomeriestoun. By the C18 its industries, such as brewing, were challenging the monopolistic powers of Ayr's burgesses, and in the early years of the C19 it became the subject of a still-born attempt at

98

planned formal development. But in 1854 John Miller pur-
chased the land, had the tower of the old church enlarged as
his house, and developed the remainder of the area within the
Citadel walls (broadly corresponding to modern Eglinton
Terrace, Montgomerie Terrace and Bruce Crescent, with Ailsa
Place and Arran Terrace) as a quiet residential suburb.

The 1850s feu plan was prepared by *Clarke & Bell*, and
included the laying out of CITADEL PLACE, which runs W
from Fort Street with, on both sides, presumably contemporary
houses, similar to those in Fullarton Street (*see* above), and, at
its W end, within a wooded enclosure, ST JOHN'S TOWER. This
is the substantial surviving fragment of the medieval parish
church, first recorded in 1233, and mostly dem. *c*. 1726. The
tower itself is *c*. 1400, square, ashlar-faced, with a few irregularly
placed square-headed openings, and lancet bell-openings. On
the E elevation, evidence for the church itself: a gable raggle, a
circular window with double chevron decoration, and a round-
headed entrance, with a similar recess, with moulded capitals
and a worn capital, above. Scanty remains of the nave's W wall,
the springing of the first arch of the N arcade, and, to the E
pier bases found during C20 excavations. The tower was used
as a look-out and sea-mark until its conversion to a house, Fort
Castle, for Miller by *John Murdoch*, *c*. 1855, with a corbelled
parapet and crowstepped caphouse. Other additions were
removed by *J. K. Hunter* in 1913–14, following its purchase by
the 3rd Marquess of Bute in 1913 and archaeological investigations carried out by him for the Marquess. The ground floor
has a stone barrel vault and a N window in a stepped recess; a
spiral stair, with wooden treads, in the SE angle leads to the
first floor, whence a similar stair, in the SW angle, links the
upper floors, caphouse and roof-walk. The rooms have fireplaces, closets (absent on the third floor) and wall cupboards;
the uppermost room is open to the roof and divided by two
timber roof supports. It has a cell in the SE angle.

The tower and its enclosure provide the green heart at the
centre of Clarke & Bell's suburb, but its physical heart, which
provides a backdrop to the tower, is the palatial EGLINTON
TERRACE, composed of twenty-six houses, of three bays each,
with a principal block of four in the centre, and at the S end two
houses in a pavilion, both of these parts with fine wrought-iron
balconies. Late Neoclassical, with windows in architraves, first-
floor cornices and a modillion cornice. In spite of having been
built piecemeal from 1861 to 1882 it is remarkably harmonious,
although there is no echoing N pavilion, and the symmetry is
further spoiled by an addition of 1925 by *J. K. Hunter*.

Facing this, curving round the E and N sides of the green
space are BRUCE CRESCENT (S) and MONTGOMERIE
TERRACE (N), both with detached and semi-detached villas,
but little uniformity of scale or treatment, e.g. Jacobethan of
1860 at Nos. 1–2 and Nos. 4–5 Bruce Crescent, while, further
N, Nos. 17–20 Montgomerie Terrace are red sandstone of 1902
by *Quintin Clark*; remains of vaulted cellars found during

construction have been associated with Ayr Castle. Nos. 30–31, a well-preserved plain villa of *c*. 1860 with a Doric porch, sits slightly back from the rest on the NW bastion. A complete section of wall is also visible running S to the W of ARRAN TERRACE, while to its N, Nos. 2–3 SEABANK ROAD was originally a three-bay single-storey cottage of *c*. 1860, unusually extended *c*. 1876 with a gabled bay to the r., with a canted bay surmounted by a two-light bow, both with a crenellated parapet; big dormer to the l., also bowed, with a swept back gable with curving eaves. More bowed slate-hung dormers to the rear. The houses in Montgomerie Terrace have their gardens enclosed at the rear by surviving sections of the Citadel WALLS (well seen from SOUTH BEACH ROAD), while in SOUTH HARBOUR STREET, to the N, the remains of the N bastion have a corbelled bartizan, a romantic addition of *c*. 1855 by *Murdoch* for Miller.

Now for the area to the S, outside the Citadel, which was gradually developed from the late C18 as a W suburb for Ayr itself. The streets form a typical Late Georgian grid, and have as their centrepiece WELLINGTON SQUARE. The square is built up on three sides, with the E end, facing the old town, open and the Sheriff Courthouse providing an enormously impressive full stop at the W end (with the Pavilion further back to the S). A square was first proposed by *John Robertson* in 1799 as part of a wider scheme for replanning the Citadel area, and was to have palace-fronted terraces. Building of individual houses began *c*. 1803 and continued into the early 1820s, explaining the wide variety in detail and size within a broader conformity. The terraces are of two storeys, raised above a basement, with the occasional dormer, the houses variously painted or harled. That to the S, of 1808–14, is the earlier, with an eaves line that drops in three stages from E to W. All the houses are of three bays, and recurring features include Doric doorpieces, three-light windows (e.g. at Nos. 18 and 23) and polished painted margins. No. 21 is of 1814, by *Robert Johnstone* of Kilmarnock. At its E end the terrace abuts No. 25, the grandest house in the square, of 1804–6 in a style suggestive of *David Hamilton*, with paired Doric columns, segmentally headed ground-floor windows with deep aprons, and first-floor windows with lengthy consoles. The N terrace is of *c*. 1815–21, with a continuous eaves (apart from No. 1, of 1815), but has considerable variation in the width and external treatment of the individual properties. Doric columns again, but also bracketed doorheads and original fanlights (e.g. at Nos. 10–11, of 1821 by *James Paton*). The central area was enclosed in 1824, to plans of *James Paton*, and in 1860 *John Murdoch*, with *Davidson*, head gardener at Culzean, laid it out as gardens to accompany the erection of the first memorial. It is now edged with hedges, and the garden plans have been simplified and modified to accommodate the additional monuments, but it remains the most important green space within the town centre and a model of understated early C19 design.

Of these memorials and monuments, the earliest is, in the centre of the E side, the gunmetal STATUE of General James Smith Neill, †1857 at Lucknow during the Indian Mutiny. Of 1859, by *Matthew Noble*. The 3-m.-high statue shows how he 'might be supposed to have looked when stopping the railway train at Calcutta', as he hurried his troops to Lucknow. Dalbeattie granite pedestal, with a bronze bas relief, also by *Noble*, showing Neill in his last act of kindness, offering his water-bottle to a wounded officer. – In the centre of the W side, a bronze STATUE of the 13th Earl of Eglinton by *Matthew Noble*, 1865, cast by *Robinson & Cottam* of Battersea. The plinth, by *Field*, of *Alexander McDonald, Field & Co.* of Aberdeen, is of white Aberdeen and pink Peterhead granite, and has chamfered corners. – In the NW corner, a bronze STATUE of Sir James Fergusson of Kilkerran (†1907), in robes and collar, of 1908–10 by *W. Goscombe John*, cast by *A. B. Burton* of Thames Ditton, on a granite pedestal designed by *Goscombe John*, sculpted by *Kirkpatrick Bros* of Manchester. – In the centre of the gardens, the simple and effective AYR WAR MEMORIAL, of 1920–4 by *J. K. Hunter*; a Creetown granite obelisk on broad shallow steps with a pedestal with bronze plaques by *H. H. Martyn & Co.* of Cheltenham. – In the NW corner, the granite KENNEDY FOUNTAIN, 1868, obelisk and pedestal, by *McDonald & Field*, and erected by *Andrew Hunter*; moved here from the junction of Sandgate and Fort Street, *c.* 1995. – Lastly, in the SW corner, centenary MEMORIAL to J. L. Macadam,* road engineer, 1936. A rough-hewn granite monolith with a bronze portrait medallion by *Robert Bryden*.

To the N, laid out at the same time as the square, is a grid formed by Cassillis Street, running N from the NW corner of the square to join Eglinton Terrace, Queens Terrace, which parallels this to the W, and Charlotte Street, which crosses these streets E–W. The streets are broad, but there is not the same consistency of treatment which characterizes Wellington Square. In CASSILLIS STREET, Nos. 6–14, two-storey-and-basement terrace of 1853 by *Henry Sym*, rubble, the front elevation mostly painted, with pilastered entrances, railed steps and windows in architraves. In QUEENS TERRACE, on the W side, two attractive and unusual terraces of single-storey cottages on raised basements. That to the S (Nos.1–17) is of 1844–51, that to the N (Nos. 19–33) of *c.* 1855–61. The feuars included the builders *James Paton* and *Henry Sym*; the architect probably *Robert Paton*. Each house is of three bays with a central entrance with railed steps and painted architraves; the windows with bracketed sills. Railed front gardens, and some original twelve-pane and lying-pane glazing. The earlier terrace is slightly grander, with pedimented end gables, a continuous mutule cornice, and bowed rear bays; the other has plain end gables and canted rear bays, and only intermittent mutule cornices. On the E side Nos. 8–16, of *c.* 1877, each gaily painted,

*So spelt; the preferred spelling is McAdam.

of two bays, with full-height canted bay windows, except No. 12, which is of three plain bays. They form an effective foil to the mid-C19 terraces opposite. The s side of the w end of CHARLOTTE STREET is dominated by the two-storey BUCK-INGHAM TERRACE (Nos. 19–37), of 1870, built by *William McFadzean*, with contrasting Ballochmyle red margins and shallow ground-floor oriels with rosette mullion decoration. Opposite are the former County Police Headquarters (*see* Public Buildings, above) and the well-composed former Lady Jane Hamilton School of 1840–3 by *Robert Paton*, with a stepped gable to the projecting central bay, and similarly treated flanking half-dormers. Charlotte Street's e end is dominated by a N-facing early C19 terrace (feus of 1813): Nos. 3–15. Invariably two-storey, but of varying eaves height, and usually of three bays with a central entrance, often with a cavetto reveal, they are mostly harled or painted. No. 11 is the smartest of the group, with a broad pilastered doorpiece, while No. 13, of painted coursed rubble, has neatly done thin margins, including an entrance of austere simplicity. At the w end of the terrace, No. 17, of 1857, three-bay, plastered, with a round-headed entrance in the l. bay, beneath a consoled head.

The grid pattern established by Wellington Square and the streets to its N also influenced the early to mid-C19 development of the areas to its e and s, where a number of small estates took advantage of the growth of the town. The estate immediately s of the town was Barns. The proprietors, the McNeights, began to feu land *c.* 1800, and a street, BARNS STREET, in line with the s terrace of Wellington Square, was opened through their lands. The earliest house is also the grandest: No. 1, at the sw corner. Of 1803, with a projecting pedimented entrance bay, and an Ionic porch. The three-light window above has blind sidelights; circular panel in the pediment. Painted plaster, hipped roof. A long single-storey mid-C19 office wing to the rear, and other, less attractive, extensions to the se, which do not affect the house's visual impact, or its importance as a hinge between the town's western and southern suburbs. The N side of Barns Street (Nos. 2–26), with its s-facing aspect, was completed first, and was almost fully developed by 1818. A terrace of two-storey houses, thoroughly Late Georgian classical in manner, and mostly three-bay, apart from Nos. 22–4, which are a four-bay pair, and given unity by the continuous cornice and roof-line, which also disguise the narrow passage bays between houses towards the w end. The houses exhibit considerable difference in details, with some displaying exposed stone, others plastered. Development of the s side was patchier. Nos. 3–5 are of *c.* 1814, with pilastered doorways and ground-floor windows in lugged architraves. The remainder, Nos. 7–29, ashlar-faced, are mid-C19: partially shown on the 1858 Ordnance Survey map, but the final feus were not granted until *c.* 1870. More ambitious, with a continuous rusticated ground floor, paired porches with fluted Greek Doric columns, and recessed apron panels in the first-floor sill course. Paired houses of four bays, apart from one of three bays with its own porch, but otherwise conformist.

ALLOWAY PLACE runs s from the junction of Barns Street with Wellington Square, flanked by the return elevations of No. 1 Barns Street and No. 26 Wellington Square. This land belonged to the Cathcarts of Alloway. On the w side, three short terraces (Nos. 1–14), of five, four and five houses respectively. The two outer terraces mostly of exposed ashlar, the other is painted. All have rusticated ground floors, and Greek Doric doorpieces, in the l.-hand bay of each house in the first terrace, centrally placed in the others. The N terrace is the youngest, of as late as *c.* 1842, while the others are of *c.* 1818–23; No. 8 was built by *Robert Andrew*, mason, and *Thomas King*, wright, to a feuing plan by *James Milne* of Edinburgh, who may also have provided elevations. To the w, and behind Alloway Place, PARK TERRACE, with a terrace of *c.* 1873, a lively mix of canted and rectangular bays, chamfered windows and round-headed doorpieces with keystones and segmental cornices, and GREENSIDE and REIGATE, two painted stone L-plan villas of 1863 with views across the Low Green and the sea. Probably by *John Murdoch*, with deep window architraves and round-headed doorpieces in the entrance porches. Reigate has been quirkily aggrandized, 1896, probably by *H. E. Clifford*, with a first-floor balustraded balcony and a tall square look-out tower, with startled window heads and slightly raised centres to the wall-head. In ALLOWAY PARK, two large late C19 paired villas: Nos. 1–2, of *c.* 1887, hipped, with semicircular bays, and Nos. 3–4, of *c.* 1873, also hipped, but with canted bays.

On the E side of Alloway Place, BARNS TERRACE, of *c.* 1857–60 by *James Paton & Sons*.* A shrewdly composed, agreeably articulated fourteen-house late classical terrace, still very Georgian in its manner, the culmination of terrace development in Ayr, and set back, with a communal garden in front, a low boundary wall, and entrances at either end, now shorn of gates and railings. Two-storey, of seven pairs of double houses, ashlar, with channelled ground-floor and first-floor architraves. Four bays at either end, and in the centre, are slightly advanced, with their own outer bays given further shallow projection and three-light windows. To the N is DEREEL, a generously detailed red sandstone Italianate villa of 1875; between them BARNS PARK runs W, with, on its N side, a short terrace of 1875, with a channelled ground floor and Doric porches, in the manner of the S terrace in Barns Street. At the junction with Barns Crescent, behind curving boundary walls and late C19 square-panelled gatepiers, BARNS HOUSE, a well-proportioned artisan Georgian house with a painted ashlar main front of 1814, and a dainty porch with fluted Doric pilasters and an arched fanlight. To the N a lower, and earlier wing, of *c.* 1725 and probably incorporating earlier

102

* The architect may, therefore, have been *Robert Paton*.

work, creates an L-plan. Restrained interiors: the central stair
with an open cast-iron balustrade and another arched fanlight.
The ground-floor dining room retains an original fireplace
with fluted pilasters, and a simple cornice; a fancier cornice in
the first-floor drawing room. In BARNS CRESCENT, late C19
cottages: one pair (Nos. 6–8), of 1879 by *John Grant*, mason,
are, from the consoled doorheads to the shell panels above the
windows, rich in stonework detail.

MILLER ROAD runs E–W, linking Racecourse Road (*see* below)
and Burns Statue Square. It now acts as an informal boundary,
13.7 m. wide, between the commercial (N) and residential areas
(S), and was laid out in 1852–3 by the Town Council to improve
communications between the S suburbs and the proposed new
station. Feuing began, on the N side, in 1858, and here still the
dominant form is the terrace. HAVELOCK TERRACE (Nos.
10–24) is of 1858 by *James I. McDerment*. Four pairs of double
houses in painted ashlar, with (mostly) paired Roman Doric
porches. The outer bays of each pair gently advanced, with
channelled ground floors and three-light windows under pediments. No. 8, of *c.* 1865, abuts to the E, with a heavy consoled
doorpiece and a round-headed window above, while No. 6, E
again, of 1859 by *Andrew McLachlan*, builder, has a modillion
cornice and a fluted Greek Doric porch, behind which is a
slightly tapering doorcase, with a rectangular disc-patterned
fanlight, more Egyptian than Greek, with echoes of Alexander
Thomson. Further W, later grander houses, e.g. ELLERSLIE
(No. 30), of *c.* 1871, which has a central porch with coupled
Corinthian columns and a balustraded balcony, with a round-
headed entrance behind; full-height canted bays to either side,
with rope-moulded mullions, Corinthian capitals and panelled
sill courses. Hipped slated roof, over bracketed eaves, and a
flanking screen wall to the l., channelled, with one two-light
window. On the S side, KENSINGTON TERRACE (Nos. 33–43),
of 1858–9, by *James Paton & Sons*, Georgian classical in spirit,
two pairs of semi-villas with low flanking screen walls by *John
Murdoch* (Nos. 29–31 of 1869, and the later, more elaborate
Nos. 25–27 of 1870–1) and a series of mostly hipped villas from
the 1870s, many of which were originally manses; many have
subsequently served as hotels, occasioning linking blocks and,
in one case, a substantial rear addition of industrial ugliness.
Largely quotidian, the villas require little individual comment;
No. 23, of 1872, has colonnettes and basket-arched first-floor
windows, No. 19, of 1875, has a heavy canted porch on Corinthian columns, and No. 17, of 1874, by *Andrew McLachlan*, has
a good pilastered doorpiece with a triglyph frieze and an
arched, keystoned fanlight.

3. *South of the centre: Racecourse Road, Midton Road*

Ayr's premier, and most rewarding architecturally, residential
area lies S of Miller Road. Two N–S streets, Racecourse Road (W)
and Midton Road (E), form its core, while E–W streets link these,

and others continue to the area's boundaries (the sea to the W, Carrick and Monument Roads to the E).

RACECOURSE ROAD is the continuation of Alloway Place, S of Miller Road. It was one of the main routes from the old town, runs for 1.25 km. and is now a street of large, though rarely substantial, late C19 villas, interspersed with earlier ones. The varying architecture of this sylvan street reflects the gradual break-up of the smaller, semi-rural properties which initially lined it. The first houses on the E set the tone for much that is to follow; a series of pleasantly scaled and detailed villas, and semi-villas of the 1850s to 1870s, such as the GLENPARK HOTEL, of c. 1857, with a channelled ground floor and pedimented Doric porch, No. 7, of 1863, with a rusticated ground floor and shouldered flat-arched openings, No. 9 (with No. 1 Park Circus), of 1879, characterized by wrought-iron balconies on heavy consoles, and good wrought-iron finials. Beyond Bellevue Crescent are the Italianate KENSAL TOWER (No. 65 Bellevue Crescent) of c. 1874, tall and rather compressed, with a tall basement, N entrance tower and diamond-pierced balustrade, and the ashlar-fronted asymmetrical ELLISLAND, of c. 1845, possibly by *William Clarke*, with solid bargeboards. It was extended in a simplified classical style by *James Scott Hay*, for himself, in 1927, and restored after a fire in 2004. SOUTH LODGE is a hipped two-storey house of c. 1820, with a fluted Ionic porch, rebuilt anew behind the façade in 1987–8 by *McLean Gibson & Associates*. It sits well back within its grounds, behind a sympathetic sheltered housing complex of 1971–3 by *Charles Eddie*, for Ayr Town Council; dark brick, with broad rendered bands and projecting windows. The AYRSHIRE HOSPICE occupies two of the grander C19 villas. The first, GARGOWAN (in-patient wing), is c. 1813, with a fair amount of swagger: a pedimented Greek Doric porch, and single-storey wings to either side, terminating in gabled bays with niches and finials. SOUTHPARK (day hospice) is c. 1842, plainer, with a fluted Doric porch. The two houses are linked by a glazed entrance and corridor block of c. 1999, incorporating Gargowan's pedimented former stables of c. 1813, while the Day Hospice is extended to the S with a tall, hipped, rectangular block, with a continuous eaves band of windows, also c. 1999. In the grounds to the N a pretty little garden outhouse, again of c. 1813, with a ball-finialled pediment with flight-holes. Finally, beyond Racecourse View (*see* below), the former VIEWHOUSE (now changing rooms) of the original racecourse, of 1867 by *James I. McDerment*, built with refreshment, jockeys' and reporters' rooms on the ground floor, and a ladies' room and smoking room above. Coursed rubble, and rather severely functional.*

---

*Horse racing on the, then, unenclosed lands to the S of Ayr became increasingly formalized in the late C18, and the first viewhouse was built in 1787, and the lands enclosed with a stone wall in 1788, for which *Alexander Stevens* was the successful tenderer. Races ceased when the new course was opened, and the ground is now used as a public sports field.

Ayr, Savoy Park Hotel, formerly Red House. Proposed extension.
Engraving, 1898

There is a wider variety of styles on the w side of Racecourse Road, beginning with the well set-back (and hidden behind late C20 flats) THE SHIELING of 1934 by *Alexander Mair*, a harled and gabled stripped Arts and Crafts house (on the site of an early C19 house whose crowstepped mid-C19 lodge remains) with an expansive garden front with square, hipped projecting bays flanking a central bay with swept-down roof. The SAVOY PARK HOTEL (originally Red House*) is of 1885 by *James A. Morris* for the Glasgow engineer Charles Alston. A large asymmetrical villa, the largest in the road, in Morris's trademark individual and thoughtful Arts and Crafts style. Tall gabled entrance bay, to the r.; one bay to the l. delineated by shallow pilasters; a hipped wing projects forward to the r., linked to the main elevation by a round tower with a slated roof and ball finial. Simple windows, two with eleven-pane upper-case glazing. Much of the charm of the house lies in such details, and others such as the incised decoration to the r. of the entrance, and the shields and monsters on the s elevation, while Morris's enjoyment of prominent rainwater goods is also in evidence. Nor is the steeply pitched roof neglected, with big wooden dormers, two with platform gables, and inventively detailed stacks. The s elevation is mostly obscured by a two-storey service wing, while the w (garden) front has full-height canted bays and a lower, central, crenellated semi-circular bay. The castellated projection to the s on the main elevation is perhaps of 1906–7 by *J. K. Hunter*, while the attractive iron and glass entrance porch is a later, but pleasing addition. Many of Morris's interiors remain, e.g. the wood-panelled dining room, though the homilies on the boarded beamed ceiling have been painted over.

The harled and hipped WHEATFIELD HOUSE is one of the earliest houses in Racecourse Road. It is of *c.* 1790, probably by *Hugh Cairncross*, who owned the property between 1790 and 1803. A conventional three-bay, two-storey house with a slightly advanced central bay with a Doric doorpiece. A low single-storey wing projects l.. DERCLACH (No. 24) is of *c.* 1904, in the style of *James A. Morris*. Arts and Crafts, mostly red sandstone, but with extensive harled sections, and many shaped dormerheads. L-plan GLENFAIRN (No. 28) is of 1873, with a big blind balustraded porch and extensions to r. (of 1897) and l. (of 1904, the chapel-like billiard room) by *J. K. Hunter*. Now follow some of the earliest villas, all of 1828–9, such as the substantial asymmetrical Jacobethan FAIRPORT (No. 34) by *James Paton*, builder, for himself, as a cottagey confection of decorative bargeboards and long contilevered brackets; CUMBERLAND LODGE (No. 36), with lying-pane glazing and a superb filigree Neo-Grec ironwork porch and balcony; and BLAIR LODGE (No. 38), very plain by comparison, wholly

---

* Much of Morris's oeuvre uses red Ballochmyle sandstone, as here. The reference here, however, to Philip Webb's house for William Morris is surely not coincidental.

Georgian in manner, with broad end pilasters and a fluted
Greek Doric porch. The neatly detailed TEMPLETON HOUSE
(No. 40), of 1845, is overshadowed by the dramatic harled
extension to the l., of 1974–6, initiated by the *Glasgow City
Architect's Dept.* The drama comes from the projecting stair-
tower, curved and upswept, and the recessed slate-faced
entrance in the linking bay. GARTFERRY (No. 44) is an impressive Italianate villa of 1865 with an Ionic screen entrance, and
round-arched windows in groups of three. Converted to flats,
c. 2005; the harled and metal-clad blocks of flats to the rear
contemporary. Not without merit, they seem alien to this territory. SEATOWER (No. 46), of 1872, attributed to *David Mac-
Gibbon*, is a tall, much crowstepped Baronial villa with
strapwork window heads, a lower projecting wing to the r. and
a rear tower, culminating in a tall French pavilion roof and
wrought-iron vane. Tall E staircase window of three trefoil-
headed lancets, within a segmental arch and below a sculpted
tympanum. Subdivided and extended to the rear in brick and
concrete in 1973–7 by *Robert Allan & Partners*. The CHEST-
NUTS HOTEL (No. 52), of 1863, is an asymmetrical painted
villa, with a rusticated ground floor, a late C19 porch and, to
the N, offices of 1893 by *James A. Morris & Hunter*, forming
an inner courtyard with pleasing details such as the banded
and ball-headed gatepiers.

Beyond the junction with Seafield Road, SEAFIELD, a
substantial light brown ashlar Italianate villa with a prominent
SE entrance tower, of 1888–92 by *Clarke & Bell and Robert
A. Bryden*, for Sir William Arrol, who lived here until his
death in 1913. Badly damaged by fire in 2008. The tower has
deeply recessed round-headed windows, with Corinthian
shafts, a low pyramidal roof and a circular NW stair-turret
capped by a wrought-iron parapet. Entrance porch at the S
end of the E elevation, with a balustraded parapet. Contemporary L-plan LODGE, by *Clarke & Bell and Robert A. Bryden*,
with a shouldered open porch in the re-entrant, bracketed
cornice and one prominent panelled chimneystack on the W
elevation.

Returning to the N end of Racecourse Road, the first street on
the W is FAIRFIELD ROAD. Fairfield House, the C18 house of
the Campbells of Fairfield (Monkton) has been replaced by
concrete and Fyfestone flats (of 1968–72 by *T. M. Miller &
Partners*). Feuing of its lands began in 1882 when *David Paton
Low* of Glasgow acquired the N portion of the land and built
for himself the present FAIRFIELD HOUSE HOTEL, an Italianate villa with a symmetrical W front with two outer canted
bays, and an elaborately detailed tower at the SE. This has a
prominent window in a pedimented architrave with balustraded balcony and deeply recessed pairs of round-headed
windows beneath broad bracketed eaves. These heavily bracketed eaves are a feature throughout, and are replicated in the
respectful late C20 additions to the E.

To the s the lands of Savoy* were acquired in 1875 by the Ayr merchant banker James Morris (†1876) and passed in 1882, under the terms of his will, to his grand-nephew *James A. Morris* on his twenty-fifth birthday. In 1880 Morris proposed a road 'which will take an easy turn to the centre of the field, and run directly down to the Low Green, thus forming a new means of access to the beach', with, on the N, 'one or two good villas' and on the s a 'handsome double terrace of a free Greek treatment' (*Ayrshire Post*). SAVOY PARK is recognizably the road, but it developed with a single large villa to the N (Savoy Park Hotel, *see* above) and two to the s, all by Morris, all in red sandstone, giving a wonderful opportunity to study the work of this inventive, if self-effacing, Arts and Crafts architect. SAVOY CROFT is *Morris*'s own house, and a marvel of inventiveness. Plans appeared in *Academy Architecture*, 1897, but approval was not sought from the town's Dean of Guild Court until 1899, work beginning that year. Rectangular, with a gabled and slated roof and big stone stacks. The E front is severely plain, with almost all the decoration carried by the projecting entrance bay, beneath its shaped gable, with slim diagonal shafts at the angles. The door is deeply recessed, within chamfered reveals, framed and decorated with block panels in the upper part only. To the r. two deeply set square windows, to the l. a taller sidelight; above, a straight cornice, and a blind semicircular panel above. The sea-facing garden (W) elevation is more open, more relaxed, with a harled central projection with corbelled features and a heavy parapet. The oriel to the l. was added by Morris in 1914; the blank s wall and stone raggle indicate unfulfilled intentions to extend the house. Morris lived here until his death in 1942, and it remained in the family until the 1990s. His interiors remain remarkably unaltered. The expansive, dark, wood-lined and complex stair hall is carefully planned, with the kitchen corridor reached beneath the first flight of stairs. These have flat-headed newels, while one small window has stained glass by *Oscar Paterson*, and a smaller window of 1993 by *Paul Lucky*; both use puns on surnames. To the l., the drawing room, in startlingly bright contrast. An Adam-style fireplace, with a stepped mantel above, seats and a slender columned screen to one window, built-in corner display cabinets. A door at the foot of the stairs leads into the dining room, again lined with dark wood, irregularly shaped, with a bowed alcove, and dominated by the full-height fireplace, with a painting by *William Strang*. On the first floor, a lounge, with the oriel window, and Delft-tiled fireplace. Many of the bedrooms on this and the upper floor have creatively styled wooden fireplaces with tiled inlays.

The third house in the group is the L-plan WELLSBOURNE, begun in 1894, i.e. before Savoy Croft, for Robert Bennett, a

*With the *cottage orné*-style Savoy Cottage, of *c.* 1844, replaced with flats in 1972–5 by *J. & J. A. Carrick*.

Glasgow master painter, in an elaborate Free Style, very unlike much of Morris's work. Two storeys on a raised basement, with the entrance on the E elevation, allowing the W front to command the extensive views; its three bays seemingly all glass, with a central semicircular window above a mullioned-and-transomed five-light window. Subdivided in 1970 by *Edward A. Darley*. Unusual cast-iron POSTS at the entrance from Savoy Park into the Low Green; they exist, too, at other access points, and look *c.* 1910.

WHEATFIELD ROAD divides the former grounds of Wheatfield House into two; feuing began *c.* 1888. Of this date, SHENINGHURST (No. 2), a raffishly jaunty red sandstone villa, with a corner tower which begins circular, corbels out to be octagonal, and has an over-sized triglyph frieze entablature beneath a very broad coolie's-hat roof and finial. The architect is unknown, but the style suggests *W. J. Anderson*. The adjacent Nos. 4 and 6, both of 1897 by *H. V. Eaglesham*, have an equally dramatic exuberance. They are harled and slated, with stone details and, in one case, much applied and decorative timberwork. S again, BLACKBURN ROAD; at its far W end, three dramatic Baronial villas, all now unified in the ownership of Wellington School. They were built from 1879 by *John Murdoch* for David Reid, upholsterer, and, when new, stood in splendid sand-blown isolation. Two (CARLTON TURRETS and CRAIGWEIL, to the N) are almost identical, their plans reversed, with many crowstepped gables, conical-headed round entrance towers and corbelled turrets. The main halls are lit by large mullioned-and-transomed windows. WESTFIELD (now Drumley House), the third of these behemoths, to the S, was probably begun *c.* 1882. It retains the crowsteps, the round tower and the turret, but has a slightly more measured feel, especially on the main (E) elevation, which has, to the l., an advanced bay with a pretty semicircular pedimented and shafted window in the gable. In the grounds of Carlton Turrets, the school ASSEMBLY HALL, of 1969 by *J. & J. A. Carrick*, single-storey, square, generously glazed, with a tall pyramidal roof. It works surprisingly well. S of Westfield, crowstepped L-plan STABLES, now adapted for use as a nursery school.

The first estate on the E side of Racecourse Road, immediately S of Miller Road, was Bellevue,★ acquired in 1860 by Arthur Lang, but feuing only began in earnest in 1874. Bellevue was a larger estate than many, and Lang was able to create three E–W roads, two of which, Park Circus and Bellevue Crescent, curve towards the W to form a deep U-shaped crescent, with a single short connecting street at the E. The other street, Bellevue Road, runs E–W to their S. These are remarkably wide, delightfully tree-lined streets flanked, mostly, by terraces, such as the spacious ones of the late 1880s and early 1890s on the N side of PARK CIRCUS. Here too, large villas, such as No. 27

★ The house, regulation early C19 three-bay two-storey with a central pediment, survives, considerably altered, in MARCHMONT ROAD, off Bellevue Road.

(of 1893) and No. 29 (of 1895), both by the resourceful *H. V. Eaglesham*; the latter has a three-bay Ionic colonnade and balustraded balcony, first-floor windows with Ionic columns at the angles, rising from shell-decorated corbels, and delicate naturalistic friezes in the entablature. More long terraces in BELLEVUE CRESCENT, such as Nos. 45–63, of 1893, canted bays giving percussive articulation, but perhaps more notable for their unusual deeply channelled and cushion-headed square gatepiers; towards the W end, a number of semi-detached villas from 1878–80, such as Nos. 5–7, with basket-arched doorheads and Burnian shaped gables, and Nos. 1–3, with brief flurries of nailhead in its basket arches. Further terraces in BELLEVUE ROAD, and the occasional detached villa such as Tighnagrain (No. 16), 1879, with a full-length front veranda, and Blendon (No. 18), also of 1879, with a neat tripartite doorpiece beneath a consoled balustraded balcony.

s again, RONALDSHAW PARK, where feuing began in the 1850s. On the N side are: NETHERBY (No. 16), of 1884 by *John Murdoch*, with big half-hipped gables and an unusual gabled and canted wooden oriel in the r.-hand gable; THE BIELD (No. 12), of 1905 by *James A. Morris*, all white harl and tiled roof, with small windows and the entrance in a red sandstone doorpiece; and the delightful ST OLA (No. 2), of *c.* 1890, with a curved ground window to the l., a rectangular window to the r., linked by a delicate wooden porch and balustraded balcony. It has round-headed first-floor windows with half-frames. In SOUTHPARK ROAD feuing began in the 1850s, but most feus were taken up in the late 1870s and early 1880s, giving the street a uniformity which makes it the most attractive of these cross streets. Tree-lined and retaining a number of Ayr Town Council's crescent-headed LAMP STANDARDS. The best house is SHONA (No. 7) of 1882, with circular two-storey bays on both the N and W elevations, and a Tudor-Gothic stair window on the N elevation. Elsewhere NEWSTEAD (No. 6) of 1880 by *John Murdoch* has ground-floor bays with good cast-iron brattishing, while ANNICKDALE (No. 5), of 1881, has a decorative panelled doorpiece, with swags in the entablature.

VICTORIA PARK, which had fewer houses and bigger gardens, has, as a result, fallen victim to flat building, and consequently presents a much more open, and much less pleasing aspect. Of the original houses, those most worthy of note are, on the N side, AIRLIE of 1876, possibly by *MacGibbon & Ross*, Renaissance-detailed with channelled angle pilasters, the substantial ROSE VILLA, of 1850, with pretty circular stacks linked by a roof balustrade, and, on the s side, OLD RACECOURSE HOTEL, 1868, with canted ground-floor bays with Jacobethan crenellated heads, a consoled doorpiece, and a single-story wing with a shaped gable to the l..

The final cross street is RACECOURSE VIEW, which was part of the same small estate as Victoria Park, and has the wide expanses of Belleisle estate to its s (*see* Belleisle House, Alloway). The houses are, consequently, on the N side, and

often of high quality. At the corner with Racecourse Road,
HARTFIELD, of 1850–1, a particularly fine example of a larger
villa, with sophisticated late classical detail. The main three-bay
elevation has broad end pilasters, a channelled ground floor,
and a central porch with coupled square pillars, elaborate
decorative capitals and a central scroll-mounted acroterion.
There is a neatly detailed eaves frieze. INVERDON is an Italianate villa of 1847 by *Clarke & Bell*. To the s, it projects a
stepped regression, with a gabled bay to the l., with a good
upper-floor oriel, a hipped bay, with a two-storey canted bay,
and, to the r., a square tower, with a three-light round-headed
window in the upper floor, capped by a shallow pyramid. The
porch extends to the E of this, with shouldered openings and
a balustraded balcony. Another pyramid-roofed tower dominates the W elevation, balancing that to the E, and rising above
the gabled l. bay. St LEONARDS, another Italianate villa with
broadly similar details, also by *Clarke & Bell*, was feued in
1846, but is larger, with a rusticated basement, and retains
more of the original lying-pane glazing. E, beyond Midton
Road, ABBOTSFORD, a large white-harled house of *c.* 1904,
faintly Arts and Crafts in its detailing, and then, on the l. as
the road curves S, No. 14, perhaps Ayr's best Modernist house,
of 1965 by *Norman McLean*. Flat-roofed, with the living spaces
on the first floor, faced in dark concrete, with a large picture
window. The recess to the r. is a delightful touch. Beyond are
SHALIMAR, of 1868, a huge and idiosyncratic Scots Baronial
pile, awash with crowstepped gables, turrets, crenellations and
ball finials, and HARTLEY HOUSE, almost equally huge, Italianate of 1869, with a squat tower, a Corinthian doorpiece and
some details which suggest inspiration by Alexander Thomson.
From Racecourse View, MIDTON ROAD runs N to Burns Statue
Square, and has its own identity, quieter and leafier than Racecourse Road. On the E side, THE KNOWE, a complex and
rewarding building. Originally built *c.* 1841, in a Jacobethan
style with shaped and decorative dormers and an etiolated
bell-cast slated turret, and substantially extended in the same
style in 1895 by *Robert Thomson* of Glasgow, the new, much
more ambitious, work extending the house to N and W. Thomson's is the balustraded and richly ornamented porch and the
bay to the r. with decorative apron panels. Good octagonal
GATEPIERS with octagonal caps with alternate shields; the
LODGE survives, Jacobethan, of *c.* 1841, with shaped gables,
finials and a tall stack; uncompromisingly, but well, extended
in 1963 by *R. F. Bluck, Drummond & Associates* of Glasgow.
They were responsible for No. 88, the best of the early 1960s
houses within the grounds. On the W side, EDENDARROCH, a
splendidly Gothic wonder of 1882, attributed to *J. Hippolyte
Blanc*. Two-storey, of coursed rubble, on an irregular plan.
Prominent big gables dominate the two main fronts, to E and
S, with highly individual bargeboards, with trefoils, pendants
and arches. Each gable has a big three-light window with a
delicately carved semicircular tympanum above. To its N,

BROWNHILL COTTAGE (No. 63), of 1848, a classical single-storey cottage-villa with a pedimented pillared porch, lying-pane glazing and a lower wing set back to the r. MIDTON COTTAGE, opposite, is a pretty two-storey *cottage orné* of 1834–5, with a central projecting entrance bay and bargeboards with foliated pendants. Now follows a series of mid to late C19 semi-villas and villas E and W, e.g. MELLING (No. 57), an asymmetrical single-storey villa of 1870, derived from illustrations of Alexander Thomson's Seymour Lodge of 1850, and CLOVA LODGE (No. 54), a crisp late classical double villa of *c.* 1850 showing a balanced symmetrical front to Broomfield Road, with advanced hipped outer bays, and verandas on paired cantilevered brackets.

In CARRICK AVENUE, DOON TERRACE, dated 1882, by *Allan Stevenson & Kerr*, a short asymmetrical terrace in coursed rubble, its outer bays with big hipped dormers rising above corbelled balconies. Also in Carrick Avenue, THE COACHHOUSE, the asymmetric former gatehouse and staff accommodation for Carrick House (dem.). Of *c.* 1900, and in the style of William Leiper. Single-storey-and-attic, with applied timberwork, tiled roofs, a semicircular pend, now blocked, with a pedimented dormer above, and a row of harled cottages, with square-headed dormers and projecting stone door frames. On the r. St Columba's church (*see* Churches, above), then, on the l., ELGIN HOUSE (No. 29), a crisp single-storey-and-attic cottage of 1859, in coursed rubble with painted dressings, a three-light window to the r. and a gabled bay to the l., and DOLPHIN HOUSE (No. 25), of *c.* 1809, a delightful rubble-fronted three-bay, gabled L-plan classical house with a slightly advanced centre bay with a pediment with circlet and a fluted Doric porch.

NEWTON-UPON-AYR

The royal burgh's transpontine twin has its own history of growth and development. A settlement for those without burgh qualifications probably sprang up the N bank of the river, almost as soon as the burgh was established, and grew as it grew. Road links between Ayr and the N and E passed through Newton, and it benefited accordingly. Newton itself became a burgh in the C14, traditionally held to be a reward for support offered to Robert Bruce at Bannockburn. It continued to thrive, providing trades and services for the burgh on the S bank, and participating equally in the development of the harbour on both shores of the river mouth. With the extraction of coal, and the development of modern industry, Newton grew significantly from the C18, becoming a separate parish in 1776, and experienced further growth in the C19, particularly to the W of the Main Street, where a grid-pattern new town was laid out on former common land, close to Ayr's first railway terminal. Newton's broad Main Street remains largely intact, mostly C19 and early

C20 in character, while the planned town to its W, centred on Green Street and York Street, has gradually changed from an area of mixed housing and small-scale industrial into an area almost wholly industrial, a world of modern sheds, with only a few ephemeral remains – a stone wall here, a setted lane there – and the street pattern as evidence of this often overlooked early C19 planned settlement.

CHURCHES

Former DARLINGTON PLACE U.P. CHURCH, Main Street. 1858–9 by *Clarke & Bell*; simplified Gothic. E front with a projecting gabled porch and flanking lancet panels; recessed entrance with trumeau and cusped decoration in the head; stepped five-light lancets above, the wider central lights with Y-tracery. Octagonal SE stair-turret. Clasping buttresses with splayed bases and truncated pinnacles. Five-bay side elevations, the outer bays gabled with squat three-light windows below and two-light windows with decorative tracery heads above. Lower shallow chancel, and attached transverse hall. The interior divided horizontally in 1986–8 by *John Wetten Brown*, forming a theatre in the gallery, with offices below.

Former MISSION HALL, 120 New Road. Disused. 1907 by *Speirs & Co.*, a corrugated-iron chapel with a gabled front and a hipped porch.

Former MISSION HALL, River Street. Now residential. 1887–8 by *James Jardine*, completed by *John Mercer*. E.E. Three-bay front: projecting porch with shaped gable and round-headed entrance, flanked by two-light pointed windows under semi-circular moulds with label stops. Two-light windows under pedimented gablets in the outer bays.

NEWTON WALLACETOWN CHURCH, Main Street. Former Free Church of 1861–2 by *William Clarke* (of *Clarke & Bell*). Dec, with all the rather thoughtful decoration on the main (W) elevation, which is set well back from the street behind a complex of church halls (of 1969–71). Central gable, flanked by pinnacle buttresses and single bays to either side, that to the S terminating in a short octagonal turret. Central gabled door-piece, slightly recessed cusped entrance, with blind cusped arcades to l. and r., and a five-light window, with wheel tracery in the head, above. Two lancets and a circular window with root-like tracery in the E gable. Neat plastered INTERIOR, with continuous gallery on three sides, with a panelled wooden front; and supported on stone columns. Further columns rise from the gallery front; these have fancifully carved naturalistic heads, and support the ribs of the vaulted plaster ceiling. Light oak Gothic platform furniture, probably coterminous with renovation in 1899, including a broad PULPIT and PLATFORM RAILS. – MONUMENT. Jane Fullarton †1819, by *Mossman*. – WAR MEMORIALS (vestibule). That from the former Parish Church is of 1921, by *James A. Morris*. Cast bronze, with a burning bush, and text by Morris, within a Pavonazzo marble surround. Bronze modelled by *Holmes & Jackson*, marble by *Galbraith & Winton*.

ST JAMES PARISH CHURCH, Prestwick Road. 1883–5 by *John Murdoch*; E.E., in a distinctive soot-stained red sandstone. Nave and aisles, gables with the main (E) gable flanked by a squat square SE tower. Pointed entrance with double-chamfered reveals, flanking quatrefoils, and three tall paired lancets above, with a wheel window above again, a diapered panel in the gable-head and a cross finial. Stepped angle buttresses, echoed in the tower, which has windows with Y-tracery, paired louvred bell-openings and a battlemented parapet with a pinnacle at the SE corner. The galleried INTERIOR has plaster walls and a pitched plaster ceiling with thin ribs. Boarded gallery fronts, supported on columns with decorative heads, and supporting, in turn, similar columns from which spring the pointed arcades. Shallow chancel recess, largely filled by the organ and a cusped SCREEN. – In the vestibule, a bronze First World War MEMORIAL by *Mary R. Henderson*; the subsidiary plaque below is by *C. d'O. Pilkington Jackson*, 1949.

To the r. of the church the contemporary MANSE, also by Murdoch, all gables and wooden eaves, while behind is the severe stone-faced CHURCH HALL of 1933 by *Alexander Mair*. C19 cast-iron lantern-holders on the main gate piers. The GATES and railings a Second World War memorial of 1949, by *James Thomson & Sons* of Ayr.

Former SALVATION ARMY CITADEL, New Road, 1905–6 by *Arthur Hamilton*, of *John Hamilton & Son*. Free Style, in red sandstone; its severity counterbalanced by the pretty Art Nouveau inscription under the central eaves. Asymmetrical, with a segmentally arched doorpiece to the r., under a gable, two groups of three-light windows in the centre part, separated by a low buttress, and a taller advanced bay to l., with a wavy moulded parapet.

PUBLIC BUILDINGS

CARNEGIE PUBLIC LIBRARY, Main Street. 1890–3 by *Campbell Douglas & Morrison*.* Free Italian Renaissance, with two storeys above a sunk basement; symmetrical with advanced outer bays. These have three ground-floor windows and a wide first-floor window with a semi-elliptical tympanum and narrow flanking windows. In the upper floor of the five-bay centre, square-headed windows with inscriptions in the tympana – 'History', 'Science', etc. – are recessed behind an arcade of Doric columns and semi-elliptical arches. The columns continue below as semi-octagonal piers framing the ground-floor windows and entrance, with its carved spandrels and iron

* Won in competition; the assessor was Robert Rowand Anderson. A sketch in Greenwood, *Public Libraries*, London, 1893, shows a tall central tower and pediments to the advanced outer bays.

fanlight. The parapets are plain to the outer bays, inscribed above the central three bays, otherwise balustraded. Some original INTERIORS survive, including the tiled vestibule and the entrance hall, which has an Ionic screen, and a big nine-panel STAINED-GLASS window by *Stephen Adam & Co.*, with 'Knowledge' in the lower central panel, and Carnegie in the upper central panel. The former Reading Room, now Local History, is classically detailed, with paired Corinthian columns and a coved ceiling. Two bright red brick rear extensions, with simple classical details in stone, both by *H. S. McNair* and *Alexander Douglas* of *James K. Hunter Architects*: the Children's Library (now part of the lending library), built 1929–30, and the Lecture Theatre (now Reference Library), built 1932–4.

LIBRARY SERVICES HEADQUARTERS, Green Street. School of 1874–5 by *John Mercer*. Single-storey, of light brown stone. A broadly symmetrical T-plan; the wings of the main (w) front have one hipped and one narrower pedimented bay. The rear wing may incorporate *Robert Paton*'s earlier school of 1845–6.

Former NEWTON ACADEMY, Green Street Lane. Mannered Free Style with mullioned-and-transomed windows of 1910–11 by William Cowie in red sandstone. Large, and no doubt originally dominant among streets of two-storey houses, but now surrounded by drab industrial buildings. Two-storey; H-plan, with flanking projecting wings under pediments on the street front; the shallow entrance porches beyond. Neatly lettered inscription and date at first-floor level.

NEWTON STEEPLE, Main Street and King Street. A harled square clock tower of five stages, the uppermost intaken, with ball finials at the corners, and topped by a squat octagonal spire. Built in 1795 by *John Neill*, builder. It formerly stood between buildings in Main Street and provided the entrance to the Parish Church (1777, dem. 1967), but it is now isolated on the busy road junction. Roderick Lawson, a Maybole minister, described it in 1891 as 'severely chaste in its simplicity, very insignificant in its littleness and awfully plain in its ugliness', likening it to a gin bottle topped by a glass.

DESCRIPTION

Newton's MAIN STREET begins at the N end of the New Bridge with, on the w, the former Darlington Place U.P. Church (*see* Churches, above). Opposite, at the junction with River Street, is the NEWTON MERCAT CROSS, a chamfered stone shaft with a plain entablature and ball finial, on original square base and broader modern base. Inscribed NEUTOUN 1675 REBILT 1775. Main Street itself is broad, very broad, partly accounted for by the infilling of the mill lade which ran N from Newton Mill, which stood near the New Bridge, to Damside, at the N end the street. The width also reflects civic pride in the late CI8 when parochial status meant a new church (dem.) and

a new manse (also dem.; at the N end of the equally wide
Peebles Street) – the streets seem to have been widened and
straightened at about the same time. The buildings are mainly
mid-C19 in character, with many simple two-storey buildings
of that period. Apart from the Carnegie Library, the Newton
Steeple and Newton Wallacetown Church (for which, *see*
Public Building, Churches, above), only the following deserve
mention: the late C19 former OFFICES of Walter Mitchell &
Sons, ham curers (E side), red sandstone, two-storey, with a
central pedimented gable and balustraded balcony, probably
by *Allan Stevenson*; and, on the W side, directly opposite the
steeple, the former ORIENT CINEMA, by *Albert V. Gardner*,
1931–2, its screen front with a canted central tower rising to a
bell-like cap; the interiors which justified the name are long
gone.

   Main Street divides into the architecturally barren PEEBLES
STREET and NEW ROAD, which was laid out from the 1830s
to improve communication from the N. At the junction of the
two streets, Nos. 1–3 New Road, a two-storey gusset building,
its S-facing pedimented bay with a pilastered C19 shopfront.
On the E side the light brown sandstone former UNIONIST
WORKING MEN'S CLUB of 1890–2 by *James A. Morris &
Hunter* (now housing, converted 2007–8). Its main three-bay
elevation, in a rather mannered C18 vernacular, neatly closes
the vista of Main Street with three tall square-headed first-floor
windows, beneath a central gabled half-dormer, and above a
central canted bay, with a memorial stone to the l. Adjacent to
its N, the former Salvation Army Citadel (*see* Churches, above)
and Nos. 8–10, late C19, also red sandstone, with canted bays,
broad pilasters and a balustraded parapet between outer
gables. Delightful, unusual brick single-storey rear elevation to
Weaver Street, with a railed parapet, and an off-centre entrance
under a lunette, above which rises a finely detailed harled
rotunda with a slated conical roof and wide eaves. Further N,
on the W side, N of Waggon Road, the C18 entrance into the
former Manse and glebe, two panelled GATEPIERS with a
pretty shaped wrought-iron head, with a thistle finial and
curlique pendants.

RIVER STREET, between New Bridge and the Auld Brig, was the
main road into Ayr after the building of the New Bridge. Nos.
9–10 have a harled façade with small second-floor windows on
both elevations; late C18, and probably earlier, the evidence
hidden behind the all-encompassing harl. To the E a former
Mission Hall (*see* Churches, above), and the BLACK BULL,
opposite the Auld Brig, is a reminder of coaching days; largely
rebuilt in 1821, with to the l. a hip-roofed wing containing a
ballroom (some of its deep windows now reduced) above a
segmentally headed pend which gave access to the stabling. At
the NE corner of the Auld Brig, Nos. 2–4 RIVER TERRACE, a
simple gabled and painted four-storey two-storey house of
perhaps *c.* 1755, with a canted lower bay to the W; exposed
stone elevation on the river side.

WALLACETOWN

Wallacetown, which lies to the E of Newton, has a similar history. It was never incorporated as a burgh, and by the mid C19 came to stand for the people of Ayr as a byword for all that was illegal, irregular and unregulated. The two settlements were incorporated into Ayr in 1873, by which time they had a greater combined population than the royal burgh.

The attritional redevelopment of Newton can be contrasted with the council-planned and council-led comprehensive redevelopment of Wallacetown from the early 1960s. Wholesale clearance and the creation of new roads, especially the inner bypass (Allison Street, John Street), and houses have produced a very different result. The initial plans were prepared by *J. C. Holmes* and *A. A. Wood*, of the *Holmes Wishart Planning Group*, incorporating a mix of housing density and car–pedestrian separation. Implementation, however, was carried out by *Cowie & Torry*. Very little of old Wallacetown survives.

CHURCHES AND BURIAL GROUND

FREE CHURCH, George Street. Former Reformed Presbyterian church of 1832. The wright was *Alexander Davidson*. Free Church since 1876. A simple gabled box, with a pedimented front, set slightly back behind square gatepiers and a low railed wall. Coursed rubble, painted to the front, exposed at the sides. Front windows in frames, the lower ones with cornices; central pedimented double entrance with flat pilasters. Round-headed windows in the rear gable. Austere, unspoilt interior: a cube, with a gallery around three sides on cast-iron columns. It has an attractive panelled front; the end and corner panels filled with nymphs and foliage. Boarded ceiling with a quincunx of small plaster roses. Panelled PULPIT and octagonal sounding-board. Bench pews. Plain harled and hipped halls to the rear.

Former MORRISON CONGREGATIONAL CHURCH, George Street. Disused. Anti-burgher church of 1770; additions of 1901 by *J. K. Hunter*. Two-storey rectangle under a hipped roof, and thickly harled. Slightly advanced pedimented central bay on S elevation, with a pair of tall round-headed windows. The two-storey recessed extension to the W has its entrance beneath a round-headed tympanum with typically Hunterian simplified Art Nouveau detailing, repeated in the gates and railings.

RIVERSIDE EVANGELICAL CHURCH, John Street. Former Free Church of 1855 and 1859–60 by *Campbell Douglas*; halls to the rear added *c.* 1910. Acquired by the Christian Brethren in 1952. Starkly plain lancets. Restored and rebuilt internally in 1976. The corbels and cross-beams of the original ceiling are evident; a rear gallery is now enclosed. Odd dark and light wood veneer backdrop to the platform, the sides reminiscent of Victorian fire-screens, and supporting a big cross-piece which increases in size in two steps. The falling site allows a substantial basement suite of halls, with a harled w extension of *c*. 1910.

Former ST JOHN (Episcopal), James Street. Hall, 1893, by *James A. Morris & Hunter*; at right angles to the church of 1933–4 by *James Carrick*. Now disused. Budget Gothic.

ST MARGARET'S CATHEDRAL (R.C.), John Street. The former St Margaret's Parish Church, elevated to cathedral status in 2007. Gabled-fronted Dec, with crenellated octagonal buttresses and angle buttresses with rich crocketed finials, of 1825–7 by *James Dempster* of Greenock, heavily influenced by Gillespie Graham's St Andrew's Cathedral, Glasgow (1814). Ashlar front, rubble sides. Four-centred aisle windows with Y tracery. Shallow chancel; the short transepts with round windows by *Goldie & Child* of London, executed by *John Mercer*, 1877. Spacious INTERIOR, with a simple plaster rib-vault, and a rear gallery, with a painted cusped panelled front, supported on cast-iron columns. Four-centred chancel arch, ribbed chancel ceiling. Reordered in 2000–1 by *Wren Rutherford Austin-Smith:Lord*; the pews rearranged, with a central aisle, stripped and laid out more spaciously. The respectful CHAPTER HOUSE is of the same phase. STAINED GLASS. In the chancel and transept of 1877, probably German. Two ethereal, bubbling blue windows, one on either side of the nave, of *c*. 2000 by *Susan Bradbury*, replacing original darker painted glass. Also by *Bradbury*, and also of *c*. 2000, the startling, framed glass STATIONS OF THE CROSS. The HALL of 1986–9 by *Charles Toner* is harled, on a stone base, gabled, with canted sides, a slated porch and big wooden-framed small-pane windows. Blockwork interiors, under a boarded ceiling, like an upturned boat. The PRESBYTERY of *c*. 1970 by *Cowie & Torry* is unusual, and effective: grey-brown brick, flat-roofed, with wooden fascias and projecting window frames. One of Ayr's best late C20 houses.

Former WALLACETOWN PARISH CHURCH, John Street. T-plan Tudor Gothic in local (Content Quarry) grey-brown stone, of 1834–6 by *John Kay*; a scaled-down version of St Augustine's Gateway, Canterbury, with a tripartite ashlar front under a crenellated gable, divided by octagonal buttresses with crenellated tops (reduced in height, 1949–50), and with diagonal buttresses at the angles rising to gableted finials. Two- and three-light windows. To l. and r., infilling the angles, stair-towers added by *J. K. Hunter* in 1903, their sharply pointed windows with sinuous decorative heads. Rubble-built side elevations, with two tall windows in square-headed and deeply splayed frames. INTERIOR with flat plaster ceiling, with galleries on two sides, their panelled wooden fronts supported on cast-iron columns. A third gallery, above the vestibule, also with a panelled front, and the repositioning of the stairs are due to Hunter's 1903 reordering, so too the PLATFORM, in light oak, with its fence of broad boards, the head of each with an ovoid opening, filled with cloth. Piers have tall pyramidal heads, while the back screen has dentil cornices and tall flat pilasters rising to flattened heads. Original bow-fronted PULPIT, dark pine. – STAINED GLASS. Either side of the pulpit, late C19, richly coloured if conventionally drawn. – MONUMENTS. Rev. George Scott †1905, of 1908 by the *Bromsgrove Guild*: bronze, with the minister's luxuriant beard overflowing the laurel wreath of his portrait medallion. – Good First World War MEMORIAL of 1920, bronze in a wooden frame. HALLS of 1935 (N) of stone and harl, and generously top-lit; further halls of 1976 (W) of brick, with deep boarded fascias.

WALLACETOWN BURIAL GROUND, Russell Street/King Street. Two irregularly shaped stone-walled enclosures. That to the W probably early C19, the other completed in 1858. – STATUE of Dr John Taylor †1842, Ayr's firebrand Chartist. 1858, by *James Shanks* of Glasgow, on a pedestal by *Peter Wilson* of Ayr. The pedestal is square, with chamfered corners; the full-length life-size statue catches a pensive bearded Taylor, scroll in one hand, in crumpled knee-boots, jacket and waistcoat.

PUBLIC BUILDINGS

AYR COLLEGE, Content Avenue. 1961–5 by *Robert G. Lindsay*, County Architect. The original building is concrete-framed, with a long asymmetrical three-storey S front, all window bands and tile facings. The recessed entrance is towards the l., with a projecting porch added 2000–1; of the same date, and set at right angles, a dramatic and decisive wedge-shaped four-storey building by *Boswell, Mitchell & Johnston*, with an over-sailing monopitch roof supported on outward-leaning steel columns. – AERONAUTICS BUILDING, 2010–11, by *Taylor Associates*.

DAM PARK STADIUM, Content Avenue. GRANDSTAND of 1961–3 by *Maurice Hickey*. A dramatic and effective statement. Concrete, the wedge formed by the tiered seating and roof wrapped around by prominent ribs which run from the under-side of the seating and fade into the roof. A brick ground floor has offices and changing rooms.

POLICE STATION, King Street. 1972–5 by *Ayr County Council*. A large complex on a prominent site, mostly clad in brick, and flat-roofed. L-plan, with the public entrance in the hinge. The lower and shorter wing, fronting King Street (S), the more interesting, with tall windows projected forward in one section, and in another, tall narrow windows hidden behind projected brick panels.

RIVERSIDE HOUSE. *See* Description.

WALLACETOUN HOUSE. *See* Description.

WALLACETOWN NURSERY SCHOOL, Queen Street. 1873–6 by *John Mercer*. Broadly symmetrical Board School with flanking projecting gabled end bays with stepped lancets and prettily detailed porches in the re-entrants. Made L-plan by projecting SW wing of 1935 by *William Reid*, County Architect.

DESCRIPTION

Wallacetown's main thoroughfares, Wallace Street and GEORGE STREET, have been almost wholly extinguished, the latter cut in two at its w end by the inner by-pass (John Street). Ayr Free Church (*see* Churches, p. 166) clings on to the w side, and from here down to the Auld Brig is a run of mid-C19 buildings. JOHN STREET runs SE, parallel with the river, with post-war housing intermingled with C19 churches (St Margaret's Cathedral and Wallacetown Parish Church on the N side, Riverside Evangelical Church on the S) and WALLACETOUN HOUSE, very long and very dull Government offices of 1953–7 by *Stewart Sim* of Edinburgh with a brick extension of *c.* 1990. Immediately behind it, however, is RIVERSIDE HOUSE of 1972–5 by *Cowie Torry & Partners*, a successful solution to a cramped site. Harled local authority offices with flanking tall stair-towers, semicircular to the l., square to the r. On the main (S) front, the ground- and second-floor windows project as a series of rectangular bays with wooden aprons; one first-floor window identically treated. To its E good late C20 social housing in STRATHAYR PLACE and QUEENS QUADRANT and, beyond Turner's Bridge, RIVERSIDE PLACE: three well-sited fourteen-storey tower blocks of 1968–71 by *Cowie & Torry* for Ayr Town Council in a staggered pattern along the river; given pitched roofs and re-clad *c.* 2000.

NE of John Street, the first phase of post-war redevelopment (MACADAM SQUARE, etc.), of 1965–9 by *Cowie & Torry*, all distinctly neglected. Two- and four-storey blocks, harled, with wooden fascias, and the firm's characteristic punched-out windows; laid out around small spaces to create neighbourly enclosures and a sense of place. Original lettering and the street furniture also by *Cowie & Torry*, in a manner influenced by the pioneering work of the Scottish Special Housing Association and Irvine Development Corporation. The Civic Trust's view (Awards, 1969) that 'this very good scheme will grow in environmental quality' now has a hollow ring.

NORTH AND NORTH-EAST AYR

CHURCHES AND PUBLIC BUILDINGS

DALMILLING CHURCH, Thornyflat Road. Simplified Gothic of 1952–3 by *Cowie & Torry*. Nave, narrower chancel and prominent gabled NW porch. Round-arched W window.
Former GOOD SHEPHERD CATHEDRAL (R.C.), Dalmilling Road. 1951–7 by *Cowie & Torry*, demolished in 2010 except for the NE tower; the site redeveloped for Ayrshire Housing to a plan of *Gordon Fleming* of *ARPL* (won in competition in 2002).
LOCHSIDE CHURCH, Lochside Road. Simplified Romanesque of 1934 by *William Cowie*. Disproportionately large NW transept, and hall at the SW end. Stepped round-headed three-light windows in the main gables. Barrel-vaulted plaster ceiling, with

broad ribs, and a deep chancel with a round arch. Internally reconstructed, 1980 and 2008.

NEW PRESTWICK BAPTIST CHURCH, Prestwick Road, close to Heathfield Road. 1900–1 by *William Kerr*. A simple harled and slated gabled rectangle with lancets; shallow porches with scooped pediments at the SW and NW corners.

UNITED FREE CHURCH, Kirkholm Avenue. 1930 by *James Pollock*. Harled, with applied timbering in the gables. Detached hall to the w.

AYR RACECOURSE, Whitletts Road. Laid out 1905–7 by *W. C. & A. S. Manning* of Newmarket, execution by *Allan Stevenson*. The CLUB STAND is of 1913–14, by *A. S. Manning* (again with *Stevenson*), replacing the original, burnt by suffragettes. EGLINTON STAND. 1967 by *J. & J. A. Carrick*, presenting its best side to the outside (N), with the entrance behind slender pilotis. WESTERN HOUSE of 1923–4 by *H. O. Tarbolton*, was the house for the clerk of the course; now a hotel. Luxurious late Arts and Crafts inside and out.

HEATHFIELD CLINIC, Heathfield Road. 1960–2 by *Keppie Henderson & Partners*, as the Outpatient Department of Heathfield Hospital (1901, closed 1981, dem.). Courtyard plan, two storeys facing Heathfield Road; the rest single-storey. Faced in brick, with a full-length veranda on slender pilotis. To the E, HEATHFIELD HOUSE, an administrative building of *c.* 1930; hipped, with stone dressings and stepped end stacks. To the w is the SCOTTISH AMBULANCE SERVICE SOUTH WEST DIVISIONAL HEADQUARTERS, of 1992–3, three storeys, stone-faced, with asymmetrical gables.

HEATHFIELD PRIMARY SCHOOL, Heathfield Road. Red brick stripped classical of 1928–31 by *J. S. Williamson* of the County Architect's Office. Two-storeys, with stone details. Asymmetrically placed main entrance. Extended, 2009–11, by *Holmes*, Glasgow. Earlier free-standing gabled brick and stone addition of 2002 to the SW.

JOHN POLLOCK CENTRE, Mainholm Road. 1962–6 by *Eric W. Hall & Partners* (*W. Fraser*, project architect) for Ayr County Council, as two secondary schools (one denominational) and one primary school on a shared campus. This is expressed architecturally as two tall four-storey teaching blocks,[*] linked by square two-storey blocks, each built around a central court. Concrete-framed, faced in brick between continuous window bands. Mostly disused, although partly converted for community use *c.* 1999; see the undulating boundary WALL.

UNIVERSITY OF THE WEST OF SCOTLAND (AYR CAMPUS), University Avenue. 2008–11 by *RMJM*. Conventionally planned around two atria, clad in ceramic granite, timber and copper, with the elevation to the river emphasized by prominent horizontal wooden slats. The predecessor buildings, originally the Craigie Teaching Training College (1964, *A. Buchanan Campbell*), are to be demolished.

[*]Demolition of these began in early 2012.

CRAIGIE HOUSE (Ayrshire Management Centre), NE of the campus, was built *c.* 1730 for Sir Thomas Wallace, and sold in 1783 to William Campbell, who had made a fortune in India. Two-storey symmetrical Palladian house, with basement, attic, and hipped roof. Coursed rubble, with raised quoins. Seven-bay front, with the central three advanced beneath a pediment with round-arched windows. To l. and r., curved links (E one higher and fronting a curved corridor block) to lower two-storey, three-bay pavilion wings, similarly detailed to the main house. The central porch was added, possibly by *W. H. Playfair*, 1838–9 (builder *James Paton*), and advances in line with the wings. Portico with paired fluted Greek Doric columns, a balustrade parapet and urn finials. The balustraded wall between it and the wings is contemporary. At the rear of the house, facing the river, the central block has a full-height ashlar bowed projection with a deep parapet, probably added after 1783. Behind the w screen wall on this side is a rectangular two-storey block by *J. K. Hunter*, 1921, and a single-storey one to the E, with tall narrow round-headed openings.

Considerably altered inside, most recently during conversion by *Frank Burnet Bell & Partners*, 2005–9. Square balustraded galleried hall has a *c.* 1750 cantilever stair with alternate slender twisted and turned balusters, carved tread-ends and timber handrail. Good plaster entablature with husked triglyphs, fluted metopes with rosettes, egg-and-dart moulding and modillions alternating with rosettes. Bowed room at the first floor (Keir Hardie Room) has a good *c.* 1783 plaster ceiling with a pretty modillion cornice, swagged husks within a moulded circle surrounded by delicate, flowing scrolls, posies of flowers and leaves, the latter tied with ribbons. The centre is late C19. A retractable screen opens to the Shaw Room with a timber and composition painted chimneypiece with Dutch tile inset. The Campbell Room is the whole depth of the house, with an anthemion cornice and a timber and composition chimneypiece with Ionic pilasters anthemions, swags and urns with late C19 Persian-style tiles bearing horsemen inset. In the w pavilion room, a good white marble chimneypiece of 1835 by *David Ness* with inset featured grey stripes imitating flutes, vases and a central urn.

WAR MEMORIAL, High Road, Whitletts. Celtic Cross of 1921 by *J. C. Kennedy*.

EAST, SOUTH-EAST AND SOUTH AYR

CHURCHES AND CEMETERY

CASTLEHILL CHURCH, Old Hillfoot Road. Brick complex of hall (originally a hall church) of 1956–8 by *J. & J. A. Carrick*, and their church of 1962–4, built for the expanding suburban population. The hall grabs the attention at the corner with Castlehill Road by the use of full-height windows in truncated triangular projections this side and, at the NE, a low but highly

effective brick tower, topped by a tall open metal and concrete
lantern and equally tall cross;* under the tower a single-storey
link with the CHURCH. This has an eaves-height window band,
above which the shallowly pitched roof hovers, and forms an
elongated hexagon, a form repeated in the windows and blind
panels in the rendered sections. More hexagonal panel decoration in the spacious INTERIOR, with two slanted wooden-
fronted galleries and contemporary furnishings including an
unusual PULPIT and SOUNDING-BOARD.

CHURCH OF JESUS CHRIST OF LATTER DAY SAINTS, Orchard
Avenue. 1962–3 by *John Easton* of Glasgow. On the front,
two decorative tiled panels; the entrance recessed. Cross-
plan tower with spike finial, the usual motif of the Mormon
churches.

ST LEONARD, St Leonard's Road, at the junction with Carrick
Road. 1884–6, by *John Murdoch*. The first of the big new
churches for the town's S suburbs (cf. St Andrew and St
Columba, p. 128). Dec, in light grey stone, consisting of nave
and aisles, transepts, a four-light reticulated window in the
front, and a NW tower with a spire that has lucarnes and angle
finials. Very plain flanks with two-light and three-light windows;
in the transepts stepped lancets and a vescia. The chancel and
halls are of 1909–10 by *Peter Macgregor Chalmers*, and built in
Giffnock stone.

The lofty interior, of nave, aisles and transepts, has a low
boarded dado, plaster walls, and a coved plaster ceiling, with
a simple but attractive kingpost roof. The tie-beams and vertical supports have unusual carved and painted wooden decoration. The beams also rise from corbels with decorative heads.
Short rear gallery, panel-fronted, and pointed aisle arcades on
elegant columns with decorative heads. Pointed chancel arch;
boarded barrel roof, and stone S wall above elaborate cusped
wooden screen: this all Chalmers; his, too, the oak COMMU-
NION TABLE. – STAINED GLASS. Chancel, a deeply hued Resurrection, 1910 by *A. Ballantine & Son*; theirs also the 1921
Nativity, a First World War memorial, in the E transept. – W
wall, first from the N, Christ Walking on Water, *c.* 1968, possibly
by the *City Glass Company*; third from the N, The Good Shepherd, 1904, by *A. Ballantine & Gardiner*. – In the E wall, third
from the N, Faith, Hope and Charity, 1907, also by *Ballantine
& Gardiner*, and fourth from the N, a fine Baptism of Christ
of 1951 by *William Wilson*. – Many brasses, usually plain, one
in the NE corner to Murdoch, who was an elder here. – In the
gallery, a wooden WAR MEMORIAL of 1921 by *J. K. Hunter*,
brought here from the former Boys' Industrial School: a lugged
frame with a cushion entablature and semicircular head. In
Chalmers's HALL a well-proportioned queenpost roof.

ST PAUL (R.C.), Peggieshill Road. 1964–7 by *William Cowie &
Torry*; a thoughtful and good design which needs a higher,

---

* The support structure for the cross was heightened in 1962–4 to enable it to match
the scale of the new church.

more dominating site. Tall, white octagon with concave angles under a shallow copper roof and flèche; full-height s chancel with a screen of geometric concrete panels. Lower Fyfestone vestibule and porch on the N front; both these have segmental copper roofs. Mostly tall, concrete framed windows, on the W face with projecting triangular heads; repeated on the E face, but with windows omitted. Light, uncluttered interior; plaster walls and ceiling. Contemporary presbytery to the E, with asymmetrically pitched roof. To the N a hall of 1973–4 by *Charles Toner*.

AYR CEMETERY, Holmston Road. 1861–2, by *John Murdoch*, and much expanded. Neo-Tudor archway, of painted stone, with octagonal buttress piers with stumpy pinnacles and crenellated centre with the burgh arms. Pedestrian entrances with shouldered heads. To the r. the simple single-storey-and-attic superintendent's house, and a lower range of offices with a stepped gable over the central entrance. The original part is bounded by walls of stone and rail, and laid out as a series of mostly teardrop-shaped plots in an informal pattern. The MONUMENTS display a distaste for overt show, perhaps reflecting Ayr's strong Covenanting, Calvinist history. In the original cemetery, the grandest, if not the most attractive, is the large Grecian memorial to the Morris family (including James A. Morris, but not designed by him). The classical Greek monument to Rev. James Stevenson, with a polished granite sarcophagus beneath a star-encrusted arch, is by *William Clarke* (of *Clarke & Bell*), 1867.

PUBLIC BUILDINGS

AYR HOSPITAL. *See* AILSA HOSPITAL, below.

BELMONT ACADEMY, Belmont Road. 2005–8 by *Ryder HKS* for South Ayrshire Council. Large, faced in brightly coloured metal panels, the main entrance in a nodal drum tower.

Former BOYS' INDUSTRIAL SCHOOL, St Leonards Road. Tudor-Jacobethan of 1874–6 by *John Murdoch*, subsequently extended and now residential.

FOREHILL PRIMARY SCHOOL, Cessnock Place. 1962–4 by *Ayr County Council Architects Dept*. Brick-faced, with wooden fascias painted red. One two-storey block of butterfly plan (*see* also Mount Carmel Primary School, Kilmarnock).

HOLMSTON HOUSE (Social Work Offices), Holmston Road. The impressive former poorhouse for the Kyle Union in Neo-Jacobethan of 1857–60 by *W. L. Moffat*, a specialist in such buildings. H-plan, with the main elevation facing s. Twenty-one bays long, broadly symmetrical, and animated by advanced and gabled bays, of which the central pair, to the entrance block, have shaped gables and finials. Ogee-headed open bell-turret. Other elevations much plainer, especially on the rear wing, for the dormitories. In front the former GOVERNOR'S HOUSE (W), of 1902 by *William Kerr*, the WEST LODGE, of 1939 by *Ayr County Council*, a hipped bungalow, and the EAST

LODGE, dated 1858, by *Moffat*, a simple single-storey house
with tall stacks.

HOLMSTON PRIMARY SCHOOL, Holmston Road. 1883, by *John
Murdoch*. H-plan single-storey in Ballochmyle red sandstone,
with sparse Gothic detailing. The E wing has a tall bellcote on
the gable; the other gables to E and S have stepped projections,
hipped roofs and stepped three-light windows. S additions of
1996–8 by *South Ayrshire Council*.

KYLE ACADEMY, Overmills Road. 1974–9, begun by *Ayr County
Council Architects Dept*. Long three-storey teaching block,
brick-faced with continuous window bands. The free-standing
LECTURE THEATRE of 2005–7 by *Ryder HKS* is a rotunda,
harled, with big windows, with a lower, semicircular service
wing and entrance. Drum features are a motif of many C21
Ayrshire schools, but here it appears at its most successful. The
path is marked by two metal SHELTERS, like sheets blowing in
the wind.

QUEEN MARGARET ACADEMY, Dalmellington Road. 1972–7
by *Clark Fyfe*, County Architect. Sprawling steel-framed
and brick-clad secondary school, mostly two-storey, arranged
around two courtyards.

DESCRIPTION

Late C19 and early C20 houses line the main routes through this
area, such as Castlehill Road (SE), St Leonards Road (SE) and
MONUMENT ROAD (S). In the latter, at the junction with
Corsehill Road, THE GABLES, harled Arts and Crafts of 1905
by *J. K. Hunter*, with a heavy corner bartizan, and in ROSE-
BANK CRESCENT, N of Corsehill Road, ROSEBANK HOUSE,
three-bay Georgian classical of *c*. 1822, with a semi-elliptical
advanced centre bay and a Roman Doric porch. To the S, in
EWENFIELD ROAD, the harled CHAPEL PARK (No. 16), of
1916 by *H. E. Clifford & Lunan*, with a prominent undecorated
tower and strong horizontals.

OTHER BUILDINGS

AILSA HOSPITAL, 4 km. SE of the centre. The former County
Lunatic Asylum, of 1865–9 by *Charles Edward* of *Edward &
Robertson* of Dundee. One of the few C19 mental hospitals still
in use, and an important survival. Many free-standing additions, demonstrating changing philosophies of psychiatric
medicine. The original form of the asylum is clearly visible on
the S front. Cross-shaped plan, with a central administrative
block and single-storey axial wings linking to wards at either
end. Little architectural show, except for four square towers at
either end and flanking the canted central block, with round-
headed windows and squat pyramidal roofs. Slated roof rising
to prominent cast-iron brattishing. Sympathetic enlargement
in 1879–80 by *Allan Stevenson* included the raising of the

Ayr, Ailsa Hospital, New Hospital.
Engraving, 1905

corridor links to two storeys and the addition of a large block on the NE front.

Within the grounds, late C19 two-storey and single-storey VILLAS for patients, following contemporary practice, also rather severe, faintly Baronial in appearance, e.g. ALBANY HOUSE, S of the main building, of 1899 by *Allan Stevenson & Kerr*. Similar isolation hospital (now BRUNSTON HOUSE) by *Stevenson*, 1894.

At the NE corner of the site is the NEW HOSPITAL (now offices) of 1903–6 by *John B. Wilson* for Dr Charles Easterbrook, Medical Superintendent, who understood that psychiatric patients responded to exercise and fresh air, and who subsequently developed his ideas on a much larger scale at Crichton Royal Hospital (Dumfries and Galloway). Originally conceived as a series of single-storey wards, with canted ends, arranged singly or in pairs, linked by a spine corridor, alongside which runs an open cast-iron veranda. At the W end is the administration block, with shouldered gables and a central pedimented entrance.

AYR HOSPITAL, 300 m. SE of Ailsa Hospital. 1987–92 by *Keppie Henderson*. Substantial, in pale brick with red tiled roofs, with a central four-storey nursing block. Functional, an exercise in seeing how far this brick-and-tile vernacular can be pumped up. In the chapel, STAINED GLASS by *Oscar Paterson*, 1906, from the Biggart Hospital, Prestwick (q.v.). Well composed but the subject, Suffer Little Children, encourages sentimentality, even in Paterson.

MASONHILL CREMATORIUM, Old Toll, 3 km. ESE of the town centre. 1960–6 by *Ayr County Council Architects Dept* (project architect, *Douglas R. C. Hay*). Harled and slated, and modishly styled. In the chapel STAINED GLASS, 1965 by *Pierre Fourmaintraux*. Abstract.

MOSSHILL INDUSTRIAL ESTATE, 2 km. SE of Ailsa Hospital. A group of Scottish Development Agency factories from the 1970s, the best the brick-clad former DIGITAL EQUIPMENT plant of 1976–8 by *G. R. M. Kennedy & Partners* of Edinburgh. It has full-height window panels, and a glazed first-floor dining area which capitalizes on the views across the Firth.

BALBEG HOUSE

3000

2.4 km. S of Straiton

Close to the Girvan and with hills rising steeply to the S. Simple early C19 two-storey farmhouse expanded into an asymmetric, rambling L-plan sporting lodge by *James Purves* of Portpatrick for Sir Charles Fergusson in 1908 and further altered by him in 1923 for Sir Gerard Chadwyck Healey. To the rear of the house, RABBIE BURNS LODGE, of 2000 by *Charles Gulland*, a dramatic roundwood timber pole building on a more extensive raised basement. Three parallel wings, shaped like upturned keels with prow-like projections, and linking blocks of similar profile, built originally as a dormitory for the charity for disadvantaged children that occupied Balbeg, 1992–2003.

BALKISSOCK

1080

5 km. E of Ballantrae

A small country house situated high above the Stinchar Valley. 1933 by *James Miller* with *Richard Gunn* for Reginald Hughes-Onslow (*see* also Auchenflower). In a *Moderne*-cum-Arts and Crafts style. Gently splayed walls in white render with a thin tile string above the ground floor, tiny flat-roofed dormers and tall stacks. The main rooms, N-facing, have large horizontal metal-framed casements.

BALLANTRAE

0080

A small village strategically placed where the main coastal route from Stranraer to Ayr bridges the River Stinchar close to its mouth, the crossing guarded by Ardstinchar Castle. Single and two-storey houses line the main road, the earliest group clustering around the church. A single-storey terrace of small fisherman's houses, akin to those in the fisher villages of NE Scotland, look out towards the harbour.

PARISH CHURCH. 1819. A pebbledashed box with elementary Gothic windows still with shutter hooks and cast-iron diamond glazing. Adding vital, if somewhat incongruous, interest a fussy red sandstone clock turret on the front gable with gables, finials and a tiny lead flèche of 1891 by *David MacGibbon*, whose family owned Laggan (*see* p. 491). Inside elegantly curved U-plan GALLERY, supported on slender cast-iron columns, retains its original high-backed seating; the rest improved in

25

1893. – PULPIT between the two W windows. An unusual Gothic design of 1819, nearly circular with an elongated niche at the back decorated with husk detail and framed by two delicate colonettes. Above, a frothily detailed sounding-board with a domed roof and pinnacles. The centrepiece of its ceiling is a finely detailed rose. Detracting from the composition, stairs curving around in front added in 1899. – STAINED GLASS. W windows of 1873: the Resurrection and the Three Maries at the Tomb. – MONUMENTS. David MacGibbon, architect (of MacGibbon & Ross) †1902. Bronze. – Among other marble wall monuments two commemorate men killed in snowstorms: James Hendry, gamekeeper, †1891 and Robert Cunningham, postman, †1908, the latter by *Scott & Rae*. – Donaldson family of Auchairne. 1887 by *J. Whitehead*. – First World War memorial, 1922 by *James A. Morris*, executed by *Alexander Carrick* of Edinburgh. Bronze and pavonazza marble with a very delicate figure of St Michael slaying Satan.

s of the church, in the Old Kirkyard, the KENNEDY AISLE, all that remains of the church built 1604 by the Kennedys of Bargany as a memorial to Gilbert Kennedy of Bargany who was killed in 1601 by the Earl of Cassillis. Lady Bargany died in 1605 and both were buried in the new vaulted aisle. It is a remarkable if somewhat untutored monument in Renaissance style but following late medieval traditions. A large canopy is supported on three receding orders of columns of idiosyncratic design, over-sized finials crown each capital and the front ones flank a stylized consoled and pedimented frame with the Bargany arms in the panel (cf. the Glencairn monument at Kilmaurs, q.v.). This centrepiece is supported at the centre by a rather clumsy square-section baluster rising from the tomb-chest itself in a most unorthodox manner. The chest has strange console-like projections, and three stylized weepers project above them. Recumbent figures of Gilbert Kennedy in armour and his wife Janet Stewart.

Adjoining the aisle an open enclosure, possibly incorporating part of the walls of the earlier church. Within, an early C19 diamond-shaped MONUMENT to David Ferguson Kennedy of Finnart. Against the E wall of the Kennedy aisle several interesting but much eroded memorials, some C17.

PUBLIC HALL, Main Street. 1925 by *Allan Stevenson* of *Allan Stevenson, Mair & Cassels*. Harled with brick pilaster quoins; the low front block has a red sandstone simplified triumphal arch-type entrance, possibly influenced by the drawing provided by Lorimer in 1920 for a frontispiece. The taller rear range has battered brick buttresses and alternate windows breaking the eaves.

HARBOUR. L-plan, constructed *c.* 1845 using a rocky outcrop to form the foundation of the sandstone pier and costing around £6,000. Improved *c.* 1860. Battered protective walls on the outer limb and the inner face of the s wall. A number of simple stone stores on the shore.

STINCHAR BRIDGE, s of Main Street below the castle from whose stones it is said to have been built in 1776. An elegant two-arched ashlar design with curved central refuges. The foundations for the piers required a 'great sum of money', wrote John Hamiliton to the 5th Earl of Stair. At the N end a much-extended and altered C18 toll house and C19 Stinchar Cottage. Closed to traffic with the opening of the single span, concrete bridge in 1964.

DESCRIPTION. MAIN STREET begins at the WAR MEMORIAL of
1920 by *James A. Morris*: a Celtic cross raised on a series of
blocks and a rubble plinth. On the N side the ROYAL HOTEL,
early C19, is the marker at the start of a long curved terrace of
cottages, *c*. 1800; a similar terrace faces it and adjoins the walls
to the Old Kirkyard. Opposite the church the ROYAL BANK
OF SCOTLAND, a standard mid-C19 villa of red sandstone
ashlar with yellow dressings and a Doric porch. In Vennel
Street W of the Kirk, in a walled garden, the MANSE incorporating a building of 1726, as remodelled 1844 to a plan from
James Adair, joiner. Porch added 1875. Fronting the sea in
FORELAND, council housing of four flats in a two-storey block
pattern. Continuing N towards the harbour, a long terrace of
small single-storey, brightly painted former fisherman's houses
are probably later C19. Behind the seafront in ARRAN AVENUE,
an interesting development for the Carrick Housing Association at CRAIGIEMAINS by *ARP Lorimer*, 2003. Two informal
courtyards combining traditional materials and forms with
energy-efficient design; the sun spaces like narrow glasshouses
on the S elevations of the southern blocks are a striking display
of the new technology. It is a pity the original plan to build in
one terrace, in sympathy with the traditional buildings of Ballantrae, had to be abandoned.

ARDSTINCHAR CASTLE. A jagged ruin perched on a bluff on
the river's N bank. Thought to have been built by Hugh
Kennedy, who led the Scots contingent under Joan of Arc in
1429. He granted it to his brother Thomas *c*. 1429. The original
three-storey tower, occupying the highest point of the steep
site, was heightened and an irregular courtyard was added with
a smaller tower in the middle of the W wall. It was occupied
for little more than a century and now only a fragment of the
small tower remains. The entrance was at the NW angle. The
surviving angle of the three-storey keep exists for its full height
making it possible to see its construction; the walls were relatively thin and each floor was vaulted at right angles to the
next, presumably for stability. The parapet has elementary
corbelling of just one row of stones. Windows survive on both
faces and although robbed of their dressings, give a clear indication of their small and irregular sizes.

WINDMILL, 1 km. NE. Clearly visible on the raised beach above
the A77, a well-preserved, vaulted, rubble-built tower, probably
early C18.

AUCHAIRNE HOUSE, 2.6 km. ESE. A simple early C19 three-bay
farmhouse with wings, given diamond flues and pedimented
dormerheads *c*. 1840 for the Donaldson family, who also
added a more stylish, deeply eaved three-bay range at right
angles.

BALNOWLART, 3 km. NE. The desolate ruin of a compact, Scots
vernacular country house 1905 by *J. Jerdan & Son* of Edinburgh for Dr George Kerr. A tall asymmetrical design with a
low service court.

CORSECLAYS FARM, 2.8 km. NE. Relatively unaltered hip-roofed and harled two-storey farmhouse of 1819–21.

CUNNINGHAM MEMORIAL, 4.5 km. S in boggy wasteland, W of the A77. A Celtic cross to Robert Cunningham, who died in the snow in December 1908.

CAVE CAIRN, Arecleoch Forest, 10 km. E. Now subsumed deep in the plantation. A Bargrennan-type round-chambered cairn, 20 m. in diameter. Robbing of it to build sheepfolds has revealed two chambers set back to back, that on the W with its roofless passage approaching from the margin of the mound.

AUCHENFLOWER. *See* p. 107.
BALKISSOCK. *See* p. 176.
GLENAPP CASTLE. *See* p. 350.
LAGAFATER LODGE. *See* p. 491.
LAGGAN. *See* p. 491.

BALLOCHMORRIE HOUSE   2080
3.5 km. NW of Barrhill

Built in 1833 for William MacAdam, grandson of John Loudon McAdam, the renowned road surveyor. The house stands on a raised knoll above the S bank of the River Duisk. It is a T-plan, the rear service wing possibly incorporating an earlier house. The main façade is dressed ashlar and has two full-height canted bays which flank the columned portico. Two rooms have elegant plaster cornices. Cantilevered stair with delicate cast-iron balusters. The stable range has the MacAdams' emblem. Crowstepped lodge of 1909.

BALLOCHMYLE HOUSE   5020
1 km. NW of Catrine

Begun *c.* 1760 for Allan Whitefoord, by *John Adam.* Claud Alexander acquired it in 1786 and extended it, further additions were made in 1835–6 before thorough reconstruction in the style of a French chateau in 1886–90 for Sir Claud Alexander by *H. M. Wardrop* with *George Mackie Watson* of *Wardrop, Anderson & Browne.* A hospital from 1940 to 1969, but restored and brashly scrubbed, after long neglect, as apartments by Ardgowan Homes, completed 2010.

Adam's villa was a modest version of Dumfries House (q.v.) and its plan essentially one end of that house with the projecting pedimented central bay of the side elevation of Dumfries House forming the centre of the rear elevation here. Wardrop's red sandstone house is wrapped around this, the W front a nearly symmetrical composition of two storeys and attic above the raised basement. An enormous ornate three-storey porch dominates the central bays decorated with applied orders:

Doric, Ionic and at the top, panelled pilasters supporting an open pediment. Above the door a coat of arms crowned by an elephant, highlighting the Alexanders' Indian connections. To the r. of the porch paired tall windows originally lit the main stair. Flanking pavilions break forward from the main front with square turrets in the angles that turn octagonal above the eaves and terminate in ogee roofs; their greenish-grey slates only emphasize the dull monotony of the slates on the extensive main roofs. Large canted windows break forward from the w elevation of the pavilions and, set into the steep roof, big dormers with boldly panelled stone frames. A similar canted bay overlaps the C18 house on the s elevation and a smaller bay projects from the pavilion.

At the SE corner of the rear elevation, the E front of John Adam's villa can still be detected in the paler red sandstone masonry with diagonally tooled droving. But the central, pedimented stair projection is Wardrop's rebuilding and he inserted also the Venetian window to the r. of the centrepiece. Abutting N, a large plain range which subsumed a nursery wing of 1791, the only trace of which can be seen in the much-altered, N-facing wall onto the low Victorian service court at the E, the latter entered through a large archway.

Inside, everything is of 2010.

With the exception of the WALLED GARDEN, the house is bereft of any meaningful landscape. The sea of new houses to the w in pick 'n' mix styles bear no relationship to the history of the site or local building traditions.

BALTERSAN CASTLE

2 km. SW of Maybole

2000

A roofless L-plan tower house standing on raised ground above the Abbeymill Burn which fed the mill pond of Crossraguel Abbey, to which the property once belonged. The Kennedys' association begins in the 1470s and there was a house on or near the site in 1530 where Egidia Kennedy died. The tower is unusually large and sophisticated and according to a C19 recording of the worn stone over the door, '. . . was begun the First day of March 1584 by John Kennedy of Pennyglen and Margaret Cathcart his spouse'. The framed arms panel above, now indecipherable, contained a quotation from Proverbs 18, also used by Kennedy's brother-in-law at Killochan Castle (q.v.). But John's lack of wealth and standing have made the enterprise something of an enigma and recent research suggests that instead of being an archaic design of 1584, the tower was built *c.* 1548 by Quentin Kennedy, Abbot of Crossraguel. He was well connected and may have felt that the C15 accommodation within the Abbey did not suit his standing. Certainly he was well placed to build such a smart and up-to-the-mark house. Did Kennedy simply update the tower in 1584? Was the date stone a marriage stone? Or was it simply misread in the C19?

The tower is imposingly solid, built of local sandstone rubble, formerly harled and limewashed, comprising a main block (15.8 m. by 8.5 m. with walls 1.2 m. thick) and square stair-tower. If the date is 1548 then this is a very early example of a square stair-tower, which is also found at Pinwherry (q.v.), as here with a turnpike stair (late C16), and at Killochan (1586, q.v.) and Kirkhill Castle, Colmonell (1589, q.v.), both sporting very fashionable scale-and-platt stairs. But it could be that John Kennedy, a stepson of the 3rd Earl of Cassillis, added the stair-tower. Baltersan was clearly built to be defended; it is spattered with loops. Archaeological investigation suggests that there were a series of small courts protecting the entrance, and these gunloops should be seen in the light of such arrangements. High at the NW and SE angles of the main block, at the same level as the upper caphouse room and originally with conical roofs, were more conventional rounded and corbelled turrets. They are almost completely lost at the SE but at the NW the subtly tapered ashlar walls survive (accurately drawn by Charles Rennie Mackintosh in 1895). A drainage system was devised from these turrets, providing rainwater to the kitchen. The wall-head dormers, now all vanished, provided further high-level vantage points. Less defensive are the three large windows with moulded jambs and lintels at first-floor level on the N, S and E. All the gables were crowstepped.

The entrance is at the base of the stair-tower in the W-facing elevation and opens onto the turnpike stair; the doorway is checked for a yett and a door and there is evidence of seatings for drawbars. The stair is set within the square turret and rises to the second floor. A secondary corbelled square turret within

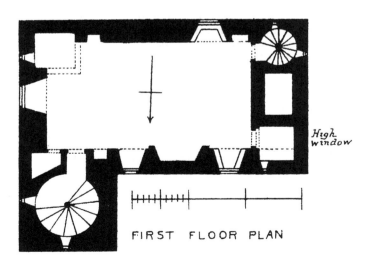

High window

FIRST FLOOR PLAN

Baltersan Castle.
Plan

the re-entrant angle houses the stair to the two-storey, gabled caphouse. The positioning of the upper room poses some interesting questions. There is still corbelling as though to support a wall-walk, but breaking through this corbelling is an unusual corbelled window. The room is rectangular in form and the window opening relates closely to the design of the more elaborate window at Maybole Castle (q.v.), which is probably slightly later in date. The window faces N with good sight lines up the valley. Did it begin life as a valuable look-out point but made rather more comfortable than the open wall-walk?

Inside the entrance, the remains of the wide turnpike stair at the l., to the r. the cellar area on the S, with two stores, originally barrel-vaulted with square ashlar blocks, the eastern one with a stair to the first-floor hall. N of the stores a passageway lit from a heavily barred window in the E wall leads to the kitchen with a serving hatch from it into the passage. On the W wall of the undersized kitchen a deep fireplace ingle lit from a small S window with a slops drain in the W wall. Above this level all the floors and roof have gone. The first-floor hall was originally entered from a screens passage: sockets by the door indicate the position. In the SE angle is the stair to the ground floor and a curious compartment above it rising the full height of the hall and cut back into the E and S walls with no obvious means of access; the position of two narrow joists (unlike the slots for other floor beams at the second floor), possibly indicate some form of hatch. The hall has three tall windows, with roll-moulded jambs, on the N, S (with bench seats) and E. In the NW corner of the hall is a small mural chamber, and above this chamber a very deep ingo opens to a square window (this relates to windows at Killochan and the Castle of Park (Dumfries and Galloway) although in both those instances the very deep ingo is to the exterior). The only evidence of the large fireplace on the N wall is a gaping space and a small salt bole. The turnpike stair led up to the two second-floor chambers, and in the SW a mural turnpike linked the hall to the floor above, where very unusually the two S windows had glazed upper sections and lower shutters which slid into the wall thickness; this detail is emphasized on the external wall by three courses of finely cut ashlar to the left of each opening. Also on the S wall two garderobes. Off the W chamber a small barrel-vaulted chamber which may have been a charter room. Although no floors or internal partitions remain the wealth of detail surviving in the outer walls may yet provide better evidence of the internal disposition of the tower.

BARASSIE

A barren area of whins and dunes until the Kilmarnock & Troon Railroad opened in 1807 and weekend and summer houses for Kilmarnock merchants followed. These are in BEACH ROAD. Least altered are THE COTTAGE (No. 24) and THE NEUK

(No. 25) both of *c.* 1835, but with mid- and late C19 embellishments. THE TOWER HOTEL also began as a single-storey
dwelling, but was extended *c.* 1859 with a two-storey wing at
right angles and an Italianate tower.

The land N of Hillhouse Road was planned as BARASSIE
GARDEN SUBURB from 1911 by *James Chalmers* but aborted
by the First World War. There were to have been three N–S
arteries, a wide central E–W boulevard, and other roads running
SW–NE. An area at the NE corner, set aside for 'practice greens',
identifies the prospective market. Also proposed were shops, a
hotel, a boarding house and a steamer pier. Associated with this
is No. 51 BEACH ROAD, now much altered, which had a gabled
front, a parapeted tower and mullioned-and-transomed windows.
Also by Chalmers are No. 49, with its tile-hung gable and first-
floor balcony with stumpy columns, and Nos. 2–4 GAILES
ROAD, harled and tiled, with tall strongly battered stacks.

BARASSIE PRIMARY SCHOOL. *See* Troon.

KILMARNOCK (BARASSIE) GOLF CLUB. Harled and tiled clubhouse of 1905 by *James Scott Hay*, swamped by subsequent
additions.

BARDROCHAT HOUSE   1080
0.8 km. SE of Colmonell

Begun in 1893 by *George Mackie Watson* (still working from
Rowand Anderson's office) for Robert Finnie McEwen. He was
an advocate, but also a musician and patron of the arts and in
1906–8 had the house extended by *Robert S. Lorimer*, who latter
remodelled Marchmont House (Borders) for him. Some of the
detail here was designed for Rowallan.

The house sits high on the steep hillside rising from the S bank
of the Stinchar, exploiting the wonderful prospects down and
across the river valley, and although large blends subtly into
the sloping ground. Its form is now roughly rectangular, of
browny-grey harl (now painted cream) and red sandstone
dressings, the latter with little roll mouldings framing the
windows, and Westmorland slate roofs. The design is a particularly sophisticated mingling of Scots vernacular with Arts and
Crafts motifs and full of quirky detail. The asymmetrical
entrance front is Watson's, and has a shallow projecting porch
with big segmental pediment and lugged door frame. This is
one of the few straightforward historical details on the whole
exterior, perhaps unsurprising from the man who went on to
re-create Eilean Donan Castle (Highland and Islands). The
full-height canted window to the E of the doorway with a segmented bellcast roof, and the chimney-breast projecting to
provide an inglenook for the drawing room to the W would be
quite at home in an Edwardian villa.

The W elevation is very different; of the first build the
big canted bay at the N end is unaltered but the two bays to
its r. have been subtly blended into the extension. This was

originally to include an enormous music room on the scale of Lorimer's dining room wing at Hallyburton House (Perth and Kinross), but as built is more modest. Nevertheless it still creates a very long W elevation which is ingeniously divided up to soften the link with the earlier house and to give the appearance of gradual growth. This is achieved by fractionally raising the height of the music room and introducing crowstepped skews to provide visual breaks. The individually detailed dormerheads with scrolls, curlicues and geometrical forms give the elevation real distinction, and the advanced gabled bay at the S emphatically completes it. The hall and public rooms form an L-plan facing N and W. In the angle created to the S and E Lorimer created extensive service accommodation with bellcast roofs over the stairs, and over the kitchen a square-plan piend roof with a bold apex stack, a detail reminiscent of Nesfield. A virtually detached laundry wing is visible from the drive and its bellcast roof announces Lorimer's presence.

Lorimer accommodated Watson's exterior, but inside he showed no such deference. The galleried Entrance Hall is fully panelled with yellow pine and beautifully featured pitch pine lines the stair walls. All of this is under a ribbed plaster barrel vault; to the l., the Dining Room with a geometrically patterned plaster ceiling and arched frame to the bay window; to the r. the Drawing Room with another patterned ceiling and a delightful balustered screen leading to the garden door. Similarly detailed woodwork originally decorated the inglenook at the N end of the Drawing Room; this was removed c. 1960 when the chimneypiece was resited on the E wall backing onto the hall flue, and a window inserted in its place. Further remodelled in the 1980s by *Patrick Lorimer* of *ARP Lorimer & Associates*. Most distinctive is the passage to the Music Room with entwined vines in the plasterwork, and the Music Room with oak linenfold panelling over the chimneypiece and a coffered ceiling festooned with vines.

2090

BARGANY

2 km. ENE of Old Dailly

The house, situated in one of the best-designed landscapes in Ayrshire, sits on a low eminence overlooking the River Girvan, and replaced Bargany Castle, a Kennedy stronghold which stood on the edge of the river to the N. The estate was acquired in 1631 by Sir John Hamilton of Letterick and the new house was begun c. 1680 by his grandson, the 2nd Lord Bargany (†1693), and its plain original appearance is clearly visible on the entrance front in spite of later additions. Three storeys with attics and crowstep-gabled wings forming a half H-plan. Above the ground floor, narrow windows, symmetrically arranged, and smaller openings in the gables of the wings which also have panelled gable stacks (seen again on the SE gable and on the ridge of the SE wing). In style it compares closely to Gallery (1677–80; Angus) and Bannockburn House (*c.* 1680; Stirling) and is remarkably early for an unfortified house in the Kennedys' fiefdom of Carrick. Across the centre of the ground floor an entrance hall with pedimented door, given this form in the late 1980s when the house was restored to a welcome orderliness by *Patrick Lorimer* of *Anthony Richardson & Partners*. Flanking this are frequently remodelled service wings, made symmetrical in the 1980s. Joining the range was an additional single-storey curved wing *c.* 1845–50 for stables and a coachhouse much in the manner of Cloncaird Castle (q.v.).

The long garden front (NE) was recast *c.* 1747 as a regular five-bay façade with chamfered window surrounds. The second-floor windows breaking the wall-head have reused C17 pediments of which the central one, very worn, is dated 1681 with 'HB' (Hamilton of Bargany). The central first-floor window became a door with steps to the garden. Evidence in the walls can be seen also for a pedimented doorcase no longer *in situ*. On this façade and on the NW and SE elevations there is also evidence of stonework reused from the old castle, particularly in the window surrounds and the wall-head pediments with very worn initials and emblems. The SE gable has been doubled in width, resulting in deep window ingoes, and a huge buttress added at the SE angle all to aid stability. At the N angle a large three-storey addition (for a drawing room), almost certainly by *William Burn*, of *c.* 1862–78 for the Duc and Duchesse de Coigny (she inherited Bargany in 1834). Rubble-built with freestone dressings, it has crowstepped gables and wide bay windows to the principal floor at the NE gable and on the park-facing elevation.

Inside is some of the best interior decoration in Ayrshire. The two principal rooms on the NE front have elaborate mid-C18 decorative schemes including plasterwork reminiscent of Thomas Clayton's decorations at Chatelherault (Lanarkshire), undertaken for the 5th Duke of Hamilton. The original DRAWING ROOM is the most sumptuous, the panelling with moulded frames of egg-and-dart and guilloche, some with lugged details or scrolls, a cornice of egg-and-dart and modillions, a cove and on the corners of the ceiling fretted panels with rosettes. The overmantel has a lugged picture frame under a pediment filled with later C19 embellishments, and there was much augmentation in the 1860s with vases, cartouches, masks etc. The DINING ROOM is the best room in the house with its barely altered C18 decoration, its grand doorcase surmounted by a deep bracketed frieze and a broken pediment enclosing a fluted pedestal. The fireplace appears to have an inserted shelf, which has the effect of shunting the elaborate carved overmantel too close to the cornice. This overmantel sits on a palmette frieze with a gadrooned band and is made up of cornucopias generously overflowing with fruit and flowers supporting a scrolled circular panel, suspended from a bowed ribbon, which contained a portrait medallion.

The LIBRARY was lined out *c.* 1740 with raised and fielded panelling divided by narrow cusped-headed panels and bookcases. Prominent cornice and coved ceiling. Mid-C19 yellow veined-marble chimneypiece. Most of the other rooms on the principal and second floor have raised and fielded panelling, egg-and-dart mouldings and panelled shutters. The NEW DRAWING ROOM added in the 1860s, however, is in the Louis XV manner with decorated framing to the walls, all with scrolled details to top and bottom and foliage detail, more elaborate in the large panels and the overdoors, this detailing reminiscent of the inserted plaster details in the drawing room. A coved cornice with an open-work frieze in bold relief.

To the NW of the house, crossing the Girvan, DUKE'S BRIDGE of *c.* 1753. An elegant shallow curved arch with ashlar voussoirs and balustraded parapet rising to a point in the centre.

George Robertson drew up a plan for the Bargany POLICIES in 1774. The most successful aspect of the design was the thick shelter belts beyond the Girvan, and specimen trees along the bank transforming the periphery of the estate into an effective enclosure and creating perspectives. In 1802 *Thomas White Jun.* undertook probably his first independent commission in Scotland and suggested a clean sweep, including rebuilding the house, but little was implemented and in 1826 the park was decisively shaped by *W. S. Gilpin* in the Picturesque style with open parkland and densely wooded areas around the enlarged lake, on its N bank a rustic SUMMERHOUSE (mid-C19) with the roof supported on slender tree trunks and decorative timber-panelled walls, and a BOATHOUSE similarly detailed but without rustic columns. The park now has an important collection of rhododendron and trees. Under Gilpin's watchful eye the E and W drives were laid out and a gate lodge was built 1824–5. – COTTAGE and STABLE BLOCK mainly 1824 with segmental-arched carriage bays off the S drive. – Further E a large brick-lined WALLED GARDEN, in two sections, one end curved, with a huge oculus opening and an urn above.

BARNWEILL

4020

In the craggy hills S of Kilmarnock.

BARNWEILL CHURCH. The parish, which belonged to the Abbey of Fail, was suppressed in the late C17 and the church fell into disuse. According to Wodrow, in 1712, the people of Barnweill 'besides their attempt to burn the new erected kirk of Stair they are now resolving to rebuild the old kirk of Barnwell.' Little more than the W and E gables remains, the latter with a square opening, with sufficient of the side walls to reveal entrances in both.

BARNWEILL HOUSE, 0.6 km. NE. Built *c.* 1783 when the property was acquired by the Neills on the break-up of the Craigie estate (q.v.). Two-storey-and-attic house of three bays, with low wings facing S. Restored by *Ronald Alexander* in the 1970s, when a galleried drawing room was created in the former coachhouse range. Handsome chimneypiece with maritime decoration. It came from Holmston Farm (dem.), near Ayr.

WALLACE MONUMENT, 0.75 km. SW of Barnweill House. A prominent Tudor Gothic tower topped by a corbelled, castellated parapet with bartizans. Of 1855 by *Robert Snodgrass* of Beith, the project driven by the Beith historian William Dobie, who also suggested alterations to the designs. A monument to William Wallace, claimed as a native of Ayrshire, had been proposed as early as 1819 for a site on Craigie Hill. On three faces, bronze inscriptions of deathless prose, e.g. '. . . ever animated by the noblest patriotism he continued warring with the oppressors of his native land, until his foul betrayal . . . by the execrable Monteith' and 'From Greece arose Leonidas, from Scotland Wallace, and from America, Washington, names which shall remain through all time the watchwords and beacons of liberty.'

BARR

2090

The village is set high up in the Stinchar valley at the river's confluence with the Water of Gregg and developed around a modest three-way road junction that formerly had more significance than now. Vernacular cottages and small two-storey houses face the Water of Gregg and range in a picturesque manner up the steep hill on the E. Across the Water of Gregg, which flows parallel with the main street, a group of sympathetic single-storey council housing.

Former ANGUS MEMORIAL CHURCH, The Avenue. 1892 by *Alexander Petrie*, replacing the original Free Church, now sensitively converted to a house by *Patrick Lorimer*. The bold red sandstone tower is a prominent feature with a clock in the upper stage.

PARISH CHURCH. Picturesquely sited at the W end of the village with a backdrop of trees and the open meadowland of the glebe. Built 1877–8 to replace the church of 1653. By *Allan Stevenson*, selected perhaps because he was rebuilding Pinmore House (dem.) at the time for Hew Hamilton, one of the heritors. A simple gabled and buttressed rectangular box with undemonstrative Gothic detailing. The W gable, S porch and S elevation to its l. are built of neatly squared whinstone; the other walls are rubble, possibly partly of stone used from the old church. In 1891 *William Tennant* replaced the original gable-head bellcote with a cross finial and created a new bellcote by extending the SW buttress upwards. A Gothic-arched porch leads into a vestibule, formed under the gallery in 1978 by *Patrick Lorimer*. The gallery itself was inserted in 1888, *Stevenson* again. Simply pewed interior with two aisles and a

boarded, open arch-braced roof into which tie-rods were
inserted in 1891. Windows of clear, leaded glass in bands of
square and diamond kames, creating a very light interior. –
Carved wooden C20 COMMUNION TABLE and marble FONT,
both from the former Angus Memorial Church, introduced
when the congregations were merged in 1953; the font probably dates from its 1892 rebuilding. – Gothic detailed PULPIT
on the E wall. – BRASS. Resited from the former church. Henry
Hughes Onslow †1871.

NE of the church is BARSKAIG HOUSE, formerly the manse
of 1803–5 by *Robert McCord* (architect) and *Alexander Jardine*
(contractor). It is traditional, of two storeys with service additions of 1820 and two-storey bay windows added in 1906.
Beside the entrance drive a long barn range, probably C18.

OLD KIRKYARD. In the centre of the village. A large walled
enclosure with a whinstone memorial gateway of 1911–12
by *J. K. Hunter*. Fine collection of headstones and chest
tombs from the C17 onwards, one HEADSTONE with an
hourglass set in a spectacular display of deeply carved scrolly
sub-Renaissance grotesque detail.

BARR VILLAGE HALL, below the Old Kirkyard, is low and
gabled. Built in 1913 with funds from the Carnegie Trust. The
architect was *John Arthur*, a native of the village. A large dull
addition of 1959–60, and a smarter extension, harled with
wooden panelling, of 2000, by *ARP Lorimer*, similar to their
work at the St Magnus Centre, Kirkwall, Orkney.

S of the Village Hall a cast-iron DRINKING FOUNTAIN
of 1902, one of the excellent standard designs by *Walter Mac-
Farlane & Co.* (*Saracen Foundry*), Glasgow, with exotic filigree
dome, over a central pelican and still retaining its chained
drinking cup. Adjacent to this the WAR MEMORIAL, a granite
Celtic Cross, 1923, by *Henry McLachlan* of Ayr.

The Water of Gregg is crossed by several bridges, including the
mid-C19 stone GREGG BRIDGE with a high parapet and,
opposite the Primary School, a tubular steel FOOTBRIDGE by
Tubewrights Ltd, of Newport. W of the Church, the stone STIN-
CHAR BRIDGE, dated 1787: a segmental arch with low flat
parapets, rusticated end piers and long abutments.

ALTON ALBANY, 0.3 km. SW beside the river. Originally a farmhouse then *c.* 1830 made into a modest villa, white-rendered
with black-painted quoins and margins but given bulky gabled
wings by *John Murdoch*, 1861, contemporary with canted
windows and a large arcaded front porch. 2005 extensively
remodelled by *Patrick Lorimer* of *ARPL Architects*.

WALLED GARDEN with ancillary buildings to NE. LODGE
c. 1860, close to the road bridge over the Stinchar in a simple
Neo-Tudor style.

GLENGENNET, 2.5 km. NE. Set on the hillside N of Barr on
the road to the Nick of the Balloch. Possibly built as a plain
three-bay farmhouse and extended to make a shooting lodge
c. 1860. Two storeys, cement-rendered main S façade with a

semicircular three-window projection at the E. All this with a crenellated parapet and piended roof behind. Plain set-back wing to the E.

MINUNTION, 5.5 km. SE. An upright, well-built farmhouse, perhaps more accurately described as a neat villa, built 1857 probably for Sir Gilbert Blane and extended in 1988–9 by *Patrick Lorimer* of *Anthony Richardson & Partners*. Stone-built with a central gabled porch. To the rear a low wing providing kitchen, service areas, a studio and bedrooms. Its E elevation gives the impression of a service range or part of the steading, but the W elevation a joyful gathering of projecting rectangular oriel windows, swept roof and canted, finialled dormers with a gabled bay for the door and steps to the garden.

BARRHILL

2080

The last village before the high moorland dividing Ayrshire and Wigtownshire. Barrhill grew up in the early C19 by the bridge over the Cross Water and owes its development both to its strategic position on the road to Newton Stewart as it crosses the Duisk, opened by 1838, and to the opening of a station on the Girvan & Portpatrick Junction Railway in 1877. A single street with simple one- and two-storey cottages, some harled, others built in granite but all built up to the pavement and with many alterations.

ARNSHEEN–BARRHILL CHURCH. Now redundant. On a rise on the E side of the main road at the village edge. Built in 1887 by *R. S. Ingram*. Muscular Gothic with touches of the architect's favoured Baronial style in the crowstepped gables and the dominant, two-stage tower crowned with an uncomfortable asymmetrically crenellated parapet; in the main gable above the vaulted narthex, a wheel window, mirrored at the E. Open interior with E transepts and a shallow eastern projection for the panelled pulpit. To its r. an organ in a panelled case. A crenellated panelled screen at the W. Kingpost timber roof with cross-ties to the central kingpost at the crossing. Coloured glass windows of floral and geometric stylized designs.

BARRHILL PRIMARY SCHOOL. 1880 by *Allan Stevenson*, probably incorporating the school of 1851. Typical single-storey gabled range with stepped windows in the gable-ends, with inferior post-war N addition. Former schoolmaster's house of 1907 by *J. & H. V. Eaglesham*.

MEMORIAL HALL. 1920–4 by *James Miller* with *Richard Gunn*, roughly contemporary with Miller's Kildonan (q.v.). Very restrained Arts and Crafts manner, simpler than his hall at Kirkoswald (q.v.); its character owes everything to the massing of the main hall and ancillary accommodation, and the clean lines.

BRIDGES. Over Cross Water, 1811, a single arch. BARRHILL BRIDGE crossing the Duisk, of *c.* 1838.

CEMETERY by Barrhill Bridge, early C19 partly walled enclosure. Wason burial enclosure. Rigby Wason epitaph, 1875, records he built Drumlamford (q.v.) and Corwar (q.v.), farms, cottages, roads and bridges and improved moorland 'conferring many public benefits in this district'.

WAR MEMORIAL. A granite Celtic cross set high above the road. 1922 by *Scott & Rae*.

MARTYRS TOMB. 600 m. uphill w of Main Street. Commemorating the Covenanters John Murchie and Daniel Meiklewrick, shot in 1685. A small stone enclosure with walls ramped up to a simple pedimented end wall with a ball finial, built *c.* 1840 by the parish and Rigby Wason (*see* Drumlamford and Corwar), who advertised for locals to contribute to the work, writing in an address to the Reformers in the District of Carrick, 'Thanks be to God alone, we live in times when we cannot be *murdered* because we will not change our opinions.'

STATION. 0.6 km. SW on the road to Glen Luce and built into the slope of the hill. Opened 1877. Simple functional block of local whinstone with granite quoins. Free-standing SIGNAL BOX of 1908, brought from Portpatrick in 1935 but containing the original eighteen-lever frame from the earlier signal box here.

BLAIR FARM, 1.1 km. SE. *c.* 1840. A superior one-and-a-half-storey farmhouse, neatly snecked whinstone with windows in bold ashlar frames. Low flanking service wings. U-plan court to rear, cart bays in outer E wall. Later C19 tall byre range against N wall supported on ashlar piers, alternate bays with tall gabled heads, an unusual design perhaps intended for improved ventilation.

CHAMBERED CAIRN, 3.5 km. NE in a clearing in a forestry plantation about 0.5 km. NW of Balmalloch farm. A Bargrennan-type chambered round cairn, measuring about 18 m. in diameter by 2.4 m in height; the ruins of two chambers set roughly at right angles to each other can be seen within the body of the cairn.

BALLOCHMORRIE. *See* p. 179.
BLACK CLAUCHRIE. *See* p. 200.
CORWAR. *See* p. 226.
DRUMLAMFORD. *See* p. 295.
KILDONAN. *See* p. 407.

BARRMILL

3050

The Crawford brothers, whose family had begun spinning linen thread in Beith in 1775, built a mill here in 1836. It became one of the largest thread manufactories in the world, but now demolished apart from the late C19 offices (now residential). The village lies to the w, separated by a railway bridge of 1888.

GIFFENMILL VIADUCT, 0.3 km. S. Seven arches, of rubble-faced concrete. Built 1898–1903 for the Lanarkshire & Ayrshire Railway; *Robert McAlpine & Sons*, engineers.

DRUMBUIE HOUSE, 1.5 km. SW. A small vernacular farmhouse, its lower walls probably late C18 but raised in the mid C19 when one window was enlarged and dormers inserted. The crow-stepped gables are C19 replacements. Low wing to r. and a wall which was once part of further buildings attached; two-storey wing at rear. Behind the house an C18 BARN, painted rubble with crowsteps to gables. On the door lintel, the initials RB and IM.

Immediately S is DRUMBUIE FARM, an interesting survival built, according to an inscription, in 1736 by Hugh Patrick and rebuilt by James Patrick in 1843. The earlier date might refer to the small building in the centre of the present composition, just two bays wide with crowstepped gables and stumpy chimneys with thacking stanes. One original tiny first-floor window. The single-storey block attached to its E end is of the later date. Saw-toothed skews. Additional low outhouse. Further addition at right angles to the W.

BARSKIMMING HOUSE

2.3 km. SE of Failford

An unexciting Neo-Georgian house, of three storeys with an attic and five wide bays to the front, four to the side. This is mostly a rebuilding of 1882–5 by *Wardrop & Reid*, after a fire, but may incorporate some fabric from the previous house, a competent Neoclassical design of 1771–4 for Thomas Miller, Lord Chief Justice of the Court of Session. On the entrance front the barely projecting centre is pedimented, with an oculus in the centre, emphasizing the height in a way that is wholly Victorian in its manner. Other incongruities are the Frenchly shaped and pedimented gables which break the balustraded parapet on the return W elevation. Good, solid Greek Revival porch, very probably by *David Hamilton*, who designed *c.* 1816 the pair of low rear wings (the E one for a library) which are linked by service buildings and an arched and pedimented entrance pend to the rear court. This is neatly shielded from the main front by a N-facing blind arch under a pediment, reminiscent of an entrance to a London mews. Inserted into the rear wall of the house is a datestone, 1642. Interior altered in the 1920s. Large well stair, galleried at second floor, said to have come from a Glasgow house. The ground floor extensively remodelled by *Patrick Lorimer* of *ARPL Architects* 2009.

The C18 house took advantage of a romantic prospect of the spectacular gorge of the Ayr. James Boswell was 'much pleased with the beauties of nature and art at Barskimming'. Spanning the gorge, and carrying the main drive, is the NEW BRIDGE of 1788, commemorating Miller's baronetcy. Handsome single arch of red sandstone, flanked by buttresses terminating in obelisks. Set below to the W and reached by a ramp, are picturesquely set COTTAGES and beyond them a crenellated

Barskimming New Bridge.
Engraving by W. Angus, 1791

VIEWING PLATFORM built over a cave with ogival windows (cf. Stairaird and the gazebo, Mauchline, qq.v.). Walkways, carved from the rock face, lead to grottos and tunnels and offer spectacular and awesome views, an essential part of this romantic elaboration of nature. Further w a simpler bridge and picturesque L-plan, single-storey LODGE with a wide bay fronting the carriageway, its over-large pediment supported on Doric pilasters. Gothic arched windows with intersecting glazing bars.

STABLES, 200 m. N of the house across the gorge. Converted 1946–8 by *Alexander Dunlop*, mainly for domestic use. Weathervane dated 1774. Grand front elevation with entrance tower and wide, outer pedimented bays giving a taste of the quality of the house for which they were built. Entrance through a basket arch in the tower, above it a Venetian window, and an oculus, all under an ogee roof with a diminutive domed cupola. The same details occur in the outer bays where the carriage arches have been glazed.

BEITH

The town lies on the E hillside of the s-flowing Upper Garnock, close to the low pass between it and the NE-flowing Black Cart, and was thus a vital staging and trading post on what was the least challenging route from Glasgow into Ayrshire and s w Scotland. In the C19 it became a major centre for cabinetmaking and furniture, supplying, among others, many designers associated with the Arts and Crafts movement in Scotland. Today it is a growing, predominantly residential town, but one that at its core is recognizably medieval, with many good buildings from its Late Georgian growth.

CHURCHES AND CEMETERY

AULD KIRK, The Cross. One gabled arm survives of the cruciform church of *c.* 1593, converted to a mausoleum in the early C19. Roll-moulded, square-headed entrance. The crowstepped gable, ogee-headed bellcote and round-headed windows are *c.* 1754. – MONUMENT. John Spiers (outer N wall). By *F. T. Pilkington*, 1887–8,* it has an elaborate Dec surround framing a marble effigy of Spiers with weeping widow at his bedside and above him, in relief, his family in mourning and a host of angels. Smaller memorial to his family to the r. Small churchyard with a number of C18 headstones, and the square C18 Cochran–Patrick MAUSOLEUM, with a bolection-moulded entrance under a pulvinated frieze, now blocked.

BEITH HIGH PARISH CHURCH, Kirk Road. Built 1806–10 by *John Connell*** and *William Harvie*, masons, on a prominent hilltop site to the SW of the Auld Kirk (*see* above); clear evidence of the shift in focus of the Georgian town. Gothic, T-plan with geometrical windows, crenellated gables, pinnacles at the angles and a N tower with latticework parapet. In the wide S gable a well-wrought entrance with ogee-headed moulding, blind arcading in the spandrels under a billet moulding and flanking buttresses. The blind quatrefoil in the gable is by *William Railton*, who restored the church in 1884–5 after storm damage. Geometric windows to l. and r. Similar windows on the return elevations, and the other wings similarly treated. Three-light windows flank the projecting square five-stage tower. Wide S vestibule, with stone stairs and wooden banisters to either side, meeting at a central half-landing.

Dignified and numinous galleried INTERIOR, with dark-stained woodwork. Plastered walls with an unusual flowing zigzag cornice, and a heavily panelled boarded ceiling. Panelled gallery front, supported on cast-iron columns; re-set heraldic panel dated 1596, from the Giffen Loft in the previous church. The FITTINGS showcase the town's cabinet-works, and are dominated by the wide ORGAN CASE, of 1885, designed and executed by *John Pollock*; the tall Gothic PULPIT and the LECTERN are of 1928 by *George McKechnie* of *Beithcraft*; the FONT and COMMUNION TABLE are of 1896, by *Osborne*. – STAINED GLASS. A fine collection by *Gordon Webster*, with his characteristic use of much blue glass and rather stylized, angular figures. – In the W wall, Crucifixion, centre, of 1950,

---

* Originally at Spiers School (1887–8 by *James Sellars*; dem. 1986).
** Probably the *John Connell* of Hamilton who later built *David Hamilton*'s tower at Kilwinning Abbey and Burns Monument, Alloway. Proposals for a new church on a new site had first been aired in 1802, its plan 'taken from' that of *Robert & James Adam*'s Lasswade (Lothian) church of 1793.

and Love One Another, N, 1962. – In the E wall, the Three
Kings, 1942, N, and He is Risen, centre, of 1929 by *G. Maile
& Son*, pallid in comparison with Webster's vibrant blues. – In
the gallery, two roundels by *Webster* of 1936: The Ascension
(W), and Jesus with Mary Magdalen (E).

Octagonal panelled GATEPIERS to the S with ogival heads
and ball finials brought from Trearne House (1868, dem. 1954).
To the SW, HALLS of 1899 by *John Snodgrass*: semicircular shell
panels above the main door and flanking windows.

CHURCH OF JESUS CHRIST OF LATTER DAY SAINTS, Auldlea
Road. 1995 by *Abrahams Sagasti Architects*, Glasgow. A landmark, dramatized by a tall fibreglass flèche.

OUR LADY OF PERPETUAL SUCCOUR (R.C.), Mitchell Street.
1893 by *W. H. Howie & H. D. Walton*, as a United Presbyterian
church. Rock-faced rubble Gothic. The gabled S entrance front
has an octagonal SE tower and three stepped lancets; the
entrance is flanked by narrow cusped lights and stepped buttresses. The tower has one nicely conceived stage of narrow
lancets with pointed hoodmoulds and gargoyles.

TRINITY PARISH CHURCH, Trinity Crescent. 1882–3 by *Robert
Baldie*, though the site and plans had been agreed in 1875.
Simple Pointed Gothic. The S front has a narrow gable with
an octagonal four-stage SW angle tower and tall octagonal
stone spire. Pointed arch entrance between narrow lancets (cf.
Darvel Free Church, q.v.). A subsidiary entrance, under a
triangular pediment, on the buttressed W elevation. The polygonal buttressed apse is of 1924–6 by *Fryers & Penman*, who
rebuilt the church after a fire in 1917. Theirs is the bright,
spacious interior with panel-fronted galleries, plaster walls and
coved wooden queen-strut roof. The chancel has a plaster
ceiling, and contemporary FITTINGS, mostly made in the
town. Particularly impressive is the octagonal Gothic PULPIT
carved by *James Macneill* and *Andrew Jamieson*. The PANEL-
LING (a war memorial), COMMUNION TABLE and ELDERS'
CHAIRS all designed and executed by the congregation's Men's
Working Party, convened by *James Guy*. – STAINED GLASS.
Chancel, unshowy war memorial, 1926 by *John C. Hall & Co.*
of Glasgow. – Transept, N wall, a richly hued St Stephen, Mary
and St Paul by *Guthrie & Wells*, designed by *Davidson* (perhaps
Nina Miller Davidson). – S wall, a single light, a Second World
War memorial, *c.* 1946, a soldier praying. At its base a finely
carved wooden memorial plaque, designed by *Andrew Jamie-
son*, and executed in the works of *Macneill Brothers*.

CHURCH HALLS also 1924–6 by *Fryers & Penman*. Elements
of Lorimer mixed with Cotswold vernacular.

Former U.P. CHURCH, Head Street. Built 1784, classical, rectangular. Originally rendered, the stone now exposed. S front
with four tall round-headed windows and prominent pedimented two-storey porch. This has a pilastered entrance, with
flanking lights, within a shallow segmental recess, with broad
end pilasters and a (now blocked) round-headed pilastered
window above.

UNITED REFORMED CHURCH, Kings Road. 1863–4 as an Evangelical Union church, by *Robert Smith* of Beith. Simple Gothic. Gabled s entrance front with pointed windows under hoodmoulds with bell-like stops. Finialled end buttresses and an apical finial.

BEITH CEMETERY, Kings Road. 1863 by *Robert Snodgrass*. Spacious and well laid out burial ground, with views across the valley towards the hills. Many obelisks and shrouded urns. At the entrance a single-storey crowstepped LODGE and ornate gatepiers with stepped caps. Ahead, and to the r., of the entrance is an oval area, partially fringed with hedges, which shield the CHEST TOMB of the Ralston-Patricks of Tearne, with half-urn corners and well-lettered bronze plaques. Possibly of *c.* 1920. Around this are arrayed a number of other prominent MONUMENTS, including the broken pillar of the Dobie family, 'Designed And Erected By *W. Dobie*, 1866'; the three linking tapering columns, with an octagonal finial head, of John Foster of the Beith Academy, and his family, of *c.* 1891; and an obelisk on a plinth decorated with many trumpet-like details to the architect *Robert Snodgrass* †1897. – On the E wall, the crowstepped MONUMENT to John Muir, tanner, †1879, and family, by *Robert McLachlan*. – Close to this, the MacNeills' late C19 MONUMENT, an urn on a circular pedestal, is warmly embraced by its neighbouring yew.

PUBLIC BUILDINGS

BEITH COMMUNITY FIRE STATION, Kings Road. 1955 by *Robert G. Lindsay*, Ayr County Architect. Brick Modernism.

BEITH LIBRARY, Main Street. *See* Description, below.

BEITH PRIMARY SCHOOL, Barrmill Road. 1996–8 by *North Ayrshire Council*. Broadly symmetrical, with a brick base and sheet-metal upper floor, rising to a central ridge. Sheet-metal roofs of varied pitch sweep down to provide broad eaves over the bands of ground-floor windows. Decorated inside and out, the fruits of the authority's first collaboration with *Bruce McLean* (*see* also Dalry Primary School). – ARTWORK. *Mohammed Shadewi*'s 'Journey into School'. – STAINED GLASS by *Susan Bradbury*.

ORR PUBLIC PARK, Muirpark Road. Gifted to the town in 1870 by Robert Orr (†1874), a wealthy Beithonian in Croydon. The low boundary walls with unusual ogee-headed pottery copes presumably contemporary.

TELEPHONE EXCHANGE, Kings Road. *c.* 1962. Brick and tile-hung, with big windows in the side bays, allowing a clear view of the internal machinery.

TOWN HOUSE, The Strand/Eglinton Street. Dated 1817, by *William Dobie* as court house and public reading room, on first floor, above shops and a lock-up. Classical, of painted ashlar. Three bays to The Strand, and four-bay return elevation; ground-floor openings have segmental heads; upper windows

in frames; string course and end pilasters. Pedimented E gable
with open ogival-headed bellcote and slender weathervane.
WAR MEMORIAL. Janefield Place. 1920 by *Robert McLachlan*.
Foliated cross. The shaft has Celtic patterns.

DESCRIPTION

The ill-considered inner ring road, planned from 1959, badly
damages the historic core of the town, and effectively isolates
THE CROSS, a paved area in front of the Auld Kirk, from the
pattern of medieval streets to its E. The varied Georgian townscape on the W side and continuing into Eglinton Street has,
however, been admirably recovered by restoration and rebuilding of the houses by *Robert Potter & Partners* in 2003–8 as part
of a Townscape Heritage Initiative. At the corner, a two-storey
curved domestic frontage with a low wall-head gable (No. 32)
is mid-C18, revitalized by coloured render and stone dressings;
its harled neighbour to the r. is contemporary, but lower and
with a wall-head gable with a panelled stack and scrolled
skewputts. Nice central Tuscan doorway. Much larger is the
handsome classical three-storey Nos. 20–22; it is mid-C19, with
wide end pilasters to the upper floors, and an entrance to the
r. under a bracketed cornice.

The core of the medieval town is represented by REFORM
STREET and MAIN STREET, which run NE from The Cross;
both are narrow with the buildings pressing in on both sides.
Outwardly late C19 and later, though undoubtedly concealing
older structures. Many have been restored by *Robert Potter &
Partners*, often with wooden shopfronts with heavy panelled
pilasters. In Reform Street the harled five-bay former OLD
DEER INN is mid-C18 and has a central wall-head gable with
end pilasters, a curved bay to the r., and a gabled mid-C19 rear
wing. Main Street is predominantly Late Georgian on its l.
side, e.g. the five-bay Nos. 15–19, and the rendered six-bay
Nos. 35–41 (including Beith Library), with a pilastered shopfront to the r., and moulded skews to the lofty pitched slated
roof. The SMUGGLERS TAVERN, however, is mid-C18, with a
harled upper floor, a wall-head gable stack, rolled skews and
end pilasters, but its extravagant pub front is late C19: three
segmentally headed openings, flanked by pilasters, with a
bracketed cornice above. Less of interest on the opposite side,
but Nos. 26–30 are mid-C18, with a big central wall-head gable
stack, end pilasters and rolled skewputts, and an entrance in
cavetto reveals beneath a shallow bracketed cornice. Nos.
44–48, mid-C19, have one original shopfront, and a pend, with
a late C19 sign for 'Archd Dale Plumber'.

EGLINTON STREET, W of The Cross, provided the late C18 and
early C19 town with its main thoroughfare, and its relatively
unaltered urban character has been much enhanced. On the S
side, Nos. 1–7 of 1906–7 by *John Snodgrass*, with pedestal
skews, two parapeted oriels, one over the bracketed entrance,
with a pedestal pinnacle rising above it to the r., and the return

elevation of Nos. 1–3 The Strand. THE STRAND itself forms
the rather low-key heart of the post-medieval growth. A rectangular open space, given some additional emphasis by its
gentle upward slope, with at its head the CLYDESDALE BANK,
of 1902–6 by *Baird & Thomson*, a red sandstone free Baronial
confection which imposes its will on its surroundings.

On the N side of Eglinton Street, Nos. 2–8 have reinstated
late C19 shopfronts and sympathetically reconstructed slate
roofs with dormers. Adjoining are two late C18 buildings with
wall-head gables, the first of which is the remarkably unaltered
SARACEN'S HEAD, white-painted harl with painted margins,
two pilastered doorways with raised curved heads to their
cornices, original window openings, and in the gable, two small
windows and a central stack. More improved frontages further
on, and after those, the five-bay ashlar HALIFAX BANK. Late
C19, with rusticated quoins, dentilled cornice, panelled parapet,
and door and window with acroteria. The rendered Nos. 40–42
are *c.* 1800, with a simple central wall-head stack, while the
three-bay painted plaster No. 44 is late C18, with end pilasters,
and a neat wall-head stack on a small pedimented gable; its
doorway has Ionic half-columns, the entrance itself recessed
with pilasters and fanlight.

The S side also has another good group of buildings mostly
of *c.* 1800, beginning with the side elevation of the Town House
(*see* above), and two painted ashlar buildings of *c.* 1800, the
ANDERSON HOTEL, and its neighbour. The POST OFFICE is
the significant interloper, but in keeping for the date, 1897, with
an ashlar top storey that has shallow bows and a charming wall-
head gable, of two stacks connected by an arch framing a carved
and painted royal coat of arms. Among the following buildings
some pleasantly unaltered frontages, notably Nos. 37–39, in
well-presented cherry-cocked whin, with painted sills, margins
and base course, and a central entrance with cavetto reveals.

The residential continuation of Eglinton Street has a group
of attractive houses on the N side, following the curve of the
road. Mostly of *c.* 1810–25, of two storeys and three bays, all
with good details. The highlight is the gabled painted ashlar
one-and-a-half storey HILLSIDE (No. 76), of *c.* 1840. It has a
channelled basement, and steps leading to a recessed door with
Doric columns *in antis* and flanking pilasters. End pilasters,
panelled parapet and ground-floor windows with moulded
architraves. Three pilastered dormers, the outer ones with triangular pediments; the other with a segmental pediment and
scrolled brackets. On the l., No. 87 is a rubble-built cottage of
c. 1800, hipped at one end; four-centred windows in square
heads.

VILLAS etc.

ARRAN CRESCENT. – THE MEADOWS. Of *c.* 1880 and substantial: all crowstepped gables, and a central French tower with
wrought-iron balustrade.

BARRMILL ROAD. – KNOCKBUCKLE. Of *c.* 1840. A three-bay painted stucco hipped Tudor Gothic villa with lying-pane sash glazing throughout. Slightly advanced central bay, with stepped buttresses and blind lozenge parapet; the entrance has flanking windows, a hoodmould and a crenellated cornice. Battlemented parapets to the flanking bays and octagonal angle buttresses. Additional late C19 gabled bays to l. and r.; also to the l., single-storey offices, with segmental-headed cart entrance, and stone partly painted boundary walls. – TAYNISH. Ashlar and classical. Gabled, end pilasters, Doric porch: ground-floor windows in bolection frames; pediments with acroteria to door and lower windows, upper windows in lugged architraves.

BIGHOLM ROAD. – HAMILFIELD. *c.* 1850. A substantial and boldly detailed villa, with Italianate details. Of squared rubble; the porch in the re-entrant plastered with a round-headed entrance below a fanlight, with a two-light round-arched window above; a Venetian window on the other elevation.

JANEFIELD PLACE. An irregularly shaped area around the war memorial (*see* Public Buildings). Mostly late C19 terraces and tenements, also found in neighbouring streets such as Kings Road and Muirpark Road. One delightful exception: SCAPA COTTAGE, single storey with pedimented porch and canted bays l. and r. Stone, each block with deeply incised, seemingly random decoration. This extends to the side elevation and to the low boundary wall. Presumably late C19 and strikingly similar to the decoration on the String Road postbox on Arran (*see* Machrie, p. 715).

LAIGH ROAD. Some good COUNCIL HOUSING of 1926 for Ayr County Council by *James Houston*. The very smart Baronial three-bay VICTORIA VILLA is dated 1874 and was built for Matthew Pollock, one of the town's leading cabinet manufacturers. It has highly decorative bargeboards to gables and dormers, perhaps an advertisement for Pollock's business. It is indeed surprising that one sees so little evidence of the local carpentry and joinery skills in the town's buildings.

GEILSLAND SCHOOL, Geilsland Road, 0.5 km. SE. A well-detailed, asymmetrical, multi-gabled Gothic villa, built in 1867–8 for William Fulton Love, a local author. Converted as a Church of Scotland approved school in 1964. Open gabled porch with finials and a hoodmoulded, dwarf pointed arcade. Octagonal turret with bracketed dentilled cornice and fish-scale slate roof adjoining lower N range. Interior remarkably well preserved. Central top-lit well stair with highly decorative open Gothic arcade at the landing with a different coloured marble for each squat column, square stone caps and pointed arches. Stained glass in top light of *c.* 2000 with images of the house and other buildings in the grounds as well as illustrations of activities. Very decorative deeply moulded plasterwork in the entrance hall and main rooms, with leaves, scrolls, lattices and rosettes. Original chimneypieces.

Within the grounds a simple CHAPEL, created in 1973–6 from a former estate building. Furnishings from a chapel at Millport. Stained glass by *Gail Muir* (made by the *Lighthouse Glass Co.*, Irvine). – LISMORE HOUSE, of 2000, is an accommodation block with an unusual top light, a gable breaking the eaves over the entrance, and a circular tower on the w gable with a faceted slate roof. An original if not very coherent design.

GRANGEHILL, Threepwood Road, 1.1 km. NE. Built 1804 for John Fulton. A well-proportioned three-bay house, painted render with stone quoins and a Doric-columned doorpiece. Single-storey wings added to l. and r. in similar style, the r. extended again *c.* 1900 when the house was substantially remodelled and a large, ashlar three-storey bowed bay inserted to the r. of the door, each storey slightly jettied and with a deeply overhanging coolie-hat roof, in the Glasgow style. Large drawing room extension at rear. Remodelled inside (*c.* 1900) with plenty of panelling, decorative plaster ceilings and marble chimneypieces. STABLE COURT of 1868, rubble-built with pediment over (blocked) elliptically arched entrance, and small arched windows in the outer gabled bays of main front, now converted for residential use.

GIFFEN HOUSE. *See* p. 334.

BELLSBANK
4000

Almost wholly mid-C20 *Ayr County Council* housing, succeeding the many isolated and inadequate miners' rows of the Doon Valley.

BELLSBANK PARISH CHURCH, Shalloch Place. 1956–8. Simple hall church with regularly spaced flat-headed openings and a later wide-eaved hall to the s.

BELLSBANK PRIMARY SCHOOL, Craiglea Crescent. 1952–5 by *Robert G. Lindsay*, County Architect, using the prefabricated aluminium system developed by the Bristol Aircraft Co.; a rare survival. Later additions and alterations.

CRAIGENGILLAN. *See* p. 229.

BENSLIE
3040

One of several miners' villages developed in this area in the early C19 but abandoned and deserted after coal was exhausted by the late C19. The area has largely reverted to agriculture, and despite being so close to Irvine, it feels remote and other-worldly.

Former FERGUSHILL PARISH CHURCH. 1878–9 by *William Railton*. Closed 2009. Gothic with a tower and octagonal spire. Five-light window above a trefoil-headed door.

MONTGREENAN HOUSE. *See* p. 545.

BLACK CLAUCHRIE

3080

6.3 km. NE of Barrhill

The epitome of a luxurious sporting lodge, in the little-known wild moorlands close to the Dumfries and Galloway border. Built for the Austen family in 1898–1901 by *J. K. Hunter* (assisted by *Matthew Adam* and *James Carrick*) in a restrained asymmetrical Arts and Crafts manner, austerely harled with red sandstone dressings (*see* also Templetonburn, Crookedholm). Tall, of two storeys with an attic and a raised basement, with a cross-wing the width of the main block at the NW end. Much of its character is imparted by the gables, some with ashlar heads and others with crowsteps. The entrance has a red sandstone doorpiece with a semicircular pediment, reached by steps from the court. This was a late modification caused by the addition of the billiard room (by *Carrick*) to the SE and its link with the house. The billiard room has a six-light mullioned window and a big canted bay in red sandstone. Of the loggia which formerly embraced this block's lower level only the decorative cast-iron uprights remain.

Interior predictably full of stained panelling, both plain and moulded, and beaten metal decoration to chimneypieces and door furniture. Many original light fittings. The best decoration is in the billiard room which has panelled walls. A large conservatory projects NW.

An extensive NE service range has been demolished but to the N are other ranges including kennels, game larder, laundry etc. Large WALLED GARDEN brick-built with tall gatepiers capped with ball finials, the latter used in the service court too, and gardener's cottage.

BLAIR CASTLE

3040

1.8 km. SE of Dalry

49   Among the most important estates in Ayrshire, this was the seat of the Blairs of Blair from *c.* 1205, when William de Blair appears in a contract, and, in Paterson's words, 'this very ancient family is connected by intermarriages with the best in the west of Scotland, and has enjoyed a high rank in Ayrshire'. The Castle remained in the family until 2011.

Built on a semicircular whinstone platform above the steep banks of the Bombo Burn, Blair is a large mansion of three and four storeys. The irregularity of its multitude of roofs is clear evidence of its complex evolution, further suggested by the details of masonry and fenestration, and underlined by the variety of wall thicknesses. The earliest part of Blair Castle is the tower house which Pont (1604–8) described as an 'ancient castell and strong dominioun veill beautiful with gardens orchards and partiers'. But seen from the SE approach its character is essentially C17, the consequence of the addition in 1688 of the three-storey SW range, forming the stem of the present T-plan, and a four-storey stair-tower in the inner SE angle containing the

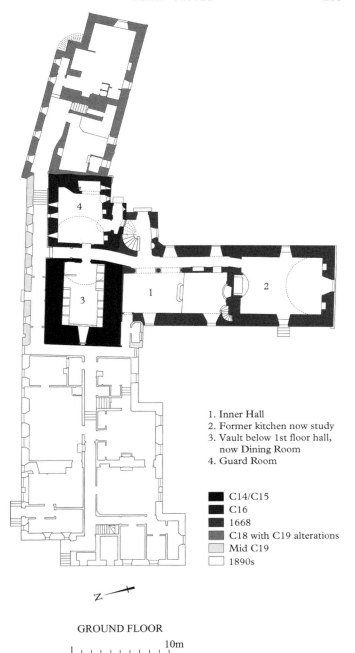

1. Inner Hall
2. Former kitchen now study
3. Vault below 1st floor hall,
   now Dining Room
4. Guard Room

■ C14/C15
■ C16
■ 1668
■ C18 with C19 alterations
□ Mid C19
□ 1890s

GROUND FLOOR

⊢ ı ı ı ı ı ı ı ı ı ı ⊣ 10m

Blair Castle.
Plan showing phasing

entrance. The large NW wing, added in the 1890s by *Thomas Leadbetter* of *Leadbetter & Fairley*, continues the C17 character.

The TOWER HOUSE, probably C14, embedded at the head of the T-plan, is rectangular, of 8.23 m. by 7.62 m. with 1.8-m.-thick walls. Some fragments of the walling of the two upper floors are still visible on the NE front, and both alterations to the windows and the mutilated wall-head (now concealed in the roof space) suggest that at some point, the tower was lowered to make its height consistent with the roof of the C17 wing. Adjoining the tower to the SE, a rectangular extension of similar height, slightly set back on the SW front and in line at the rear. It is probably mid-C15 and perhaps accommodated the kitchen, now known as the Guard Room (a stone water pipe was found in the large chimney on its E gable). Its entrance is concealed by the C17 stair-tower and is reached instead via a narrow passageway behind the new stair through an inserted porch-tower to the r. of the main entrance. This porch has a carved lintel, dated 1617, with the initials of Bryce Blair and Anabel Wallace, and an even earlier reset ogee-headed lintel with the initials of Roger de Blair and Mary Mure above. The original tower probably had its entrance at the first floor but any evidence is now hidden by later reordering. A small projection at the W angle of the original tower, now greatly remodelled, may have housed a stair and appears to have been cut down in height.

William Blair's late C17 SW WING extends for four irregular bays and has a substantial stair projection, probably replacing an earlier newel stair-tower, but does not join the Guard Room's SE wall because to do so would have blocked its entrance. Above the simply pilastered doorway of the late C17 entrance, a shield bearing the arms of William Blair and Lady Margaret Hamilton (daughter of the 2nd Duke of Hamilton) impaled and framed with flat Baroque scrolls originally with a pediment. Above this again in a simple bolection-moulded frame is a further simple escutcheon with the initials BB and a date 1203, but of doubtful origin. The addition has ogee-pedimented dormerheads, sporting Blair and Hamilton initials. On both long elevations there are substantial wall-head stacks, more than are apparently necessary. In the wing's SW elevation is a blocked doorway, and the varied dressings of the windows, particularly on the SW gable, indicate other later alterations.

SE of the mid-C15 tower is a simple three-storey range of five bays, added in the C18 but raised over the W three bays and given a C17 appearance by *Thomas Leadbetter* in 1891–3. At the same time he erected the substantial four-storey NW WING, a gaunt block with self-conscious corbelling below crowstepped gables and pedimented wall-head dormers. Elaborate dormerheads also dominate the two-storey projection (1890s) built over the mid-C19 linking passage between the SE wing and the service court, across the NE wall of the original tower house;

the windows light the dining room created by removing the NE wall of the tower at first-floor level (its hall), and Leadbetter embellished them with more initials and carved coats of arms.

The INTERIOR has been substantially altered. The stair of 1668 rises in a semicircular flight around a small open well reusing some stone treads but with C18 twisted balusters. At ground-floor level the inner hall, with a stone arched screen and panelling by Leadbetter, gives access, via a passage, to the vaulted SW room, the former C17 kitchen but remodelled 1892 by Leadbetter as a study for Col. Frederick Blair and given a plaster-panelled barrel vault and a bombastic medieval-style chimneypiece with a pedimented hood elaborately carved with thistles, and a framed coat of arms. Leading NE from the inner hall there is a passage cut into the thickness of the original tower wall c. 1845 by Captain William Fordyce Blair, providing access to the vaulted chambers of the tower, the Guard Room at ground-floor level and via the rear passage to the C18 wing. The Guard Room has a disused door, to the earlier lost stair-turret, various defensive slots or ventilation openings, presses or storage recesses as well as the drain suggesting it has been used as a kitchen.

On the first floor, the principal rooms are entered from a wide landing. The two rooms of the late C17 SW wing have been united to give a large drawing room, created in the later C19 when a fluted Ionic-columned screen replaced the dividing wall (creating a hazardous route for the flue for the study fireplace below and also partially screening a small mural stair). The door is Neoclassical, set in a broken pedimented frame with rinceau in the frieze and flanked by similarly detailed bookcases. But, surprisingly, the ceiling has Jacobean-style geometric plasterwork with inserted coats of arms oddly mixed with classically detailed cornices. On the SW wall a high-quality marble chimneypiece and on the SE wall, towards the N end, another with eagles carrying the mantelshelf on their wings, both brought in, the latter said to come from a house in Rutland. The former great hall of the tower was first altered as a chapel in the C18 and in 1782 remodelled as the dining room. Enlarged in the general remodelling by Leadbetter in the 1890s when the NE wall of the hall was removed and given half-height oak panelling and a huge wooden chimneypiece with twisted columns.

The rooms in the Guard Room tower and in the 1668 tower still have C18 fittings, particularly shutters and some chimneypieces. Elsewhere all is 1891–2, either remodelled or as designed by Leadbetter mostly in C18 style but with some flattened Jacobean-style plaster ceilings. The half-lapped collar-beamed roof over the 1668 wing retains its wooden pegged sarking.

STABLES. S of the house. A delightful Gothick front, c. 1800, with castellated parapet and towered middle, over the pend, that has a pair of quatrefoils. Now attractively altered to form a dower house by *ARP Lorimer & Associates* and *Ronald Alexander*.

NORTH LODGE. 1858 and single-story, SOUTH LODGE early C19 and one-and-a-half storeys. FORESTER'S COTTAGE and SMITHY COTTAGES, early C19 with Gothick detailing to some windows.

POLICIES. Enclosed within park walls of 1840 and mainly laid out in the C19 with shelter belts and woodland, nearer the house some fine specimen trees and many rhododendrons. To the N of Bombo Burn, a WALLED GARDEN with C18 Italian wrought-iron gates in one entrance.

BLAIR HOUSE
2.75 km. NNE of Old Dailly

2000

Remotely set high on the S-facing slopes of the Girvan valley. Originally a three-bay house expanded in 1883–5 by Eugene Wason into an asymmetrical villa of incongruously suburban character. Tough rock-faced red sandstone with applied timber framing in the gables. Billiard room extension to the E, *c.* 1900 with large mullion-and-transomed windows. Steading court to the E, probably early C19.

BLAIRQUHAN
1.5 km. NW of Straiton

3000

71   One of the finest country houses in Ayrshire, with a parkland setting to match. The estate had been acquired in 1798 by Sir James Hunter Blair, banker and some time Lord Provost of Edinburgh, from the Whitefoords who had been ruined by the failure of the Ayr Bank.

The present house is of 1820–4 by *William Burn* for Sir David Hunter Blair, replacing a castle built *c.* 1570 for John Kennedy, which may have stood where the lawn now is. Burn's commission followed an unsuccessful proposal for remodelling the old castle in 1813 (by *James Gillespie Graham*) and a scheme of 1818 for a new house by *Robert Wallace*, the architect of neighbouring Cloncaird (q.v.).

EXTERIOR. From the W and S the house has an assured presence created by Burn's mastery of subtle asymmetry and the beautifully detailed grey sandstone masonry. Hoodmoulded mullion-and-transom windows predominate, and crenellated parapets, detailed to correspond with the importance of their position, surround the entire wall-head. The front elevation illustrates clearly the hierarchy of planning. Firstly, at the W end of the S entrance elevation, is the imposing two-storey block containing the public rooms. The entrance is off-centre in a wider bay with the most detailed Gothic decoration. It is given drama by the massing of the large vaulted *porte cochère*, two elegant octagon turrets with Gothic panelling that rise through the main parapet, and behind this, the lantern tower rising high above the central saloon. At its angles are turrets which rose higher still before their chimneys were capped. Slender octagon turrets also clasp the angles of the house and give emphasis, e.g. on the W front to a tall canted window which has a bold frieze of stylized roses and a free-standing gable at the top. This curious motif, so out of character with Burn's usual practical logic, derives from Dalmeny House, Lothian (by Wilkins, 1814–17), and appears also at Burn's Carstairs (Lanarkshire, also begun in 1821 and of which Blairquhan is a variation). The asymmetry of the composition is most marked on the N elevation which, because of the fall in the ground, is of three storeys and has a restlessness produced by a double-height bay at the r., and a large oriel which lights the stair. On the main front the plainer and lower family wing extends E and is anchored by a squat crenellated tower with a first-floor oriel. Dropping down again is the barely visible kitchen court (part converted into estate offices by *Michael Laird* from 1967). This is entered through an arch on the E elevation and within the court Burn skilfully incorporated flamboyant carved decoration from the old castle. The motifs, particularly the robust rope mouldings, are reminiscent of decoration at Seagate Castle, Irvine (q.v.). The doorway to the family wing is the reused entrance archway from the great C16 or early C17 frontal range of the old castle.

INTERIOR. Inside, the attention to detail and the very high quality is maintained. The emphasis on Gothic detail seen on the outside of the entrance bay runs through the Entrance Hall, the Saloon and the Stair compartment. The low plaster-vaulted ENTRANCE HALL opens into the high drama of the Gothic SALOON, rising 18.2 m. into a lierne-vaulted lantern, and encircled by a gallery with a refined Gothic cast-iron balustrade. The inspiration is the larger and classically detailed hall at Kinmount House, Dumfriesshire (by Robert Smirke, 1812–18), but displays Burn's control of proportion and detail. Strong symmetry in the disposition of the Tudor-arched doorways, some of them dummy, all hoodmoulded with stiff-leaf label stops and with expertly crafted Gothic panelling. Stone chimneypieces flank the large archway to the STAIR HALL, which has an imperial stair rising to a half-landing in the big oriel window. The tracery pattern of balustrade repeats that of the saloon gallery, and over the stair is another lierne vault with more splendid bosses.

The public rooms entered from the Saloon are in contrast classically detailed, a stylistic separation also reflecting the influence of Wilkins at Dalmeny. SW of the hall the SMALL DRAWING ROOM, designed as a billiard room, well-proportioned architraves and cornices to the doors. Cornice of standard classical mouldings with a bold Greek key on the flat of the ceiling and a striking large leaf design to the central rose. Same details in the interconnecting DRAWING ROOM, which is lit from two sides, and also in the DINING ROOM (SE) which has a black marble chimneypiece. The LIBRARY, NE, is plainer. Burn's bookcases are now painted white. From the centre of the E side of the Saloon at each floor a doorway opens into a

long central passageway serving the family rooms. The basement is stone-vaulted on the S side but on the N fully above
ground level and originally devoted to service and servant
accommodation.

The STABLE COURT lies immediately E of the kitchen court. A
fully developed Jacobean design, the big shaped gable over the
entrance arch being a very early example of this revived style.
To the E again the ICE HOUSE, c. 1823, constructed with an
unusually wide opening. Inside it is a deep, curved square-plan
chamber rising into a domed roof with a central drain at the
bottom. Uphill to the S the large WALLED GARDEN, enclosed
on three sides. Along the N wall a wide terrace with a strong
brick retaining wall, raised up above the garden, and steps to
the garden with urns crowning the piers. The GLASSHOUSE,
probably late C19, had an entrance gable supported on unusual
stone columns with acanthus mouldings at top and bottom,
presumably reused. The KENNELS are 1820s, with a five-bay
cottage with central door and piended roof flanked by two
ranges with single-slope roofed kennels and cast-iron fenced
dog runs.

In 1803 a scheme for improving the PARK was commissioned
from *Thomas White*. While White may have stimulated ideas it
was *Sir David Hunter Blair*'s own scheme for the landscape that
was implemented while the old castle still stood. The house is
sited on the edge of a very substantial platform which drops
down steeply N to a picturesque bend in the River Girvan
which was created by Sir David by diverting the river to its old
course. Views extend across the parkland to hills beyond. To
the S of the house are extensive lawns and gently rising land
framed by mature planting. Long drives wind through the
wooded policies, and the one from the Ayr Lodge provides
picturesque glimpses of the house worthy of *Northanger Abbey*.

The lodges are 1820s, single-storey with shallow gabled bays,
with Burn's hallmark. GIRVAN LODGE the best, an irregular
cruciform with overhanging gables in the form of open pediments, a porch in the angle with a bold octagonal pier anchoring it. Beside Ayr Lodge, a pleasing BRIDGE by *Burn*, c. 1821,
with a wide Tudor arch. The design said to be a present from
Burn to his patron.

MILTON HOUSE, 1 km. E of the house by the Girvan. The dower
house, built c. 1885, and in style like a mid-Victorian suburban
villa with a French-roofed tower. Joined to an earlier cottage
and steading-like range, in an informal U-plan; a long detached
range at right angles with three cart arches and domestic
accommodation at one end. Close by, OLD MILTON MILL,
early C19, now converted for residential use.

BLANEFIELD
1 km. W of Kirkoswald

A country house in refined Arts and Crafts style built for Sir John
Richmond by *James Miller*, 1913–19. Richmond was the first

captain of the Turnberry Golf Club and would have known Miller's work for the Turnberry Hotel (q.v.).

The house is a Z-plan set on a gentle hill with broad vistas to the coast and Ailsa Craig, currently obscured by planting. Broad sweeping dark slate roofs contrasted with Voyseyish chimneys, the white-harled first floor and cream stone ground floor. On the entrance front the stone facing is carried up to the full height of the two-storey gabled bay at the r. and the tall, parapeted porch. First-floor windows nestle under the eaves in the inner bays. The garden front is altogether sleeker, the materials giving a strongly horizontal emphasis, a theme continued in the bands of small casement windows, stone-mullioned for the ground floor, timber above. On this front also a pleasant asymmetry of one bay projecting under a gable and the other with a half-hipped roof. The hierarchy of the internal planning is expressed in the varying scales of the ranges, the lowest of these being the service wing to the S, returning to form a small open court.

Inside, the plan segregated family and guests from the servants. The vestibule, lined with panels of warm red herringbone brickwork, opens into a stone-floored and panelled outer hall. To its N, the LIBRARY, originally fitted with walnut bookcases and a walnut and tiled chimneypiece (now painted as part of redecoration in 1996 by *Michael Priest*). Opposite the front door, in the centre of the W front, the large, oak-panelled HALL which has a ceiling framed with a plaster band depicting birds pecking grapes. This room connects by large double doors to the well-lit DRAWING ROOM at the NW which has an elaborate cornice modelled with garden flowers. The hall connects via the stair hall to the DINING ROOM towards the S end of the house and with another elaborate frieze, this time of hunting scenes. A spine corridor runs behind this sequence of rooms to provide discreet circulation and access to the service rooms along the E front and in the S wing (now altered).

MOTOR HOUSE. Spacious U-plan with a covered inspection area and chauffeur's house. Continuing the harled streamline appearance of the house with big slate roof and slate-hung gables. Further S a large WALLED GARDEN attached to the earlier steading buildings at the E. Further E again, a pair of semi-detached COTTAGES with half-piended projecting gables and open porches in the re-entrant angles. The rear elevation opens onto a court, formerly part of the steading.

BOURTREEHILL

3030

Irvine

Originally a small landed estate with a late C19 country house by *R. S. Ingram*. This was demolished in the 1970s, and the area identified in the Irvine New Town Plan for major residential growth. Almost all of the housing is by the *Irvine Development Corporation*, and shows their fondness for simple vernacular styles. The layout of the estate is based on pedestrian–traffic separation, while a perimeter bus-only road provided easy access to public transport.

In a determinedly ecumenical piece of urban planning, the parish and Roman Catholic churches face each other across the narrow North Vennel.

RELIEF (BOURTREEHILL) PARISH CHURCH. 1976–8 by *Hay Steel & Partners*. Blockwork with a sheet-metal fascia, projecting windows in angled reveals and a stumpy triangular belltower, all rather irregular and unsettled. More cohesive interior; church (r.) and hall (l.), separated by a demountable wall (cf. St Kentigern, Kilmarnock). Bold ORGAN CASE and PULPIT, with overlapping timber boards.

ST JOHN OGILVIE (R.C.). 1977–9 by *Douglas Niven & Gerard Connolly* of Glasgow. Octagonal, with a priests' house to the l., a hall to the r., and a linking vestibule running along the NE (North Vennel) elevation. Boldly massed wooden framed glazing, especially at eaves level in the church and along the NE elevation. From the NE vestibule one descends into the arresting interior, distinguished by a complex open roof of principal beams with prominent pegs, and ceilings crisscrossed by paired beams creating a rich lozenge pattern. – Tiled FONT and PULPIT. – STAINED GLASS by *Paul Lucky*, 1994, including a Burning Bush, and a rich skull-like Crown.

Bourtreehill is not immune to the vicissitudes which bedevil all mass housing developments, but the strengths of the design remain apparent. Some of the most characteristic early *Irvine Development Corporation* HOUSING is in MOORFOOT PLACE, and other streets (1977–8, *David Simister*, project architect) close to the two churches. Paved and setted footpaths, tall harled blocks, of various heights, with broad raised dressings and some monopitched roofs, and a wide variation in colourwash, from white to dark olive green. In and off FENCEDYKE WAY, some 400 houses (*Sue Thornley* and *Jenny Smiley*, project architects, *c.* 1976–80), in varying combinations of types, thoughtfully composed, creating a distinctive identity for each group. Particularly attentive landscaping. In GIGHA TERRACE the house numbers, where they survive, are a good example of I.D.C.'s eye for graphic detail.

BRISBANE

3.2 km. N of Largs

BRISBANE HOUSE of 1636 (known as Kelsoland until 1671) was destroyed during the Second World War. 100 m. W of its site is a ruinous OBSERVATORY, erected in 1808 by *Sir Thomas Brisbane*, who inherited the estate in 1812*. It has a semicircular S

---

* As Governor of New South Wales from 1821, Brisbane built a similar observatory at Parramatta and produced the first major catalogue of southern hemisphere stars. In 1826 he returned to his wife's estate of Makerstoun (Borders), where he built a further observatory.

projection, doubtless for telescopic observation, and formerly a domed roof and hexagonal porch. The observatory and two circular stone MERIDIAN PILLARS, 300 m. N and S respectively, are aligned with the Three Sisters in Largs (*see* p. 508).

BRISBANE MAINS FARM, 200 m. N. Symmetrical painted stone classical farmstead of *c.* 1812 by *James Gillespie*, with a tall central pend and two storeys of flanking windows beneath a pedimented gable. A 1622 date stone is re-set on the inner face of the pend. Late C19 wings enclose a rear courtyard.

BRUNSTOUN CASTLE see DAILLY

BRUNTWOOD
3.5 km. S of Galston

5030

A heavily restored laird's house of *c.* 1700 with the Moor family coat of arms set into a steeply pitched pediment over the bolection-moulded main entrance. It is rectangular, of two storeys and three windows wide, rubble-built with dressed margins and a steep crowstepped gabled roof. Low wings form a N courtyard. There appears to have been a projecting wing on this front of the house, perhaps as at Sornhill (q.v.). By 1778 when James Boswell visited its estate was very reduced in size.

CAPRINGTON CASTLE
1.5 km. E of Gatehead

4030

The seat of the Cuninghame family, set in extensive parkland overlooking the partially canalized River Irvine. It is a muscular essay in Adam's Castle Style, the result of a major recasting 1829–30 by *Patrick Wilson* for J. Cuninghame-Smith W.S., who inherited the estate in the earlier year through his wife. Wilson was dressing up a genteel remodelling of 1797 (made after proposals of 1780 for a Neoclassical house by *David Henderson* were abandoned) which incorporated a tower house (approximately 14.6 m. by 10 m.) probably of C15 date to which a substantial wing, containing a newel stair, had been added in the early to mid C17.

72

The house has a big, full-height, canted bay in the centre of its SE front, introduced in the 1797 Georgianization and raised by Wilson to form an imposing tower with bold crenellations. The fortified character is further emphasized by its elevation on a terrace with strongly battered walls and a rib-vaulted *porte-cochère* in the form of a gatehouse with chunky angle turrets and a machicolated bartizan over its Tudor-arched entrance. The angles of the main house are clasped by conspicuous, buttress-like crenellated turrets, set diamond-wise and sporting mock slit windows; in contrast SE-facing canted windows introduced in the principal floor are purely domestic. The C15 work is now concealed in the S end: see the rubble masonry on the SW elevation and the blind windows on the SE front concealing the 2.1 m. thickness of the keep walls. Wilson raised the drum of its stair-tower into a tall, crenellated cylinder, which effectively links the main block to the asymmetrical massing of the low service wing of the same date to the NW. This is more characteristic of its period and has a fine, hood-moulded Gothic window under a pointed gable housing the larder and servants' quarters, and ends in a big square, squat tower with crenellated parapet and octagonal angle turret. The details are varied and done with some relish. The restrained NW extension to the house is *c.* 1900 by *Basil Slade* of London and has a prominent recess with a wilfully Moorish arched head, a motif found again on the W front where Slade created an oriel-like link from the house to a dining room made in part of the service wing.

The INTERIOR is firmly early C19 Gothic, with pointed-arched doors and rib-vaulted ceilings. A generous flight of stone steps, with an elaborately arched balustrade with fleur-de-lis detail, leads up from the confined lower hall to the principal HALL. Four-centred Gothic arches with attached colonnettes and stiff-leaf capitals frame the panels on the side walls, and in the canted bay two-light round-arched windows set into square-headed openings have blind intersecting arched panels below. The colonnettes flanking these windows and the wall panels rise into the rib-vaulted ceiling with a central pendant and elaborately moulded bosses with naturalistic leaves, birds and animals. More crisp and inventive leafy plaques in the cornice. This medieval hall leads to the *tour de force*, the vast, full-height, open-well STAIR rising through three galleried floors to the tall, panelled and ribbed top-lit cupola. Each of its walls is filled with a pair of romantic paintings illustrating the seasons. The high-quality balustrade of the lower hall continues with yards of mahogany handrail. To the l. of the hall, occupying the position of the C15 hall, the DRAWING ROOM. Plain ribbed ceiling, a replacement of *c.* 1900, and a probably contemporary white marble chimneypiece with ormolu panels. Off the hall to the l., a plaster-vaulted corridor with the DINING ROOM to the N and LIBRARY to the S, both with plaster rib-vaults, decorative bosses and corbels, and with white marble chimneypieces with eagles peering out from the Corinthian capitals of their pilasters. BOUDOIR on first floor in the centre with bay window with bold vine cornice and anthemion moulding above. Sinuous French-manner chimneypiece of *c.* 1900 with female caryatids and frothy central panel with musical instruments, elaborate gilded wallpaper also French in style.

To the SW, a handsome, two-storey STABLE, square with a pedimented entrance arch. Picturesque early C19 GARDEN COTTAGE to S, the windows in squared recesses with intersecting Gothic glazing. Two diminutive simple pedimented LODGES with pedimented tripartite windows; linked by a low retaining walls, pairs of solid square gatepiers and decorative cast-iron gates.

CARLUNG HOUSE   *1040*
1.5 km. N of West Kilbride

A Neo-Elizabethan manor house (now flats) of 1930–2 by
J. Austen Laird for his uncle Robert Barr, a whisky and shipping
magnate. The previous house burnt in 1902. Elizabethan
double E-plan with a lower service wing to the N, the masonry
stippled red sandstone ashlar, with contrasting creamy-grey
dressings, including diamond-shaped stacks. The wings have
curved angles, corbelled to square above. Over the door a
carved Viking ship, and to the l. a quatrefoil panel with a
dolphin flanked by narrow windows. The same motif appears
on the S elevation, which is perhaps the most pleasing in its
simplicity. The W (garden) front is the grandest, raised above a
basement with a smart balustraded perron rising to a terrace.
In the wings on this side, massive two-storey canted oriel
windows, supported on bulbous corbel tiers with corbelled
parapets. Handsome carved Chinese lions guards the SW corner
of the terrace parapet. Inside, stair and gallery survive with
much panelling, pilaster decoration and beamed ceilings.

CARNELL   *4030*
4 km. E of Craigie

The house stands on a bluff on the S bank of Cessnock Water.
Its present appearance is strongly Victorian, the consequence of
two major phases of enlargement in 1843 by *William Burn* and
David Bryce, for Colonel John Ferrier Hamilton, and 1880 by
Charles Reid of *Wardrop & Reid*. But on the W approach its evolu-
tion from a small late C15/early C16 tower house built for the
Wallaces of Cairnhill (Carnell) becomes clear.

The tower is simple, rubble-built, of three storeys and in character like Craufurdland (q.v.), but probably earlier. Continuous
corbelling with putative open bartizans supports the wall-walk,
but the original plain parapet crudely replaced in the mid C20
in red sandstone with crenellations, an unnecessarily fortified
conceit. Crowstepped gables behind, with big gable-end stacks
probably rebuilt by Burn. The central door in this elevation is
C20 and all the windows C18 enlargements. Peeping up behind
the roof is the crowstepped caphouse of its square stair-turret;
this was probably built in 1569 by Hew Wallace and Isobel
Mure, on the evidence of a datestone with their initials.*
Burn's substantial two-storey-and-attic additions form an
L-plan range to the S and E. The symmetrical S front has three
dominating crowstepped gables, the central one advanced. At
the angles bold square corbelled turrets with pyramid roofs of
the type used by Burn and Bryce at Tollcross House, Glasgow.
In the centre, however, a rather incongruous Neo-Georgian

---

* This was removed by Burn but survives. It is inscribed 'Wt. out the lord be maister
of the wark. He bigis in vain tho ever so strong.'

doorway with pilasters, sidelights and an overarching fanlight. It superseded the former entrance in a smartly gabled bay at the s end of the e front which retains its Renaissance-detailed swan-necked pedimented doorcase. On this front more of the angle turrets, but nestling against them also pedimented dormers to the first-floor windows, a deliberate design and not indicating, as some have suggested, that the turrets were added. N of this part is the 1871 addition, also L-plan, linked at its rear to fragments of C17 courtyard buildings associated with the tower, the most obvious survival a curved stair-turret corbelled to square at the first floor and finished with a crowstepped gable.

The placing of the doorway on the s front made possible a successful internal rearrangement that included the creation of a large hall with glazed bookcases and a large chimneypiece. From it the square stair compartment is entered and makes a link with the tower. Adamesque chimneypieces in the main rooms may have been inserted by Reid. Off the stair hall an entrance to the vaulted ground floor of the tower. Off the main stair the newel stair to the barrel-roofed attic gallery with access to bedrooms remodelled in the C18.

WALLED GARDEN. 1843, with an arched gateway to the old quarry water garden. Garden house built on the N wall, 1973. Extensive ornamental gardens laid out by Georgina Hamilton Findlay, 1906–14. Opposite the C20 entrance, beyond the immediate garden a lime-tree plantation representing two squares of Scottish soldiers at the battle of Dettingen, 1743. Four stalwart square-plan GATEPIERS c. 1843 with later ornamental metal gates; LODGE by *James Cairns*, 1907.

CARNELL HOME FARM. Mid C19. Imposing roadside range in neatly coursed rubble with slate roofs. Two-storey four-bay house at the centre, low dairy buildings attached to N, further low range s of house, and byre and storage ranges at right angles and parallel to the rear.

CARWINSHOCH *see* SAUCHRIE

₃₀₁₀ ## CASSILLIS HOUSE
2.5 km. sw of Dalrymple

A substantial late C14 tower house, most probably built for John Kennedy of Dunure (q.v.) who acquired the estate from Marjorie de Montgomerie and her cousin. David Kennedy became Earl of Cassillis in 1509. Substantial remodelling took place in the later C17, when a stair jamb was added and the upper works remodelled, with advice from *Sir William Bruce* with whom the 7th Earl was in correspondence in 1673–4. Further alterations were planned in the 1780s but only partially completed, probably by *Hugh Cairncross*, the clerk of works for the 10th Earl at Culzean Castle (q.v.) and an able designer. Finally, c. 1830–2, a considerable addition in an embryo Baronial style by *David Bryce*, while he was still in Burn's office.

The castle commands a prominent position high above the S bank of the Doon and is set in well-wooded policies. In the picturesque ensemble seen on the approach, all three main phases are easily recognized. The FRONT RANGE is Bryce's, built of lightly stugged pale pink masonry and of two storeys over a basement. Its principal, E-facing elevation is asymmetrical with, off-centre, an advanced, crowstepped bay containing the entrance. This has a heavily bracketed, open pedimented canopy with Jacobean decoration, bearing close resemblance to the additions made at Belleisle (Alloway, q.v.) in 1830–1, by Bryce. To the r. another wide crowstepped bay and to the l., set back, a lower wing with an elongated, corbelled angle turret with candle-snuffer roof and pedimented wall-head dormers. On its N face, this part has a six-light canted window in the principal floor with a simply corbelled chimney above and more pedimented dormers. A plain, self-effacing bay links this range with the later C17 STAIR-TOWER added to the earlier castle. This is crowstepped and has two corbelled turrets flanking its E gable. It is linked into the upper level of the original tower by a square-plan turret with a pyramidal roof (probably C17) above the original stair, replacing a former bartizan, part of its curved corbelling visible as a bulge.

The rectangular-plan (18.2 m. by 9.1 m.) late C14 TOWER has three tall storeys and an attic above a raised basement; its walls entirely harled except for the quoins, corbel table (probably C16), window margins and the pilasters supported on individually rustic carved heads framing the windows in the angle turrets, these all C17 (*see* Maybole Castle). The elevations are severely plain below the continuous corbelling, as one finds in several Ayrshire towers, with asymmetrically placed openings – a number of which have been enlarged. On the W elevation facing the river, there is a pointed-arched door at raised ground-floor level, probably reached originally by a timber stair but now by a flight of late C19 stone steps. The remodelling of the upper works of the tower and the addition of the stair jamb puts Cassillis into a league of its own in Ayrshire. The parapet-walk above the continuous corbelling was enclosed in the C17 and now has four windows to the W and three to the E, the latter with the same decorative pilaster detail as the candle-snuffer roofed turrets of the stair jamb. At the gable-ends the parapet has been replaced with balustrades but the open wall-walk and the cannon waterspouts still exist.

A COURTYARD, enclosed at the SE by a semicircular wall, has a functional low service range at the W, in the re-entrant angle of the 1830s range. It is late C19, probably by *H. M. Wardrop* who was employed in 1886–7. There is also a low lean-to projection, linking the 1830s work to the tower, which conceals the entrance made after the addition of the stair jamb in the late C17.

Inside, the house is in two distinct parts, the entrance range and the tower. The partly panelled ENTRANCE HALL has Jacobean-style balustraded steps, and a large pedimented doorway

leading to the INNER HALL, which is lit from above with borrowed light. Late C17-style corniced and lugged architraves to
the symmetrically placed doors (some blind) and the chimneypiece. S of the inner hall, the DINING ROOM with a rect-
angularly panelled ceiling and pendant mouldings, dado
panelling with plaster panels above and a smart mid-C18-style
chimneypiece with marble slips; to the N of the inner hall, the
DRAWING ROOM with a geometrically panelled ceiling, dado
panelling and an C18-style swagged chimneypiece. A compact
well stair leads to bedrooms mainly with combed ceilings.

54   A passage from the front range leads to the great marvel of
Cassillis: the spacious late C17 NEWEL STAIR between the
raised ground floor and the ballroom on the second floor of
the tower. Built of immaculately cut red sandstone, it is exactly
as Abercrumbie described it in 1696: 'a fine stone stare turning
about a hollow casement, in which are many opens from the
bottome to the top, that by putting a lamp into it gives light
to the whole of the staires'. This arrangement is very rare, if
not unique.* Delicate wrought-iron panel on top landing with
thistle design. The remains of an earlier newel can be seen in
the bay to the W, now used for plumbing.

The TOWER has a partly vaulted BASEMENT, the remaining
part with massive timbers on a wall-plate supported by substantial stone corbels. Gothic door towards the N. Various passages and rooms are contained within the substantial walls,
which are 4.8 m. thick at this level, but only 3 m. above. On
the W, at raised ground-floor level, the original ENTRANCE
with outer and inner doors within the wall thickness with slots
for a portcullis operated from a mural chamber. Stairs rise to
l. and r., the latter possibly of later date, and on the walls and
vault of the former, remains of monochrome wall painting
including the figure of a guard protecting the entrance and
some lozenge patterns on the vault, probably early C17. These
paintings and the whole compartment would repay thorough
analysis.

Within the tower, two sizeable rooms on each floor except
for the second floor where there was the hall (now divided into
ballroom with a retiring room/library off it). At raised ground
level they are low and simply detailed, one with a later entrance
to the base of the mural stair. The two first-floor rooms and
the mezzanine bedroom all have early to mid-C18 panelling
and chimneypieces with basket-arched lintels. The first-floor
rooms have veined marble chimneypieces with later C18 Adam-
style surrounds, probably part of works planned by the 10th
Earl but not undertaken until 1798 by the 12th Earl. It is likely
that *Hugh Cairncross* had a hand here. The second-floor BALL-
ROOM is also probably a late C18 creation. Large arched niche
on the W and a deeply recessed arched window opposite; at

---

* It was also used in the early C18 in the Strathmartine Lodgings, Dundee (dem.).
An early C17 hollow newel at Glamis (Angus) directed hot air into the castle's upper
floors.

the N a classically detailed chimneypiece with tapered, fluted columns supporting hourglass-like urns with swags and leaves in the frieze. From the S end of the Ballroom a lobby to the LIBRARY, fitted out in 1886–7 by *Wardrop* (and not in a new wing as first proposed), with bookcases and a period chimneypiece with tall, thin Corinthian columns framing a mirrored overmantel. The tower's upper level was created in the C17 with a wide E corridor replacing the wall-walk. In some of the turrets and stair-tower garret are rooms with bolection and raised-and-fielded panelling, box-moulded cornices, and sash windows with heavy glazing bars. The BARTISAN ROOM has a fireplace set in a bold quarter-round stone moulding with a wooden chimneypiece and a big overmantel panel, doors in lugged frames with cornices, and above the main cornice a cove.

Below the castle's W elevation, a river walk and a crenellated platform high above the river. Abercrumbie in 1696 records high stone-walled enclosures which yielded apricots, peaches, cherries and all other fruits. Some may be incorporated into the *c.* 1830 walled garden (walls much reduced) and a gardener's cottage to the W.

CATRINE

5020

A late C18 planned industrial village on the River Ayr, the most significant such development in Ayrshire, and one of national importance. Only a corn mill and a smithy had occupied the site, haugh land on the N bank, before 1787 when the proprietor, Claud Alexander of Ballochmyle, and the Glasgow merchant David Dale, commenced the construction of a cotton spinning mill. They were encouraged by the M.P. George Dempster and Richard Arkwright, with whom Dale had previously been associated at New Lanark. Their village had the mill in a central square, with houses around the outer sides, and streets orientated on the centres of the mill's façades. Dale had learnt, from his father-in-law Robert Owen, the importance of decent housing but did not replicate Owen's other social innovations.

The MILL (destroyed shortly after its closure in 1963) was architecturally much more sophisticated than its contemporaries at New Lanark, Deanston and Stanley. Of five storeys, its main façade had a pediment and belfry, and Venetian windows. Water for the mill-wheels was brought from Glenbuck (q.v.) by a series of conduits to holding reservoirs in the village (The Voes, *see* below), which regulated the flow. The mills were acquired in 1801 by James Finlay & Co. of Glasgow, with whom they remained until closure. A pair of giant cast-iron wheels of 1827 by *Fairbairn* of Manchester remained in use until 1945. The mill was extended and altered many times, and a substantial new mill (also dem.) was added to the W in the 1950s.

CATRINE PARISH CHURCH, Chapel Brae. Built 1792–3 and financed by Claud Alexander. Classical; rectangular, with a big

hipped roof, but with pointed windows in pairs on the S front
which has a projecting centre under a wide pediment with urns
and a swagged circular window. Open bellcote of 1898, with
leaded ogee roof. The side elevations have two tiers of round-
headed windows. Galleries inside, added in 1837–40. Central
area rearranged in 1958–60, the pale wood-panelled REREDOS
and matching PULPIT of this date. – STAINED GLASS. N wall,
Girls' Guild (l., 1966), and war memorial (r., 1967), both by
G. Maile & Son.

Former FREE CHURCH, Ballochmyle Street. 1844–5 by *Robert
Barclay.* T-plan, dark pink sandstone. Stepped and skewed
gables, and tall square-headed windows. The main front has a
single window in the gable and the entrance below, beneath a
pentice porch, its brackets like inverted Js, ending in small
pyramids.

ST JOSEPH (R.C.), Ballochmyle Street. 1960–3 by *Charles W.
Gray* of Edinburgh. Boarded wooden exterior and shingle
roof.

Former UNITED PRESBYTERIAN CHURCH, Ballochmyle Street.
1836–7; residential since *c.* 2002. Gaunt dark pink sandstone
preaching box with a hipped roof. The front is dominated by
a tall gabled projection. Entrance with a four-centred head and
cavetto reveal, two-light pointed window above.

A. M. BROWN INSTITUTE, Institute Avenue. 1897–8 by *R. S.
Ingram.* Scots Baronial with crowstepped gables, dominated by
an out-of-scale octagonal corner turret, with battlements and
towerlets (cf. the institutes at Cumnock and Muirkirk). Inside,
a marble BUST of the donor, a partner in James Finlay & Co.

WAR MEMORIAL, Chapel Brae. 1922, builder *John Reid* of
Catrine. 10.6-m.-high obelisk in rock-faced granite from the
Sorn Castle estate, with Creetown granite panels.

Catrine, view from the west.
Drawing by J. Black, 1819

DESCRIPTION

The site of the mill (*see* above) in MILL SQUARE is now land-scaped. On the s side, some of the houses provided *c.* 1788, two-storey with polished and painted dressings and, mostly, twelve-pane glazing, but with a grey-harled uniformity dating from restoration by Ayr County Council in the early 1970s. Another late C18 grey-harled terrace in BRIDGE STREET, which runs s from the square and ends in a cast-iron FOOT-BRIDGE spanning the Ayr, of 1879, made in the workshops of *James Finlay & Co.* MILL STREET runs w from the Square. The grassed area on the s was the site of the Jeanie Mill (fur-nished with sixty-seven spinning jennies) of *c.* 1790. In BAL-LOCHMYLE STREET is AYRBANK HOUSE, the mill manager's house of *c.* 1790. Classical, two storeys of cheerful pink sand-stone, with a hipped roof and shallow segmental heads to the ground-floor windows. Single-storey wings to either side, with round-headed openings: that to the r. of one bay only and merging into a curving screen. Mid-C19 rear wing. Beyond is the early C19 former EAST LODGE to Ballochmyle (*see* p. 179).

ST GERMAIN STREET runs e from the square. This was, and remains, the commercial centre of the village, and dates from the late C18. On the N side, two red sandstone properties reflect the village's prosperity in the late C19 and early C20: the ROYAL BANK OF SCOTLAND, of 1873 by *Peddie & Kinnear*, and the CATRINE CO-OPERATIVE STORE of 1902–3 by *Andrew & Newlands*. Between these two, grey-harled infill of 1994 by *Meikle Kleboe Architects*, with polished red sandstone dressings and articulated by regular projecting gabled entrance bays.

In TOWNHEAD, the over-restored NETHER CATRINE HOUSE, almost anonymous as the middle block of a symmetri-cally disposed housing development of *c.* 1998. It is probably late C17, but the pedimented harled projection which adorns the former front elevation (now to the rear) must be mid-C18. It has a round-headed niche in the pediment, and chubby over-sized urns. Beyond is AVONLEA, probably of 1904 for the local master builder *John Reid*, an attractive and understated harled Arts and Crafts house, with sandstone dressings to the wide entrance and window above.

From the e end of St Germain Street, AYR STREET, also part of the original late C18 scheme, runs N and e to become ST CUTHBERT STREET, which had, on its N side only, single-storey stone cottages (many altered and raised to two storeys), facing THE VOES, the former holding reservoirs, restored and landscaped in 1992 by *Meikle Kleboe Architects*. Stone-lined, and linked to the mill site by a brick-lined tunnel; they are fed by a weir on the river, and a wooden sluice which controls the lade which feeds the voes. In LAIGH ROAD, to the s, the pretty red sandstone early C19 AYRVALE COTTAGE with mid-C19 rustic porch, and the former CATRINE BLEACHING WORKS, now a bonding and bottling plant; of the original buildings only the single-storey hipped mid-C19 gatehouse survives. It has an

C18 wing to the rear with steeply pitched gables which suggest that it was once thatched; this was the pre-existing corn mill.

DALDORCH HOUSE SCHOOL. In a small estate E of the river, linked to St Cuthbert Street by a bridge. Originally Catrine Bank. Built in 1801 for Archibald Buchanan, manager and principal partner of the cotton mill after its acquisition by Finlay & Co. Buchanan had trained under Arkwright at Cromford and his family's mill at Ballindalloch had been bought by Finlay in 1798. The house began as a compact two-storey, three-bay design over a basement, reminiscent of David Dale's house at New Lanark. Built in local red sandstone, the front and rear elevations have shallow set-backs at the angles. It is remarkable for the proportion of window to wall; the long ground-floor windows with slender consoles supporting cornices are set in panelled frames. Arched windows light the basement. Bulky porch of c. 1850, contemporary with the tall NE addition in polished pink ashlar. It is only one room deep and has a curious skinny pilaster on the return elevation which relates to nothing. Was the top storey an afterthought?

In front, a semicircle of simple paired residential units by *Miller Partnership*, 2007. Below the house to the W, the smart pedimented STABLE COURT of c. 1850, neatly converted to institutional use.

BALLOCHMYLE HOUSE. *See* p. 179.

5030

CESSNOCK CASTLE

1.5 km. SE of Galston

An interesting example of a medieval keep enlarged into a Scots Renaissance mansion. Built on a steep bluff overlooking the Burnawn Burn, Cessnock came to a branch of the Campbells of Loudoun c. 1527. At the end of the C16 Sir George Campbell appears to have begun extensions, of uncertain extent and more domestic in character. The L-plan wings creating the quadrangular plan are chiefly due to his grandson Sir Hew Campbell. Constantly under suspicion of political intrigue, he occupied himself with almost continuous building from the mid C17 to 1686. Repairs to the old tower were made, after a decision not to demolish, in the 1720s for Lord Polwarth (2nd Earl of Marchmont from 1724). His builder in 1727 was Mr Williamson, probably *James Williamson* who built the dovecot at Marchmont (Borders). Major restoration by *Thomas Leadbetter*, 1890, for the Duke of Portland. After subdivision in the C20 it has been carefully reinstated as a house.

Enclosing the courtyard is a mid-C20 low wall and archway. At the SW corner, the harled five-storey tower, C15 but probably incorporating earlier fabric. Massive walls at ground level, particularly on the NW and SE gables, which even on the upper floors are 1.5 m. thick. On the NW gable, the roof raggle of a later two-storey building. The tower has been much altered, most noticeably at the upper level where a parapet and wall-walk have been replaced by a crowstepped, gabled roof. At the apex of the NW gable, evidence of a birdcage bellcote. At the W corner the chamfered angle is corbelled to a square above the second floor; was it formerly joined to another range? The tower is studded randomly with windows, mostly altered, but to the basement on the NW gable is an arrowslit. Another small window on the SW, and high above in this wall also tiny lights for the third- and fourth-floor closets. Windows to the former turnpike stair at the SE are obvious although enlarged. Close to this stair was the first-floor entrance. A separate door at the NE served the stores below but this now opens within the stair-turret added in 1666 by Sir Hew. This is of four stages, rubble-built with moulded strings between each floor and a cavetto-moulded doorpiece with a steep pediment, breaking the pediment a diminutive pilaster supporting a ball finial. The stair was built to improve circulation between the tower and the three-storey SE wing (much enlarged windows), which links at right angles to the NE wing built in two stages during the C17.

Filling the inner angle between the wings, a semi-octagonal stair-turret added *c.* 1690. This is Scots Renaissance, its door modelled on the other turret door but wider, with fluted pilasters and bolection-moulded frame, string courses between the floors broken by later window enlargements; in the first stage a framed panel with the Campbell arms and over the upper window a strapwork pediment. A balustrade of rectangular-section balusters, linked to the large stepped chimneystack on the NE wing, completes it. The two bays of the wing to the l. of this have a mid-C17 pedimented doorpiece set in a bolection-moulded lugged frame with a delicate dentil cornice, the elaborate carving of the pediment now sadly eroded. Again there has been much alteration to the windows. The carved dormerheads above the wall-head are by *Leadbetter* in C17 style. These bays were extended in a slightly pinker rubble in 1675 (dated on the string course). Of the same date is the lower NW range, which has Sir Hew Campbell's initials. This has also been much altered, notably in the 1890s, see the heavily windowed SW gable. The same period saw the reconstruction of the roofs with dormers and the tall chimneystacks. The courtyard elevations are the most architectural, in contrast the outer SE- and NE-facing ones, which are harled and austere except for the pedimented first-floor door, balcony and stair wrapping around the E angle, a favourite device of Leadbetter.

The tower's vaulted ground floor and the tall vaulted space above it, into which an additional floor was inserted, survive. Also mural chambers, but not the turnpike stair. The C16 and C17 ranges have some vaulted rooms below the principal rooms which are reached by the generous spiral stair. The Study at the E angle is the room probably remodelled in 1723 when windows were inserted to be symmetrical with those below.

The most important mid-C17 survival is the painted ceiling of the GREAT HALL. Bands of scrolled leaves, flowers in roundels and grotesques and urns all in ribbon-framed panels, the colours now faded to grisaille effect. The hall is two-thirds panelled, with a large fireplace on the courtyard wall and arched windows. In the later C17 extension (former drawing room), a 1680 panelled plaster ceiling with strips of vines and sprays of oak leaves.

CHAPELTOUN HOUSE

4040

3.2 km. NW of Kilmaurs

A big Free Style mansion of 1908–10 by *Alexander Cullen* of *Cullen & Lochhead,* for Hugh Neilson, owner of the Summerlee Iron Works. Built on a slope overlooking Annick Water, the house steps along the hillside in three blocks of diminishing height, cream-painted harl with grey polished sandstone dressings, the gables with distinctive stone apex triangles. The N door has an elaborately carved surround, its hoodmould stepped up over a decorative panel in the balustraded parapet. The parapet sill continues into the W gabled bay, giving the illusion of a shallow jetty; this gable also has flower-decorated skewputts and a large, leaded mullion-and-transom window to the ground floor. The garden front has a symmetrical main block with big full-height canted windows in the gabled bays and a single-storey curved bay at the centre with a balustrade. – LODGE and GATES. 1918 by *Cullen, Lochhead & Brown.*

CLONBEITH CASTLE

3040

4 km. NE of Kilwinning

The ruins of an early C17 mansion stand forlornly in a farm courtyard. It was a stone-built oblong, of which three thinly built walls remain to first-floor height. The entrance front has a central Early Renaissance entrance, on which the date 1607 could once be read. Above this, corbels which supported a bow window similar to those of *c.* 1600 on the Earl's Palace, Kirkwall (Orkney). This lighted a first-floor hall (8.5 m. by 5.5 m.), which was approached by a straight stair to the r. of the entrance. The ground floor was vaulted, and a wheel-stair in the NE angle gave access to the upper floor.

CLONCAIRD CASTLE

3000

2 km. E of Kirkmichael

A C16 L-plan tower house built for the Mures, transformed 1810–19 into a toy fort, which was begun for Francis Cunynghame but completed for his brother by *Robert Wallace.* Wallace was only twenty in 1810, however, and the design might be attributed to *J. Gillespie Graham*, given the resemblance to Culdees Castle, Perthshire (*c.* 1810) and sketches of similar character produced for Blairquhan (q.v.) in 1813.

The tower house, concealed behind the additions, is perched over a steep gorge where the Girvan joins a tributary, a position similar to Penkill Castle (q.v.). The present house, however, turns its back on the river and overlooks gently rising meadowland and the steeper hills to the E. It creates its own drama as a theatrical set piece in the views along the E approach, the whole composition dominated by a large four-storey drum tower, which has at its base a projecting stocky porch, with a coat of arms. Three very large basket-arched windows in the tower's first floor. Two unequal three-storey wings extend from the tower, both screening and enclosing the C16 tower at the rear. All of this is castellated and the crenellations for the tower are corbelled out. Diminutive turrets mask the angle between the drum tower and the wings. In the shorter S wing the three windows are grouped, a configuration that is emphasized by the continuous hoodmould over the first floor's segmentally arched windows. A pencil-like square turret clasps the SW angle. On the E elevation this arrangement is spaced out, all the windows have squared hoodmoulds and at the NE angle the turret is octagonal with pointed windows and corbelled crenellation. The C16 tower appears to have been L-plan but only the N façade and a little of the E wall are visible. It is probable that this tower is not all of one date but that the E section with the dogtooth moulding in the corbel table is later; a datestone in the rear court of 1585 could record the addition. Added to this, on the E there is a small, much-altered wing, probably C18. The rear elevation is enclosed by an early C19 semicircular service court. At its centre a two-storey crenellated dwelling flanked by larders, storage etc. under a single-pitch curved slate roof.

Hugh Robert Wallace inherited in 1885 and in 1905 sold the house to Isabella Dubs (but regained it by marrying her in 1908). She instigated the thoroughgoing makeover of the INTERIOR, the only clue to which externally is the small-pane glazing of the first-floor windows on the main elevations, reminiscent of Lorimer's style. But whom she employed remains unknown. Much of the detail is quirky, e.g. delicate oak-leaf brass window lifts and a recurring motif of parakeets in wood and plaster. There is also excellent door furniture and light fittings, from hanging lights to swinging-arm lamps.

The drum tower houses an octagonal ENTRANCE HALL with heavy Doric columns on big plinths and red oak panelling. The circular plaster wreath of fruits and flowers is so realistic, apart from the pastel colours, that they ask to be picked. Off the stair hall, the fully panelled DINING ROOM, with very low stone-surrounded chimneypiece and its integral fender seat set in a shallow curved wall with elaborate marquetry panels above. The STAIR HALL is dominated by a sea of grey-figured marble and dark panelling and half filled by the fan-shaped lower flight of the imperial stair; a darker-shaded marble leads the visitor forward, a variation on the red carpet. The oddest feature of the design is that this flight leads straight into a plain right angle with nothing but the balustrade to encourage ascent. The balustrade itself is a complex and highly crafted heavy wrought-iron confection of scrolls and Tudor roses with an oak handrail. On the eastern wall a big open timber grille provides light for the stair to the upper floor in the compartment to the E. This stair is modest but does have charming animal and human figures perched on the newel posts. Above the main stair there is a coffered ceiling with a central decorated plaster dome with Father Time over the door to the saloon.

The SALOON is flooded with light after the rather sombre stair. The central circular area supported on Ionic columns with complementary pilasters is screened from the Billiard Room and the Boudoir, the screens demountable to allow for one large V-shaped space to be created. The screens themselves are filled with tiers of decorated colonnades. Over the door in a circular oak frame is a portrait of little Miss Dubs, as though she were peering through a porthole. The ceiling in this circular compartment has a central sun surrounded by the Signs of the Zodiac and yet more luscious grapes. The BILLIARD ROOM to the l. is the most sober compartment and is dominated by a large bolection-moulded, lugged panel over the simple moulded marble chimneypiece, the only piece of early C18 style in the castle, but even this bold detail is lightened by the inlaid work and Frenchified frames to the flanking cupboards. The geometric-patterned plaster framework on the ceiling is swagged with vines and grapes. The billiard table was constructed for the room and has strong fluted legs and brackets in the form of putti supporting the frame. The scoreboard carries the motto, 'He that is of a merry heart hath a continual feast.' Off the saloon to the r. is the BOUDOIR with the emphasis on the end wall, where the handsome lugged marble chimneypiece is set in the middle of three full-height pilastered panels each richly panelled in oak with framed marquetry inset medallions and crowning swags; the medallion on the chimney-breast is supported on a colonnette almost as though it were a fan. The ceiling has intersecting plaster circles, the central one composed of flowers and with loops of roses and parakeets in the angles.

A door from the half-landing leads into the old tower and the lower-ceilinged LIBRARY. This is much more C17 in character, with fully panelled walls and a form of entrance lobby with a densely carved screen full of parakeets and grapes from which steps descend to the library, which has a stone chimneypiece with turquoise tiling and another painting of Miss Dubs, this time with doves and pigeons in a boldly lugged frame. Flanking the chimney-breast are two rooms/closets in the turrets, and a big shelved recess on the long wall has a large window with yet more vines and parakeets in vivid colours. The ceiling is in a C17 style with ribbed geometric compartments, some of the ribs dissolving into foliage.

To the N, the STABLE COURT in a similar crenellated style. GARDENER'S COTTAGE, *c.* 1900 Arts and Crafts manner.

COLMONELL

1080

Strung along the road from Pinwherry to Ballantrae. The *New Statistical Account* (1838) reported that the 'the village of Colmonell, merely a row of thatched cottages a few years ago, has been almost rebuilt'. Feu dates of 1818 and 1825 are known. There are a mixture of single- and two-storey elevations.

PARISH CHURCH. 1847–50 by *David Bryce*, replacing the 1772 church, but altered in 1899 by *Robert S. Lorimer*, who 'Was up at five and down to Ayrshire to a little alteration to a church. Ten hours on the going and coming and forty minutes on the job.' Restored 1980 by *Anthony Richardson & Partners* (project architect, *Patrick Lorimer*). A rectangular granite box, oriented E–W but not liturgically, with simple Gothic hoodmoulded windows and three stepped lancets in the W (liturgical E) gable wall. Traditional gabled N porch (possibly the original entrance) and on the S side a stair to the choir gallery added by Robert Lorimer with C17-style squat balusters. Imposing, nearly full-height E porch; only a blind oculus breaks the surface. Could the original plan have been to have a tower here? The character of the interior is partly due to Robert Finnie McEwen of Bardrochat (q.v.), who commissioned Lorimer to provide the shallow E choir gallery and a fine ORGAN, its case carved by Lorimer's usual collaborators *W. & A. Clow.* They also carved the PULPIT, in 1909, which is set on the W wall, below the windows, with flanking oak panels. Square-plan with linenfold panels and angles chamfered for carved angels. Small carved oak FONT and COMMUNION TABLE of 1943 and 1945 by *Scott Morton.* – ELDERS' CHAIRS. An excellent set possibly designed by *Bryce.*

STAINED GLASS. Of particular note the three W lancets by *Louis Davis*, 1909–10: the Sacraments, Praise with the Ascent of the Blessed to Heaven accompanied by Banners of Music and All the Works of the Lord. Much emphasis on sweeping diagonal lines and subtle blue and grey-brown hues streaked with vivid colour. Davis was favoured by Lorimer, who must have recommended him to McEwen. The donors are depicted at the bottom of the sidelights. – Also by *Davis* the war memorial window (S wall) of 1919–20, made by Powells with a beautifully inscribed list of names below by the same. The N side W window, 1903, a Nativity with very real, child-like angels from *Davis*'s studio. – Also on the S side, St Colmonella set against an opaque glass sky, by *H. B. Powell*, 1952, with Craigneil Castle and a fisherman in the background. Next to it, I am the Resurrection and the Life by *Ballantine & Gardiner*, 1895. – One N window by *Douglas Strachan, c.* 1925, using luminous colours to portray the Good Shepherd and more muted colouring in the background which includes Knockdolian Castle. – Strikingly different NE window using dramatically vivid colours to depict the Dream of the Rood. Dedicated by the Duchess of Wellington to her parents, Douglas and Ruth McConnel, and designed by the *Marchioness of Douro,* executed by *Maria McClafferty,* 1994. – In the gallery, flanking the organ, two E windows of 2000–1 by *Catriona R. McKinnon* depict Grace and Praise in watery, wistful colouring skilfully complementing Davis's work.

MONUMENTS. John Snell †1679. Handsome Baroque aedicule in appropriate C17 style, by *Lorimer c.* 1915. Hoptonwood stone with green marble pillars (cf. Almont, Pinwherry, p. 573). The McFadzean Memorial is also by *Lorimer.*

In the KIRKYARD, Arts and Crafts-style lamps of 1914 by *Lorimer* (now missing their lamp heads) of a type also provided for the church. Some remarkably lively C18 HEADSTONES crammed with symbols of mortality, e.g. *inter alia* the headstone to James McCracken inscribed on the back to Matthew McIlwraith, a Covenanter shot in 1685, and *c.* 1758 the Mckilsock stone. Fine early C18 BURIAL ENCLOSURE for the McCubbins of Knockdolian, later taken over by the McConnels. Squat balustrade and slender, somewhat rustic Composite columns flanking a bolection-moulded doorcase with a coat of arms above and initials FM and FK incised in the frieze. Unusually there is an inscription beside the doorway 'This was by masoune vork vroget John Dicon Ayr.'

The former MANSE lies W in substantial grounds overlooking a big sweep in the River Stinchar. Built 1820–2, a smart three-bay, two-storey house raised on a basement with railed steps to the front door. Additions and alterations by *Allan Stevenson,* 1908–10, probably including the dormers.

N of the kirkyard is the CHURCH HALL of 1910–11 built at the expense of Robert Finnie McEwen and probably by *Allan Stevenson* with *Thomas McGill Cassels.* Crowstepped gabled, with an ogee-domed porch.

COLMONELL PRIMARY SCHOOL, Main Street. 2009–10 by *ARPL Architects.* Stylish, and incorporating many environmentally sensitive innovations including a living green roof.

DESCRIPTION. E of the church in MAIN STREET, the BOAR'S HEAD HOTEL of 1899–1900 by *Allan Stevenson,* a rebuilding of an earlier pub. Further along on the N side of the street, the PUBLIC HALL and LIBRARY, also by *Stevenson* in 1890. On the front, the Hall and Library end in gables with the entrance in between under a tall Jubilee clock tower added 1897 by Stevenson. Further E the former FREE CHURCH by *Alexander Petrie,* 1898. Solid tower with a pyramid roof.

In CRAIGNEIL ROAD, S of Main Street, some County Council housing of 1921–2 by *Ingram & Brown.* Pairs of single-storey harled cottages in a crescent, externally little different from C19 vernacular. Opposite, dramatically elevated on a bluff, the WAR MEMORIAL of 1920–2 by *Lorimer*. A very tall shaft supports a square capital with lions rampant on shields. Plinth flanked by three stone walls at angles, forming shelters for seats.

COLMONELL BRIDGE, over the Stinchar. 1867. Graceful, of two shallow segmental arches with a central rounded cutwater.

KIRKHILL, N of Main Street. A neat Tudor Gothic gabled mansion of 1843–5, possibly by *David Rhind* (cf. Knockdolian) or *David Bryce* and built for Alexander Barton whose coat of arms is placed over the door. Altered by *James Carrick* and again by *A. C. Wolffe*, including the ballroom inserted in the 1920s between the former coachhouse and the lower rear service wing. Remarkably untouched interior of waxed wood-work, well-detailed cornices and some elegant marble chimneypieces. The ballroom, now converted to a studio, retains streamlined radiator covers doubling as window seats and a good Art Deco chimneypiece.

The house is closely watched over by the the shell of KIRK-HILL CASTLE, built for Thomas Kennedy. Datestone of 1589 over one window. It is built in whinstone rubble with dressed stone quoins and crowsteps to the gables; unlike earlier towers it has comparatively thin walls. It was entered in the re-entrant angle directly into the jamb, which was filled with a fashionable scale-and-platt staircase leading to the first floor (*see* also Killochan Castle). The upper floor was reached by a newel stair corbelled out in the NE angle, now mostly collapsed. The kitchen in the ground floor had a large chimney on the E wall which passed through the E end of the first-floor hall providing alcoves for small flanking closets. There do not appear to have been any vaulted rooms.

CRAIGNEIL CASTLE, 0.7 km. S. A most romantic ruin in a commanding position on a rocky bluff S of the river and perched precariously over an old quarry into which its NW angle fell in 1886. Rectangular, rubble-built, with roughly dressed quoins. 1.8-m.-thick walls. Probably late C15. There was a newel stair in the thickness of the wall at the SE near the ground-floor entrance. Unusually the only vault was over the second-floor hall, and there are traces of a large fireplace at this level.

THE CRAIG. *See* p. 228.
KNOCKDOLIAN HOUSE. *See* p. 488.

COODHAM

2.25 km. NW of Symington

3030

An imposing Greek Revival house built *c.* 1826 for Mrs William Fairlie, widow of a merchant and banker in Calcutta. It cost over £20,000 and may be by *Robert Smirke*. Tall, three storeys with a basement exposed at the rear, of beautifully polished

82

pinkish-cream sandstone ashlar. The two central bays of the six-bay entrance front are slightly advanced with a powerful Greek Doric portico. Flanking architraved windows with consoled pediments, a band course above. Moulded sill courses to first- and second-floor windows, the former architraved and corniced. Balustraded parapet. On the plain garden front, a shallow two-windowed curved centrepiece. A balustraded parapet fronts the basement area.

E and W are additions in a stronger pink sandstone. First in date are those to the W, of 1871–9 by *Alfred Waterhouse* for Sir William Henry Houldsworth, the Lancashire cotton miller.* Adjoining the S front are low classical ranges, also balustraded, designed as a music room and orangery (later a ballroom) with a Corinthian portico and pedimented doorpiece. Behind these, and altogether more typical of the architect, is the CHAPEL, in Romanesque style with a narthex at the W end. Five bays of paired round-arched windows with linking hoodmoulds, and an arcaded corbel table above raised over a plainly detailed crypt. Chevron-patterned slate roof. Of the same date the GAME LARDER at the NE end of the garden terrace, with its steep Germanic helm roof of fish-scale slates; on its N a shouldered recess probably once with a seat to view the gardens.

The two-storey E wing, added 1911, is set back one bay from the main front of the house and stepped in three stages; it is two storeys and adjoins an earlier low wing (raised to two storeys) extending from the garden front. In the upper floor of the bay linked to the main house, an aedicule, inscribed NISI DOMINUS AEDIFICAVERIT DOMUM IN VANUM LABORAVERUNT QUI AEDIFICANT EAM ('Unless the Lord have built the house, they have worked in vain who built it').

The house was gutted by fire but restored and lavishly converted to six apartments in 2006–9 by *CDP Architects* of Glasgow. Central top-lit circular Italian marble stair, with bold bombé-section wrought-iron balusters, rising the full height from the black and brown patterned marble hall floor, is theirs.

2080

CORWAR
4.8 km. ESE of Barrhill

A neat, uncompromising three-bay, two-storey house, formed in the 1940s from the demolition of a mansion begun in 1838 for Rigby Wason M.P. He built Drumlamford (q.v.) nearby at about the same time. No doubt *W. & W. Fraser* were his architects here also. Why Wason needed another house in such close proximity is difficult to imagine – perhaps the slightly less exposed position appealed. The porch has been retained but

---

*Houldsworth subsequently employed Waterhouse at Reddish, Lancs., where he had his mills. Stained glass commissioned for the chapel at Coodham is in the church there.

the body of the house is adapted from the wing added in 1892 by *Richard Park* for the Hon. Hugh Elliot. Exemplary granite masonry, rough-hewn for the plinth but neatly cut and regularly coursed above, the polished dressings similarly well executed. The end stacks and the long-and-short quoins are more boldly cut to give them prominence. Windows of lying-pane glazing, the ground-floor ones dropping to floor level. Low later C20 SW extension with thin horizontal bands of granite. – LAKE made by Wason to provide a curling pond and to recreate in a modest way the juxtaposition of Drumlamford with Loch Dornal. The plantations were made in the 1820s by a previous owner.

CORWAR OLD SCHOOL, 1 km. NE, by the A714. Late C19 for the isolated hill-farming community. Very domestic, the former schoolroom with a large three-light window.

COYLTON

A tripartite village: Laigh Coylton, the original settlement by the Water of Coyle, Hillhead with the church, and Joppa lying astride the Ayr–Cumnock turnpike. Dependent on coal in the late C19 and early C20, but since the mid 1960s increasingly a commuter dormitory for Ayr.

COYLTON PARISH CHURCH, Hillhead. Turreted Gothic Revival preaching box of 1829–32, by *David Bryce*, an early commission and, like his parish church for Prestwick & Monkton (*see* p. 577), not very rigorous. T-plan, with a projecting entrance tower flanked by two tall arched windows. Similar windows to the other elevations. Equally unassuming plastered and galleried interior.

Former PARISH CHURCH, Laigh Coylton. Scant remains of the rectangular gable-ended pre-Reformation church, which had projecting aisles to N and S. What survives, after a sale of the materials in 1832, is the W gable with a small C17 bellcote, the N aisle used as a burial vault by the Hamiltons of Sundrum, and, lengthened later in the C19, the arched entrance to the S aisle, and a fragment of the N wall, with a richly moulded arched tomb-recess. This wall fragment now forms the N wall of the C19 burial vault of the Chalmers of Gadgirth.

CLAUD HAMILTON MEMORIAL HALL, Hillhead. Harled Arts and Crafts of 1909 by *A. C. Thomson*, with Renaissance details, e.g. the red sandstone doorpiece. Large hall, with open timber roof.

COYLTON PRIMARY SCHOOL, Joppa. Of 1964–6, by *Ayr County Council Architects Dept.* Inside, a bronze portrait medallion of George Douglas Brown, 1920, sculpted and gifted by *Robert Bryden*. Both Bryden and Brown, author of *The House with the Green Shutters*, were educated at Coylton.

WAR MEMORIAL, Hillhead. 1920. Stone Celtic cross, with bronze plaques in the plinth, by *Bryden*.

DESCRIPTION. At Laigh Coylton, beside the kirkyard, the COYLTON ARMS, a largely C19 assemblage, based on a two-storey, three-bay centre, with single-storey former cottages now incorporated. Towards Hillhead is LOW COYLTON HOUSE, the pert former manse of 1838–9, with a central pilastered doorway. Joppa begins with the school on the S side, then GLENHEAD COURT of 2004–5, by the *Alistair Murdoch Partnership* for Carrick Housing Association. Striking courtyard development, with harled walls, exposed wooden panels and monopitch roofs.

CARBIESTON, 3 km. W. Of 1894, for Claud Hamilton of Sundrum. Asymmetrical, unusually of red brick, with red sandstone dressings. Prominent projecting entrance tower terminating in a French manner, with a steeply pitched slate roof and cast-iron balustrade. To its l. a projecting bay with a crenellated parapet; otherwise, crowstepped gables. Classical interiors, including an L-shaped drawing room with an elaborate cornice.

DUCHRAY, 0.3 km. E. Four-square late classical house of *c.* 1840, harled, with exposed dressings, beneath a broad eaves. Three-bay entrance front, the door with a bracketed head, the ground-floor two-light windows with raised heads; a similar treatment to the three single lights on the side elevation. To the W, DUCHRAY FARM, a relatively unaltered single-storey harled courtyard farm, probably with a late C18 core.

THE CUSHATS. *See* p. 267.
GADGIRTH. *See* p. 327.
SUNDRUM CASTLE. *See* p. 644.

1080   THE CRAIG
                            2.5 km. E of Colmonell

Tall and simple three-bay harled laird's house of several dates, facing S over the River Stinchar. The proportions of the ground floor and the rear wing suggest work of the mid C17 when the estate was owned by John Fergusson, but the symmetrical character is due to the substantial rebuilding of *c.* 1783 by David Kennedy, when the first-floor windows were also enlarged. Small sash windows in the ground and rear first floor. Various C19 and C20 additions including the attic storey raised in the 1920s. Inserted into the rear cottage wing is a lintel dated 1658 with 1783 inscribed later. The wing is linked by a curving passage to the house.

3030   CRAIG HOUSE
                            1.5 km. ENE of Gatehead

Symmetrical N front, with a late C18 house embedded at its centre, dominated by a giant Ionic portico rising from a sweeping perron stair. This classical grandeur was provided by *James Ingram c.* 1835, along with the two large wings that have shallow projections, consoled first-floor windows, a bold cornice and panelled parapets broken at the angles in a mannered treatment. Rear elevation similarly detailed but with a simply pedimented central bay, and on this side the W wing has been enlarged in ungainly fashion by *Allan Stevenson,* 1882. At the SE, a colossal WINTER GARDEN, of 1902 for Robert Pollok-Morris by *J. J. Burnet,* is the most arresting feature of the house. Glazed on two sides between bold sculptured piers breaking through the eaves (cf. Burnet's winter garden at Baronald (Cartland Bridge Hotel), Lanarkshire), with elaborate swags supporting male and female masks, the style surely influenced by Burnet's visit to North America in 1896. Converted into a residential school in 1947, and into apartments in the 1990s, after a period of dereliction and some demolition, and covered in smooth cream render, the house is devoid of its landscape and partially surrounded by very dull villas and semi-detached houses of 2007–8.

CRAIGENGILLAN
2 km. S of Bellsbank

4000

Remotely situated at the head of the Doon valley in well-matured policies, with extensive views of the hills to the E and S towards the dramatic Ness Glen which opens out of Loch Doon.

The house, sometimes prior to 1900 called Berbeth, is long and thin, aligned N–S with low E ranges projecting around an entrance court. The earliest part is at the N end of the main range and this appears to be the laird's house remodelled in the 1770s by John McAdam, whose family acquired the land in the C17. Its roof is slightly taller than the rest and has all the hallmarks of having been thatched. The full-height canted bay on the W elevation is mid C19. Next comes the five-bay S addition, made *c.* 1802–5 by Quinton McAdam and in a similar style. Its ground storey is taller than normal and at the centre of its W front is a pencil-like turret with a candle-snuffer roof, possibly also mid-C19. Then, *c.* 1827, after the marriage of Jean McAdam to the Hon. Frederick Cathcart, the house received the trappings of a fashionable gentleman's residence. Of this time are the two projecting bays on the E front, with crow-stepped gables and diamond flues on corbelled blocks at the apex, linked by a glazed passage with Tudor arches – all motifs from David Hamilton's vocabulary. Probably of the same date, and also Hamiltonesque, is the elongated, square crenellated tower rising from the SE corner of the SW wing (the wing itself incorporates traces of a pre-1780 cottage).

None of this is any preparation for the remarkable French C18 Revival interior, executed *c.* 1905 by *Jansen* of Paris for Charlotte McAdam, who was widowed in 1901. To find such

Parisian urbanity in the depths of rural Ayrshire is astonishing. From 2001–3 the house was sensitively repaired. The ENTRANCE HALL opens through a wide panelled arch into the large STAIR HALL. This is the hub of the interior and elegantly panelled with a marble floor and painted overdoors in the style of Boucher. The stair itself, cleverly fitted into a very tight space, is a sensational confection of beautifully formed woodwork and a most elaborate Baroque wrought-iron balustrade with gilded decoration and iron handrail covered with sensuous velvet. Two wide sliding doors, set into shallow arched panels, open from the Stair Hall into the SALOON; although some of the panelling was lost to dry rot it still has a handsome First Empire marble chimneypiece with the motif of a bow and arrows subtly woven into the form of fasces. The mirrored overmantel has another painted panel in a delicate Boucher style. Beyond the stair on the l., the *bibliothèque*, fitted out with narrow shelved cupboards, not intended for British books, all white and gilded. The door from this room leads into the coved ceilinged MORNING ROOM, again with elaborate woodwork and panelled doors with hunting scenes over. The N wall is filled by a grand Aubusson tapestry (*c.* 1700). The Louis XV-style marble chimneypiece on the S wall has the ingenious feature of a large window over it in place of a mirror, although it is curious that the view which it frames is not a romantic landscape but the Stable Court. A crank in the panelling closes its outer shutter in true Parisian style.

Almost adjoining, S of the house, is the magnificent STABLE COURT, which Quintin McAdam erected in 1802. This is of a far greater ambition than his enlargement to the house. Ashlar-built tall arched entrance with a domed clock tower, a grander version of Barskimming's stables (q.v.) and a feature more familiar in smarter East Lothian steadings. Low rendered rubble ranges with ashlar margins attached. The first stage above the entrance has a Venetian window to the outer and inner faces, the former set into an open pediment. Next stage with chamfered angles, the chamfers simulating pilasters below an entablature. Clock in a circular moulded frame. The upper octagonal stage, with pilasters clasping the angles and arched openings, supports a finely wrought segmented dome and weathervane. Within the two-storey courtyard a substantial range of boxes for forty horses remain some with classy arcaded screens, tongue-and-groove linings and cast-iron mangers and water troughs. Former smithy close by.

GARDENS. Reworked in 1909–10, they include a spectacular ROCK GARDEN (being restored) by *James Pulham & Son*. The wider LANDSCAPE was greatly improved in the 1780s with extensive planting by John McAdam and further enhanced by his son, and again after 1827 when the Ness Glen was incorporated and landscaped as a Romantic attraction. There are still remnants of ESTATE BUILDINGS including the ruinous GAS WORKS; unusually close to the house is the ICE HOUSE, a subterranean chamber (approx. 7 m. square) reached by a well-constructed vaulted passage, with a drain for meltwater from the chamber to an elaborate tunnel, part of a sophisticated drainage system. In the garden a domed WELL-HEAD, its details like the stable tower. Various cottages have been restored, all part of a careful regeneration of the wider landscape.

The elegant LINN BRIDGE carries the drive over the Doon, and close to the drive entrance is MUCK BRIDGE, with cast-iron parapet railings capped with urns. – LODGE. 1804. Ogee-headed windows. – HOME FARM, c. 1800. Two-storey farmhouse; the octagonal chimney flues suggest additions c. 1840.

On the hills to the E of the house a timber mock CRUSADER CASTLE, created 2009, and an OBSERVATORY, 2010–12 by *G. D. Lodge Architects*, created to take advantage of the Galloway Forest Dark Sky Park.

CRAIGIE
4030

A tiny village lying amid the rugged hills S of Kilmarnock, in the shadow of an exposed stone ridge.

CRAIGIE PARISH CHURCH. At the SW extremity of the village. Simple T-plan of 1776 with a tall ogee-headed bellcote on the stepped E gable, above a gabled porch. Two pointed windows on the S elevation, and another with Y-tracery in the gable of the N wing, which also contains an entrance in its E elevation. Cosy and comfortable interior with plaster walls, coved ceiling and panel-fronted galleries, E and W. The Cairnhill Loft, slightly raised, has a blind balustraded front, a boarded ceiling and a well-executed bronze MEMORIAL to John Findlay-Hamilton †1918: an angel and a soldier gaze at each other across the inscription.

S of the church, a MONUMENT to Rev. Campbell †1920. It utilizes a small rectangular stone structure, a few courses high, which may represent some part of the previous church. Its W wall is raised up, in whin, and given red sandstone crowsteps. Also a TABLE TOMB with balustraded sides, quatrefoil panels and dentil moulding.

At the church gates, CLACHAN HOUSE, a harled two-storey house with plain dressings, c. 1807. Opposite are the WAR MEMORIAL, a granite Celtic cross of 1920 and the T-plan former SCHOOL, 1874, its central gable with a trefoil datestone. The village runs NE, with most of the interest on the NW side. Feus were advertised in 1818: 'from its vicinity to Kilmarnock, it is worthy the attention of tradesmen, and as the feuars have the liberty to raise whinstone, the rate of building is moderate'. Of about that date some short rows of vernacular cottages (one dated 1819) whose pitched roofs with tall skews suggest that they were originally thatched. Beyond these, a group of surprisingly welcome houses of the 1970s. The best is No. 23, of 1974, on the NW side of the street, a busy and successful pile of monopitches, using the fall of the land, and finished in stone, render and slate-hanging.

HOUSE OF CRAIGIE, 0.5 km. SW. 1807–8, as the parish manse. An austere two-storey gable-ended house, with a single-storey wing to the l. To one side of the low rushy field to the S, a roofless unicellar brick building with a chimney-breast at one end. This was the village's CURLING HOUSE, where the stones were kept and warmth found. Probably early C20, and a rare survival.

CRAIGIE CASTLE, 2 km. SW. A very significant building, incorporating some of the earliest built remains in the county, and one which should be better known and understood. It is not at first sight a particularly fortified site, for the boggy morasses originally to either side have been substantially drained, and of ditches N and S only the southern is readily detectable. The surviving buildings stand on a mound, and Cruden suggests there may have been a motte at the centre. Two distinctive building phases are evident in the keep: Cruden recognized the first as a hall house of the late C12 or C13, onto which was raised an elaborate vault for a new hall and upper floors in the C15 for the Wallaces of Craigie.

The complex covers a large site with the hall house/keep at the centre and courtyards E and W. Substantial fragments of rubble walls survive and there is some evidence of associated buildings. The heavily overgrown and inaccessible nature of the site makes it difficult to separate built remains from large sections of fallen masonry. From the plan made by MacGibbon and Ross it appears that the entrance was by a pend in the NW angle with a protecting tower. The hall house/keep was a substantial building *c.* 18.3 m. by 11.6 m. The two long rubble-built walls survive, at its wall-walk level a crenellated parapet constructed from dressed sandstone can be detected, with drainage holes along its length, all best preserved on the E wall. The C15 work uses the wall-walk as its base and the merlons are infilled. The hall raised at that time was of exceptionally high quality, its three wide bays faced with ashlar and with groin-vaults springing from delicately carved corbels set into the original wall-walk. The wall ribs of the vaulting enclose the tall arched openings, the latter with simple nook-shafts which frame high-stepped, square-headed windows. Small square openings are centrally placed in the arched heads (what is their purpose?). One complete and two part bays survive on the E; only a single bay survives on the W. At the SE at the ground level a wide chimney opening, probably from the first building period but given clustered column jambs and moulded caps in the C15, of which one survives. No window openings of the first period are obvious but there may have been something in the lost S gable, while archaeological investigation may reveal others. Fragmentary remains of the two upper floors include some simple chamfered window openings.

CARNELL. *See* p. 211.

CRAUFURDLAND CASTLE   *4040*
2 km. S of Fenwick

A house of striking contrasts, built on a steep bank overlooking
Craufurdland Water. It has been the seat of the Craufurds of
Craufurdland since the C13, and they have left very individual
marks on it.

The earliest visible part is the rectangular late C15 or early C16
tower at the W end; it possibly stands on earlier foundations.
It has a stair projection at its NE angle. Its walls are approximately 1.2 m. thick and harled. Above the second floor a continuous moulded corbel table curving round the barely
projecting bartizans and, a curious feature, slightly stepped up
over the S window in the second floor, a detail found also at
Sorn Castle (q.v.). Cannon spouts in the crenellated parapet.
Crowstepped gabled roof within the wall-walk and a substantial chimney at the S. A crowstepped caphouse over the newel
stair. Windows enlarged in the C17. Doorway inserted in the W
elevation by *Patrick Lorimer* of *ARP Architects*, late C20 when
the house was extensively remodelled internally and made into
two dwellings. At the E extent of the building is a domestic C17
wing which began as a detached house with crowstepped
gables and embryo catslide dormers but which by several additions was gradually linked with the tower, notably in 1824–5
with the two-storey addition S of the tower (for library and
drawing room) for William Houison Craufurd.
  Accretive expansion left the house with no grand or indeed
obvious entrance. To address this, *c.* 1830–40 Houison Craufurd commissioned the imposing and theatrical Gothic Revival
façade which brings some unity to the N front. No architect is
known. The scale is disconcerting, with a very low ground
storey and a massive upper one concealing the three-storey
medieval tower. The elevation is symmetrical, of two wide bays
flanking the imposing central tower and two narrower outer
bays, the divisions marked by square shafts with pyramid caps.
Small bartizans mark the outer angles and the front angle of
the central tower, which breaks the corbelled and crenellated
parapet of the lower bays and is finished with an arcaded corbel
table and evenly crenellated parapet. At its base, the entrance
is set into a wide Gothic moulded surround with triple nook-
shafts supporting the outer mouldings and continuous mouldings framing the Gothic panelled door. Above, a framed
armorial panel and four identical tall lancets filled with lattice
glazing and intersecting leaded lights in the heads, all under a
two-centred, arched hoodmould. The other windows in the
upper storey might almost appear to be randomly picked from
a pattern book: in the wider bays paired lancets with triangular
heads under a square hoodmould, in each narrow bay a four-
centred arch-headed opening under a sharply pointed hoodmould. Even the leaded glazing patterns differ. Large shouldered
chimneystacks originally appeared like jack-in-the-boxes from

behind the parapets of the flanking wings. None of this bears any relationship with the earlier parts of the house.

The INTERIOR is equally disjointed. The stair hall has a plaster groin-vault and Gothic detailing in the big arch over the four windows with heraldic stained glass. The plaster details are mirrored in the cornice. A large well staircase and an intersecting three-light Gothic window on the S. Library, SW of the hall, lined with bookcases and with an ornate marble chimneypiece. The drawing room above with an elaborate cornice and a yellowish marble chimneypiece, both of the 1820s. Within the old tower a vaulted ground floor, now the dining room, and former hall above reached by a newel stair, given raised and fielded panelling when the windows were enlarged, probably in the early C18. On the E wing's first floor, the King's Room with a fine plaster ceiling dated 1648. It has geometric panels with decorative frames enclosing a royal coat of arms, the lion and unicorn sporting the flags of St Andrew and St George, royal beasts and foliage patterns, all surprisingly sophisticated. A specific grant enabled all the small heraldic lions to be re-manned! The room is partially panelled and has a simple stone bolection-moulded chimneypiece. The remaining rooms on this floor have been subsequently subdivided but small remnants of C17 plasterwork remain, now much cut about.

In the grounds two mutilated stone EFFIGIES, thought to be Mures of Rowallan and formerly in the Laigh Kirk at Kilmarnock. Possibly medieval.

On the NE drive the remains of a walled courtyard to the rebuilt Craufurdland Mains. It has a series of pointed-arched niches. Was it once part of a walled garden? – GATES. Classical gatepiers with banded globe finials.

CROOKEDHOLM

4030

Roadside hamlet between Kilmarnock and Hurlford. It developed in the C18 around a woollen mill and dissenting chapel, and remained an essentially industrial settlement into the C20. Now mostly residential, at the S end it merges imperceptibly into Hurlford on the other side of the Irvine.

HURLFORD PARISH CHURCH, Main Road. 1856–7 by *William Railton* as a Free Church.* Simple Gothic in pink sandstone, with octagonal three-stage SW tower with narrow lancets, a shallow cusped corbel table and a slated spire with lucarnes and, on alternate faces, stone panels for clocks (absent) with crocketed pediments and colonnettes. W gable with a five-light window with Y-tracery, above a recessed and pointed-headed entrance. Single lancets in the side elevations. The windows in

* It was known as the Reid Memorial Church between 1929 and the local union of 1995.

the gable, tower and vestibule have small diamond-pattern
cast-iron glazing bars. To the rear, gabled red sandstone halls
of 1904 by *Andrew & Newlands*, and further harled brick
monopitched halls of 1972–3. The galleried interior has
plastered walls and a plaster ceiling with crocketed ribs. –
Gothic PULPIT with balustraded steps to l. and r. – ORGAN.
A glorious piece of 1874–5, from the former Parish Church
(*see* below); case probably by *James Ingram*, the instrument
by *Forster & Andrews* of Hull. Given by William Weir of
Kildonan. Pipes, brightly painted in blues and golds, browns
and reds, rise above the glowing red wood of the case, which
is a riot of incised and fretwork Gothic decoration, culminating
in the many brackets which support the pipes at either end,
themselves supported on attached columns. – STAINED GLASS.
l. and r. of the pulpit, two bright cheerful windows, of The
Good Shepherd and John the Baptist, 1937 by the *Abbey
Studio*.

Former HURLFORD PARISH CHURCH, Main Road. 1873–5 by
Robert Ingram (of *J. & R. S. Ingram*). Closed 1995, and now in
residential use. Powerful, almost intimidating E.E., in smoke-
stained and prominently pointed Ballochmyle stone, with a tall
square two-stage SE tower terminating in a balustraded parapet.
The buttressed W gabled front has the main entrance of two
arches beneath a spandrel with a central sandstone roundel of
Christ in Majesty, all recessed within a taller pointed arch,
below a three-light window. Four-bay side elevations, with
pointed deeply recessed two-light gallery windows and paired
aisle windows, and transepts with three-light gable windows.
– STAINED GLASS. Sumptuous W window of 1970 by *Sadie
McLellan*: an extraordinary symbolic discourse on The Natural
Power God Gave to Man. Gabled former MANSE, of 1874–6
by *J. & R. S. Ingram*.

Former CROOKEDHOLM PRIMARY SCHOOL, 0.8 km. NW.
Tudor Gothic of 1873–6 by *Alexander Adamson*. Good, large
and mostly single-storey example of early Board School form.
Now disused.

WAR MEMORIAL, on the main road towards Hurlford. 1922.
Sandstone, with octagonal steps and base, and a square shaft
surmounted by a complex head with scrolled brackets supporting a shallow square block, above which there is a cube with
rosettes, further scrolled, but uncurving, brackets and a ball
finial.

TEMPLETONBURN, 1.2 km. NE. The house, harled Arts and
Crafts with Scots Baronial details of 1901–8 by *J. K. Hunter*,
was badly damaged by fire in the 1960s, leaving only a neat
stepped circular garden seat recess and a stone loggia, incorporated into the respectful replacement of *c.* 2000. The very
mannered U-plan former STABLES survive, with an ungainly
castellated central bay; there are also a LODGE, where the
Baronial elements dominate, and a conically headed DOOCOT,
similar to that at Monktonhead (q.v.).

2040

CROSBIE TOWER
2 km. NE of West Kilbride

A former mansion of the Craufurds, ruinous since a fire *c.* 1992, and the grounds occupied by a substantial caravan and holiday home park. Long, narrow rectangle, dated 1676, with crow-stepped gables and a projecting stair-tower on the S front containing a pilastered entrance. Decorative gabled heads to the attic half-dormers, of 1834 when it was restored as a shooting lodge. Further embellished for Dr James Graham, 1896 (see the dormers on the S front) but his additions to the E were demolished in 2007. Effective panelled GATEPIERS, late C19, with swags, topped by broken pediments and ball finials. The LODGE looks early C20, with a contrasting English Domestic air.

3000

CROSSHILL

The least altered example in Ayrshire of a weavers' village, planned from *c.* 1808. Feus were offered to handloom weavers, many of whom came from Ireland. In the mid C19 it gained a reputation as an 'exciting neighbourhood' (Cuthbertson), with inhabitants 'indolent, improvident and passionately addicted to spirits and tobacco' (*Second Statistical Account*). Modern Crosshill is essentially a dormitory village for Ayr and Maybole.

CROSSHILL PARISH CHURCH, Milton Street. 1838, as a chapel of ease to Kirkmichael. Three-light four-centred windows on the main elevations, to the front above a hipped porch of 1907, to the side above projecting arched niches. Simple plastered interior, reordered in 1975–7 and divided by a screen. – PULPIT with its attractive tester now against the S (short) wall. GATES, 1907 by *A. & J. Main & Co.*, of Glasgow and London.

DESCRIPTION. King Street and Dalhowan Street form the spine. KING STREET is part of the early C19 plan, and has single-storey cottages from that date as well as an effective WAR MEMORIAL of 1920–1 by *Hugh R. Wallace*, executed by *Matthew Muir*, in the form of a stone cenotaph with Celtic decoration, inscriptions and crosses on the faces. DALHOWAN STREET is predominantly single-storey early C19 cottages, originally thatched. On the l. a long gently curving group, remarkably unified. At the corner of No. 15 the street name is incised. Two nice *Glenfield & Kennedy* lion-headed WATER PUMPS. At Nos. 83–87, notable infill of 2004–5 by *ARPL Architects*, a sympathetic front building with irregular glazing, and a tall wooden studio behind. More early C19 cottages in NEWTON STREET and, on the r., the ruinous former FREE CHURCH of 1848 by *Alexander* of Ayr, with a gabled porch and solid bellcote, and a good four-bay two-storey early C19 house with a four-centred pend to the r.

DAILLY ROAD begins with an early C19 MILESTONE, the lower part crassly lost in tarmac, and an Ayr County Council FINGERPOST, possibly 1930s, made by the *Royal Label Factory*,

Stratford on Avon. In Kirkmichael Road, EBENEZER GOSPEL HALL; 1932 by *Allan Stevenson & Cassels* and the former SCHOOL (Crosshill Community Centre) of 1881; the single-storey H-plan and wooden veranda make it look like a country railway station.

KIRKBRIDE HOUSE. *See* p. 480.

CROSSHOUSE

3030

Developed in the C19 to serve long-vanished collieries, the miners' rows superseded by local authority housing.

CROSSHOUSE PARISH CHURCH, Kilmarnock Road. 1880–2 by *Bruce & Sturrock* of Glasgow. Red sandstone, with a prominent shouldered central gable containing a big Perp window which has a broad central transom with quatrefoil decoration. Entrance tower to the r., with square-headed bell-openings set within recessed panels, short top stage of stepped parapet and filleted angle shafts now shorn of finials. ORGAN (N wall) of 1901, with pulpit in front. – STAINED GLASS. W wall. One window a dramatic memorial to Rev. William White, 1948 by *Douglas Strachan*. To its r. Blessed are the Pure in Heart *c.* 1955 by *John Blyth*; particularly effective the working collier in the bottom panel. E wall. The Good Shepherd, 1911 by *William Meikle & Sons*; the figures unusually expressive, caught in mid-conversation.

MANSE, 1887, also by *Bruce & Sturrock*. Naturalistic decoration high in the gable, and triangular first-floor windows, matching those of the church. – WAR MEMORIAL, of 1921 by *Matthew Muir & Co.*, after St Martin's Cross, Iona.

CROSSHOUSE HOSPITAL, 1 km. E. Planned from 1966, built 1973–7. By *Boissevain & Osmond*, of Glasgow. Strong horizontal lines, bright white colour, and situation in the bowl of the Irvine valley make it a prominent presence in the landscape. Steel-framed, concrete central block of five storeys; long, with continuous bands of horizontal windows. Lower wings projecting and taller square towers towards either end. Originally flat-roofed, contributing to the stark aesthetic. Of the various subsequent additions and alterations only the following stand out: LISTER CENTRE, *c.* 1985, in the style of the main hospital, and the bold brick harled and timber-clad two-storey MATERNITY UNIT, 2005–6, by *Keppie Design*. One wing of this continues the hospital frontage, while a curving rear wing encloses two courtyards; entrance and spacious reception area in a drum tower. Arranged on the hill to the E, and evoking an Italian hill village, STAFF HOUSING of 1973–82 by the *Scottish Special Housing Association*, demonstrating their ability to work equally well with four-storey flats and two-storey terraces, using changes of level, the contours and curving roads to create a sense of place.

CROSSHOUSE PRIMARY SCHOOL, Playing Field Road. 1930s Neo-Georgian by *Ayr County Council* (*William Reid*, County Architect). The outer bays of its long block ape pavilions and have stone cornices.

CARMELBANK, 0.8 km. SW. A farmhouse or small mansion of greater than usual pretension, probably built *c.* 1800 for John Cunninghame of Carmelbank. Distinguished arched entrance incorporating a fanlight; an alcove of corresponding form in the hip-roofed pavilion to the l.

THORNTOUN, 1.5 km. W. A small estate, in the possession of the Cunninghames of Cadell from *c.* 1700. The house built for them *c.* 1800 was demolished *c.* 1967 when ownership passed to Dr Barnardo's; on the site a large, assured RESIDENTIAL SCHOOL, mainly two-storey, in dark brown brick, with tiled panels: 1969–72 by *H. Hall* of London, with *Stanley Poole, Brand & Associates* of Edinburgh. A classical mid-C19 single storey LODGE, with curved screen railings, survives.

CROSSRAGUEL ABBEY★

2000

2 km. SW of Maybole

Seen from the road that now bisects the precinct, the buildings present a highly attractive image of a medieval rural monastery of moderate scale. The abbey was the second of Scotland's two Cluniac houses, with its origins in a grant made to Paisley Abbey by Duncan, who was made Earl of Carrick in 1214–16. His intention was to found a monastery, but Paisley was reluctant to relinquish the endowment and initially made provision for no more than an oratory served by some of its own monks. In 1244 a ruling was made by Bishop William de Bondington of Glasgow that a monastery exempt from the control of Paisley must be established. Despite Paisley's protests, it was in existence by a date between 1274 and 1292, when an abbot is first recorded. The house possibly suffered in the early stages of the wars with England, because in 1329 there was a grant of the king's penny for repairs, and there is some evidence of works on the nave from around this time. According to Fr Richard Augustine Hay, writing *c.* 1700, albeit on the basis of no currently known documentation, Abbot Colin Kennedy (1460–90) carried out major building works, which can probably be associated with a new choir, the adjacent parts of the E conventual range, and parts of the S range. Hay also says that works were carried out by Gilbert Macbrayer, who was buried in the abbey in 1547, but these cannot be identified. The abbey is said to have been partly destroyed by the reformers in 1561, though in the following year Abbot Quintin Kennedy, a well-qualified theologian who was fostering recusancy in Ayrshire, dared to conduct a disputation with Knox over a period of three days. The first systematic repairs of the buildings

★ The entry for the abbey is by Richard Fawcett.

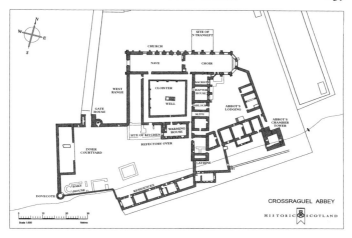

Crossraguel Abbey.
Plan

were carried out in 1897–9 by *James A. Morris*, and there were
further works after the abbey was taken into state care in 1913.

In its final form the PLAN of the church was an elongated rectangle terminating in an E apse, though excavation has shown
that in an earlier state it was cruciform, with transeptal chapels
on each side towards the E end, and possibly with a sacristy in
the re-entrant angle between the S chapel and the choir. The
cloister was to the S. There was also an inner courtyard, S and
SW of the cloister, and another range along the S side of that
courtyard, evidently of a relatively late date, which was subdivided into individual residences. E of the cloister was the
abbot's residence, extending around two sides of its own
courtyard.

The CHURCH is aisleless, and of thirteen bays terminating
in a three-sided E apse; some of those bays are irregularly
spaced and, although the nave and choir are of almost equal
length, the former is of eight bays and the latter of only five.

Despite the simplicity of its plan, the NAVE, which is constructed of a variety of types of ashlar and rubble, is difficult
to understand. It has a base course of slightly varying form,
stepping up towards the W end, which probably originally
consisted throughout of two levels of chamfers below a pronounced roll. This runs along the N flank, including the W bay
of the choir, and turns along at least the W side of the excavated
N transeptal chapel. It also runs across the W front and along
the S flank for a length equivalent to slightly more than two of
the bays on the N side. However, the only masonry that appears
to be contemporary with it is the buttresses at the W corners,
the wall to either side of the W door, and possibly some of the

masonry below the windows along the N flank. All of this is
likely to be mid-C13, and the S wall may be of the same date.
The W doorway has a depressed two-centred arch with three
continuous orders of flattened wave mouldings rising from a
chamfered sill. This could be an earlier C14 insertion, perhaps
after the grant of 1329. The upper parts of the N wall have been
entirely rebuilt. The new buttresses have chamfered base
courses; but below them are the retained lower parts of the
earlier base courses, which would presumably once have been
covered by raised ground levels. The N doorway, in the third
bay from the W, may have been assembled from earlier fragments, perhaps in the C15. The jambs have a variety of keeled
or filleted rolls separated by hollows, but with no bases, and at
the top they have been cut back below capitals that are little
more than moulded imposts; the arch, consisting of four orders
of cavettos, pays little obvious regard to the jambs. Above the
door is a re-set deep, trifoliate-headed C13 niche. Inside, E of
the door is a cut-back holy water stoup. Windows were provided in only the five E bays of the nave. Their reveals, with
sequences of cavettos inside and out, point to a date not before
the earlier C15 (cf. the window at the W end of the N nave
aisle of Dryburgh Abbey). At an unknown date they were
modified by the insertion of transoms at arch springing level
for rectangular glazing frames. Only the second window from
the E retains tracery, but this is of c. 1530 and is associated
internally with the tomb of Egidia Lady Row (she gave orders
that she was to be buried before the Lady altar in 1530, and
that altar was therefore presumably in the nave's NE corner).
This window is of two lights, with an encircled sexfoil between
the trifoliate light-heads, and transoms at arch springing level
that are of flattened V-shape. It compares with the window in
the chantry chapel at Straiton church (q.v.), and was presumably the work of the same mason. Lady Row's tomb-slab
survives inside, below the window, and there appears to have
been a canopy over it, of which the bases and the lower jambs
on the E side survive. The easternmost window is partially
blocked by the cross wall built in the later C15 to divide the
nave from the rebuilt choir. At the centre of that wall is a
round-arched doorway with continuous mouldings of a filleted
roll between hollows. To its N there is a segmental-arched
recess that was probably associated with the altar of the Lady
Chapel. S of the door, the wall is thickened on the E side to
accommodate a spiral stair from the choir to a rood loft, of
which nothing more survives than an upper doorway and
pockets for the timbers that supported the loft. Also S of the
door are traces of an altar platform. Surmounting the gable of
the cross wall is a bellcote, with openings for two bells below
a gabled apex and a cross finial.

By contrast with the much-remodelled nave, the CHOIR is
altogether more elegant, and appears architecturally homo-
geneous, despite earlier masonry having been retained within
its W bay. The aisleless apsidal plan may have drawn inspiration

Crossraguel Abbey, east end of the choir.
Engraving, published 1852

from that of the French-inspired chapel at St Salvator's College in St Andrews (built 1450–60 for Abbot Kennedy's presumed kinsman, Bishop James Kennedy). Constructed mainly of ashlar, the buttressed walls of the choir rise from a chamfered base course, except (as already noted) in the w bay on the N side. There is a chamfered string course below the windows that is reflected in a chamfered intake below a mid-height offset of the buttresses, at a level corresponding with the window arch springing. Along the flanks, the window reveals are composed of orders of broad chamfers, but around the apse prominence is given to the site of the high altar by considerably richer mouldings, with two shafted orders both internally and externally. As in the nave, transoms for modified glazing have been inserted.

A scroll-moulded string course runs below the inside of the windows, except in the second and third bays from the w, where it has been cut back. The bays are marked by triplet wall-shafts; in the presbytery these rise from bases at ground level, but in the choir they rise from the string course, presumably to avoid interfering with the choir stalls. The windows in the two w bays on the N side are narrower than the others, and that in the w bay has a lower sill, perhaps partly because it was in the area of the ante-choir where there were no stalls, but probably also because earlier masonry was retained in the lower and w part of the wall. The upper walls are slightly thickened above the window heads, beyond a hoodmoulding that extends across horizontally to interconnect the windows at arch springing level, and the wall-shafts are reduced to single shafts at that upper level. On the S side is a door to a dog-legged passage to the sacristy; that passage crosses the base of a stair to the rooms above the sacristy and chapter house. The doorway has a three-centred arch with mouldings consisting of a continuous filleted roll flanked by hollows. The doorway in the W bay, with similar mouldings but a depressed two-centred arch, gave access to the cloister. The way in which the internal string course is arched upwards, together with the external survival of a single jamb stone, shows that this doorway was initially to have been located a little to the W. A post-Reformation doorway directly into the sacristy from the choir has been blocked.

The furnishings must have made a major contribution to the internal impact of the choir and presbytery, though we can now only imagine the appearance of the high altar and choir stalls. At a later date, a platform for the altar approached across three broad steps with edge-rolls was constructed; the altar would then have been placed against a wall across the apse, which presumably supported a retable. In the wall of the SE angle of the apse is a two-basin PISCINA and narrow CRE-DENCE SHELF; it is set within a recess capped by a three-centred arch below a crocketed ogee super-arch flanked by pinnacles carried on miniature buttresses. W of this is a four-seat SEDILIA, the seats surmounted by arches and elaborately crocketed gablets punctuated by pinnacles; within the wall thickness are four half-bays of miniature vaulting. E of the door from the ante-choir to the cloister is a Holy Water STOUP, a rectangular recess with a broken basin, and with the arcs of an inverse arch cut into the lintel.

It is evident from the continuity of the base courses that the parts of the E CONVENTUAL RANGE adjacent to the church, on the site of the earlier S transeptal chapel, were built along with the choir. There was evidently a significant change of plan in the earlier phases of the work, however, since, along the N wall of the sacristy and the stair vestibule to its E, three wall-shafts were built with the lower parts of the wall, and the easternmost is in a position that suggests the sacristy was initially to have been wider from W to E. The intention at that stage must have been to reuse the E foundation of the demolished chapel. Instead a small lobby was formed between the sacristy and the stair to the upper floor. The jambs of the door from the sacristy to the stair, with mouldings in the form of a slender roll and hollow, were also left unfinished. Covering the sacristy is a sexpartite vault rising from corbels carved with heads or animals. Sexpartite vaults enjoyed a limited revival in late medieval Scotland (see e.g. the choir of St Monans church (Fife), as remodelled around the 1470s, as well as a number of late towers). In the S half of the E wall is a three-light window, and there are two similar windows in the adjacent chapter house, each with a large quatrefoil at the head of the tracery field (extensively but correctly restored in 1899). Such tracery is an illustration of a renewed interest in mid-C13 types, and amongst related examples of the revival of earlier tracery forms is the E window of St Mirin's Chapel at Paisley Abbey (Renfrewshire), of *c.* 1499. Here it is the pointed head of the quatrefoil and the ogee curves of the dagger forms in the side spandrels that confirm the windows' mid-C15 date.

The CHAPTER HOUSE is square, with four compartments of quadripartite vaulting carried on a heavily weathered octofoil clustered-shaft pier with a moulded capital. Chapter houses of this plan had been favoured in Scotland from the mid C13, whether within the body of the range, as at Cambuskenneth Abbey (Stirling and Central Scotland), or attached to the side of the building, as at Glasgow Cathedral, and were again in favour in the late middle ages, with the closest parallel for Crossraguel's at Glenluce Abbey (Dumfries and Galloway). Unusually, the chapter house is entered from the cloister by an asymmetrically placed doorway, in the NW compartment. At the centre of the E wall is an ogee-arched recess for the abbot's seat, and there were stone benches around all four walls. That there was no intention of simply extending the dormitory over these parts is demonstrated by the higher levels of the vaults over the sacristy and chapter house than over the rest of the range, and by the way that the chamber above the sacristy and chapter house was separately enclosed.

The mainly rubble-built S parts of the E conventual range appear to have been extensively modified internally, perhaps at the same time that the N parts were rebuilt, and it is no longer possible to identify the functions of everything now seen. The room immediately adjacent to the chapter house was contracted when the latter was built, and a day stair to the dormitory was built within it. The passage of the PARLOUR can be identified from the stone benches along each side. Further S is a SLYPE that gave access between the cloister and the courtyard of the abbot's lodging and at the end of the range is a narrow latrine block over the main drain. Several ground-floor rooms now house displays of grave-slabs and architectural fragments.

The ashlar-constructed E part of the S CONVENTUAL RANGE was evidently rebuilt at the same time as the sacristy and chapter house. Only the lower storey survives and the large fireplace within it suggests the warming room was located here. Above it would have been the refectory, which was reached by a stair immediately S of the warming room, and thus at the centre of the range. The stair doorway has very similar mouldings to those of the doorway from the sacristy to the stair to its E. The W part of the S range, which appears to have remained structurally relatively unchanged, housed the kitchen; it was perhaps separately roofed from the rest. At first the cloister was probably enclosed to the W by no more than a wall, but later a W CONVENTUAL RANGE was built, presumably housing cellars and an outer parlour adjacent to the church.

The lower walls of the CLOISTER walks survive, and these show that on the N and W sides they were of four bays demarcated by shallow buttresses. The corbels that supported the wall-plate of the roofs over the walks are in place along much of the N and E sides and along part of the S side; at the junctions of the N walk with the E and W walks the roof was supported by diagonal arches. At the centre of the garth is a sunken WELL approached down a flight of steps; an inscription on one of the lower steps records that they were made for Sir John Boyd, presumably in the late C15 or early C16.

The INNER COURTYARD, to the S and SW of the main claustral complex, is entered through an imposing GATEHOUSE in its N wall. This is of rectangular plan with a prominent circular stair-turret at its SE corner. The lower part of the stair, together with the adjacent stretches of precinct wall, is pierced by loops of dumb-bell form. At ground-floor level of the gatehouse is the barrel-vaulted entrance passage, with a narrow porter's lodge on its W side. Above this are two levels of chambers, each equipped with a fireplace, aumbry and latrine closet, and with windows furnished with seats in both the N and S walls. At the top a wall-walk is surrounded by a parapet carried on corbels, with projecting rounds at the two N corners. There would have been a garret within the roof, and at this level the stair-turret was topped by a square caphouse with a saddle-back roof. The checkered corbelling of the outer face of the gatehouse suggests a date of construction no earlier than *c*. 1500. The buildings around the courtyard included what may have been a barn to the W and a bakehouse with a projecting bread oven to the SW. At the SW angle of the courtyard wall is a round tower with gunloops of inverted keyhole form; a C16 DOOCOT of beehive type has been added on top of it. Along the E part of the courtyard's S side are the footings of what appears to be a row of five small individual residences, with a sixth on the S side of the enclosure in front of the entrance to the Abbot's Lodging. It has been suggested these were built for corrodians, individuals who had acquired or bought the right to live within the abbey and to be fed at its expense. If they are indeed of medieval date, it may be more likely either that they were residences for some of the monks at a time when conventual life was being pursued less communally, or houses for lay officers of the abbey.

The ABBOT'S LODGING could be approached through the inner court by way of the smaller enclosure at its E end, or by the slype within the E claustral range; there may also have been direct access from the wider precinct to the E. The rubble-built main part of the residence was set at an angle along the S side of the abbot's courtyard and abutted the monastic dormitory, so that the letter of the rule that the abbot should live in common with his monks could be observed. Only the ground floor of this survives, but it was originally divided into two unequal parts, the larger to the W presumably corresponding to the Abbot's Hall on the upper level, and the smaller to the E corresponding to his chamber. Both of those parts at the lower level have been later subdivided, with barrel vaults built over them, and a latrine block has been added over the drain on the S side of the range. The lower part of the external stair that led up to the first-floor rooms of the lodging survives against the N wall. On the E side of the abbot's courtyard is a range of domestic offices, including a kitchen. Off the SE corner of the main range is the later CHAMBER TOWER, perhaps added in the time of Abbot Kennedy, since there are masons' marks matching those found in the rebuilt part of the E conventual range. It is essentially a smaller version of the type of later medieval tower house built by large numbers of land-owners. It rises through three main storeys above a barrel-vaulted basement, and there would also have been a garret within the roof behind a wall-head parapet. There was a doorway into the basement on the W side, but the main entrance was at first-floor level, by way of a vaulted vestibule that linked with the earlier part of the abbot's residence. The single chamber on each main floor of the tower was fitted out with a fireplace, closets and generously scaled windows. A spiral stair within the wall thickness at the SE corner connected the basement and first floor, and the levels from the second floor upwards; but access between the first and second floors was presumably at the NE corner, which has collapsed.

CULZEAN CASTLE   2010

Perched sensationally on precipitous cave-riddled cliffs S of Culzean Bay, the Castle could belong to the stuff of legend with its bold circular tower and crenellated silhouette set against a forest backdrop. It symbolizes on the one hand the ancient power of the Kennedy family and on the other their cultural presence in late C18 Scotland. This romantic and powerful statement is *Robert Adam*'s masterpiece and the most complete example of his Castle Style. Designed in 1776 and completed after Adam's death in 1792, the Castle was created for the 10th Earl of Cassillis. Unlike Dalquharran (q.v.) or Seton (East Lothian), the evolution is more complex than appearances suggest.

The earliest known building on the site was Coif, or Cove, Castle, acquired in 1580 by Thomas Kennedy and rebuilt in 1590 at 'grate coste and expensse' to withstand the ceaseless feuding of the Kennedy clan and their neighbours. Pont's survey (1585–95) almost certainly shows Sir Thomas Kennedy's 'Koif', set within a barmkin, as the most substantial building in the area. In the mid C17 the defensive barmkin wall was breached and three terraces constructed as fashionable hanging gardens; these, mod-ified, can be seen in the surviving terraces S of the Castle. Aber-crummie (the Episcopal minister of nearby Maybole) described the castle in 1696 as 'standing upon a rock above the Sea, flanked upon the South with very pretty gardens and orchards adorned with excellent tarrases, and the walls loaden with peaches, apri-cotes, cherries, and other fruits; and these gardens are so well sheltered from the north and east winds, and ly so open to the south that the fruit and herbage are more early than at any other place in Carrick'. Sir John Kennedy, one of the earliest landowners in Scotland to introduce enclosure on his estate, from *c*. 1705 greatly improved its agricultural output and the estate's finances. Improvements to the Castle were made in the 1740s, 1750s and 1760s by Sir Thomas Kennedy, despite his absence 1748–54 on the Grand Tour. For instance in 1750 a new dining room (now the Library) was made in the ground floor of the tower with views to the terraces. Upon his return, in 1755 he approached *James Adam* to design a villa but did not proceed further and *Sir William Chambers*'s drawings for a Doric 'Casine', or banqueting house, also went unrealized in 1759. In that year Kennedy claimed succession to the title and estates of the Earl of Cassillis (he succeeded, after a protracted challenge in the courts, in 1762). A second visit to the Continent followed in 1764–5, during which time Kennedy commissioned a set of drawings (dated 1765) for a country house from I. Aulagnier, a little-known Marseilles architect, but these too were unbuilt. Instead in 1766–8 a detached, plain, barrack-like 'Office House' was built along the cliff edge N of the L-shaped tower house. It was set at an angle to the castle and housed not only service and bedrooms but also a billiard room. The presence of this range had an undue influence on the major developments initiated from 1775 by the 9th Earl's brother and successor, Sir David Kennedy, who in 1776 commissioned *Robert Adam* to create a major country house from the existing hotchpotch of buildings, illustrated in a picturesque view (attributed to Robert Adam) of 1776. This commission was a huge challenge. The old tower and the office house were to be retained together with the stable range to the E leaving little space for new building because of the steep fall of the land to the S and W.

From 1776 to 1782 Adam and his clerk of works, *Hugh Cairncross*, undertook the first phase of transformation. This included the recasting and enlargement of the tower house into a regular rectangular plan with the earlier part flanked by lower wings animated by corner turrets. In remodelling the 1760s range Adam also planned a separate kitchen block for the area between this and the E end of the castle. A laundry tower was proposed for the W end of the 1760s range but was quickly replaced by a more adventurous design for a circular brewhouse and offices in a butterfly-like plan. The position of these service buildings, along with the retention of the tower house, dictated that the principal rooms of the house faced S, overlooking the gardens. For a house intended to impress visitors the lack of a sea view was serious. The second phase, proposed in 1784, was intended to remedy this and envisaged demolition of most of the angled 1760s range and its replacement by a straight link between Adam's kitchen and brewhouse with a large three-storey drum tower at its centre. The bold form of this feature was influenced perhaps by designs of 1759 for Kedleston by James Paine (published in 1783) but also show a debt to Adam's design for Dalquharran (1782–5, q.v.), built for a relative, Thomas Kennedy of Dunure, and

Adam's niece. His scheme for Culzean failed, however, to resolve the link with the existing castle and in 1787 the earl decided to encourage Adam 'to indulge to the utmost his romantic and fruitful genius' in the wholesale reconstruction of the N and E fronts.

The revised proposals would transform Culzean into a spectacular country seat. All the pre-1776 works were swept away and the N front of the castle taken down. In its place rose a grand three-storey addition with a symmetrical centrepiece for the sea front of a drum tower, containing a circular Saloon (interestingly such a room had also been planned in Aulangier's unrealized designs of 1765) flanked by set-back towers of equal height. Inside, uniting the N and S halves of the building, Adam introduced a grand oval columned stair compartment. From the accounts, the creation of Adam's Culzean cost approximately £2–3 million in today's money, and even then much was unfinished when Adam and the 10th Earl died in 1792.

Subsequent generations continued to work in the Adam spirit; in 1877 *Charles Reid* of *Wardrop & Reid* added the nursery wing and undertook some interior remodelling. In 1945 the house and a part of the estate were handed over to the National Trust for Scotland. The Trust embarked on major conservation work and under the agreement with the Kennedy family created a guest flat at the top of the house, which was offered to General Dwight D. Eisenhower for his lifetime.

But the question remains: why did two bachelor brothers, the younger of whom spent much of his time at Newark Castle (*see* below), need such a magnificent house? The influence of the Grand Tour must, as noted, have played a part and this experience, in concert with the inheritance of the Cassillis estate and the title, would have been a powerful incentive to underline the continued importance of the Kennedy family in Ayrshire and beyond. To this end Sir David (10th Earl) devoted his energy and fortune.

EXTERIOR

The account of the castle and its setting should begin with the Cat Gates (SW) or the Hoolity Ha' Bridge (SE) and their drives from which all drama is denied until they meet at the RUINED ARCH AND VIADUCT. But since the division of the estate in 1945 and realignment of the roads, the modern visitor is denied a grand entrance, a utilitarian kiosk being no substitute. The present drive snakes from a high level down through the parkland, offering a distant, tranquil view of the castle devoid of excitement and romance. At the ruined arch and its flanking asymmetrical towers the excitement begins. They are built in pinkish sandstone rubble and belong to the dramatic final phase of work begun 1787 and unfinished at Adam's death. The long, unadorned, serpentine viaduct, replacing an earlier simpler construction, was conceived in 1780 and mainly built by *c.* 1784 as a symbolic gesture to resolve a functional problem of spanning the glen. The viaduct, supported on big plain

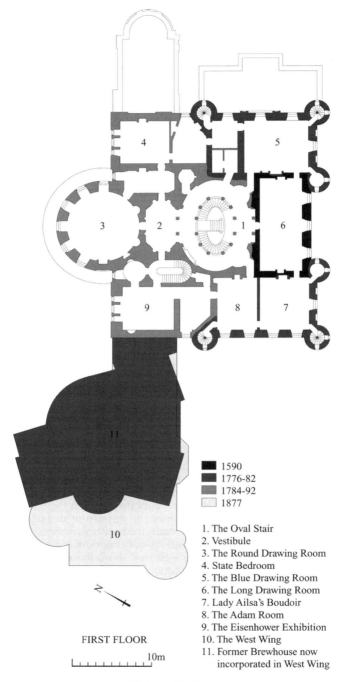

1590
1776-82
1784-92
1877

1. The Oval Stair
2. Vestibule
3. The Round Drawing Room
4. State Bedroom
5. The Blue Drawing Room
6. The Long Drawing Room
7. Lady Ailsa's Boudoir
8. The Adam Room
9. The Eisenhower Exhibition
10. The West Wing
11. Former Brewhouse now
   incorporated in West Wing

FIRST FLOOR

10m

Culzean Castle.
First Floor Plan

Roman arches with an Italianate corbelled parapet and heroic fortifications symbolize an unsettled past, while through the arch, a romantic vista to the transformed castle, now outward facing with only sham defences, looks to the future. An egg-shaped ice house is, rather surprisingly, sunk into one of the viaduct piers.

At the head of the viaduct, set into the forecourt wall is the FORECOURT ARCH, proposed in 1784, a classical triumphal arch symbolic of the new era and originally providing a stark counterpoint to the Ruined Arch, although its form is now mellowed by the scarring effect of salt winds on its stonework. Set in its crenellated parapet a bold panel with the Kennedy arms and motto *Avise La Fine* and crowned with a boy astride a dolphin, possibly added in 1811. The piers match those to the s front terrace. The large, roughly circular FORECOURT is enclosed by low crenellated walls, broken at the s to provide an entrance to the top E terrace, itself retained by yet more crenellated walls and, on the N, by the MORTAR BATTERY. The last was constructed 1829, possibly by *Thomas White Jun.* as part of comprehensive improvements to the policies (*see* p. 254), as a platform from which to admire Ailsa Craig and Arran, also providing a base for two symbolic mortars and a sundial mounted on a sculpted characterful head. In the centre of the court an octagonal plinth provides the base for a further mortar. Beyond the forecourt on the seaward side, an outer retaining wall clings to the edge of the cliff and hides a servants' passage to the Castle. On the E side of the court, opposite the entrance to the castle, are two squat square guard towers and conically capped, crenellated drum piers framing the entrance to the TOWER GATE, the centrepiece of a stable range of 1750–3 (i.e. for Sir Thomas Kennedy) reusing materials from a demolished building on the cliff top, but radically revamped in 1779 by Adam to bring it stylistically into line with the Castle (although the outline of an earlier pediment can still be seen in the masonry). He introduced a Venetian window over the archway and a Diocletian one above, a clock in the upper stage and a crenellated parapet with diminutive bartizans at the angles. The flanking ranges were parapeted at the same time and tall, anchoring angle turrets added at the outer angles. (For stable courtyard beyond *see* Policies and Estate Buildings, below.)

The culmination of the theatrical build-up which began at the Ruined Arch is reached at the s FRONT of the Castle itself. This shows most clearly the evolution of the first phase, the reconstruction and enlargement of the existing buildings. The earlier tower house, raised in 1760 to provide an attic storey, forms the central section of this elevation, but refaced by Adam in warm-hued sandstone from the Blanefield quarry. Large, regularly spaced windows were introduced into the ground and first floors, set within a balustraded, pilastered and arched frontispiece creating an unexpected articulation. The corbelled frieze above this section with terracotta lozenges filled with Kennedy emblems emphasizes the trophy nature of this house. 59

The two lower wings added to E and W clasp the tower but have none of the articulating detail of the centrepiece, interest being created from the pattern and sizing of the unarchitraved windows: forms that Adam later used over the entrance at Seton House (East Lothian). The W wing wraps around the tower to infill the angle created by the L-plan. This and the E and S elevations are given movement by the tall turrets housing newel stairs or closets – Adam's subtle interpretation of castle-like elements – that mask the junction of his wings with the tower house and clasp all the angles. Each turret has a simple, cross-shaped window, a motif adopted in many estate buildings, additional narrow-arched windows and a crenellated parapet. This crenellation continues in all the parapets, given diminutive angle bartizans over the old tower.

Similar crenellations continue across the E FRONT of the E wing. Adam was forced by lack of space for a carriage drive on the S and the constraints of internal planning to maintain this as the entrance front. The door is now concealed behind a bulky single-storey porch of 1877 but above this is a blind screen, in the form of a triumphal arch, rising to the sill of the second-floor window, underlining the impact this house was intended to make. N of the entrance is the kitchen range of 1779, single-storey but tall and chapel-like, with a semicircular E end (the model for the tea house at Auchincruive) and high, arched upper windows set in full-height blind arches. Originally virtually free-standing, only linked to the E front by a wall. The bartizaned linking block with a Diocletian window, mirroring the window in the Tower Gate, was built in the second phase c. 1790.

The extraordinary theatrical composition of the N FRONT is best seen from the sea, although it is no longer exactly as Adam left it, having been partially obscured by the W wing added in 1877. It is Adam's dramatic three-stage drum tower, begun soon after 1785, which still dominates, with seven curved bays projecting from the main elevation. It stands on a solid, battered masonry drum growing from the cliff face; at ground-floor level deeply recessed openings framed by splayed piers support the balcony in front of the first-floor, full-length windows set in arched panels. In the storey above, alternating arched and flat-headed windows below a boldly corbelled parapet enclosing a low conical and finialled roof. The whole is not as Roman as the elevation produced in 1785 and instead draws elements from the frontispiece of the S elevation. To either side of the drum are wide, full-height bays with variants of a Venetian window in the principal floor and crenellated parapets with tiny bartizans over the second. The E of these bays required the partial refronting of the kitchen range. The W bay now links to the 1877 reconstruction of the W service buildings (*see* below). The remodelled circular brewhouse still has an important articulating presence at the W of the N front.

NURSERY WING added in 1877 by *Wardrop & Reid* (mainly *Charles Reid*) who expanded and raised the low, butterfly-plan

service wings and brewhouse to provide better family accommodation. The character of the work is sympathetic with symmetrical W and S elevations enlivened with round towers, a
turret and crenellations. The W FRONT of Adam's extension to
the tower house is a simple composition with, as on the E front,
battered stair-turrets anchoring the angles.

INTERIOR

The classically conceived interior contrasts with the Castle Style
exterior. Recent research has revealed that the process of
change continued through the C19, albeit powerfully influenced by Adam's vision. The interior at Culzean should no
longer be seen as purely the work of Robert Adam. The 1877
alterations, in particular, are perhaps the earliest example in
Britain of Adam Revival in a genuine Adam house and thus
very important in the history of taste. These subtle changes
and introductions will become clear as the rooms are described.

The layout of rooms is entirely unconventional for a country
house, the consequence of constraints imposed by the reuse of
the existing tower and by the site itself, which means that the
principal rooms are not on the same floor. Dining Room and
Library were confined to the ground floor with Drawing
Rooms and best bedrooms on the first with little in the way of
family accommodation; little wonder that they required the
extensions of 1877 by Wardrop & Reid. Also of that date the
PORTICO which incorporated to l. and r. offices and plan
rooms for the 3rd Marquis of Ailsa's boat-building enterprise;
part of these are now incorporated into the ENTRANCE LOBBY,
the former S division marked by an Ionic screen. The bookcases
were installed in 1877 from the original Library (*see* Dining
Room, below). The original front door with fanlight is preserved as the entrance into the stone-floored ARMOURY,
Adam's entrance hall, restyled in 1812 for a display of weapons
acquired by the 12th Earl. It is now as enlarged in 1877, incorporating the former Buffet Room to its S, when the Doric
screen was inserted. Consoled stone chimneypiece, 1778, with
a dolphin and coronet. Opposite the entrance a door leads to
the Stair Hall, at the heart of the plan, and from there to the
first-floor Drawing Rooms, but at the opposite end of the
Armoury, there is a deep angled doorway cut through the wall
thickness of the 1590s tower, the ground floor of which is
occupied by a single room, called the LIBRARY since 1877; but
created in 1750 as a S-facing 'eating room' for Sir Thomas
Kennedy, under the supervision of *Thomas Clayton* (possibly the
plasterer who worked extensively for the Adam brothers), to take
advantage of the views over the C17 terraces and garden. It was
maintained as the Dining Room by Adam in 1778–9, but charmingly remodelled with apsidal ends and redecorated, using fruit
and vines to reflect its use and given symmetry with opposing
curved mahogany doors in the bowed ends. To the r. of the
chimneypiece, a door to the Stair Hall and matching dummy to

the l., all with consoled cornices. White marble chimneypiece,
with swagged frieze and decorative pilasters. Delicate plaster
ceiling, with high-quality inserted painted roundels of nymphs
in classical settings, the central one set in an anthemion-moulded
frame, by an unidentified artist (*Antonio Zucchi* has been suggested); circles, swags, urns and rosettes make up the pattern
with swagged panels at the angles of the central square filled
with gryphons, all coloured in shades of green.

The DINING ROOM, adjoining to the W, was formed in 1877
from the late C18 Library (S) and Dressing Room (N) to be
closer to the kitchen in the new W wing. *Charles Reid* retained
only a fragment of Adam's decorative scheme on the S wall,
which has three segment-headed windows flanked by stucco
roundels and tablets above the doors to the stair-turrets at the
angles. The bucranium frieze, however, was reproduced on the
other walls, part of Reid's scholarly revival of Adam's classical
style which included the papier mâché ceiling copied with
subtle modifications to fit the space from Adam's design for
the Music Room at No. 20 St James's Square, London (1772–
3). It is in higher relief than the C18 plasterwork and not
coloured. The chimneypiece and consoled doorcases are
copied from the old Dining Room (*see* above). At the N end, a
Corinthian-columned screen marks the buffet.

61   The OVAL STAIRCASE provides the showpiece at the heart
of the house. Designed 1787 but still undergoing modification
in 1790 and probably completed *c.* 1810 under the supervision
of *Cairncross*. This *tour de force*, inspired by the Temple of
Jupiter at Spalato, not only resolved, in a very theatrical
manner, the awkward junction between the old tower and the
new W-facing drum but also transformed the circulation for
the main rooms. The stair hall with the colonnades fronting
the ground-floor circulation space and the galleries has a rare
distinction, linking the rooms on all sides. The weighty Doric
piered arcade at ground floor; above, an unusual reversal of
the Orders, with the Corinthian on the *piano nobile* and the
Ionic for the upper gallery. This reversal of the conventional
hierarchy is both practical, emphasizing the importance of the
piano nobile, and visually effective, exaggerating the sense of
height. The decision may have been the 12th Earl's (his portrait
shows him against a more elaborate but similarly detailed
colonnade) but Adam used such a strategy for effect at Osterley
and elsewhere. The grand imperial stair with its elegant metal
balusters of pedestalled urns, made of brass, gunmetal and
wrought iron, rises to the *piano nobile*. The stair was designed
for access to the State Apartments on the S front, created by
Adam in his first building campaign, and the Round Drawing
Room and the (planned) suite of State Rooms on the N.

The S State Apartments Rooms, arranged *enfilade*, all have
delicate friezes to the doorcases mirrored in the main entablatures. The first of two drawing rooms is the BLUE DRAWING
ROOM (SE) with a white statuary marble chimneypiece of
1778, overdoors and frieze with winged gryphons and urns,

and a delicately ornamented and finely detailed plaster ceiling with a central painted panel and, surprisingly, four sculptured bas reliefs set within the central circle, all delicately tinted. The LONG DRAWING ROOM at the centre of the s front occupies the space of the former Great Hall of the 1590s tower. Adam redesigned it as the Picture Room for the 9th Earl's Grand Tour collection In 1787 he moved the original chimneypiece from the centre of the long N wall to the E wall to accommodate the door onto the gallery, creating a striking uninterrupted vista N across the stair hall, through the vestibule and the Round Drawing Room to the Firth of Clyde. This white marble chimneypiece is a fine example of Adam's design, with tapering pilasters and stylized capitals flanking the frieze and central panel. The overmantel was originally designed in 1782 for the 10th Earl's Dressing Room (*see* Dining Room, above). The frieze and overdoors have patterns of vases and festoons. The ceiling here is an ingenious composition based on a design of simple diagonal lines and in buff/green tints. Eileen Harris has pointed out the Jacobean spirit relating it to ceilings at Syon and Audley End, with Serlio the common source: 'the nearest Adam came to bringing Culzean's medieval castle-style architecture to bear on its interior decoration'.

LADY AILSA'S BOUDOIR (SW) was the 'best bedroom' in the 1777 scheme with the witty inclusion of poppyheads, symbolic of sleep, in the overdoors and cornice. The white marble chimneypiece, with a classical scene in the central panel, is of 1778, but originally in the Library (*see* Dining Room, above). It is a simpler version of that in the Long Drawing Room. The adjoining DRESSING ROOM also has poppyheads and a chimneypiece with swans. The planned progress to the rooms of Adam's second campaign is around the gallery and N through a Corinthian-columned screen into a low, dimly lit alcoved VESTIBULE – a subdued preparation for the explosion of light in the ROUND DRAWING ROOM – the climax of the drama that began at the Ruined Arch. This room perfectly reflects Adam's concept of the sublime, with the wildness of the Firth of Clyde and mountains of Arran outside and calm and order within. From these windows the N elevation can be glimpsed. As with the oval stair, neither the 10th Earl nor Robert Adam saw this room finished. The 12th Earl with *Hugh Cairncross* completed it, respecting Adam's concept but interpreting his circles, swags, rosettes, fans, gryphons and pedestals in sympathy with Regency taste: as seen in the stronger and less fussy plaster decoration for the ceiling (apparent when compared with Adam's drawing) and the bolder style adopted for the carved marble chimneypiece. The taste was for light and shade rather than subtle Adam tints. The frieze and overdoors with vase details are much more delicate, suggesting that drawings existed for their execution. The niches flanking the main door also show a bravado not found in the earlier rooms. E of the Round Drawing Room, the 12th Earl's STATE BEDROOM. Adam's plans of 1787 proposed a bow-ended library here taking in the first of the current ante-rooms on the E, to be a miniature version of the library at Kenwood; instead it became part of the modifications under-taken after the 12th Earl became the 1st Marquis of Ailsa in 1832, and is very simple, lacking the expected plasterwork and marble chimneypiece.

To the W of the vestibule a plain service stair set in a rect-angular compartment with curved ends and simple curved wrought-iron balusters. The BEDCHAMBER and DRESSING ROOM to the W of this stair are part of a display about Dwight D. Eisenhower.

Throughout these public rooms there are good examples of furniture and decorative artifacts designed by Adam although many have moved around the building. On the ground floor, in the E projection, is the former KITCHEN – superseded in 1877. A tall room with a large range, spit, bread and baking ovens and a battery of simmering and warming plates. Tall dressers line the walls below the high-level windows.

THE POLICIES AND ESTATE BUILDINGS

In the C17 there were S-facing terraces and orchards in the imme-diate vicinity of the Castle with enclosed park areas beyond for stock. During the C18 shelter belts were planted and late in the century the landscape designer *Thomas White Sen.* made propos-als for further extensive planting peppered with picturesque buildings and the Swan Pool; his contract, put on hold during a period of belt-tightening in the 1790s, was nevertheless the basis for the extensive C19 enhancement with *Thomas White Jun.* being consulted. Additions and modifications continued up to the First World War.

TERRACES. Laid out on the steep slope below the castle's S front in the C17 for Sir Archibald Kennedy; further embellished 1710 and made the focus of the 8th Earl's 'eating room' in 1750 (*see* above, p. 246). The top terrace and flight of steps from the house were removed *c.* 1787 when the walls were crenellated in keeping with the forecourt. Tiny square, corbelled and cas-tellated turrets added to mark the steps at either end of each terrace. Lower terrace wall brick-lined. ORANGERY/CONSER-VATORY, added at W in 1792, based on proposals from *Thomas White Sen.* Implemented by the estate architect, *Thomson* (pos-sibly *James Thomson* of Dumfries). Restored 1987 by *Geoffrey Jarvis.* Stone-piered, with large rectangular sash windows and a crenellated parapet concealing the double-gullied, formerly glazed roof supported on cast-iron columns. Low-arched troughs on N wall with shelf above. Below the terraces, FOUNTAIN COURT, in the C18 a walled garden, created with material excavated during the construction of the Viaduct. Its walls were demolished in 1877 and a sunken garden created with the large elaborately shaped pond and FOUNTAIN from *Austin & Seeley*, a huge, circular scalloped-shell bowl on a

granite base with entwined dolphins supporting another scalloped shell and figure with waterspout.

The STABLES, on the E side of the forecourt, are reached
through Tower Gate (*see* Exterior, above). Originally a three-
sided court; the S side incorporates mid-C18 buildings built on
two levels, the five basket-arched and vaulted coachhouses
entered from the exterior at the low level. Within the stable
court, opposite the main entrance, a piend-roofed COACH-
HOUSE (now giftshop) of 1807 by *Robert MacLachlan*, overseen
by *Hugh Cairncross*; two segment-arched coachhouses with a
bold pilastered centrepiece breaking through the parapet and
with the door set in an arched opening, itself within a tall, blind
arch. Two diminutive arched windows are punched into the
pilasters. A crenellated wall links to the S range. On the N,
ARTILLERY HOUSE – converted 1951 with funds provided by
the Royal Artillery to accommodate disabled artillerymen.
Beyond the rear carriage drive is the crenellated, triangular-
shaped LOWER COURT, its N wall clinging to the cliff top and
with a crenellated, bowed and pilastered gazebo-like tower
built up from the cliff at the extreme E point, with a semi-
conical roof. Possibly built as abattoir but since altered; on the
S side a converted stable range with bull's-eye ventilation openings on the SE elevation. The E tower seen from the Home
Farm range is the start of the great cliff-top drama opening to
the W.

HOME FARM, 0.75 km. E of the castle on the cliff top. A continuation of the romantic ensemble created by the Castle and the
stables. It is a model complex, erected at the instigation of John
Bulley, the farm manager recruited from Essex in 1773, who
wrote in 1778, 'I have not a proper farm-yard, nor a house or
shed for feeding cattle, or for the conveniency of raising near
so much dung as might be made; but these things will come
in course . . . Lord Cassillis has an extensive and very commodious plan of offices, which he intends to build soon.'
Designed by *Robert Adam*, built 1788–9. Approached from any
direction it is like walking into an architectural capriccio. Adam
adopted a simplified castle style appropriate to its status, again
using honey-coloured Blanefield sandstone. It is composed of
four T-plan ranges around a large court, all crowstepped, and
linked by angled archways with turreted parapets. The single-
storey courtyard ranges have dumpy corner turrets with funnel-like bartizans at their outer angles, and each range has a
two-storey central rear wing, one originally planned as a house,
three as barns, all with crowstepped gables and tiny bartizans
and cross finials; on the long elevations full-height blind arches
frame the central bay, in the upper floor small oculi. The N
wing is three storeys at the N where the cliff slopes away, on
its E side a forestair. Originally the wings were planned with
linking retaining walls to form outer courts; a reduced enclosure still survives at the SW. Converted to the Visitor Centre
by *Geoffrey Jarvis* of *Boys Jarvis Partnership*, 1971–3. Within the
courtyard the W range is unaltered, while the N side has had

the arched cart openings extended for the full length with set-back glazing; the E side, originally the stables, has been re-created with arches to form the restaurant and the S side has had openings infilled. Stone from Blaxter, Darney, Stainton and Prudhoe quarries was used where necessary to give the variety of colour found in Adam's work. The complex was adapted to provide a new kitchen, a shop and an information centre with an added auditorium. The centre extensively remodelled 2003 by *ARP Lorimer & Associates*.

NEW STABLES, just to the W of the Home Farm. Built 1868–9, a substantial U-plan range facing N, red sandstone, two-storey with wall-head gablets to the court and crowstepped gablets over the doors at the head of the forestairs on the outer E and W elevations. Now converted to commercial and domestic use. Beyond, to the W, a pair of plain rendered COTTAGES: one built for the Scottish Veterans Garden City Association, the other for the Scottish Women's Rural Institute, both of 1953 by *James T. Gray*, in memory of the fallen.

GAS HOUSE. On the shore NE of the Castle, built *c.* 1850. It comprised a gabled retort house, with arched entrance in the simply pedimented gable-end, and attached to this a tall, banded and corniced brick chimney; a circular gas holder (of which the tank survives) within the walled compound, entered past outsized crenellated drum gatepiers with conical tops and ball finials. To the E the manager's cottage, single-storey with crowstepped gables, blind oculus and mock angle bartizans. Comprehensively restored by *Bob Heath*, early C21, as a memorial to James Murdoch.

The DOLPHIN HOUSE. On the shore W of the Castle. Built as a laundry in 1840. Two-storey house, with a simple Venetian window in the centre and flanking low wings, with crow-stepped gables, mock angle bartizans and cross finials in the estate fashion. Oculi at first-floor level at rear (*see* also Home Farm, above). Converted to Educational Centre by *ARP Lorimer & Associates* 2003. To its W along the shore, the remains of the PLUNGE BATHS, of *c.* 1816, two square, rubble-built compartments (for hot and cold baths) each with door and paired arched windows. It replaced the bath house at the Castle. Beside it is the ROUND HOUSE, of similar date, built as a changing room for sea bathing. Circular structure with big ashlar dome, ball-finialled and reminiscent of metal domes for covering hot meat dishes.

The influence of Thomas White's 1780s Picturesque design to enrich the gardens and park with ornamental buildings is best seen in the extensive area W of the Castle and was mostly initi-ated in the early C19. The WEST BATTERY, W of the Castle on the West Green, proposed 1812, completed 1815, consisting of geometrically sculpted, grassed mock fortification and nine guns. At the W end of the battery an octagonal rustic SUM-MERHOUSE of 1908 with a veranda supported on timber posts.

0.25 km. SW of the castle, off the cliff walk, the ruin of the POWDER HOUSE, erected *c.* 1880 to store powder for the gun at one time fired at 8 am daily. Solid rectangular block with hefty clasping angle pilasters and tall parapet with mock gun-loops in s face and octagonal tower to seaward. 0.25 km. SE of the Powder House is a second ICE HOUSE (*see* Viaduct above for first), probably early C19, a simple square building with egg-shaped chamber, missing its outer doors. Set into the slope and reached by steps.

Further W is the SWAN POND, created partly as a means of draining marshy land in the Cow Park and bringing it into the policies in 1815–23, with an artificial island and arcaded, semi-octagonal duck house added *c.* 1880, safely away from preda-tors. Inside, twenty-four nesting boxes but missing pens. In 1900 stepping stones were provided to the island, which was enlarged 1903 when the pond was given a stone retaining wall with stubby pedestals supporting urns and flanking the shallow steps to the mooring point. On the pond's s side is SWAN COTTAGE, a Picturesque Gothick *cottage orné* with courtyard and aviary. Based on a design by *Robert Lugar c.* 1815 for the 12th Earl, itself modelled on a rustic lodge designed for the Earl at St Margarets, Twickenham Park, Middlesex. It is a two-storey octagon with a gabled porch projecting N (the design was repeated for Pennyglen, Glenside and Morriston Lodges (all demolished)) and surrounded by a veranda that links with low, angled ranges enclosing the semi-octagonal courtyard behind. Porch with a moulded four-centred arched entrance under a square hoodmould with an arcaded corbel table supporting the gable. The eaves to the octagon and the veranda have timber valances. Paired Gothick windows to the ground floor, Gothick detail in the rectangular windows above. The side ranges project forward with open-arched shelters. Across the s of the court is the former aviary, a long low, free-standing building with pedimented end bays and eleven pilas-tered openings with inset ogee-arched heads fronting the bird cages; completed 1820. Continuing the Picturesque theme is the PAGODA, seen on a rise to the w also *c.* 1815, rebuilt by *Bob Heath* 1990. Octagonal staged pagoda, with ochre-coloured walls and copper roofs. Spreading lower stages form the animal/bird shelters and cages. Above, two diminishing tiers with ogee openings and deeply overhanging roofs, the upper gently bellcast. The elegant horseshoe stair has balusters mim-icking monkeys tails; it rises to the second stage and continues as a single flight to the door to the tearoom.

CAT GATES, on the Swinston Drive. By *John Thin* who in 1796 provided the 12th Earl with two designs for gates and lodges, both stylistically very different from the Adam Picturesque. Piers in the form of two simple triumphal arches with paired Tuscan pilasters each with pedestrian gated archways and sup-porting swept cast-iron gates to the drive. Two recumbent Egyptian lionesses, of *Coade* stone, 1802, scowl at each other across the drive. The adjoining lodges have been demolished.

WALLED GARDEN, 0.25 km. SW of the Castle. Begun 1782, improved 1815, enlarged 1820 and 1833–6. Tall brick-lined and coped walls with curved corners. In three compartments. Smart arched entrance on E to central section, piers rusticated below springing, above blind niches and supporting cornice with large urns on parapet; smaller urn at centre, possibly later; *Coade* stone inset panel on E side and blind cross design dated 1786. Is this Adam or Cairncross? Along the N wall is a VINERY with lean-to potting sheds dated 1815 at the rear; vinery recreated by *Mackenzie & Moncur*, 1889, demolished 1946 and rebuilt by *Gordon Fleming* of *ARP Lorimer & Associates* 2003. Garden enlarged to N *c.* 1820, when GARDEN HOUSE on N wall looking onto Pipers Brae was probably built. Further expanded to SW in 1833 with a new entrance flanked by handsome panelled piers and plain urns. To its S at this time further gardener's accommodation and stores built against the outside of the W wall, with an arched entry to the garden to their S and a bell above, moved here from Morriston in the 1870s. The original garden enclosure was altered in the 1880s with a RUSTIC SUMMERHOUSE of 1886 for Lord Charles. Timber-framed on a cobbled base, with panels made up of sticks, deeply overhanging eaves supported on rustic tree trunks and a piended, thatched roof originally with a doocot on the top. Panelled frames and wall bench inside with coved ceiling. To the SW of the summerhouse grotesque-like ROCKERIES, 1903, created with rustic walling and niches within an arch over the path. C17 lectern-type sundial near Garden House.

Beyond the gardens to the SW, striking and functional MASONS' YARD, 1991; timber-boarded on brick base with large double doors made up with diagonal cross panels between shouldered posts. Returning towards the Castle from the E entrance to the gardens along a tree-lined avenue, on the l. the CAMELLIA HOUSE. Designed in 1818 by *James Donaldson*, retained as estate architect. Completed 1823 and rebuilt by *Bob Heath* 1995. Built as an orangery but never satisfactory and used as a conservatory. The most picturesquely Gothick building on the estate. The tall central canted section with two tiers of windows: ogee-headed for the lower; square-headed with Gothic tracery for the upper, the latter pattern also used for the full-height windows in the lower wings. Crenellated parapet with pinnacles at all the angles. Inside divided into three by triple ogee-arched, stone screens supported by clustered columns.

HOOLITY HA' LODGE AND BRIDGE. On the E drive, *c.* 1816. Tall single-arched masonry bridge rebuilt by *Bob Heath* 1998, at its W end four clustered column-gatepiers with ornamental cast-iron gates. To S between the gates and the bridge the Gothick lodge. Simple rectangular-plan, gable-end to bridge with finial and tiny conical bartizans. Big blind pointed arch in gable with triple ogee-headed window. Restored by *Patrick Lorimer* of *ARP Lorimer & Associates* 2002.

ENOCH LODGE at the junction of the B7023 and the A719. *c.* 1840, simple estate-style single-storey lodge with crow-stepped gables, cross finals and tiny cylindrical bartizans.

CUMNOCK

5020

On the s bank of the River Lugar, at the junction of the routes into Ayrshire from Dumfries and Edinburgh, and always an important centre for the upper part of the province of Kyle. It is first recorded in 1297, and became a Burgh of Barony in 1509. The small market town that developed, of which the medieval street pattern remains relatively intact, was transformed in the C19 by the industrialization of the surrounding area, especially through coal extraction and iron-working. The railway arrived in 1850 and Cumnock grew as a commercial centre, with banks and public buildings to reflect this. At the same time it remained an important agricultural focus, particularly as it was the main settlement on the extensive estates of the Bute family (*see* Dumfries House). From the 1950s the Burgh Council embarked on an ambitious redevelopment project, working with *Robert Matthew* of *Robert Matthew, Johnson-Marshall & Partners* (*RMJM*), and if

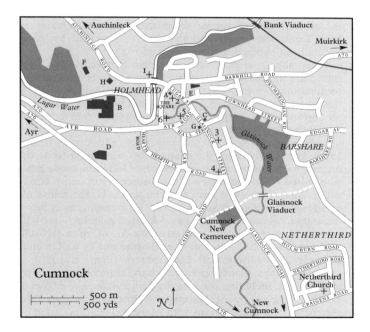

Cumnock

1	Congregational Church	A	Baird Institute
2	Old Cumnock Old Parish Church	B	Cumnock Academy
		C	East Ayrshire Area Office
3	St Andrew (U.F.) Church	D	East Ayrshire Community Hospital
4	St John (R.C.)		
5	Trinity Church	E	Greenmill Primary School
6	Former West Church	F	Sports Pavilion
		G	Town Hall
		H	Visions Leisure Centre

the results are now regarded with ambivalent emotions, the proposals were, at the time, seen as radical and forward-looking. Inevitably the plans, especially those for the reconstruction of the town centre, were scaled down, while those that were implemented came to fruition just as the underpinning industrial economy began to decline.

CHURCHES AND CEMETERIES

CONGREGATIONAL CHURCH, Auchinleck Road. 1882–3 by *John Murdoch*. Dec, with a four-light Geometrical window in the s gable, pinnacled buttresses, bellcote and prominent octagonal flèche. Nave and shallow transepts plan. The side elevations have single lancets, and the gabled transepts triple lancets. Roof braces prettily conceived with gentle curves and pendants. Decorative coloured glass, including a Star of David in the circular N gable window. Attached MANSE of 1884.

OLD CUMNOCK OLD PARISH CHURCH, The Square. Early Dec of 1863–6 by *J. M. Wardrop*, of *Brown & Wardrop* of Edinburgh. A busy, bold and striking concatenation of gables in snecked yellow rubble from the Coalburn Quarry at New Cumnock. It replaced the church of 1753–4 by *James Adam*, itself succeeding the church of 1647.

Externally apparently traditional plan of nave, double transepts, and apsidal chancel with a chunky buttressed SE tower, terminating in a pyramidal wooden bellcote (added in 1872, the proposed spire remaining unbuilt). The central porch has an entrance with deep reveals, and a strongly foliated finial, and stair-tower to its l. In the twin gables of the sides three-light Dec windows to the galleries inside and lancets below. Lively big gargoyles on the N apse; this was designed as the retiring room for the Butes, behind their loft, and inside has a rib-vaulted roof. Flanking this the former vestry and a family vault. Waggon roofs to nave and transepts. To the transepts, arcades of four-pointed arches carried on extraordinarily heavy decorative columns, beneath panel-fronted galleries. – MONUMENTS. Gauche Gothic WAR MEMORIAL of 1920 (N wall, below the Bute Loft) and another simpler one (E wall, S end) formerly at the Memorial Hall, Skares (dem. *c.* 1980). – STAINED GLASS. Contemporary with the church, the windows in the s wall, including the rose, by *James Ballantine & Son* of Edinburgh, given by the Marquess of Bute, who prepared the sketches. – NW gallery (Jesus with Mary and Martha) again by *Ballantine & Son*, 1912. – NE transept, two windows by *James A. Crombie* for the *Abbey Studio*, 1960. – SE gallery, an impressively busy and rich set of three lights: Healing the Sick, Suffer Little Children and the Raising of Lazarus, 1906 by *A. L. Moore* of London. Two quatrefoil lights in the porch filled with naturalistic designs of 1987 and 1989 by *Susan Bradbury*, in her trademark blue, with clear glass lenses.

ST ANDREW'S UNITED FREE CHURCH, Glaisnock Street. Late C19 Gothic, with a broad gable and bellcote, a three-light round-headed window in the gable, and single lancets either side of the central entrance.

ST JOHN (R.C.), Glaisnock Street. Early Dec, 1878–80 by *William Burges*, a simplified version of his church at Murston, Kent (1873–4), and completed, to slightly different designs, by *J. F. Bentley* and *N. J. Westlake*. The presiding genius was, of course, the 3rd Marquess of Bute, and while it cannot compete with the decorative hyperbole that Burges and Bute in tandem were capable of at Cardiff Castle and Castell Coch, it brings something of their bravura to this corner of Bute's Ayrshire estates.

Four-bay nave, with flanking aisles, an apsidal chancel and an incomplete SE tower. Three gables to the main (N) front, that to the nave taller with rose window with plate tracery; a central elaborate quatrefoil and a ring of eight quatrefoils. Below this a lean-to wooden vestibule; this and the rose window particularly echoing Murston. Four-bay side elevations with trefoil-headed windows, and round-headed windows in the chancel. The tower terminates in a wooden bellcote.

The INTERIOR has a kingpost roof, boarded as a waggon roof, while the aisles are separated by arcades on square pillars with uncut capitals. Painting in the spandrels of the pointed chancel arch, with the Last Supper above, David to the l. and Solomon to the r. The glory is the chancel, with an arcade, with ring-shafts, running in front of the windows, and a resplendently painted boarded ceiling. This consists mostly of a starry firmament, but there is a frieze of angels, each with a scroll, carried as if it were a football scarf. – REREDOS. E aisle. Rich Late Gothic by *Bentley*, executed by *Westlake*. – LIGHT FITTINGS. Electric light was introduced in 1898–9, the pendant fittings of two concentric metal rings linked by elongated S-brackets probably by *R. Weir Schultz*. – STAINED GLASS. By *Westlake*, the w window (St Ninian, 1883), commissioned by Bute, also the eight saints in the chancel (1884) and St John and Mary in the s window of the w aisle. All but the first have lost their facial expressions. Harled presbytery of 1913 by *Reginald Fairlie* (cf. Our Lady & St Meddans, Troon).

TRINITY CHURCH, Ayr Road. Built as a Free Church in 1896–9 by the otherwise unheralded *Duncan Menzies* of Edinburgh. *William Richmond* of Cumnock, mason. Of Ballochmyle sandstone and very accomplished, its four-stage SE tower and spire with tall lucarnes and octagonal pinnacles a prominent landmark. In plan, a truncated cross, with the longer arm facing Ayr Road. This has a broad gabled front, flanked by the stair-tower (l.) and tower (r.). Central doorway with three orders of granite shafts and gables with crocketed finials. Two-light windows and a rose window in the gable, all with flamboyant Dec tracery like those of three and four lights in the transepts. Spacious and dignified plastered interior. Shallow s gallery with a panelled wooden front. Otherwise only two tall columns with decorative heads disturb the space, supporting the

29

complex collar-beam roof, which springs from stone corbels.
– Pretty Gothic COMMUNION RAIL with foliated heads. –
STAINED GLASS. A unified scheme of 1906 in the four principal windows, the style suggesting *James Ballantine & Son*:
Suffer Little Children (nave N), Old Testament figures (N transept), Sermon on the Mount (nave S) and the Evangelists (S
transept), all in memory of the Crichton family; the church
was the gift of Miss Crichton of Hillside, the daughter of Hew
Crichton, factor on the Dumfries House estate.

Former WEST CHURCH, New Bridge Street. 1831, for the United
Associate Church. Rectangular, with a classical W façade to the
road. Tall central entrance bay with Tudor hoodmoulds over
the splayed entrance and two-light side windows.

CUMNOCK NEW CEMETERY, Glaisnock Street. 1876, by *John
Murdoch*. Big ball-finialled gatepiers. WAR MEMORIAL, 1920–1
by *Matthew Muir & Co.* Creetown granite column, 2.7 m.
high, with bronze panels, terminating in a stylized martyr's
crown and a ball finial, 'emblem of a new world'. – James
Keir Hardie †1915, the pioneer Labour M.P. Very simple. –
James Gray, coalmaster †1904. Low dark granite enclosure
with urns.

OLD CHURCHYARD, Barrhill Road. Formally laid out in 1756
on the original site of the parish church, which had been abandoned in 1647 for the new church in The Square (see Old
Church above). Walls and gatepiers of 1804. At the entrance,
a separate railed enclosure contains the grave of the Covenanting minister Alexander Peden †1686 (now with a C19 headstone), and late C17 or early C18 lettered memorials to other
Covenanters. Also a Gothic MONUMENT with a spire to Peden,
'who was hunted for his life in the surrounding mountains and
moors'. 1891–2, by *R. S. Ingram*, and *Andrew Murdoch* of
Cumnock, sculptor.

PUBLIC BUILDINGS

BAIRD INSTITUTE, Lugar Street. 1889–91 by *R. S. Ingram*;*
Scots Baronial library, museum and reading room. Mostly
single-storey, and quite eccentrically detailed, with crowstepped gables, and a polygonal turret entrance with corbel
rounds beneath a string course and toytown battlements (cf.
Kames Institute, Muirkirk, and A. M. Brown Institute,
Catrine). The original panelled rooms survive largely
unaltered.

CUMNOCK ACADEMY, Ayr Road. 1967–70 by *Ayr County Council
Architects Dept.* A large but unfocused group of buildings, steel-
framed, mostly two-storey, with brick skins. Subsequent additions increase the shapelessness.

---

* At the official opening it was said of Ingram 'that it was a difficult matter to get
the detailed plans from the architect. But this only proved the architect at his best
– the genius is very like the prophets of old, the mood – the divine afflatus – is not
always on him.'

EAST AYRSHIRE AREA OFFICE, Greenholm Road. 2009–11 by *CDA*, Glasgow.

EAST AYRSHIRE COMMUNITY HOSPITAL, Ayr Road. 1997–2000 by *Maclachlan Monaghan*. Generously scaled, predominantly single-storey, in pale brick with slate-grey tiles. Tall angular entrances with 1950s-style lettering.

GREENMILL PRIMARY SCHOOL, Barrhill Road. 1924–6 by *William Cowie*, extended to form a U-plan with the addition of a wing in 1937–9 by *William Reid*, County Architect. Harled, plain and unfussy, with red sandstone margins to windows. – BELL by *Quirinus de Vinscher* of Rotterdam, 1697. It hung originally in the parish church.

Former ST JOHN'S R.C. PRIMARY SCHOOL, Bank Avenue. 1906–7 by *Thomas McGill Cassels*, as managing assistant to *Allan Stevenson*. Harled brick, with an ogival-headed porch and red sandstone dressings.

SPORTS PAVILION, off Auchinleck Road. 1965–7 by *Robert Matthew, Johnson-Marshall & Partners*. Very dramatic. Between a single-storey brick rectangle and a first-floor viewing gallery raised on pilotis, an over-sized but expressive enclosed stairwell, concrete with a curved end to the first landing.

TOWN HALL, Glaisnock Street. A striking expression of civic pride of 1883–5 by *R. S. Ingram*. The masons were *Smith & McMillan* of Cumnock. Mixed Italian and French Renaissance. Two-storey three-bay front, with full-height projecting central porch with two orders of columns in couples, Roman Doric below with banded rock-faced rustication and Corinthian above. Venetian windows at first floor. Balustraded parapet and a domed French roof with cast-iron brattishing. Inside, the MAIN HALL has a panelled plaster ceiling, springing from elaborate plaster corbels (plasterer *Falconer Elder* of Kilmarnock), and a gallery wrapped around one end, supported on over-sized cast-iron brackets. To the l. of the entrance, the COUNCIL CHAMBER, thoroughly remodelled with a suspended wooden ceiling in 1971. On the first floor, the LESSER HALL, also with a plaster ceiling. – SCULPTURE. Keir Hardie, a heartfelt bust by *Benno Schotz*, 1939 (Hardie lived at Cumnock from 1881).

VISIONS LEISURE CENTRE, Auchinleck Road. 2003–4, by *Barr Construction*. To the l. a glazed swimming pool, to the r. a prominent harled prow under a sloping slate roof, making a bold and positive statement.

DESCRIPTION

THE SQUARE is the traditional centre of Cumnock and since 1966 has been partially pedestrianized,* though the N and E sides are still busy with through traffic. Dominant in the centre is the Old Parish Church (*see* Churches, above) and, in front,

* Pedestrianization of The Square was first suggested by *George Pease* of *Robert Matthew, Johnson-Marshall & Partners* in 1962.

the MERCAT CROSS, with a chamfered shaft, stone cube
sundial with the Crichton arms, the dates '1703, repaired 1778'
and a ball finial. On the S side of The Square a remarkable late
C19 shopfront, with wooden shutters, columns and a bracketed
cornice: a rare survival, while to the rear Nos. 3–5 display well-
preserved rubble, and No. 6 a round stair-turret. In the open
angle of the buildings along the S and W sides, the VICTORIA
FOUNTAIN of 1898. On the W side, the SUN INN, two long
plastered, two-storey early C19 pubs, now run as one establishment, and No. 26, probably 1930s, with a splayed corner and
a tiled entrance and stall-riser.

The CLYDESDALE BANK, on the N side of The Square, is
very capable Free Renaissance, in red sandstone, of 1882–4 by
John Murdoch. It has a central entrance, with paired consoles
either side, supporting a blind balustrade, and a pedimented
window behind this. To the r. of the bank, No. 38 is early C19,
with a projecting late C19 timber shop. The single-storey rear
wing has another good late C19 shopfront with twisted iron
columns. Then, on the E side, the MERCAT HOTEL, probably
C18 and originally with gabled wings projected forward (now
infilled between) and of two storeys, but the centre was raised
to three storeys *c.* 1800. The S wing retains its original appearance, the N wing made over in 1906 with crowstepped gables
and a bowed return, contemporary with the infilling of the
ground floor of the centre. Its neighbour, the ROYAL HOTEL,
occupies two distinct buildings. The first is mid-C19, with
pedimented windows, the other of red sandstone, *c.* 1892, with
a nice corner oriel, and its main elevation to Glaisnock Street.
Round-headed door beneath a segmental head, with a head
keystone and scrolled consoles. In TOWER LANE, running
behind the S side of The Square, the CUMNOCK SENIOR
CLUB, a neat simple harled box of *c.* 1969, by *Robert Matthew,
Johnson-Marshall & Partners*.

GLAISNOCK STREET bends, drops, turns again and then steadies
itself for the climb past the Town Hall. At the start, two good
two-storey rubble buildings of the C18, both with their gables
facing the road, but also the unforgivable CUMNOCK SHOP-
PING CENTRE, opened in 1971. On the opposite side of the
street, No. 18, late C19 Scots Renaissance with decorative finials
and an impressive keystoned central entrance in the channelled
ground floor. As the street climbs, at the junction with Ayr
Road is the former BANK OF SCOTLAND, Scots Baronial of
c. 1871, probably by *William Petrie*, with crowstepped gables
and a curving corner entrance bay with a semicircular corbelled
turret. Opposite, an impressive group of three commercial
buildings. The first of *c.* 1905, castellated and crowstepped,
with a parapet balustrade linking corner towers, and first-floor
windows in big basket-arched recesses; the next of *c.* 1880, with
shaped gables to the outer bays, a linking lozenge-patterned
balustrade, and a doorway with large consoles; finally, the
ROYAL BANK OF SCOTLAND, 1866 by *Peddie & Kinnear*, and
distinguished by crowstepped gables to the outer bays.

AYR ROAD runs SW from Glaisnock Street. On the r. the former MASONIC TEMPLE of 1911–12 by *William Cowie*, of three bays with round-headed dormers and a fourth bay to the l. with a round-headed pediment. No. 30 is probably late C18, with a late C19 forward extension with a good shopfront, and then Nos. 36–42, with mostly unaltered single-storey late C19 shops with decorative cast-iron Gothic window frames. Beyond Trinity Church (*see* Churches, above) two well-mannered houses. No. 48 is mid-C19 of one storey and attic, while No. 50 is a big villa, unusually in whin and red sandstone, probably of *c.* 1890. A big central gable over a low splayed porch with neatly chamfered and corbelled corners. The grounds are enclosed by spear-headed railings and two sets of gatepiers. The other side of Ayr Road is dominated by five villas elevated above the road facing the church. The first three, two of which are dated 1874, have gabled bays, while the fourth, BEECH-BANK, has shaped gables with ball finials, and the fifth, THE BRAE, of *c.* 1869, has crowstepped gables and a tall pyramidal tower over the entrance.

LUGAR STREET runs out at the NW corner of The Square. Immediately on the l., set back, the Baird Institute (*see* Public Buildings, above) and, forming a right angle with it, an early C19 three-bayed house, with a big crowstepped gable, matching the Institute, and probably contemporary. Nos. 7–13 are of *c.* 1860, probably by *John Baird*, with a lively roofscape of urns, tall stacks and decorative chimney-heads. The red sandstone POST OFFICE is of *c.* 1911, with a strongly channelled ground floor and a swagged and shouldered wall-head gable. On the r., RIVERSIDE HOUSE. This is late C18, with three widely spaced bays, and an architraved doorway. A canted bay to the l., and the rear wing with its finialled gable, are probably of *c.* 1867. Behind is MILLBANK HOUSE, of *c.* 1840, with a consoled doorpiece and lying-pane glazing. Well-detailed single-storey extension of *c.* 1986 to the r. Spanning the River Lugar is a wide red sandstone single-arch BRIDGE with channelled voussoirs and a low parapet. It is early C20.

After the bridge, in AUCHINLECK ROAD, the Congregational Church (*see* Churches, above) and two very contrasting houses. No. 4a of 1963–4, low and flat-roofed with big glazed walls, and STEPENDS HOUSE, mid-C19, with a simple pedimented entrance and a full-height bay to the r. Elsewhere in Auchinleck Road (and in Holm and Holmside Road), some good C19 and C20 houses, including, on the l., No. 33, a Gothic former manse of *c.* 1857, and No. 47, LOCHNORRIS, the many-crowstepped house built in 1891 for James Keir Hardie. No. 40 is well-hidden on the N side, *c.* 1904, probably by *J. K. Hunter*, harled with a central tower and a stone porch. KINGARTH is late C19, with castellated bays to l. and r. BROOMFIELD (Cumnock R.U.F.C), is a late C18 two-storey farmhouse with symmetrical lower wings to either side.

Hamilton Place leaves The Square at the NE corner, connecting it with BARRHILL ROAD. On the l. the former Mission

Hall, and in ROBERTSON AVENUE the former PARISH MANSE
(Nos. 1–3) of *c.* 1750 but extended in 1838, with quirkily shaped
dormerheads, the masons were *William Gibson* and *John
Richmond*. The original façade now to the rear, with a full-
height late C19 porch. On the E side of Barrhill Road, after the
long façade of Greenmill Primary School (*see* Public Buildings,
above), is RICHMOND TERRACE, two-storey, timber-boarded
houses of 1964–6 to designs of *Robert Matthew*. With the Sports
Pavilion (*see* Public Buildings, above) they are perhaps the most
successful of his interventions in the town and remain attractive. The climbing site both gives them a wide outlook, and a
prominence in distant views of the town.

HOUSING ESTATES

BARSHARE, 1 km. SE of the centre, is the largest estate with 550
houses planned in 1957 by *Robert Matthew*, and built in phases
1959–66 by *RMJM* at a cost of £1,000,000. It was one of the
first in Scotland to be built with vehicle–pedestrian separation,
with the houses built in terraces at right angles to the roads
(cf. Bannerfield, Selkirk (Borders), begun in 1945). The houses
are linked with each other, and with the local facilities by a
series of wide paths. Matthew also planned for a wide variety
of houses, including flat-roofed houses and houses with
exposed timber boarding. Wall finishes include brick and harl,
as well as timber, and stone reused from previous buildings on
the site. DRUMBROCHAN, to the N of Barshare, is a more
conventional layout of the late 1960s and early 1970s, also
designed by *RMJM*.

NETHERTHIRD, 1.25 km. S of the centre, lies outwith the old
burgh boundaries. The houses and primary school (1959) were
provided post-war by *Ayr County Council* and the *Scottish
Special Housing Association*. NETHERTHIRD CHURCH, Craigens Road, is of 1953–5 by *W. E. A. Hurcomb* of Kilmarnock.
CRAIGENS, to its E, is a smaller, distinct scheme sharing the
same characteristics.

KNOCKROON, 1 km. NW of the centre. Planned from 2008, and
perhaps the most innovative and important C21 mass housing
development in Scotland, though it is too early to assess its
success, either as a development *per se* or as a catalyst for future
schemes. Designed by *Lachlan Stewart* and *Ben Pentreath* for
the Great Steward of Scotland's Dumfries House Trust, with
input from the Prince's Trusts. The underlying holistic concepts, such as the desegregation of uses, and the emphases on
traditional materials and designs, derive from Leon Krier's
plans for Poundbury (Dorset), but here the scale is smaller (the
ultimate plan envisages 770 houses), and the traditions evoked
Scottish. The first houses were completed in 2011 by *Hope
Homes Ltd* of Drongan.

BANK VIADUCT, 0.7 km. NE, crossing the Lugar. 1847–9 by *John
Millar* (builder, *James McNaughton*) for the Glasgow, Paisley,

Kilmarnock & Ayr Railway. Thirteen mighty arches, standing 44 m. above the river. The nine central arches have panelled pedimented pilasters and rock-faced piers with simple capitals and channelled voussoirs.

GLAISNOCK VIADUCT, 0.7 km. SE, 1870–1 for the Glasgow & South-Western Railway by *Andrew Galloway*, engineer, and *Charles Brand & Son*, contractors. Thirteen segmentally headed arches, with piers, parapets and spandrels of rock-faced rubble and red ashlar intrados. Converted into a footbridge in 1964.

TERRINGZEAN CASTLE, 1.2 km. NW, on a steeply sided bank overlooking the Lugar. Fragmentary remains of what appears to have been a walled broadly square enclosure. The most telling element is an irregular hexagon corner tower, with a spiral stair in one angle, where a length of wall survives. Said to be of *c.* 1400, the tower contained a room 3.6 m. square. The foundations of other structures, described by MacGibbon and Ross, can no longer be distinguished. By *c.* 1700 it was possessed by the Crichtons, Earls of Dumfries, who had acquired Leifnorris (*see* Dumfries House) in 1638.

DUMFRIES HOUSE. *See* p. 295.
GLAISNOCK. *See* p. 348.

CUNNINGHAMHEAD

3040

Roadside hamlet midway between Irvine and Stewarton.

CUNNINGHAMHEAD HOUSE, 1 km. W. Built in 1745–7 for John Snodgrass. It was then considered one of the most elegant in the county. Demolished *c.* 1955; the estate now a caravan park. Perjink STABLES of 1820. Advanced centre with an arch in a rusticated and pedimented surround and hip-roofed end bays with windows in tall round arches. Square-headed windows in segmental-headed frames.

GIRGENTI. *See* p. 337.

THE CUSHATS

4020

1.7 km. N of Coylton

A gingerbread house of complex asymmetrical form, whose origins lie in an early C19 *cottage orné* built as a dower house for the Hamiltons of Sundrum. It appears to have been extended, in similar style, in the late C19, and was extensively modernized *c.* 1934–6 for Frank McPherson, an Ayr solicitor. The original house is set back to the r. of the present main front, and is distinguished by its painted stone finish. The rest is harled. This front is of three bays, with a slightly recessed entrance bay to the r. Here, as on all elevations, large gabled dormers with well-finished pendant bargeboards that repeat in the many gables. 1930s panelled interiors.

Large late C19 STABLE, N, with broad gabled eaves and applied timber decoration. Also early C20 GARAGES. Plain mid-C19 LODGE, with a Palladian window.

2000

DAILLY

The village, on the l. bank of the Water of Girvan, dates from the erection of a church in 1696, succeeding Old Dailly (q.v.). The straight Main Street, roughly parallel to the river, is evidence of an associated planned settlement. The fertile river valley was exploited for coal from the C15.

DAILLY PARISH CHURCH, Main Street. An excellent design of 1766–7, replacing the late C17 church. T-plan with a tower rising through the front gable. Its first stage has a tall cavetto-headed niche, with a pediment above, a second storey of big rusticated quoins and urns at the angle, and a top stage with ball finials. In the wings l. and r., two tall round-headed windows and in the SE gable three more, the centre one slightly raised above a pedimented and bracketed wall monument (Rev. William Patoun †1755). On the NE elevation of the SE arm, one full-height window and another to its r. with an ogee arch. Painted stucco COAT OF ARMS (SE gallery), inscribed 'Bargany 1767'. – FITTINGS (NW wall) by *Peter Macgregor Chalmers* who restored the church in 1913–15. – REREDOS (war memorial) designed as a series of panels. – PULPIT and COMMUNION TABLE, with Ionic columns, made by *Mackay* of Glasgow. – STAINED GLASS. NE aisle, Suffer Little Children, a thanksgiving for the return of Eugene Wason's son from the Boer War, 1901, by *Powells*, designed by *Henry Holiday*; neat tiled panel below, probably by the same. NW wall, either side of the pulpit: Ascension (l.) designed by *Macgregor Chalmers* and executed by *Stephen Adam*, 1922; Christ with the Cross (r.) by *Heaton, Butler & Bayne*, 1927. Effective use of clear glass. SE wall: Dorcas, 1921, the designer unknown, flanked by Faith (l.), 1937–9 by *Douglas Strachan*, and Hope (r.), 1942 by *Alexander Strachan*. SE aisle, NE side: The Sower, 1948, by *Guthrie & Wells*, making bold use of colour. At the head of the tall window, a copy of Holman Hunt's The Light of the World, *c.* 1913, and an anachronistic Charity of 1929.

Close to the church's SE corner, and in awkward juxtaposition with it, the imposing pedimented and gabled MAUSOLEUM of the Fergussons of Kilkerran. Finely tooled cyclopean ashlar. Simple entrance with moulded architrave, with a square recess above, and an elliptical opening in the pediment; tall square-headed recess on the side. Possibly by *William Adam* (cf. Kilkerran). Many C18 GRAVESTONES in serried ranks. James Wiggam, †1704, has skull and crossbones emblems. Cornelius Campbell, *c.* 1735, combines these reminders of mortality with a mason's tools.

DAILLY PRIMARY SCHOOL, Main Street. All the characteristics of a Board School. Rear extension by *J. R. Johnstone*, 1909–11.

DAILLY BRIDGE, Main Street. 1873, possibly incorporating
parts of an earlier structure. Single arch, stone, with dressed
arch-ring and low stone parapets.

FOOTBRIDGE across the Water of Girvan. Bold, imaginative
design of 2002 by *Steve Dilworth*, with *Ian McLeod*; engineered
by *Charles Scott & Partners*. Single span, with a skeletal superstructure of triangular tubular metal arches, with bracing
struts; the arches are gracefully bowed like the sails of yachts
in a regatta.

DESCRIPTION. SW of the church, a small square, little more than
a widening of MAIN STREET, with the WAR MEMORIAL of
1921 by *James A. Morris*. A panelled octagonal plinth with
alternate bronze panels, with a tapering octagonal column and
a stylized Celtic cross on a scrolled tripod. At the junction of
GREENHEAD STREET and Back Street, a group of sharply
detailed brown sandstone cottages, apparently built as the
Working Men's Club in 1876. To Back Street an entrance
with a shaped pediment, like three strips of toothpaste, and
a Lorimerian thistle-headed gable above. Also in BACK
STREET the classical COLUMBA MANSE, dated 1860, of
three bays, two storeys with a big porch (later) and a hipped
rear wing, and No. 9, late C19 Baronial with exposed rafter
ends and a big glazed porch. Opposite, KILMORY, also late
C19 but with a rubbly early C19 stable to its l., and the odd
rather stark classical MASONIC HALL of 1930 by *George P.
Greenlaw*.

Former MANSE, Linfern Road, 1802–3 by *James Rutherford*
of Ayr (builder, *Andrew Balfour* of Dailly). Gabled, two-
storey, of coursed stone with rusticated quoins. Late C19
wing.

BRUNSTOUN CASTLE, 0.25 km. W on the Golf Course. Early
C17 fragment of a former Kennedy house on the N bank of the
Girvan Water and probably not the first on the site. Rectangular plan with an octagonal stair-tower projecting from the wall,
enough of which survives to show that it was canted to square
at the top stage. Vaulted ground floor with a few horizontal
gunloops, possibly incorporated from something older. Rudimentary remains of C18 additions on the S wall. The club's
chalets seen from a distance appear like a giant outcrop of
mushrooms in the tranquil valley.

LOCHMODIE CASTLE, 1.1 km. NW. The tilting remains of the
NE stair-turret of what was probably a rectangular castle, probably early C16 and first mentioned in 1536, on a defensive site
above the Quarrelhill Burn. 700 m. SW, equally neglected, the
rather more castle-like ruins of the ENGINE HOUSE of the
Bargany Colliery; of perhaps *c.* 1830, as suggested by the broad
pointed openings.

DALQUHARRAN CASTLE. *See* p. 273.
DRUMBURLE. *See* p. 293.
KILKERRAN. *See* p. 410.

DALGARVEN

3040

DALGARVEN MILL (Museum of Ayrshire Country Life). A grain mill, rebuilt on a grand scale after a fire in 1869 and restored from 1984 by *Robert & Moira Ferguson*. C18 and earlier stonework can still be identified. Main building of three storeys, taller to the l., with two tall gabled granary wings projecting behind; all are rubble-built, with dressed openings and simple gables. At the W end a timber and iron undershot 6-m. paddle wheel. The floors are mostly supported by wooden posts with cast-iron capitals. The machinery is from Lindean Mill, Galashiels (Borders), while other items, such as the stairs, were salvaged from demolition sites in Glasgow and Renfrewshire. The MILLER'S HOUSE projects forward at right angles. Opposite are byres and stores, also rubble-built, and a square brick chimney and boiler house lie to the W.

DALLARS

4030

3.25 km. S of Hurlford

Formerly Auchinskeith. A mid to late C18 villa, built for the Cuninghames. The elevation and plan are somewhat old-fashioned: tall, of three storeys with bays 1:3:1, the central three advanced and with rusticated quoins, under a pediment that has urns at the base and apex (cf. Old Auchenfail Hall). Early C19 Doric pedimented porch with smart triglyph frieze; reverting to the C18, a keystoned niche over it in the first floor, blind concave oculus in the second, and a simply lugged attic window in the pediment. The only blot is an oriel window of *c.* 1900 at the second floor to the r. of the centre. Set-back shallow wings, C19 but not of identical date, the W with rusticated angle quoins, the E plain but both with slightly bellcast roofs. At the rear, a full-height canted three-window bay (cf. Perceton House), with a terracotta balustrade probably also *c.* 1900. The *piano nobile* is reached by a shallow stair curving up the rear wall of the entrance hall with bull-nosed treads. The room projecting into the rear bay has a shallow domed ceiling.

STABLES AND COTTAGE, on axis with the house. Two low parallel ranges, possibly with C17/early C18 origins but altered to accommodate services for the house. – WALLED GARDEN. Brick, with rusticated stone piers topped by large ball finials. Garden shed dated 1779 on gable skew and in brickwork over entrance.

DALMELLINGTON

4000

Compact village at the head of the Doon Valley; a remote hill settlement until the exploitative industries arrived in the C19. Lord Cockburn's comments of September 1847 are hard to better: 'I grieve for Dalmellington . . . it is now to taste of manufactures in an *improved* state. The devil has disclosed his iron, and speculation has begun to work it. There seems to be about a dozen of pits striking within half a mile of the village, and before another year is out those now solitary and peaceful hills will be blazing with furnaces . . .'

CHURCHES AND PUBLIC BUILDINGS

DALMELLINGTON PARISH CHURCH, Knowehead. Severe Neo-Norman of 1845–6 by *Patrick Wilson,* its four-stage w tower with angle buttresses and octagonal pinnacles commanding the view down the valley. Inside, E gallery and arcades on tall cast-iron columns. The nave ceiling and ribbed aisle ceilings with pretty corbels, much enlivened by the blue, green, silver and ivory paintwork. Reconstructed 1937–8 by *Leslie Grahame-Thomson*; he introduced the glazed partition beneath the gallery, the REREDOS and the PEWS (from Old Greyfriars, Edinburgh). – PULPIT. 1926 by *G. Maile & Son.* – STAINED GLASS. N aisle, second from the E, The Agony in the Garden, 1893, and Charity and Faith (l. and r. of the reredos), 1902, both by *A. Ballantine & Gardiner.* – s aisle, second from the E, Mary, Elizabeth and Zacharias, 1971, by *Gordon Webster,* very assured in his trademark lush blue. – In the vestibule, two windows of considerable character: St Paul, by *Marjorie Kemp,* 1947, stylish and measured, and a busy King David playing a lyre, by *Gordon Webster,* 1958–9. – MONUMENTS. N wall, Captain John Woodburn †1841 in Afghanistan, marble with military honours against a black background. Sir John Woodburn †1902. Gothic with coupled columns with shaft-rings, a facsimile of monuments to him in Fyzabad and Lucknow.

CHURCH HALL, Knowehead. The previous parish church of 1766, by *James Armour* of Mauchline. Converted 1888 (porch and rear addition) and reconstructed 1938 by *Alexander Mair,* who inserted the tall, square-headed openings.

Former FREE CHURCH, Main Street. Now Scout Hall. Plain Gothic of 1851 by *David Millar, Jun.*, of Glasgow.

OLD CHURCHYARD, Townhead. Stone-walled enclosure on the site of the medieval church (the parish was given by James IV to his re-established Chapel Royal at Stirling in the early C16). Early C19 stone watch house, now a roofless shell. Greek Revival MAUSOLEUM of the MacAdams of Craigengillan. HEADSTONE of 1682, with a skull and crossbones below the date and between the initials AA and CMM, another of 1721 to TS and IM with an inscription (partially buried) which begins THE REMNANTS WC REMAINE OF MAN UNBURIED IN THE GRAVE BECOME AS GODS & IN THE HEAVENS.

CATHCARTSTON VISITOR CENTRE, Cathcartston. A row of four mid-C18 harled cottages, converted 1984–5. Pretty datestone with a scrolly floral border: A MC 1744. DALMELLINGTON AREA CENTRE, Main Street. A 1960s textile mill converted in 2001–2 by *East Ayrshire Council.* The form of the weaving sheds is still very obvious. Striking entrance porch with an upswept timber and steel roof suspended from tall steel columns.

DALMELLINGTON LIBRARY, Townhead. 1986 by *Cumnock & Doon Valley District Council*. Neo-vernacular L-plan group of asymmetrically arranged brick-harled blocks of varying height, a successful use of traditional forms and materials.

DOON ACADEMY, Croft Street. 1973–8 by *Ayr County Council Architects Department*. Amorphous and undemanding.

WAR MEMORIAL, Bellsbank Road, on a commanding site overlooking the village. 1921–2, by *J. S. Glass* of London, a native of Dalmellington. Cullaloe stone obelisk, with a bronze panel by *J. L. Emms*.

DESCRIPTION

In the open space at the centre of the village, the DALMELLINGTON INN, perhaps late C18, and the unusual MERRICK CAFÉ, with a front of *c.* 1935, with stepped parapet, painted brick pilaster strips and a prominent porch with solid curvy brackets. On the N side, Nos. 7–11 MAIN STREET, mid-C19 ashlar with moulded first-floor windows, a parapet, a wall-head stack and stepped gables. Little else of note in Main Street, except the ROYAL BANK OF SCOTLAND, of 1875 by *Peddie & Kinnear*, and DALMELLINGTON HOUSE, *c.* 1860, the village's grandest house, with big coupled end stacks, channelled quoins, and a prominent porch with paired pillars and a partially balustraded parapet. It is set slightly back behind good gatepiers and a low stone wall and railing. On the same side, a row of mid-C18 properties, including the painted stone EGLINGTON (*sic*) HOTEL, of painted stone, with a big doorpiece with the late C19 painted inscription T MCCUBBIN LICENSED TO LET POST HORSES. Main Street becomes AYR ROAD. The best of its late C19 and early C20 villas and cottages is GLENAUCHIE (No. 10), of *c.* 1910 with Arts and Crafts details in the canted bay to the l., and the finely detailed porch dying into imposts. No. 14 is the former Police Station, Baronial of 1876–7, by *John Murdoch* in mixed red and yellow sandstone.

HIGH MAIN STREET running N and upwards from the centre culminates in the smooth red sandstone of the POST OFFICE (1930s). In CHURCH HILL, among other early C19 houses and cottages, the Church Hall (*see* above, with a mixed harled early C19 row of houses to its l.), and SEAN BOILE HOUSE (No. 17) dated 1838. The advanced central bay has a moulded door frame, with a wedge-like keystone and broad lintel, and a shouldered gable.

HIGH STREET runs SE and E from the village centre. It has the early C19 DOON TAVERN with fretted doorhead on scrolled brackets, and the SNUG BAR (No. 16), a conservative design of 1958, with a stone base and a harled upper floor, for Maclays of Alloa (their thistle emblem carved in the deeply recessed entrance). To its r., the mid-C19 BLACK BULL HOTEL has been stripped back to its random rubble walls so that the shouldered red sandstone window and door frames of 1894–5 by *Allan Stevenson* stand well proud.

RATHAN, No. 19 Carsphairn Road. A harled gently Arts and Crafts house of *c.* 1905, with an etiolated urn on one gable.

LOCH DOON CASTLE. *See* p. 511.

DALQUHARRAN CASTLE   2000
1 km. N of Dailly

The stunning, pristine ruin of one of *Robert Adam*'s finest essays in the Castle Style, originating from his fascination for Roman military architecture. Designed in 1782–5 for Thomas Kennedy of Dunure and his wife Jean, Adam's niece. The work, supervised by *Hugh Cairncross*, was complete in 1789–90. The site commands the Girvan valley as it narrows to the E of Dailly, and on its S front the castle is given exaggerated dominance by matching wings added by *Wardrop & Reid* in 1880–1. It was unroofed in 1970 but remains an imposing sight, like a massive sculpture in a neglected landscape.

A gently sloping drive curves down the hillside to a turreted and walled FORECOURT, and it is here that the design's Roman ancestry is best appreciated. Adam originally envisaged a very large entrance forecourt in the manner of Vanbrugh's castle complex (albeit diminutive) created at Blackheath, but this and the associated buildings were reduced in scale once work was under way. So instead of the intended grand archway, there are bold square turret-like GATEPIERS opening into the courtyard. The imposing house is on the S side with the low service range opposite set into the hillside. The latter, although reduced in scale from the original plan (seen in the drawing) is still boldly turreted and with a pilastered centrepiece crowned with small crowstepped gablets. The elongated blind crosslets, familiar from Culzean's estate, stylized blind gunloops and blind oculi are constantly repeated details throughout this whole scheme.

The CASTLE is symmetrical in design, raised on a heftily battered basement. A flight of steps spanning the basement area leads to the central door and its two small sidelights, the latter simply set but with a huge overarching, semicircular fanlight. This central bay is recessed into a very shallow, full-height arch with the corbelled parapet above. Two full-height rounded towers anchor the centrepiece and are balanced by square towers at the original corners. In the ground floor round-arched recessed panels with rectangular windows punched through the masonry are used; the same pattern but the arch pushed up into the second floor is used above. At first-floor level a deep band of masonry ties the elevation together; below the windows blind balustrades. A string course marks the second floor. These strongly geometric forms are the

only decoration; the walls are severely plain with window openings precisely carved out without a hint of an architrave. The
two later, lower bays added at either end of the elevation are
politely subservient, and the lower and smaller angle towers
equally plain. They replace the original turreted wall. Their side
elevations reflect Adam's design, the only change being the
insertion of a canted bay window in the centre.

The greatest drama is reserved for the S show front with the
powerful central drum tower, used again so brilliantly at
Culzean, and which derived from Adam's second scheme for
The Oaks at Sutton, Surrey, for the Earl of Derby. The ground
and second floors are emphasized by tall, round-arched
windows. There is no superfluous stone carved decoration in
the large ground-floor windows; only the refined guilloche
moulding of the timber frames softens the austerity, and then
only when viewed from close up. The central window is at the
head of steps from the garden terrace, with sashes arranged to
allow easy access and a carved balustrade in looped design. As
in the central bay of the entrance front, the top two floors are
united by a big pilastered arcade, apparently supported by the
ground floor and framing recessed arched panels into which
the windows are set. The vertical emphasis is broken only by
a string course at second-floor level. The drum breaks through
the cornice and is completed with a confidently corbelled,
machicolated parapet, but the conical roof and ball finial that
originally crowned this tower have collapsed. The 1880s wings
turn this elevation from a compact vertical form to one with a
horizontal emphasis, and, unlike the N front, the symmetry is
also broken by the inclusion of very simplified Venetian
windows in the eastern wing.

Within, it is still possible to ascertain the plan, an intricate
piece of geometry. Above the brick-vaulted basement the main
rooms are on the raised ground floor. It is a three-part plan
with a central axis. This axis forms the main communication
through the building. The octagonal entrance hall on the N has
two circular towers flanking the doorway, the one to the E
housing a secondary stair. A door leads directly from this hall
to the central small circular hall housing the sophisticated
cantilevered stair which curves up the drum; it is partially
removed and without a handrail. From the stair hall a door
leads to the large drum tower which provides a big circular
room on each floor; at the ground floor it was the drawing
room and has an access to the dining room which filled the
entire depth of the house on the E. No interior decoration
survives.

OLD DALQUHARRAN CASTLE lies below, 300 m. SE by the bank
of the Girvan, on a man-made platform. An elegiac ruin,
heavily concealed by overgrown yews, limes and sycamores,
the remnants of former landscaping. The S block is the earliest
part, built for a branch of the Kennedy family. It is rectangular
(18.2 m. by 9.1 m. with walls 1.5 m. thick), with an unusually
large footprint. The masonry suggests at least two phases of

construction. Up to about 3.6 m. high the walls are in neatly squared rubble and may have begun as a hall house; modest provision for defence in the form of inverted keyhole gun-ports, signifying a later C15 date, maybe inserted. The rubble upper walls are more randomly coursed with greater use of pinnings, which may simply indicate that they were to be rendered, but most likely there was rebuilding *c.* 1540 after the return of Sir Hew Kennedy from France, as a result of which was adopted the local fashion (found formerly also in the Girvan valley at Blairquhan and Bargany castles; both demolished) for horizontal planning, distributing accommodation over only two main floors. Most arresting is a corbelled parapet with the corbels uniquely linked by diminutive ogee-headed arches. The corbels circled the open rounds, only one surviving at the SW angle. The large ashlar-built tower at the SE angle, a small version of the great tower at Huntly Castle (Aberdeenshire, *c.* 1553) is clearly an addition, but not much later, providing superior closet accommodation. It continued the arched corbelling, surprisingly crudely joined to the E gable and the S wall; each floor was vaulted and a garderobe installed at first-floor level. It is possible it superseded a smaller stair-turret providing access to the upper floor. The SW angle has stepped buttressing suggesting a problem with settlement, and the large cracks in the SE tower indicate that the foundations are not stable. On the N front a tower for a newel stair was added, possibly concealing the original first-floor entrance. Unlike the round tower the corbelling did not continue round this tower, which appears to have been linked into a courtyard wall extending from the N face.

The N front was radically altered in 1679, the property having been acquired by Sir Thomas Kennedy of Kirkhill, Provost of Edinburgh. He added a large, three-storey wing to provide more convenient living accommodation. This wing was offset from the tower on the E side in order to gain sufficient width, and the corbels of the tower were cut back to make a flat wall for the inner face of the wing. At the same time a new tower for a spacious newel stair, as at Blair, was added in the newly created re-entrant angle. It had rusticated quoins, seen also at the NW angle of the wing. Incorporated into the stair-tower, a fashionable pedimented doorcase, dated 1679. The moulded architrave of the doorcase has chamfered angles with tiny corbels, a cyma reversa moulding, and the pediment has splayed ends in the manner of James Smith. Within the pediment the entwined initials JSKMD (oddly not the initials of Sir Thomas). Above it a red sandstone panel set into a bolection-moulded frame with the emblazoned Kennedy arms. The well-lit stair-tower has a gable detailed as the door pediment but with a flat top. The earlier stair-tower to the W appears to have been given a similar gable detail. All that remains of the NE wing is the E wall and N gable, with the tall circular NE turret mirroring the turret at the SE angle of the tower. The S wall had vanished in the late C19. The wing had large windows to

provide well-lit rooms; at first-floor level towards the s a handsome bolection-moulded chimneypiece with the initials JSK
and MDK and a central escutcheon now stranded on the E
wall. The NE turret had a single room (closet?) on each floor
each with a fireplace, the flue emerging from the half-roll
mould of the tower coping in an elegant, curved trapezoid
stack and a smart moulded cope.

Scars at the NW corner of the C17 wing and on the first stair
addition indicate a former walled courtyard, entered opposite
the C17 door. Beyond to the N two dramatic GATEPIERS to a
lost outer court with banded, vermiculated rustication, bold
entablatures with egg-and-dart mouldings, mannered broken
pediment-type details above with mask-heads at the angles and
originally supporting lions.

The interior of the early tower has vaulted compartments at
the lowest level with ventilation and drainage openings as well
as random gun-ports. The principal floor appears to have been
divided into the hall at the W end with a large chimneypiece
on the N wall, and chamber at the E; within the latter there is
an elaborate aumbry on the s wall set into a cusped frame with
floret detailing and a coat of arms, a hearth on the E wall. It is
not clear how communication between the floors was achieved
but it is probable that there was a newel in the SW angle.
Various mural closets and garderobes occur at both upper
levels. After the new mansion was built, one of the vaulted
chambers appears to have been brick-lined, given double doors
and used as an ice house.

DALRY

2040

Parochial centre and large village in the Garnock valley, which
developed as a staging post on the route from Ayrshire towards
Glasgow, and remained an important transport hub when in the
late 1830s the Glasgow, Paisley, Kilmarnock & Ayr Railway
selected this valley for its lines. The branch line to Kilmarnock
was opened from Dalry in 1843. Commercially, an important
agricultural trading centre in the C19, but lightly touched by
mining (being on the northern edge of the N Ayrshire coalfield)
and industry. Since the mid C20 the town has been dominated
in views from the s by the chemical works (DSM, originally
Roche Industries, established here 1955–8, designed by *Wilson,
Hamilton & Wilson*, with *David S. Paterson*, and substantially
expanded 1979–83).

CHURCHES AND CEMETERY

ST MARGARET, The Cross. 1870–3 by *David Thomson* of Glasgow,
on the site of the church of 1608.* One of the best late C19

* In July 1870 the heritors agreed that the new church should be based on the new
Eastwood Parish Church (Renfrewshire), and that *Thomson*, the architect of that
church, should be engaged.

churches in Ayrshire, confidently executed in late C13 Gothic style, cruciform with a soaring E entrance tower with a broach spire with lucarnes. To its lower stages, angle buttresses and paired belfry openings with clustered shafts. The flanking bays of the front have two-light pointed windows under gabled heads, with the gable of the church rising behind, while the central arched entrance has a cross finial and skilful triple-gabled lights. Side elevations of three gabled bays; two-light windows, the upper tier much taller. To the transepts, three-light windows with Geometrical tracery. To the s side, four pretty stepped windows to the gallery stairs, in recessed panels with corbelled heads.

Masterly and harmonious galleried interior, the result of assured reconstruction by *Gabriel Steel*, 1951–3, after a severe fire: exposed stone wall, a panelled timber roof divided by simple trusses on big wooden corbels, and a rich panelled gallery front, curved at the junctions of nave and transepts. – FURNISHINGS all of *c.* 1953, made in Beith, including the pews, Elders' chairs and neatly decorated reredos spanning the chancel recess. – STAINED GLASS. Bavarian glass of 1873 in the chancel, the E gallery and N transept. In the s transept is the well-judged Peace, Be Still, by *Charles Payne*, executed by *Guthrie & Wells*. Also four windows designed by *R. Anning Bell* for the same firm: The Lord is my Shepherd and Suffer Little Children (N transept, W wall) and Flight into Egypt – the hurrying, worrying figures well captured – and In the Temple (s transept, W wall). – Two windows of 1953 by *Nina M. Davidson* in the N wall of the nave: Dorcas and Cecilia, and Miriam and Naomi; the war memorial (nave s wall) is by *Charles Davidson*, 1925. – Latest are two designs by *Rona H. Moody*: in the s transept, St Margaret, 1986, and in the N transept, Creation, 2006, its design based on the DNA double helix. – MONUMENTS. In the vestibule, a pair of carved and painted heraldic shields above the N gallery entrance, and another, dated 1604, on the wall opposite. Also, one with the enigmatic request to 'Remember Lot's Wife'.

To the N, CHURCH HALL of 1887–9, also by *David Thomson*. Free Gothic. T-plan, with a low two-stage tower with a broach spire in the s re-entrant. Within the large CHURCHYARD, HEADSTONES from the C17 and C18, e.g. Alexander Boyd and his wife, 1712, with a primitive cartoon face on the reverse.

ST PALLADIUS (R.C.), Aitken Street. Gothic of 1851 and assertive for a Catholic church of the period. Probably by *Robert Snodgrass Sen.* (cf. Trinity Parish Church, below). Gabled s front with central entrance (now blocked) under an ogee hoodmould with a fleuron, a corbelled open bell-turret, two-light windows with vesica-shaped heads, and stepped angle buttresses with octagonal pinnacles. Three-bay side elevations, two-light windows with Y-tracery. Plain, plastered interior, restyled by *James Houston & Son*, 1961–2. Gallery of 1858, the glazed vestibule below of *c.* 1970. Attached NW the contemporary PRESBYTERY, which has an advanced gabled bay to the l., a lean-to porch and lying-pane glazing.

ST PETER (Episcopal), Tofts. E.E. by *John Armour Sen.*, 1888–9. Small, in a bosky enclosure. Three bays of rock-faced ashlar, with half-dormers. Three-light E window and pointed SW entrance. Exposed stone interior with a pitched wooden roof on simple trusses; the W bay divided off, *c.* 1985, to create a small hall.

TRINITY PARISH CHURCH, The Cross. Tudor Gothic of 1857 by *Robert Snodgrass Sen.* Gabled street front, divided into three by angle buttresses with offsets and pinnacles, and in the middle a corbelled open bellcote with stumpy broached spire-let. Tudor arched entrance with moulded reveals and quatrefoil decoration in the spandrels, below a big window with panel tracery and ogee hoodmould with a fleuron and stiff-leaf. Outer bays have two-light windows. Starkly plain side eleva-tions of six tall lancets. Steps, with elaborate naturalistic wrought-iron railings, and torchères to two of the piers. The cosy interior has a gallery with a curving wooden panelled front, plaster walls above, and a shallowly pitched ribbed plaster ceiling. Platform added in 1877–8 by *William Railton*, but the plainly panelled light oak PULPIT, COMMUNION TABLE and other fittings are of *c.* 1968. – STAINED GLASS. Strongly coloured if conventional interpretations of Christ, John, Abraham and Isaac by *W. & J. J. Kier*, of 1877.

Also by *Railton* the accomplished Tudor Gothic MISSION HALL of 1876–7 which adjoins to the E. Internally two halls, both of an unsuspected flamboyance. The larger room has a shallowly pitched timber roof, divided into bays by unusual steel trusses busy with cusped open decoration. Excellent strapwork decoration over the main door. – STAINED GLASS. Jesus with the Widow's Son, a circular window by *W. & J. J. Kier*, 1877, much livelier than their work in the church. The smaller hall has delightful decorative timber ribs.

DALRY CEMETERY, West Kilbride Road. 1866 by *David Kyle*. Single-storey painted stone LODGE with a crenellated parapet; the adjoining GATEPIERS have cusped panels and urn finials.

PUBLIC BUILDINGS

DALRY LIBRARY, New Street. The Town House of 1853–5. A handsome classical front, neatly pointed ashlar, of five bays, the three central bays expressed as an attached portico with Ionic columns *in antis* to the upper floor under a dentilled pediment with foliated carving and a central clock face. Square round-arched cupola with a lead dome and acorn finial above. Round-arched windows, except for wide segmental-headed openings in the outer bays of the ground floor. The building was in other use from 1881, and converted *c.* 1980.

DALRY PRIMARY SCHOOL, Sharon Street. 2006–8 by *North Ayrshire Council* (project architects, *David Watts*, *Irene Farish* and *Peter Togneri*), the design evolved from 1998 with a team led by the artist *Bruce McLean* (cf. Girdle Toll, Lawthorn Primary School), and expressing his concept of 'imbedded intelligence', i.e. the projection of concepts, ideas and data through the fabric of a school building, externally and internally. Broadly symmetrical S elevation of three low glazed and sheet-panelled projections, with the bulk of the school hall to the rear. To the r., though, McLean's input becomes apparent: a sprouting roller-coaster-like steel mesh, with coloured circular voids within, and plant room clad in black and white glass panels, resembling a crossword: the aim to develop children's analytical and numerical skills. The panelled hall dominates the back, with a footbridge to the first-floor entrance to the l., and the Community Wing, monopitched, to the r.

DALRY PUBLIC PARK, North Street. 1892–3, by *James Johnstone*. The gift to the village of John Blair, W.S., of Edinburgh; his likeness adorns some of the elaborately stepped gatepiers in North Street. Within the park, the impressive WAR MEMORIAL, of 1927 by *Kellock Brown*. Sandstone cenotaph, with a tall simple cross rising above it, fronted by a bronze angel with wreath and sword.

HEALTH CENTRE, Vennel Street. *c.* 1978 by *Strathclyde Regional Council*. A large complex of many asymmetrically disposed monopitched blocks, and rather good for its date.

PUBLIC HALLS, Aitken Street. Italianate of 1883–5 by *R. S. Ingram*. Two storeys, ashlar, with a channelled ground floor. Five bays, divided by pilasters, paired in the upper storey and with Corinthian capitals. The two l. bays are advanced and the inner of these is also pedimented. It contains the entrance, flanked by Doric columns, the window above set between Corinthian pilasters. At the apex of the pediment, a carved deer. Upper-floor windows with bracketed cornices, mansard roof with fish-scale decoration and iron brattishing.

DESCRIPTION

The compact centre is focused on THE CROSS, where two sides are dominated by St Margaret's and Trinity churches (*see* Churches, above). FOUNTAIN of 1876 by *Adam Mitchell* of Aberdeen, given by Thomas Biggart of Baidland. Three tiers of basins in polychrome granite, the middle basin carried on columns with decorative capitals. On the E side of The Cross, the nice ensemble of the Baronial-style former CLYDESDALE BANK, asymmetrical with a crowstepped gable, and the former Town House in New Street (*see* Library, above).

MAIN STREET'S name and twisting shape, which may echo the boundaries of the church lands, are significant. In the first stretch, two late C18 two-storey blocks and then a frontage of *c.* 1800 curving with the street line. Then a compact, coherent group of mostly mid to late C19 date, ending abruptly at the 1960s inner by-pass, destroying the street's relationship with the C19 suburbs beyond.

The line of the initial stretch of Main Street is continued as
NORTH STREET, towards the entrance to the Public Park.
Buildings on the W side mostly two-storey, beginning with the
ashlar late C19 corner block with a wall-head stack with scroll
supports. Beyond it, a painted block of *c.* 1800, detail confined
to scrolled skewputts, and Nos. 28–30, late C18, harled, with a
stilted wall-head gable and pilastered C19 shopfront. To the N,
on the r., the long gently harled and tiled façade of REGAL
COURT, *c.* 1979–81 by *Cunninghame District Council*; given
character by asymmetrical placed glazed gabled bays and
oriels. NEW STREET, running SE from The Cross, has most of
the interest. The first stretch is short, straight, and was probably laid out *c.* 1840–2, acknowledgement that the coming of
the railway was changing the focus of the village. After the
former Town House, the powerfully impressive former CITY
OF GLASGOW BANK of 1877–8* by *H. & D. Barclay*. Of polished red sandstone, with a gabled central projecting doorpiece
with Ionic columns and a pediment. The flanking ground-floor
windows have apron panels and banded pilasters. The outer
first-floor bays have three-light windows with panelled pilasters
and segmental pediments, which rise in front of the parapet,
pierced behind the pediments with pedimented dormers
behind. Opposite, the DALRY CO-OPERATIVE SOCIETY,
built in 1916. Its centre is a Baroque pediment, a cartouche
with swags supported by decorative amphorae, an open segmental pediment and an inscribed carved stone, its lines of
text justified by a superfluity of beehives. Further on, on the
NE side, the ROYAL BANK OF SCOTLAND, dated 1887, with
nice bell-shaped gable, and No. 62, a three-bay mid-C19
cottage, of exposed rubble, with ashlar dressings, an entrance
with cavetto reveals in an advanced gabled bay, and two fluted
columns in the recessed bay to the r.
TOWNEND STREET runs SW from New Street. On its N side, the
former POST OFFICE, a delightful piece of Gothic, originally
designed *c.* 1845 as a Free Church school but converted and
refaced at its E end in 1934. Ten bays, originally fourteen, of
lancets under a continuous moulding, their sashes with Y-tracery. Slightly advanced gable with oculus, now off-centre.
Shorter rear wing with a wooden bellcote. Opposite, Nos. 4–6
an especially well-composed and well-preserved terrace of late
C19 single-storey cottages with paired round-headed windows
in lugged frames, and an advanced pedimented centre. Good
contemporary front railings. S from Townend Street, AITKEN
STREET has the outstanding Public Halls (*see* Public Buildings,
above) on its E side. No. 1 to its N, of 1883–4, is so much of a
piece with it architecturally that it must be *Ingram* too. It is
plainer, more Italianate, of ashlar with an advanced hipped bay
to the l., and a Roman Doric doorpiece with a balustraded
parapet. After the hall, and set back, No. 5, a well-proportioned

---

* Completed almost contemporaneously with the collapse of the bank. Acquired in
1879 by the British Linen Bank.

mid-C19 former manse, with a block-pedimented and pilastered entrance, raised painted margins, good panelled gatepiers, and a gabled stable block recessed to the l. No. 7 is also mid-C19, and set back; it differs by being hip-roofed (an instructive contrast), and has end pilasters. This compact group is completed by the gabled and ashlar No. 9, also mid-C19, with a pilastered entrance under a bracketed pediment and recessed door and fanlight.

VILLAS etc.

BRIDGEND HOUSE, Bridgend, 0.7 km. E. *c.* 1830. Central recessed Roman Doric entrance, flanked by windows in frames with entablatures. Shallow hipped roof behind low parapet, and flanking screen walls.

BROADLIE HOUSE, 1.2 km. NW. 1891–2 by *T. G. Abercrombie.* Restrained red sandstone English Manorial, with Baronial dormerheads, ball finials to the gables, and one window with an unusual glazing pattern.

DOGGARTLAND HOUSE, Drakemyre, 0.8 km. N. 1871, Italianate, with a stilted, segmentally headed porch, the foliated capitals of which are echoed in the windows to the r. Broad eaves with paired brackets. To the S a single-span cast-iron BRIDGE with elaborately detailed balustrades. Unusual GATEPIERS in pairs, one tall, one stumpy, all octagonal with panelled heads, like two pairs of harbour leading lights.

HILLEND HOUSE, 1 km. N. 1863, in a swaggering Scots Baronial similar to that employed two years later at Swinlees (*see* below). Grey stugged ashlar, with a conically capped round tower in the re-entrant, crowstepped gables and two sharply delineated pedimented and finialled dormerheads.

NETHERLYNN, No. 13 West Kilbride Road, 0.5 km. W. 1896, perhaps by *T. G. Abercrombie.* English Domestic in red sandstone, with a wooden porch with a half-barrel head, and a shaped dormerhead. Restful two-gabled garden front, with a projecting square bay and balustraded balcony; the other bays have large basket-arched ground-floor windows, and small-paned three-light upper windows.

PARKHILL HOUSE, off Courthill Street. Three-bay house stylistically of *c.* 1800, but called 'lately built' in 1820, with flanking single-bay wings of 1900 by *Leadbetter & Fairley.* Harled. The original house has a raised, advanced central pediment and a doorpiece with paired Roman Doric columns. Canted ground-floor bays to the wings, with parapets and pedimented dormerheads. On a side elevation, a reused marriage stone JR 1732 JR.

RYEFIELD HOUSE, Drakemyre, 0.8 km. NW. Asymmetrical hipped two-storey painted ashlar classical house, called 'almost new' in 1851, with a projecting Doric porch and a wide projecting canted bay to the l. Extended to the l. in the 1920s with a quietly assured single-storey bow-fronted ballroom.

SWINLEES, 3.5 km. N. Small, L-plan two-storey house built 1857 for Theophilus Paton, with tower-like porch in re-entrant

angle. Extended s in 1865. The addition's w elevation is enthusiastically Baronial with a large circular tower in the sw re-
entrant angle which has a fish-scale slate roof with a ball finial.
New main entrance to its s with an initialled and dated panel
over it and rope moulding, and a tiny, much decorated corbelled bartizan with a conical stone roof. After this set piece
all subsides into mediocrity.

TEMPLAND COTTAGE, Braehead. Charming, painted three-bay
Gothick cottage dated 1828. It has pointed windows with
Y-tracery in the upper sashes, and similar tracery to the fan-
light in the pedimented porch with an urn finial.

FARMS

BAIDLAND MANOR, 2 km. NW. A C17 single-storey-and-attic
farmhouse with a crowstepped two-storey C18 wing at right
angles. Plain skews, slate roofs, but also much C20 render and
additions, so that few C17 or C18 details remain inside or out.

BURNHOUSE, Sharon Street. A traditional early C19 three-bay
two-storey farmhouse close to the village centre, yet in a surprisingly rural setting by the Putyan Burn.

FLASHWOOD, 1.7 km. NW. Reconstructed *c.* 1878. A good
example of a late C19 two-storey farmhouse, with a wooden
porch and prominent window frames; earlier single-storey
farm buildings to the r., stepped with the slope, with a further
range projecting to the rear.

GIFFORDLAND, 2.1 km. W. Late C18 two-storey harled crowstepped farmhouse with, on the N front, a raised pedimented
central bay and apical stack. A later porch covers the s door,
which gives onto a surprisingly spacious and elegant open-well
stair.

MUNNOCH, 3.8 km. W. Two-storey farmhouse of *c.* 1860, originally plastered, with a simple pilastered doorpiece, and a U-plan
courtyard complex to the r., which incorporates an earlier
farmhouse. Converted and subdivided 2007–9 by *Frank Hirst*,
who also designed the spectacular boarded and glazed detached
house to the r., with its oversailing roof supported on rows of
reused cast-iron columns.

PITCON. *See* p. 573
SWINDRIDGEMUIR. *See* p. 646

DALRYMPLE

A small village on the Doon in pastoral country s of Ayr. Prior
to *c.* 1800 it consisted 'of a few thatched cottages huddled
together round the churchyard' (*New Statistical Account*), but was
then rebuilt by the 1st Marquis of Ailsa.

DALRYMPLE PARISH CHURCH, Church Street. 1848–50 by
David Cousin (builder *Andrew McLachlan* of Ayr), on the site

of its medieval and C18 predecessors. Nave and lower chancel,
E bellcote. Dec E and W windows and gabled SE porch. Low
vestry and session room of *c.* 1930. Inside, an oppressive hammerbeam roof. Panel-fronted E gallery added by *Cousin* in
1851. – STAINED GLASS. Chancel. Abide With Us of 1895 by
Stephen Adam. In the centre light, Christ, with a single disciple
in each of the outer lights. A fine example of Adam's design
and full of the rich colours that he exploited so well. Given by
William Hammond (†1898), whose memorial window in the
N wall (The Meeting of Abraham and Lot) by *Stephen Adam
& Son,* is a much more muted composition.

Close to the SW corner of the church, a deeply cut and well-
modelled HEADSTONE of *c.* 1725, with scrolls, a winged angel,
crossed bones behind an hourglass, a skull and, in the lower
half, a finely sketched plough team and the inscription: 'No
man having put his hand to the plough & looking back is fit
for the kingdom of God.'

WAR MEMORIAL, Barbieston Road. 1922 by *James Miller,* executed by *William Vickers* of Glasgow. Square pedestal, with
octagonal granite plinth, octagonal shaft and circular cross-
head with floral carved decoration on both faces.

The early C19 planned layout is two streets (Garden Street and
Main Street) at right angles, with Church Street joining at the
inner angle. The earliest known leases are dated 1799, and most
of the cottages must have been completed by *c.* 1820. They are
invariably single-storey, with a central entrance, mostly of
painted rubble with contrasted dressings. In GARDEN STREET
one interloper – the red sandstone Nos. 4–8 of 1901–4 by *John
Eaglesham,* with applied timber dormer gables. No. 10, of
exposed stone, retains its small, chamfered windows. In MAIN
STREET there is also the asymmetrical and picturesque
KIRKTON INN of 1906 by *Thomas Smith,* with a nice variety
of roofs and tiled pentice, and the cottagey former VILLAGE
HALL of 1894 by *Allan Stevenson,* of red sandstone and half-
timbering. After this pair, on both sides of the street, comes
the best, and most complete, part of Ailsa's planned village,
including CRIBBS COTTAGE (No. 5) with pretty detailing, like
the edges of a lace tablecloth, to its dormers. At the S end of
Main Street, DALRYMPLE BRIDGE, a single flat segmental
stone arch, dated 1849.

In CHURCH STREET the former MANSE of 1799–1801,
a hipped two-storey house with a ground-floor bay to the l.
and a bracketed tripartite window to the r. The tall central
porch, with string moulding, was added in 1852. BARBIESTON
ROAD runs NE from the junction of Garden and Main Streets,
before quickly turning E. On the l. the former SMITHY,
dated 1868, a low single-storey row in big whin blocks, with
yellow sandstone dressings; to the r. its associated house, with
a central gable, of smaller coursed whin. Beyond are the
war memorial (*see* above) and the WHITE HORSE INN, the
former Free Church manse of 1867–8, perhaps by *Campbell
Douglas.*

BURNTON VIADUCT, 1.8 km. NE. 1855–6, for the Ayr & Dalmellington Railway. Impressive, tall and gently curved with sixteen
semicircular stone arches.

BURNTON FARM, S of the viaduct. Sturdy late C19 farmhouse
with a detached courtyard steading (c. 1840?) of rubbly yellow
sandstone with red sandstone dressings. Four round-headed
openings in the NW range. A rare, relatively unspoilt and
unaltered example.

CASSILLIS HOUSE. *See* p. 212.
SKELDON. *See* p. 609.

3030   DANKEITH HOUSE
                          1.8 km. N of Symington

At the centre of a caravan park. Begun in the late C18 for William
Kelso as a symmetrical three-storey house with a projecting
bay, a familiar Ayrshire pattern. But nothing substantial of this
is visible, following enlargement in 1881, in Tudor Gothic for
J. L. White, and even grander extension in 1893–5 for J. Mann-
Thomson – on both occasions by *Allan Stevenson*, assisted in
the later phase by *Thomas McGill Cassels*. The entrance front
is the product of both stages and steps up from r. to l. At the
r. is the original house as remodelled in 1881 as an asymmetrical three-bay elevation with a central, crenellated entrance
tower and higher stair-turret in its angle; tripartite Tudor
arched windows in the ground floor, band of crests under the
first-floor windows. Porch with a pinched Gothic doorway
(dated 1893). At l. the taller and plainer range of the second
phase, with canted bays and a tall octagonal tower at the
corner, the high point of the composition. On its SW front a
pretty cast-iron double stair to a balcony. Some late C18
masonry at the rear but many alterations and additions including a large mullion-and-transom window, part of reconstruction in 1930 after a fire, by *Richard Gunn*, assistant to James
Miller. Some elaborate late C19 interior decoration survives.

STEADING. NW, below the house. Unusually well-preserved,
courtyard group still essentially of c. 1800. SE range with tower
over the central arch, the outer bays shallow projecting blocks
with piended roofs and arched recesses. Improved in 1882
when windows were enlarged, ridge ventilators inserted, and
the house opposite the arched entrance given a gabled projecting bay and porch in the re-entrant angle. A clock in a pretty
shaped frame inserted into the entrance tower.

5030   DARVEL

At the upper end of the Irvine valley, developed as a weaving
village in the late C18. Machine weaving of lace and muslin pre-
dominated from the 1870s. Behind this was Alexander Morton,
a local weaving agent, who built the first lace factory, importing

machines and skilled men from Nottingham. His enterprise paid off, and the lace industry expanded rapidly here and in neighbouring Newmilns (q.v.). It declined in the late C20 and most of the mills have been closed and demolished. A grid pattern of streets developed, especially at the W end of the town, but this seems to have been a matter of accident rather than design; the main axis is Main Street, focused on the far distant volcanic plug of Loudoun Hill (*see* Priestland).

CHURCHES

DARVEL PARISH CHURCH, Hastings Square. 1887–8 by *R. S. Ingram*. E.E., on a cramped site, with the tower in the centre of an asymmetrical N front, topped by an elongated belfry and needle spire. Inside arcades to the E and W aisles and 'transepts' on squat columns with foliage capitals. Circular windows to the clerestory. Above each arcade, CLOCKS, probably late C19, evidently re-set. The fittings: N GALLERY, PULPIT and large ORGAN CASE (of *c.* 1908) at the S end have the same nicely finished woodwork. – STAINED GLASS. E 'transept', a window of 1923 by *Douglas Strachan*, originally at Gowanbank (*see* Description), introduced 1958. Suffer Little Children, beautifully executed, with the central panel surrounded by others, especially well composed, depicting agriculture and industry. Opposite, Boys Brigade window, 2007, *Moira Parker*.

Former EVANGELICAL UNION CHURCH, West Main Street. Now Guide Hall. 1889 by *Robert Boyd* of Stewarton. T-plan, the central gable with finialled buttresses and a window with basic geometrical tracery.

Former FREE CHURCH, West Main Street. 1884–5 by *Baldie & Tennant* of Glasgow. In the style of *c.* 1300, with large main gable and a two-stage square tower to its l., with octagonal spire and spirelets. Five-light window of intersecting tracery above pointed-arched entrance with angle shafts and, l. and r., narrow lancets. To r., a lower bay, with chamfered corners, a row of small spherical triangular windows and square openings above. Now residential.

OUR LADY OF THE VALLEY (R.C.), West Donington Street. Original Secession Church of 1883 by *Boyd & Forrest* of Kilmarnock. Red ashlar front, with a central entrance and round-arched windows with quoins.

Former UNITED PRESBYTERIAN CHURCH, Ranoldcoup Road. Now Scout Hall. 1884–5, probably by *John Macintosh*. Gothic, in red sandstone. Lancet windows.

DARVEL OLD CEMETERY, Causeway Road. Opened 1858. MONUMENT. Rev. Matthew Easton †1894, by *Matthew Muir*, Kilmarnock. Inscription in a circular-headed foliated frame, with detached columns and grieving angels.

PUBLIC BUILDINGS

Former BROWN'S INSTITUTE, Ranoldcoup Road. Of 1872, provided by the Browns of Lanfine (cf. Newmilns and Galston).

Low and wide, with a broad four-light window under a classical entablature to the gabled central bay. The flanking bays
each have a segmental-headed door and window. The door to
the r. leads to the READING ROOM, that to the l. promises
'Conversations'.

DARVEL NURSERY SCHOOL, Ranoldcoup Road. Mair's Free
School of 1863–4 by *William Railton* of Kilmarnock (*J. R. &
G. Anderson* of Galston, masons). Pink ashlar; a little gem 'in
the Italian style, showing an ornamental gable to the front, with
a three-light window and clock above flanked by porticoes of
the Roman Doric order, under one of which is the entrance to
the school' (*Ardrossan & Saltcoats Herald*, August 1863). The
clock has gone; the pediments have acroteria. Segmental-
headed windows to the five-bay side elevations. Former head-
master's cottage to the l., raised to two storeys in the late C19.
Entrance with a triangular pediment and block acroteria.

DARVEL PRIMARY SCHOOL, Jamieson Road. Neo-Jacobean of
1901–4 by *Henry Higgins Jun.* of Glasgow, won in competition,
for the School Board. Symmetrical and mostly two-storey, with
the name inscribed along the main façade. Gabled end bays
and covered pupils' entrances in the angles. The playground
bites into the hillside, with two contemporary toilet blocks in
the NW and NE corners.

MORTON MEMORIAL, Gowanbank. *See* Description, Gowanbank House, below.

Former PUBLIC SCHOOL, West Donington Street. Of 1874 by
Harry Blair of Glasgow. Single storey of red sandstone with
three triangular-headed lancets in the central gable. Flanking
wings set back, that to l. the schoolmaster's house. Jaunty 1930s
public conveniences (now disused) adjoin.

TOWN HALL, West Main Street. 1904–5 by *T. H. Smith* of
London. Freely interpreted Italianate, and unambitious for its
period. It could easily belong to a London suburb. Two symmetrical storeys of red ashlar, five central bays separated by
paired pilasters on panelled bases, and narrower flanking bays.
Central round-headed recessed entrance; subsidiary entrances
in the outer bays. Big three-light windows on first floor with
stone mullions and transoms above a broad panelled sill
course, interrupted by a balustraded balcony.

WAR MEMORIAL, Hastings Square. *See* below.

DESCRIPTION

HASTINGS SQUARE, opening along the s side of Main Street, is
the heart of the town and impressively formal with the WAR
MEMORIAL, a Creetown granite obelisk of 1923, by *Hay &
Steel*, at its centre and Darvel Parish Church as its backdrop,
flanked by L-shaped two-storey C18 ranges (one with big fluted
Neoclassical doorpieces, the other with an early C18 classical
doorcase) which were restored by *Ayr County Council* in the
early 1960s. Opposite is the Town Hall (*see* Public Buildings,
above) and the harled BLACK BULL HOTEL, dated 1860 on

its squat-shouldered wall-head stack. EAST MAIN STREET begins on the s with the former premises of Darvel Co-operative Society, including a classical corner block of 1931–2 by *Cornelius Armour*, and its neighbour, dated 1880, with crow-stepped gables. Otherwise, there are many more-or-less altered harled or plastered late C18 and early C19 cottages, intermixed with later buildings such as Nos. 81–89, five five-bay linked blocks of respectful infill for Darvel Town Council. More tactful infill of the 1950s on the s side of the street at Nos. 108–110, in a Scots vernacular style concluding with a round tower and stepped SE gable.

In the other direction from Hastings Square, WEST MAIN STREET has a similar mix but also the Evangelical Union and Free Churches (*see* Churches, above), and the TURF HOTEL, of *c.* 1840, with a channelled ashlar ground floor and doorcases with fluted columns. Then, at about 500 m. from the square, begins a satisfying group of late C19 and early C20 villas, the biggest and best of which stand to the s, in secluded grounds: LINTKNOWE, *c.* 1901 by *J. G. Morton*, a large white-harled villa asymmetrical planned, with many small simple windows and a slate roof, and THE GRANGE, *c.* 1906, also of white harl, but the windows, including one big tripartite window with stone mullions and transoms, dressed in red stone.

In JAMIESON ROAD, DUNARD, of 1913, possibly by *Whyte & Galloway*, in red ashlar, with a corner turret and three-light gable window with a raised head. Higher up the road, the harled and tiled OAKMOUNT, 1903, the Serlian E entrance in red sandstone. In BURN ROAD, the continuation of this road N, THE BRAES of 1890–1, for the mill-owner Alexander Jamieson. A huge red ashlar confection with half-timbered gables. The former stables form a courtyard behind a harled entrance wall with quirkily jerky coping.

FRIAR'S CROFT, Mair's Road. Rock-faced red sandstone L-plan Baronial villa of 1911–12 by *William Newlands*. A crowstepped gable to l., the canted bay below with a crenellated parapet. Re-entrant porch with dwarf wall and Doric column. Round-headed dormers with fan tympani.

GREENBANK, East Main Street. Five-bay two-storey harled house of *c.* 1800, with a wide central door and channelled long-and-short quoins. Restored *c.* 2002, when symmetrical hip-roofed wings were added to l. and r.

KIRKLAND PARK, Kirkland Road. Late C19 two-storey three-bay cream ashlar villa with a Roman Doric porch in the re-entrant angle, and presently (2012) derelict and roofless. To its rear, a blue Nellfield (Edinburgh) brick VIADUCT built in 1897–1905 to carry the Caledonian Railway's Strathaven branch. *Mathieson*, engineer; *James Young & Sons*, Edinburgh, builders.[*]

GOWANBANK HOUSE. At the w edge in wooded grounds above the road. Built *c.* 1881–4 as two houses for Alexander Morton,

<hr>

[*] The Darvel Viaduct is a smaller version of the thirteen-arch Loudounhill Viaduct which crossed the valley E of Priestland, and was demolished in 1986.

textile industrialist, and his brother Robert. Scots Baronial house in grey ashlar. Nearly symmetrical. Four-bay two-storey s elevation, with large crowstepped gables to the outer bays. The E entrance has an octagonal and crenellated tower, that to the w a flat-headed round tower.

sw of the house, on the roadside, the substantial ALEXANDER MORTON MEMORIAL of 1926–7 by *Lorimer & Matthew* (*Robert S. Lorimer*), with *C. d'O. Pilkington Jackson*, sculptor. A bronze bust of Morton in a niche forms the centrepiece. Splayed pink sandstone walls, terminating to l. and r. with statues of young girls, in 1920s garb, one with a sickle harvesting cotton, the other carrying a spindle. Low-relief panels depicting (l.) traditional hand weaving and (r.) the machine weaving introduced by Morton to Darvel and the Irvine Valley. The simple coping bears the legend: THE WONDER OF THE WORLD: THE BEAUTY AND THE POWER: THE SHAPES OF THINGS THEIR COLOURS LIGHTS AND SHADES: THESE I SAW: LOOK YE ALSO WHILE LIFE LASTS.

WATERHAUGHS, 0.75 km. SW. Close to the town, though the tree-lined river accords it a sense of rural remoteness. A delightful, well-proportioned early-to-mid-C18 vernacular house. Painted stone front, with polished dressings, and projecting centre with shouldered architrave to the entrance, a similarly framed window above with a triangular pediment, and a stone panel below a roundel in the gable. The hips of the roof descend to end stacks rising from miniature gablets to produce an unusual roof-line. Stair wing at rear. To the r., a single-storey pentice; to the l., a byre, both probably mid-C19. Good C18 stair with barley-sugar balusters.

FARMS

To the N, amongst the hills and impressively deep glens, a number of relatively unspoilt C19 courtyard farms, usually with the courtyard behind the farmhouse. They include HENRYTON, 2.1 km. NE, crowstepped, with a projecting centre bay, a gabled porch with a ball finial and single-storey wings, and the simpler LOCHFIELD, 4.2 km. NE, single-storey throughout with a gabled central bay and later dormers, and where a rough-shaped polished granite MONUMENT, erected in 1957, records that Sir Alexander Fleming was born here in 1881.

LANFINE HOUSE. *See* p. 491.

DINWOODIE *see* HOLLYBUSH

DOONFOOT

Almost wholly residential settlement on both sides of the Doon. Separation from Ayr and Alloway is maintained, just, by the surrounding parklands of Belleisle and Cambusdoon (*see* Alloway).

At the heart is DOONFOOT BRIDGE, of 1860, by *H. H. McClure* of Glasgow, replacing a bridge of 1772. 300 m. downstream the attractive MILLENNIUM FOOTBRIDGE of 2000–1 by *Barr International*. Steel and concrete with a balustrade of sail-like steel balusters curving gracefully inwards.

s of Doonfoot Bridge, in DUNURE ROAD, a few late C19 red sandstone villas, e.g. CRAIGDOON, Burnetian of 1896, with a harled extension of 1919, and REDFORD, 1893, with an elaborate door frame incorporating a Diocletian fanlight. The best, and biggest, is BALGARTH (now a hotel) of 1892 by *James A. Morris*. Asymmetrical, with two severe gables on the main façade, tall stacks and one unmistakably Morrisian dormerhead. Many unsympathetic additions; the original interiors also lost.

The other buildings of interest are scattered among the housing developments:

DOONBANK COTTAGE, Glenalla Crescent. By *Alexander Mair*, *c.* 1934. Something of an oddity. Large, if conventional, house transformed by a thatched roof, carried out in a traditional English style.

GEARHOLM, Abercrombie Drive. A harled, hipped, three-bay classical villa of *c.* 1820, for William Stewart, a returned Indian nabob. Slightly advanced central bay, and unusually smart details, such as the elegant doorpiece, with pilasters and slender sidelights, and the consoled and corbelled ground-floor window frames. Lying-pane glazing; low flanking wing to the N. Now subdivided.

GEORGE PLACE. An appealing group of social housing of 2005–7 by *Wren Rutherford Austin-Smith:Lord*. Twenty-four houses, harled, with corner windows and deep eaves. Fourteen have a tall front block, with a steep monopitch running back to a more conventionally realized single-storey rear building, with an internal patio between. They are designed with the needs of disabled residents and their carers in mind.

MOUNT CHARLES, Mount Charles Crescent. One of the estates formed after the lands of Alloway (q.v.) were sold in 1754. The straightforward three-storey hipped box built at that time for Charles Dalrymple survives to the rear of a severely classical mansion designed for John Hughes of Balkissock in 1829, probably by *James Patton*. This is two-storey, with end pilasters, and a slightly advanced central bay, and a pedimented porch with paired Ionic columns; lying-pane glazing in the upper windows. The bowed rear projection also of 1829. OBELISK, with a damaged inscription, to Dalrymple, †1781. Late C18 former STABLES, with a central pend, now blocked, beneath a pediment with a pierced cusped panel. Residential conversion of 1973 by *Hay Steel MacFarlane & Partners*. In Greenfield Avenue, the former LODGE, of 1829, a delicate single-storey house with a distyle Doric porch set back beneath a projecting bay.

WHITEPLAINS, Longhill Avenue. 1939 by *Alexander Mair*. Two-storey *Moderne* house, with a central porch and, originally, a flat roof (pitched since 2000).

GREENAN CASTLE, off Greenan Road. A picturesque ruin, dramatically perched on the cliff top, a secure site overlooking the
bay of Ayr. Late C16 appearance, probably a remodelling of an
earlier tower by John Kennedy of Baltersan. MacGibbon and
Ross record a very worn lintel initialled JK and dated 1603.
Rectangular, rubble-built, four-storey tower, 10.6 m. by 8.5 m.,
with a vaulted ground floor. Entrance on E gable into passage
with right-angled bend leading to the foot of the newel-stair in
the thickness of the wall at the NE angle, replacing a first-floor
door, possibly the blocked door on the S face. Two narrow
gunloops on N wall. Hall above with chimney on W wall, top
floor with wall-head dormers, some sills only surviving, and
remnants of corbelled angle bartizans except at the NE angle.
S additions were made in the late C17 (some scars in the
masonry of the S wall). Ruins stabilized by *James A. Morris* in
1899 using brick 'according to the most approved methods
where preservation as opposed to restoration is the aim'.
CRAIG TARA, 2.2 km. W. 1941–2 by Billy Butlin (perhaps with
L. H. Fewster, architect) as a Naval Training Station (HMS
Scotia), capable of being transformed, as it was in 1947, into a
holiday camp. Substantially re-constructed and expanded
subsequently.
PERRYSTON HOUSE, 2.5 km. W. By *Ninian R. Johnson* for
Archibald Newall, 1939. Rambling two storeys and gabled in
sub-Arts and Crafts manner with a hierarchy of subdued red
tiled roofs and some charming decorative leadwork. Unpleas-
ant ruffled icing-sugar finish to the roughcast walls. Lodge in
similar vein.

HIGH GREENAN HOUSE. *See* p. 365.

DOONHOLM *see* ALLOWAY

3030   DREGHORN

Situated on a ridge between the Irvine and the Annick Water.
One of the few sites in Ayrshire where evidence of settlement
from the Neolithic and medieval period has been excavated.
Weaving was predominant in the C18, and the village served as
the model for Dalmailing in John Galt's affectionate satire on
Ayrshire village life, *Annals of the Parish* (1821). Increasingly
industrial in the C19 and early C20, with coal mines and brickworks, it was much developed by Irvine Development Corporation in the later C20 as part of the New Town.

CHURCH AND PUBLIC BUILDINGS

DREGHORN PARISH CHURCH, Station Road. An unusual
design of 1780, a rubbly brown stone octagon with a S entrance
tower, very probably by *Archibald Montgomerie*, 11th Earl of
Eglinton (and the major heritor) who 'obtained' the designs

(cf. his similar church of 1788 on his property at Eaglesham (Renfrewshire)). The tower has pediments to its first and third stages, a bell-stage with corner urns, octagonal spire and gaily painted weathercock. Two tiers of windows on each face of the church, mostly with interlaced tracery. Plastered interior, altered by *William Railton* in 1864 and 1875. Continuous panel-fronted gallery on seven sides of the octagon, supported on stone columns. Further columns extend from the gallery to the ceiling. They begin as fluted columns, have a capital midway and then continue as pillars to decorative capitals. This super-fluity of columns, coupled with the shape, makes the interior resemble a wedding cake. – Dark Gothic panelled PULPIT of 1864 by *Railton*. – STAINED GLASS. Jesus with the Elders, striking design by *Gordon Webster*, 1965; a well-executed but unattributed Ascension, of *c*. 1905; and, in stark contrast, a naturalistic window of 1982 by *Susan Bradbury*, with blues and greys predominating.

The church sits within an extensive walled churchyard, its GATEPIERS with ball finials. To the l. of the gateway, the former SESSION HOUSE, built 1774 (as a school house), three bays, harled with dressed stone finishes. There are a few C18 carved HEADSTONES, notably SW of the church, including reliefs of a plough team, and a skull and cross-bones.

CHURCH HALLS, Townfoot. 1903 by *J. & J. Armour* of Irvine. Big, gauche, mixing Baronial and Gothic. Five-bay rock-faced red sandstone front, with a dumpy tower to the l., a central pediment and a pointed doorway between buttresses. Windows mostly square-headed.

DREGHORN PRIMARY SCHOOL, Main Street. 1907–8 by *J. & J. Armour*, of Irvine, a symmetrical design in red sandstone with a wide projecting centre under a straight gable with segmental gablet. The outer bays have ogival gables. Large rear extension of 1934–7 by *William Reid*, County Architect, faced in red sandstone and harl. Perky freestanding DINING HALL of 1946. SCHOOL HOUSE of 1874 by *William Railton* alongside: Gothic, with bargeboarded gabled dormers and a sinuous wooden porch with finials.*

DUNLOP MEMORIAL HALL, Main Street. 1957–60 by *R. G. Lindsay*, Ayr County Architect, and very straightforward. John Boyd Dunlop (†1921) was the Dreghorn-born inventor of the rubber tyre. Later extensions; that to the l. (library), 1995, harled with a large SW window.

FIRE STATION, Corsehill Mount Road. 1978–80 by *Strathclyde Regional Council, DARS* (*A. Boyd*, project architect). Red brick; the garage dominant with administrative wings either side. Brick hose tower.

GREENWOOD ACADEMY, Irvine Road. 2006–8 by *Keppie Design*. Large and panel-clad, with the obligatory drum tower hinge.

HOLMSFORD BRIDGE CREMATORIUM, 1 km. SE. *Critchell Harrington & Partners*, 1996–7. A simple design in harl and

*Construction of a new school, in Dundonald Road, began in 2011.

grey tile, the chapel marked by a tall gable. Covered passages at the entrances, and a trim landscape setting.

TOWNEND COMMUNITY CENTRE, Townfoot. Single-storey former farmhouse of *c*. 1840 with catslide dormers, and hip-roofed rear wings. Sinuous slate-hung and glazed rear veranda added during conversion by *Park, Rowell, Baird & Partners* of Irvine, 1971–4.

DESCRIPTION

MAIN STREET, the heart of Dreghorn, runs E–W between the church and the Primary School. It is mostly two-storey, largely late C19 in the local brown stone, but with earlier cottages of *c*. 1810–20 at the E end on both sides. Opposite Dunlop Memorial Hall (*see* Church and Public Buildings above) is LEGGAT FARM, of *c*. 1840, a two-storey three-bay dwelling house with pilastered four-centred arched entrance and oddly raised spandrels. The CROWN INN, *c*. 1800, is set back. Five wide bays with a gabled rear wing forming an L-plan.

TOWNFOOT runs W from the Cross. It is more open than Main Street and falls away below the church. Single-storey cottages of *c*. 1800 predominate, but No. 57 is an odd Arts and Crafts cottage, *c*. 1894, with a pilastered doorway and bracketed wooden porch, and Nos. 89–107 harled infill of 1975 by *Irvine Development Corporation*, with one carefully shaped pend. Off Townfoot (in TIREE COURT, STAFFA COURT, etc.) are *I.D.C.* flats of 1969–72 (*G. Hesketh*, project architect) arranged around pedestrian courts, segregated from the traffic. Two- and four-storey blocks with single pitched roofs, and timber panelling at eaves level. Nos. 1–19 CAMPBELL COURT, 1922–4, are by *J. & J. Armour* for Ayr County Council, five semi-detached blocks, harled with big splayed slate roofs; first-rate early local authority housing.

DUNDONALD ROAD runs S from the Cross, mixing red sandstone cottages, such as No. 2, of 1914 by *Robert Frew*, with one half-timbered gable, and late C19 tenements. No. 33 is of 1895, but still of painted ashlar with quoins and square-headed windows with dripmoulds tightly attached. In THE GLEBE, Nos. 25–36, *c*. 1950, two long *Ayr County Council* terraces given structure by two symmetrically placed gables, and Nos. 1–22, *c*. 1939, also *Ayr County Council*, timber-clad houses, mostly single-storey, neatly set out in a spacious T-plan, the harmony ruined by one crass piece of refacing.

CORSEHILL MOUNT, 0.75 km. E. Two former manses: No. 116 MAIN STREET, for the Free Church, 1877, and perhaps by *Robert Baldie*,★ and No. 118, for the Evangelical Union Church, 1895. The former of grey sandstone, the latter red, with a full-height canted bay to the l., and half-timbered gables.

★ *Baldie* was the architect for the contemporary Free Church, which stood adjacent. Demolished *c*. 2001, subsequently re-erected in Japan.

DRONGAN   4010

A substantial village, the one completed neighbourhood of an uncompleted town conceived by Ayr County Council in late 1946 to stand midway between Ayr and Cumnock, coupled with new coal mines at Killoch (*see* Ochiltree) and Bonnyton (s). Work began in 1947, but the plan stuttered and died. Killoch was beset with geological difficulties, and the other pit never materialized. Almost all the housing is by the Council, some of it using well the natural contours.

THE SCHAW KIRK, Glencraig Street. 1954–6 by *William Cowie & Torry*. Conventional hall church, brick with round-arched windows, a SW porch and a narrow chancel. Spacious interior, the ceiling painted a cheering bright red.

DRONGAN AREA CENTRE, Ladies Walk. 2001–3, by *Wren Rutherford Austin-Smith:Lord*. A striking and bold combined neighbourhood office for the local authority, health services and police, with a central public area, flanked by offices. The harled exterior has a tall glazed entrance and clearstorey lighting to the N, while the roof pitch changes from N to S as it spirals round a cupola set back from the semicircular W end.

DRONGAN HOUSE, 1.5 km. NE. A neat coursed stone classical house of 1776, for Mungo Smith, one of the county's leading agricultural improvers. Of two storeys, on a raised basement, with pediments to the central bay of each of the elevations, that to the main front slightly projecting, its pediment having an elliptical panel and apical stack. An earlier crowstepped house is incorporated to the rear.

DRUMBURLE   2000
2.6 km. N of Dailly

A small but architecturally sophisticated country house originally belonging to the Kennedys of Drummellen, coming to the Kilkerran estate in 1825. Its date is a puzzle but in 1731 Alexander Kennedy was forced to sell parts of his estate and by 1736 Lord Kilkerran had purchased lands S of the Girvan Water. Did Kennedy over-reach himself by building Drumburle in the 1720s?

Rectangular plan, of five bays, given a powerful presence by its scale and particularly by its huge piended roof with swept eaves and symmetrically placed panelled stacks on the cross walls. On the entrance (E) front the first-floor windows are larger than those below, and on the ground floor to the N of the door these are asymmetrically placed, perhaps indicating constraints imposed by a previous building. Smart Doric doorpiece with an ogee-arched pediment. At the angles very pronounced rusticated quoins rising to an eaves band and a deep, moulded eaves cornice. The scale of the rear elevation is exaggerated by division into three bays with a large arched stair window at the centre. The walls here are rendered and lined as ashlar under-lining the sense of sophistication.

The interior fulfils the promise of the stylish exterior. Central hall with four symmetrically placed doors opening l. and r. through the very thick cross walls. These have double doors with raised and fielded panels and reveals, a pattern found throughout the house. Rooms to the s have chunky box cor-nices. The doors to the two rear rooms are squint to accom-modate the bottom of the stair. The newel stair rising around a central wall is surprisingly generous and the risers are framed with nosings. The sensation of this house is the tall Greek Doric pilaster masking the central stair wall on the first floor landing. It seems to have come directly from a print of the classical Orders, the only quirky detail being the angle cham-fers which once had carved details at the head and base of the shaft. The two rooms to the r. of the landing were formerly the public rooms, the rear, smaller room perhaps an ante-room. They are much taller than the ground-floor rooms and both have finely detailed cornices that include modillions inter-spersed with alternating floret design and a deep egg-and-dart moulding. No chimneypieces survive on this floor and only one less ornately corniced room has retained its dado panel-ling. The capacious stair continues to the attic, and the newel wall and its coping retain dark greenish marbling. Topping the newel wall and also across the stair window on the lower flight, there are sophisticated turned balusters. The attic floor too has its surprises: box bed recesses survive, three in the l. room, two in the r.. They are set within pilastered and key-blocked basket-arched recesses, and some contemporary cupboards with raised and fielded panelling remain. The three-bedded room also has a chunkily moulded cornice at the point where the coomb meets the flat ceiling.

The COACHHOUSE and STABLE mimic the features of the house, although only a single storey. This range is entered from the N through a small courtyard and the only openings on the long walls are central opposed doors, the carriage house being at the end and now altered. In the NE corner of the yard a diminu-tive square-planned DOOCOT.

DRUMELLAN
I km. E of Maybole

The core is C18, when it was the property of the Binning family, but a building is also shown on Pont's survey. Radically remod-elled in 1923 for Charles Crawford, the Maybole shoe manu-facturer, with two-storey extensions to either end, that to the E taller and providing a grand drawing room with a large square bay window. 2010 new rear extension, big conservatory on upper level. A ruined garden room appears to have used older materials.

DRUMLAMFORD   *2070*
7.5 km. SE of Barrhill

A country villa, in Dalbeattie granite, in a remote setting with
spectacular views over Loch Dornal and the surrounding
moorland. Designed by *William Fraser Jun.* and built by his
father, *William Fraser Sen.*, in 1838–41 for Rigby Wason M.P.,
who erected the larger house at Corwar at the same time.
Emasculated by the replacement of piended roofs with flat
rendered gables, dinky half-oculi light attic. An inkling of its
smart, restrained, original character in the porch with pilasters
and Doric columns *in antis*. The garden elevation has a wide
three-bay projection at the centre with a gabled head like those
on the entrance front.

DRYBRIDGE   *3030*

BRIDGE, of 1809–11, probably by *William Jessop*, engineer for the
Kilmarnock & Troon Railway. Single stone arch with curved
abutments, carrying the road over the line, hence the name.
HOLMES FARM, 0.7 km. N. Late C18 T-plan farmhouse, of two
storeys; harled, with a pedimented porch, painted dressings
and rolled skews to the gables. A small square window high in
the W gable supposed to be a smugglers' look-out. To the N a
square of single-storey stone steadings, probably also C18; the
central block raised in the C19.

DUMFRIES HOUSE   *5020*
2 km. W of Cumnock

The elegant mansion of the 5th Earl of Dumfries, not only   56
an important and largely untouched example of mid-C18 Neo-
Palladianism in Scotland, built to the designs of *John* and *Robert
Adam* at an early stage of their career, but celebrated also for its
unique collection of contemporary furniture, some of which was
designed for the house by *Thomas Chippendale*, *Francis Brodie*,
Alexander Peter and *William Mathie*. In 2007 the estate was dramatically rescued from sale and dispersal by a consortium of
organizations and trusts led by the Prince of Wales. It is now
managed and maintained by the Great Steward of Scotland's
Dumfries House Trust and open to the public.

William Dalrymple-Crichton inherited his title and the Leifnorris estate in 1742; it had been in the family since 1635 and
had a 'tower, fortresse, mansion place, orchards, yards and per-
tynences' on the banks of the Lugar, lying E of the present house.
He served at the battle of Dettingen in 1744 under the command
of his uncle, Lord Stair, returning in 1747 when he embarked on
plans to replace the old house (dem. 1771) and landscape the
estate. Lord Stair, a patron of William Adam, probably influenced his nephew's choice of architect. Indeed, there exists an

undated drawing for Leifnorris House, as it was then, in *William Adam*'s late style, but possibly drawn by his clerk Andrew Whyte or by John Adam. After William's death in 1748, however, discussions continued with John Adam. Estimates for four schemes were scrutinized by the Earl of Hopetoun, another of the Adam brothers' patrons, as adviser to Lord Dumfries. One of these designs he showed to the Earl of Burlington and gained his approbation. The 5th Earl's neighbour Lord Auchinleck was also closely involved. A design submitted in 1751 was modified on the grounds of cost and redrawn by Robert Adam before it was accepted in 1753. The plan, of a central *corps de logis* with pavilion wings, and in particular the position of the staircases inside, bears comparison with plate 58 in James Gibbs's *Book of Architecture* (1729) to which William Adam had subscribed. The contract with John, Robert and James was signed in 1754; the contract drawings are in Robert's hand. The roof was complete in 1757, the quadrants and pavilions a year later and the interior by 1759. The 5th Earl died in 1768 when the estate passed to his nephew, whose grandson became the 7th Earl and through his paternal grandfather 2nd Marquess of Bute. The main house was little altered until 1894 when the 3rd Marquess commissioned *Robert Weir Schultz*, who was then at work on alterations for the Marquess at Falkland Palace, to provide the chapel and tapestry gallery. But the Marquess died in 1900 and the work was completed in 1908 for his son. These additions, although substantial and radically altering the wings, are remarkably sensitive to the C18 work.

The EXTERIOR, with its strongly horizontal emphasis and suave simplicity, was built under the careful direction of John Adam (Robert was in Italy 1754–8). The creamy-pink sandstone came from the Templand quarry on the estate. The masonry to the S, entrance, front of the house is impeccably detailed; on the remaining elevations it is less evenly coloured with nuggets of mineral deposits flecking the surface. On each elevation the ground floor is rusticated, with ashlar above, polished on the S front and finely droved on the others. The principal elevation fronts a spacious court and is of nine bays, with its three central bays advanced and pedimented, the latter remarkably crisp and filled with a coat of arms and supporters, the motto 'God send Grace' and emblems of the family and the Order of the Thistle to which the 5th Earl was admitted in 1752. A bold pulvinated frieze surrounds the entire block. Rising to the simply pedimented doorpiece and as wide as the centrepiece are steps, akin to those at Hopetoun (Edinburgh) and Auchinleck (q.v.). All the principal-floor windows have cornices, those in the first floor with lugged architraves like picture frames. Alas the shallow piended roof was re-covered with dull Welsh slates in 1913–15 (when the roof structure was replaced by *Allan Stevenson*). Linking the house to its five-bay pavilions are blind-arcaded and balustraded quadrants. The low pavilions, also facing S, originally had low service courts beyond, screened by walls with shallow pediments and mannered ball finials, but the courts were gradually subsumed into the house. The wings were deepened northwards by Weir Schultz who also created the passage links to his additions that can just be seen behind the quadrants together with the charming colonnaded, domed cupolas over the new stair-turrets.

The side elevations of the main block are articulated by a wide, advanced, pedimented bay in the centre. The windows in these bays light the two staircases; at principal level by a Diocletian window with a big Venetian above. Cut into the pulvinated main frieze are plain rectangular windows which light the mezzanines at either end of the house – a feature used much earlier by William Bruce. The N elevation, its three central bays advanced, is smartly austere, the only decoration to the principal-floor central window, which has a consoled pediment and a blind balustraded apron below. The 1751 estimate described a window in the main pediment (*see* also Auchinleck) but this was abandoned in execution. The N elevation of each wing illustrates the great care taken by Weir Schultz to integrate his extensions sympathetically with the earlier building. The masonry is slightly pinker but the detailing is as before and in spite of more than doubling the size of the original pavilions they contrive to be politely subservient to the main building. The N elevations have slightly advanced central bays with Venetian windows rising into pediments, a detail repeated on the W elevation of the W addition but omitted on the E. The E has a small arched window lighting the Lady Chapel and a delightful lead down-pipe and hopper decorated in a purely Arts and Crafts manner with geometric patterns and dated 1899; these tiny breaks with symmetry are typical of Weir Schultz's approach to classicism.

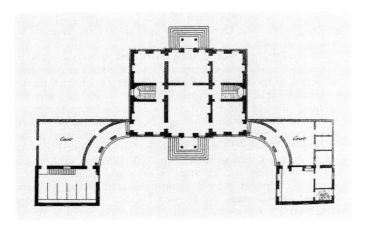

Plan by James Gibbs, 1728, for a six-room house, possibly influencing the plan for Dumfries House

By contrast with the unembellished exterior, the public rooms in the INTERIOR display some excellent Rococo plasterwork of the period prior to Robert Adam's visit to Italy. The plasterer's name is unknown; *Thomas Clayton* has been suggested but perhaps more probable is *Philip Robertson*, a cousin of the Adam brothers and former apprentice of Joseph Enzer; he had worked for the Adams from 1736 and was at Auchincruive in the 1760s. *David Robertson*, his brother, provided the high-quality firegrates, steel fenders and other fireplace furniture.

Entering from the platform at the head of the outside stair, the general PLAN is readily understood and little altered. On the ground floor, i.e. the *piano nobile*, above the service rooms in the basement, the square entrance hall is matched by a parlour to the N, and the two are divided by a central lateral corridor which links the two great staircases, making a cross plan with the angles filled by the drawing room, the dining room and two suites of family bedrooms. The stone-flagged ENTRANCE HALL with black diamond-shaped insets, is strongly C18 in form. Separating it from the passage is a screen of Doric columns and triglyph frieze with the metopes filled with the Order of the Thistle and wyverns (the Crichton family crest). The grey marble chimneypiece with a small central pediment over a block frieze is a simplified version of plate 2 in Isaac Ware's *The Designs of Inigo Jones* (1731), a source from which the Adams mined many of their interior details. The fireplace also has a blue and white Dutch tiled interior, a finish found in all the public rooms. The bold colouring and gilding of the hall is due to the 3rd Marquess, however, who *c.* 1877 commissioned *C. Campbell & Smith*, his decorators at Cardiff Castle, to emblazon it with arms and undertake 'gilding and colouring fascia as instructed by His Lordship'.* The two romantic scenes and the hounds in Rococo frames in the S, E and W coves and the brightly painted vase of flowers in the alcove may be of 1895 when Weir Schultz supervised further painting work. The Doric cornice appears to have been modified at this date.

E is the DINING ROOM, with the richest Rococo decoration in the house in plaster and painted timber, a restless collection of details as though it were itself a pattern book with motifs selected to celebrate the earl. On the N, E and W walls are ornately detailed and varied panels designed for paintings, as shown in the contract drawings. Set into the large broken pedimented frame above the chimneypiece, the portrait of the 5th Earl by *Thomas Hudson*. The huge frame designed by *John Adam* on the E wall with swan-necked pediment enclosing a basket of flowers and garlands of vines and grapes, was too large for the painting by Bassano purchased by the 5th Earl, *William Mathie* made the Rococo fillet to make it 'fit more comfortably'. Opposite, another ornate pedimented frame with the Order of the Thistle. These frames are reminiscent of

57

* William Railton completed a coloured sketch for redecoration as early as 1867.

James Paine's earlier work in Yorkshire at the Doncaster Mansion House and Nostell Priory. Flanking the portrait overmantel delicious sinuous *Chippendale* girandoles, and between the windows gilt pier glasses, again by Mathie, incorporating the earl's coronet, a wyvern and thistle. The chimneypiece, soberly Neoclassical, supplied by *George Mercer* of London in 1757, is supported by elongated consoles, varying slightly from the drawing but of a pattern used by Robert Adam in several later houses. Mercer also supplied the pier tables. The doorcases do not follow the pedimented form proposed by Adam but have heads remarkably similar to the hall chimneypiece, with an inset pedimented block here with festoons of fruit in the frieze. Carved drapery swags are pinned to the wall over them, and above again, an exuberant modillion cornice of vine leaves, grapes, rinceau and shells. The flourish of the wall decoration is completely absent from the ceiling, for which no design appears in the contract drawing. The executed design is a distant relative of the decoration illustrated by Robert Wood in *The Ruins of Palmyra* published in 1753. It has none of the connectivity of Robert Adam's later use of the model or of its antique original, instead it is composed of octagonal plates filled with identical acanthus leaves around a circular centrepiece enclosed in a square from which little floral bosses project and are replicated to fill the gaps between the octagons. Was it an afterthought, perhaps by another plasterer? It is tempting to think that it is a much later replacement although no evidence exists.

On the opposite side of the hall is the BLUE DRAWING ROOM (formerly known as the White Drawing Room) with large plain wall panels, originally designed to take Gobelins tapestries given in 1715 by Louis XIV to the Earl of Stair and purchased from him by the 5th Earl. The effect must have been sumptuous before they were removed to Weir Schultz's Tapestry Room (*see* below). At that time the creation of a passage to the w wing led to the addition of two doors, one mock mirroring the opposite wall. George Mercer supplied the chimneypiece, an Adam design again drawn from Ware, with a large portrait panel above sporting another inset pediment, elongated console brackets, a floral swag and plenty of rinceau, husks and egg-and-dart moulding. The free swirling style of the foliage and baskets of flowers in the frieze relates to the ceiling plasterwork, a *tour de force* of the plasterer's art with the thistle prominently displayed. Its enormous central feature bursts with exuberance, reaching to the low-relief, sinuous border.

N from the hall the PARLOUR is similarly proportioned with three windows facing N and simply panelled with a dado moulding. On the E wall an elegant grey marble chimneypiece with inset white panels with grapes (possibly a later insertion). Opposite, a niche with plasterwork vines and a mask of Bacchus in the head with a floral swag on the wall above. As in the hall this room has a deep cove and the plasterwork flows from it into the ceiling. Vines feature prominently with swirling foliage with hunting horns, pipes and bows and quivers all leading to a rich central ceiling ornament. To the E is LORD DUMFRIES'S study, originally 'my Lord's dressing room', the Charter Room and closet, with coved ceiling and simple grey marble chimneypiece but all plainly decorated. W of the parlour is LADY BUTE'S BEDROOM, with dressing room and closet, and a decorative chimneypiece.

E and W of the hall opening into the central passage are SCREENS, inserted in 1818 with paired doors and fanlights over. Beyond these are the two grand scale-and-platt STAIRCASES. Both have simple column balusters but the treads of the W stair are wooden, to the E stair stone. It is interesting that there is no specific service stair.

On the first floor a top-lit GALLERY extends between the staircases. It was planned originally to have this gallery aligned N–S in the centre with bedroom suites at the four corners. As built the gallery was supplanted by more bedrooms entered through large arches. The doors to the four corner bedrooms have the emblem and motto of the Order of the Thistle or of the Garter above them, and inside the BEDROOMS have coved ceilings and elegant but plain figured marble chimneypieces. Both staircases lead to the attic storey but with stairs off the half-landings leading into the mezzanine rooms, originally for servants, at the E and W. At the end of the C19 Lord Bute created a temporary chapel in the attic before work on the new chapel in the E wing began. Access from the stairs, at the first half-landing level, leads into the upper corridors introduced by Weir Schultz.

The E and W CORRIDORS, added in 1897 to link to the new rooms in the wings, have three bays divided by arches and each with a saucer-domed ceiling on squinches, the pilasters with leaf decoration. The W corridor link and the longer Tapestry Corridor have delicate arabesque decoration, restored 2010. The E WING was designed to contain the chapel – an essential feature of all Lord Bute's houses – conceived, as was his preference, in an imposing Byzantine style. It was to have been double-height with galleries, but only its structure was completed in 1905, after the death of the Marquess. The upper storey (at the level of the ground floor-rooms) was made into a new DINING ROOM 1935 by *A. F. Balfour Paul* of *Rowand Anderson & Paul*. At its N end it has a coffered, arched recess remodelled in 1968 by *Watson, Salmond & Gray*, and lit by the Venetian window. A shallow recess at the S end is framed by giant pilasters which continue round the room. The large marble chimneypiece is by *Robert Adam*, but came via Mount Stuart, Bute, from Luton Hoo in Bedfordshire. The lower level of the former chapel was turned by *Balfour Paul* into the CHAPEL LIBRARY in 1936. The most visible part of the Weir Schultz design is the Lady Chapel, a small domed compartment off the NE corner. This has a small window of 1892 from Lord Bute's London mansion, St John's Lodge, Regent's Park, for which Weir Schultz also designed the chapel.

The W WING contains the Bachelor Wing, and on the first floor, accessed from the main house by the corridor, the TAPESTRY ROOM, Weir Schultz's best surviving interior, completed in 1908 to house the Gobelins tapestries portraying scenes from Greek mythology previously in the Drawing Room. It is large, running N–S and sumptuously panelled in American walnut, with a dentilled cornice and deep coving and eighteen domed roof-lights. At the N end an Ionic screen with a very deep frieze carved with vines, grapes, cherubs and birds, and behind this a Venetian window flanked by carved shell-headed niches. At the opposite end of the room is an Adam-style white marble chimneypiece (could it too have come from Luton Hoo?) with a decoratively consoled frame above with a portrait of the Earl of Stair. Over the elaborately panelled door the Bute coat of arms. All the carved woodwork came from the family workshops in Cardiff.

To the W of the Tapestry Room two panelled bedrooms with coved ceilings, reached by a private stair in the NW angle of the wing. The ground floor, which was arranged mainly for Bachelor pursuits, is entered through an arched door on the W of the extension into a passage leading to the TOBY JUG ROOM, formerly the Book Room and then the Gun Room, panelled in oak with a beamed ceiling and delicate plasterwork. Fitted out with a blind arched overmantel with curved shelves, above a large figured white marble chimneypiece, and glass-fronted bookcases. The SMOKING ROOM/BILLIARD ROOM, created by Weir Schultz for the 4th Marquess, occupies what was the Laundry in the C18 W pavilion and the service court, part of the latter having become a Turkish Bath in 1867. On two levels, the change marked by a paired columned Doric screen. Completely lined with walnut bookcases. Above them a frieze with thistles and roses and low-relief plasterwork on the ceiling. A large red figured marble chimneypiece with Vitruvian scroll frieze and old Dutch tiles at the E and a domed light above the billiard table.

The POLICIES, formed in the C17 from the Leifnorris and Waterside estates, were planted with an eye to commercial value rather than dramatic landscaping. The earliest surviving building associated with them is Terringzean Castle (now within Cumnock, see p. 267). Of proposals executed in 1756 a number of wooded mounds remain, including Stair and Dettingen Mounts S of the house. The policies around the house were modest, planned to the E with allées, possibly of earlier C18 date and associated with William Adam's design for the house, which appear to have been overtaken by 1772 by more fashionable informal clumps, scattered single trees and a bowling green, now planted over. In keeping with this approach new W and E drives were created, possibly as early as 1803, allowing romantic glimpses of the house. The landscape today owes much to the 3rd and 4th Marquesses who restored the allées to the E of the house and planted belts of trees to screen the Mains Farm and the coachhouse and stables, leaving the house to be seen unencumbered. In the immediate vicinity of the house there was little ornament except for four tall obelisks (only two were specified) designed by *John Adam* in 1761, two flanking the broad steps to the front door and two set out towards the park and aligned to the E and W extent of the house.

The entrance courtyard remained as a plain gravelled area until 1878 when the sunken garden was created in front of the house; it was modified by Weir Schultz in 1896. His sculptured forms remain. He also provided designs for a formal garden, never completed, W of the western ha-ha called New Chiswick with a casino, embodying the essence of the gardens of Chiswick House (where the family had lived for a time) in tribute to Lord Burlington. All that is now visible is the entrance made through the WEST HA-HA, the latter being a mid-C18 creation. The fragmentary masonry remains of an EAST BOUNDARY, of C16 or C17 date, can be detected extending N from the Stockiehill lodge and were possibly associated with the Leifnorris estate; it may delineate the boundary of a deerpark. To the NW of the house is a crowstepped DOOCOT, dated 1671 and built for Leifnorris. Continuous rat course below the top third of the wall, on the S wall a door in a smartly moulded frame with dated lintel and carved panel above with a lion rampant and an earl's coronet with a rope-moulded frame. N of this, the modest COACHHOUSE and STABLES, 1761 in an informal courtyard, the coachhouse of five bays with a pedimented centre and five arched carriage openings, the upper floor given pedimented dormerheads when it was turned into service accommodation by Weir Schultz.

To the N, in what was the SE corner of the garden of Leifnorris, now surrounded by woodland, the ruined shell of the simple two-storey WASH HOUSE, 1761. NW of the coachhouse and of the same date, the AVENUE BRIDGE, by *John Adam*, influenced by Roger Morris's Garran Bridge at Inveraray which Adam built. A central semi-elliptical arch with two smaller flanking arches. A long graded slope to the apex with a stone parapet and four tall obelisks, the original balustrades destroyed by troops during the Second World War and replaced with timber saltires.

N of the house is a ruinous and overgrown GATEWAY built by 1768 and a modification of *Robert Adam*'s design of 1760 for a thoroughgoing Gothick conceit of '. . . Gateway, Porter's Lodge, a Temple & walls adjoining . . .' When the Earl was unable to acquire the land between it and the Barony Road to the N it became truly a folly, a gateway to nowhere. Blind pointed arches and the clustered columns of the entrance are readily detectable amongst the overgrowth. In 1784 *Robert Adam* produced a design for a gateway probably at the Auchinleck entrance, but only a single lodge was built *c.* 1803 by the 6th Earl and now irredeemably altered. The Auchinleck gates went with the construction of the by-pass, which also destroyed the eastern designed landscape.

The paired, harled lodges at STOCKIEHILL and the WEST GATE, linked to the early C19 drives (*see* above) share a discreet L-plan design each with a Palladian window in the gable projecting to the road and a band course at the springing level. Each pair is linked by a low wall with railings, plain gatepiers and wrought-iron gates. The Stockiehill Gate lost its importance as an entrance when the Ayr–Cumnock road was moved s in 1837, and its gates have gone. It was replaced by the CUMNOCK GATE which entailed a longer drive, built *c.* 1840, the lodge (*John Murdoch*, 1874) a grander version of the earlier ones with channelled ashlar and a variant of the Palladian window with arched lights in the overarch and deep bracketed eaves; panelled gatepiers, also *Murdoch*, and stalwart cast-iron gates.

THE MAINS. Built in the mid C18, before 1756, as a model farm, a simple three-bay two-storey house with an elongated courtyard to the N and facing the Polcalk Burn to the W. Much altered and added to. A bolection-moulded chimneypiece and a reused window of C17 date are possibly from *Leifnorris House*.

WALLED GARDEN. W of the Avenue Bridge on the sloping bank of the N side of the Lugar. The W part appears to be the walled garden for Waterside (the house demolished 1763), the E part was its orchard. Walled on three sides possibly in 1766 when the gardener's house in the N wall was built (now altered and raised). By 1818 the E part had been divided by an E–W wall, evidence of which is still visible. A small wrought-iron gate with oval detailing leads to the E. On the slope E of the wall, a late C19 GARDENER'S HOUSE, a gabled one-and-a-half-storey building with decorative bargeboards.

In the woodland E of the house a MONUMENT to the 3rd Marquess of Bute (†1900). A crucifix, its plinth is inscribed 'The Wounds are my Merit' and HAEC SACROSANTA IMAGO JUSSU JOANNIS MARCHIONIS III BOTHAE ERECTA EST PROPE LOCUM UBI IPSE ANIMAM DEO REDDIDIT DIE IX OCTOBR ANN MDCCCC. (This sacred image was erected on the wishes of John the 3rd Marquess of Bute near to the place where his spirit returned to God on 9 October 1900.)

DUNDONALD

A sizeable village between a broad flat plain to the N, and craggy hills to the W, and dominated by its royal castle, which looms over the long, wide main street. The village belonged to the Stewarts from at least the C12, and was initially granted to the short-lived Gilbertine convent at Dalmilling, Ayr, and re-granted in 1238 to the abbey of Paisley, which retained it until the Reformation. Settlements must have existed close to both castle and church, but the present village dates from a planned resettlement of *c.* 1775 and after. Only in the late C20 and C21 has it witnessed significant growth.

DUNDONALD PARISH CHURCH, Main Street. Classical, rectangular, hip-roofed preaching box of 1803–4, with a finely conceived steeple of 1809 that has an octagonal bell-stage with flat
corner pilasters and ogee caps, and a spire with a rhomboidal
finial. Windows in two tiers, square-headed below, pointed
above. Long-and-short quoins. The contractor and architect is
recorded as *James Hodge*, mason in Dundonald, but the similarities to the churches at Riccarton and Tarbolton (qq.v.)
suggest *Robert Johnstone* may have been the designer. Pedimented porch of 1817, by *William Thomson*, wright of Dundonald. Shallow dark stone chancel added in 1904–6 by *R. S.
Ingram*, with a big five-light Dec window. Uncomplicated interior, with a panel-fronted gallery supported by fluted pillars.
Round-headed chancel arch, on panelled pilasters with triglyph-like heads. ORGAN CASE, with gentle Gothic details, and
PULPIT by Ingram. – Oak panelling of 1919. – STAINED GLASS.
Chancel window. Outstanding Last Supper by *Morris & Co.*,
1906. Across the lower part of five main lights the feasting table
set in a plain architectural setting, designed by *J. H. Dearle*. In
the upper lights, angels (to *Burne-Jones*'s design of 1880, first
used at Brampton, Cumberland), and central Agnus Dei, by
W. H. Knight. In the terminal quatrefoil, a Christ in Majesty,
with pink and red angels clamouring about the white-cloaked
Christ; also by *Burne-Jones*, and first used in 1865 at St Stephen,
Guernsey. His too the piping angels in the teardrop lights. –
Nave, SE, magenta-winged angel by *Gordon Webster*, 1953. – NW
gallery, an armoured and stern-faced St George, of *c.* 1918.
    S of the church some late C18 HEADSTONES, e.g. a deeply
carved coat of arms in a ringlet with ball detail, surmounted
by a wheel and angel, with flanking scrolls. Also, half-hidden
beneath a yew tree, a pale white early C19(?) stone with a
remarkable angel with an encircling wing, above a skull and
uncrossed bones, all within panelled pilasters and a round-
headed arch.
MONTGOMERIE HALL, N of the church. The school of 1802,
substantially rebuilt *c.* 1910–13, with five tall windows piercing
the harl, and flanking porches with red sandstone parapets.
GLENFOOT HOUSE, N of Montgomerie Hall. The manse of
1783–4 by *John Swan* of Kilmaurs. It has rolled skews, hipped
dormers and a pretty, if incongruent, late C19 porch. LODGE,
of *c.* 1845.
CHURCH HALL, off Main Street. Former Free Church of 1843
(the first completed in Ayrshire), substantially enlarged in 1885
by *Robert Park* of Kilmarnock. W bellcote, square-headed side
windows. Poor 1960s addition. Behind, in parallel, the manse
(now PARISH MANSE) of 1849, with hipped roofs and end
stacks.
DUNDONALD PRIMARY SCHOOL, Castle Drive. 1998–2000 by
South Ayrshire Council. A broad stone-faced L-plan under
sloping steel roofs with irregular fenestration. It is attached to
the activity centre of *c.* 1990 by *Barr Construction*, with see-
sawing V-shaped roofs.

WAR MEMORIAL, Main Street/Kilmarnock Road. 1921 by *Laura Loudon* (executed by *Matthew Muir & Co.*). Whinstone base, granite plinth and Celtic cross with knotwork and a basket-handled short sword on the shaft.

DESCRIPTION. MAIN STREET runs SE from the war memorial, uphill towards the church. It retains a pleasing unity, despite some losses. This is especially so on the SW side, which has a run of small cottages (Nos. 8–18), probably late C18, each with a door to its far l., and a single window. Walls of local whin, mostly painted and harled. Beyond, two-storey houses are mixed with the cottages: e.g. No. 24, *c.* 1830, in neatly bedded whin, with vermiculated stone dressings and a simple chamfered doorpiece. On the opposite side CARRICK COTTAGE (No. 15), of *c.* 1820, with chamfered openings and vermiculated dressings. RICHMOND TERRACE, which runs at right angles from its nicely curved corner bay, is mid-C19. This side terminates with an unusual group of four single-storey houses of *c.* 1815 (Nos. 31–41). Each has a big central attic gable and chimney-head, but varied in the details of gable shapes, dressings etc.

FINGERPOST. At the junction of Main Street, Tarbolton Road and Old Loans Road. Made *c.* 1930 by the *Royal Label Factory* for Ayr County Council (*see* also Crosshill).

EARL RISE, E of Main Street. One of the largest and best social housing schemes by *Wren Rutherford Austin-Smith:Lord* for Carrick Housing Association, 2001–2. It has all the elements (bright harl, monopitch roofs, square corner windows) which characterize the firm's work for this client.

DUNDONALD HOUSE NURSING HOME, Old Loans Road. 1882–3 by *Allan Stevenson* as a children's convalescent home. The original building is red sandstone, with a tall gabled bay to the r., and a ground-floor bay window to the l.; mostly tripartite fenestration, and a seemingly disproportionate amount of wall to window, especially in view of its purpose.

DUNDONALD CASTLE
0.3 km. NNW of the church

A powerful hilltop site, with expansive views in all directions, that has been shown by excavation (1986–8) to have been occupied since about 3000 B.C. The first medieval castle was probably of motte-and-bailey type, but the present castle was begun *c.* 1280 by the Stewarts, at the heart of their Ayrshire Barony of North Kyle, as a large curtain-walled courtyard castle with twin-towered gatehouses, E and W, comparable to Edwards I's castle at Rhuddlan in Flintshire (1271). It suffered during the Wars of Independence and Robert II rebuilt it *c.* 1371, abandoning the E gatehouse and reducing the area of the courtyard but building on the remains of the W gatehouse. It became his favourite castle and he died there in 1390. In later times the castle was granted to supporters, including the Cochranes who robbed stone to build nearby Auchans in the early C17 (*see* below).

41

The surrounding walls, remnants of the E courtyard buildings, and at the W, the dominating shell of the great TOWER
remain. The walls are rubble with creamy freestone quoins.
Incorporated within the austere W front there is still evidence
of the drum towers and central arched entrance (blocked) of
the late C13 gatehouse. At the NW angle some strengthening
corbelling demonstrates how new and old were interwoven.
The SW angle is chamfered, and a little set back from it is a
slightly later service wing, standing almost to the same height
as the rest. In the W elevation, above the ground storey each
storey has one opening: at first floor a tall pointed arch window
to the S, in the entresol a near-central small flat-headed window,
and in the upper storey a larger segmental-arched window. Set
high into this wall at intervals are an unusual series of shields,
two of which contain the royal arms and the Stewart arms with
some heraldic beasts below. The E wall, facing the courtyard,
is articulated as two broad tower-like sections linked by a
narrow recessed bay. Pointed-arch entrance at first floor in the
S part. At the same level in the N part another opening, its arch
altered. Two windows in the upper floor. On the S wall, round-
arched doors have been made into the S addition. A newel
stair-tower in the SE angle indicates that there was probably a
further storey and wall-walk. The castle must have been of an
unusually imposing height comparable to other late C14 castles
such as Threave (Dumfries and Galloway), Alloa (Clackman-
nanshire) or Borthwick (Lothian).

The rectangular plan (25 m. by 12 m.) and the internal
arrangements resemble Carrick Castle, Argyll (late C14). Inside
Robert constructed two vaulted halls. The LOWER HALL is
lofty, but originally had a basement, linked to the hall by a
mural stair at the NE. The original floor level is indicated by
the modern gallery. There was also an entresol at the N end.
Into the hall's pointed barrel vault some window openings were
rather oddly inserted, and shafts to funnel the smoke from
braziers to mural chimneys were created. Above is the GREAT
(or KING'S) HALL, an impressive chamber despite the loss of
its pointed barrel vault. This was originally in two sections
decorated with ribs, the corbelled springers for which survive,
linked by segmental lateral arches. The ribs were set out on a
diagonal pattern, imitating, as Richard Fawcett has pointed
out, the ribs which defined the intersections of quadripartite
vaulting. Segmental lateral arches which linked the sections
remain. This form of pointed, ribbed barrel vault is a significant development in later Gothic Scottish architecture (e.g. the
vaults of the western choir aisles of St Giles, Edinburgh,
c. 1385). In the N wall, remains of the pointed wall arch and a
pointed arch doorway. Set within the wall thickness at the N
end are several vaulted closets and garderobes with shoots. On
the W wall fragmentary remains of the chimneypiece. At the S
a former servery.

The BAILEY WALL extends E from the extension to the tower
for approx. 36.5 m. and the breadth of the bailey is about

Dundonald Castle, view of the Great Hall.
Engraving

36.8 m. The entrance was at the E and evidence survives of
outworks beyond the site of the gate. Footings of a building
near the NE of the tower are thought to have been a chapel.

VISITOR CENTRE. 1999 by *Page & Park*. A simple structure
in sheet metal with big windows and a shallow segmental roof.

OLD AUCHANS CASTLE
1.25 km. NW

The melancholy overgrown ruin of a complex building, enlarged
by the Wallaces of Auchans, to whom James V had transferred
Dundonald Castle (*see* above) and its estates in 1527, using stones
raided from the castle. It became a baronial showpiece only after
its acquisition in 1638 by Sir William Cochrane, later the 1st Earl
of Dundonald (†1686). Like Innes (Moray), Auchans was purely
domestic with tentative Renaissance decoration. In 1726 it passed

from the Cochranes to the 9th Earl of Eglinton, but he died 1729 and the house was inhabited by his widow and third wife Susannah, daughter of Sir Archibald Kennedy of Culzean; in 1773 she entertained Dr Johnson and James Boswell at Auchans. After her death in 1780 the family abandoned Auchans, probably because the internal planning of intercommunicating rooms no longer suited domestic needs. Subsequently used by the estate factors until Auchans House was built (*c.* 1819, now dem., possibly by *William Wallace* who exhibited designs at the Royal Academy). After that the old mansion slowly declined, being divided into workmen's houses, ultimately abandoned in the early C20.

The structure is L-plan, C17 in character but begun C16 and with a small C18 addition, its upper levels now seriously depleted. The long S elevation is the best-preserved and has the appearance of a palace range. As illustrated by Billings, the house had four storeys originally (now reduced to no more than three) with gablet dormerheads to light the upper floor. Built in random rubble with local pink sandstone dressings, it was almost certainly lime-rendered and washed (see especially the traces on the SW tower), which would have created a unity out of the muddle of masonry joints.

  Understanding of the castle's development would benefit from thorough archaeological investigation. The earliest part appears to be the SE corner, which on its E front has an arched door leading to a vaulted ground-floor room. Evidence in the internal masonry suggests that in the late C16 it was recast and raised to three storeys with a door in the N wall of this block

Auchans Castle.
Engraving, published 1852

connecting probably to a stair jamb, later altered. The first- and second-floor windows of this part all have fillets and shallow roll mouldings, the hallmark of a thorough remodelling. On the S front, the W extent of this building is indicated by quoins to the l. of the first-floor window. These quoins stop above first floor, and there is clear evidence that there was originally a gable here that was then built up to provide the full second storey, again possibly in the later C16. An apex stack (the flue visible on the inside of this wall) has been extended upwards to provide a second-floor hearth. Everything above second floor is mid-C17, contemporary with the addition of Cochrane's hall range (*see* below) and the gallery in its upper storey (now lost) which was carried over the earlier part. Associated with this phase, in the crowstepped E gable is the surprising feature of a Y-traceried Gothic window originally lighting the gallery, placed uncomfortably off-centre to accommodate the existing flues in this wall; its S jamb sits awkwardly some courses over the relieving arch for the chimney-breast in the room below. It was perhaps an expedient rather than stylistic choice, to achieve the largest window possible in the given space (but *see* the similarly placed C16 window in Old Rowallan Castle). To the r. of the gable the remains of a small drum stair-tower, created at about the same time to provide private access to all floors. One simple C17 chimneypiece in the second floor.

W of the L-plan is the hall range; on the S front it has two widely spaced bays and its extent is defined by a straight joint with less robust quoins. The N front mirrors the S elevation; all the windows had plain flat architraves and there is a simple eaves cavetto cornice, broken by gabletted dormers, the latter now gone. The W end must have followed shortly after and was almost certainly designed to provide a kitchen in a more convenient position with access to the W end of the new hall. A ragged gap in the masonry to the W of the straight joint with the hall range was formerly filled by a carved panel, but what it depicted is unrecorded. Projecting from the SW corner is a generous drum tower which is corbelled to square at the gallery level; it contained at the top a small room, with its own fireplace (*see* Baltersan and Maybole Castles). Its gables are partly preserved along with a vestige of its W window, which was tucked originally into the eaves. At the W a fragmentary but large crowstepped gable incorporates the large chimneystack serving the ground-floor kitchen. The drum room adjoining the kitchen had a drain to the S. Windows offset to the l. above ground floor lit bedrooms that had closets and garderobes in the SW tower.

On the N front of this part, at the junction with the hall block, is a third drum tower, originally conical-roofed, with a newel stair serving the rooms at the W end and providing access to the hall range. It had a baffle entry shared with the kitchen and evidently failed to provide a suitable entrance to the reception rooms. The solution was the tall square entrance tower in the re-entrant angle of the hall range and the older E range; it

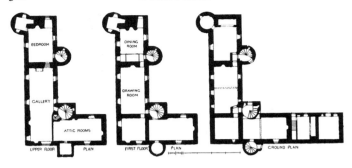

Auchans Castle.
Plan

butts up uncomfortably close to the windows at the E end of the hall range, emphasizing its slightly later date. Though partially preserved on its W face nearly to parapet level, Billings shows that it also had a handsome doorpiece, comparable to the doorway to the N wing at Rowallan (c. 1650, q.v.), with fluted pilasters, a broken segmental pediment with a crowning stumpy obelisk and more ornate obelisks, reminiscent of the finials on the Montgomerie monument at the Skelmorlie Aisle, Largs (q.v.), sitting uneasily over the projecting ends of the entablature. Above the door a panel contained family arms, and at gallery level there was a red sandstone, rolled string course with one window above. The top window, the distinctive Renaissance balustraded parapet and the conical cap of the stair-turret leading to the crowning platform roof have all gone.

The lower N wing also represents more than one build. That part abutting the N side of the C16 tower must have followed on quickly from the entrance tower – a datestone of 1644 was formerly above one of its windows – and had a raised wallhead crowstepped gable and apex stack. Its N extension is only two storeys, and seems to have been built after 1726 to improve the services for the house, for the Countess of Eglinton. It incorporated a second kitchen to supply food for the retainers. Of the interior nothing remains.

FORTS, Wardlaw and Harpercroft, 2 km. SSW. Two forts, probably Late Iron Age, standing side by side, one comprising a single rampart enclosing an area some 60 m. in diameter on the summit of Wardlaw, the other forming a much bigger enclosure on the adjacent summit, the outer of its two wide-spaced ramparts taking in about 6.5 ha.

FAIRLIE HOUSE. *See* p. 322.
HILLHOUSE. *See* p. 366.

DUNDUFF *see* FISHERTON

DUNLOP   *4040*

One of the most attractive villages in Ayrshire, set in the rolling
hill country of the north. The parish, which is first recorded in
the mid C13, belonged to Kilwinning Abbey. It has always been
primarily an agricultural centre – the lands and climate of the
parish ideal for growing grass and raising cattle – and Dunlop
was later synonymous with cheese-making, a craft brought to the
parish in the late C17 by Barbara Gilmour, a migrant from Ireland
(†1732, her headstone is in the churchyard).

DUNLOP PARISH CHURCH, Main Street. Largely rebuilt in
  1835. T-plan, ashlar, with a square battlemented E tower that
  has stepped angle buttresses, a big four-centred arch window
  with tracery, and tall round-headed bell-openings. The other
  elevations have tiers of windows, the upper ones usually with
  aprons. The N aisle has reused strapwork details from its predecessor of 1643, itself an addition to the medieval church.
  Bright spacious interior with panel-fronted galleries in each
  wing, supported on cast-iron columns. Plaster walls and
  pitched plaster ceiling with simple ribs and cornice. The
  Dunlop of Dunlop Aisle (N) is distinguished by an arch supported on paired corbels; this too is a retained C17 detail.
  Thoroughly renewed inside in 1884 by *John Small* of Beith, the
  dark oak Gothic woodwork by *Robert Balfour* of Beith. –
  STAINED GLASS. A superb collection, mostly of 1884, including armorial glass by *James Ballantine & Son* and, in the S wall,
  Old Testament prophets, apostles and Holy Women, all by
  Powells of London. These are of high quality: the best those
  where the figure is allowed to escape the backcloth, such as
  the languid David, the muscular Isaiah and the restful, watchful Priscilla in her well-realized bottle-green dress. – N aisle,
  Faith, Hope and Charity by *Henry Holiday* for *Powells*. – W wall,
  by *Alfred Webster*, with a particularly painfully dejected Adam
  in one light; designed in 1914, but only installed in 1927, as a
  memorial to the artist, who was killed in the First World War.
  – Several characteristic windows by *Gordon Webster* (1947, 1966
  and 1972), but also a naturalistic, ascetic E window by him,
  1968, in marked contrast. N wall, a Millennium window by
  JMJ Stained Glass Design (Judith Johnston) of Glasgow, 2000,
  designed by *Charles Jamieson*: named tree leaves, like a page in
  an Observer's Book.
Former CLANDEBOYE SCHOOL, E of the church. Erected in   89
  1641 by James Hamilton, Viscount Clandeboye, whose father,
  Hans Hamilton (†1608) had been minister here. Two-storey,
  of randomly laid stone, with small windows in painted stone
  frames, either side of a central doorway. Steeply pitched slate
  roof, with crowstepped gables. Single-storey S extension by
  David M. Brown (of *Ingram & Brown*), 1925, when converted
  as the Church Hall. Interior of the same date, tall and narrow
  with a plaster barrel vault. Attached to the W wall, HANS

HAMILTON'S TOMB, built by his son in 1641. Ashlar, with a steeply pitched flagstone roof and crowstepped gable. Central framed entrance, with two panels above, the upper one with a decayed skull and cross-bones. The monument itself has figures of Hamilton and his wife, Janet Denham – the 'painfull pastor and his spotless wife' of the inscription. They kneel on a sarcophagus, facing each other across a stool, praying. Above and about them rises an arched recess carried on panelled pilasters, with flanking columns with decorative caps supporting a cartouche; another cartouche at the head of the arch. The arch

Dunlop, Hans Hamilton's Tomb, elevation and plan
1884

decorated as though it were a curtain, drawn back by hands which reach out from behind the lower cartouches to reveal the lengthy inscription in the tympanum.

CHURCH HALL, Main Street. Free Church of 1845, converted 1958. Neo-Tudor hoodmoulds and a nice big bellcote. – STAINED GLASS. Two brightly coloured windows of *c.* 1933. In each an angel; in one a shipwreck behind, in the other a lighthouse.

VILLAGE HALL, Main Street. 1891. Given character by an eccentrically detailed tower with corbelled buttresses beneath an octagonal slate-hung upper stage and a spirelet. Extended 2007 by *Austin-Smith: Lord* in glass and steel, a provocative and positive statement.

DESCRIPTION. The village has largely avoided C19 and C20 development; its core remains the narrow MAIN STREET, running E from the church, its gentle twists creating varying vistas. Lining it are mainly late C18 and early C19 cottages. Of these, the first group on the S side (Nos. 89–95) illustrates the variety: one is dated 1782, one has its stonework exposed, one is plastered, one harled and one of painted stone. The windows are also variously treated and there is a pretty little late C19(?) semicircular oriel in the W gable. Oddly curving skews to No. 89. The rendered and crowstepped MANSE COTTAGE (No. 75) is set at an angle to its neighbours. Set back is the harled and gabled two-storey OLD MANSE, of 1781, with windows in painted frames and moulded eaves. Its porch may be of 1894 when *Robert Turnbull* (of *A. Thomson & Turnbull*) carried out improvements. Single-storey wings, one late C18, the other of *c.* 1814, dominate the view from the street.

On the N side of the street is KIRKLAND. This is the early C16 manse, later a farmhouse. Exposed rubble L-plan with a stair-tower in the re-entrant angle and crowstepped gables. A stone drainage spout, carved mask corbel and a small aumbry close to the original entrance are original. L-plan addition of 1935 forming a courtyard; many of the details are of this date, e.g. the simple square-headed openings, the gabled half-dormers, pyramidal tower roof and panelled interior. MAIN STREET continues, increasingly wider and open, the cottages becoming fewer, with more C19 two-storey buildings and the village's other public buildings, such as the Village Hall (*see* above) and the Primary School (*c.* 1930) on the l. On the r. is THE OLD SCHOOLHOUSE, an L-plan two-storey three-bay house of *c.* 1800 with a harled front, and a shouldered triangular pedimented doorpiece. At the junction with Stewarton Road, the painted stone two-storey VILLAGE INN, of *c.* 1830, with a curved corner bay and some lying-pane glazing. The main entrance has a lozenge-pattern fanlight and panelled Doric pilasters.

LADYSTEPS MILL, 0.5 km. SE. Early C19. Harled and slated former mill lying close to, and below, the road. Simple openings and stumpy chimneystacks; unusual stepped skews, each step with its own protective slate.

THE HILL, 1 km. SE. Remarkably fine and compact U-plan vernacular house, somewhere between a farm and a mansion; this was the farm of Barbara Gilmour, who brought to Dunlop the art of making hard cheese. The earliest part, however, is the wing to the l., a single-storey farm and byre, dated 1740 and 1748, but raised *c.* 1760, probably at the same time as the present gabled three-bay two-storey main house was built. The r. wing, built as stables, was added in the later C18, and the house was aggrandized *c.* 1817, when the doorcase with its carved ornamental heraldic head was added. Interiors also largely of this date.

DUNLOP HOUSE
2 km. E

On the N bank of the Clerkland Burn in well-wooded policies. Built in 1831–4 for Sir John Dunlop, M.P. for Ayrshire, by *David Hamilton*. The third building on the site, it replaced an earlier tower. In its style, compact plan and verticality it is a conscious, and early, attempt to emulate the character of a tower house. The Jacobean style was new for Hamilton (although reprised for his competition entry for the Houses of Parliament in 1834), and the detailing of strapwork etc must be influenced by the Dunlop Aisle at the Parish Church (*see* above), and the Skelmorlie Aisle and Montgomerie monument at Largs.

Built of droved sandstone ashlar with polished dressings, it has three storeys and an attic. The asymmetrical E and S fronts are full of panache, particularly in the roof-line of corbelled and domed bartizans, decorative dormerheads, finialled gables and, originally, tall chimneystacks. Elaborate strapwork pediments to several of the windows. Near to the centre of the E front the entrance tower, and to the NE corner of this front a slender four-storey tower with a leaded roof and lantern finial recalling the Glasgow Tolbooth steeple. The W elevation is in two sections, like a tower house with an added wing. The r. part is the full three storeys and attic with a big three-light window and balustraded steps leading from the principal floor to the ground. The lower range to its l. is advanced and emphasized by a large two-storey canted bay with an open loggia at the ground and a five-light window above, its balustraded parapet forming a balcony with an elaborate strapwork pediment. The N elevation is a shallow U-plan, mainly infilled at ground level, with a high-walled service court in front evoking a barmkin; basket-arched entrance with a dramatic Baroque bellcote.

Interior altered *c.* 1860 after the house was sold to Thomas Dunlop Douglas, a distant cousin of Sir John, and again after 1933 when it was converted for use as a convalescent home. In 2011, conversion to flats is awaited. The *Minton*-tiled entrance hall has a decorative framed stone dated 1599 from the previous house. At ground floor a number of service rooms including a groin-vaulted strongroom and wine cellar. Main rooms on the principal floor. The main stair was removed from the centre of the house after 1933 but the decoration has, remarkably, survived. At the W end of the house are the former dining and drawing rooms, entered from a bowed ante-room at the head of a long corridor. The drawing room has a compartmented, geometric ceiling with guilloche mouldings and leafy bosses. Marble chimneypiece and elegant, fretted pelmets. The dining room has a simpler ceiling, panelled dado and a French-inspired marble chimneypiece with cartouche-like decoration at the angles and in the centre. In the sitting room, another compartmented ceiling and Jacobean motifs in the cornice. On the second floor at the E the top-lit gallery, now floored, can be appreciated but the elaborate ironwork balustrades have gone. – WEST LODGE. Also by *Hamilton*.

AIKET CASTLE. *See* p. 87.

DUNURE   2010

Small, charming fishing village on the Carrick coast, essentially a C19 creation of the Kennedys of Dunure, squeezed tightly in between the sea and cliff. The HARBOUR is natural, but developed in 1810–11 by *Charles Abercrombie* for the Kennedys. Partly rock-cut and partly rubble-built quays on the S and E sides; on the N and W sides rubble-built piers form a rectangular basin with its entrance at the NW corner, where the W pier terminates in a cylindrical beacon pillar, its stone now weathered sculpturally. Beyond the N pier, the decayed remains of a second pier. S, a stone breakwater giving shelter from NW winds. Deepened, and the entrance widened, in 1897 by *H. V. Eaglesham*. Beside the harbour, three rows of COTTAGES – building plots were advertised in 1819.

DUNURE CASTLE, 200 m. SW of the village on a rocky headland commanding the Firth. The Kennedys were in Carrick by the C13, and Dunure was the chief residence of the main branch. Of the family's many castles and towers, none is such a bold and aggressive architectural statement of power. It was here in the mid C16 that Gilbert Kennedy attempted to gain ownership of the lands of Crossraguel Abbey by the simple expedient of roasting Allan Stewart, the Commendator of the abbey, on a spit. Ruinous by the mid C17; archaeological evidence suggests it may have been destroyed by fire.

Mostly built of the local hard black whin, with sandstone dressings. The castle, of C13 or C14 date, appears to have been a keep of irregular shape, the shape dictated by the rock on which it is built. MacGibbon & Ross characterized the style and outline of this first phase as recalling 'the form of the primitive fortresses of the West Highlands'. It has an enceinte wall, 1.5 m. thick, with a central passageway, and vaulted rooms to either side. Only on the seaward (W) and S sides do

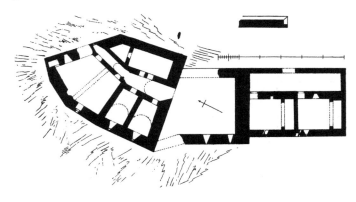

Dunure Castle.
Plan

the walls remain to any height, displaying a number of irregularly placed windows – 'a tall gable honeycombed with
windows'* – though none of these is likely to be original, the
walls having been raised at a later date.

Extended to the SE, probably in the C15, as suggested by the
large corbels which support the parapet on the S elevation; two
tiers of regularly spaced small square windows are set below
this. This section of the castle sits lower than the original tower,
and was intended to strengthen the landward defences. The
interiors have mostly been robbed, but it seems to have consisted of an entrance passage with two right-angle turns, with
a NW guardhouse. The third and final phase of building is
probably late C16 in date. Now the best preserved, it consists
of a rectangular block, again extending the castle in a SE direction. This range is more domestic, gable-ended, originally with
crowsteps; it seems to have been built with reused stone, and
may have replaced the chapel that is known to have existed in
the late C16. Long, wide gallery passage along the NE elevation,
giving access to a kitchen (r.) and a bakehouse (l.), each of
which has a large fireplace, and small square windows, echoing
those in the C15 work. At its NW end the passage connects with
the C15 phase, and there are the beginnings of a stair. In
1996–9, archaeological investigation was carried out, followed
by conservation and consolidation of the ruins. This work was
done for Strathclyde Building Preservation Trust by *Page &
Park*; the steel stairs and entrances date from this period, and
are designed to be non-intrusive to the historic fabric.

42   NE of the castle, an excellent circular beehive-type DOOCOT.
Probably C15, and in a very good state of preservation. A simple
entrance, and three prominent roosting ledges running round
the upper part of the structure.

*R. L. Stevenson, writing in 1876.

DUNURE HOUSE, 100 m. N of the harbour by the sea. Early C19, for the Kennedys. On the seaward side, a big projecting bow, with flanking bays. On the entrance front a wing, perhaps of *c.* 1868, with a pedimented porch.

LIMEKILN, at the S edge of the village. Two single-draw kilns with segmentally arched draw-holes (blocked). Atop is a house, originally a shop and tearoom, built in the C20.

DUNURE CEMETERY, 0.5 km. S, on the A719. 1912 by *James Russell* of Maybole. Attractive red sandstone lodge. A number of war graves and *Reginald Blomfield*'s Cross of Sacrifice.

DUNURE MILL, 1 km. S. Late C18. In the Culzean estate style. Three storeys, with crowstepped gables terminating in crosses. Gothic openings, paired on the S elevation, clustered together on the W elevation, and on the upper floor of the otherwise blind N elevation.

EGLINTON CASTLE *see* KILWINNING

ENTERKINE HOUSE
1.5 km. NE of Annbank

4020

A country house of 1939–41 by *W. J. Fairweather* of *John Fairweather & Son* for James Houston, a Scottish businessman who had made a fortune in American shipping. It is the third house on the site. Extensively remodelled in the 1950s for Alan Mackay. Converted to a hotel in 2000. A strange design with an elongated plan entered at the W end, no doubt dictated by the narrow site with a dramatic drop to the River Ayr to the S. White walls of painted brick and render, the brick parts probably originally exposed like the chimneystacks. N and E fronts give a hint of the original sleek appearance. Inside, the main rooms lead *enfilade* from the stair hall influenced by contemporary American design. The interior is light and spacious using both Oregon and Canadian pine for panelling and woodwork. The dining-room Adamesque chimneypiece possibly reused from the late C18 house. – CHAUFFEUR'S HOUSE. By *J. Carrick*, 1937, setting the style for the main house but with touches of Arts and Crafts charm. – LODGE. Mid-C19, typical, with a canted central bay, pilasters and segment-headed windows.

FAILFORD

4020

Roadside hamlet.

HIGHLAND MARY MONUMENT. 1920–1 by *James S. Hay* of Kilmarnock. A red sandstone pillar on a square base, with a globe finial. Near this spot Burns and Mary Campbell ('Highland Mary') had their 'day of parting love'.

PEDEN'S COVE, 0.4 km. SE. Steps, carved into the soft Permian red sandstone of the Ayr Gorge, lead to a cave from which the Covenanting minister, Alexander Peden, is said to have preached in the late C17. Probably, however, early C19, and comparable with the carved passages and rooms at Barskimming (q.v.).

RAILWAY CROSSINGS. The Glasgow & South-Western Railway line between Ayr and Mauchline, built in 1869–70, passes to the W and N of the hamlet. The engineer was *William Johnstone*. It crosses the road 0.5 km. W by an elliptical single-arch BRIDGE with flat pilasters and panelled haunches; the Water of Fail 0.4 km. NW by a VIADUCT of nine tall arches; and the Yonderton Burn 2 km. NE by a similar six-arch VIADUCT.

STAIRAIRD, 1 km SE on an idyllic site above the Ayr with extensive grounds sloping down to the river. It began as a farmhouse and steading, probably built in the 1770s, for the Barskimming estate. The U-plan with rear courtyard is typical for an Ayrshire dairy farm, but the two-storey house is unusually large and may have been built as a dower house. The striking ogee-headed windows (a motif of the estate's buildings) and evidence that the roof was formerly thatched also suggest that it was positioned as a romantic eyecatcher in views from Barskimming House. Ground floor and interior substantially altered in the 1920s, and the low S range, linking to the farm court, remodelled in simple Arts and Crafts manner for domestic use. The N range of the court, formerly the byre, was converted to stables. Entrance/stair hall in the same Arts and Crafts style.

BARSKIMMING HOUSE. *See* p. 191.
OLD AUCHENFAIL HALL. *See* p. 565.

FAIRLIE

Coastal village, tucked between the shore and the cliffs. Development began in the early C19, when 'marine villas' were built on feus granted by Lord Glasgow of Kelburn. In 1842 Lord Cockburn found 'the best village of the wealthy in Scotland' with 'excellent houses, capital gardens, umbrageous trees, the glorious Clyde, backed by Arran and its dependencies stretched out before them, a gravely soil, and a mild western climate'. The steamer pier accelerated growth in the late C19, and there is also much from the 1920s. For much of the C19 and C20 it was also renowned for the elegant yachts built by William Fife & Son.

Former FAIRLIE FREE CHURCH, Main Road. Now residential. An idiosyncratic design of 1879 by *William MacChlery*, incorporating the lower courses of its predecessor (of 1843). The N gable, with a bellcote, four-light window with Y-tracery, and gabled porch, is flanked by square-headed windows with round-headed niches above. Side elevations with pointed windows between buttresses below, and unusual circular windows above, separated by flat pilasters.

FAIRLIE PARISH CHURCH, Main Road. Of 1833–4, but enlarged and improved out of all recognition in 1894–5 by *J. J. Stevenson*. Simple Gothic, with a N tower and E and W transepts. The nave marks the old church, a single cell with lancets, but the coursed rubble walls have been raised and pairs of pointed windows inserted. Crisper stonework to the transepts, with three-light gable windows, and the tall square three-stage tower, which has Y-tracery bell-openings, a castellated parapet and a tall broach spire. The weathervane, 1951 by *James S. Howie Ltd*, is a model of the yacht *Latifa*.* A narrower gabled S extension contains a hall and the vestibule, with a gabled porch. On the W (rear) elevation an unassuming suite of halls, of 2000.

The highlight of the interior is the timber roof, a joyous celebration of the skills of the village boat-builders. The central feature resembles an upturned yacht keel, with cross timbers and simple ribbing, and side panels decorated with wooden members shaped like the cross-section of a keel. The ceilings otherwise of flat timber panels. Pointed chancel arch, and a canted boarded ceiling to the chancel. – COMMUNION TABLE, 1915, by the minister Rev. *Arthur Allan*, modelled on an elaborately carved cassone. Also by him the LECTERN, 1936. – STAINED GLASS. A fine assortment. – W wall, S–N, St Christopher, and St George, 1900 by *James Powell & Sons*, designed by *John William Brown*; a vibrant Good Shepherd by *Gordon Webster*, 1932; and Sir Galahad and the Holy Grail, *c.* 1918, by *J. H. Dearle* for *Morris & Co.* – Dearle for Morris too in the E wall: Courage and Endurance, of 1917, and St Michael and St David. The rather stiff 'Mary hath Chosen the Better Part' is of 1934 by *Heaton, Butler & Bayne*. – W transept W wall, St Kentigern and St Margaret, by *James Powell & Sons*; well-judged Gothic thrones and a consummate use of colour and light. – In the chancel, Ascension of 1930, designed by *Alfred A. Webster* from a sketch by Rev. Allan, and executed by *Gordon Webster*. – MONUMENT. Lady Glasgow (S wall), 1927 by *Robert S. Lorimer*.

In the vestibule, the FAIRLIE STONE, purportedly Pictish. Found at Chapel House Farm, Fairlie. It depicts a human figure with a shield and sword confronting two beasts, the second of which appears to have the tail of the first in its mouth.

Former FAIRLIE PRIMARY SCHOOL, School Brae. 1887 by *J. J. Stevenson* in an eclectic Scots Baronial, diverging successfully from the Board School template, and owing much to Stevenson's involvement with London schools. T-plan with crow-stepped gables and ashlar walls, the basement with a curious facing akin to crazy paving. Datestone with thistles, clasped pilasters and strapwork fleur-de-lis, and a dainty bellcote, which seems hardly to be attached to its gable.

FAIRLIE VILLAGE HALL AND LIBRARY, Main Road. 1892, again by *J. J. Stevenson*, in an attractive Tudor Gothic,

*A Bermudan cutter, commissioned in 1935 from William Fife & Son.

thoroughly transforming the simple parochial school of 1871. Two-storey, with a gabled N wing, and an octagonal s addition of 1928 by *Fryers & Penman*. The lighter stone of the main block's ground floor betrays the original school; ogee-headed windows here, otherwise square-headed, those in the N wing with simple tracery.

DESCRIPTION. BAY STREET runs s and down from the Parish Church. The w side is multi-hued harled Neo-vernacular of 1985 by *Philip Cocker & Partners*, built on the site of the Fifes' yard. A wider variety of styles on the E side: typical are the C19 cottages and houses in rubble stone and ashlar, e.g. the Village Inn, called 'lately rebuilt' in 1878, plastered with four pretty dormers, and Nos. 28–30, early C19, quite classy, single-storey with jolly bargeboarded porches and square mouldings to the windows. ALLANTON PARK TERRACE extends Bay Street N; two late C19 terraces, one with French towerlets at either end and canted bays.

MAIN ROAD runs s from the church, and has an enclosed, urban ambience, accentuated by the traffic and the backdrop of the cliffs. On the w, harled infill of *c.* 2001, of varying height, with prominent glazed fins, the mid-C19 POST OFFICE, harled with bargeboarded gables, and Nos. 81–83, late C19, with flanking dainty wooden porches that double as bridges, providing access via the middle floors. Where the cliffs relent development has been possible on both sides of the road. The original marine villas occupy spacious grounds between road and sea, their privacy guarded by stone walls. After the junction with Jetty Road, BEACH HOUSE, of *c.* 1820. Three bays; the tall circular bay to the r., with a slender balustrade, and the shallow veranda to the l., are early C20 additions. FAIRLIE LODGE is an early C19 enlargement of a nepus-gabled cottage, dated 1763, again with a rounded bay facing the sea, given character by windows with small-pane glazing in an astonishing variety of patterns. Sitting proud on the rocks of the shore, PINE HOUSE is timber-clad and bow-ended, *c.* 1927 by *James Miller*, something between a house and a boathouse.

THE CAUSEWAY begins with THE PARAGON, Tudor Gothic, dated on a keystone 1876, with a carving of a yacht, and ends with ROCKHAVEN, a white-harled and crowstepped two-storey C18 house with small windows, a curving boundary wall and contemporary offices. Extended to the s in the early C19, with a canted and hipped bay, segmentally headed dormers with panelled pilasters, and a pedimented and bracketed doorpiece. To the N of The Causeway runs FERRY ROW, as brashly sea-sidey as Fairlie gets, with mostly altered two-storey mid-C19 cottages. s again the harled two-storey classical FAIRLIE HOUSE, of 1812, one of the original and best 'marine villas'. It has a big central semicircular bay and tall castellated sea walls.

Landward of the road, mostly interwar and post-war bunga-lows and houses, with occasional highlights. In CASTLEPARK GARDENS, No. 28, THE PLACE, 1904–5 by *Allan Stevenson*,

harled with shouldered gables, painted stone dressings and
a big stone bay to the r. of the main entrance, and in
CASTLEPARK DRIVE, No. 12, a crisp Late Arts and Crafts villa
of *c.* 1920, broadly symmetrical about a central tile-hung gable;
to the r. the tiled roof sweeps down to form a narrow covered
porch. Off GLEN ROAD, THE ROUND HOUSE, two linked
canted pavilions with ogee-headed roofs. An oddity: it looks
late C19 and isn't round. Also in Glen Road, FAIRLIECRAIG,
a spreading and amorphous harled house of 1899. In
BURNFOOT ROAD, BURNSIDE, a delightful rubble-built
Tudor-rustic cottage, originally early C19, with the main elevation facing W. The projecting rear wing has a rustic timbered
and slated porch and catslide dormers. Raised *c.* 1900, possibly
by *J. J. Stevenson*, with a long timber panel below deeply projecting eaves. The early C19 (perhaps late C18) harled ARGYLL
COTTAGE sits in an impossibly romantic position beside the
Fairlie Burn.

FAIRLIE CASTLE, 0.7 km. S, set on the hill above the railway
line and close to Fairlie Burn. One of the best examples of a
series of C16 towers found along the county's coastline and in
its immediate hinterland (Little Cumbrae; and also the Abbot's
Tower at Crossraguel, qq.v.). Described by Pont in 1608 as a
'strong tour and werey ancient'. Square plan, built in a striking
combination of carefully matched local pink and yellow
sandstone with yellow quoins. In the S wall a round-arched
roll-moulded entrance with a blind panel high above. No regularity in window sizes or arrangement. Sophisticated chequered
corbelling at the wall-head, supporting a parapet, and
putative corbelled-out angle bartizans. Inaccessible interior –
MacGibbon & Ross record two vaulted chambers on the
ground floor, with a spiral stair towards the SE corner. First-
floor hall, with a kitchen and fireplace at the E end, separated
by a stone partition.

SOUTHANNAN CASTLE, 1.5 km. S. Remains of a square tower
house, which may have been similar to the C16 castles at Fairlie
(*see* above) and Portencross (q.v.). Ambitious entrance arch,
almost entirely preserved, dating from a remodelling of *c.* 1600;
the design, according to one source, 'procured [by Lord
Semple] in Italy, and was one of the most ambitious buildings
built during the reign of James VI'. Projecting forward to the
l. of the arch is SOUTHANNAN HOUSE. Its genesis is a plainly
detailed L-plan two-storey house of *c.* 1800, remodelled, rather
inelegantly, in 1902–3 by *Allan Stevenson*. The main front has
projecting curved outer bays, with crowstepped shield-like
gables, and a battlemented single-storey porch. Conically
headed tower at the junction with the castle. In institutional
use for much of the C20, and converted to flats in 2001–2 by
Stuart Duncan Partnership.

HUNTERSTON POINT, 3.5 km. SW of Fairlie, juts out towards
the deep-water Fairlie Roads, where one channel of the Firth
narrows between the mainland and the Cumbraes. The site was

identified in the the mid C20 as suitable for two nuclear power stations, which could be cooled by sea water. Neither makes much attempt to blend in or to ameliorate its bulky presence. They are:

HUNTERSTON 'A' POWER STATION. Planned from 1953, built 1957–64, the design by *Howard V. Lobb & Partners* (contractors, *Mowlem*). Twin 'Magnox' reactors sheltered within curved-sided glazed boxes. The verticality is the result of elevating the reactors to permit refuelling from below. The concrete-framed ancillary buildings (including the 213-m. long turbine hall) have grey brick panels and sandstone and slate facings. Closed 1989. Now being decommissioned.

HUNTERSTON 'B' POWER STATION. An advanced gas-cooled reactor (AGR), one of the first of its kind, constructed 1967–76, the designs by *Robert Matthew, Johnson-Marshall & Partners*. Single envelope for the reactors, turbine hall, etc. Due for decommissioning in 2016.

ORE TERMINAL, 2.5 km. N of the power stations. 1979 by *Frank Mears & Partners*. The main element is the long hammer-headed pier which stretches out into the Fairlie Roads. At the landward end a large functional barn, with a tall administrative block in the shape of the figure 'I'. Associated with the terminal are covered conveyers which carry the ore to waiting trains. The landscaping, by *Scottish Landscaping Ltd*, is ground engineering on a vast scale, with bunds and considerable tree planting.

HUNTERSTON CASTLE. *See* p. 368.
HUNTERSTON HOUSE. *See* HUNTERSTON CASTLE.
KELBURN. *See* p. 392.

FAIRLIE HOUSE

3030

2.5 km. NE of Dundonald

64   Designed by *David Henderson* and built 1781–7 for Alexander Fairlie, a leading agricultural improver in the county. *Thomas Clayton Jun.* 'offered to finish the principal floor' in 1782, but the house was not completed until 1787 after a court case between Fairlie and Clayton was resolved.

George Robertson in 1823 called it a 'shewy modern mansion' and it is indeed an elegant villa, known as 'the house of the five lums' after the line of five prominent stacks placed across the centre of the roof. Two storeys with a sunk basement to the front, an attic, a band course to the principal floor and a bold modillion cornice. Five-bay entrance front, the centre three advanced. At the outer angles wide pilaster-strips. All very plain except for the doorpiece, which has an arched, fanlit door and sidelights, set *in antis* with pairs of Roman Corinthian columns and outer pilasters of a similar order. Within the sides of the recess, tall niches. The retaining wall in front of the

basement area is unusually sophisticated with an attached colonnade of Roman Doric columns each with two square blocks
in the manner of Giulio Romano, supporting a cornice and
with alternating bays with doors and oculi. Henderson's son
John had recently returned from Italy. Could this be his
influence?

The side elevations have two windows in each floor; at the
rear two windows at each side flank an advanced centre bay, a
narrower projection than at the front, dominated by a large
Venetian stair window sitting on the band course and set within
an arched panel as used by Lord Burlington at his Chiswick
villa. Below the window a key-blocked *œil de bœuf* at mezzanine level. Two late C19 pedimented dormers above the outer
bays.

The interior is equally smart although the grand imperial
oak stair is a replacement, probably late C19. The plan plays
with geometry: at the front, two oval rooms in the outer bays
with a stone newel in a compartment to the l. of the door which
rises from basement to attic, while a small balancing compartment to the r. acts as a lobby to the dining room. Two large
rectangular rooms, symmetrically planned, flank the stairs.
They have fine plaster cornices (not exactly matching the
designs submitted in court). Good white marble chimneypiece
in the drawing room.

LODGE. Single-storey with pedimented gable-ends. Blind
oculi in the gables. Doric-columned gatepiers with ball finials.
– Extensive WALLED GARDEN AND POTTING SHEDS, one
dated 1776; the vine house, designed by Henderson in 1783,
has gone. Tall, coped rubble walls, two inner dividing walls.
Segmentally arched gateway and flat triangular-topped buttresses to inside and out. U-plan court of sheds to E. Robert
Burns's father was a gardener here. N end of E wall, a gardener's
cottage overlooking the garden.

FAIRLIE MAINS, SW. A courtyard range, formerly including
stables but now domestic. Entered through a central pedimented arched opening with an octagonal tower and spire
over.

FENWICK

4040

Attractive small village and parochial centre on the southern
slope of the moorland that isolates Ayrshire from Glasgow and
the Central Belt.

FENWICK PARISH CHURCH, Kirkton Road. An elegant Greek
cross-plan church of 1643. Stone, harled, with crowstepped
gables to all arms, the irregular pattern to the margin between
the crowsteps and the harl especially picturesque. S doorway
with a dated lintel, and a neck-iron or jougs attached to the
wall. On the E arm a stone stair to a round-headed moulded
entrance dated 1649 with the arms of Mure of Rowallan.

17   Blocky multi-staged w steeple of 1660 by *John Smith* of
Kilmaurs topped by a bellcote of 1864 by *William Railton*.
Restored 1930–1 by *Gabriel Steel* after a fire; the metal-framed
small-pane windows and the roof, with its unusual tonal variation and two crosses picked out in the slate, are of that date,
as is the plastered interior, with prominent corbelled wooden
cross-beams, and three panel-fronted galleries. A tall panelled
reredos partitions off the N arm, used as a vestry. – COMMU-
NION TABLE and PULPIT with sounding-board, a simplified
version of the elaborate C17 pulpit lost to the fire; the original
wrought-iron SAND-GLASS HOLDER is reused.

Walled CHURCHYARD with simple gatepiers and small hexagonal stone WATCH HOUSES erected in 1828 to deter body-
snatchers. MONUMENTS from the late C17 onwards.* The
earliest often flat and crudely decorated, e.g. James Brown
†1691, where the decoration resembles a childish view of a
dog's-bone, but may be a spade. One nicely carved early C18
stone, Jean Taylor, wife of James Tannahill, †1727; on the
reverse an adze, awl and square, beneath drapes, angels with
trumpets l. and r. There is a wealth of nicely lettered stones
from the early C19, with cursive script, such as those of James
Craig †1806, and John Fowlds and family, *c.* 1808. The parish
was a centre in the C17 for the Covenanters, hence several
COVENANTER MEMORIALS. Probably erected *c.* 1700, they
are often fairly crudely done, though the inscriptions are both
touching and telling. That to James White, †1685, has this verse
on the reverse:

> This martyr was by Peter Ingles shot
> By birth a Tyger rather than a Scot
> Who that his monstrous Extract might be seen
> Cut off his head and kick'd it o'er the Green
> Thus was that head which was to wear a crown
> A football made by a profane dragoun.

Equally poignant, the memorial to Peter Gemmell, 'who was
shot to death by Nisbet and his party 1685', e.g. '. . . Blood
thirsty redcoats cut his prayers short, And ev'n his dying
groans were made their sport . . .'

Directly SE of the churchyard, the former MANSE, of 1783.
Three-bay and two-storey, harled. The rear elevation, facing
the church, has flanking byres, and a reused 1645 datestone.
NE, the harled KIRKTON COTTAGE of *c.* 1975, with timber
boarding and a tiled roof, a pleasing reinterpretation of the
traditional cottage.

JOHN FULTON MEMORIAL HALL, Main Street. 1844 as a Free
Church; later pilastered and pedimented porch.

DESCRIPTION. One long single street (Main Street). At the N
end, in High Fenwick, the WAR MEMORIAL of 1921, a grey
granite replica of the Inveraray Cross. There is a characterful

---

*A useful guide to the churchyard, produced by the Lochgoin and Fenwick
Covenanters Trust, is sold in the church.

mix of houses throughout the village, much of it late C18 and early C19, typified by the row of single-storey cottages on the E, mostly harled, with painted stone dressings, that terminates with a two-storey house of exposed stone with a pilastered doorway and lying-pane glazing at first floor. Another two-storey house (Nos. 101–103) is dated 1824 in an elliptical ropework-edged panel in the wall-head gable; a carved heart above the date. To the village vernacular the KINGS ARMS HOTEL of c. 1900 is totally alien, if not unattractive, with fictive half-timbering and excessively ornate castellated wooden porch. Also on this side, a good group of two-storey houses of c. 1820, originally harled. One has a Doric-pilastered doorway, and, in the wall-head gable, another elliptical panel with ropework surround; weathered, but showing a man and pair ploughing. At the Laigh Fenwick end of Main Street, No. 52 is very neat early C19 with scrolled skews. It was a pioneering restoration in 1949 by *Stuart Harris*, for the actor Moultrie Kelsall. Finally, HALLHOUSE LODGE (nursing home). 1833 by *John Thomson* of Glasgow. Porch with Greek Doric columns.

Off Main Street's E side, and turning N, is narrow twisting MAUNSHEUGH ROAD, the epitome of a country lane, with a number of interesting houses, especially RETREAT COTTAGE, of c. 1840, well presented with Gothick tracery and strong mouldings. Also No. 7a, of c. 1965, very striking, mostly harled, with a large central window taking up most of the front elevation. No. 11a, 1967, has two monopitches abutting. Then BRAEHEADS, dated 1908, and very English in style: red brick, harled with tiled roof and glazed wooden porch. At the very far end, C18 cottages (Nos. 20–22 POLES ROAD); one dated 1740 on the lintel, on which are also carved a square and dividers.

CRAUFURDLAND CASTLE. *See* p. 233.
HILLHOUSE LODGE. *See* p. 367.

FISHERTON

2010

FISHERTON PARISH CHURCH, 1.2 km. NE of the hamlet. Built 1838–9 to serve part of Maybole parish; comprehensively rebuilt after storm damage and given a chancel and crow-stepped session house in 1912 by *J. & H.V. Eaglesham*. Ashlar entrance gable (E) with angle buttresses, a pedimented porch with a finial, and pointed-headed windows. Rendered side elevations with widely spaced bays. – FONT. Made in 1912 from the pinnacle of the 1830s bellcote and a holy water basin from the medieval church at Kirkbride (q.v.). – STAINED GLASS. Chancel. Brightly coloured with well-drawn faces, by *James Wright*, executed by *St Enoch Stained Glass Works*, 1933.

In the hamlet, FISHERTON SCHOOL, of 1875–6 by *Fulton*; extended by *J. K. Hunter*, 1910, and 1926–7. Single-storey U-plan, with gable-ended wings, and a gabled stone rear wing.

In STATION ROAD, two classics of bow-fronted seaside domestic architecture: No. 28, with single-storey drums either side of a two-storey drum, and No. 34, mostly flat-roofed and single-storey, with a bow to the l., to the r. a two-storey drum front. Both are of 1970.

DRUMBAIN, 0.3 km. w. Neat, pretty farmhouse altered and extended by *Stuart McPherson*, of *Lawrence McPherson*, Ayr, 2009.

KIRKBRIDE CHURCH, 0.6 km. s. Ruinous, small rectangle, almost nowhere higher than one or two courses of stone. The parish merged with Maybole before the C16.

DUNDUFF FARM, 0.6 km. s. Large, handsome and well-sited stone farmhouse of *c.* 1800, with a semicircular projection on the w front. To the s and e, early C19 farm buildings, including (to the s) a former mill, enclose a generously proportioned courtyard.

DUNDUFF CASTLE, 0.8 km. s. The castle stands on a platform on bleak hillside but with astounding views. Apparently begun in the C16, and of an L-plan with a stair-tower tucked into the re-entrant angle. Described in 1696 as 'near finished' but may never have been completed above the first floor. The rubble walls had dressed stone quoins and mouldings. Restored by *Ian Begg* and *Patrick Lorimer* of *ARP Lorimer & Associates* in the 1990s into a tower of three storeys and an attic, finished with a buff harl. The door at the foot of the stairs is set in the surviving roll-and-double-fillet moulded doorpiece. A narrow arrowslit guards the entrance and others are scattered around the ground floor. In the first floor mainly larger windows with original reveals and curving mortices for defensive bars. Some smaller windows in the stair-turret, also original. For all the other openings the harl returns into the ingoes. The new upper storey is finished with blunt concrete skews and chimney caps.

FULLARTON HOUSE
0.7 km. N of Southwood

3030

The house built in 1745 for William Fullarton was demolished in 1966. It was a tall, symmetrical box with a bold pedimented frontispiece, urns anchoring the pediment and a segmental window piercing it, as at Auchinleck (q.v.). It also had a forecourt, enclosed by a curved screen wall extending from the house and continuing as straight walls to a pair of diminutive pedimented lodges. The monumental cream sandstone PIERS which terminated the straight walls survive. They are square with channelled angles at the base supporting on the principal face fluted Doric columns framing a shell-headed niche. Triglyph entablature with shells, thistles, fleurs-de-lis and roses in the metopes, block modillions framed by guttae and a urn on a plinth supported by volutes. The motifs sit unhappily with the house's mid-C18 date but are hallmarks of *Robert Adam*, who

submitted designs for a castellated house in 1790, of which only
the stables were built (*see* below). There is nothing of this style
about the Neoclassical piers, so was Adam at Fullarton earlier?
    STABLES, W of the site of the house, are *Adam*'s and on the
S and W elevations are in the castellated style of his unrealized
design for the house, the other fronts simply harled. Converted
to housing in 1974 by *Hay, Steel & Macfarlane*. The long S
elevation is the more impressive, with a tall arched central
entrance clasped by drum piers with corbelled parapets. The
corbel course continues along the ranges l. and r. that terminate in three-bay pavilions, each with an advanced centre,
turrets to the parapet and arched attic windows in a crowstepped gable. The W elevation also expresses its centre in the
form of a gatehouse with arched openings (now glazed) in
the centre and taller flanking bays that end in corbelled turrets
and crowstepped gables. The outer bays of the wings also have
crowstepped gables with turrets and large arched windows.

Crosbie Church. Roofless medieval rectangular-plan set within
high walled kirkyard.

GADGIRTH

3 km. NW of Coyton

4020

A substantial house of 1808, demolished in 1968.

GADGIRTH HOLM. Terrace of eight estate cottages of 1906, in
    a gentle harled and red sandstone Arts and Crafts idiom, pos-
    sibly by *J. K. Hunter*, although *Honeyman Keppie & Mackintosh*
    made alterations to the mansion in 1903.
GADGIRTH MAINS. Courtyard farm, possibly that advertised to
    let in December 1807, with the promise that 'a suitable set of
    farm offices will be built, next summer'. Central arched
    entrance with a pigeon house in the gable above. Flanking
    wings gabled too, with raised quoins; that to the l. has a
    blocked arched window beneath a circular panel.
GADGIRTH VIADUCT, 0.6 km. NE. 1869–72 for the GSWR line
    between Ayr and Cronberry (Lugar). Probably by *William John-
    stone*. Dramatically high, ethereal stone and wrought-iron edifice.

GAILES

Irvine

3030

A windswept area of sand dunes and whin knolls to the S of
Irvine, largely devoted to golf.

IRVINE (GAILES) PUMPING STATION. 1979–81 by *Strathclyde
    Regional Council DARS*. Tall, harled, with a stepped profile.
GLASGOW GAILES GOLF CLUB. 1894 by *Peter Macgregor
    Chalmers*, largely rebuilt in 1931–2 by *Keppie & Henderson*. Red
    sandstone, with stepped gables, big mullioned-and-transomed
    windows, and a battlemented entrance.

WESTERN GAILES GOLF CLUB. Clubhouse of 1908 by *James Chalmers*. Harled Arts and Crafts, with applied timber gables, canted bay windows and a low square parapeted tower behind. Substantially extended to the r. in 1931–2 by *William J. B. Wright*.

GALSTON

5030

A burgh since 1864 with a tight medieval urban core around the church, early C19 development to the E, and mid-C19 expansion to S and W. The Burgh Council enthusiastically embraced urban redevelopment in the 1960s, so that much was lost to comprehensive clearance.

CHURCHES AND CEMETERY

Former ERSKINE CHURCH, Wallace Street. 1859 by *J. M. Dick Peddie*. Simple Romanesque, with a broad gabled front with corbelled eaves, bellcote and a triplet of round-arched windows in the centre above an arched entrance with angle shafts and roll moulding. The lower tier of windows on each side have Caernarvon-arched heads and colonnettes. Converted to flats, 2006.

GALSTON PARISH CHURCH, Brewland Street. Gabled preaching-box with E tower of 1807–10 by *John Brash*. The raised site is that of its predecessor, its stone also reused; the mason was *Peter Menzies*. Three-bay front with an overall pediment. The tower rises from the apex of the pediment, and has two square stages, with corner urns, an octagonal bell-stage and octagonal spire. Below it the main entrance, with paired pilasters to either side. Subsidiary doors l. and r. in moulded surrounds. Round-headed windows above, and in two tiers but on the side elevations, the upper tier smaller. SW porch of 1879 by *R. S. Ingram*; narrower pedimented chancel of 1913 by *Gabriel Steel*, very much in keeping. The interior has painted plastered walls, a panelled ceiling and a wooden panel-fronted curving gallery supported on stone pillars. The chancel has exceptionally lush Neo-Georgian decoration; tall round-headed chancel arch, with Ionic columns *in antis* and a panelled soffit and panelled barrel-vaulted ceiling, and two round-headed W windows within a bigger overarch, with swags in the spandrel. Circular window in the S wall, again with swags. – FITTINGS, including the pulpit and choir stalls, mostly of 1913; the Portland stone FONT of 1936 also by *Steel*. – SCULPTURE. In the gallery stairwell, two attractive wrought-iron pieces, Crucifixion to l., and Flight into Egypt to r. Unmistakable work of the 1960s, and brought here from the Erskine Church. – STAINED GLASS. Chancel W wall, 1920, by *Oscar Paterson* (war memorial). – MONUMENTS. Black and white marble tablet of 1809 to the Campbells of Cessnock (nave). Col. George Hutchinson, †1787, has a tablet beneath a draped urn.

In the churchyard, a MONUMENT to Andrew Richmond, Covenanter. First erected in 1823, but all that survives is a 'miserably-executed' (Paterson) bas relief of Richmond's martyrdom, showing two armed men and an hourglass. Frequently re-cut and restored, most recently in 1994. In the CHURCH HALL (2004–5, *Munro Architects* of Kilmarnock), STAINED GLASS from the Erskine Church and a window, by *Paul Lucky*, 2005, with two figures entwined to form a cross.

ST SOPHIA (R.C.), Bentinck Terrace. 1884–6 by *Robert Rowand Anderson*, in a dramatic and early example of Byzantine Revival. The church's genesis lies with the 3rd Marquess of Bute, whose conversion to Catholicism caused shock waves in late C19 Britain. Bute's artistic interests not only led him to a study of Byzantine architecture; he was also a generous supporter of Catholic churches in those areas where he had influence, and after an earlier proposal for a Byzantine church in Troon came to naught, these threads came together in Galston. The original proposal was closely modelled on Hagia Sofia, before practical considerations forced many changes, though the church, as built, still presents a powerful, if unlikely, whiff of the orient in this quiet Ayrshire side street. *Robert Weir Schultz*, then with Anderson, but who later worked extensively for Bute, may have been responsible for some of the design. Full restoration, 2002–3 by *W. I. Munro* of Kilmarnock.

Of Greek cross-in-square form, and polychrome in appearance, using a simple pink-red brick, white freestone and red tiles. The central rotunda, with conical roof, rises above the gabled roofs of the transepts, which in turn rise above the corner blocks, each with a hipped roof. Openings all round-headed. On the front (N) elevation, approached up steps, and behind railings and gates with two good contemporary lanterns, three-arch doorway with Romanesque zigzag ornament. Flanking taller round-headed recesses, each with a small window. Above the door a large circular window, and in the gable a roundel with an inset cross; apical stone Celtic cross. At the NE corner a stone minaret. The E and W elevations have two tiers of three windows: to the W above a long five-bay single-storey projection, to the E elevation above a corridor link to the Presbytery. Disappointingly plain interior with nothing to compare with the exterior polychromy. Walls of plain white plaster; tall pillars rise to the dome. A brick arcade between the body of the church and the vestibule; lower brick arcades incorporate the link with the Presbytery, and the confessionals. STAINED GLASS in the chancel, of 1962, by 'a French artist'.

The contemporary gabled two-storey PRESBYTERY uses similar motifs and materials, with a big plate-tracery first-floor window. Former SCHOOL also of 1884, but very plain and straightforward, and now painted in an aggressive shade of dark orange.

GALSTON CEMETERY, Cemetery Road. 1858–9; extended in 1896–9 by *Allan Stevenson*. Large, stone-walled and characterized by a good number of well-grown yew trees. Simple brick lodge with red sandstone dressings.

GALSTON COMMUNITY EDUCATION CENTRE, Orchard Street. 1937 by *James Hay & Steel*. *Moderne*. Two storeys, harled, with steel-framed windows; the central upper window with fin-like brick surround. Deeply recessed entrance in return elevation, with stair window above. Big hall to rear.

GALSTON PRIMARY SCHOOL, Western Road. 2007–8 by *East Ayrshire Council*. A spreading, mostly single-storey, brick and tile complex, with no obvious focus, and enlivened only by two lantern windows on one wing.

Former GALSTON PRIMARY SCHOOL, Glebe Road. Two red sandstone buildings on either side of the road. The older (now residential), of *c.* 1875 by *William Railton* of Kilmarnock, is single-storey and H-plan, with flanking gabled wings, that to the l. having balustraded shoulders. The other, much grander in scale, is the former Higher Grade School of 1908–10 by *J. & J. Armour*. Edwardian Baroque, the three-bay two-storey centre, with columns *in antis*, flanked by wings with first-floor Venetian windows. All five bays gabled, their varying height holding the composition together.

LOUDOUN ACADEMY, 0.8 km. N in parkland s of Loudoun Castle. 1968–70 by *Gilbert-Ash Ltd* for Ayr County Council. Informally composed group of steel-framed and brick-faced buildings around a four-storey block that has pilotis in entrances to an inner courtyard.

Former POLICE STATION, Church Lane. Red sandstone, originally single-storey by *James I. McDerment* in 1860, raised in 1897–8 by *John Murdoch*.

TOWN HOUSE, Cross Street. 1925–7 by *James Hay & Steel*;★ an accomplished 'Old Baronial Style' piece in Ballochmyle stone. Square-headed ground-floor windows, with a balustraded balcony and chunky bartizan turret above. Triangular-headed dormers with rose or thistle finials and a similar window, fleur-de-lis-headed, in the crowstepped gable to the r.

WAR MEMORIAL, Duke Street. 1922 by *Robert S. Lorimer*. Octagonal Aberdeen granite plinth, cross-shaft decorated with sword and wreath, and floriated Celtic cross. The plinth alternates bronze dedicatory panels and carved shields.

BARR CASTLE
Barr Street

Also known as Lockhart Tower, and originally the possession of the Lockharts of Barr, who are recorded from around 1400. The tower probably dates from *c.* 1500; it passed to the Campbells of Cessnock in 1670. Built of coursed rubble sandstone,

★ Gabriel Steel was the son of Galston's Burgh Surveyor.

rising through five storeys to the parapet corbelling, with a number of irregularly placed window openings in the 2.1-m.-thick walls. The original roof has been replaced with a low hipped roof, reaching to the wall-heads. The original entrance is on the first floor. It had been 'much modernised' and was in use as a wool store when surveyed by MacGibbon and Ross in the C19 but became a Masonic Hall *c.* 1899, of which date the castellated entrance porch and the wood-panelled rooms.

DESCRIPTION

The cross-roads at the heart of the town is known as the Four Corners (Polwarth Street, Henrietta Street, Bridge Street and Wallace Street) and only for 100 m. or so in any direction is the pre-1960s character of the town maintained with some early, mid- and late C19 buildings. POLWARTH STREET leads N to the River Irvine (the BRIDGE by *Laughlen*, of 1838–9), with on the W side two-storey houses of *c.* 1800 (one dated 1803), some with wall-head gables and chimneys. The two buildings of principal interest are the classical red sandstone former BROWN'S INSTITUTE, of 1873–4 by *James Stark* (*see* also Newmilns and Darvel), which has a tall balustraded slightly projecting centre, with a big four-light window, flanked by wings with round-headed windows and panelled corner pilasters, and the former BLAIR'S SCHOOL, opposite, erected in 1840–1. Also *c.* 1840, Nos. 21–23, a house by *James Ingram*, with a triangular pediment to the doorcase, with floral detailing (similar to a monument in Tarbolton churchyard (q.v.)). Wide corner pilasters, upper-floor windows with aprons. Just to the E, in BARRMILL ROAD, No. 7 (formerly Longhouse Farm) is of *c.* 1860 but has the rare survival of a coursed rubble earlier farm building, with a steeply pitched slate roof, and splayed corners to the N gable. It may be late C18.

WALLACE STREET runs S from the Four Corners towards Barr Castle, past the former Erskine Church (*see* Churches). Opposite this Nos. 32–34, a fine three-bay red sandstone Arts and Crafts house of 1911. Projecting bay to the r., and contemporary glass in the porch. W along BRIDGE STREET towards the Parish Church, there is little of note until BREWLAND STREET commences with Nos. 4–12, the former offices of the Galston Co-operative Society Ltd. This is Galston's grandest commercial property and a fulsome expression of the Society's confidence. The architects were *Andrew & Newlands* of Kilmarnock, 1900–1. Three storeys and seven bays in red sandstone, the style Free Renaissance. On the upper floors the bays are divided by broad pilasters, and the floors by an equally broad and partly panelled string course. Wider central bay with two round-headed windows on the first floor, a corbelled-out window above and, at roof level, a grand entablature of volutes and urns. The inner flanking bays have two round-headed windows to the first floor, and three square-headed mullioned windows above, while the outer bays terminate in small Dutch gables with framed circular windows. A further narrow bay has been squeezed in at the E corner, finishing in an attached octagonal turret and a complex roof with a finial.

As the street turns SW, late 1960s local authority housing dominates along the NW side, by *Stewart Hume* of *Hay Steel MacFarlane & Partners* of Kilmarnock. A series of three-storey deck-access flats in Chapel Lane and Manse Place were demolished in 2008–9, but more conventional two-storey houses remain, set obliquely to the street and in a staggered line, along with undemonstrative three- and four-storey blocks of flats. The relationship between the flats and the houses is carefully thought through, the contrasting materials and shapes blend well, a commendable resolution in a difficult, and sensitive, location. More or less opposite, Nos. 26–58, of 1890–8, speculative housing by *Robert Anderson* for the Galston Co-operative Society.

E of Brewland Street, in GLEBE ROAD, No. 10, a former manse of *c.* 1901, with a balustraded entrance tower, and a big wooden porch, the equally large No. 12, of *c.* 1902, dominated by two bargeboarded gables and, opposite, the three-bay single-storey No. 23 (Nelville), of 1868, its entrance with pilasters and heavy entablature.

CROSS STREET, N of Bridge Street, begins with the PORTLAND ARMS of 1863–4, which turns the corner in well-done channelled pink-red ashlar; lying-pane glazing and squat wall-head stack to the l. elevation. The street widens out to form a small square, with the Town House (*see* Public Buildings) on the r. and the buttressed stone wall of the churchyard on the l., adjoined by a former school (No. 6) of 1787–8 built by *Matthew & Hugh Hunter*, reconstructed as houses in 1880; three bays, the windows with dressed stone surrounds. Beyond, in TITCHFIELD STREET a mix of single-storey cottages (No. 11 is dated 1797), the BURNS TAVERN of 1952 by *Robert Hurd*, respectful period infill, and the domestically scaled POLICE STATION of 1964–5. In GAS LANE, Nos. 1–3, well-restored early C19 cottages, harled, with big slate-hung dormers. S from here runs ORCHARD STREET, a long straight road climbing sharply at its S end, enhancing its visual appeal. It has the most coherent C19 townscape in Galston. The N section is mostly single-storey cottages, from *c.* 1820–40, usually of three bays with a central doorway, harled or painted stone, with stone dressings to the openings. No. 13 (Orchard Cottage) is earlier, three bays, painted stone, dressed quoins. Beyond the Community Education Centre (*see* Public Buildings, above) the street begins to climb. Here the dominant elements are paired cottages with red ashlar front elevations, of *c.* 1890–1900, stepping jauntily up the hill. The usual pattern is four bays, with the doors in the middle; rear access through paired entrances, with stone lintels, some of these pairs stepped to suit the contours.

In MAXWOOD ROAD, E of the centre, Nos. 1–3, a standard terrace of *c.* 1905, with one shallow bowed window on the upper floor, No. 6 (BELLEVUE), a superior early C19 house of three bays and two storeys, in grey-red ashlar, with a simple consoled porch, and Nos. 10–12, a compact red sandstone villa of *c.* 1890 with decorative ridge tiles, big dormers and applied-timber detail, and a large circular-headed window and door.

More C19 and C20 villas in Cessnock Road and Clockston Road, notably No. 9 CESSNOCK ROAD, which has a smart addition in small dark brown bricks, of 1931, probably by *Gabriel Steel*; also THORNBANK of *c.* 1890, with a round central bay and arrowhead bargeboards; ROSLYN, of *c.* 1925, a red sandstone single storey with a wide-brimmed conical corner tower; and WESTWOOD, also of *c.* 1925, white harl with grey stone dressings, a slated roof and a fat column forming a porch. Opposite, No. 24, of *c.* 1968, is a complex of monopitched blocks in dark brown brick and dark-stained wooden panels, nestling comfortably amid trees below the road. In CLOCKSTON ROAD, some big red sandstone villas, e.g., on the r., BROOM-PARK of *c.* 1885, with applied timbering to gables and window panels, and, on the l. and on the very edge of the countryside, the assured GREENBRAES of *c.* 1908, with crowstepped gables, a curving corner window, and a turreted entrance tower.

HOLMES HOUSE, 2.5 km. w. Demolished. Tudor Gothic of *c.* 1825, echoing strongly William Burn's Blairquhan (q.v.). LODGE and octagonal ball-headed GATEPIERS survive.

SORNHILL HOUSE, 2.6 km. s. A rare survival of a C17 laird's house, repaired in 2008–10 after a long period of dereliction. Three storeys, L-plan with one long range, a shorter N wing and a separately roofed stair-tower in the angle, all with crow-stepped gables. Various dates are inscribed: on the stair-tower a (reused?) window lintel dated 1660 and a panel with the initials MN MK, suggesting the house was built for the Nisbets of Greenholm. The s elevation is feeling towards symmetry, if the inserted first-floor window is ignored. Simple quarter-round eaves cornice. Windows have roll-moulded arrises and in the roof there is evidence that the top-floor windows may have had raised lintels, as at Stair House (q.v.). At ground floor and above there are also traces of diamond-section security bars. The door opens directly into the stair compartment; the stone turnpike and the roll-moulded doorways leading from it remain virtually unaltered. Otherwise remodelling has left only the substantial arched fireplace on the ground floor in the E gable, with two windows within it (the E one possibly inserted in the late C18 – a scratched date 1799 and the initials AN are close by), and a crisply carved fireplace lintel on the floor above. This has a central panel with carved buckle detailing, like handles, on the sides and the initials RN BN 1683. It could be that this replaces the lintel noted on the stair-turret. To the E a range of low farm buildings with a courtyard. Early C19; s elevation unusually sophisticated with Palladian details, the symmetry now lost by the raising of the E end and later openings.

BRUNTWOOD. *See* p. 209.
LOUDOUN CASTLE. *See* p. 512.
LOUDOUN OLD KIRK. *See* p. 514.

GATEHEAD
3030

Small hamlet between Troon and Kilmarnock.

95   LAIGH MILTON VIADUCT, 1 km. N, over the Irvine. 1809–11 for
the Kilmarnock & Troon Railway (*William Jessop*, engineer;
John Simpson, contractor) that carried coal from the Duke of
Portland's estates around Kilmarnock to his new port at Troon.
Perhaps the earliest surviving example of its type. Coursed
rubble, with rusticated dressings. Four round arches, with
round-section cutwaters, rising to half-column buttresses. Low
parapet. Abandoned in 1846, but restored for pedestrians in
1995–6 (contractors, *Barr Construction Ltd*).

CAPRINGTON CASTLE. *See* p. 209.
CRAIG HOUSE. *See* p. 228.

GATESIDE
3050

Roadside hamlet between Beith and Lugton.

SCHOOL. 1903, with prominent bellcote. Pretty crowstepped
VILLAGE HALL, 1897, given in memory of Isobel Patrick of
Trearne. Attributed to *Charles S. S. Johnston* (Listed Building
Register).
CHAMBERED CAIRN, Cuff Hill, 2.75 km. NE. 45 m. long, with
the remains of three chambers exposed, each set transversely
to the axis of the cairn and comprising a single compartment
of slabs approached by a narrower passage.

GIFFEN HOUSE
3040

4.25 km. S of Beith

76   An archetypal Scots Baronial mansion built for Henry Gardiner
Patrick in 1868–9 by *Andrew Heiton Jun.*; the design probably
contributed to by his senior draughtsman *John Murray
Robertson*. It replaced an earlier tower house nearby.
     Built of a creamy-grey sandstone laid in regular but narrow
courses, two storeys above a raised basement acting as a plinth.
There is a set-back above the basement and string course at
second floor. Roughly rectangular plan with shallow rear wings
and lower service court at the NE.
     The entrance is in a projecting bay at the l. of the SW eleva-
tion, below a corbelled oriel, and to the r. is a substantial round
tower, finished with a fish-scale slated conical roof and two
bold gabled wall-head windows, characteristically subtle
French details of the type introduced to Heiton's office by

William Leiper and which defines this period of the firm's work. The composition is the same on the NE side, although here the tower rises higher. On the garden front two canted projections with tourelles at their outer angles, and in the SE re-entrant angle a full-height turret. Linking these bays, a balcony with pierced balustrade. Shallow rear wing, forming a U. A pyramid-roofed turret breaks through the roof-line to the W of the triple-arched stair window.

Inside, a door with fine STAINED GLASS, depicting a shepherd boy piping to his sheep with the setting sun behind, all in vibrant hues of red, orange, green and blue with inset armorial panels and texts (FREE FROM YE BREESE AND DWELL IN SOOTHFASTNESS). The style suggests *Stephen Adam*'s studio. The interior plan has a rear spine corridor, with a curved vestibule at the SW end and the three principal rooms opening to the SE. A large imperial staircase leads from the NW with turned balusters and dramatically carved thistle finials. The thistle, in silhouette form, features again in the cornices.

GILMILNSCROFT   *5020*
1 km. S of Sorn

A late C17 laird's house, built by the Farquhars on lands formerly belonging to Melrose Abbey. It was formed into an L-plan in 1708 by the enlargement of the W wing and an addition to the N. Further enlarged in the early C19, then dressed up in Gothic and Baronial style in 1888, but almost all of this was carefully unpicked by *David Somervell* in 1968 to reveal the three-storey house created in the first two campaigns.

The W front faces the drive and was revealed by demolishing the three-storey early C19 additions which overlaid this and the N front. It has survived remarkably well, except for the size of second-floor windows, the result of raising the roof in the early C19. They have also lost their chamfered reveals which are seen elsewhere. In the re-entrant angle, the porch of 1968 incorporating a lintel depicting a hunting scene. Within, a surviving C17 door-jamb indicates the original entrance, and a narrow window, now opening into the W wing, is evidence for the original T-plan (*see* Crosbie Tower, p. 236). Extending from the W gable of the W wing, and of the same width, a two-storey canted bay, remodelled *c.* 1900 from a single storey that probably contained the kitchen. Distinctive eight-pane glazed windows, the W one with a hoodmould and over it the Farquhar crest, reused from the remodelling of 1888. Projecting from the house's N end is a piend-roofed wing. This is all that remains of the early C19 enlargement. Somervell reduced it to a single storey and neatly remodelled it with a big canted bay overlooking the garden at the E. The garden front itself is punctuated by two turrets, one uncomfortably thin of *c.* 1900 and another clasping the SE angle of *c.* 1909. To the l. of the central turret the ground- and first-floor windows retain their *c*. 1700 scale. At the extreme r. of the three-storey section a small slit opening, possibly originally lighting the kitchen.

The s elevation belongs to a Baronial-style extension of 1909–14, probably by *J. K. Hunter* who is known to have been working here at that time. It has a big three-storey crowstepped projection with curved angles corbelled to square above the first floor. The gable is dominated by a double-decker oriel. This combines the detail of the diminutive oriel at Baltersan (q.v.) with a Bryce-like corbelled canted window lighting a big second-floor room. Walling is all that remains of the service wing to the s. Into this a GATE has been inserted, crowned with a reused Jacobean-style scrolled pediment with the initials GH. In the garden other scrolls, of 1888, are reused as sides to shallow steps leading to the first of a series of wide terraces.

The most important survival inside is the scale-and-platt STAIRCASE with bold roll-moulded treads. It was introduced in 1708, the date on primitive pilasters which mask the ends of the newel walls. The pilaster heads include the initials IF and IP and some untutored carved detail representing capitals. Also in the house but resited in the 1960s remodelling is a lintel with the date 1682 which may have come from the first-floor hall. Raised and fielded panelling survives although it too may have been reused. Introduced during the remodelling, several chimneypieces, one smart grey marble and another white, reminiscent of Burn's early C18 French-style designs.

3040

GIRDLE TOLL
Irvine

Much mid-C20 Ayr County Council housing succeeding miners' rows in the locality. Expanded substantially after 1975 as part of Irvine New Town; the many variations of the Development Corporation's housing designs are demonstrated within a small compass.

GIRDLE TOLL PARISH CHURCH, Bryce Knox Court. 1989–90 by *John Hepburn Associates* of Glasgow. A simply but effectively detailed harled octagonal Neo-vernacular church, with a slate roof and gabled dormers, forming a fourth side to the courtyard of the former Littlestane Farm (now the Manse). Glazed entrances in the wings linking it to the former byres on either side. – FITTINGS by *Johannes* of Sweden; the COMMUNION TABLE and FONT particularly good. – Late C19 Gothic PULPIT from the Lockhart Memorial Church (Edinburgh). – Bright flowing STAINED GLASS by *Moira Parker*: The Burning Bush, 2000, and The Flood, 2005.

BRYCE KNOX COURT is sheltered accommodation of 1989–90 by *Irvine Development Corporation* (*H. Roan Rutherford*, project architect): harled, with exposed blockwork interiors; it looks back to Cornerstone Church (Kilwinning, q.v.), and forward towards spikier I.D.C. work, such as Cochrane Street, Irvine (p. 388).

LAWTHORN LOCAL CENTRE, Cardow Crescent. 1989–91, by *I.D.C.* architects. A dramatic if uncompromising semicircular development of shops, with maisonettes above, partly faced in large panels of rough-finished concrete.

LAWTHORN PRIMARY SCHOOL, Lochlibo Road. 2000–1, by *North Ayrshire Council Architects Dept (David Wadsworth*, project architect). Broad-gabled single-storey brick front, with a panelled flat-roofed hall rising behind. The N wall is designed by *Bruce McLean*: a dynamic learning feature, calibrated in metres and centimetres, and decorated to identify the functions of the rooms behind. This is based on McLean's concept of 'imbedded intelligence', developing his work at Beith Primary School and presaging that at Dalry Primary School (qq.v.). 125

BRAEHEAD is a small estate of 137 white-harled, nicely detailed and frequently imaginatively planned Irvine Development Corporation houses of 1977–9 (*H. Roan Rutherford*, project architect) with varied roof-lines. They are concentrated on the crescented ridge behind the mid-C18 Gothick entrance GATES to Eglinton Castle (*see* Kilwinning), which have a round arch, with flanking low screen walls and two-storey lodges with round-headed windows and battlemented parapets on continuous corbel arcades. STANECASTLE, opposite, was restored and re-roofed by the Corporation *c.* 1989. This is a small rectangular early C16 tower house built for William Montgomerie, who inherited the estate of Stane by marriage in 1508. Parapet with rounded angles, supported on two rows of corbels. Gothicized in the mid C18 as an eyecatcher in the landscape S of Eglinton Castle (*see* Kilwinning).

HIGH ARMSHEUGH, 0.7 km. NE, outside the built-up area. A well-composed courtyard farm complex, probably mid-C18. Generously proportioned stone farmhouse with rear wings, apparently heightened (*c.* 1800?), with a raised wall-head gable on the front. One wing has been extended in brick, probably in the late C19; the other retains an open-fronted cartshed, and stone steps at the gable.

GIRGENTI 3040

2 km. NW of Cunninghamhead

John Cheape, a widely travelled former army captain, acquired the lands of Muirhead in 1827 and renamed them after Girgenti (Agrigento) in Sicily. The house, begun in 1829 'in a somewhat fantastical order of architecture', was demolished in the 1940s. Quirky HOME FARM, of 1843, a single storey with an impressive range of segmentally headed cart openings and a prominent octagonal bell-tower. Two LODGES, each with a central chimney and, originally, the eaves extended at the corners on columns.

GIRVAN

'Home of Ailsa Craig', as the rather gauche decorative sign says
at the S end of the town. The harbour, whence trips leave for the
island, is the essence of Girvan. It developed at the sinuous
mouth of the Water of Girvan, one of the few safe anchorages on
the Carrick coast. The early village, originally known as Inver-
garven, developed on higher ground to the E above one of the
curves in the river, its location now represented by the Old
Churchyard and High Street. In 1668 Robert Boyd of Ballochtoul
obtained a burgh charter, which was renewed in 1696 for
Alexander Muir, but only put into execution in 1785, by which
time the superiors were the Dalrymples of Bargany. They conceived a roughly grid-plan new town on the lands of Doune, S of
the old town, with two main N–S axes, represented by Dalrymple
and Henrietta Streets. The new town was populated by weavers
and seafarers, and in parts still retains something of a separate
identity and character. Once the railway had arrived in 1860, the
town developed into a 'delightful and health-giving resort [with]
numerous commodious guest houses' (Groome) and, as a result,
is principally late C19 in appearance. In the early C20, another
settlement was introduced to Girvan, when the local coal
company built, in essence, a mining village on the town's N edge.

Contemporary Girvan bears witness to all these aspects: the
sea town and the mining village remain, as does the working
harbour and the sandy beach which used to attract the summer
visitors. They still come, though in fewer numbers, and Girvan
is perhaps the most 'kiss-me-quick' of the Ayrshire resorts.
Tucked in between the sea and the hills of Carrick, Girvan has
a stunning setting. It is to be hoped that current regeneration
proposals for the harbour area bring back to the town the vibrancy
it needs.

CHURCHES

Former BAPTIST CHURCH, North Park Avenue. 1959–60 by
George A. Cassells; harled with a base course of granite reused
from Corwar House (q.v.). Disused since 2005.
Former METHODIST CHAPEL, Ailsa Street West. 1820, restored
in 1879, and closed in 1903. Rubble-built with raised stone
dressings.
METHODIST CHURCH, Dalrymple Street. 1902–3 by *Watson &
Salmond*. Reordered and restored by *ARP Architects*, 1995–
2000. Attractive Arts and Crafts Gothic in red sandstone. Nave
and S aisle, under a single roof; gabled W front with a stepped
parapet, big five-light Perp window and SW porch with a half-
timbered gable. – REREDOS. Panelled, with inlaid decoration.
– Good but anonymous STAINED-GLASS E window. – HALL of
1925 by the pastor, *Rev. A. B. Cannon*.
NORTH PARISH CHURCH, Montgomerie Street. 1882–4 by *W. G.
Rowan* of *Rowan & McKissack* of Glasgow. Won in competition,
and replacing the previous parish church in Church Square.

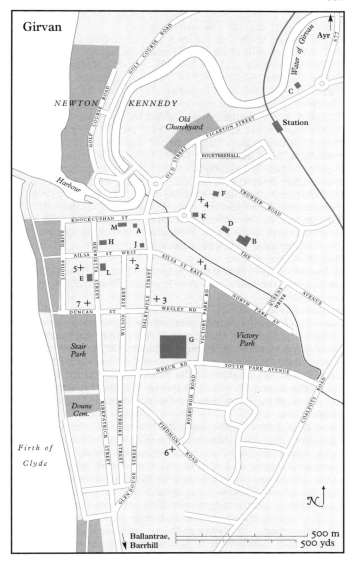

Girvan

1	Former Baptist Church	C	Girvan Community Hospital
2	Former Methodist Chapel	D	Girvan Bowling Club
3	Methodist Church	E	Former Girvan High School
4	North Parish Church	F	Girvan Library
5	Sacred Heart (R. C.)	G	Girvan Primary School
6	Former St John (Episcopal)	H	Innergarvan School
7	South Parish Church	J	McKechnie Institute
		K	Police Station
A	Auld Stumpy	L	Sacred Heart Primary School
B	Davidson Cottage Hospital	M	Knockcushan House

Large and assured, on a commanding site. The style of *c.* 1300: nave, aisles, shallow transepts and a very tall SW tower with splay-footed spire with lucarnes and angle pinnacles.

Shallowly projecting central entrance on the W front with moulded reveals and nook-shafts, below a Geometric four-light window, and flanked by stepped buttresses terminating in octagonal turrets. Three-bay side elevations and shallow, buttressed, full-height transepts. Tall windows with Y-tracery. To the rear a contemporary gabled hall, and to the r. a later hall, much lower and rendered, of *c.* 1977. Galleried interior; the panelled gallery front carried on cast-iron pillars and brackets. Roof trusses with foliated openwork decoration. The glorious panelled ceiling is to Rowan's design, painted a rich deep blue, littered with uncountable stars, with a layered frieze of the earth (the flowers of the field), the sea (a pattern of undulating lines) and the seabed (scallops and seaweed). The N transept was reordered to form a memorial chapel in 1987. ORGAN LOFT at the E end, behind the low Puginesque PULPIT. – Conventional STAINED GLASS in the transepts, all of 1890 by *Ballantine & Son.*

In front the WAR MEMORIAL of 1920 by *Robert Gray* of Glasgow, modelled on *Sir Reginald Blomfield*'s Cross of Sacrifice.

SACRED HEART (R.C.), Harbour Lane. A chapel of 1860 by *George Goldie*, its façade overlaid by a gabled projection of 1958–9 by *Stevenson & Ferguson* of Ayr, containing the entrance and window above in a single tall arch. Of the same date the side windows, angled out from the wall of the earlier building, the thin metal balusters of the gallery stair, and the open roof with big scissor trusses. The former ST JOSEPH'S CONVENT is of *c.* 1879, in rubbly sandstone, extended 1921 in red sandstone.

Former ST JOHN (Episcopal), Piedmont Road. In a cramped position. 1857–9 by *Alexander George Thomson* of Glasgow. Only the nave was built, in blue whinstone, with four simple buttressed bays and W bellcote, a model of E.E. simplicity. The sandstone tower, of 1911 by *James Chalmers*, appears to be based on Thomson's original intention,* but it, too, is incomplete, terminating at the nave roof, and has big harled arched openings anticipating the unexecuted transepts. Equally meagre interior of plaster walls, an open timber roof and tall stone chancel arch, with dying mouldings.** – STAINED GLASS. Chancel window, Christ in Glory by *Gordon Webster, c.* 1961.

SOUTH PARISH CHURCH, Henrietta Street. 1841–2, restored and redecorated 1959–62; the unpretty Fyfestone and thick

---

*There was formerly a sketch of the proposed building in the church.
**Now lost from the church is a remarkable chancel screen assembled in 1934 from woodwork of C16 Italian, possibly Sicilian, provenance formerly at Brougham Hall (Westmorland) which was reassembled by *Harvey Paterson* of Girvan, with supplementary work by *Ernest Johnstone* of Penrith. The sanctuary panelling was made up in 1948 and the fittings also enriched with salvaged medieval work. To be re-erected at Holy Trinity, Ayr.

harl exterior speaks of that date too. Warm and unified interior, with the gallery on cast-iron columns, the walls and panelling in attractive shades of green. – PULPIT. Elaborate, with a wooden sounding-board and a plethora of cast-iron balustraded steps. The windows mostly of ETCHED GLASS with a geometric pattern, 1959–62, but STAINED GLASS l. and r. of the pulpit: I Am the Good Shepherd, after 1887, perhaps by *W. & J. J. Kier*; Blessed are the Peacemakers, 1890, decorative rather than figurative, the different styles of the windows creating an odd imbalance. – WAR MEMORIAL. Copper and enamel, in an oak frame, by *Mary Henderson* of Glasgow.

HALL of 1905–6 by *William Kerr* of Ayr, completed after his death; quite a little gem. Harled, with an entrance porch topped by a tiled Burnet-esque tower. Wooden barrel-vaulted ceiling, and panelled dado.

CEMETERIES

DOUNE CEMETERY, Henrietta Street. 1861–2 by *John Murdoch*; extended by *H.V. Eaglesham*, 1898–9. The original entrance a stone arch with octagonal turrets and an openwork balustrade. Eaglesham's entrance gates have ogee-headed piers, with subsidiary pedestrian entrances to either side; hipped roofed red sandstone lodge with tall battered chimneystacks.

OLD CHURCHYARD, Old Street. The site of the first parish church, in its final form probably mid-C17. After the new church was built in Church Square, the graveyard was retained and its present appearance is due to Alexander Johnstone of Ayr for whom in 1907–8 *James A. Morris* added new walls and entrance as a memorial to his parents and brothers. The balustraded red sandstone wall is conventional enough, but the commanding ENTRANCE takes the form of a triumphal arch and is set back behind an outer entrance with square gatepiers, and side walls with bold obelisks. At the centre of the arch a pilastered archway, flanked on both elevations by widely spaced pairs of engaged Doric columns; there are further pairs on each short elevation. Decorative wrought-iron GATES (now in poor condition) designed by *Morris* and made by *George Wragge* of Salford. Within the arch two BRONZES, that to the l. with a lengthy inscription, that to the r. 'He is Risen', with a seated angel, by *Robert Bryden*, 1908. – Several early MONUMENTS, including two with the inscriptions within floriated frames, one of these of *c.* 1691. Another stone of *c.* 1735 has a very elaborate carved back. The table tomb of Mary Anne Hosack (Mrs John Bell), †1838, is decorated with a profusion of carved ivy leaves. That to Thomas Davidson, †1924, has thistle decoration and a wealth of biographical detail.

PUBLIC BUILDINGS

AULD STUMPY (GIRVAN STEEPLE), Knockcushan Street. *See* Description.

DAVIDSON COTTAGE HOSPITAL, The Avenue. 1919–22 by *John Watson* of *Watson, Salmond & Gray*. Scots Renaissance, in Auchenheath (Lanarkshire) stone. A highly attractive and accomplished piece of work. Single-storey and symmetrical about its central three-bay block. Door with moulded architraves, bracketed name panel and scrolled and broken segmental pediment. Three upper-floor windows with shaped gables. Semicircular outer bays with piended roofs, linking blocks of one bay. To the l., at the rear, a small building in similar style, originally the MORTUARY. To the r., sympathetic extension of *c.* 1938 by *J. & J. A. Carrick*. Closed in 2010.

GIRVAN BOWLING CLUB, off The Avenue. Greens laid out in 1898–9, the CLUBHOUSE by *James Kerr* of Lanark, replaced in 1959–60 by *T. K. Irving* of Stranraer, and remarkably unconservative. Big lounge to the r., and to the l., a flat-roofed semicircular first-floor committee room raised on two pilotis, matching the supports for the veranda which fronts the lounge.

GIRVAN COMMUNITY HOSPITAL, near BRIDGE MILL, a large grain mill to its N, C18 in origin, a new mill house, kiln and seedhouse added in 1835, later alterations. 2007–10, *Austin-Smith: Lord*. Stylish, welcoming, spacious and environmentally aware.

Former GIRVAN HIGH SCHOOL (now AYR COLLEGE), Henrietta Street. 1911–12 by *William Cowie*. E elevation of red sandstone, two storeys, with the six-bay centre projected slightly forward, under two gables with carved decoration and a linking balustrade; over-size urns at either end. Three bays to either side, with harled returns; that to the s with two segmental-headed dormers, that to the N with a big first-floor window lighting the art rooms.

GIRVAN LIBRARY, off Montgomerie Street. 1973–6, by *Ayr County Council Architects Dept.* A flat-roofed box of rustic brick. Original signage.

GIRVAN PRIMARY SCHOOL, Wesley Drive. The former High School, planned 1939 and built 1953–5 to succeed the earlier High School (*see* above). The architect was again *William Cowie*, but the style entirely of the streamlined 1930s, low and horizontal with a flat roof, strips of windows and an entrance recessed between two round towers.

GIRVAN STATION, off Vicarton Street. Opened in 1877, on the new through line to Portpatrick.★ The station buildings of 1948–9, probably by *W. Y. Sandeman*, ably demonstrate how 1930s design re-emerged in the thin years before the Festival of Britain. Largely symmetrical in brick and cement render, with curved corners to the recessed entrance, and a pronounced horizontality.

INNERGARVEN SCHOOL, Henrietta Street. Originally of 1832, though its present crowstepped harled and multi-gabled appearance is probably late C19. The l. gable has an open stone bellcote.

★ The previous station, opened in 1860, was in Bridge Street; it became the town's goods station.

McKechnie Institute, Dalrymple Street. Provided for the town by Thomas McKechnie (†1886). 1887–8 by *John McKissack* of *Rowan & McKissack*. Scots Renaissance in Ballochmyle sandstone with a prominent corner tower at the junction of Dalrymple Street and Ailsa Street West. Entrance in the r.-hand bay, in a deeply recessed round-headed arch; two round-headed windows with aprons to the l. Above these a corbelled balustrade, and above again two windows headed with broken pediments, each with a crowstepped gable with decorative quoins. The tower's ground-floor windows have mullions and transoms, pedimented windows above, and scrolled Jacobean heads to the windows on the second floor, and a balustrade with ball finials. The return elevation has the gabled end elevation of the former library, with square-headed windows below and a large Venetian window above. Crowstepped gable; in the ancillary buildings to the rear more crowsteps and also wall-head dormers, with carved coats of arms and terracotta elves, bringing a surprising levity to the building.

The interior originally contained a library, separate reading rooms for men and women, a billiard room and a committee room. On the ground floor is the former LIBRARY, now museum, with a flat panelled roof, and stencilled decoration. What one sees first, however, and perhaps secondly as well, is the forest of Tuscan pillars supporting round-headed arcades. The pillars have dramatic large abaci, with anthemion-like decoration. The abaci are not square, but have their corners cut back to the column, providing further surfaces for decoration. A door at the rear leads to the former men's READING ROOM, and a stair to the main room on the first floor, originally a BILLIARD ROOM. Both of these rooms have open timber roofs, again with some stencilled decoration, but lack the panache of the library.

Police Station, Montgomerie Street. 1921–3 by *A. C. Thomson*. Remarkable late-flowering Arts and Crafts, almost Art Deco, looking nothing like a police station. Long, of two storeys, originally for police office and houses for the men. Brick, harled, with brick decoration, including the corners of the projecting end gables and a sill course with bricks set at an angle.

Sacred Heart Primary School, Henrietta Street. Board School of 1874–5 by *William Murdoch*. Symmetrical single storey with gabled bays to either end and centre. Square-headed windows, those in the gables with pointed tympana and disc decoration.

DESCRIPTION

An obvious place to start is at GIRVAN STEEPLE ('Auld Stumpy') in Knockcushan Street, close to the junction with Dalrymple Street (s), Bridge Street (N) and Hamilton Street (E). It is the landmark of the town and was built in 1825–7 (contractors were *Denham, Davidson & McWhinnie*) as an addition to the Town Hall of 1822 (dem. 1909) and subsequently incorporated into the side elevation of the McMaster Hall (1909–11, by *W. J. Jennings* of Canterbury*) which was destroyed by fire in 1939 leaving the tower to stand in a small open square. Ashlar, roughly square with a pronounced batter and a corbelled parapet. Pend, now blocked, from N to S, with segmentally headed openings and thermal windows in the stages above. Square clock stage, with the clocks within open pediments on Tuscan pilasters, octagonal bell-stage and spire and ship weathervane. Vaulted ground floor, with three barrel-vaulted chambers above, all linked by a SE newel stair.

Looking W, KNOCKCUSHAN STREET is slightly raised and open on its N side to the river. Here the successful synthesis of the buildings of the town and harbour can be appreciated. Along the S side, a late C19 Italianate commercial range, a pair of mid-C19 cottages and KNOCKCUSHAN HOUSE (Council offices), which is mid-C19, of three bays and two storeys, thinly pilastered, with a central pilastered doorway and a two-storey bay window to the l. Between the road and harbour, RNLI OFFICES, Neo-Scots vernacular, 1993, with a battered stone base. Further on, a public seating area, with metal railings, built on top of an array of fishermen's sheds. The HARBOUR itself has stone-faced quay walls, and was reconstructed in 1869–70 by *James I. McDerment*, and further improved in 1881–3. Works from this period include the PIER on the S side, with a small LIGHT TOWER at its far end. S of this, the large Creetown granite CLACHAR FOUNTAIN of 1926–7 by *Scott & Rae* of Glasgow. The centrepiece is a chained anchor, guarded by four alert lions holding shields. S, running between the beach promenade and the little villa houses along LOUISA DRIVE, a BOATING LAKE of 1938, created by *A. G. D. Grant*, the Burgh Surveyor. The lake, its island and bridge re-create the design of Willow Pattern plates, following the suggestion of the town's artistic adviser, the Girvan-born artist *James Wright*.

HARBOUR STREET, next inland from Louisa Drive, marks the beginning of the early C19 sea town. Its cottages are mostly single-storey. It leads to Ailsa Street West, which with Duncan Street and Duff Street forms one of the short E–W axes of the area. The N–S axes are Wilson Street and Greenside, both largely of *c.* 1835, and perhaps, too, the least spoilt, where the bustle of the town and the beach can seem far away, while Henrietta Street forms the W boundary. All of these streets contain single-storey cottages, usually harled and slated, though there is tremendous variation in detail.

Besides the cottages, little of note, though the striking HOUSING complex at the junction of AILSA STREET WEST with Harbour Street, with its bright white harl, and big glazed prows, cannot be ignored. 2004–6 by *Austin-Smith:Lord* for the Ayrshire Housing Association. To the W, at the junction with Henrietta Street, ALLERTON, a conventional three-bay C19 house which has been altered in the early C20, perhaps *c.* 1925, suggested by square bays on the front elevation, the harled semicircular rear stair-tower with stone-dressed window and low parapet, and the stone-framed doorway.

s on HENRIETTA STREET is the Sacred Heart School (*see* Public Buildings, above) and MERLINDALE (No. 19), of *c.* 1883, red sandstone with a stilted doorpiece and a large cast-iron-faced circular dormer. Further s, the late C19 villas are open to the sea with STAIR PARK in front. This was originally part of the Green of Girvan, handed to the public by Lord Stair in 1875. Late C19 PAVILION with an attractive cast-iron veranda and, in the centre, raised on a knoll with low stone steps, is the WAR MEMORIAL of 1921–2 by *James A. Morris*. An impressively tall granite obelisk, divided into panels for the names of the fallen, set upon a high plinth with massive volutes at the angles framing inscribed bronze panels. Beyond the Doune Cemetery (*see* Cemeteries, above), on both sides, Girvan's first COUNCIL HOUSES, indeed, among the earliest in Ayrshire. 1919–21 by *Thomas Taylor* of *Taylor & Hutton* of Glasgow to an 'English style of street planning' (*Ayr Advertiser*), i.e. a spacious Garden Suburb-style layout of harled two-storey houses with decorative details. Typical of this period of council house building, before financial considerations took precedence.

Now to the area of the late C18 'new town' and DALRYMPLE STREET, the principal commercial street. Its urban character is now primarily late C19 up to the crossing with Ailsa Street west, culminating in the McKechnie Institute (*see* Public Buildings, above). The buildings along the E side are two-storey with moulded architraves to the first-floor windows, sometimes with apron panels, and of the local grey sandstone. Breaking this pattern are No. 9, of red sandstone, with recessed upper-floor bays, of 1915 by *J. K. Hunter*, and the former BRITISH LINEN BANK of 1879, with a big hooded and bracketed door-piece, rusticated outer pilasters and obelisk finials. On the opposite side of the street from the top, the unmissable former KINGS ARMS, rebuilt in 1848. Four storeys, the harled front elevation with a big Doric porch and canted bay window, with a carved coat of arms above. Extensively altered in 1912 and 1923 by *Clarke & Bell* and *J. H. Craigie* and converted into flats, 2005–6. Then the Scots Baronial ROYAL BANK OF SCOTLAND of 1863–4 by *David MacGibbon* for the National Bank. Five bays, red sandstone with yellow stone dressings, the central bay with a first-floor oriel, above which is a two-light window with a tympanum with a foliated panel and two rosettes. The effect of the whole is all string and sill courses, and a final profusion of crowsteps; it was, according to the *Kilmarnock Standard*, 'after no particular style of architecture, being what some term a mongrel, but will be one of the finest, if not the finest, bank in the West of Scotland'. Of the standard late C19 properties, the CARRICK GAZETTE retains an early shopfront and there are also very good shopfronts with curved windows and recessed doorways at Nos. 34–42, of 1910. s of Ailsa Street there is much less to single out apart from, on the W side, a red sandstone group, dated 1896 and 1897, with an ogee-headed round turret, and the narrow faience Art Deco front of the former Regal Cinema (now OMEGA BINGO) of 1933 by *Stellmacs* of Glasgow, and, on the E side, opposite the Methodist Church, the CO-OPERATIVE SOCIETY store of 1935 by *Alexander Skirving*, with a central fin.

HAMILTON STREET runs inland from Girvan Steeple along the N edge of the late C18 grid. At the junction with Bridge Street a former ROYAL BANK OF SCOTLAND, 1856 by *Peddie & Kinnear*. Very severe Italianate, with a canted corner bay, round-headed windows, a pilastered entrance and wide over-sailing eaves. On the S side, the former COMMERCIAL BANK of *c.* 1870 stands back, proud and solitary. Bold French Renaissance in red sandstone, with yellow dressings and quoins. Perhaps by *David Rhind*. To its E, MILLBANK, also of *c.* 1870 for the City of Glasgow Bank. Central round-headed and pilastered doorway, beneath a blind balustrade and a single central first-floor window. Balustraded parapet, and a further narrow recessed bay to the r. Finally on the N side, KIRKBRAE, again for the Ayrshire Housing Association by *Austin-Smith: Lord*, of 2004–6. Again, dramatic use of white harl and much glazing, and thoughtful management of the changes in level.

At the E end of the street is CHURCH SQUARE, the site of the parish church from *c.* 1770 to 1883. The central feature is now the McCUBBIN FOUNTAIN of 1911–12, executed by *Scott & Rae* to a design by *Robert Wright*, of the Liverpool City Architect's Department. Peterhead granite. Large centrepiece with fluted buttresses, and a broad flat head, with a finial on top. Two drinking basins, and four approaches with low granite walls and piers.

From here THE AVENUE runs arrow-straight SE between the Police Station (*see* above) and ST ANDREWS COURT, *c.* 1985 by *ARP Lorimer & Partners*, a polychrome brick housing development consciously trying to echo the form of the church (1870 by *Clarke & Bell*: Gothic) which had previously stood here. The Avenue contains Girvan's finest display of mid- to late C19 villas. A couple on the NE side, including ORCHARDLEA, Scots Baronial dated 1875. The SW side begins with early C19 cottages, and then nine big C19 villas, Nos. 18–34. Particularly noteworthy are No. 18, SOUTHFIELD, of 1833, with a Greek Doric porch and a pediment; the crowstepped No. 20, MONTROSE, of *c.* 1862, with a crowstepped stable block to the l., the quirky L-plan No. 24, ROZEVILLE, of *c.* 1852, with a dainty wrought-iron balcony on the first floor, and No. 34, *c.* 1872, with a fluted Doric porch, and two sets of gatepiers with channelled semi-circular decoration and raised pyramidal caps. At the far end of The Avenue, and closing the vista, EASTBURN, a hipped villa of *c.* 1872. It stands in its own walled grounds, with a cottagey stable block at one extremity, a country estate in miniature.

MONTGOMERIE STREET, N from Church Square, has two villas, both of *c.* 1877: ASHFIELD is pink-harled with quoins and a stilted round-headed door, while KIRKHILL is harled with a prominent string course and a three-light window to the r. The painted stone QUEENS HOTEL, opposite, is mid-C19, with a pilastered doorway and a subsidiary entrance neatly chamfered out of the r.-hand corner. The historic site of the old village lies beyond the North Parish Church (*see* Churches, above), but is now largely overlaid by low-rise local authority housing such as MCCONNELL SQUARE, the result of a comprehensive redevelopment scheme begun in 1959 and completed in the mid-1970s; the consultant was *T. Findlay Lyon*. The architects were *Cowie Torry & Partners*.

Due E, BOURTREEHALL and KILLOCHAN STREET form the core of the mining 'village' built here *c.* 1915–16 for South Ayrshire Collieries Ltd. Houses are invariably single-storey, and of brick, harled. One block, at least, is by the Ayr builder *Robert Hutchison*. Some blocks have gables, others only end gables, and others have none; perhaps representative of a hierarchy within the workforce. The company had planned to sink a pit near the station to the N but this never materialized. The station (*see* Public Buildings, above) must instead have proved useful in transporting the men to the company's mines at Dailly.

Finally, BRIDGE STREET dropping N downhill from Girvan Steeple towards the riverside. On the E side Nos. 6–8 of *c.* 1860, angled to the site, with some original consoled shopfronts, and an eaves balustrade which disguises two chimneystacks. The two-storey HAMILTON ARMS, of *c.* 1862, with a channelled ground floor, and narrow end pilasters. Its big extension is of *c.* 1920, perhaps by *William Cowie*, for a ballroom with hotel rooms above, set behind a brash semicircular pediment, flanked by tall chimneystacks. Long side elevation, quite assured. Bridge Street now opens out and the snaking river comes close. This low-lying area, known as The Flushes, must originally have been reedy marsh. That would be an improvement on the dreadful former TOURIST INFORMATION CENTRE (on the r., 1973) and the former PAVILION CINEMA, now Le Mirage nightclub, of 1914 by *J. R. Johnstone* of Troon, reconstructed in 1934 by *William Morrison* of Glasgow as a harled box with twin towers on the W gable, and largely shorn of detail since it closed in 1959.

Newton Kennedy

A separate settlement on the river's W bank. In the street of that name, and also in NEWTON TERRACE, are early C19 single-storey cottages. Many are now occupied as part of the big BOAT REPAIRING YARD of Alexander Noble & Sons, established here 1946, whose sheds, placed in a curve of the river, dominate many Girvan views. GOLF COURSE ROAD follows the river upstream. Here the late C19 houses turn towards the sea for the views across the Firth of Clyde towards Ailsa Craig, presenting to the road only their extraordinary and remarkably unified back boundary wall, built for the most part from large boulders, perhaps from the river bed. It is punctuated with stone-framed and lintelled back entrances, often with the house name on the lintel. The houses are pallid by comparison. At the N end of this group, set in a raised position, is KNOCK-AVALLEY of 1934 by *Hutton & Taylor* of Glasgow. A fine piece of domestic architecture, harled with a semi-octagonal tower in the re-entrant, and above the main door a stone panel with Celtic decoration. The sylvan views E across the river have as their object the former MANSE (now in the Strathavon Caravan park) of 1818 by *Alexander Jardine* (*see* Barskaig House, Barr). Quadrant walls link with flanking single-storey outbuildings, forming a broad courtyard for the main house with its central flight of steps. House and wings do not quite cohere, but it is an enjoyable piece of artisan design.

DOUNEBURN CRESCENT, 1.2 km. S of the centre. 2005–6 by *Robert Potter & Partners* for Ayrshire Housing Association, and a visual treat: arranged in a big two-storey semicircle, the courtyard hidden from the road; at the SE corner of the block a round tower accommodating further flats of four storeys, the final storey cut away like a sponge cake to provide a balcony. A dramatic contribution to the townscape.

ARDMILLAN CASTLE, 4 km. SW. Once an estate of some importance, occupied by the Craufurds from the mid C17 until the late C19. The house (dem., after a fire, 1991) consisted of a late C16 tower, with a mid-C18 wing at right angles. – Scots Baronial LODGE, 1908. – OBELISK (after 1856), on the hill behind. Weathered into sculptural abstraction.

BURNSIDE FARM, 3.2 km. N on the E side of the A77. On a slight rise with the banks of the raised beach immediately behind. These were once terraced for growing early potatoes and the flat coastal plain W of the road is still so used. Farmhouse erected *c.* 1860 for Mr Kerr of Kerr & McBride of Greenock, its lower rear range formed from a house of *c.* 1800. A low office range extends N of the rear and links to one of three parallel ranges of storage barns and lofts. To the N, a substantial former BOATHOUSE, once a common feature of coastal farms. Red sandstone rubble, possibly raised in a second phase, with a segmental arch facing the road and a loft above.

GIRVAN MAINS, 0.75 km. N. On site of earlier dwelling, courtyard steading *c.* 1835 with two-storey house at centre of S range, its S elevation a large three-bay bow.

GLENDOUNE HOUSE. *See* p. 352.

GLAISNOCK
                   2.5 km. SE of Cumnock

A substantial Tudor Gothic mansion of two main phases, restored in 2006–7 after a long period of institutional use but now empty. The first part, of 1835 by *James Ingram*, is asymmetrical copybook stuff, two storeys over a raised basement, with a nicely finished porch on the E front. To its rear, a two-storey projection with full-height windows at first floor. This is over-shadowed by late C19 additions to the S, and in the angle between the two a walled courtyard has been created. A circular stair-tower rises above the rear of the original house. It looks *c.* 1900. The octagonal raised base N of the house supported a late C19 conservatory. Inside, facing the stair, a flamboyant late C19 wooden fireplace, with two brass panels with putti (or babies) playing, e.g. at leapfrog. Congruent LODGE of 1900.*

GLENAPP

GLENAPP CHURCH. A chapel of ease to Ballantrae of 1849–50, known as Butter's Chapel after the donor Mrs Isabella Butter. It is a Gothic box, granite-built, its w window of three narrow lights, and lancets in the side walls. Tiny w bellcote. *P. Macgregor Chalmers* restored the church in 1909, adding the w porch and chancel. In 1929–30 *Thomas McGill Cassels* raised the chancel to accommodate the three round-headed E windows. The entrance vestibule is panelled and fitted out with fumed oak and has Late Arts and Crafts-style door furniture of 1929–30. The nave has an open timber pitch-pine roof of 1909, the oak dado panelling and furniture by *James Bowie & Co.* of Ayr, 1929–39. Round-headed chancel arch, a form favoured by Chalmers, in red Ballochmyle sandstone. – PULPIT on a base of Ballochmyle stone. Austrian oak upper part, with cusped detailing, 1909. – LIGHT FITTINGS. Probably *c.* 1929. – ELDERS' BENCHES. Handsome, probably 1929–30. – COMMUNION TABLE. 1909, more traditional with open arcading. – STAINED GLASS. – In the E window Christ Stilling the Tempest, donated by the Earl and Countess of Inchcape in memory of their daughter, Hon. Elsie Mackay, who died in 1928 attempting to fly the Atlantic with Captain Hinchcliffe. – On the s wall a window by *Douglas Strachan*, 1933, a memorial to Lord Inchcape (†1932), the calling of Peter and Andrew; the strikingly elongated figures have prominent Roman noses and there is plenty of delicate change of tone in the coloured glass. – Another more recent *Strachan* window at the w, with three archangels watching Christ appearing to the disciples in their boat.

– MONUMENT. 1st Earl of Inchcape †1932, and his wife †1937. Very probably by *Herbert Baker*, who designed the Inchcape memorial church at Woldingham, Surrey. Magnificent

---

*Opposite this there was a private Episcopal chapel, of 1885 by *R. S. Ingram* for Robert Campbell of Auchmannoch in an E.E. style, the details taken from the abbeys at Whitby, Bridlington, Fountains, Netley and Rievaulx. Demolished mid C20.

polished granite sarcophagus on a rubble-faced plinth with
acanthus leaves as angle finials, with, at the four inner corners
of the enclosure, two stylized lions and two eagles. Enclosed
on three sides by yew hedges.

THE OLD MANSE, to the S. Built 1850. Plain, handsome two-
storey, three-bay, granite-built T-plan, with rear offices and
stabling.

0080   GLENAPP CASTLE
                        2 km. S of Ballantrae

78   A substantial asymmetrically planned house in a pared-down
      Baronial style, built in 1870–6 by *David Bryce* for James Hunter,
      an ironmaster, who purchased the estate in 1865. This had been
      created when the lands of Ardstinchar (Ballantrae) were broken
      up in 1816. Enlarged in 1922–4 for James Lyle Mackay, 1st Earl
      of Inchcape, with further service additions for him by *James
      Bowie* in 1929. Massing rather than decoration gives this house
      character, there is none of the swagger of Bryce's Ballikinrain
      (Stirling) or The Glen (Borders). Only the roofscape with its
      towers, candle-snuffer-roofed turrets, bartizans, crenellated para-
      pets and crowstepped gables provides drama. Now a hotel, and
      extensively restored since 1994.

      The house is principally of two storeys and an attic over a raised
      basement with the main public rooms facing NW over the Firth
      of Clyde. The walls are of pinkish sandstone ashlar cut into
      narrow rectangular blocks; the similarly detailed SW addition
      of 1922–4 in grey sandstone. The SE front is asymmetrical and
      articulated with a variety of well-tried Baronial details, most
      successful at the E end where the elements are massed into a
      bold towered composition containing the entrance. The lowest
      section is three-storey with chamfered angles and a corbelled
      and crenellated parapeted wall-walk. A crowstepped gable rises
      within it. At its base, the entrance is set into the 1920s porch
      that has a round-arched door mimicking the original with a
      knotted rope moulding above, this detail taken from the
      moulding in the parapets. Above the first-floor window a
      sundial set in a panel with the inscription 'lux et umbra vicis-
      sim sed semper amor' ('Light and darkness in turn but always
      love'). A corbelled turret in the re-entrant angle links this
      entrance tower to the slightly lower and plainer range to its r.,
      and rising behind the tower two taller square towers of five
      and six storeys, similarly parapeted but the lower with open
      bartizans. The taller tower has a circular turret in the centre of
      its SE elevation, breaking through the parapet and climaxing
      with a dome-roofed caphouse and a weathervane – a com-
      position derived from Midmar (Aberdeenshire). The 1870s
      entrance front concludes with a double-pile projection with
      an M-roof and little angle bartizans; in its re-entrant angle, a
      big stair-tower with conical roof. The 1920s S addition has a

basket-arched loggia in the basement and continues the theme of the earlier part, the bold angle turrets giving particular emphasis. The NW elevation is composed of three stepped ranges culminating in the northern towers. It is simply detailed apart from quirky curved windows on the angles of the two- and three-storey northern section, and squared window bays projecting SW and NE from it.

The interior was subject to much change before 1994, its Victorian appearance largely re-created since then. The main details to survive are the cornices, plaster ceilings and oak panelling. Jacobean-style entrance hall, fully panelled in Austrian oak. At its far end a staircase, modelled on Bryce's entrance stair at Cassillis (q.v.), with arcaded balustrade and finials of a similar style. This breaks l. and r. to the principal floor and the public rooms. The drawing room was created c. 1950 from the former inner hall and library, both with geo-metric Neo-Tudor ceilings. Dividing them, Ionic columns. Beyond this, a compact Jacobean-style staircase in a partially panelled compartment of limewashed oak. On the garden front two dining rooms on either side of the drawing room, both with modillion cornices in C18 style but one with a simple Jacobean-style plaster ceiling. The former smoking room is now the library, with raised and fielded panelling and a built-in bookcase (possibly resited). The C20 wing is essentially two large rooms one above the other, the one on the principal floor formerly Lord Inchcape's morning room, with a Wrenaissance plaster ceiling and an C18-style mantelpiece. A spiral stair in a corner turret connects to the room above, which has a late C18 type plaster ceiling and a French effect marble chimneypiece.

WALLED GARDEN. Re-created, its 45-m.-long Victorian glasshouse with a projecting conservatory section carefully restored. – GARDENS below the house terrace and to the S. *Lorimer* provided plans in 1904 and *Gertrude Jekyll* offered planting advice, but how much of this was implemented is unknown.

GLENBUCK   7020

The village, first associated with an iron works established in 1796 and subsequently with blackband ironstone mining, has been erased by opencast coal workings.

MONUMENT. Bill Shankly †1981, Liverpool F.C. manager, who was born at Glenbuck. Erected 1997.
GLENBUCK HOUSE. Demolished. Scots Baronial of 1878–9 by *John Murdoch*. Contemporary crowstepped STABLES and an attractive broad-eaved LODGE survive.
GLENBUCK LOCH. The upper reservoir of a complex system created from c. 1802 to provide an adequate head of water for the cotton mills at Catrine (q.v.) by damming the upper reaches of the Ayr.

GLENDOUNE HOUSE
1 km. SE of Girvan

A neat villa of 1792–1800 for Spencer Boyd by *John Paterson* and the modest sole survivor of a known trio of houses by him in Ayrshire (Eglinton and Montgomerie House have gone). It must have looked altogether suaver before its render was removed. Sophisticated Italianate SW wing of *c.* 1845, in the manner of David Hamilton. The matching wing to the NW, depicted on a Rockingham china plate, was never built.

The entrance front of the original house is two storeys over a raised basement with a boldly projecting central bay under a piend roof framed by the chimneystacks. Mid-C19 porch. Ashlar band courses, the lower one on the entrance elevation lost when the balcony, which spans the flanking bays, was built *c.* 1845. Tripartite arched window in the wing with balconette to the first floor. Side elevation articulated by shallow projecting stacks with ashlar quoins that frame tripartite windows at each floor, that in the raised ground projecting with a pierced parapet. Because of the fall in the land the basement is virtually above ground on the garden front and the wing seems tower-like. In the centre is a full-height bow with three windows.

Compactly planned interior with two of the original reception rooms remaining on the ground floor: a library in the bow, and the drawing room at the NE, lit from two sides. Both have cornices and chimneypieces owing much to the style of the Adams, whose business Paterson managed from 1789 until 1791. Stair-hall created *c.* 1845, incorporating the former dining room and probably the stair compartment. The C19 wing contains a large dining room with bold cornice.

GLENGARNOCK

Developed in the C19 as a mining and mineral processing settlement, known as Kilbirnie Ironworks Village. It remains predominately industrial.

HEBRON HALL (Christian Brethren), Grahamston Avenue. Dated 1921. Stone-faced gabled front.

GLENGARNOCK PRIMARY SCHOOL, Grahamston Avenue. 1991–2 by *Strathclyde Regional Council.* Brick; a central hall surrounded by lower teaching blocks.

GLENGARNOCK STATION, Main Road. Simple mid-C19 two-storey station house with an external stair similar to that at Waterside by Patna (q.v.).

Former CO-OPERATIVE STORES, Main Road. 1899 by *John McLelland*, its canted corner given emphasis by a semicircular pediment, and a circular clock face in a decorative panel. To its W, mounted on brick, a pyramid-headed BELLCOTE, all that remains of *Robert Baldie*'s U.P. Church of 1872–3.

GLENGARNOCK BUSINESS PARK AND INDUSTRIAL ESTATE.
On part of the site of the massive iron and steel works established in 1843 by Merry & Cuninghame and from the earlier
C20 owned by David Colville & Sons. When it closed in 1986
it covered 750 acres (303.5 ha.). Preserved are the former
works offices of c. 1925. Gabled four-bay central block, and
flanking hipped wings with big three-light windows. On one
wall, a bronze FIRST WORLD WAR MEMORIAL. Next to it, a
long brick workshop, and opposite, further offices of c. 1935,
with flat roof, a raised centre projected forward, and porthole
windows in the flanking bays. Elsewhere is a mid-C19 brown
stone WORKSHOP (now MOT centre) with square-headed
windows and wooden boarded gable-ends.

GLENGARNOCK CASTLE

3050

3 km. N of Kilbirnie

Dramatically situated above a steep ravine in the River Garnock
which almost encircles its narrow promontory site. There is
clear evidence of a defensive ditch cutting through the neck of
the promontory at the E. The Cuninghame family acquired the
lands of Glengarnock by marriage in the C13 but the building
is probably late C15 or early C16. It was in existence in 1539
when William Cunynghame was granted a charter of confirmation by James V. Abandoned in the C18, it suffered serious
damage in storms in 1839, and the ruin was stabilized by
William Cochrane Patrick of Ladyland in 1842. The keep is
40 m. by 10 m. and rubble-built; so perilously close to the bluff
edge that the well-constructed dressed quoins were vital to its
stability. Three walls survive on the N, S and W to roughly their
full height but have lost parapets. Originally with a vaulted
ground floor with no openings in the extant fabric. Above, a
very high vaulted hall. It does not appear to have had an entresol, and at its SW angle is evidence of a tight turnpike stair
rising to the upper levels. At the S end of the hall a precarious
bridge of vaulting survives. On the W wall an arched window
overlooking the burn 18 m. below, further windows on the S
wall. MacGibbon and Ross suggest the entrance was through
a high door on the N gable accessed from an adjoining building;
the lost E wall must have had the hall chimneypiece. The
attached courtyard was entered through an arched gatehouse
set into its E wall, to its N a two-storey building with an arched
window looking E; further buildings to the S. Within the court
traces of other buildings lurk under the nettles and line the
relatively narrow court leading to the keep. On the S a low
vaulted structure which has the remains of a fireplace; it seems
barely large enough for a kitchen as suggested by MacGibbon
and Ross. The outer courtyard walls with remnants of corbelled bartizans, like the keep, rise from the top of the steep
river banks; on the N various additional projecting walls to aid
defence, and one shielding a postern gate.

GLENLOGAN HOUSE
5020

2 km. E of Sorn

Formerly Burnhead, renamed shortly after its acquisition by George Ranken of Whitehill in 1802. On the site of a tower house, which survived into the mid C18, by which time it belonged to the Logan estate. The house is late C18, designed for a minor laird but only slightly grander than the typical Ayrshire courtyard farm, with the house (three bays and two storeys with a stair-tower at the rear) flanked by narrow links to projecting gabled E wings. Some C19 embellishments, e.g. pedimented Doric porch (probably early C19) and shallow pediments (mid-C19?) at the first floor. Two early C19 Gothick windows in the NE wing.

GRANGE HOUSE
3010

1 km. W of Minishant

Part of the lands, known as Maybothelbeg or Little Maybole, that were granted to Melrose Abbey c. 1193 by Duncan, later 1st Earl of Carrick (see Monkwood etc.). The name is suggestive, and the remains of a wall in the stable complex may relate to a large granary. Post-Dissolution the land passed through branches of the Kennedy family. In 1752 it was sold to Gilbert McMikin. The present modestly sized and charming house was built either for him or his son John (†1789) who married a daughter of Craufurd of Ardmillan in 1763.

The setting is landscaped parkland, with the house placed in the slope so that its basement is partly sunk to the front but a full storey to the rear. Two storeys above, all built of pinky-cream squared sandstone rubble with polished ashlar margins to the windows, angles and eaves. Wide steps splayed at the base rise to the smart Tuscan-columned doorpiece. Rear elevation dominated by the very tall arched and key-stoned stair window. The windows are carefully balanced to front and rear. All the first-floor windows use the eaves band for their lintels. Inside, a wide newel stair with moulded frames to the risers, bucking contemporary fashion, but also up-to-the-minute panelling for doors and shutters with a beaded inner panel.

GRANGEHILL see BEITH

GREAT CUMBRAE
1050

Modestly sized island, 4 km. in length (N–S), and 2 km. across at its widest. Although part of Buteshire, it is geologically and topo-graphically closer to the mainland, with raised beaches on the W coast, and a rocky summit, the Glaidstone, rising to 127 m. Traditionally associated with the Celtic St Maura, and also said to be where King Haakon of Norway prepared for the battle of

Largs (1263). For much of the modern period the W part was
part of the estate of the Marquesses of Bute; the E part of the
estate of the Earls of Glasgow. The population of *c.* 1,250 lives
mostly in the main settlement, which spreads around two bays
at the S end of the island.

MILLPORT

A burgh since 1864, it has the timelessness of all island towns.
Before the late C18, there was little here other than the quay, with
a few houses at the quay head, a mill and a church, in a line
running NW from the sea. A village was planned by the Earl of
Bute, 1780, principally to provide accommodation for the crews
of the anti-smuggling revenue cutters that patrolled in the Firth
of Clyde. The village saw modest growth through the C19, particularly in the latter half, when strings of villas struck out to E
and W along the shore. This was Millport's heyday, reinforced by
the decision of the Earl of Glasgow to develop the island as an
Episcopalian Iona.

CATHEDRAL OF THE ISLES
AND
COLLEGE OF THE HOLY TRINITY
College Street

The town's outstanding architectural feature. Geometrical   26
Gothic of 1849–51 by *William Butterfield*. The church and associated buildings are the result of one man's fervour, kindled by the
teachings of the Oxford Movement. There is, indeed, nothing to
match it in Scotland; here Butterfield, who through his buildings
has become closely associated with the Oxford Movement, could
synthesize his ideas. The Oxford Movement, led by Pusey, Keble
and Newman, arose in the 1830s, and was an attempt within the
Church of England to reconnect with both national issues of
social concern and the Church's pre-Reformation past. George
Boyle, later the 6th Earl of Glasgow* (of Kelburn, p. 392), a
Scottish Episcopalian, was at university at Oxford in the 1840s
and embraced the agenda of the movement. Returning to Scotland, he envisaged a collegiate establishment through which his
Church could be reinvigorated through close association of training for the ministry, theological research, choral work and monas-
ticism. He was encouraged in this by, especially, Keble. Cumbrae
was chosen as the site partly due to its island isolation: the land
required was already in the family's ownership and control. In
choosing for his architect Butterfield, Boyle was turning to a man
who had already, through his work with the Camden Society,
demonstrated his wish to achieve in church art and architecture
what he sought to achieve in theology, and whom Boyle had
previously commissioned (in 1848) for St Ninian's Cathedral,

---

*He succeeded to the title in 1869, on the death of his half-brother.

Perth. Work on site began in 1849, the colleges were in use by 1850, and the first service was held in 1851.*

The church was raised to cathedral status in 1876, serving the diocese of Argyll and The Isles. However, in 1886, because of his own worsening financial position, Boyle's support of the college ceased and, in 1890, he died. In straitened circumstances the project continued, although there has been no collegiate body since; it has relied on private support, most notably from the first Bishop, Alexander Haldane-Chinnery. In the C21 the cathedral remains, with its flourishing musical tradition, while the college buildings have adapted as a retreat and conference centre for the Scottish Episcopal Church, following a thorough restoration, begun in 1989, by *Gray Marshall & Co.* of Edinburgh.

26 The complex consists of three main buildings: the cathedral itself, the attached South College and the separate but adjacent North College. They form a broad T-plan, with the main (W) front of the cathedral at the base, on raised ground which falls steeply away to the W and N, so that their full power is seen on entering the grounds from College Street.

The CATHEDRAL has a gabled W front with a three-light Geometrical window above a central buttress, a SW entrance tower, two-bay nave, narrower two-bay chancel and a NE Lady Chapel, all built from local light grey stone, with slate roofs. It is much less 'experimental' than Butterfield could be; his innate ruggedness tempered. Pointed entrance in the S tower elevation, approached by a flight of steps with low stone walls, and between stepped angle buttresses; the tower's final stage has three lancet bell-openings with Y-tracery on each face, surmounted by a tall stone spire with gabled lucarnes at the base. Deep buttressed basement to the S elevation: two-light windows in the nave, three-light windows with Y-tracery in the lower chancel. Startlingly severe N elevation, again buttressed, but virtually windowless. Three-light Geometrical window in the E gable, with a five-light window of stepped lancets with etiolated cusped heads in plate tracery in the E gable of the projecting Lady Chapel.

27 Butterfield's inventiveness is on much greater display in the numinous INTERIOR. Vestibule, with heavy inner doors with flowing floriated hinges and a quatrefoil window above. Beyond, the immediate contrast is between the dark nave and the lighter chancel. The NAVE, whose plainness symbolizes the world, has a tiled floor, very low boarded dado, and plaster walls to the foot of the window reveals, exposed polished ashlar above, with polychromatic grey and red stone window dressings. Simple pitched open timber roof. The change in tone between here and the chancel is dramatic, introduced by the pointed chancel arch, with some red and green tile decoration, which is fully filled by a tripartite rood screen, based on that

---

*Perry (in *The Oxford Movement in Scotland*) has called the ensemble 'modest, shy, retiring', as if 'part of an Oxford College' had been brought to this tiny island.

of the late C14 at Great Bardfield (Essex), with stone tracery
and above the four-centred central arch a decorative cross. The
screen base a low wall; in the centre, steps up to the chancel.
The richness of the CHANCEL and SANCTUARY symbolizes
heaven. They have tiled floors, colourfully patterned, and this
is echoed in the walls, with their remarkable and exuberant
tiled display, mostly in red and green, in a variety of geometrical designs. This joyous display of Butterfield's 'constructional
polychromy' is carried through to the stencilled decoration in
the ceiling. In the N wall an arched opening for the organ, with
access to the Lady Chapel to the r.; in the s wall, a door into
the link with the South College, and a pointed sedilia, filled
with more tiled decoration. The space linking the chancel with
the Lady Chapel has another stencilled wooden ceiling. The
LADY CHAPEL is plainer, severely austere with only the E
window and a trefoil in its w gable; plaster walls, a stencilled
scissor-truss roof, and a tiled floor. There are appealing low
stone screens at the entrance to the chapel.

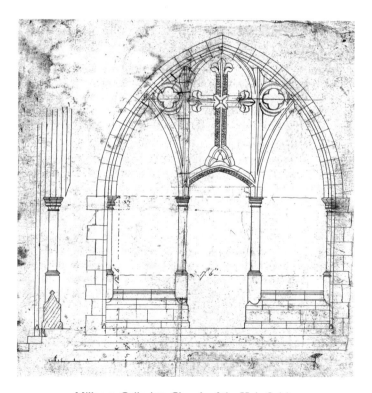

Millport, Collegiate Church of the Holy Spirit,
later Cathedral of the Isles. Chancel screen, elevation and section.
Drawing by W. Butterfield, c. 1850–1

– FITTINGS. – ALTAR within a tall wood and fabric screen, topped by angels bearing candles. – An AUMBRY in both N and S walls. – Bronze CANDELABRA. – Wooden Gothic CHOIR STALLS with foliated bench-ends, a band of nailhead decoration and brass nameplates. – In the chancel arch, gleaming bronze RAILS and GATES; the gates Gothic with large trefoils and nailhead borders, the rails with trefoils under fleur-de-lis. – Octagonal FONT of 1880 by *Ernest Geldart*: marble basin with granite feet. – Octagonal wooden PULPIT with cusped panels. – The ORGAN, installed *c.* 1930, is squeezed uncomfortably behind a wrought-iron screen, almost filling the space between chancel and Lady Chapel. – STAINED GLASS. – Nave W gable and Lady Chapel E window by *William Wailes*, 1851. The rest are mostly by *John Hardman & Co.* Bright primary colours, the figures conventionally drawn, and strongly influenced by Bavarian glass. – In the nave, from E to W, SS Polycarp, Ignatius, Catherine, Cecilia, Augustine, Gregory the Great, Jerome and Ambrose. – Chancel S, Crucifixion and Resurrection; the E window is simpler, with more uncoloured glass, with St Columba, St Augustine and the four Evangelists. – Two good, unsigned early C20 windows in the ante-room to the Lady Chapel: St Michael and St Gabriel; much livelier than Hardman's work. – MONUMENT. N chancel wall: Bishop Chinnery-Haldane †1906; tiled and marbled.

Attached at the SE corner of the cathedral is SOUTH COLLEGE, an L-plan of one long range extending S and a shorter range (for the refectory) projecting E, with a cloister in the angle between the two. The longer range, containing the common room and library on the ground floor, and cells above, has on its W front a half-octagonal stair-tower in the centre with spire. Ground floor of large plate-tracery openings of two lights with cusped heads and a trefoil in the head of the arch. Gabled dormers above. At the S end, where the fall of the ground allows for a basement, is the master's accommodation, with single-light openings, and on the S front a very typical Butterfieldian elevation of a half-hipped gable, windows in pointed-arch surrounds, and a projecting oriel. Big chimneystacks on the flanks. The cloister of five (W) by three (N) bays also has paired openings with trefoils in the arches but of a slightly greater enrichment. Its roof is pitched with saltire bracing carried on posts rising from stone corbels. In the common room a timber mantelpiece, Gothic. In the upper corridor, two STAINED-GLASS windows of *c.* 1965, of Mary with the Infant Jesus, and Our Lady's Tumbler.

NORTH COLLEGE, providing more residential accommodation and separate common room, repeats several of the motifs of the South College but is more distinguished. A single range, with its principal front to the W. It most approaches that feel of an Oxford college; on its own it would be one of the best mid-C19 buildings in Ayrshire. It is mostly two-storey, with dormered bays at either end; trefoil windows, and prominent W and E stacks. Tall octagonal flèche with a pyramidal head.

The cathedral grounds are bounded on the w by a long stone WALL, with a Gothic-arched pedestrian GATE; within the grounds many simple stone flights of steps, with low walls, between the many terraced layers and buildings. To the w of the cathedral, a GRAVEYARD within an enclosure with a walled w gate; among the headstones many Celtic crosses: the tallest, a stone WHEEL CROSS commemorates George Boyle, the fervent idealist to whom this whole extraordinary complex owes its existence, and who has, through its existence, the only monument he truly needs.

CHURCHES AND CEMETERIES

Former BAPTIST CHURCH, Howard Street. 1855. Now used as a store. Gabled, with polished window dressings.

CUMBRAE PARISH CHURCH, Bute Terrace. Typical Tudor Gothic of 1837, with a standard tripartite front of projecting and battlemented tower in the centre and gabled sides. Simple rectangular plan, nice tall Perp windows under hoodmoulds, with a narrower N chancel and behind this a hall of 1894. Inside, GALLERIES on three sides, supported on cast-iron columns; Gothic panelled fronts. – PULPIT. Gothic; enlived by a leafy brass LAMPHOLDER. Above the door to the hall, a red sandstone TYMPANUM, with an inscription in Hebrew, said to have been found at the site of the previous church (*see* Old Kirkyard, below). Panelled GATEPIERS complete the ensemble.

Former EAST CHURCH, Glasgow Street. 1858, as a Free Church. Disused. Gothic, with a bulky bellcote on the main (S) front. This is set back from the street, and now partly obscured by later buildings. Central paired entrance, divided by a granite column on a tall base; shouldered heads, below a pointed tympanum with burning bush. Pointed head, with orders dying into the responds. Four-light Geometrical window in the gable, below the tall, stepped bellcote and its gabled head. Pretty low boundary wall of Gothic openings. Lancets on side elevations and rear gabled hall below stepped lancets.

OUR LADY OF PERPETUAL SUCCOUR (R.C.), College Street. 1956–8 by *Robert Rennie* of Saltcoats. Fairly traditional, with a slender bell-tower, a w vestibule and flat-headed porch on spindly, tapering legs. Grey harl walls. Simple interior. Impressionistic STAINED GLASS of after 2001 in the chancel.

Former ST ANDREW (EPISCOPAL), George Street. *c.* 1850 by *William Butterfield* for George Boyle as a chapel for the small Episcopalian congregation on the island not associated with his collegiate church. Now residential, the fenestration much altered. Grey sandstone, with a s gable of varying pitch under a simple bellcote, and a stumpy stack on the w elevation.

MILLPORT NEW CEMETERY, Kirkton Road. *c.* 1935. One charcterful MONUMENT: Roy Dingley, designer, †1993; columnar, the inscription on three steel bands, with bronzes of a fish and the moon inset above.

OLD KIRKYARD, Kirkton Road. The site of the pre-Reformation
parish church, in existence by 1330, and rebuilt in 1602. No
remains. – MAUSOLEUM for the Crawfords of The Garrison.
Square, with a Gothick battlemented frontispiece, and a barrel
vault. Dated 1807 on the frame of the scrolled crest above the
entrance. Otherwise, mostly late C18 and C19 HEADSTONES,
some with neatly and deeply incised lettering, e.g. John McCal-
lum 'who Dyed of the Smallpox' and his father, also John, who
'parish^d in Larn Loch' in 1788; and that adjacent, of John
Hunter, farmer in Portray, †1785.

PUBLIC BUILDINGS

CUMBRAE PRIMARY SCHOOL, Bute Terrace. A well-preserved
early Board School of 1875–6 by *Alexander Watt* of Glasgow.
Single-storey H-plan, with central hall and classrooms in the
gabled main elevations. Mullioned-and-transomed windows.
Contemporary schoolmaster's house with decorative wooden
bargeboards. Equally interesting detached wing of 1961–6 by
Baron Bercott & Associates (*George Horspool*, project architect;
cf. Whiting Bay School, Arran). Harled, with big bands of
windows between coloured panels. Impressively scaled boiler
house, with play shed attached.

THE GARRISON, Guildford Street. A house of *c.* 1819–20, for
the Earl of Glasgow, in a curious, but playful, crowstepped
Tudor Gothic, in a prominent position on the seafront. Council
offices from the mid C20. Badly damaged by fire in 2001, and
restored by *Lee Boyd* of Edinburgh, 2003–8 for North Ayrshire
Council, with surgery, library, etc. It has its origins in a barracks of *c.* 1745 built for James Crawford, commander of the
revenue cutter based in the Clyde, that was remodelled into
its present form for Lord Glasgow. In the late C19 it passed to
the Crichton-Stuart family, for whom *R. Weir Schultz* did work
in 1908–9. Broadly symmetrical two-storey s elevation, with
crowstepped gabled bays projecting towards either end. Four
half-dormers between, two with crowstepped heads, above a
single-storey loggia with a crenellated parapet and pinnacle
buttresses; the main entrance in the central bays. Similarly
detailed porches in the re-entrants at either end. The N front
is much less cohesive; its most interesting feature the single-
storey service courtyard, which has a Gothick w screen wall
terminating in an octagonal, battlemented SUMMERHOUSE.
This has a tiled floor and dado, perhaps added by Weir Schultz.
    Of the original interiors only a few Gothic doors and simple
fireplaces survive. The tiled fireplaces in the main entrance may
be by Weir Schultz. New spacious top-lit interior, with a
museum–exhibition space serving as a common access to café,
library and council services; helical stair to upper levels.
    In front of the s elevation, a SUNKEN GARDEN, designed by
Weir Schultz, with a low retaining wall, and regularly arranged
flowerbeds, paths and a pond, now restored. The house sits in
spacious walled grounds, with a low wall to the s, to the w and

E castellated GATEWAYS; at the W entrance an L-plan LODGE. In the NW corner of the grounds, a U-plan courtyard group, probably mid-C19, with a two-storey L-plan house, and a chapel-like N wing, all with triangular-headed windows. The courtyard is enclosed by a low stone wall with a central entrance beneath a shaped gable and a late C19 barley-sugar weathervane.

LADY MARGARET HOSPITAL, College Street. 1899–1901 by *Fryers & Penman*. The epitome of a cottage hospital: a two-storey red sandstone villa with a gabled bay to the r. and a substantial rear wing creating an L-plan. Dormers with applied timberwork in the gables. Similar, but single-storey, pavilion to the rear, with a big timbered gable. Between the two original buildings late C20 hipped brick free-standing blocks.

POLICE STATION, Millburn Street. Late C19, purely domestic: a rendered cottage with a gabled porch and big dormers with heavy bargeboards; gabled C20 police office to the l.

TOWN HALL, Clifton Street. 1877–9, by *John Kay* of Rothesay. Stone, gabled, on a tight site; a flurry of shouldered openings, from the chamfered E entrance gable to the stepped upper side windows. Gableted skews, repeated on the lower S wing (1894–5).

WAR MEMORIAL, Guildford Street. 1922 by *Robert Gray*, builder. In the style of a Scots market cross with a battlemented octagonal plinth and chamfered shaft supporting a lion with a shield. Projecting from the cornice below the battlements, heads of a soldier and sailor.

DESCRIPTION

The heart is QUAY HEAD. It is broad, roughly square with buildings on three sides, and partly created by C20 infilling of the inner section of the OLD HARBOUR on the fourth side. The harbour was begun *c.* 1750, and reconstructed in 1797. Stone piers extend NE from Quay Head and SE from Stuart Street to form a sheltered enclosure, now reduced in size. The PIER, of 1883, projects SE from Quay Head; stone pierhead, with a small brick WEIGHBRIDGE HOUSE, probably of *c.* 1955, with a stumpy plastered flat-headed clock tower. The pier itself is supported on wooden piles. Cast-iron LEADING LIGHTS by *MacFarlane & Co.*, of Glasgow.

The buildings of Quay Head are mostly C19 in appearance, though possibly concealing earlier structures, for this is the original landing point, and the small pre-late C18 village would have been here. On the SE side, the ROYAL GEORGE HOTEL, harled, mid-C19, given a big mansard roof in 1934 by *Southern & Orr* of Glasgow. From Quay Head, CARDIFF STREET runs uphill NW, away from the sea. This is noticeably wide and was laid out from 1780, as the centrepiece of the new settlement planned by the Earl of Bute. Some of the buildings, especially on the NE side, date from this period: two-storey tenements, plastered, with painted stone dressings. The head of the street is closed by MILLBURN, a neat and pleasingly proportioned L-plan harled two-storey house of *c.* 1800, within a walled enclosure. BUTE TERRACE, which runs NE from the head of Cardiff Street, forms the other major element in the planned settlement: a succession of big VILLAS, lying below the road, with terraced gardens dropping down towards Howard Street, facing SE towards the ever-changing view of sea, sky and land. They are mostly mid to late C19, often quite substantial, but many have now been divided, and their glory days are behind them. The first group, as far as Church Street, is of after 1860; the best the last (No. 8), with a double-gabled S front, with a two-storey bow window to the l., and a wide porch with simple columns, shouldered heads and an iron balustrade. To Bute Terrace, it is L-plan, hipped, with Greco-Egyptian gatepiers. Beyond Church Street, earlier villas, e.g. the classical SPRING-FIELD and SEAVIEW, with porches, that of the latter with Ionic columns. It also has a circular rear stair, as does CROSSBURN, which lies much lower below the road. Broad S elevation, of *c.* 1845, with canted gabled bays to l. and r., and single storeys beyond, with canted bay windows and dormers. It has a bracketed doorhead, the entrance off-centre in the central bay, and retains much of its terraced gardens. The original house at STRAHOUN is less decorative, but has a taller W wing which has a dentilled pediment frame, while the final house (No. 24) has square projecting bays and a neat octagonal Gothick summerhouse in the garden.

From Quay Head, STUART STREET runs NE with the curve of the bay and open to the water. With Guildford Street, into which it seamlessly merges, it forms the commercial heart of the town. The pattern established in Quay Head is repeated here: a cheerful C19 seaside ensemble, starting rather well, with Nos. 1–5 (late C19) with much nicely proportioned decorative stonework but also including some good survivors from the beginning of the century (e.g. Nos. 30–32), mostly in a vernacular idiom: two-storey, harled or rendered, with slate roofs. In ever-broadening GUILDFORD STREET late C19 and early C20 tenements are commoner, e.g. AILSA VIEW (Nos. 20–27), dated 1907. No. 18 has chunky rusticated ground-floor window frames against exposed brick walls. At the far end of Guildford Street are The Garrison and war memorial (*see* Public Buildings, above). After that, the shore road (now GLASGOW STREET) is predominantly late C19 in character. Here is a good stretch of beach, and catching the 'beside-the-seaside' mood is CROCODILE ROCK on the foreshore, first painted in 1913 by *Robert Brown*, a retired Glasgow architect. As the road passes around KAMES BAY there is a change of atmosphere, with the appearance of villas, set back and in relatively spacious grounds, including a good early C20 terrace in rock-faced red ashlar and the stylish early C20 English Domestic FERNBANK. The best houses, however, are in MARINE PARADE, running down the E side of the bay towards Farland Point, which are set against a wooded backdrop, e.g. EASTWOOD (No. 10), of 1862, with all its windows, including those in the bowed outer bays, an ebullition of cast-iron colonnette transoms and bracketed balconies. The bows are topped by conically roofed dormers.

Finally the area s and sw of Quay Head and Cardiff Street. Here CLYDE STREET, MILLER STREET and CRICHTON STREET create a tightly knit grid, mainly of early C19 cottages and later, larger houses, some perched above the rocky shore, all nicely varied. In Clyde Street also a house of 2003 by *David Boyle*: harled, behind garages, with wooden prow-like gables; a fine approach to a difficult site. WEST BAY ROAD, running sw with the curve of the bay, has more late C19 marine villas, mostly detached, two-storey, and in grey stone, stretching for 0.75 km. or so. It begins with Nos. 4–6, a matching set of three, with canted outer bays beneath gabled dormers; they have gravitas, a determination to have a serious seaside holiday. The faintly Gothic THORNBANK, 1880, has good square gatepiers, with pedimented heads and ball finials. It, and GARNOCK to its l., have curious series of carved corbel-like heads at eaves level. The significance is not clear.

KIRKTON HOUSE, 0.7 km. NW. Originally the parish manse; early C19. Three-bay, two-storey over a raised basement, gable-ended and harled. Windows in frames on the main (E) elevation, which has a central gabled porch, a straightened flight of stairs and round-headed side windows.

WESTBOURNE HOUSE, 1.1 km. SW. Large otherwise conventional late C19 marine villa given character by the glazed belvedere with bracketed eaves, which rises above the hipped slated roof.

UNIVERSITY OF LONDON MARINE BIOLOGICAL STATION, Keppel Pier, 1.4 km. SE. 1896–7 by *Peter Macgregor Chalmers*; addition of 1936–9 by *J. B. Wilson, Son & Honeyman*. Functional, but with gravitas. Built to provide a permanent successor to a boat, the *Ark*, from which marine biological research had been conducted from 1885, initially at Granton (Edinburgh), and at Millport from 1894. Chalmers was asked for a 'small but elegant and convenient structure': his building is L-plan, red sandstone, with a semicircular window over the main entrance in the s gable almost the only decorative detail. Top-lit first-floor library with a wooden roof and tie-beams; the virtually windowless ground floor is a museum and aquarium. The 1930s wing converted the L into a U, and is fully respectful of Chalmers's work. – STAINED GLASS. 1983–4, by *Joanna Scott*, including the l. semicircular window. The inspiration the land-sea transition, and its life forms; two of the windows are in ceiling lights, enhancing the effect of looking up from below, with pelagic colepoda bouncing against the surface film of the sea. HALLS OF RESIDENCE, 1972–4, by *J. L. Gleave & Partners*.

CUMBRAE SLIP, 4.5 km. NE. The island's workaday link to the mainland via ferry to Largs (q.v.). NATIONAL WATER SPORTS TRAINING CENTRE. 1974–6 by *Frank Burnet, Bell & Partners*

(*James Rennie* and *Robert D. McPhail*, project architects). A neat
cruciform gathering of interlocked spruce and pine log structures, with grey tile roofs, of varying heights and scales. Simple
and functionally designed, with one neat downswept dormer.
The inspiration Nordic, the result a well-mannered contribution to the Cumbrae landscape. 100 m. s, a remarkably wide
early C20 stone-walled JETTY, now grassed over between the
walls.

OBELISK, Tomont End, at the island's N tip. To two midshipmen
from HMS *Shearwater*, who drowned near here in 1844.

GREENAN CASTLE *see* DOONFOOT

HARESHAWMUIR LODGE
5040
2 km. E of Waterside

Begun *c.* 1875 as a small shooting lodge for the Earls of Glasgow,
substantially enlarged for A. B. Paton from 1894 onwards, the
Billiard Room added *c.* 1920 for E. R. Paton. Low, rambling
and gabled, sprouting numerous bay windows. A squat, crenellated tower (dated 1900) has a faceted slate roof and weathervane finial.

HAUGH *see* MAUCHLINE

HESSILHEAD
3050

Little more than a farmtoun, centred on a single-arch stone
BRIDGE crossing the Dusk Water, which here descends in a series
of shallow falls.

HESSILHEAD CASTLE stood 0.4 km. NW, but of it, and its
grounds, which in the C17 were considered among the best in
the district, there are but a few mute remains. Unroofed
c. 1776. MacGibbon & Ross recorded a vaulted ground floor,
and a later addition, also vaulted.

HIGH GREENAN HOUSE
3010
1 km. SW of Doonfoot

Small country house of 1910 for James E. Shaw, County Clerk.
By *J. K. Hunter* (or more likely his assistant *James Carrick*) in
a sparing Arts and Crafts manner. Grey drydash with a variety
of small-pane windows made up from one modular size for
each floor. Asymmetrical T-plan with gables of varied size.
Bold, projecting gable to the N (entrance) front with a flanking
stepped buttress and a wide basket-arched inset porch; deeply
recessed timber door with wrought-iron fittings and inscription, 'Here we have no continuing city'; tall stair window to l.
with small closet window below. Further service stair set back

to the r. Garden front with two big gables, the E with a two-storey canted bay and a stepped buttressed stack at its r. Slightly overhanging swept eaves and grey slate roofs. Simple Arts and Crafts-style interior with dark panelling in Jacobean manner and contemporary brass light fittings. Small LODGE in same style integrated with stables.

HIGH WILLIAMSHAW

4040

3 km. NE of Stewarton

Late C18. Pretty, of three bays, two storeys and an attic, with painted walls and stone dressings. A neat mix of traditional and classical idiom, possibly built by *James Donaldson*, the minor London architect, after he inherited the estate. One gabled wall-head dormer in the centre with an oculus and chimneystack, the other attic windows set in the gables. Serlian doorpiece, its form echoed in the windows of flanking single-storey wings which run back to form a spacious courtyard. These were added in 1862 for Donaldson's son *T. L. Donaldson*, whose initials appear on the porch door lintel. Restored in the late C20, retaining some original features such as the horseshoe stair and simple plasterwork.

HIGHFIELD

3050

A roadside hamlet between Dalry and Beith in an area populated from the mid to late C19 by villages of miners' rows. From the mid C19 seams of coal and ironstone were exploited, and there were numerous row villages in the area. The seams were largely exhausted by the late C19, and the population moved away.

KERSLAND, 0.7 km. NW. A courtyard farm, on a defensible site above the Garnock, that has the remains of an L-plan TOWER HOUSE filling the NW corner of its courtyard (the re-entrant angle unfortunately obscured by C20 infill). Where the tower abuts the present mid-C19 farmhouse it appears to have been reduced in length. Both this part and the lower wing of the tower are crowstepped and have vaulted ground-floor rooms. A vaulted corridor separates it from the house and appears to represent the original entrance. The date for this is 1604, on the evidence of the datestone, with name, possessor (Daniel Ker) and heraldic shields, that is re-set in the farmhouse. It is carved with relish, with a border of two bands of roll moulding, separated by dogtooth, reminiscent of the late C16 work at Seagate Castle, Irvine (q.v.). The farmhouse itself faces S and is flanked by projecting wings. It is of notably large stonework and has prominent scrolled skewputts. A substantial portion of the BARMKIN WALL is also preserved, presumably also of 1604. It is 3.6 m. high and extends W of the house to a circular tower, from which it runs S for a short distance.

GRAZE RESTAURANT, The Den, 2 km. NE. 2004 by *Victor Swindall*. Stone and harled, with a bold circular dining room, open timber roof and bright decoration. Far above the average for such enterprises.

MAULSIDE, 2.5 km. NE. Classical villa of *c.* 1833 (called 'excellent, modern' in 1851, but recorded in 1836), given some distinction by block modillions unifying pediments and eaves. It had wings N and S, but the S one has been demolished. The service stair on the rear is carried within a circular tower. Surviving interiors include an oval stairwell. 100 m. NE, MAULSIDE MAINS has a folly-like side façade, which is symmetrical about a pedimented entrance. It would have been visible from the main drive, and is presumably coeval with the house.

3030

HILLHOUSE

2.5 km. SW of Dundonald

One of a group of smart, classical villas built in the county in the later C18 (*see* also Skeldon and Old Auchenfail Hall). Built *c.* 1790, for John McKerrell of the Paisley silk weavers, who inherited the estate from his brother in 1782. To this has been added a large S wing, probably by *Leadbetter & Fairley* who made plans for additions in 1896. Further additions to the rear, of 1911, were removed during restoration in 2003–4 by *Ronald Alexander*.

The house stands on an elevated site surrounded by strategic planting. Of three bays with a raised basement, two principal storeys and an attic, with advanced pedimented bays at the centre of the front and rear. The façades are neatly defined by narrow ashlar margins but its uniformly grey harling is less appealing. Flying stair (rebuilt in 1911 for a porch, now dem.) to the handsome semicircular-arched doorpiece. This has wide panelled pilasters supporting a cornice with a small fanlight set in an unusually deep ashlar panel. Simple bull's-eye window in the tympanum. The rear pediment is open with the upper arched stair window rising into it. Behind this pediment a curious half-octagon inserted to conceal the top light added to the stair when the Edwardian wing blocked all the rear windows.

The main block's interior is conventional with an entrance hall with an Edwardian pedimented opening leading through to the circular stair compartment. The hall retains its C18 ribbed moulding to the front doorcase and Adamesque modillion cornice with scrolls and urns. Below this cornice a deep papier mâché Neo-Adam frieze, probably *c.* 1896, sandwiched between deep plain bands with rosettes. The drawing room retains an C18 cornice but the chimneypiece, mahogany doors and the Frenchy C18-style wall panels are all *c.* 1900. The late C18 dining room sporting a delicate frieze with urns, husks of wheat and sprays of flowers, dado mouldings and an unusual beaded decoration around the shutters. Late C18-style chimneypiece. The S wing of 1896 is almost a separate house with a spacious dog-leg stair with twisted balusters and a Neo-

Adam domed ceiling. The s drawing room has an elaborate carved chimneypiece in natural wood.

STABLE COURTYARD. Possibly related to an earlier house. It has some surprising Gothick details in blind ogee-headed panels and finials. To its E a large partially WALLED GARDEN with a stone inserted over the entrance: 'J McK 1671'.

HILLHOUSE LODGE

4040

1.8 km. SE of Fenwick

Spectacularly sited small Picturesque Gothick mansion house which has its origins in an earlier tower house. This is said to have been a lodge of the Earls of Glasgow, and forms the l. part of the front elevation, with its lower storeys fronting the defile above which the house sits. It may be C17, but its present features are contemporary with the additions of *c.* 1840 that wrap around two sides of the tower. Front elevation enlivened by a heavy porch with ball finials and gableted turret l. of the main gable. Bargeboards and haunched arches abound. The contemporary interior, which integrated a thorough reworking of the tower, includes a tidy horseshoe stair and some original plasterwork.

HOLLYBUSH

3010

Small hamlet which grew up in the C19 around a toll house on the turnpike between Ayr and Dalmellington. TOLL COTTAGE, tightly placed between the road and the railway, is of 1926–7 by *J. K. Hunter*. Stone, with a deeply overhanging steeply pitched slate roof, and two big triangular dormers.

HOLLYBUSH HOUSE. A large and sparse Elizabethan-style mansion begun *c.* 1853 by *Robert Paton* for Frederick A. Eck, partner in the mining company of Anthony Gibbs & Sons. His collection of minerals is now in the Hunterian Museum, Glasgow. Subtly variegated pinkish sandstone. Cross-windows with sashes behind. Sympathetically, if slightly mechanically, remodelled and enlarged by *James Carrick* in 1926 for Mrs Laird with a new entrance and set of public rooms, the decoration of these rooms also 1920s. Hall lined with three-quarter plain rectangular panelling finished with a projecting dentil cornice. Big stone chimneypiece. Arched recess at the SE. The ceiling coffers are smothered with shallow plaster foliage decoration. The DRAWING ROOM at the SE has classically inspired decoration with geometric plaster decorations on the ceiling. Two tall Doric pilasters flank the lugged and corniced chimneypiece.

SKELDON MILLS, 1 km. SW by the Doon. A meal mill until 1824 when William Templeton converted the site to produce blankets. It was expanded by his grandson William Hammond *c.* 1860. Production ceased after a fire in 1955. The stone walls of early buildings can still be made out among later brick structures.

AUCHENDOON, 1 km. SSW. 1892, by *John Murdoch*, for W. T. Hammond, owner of Skeldon Mills. Large and unfussy red sandstone villa of suburban character.

BALGREEN, 1 km. W. 1883 by *R. S. Ingram*. A model farm for the Duke of Portland, red sandstone, built around an internal courtyard, approached through an arched entrance.

DINWOODIE, 1.5 km. NE. Predominantly of 1857–8 but an enlargement of an earlier building, which seems to have been associated with Martnaham Moor sawmill. The mid-C19 work is of whinstone with granite dressing and comprises the upper floor, a wide gabled bay on the W front and a square pyramid-roofed turret set against it to the N. Substantial C20 additions, in two phases: first probably *c*. 1909, with a single-storey N addition (now drawing room) and wide corridor and new staircase at the rear. Of this period some solidly made Arts and Crafts details inside. The top-lit billiard room, E, adjoining the S wall of the service court, and a squash court linked to the rear quarters by a covered walkway are 1920s.

The service court's W range appears to have been the first house on the site, a late C18 or early C19 cottage with boulder footings. Stables, a hayloft, domestic quarters and later garage accommodation fill the remaining sides.

2040

HORSE ISLAND

Flat rocky island, close to the shore N of Ardrossan.

BEACON TOWER. Erected 1811 by the 12th Earl of Eglinton, following a suggestion made by the Arctic explorer Sir John Clark Ross. The tapering stone tower warned of low rocks and marked the entrance into Eglinton's Ardrossan harbour.

1050

HUNTERSTON CASTLE
4.25 km. S of Fairlie

The castle began as a small tower of C15 or early C16 date for the Hunters of Hunterston, replacing earlier buildings. It was once protected by marshland. Originally a tower of three storeys with a garret. S wing added, apparently in two stages, in the years either side of 1600. Offices which extended to S were replaced or incorporated into a farm court in 1847, altered in 1884 and again by *Robert S. Lorimer* whose work on the castle and courtyard was planned *c*. 1913 and undertaken in 1926. The result is a picturesque grouping.

The tower is rectangular in plan (7.5 m. by 6.5 m. with 1.5 m. thick walls), built in pinkish rubble with ashlar dressings, some belonging to later enlargements. The walls rise sheer to a tall corbelled and crenellated parapet with elementary drainage shoots. On the S elevation a small curved projection with continuous corbelling at the point where the turnpike stair opens onto the wall-walk. This detailing and the corbelling on the S gable are not illustrated by MacGibbon and Ross and may belong to Lorimer's restoration. Steep slated roof behind with crowstepped gables and end stacks with chamfered coping. The entrance was originally in the S wall, at first floor. In the storey below, a narrow arrowslit (W) and drainage shoot (E). In the N wall, any early openings were lost when double doors (now blocked) were inserted to give access to the vaulted chamber; it had no access to the floors above.

S of the tower is the two-bay, rectangular, rubble-built addition, the first phase of which appears to be late C16 and has a crowstepped stair-turret projecting from its W face at the junction with the tower. The ashlar work on this simple turret is probably due to Lorimer, who removed a courtyard wall formerly adjoining its NW angle and inserted the trademark boat-shaped N dormer. Above its S door is a square dormerhead. S of the turret, a clear straight joint and disturbance in the walling suggest that the first addition was raised when the second part of this wing was completed in the early C17. The windows here and on the E elevation are as enlarged by Lorimer; he added the E dormers with Hunter emblems.

Inside, a wide stone newel stair leads to the Great Hall in the addition to the tower. Large chimneypiece installed by Lorimer with carved panel over displaying the achievement of the Hunters with the clan motto 'Cursum Perficio' ('I will complete the course') below. There are recesses to either side, that on the W originally a window. The original hall in the tower has a chimneypiece with columned jambs. On the floor above, reached by the tight newel in the depth of the wall, a room with a C17 bolection-moulded chimneypiece set into an earlier recess, an aumbry on the W wall and a garderobe set into the NE corner. Above, the garret with a small fireplace and exposed roof trusses of pegged couples with carpenters' marks to aid assembly.

Opposite the W front a two-storey cottage range with every gable crowstepped, full-height projection and outside steps to first floor, dormers, decorative pedimented window head in N gable. Attached to the S of the tower range the courtyard STEADING of 1847. In 1884 it was altered and the mildly Baronial-style range added to its E side. It has chimney-like bartizans, an external stair and balcony, crenellations and an angle turret at the SE with a candle-snuffer roof. All this was adapted by Lorimer in 1926 as service accommodation. The courtyard windows and the deep crenellated parapet belong to this period.

Opposite the castle complex a large WALLED GARDEN with arched entrance on the E and wrought-iron gates.

HUNTERSTON HOUSE, 0.25 km. N, was built c. 1800 for Eleonora and Robert Caldwell Hunter to provide better accommodation than the castle. Symmetrical with shallow advanced outer bays and a recessed entrance, a shallow projection for the stair at the rear. Added to c. 1835 and substantially remodelled in 1883 for Col. Gould Hunter Weston by *John Honeyman*, with additions, enlarged windows, mansard roof and a large low service court. But none of this has his usual flair. Inside, some good panelling and carved work together with delicate plaster decoration in the dining room and the drawing room. This work dates from 1883 and *c.* 1913, the latter by *Robert S. Lorimer* for General Sir Aylmer Hunter-Weston. – WELL-HEAD, with wrought-iron standards. A copy of that at Château de Bucy, seen by Hunter-Weston during his service at the Battle of Aisne in 1914. Grounds extensively landscaped by Hunter Weston's regiment post WWI as part of a make-work scheme.

HURLFORD

4030

Late C18 and early C19 coal and iron mining village, which later became home to the engineering works of the Glasgow and South-Western Railway, and Andrew Strang & Co., who specialized in marine propellers (the last to be produced now marks the village centre).

HURLFORD PARISH CHURCH. *See* Crookedholm.
Former HURLFORD PARISH CHURCH. *See* Crookedholm.
Former MAUCHLINE ROAD CHURCH, Mauchline Road. Workaday Gothic of 1897–8 by *Gabriel Andrew*. Converted to flats, 2007.
ST PAUL (R.C.), Galston Road. 1882–3 by *J. & R. S. Ingram*. Ambitious, in brick, with transepts and chancel. The openings dressed in brick, the windows triangular-headed. To the r., no less ambitious PRESBYTERY, of 1966–7, perhaps by *Charles W. Gray*, who worked on the church 1960–3. A boarded trapezoid, with a sunken harled lower floor. On its w flank, two lower harled lean-to blocks face the church; one connected with the church grounds by an enclosed wooden bridge/porch.
HURLFORD PRIMARY SCHOOL, Academy Street. 1902–5 by *Andrew & Newlands* (*Gabriel Andrew*) for Riccarton School Board. A strong Free Renaissance exercise in red Ballochmyle sandstone; close in spirit to the Glasgow Board Schools: unified main (w) elevation of two storeys, four bays of Gibbsian Venetian windows in the upper storey, the outer bays advanced as gabled end pavilions with broken ogee pediments with finials. The heads of the windows of the inner bays form dormers with tympana carved to represent science and art. The square SW tower has a solid parapet broken by Gibbsian niches, with, between them, lower simple niches forming an octagon, from which rises the lead-roofed ogee cap.

The centre of the village is a crossroads, now a roundabout, from which the buildings have shrunk back. To the N, HURLFORD BRIDGE of *c.* 1836, a wide flat two-arched bridge with low stone parapets, triangular cutwaters, segmental arches and polished ashlar voussoirs. In RICCARTON ROAD on the l., the former CO-OPERATIVE STORE of 1904 by *J. B. Fulton*, red sandstone with shallow first-floor wide-eaved coolie-hatted bows. Alongside, No. 9 of 1903–4 by *Andrew & Newlands* has a big pilastered doorpiece and semicircular dormerheads with square finials. Opposite is the red sandstone former MASONIC HALL, 1907 by *James S. Hay*; a single-storey block, with a central shaped gable flanked by balustrades to the l., to the r. a two-storey block with crowstepped dormer gables.

SHAWHILL HOUSE, 1 km. NNE above the E bank of the Irvine. The grand five-bay frontage is an addition, one room deep, to a conventional late C18 two-storey three-bay house whose rear elevation and gables can still be seen. The addition was built for Col. Clark who acquired the estate in 1822. Set on a platform, it is intended to make a statement. The flat façade, reminiscent of Sauchrie or Doonholm (qq.v.), is relieved by minimal Doric pilasters framing the end bays and supporting a simple eaves cornice. At the centre a dramatic Greek Doric columned porch and above the main cornice, a stepped and consoled parapet supporting five fluted chimneystacks. In the remains of the walled garden a small SUMMERHOUSE with overhanging eaves and Gothic details to the windows.

KAIMSHILL CEMETERY, Riccarton Road, 0.9 km. SW. 1863. One exceedingly long and mannered memorial to the Cuninghames of Caprington: a stone wall book-ended by tall monuments with shouldered pediments, with a similarly detailed triple memorial at the centre. – Mrs Andrew Miller †1886. Back panel of glazed brick.

HURLFORD VIADUCT, 0.9 km. W, spanning the Irvine. 1848, for the Glasgow, Paisley, Kilmarnock & Ayr Railway Co. Seven semicircular arches, with polished ashlar voussoirs, and coursed rubble piers and spandrels.

KIRKLANDSIDE HOSPITAL, Riccarton Road, 1.1 km. SW. Isolation hospital of 1892, by *R. S. Ingram*, the original buildings brick and plain.

H.M.P. KILMARNOCK, 2.7 km. SE. 1996–9 by *John Seifert Architects*, the first privately run prison in Scotland. Main buildings harled and tiled Neo-vernacular, of one and two storeys.

DALLARS. *See* p. 270.

IRVINE

INTRODUCTION

Modern Irvine is primarily associated with the late C20 New Town, the development of which made Irvine the third largest town in Ayrshire, with a population, of 40,000; if the other settlements* within the New Town designated area are included the population is closer to 60,000, exceeding both Ayr and Kilmarnock. Beneath this modern façade, there is an ancient settlement with a varied history and fortune, epitomized by the three spires (Town House, Parish Church and Trinity Church) which signal Irvine from afar.

The shared estuary of the Irvine and the Garnock provided an obvious natural harbour, and the original settlement developed

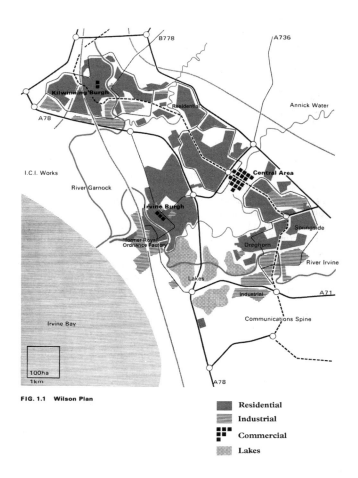

FIG. 1.1   Wilson Plan

Residential
Industrial
Commercial
Lakes

---

*These settlements have their own pre-New Town histories, and are described separately: *see* Bourtreehill, Dreghorn, Girdle Toll, Kilwinning and Springside.

on the r. bank of the Irvine on a low ridge from where an exten-
sive freshwater loch extended inland to the NE. Irvine is first
mentioned in the mid C12, and a castle is recorded from 1184.
This was held by the de Morvilles, Norman liegemen to the
Scots kings. The town grew, and in the mid C13 was created a
Royal Burgh by Alexander II (1214–49). Its main street ran
NW–SE along the ridge – the line of High Street and Seagate
today – with the church at the SE end and, probably, the castle
at the other (no doubt close to the site of the C16 Seagate
Castle), protecting the original harbour. The town grew slowly,
if steadily, through the early medieval period, helped by its
convenience as a port for Glasgow. The loch restricted growth

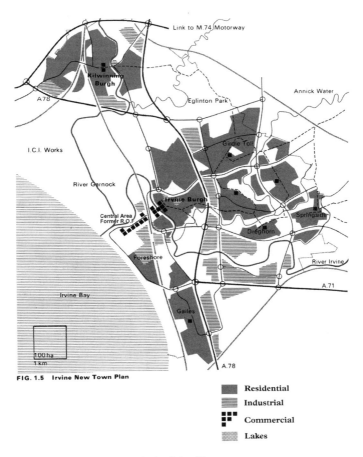

FIG. 1.5 Irvine New Town Plan

Residential

Industrial

Commercial

Lakes

Irvine New Town.
Original plan by Wilson & Womersley (1966–7) (l.)
and revised plan, as adopted (1969–71) (r.)

to the NE, but to the SW, crossing the head of a meander in the Irvine, there grew up an unregulated suburb in the parish of Dundonald (known as Halfway and, from 1707, as Fullarton, a Burgh of Barony; incorporated into Irvine, 1881). The harbour, however, became increasingly harder to reach, partly because ships were of an increasing draught, but also because the sea was gradually retreating. In response, the Glasgow merchants founded Port Glasgow (Renfrewshire) in 1662.

The loch was successfully drained in the late C17 by the Rev. Partick Warner, who had acquired the necessary engineering knowledge while in exile in Holland. At this time a new direct route to Glasgow, via Glasgow Vennel and Ballot Road, was created. The problem of the harbour was addressed in the late C18, when new wharves were created on the l. bank of the Irvine, downstream and SW of Fullarton closer to the river mouth. The wharves were improved and added to during the C19, but the harbour suffered from competition with Troon and Ardrossan, which took most of the coal export trade on which it depended. Although from 1840 Irvine was on the Ayr to Glasgow railway, its importance to N Ayrshire was increasingly challenged by Kilmarnock, and Victorian Irvine saw neither large-scale industrialization nor substantial growth as a town. There was more industry at Fullarton, especially after the arrival of the railway.

In 1917 a Royal Ordnance Factory was built s of the harbour, as an adjunct to Nobel's dynamite factory at Ardeer (Stevenston, q.v.), which lay immediately across the river to the N, and this became the town's major employer until the mid C20. Its closure in 1957 prompted the Town Council, with some commendable foresight, to reinvent Irvine as an overspill town for Glasgow, actively and successfully promoting industrial units (on the site of the ordnance factory) and social housing. The creation of Irvine New Town, administered by Irvine Development Corporation, in 1967, was thus a natural extension of this policy.

The plan for the designated area of the New Town was prepared by *Hugh Wilson*, of *Hugh Wilson and Lewis Womersley*, in 1966–7, and revised in 1969–71. Wilson's plan has a N–S spine road, with discrete residential and industrial areas linked to it and to a parallel distributor road. The residential areas are characterized by a clear segregation of traffic and pedestrians – community roads through the residential areas were designed to carry only public transport. To that extent the plan, for its date, is conventional, but in the details of the architecture there is much radicalism, and of a kind that has proved far more enduring than the aggressive megastructures of Cumbernauld. The Corporation was well served by its Chief Architects: successively *David Gosling* (1968–72), *John K. Billingham* (1973–9) and *Ian C. Downs* (1979–96) who with their staff pioneered many solutions to late C20 planning issues which were adopted nationally. These included terraces of rentable factory and industrial units, social housing of a vernacular inspiration, a multi-function leisure centre, and the careful integration of historic buildings into new developments. Radical solutions, too, were adopted in the town centre, most memorably the shopping centre which crosses the river.

Since the disbanding of the Development Corporation in 1996, the town has continued to expand, especially to the N and E, but now with unremarkable private developments predominating. The town centre retains a small-town feel in the original High Street, with a forceful and memorable dissonance between old town and New Town at Irvine Cross. It is a pragmatic, workmanlike place, but one with a complex, if not easily glimpsed, history, and a succession of important buildings from all periods.

CHURCHES AND CEMETERIES

EMMANUEL CHRISTIAN CENTRE, West Road. Former Relief Church of 1773. Simple classical hipped preaching box, with

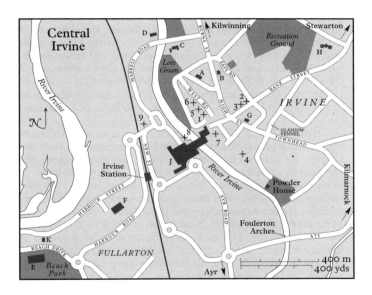

1	Emmanuel Christian Centre	A	Seagate Castle
2	Former Good Templars' Hall	B	Burns Museum
3	Irvine Baptist Church	C	Former Irvine Royal Academy
4	Irvine Parish Church	D	Irvine Sports Club
5	Mure Church	E	Magnum
6	St Mary (R.C.)	F	Scottish Maritime Museum
7	Former Trinity Parish Church	G	Town House
8	Former Fullarton Free Church	H	Woodlands Primary School
		J	Rivergate Shopping Centre
9	Fullarton Parish Church	K	Harbour Arts Centre

tall round-headed windows. The large projecting frontispiece has a central pediment, paired flat pilasters and lower flanking entrance bays recessed to either side. The interior has been subdivided to provide a hall on the upper floor, and ancillary accommodation beneath.

Former FULLARTON FREE CHURCH, Waterside. 1872–3 by *Robert Baldie*. Gothic, with the church raised above a suite of halls, but not seen to advantage in its present position between the road and the river, with its nose pushed into the flank of the shopping centre. Gabled, with a SW tower and N transepts; pointed windows and buttresses. The tower has pilasters above the first stage, paired bell-openings and a truncated octagonal spire: the main (S) entrance elevation has a pointed-headed door with colonnettes in the reveals, flanking sharply pointed lancets, three stepped windows above and an oculus in the gable. Steps with low stone walls and iron torchères; these latter perhaps of *c.* 1900.

FULLARTON PARISH CHURCH, Church Street. 1837–8 by *James Ingram*. Tudor Gothic. Coursed rubble (the W wall harled); the main (S) elevation gabled with an open octagonal bellcote, tall square-headed openings and corbelled finials. Panel tracery in the centre window. Austere galleried INTERIOR. Plaster walls and ceiling. PULPIT, with a Gothic screened and raised enclosure behind, probably original, below the wall-mounted ORGAN. Pair of flanking windows with STAINED GLASS of *c.* 1937: the Good Shepherd to the l., Suffer Little Children to the r. Conventional, though the children have brought their toys.

CHURCH HALL of 1907, attached to the N, and, to the E, the former PARISH SCHOOL, probably contemporary with the church. Its details are domestic, with lying-pane glazing; the shouldered gabled porch on the E elevation probably later.

Former GOOD TEMPLARS' HALL, Bank Street. 1871–2 by *John Armour Jun*. Stone, with three linked round-headed windows with prominent keystones to the shouldered S gable.

IRVINE BAPTIST CHURCH, Bank Street. 1877–8 by *John Armour Jun*. Romanesque. Polished ashlar façade with tall windows in the outer bays, paired central entrances, and a three-light window above with columns and decorative caps. The heads all have incised carving, imitative of channelling, but finished short of the outer moulding. Acroterion finial to the gable. Simple interior. – Elaborately detailed cast-iron PULPIT.

IRVINE PARISH CHURCH, Kirkgate. Imposing four-square preaching box of 1772–3 by *David Muir* of Irvine with a spectacular six-stage steeple added in 1775–6; the whole design closely modelled on the High Church, Paisley (John White, 1750–6). Repaired in 1830, when the roof was rebuilt.

As befits the parish church of a proud and ancient Royal Burgh, the finishes and details are of high quality. The exterior is of light brown ashlar, except the principal N elevation, facing down Kirkgate, which is harled l. and r. of the steeple. This is a finely massed and detailed design, with a round-headed

entrance beneath a Venetian window; the next stage with dentil
pediments and Doric columns, its N window with swags.
Square clock stage with angle pilasters and urns. The upper
stages are octagonal and recede: the first with bell-openings
and Ionic pilasters and a domed roof carrying the next stage
with a balustrade parapet, and the final one topped by the spire
with series of blind oculi on alternate faces. Two bays of
windows on this front, the inner ones with full-height round-
headed windows, the outer ones with round-headed windows
above segmentally headed openings. Six similar bays on the S
elevation, the lower tier more closely spaced to permit an
entrance. Five-bay E and W elevations, with two tiers of round-
headed windows – the middle bays have entrances, also
round-headed.

Vestibule with a tiled floor and dado, and a flat ribbed plaster
ceiling. The present appearance of the very elaborate INTER-
IOR is due largely to *John Armour Sen.* in 1896–7. Plaster walls
and shallow coved ceiling, with large central rose and four
subsidiary ones, painted by *John Gilfillan* of Irvine. Three-sided
gallery with canted corners supported on two rows of cast-iron
columns and with a wooden-panelled front to the central magistrates' loft, which has seats not pews; it was a 'seedy and
rotten ruckle of benches' (*Troon Times*) prior to 1896. The N
wall is dominated by the subdued classical ORGAN case (1878).
– PULPIT, with two stairs with delicate wrought-iron handrails,
and COMMUNION TABLE, both of 1877–8. Contrasting High
Victorian FONT of 1873, by *Robin* of Paisley; granite and white
marble, claw feet, columns with decorated heads, the bowl in
a granite surround, from which projects the marble head of a
child 'with short clustering curls, and a face – not of the dump-
ling and cod liver oil order, but of the most tender beauty'
(*Ardrossan & Saltcoats Herald*). – STAINED GLASS. Twenty-two
different stained-glass windows, mostly by *W. & J. J. Kier* of
Glasgow, whose roots were in Irvine. The earliest are the two
full-height N windows (1861 and 1866). Others in the lower
tier include a laboured version of Holman Hunt's The Light
of the World, 1909, and Christ and the Woman at the Well
(1904, E wall, second from N). – Six windows in the S gallery,
I was a Stranger, and Ye took Me In, etc. – The W wall, N
window, is in memory of J. J. Kier himself, The Three Kings,
1907. – From the mid and late C20: S wall, second from E by
Guthrie & Wells, Christ with Andrew and Peter, 1938, escapes
the conventions. – In the E gallery wall, a pensive St Inan, surrounded by the badges of the Incorporated Trades of Irvine,
by *W. Blair & J. Blyth*, 1975 (second from N) and a fluid Tree
of Life (N window) by *Susan Bradbury*, 1996, both in sharp
contrast to the style of the Kier windows. – MONUMENTS.
David Frew, mason, †1764, within a frame with a swan-neck
head above a square and compass. Andrew Cunninghame,
1887 by *J. & G. Mossman*: black Belgian marble pillars to either
side and an anthemion in the semicircular head. On the N wall
of the W gallery, First Lieutenant Bryce Gulliland, killed at

Trafalgar: obelisk and draped urn. On the adjoining w wall a plaque of 1880 with a three-master in full sail proclaims the Sailor's Loft, and in the window to the l., a MODEL, presented in 1873, of the Irvine lifeboat *Isabella Frew*. Outside, big bronze WAR MEMORIAL panels either side of the door.

Large, extended CHURCHYARD with the river on its SW boundary. Inset into the walls of the original enclosure some C16 and C17 PLAQUES. Several carved C18 HEADSTONES, e.g. John Turner and family, *c.* 1786 (SW of the church), with a skull and what appears to be a seated figure, somewhat surprised by the two angels carrying him upwards. Angels with encircling wings are a favourite motif, see Robert Allan †1770 (S of the church), which also has a three-masted sailing ship and verse.

Immediately outside the church gate, in Kirkgate, PARISH CHURCH HALLS of 1894–6 by *John Armour Sen*. Ashlar front, with a first-floor Venetian window to the l. under a big Dutch gable with broken segmental pediment and finial and decorative carved panel. Slightly advanced entrance with channelled voussoirs to the r. under a raised broken pediment.

MURE CHURCH, West Road. Former Free Church, 1848–9 by *Black & Salmon* of Glasgow. Gothic, with gables and corner pinnacles and originally with a spire, now reduced to a bell-cote, on the decorative w front which also has a projecting centre and three-light geometric window. Behind the church, and making a substantial low forework to it on the approach from West Road, are halls of 1902–3 in an odd Free Gothic with a cupola, lancets and gablets with quatrefoils. Between these two parts, a single-storey link, probably of 1848–9, but with a clearstorey that lights stairs to a gallery added during alterations in 1876 by *John Armour Sen*. Simple nicely detailed plastered INTERIOR. The GALLERY has cast-iron columns and an attractive wooden front with a long cusped arcade; matching double-stair PULPIT and panelled screen. Decorative GLASS in the w window, attributed to *David Kier*. The main HALL has a complex hammerbeam roof.

ST ANDREW, Caldon Road.* 1951–7 by *Robert Rennie*. Dumpy stone-faced SW entrance tower and interesting semicircular flat-roofed 'transepts' that are almost wholly glazed with vertical concrete mullions. Unusual E window of five square lights, linked by a circular moulding, like a Celtic cross. Businesslike w extension of 1968–70; more rewarding s addition of 1980–1 by *Robert L. Dunlop* with a new entrance in a broad timber and glass porch between two solid canted but dissimilar blocks. Inside, the side walls have been painted and plastered to resemble arcades; chequerboarded chancel roof. – Nicely carved early C20 light oak PULPIT. – STAINED GLASS in the small E windows: The Lamb of God and the Evangelists, 1957 by *Mary Wood*, Edinburgh. – In the main corridor an odd window by

* Originally built for the Church of Scotland, but since 1973 shared with the Scottish Episcopal Church.

Ann Marie Docherty of Milngavie, 1998. – The various additions have created an internal courtyard; in this a very stylized
CARVING of St Andrew, of 1957, by *Thomas Whalen*.

ST MARGARET (R.C.), Castlepark Road. 1975–6 by *Clunie
Rowell*; addition of 1982 by *Sam Gilchrist*. Rowell's original,
now used as a hall, is harled, with a brick interior, and a steeply
pitched roof – a child of its time. The addition is straightforward, with a timber gable, and composite stone interior walls
to the low-ceilinged sanctuary.

ST MARY (R.C.), West Road. A big church and presbytery of
1882–3 by *J. & R. S. Ingram*, befitting one of the largest C19
R.C. congregations in the county. It functioned as church and
school until 1928. The style is E.E., quite simple, with a gabled
E front that has a wheel window, stepped buttresses, small
lancets and an image niche. The central door within a moulded
square recess, with corbels and decorative panels, is of *c.* 1928.
Paired square-headed windows on the side elevations. Plaster
walls and an unusual plaster ceiling, with soft longitudinal ribs,
like creases in cloth. Chancel arch with imposts and short
columns. Gallery and vestibule of *c.* 1928, when the interior
was reordered by *Robert Thomson* of Musselburgh. – Creetown
granite FITTINGS, *c.* 1963, including a delightfully tactile egg-
like FONT and a triangular ALTAR. – STAINED GLASS of *c.* 1928,
saints conventionally rendered, and said to be Belgian. Set
back to the N, the late C19 PRESBYTERY, with unattractive late
C20 additions. Adjoining to the S, and with a shared vestibule,
HALL of 2004 by *Sam Gilchrist*. Gable front, stone-faced, with
low square-headed windows.

SEVENTH DAY ADVENTIST CHURCH, High Street. *See* Description 1, below.

Former TRINITY PARISH CHURCH, Bridgegate. United Pres-   28
byterian church of 1861–3 by *F. T. Pilkington*, in the individually
conceived Ruskinian Gothic of which he is the acknowledged
master, and which here produces, on the most commanding
site in the town, perched high above the river, one of his finest
buildings, rivalled only by Barclay Bruntsfield Church
(Edinburgh). The polychrome stonework, the steep and vari-
ably angled roofs, the many finials and the steeple give the
church, even in its present disused state, a haunting, mystic
presence. The builder was *Archibald Wilson*, the slater *John
Kier*. Nave, chancel and transepts, with a NW entrance tower.
Canted bays in the angles between the chancel, nave and transepts, a session house attached to the E transept, with angled
sides. The walls of brown freestone, the quoins of white stone,
and the window dressings a polychromatic white and Ballochmyle red. Tall lancet windows throughout, stepped in the transepts, with a pair, with decorative caps, below a finely conceived
vesica in the nave; this pattern repeated in the chancel. Red
sandstone columns to many of the windows, such as the three-
light arcades in the angle bays. The session house is semi-
conical, with a steeply pitched roof terminated by an equally
steep conical slated lantern. The masterly octagonal spire rises

from four tall lucarnes, with Florentine heads, and paired windows with elongated cusped heads, red sandstone columnar transoms and more columns in the reveals. At the angles baldacchino-like finials, with more red sandstone columns and elongated cusps. The entrance, by comparison, almost restrained, with a haunched head and corbelled columns with finely executed decorative caps. Subsidiary entrances are similar, but smaller. Discarded by the Church of Scotland in the 1970s, Trinity has yet to find a new use, and the interiors have been lost. Conservation and conversion began in 2011: *ARPL Architects.**

KNADGERHILL CEMETERY, off Bank Street. 1925–7 by *J. & J. Armour.* Low brick and railed walls, pyramid-headed stone gatepiers and a crowstepped lodge. In front of the gates a much weathered granite MONUMENT of 1929 records that the Scots Army assembled here in July 1297.**

SHEWALTON CEMETERY, Ayr Road. 1866. Stone walled enclosure, with a Tudor-Gothic L-plan single-storey lodge. The panelled gatepiers have stepped pyramidal heads with ball finials.

SEAGATE CASTLE
Seagate

The ruins of a late C16 castle, whose former strategic importance is now hard to visualize. There has probably been a fortified building on this site since the C12, for at the foot of Seagate was the original harbour, and the castle guarded entry to and from the town by sea. The existing structure may incorporate materials from earlier building campaigns, but what is seen today probably dates from the time of Hugh, 3rd Earl of Eglinton, married in 1562. The castle seems to have been occupied until it was de-roofed in 1746.***

The castle is built of local stone. The main block is roughly aligned with Seagate and has a broadly symmetrical elevation with a central pend; on the interior face, three towers, two round and one triangular projected into the inner courtyard. The w half still survives to wall-head height. The w gable also survives, and is crowstepped. The e half has been considerably robbed out and reduced, as has the tower which projected here and the interior faces, but the other two towers survive: one round and one square. The wide entrance has a moulded semicircular arched head, with plain caps, and dogtooth and

---

* Some of the stained glass has survived and is in the People's Palace, Glasgow, and in the Stained Glass Museum, Ely, where two panels are displayed, one designed by *Daniel Cottier* (1864) and one by *James Tennant Lyon* (1865), both executed by *Field & Allan* of Edinburgh.
** The decision of the Scots nobles encamped here, including Bruce, to surrender rather than attack the English troops, who were supporting John Baliol, in Seagate Castle, is said to have been a major cause of the rift between Bruce and Wallace.
*** A bronze plaque of 1930, in a panel to the l. of the door, records that the Treaty of Irvine was signed here in 1297, and that Queen Mary lodged here in 1563.

star decoration to the moulding in the arch and reveals. Above the entrance is a large empty three-part recess for panels, with moulded frames. Two large windows with rope-moulded frames light the main hall, with smaller windows elsewhere, especially on the ground floor.

Vaulted pend; bosses with the arms of the 3rd Earl and his wife, Agnes Drummond of Innerpeffray. It gives access only to the courtyard, and to a vaulted guardroom on either side. To the l. (seen from the courtyard) of the pend, the round tower rises to the remains of a corbelled and crowstepped caphouse; to the r. a low entrance to the vaulted ground floor, and a further low entrance within a tall arched recess. Another rope-moulded window on the W first floor. A raggle in the square tower shows that ancillary buildings ran along the boundary walls. Access to the first floor was by a wheel-stair in the round tower. The interiors, which include a large arched fireplace in the kitchen in the N basement, have become seriously overgrown.

PUBLIC BUILDINGS

AYRSHIRE CENTRAL HOSPITAL, Kilwinning Road. A large general hospital on a generous site, designed 1935–41 by *William Reid*, County Architect, and built 1937–41. Many of the original progressive Modernist buildings remain; very much of its time, and a rare and under-appreciated example of a public building of that time, still serving its original purpose. There were originally three main blocks, all flat-roofed and faced in bright white harl, of which two survive. That to the N is now ADMINISTRATION AND OUT-PATIENTS and is in the form of a three-sided courtyard. Its side wings are of mixed height (two- and three-storey), with taller semi-circular fronted stair-towers; the other wing is single-storey, with a tall central feature with the arms of the county. The other main block is towards the S boundary of this large site; with the same design features as the other, but the side wings have been turned back to form one long façade. Now unoccupied. The third, and central, main block, the MATERNITY UNIT, was demolished *c.* 2006. Other original buildings include the swarm of butterfly-plan nursing PAVILIONS, the LODGES and former STAFF HOUSES.

BURNS MUSEUM, Eglinton Street. A house of 1901–4 by *John Armour Jun.*, red sandstone with crowstepped gables and a rectangular strapwork panel above the entrance. Bequeathed to the Irvine Burns Club in 1962, and converted into club rooms and a museum, 1967. One ground-floor room is a re-creation of the heckling shop in which Burns worked, and has interesting MURALS of 1965–6 by *Elizabeth & Edward Odling* with notable Munch-like figures of Poverty and Obscurity. The sumptuous stair leads to a large first-floor meeting room, with a STAINED-GLASS window by *Paul Lucky*, 2001, the subjects of Burns and Irvine explored through documents and maps. Another window has re-set C19 PAINTED GLASS panels (Burns Monument, Tam and Cutty Sark, Brig o Doon, Burns Cottage) rescued from a shop in Kilmarnock. Incorporated into the walls are several PLASTER RELIEFS, purportedly from the original Mercat Cross of Irvine (*see* the war memorial, below, p. 384). These include a crown, a lion and a further, irrefutably male, lion, flanked by scrolls and putti. This latter early C17, the others later.

CUNNINGHAME HOUSE, Friars Croft. *See* Description 2, below.

FOULERTON ARCHES, 0.4 km. SE. A tubular steel bridge with tall incurving open-arched parapets, designed by *URS*, Edinburgh, 2008–10. It succeeds a Bailey bridge of 1973 required after the demolition of Irvine Bridge.

Former IRVINE ROYAL ACADEMY, Academy Road.★ 1899–1902, by *John Armour Sen*. Classical, of red Ballochmyle sandstone. Now in mixed commercial and residential use. Symmetrical, two-storey, with a parapeted central block, and hipped end pavilions. Ionic columns to the central entrance, and to the recessed three-light window above. Big drum domes on square bases with finials behind the pavilions.

IRVINE ROYAL ACADEMY, Kilwinning Road. The former Ravenspark Academy of 1967–9 by *Ayr County Council Architects Dept*. A large four-storey system-built design, the ground floor on the front elevation set back behind arcades, with the main entrance in the centre.

IRVINE SPORTS CLUB, Waterside, Fullarton. 1974–5, extended in 1995, by *I.D.C.* (*Robin Wilson*, project architect for both). A big harled and single-storey clubhouse, flat-roofed, with one tall monopitch; neatly composed and at ease in its surroundings. Minimal glazing on the front, restricted to a band at eaves height. Glazed lounge windows on the opposite elevation.

IRVINE STATION, New Street, on the Fullarton side of the river. First opened in 1839 by the Glasgow, Paisley, Kilmarnock & Ayr Railway, but mostly of 1876. Stone-built with offices and, on the w, former stables at street level. The platforms are linked by a subway, also of 1876. The E buildings are the more formal; the dark stone of the former stables suggests some reuse of the 1839 building. 2 km. N, the QUEEN'S BRIDGE, over the Irvine, of 1838–9 by *John Miller*, is a six-arch viaduct with low segmental arches.

MAGNUM, Beach Drive. Opened 1977. A big beast, without architectural pretension, but nationally one of the first all-inclusive leisure centres, popular if not pretty. Planned by *I.D.C.* from 1970, the inspiration the Forum, Billingham (Co. Durham, by Elder, Lester & Partners, 1965–7). The large spaces (sports hall, bowling green, swimming pool and ice rink) are on the ground floor; access via a pedestrian bridge at first-floor level, with offices and other facilities at this level.

Former POST OFFICE, High Street. *See* Description 1, below.

POWDER HOUSE, Golffields Road. 1642, a simple harled octagon (restored 1992) with a slated roof and a weathervane. It was built 'following an edict by King James VI instructing the

---

★ On the site of its predecessor, of 1814–16 by *David Hamilton*.

provision of 'Pouther magazines' in all Royal Burghs', for use by the army.

ROBERT BURNS STATUE, Irvine Moor. Unveiled in 1896, the gift of John Spiers, a Glasgow underwriter who was born at Irvine and retired to Seamill. Bronze, 2.75-m.-high figure by *J. Pittendreigh Macgillivray*. The poet is shown facing S, with one foot resting on a stone, a hand on his thigh. On the Aberdeen granite pedestal, itself 3.6 m. high, a decorative thistle frieze and three bronze panels show Burns's Parting from Mary Campbell; the Cottar Returning; and Burns with the poetic Muse (her well-turned calf a possible distraction). The other panel is decorative, with Burns's name in a cartouche.

RED CROSS HOUSE, Tarryholm Drive. 1989–93, *I.D.C.* (*H. Roan Rutherford* and *Allan Stewart*, job architects). Well-thought-out single-storey disabled housing and day centre complex.

SCOTTISH MARITIME MUSEUM, Linthouse Vennel. *See* Description 2, below.

TOWN HOUSE, High Street. 1859–61 by *James Ingram*. An Italianate palazzo, but in typically Scots fashion given an elegant, preternaturally tall landmark tower. A remarkable statement of local pride, but one in need of sympathetic restoration. Symmetrical seven-bay front with in the centre a two-storey portico with paired Doric columns, round-headed windows, channelled quoins, a heavily bracketed cornice and open parapet. Above this rises the tower, its lower stages square, the first with big square panels and a corbelled cornice, the second with single round-headed windows and paired pilasters. Volutes support the base of the tall octagonal lantern with its heavily bracketed cap, and ship weathervane. Side elevations much simpler: tall round-headed windows to the first-floor Council Chamber. This was subdivided *c.* 1973, but its ornately panelled ceiling, and much else remains above the suspended ceilings.

WOODLANDS PRIMARY SCHOOL, Woodlands Avenue. 1996–8 by *North Ayrshire Council Architects Dept* (*David Watts*, project architect). Large, broadly L-plan, of brick, with sheet-metal roofs of varying pitch, all rising to a taller block at the angle, with a shallow curved roof over glazed recesses.

DESCRIPTIONS

1. Irvine town centre

The heart of Irvine is the junction of High Street, running NW–SE, with Bridgegate (SW) and Bank Street (NE). Here the old burgh and the New Town meet with a vengeance in BRIDGEGATE HOUSE of 1973–4 by *David Gosling*, chief architect to the I.D.C., the piloti-supported end elevation of which thrusts itself into and between the earlier, mixed buildings of the High Street. What remains of the S side of BRIDGEGATE is largely undistinguished C19, and at its W end it widens into a rather formless open space, dominated by the former Trinity Church (*see* Churches, above) to the S and the RIVERGATE SHOPPING

CENTRE to the W. This is of 1975–6 by the *I.D.C. Architects Dept* (*David Gosling*, chief architect, succeeded by *John Billingham*), replacing *John Herbertson*'s four-arch bridge of 1825–7, whose demolition in 1973 is still an emotional issue for Irvineites. Originally as direct as Bridgegate House, but softened by new entrances, *c.* 1998. In another bold and uncompromising move, the centre spans the river; the intention being to bring closer together the two sides of the river, but also reinforcing the fact that the New Town was a new broom. The full impact of the shopping centre is better seen from afar, especially from the N; the interior, however, could be anywhere, apart from the glazed section where the national chain retailers are replaced by views down the river. These two buildings are not architecturally meritorious, now, indeed, deeply unfashionable, but the vision and the planning that they represent is unique in British new towns, a can-do pragmatic approach with its inspiration, surely, in the United States.

HILL STREET, pedestrianized 1975–6, runs S from Bridgegate, and immediately offers a different image of I.D.C.'s relationship with the town in the form of nicely restored late C18 and early C19 two-storey and harled buildings. *D. L. Brice* was the architect; his too the necessary polite infill. At the S end, KIRKGATE, a wide relaxed rectangular space with Irvine Parish Church (*see* Churches, above) at its S end. The excellent, organically composed group of two-storey houses on the W begins with the Parish Church Halls. To their r., Nos. 45–47 the most formal, harled, with windows in raised frames, and a central entrance with simple columns. The three bays squashed into the centre of the front, allowing a subsidiary, lower, pilastered entrance to the r. To the r., again, No. 49, late C18, harled with a steeply pitched slate roof, and Nos. 51–53 of *c.* 1820, of dressed whin with prominent quoins, while the mid-C19 No. 55 is painted stone. The E side of Kirkgate consists of *I.D.C.* flats of *c.* 1980–2; on the N side, the two-storey hipped OLD MANSE, of 1820 by *Robert Johnstone*, with moulded frames, thin margins and a simple door entablature; late C19 dormers and lifelessly harled. The late C18 harled No. 26 has a single raised skew suggesting that it was initially thatched.

To the E Kirkgate joins HIGH STREET with, on the E, the Town House (*see* Public Buildings, above), and to its S the WAR MEMORIAL of 1921 by *A. F. Balfour Paul*, architect, and *Thomas Beattie*, sculptor. A fanciful re-creation, from contemporary written accounts, of Irvine's medieval Mercat Cross, taken down in 1694. Of Ravelston (Edinburgh) stone; an octagonal base with a moulded cope carries a bronze memorial panel, from which rises the octagonal cross finishing in four heraldic shields beneath the burgh crest, a crown supporting a lion sejant with a sword and sceptre. Turning N, the street begins on the W with the harled, richly red-painted mid-C18 Nos. 57–59, with a big central wall-head dormer and curvy gable. No. 65 is mid-C19, ashlar, with stilted ground-floor openings, a chequerboard frieze and an arcaded corbel table. Also an impressive five-bay ROYAL BANK OF SCOTLAND, dated 1858, by *Peddie & Kinnear*. Italianate, with decorative brackets and spandrels to the doors in the outer bays, and oversailing eaves: 'for chastity of style, richness of design and excellence of work-manship [it] proves quite an ornament' (*Ardrossan & Saltcoats Herald*). The tall, harled and painted Nos. 85–93 are of 1982–6, crisp infill by *I.D.C.*, a simple Neo-vernacular given character by the stepped reveals to the ground-floor doors and windows. Opposite, one painted stone late C18 house, but otherwise mostly the buildings of the former IRVINE & FULLARTON CO-OPERATIVE SOCIETY: late C19 Scots Baronial at the junction with Bank Street with good cast-iron dragon rhones, and a long stone-faced range from 1932 by *William F. Valentine*, its centre bay with a crowstepped gable and flanking towerlets. The monogram below in a good-mannered 1930s idiom.

High Street continues NW of Irvine Cross. This stretch is much less cohesive. Most of the buildings are late C19 or C20 commercial; towards the N end the C20 begins to dominate. However, this is the heart of the early medieval burgh, and many of the façades may disguise much earlier structures. But the visible earliest buildings are mostly Georgian, e.g. the KINGS ARMS (on the W side) with a plastered façade of *c*. 1825, and, on the E side, the late C18 former EGLINTON ARMS, also relatively unaltered, with painted harl, heavy flat door surrounds and early C19 dormers. Other late C18 façades on the E side, such as Nos. 148–150, of two wide plastered bays, and the CROWN INN, with flat-headed dormers and small ground-floor openings. On the W side, the mid-C19 three-storey CLYDESDALE BANK, with a big bracketed head to its first-floor windows. Two early C20 red sandstone buildings of note are (on the W) the former POST OFFICE of 1909–10, with a canted oriel and corbelled pediment, and (on the E) the UNIONIST CLUB of 1913, with a bowed oriel and shaped gable. High Street continues N as EGLINTON STREET. This is a broad street, again mostly late C19 and C20 architecture, with the Burns Museum (*see* Public Buildings, above) and, at the far end, the vernacular early C18 façade of the TURF TAVERN seeming to sink into the ground.

SEAGATE, running NW, once formed the main route to the harbour. Well restored, with judicious infill, *c*. 1993 by *I.D.C.* (*H. Roan Rutherford* and *Karen O'Sullivan*, project architects). The houses on both sides are mostly C19, of one and two storeys, with the obvious exception of Seagate Castle (*see* above), and an occasional earlier house, such as the harled steeply pitched mid-C18 No. 11; its painted whin neighbour to the l. is mid-C19. Beyond the castle, a good crowstepped house of *c*. 1900. From the NW end of Seagate, Castle Street runs E and w, passing the STATUE of Lord Justice Boyle of 1865–7 by *John Steell* (commissioned in 1861). Full-height bronze of Boyle (†1853) in his robes of office, one hand holding a scroll. Equally tall, but very restrained red granite pedestal. To the E three good houses: ACADEMY COURT, of *c*. 1840, with channelled ashlar ground floor and a porch with fluted columns; the dapper CASTLE GRANGE of c. 1820, harled and painted, with its pilastred entrance approached by a straight flight of steps; and ANNFIELD, an L-plan house of c. 1840, again with a channelled ground floor, raised quoins elsewhere and a later balustraded porch with Ionic columns in the re-entrant.

WEST ROAD turns s from Castle Road's w end, on the line of the back lane of the original burgh (there is a corresponding East Road on the other side of High Street). Below and to its w the communal Low Green along the river bank. On the green, a KIOSK AND TOILETS of c. 1988 by *H. Roan Rutherford* for I.D.C. Harled, elliptical, with a hull-like finialled roof, and further s, the INCORPORATED TRADES MONUMENT of 1996. Octagonal, like a well-head, with bronze representations of the arms of the trades, and a fearsome lion, holding his sword and sceptre. In West Road itself a variety of C19 houses, such as the hipped and painted early C19 VIOLETBANK, with its panelled pilasters and neat panelled and pyramid-headed gatepiers, and the T-plan mid-C19 No. 19, facing w to command the view. At the s end of the street is a cluster of churches (St Mary, Mure Church and the Emmanuel Christian Centre; for which, *see* Churches, above) and social housing of c. 1990 by *I.D.C.*, hip-roofed and harled Neo-Georgian, providing a foretaste of the film-set architecture of Linthouse Vennel (*see* below).

BANK STREET, NE from Irvine Cross, is mostly C19 and C20 commercial in character. On the s side the five-bay three-storey LODGE IRVINE ST ANDREW of 1903–4 by *J. & J. Armour*, with canted oriels and a classically detailed entrance with fluted pilasters, a blind semicircular fanlight and bracketed cornice. Still on the s side, Nos. 20 and 22 also by *Armour & Son*, two good red sandstone blocks. The first was built as the Parish Council offices in 1904–5, and is Jacobethan, with a strapwork balustrade, banded quoins, bracketed open segmental door hoods, a central bowed oriel and first-floor windows with decorative heads. Its neighbour is slightly earlier, much plainer, with a castellated canted oriel supported on a bracket. On the N side, mostly early to mid-C19, but also one long, harled and painted mixed-height range of *I.D.C.* infill of c. 1988–90. Glazed façades to the central pend, the busy rear elevation a contrast to the quieter front. Beyond is a wide early C19 house with end pilasters, the Irvine Baptist Church, the former Good Templars' Hall (for these *see* Churches above) and, on the far side of East Road, one early C19 house with a basket-arched head, raised quoins and a carved shield in a recessed panel above the door, heralding a range of plainer two-storey houses. For the villas further out, *see* Other Housing and Villas, below.

EAST ROAD, like West Road, marks the rear lane of the original burgage plots but is much less intact and is now part of the inner ring road around the town centre. Accordingly, Nos. 33–45 at its E end, following the curve of the street SW back to High Street, is very severe stone-faced *I.D.C.* social housing of 1987–9 with few windows to the road but less harsh behind. No. 65, of *c.* 1905, has an attractive Gibbsian entrance surround.

East Road rejoins High Street at the war memorial. S E of here the street quickly becomes TOWNHEAD. On the r. (S W side) is PARTERRE, attractive harled and painted I.D.C. housing of *c.* 1984–6, two-storey, with simple dressed openings, and given character by the recessed curved shield-like corner block. Behind this is the VOLUNTEER ROOMS, a former drill hall of 1906 by *J. K. Hunter* in a pleasing Arts and Crafts style with a round-arched entrance and red sandstone dressings. Still in High Street, the SEVENTH DAY ADVENTIST CHURCH occupies a stone mid-C19 block with Thomsonesque details, while the PORTHEAD TAVERN, opposite, is infill of *c.* 1979 by *James McKelvie.* Harled with small-pane windows and thin dressings. To its r., GLASGOW VENNEL begins. At one time this was the principal entry into the town from Glasgow and it was to this street that Robert Burns came in 1781 to learn the trade of flax-dressing (heckling). He lodged at the house of William Peacock (No. 4), a late C18 exposed stone single-storey cottage cottage with round-headed entrance and flowing fanlight. The other COTTAGES on either side of the cobbled and setted street are mostly early C19, harled and single-storey. On the r. is another C18 cottage, of rubble stone, with simple dressings and a slate roof. Behind this is the HECKLING SHOP, similar in style, but with a thatched roof and stepped skews. On the l., the two-storey house of exposed stone, distinguished by rough-hewn dressings and a late C19 porch, was used as a MEETING HOUSE in 1783–4 by the followers of Elspeth Buchan, a charismatic preacher, until they were driven from the town. All this was restored and conserved by *I.D.C.* 1984–6, and accompanied by the construction of unassuming, well-scaled Neo-vernacular social housing, such as Nos. 8a–8d, behind the Heckling Shop. In BALLOT ROAD, the continuation of Glasgow Vennel, a nine-bay single-storey brick WEAVING SHED survives, of *c.* 1900, most bays with round-headed windows in pairs.

2. Fullarton and the harbour

The heart of Fullarton was destroyed in the late C20 by the W end of the Rivergate Centre (*see* p. 383), other retail units and car parking. The removal of the earlier urban landscape has given the embanked railway an undue prominence, and the relationships between the pre-C20 buildings have been lost in a flurry of roads and roundabouts. N of the shopping centre, strikingly long but dull four-storey block of COUNCIL OFFICES (CUNNINGHAME HOUSE, completed 1976), with end pilotis, and to its N MARRESS HOUSE of 1990 by *P.S.A. (Scotland)*, which has a canted and sloped N W front, almost wholly of reflective glass, the entrances in harled porches with glazed pyramidal heads. The sloping walls were designed to minimize any damage in the event of an accident at the Ardeer explosives works, a safety feature introduced after the explosion at Flixborough (Lincolnshire), 1974. Near to the station a former TOURIST INFORMATION CENTRE of 1993 by *Crichton & Crotch*. Metal-clad throughout, with the gently curved roof supported on thin detached columns. S of the shopping centre an area of housing with four tower blocks, completed in 1966–7, as its key landmarks.

The surviving buildings of the harbourside settlement are concentrated in Montgomerie Street* and Harbour Street to the w, but little of this is encountered in the approach from the station along MONTGOMERIE STREET, which begins with THE BOOKENDS (Nos. 78 and 101) of 1977, by *I.D.C.* (*William Crichton*, project architect), a typically well-imagined and innovative design of two blocks making a formal entrance to the area. Each is of stone blockwork, with asymmetrically placed windows and an E gable projecting forward like the prow of a ship. To the N, in COCHRANE STREET, *I.D.C.* social housing (*H. Roan Rutherford*, project architect) of 1995–6,** a narrow, stepped, curving block of twenty-two houses. Windows with dressed sills, flat projecting window- and doorheads, and big bracketed eaves, give this development ambition and articulation. A prow at one end, acknowledging the Bookends.

Further w along Montgomerie Street, off the S side, LINTHOUSE VENNEL and GOTTRIES ROAD, an extraordinary *I.D.C.* scheme of 1994–6 (*Allan Stewart*, project architect) for flats and houses in an almost infinite variety of Scottish vernacular and classical garbs, although with some inventive detailing. The high-water mark of the Corporation's intention to translate into a modern idiom a range of architectural styles reflecting the growth of the harbourside from the C17. The centrepiece, which faces the open court in front of the Scottish Maritime Museum, has three bays (with porthole windows) and is pedimented, its centre recessed behind Doric columns, with a broad flight of steps. Dramatic sculpted metalwork to the steps, while at the corners of the block the channelled quoins project outrageously, and fail to reach the skews. The terrace along one side of Linthouse Vennel has raised quoins, porthole windows and over-sized scrolled skewputts; elsewhere a crowstepped and corbelled caphouse. The centrepiece of the museum is a rare, iron-framed former MACHINE-ERECTING SHOP of 1872 by *James Spencer*, originally built for the shipbuilders Alexander Stephen & Sons at their Linthouse Yard in Govan (Glasgow). Re-erected here and re-clad in brick in 1990–1 by *Ian Downs*, I.D.C. Chief Architect, and *Lance Smith* of Ironbridge Gorge Museum, Shropshire. The frame is of two tall bays with entrances at the w end. The flanks are twenty-

---

* One of the tenement flats in Montgomerie Street has been restored by the Scottish Maritime Museum to re-create a shipyard worker's house of *c*. 1912.
** Completed by *Wren & Rutherford* after the winding-up of Irvine Development Corporation.

three bays long with side aisles of unequal length. In the steeply
pitched slate roofs are bands of glazing. Inside, the shed is   107
divided into twelve bays by thirty-five tall cast-iron stanchions,
nine weighing 9 tons, the remainder 6 tons each. Iron crane
rails run along the colonnades near roof height; timber roof
trusses and sarking. The museum OFFICES are in a late C19
two-storey brick building in Gottries Road; another part of the
museum lies on the N side of Harbour Street. This has a sharply
pointed harled ENTRANCE and BOATSHED of c. 1990, by *H.
Roan Rutherford*.

HARBOUR STREET has houses on the l. side only, facing the
river. They are mostly two-storey, mixing C19 with complementary late C20 *I.D.C.* infill, such as the initial painted blocks,
in a well-mannered and well-assimilated whole. The fronts are
mostly painted, from a wide palette, with the occasional simple
pilastered doorway, while the wide setted promenade allows
the group to be seen to advantage. Further W, at Nos. 68–108
and in the streets behind, more dramatic *I.D.C.* social housing
(*H. Roan Rutherford*, project architect), of 1994–6: gently
curving terraces, harled and slated, with the occasional gabled
bay. The details similar to the smaller development in Cochrane
Street (*see* above). The MARINA INN is two-storey, of painted
stone, with flat broad skews; early C19. Beyond is the HARBOUR
ARTS CENTRE, built in 1888 as a Seaman's Bethel and converted 1973–4 by *I.D.C.* (*Doug Stonelake* and *Digu Nerukar*,
project architects). Extended and altered internally 2006–7 by
North Ayrshire Council. So now its appearance is largely late
C20, Neo-vernacular, harled and slated, with a steeply pitched
bay to the r. Beyond again, the pedestrian bridge access to the
Magnum (q.v., above) and, opposite, an approachable figurative SCULPTURE, The Carter and his Horse, by *David Annand*,
c. 1996. On the l., the SHIP INN, harled, one two-storey block
of c. 1830, with heavy finialled gables to its half-dormers, with
an earlier single-storey C18 cottage to the l., and the harled and
painted single-storey COURTYARD STUDIOS, stables and cottages of c. 1860, converted in 1993–4. Beyond, a simple C19
cottage was the harbour office, but only a late C19 TRAVEL-
LING CRANE by *William Morgan & Co. Ltd*, of Kilwinning
(removed in 2011) was a clue to the harbour's past importance.

C19 Fullarton survives elsewhere only in WATERSIDE, which
faces Irvine across the river and the Low Green. The houses
are mostly late C19, with some early C20 (e.g. Nos. 74–80). The
first house is the Fullarton Manse (No. 48), of c. 1880, two-
storey, with banded reveals to the round-headed entrance. Of
about the same date, Nos. 54–56 are mostly whin but have
unusual patterned brick front elevations.

BEACH PARK
Beach Drive

Irvine's seafront was never developed in the same manner as
other Ayrshire coastal towns, and was, in fact, occupied by

factories, many involved in the chemical industry, which
created particular problems when the area was restored in
1975–80 by *I.D.C.* (*Digu Nerukar*, project architect), with *Brian
Clouston & Partners*, landscape consultants, to create the
present pleasant area of sandy dunes, green swards and a loch
stretching out to the s of the contemporary Magnum leisure
centre (see Public Buildings, above). w of this on the s bank of
the river, an AUTOMATIC TIDE MARKER, of 1906. A square
harled roofless brick tower, enclosing a wooden signalling
mast, equipped with a series of chains and pulleys, originally
linked to a flotation chamber in the river, by which a series of
balls and ellipses (and, at night, gas lamps) were moved up and
down the mast to indicate to shipping the depth of water at
the harbour entrance. The patent for the machinery was issued
to *Martin Boyd*, Irvine's harbourmaster, in 1904. To the s,
BEACH PARK QUEST, of 1984–6 by *Page & Park*, as an aquarium. Simple gabled shed, with blockwork walls and big bracketed eaves. s again, in the dunes, a BEACH SHELTER of 1987
by *Anthony Vogt* and *Roy Fitzsimmons*; reused red sandstone in
the form of a long-tailed dragon, the seat sheltered within the
loops of the tail.* Spanning the harbour mouth from the N end
of the park is the dramatic BRIDGE OF SCOTTISH INVEN-
TION by *Bennett Associates*, 2000, a shallow curving steel arch
on concrete piers, with a retractable central span to allow boats
to enter the harbour. The names of Scots inventors, and naturalistic designs, are cut through the bridge panels and entrance
gates. It was built to serve THE BIG IDEA exhibition hall on
the other side of the river. This is of 1992–2000 by *BDP* (*Angus
Kerr*, project architect); an ill-fated Millennium project, disused
since 2003. Built on part of the site of Alfred Nobel's dynamite
factory at Stevenston (q.v.), the building was designed to showcase innovation and invention, particularly the work of Nobel
Prize winners and Scots inventors. It burrows into the sand
dunes, dune-shaped itself with only its curved roof (turf-cov-
ered, the largest in Europe, and supported on concrete ribs)
and big glazed front, the effect very similar to Duxford Air
Museum, Cambridgeshire (Foster & Partners, 1987–97). Large
domed exhibition space within.

OTHER HOUSING AND VILLAS

BANK STREET. Nos. 58–60; an imposing, and crisp, two-storey
gabled house of *c.* 1870, with a channelled ashlar ground floor
and panelled end pilasters, on a raised basement. Single flight
of steps with good iron railings, pilastered openings. Nos.
79–81, of *c.* 1880. Red rock-faced sandstone, with paired crowstepped gables, and giant knot-ended string courses. The
brown stone Nos. 87–89, of *c.* 1885, have a hipped bracketed
porch with station-like fretwork, while Nos. 99–101 are harled

---

**Jill Malvenan's jewel-like helical BEACH PARK MAINTENANCE DEPOT, of
1981–2, for I.D.C, was demolished in 2001.

above red sandstone, with paired gables, and porthole windows with etiolated keystones; of *c.* 1900, probably by *Thomas Smellie*. Finally, Nos. 110–112 are late C19, a bold pair with sculpted bargeboards and sunrise-like applied timbering in the gables, and Glasgow Style plaques above the doors, the shouldered heads of which rise from delicate carved corbels.

BURNS STREET. Fine, and unprissily restored, 'neat and tidy' range of early C19 two-storey houses on the E, some harled, others painted, some with dormers, others not; the best the first, Nos. 4–6, taller than the others, harled, with big skews. On the W mostly C19 villas, such as No. 7, of *c.* 1860, with delicate strapwork-like bargeboards.

IVYBANK, Low Green. Harled three-storey two-bay villa of *c.* 1820, with a hipped roof, single-storey hipped wings, and a flight of steps between low curving harled walls.

KIDSNEUK COTTAGE, Kidsneuk Gardens. Early C19 in appearance, but at its core a *cottage orné* built for Lady Susannah Montgomerie (†1780) and modelled on Marie Antoinette's Hameau. Built of large whin, with many gables and steeply pitched roofs, which were thatched until the 1920s, when it was altered to form a golf clubhouse. The timber porch and canted entrance bay on the return elevation date from these alterations.

KILWINNING ROAD. The largest concentration of C19 villas, and a pleasing group, with a spaciously laid out road and, generally, large feus. HEATHFIELD, the first on the W, is perhaps the grandest, undoubtedly the severest. Classical, of *c.* 1810, with a projecting pedimented centre bay, approached by a flight of steps with iron rails. Single-storey wings, and an extension of 1986–7 by *I.D.C.* (*H. Roan Rutherford*, project architect): a single-storey courtyard, well suiting its use as sheltered housing. On the E side, the most noteworthy are the gabled and painted No. 4, of *c.* 1860, and the beautifully presented No. 12, of *c.* 1800, in an olive-green colourwash with contrasting white dressings; hipped, with a pilastered doorway, single-storey flanking wings and panelled gatepiers. Also on the E, BURN-SIDE, No. 24, dated 1863, with big gables, an Italianate tower, and large C20 additions, and the heavily handled Arts and Crafts of No. 32, *c.* 1910. Formerly on the W side, Williamfield (1821, remodelled *c.* 1872–6 in a French Gothic manner, dem. 1982): its two LODGES, of the 1870s, are, with their hipped roofs, ball finials, semicircular pediments and tall stacks, little gems.

MAYFLOWER, No. 11 Annick Road. A conventional late C19 stone cottage given character by a robustly carved sculpture of two cherubim holding a shield below an odd Glasgow Style-like mask.

SOUTH NEWMOOR INDUSTRIAL ESTATE
Annick Road

1976–8 by *I.D.C.* (*David Hutchison* and *Donald Ritchie*, project architects). One of the Corporation's first industrial estates, and a template for many others locally (e.g. North Newmoor, Oldhall West) and nationally, with flexible units in simple shells. Single-storey, harled with timber fascias and sloping roofs; the individual entrances marked by harled walls and strong graphics. They are laid out in parallel rows, with broad access roads and softening landscaping.

KELBURN CASTLE

1.5 km. NNE of Fairlie

51   Kelburn nestles into the hillside above the narrow coastal plain facing the Firth of Clyde and the island of Cumbrae. It has been held by the Boyles since the C13 at least; David Boyle, a leading proponent of the Act of Union, was created Earl of Glasgow in 1703.

The four main phases of its development are easily detectable, but much more research is needed to uncover its precise evolution. Built on high ground, overlooking the deep gorge carved by the Kel Burn, is the TOWER, which is constructed in two parts and was originally approached from the SW. The E part is the original small tower, to which a charter refers in 1556. Most probably it is of c. 1500 and was presumably fortified in some fashion. If it was attached to other buildings then there is no trace of them now. Its radical enlargement and remodelling in the late C16 into a Z-plan form of tower was by John Boyle and his wife Marion Craufurd, whose fragmentary initials appear over the window, formerly the main entrance, on the SE elevation. This has an unusual lintel of a moulded double arch, and a W jamb comprising one angle-rolled arris joining a hollow moulding with pointed base stop. A C19 antiquary also recorded the date 1581 and this is replicated on the panel inserted in 1890 between the first-floor windows, which commemorates repairs made by the 7th Earl of Glasgow. At the SW angle the huge conical-roofed stair-tower, the most prominent expression of the Z-plan. Its opposing and lower tower on the NE angle is now entirely engulfed at the lower levels by later additions. Corbelled turrets at the NW and SE angles, similarly roofed, complete the lively roofscape. Flimsy weathervanes have replaced the 'ancient metallic terminations' extolled by Billings as the only old examples he had seen. Three attic windows at the W end of the SE elevation break the eaves, their plain gablet heads apparently rebuilt. On the NW elevation, to the E of the large stepped wall-head chimneystack, is a small original attic window, but it is only seen looking towards the N front from a distance. The gables are crow-stepped, an alteration to the SW one made to accommodate an additional chimney flue in the later C19. On this gable, at first-floor level, a corbelled rectangular garderobe projection. Above this, to the r. of the corbelled turret, a simple waterspout. At

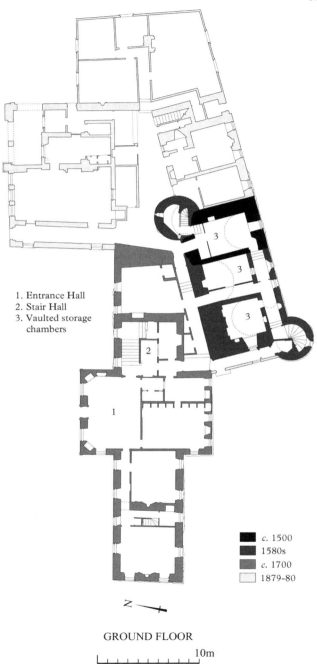

1. Entrance Hall
2. Stair Hall
3. Vaulted storage
   chambers

c. 1500
1580s
c. 1700
1879–80

N

GROUND FLOOR

10m

Kelburn Castle.
Ground Floor Plan

the time of writing, the tower is dramatically animated by colourful murals of 2008 by Brazilian graffiti artists: *Os Gemeos* (*The Twins*), *Nina* and *Nunca*, the subjects inspired by Kelburn's history. The planned removal of its canvas, the ubiquitous lifeless cement render, will offer an opportunity to test some current assumptions about the tower's history.

The spacious N COURTYARD was laid out by the 1st Earl of Glasgow to provide a grand setting for his two-storey N RANGE, which conceals all but the roof of the earlier tower. At first glance this range appears to be all of a piece, but the w end, furthest from the tower, seems to have existed by 1692, when *Thomas Caldwell*, mason of Belltrees, contracted with David Boyle '. . . to build me ane house sufficient; to the end of the east end of the new house alroaddy builded of the same wideness, the same length and same thickness of wall'. This piecemeal development is evident from the fabric, e.g. the difference in the crowstepped gabled bays at either end. Yet to create this symmetrical appearance Caldwell's instructions record that he needed to demolish 'the house that [is] adjoining to my old house and make use of the stones as they will serve'. From this it is apparent that there was already an extension to the tower before any work began on the new range, and to this may have related the angled gable that links to the tower at the E. The likely date for this is *c.* 1672 when John Boyle inherited. He held a number of public positions, including Crown Commissioner and M.P. for Ayrshire and Bute, and so may have begun remodelling the tower. The windows were sashed and glazed in 1701 and an interesting feature is that despite their thick astragals the lower parts probably opened like casements (since altered), as can still be seen on the stair windows. The imposing double-gabled centrepiece, which breaks forward on both the N and S fronts of this range, is emphasized in importance by panelled gable-head stacks and huge sash windows. Yet it seems to have been an afterthought, for the contract of 1692 makes no mention of a door or a projection of this kind. Most likely it relates to the layout of the courtyard and the approach avenue with its tall ball-finialled gatepiers. Caldwell received payments until 1703 and the change of plan may have been made *c.* 1700, the date embossed on a decorative lead panel in the pediment of the doorpiece. Above is a framed panel in which is set the family crest, a double-headed eagle and the motto 'dominus providebit' ('The Lord will provide') strung out as a lead banner. Above again is a carved stone which looks like a lintel (perhaps displaced from an earlier door) with two sets of initials for David Boyle and his first wife Margaret Lindsey (married in 1687), and a second set with his initials and those of his second wife Lady Jean Mure, whom he married in 1699. She was the daughter and heiress of William Mure of Rowallan. All this elaboration is framed by an ornamental arrangement of lead rainwater pipes draining the valley between the two gables, a functional necessity turned into an artistic virtue with decorative straps with thistles and roses all pointing to the earl's part in achieving the Act of Union. At the point of division is a larger strap dated 1722, underlining the drawn-out development of this range. The W gable, because of the fall in the land, has a full-height basement below the W rooms, and between the first-floor windows is an unframed stone panel with the double-headed eagle, the motto and the earl's coronet (i.e. after 1703 but it was re-set here after 1869). The S elevation reflects the W part of the N elevation, but the advanced bays have small windows in the ground floor and no door. The E end is placed uncomfortably close to the tower and has a triangular infill linking the two.

The 1st Earl retreated from public office in 1714, under suspicion of sympathizing with the Jacobites, and reined in any further ambitions he may have had for his house. The final addition was completed c. 1885 with the unassuming NE WING; although large it does not impinge greatly on the c. 1700 arrangement and was built to provide a new kitchen, dining room and billiard room for a tenant, Alexander Crum, M.P. for Renfrewshire. The design is possibly by *William Little* who had recast the E front of Crawford Priory (Fife) for the 6th Earl. Large corbelled rectangular oriel in the centre of the first floor lighting the dining room.

The INTERIOR is predominantly of the time of the changes made after c. 1690 but has a Baroque swagger only hinted at externally. Like the exterior it was only slowly completed; *William Caldwell* (presumably the son) was providing hewn stones for chimneypieces in 1715. The present form of the ENTRANCE HALL in the N range was created in 1870 by uniting the former hall with an ante-room to its W. Both parts have angle chimneypieces. The low ceiling emphasizes the grandeur of the panelled STAIR HALL, which fills the whole width of the two bays to the E of the hall and is entered through an arched doorway with panelled pilasters and moulded keystone. Fashionable open-well stair with bulbous turned balusters and a heavy moulded rail. Coved ceiling, above a modillion cornice rising into the attic storey. In the centre of the landing a wide pedimented lugged doorway (now blocked) is the start of a processional route that begins with the DRAWING ROOM (although the entrance is now via the triangular lobby created between the N range and the tower house). This room was originally the Great Dining Room, a monumental apartment and the most richly decorated in the house. It is approx 11.5 m. by 6.7 m., extending into the projections on the N and S front and lit by large multi-paned sash windows. The E and W doors and the chimneypieces set between windows at either end of the room are framed by giant Corinthian pilasters with entablature blocks, shadowed in the detailing of the cove above the modillion cornice. Elaborate frieze of scrolling acanthus leaves intertwined with thistles and roses, another allusion to the 1st Earl's support for the Act of Union. Originally both fireplaces had simple bolection-moulded surrounds. The N chimneypiece was introduced by the 7th Earl *c.* 1890 and is a remarkable design of *c.* 1700 with an arch at the centre over a Roman emperor's bust set against a background of oak and acanthus leaves, and framed by engaged twisted Ionic columns (cf. the Bastille Room, *see* below). Gervase Jackson-Stops compared it to the work of Daniel Marot but its provenance is unknown. Above, a large pedimented frame with panelled sides enclosing a portrait of the 1st Earl's father. The walls have panelled frames, on which portraits were originally displayed. Its present decoration with gilded stars on the panels and arabesque decoration to the doors is attributed to *Thomas Bonnar* who also worked for the 6th Earl at Crawford Priory. To the W the sequence continues with other panelled rooms, smaller in scale with lower ceilings. The LIBRARY, originally the Withdrawing Room, has a bolection-moulded chimneypiece, again framed by giant Corinthian columns with a pulvinated frieze above. Bolection-moulded wall panels. In the panel above the chimneypiece a delightfully naïve landscape painting of the late 1760s, showing that, apart from the NE wing, the house remains much the same. The large swan-neck-pedimented bookcases are thought to come from Shewalton, a house near Irvine, which was built by the 1st Earl's younger brother. It was sold by David Boyle, who became 7th Earl in 1890 and used the proceeds to rescue Kelburn. Beyond this room is a LOBBY for a stair from the private rooms below and finally at the W end the TAPESTRY ROOM, formerly the State Bedroom, with the same pattern of pulvinated frieze, enriched cornice and Corinthian pilasters framing the chimney-breast. The lugged chimneypiece, with egg-and-dart surround, has an Edwardian mantelshelf. The larger wall panels in this room are filled with flower and leaf designs in a scrolled pattern. Below are two rooms, reached from the Entrance Hall by an inserted passage and separated by the staircase to the first floor. The first room is again panelled with Corinthian pilasters but the W room was remodelled in the C19.

The ground-floor rooms of the tower are vaulted. At the first floor, adjacent to the stair-tower at the SW angle is the SOUTH ROOM. In the late C17 it was fully panelled with a cushion frieze, modillion cornice and Corinthian pilasters in a more rustic Baroque manner than the rooms in the N range. The chimneypiece has panels with decorative scalloped beading and a deep entablature detailed as the main cornice, breaking forward over the pilasters and at the centre. Bolection-moulded panel above with similar scalloped beading. In the NE angle is a modest door leading to the secondary stair-turret linking the upper floors. On the very thick E wall a large double door with more Corinthian pilasters and a bold bolection-moulded panel above. The position of this communicating door leaves no doubt that this room and the adjoining Bastille Room were used as the Great Chamber and Withdrawing Room in the late C16 and only became bedrooms sometime later. In fact, the BASTILLE ROOM occupies the hall area of the earliest tower.

It too has late C17 panelling but less elaborate than the South Room. In the SW corner, however, is an extraordinary chimneypiece and overmantel framed by paired naïve Salomonic pilasters, Doric below, Ionic above (the Raphael cartoons used by the Mortlake tapestry weavers, and known from contemporary engravings, have been suggested as the source). At the NE is a closet, occupying part of a former chimney flue. A door on the N wall leads to the passage with a mural stair to the ground floor and a newel to the upper floors. More panelled rooms in the floors above with bolection-moulded chimneypieces. On the third floor the CHARTER ROOM at the W end has panelling continuing onto the deeply coved ceiling. The roof timbers are late C16, halved and pegged with ashlar pieces and trimmed for dormers. In the Victorian wing, the long DINING ROOM has a chimneypiece with mirrored panels in the frieze and dado panelling with *Morris & Co.* acanthus-pattern wallpaper above. Simple moulded cornice, and ceiling divided into flat panels with disc mouldings in the borders. Above is the BILLIARD ROOM, detailed as the Dining Room, but with domed top lights. Willow-leaf-pattern wallpaper, also by *Morris & Co.*

Below the castle to the SW, a fine obelisk SUNDIAL, dated 1707, set diagonally on a base and three steps, the shaft divided into five with a variety of hollowed designs with the 1st Earl's coronet and initials for him and his wife, Jean Mure. Conventional faceted octagon with more hollowings and some metal gnomons, above an obelisk with six tiers of metal gnomons and a delicate wrought-iron pennon including the earl's initials and crowning thistle. The original finials on the conical roofs of the tower were similar. Second SUNDIAL of *c.* 1707 in the garden on a pedestal, the shaft set diagonally but with irregular hollowings. Also the earl's coronet and initials. Above the octagon a ball finial sits on a shaped obelisk and probably replaces an obelisk with gnomon. A series of garden compartments to the W of the castle; the Plaisance, with walls on three sides created after 1740 by the 3rd Earl, entered down steps from the W side of the entrance court with some excellent C18 wrought-iron gates. Below the castle and close to the burn the ICE HOUSE. Egg-shaped (now open at the top), and entered by steps leading down from the side.

– MONUMENT. Set into the steep valley side E of the castle. *p. 398* To the 3rd Earl (†1775), erected by his widow in 1776 at a cost of £300. By *Robert Adam*, although not executed exactly to his design. An aedicule enclosing an alcove and set into a truncated and flattened pyramid with a disc above and the family arms, motto and supporters. Within the niche a marble statue of a sorrowing figure leaning on an urn. This may be the urn known to have been carved for the Earl of Glasgow by *Giuseppe Ceracchi c.* 1774–9. Ceracchi carried out work for Adam at this time. Below, a fulsome epitaph.

THE COUNTRY CENTRE. Home Farm of *c.* 1760, converted 1979–80. Single-storey, rubble-walled buildings grouped in an

Kelburn Castle, Earl of Glasgow's Monument.
Plan and elevation, by Robert Adam, 1775

informal U. At the W a five-bay piend-roofed range, the reception, with arched and keystoned windows and doors. A pedimented loft opening is reached by a flight of stone steps on
the courtyard side. Entrances to the courtyard at either end
with ball-finalled, rusticated piers against the flanking end
gables of the long side buildings extending E. These gables with
segmental-arched openings. Irregular openings stepped up the
sloping courtyard ranges still with some internal fittings. – The
COTTAGES and former CARTSHED to the NE of the castle are
mid-C18 with late C19 additions. LODGE AND GATEPIERS.
c. 1885, when the coast road was realigned. – KELBURNFOOT.
Mid-C19 and originally two lodges linked in 1900. Pilastered
and pedimented outer bays.

KENNOX HOUSE

3.5 km. wsw of Stewarton

An agreeable small country house, above a curve in the Water of Glazert. The earliest part was built *c.* 1720 for James Somerville and named after his Lanarkshire property. It has its front to the w, is of six bays with first floor windows enlarged, probably *c.* 1820, and an advanced centrepiece with bold rusticated quoins and steeply pointed gable appearing as an embryo open pediment. It was originally thatched. The single window in the ground floor was probably the original entrance but the surrounding ground was raised to protect against flooding when the new entrance range to the s was added in 1820. This is raised on a high plinth but is otherwise a standard composition of three bays and two storeys with a simply pilastered and pedimented doorcase and an elementary Venetian window.

The 1720s house now provides the link between the entrance range and a N wing of 1762, the latter greatly altered, and the same is true of the rear of the early c18 house, where there is a tall, narrow gabled wing with a small well stair and a new entrance, possibly of 1831. A small projection suggests this was the position of a c17 turnpike stair, and in the tall window of the new wing are incorporated some panes scratched with a romantic verse, signed Will Somerville 1740. The space between this wing and the 1820s range was filled by *James A. Morris* in 1911, with a pyramid-roofed tower holding a large water tank. The interior bears the stamp of generations of change, the most recent 2001–8 by *Patrick Lorimer* of *ARP Lorimer & Associates*. Decorative cornice in the entrance hall with a frieze of rosettes and triglyphs. Big, plain 1820 well stair, like that at Monkcastle House.

KILBIRNIE

Large predominantly industrial village at the head of the Garnock valley; separated from the central belt only by the Renfrewshire hills, but with a remote, sequestered feel. It is a historic parochial centre, whose church belonged to Kilwinning Abbey until the Reformation. The surrounding agricultural land is largely s-facing, and good for cattle raising; this was one of the areas in which the Ayrshire dairy cow was developed. The c19 brought industrialization, firstly in the form of cotton thread and net manufacture (Kilbirnie was at one time Scotland's major manufacturer of fishing and trawling nets), and subsequently the Glengarnock Iron and Steel Works (*see* Glengarnock), but new transport links by road and rail between Ayrshire and Glasgow avoided the hills, and left Kilbirnie sidelined. Its fortunes subsequently rose and fell with the steel works, which closed in 1986. Efforts to revitalize the village since must be applauded; the decision to locate a supermarket adjacent to the moribund centre is to be regretted.

CHURCHES

KILBIRNIE AULD KIRK,* Dalry Road. A fascinating illustration
of how a medieval parish church might be enlarged and
adapted to meet changed needs after the Reformation. Of the
rectangular medieval church (dedicated to St Brendan), which
was appropriated to Kilwinning Abbey at a date between 1410
and 1430, there is the E wall (originally blank, but now pierced
by windows) which has a chamfered base course and a chamfered intake at the base of the gable; such details point to a
date no earlier than the C15. The simple low W tower of roughly
squared rubble is presumed to date from after 1470 since it
has the carved arms of Crawford and Barclay, relating to
Malcolm Crawford and his wife, Marjory, heiress of John
Barclay of Kilbirnie. It has small rectangular windows, a chamfered intake on the W face at one level and a second chamfered
intake around three faces at a higher level. The saddleback roof
and the arched W bellcote with a pyramidal cap date from a
major restoration in 1854–5 by *Robert Snodgrass*.

The church was expanded to a T-plan by adding lairds' aisles
N and S of the E end. The S aisle of 1597, for Sir James Cunninghame of Glengarnock, is of squared ashlar to the lower
walls and roughly squared rubble to the crowstepped gable. It
has a rectangular S window with a mullion and transom and a
heraldic tablet above, all framed by multiple roll mouldings.**
A string of similar profile continues the line of the transom
across the base of the gable. The N aisle, built for Sir John
Crawford, is dated 1642, and has a loft above a burial vault.
The walls of squared rubble are capped by a crowstepped
gable. A Y-traceried window with raised margins lights the loft
level, with a rectangular window to the vault. An E dormer
window has a semicircular pediment.

Much of the S wall was rebuilt in 1854–5, incorporating two
two-light windows, and a small porch was added to the E gable.
The gabled organ chamber, W of the Glengarnock Aisle, was
added by *Charles S. S. Johnston* in 1910 (date on rainwater
hopper). On the N side, W of the Crawford Aisle, is a large aisle
of roughly tooled ashlar, added in 1903–6 by *Johnston*, which
contains the entrance and gallery. The entrance vestibule is
topped by a round-pedimented dormer adjacent to the Crawford Aisle, and there is a round conically roofed tower with a
tangentially set porch at its base at the aisle's NW corner.
Between vestibule and turret is a crowstepped gabled section
with a tripartite echelon window to the gallery and two pairs
of windows below. The multiple rolled mouldings and other
details take their lead from those of the Glengarnock Aisle.

---

* This entry has been contributed by Richard Fawcett.
** These are identical to mouldings of 1597–9 at Newark Castle (Renfrewshire). It
has recently been argued by A. Mackechnie (*Architectural History*, 2009) that they
may be the work of *Sir David Cunningham* of Robertland, master of works from
1602, whose mother was a Cunningham of Glengarnock.

The interior is dominated – perhaps almost overwhelmed – by its FURNISHINGS and in particular by the CRAWFORD LOFT, set in front of the entrance to the Crawford Aisle. This is the most ambitious laird's loft known to have been constructed in Scotland, and must have been inserted between 1703, when the Viscountcy of Garnock was created, and 1708, when the 1st Viscount died. It is an extraordinary confection in which there is a highly creative interplay between the levels and planes. It is tripartite and of two levels, with straight side sections and a central polygonally bowed projection below a canopy that projects yet further and is supported by slender full-height Corinthian columns on plinths. The upper level is carried by a pair of columns (one in front of the other) at the front of the bow, and by another at the w angle; at the angles of the canopy are short Corinthian columns. Behind the two tiers of seats at the front of the loft is a screen of four columns demarcating an area given over to two rows of pews; at the back, behind fretted panelling, is the entrance passage and a closet. The whole structure has carved decoration of the utmost richness, with blind arcading along the front of the loft that frames an extraordinary display of heraldry proclaiming the ancestry and connections of the viscount; a full entablature with a bracketed cornice to the canopy has further heraldic display. A painting of Moses the Lawgiver is on the pier at the w end of the loft. In 1905 the loft was connected to a gallery within the new N aisle, with a decoratively carved panelled front, and also to an existing w gallery. Over the E end of the church is an C18 boarded ceiling with a flat centre, coved sides and modillioned cornices. The w end and N aisle are covered by an open timber roof of 1903 with collar-beams and queen-posts decorated with pendants, and there are tree-like group-ings of timbers at the junctions of the main part of the church and the N aisle.

– PULPIT, s wall, between the Glengarnock Aisle and organ chamber. A composite structure: late C17 pine polygonal base with enriched framing to panelling, and desk supported by volutes terminating in heads; backboard with Ionic pilasters. Arms of Crawford impaling Lindsay on cornice; canted canopy decorated with re-set C17 carved oak elements including angel, putti, olive-bearing doves, rose and thistle and foliage. Wrought-iron bracket for a pewter BAPTISMAL BASIN. – COMMUNION TABLE, on a platform angled to face into both nave and N aisle. Early C20, with arcaded front, Corinthian colonettes and bracketed cornice. – LADYLAND PEW, resited from N to E wall, a canopied seat put together from C17 and C18 elements: min-iature balustrade along front of pew enclosure; raised and fielded panelled back with armorial panel flanked by volutes and dated 1671; canopy with pediment of two volutes with anthemion finial.

STAINED GLASS. E windows, heraldry, *James Ballantine II*, 1926; war memorial window, 1948, designed by *Sydney Holmes* and made by *Guthrie & Wells*. – Glengarnock Aisle, Girl Guides window, Celtic cross, *Guthrie & Wells*, 1958; S window, foliate designs, *c.* 1892. – W window *Gordon Webster*, 1959. – N wall, children kneeling before descending holy spirit, *Arthur Spiers*, 1990. – MEMORIALS. S wall. Re-set stone plaque of 1594 with relief inscription, to Thomas Crawford of Jordanhill and Janet Ker, whose mausoleum is in the churchyard. – E wall, War Memorial, *James Houston*, 1922, oak: an angel holding a wreath and with outspread wings supporting a plaque. – W wall. James Allan. Oak plaque, 1910 by *Stephen Adam* and *Alfred A. Webster*; portrait medallion by *Olsen*. – In vault of Crawford Aisle a number of late medieval cross-slabs. – BELL. *John Milne* of Edinburgh, 1753.

S of the church the CRAWFORD MAUSOLEUM, dated 1594. Small, rectangular and ashlar-built, with dogtooth decoration to the moulded angles and to the window opening in the E wall; a flat cornice with three tiers of miniature corbelling runs around the wall-head. It contains the effigies of Thomas Crawford of Jordanhill and Janet Ker of Kersland. S of the tower a C17 TABLE TOMB with monstrous sheep shears; other memorials include some of the C18, but are mainly of the C19, including several obelisks, and some cast-iron enclosures. Many memorials have collapsed.

ST BRIGID (R.C.), Newton Street. 1862, simple gabled Gothic. E porch extended to create a baptistery in 1961–2 by *James Houston*. Presbytery, also 1862, to the l.; it has a finialled gable and prominent moulded window heads.

ST COLUMBA, Glasgow Street. Former Free Church of 1844, a tall gabled rectangle with pointed windows, enlarged 1902–3 by *John McClelland* who added the W porch and graceful three-stage rectangular bell-tower, with tall windows in the second stage, and a bellcote like a medieval canopy tomb, with shallow segmental heads to the openings, urn finials, ridge tiles and bell-cast gables. The interior has galleries with remarkable and unusual decorative plaster fronts: empty escutcheons with swirling foliage swags. Gothic dark wood ORGAN CASE and PULPIT, with nicely turned balusters to both stairs; all of 1902–3. Immediately opposite is the former CHURCH HALL, a Free Church of 1887–9 by *Alexander Petrie*. Red sandstone, rather lumpen Gothic, with a stepped three-light E window, buttresses and flanking hipped stair-towers. Divided horizontally to form two halls, *c.* 1975: in the upper hall, two STAINED-GLASS windows. In the E gable, a stepped three-light Blessed are the Pure in Heart, by *Stephen Adam*, dated 1906: a glorious display of Adam's rich hues. In the W gable, Jesus with Mary and Martha, of 1878 by *W. & J. J. Kier*, rather less dramatic.

SALVATION ARMY CITADEL, Newton Street. 1920–1, brick with concrete window frames. The main elevation has a low porch, and a stepped pediment, reminiscent of contemporary cinemas.

PUBLIC BUILDINGS

BRIDGEND COMMUNITY CENTRE, Bridgend. Former school of 1848, much enlarged in 1895; gabled and bellcoted front and two gabled bays with finials on the E elevation. Extensive rear wing of 1935–6 by *William Reid*, County Architect. Harled additions of *c*. 1978 by *Strathclyde Regional Council* with wooden fascias.

GARNOCK POOL, Bathville Road. 1967–9 by *James Houston & Son*. Brick, with a tall sheet-metal upper section, which slopes gently from one end to the other; monopitch ancillary buildings in red brick.

WALKER MEMORIAL HALL, Main Street. 1914–16 by *Robert J. Walker* of Glasgow. Bland grey stone Renaissance front but very different harled rear elevation to the river which rises to three towering storeys, with its middle storey jettied out on decorative cast-iron brackets and with one oddly continental corbelled bay with small windows and a hipped roof, almost like a watch house. Prominent roof ventilator. The exceptional interiors include the theatre-like main hall, with its curving plaster-fronted balcony, pilastered walls and proscenium arch, all decorated with wreaths. The first-floor Council Chamber has a wooden memorial overmantel and over-sized ceiling rosette, and the main stair attractive wrought-iron balustrades. In front, a stone STATUE of Hygeia by *D. W. Stevenson*, 1894. In flowing robes, the goddess steadies an overturned jar; it rests on a snake-entwined pedestal. On the plinth a bronze bust of Dr William Walker (†1885).

WAR MEMORIAL, Holmhead. 1922, by *James Houston*. The eye-catching entrance into the public park, with a tall opening with a shallow segmental head; simple deep entablature with a bold inscription and shrouded urn finials. Lower flanking wings, and bronze memorial panels.

DESCRIPTION

The centre is the junction at BRIDGEND, now little more than a roundabout, which is dominated by RADIO CITY, the dramatic former Radio Cinema of 1937–8 by *James Houston*. Impressively restored 1998–2003 by *Paddy Cronin* as a community leisure centre, its exterior is conventional Art Deco, flat and angular with the corners stepped back, but recessed within the centre and soaring high above it, an open steel pylon culminating in an octagonal lantern. Painted decoration under the eaves and at the corners impressively shiny streamlined chrome ornamental signage with flagpoles and radiating neon lightning flashes. Running S is the narrow MAIN STREET, announced on the E by the former KNOX INSTITUTE, of 1892 by *Robert Snodgrass*. Three-storey, Free Renaissance, with a corbelled corner turret, balustrade parapet, and a Venetian window on both first-floor elevations. Beyond, a pleasing, if rather neglected run of early C19 buildings, all two-storey, distinguished by wall-head pedimented stacks; they are mostly painted ashlar, with polished dressings, often with pilastered shopfronts, and octagonal stacks. Opposite a low, sleek red sandstone POST OFFICE of 1928, and former CLYDESDALE BANK, 1920–1 by *Baird & Thomson*. It is hardly cutting-edge. Main Street becomes

118

NEWTON STREET; sandwiched between the Salvation Army Citadel and St Brigid R.C. church (*see* Churches, above), is the LODGE ROYAL BLUES No. 399, of 1903–4 by *John McClelland*. Gabled, a round-headed window rising from a richly decorated semicircular bracket into the pediment. Beneath a broken pediment, the entrance has three detached columns: one Ionic, one Doric, one Corinthian!

From Bridgend, SCHOOL WYND runs N, before turning sharply to the W. On the N side, No. 2: this is early C19, harled, of three bays with a broad central pediment. A curved bay to the r., central framed entrance with cavetto reveals, and a pilastered window above. Restored 1939 by *James Houston* as a house and office for himself. School Wynd becomes COCHRANE STREET, with some interesting, shield-fronted harled houses of 1999–2000 by *North Ayrshire Council*, infilling gaps on both sides of the road.

In GARNOCK STREET, running SE from Bridgend, the main monument is the STONEYHOLM MILLS of W. & J. Knox Ltd, who acquired Kilbirnie Cotton Mills in 1864 and converted them to thread and net manufacture. Dominating the S elevation of the complex is the Cotton Mill, which was rebuilt in 1831 by George Allan after a fire. It is of five storeys and eight bays; to its r. a lower hip-roofed engine house is dated 1870; to its l., and projecting forward, a gabled block, probably of *c.* 1864–70, also of five storeys. This forms the S portion of the W elevation, and a lower gabled block connects it to a broadly U-plan late C19 block, of three storeys, nine bays in length, with the central bays advanced and pedimented: the most 'architectural' part of the complex. Eight-bay return elevations. Free-standing block of 1885, of three storeys and fourteen bays, to the r. of the engine house, and tall gatepiers with bracketed heads at the NW (blocked) entrance.

NEWHOUSE FARM, opposite the Auld Kirk, an attractive early C19 farm, stone, with a central two-storey block, and single-storey flanking wings; that to the l. is C20, that to the r., with its gable skew, and upper windows tucked under the eaves, may be late C18.

GARDEN VILLAGE, 1.25 km. S of the centre, S of Dalry Road. Laid out on Garden Suburb principles in 1916–17, to plans of *J. Walker Smith* for the Local Government Board of Scotland, to provide accommodation for workers at Glengarnock Steel Works. A central spine road (Central Avenue) and two subsidiary roads, running parallel (Western Crescent; Eastern Crescent). 250 houses, in pairs and terraces of six; they are harled and slated, with compact gardens. The pairs often have prettily shaped dormerheads, while the terrace ends have big gables rising from deep hipped roofs which drop down to first-floor level. Although much altered, their character can still be appreciated.

OLD PLACE OF KILBIRNIE, 1 km. W. Situated on high ground in a bend of the Paduff Burn. The ivy-shrouded ruin comprises

a tower house of the Barclays, thought to have been built
c. 1500, but the variation in the masonry with some neatly
coursed work, particularly on the NW, the simple corbelling
for the lost parapet, and the lack of bartizans suggest that an
earlier building may have dictated the form. John Barclay died
in 1470 and his daughter, married to Malcolm Craufurd,
inherited his property. In 1499 a charter confirmed the lands
of Kilbirnie passing from Marjorie Barklay to her son but with
no mention of a tower. About 1627 John Craufurd made the
substantial addition to the NE in a fashionable domestic
manner; of this little more than a storey remains. He was probably responsible for creating the long avenue and the large
walled courtyard of which traces remain. A disastrous fire in
1757 rendered the building uninhabitable since when it has
continued to decay.

The plain, rectangular tower, 12.8 m. by 9.75 m. and four
storeys high, stands to the wall-head except at the N angle
where the turnpike stair, constructed within the thickness of
the wall, has completely collapsed. It is partly rubble-built but
with substantial areas of squared and coursed masonry, and
wall thicknesses vary from 2.2 m. to 2.5 m. The ground floor
and hall above were originally vaulted, but both vaults have
fallen. Two arrowslits are visible in the vaulted ground floor
and the raised ground level has concealed a third. A shallow
arch visible on the exterior of the NW wall may have given
ground-level access. The hall was lit by windows on the SW
and SE walls, while on the NE wall an opening now hidden
beneath ivy may have been the first-floor entrance. Inside, the
hall appears to have been over 6.4 m. high and not to have had
an entresol. The remains of the substantial chimneypiece on
the SW wall survive, comprising the banded mouldings for the
bases and capitals of the shafts with a floral pattern carved on
the chamfer; the lintel has fallen. Within the NW wall a passage
leads from the stair to a hatch opening to a small dungeon
below; above the passage was a garderobe. The plan resembles,
on a smaller scale, that of Dean Castle, Kilmarnock (q.v.).

The C17 addition butted up to the E angle was approximately
22.5 m. by 7.6 m. and three storeys with an attic. A full-height,
well-lit stair-turret is visible at the W angle and from it an
entrance was formed into the hall (and presumably to the
floors above). The long SE-facing elevation of the wing had
boldly corbelled angle turrets rising from first-floor level, the
corbelling at the S angle still visible; at the centre is a projecting
porch containing the wide doorway, a rare survival of a type
found also at Stobhall (Perth & Kinross). The wide mouldings
are preserved but the consoled lintel (possibly supporting a
balcony) has gone and all that remains is the big relieving arch
behind. It opens onto a passage providing a through link from
a big arched entrance facing the N courtyard to the S. MacGibbon and Ross show the elevation surviving to the wall-head
and it is clear from their illustration that the addition was in
smart Scots Renaissance manner. On its NW elevation there is

a doorpiece with a roll-moulded surround set in a quarter-round moulded frame and simple Jacobean-style pilasters with a drop moulding below the moulded capital. A big, flat relieving arch above suggests that there may have been a carved inset panel. To its l. a window and an inset moulded stone with a circular hole, more like a drain than a shot-hole. The door led to a passage and r. to the stair-turret giving access to the old hall and the new drawing room. This smart C17 range is associated with extensive walled enclosures, the garden layout and a wide tree-lined avenue that is now barely detectable.

MOORPARK HOUSE, 1 km. NW. Now a hotel. A self-confident Italianate villa of urban character, despite its rural setting, built in 1860 for William Knox, owner of the local linen thread mills. On the front, canted windows flank the columned entrance; in the upper storey, windows framed by pilasters with pediments perched uncomfortably on top of the roof balustrade. Round-arched windows. The long w elevation similarly detailed, the only novelty in the angle to the s which is filled with a curved window. On the E side a huge three-light mullion-and-transom window set over a low arched window with deep plinth. Lower service wing to the N, its court now infilled.

The interior, probably re-fitted in the 1890s, is very eclectic. Hall, with dado panelling and inset mahogany chimneypiece, opening into a big, open stairwell with a full-height screen of basket arches in two tiers supported on square-section tapered columns. Carved panels between the balusters, urn finials and two scrolled, wrought-iron electroliers. The large stair window, like all the stained glass, is probably by *Stephen Adam* who was working here in 1893. Three seated figures of Lachesis, Clotho and Atropos working with textiles and threads. The Marble Room has handsome marble Corinthian columns set into a mahogany pilastered screen that has Aesthetic Movement mosaic panels in the spandrels.

The Gold Room (former dining room) is unexpectedly opulent and dark with Renaissance-style mahogany panelling with Corinthian pilasters framing mirrors and full entablature. Big inglenook to the N wall, also panelled, with coloured glass panels of Celia and Rosalind, and its ceiling with a painted strip in Morris style depicting 'Fire', 'Earth', 'Air' and 'Water'. The richness is further emphasized by the geometric-pattern ceiling gilded with stencilled intertwined curves, delicate flowers and leaves. The square panels are filled with fishes and leaves closely resembling the patterns used by de Morgan. Whoever created this room clearly had access to plenty of pattern books.

PLACE HOUSE, 1.4 km. NW, was a large but elegant Jacobethan house of 1892–4 by *Henry Lord* of Manchester, demolished in 1991. Something of its sophistication can be inferred from the contemporary U-plan stable court (GLENPARK HOUSE), whose circular entrance tower has a tall tiled conical roof and dominant Arts and Crafts lantern. Globe-headed gatepiers to the courtyard.

REDHEUGH, Dipple Road, 1.7 km. N. Large late C19 Baronial villa, possibly by *Clarke & Bell*; now subdivided. Originally an L-plan with an asymmetrical, rather unsettled melange of crowstepped gables, especially on the main (E) front. The entrance is in an advanced canted bay, and has a segmental head and roll-moulded jambs; the angles of this bay corbelled at sill height, and corbelled to square at eaves height. Both wings were extended by *John Snodgrass*; the shorter S wing is dated 1906, with a conical tower at the SW corner; a similar conical tower also on the extension to the main elevation. To the S, the Baronial LODGE and GATES with delicate thistle details in the gates and cast-iron gate finials; to the N harled crowstepped offices, now residential.

GLENGARNOCK CASTLE. *See* p. 353.
LADYLAND HOUSE. *See* p. 490.

KILDONAN HOUSE

2080

1 km. NW of Barrhill

The last of the great country houses built in Ayrshire and, as its 85 chequered history indicates, too large for a viable existence. Built in 1914–23, and thus too late for the society that produced it, by *James Miller* for Captain Euan Wallace. He married firstly Lady Sackville, daughter of Lord de la Warr, and then, in 1920, Barbara Lutyens, daughter of the architect. He gave up Kildonan in 1937 for Lavington Park, West Sussex. Since then the house has been either in institutional or commercial use.

The modest lodges and stable court do not prepare the visitor for the vast cream Northumberland sandstone spectacle that stretches out along the hillside. Planned around a large entrance forecourt facing E with raised terraces fronting the three outer elevations, it is built in an Arts and Crafts manner in everything but scale. There are echoes of Voysey, Webb, Lethaby and most strongly of Lutyens but none of their delicacy of touch. Enormous sweeps of roof punctuated with flat-roofed dormers and, apart from the N service range, almost all with the same ridge height, emphasize the horizontality of the design. But the horizontal is not allowed to dominate – instead gabled bays, canted windows and large chimney-breasts break out of the mould on every elevation and added drama comes from the tall clusters of diamond and rectangular flues banked in twos, threes and sixes with linking cornices, all harking back to and elaborating on the style of the C16 English prodigy houses. There is virtually no carved decoration, the interest being provided instead by the restless articulation of the elevations. *Crittall* steel window frames are used throughout.*

* From 1929 Miller took over the design of houses at Crittall's village at Silver End, Essex. *See* Buildings of England, *Essex*.

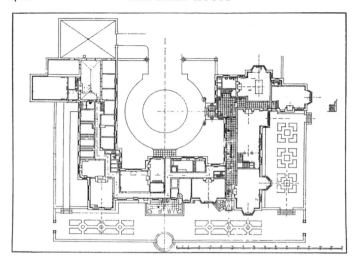

Kildonan House.
Plan, 1923

The entrance court encloses a large turning circle, but the
front door is not directly ahead, as one might expect, in
the triple gabled section of the E elevation. Instead Miller gives
the clue to the internal planning by placing a projecting gabled
porch on the S side of the court with access to the public
rooms. This wing itself could be a sizeable house. The entrance
is then at the pivotal point between the two main ranges of
public rooms. Rather less satisfactory is the entrance to the
service quarters, a plain affair, in the prominently gabled
section of the E side of the court and also off-centre. Opposite
the front door the lower service range with huge roofs stepped
down to the E and tiers of dormers. The main living rooms are
all on the southern sides of the house and these elevations are
characterized by big, one- and two-storey canted windows. At
the E end of the hall, which occupies much of the S range, there
is a full-height window suggesting the high end of a medieval
hall. The W elevation, at first glance, appears to be symmetrical
but the big central projecting gable with an arcaded loggia at
the terrace level is once again off-centre. It marks the division
between the public rooms and the service ranges, the later with
a footprint nearly as large as the main part of the house and
identified by the small ground-floor windows.

The interior was never completely finished and the *Architectural Review* (1928) described it as verging on 'monastic baldness'. From the reception hall a passage leads straight on to
the Smoking Room and Billiard Room, another at a right
angle leads to the main Hall, Dining Room and Drawing
Room. There is simple oak panelling in the Hall, and a few

Tudor-styled chimneypieces perhaps hint that more decoration was originally intended. This was a house built for entertaining on a large scale, but by the time it could have been put to such use, the way of life and the servant population required to run it had vanished.

STABLE BLOCK. A charming U-plan range also by *Miller*, at the same time as the house, with a central archway breaking through the roof-line and crowned with a clock turret, more truly Arts and Crafts in appearance than the main house.

GARDENS laid out by *Gertrude Jekyll* in 1924, but little evidence remains.

KILHENZIE CASTLE   3000

2 km. SE of Maybole

The core is a small rectangular, two-storey and attic tower built for the Bairds. It was in existence in 1542 when a charter records a tower and fortalice. To this a three-bay domestic range was added in the C17 but the house was a roofless ruin by the early C19 and only made habitable again *c.* 1856 when it was converted as a farmhouse for the Kilkerran estate. *David Bryce* was working at Kilkerran in the 1850s. Might he have been involved?

The C16 tower resembles the early part of Penkill (q.v.), i.e. crowstepped gables but no parapet and wall-head walk. Rubble-built with some random granite blocks, it is mainly sneck-harled except for the W gable which is harled. The NW, SW and SE angles at the upper storey are clasped by chunky turrets supported on tiers of continuous corbelling and with finialled candle-snuffer roofs. The original entrance is no longer visible but on the N elevation near the E there is a blocked arch perhaps indicating a doorway at first floor, and possible signs of a smaller door below. It appears that the internal stair to the upper floor was at this angle. There is evidence in the masonry of some rebuilding including enlargement of upper windows and attic dormerheads. The C17 E range was substantially reconstructed in the C19 works. High on its S gable there is a small blocked opening apparently with simple C17 moulding, but the gable has been altered here in the rebuilding and a dormerhead inserted between this range and the tower. On its E front there is also evidence of the raising of the wall-head and rebuilding of the N gable, suggesting that this block was longer. The principal C19 feature, and done with masterly understatement, is a drum tower, for entrance and stairs, set in the re-entrant angle of the earlier ranges. There is single vaulted chamber inside at ground floor. Door set in a roll-moulded architrave with carved detailing over the lintel. Above, the tower is boldly corbelled to square and capped with a crowstepped gable.

A drawing by Bryden made some forty years after the reconstruction shows the ruined tower and C17 range as part of a

courtyard complex but his source is unknown. Only archaeology would reveal the form of the enclosure.

KILKERRAN

3.5 km. NE of Dailly

Of all the country houses in the Girvan valley Kilkerran is the
one most in tune with its landscape. It sits on an artificially levelled platform overlooking lush parkland and arable fields falling
away N to the river, and with a backdrop of mature woodland
rising up the steep slopes to the moorland tops of Barony Hill to
the S.

Kilkerran has belonged to the Fergusson family since 1466, but
the name originally applied to a tower house which stands to the
S (*see* below). The present house developed instead from a tower
built on the neighbouring estate of Barclanachan, which was
acquired through marriage in 1686 by Sir John Fergusson and
renamed in 1700. It was probably rectangular in plan with a long
E–W range and a stair projection (cf. Old Dalquharran, p. 274)
but was augmented into a U-plan classical form in the early C18
with the addition of two cross-wings extending N and S to form
an H. A survey of the estate dated 1721 shows the house as
H-plan, but this plan may not have been implemented until Sir
James Fergusson inherited in 1729. He was a judge in Edinburgh
and it is likely that he sought advice from the city's architectural
establishment. The constraints of the tower house meant that the
entrance was awkwardly placed in the angle with the W wing, and
this may have been what led Sir Adam Fergusson *c.* 1760 to
reorient the entrance to the W front, at the same time as com-
missioning major changes to the landscaping of the park by *John
Hay*. The C19 saw several important alterations and additions:
first, in 1814–22 by *J. Gillespie Graham*, who added bowed extensions to either end of the W front, but his ambitious plan for
infilling the N court was not acted upon, then in 1855 by *David
Bryce* and finally in 1873 by *Brown & Wardrop*. They too intended
major enlargements, in an Italianate style, again abandoned in
favour of simpler alterations.

The approach to the W FRONT conveys an impression of
Georgian unity and symmetry that belies the complex evolution. It is of seven regular bays with the centre bay projecting
under a pediment that has an oculus and urns. Rusticated
quoins at the angles. Single bays to l. and r. of this and then
at the ends two bay square projections rising to the full height
with hipped roofs. On the flanks N and S are tall elliptical bows.
The centre three bays date from the remodelling *c.* 1760 of the
earlier C18 N-facing wing. The curiously off-centre position of
the windows under the pediment must have been dictated by
the existing internal planning (the present windows are in fact
replacements for a Venetian and tripartite window in the same
position). Pedimented timber and glass porch of 1873. The S

square bay and the bow were added in 1815 by Gillespie Graham. The bow has one central window with narrow side-lights and two blind windows flanking, but was conceived with three identically sized windows. It housed the drawing room and the kitchen below, intended originally as a temporary arrangement until the N court was infilled. The corresponding N extension of the W front followed in 1817 and here the bow fits uncomfortably across the N end of the early C18 wing, overlapping it in a manner which shows his anticipation of further extensions.

The shallow open court between the wings on the N FRONT has been infilled by a single-storey Billiard Room of 1855 by *Bryce* but above and behind this the upper part of the early C18 refronting is visible. It is six bays wide, the W window masked by Gillespie Graham's extension, the centre four bays flanked by single giant Tuscan pilasters; their detailing suggests that the pediment (now gone) straddled the eaves in a manner adopted by James Smith and seen at Ardmillan (dem.) and Craigie House, Ayr (q.v.). Because of the thickness of the tower walls at ground level a central doorway was impossible, and the solution was to have two doors in the bays flanking the centrepiece (the eastern one was blind and survives, although concealed by Bryce's addition). For the character of the early C18 wings one must look to the E WING to see the refined ashlar work, rusticated quoins to the N angles, neat lugged architraves to the windows and piended roof with elegantly swept profile. The S FRONT is a muddle, at the r. the plain end of the early C18 wing, partly concealed by a big projection to its r. by *Brown & Wardrop* (1873–4) for a dining room and small service rooms. This was an enlargement of the dining room added *c.* 1819 and has a cast-iron balcony with steps leading to the garden relieving its austerity. Further W Gillespie Graham's bow-ended wing. Also by Brown & Wardrop the E SERVICE COURT. Cobbled with game larders etc. The GAS HOUSE is a piend-roofed square tower with louvred vents.

INTERIOR. The front hall is part of the *c.* 1760 reorientation and is a gathering place from which to rise to the *piano nobile* and the main rooms. From it a door leads into the passage that was formerly part of the lower floor of the tower house. It provides access to vaulted storerooms as well as to the steps to the cellars, which run under the W range. Glazed doors lead to the straight flight of stairs (probably early C19) rising to the first floor, a replacement for the earlier C18 scale-and-platt stair that led from the W door in the N front to an ante-room on the first floor. This room was lost in the C19 rearrangement and became a landing with two fluted, Ionic cast-iron columns inserted to support a beam and the chimneystack on the floor above on the line of the W wall of the tower house. The resulting upper hall provides the circulation around the balustraded stairwell for the central and western part of the house, access to the stairs connecting to the upper floor and by a passage to the E wing.

In the SW corner, i.e. in the bow of the S addition of 1815, is the DRAWING ROOM but it is now as reconstructed after a fire in 1994. However, the the SMALL DRAWING ROOM to its N preserves its early C19 delicate Vitruvian scroll cornice and a Neoclassical marble chimneypiece with a sphinx in the central panel. The LIBRARY in the central projection probably designed for Sir Adam Fergusson's important collection of books. It is possible that the off-centre position of the windows outside was dictated by the wish to accommodate the bookshelves and retain the effect of internal symmetry. The delicate cornice, marble chimneypiece and black and gold decorated shelves were being finished in 1821. The DINING ROOM was created by Gillespie Graham from part of the original hall of the tower house and, as noted outside, extended by Brown & Wardrop. It is a very wide room with supporting cast-iron beams in the grid-patterned ceiling, huge plate-glass windows, a bold cornice and handsome marble chimneypiece: all of 1873–4. From the NE of the landing a wide passage leads E to two remarkable rooms, the PARLOUR and the room to its N in the early C18 wing. They have full-height panelling, low dado rails and lugged architraves to the doors; the two marble chimneypieces probably those provided by *William Adam* in 1744 and have unusual semi-bolection-moulded frames above, one painted with shell motifs in grey and gold, the other in terracotta and gold with a stylized flower motif, both contemporary with the chimneypieces.

The UPPER STAIR of *c.* 1760 on the S is in a cove-ceilinged compartment with an upper landing It has graceful balusters of alternating straight and twisted form as well as rather old-fashioned stone steps with nosings, possibly reused. One second floor room has early C18 panelling with arches to some of the upper panels. Somewhat old-fashioned in metropolitan terms but comparable with slightly later panelling in Boswell's business room at Auchinleck (q.v.).

DRUMBURLE LODGE and NORTH EAST LODGE. By *Gillespie Graham, c.* 1814. Single-storey with deeply overhanging eaves and rustic porches. – STABLES. 1875 by *Brown & Wardrop*. Courtyard closed on the N side with a wall. Dormers with over-sized consoled pediments. Clock turret and weathervane. – LAUNDRY COTTAGE. *c.* 1814, in Gillespie Graham's manner. – DRUMGIRNAN BRIDGE carries B741 across the Girvan. 1799 by *John Rutherford*. An elegant, shallow, single arch with vermiculated voussoirs.

BARCLANACHAN CASTLE, 2.7 km. SW. Called Kilkerran Castle until 1700. Maybe C15 but only part of a gable wall survives.

KILKERRAN STATION

Former KILKERRAN STATION on the Maybole & Girvan railway, opened in 1860 (engineer, *John Miller Jun.*, of Edinburgh).

Closed in the 1960s. STATION HOUSE, with crowstepped gables, now in industrial use.

100 m. NW, at the junction with the Maybole to Girvan road, a FINGERPOST, perhaps the best surviving of these signs in S Ayrshire, retaining two of its original C19 cast-iron arms.

KILLOCHAN CASTLE

2 km. N of Old Dailly

2000

'Begun the 1 of Marche 1586', according to the inscription over the entrance, 'be Ihone Cathcart of Carltoun and Helen Wallace His Spous' but added to and remodelled inside by Sir John Cathcart probably after his second marriage, in 1729, to Elizabeth Kennedy.

50

The late C16 tower house is L-plan, of four storeys and an attic, harled with crowstepped gables. There is an unusual tall drum tower at the SE angle of the main tower, reminiscent of the slightly earlier towers at Kelburn (q.v.); a square jamb projecting NE and in the re-entrant angle is a narrow square turret rising two storeys above the eaves. Killochan belongs to the small group of late C16 Ayrshire tower houses that includes Baltersan, Kirkhill and Pinwherry (qq.v), as well as Castle of Park (Wigtown, Dumfries and Galloway), in having the jamb filled or partly filled by the stairs. Access to the upper floors is by a turnpike in the re-entrant angle turret. This turret also contains at its base the entrance to the castle which is protected by a boxed machicolation in the eaves (*see* also Lochranza Castle, Arran) and a gunloop in the N wall of the main tower. Above the bolection-moulded doorpiece, the finely carved date panel and inscription 'The Name Of The Lord Is Ane Strang Tovr And The Rythteovs In Thair Trovblis Rinnis Unto It And Findeth Refuge. Proverb 18 Vers 10'. Set higher, a moulded frame with nailhead decoration with the Cathcart arms and supporters. To the r. and above, slit windows to the turnpike stair. Abutting this and rising from the wall-head of the main range is a substantial chimney. At the SW and NW angles of the main range are corbelled round bartizans with conical roofs above the eaves. A curious feature in the W wall is a large square opening at first-floor level containing a small, deeply set window, a motif also found at Baltersan (q.v.) and the Castle of Park (Dumfries and Galloway). What was its purpose? S of this three narrow windows light a mural stair. The large chimneystack on this wall serves the original basement kitchen. On the long S elevation the corbelling of the SW bartizan continues across the façade, originally supporting a wall-walk or gallery which was altered in the 1730s when the classical cornice and windows were added. The large drum at the SE breaks through the eaves to finish with a corbelled crenellated parapet, with an array of waterspouts, enclosing a candle-snuffer roof. There are good-sized windows on the SW but elsewhere the openings are small with

a scattering of shot-holes and gunloops. Small newel stair corbelled out at the E angle of SE tower to upper floors and roof.
    Attached to the NE jamb is a two-storey N WING, probably
added in the 1740s, with an unusually low ground floor and
large first-floor windows. On the E elevation it wraps round the
original N jamb with swept eaves. Its cross-wing, also with
swept eaves, forms part of the SERVICE COURT and is linked
to a two-storey C19 service range on the court's N side by a tall
wall with impressive C18 rusticated and ball-finialled gatepiers
and C19 cast-iron gates. The C18 range has STABLES with
boarded and cast-iron columned and screened loose boxes, all
C19. Unusual ladder to the former loft, a vertical plank with
alternating toe holes. The C19 range is unusually grand with a
timber balustraded stair with finely panelled soffits and a
stained-glass window in the manner of Stephen Adam including a roundel with a bust of Calliope set in delicate, floral
panels. Well-proportioned rooms inside with good cornice
details, more like a hunting lodge than a service range.
    Inside the door to the castle, a vaulted porch leads to a
handsome scale-and-platt staircase in the NE jamb. This is an
early example of this more commodious form of staircase (as
found also at Kirkhill Castle, Colmonell, q.v., 1589). Steps
descend from its first landing to a vaulted basement in the
main range. A long E–W passage leads W to the kitchen (stone-
arched fireplace) and E to a vaulted room under the stair, said
to be a dungeon but with a small fireplace and window so
possibly a former guardroom. Beside it is a back door, an
unusual feature (but *see* Kilkerran). The rest of the interior of
the 1730s, according to the contemporary fashion for improved
accommodation for entertaining. So, on the principal floor is
the former hall (11.2 m. by 6.1 m.), converted into a DRAWING
ROOM and fully panelled with a low dado rail and bolection-
moulded panels. On the N wall a big chimney-breast framed
with giant Corinthian pilasters. The chimneypiece is mid-C20.
In the W wall, l. and r., two small panelled doors, that to the
l. leading to a newel stair to the original solar above, the other
to a closet/study. This is lit by the unusual window noted
on the exterior of the W wall. At the E end of the room is a
doorway into the turret room from which a stair leads upwards.
Behind the l. shutter of the E window a small roll-moulded
door leading to a straight mural stair to a room in the N jamb.
In the N wing of *c.* 1740, reached from the main stair, is the
DINING ROOM, with dado panelling, modillion cornice and an
eared and lugged decorative frame over the altered chimneypiece. Above the former hall, two bedrooms with stone
moulded door frames, the W, once the solar, with a large stone
roll-moulded chimneypiece and a door to the mural stair at
the SW and to a closet at NW, the E with more good panelling
and a tightly lugged frame over the later chimneypiece; the
turret room entered off it. More panelled rooms in the upper
floors of the main range and jamb, with closets and one with
access to the mural stair from the former hall. At the top of

the N wing the CHARTER ROOM with a combed ceiling. Crowning the porch turret is a small room with fireplace and access to the box machicolation.

Walled enclosure to the E, and a terraced walk across the S front to the W garden. Close to the river, BRIDGE COTTAGE, a much altered *c.* 1800 U-plan. The former main GATES to the W are identical to the entrance to the service court but with smaller outer piers and pedestrian gates.

KILMARNOCK

4030

INTRODUCTION

The county's engine house, whose late C19–early C20 heyday took its name to every corner of the globe, on water hydrants, shoes, railway engines, carpets and whisky. Those days are behind it, especially with the closure of the Johnnie Walker bottling plant (2012), and the town seeks to reinvent itself for the C21, and to forget the damage the late C20 wrought on its economy, communal psyche and built environment. With a population of *c.* 45,000, it remains the second largest town in the county, recently boosted by substantial residential growth to the N, and enhanced road links with Glasgow.

The parish is an old one, occupying fertile low ground on the r. bank of the Irvine, and takes its name from a cell or chapel dedicated to St Marnock, close to a convenient crossing of the Marnock Water; the present parish church (Laigh Kirk) is probably on the site. A small settlement developed and thrived here, servicing the local rural community, though there are no written references to mills here until the late C17. By the mid

C16, the parish (which included Fenwick) contained about 300 families, and was probably of lesser importance than either New-milns or Kilmaurs, both of which were established burghs when Kilmarnock was, for the Boyds, created a Burgh of Barony in January 1591/2.

Hereafter the town began to grow more rapidly, as it stood at an important crossroads, where the road into Ayrshire from Edinburgh escaped the narrowing confines of the upper Irvine valley and met the increasingly important Fenwick Moor road between Ayr and Glasgow. By 1609 it had, according to Pont, a weekly market and a stone bridge over the Marnock, while the foundations of the town's industrial economy had been laid: mainly the leather and shoe industries based on the by-products of the agricultural hinterland. The weaving of stockings and, especially, bonnets also commenced in the C17, and the town grew rapidly under the beneficent control of the Boyds* and, after the execution of the last Boyd, Earl of Kilmarnock, in 1747, increasingly under the guidance of the townspeople themselves. Growth was accelerated by the discovery of coal seams, first exploited *c.* 1736, prompting the acquisition of the Kilmarnock lands by the Bentincks, Dukes of Portland, late in the C18. By then, however, the town was already beginning to take on the appearance of a modern town: the streets had been causeyed shortly after 1702, pumps erected and drains laid. The Tolbooth was rebuilt in 1735, and the long street (Titchfield Street, Glencairn Street) connecting Kilmarnock with the bridge at Riccarton was laid out in 1765. The late C18 saw the establishment of many industrial buildings, including the first carpet-weaving factories; these were mostly alongside the Marnock Water, both upstream of the town and downstream towards Riccarton and the confluence with the Irvine.

Town Improvement Commissioners were established by Act of Parliament in 1802 and, with their surveyor *Robert Johnstone*, they oversaw the replacement of the twisting medieval streets of the town centre with straight, broad thoroughfares, such as King Street, from 1803, and Portland Street, from 1805, radiating from The Cross, and shifting the centre of the town away from the area around the Parish Church (itself rebuilt in 1802). To these were added St Marnock Street, from 1834, the sumptuous Duke Street, from 1859 (dem.)** and John Finnie Street (planned by *William Railton* and *Robert Blackwood*), from 1864, one of the finest Victorian streets in Scotland, designed to improve communications between the station and the growing industrial and residential areas to the S of the town. The railway from Glasgow had opened in 1843, while the early C19 had seen the expansion of the town to the SW, along Dundonald Road, and E, along

*The Boyds had assigned the common good of the burgh to the townspeople in 1702, which gave them control of how these annual revenues were spent.
**Planned by *Robert Blackwood*; most of the flanking buildings were by *James Ingram*. The street ran E from the Cross to London Road, was demolished in 1973, and replaced by the present shopping mall.

London Road, with the majority of the town's grander houses. The late C19 and early C20 witnessed the completion of streets such as John Finnie Street, and the erection of new churches, commercial properties and houses worthy of the town's prosperity and sense of worth; it was fortunate, too, to have a succession of first-class architects, such as *James Ingram*, his son *R. S. Ingram*, and the innovative *Gabriel Andrew*, *Thomas Smellie* and *James Scott Hay*.

Steady growth, underpinned by a strong industrial economy, continued into the latter half of the C20, occasioning the spread of suburbs to N, E, S and W, but thereafter the economy faltered, with a succession of hammer-blow closures in the 1970s and 1980s. From the 1960s, the Town Council, succeeded by Kilmarnock and Loudoun District Council after 1975, had embarked on a comprehensive redevelopment of the town centre (by-passed from 1973), with the loss of many important buildings, such as *Johnstone*'s Town Hall of 1805. The replacement buildings are devoid of any character, but elsewhere modern Kilmarnock has many fine buildings, which reflect its earlier history, such as the Old High and Laigh Kirk churches, its industrial heritage, e.g. the redeveloped Barclay's Works, and its heyday, such as John Finnie Street, the Dick Institute and its spacious public parks, while to the N of the town the multi-phased Dean Castle truly illustrates the relationship between the town and its superiors.

CENTRAL KILMARNOCK

CHURCHES

BAPTIST CHURCH, Fowlds Street. 1869–70, simple gabled Gothic by *J. A. Rennison* of Paisley. The main (N) elevation has a central moulded entrance, tall flanking lancets and a two-light window in the finialled gable, all pointed-headed, with a small circular window high in the gable.

CENTRAL EVANGELICAL CHURCH, John Finnie Street. 1932–3 by *William F. Valentine*. A curious exercise in Italian Romanesque, recalling Valentine's Masonic Hall in London Road (*see* below, p. 444). The outer bays have three-light ground-floor windows, four round-headed lights on the first floor, and a balustrade above. The central bay is slightly recessed within a full-height round-headed arch with a keystone, with a solid parapet above. Within the recess a round-headed door, a balcony with heavy brackets, and three round-headed windows above. Tall hipped roof behind the balustrade. Simple plastered hall, with a shallow segmental ceiling, with big roof-lights, and further round-headed windows on the side elevations.

Former FRIENDS' MEETING HOUSE, Sturrock Street. *See* Description 3, p. 443.

Former GRANGE PARISH CHURCH, Woodstock Street. 1877–9 by *R. S. Ingram* (*J. & R. S. Ingram*). E.E. Cruciform church on a tight site, with a tower and spire, and linked to a contemporary hall to the E. Coursed rubbly Ballochmyle sandstone

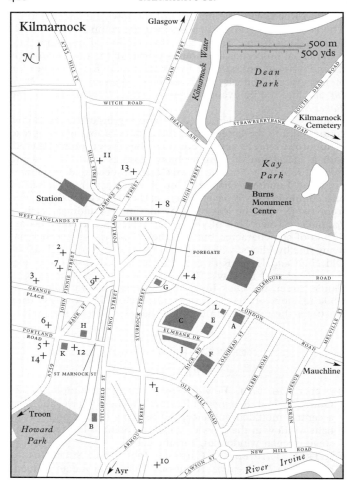

Kilmarnock

1 Baptist Church
2 Central Evangelical Church
3 Former Grange Parish Church
4 Henderson Parish Church
5 Holy Trinity (Episcopal)
6 Former Howard St Andrew's
   Parish Church
7 Laigh Kirk Mission Hall
8 Old High Parish Church
9 Old Laigh Parish Church
10 Former St Andrew's Parish Church
11 St Joseph (R.C.)
12 St Andrew's & St Marnock's
   Parish Church
13 Former West High Church
14 Winton Place Evangelical
   Union Congregational Church

A Dick Institute
B Galleon Centre
C Kilmarnock Academy
D Kilmarnock College
E Former Kilmarnock
   Technical College
F Loanhead Primary School
G Palace Theatre
H Procurators Fiscal's
   Offices
J Former St Columba's R.C.
   Primary School
K Sheriff Court House
L War Memorial

with ashlar dressings, fish-scale roofs and mostly three-light windows. The gabled main entrance elevation faces s; paired doors in moulded reveals, and an oculus above, all under a pointed arch. Geometric window in the gable. To the r., the tower: lower stage with corner buttresses, and stepped three-light windows; the upper stage with attached angle shafts and bell-openings with plate tracery; broach spire with lucarnes on alternate faces. The vestibule, with a groined ceiling and gallery stairs with cast-iron balustrades, leads to the elaborate and intricately planned High Victorian plastered interior with pews in semicircles, organ recess, transepts, splayed angles between the transepts and the rear wall, a ribbed and studded ceiling and a semicircular gallery with a bracketed and panelled front, supported on cast-iron stiff-leaf columns. Where the gallery passes into the transepts, further squat columns support pointed arches. This remarkable tableau, heightened by the Gothic furniture, all looks toward the PULPIT and ORGAN CASE of 1956 by *George Horspool*, iconoclastic in their use of light wood for simple, often unadorned panels. Behind the pulpit, a five-light STAINED-GLASS window of The Good Shepherd by *Ballantine & Gardiner*, 1896. A glazed linking block was added in 1934, connecting the church with the HALL, which has gable windows with plate tracery, saw-toothed skews, fish-scale slating and a tiled ridge.

HENDERSON PARISH CHURCH, London Road. 1906–7 by *Thomas Smellie*. A memorable Free Gothic exercise in Balloch-myle sandstone on a prominent site. Rectangular with a strong SE tower, the steep slope allowing the church to be built atop its suite of halls. A sweeping curve of steps bridges the gap between London Road and the entrance to the r. on the S elevation below the tall tower. This has two stages, the first with angle buttresses and paired windows with plate tracery. An octagonal stair-turret is corbelled out from the SE corner, and rises through the upper stage which has paired cusped bell-openings, a deep crenellated parapet and squat angle finials. To the l. of the tower, the S gable with a big reticulated window. Five-bay side elevations, that to the W with hall windows with mullions and transoms, below triple windows with four-centred heads and gallery windows with Y-tracery; the E elevation more complex, the offices and vestry forming a broad transept-like wing to the S, with a lower gabled chancel on the N elevation.

The interior consists of a nave with a narrow W aisle, chancel, NE transept and gallery, and rear gallery. Plastered walls; open wooden roof with decorative patterned paper, added in 1957 to plans of *Sir William Kininmonth*. Arcades on chamfered stone pillars, with pointed arches and irregular quoins; the chancel arch treated similarly. In the chancel deeply recessed windows and panelling painted pale green, another survival from Kinin-month's decorative scheme. – Brass COMMUNION CROSS by *Benno Schotz*, in memory of Rev. James Hamilton †1944. – STAINED GLASS. Three lights in the chancel by *Stephen Adam*,

Kilmarnock, Henderson Parish Church.
Engraving, 1907

1907; in the nave, two windows, one above the other, of 1914
by *Alfred A. Webster* in a medieval Flemish style; in the NE
transept four busy windows by *Wendy Robertson*, 1987.

HOLY TRINITY (Episcopal), Portland Road. Gothic of 1856–7
by *James Wallace* with a chancel and gabled NW porch of 1875–6
by *Sir George Gilbert Scott*. The resolutely conventional exterior
conceals a remarkable decorated interior. Wallace's original
snecked rubble church consisted of a four-bay nave with
lancets and buttresses, a small chancel and a vestry. The nave
has four bays, with lancets and buttresses, and a W window
with Y-tracery. Scott's chancel has a saddleback roof, traceried
E window and two paired lancets to the S. At its NE corner the
buttressed square base of a proposed tower, now topped with
a pyramidal roof. This stillborn feature would have formed the
most obvious evidence of Scott's involvement, for the extensions otherwise owe more to Wallace, now in the role of builder

rather than architect, than to Scott, who, in the words of the local press, 'has been much assisted by the builder Mr Wallace, that gentleman's plan for an east window having been adopted by the architect'. The nave has plaster walls, an open wooden roof with scissor trusses and carved bosses, and an internal wooden porch in a Tudor Gothic manner, all mullions and transoms, added in 1922–3 by *Paterson & Stoddart*, executed by *Craig Brothers*, both of Glasgow. The walls were painted and stencilled *c.* 1987 with texts in scrolls framing the window reveals by *Stanley Fox*.

The tall chancel arch, with an inner arch of five orders springing from high imposts, leads into another world. The CHANCEL is lavishly decorated, to a scheme presumably initiated by Scott, and designed by the London firms of *Powell & Sons* and *Burlison & Grylls*; the painterwork done by *R. C. Robertson & Sons* of Kilmarnock. It is without parallel in Ayrshire, and stands among the best examples of High Victorian church decoration in Scotland. The pitched wooden ceiling is divided into panels, each of which is painted: the two upper rows with naturalistic decoration, the lower rows with Old (N) and New Testament (S) characters. The E wall too is painted, with angels to l. and r. of the window; below sill level a panelled wooden REREDOS added in 1932. In the N wall a big recess for the organ; painted above the dado with Christ's Entry into Jerusalem below scrolled inscriptions. The ORGAN itself (*Hill & Son*, London, 1875–6) has an open crocketed case, and the pipes are painted white, with blue and gilt detailing. In the S wall, further naturalistic painted decoration, carried into the deep window reveals. There is a mosaic TILED FLOOR, made by Powells in the 'Pompeiian pattern', which increases in richness towards the altar: mostly in a polychrome pattern of squares, with stalks of wheat and bunches of grapes, and larger terrazze of green marble in the panels flanking the altar. FURNISHINGS contemporary with this work include the low COMMUNION RAIL, the crocketed CHOIR STALLS and the simple ALTAR; the PEWS with crocketed ends apparently from 1856–7. – STAINED GLASS. A mixed bag, of which the best is undoubtedly *Powell & Sons'* busy E window of 1875–6, The Life of Christ, complementing the chancel decorative scheme. Also in the chancel, in the SE window, an unsigned Resurrection of *c.* 1925. The three-light W window, Faith, Hope and Charity, is *Clayton & Bell*, 1902, while the second window from the W on the S wall, St George, is *William Aikman*, 1937. To the W the church is adjoined by its gabled CHURCH HALL, of 1859 by *James Wallace*, with Y-tracery windows and scissor-beam trusses. To the S the original vestry links with the asymmetrical Gothic RECTORY, also of 1859, but by *James Ingram*.

Former HOWARD ST ANDREW, Portland Road. 1969–71 by *Allan MacPherson* of *Alexander Dunlop & Partners*, on the site of the Portland Road U.P. church (1858–9 by *Peddie & Kinnear*). The ribbed concrete church, to the l., and hall are linked by a single-storey recessed, glass and concrete vestibule, all set back

31

from the pavement behind a well-detailed area of hard landscaping, with cobbles and a concrete cross. Internally, the
spacious vestibule forms a T; to the l., the church, an irregularly
shaped auditorium with brick walls, and a flat boarded ceiling.
The altar is asymmetrically placed, beneath an H-frame of
rough concrete uprights and a steel cross-bar, lit from above
by a deep trapezoidal roof-light. Framed and back-lit on one
wall, STAINED GLASS from the former St Andrews North
Church (dem. 1987*): Blessed are the Dead Which Die in The
Lord by *W. & J. J. Kier*, 1871. More in the vestibule, from King
Street Church (dem. *c.* 1968**): three diverse but anonymous
central panels, Christ in the Temple, Suffer Little Children and
St Luke. Now church hall (Howard Centre) for St Andrew's
& St Marnock's.

LAIGH KIRK MISSION HALL, John Finnie Street. 1883–4 by
Bruce & Sturrock of Glasgow. E.E. Three-bay red sandstone
front façade, with a central entrance with semi-octagonal piers
and a crenellated blind parapet; the gabled outer bays have
three-light first-floor windows beneath carved panels. Brick
side elevations with pitched roofed aisles and round-headed
gallery windows (now blocked). The slated roof originally had
a central flèche and cross. The main hall has pointed arches
on cast-iron Corinthian columns.

OLD HIGH PARISH CHURCH, Church Street and Soulis Street.
Harled classical five-bay rectangular church, gabled with an E
tower, of 1732–40, which hovers at the junction between polite
and vernacular architecture. The architect is unknown, though
the builders were *Robert Hunter*, mason, and *William Hunter*,
wright. The inspiration clearly James Gibbs's St Martin-in-the-
Fields (1722–6), but the closest comparison in Scotland must
be Allan Dreghorn's St Andrew's Parish Church, Glasgow,
begun in 1739, as work here was drawing to a close. Two characteristics distinguish this church from these examples: the first
is size. Although large, Old High has not the dimensions of
either, and this is underlined by the visual effect of the second:
the concentration of classical detail on the E front, leaving the
other elevations almost starkly plain. Additions and alterations
of 1868–9 by *William Railton*, while the unparalleled suite of
windows by *W. & J. J. Kier* was installed 1868–72. Thorough
conservation of the exterior in 2005–6 restored the long-lost
harling, returning this attractive building to something akin to
its original state.

   Description must begin with the E front. Central round-
headed entrance, with to l. and r. square-headed entrances,
with round-headed windows above, all these with Gibbsian
surrounds, beneath a lightly pedimented gable. From the
apex of this rises the clock tower; the lower stage is square
with urn finials, the upper stage octagonal with round-headed

---

* 1844, remodelled by *Robert S. Ingram* in 1886.
** 1832 by *Robert Johnstone*. It was classical with a steeple, similar to Tarbolton
and Riccarton.

bell-openings, capped by a leaded ogival roof and a miniature cupola. The side elevations have segmentally headed windows beneath round-headed windows, all in simple surrounds. The W front is compromised by single-storey, gabled porches added by Railton, who is also responsible for the central Venetian window.

The numinous plastered INTERIOR is a mix of the C18 and the C19. C18 the deeply coffered plaster ceiling, each panel with border strips of acanthus detail, the deeply recessed windows, the broad panel-fronted wooden gallery which fills three sides, and is supported between heavy plain columns which reach up to the ceiling with big square capitals and idiosyncratic acanthus decoration, and the matching pilasters in the E gallery and W wall. C19 the High Gothic PULPIT, and the elaborately detailed W Venetian window with Corinthian columns. – The Kiers' STAINED GLASS scheme is also mid-C19: designs were prepared from 1868, and the final window was installed in 1872. The highlight is the memorial to Lord Kilmarnock in the W window, The Sermon on the Mount, of 1868–9, while Old Testament scenes are depicted in the lower windows, beginning with Adam and Eve in the westmost window in the N wall, and finishing with Isaiah opposite. – In the gallery, New Testament scenes, from Lazarus in the NW to the Ascension in the SW. – The scheme continues in the E VESTIBULE, with four further windows, including the second from the N, The Vision of Heaven, with Christ and a multi-ethnic audience, the final window to be installed. – Some simple inscribed C18 and C19 WALL MONUMENTS; in the W porches wall tiling of c. 1900.

Large partially walled CHURCHYARD, mostly cleared of MONUMENTS except for several late C19 shrouded urns and obelisks and the classical monument of 1827 to the printer John Wilson, †1821, with its urn and acroteria, and the crocketed Gothic monument to John Mather †1836. On the E wall, a Gothic marble monument to William and James Aitken, of c. 1879, and on the N wall two cartouches of c. 1890 to Mrs James Parker and Mrs Robert Crooks, sisters-in-law. The E gateway has rusticated gatepiers and ball finials; to the l. of this, in a pilastered and round-headed niche on the exterior side of the wall, the SOULIS CROSS, a Doric column supporting an urn. Of 1824–5, replacing a decayed C15 pillar.* To the NW, gabled Gothic brick HALLS of 1899–1900 by *William Railton*, with a three-light S window.

LAIGH KIRK, John Dickie Street. The town's senior parish church, its site probably both that of the original parish church, and the preceding cell of St Marnock. Classical rectangle of 1802 by *Robert Johnstone*, but linked to an earlier tower, C17 in appearance. The previous church on the site, of 1750, was replaced after thirty members of the congregation died in

* A Lord Soulis is said to have been killed here by one of the Boyds of Kilmarnock in 1444.

October 1801, after a rumour of a collapsing roof sparked a panicked exit. Johnstone designed his church with several doors. The five-bay long elevations face NW and SE. Harled, with corner pilasters and a hipped slate roof, square-headed ground-floor windows and round-headed first-floor windows with Y-tracery. Projecting centre bays on the long façades, with triangular pediments; that on the NW has a pedimented ashlar porch, added in 1900; that on the SE an architraved entrance approached by steps with wrought-iron railings and lamps. At each angle are harled hipped stair-towers, the most obvious evidence of Johnstone's safety measures; they project slightly forward of the long façades, and stand proud of the side elevations. That at the E angle is attached to the coursed rubble earlier square four-stage TOWER, whose first two stages have small openings. The third has square moulded panels with clock faces, while the final stage is set back, with round-headed bell-openings and a leaded ogee roof. The area between the towers on the SW elevation is infilled by the hipped late C19 ashlar SESSION HOUSE.

Spacious plastered interior with a simple flat ceiling, and a panel-fronted horseshoe gallery supported on plain cast-iron columns. The platform is dominated by a big lightly classical organ, installed in 1878. – STAINED GLASS. The lower windows to l. and r. of the platform, Nativity and Resurrection, deeply coloured work by *Norman MacDougall*, 1904, the lights above, Crucifixion and Ascension, also 1904, but designed by *J. T. & C. E. Stewart* and *J. S. Melville*, and executed by *William Meikle & Sons*, who also executed the outer lower windows, Suffer the Little Children (l., 1904) and Feed My Lambs (r., c. 1906), both by *J. T. Stewart*. The r. outer upper window is also of c. 1904, The Valley of the Shadow of Death, again designed by *J. T. & C. Stewart*, and executed by *Meikle & Co.*, but that to the l. is a finely detailed St Andrew by *A. C. Whalen*, 1973, a memorial to Lord Howard de Walden; it contains symbols of his many interests, such as a riding cap in his apricot racing colours (chosen for him by Augustus John to match with the grass of the courses). In the NE wall, two windows by *Susan Bradbury*, 1992: Dorcas (to the l.) and Lydia; in the gallery, opposite the pulpit, a window of 1981 by *Whalen*: SS Collum Cille and Marnock. Finally, in the NW porch, *Bradbury*'s Millennium window of 2000, a swirling Creation using masses of clear lenses.

The church sits to one side of a neat CHURCHYARD surrounded by a low stone wall with iron railings. Entrance gates with cast-iron lamps inscribed 'Low Church'. Neatness is obtained at the expense of the monuments, of which only a few remain, their survival due to historic interest rather than artistic merit; they include the Covenanters John Ross, John Shields (both executed in Edinburgh, 1666) and John Nisbet, executed at Kilmarnock Cross 1683 (his memorial erected in 1823), and associates of Burns such as Thomas Samson †1795.

Former ORIGINAL SECEDERS' CHAPEL, Fowlds Street. Dated 1857, a simple gabled ashlar church, with tall round-headed openings on the front (N) gable.

Former ST ANDREW'S PARISH CHURCH, St Andrews Street. 1840–1 by *James Ingram*. Greek Revival. Rectangular, ashlar, with a hipped roof. The front (SW) elevation has a wide advanced central bay with twin Doric pilasters supporting an entablature and shallow pediment, above which there is a square bellcote, with curved edges above the cornice, round-headed bell-openings with pilasters and pediments, and a leaded dome. Slightly recessed entrance, divided into three bays by pilasters. The outer bays of the elevation are blank. Four-bay return elevations with two tiers of windows, and an apsidal chancel on the NE elevation. Converted into flats, 2006–7. To the l. the former CHURCH HALL of 1890–1 by *Robert S. Ingram*. Classical, dark ashlar, the main elevations with pilasters, pediments and tripartite windows. It is also now in residential use.

ST JOSEPH (R.C.), Hill Street. Spiky Gothic of 1846–7 on an elevated site. By a Mr *McIlroy* architect, and a Mr *Gallocher*, builder, both of Glasgow, and otherwise unrecorded. The church closely resembles the 1846 St Mary's, Hamilton (Lanarkshire). The main elevation faces S, divided by prominent stepped buttresses with tall pyramidal finials. Tall lancets in the outer bays, the pointed-headed entrance (now infilled with opaque glass bricks) in the middle bay, which is surmounted by a tall open feature consisting of two linked pyramidal finials with a cross between. Side elevations have buttresses and tall lancets. Fyfestone SW porch added 1970–1 by *Sam Gilchrist*. Internally, a rear vestibule with a glazed screen, below a shallow panel-fronted gallery. Very tall plastered interior, with slender cast-iron columns reaching up to the peculiar ceiling, shaped like the base of an egg box or the dugs of a well-endowed sow. The sanctuary was first decluttered by *Clunie Rowell* in 1970–1; of this date the striking abstract metal Crucifixion. The suite of marble furniture was added in 1994–5 by *Thomas & Stephen MacMillan* of Paisley. – C19 STAINED GLASS in the nave windows, and a swirling blue and pink window in the S gable, 1997 by *Paul Lucky*. At the NE the church is linked with the simply detailed PRESBYTERY of 1846–7. To the W the CHURCH HALL of 1977–8 by *Sam Gilchrist*.

ST ANDREW'S AND ST MARNOCK'S PARISH CHURCH, St Marnock Street. Mannered and scholarly Perp Gothic of 1834–6 by *James Ingram* on a huge scale. Built by subscription, the lists led by a number of prominent businessmen in the town whose attitude to increasing seat rents in the Laigh Kirk and High Church seems to have been that if money could be made from churches, then they should do so too. The scale of Ingram's building, and its position looking almost directly towards the Laigh Kirk, seems to be a deliberate snub to the established Church. After the Disruption the minister was called to the High Church after its previous minister and most of the congregation had decamped to the Free Church (*see* West High Church, below); he accepted and he and his congregation moved there. This church then remained empty until 1857 when it was acquired by the Church of Scotland and reopened under their extension scheme.

Rectangular plan in pink ashlar, with a central tower on the N gable. This is of four stages, with angle buttresses, and a panelled Gothic door within a pointed-headed recess with moulded reveals and a crocketed ogival hoodmould. Above this a tall reticulated window under a square panelled hood, with a lozenge clock panel above. The bell-openings have panel tracery and further ogival hoodmoulds; all beneath a battlemented parapet with angle pinnacles. The flanking bays are battlemented, have tall windows with panel tracery, and corner turrets with crocketed finials. Similar windows to the side elevations. Three tall stepped Geometric windows in the S gable. The interior matches the exterior in scale, beginning with the sizeable and full-height vestibule, which is divided into three bays by large pillars, and has ribbed plaster ceilings, and tiled floors. Gallery stairs to l. and r., with iron railings, meeting to form a promenade across the inner face of the space. Beyond, the church proper, with a gently pitched and ribbed ceiling in the centre, flat ceils over the steeply raked gallery on three sides; this is supported on cast-iron columns. Big semicircular scoops have been taken out of the galleries where they cross the windows, while the gallery front is wooden, with curved corners and Gothic fretwork decoration. Further cast-iron columns extend upwards from the galleries to the longitudinal ceiling ribs; these seem to have been added *c.* 1841 to strengthen the building. Excellent ensemble of Gothic FURNITURE, including the original pulpit and communion rails: the organ was installed in 1872, its organ case probably also by *Ingram*. The church was given a thorough restoration in 1885–6 by *R. S. Ingram*, the pews and the naturalistic window glass dating from this work; the remarkable large LANTERN suspended from the ceiling at the N end looks *c.* 1895; deep-hued glass panels depicting Christ, St Peter and others.

Former WEST HIGH CHURCH, Portland Road. Cheerful Free Gothic, with a polished ashlar E front. Of 1844 by *Cousin & Gale* of Edinburgh as a Free Church, the present appearance due to the alterations and additions of 1859–60 by *Alexander Andrew*, who introduced the pinnacles, and lengthened and gabled the side windows. Converted to offices in 2004–5. Gabled front elevation, with a projecting central tower. Round-headed central entrance with a pair of tall windows above; the tower itself square with circular clock faces in the third stage, and round-arched bell-openings above, the stages separated by a stepped string course. Crenellated parapet and corner finials. The bays flanking the tower are separated by flat pilasters and have angle pinnacles, pierced parapets and round-headed windows. The gable behind much plainer, with angle pinnacles; a stepped three-light round-headed window in the W gable. The side elevations have five tall windows, their gabled heads capped by urns; Andrew's work. Surviving interior, with galleries on Corinthian cast-iron columns, Gothic organ case of *c.* 1897 and elaborate braced roof; open wooden and steel stairs in front of the organ now give access to the galleries.

To the S a HALL with round-headed windows and a hipped roof, of 1849, probably again by *Cousin & Gale*; to the N a further hall, of grey ashlar, with a canted front, *c.* 1920, possibly by *Gabriel Andrew*, and also converted in 2004–5.

WINTON PLACE EVANGELICAL UNION CONGREGATIONAL CHURCH, Dundonald Road. 1859–60 by *James Ingram*. Early English, in yellow sandstone with polished dressings. E gable with central entrance recessed under a pointed arch, with moulded reveals, nook-shafts and a hoodmould with label stops, beneath a four-light traceried window. To either side, semi-octagonal piers rise through the gable to form pinnacles, while the outer bays have lancets and stepped angle buttresses. Six-bay side elevations with single lancets and buttresses. Vestibule subdivided by pointed arches; gallery stairs to l. and r.; in the central bay a marble MONUMENT of 1897 by *J. & G. Mossman* to Rev. James Morison (†1893), the founder of the Evangelical Union Church. The church proper has a pitched timber hammerbeam roof and plastered walls and deep recesses; panelled gallery on three sides, curved at the angles, and supported on quatrefoil cast-iron columns with foliated heads. Broad, light oak Gothic PULPIT, flanked by doors with pretty foliated labels to the hoodmoulds. – STAINED GLASS. W window. The middle light (the Resurrection) is of 1880 by *W. & J. J. Kier*, the outer lights (Annunciation and Ascension) are by *Ballantine & Gardiner*, 1897.

A suite of halls was added transversely across the W gable in 1892 by *Robert S. Ingram*, with gabled wings with traceried windows flanking the church on either side. The larger hall has a good panelled waggon roof.

KILMARNOCK CEMETERY

Grassyards Road

A spacious and well-ordered burying-ground of 1874–5 by *Alexander Adamson* for the Kilmarnock Cemetery Co. Ltd, with a handsome asymmetrical Scots Baronial linked lodge and gateway. The LODGE has crowstepped gables, a conical tower with square windows and fish-scale slating, and Jacobethan decoration. The buttressed GATEWAY has a haunched pedestrian entrance and a segmentally headed carriage entrance with a coat of arms and battlemented parapet. The ensemble terminates in a turret with gargoyles, loopholes and a fish-scale roof. The cemetery is surprisingly free of grandiose MEMORIALS, though that to Rev. Walter Low †1883, close to the main gate, is worthy of comment. Erected in 1894, designed by *R. S.*

Ingram, and executed by *Matthew Muir* in red Thornhill sand-stone, it was said by the contemporary press to be 'quite unique in character. Base and body and square, with intakes and pediments, containing carved panels. Above this, four granite columns, with carved capitals, support a circular canopy, which tapers to the top, and is surmounted by an ornamental cross'.

PUBLIC BUILDINGS

CENTRAL CLINIC, Old Irvine Road. By *Neil S. Sutherland*, opened 1966. The main element is an unexceptional two-storey steel-framed block with deep glazing bands. To the w, though, the roof rises gently, while the walls are mostly of concrete render, and in front of this a low brick and glazed entrance. Thoughtful.

Former CORN EXCHANGE, London Road. *See* Palace Theatre, below.

104 DICK INSTITUTE, Elmbank Avenue. Edwardian classical library and museum of 1897–1901 by *R. S. Ingram*, rebuilt to his design in 1909–11 after a disastrous fire (the blackened stone still visible), and thoroughly restored in 2006–7. The gift to their native town of Robert and James Dick, pioneers in the gutta-percha footwear business, and a superb example of municipal pride made flesh. Architecturally, it is among the finest libraries and museums in Scotland. Ashlar fifteen-bay front with the three-bay ends projecting as pavilions and to the centre bays a full-height Ionic portico topped with a pediment sculpted with a figure of Minerva between sphinxes. Behind this a dome. Channelled stone ground floor, the upper floors divided by Corinthian pilasters. Shallow parapet with dies, above a dentilled cornice. The nine-bay return elevations (NE and SW) are similarly detailed. The well-planned INTERIOR has a full-height entrance hall behind the portico with a tiled floor and an ornate oak and marble T-stair leading to an upper promenade gallery. To the l. the lending library, to the r. the former reading room (now the reference library); the lecture room behind the staircase is now a temporary exhibition space. The museum is on the upper floor; its two main spaces known as the North and South Galleries.

EAST AYRSHIRE COUNCIL OFFICES, Greenholm Street, 1928–9 by *Gabriel Steel*, of *James Hay & Partners*, as the AYR-SHIRE ELECTRICITY BOARD OFFICES. Big three-storey mansarded Neoclassical block in stone and brick, with advanced outer bays and a central porch with attached columns, flanked by piers with cartouches, supporting a simple entablature; doors under a geometrically patterned fanlight. To the l. of the offices, and at right angles, are the brown brick former TRAMWAY OFFICES of 1904 by *C. Stanley Peach*, of London, and *Charles Fairweather*, with a central pediment above a deeply recessed entrance with a segmental head, channelled voussoirs and flanking windows.

1. Firth of Clyde and Ailsa Craig (pp. 9, 89)
2. Ayr, aerial view (p. 119)

7. Kilwinning Abbey, SE processional doorway, C12 (pp. 16, 469)
8. Symington, Parish Church, E windows, mid C12, restored by
   P. Macgregor Chalmers, 1919 (pp. 18, 647)

9. Maybole Collegiate Church, 1371 (pp. 17, 528)
10. Monkton, St Cuthbert, C13 and mid C17 (pp. 18, 20, 542)

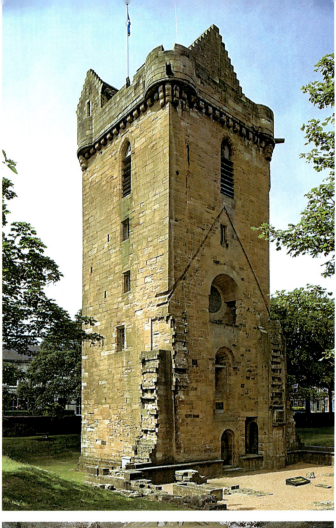

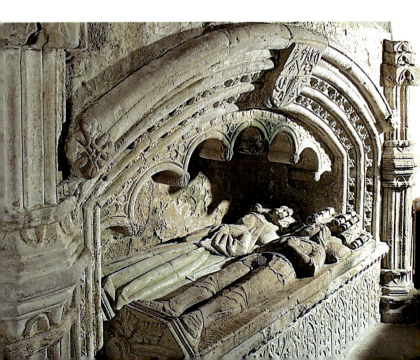

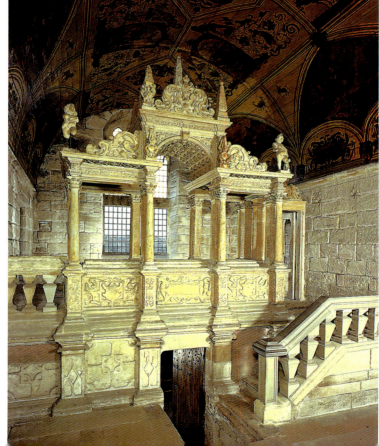

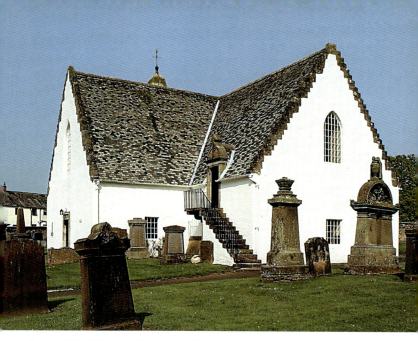

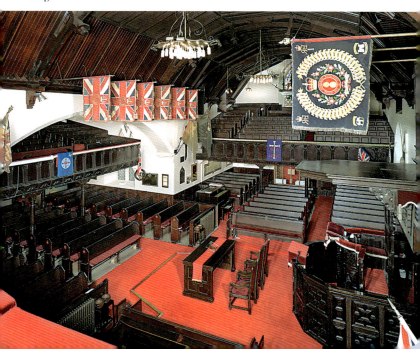

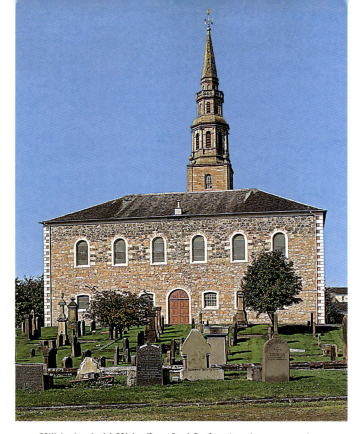

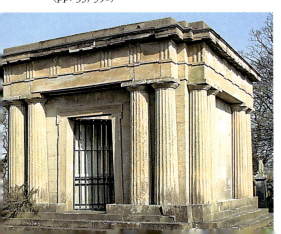

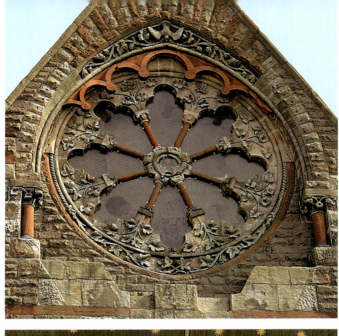

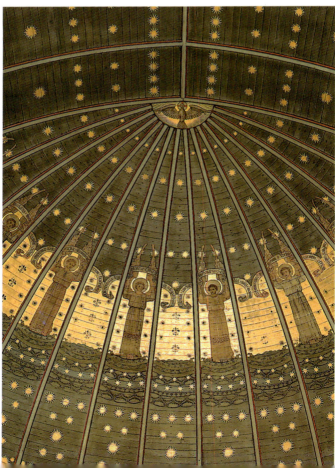

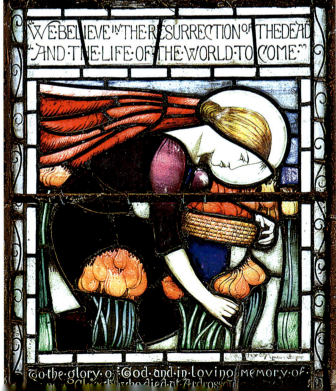

32. Troon, St Meddan's Parish Church, stained-glass window, detail, 1888 by William Smith (p. 657)
33. Ardrossan, St Andrew, stained-glass window, detail, 1894 by Harrington Mann, executed by Guthrie & Wells (pp. 31, 100)
34. Arran, Corrie Church, interior, 1886–7 by J. J. Burnet (pp. 26, 29, 683, 697)
35. Galston, St Sophia, 1884–6 by Robert Rowand Anderson (pp. 27, 329)

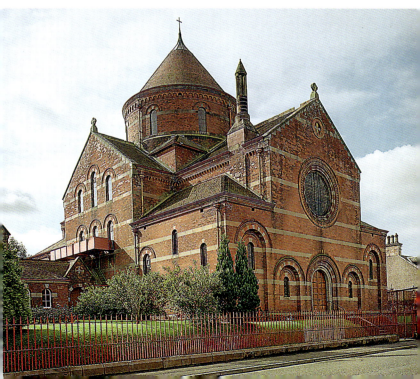

36. Arran, Shiskine, St Molios, 1888–90 by J. J. Burnet (pp. 26, 683, 721)
37. Largs, Clark Memorial Church, 1890–2 by William Kerr, working for T.G. Abercrombie (pp. 27, 493)

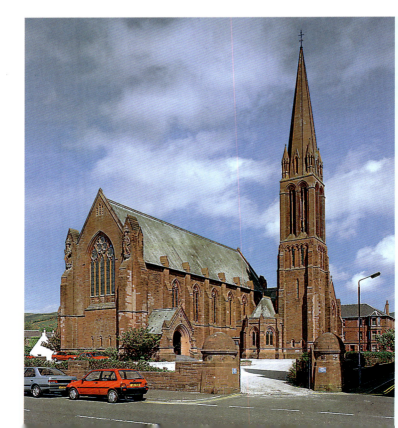

38. Troon, Our Lady of the Assumption, 1909–11 by Reginald Fairlie
    (pp. 28, 654)
39. Ardrossan, St Peter in Chains, 1938 by Gillespie, Kidd & Coia
    (pp. 32, 100)

40. Loch Doon Castle, C13, reconstructed and resited, 1933, by James S.
    Richardson (pp. 37, 511)
41. Dundonald Castle, *c.* 1280 and after (pp. 38, 305)
42. Dunure Castle, C13–C14, with doocot, C15 (pp. 51, 315, 316)
43. Kilmarnock, Dean Castle, late C14/early C15, and *c.* 1460, restored from
    1908 by Ingram & Brown and James S. Richardson (pp. 39, 41, 43, 455)

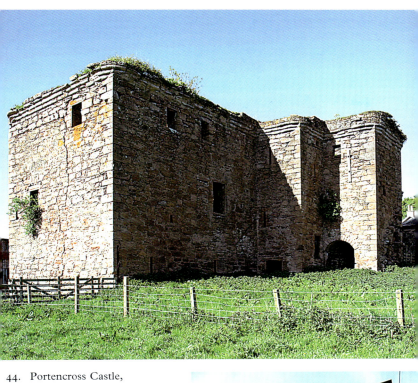

59. Culzean Castle, s façade, 1775–92 by Robert Adam (pp. 47, 249)
60. Auchincruive, Tea House, 1778 by Robert Adam (p. 111)
61. Culzean Castle, oval staircase, 1787–90 by Robert Adam, completed *c.* 1810 by Hugh Cairncross (pp. 47, 252)

71. Blairquhan House, 1820–4 by William Burn (pp. 48, 204)
72. Caprington Castle, 1829–30 by Patrick Wilson (pp. 48, 209)
73. Dunlop House, 1831–4 by David Hamilton (pp. 48, 314)
74. Arran, Brodick Castle, late C13, extended C14, C17 and, at left, 1844–6 by James Gillespie Graham (pp. 49, 681, 690)

79. Neilshill House, entrance hall, *c.* 1870 (p. 550)
80. Penkill Castle, staircase wall painting, from 1865 by William Bell Scott (pp. 49, 570)
81. Craigengillan, Stair Hall, 1905, by Jansen of Paris (pp. 49, 230)

82. Coodham, *c.* 1826, perhaps by Robert Smirke. Additions by Alfred
    Waterhouse 1871–9 (pp. 48, 225)
83. Noddsdale House, 1902 by James Miller, extended 1924–32
    by Fryers & Penman (pp. 50, 562)

84. Rowallan House, 1901–5 by Robert Lorimer (pp. 50, 594)
85. Kildonan House, 1914–23 by James Miller (pp. 50, 407)

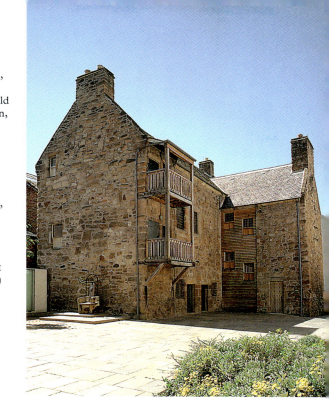

90. Kilmaurs, Town House, C18; steeple 1799–1800 by Hugh & David
   Barclay, masons (pp. 67, 463)
91. Prestwick, Salt Pan Houses, 1764–7 (pp. 57, 587)
92. Tarbolton, Bachelors' Club, C18 (p. 650)

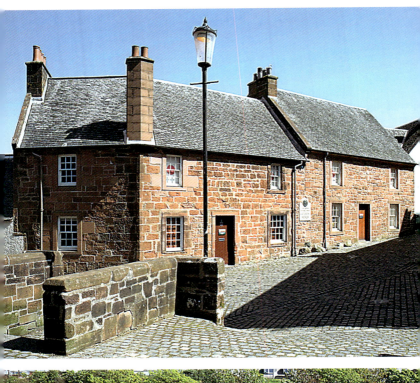

93. Mauchline, Burns House, *c.* 1760 (p. 523)
94. Dunure, Harbour, 1810–11 by Charles Abercrombie (pp. 55, 315)
95. Gatehead, Laigh Milton Viaduct, 1809–11 by William Jessop
    (pp. 56, 334)
96. Arran, High Corrie, late C18 and after (pp. 62, 681, 699)

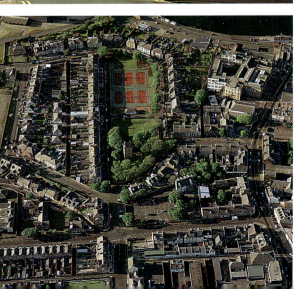

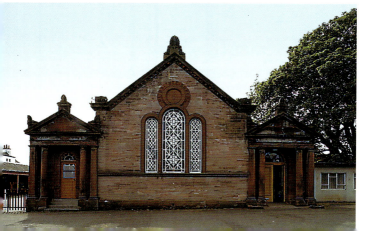

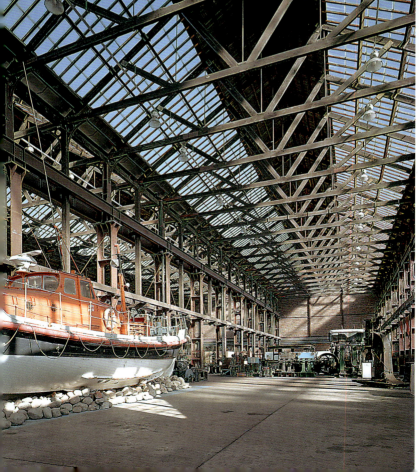

106. Waterside by Patna, former Dunaskin Ironworks, blowing engine house, 1847 and 1865 (pp. 59, 673)
107. Irvine, Linthouse Vennel, Linthouse machine-erecting shop, 1872 by James Spencer; re-erected 1990–1 (p. 389)
108. Turnberry, Lighthouse, 1871–3 by D. and T. Stevenson (pp. 55, 670)

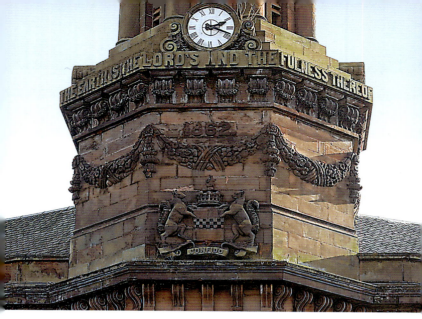

109. Kilmarnock, Palace Theatre (former Corn Exchange), detail, 1862–3 by James Ingram (pp. 71, 431)
110. Kilmarnock, John Finnie Street, planned from 1861–4 by William Railton and Robert Blackwood (pp. 70, 74, 438, 440)
111. Hurlford, Primary School, 1902–5 by Gabriel Andrew (pp. 71, 370)
112. Newmilns, Westgate House, 1898–1900 by Gabriel Andrew (pp. 74, 559)

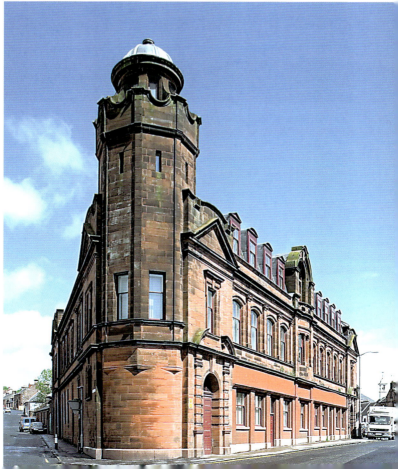

118. Kilbirnie, Radio City, 1937–8 by James Houston (pp. 84, 403)
119. Largs, war memorial, 1921 by Kellock Brown, detail (pp. 77, 503)
120. Darvel, Morton memorial, 1926–7 by Lorimer & Matthew, with
     C. d'O. Pilkington Jackson, detail (pp. 77, 288)

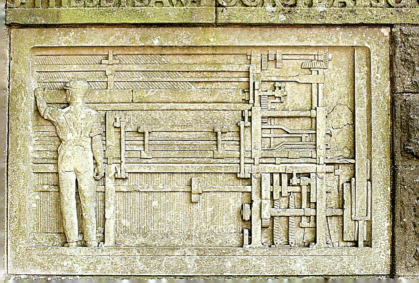

125. Girdle Toll, Lawthorn Primary School, 2000–1 by David Wadsworth
(North Ayrshire Council Architects Department) (pp. 82, 337)

126. Auchinleck, former Barony Colliery, head-frame, 1945 (pp. 58, 113)

EAST AYRSHIRE COUNCIL OFFICES, John Finnie Street. *See* John Finnie Street, below, p. 439.

EAST AYRSHIRE COUNCIL OFFICES, London Road. A red sandstone secondary school of 1930–3 by *William Reid*, County Architect, converted 1996. Big, classically detailed and broadly symmetrical about an advanced central single-storey block with carved decorative heads to the outer bays, while the flanking two-storey blocks have hipped roofs; their outer bays raised to form pavilions.

Former FIRE STATION, Titchfield Street. 1935–7 by *Gabriel Steel*. A four-storey brick structure, originally with vehicles below and accommodation above, now all converted to flats and shops. Projecting outer bays with rounded corners; the upper floors marked by strongly horizontal, but discontinuous, bands of metal windows. Two stone pilasters carry carvings of the town arms and a fireman's helmet.

GALLEON CENTRE, Titchfield Street. 1986–7 by *Crichton Lang, Willis & Galloway* of Edinburgh. A sports and leisure centre, presenting long façades of red and cream stone separated into bays by shallow paired brick pilasters: the main façade given interest by the large projecting entrance, a giant glazed T with a triangular pediment, the glazing carried back to light the central atrium.

KILMARNOCK ACADEMY, Rennie Street. 1896–9 by *R. S. Ingram* in Queen Anne style. Three storeys of Ballochmyle red sandstone. Its hilltop site to the E of the town centre makes the symmetrical main (W) façade a notable landmark. The central projecting bay has a gable with stepped skews and a clock face with scrolled consoles and a coat of arms above; below this, the round-headed, pilastered and pedimented porch and two storeys of four-light windows and strip pilasters. The flanking bays have three-light windows, the second-floor ones with pediments. The S elevation has similar details, symmetrically arranged about a five-stage square central tower, originally crowned with an observatory, with three-light windows and a balustrade to the final stage. Attractive entrance hall with two levels of galleries and a marble WAR MEMORIAL. The school has been considerably enlarged, most noticeably in 1964–7, and reduced in size in the succeeding years.

KILMARNOCK BUS STATION, Green Street. 1972–4 by *Percy Johnson-Marshall & Associates*; reconstructed 1994–5 by *Elder & Cannon*. Little of the original concrete structure remains. A glazed foyer provides a link with the town; platform finishes in granite, steel and Caithness flags. Aluminium and sheet-steel canopy.

KILMARNOCK COLLEGE, Holehouse Road. 1961–6 by *Robert G. Lindsay* for Ayr County Council, with *F. A. Macdonald & Partners*, engineers. Large but architecturally undemanding concrete-framed college on a quadrangular plan with a central courtyard.

KILMARNOCK PORTLAND BOWLING CLUB, South Hamilton Street. The club was formed in 1860, and the original pavilion with its dainty octagonal wooden and conical-headed tower is from that date and a rare survival; although the front has been altered to form a lounge, and there is a long late C20 brick clubhouse to the l.

KILMARNOCK STATION, John Finnie Street. The Glasgow, Paisley, Kilmarnock & Ayr Railway Company's line to Glasgow (via Dalry) was opened in 1843, and the more direct line via Stewarton opened by the GSWR in 1873. The station was rebuilt after this; the work completed in 1877, the architect probably *Andrew Galloway*. The red ashlar station, with its prominent pedimented Italianate E tower, sits in an elevated position; the overall character is castellated Gothic. The S façade has simple moulded square-headed windows, above a basement which increases to the W. Within the station, simple sandstone façades, while an impressive CANOPY, originally glazed, but now with clear plastic material, on simple cast-iron columns spans the island platform and the curving through platform. The filigree cast-iron canopy supports have the initials of the railway company in roundels. The accesses to the station equally fine; externally height is gained by a steeply climbing hairpin access, still with most of its original setts. Internally, steps from the platforms lead to a subway with a simple entrance to the N, and an elaborate castellated entrance and former booking office to the S.

Former KILMARNOCK TECHNICAL COLLEGE, Elmbank Avenue. 1907–9 by *Gabriel Andrew* (of *Andrew & Newlands*), converted to flats, 2002. Flamboyant Edwardian classical in red sandstone. Two storeys, on a raised and channelled basement; eleven-bay main façade with a lavishly decorated advanced central entrance bay. The doorway is square-headed, beneath a semicircular fanlight and within a huge shell hoodmould, supported on fluted brackets. Above this a mullioned-and-transomed window, flanked by paired Ionic columns above drop mouldings; above again, a raised, open pediment enclosing a semicircular tympanum with figure sculpture and spandrels with swags, the pediment capped with segmentally headed blocks at the ends and apex. The three outer bays to l. and r., also advanced, have panelled angle pilasters, pilaster-strips and strong keystones, while the other bays have windows with mullions and transoms. Twelve-bay return elevation to the S, with the outer bays advanced, and similarly detailed. Good GATEPIERS with shallow pedimented heads and drop moulding, and original iron gates.

LOANHEAD PRIMARY SCHOOL, Dick Road. 1902–4 by *J. & R. S. Ingram*. Large, austere symmetrical composition in Ballochmyle sandstone, with a channelled ground floor. The main façade has a three-storey nine-bay central projection, with a pediment over the three central bays. The other elevations similar but simpler.

ODEON CINEMA, Queen's Drive. 1997–8, by *ADF Partnership* of Glasgow. More historically conscious and memorable than many contemporary multiplex cinemas, with traditional ele-

ments of picture-house design, such as the tower with fin carrying the Odeon name and the bold exterior lighting, but
reimagined in an undeniably late C20 manner.

PALACE THEATRE, London Road. The Corn Exchange of
1862–3 by *James Ingram*, extended by *R. S. Ingram* in 1885–6
for an art gallery and a link to what was then the Agricultural
Hall, a straightforward work by the elder *Ingram*, also 1862–3.
The exchange became a Music Hall in 1903, while the Agricultural Hall was remodelled by *James Miller* in 1927 to form
the Grand Hall. At the rear, elements survive of the original
Kilmarnock Academy of 1807, probably by *Robert Johnstone*.

The Corn Exchange is Italianate, in Ballochmyle stone, of
two storeys, with nine bays to London Road and thirteen to
Green Street, each with a shallow central projection. Channelled ashlar ground floor with segmental-headed doors and
windows; upper floor with round-headed windows, separated
by panelled pilasters; some decorative keystones. Moulded
panels and blind balustrades between the floors, and a bracketed cornice and balustrade, with the central portions panelled
and topped with urns. At the angle the powerful octagonal   109
ALBERT TOWER, a memorial to the Prince Consort. At its
base three round-headed entrances, beneath a balustraded
balcony on giant console brackets; round-headed windows to
the first floor; here the keystones portray (from the l.) Lord
Clyde, Prince Albert and Sir James Shaw. Above this the first
stage of the tower proper, with wreaths, a datestone and the
town arms, and above these is carved 'the earth is the Lord's
and the fulness thereof' on a band supported on triglyph
corbels. Above, three clock faces, and then eight Corinthian
columns separate round-headed bell-openings and support a
dome with decorative slating and a bold finial. The main contractor was *Adam Loudon*, the sculptural work by *Joseph Boyd*.

The Agricultural Hall was set back from the road, and Robert
Ingram's Italianate Art Gallery extension ran in front of it. It is
of Ballochmyle stone, lower than the Corn Exchange, borrowing its details therefrom, with a channelled ground floor, and
widely spaced round-headed windows in the first floor, separated by panelled bays; most of these windows are blind.

The interiors have been made over on several occasions,
most thoroughly by *Kilmarnock & Loudoun District Council* in
1979–82 after a fire. The Grand Hall is still recognizably of
1927, with a segmentally arched roof and a gallery around
three sides. Proscenium arch with Ionic columns added by
Gabriel Steel, *c.* 1947.

POST OFFICE, No. 73 John Finnie Street. *See* Description 2,
p. 441.

PROCURATORS FISCAL'S OFFICES, St Marnock Street. The
town's first Sheriff Court House, Greek Revival style. Of 1850–2
by *William Railton* who made internal alterations and additions
in 1864. Conversion and extension, 1987–8, *Hay Steel & Partners*. Seven bays, with a round-headed blind arcade running
above single windows with bracketed cornices. The central

block has round-headed ground-floor openings and first-floor windows in eared architraves, and rises to an attic storey, temple-like, with Corinthian columns, pediments and prominent dentillation. Deep portico with square piers and round-headed keystoned arches. Flanking wings are pedimented with acroteria. Similar details to the side elevations. The interior has been thoroughly remodelled: the courtroom itself, which occupied the upper floor, has been divided horizontally and subdivided; an L-plan section of the original coffered ceiling alone remains. Excellent spear railings.

Former ST COLUMBA'S R.C. PRIMARY SCHOOL, Elmbank Drive. Renaissance of 1902–3 by *Alan Crombie* of Dumfries. Two-storey, five-bay red sandstone front elevation, with the outer bays advanced and pedimented; the entrance (now blocked) to the r. under an open bracketed pediment. The bays are divided by pilasters, those flanking the central bay paired and all banded from the first floor. The central bays have semicircular-headed windows below three-light windows divided by Ionic half-columns. Similar half-columns divide the pilastered and pedimented two-light windows in the outer bays.

SHERIFF COURT HOUSE, St Marnock Street. 1984–7 by *David N. Gregory* for the Property Services Agency. The external walls are largely windowless, big expanses of red sandstone conveying the full austerity of the law. The N-facing glazed entrance more welcoming.

WAR MEMORIAL, Elmbank Avenue. 1926–7 by *James Miller*. Classical, in the form of a shrine or temple, with a main elevation of three bays divided by flat pilasters, with a tall panelled parapet, and single-bay returns. The entrance is in the central bay with fluted Ionic columns and recessed steel and glass doors. Internally, a marble floor and bronze tablets on the walls with the names of the dead. Placed centrally is a moving bronze sculpture, The Victor, bowed in grief, by *David McGill* of London. Miller is not generally known for his war memorials, but this effective little design is an antidote to his contemporary monumental work in Glasgow.

PARKS

HOWARD PARK, Dundonald Road. Formally handed over to the Town Council in 1893 by Lady Howard de Walden, having been laid out in 1891–3 to plans of *C. & W. Mitchell & Langharne*. The wrought-iron gates with scrolled heads and scroll-headed piers date from this period. At the far side of the park, at the end of the avenue known as the Lady's Walk, the MONUMENT to Dr Alexander Marshall, erected in 1896. Elaborately detailed Gothic in Giffnock stone, with a square base, from which rises the clustered shaft with a richly carved capital, and florette decoration between the columns. The shaft is surmounted by a marble figure of Mercy on a single stumpy column, while the base has ball-capped columns at each corner, the lower halves of the columns with chequerboard decoration. Designed by *William Bone*, and executed by *Matthew Muir & Co.*, and not easily forgotten. To the N of the monument, a harled OLD MEN'S CABIN, presently disused, of 1897, 'in the English Cottage style of architecture, having an awning right round the exterior' and a hipped slated roof swept down to cast-iron columns.

KAY PARK, Strawberrybank Road. The original park was gifted to the town by Alexander Kay in 1879, and was considerably extended in 1884 when the neighbouring Strawberrybank lands were acquired. The layout was remodelled at that time by *Charles Reid*. It remains an important green space for central Kilmarnock. Of Reid's work the BOATING LAKE and the bosky avenues survive. The chief glory of the park was the BURNS MONUMENT of 1877–9 by *R. S. Ingram*, a dramatic Scottish Baronial edifice in Ballochmyle sandstone with a two-stage 24.3-m. tower. It was destroyed by arsonists in 2004. The fine Sicilian marble STATUE of Burns by *W. Grant Stevenson*, which stood in an alcove at the head of the entrance stairs, survived the fire, and forms the centrepiece of the red stone and harl U-plan BURNS MONUMENT CENTRE, of 2007–9, by *East Ayrshire Council*. To the E a fine cast-iron DRINKING FOUNTAIN, dated 1902, by *McDowall, Steven & Co. Ltd* of Glasgow. Four faces, with bowls, lion's-head fountains and, on two faces, portraits of Edward VII and Alexandra; surmounting all, an orb, and a gloved hand holding a crown aloft. To the N is the simple grey stone REFORMERS' MONUMENT of 1885, also by *R. S. Ingram*, which takes the form of a Corinthian column on a tall plinth, with an inscribed plaque in an aedicular frame on one elevation, commemorating those men of Kilmarnock who campaigned for Parliamentary Reform and 'devoted themselves with unselfish zeal to the cause of the people'. The column was originally capped with a statue of Liberty by *Charles B. Grassby*, blown down *c.* 1930.

DESCRIPTIONS

1. Town centre

The heart of Kilmarnock is THE CROSS, where King Street, Portland Street, Foregate and Cheapside Street meet. Originally five streets met here, but the Victorian exuberance of Duke Street was lost in 1976 to *Hay Steel MacFarlane*'s shopping precinct (now THE BURNS MALL), the unwarranted brick and concrete intrusion on the E side of The Cross. More successful, within The Cross, are two SCULPTURES introduced in the revitalizing improvements by *Page & Park* in 1995–6: one is *Sandy Stoddart*'s 1995 bronze of Robert Burns and John Wilson, the printer of the first edition of Burns's poetry, whose print shop lay close by. They stand back-to-back; between them at their feet two classical busts. To the N of this 'Twa Dugs' shape up to each other. The highlight of The Cross is the former

ROYAL BANK OF SCOTLAND, N, in the tight angle between Foregate and Portland Street. 1937–9 by *W. J. Walker Todd*, of *Dick Peddie, Todd & Jamieson*. A two-storey fawn sandstone Neoclassical rotunda, channelled on the ground floor, with flanking pavilions and a copper dome. The main ground-floor windows round-headed, recessed, with big stylized console keystones; the metal windows have multi-panel borders and roundels. The main entrance in the l. pavilion, a big moulded doorpiece with a narrow decorative panel above, carved with quoins and scrolls, and a dentilled head.

Kilmarnock, former Royal Bank of Scotland.
Perspective view and plan, drawing by B. Spence, 1937

KING STREET, the main shopping street, runs S from The Cross with the Burns Mall along most of its E side. First laid out in 1803–4, as part of a thorough scheme of replanning of the town by the Kilmarnock Improvement Commissioners. The plans were prepared by *Robert Johnstone*, and he appears to have also prepared elevations to accompany the feus sold to developers. There has been much rebuilding since but, above ground-floor level, much of interest remains from all periods. Now pedestrianized, and the major beneficiary of *Page & Park*'s 1995–6 townscape improvements, it has been given a quiet unity by new surface finishes, lamp standards and the occasional metal sculpture, including a quizzical diver and a fish, marking the subterranean passage of the Kilmarnock Water.

The W side begins with a canted three-storey block, of six closely spaced bays, a respectful replacement of *c.* 1930. To its l., the painted stone three-storey four-bay Nos. 9–13 are dated 1805 high in the S gable; the simple elevation might thus be *Johnstone*'s, but must in any case have been typical. Next again, the undistinguished single-storey front of Nos. 15–23 disguise a low stone building carried on a shallow segmental arch with polished voussoirs across the river. This is followed by a remarkable 1960s façade of white tiles, and tall narrow first-floor windows, and Neo-vernacular infill of 1986–7 by *Carl Fisher, Sibbald & Partners* of Edinburgh; the quoins and dressings standing proud above the harling. The former LAUDER'S EMPORIUM was built for Hugh Lauder & Co. in 1923 by *Frederick Sage & Co.* of London and is an excellent piece of early C20 Neoclassical commercial architecture, with channelled quoins, tall upper floor steel windows and a dentilled cornice. The three-storey-and-attic red sandstone VICTORIA BUILDINGS (Nos. 57–65)* are of 1901–2 by *Thomas Smellie*, with a Dutch gable above a shallowly canted bay between finialled pilasters, and an octagonal corner tower with an ogee-headed leaded roof, corbelled out above a window with podgy Ionic columns. To the l. of this tower a small window is squeezed uncomfortably in; it has an overly stilted frame, fluted corbels, more Ionic columns and an open semicircular pediment. The entrance vestibule and stairwell have Glasgow Style tiles. Nos. 77–79 are of 1956, by *Alexander Dunlop* in silver-grey bricks from the local Southhook potteries, with slightly projecting horizontal window bands. At the SW corner with Bridge Lane, three contiguous blocks which give some indication of how the street may have looked in the mid C19. Each is of three storeys, the first of three bays of exposed ashlar with moulded windows and end pilasters; the next of three bays, plastered, with moulded first-floor windows and end

---

*A contemporary observer saw this building as 'steering clear of the baldness which affected [so] many of the early nineteenth century blocks, and of the unhappy flashiness which stares out of the face of a good many that have been up-reared within the past decade'. (*Building Industries*, August 1901)

pilasters with odd capitals; the final one of six-bays, again with
end pilasters, and moulded windows on first and second floor,
the first floor with entablatures. There is a similar six-bay
return elevation to St Marnock Street. They must be of 1834,
or shortly thereafter, and the details, especially the pilasters,
suggest *James Ingram* as the architect. The E side of King Street
has little of note: only the early C19 two-storey painted stone
Nos. 84–90, with moulded first-floor windows and wide end
pilasters. Again probably by *James Ingram*.

CHEAPSIDE STREET runs SW from The Cross, and quickly
forks to form John Dickie Street and Bank Street. In JOHN
DICKIE STREET, at the entrance to Laigh Kirk (*see* Churches,
above), is a diminutive statue of Johnnie Walker of 1995–6 by
Sandy Stoddart. Walker leans nonchalantly on a top-hatted and
bearded god: 'Who are you? Vulcan god of labour. Who is he?
Mercury as Walker distiller in this town. Industry is a compact
between labour and capital.' In BANK STREET on the r., the
church dominates; on the l., firstly Nos. 2–18, a long row of
single-storey shops, with deeper stone façades to the river, of
c. 1860: No. 2 has a good shopfront with a gently curved central
entrance and cast-iron window frames and decoration. After
the five-bay early C19 Nos. 26–34, with its flat end pilasters,
are two imposing red sandstone buildings: Nos. 36–40 are of
c. 1910, with flanking recessed canted bays and a central pediment and wall-head stack, while No. 42 is of *c.* 1900, probably
by *Gabriel Andrew*, and is smartly and richly detailed. Three-
light ground-floor windows flank the Ionic-columned entrance
with its broken pediment on heavy consoles. Above this a
round-headed window in a Gibbsian frame, while, below the
corner turret with fish-scale decoration, a curved window
strains to break free from its own Gibbsian surround. Beyond
again, and set back, is the six-bay two-storey and raised basement late classical former UNION BANK of *c.* 1850 by *William
Railton*, altered by *T. G. Abercrombie* in 1904. Entrance in the
third bay from the l., with a flight of steps and a Roman Doric
porch with paired columns and decorative metopes. Recessed
flanking single-storey wings had blind round-headed openings;
that to the l. converted by Abercrombie to form a new entrance
to the agent's house. Outside is another of the quirky FIGURA-
TIVE SCULPTURES: a dumpy frowning workman sits to read
the *Kilmarnock Standard*. The l. side of Bank Street continues
with two mid-C19 two-storey blocks, both with raised quoins,
but one plastered, with oriels, the other painted and retaining
a good shopfront with console brackets. At the junction with
Nelson Street, No. 60 is another exuberant Free Renaissance
red sandstone block of 1903–4, probably by *Thomas Smellie*;
most of the decoration piled onto the rounded corner bay. This
has a round-headed entrance in a keystoned architrave, with
flanking round-headed niches, under four fluted consoles supporting a solid balcony; above this square-headed windows,
and another consoled balcony, with round-arched openings in
the balustrade; the final storey has round-headed windows,

surmounted by a solid parapet and a complex finialled and pedimented gable. Parapet with portholes, while the entrance vestibule and stairwell are beautifully decorated with Glasgow Style tilework. The r. side of Bank Street continues beyond the church with a two-storey harled late C18 or early C19 vernacular block, with its return elevation in COLLEGE WYND, where it is adjoined to the r. by a similar block, this one plastered, with a pend and a scrolled skew to the r. More red sandstone exuberance at No. 37, of *c.* 1905 by *Gabriel Andrew*: two storeys, with big semicircular gables to l. and r., and three big semicircular ground-floor windows with Gibbsian surrounds. The entrance has a large semicircular hoodmould supported by busty fluted caryatids.

In NELSON STREET, the three-storey brick façade of the former Smith's Printing Works, *c.* 1900, attributable to *Thomas Smellie*, with a big shaped Flemish gable above three linked semicircular windows in the second floor. In ST MARNOCK STREET a simple iron BRIDGE of 1867 is flanked by two impressive C19 SEED STORES, perched between the street and the river. The smaller is of 1883, for William Samson & Co., brick, of six bays, with round-headed upper-floor windows, and a red sandstone Renaissance front façade. The other was begun in 1850 for Dickie Foulds & Co., and was originally of nine bays, and extended by four bays to the N in 1858. Ashlar, with a flat-arched pend in the original first bay, a substantial basement on the river elevation, and at the N end a single-storey boiler house. It has a much grander plastered four-bay S elevation, facing St Marnock Street, with moulded curved corners and rusticated quoins at first-floor level.

Returning to The Cross, from which Portland Street runs northwards, immediately on the l. is CROFT STREET with, at the far end, on the r., the early C19 WHEATSHEAF HOTEL, rendered with painted dressings and crowstepped gables, and now part of much larger premises; opposite, filling most of the block and running the full length of STRAND STREET, are the unforgettable giant three-storey yellow brick WHISKY BONDS built for John Walker & Sons in 1879 by *Gabriel Andrew*. Fourteen bays to Croft Street and fifty-eight bays to Strand Street. Most of the simple classical detail clustered into the three curving bays at the N end: a tower with concomitantly huge channelled pilasters and pilaster-strips forming panels, and the Kilmarnock coat of arms. Elsewhere articulation given by single pavilion bays with channelled pilasters, stilted segmentally headed windows on the first floor and pilastered three-light attic windows; the other bays have second-floor windows with paired pilasters and no attic. Converted to local authority offices, 2009–11, by *iLo Design*, Glasgow, architects.

PORTLAND STREET was laid out in 1806, again by *Robert Johnstone* for the Town Improvement Commissioners, to create an appropriately imposing entrance into the town from Glasgow. Most of the buildings on either side were demolished in the 1990s, and replaced with a bland development of

standardized units *c.* 2000. At the N end the former George
Hotel, a large classical block, with a curving corner bay, and
giant Ionic pilasters framing the central bays of the main elevation. Of *c.* 1822–6, perhaps by *John Thomson* of Glasgow. In the
car park opposite, SCULPTURE: two allegorical figures of Trade
and Industry, in red sandstone, salvaged from *Gabriel Andrew*'s
premises for the Kilmarnock Equitable Co-operative Society
(1905–6), which formerly stood in Portland Street. The view N
is closed by the striding arches of the KILMARNOCK
VIADUCT, built for the Glasgow, Paisley, Kilmarnock & Ayr
Railway in 1847–8, designed by *John Miller*: twenty-three segmental arches with dressed stone arch-rings and quoins; a
bravura display of railway engineering. Beyond the viaduct
Portland Street continues with the Old High Church on the r.
and on the l. the former West High Church (for both, *see*
Churches above) and the stone boundary WALLS with
anthemion-headed piers and cast-iron railings patterned with
anthemia of *William Railton*'s Greek Thomson-influenced
Kilmarnock Infirmary of 1867–8 (dem).

Foregate and Foregate Square run NE from The Cross,
between Walker Todd's Royal Bank and the Burns Mall (*see*
above). In FOREGATE SQUARE, another laconic SCULPTURE
of 1995: four men face outwards, their heads, shoulders and
toes peeping above and below what may be a Kilmarnock
carpet. FOREGATE is of 1972–4 by *Percy Johnson-Marshall &
Associates*; when its predecessor Fore Street was included in
the town's Comprehensive Development Area in 1969, a group
of local traders came together 'to form a consortium to buy
land and build their own premises in a secondary trading area,
to avoid the high assessments likely to be met in more central
parts'. The architectural result of this unique development is
brick, chunky and rather austere: ground-floor shops with
offices above, reached by a plain bridging access. The contemporary CAR PARK, by *J. H. Routledge*, the Burgh Architect,
1972–4, deepens the austerity by virtually blocking out all
natural light from the street and shops; seen from the N or E,
however, with its many steel vertical emphases, the car park
has an architectural quality not usually associated with such a
function. At the NE end of Foregate, in PLACE DES ALÈS, the
CLYDESDALE BANK, of 1975–6 by *Hay Steel & MacFarlane*,
with a prominent circular stair-tower, glazed with concrete
verticals, echoed in the windows of the concrete first floor,
which projects beyond the dark brick ground floor.

2. *John Finnie Street and streets to the west*

The medieval core and the early C19 commercial streets described
above are bordered on the W by the grand N–S thoroughfare
of JOHN FINNIE STREET. This is easily the most dramatic
street in Kilmarnock and, as an example of a planned commercial street of the late C19, without parallel in Scotland.
Planning for it began in 1861 when the Town Improvement

Commissioners recognized a need for a direct connection between the railway station (opened 1843) at the N end of the town and the growing residential areas around Portland Road and Dundonald Road to the S (*see* p. 446). Plans were prepared by *William Railton*, architect, and *Robert Blackwood*, civil engineer, but progress could only be made after one of the major properties on the line of the new road was acquired in 1863 by John Finnie, a native of Kilmarnock and merchant in Manchester. The contractor for clearing the site and making the road was *Charles Reid*, and the street was formally opened in October 1864. Developers were slow to recognize the commercial possibilities and the buildings which line the street are mostly from the last quarter of the C19 and adopt the Free Renaissance styles of those years. Almost all of Mauchline red ashlar; they form an impressive ensemble and are, both architecturally and as a statement of Kilmarnock's late C19 pride and self-belief, matchless. In the early C21, John Finnie Street still stuns, despite its use as part of the town's choking inner one-way system, coupled with those banes of all Scottish urban centres, under-use and disuse of the upper floors and depressing shopfronts.

The street runs S, and arrow straight, from Kilmarnock Station (*see* Public Buildings, above), the Italianate tower of which closes the view N up the street. The E side of the street begins with the two-storey Franco-Italianate former OSSINGTON TEMPERANCE COFFEE HOUSE (Nos. 2–4), of 1883–4 by *J. & R. S. Ingram*. It has an oriel window in the centre of the three-bay return elevation in West George Street, and a single-bay wrought-iron balcony on the main elevation, between deeply channelled pilasters. The three plainer pedimented bays to the r. were added in 1890–1 by *R. S. Ingram*. The former OPERETTA HOUSE (Nos. 6–12), of 1873–4, was among the first buildings to be built in the street. Also by *J. & R. S. Ingram*, in an Italian Renaissance style, with a channelled ground floor and a central entrance with paired Roman Doric columns. Now merely a nine-bay façade;* the three central bays have complex Venetian windows, with outer pairs of Corinthian pilasters and inner engaged Corinthian columns. Nos. 14–28 are French Renaissance of 1880; of eight bays, the outer bays with rusticated pilasters, the four central bays framed by tall panelled and ornamented pilasters. Three tall mansard roofs, above the outer and central bays, with round-headed dormers between. The three-storey Nos. 30–38 are Free Renaissance of 1895–6 by *R. S. Ingram*, with a return elevation to Dunlop Street and a four-storey polygonal tower, capped with a faceted slate roof and an ogee-headed cupola. The main elevations busy with pilasters and pedimented wall-head dormers. Next, two mighty commercial properties fill entire blocks: converted to local government offices 1969–72

---

* Plans for restoration were brought forward by *Smith Design Associates* of Glasgow, 2010; work on site began 2011.

by *Alexander Dunlop* (*Allan Macpherson*, job architect), with
some fittings from *Robert Johnstone*'s Town Hall of 1805 (dem.).
The first, which stretches from Dunlop Street to John Dickie
Street, is the former KILMARNOCK EQUITABLE CO-
OPERATIVE SOCIETY premises of 1879–80 by *Gabriel Andrew*.
Free Renaissance with classical details, with ten bays to the
street and curved corners. Main entrance at the s corner, with
rusticated pilasters supporting a raised cornice and clock
under a shell pediment. A further rusticated pilaster in the
centre of the w elevation, and more at the N corner, which has
an octagonal turret with a scooped parapet and domed copper
roof. The thirteen-bay extension to the r. in John Dickie Street
was added by *Andrew* in 1886–7, using the same style to the
same height, but squeezing in an additional floor. s of John
Dickie Street is the equally handsome range of 1905–6 by
James M. Pearson, of *Pearson & Ronaldson* for William Wallace,
with lots of good carved details. The main façade has the
entrance in a curving corner bay to the l. with scroll carving
in the spandrels and a carved figure above the keystone. The
corresponding s corner bay similarly richly detailed. Channelled ground floor, and giant pilasters above. Windows with
segmental pediments on the first floor of the outer bays, the
central one with a carved panel above. Central pediment above
another carved panel at second-floor level, with balustrades to
l. and r. Simpler elevation to John Dickie Street, with segmentally pedimented entrance and a crowning pediment above the
parapet.

Smaller commercial premises follow, but with similar vigour.
The collegiate Gothic former ODDFELLOWS HALL (Nos.
60–62) of 1889–90 by *Gabriel Andrew* has a boldly projecting
octagonal angle turret to the l. with decorative panels of narrow
slits above eaves level and original haunched surrounds to the
shopfronts. Ground-floor pilasters support console brackets
which carry stepped buttress piers with shallow decorative
gabled niches and gablet finials. Big mullioned-and-transomed
first-floor windows, and a corbelled parapet. PEDEN'S BUILD-
INGS (Nos. 66–70) of *c.* 1880 is also Gothic, with mostly paired
windows, pointed on the first floor, with a continuous string
hoodmould; square-headed on the second floor, with a blind
arcaded parapet with terminal finials above, interrupted by a
central gable with a decorative panel and an apex stack. Next,
the mighty thirteen-bay range of Nos. 72–84, of 1879–80 by
William Railton, and firmly in the style of Alexander Thomson.
Plinth of channelled ashlar; some original ground front elevations survive, the doors with pilasters, the windows with pilasters and acanthus capitals. First-floor windows with broad sills,
architraves with anthemion details near the foot, and block
pediments with incised decoration and terminal anthemia.
Second-floor windows linked by panels with anthemia. The
only interruption to this consistent Late Victorian run is the
concrete-framed ROYAL BANK OF SCOTLAND of 1972, by
Henry Dawes & Sons (project architects *George Dawes* and

Robert Gardiner). The tall ground-floor banking hall is faced with large panels of solar glass. Finally, two earlier commercial buildings: the Italianate Nos. 100–106 with a sill course inscribed 'SMITH'S BUILDINGS ERECTED 1876', while the former KILMARNOCK ARMS is simple Free Renaissance of *c.* 1890.

Back at the N end, the opposite side begins with the Free Renaissance KILMARNOCK CLUB of 1898–9 by *R. S. Ingram*. Its four-bay front elevation is flanked by wide canted bays. Central segmental pediment with the town's arms, flanked by short balustrades; the central first-floor bays flanked by rusticated pilasters. The entrance to the club is off-centre on the brick N elevation; it is ashlar, with a central triangular pediment and brackets with grotesque bearded faces, carved by *James Rome & Sons*. Inside entrance hall with a tiled floor by *Galbraith & Winton*, paired Corinthian columns and a rich oak stair. S of John Dickie Street, a two-storey ashlar block of *c.* 1930 with a canted corner and a strong horizontal emphasis, the Central Evangelical Church (*see* Churches, above) and a plain light brown sandstone two-storey block by *J. & R. S. Ingram* for the Kilmarnock Equitable Co-operative Society, 1888. The Laigh Kirk Mission Hall (*see* Churches) is succeeded by the Tudor Gothic Nos. 39–41, of *c.* 1875. Of three bays, the first floor divided by pilasters rising to faceted finials, while the central bay has a four-light window within a square hoodmould, which rises to form a star in the middle; above this a corbelled crowstepped gable. Nos. 43–49 are of *c.* 1925, with tall first-floor glazed bays, and many fine details, especially the engaged Corinthian columns and channelled pilasters, borrowed from the block to the l.: this is the elaborate and effective Nos. 51–53, of 1873–4 by *James Ingram* for Archibald Finnie & Son, coalmasters. Classically detailed, of five bays and two storeys, with a three-bay return elevation. Ground floor with round-headed openings and channelled pilasters. Above, Corinthian columns divide semicircular-headed windows with mask keystones, while the columns themselves have lions' heads in the frieze.

Beyond Grange Place the unity of the street begins to break up, but it begins strongly with the three-storey Free Renaissance Nos. 55–57, of 1890–1 by *Peddie & Kinnear* for the BRITISH LINEN BANK. Dramatized by oriel windows in the outer bays that terminate in gables with triangular pediments; the central bay broadly similar and its pediment lower. Round-headed windows on the return elevation ground floor, the floors above echoing the central bay of the main elevation. Nos. 59–61 are of *c.* 1965, also three storeys, but much lower and with a curving twelve-bay façade, divided by concrete piers and infilled with glass and concrete panels. Finally the POST OFFICE of 1907 by *W. T. Oldrieve* of *H. M. Office of Works*, in the grand tradition of the street's other commercial buildings but in the Baroque style more typical of its date. Two-storey red ashlar block, with a splayed corner, with two-light windows,

a broken pediment above the first floor and a raised and decorative parapet. The wide pedimented flanking bays have ground-
floor Venetian windows, three-light windows on the first floor
and swagged oculi. Beyond this, GEORGE TANNAHILL &
SONS (Nos. 75–77), of c. 1894–5, retains its original shopfront
with Corinthian banded shafts and a door with a scrolled
pediment.
The laying out of John Finnie Street cut across several existing
streets, and opened up the areas to the W for development for
commercial and industrial purposes. The effect can be seen in
WEST GEORGE STREET which has a terrace (Nos. 14–20) of
c. 1850, and a pub with a corner turret and interior of c. 1903,
and opposite, a three-storey commercial range on a narrow site
of c. 1880, with an octagonal slated and copper turret, and bays
divided by prominent attached columns. Characteristic of the
post-1864 period is GRANGE PLACE. It was laid out in 1876
to plans of *William Railton*. Of that date a single-storey block
on the N side, with a tall chamfered arched and pedimented
entrance to the r., and blind openings to the l. To its l. an
Italianate two-storey three-bay block of c. 1880, with cavetto
reveals, three-light first-floor windows with colonnettes, and a
ball-finialled balustrade. To the l. again, No. 13, former GRAIN
STORES built for the Scottish Co-operative Wholesale Society
in 1881–2 by *Gabriel Andrew*. Also Italianate, red ashlar, its
nine-bay façade divided by full-height pilasters on battered
plinths. The first-floor windows have Corinthian caps to the
flanking pilasters and allegorical sculptured heads in the blind
arches above. Opposite are the two-storey fourteen-bay ashlar
former offices and printing works of the KILMARNOCK
STANDARD, of 1890–1 by *Gabriel Andrew* in French Renaissance style. Ground-floor pilasters partly fluted and paired at
the W end; Corinthian pilasters above, and a one-bay splayed
return with a figurehead keystone to the entrance, and a corbelled and pilastered three-light window above. Beyond Grange
Street (*see* below), Grange Place becomes WOODSTOCK
STREET, with the former Grange Parish Church (*see* Churches,
above) and a grey sandstone terrace of c. 1880: beyond is
LINDSAY STREET, with a short glazed-brick terrace of c. 1880,
simpler than that in North Hamilton Street (*see* below).
    GRANGE STREET runs N–S, almost parallel with John Finnie
Street as far as Dunlop Street. Towards the N, on the E, is one
earlier painted stone house of 1818, the ARTISTS' HOUSE,
built for the artists James and William Tannock. Two distinct
parts. To the l., the house is two-storey with an Ionic-pilastered
doorway to the r., and centre under a blocking course with
relief panel of a goddess reclining at an easel. To the r., a taller
gabled block contained the brothers' studio and picture gallery,
with a small segmental apical pediment, a first-floor Venetian
window and a three-light ground-floor window with a cornice.
    The major industrial enterprise in this area is the former
CALEDONIA WORKS on WEST LANGLANDS STREET, built
for Andrew Barclay Sons & Co. Ltd, locomotive engineers. The

buildings, which were converted into residential and commercial use by *Smith Design Associates*, of Glasgow, for the Klin Group from 2006, form three sides of a rectangle. They are mostly rubble-built with ashlar dressings. The oldest block is that at the junction with North Hamilton Street, of six bays and two storeys, with a big gabled return. It was built *c.* 1851; in the attic a double dormer which housed the observatory of Andrew Barclay, who was a keen amateur astronomer as well as a pioneering and innovative engineer. This block was subsequently extended a further ten bays to the l., and the whole was rebuilt internally after a fire in 1876. At the E end, the offices of *c.* 1906, in red brick, with pilaster-strips, tall eaves and a corbelled angle turret. The nineteen-bay range which faces W to NORTH HAMILTON STREET, with a six-bay return to Park Street, is late C19, probably post-dating the fire. For the early works, *Andrew Barclay* was probably his own architect. The C21 conversion has brought new elements – brick, sheet steel and copper panelling to the stairwells – to the inner faces of the blocks. The internal courtyard retains a 15-ton travelling CRANE by *John M. Henderson & Co.* of Aberdeen, while the wrought-iron sign on the ridge of the E range is both a landmark and a sign of the C19 town's pride in its industrial prowess. Opposite the SW corner of the works, in NORTH HAMILTON STREET, Nos. 21–29, a terrace of five blocks of tenements, two-storey, dated 1883, their front elevations faced with white glazed brick, probably from *J. & M. Craig & Co. Ltd*, with the dressings picked out in purply-red ashlar and terracotta.

3. London Road and the inner eastern suburbs

London Road runs E from the centre for 1.5 km., and contains many of the town's best public buildings, but is now regrettably visually separated by the inner one-way system along Green Street and STURROCK STREET, where is the Italianate CONSERVATIVE CLUB of 1887 by *R. S. Ingram*. This is in polished Giffnock ashlar, with a porch supported on paired Ionic columns, and vermiculated quoins to the round-headed ground-floor windows. By the same architect is the former FRIENDS' MEETING HOUSE of 1885: a single-storey hall with a channelled ashlar front dominated by a keystoned Venetian window in a square recess with panels below and panelled spandrels. Lower flanking entrance bays recessed to l. and r.; now offices.

LONDON ROAD proper starts with the good early C20 Henderson Parish Church (*see* Churches, above) and the proud C19 Corn Exchange (*see* Palace Theatre, Public Buildings, above) but continues in stuttering fashion before its essential character – that of a high-class mid to late C19 residential area, with substantial houses in generous grounds – holds sway. These houses mostly remain in domestic use and, especially on both sides beyond the junction with Elmbank Avenue, convey the feel of a wealthy Victorian domesticity. The earlier houses are generally on the N side; much of the S side was the glebe.

Firstly, though, on the S, the red sandstone MASONIC HALL of 1926–7 by *William F. Valentine*, a simpler and earlier version of his Central Evangelical Church (*see* Churches, above), with the same full-height central recess but with a plain round-headed entrance and without balustrades. At the corner of Elmbank Avenue, the Ravaccione marble STATUE of Sir James Shaw of 1848 by *James Fillans*;* Shaw is portrayed in his mayoral robes, on a tall Aberdeen granite pedestal. On the N side, Nos. 6–8, early C19, with Roman Doric doorpieces and canted central bays. No. 10, also early C19, with a later C19 single-storey porch; the original house has wide end pilasters and windows in crisp architraves, and may be by *James Ingram*. No. 12 is late C19, in finely cut red ashlar, with a fluted Doric doorpiece and flanking screen walls with segmental archways. The mid-C19 asymmetrical painted ashlar No. 14 is Tudor Gothic, with an advanced bay to the l., a re-entrant porch with a pediment and bracketed frieze, and canted bays with decorative parapets. Flanking late C19 single-storey wings.

The block beyond ELMBANK AVENUE is dominated by the Dick Institute, with the former Kilmarnock Technical College and the town's war memorial (for all these, *see* Public Buildings, above) facing the Institute across Elmbank Avenue. Beyond Holehouse Road, the N side begins with the gabled mid-C19 No. 18, with a pilastered doorpiece and flanking canted bays, and Nos. 20–22, of *c.* 1870, with a central porch supported by one Ionic column and a large bracket. The hipped and plastered ORCHARDHILL (No. 26), of 1818, has three wide bays with end pilasters, pedimented single-storey flanking wings and a big classical porch which may be early C20. Opposite, beyond the Dick Institute, late C19 houses built on the former glebe, mostly *c.* 1886–94 by *Charles Mitchell*, who acted as developer and architect until bankruptcy in 1894. They include No. 47, of 1895, red sandstone Tudor Gothic, all arched moulds and gables, the gabled Nos. 49–51 of 1896, with pretty flanking glazed porches with brattishing, and No. 1 GLEBE ROAD, of *c.* 1890. Its main elevation, with a canted central bay, a figurative sculpted panel above the entrance, decorative panels in the frieze and a balustrade, faces Glebe Road. The London Road elevation has a subsequent subsidiary entrance, profoundly 1960s.

The N side continues with No. 30, of 1838, its entrance and r.-hand ground-floor window with bracketed cornices, and a late C19 semicircular bay to the l.; the hipped and plastered mid-C19 No. 34 has end pilasters and a shallow fluted Doric porch. The additional single storey bay to the r., of *c.* 1880, is dominated by a huge oval window in a flamboyant frame. The classical LESLIE VILLAS (Nos. 36–38), of *c.* 1850, are probably

---

*Born in Riccarton, Shaw rose to became Lord Mayor of London. His statue was originally at Kilmarnock Cross, but became a traffic hazard and was resited in 1929.

by *William Railton*; their outer bays advanced and flanked by giant pilasters, while the entrances are on the side elevations, that to the E with an Ionic portico. The asymmetrical hipped light brown ashlar Italianate TREMOLESWORTH (No. 42) is one of the bigger houses in the road. Of *c.* 1850, by *James Ingram*, with a large central pedimented Ionic porch. On the S side, between Glebe Road and Nursery Avenue, the houses again late C19, the best Nos. 59–61, of 1896–7 by *Thomas Smellie*, an almost symmetrical pair in light brown ashlar with prominently projecting canted bays to l. and r.; the entrances are in the re-entrants, that to No. 59 under a conically headed round tower.

On the N side of London Road, between Melville Street and Walker Avenue, the houses, known collectively as NURSERY-HALL TERRACE, are set back from the road and raised above it, with a communal access paralleling the road. They begin with the Gothic mid-C19 No. 44, probably by the same hand as Nos. 20–22, as suggested by the porch on Peterhead granite columns, resembling a medieval chimneypiece, while No. 48, of *c.* 1850, is also faintly Gothic, with shouldered gables to the porch and r.-hand bay. At the E end a pair (Nos. 52–54) and a detached house (PIERSLAND, No. 56) date from *c.* 1874; a well-composed and attractive group, possibly by *William Railton*. They are of grey sandstone, with dressed red stone details and a rubbly red sandstone base course. Between them they muster one single storey and three full-height semicircular bays with exposed rafter ends and finials; the round-headed entrances have Corinthian pilasters and prominent moulded heads.

On the S side E of Nursery Avenue, i.e., beyond the former glebe land, the houses tend to be earlier C19 and the building line initially curves away from the road. HAWTHORNBANK is a painted ashlar Grecian villa of *c.* 1830 with wide end pilasters, while the Gothic Nos. 73 and 75 are of *c.* 1840, with big door-pieces and very noticeable Tudor chimneys. DEANMONT (No. 77) is a large mid-C19 asymmetrical villa built by *James Ingram* for the coalmaster James Craig, with a central Roman Doric portico and a balustraded parapet. It has a gabled bay to the r. with a three-light first-floor window with a bracketed pediment to the central light; to the l. a shallow square balustraded projection guards another three-light window. One other villa of distinction beyond Middlemas Drive: TANKARDHA (No. 79) is of *c.* 1880, perhaps by *William Railton*; grey sandstone with polished red dressings. It returns to the street line, though its faintly Thomsonesque main façade looks W down the road. This has an octagonal corner turret, a wide paired round-headed entrance with Roman Doric columns under a balustrade, and a broad canted full-height bay to the r., topped by a balustraded parapet. Good chimney pots. On the l. return one square projected bay with a ground-floor canted window projection; to the l. modest single-storey C20 additions that, with the lounge addition to the r., in a very simple classical

manner, with semicircular bays, betray a long period of institutional use.

The streets to the N of London Road are primarily residential. In HOLEHOUSE ROAD, besides Kilmarnock College (*see*
Public Buildings, above), THE KNOLL, of *c*. 1910, harled with
exposed stone details such as the panelled and moulded
entrance; Nos.11–13, *c*. 1925, also harled, but in an angular Art
Deco (possibly by *William F. Valentine*) gauchely composed,
especially when compared with the handling of the canted bays
of the light brown stone Nos. 15–17, of *c*. 1910. On the N side
of Holehouse Road, EVELYN VILLAS, of *c*. 1905 by *Gabriel
Andrew*, two pairs, harled with polished red sandstone dressings. Paired round-headed central entrances below porches,
supported from above by iron ties; above, semicircular windows
with prominent flat keystones; full-height canted bays with
eared, shallowly curved pediments. To the l. of these, DE
WALDEN TERRACE, a smart red sandstone terrace of *c*. 1900,
again by *Andrew*, with canted gabled bays with applied timbering. The return elevation features a delicate timber and slated
porch.

In WILSON AVENUE and MELVILLE STREET the town's
first local authority housing developments, built between 1920
and 1922 to plans of *James S. Hay*. Mostly semi-detached
houses, brick harled, simply detailed; spaciously laid out in line
with Garden Suburb ideals. In WALKER ROAD, No. 1, a red
sandstone villa of *c*. 1900, probably by *Gabriel Andrew*, unremarkable but for its lavishly detailed doorway: a round-headed
entrance with Gibbsian surround, flanked by tapering Corinthian pilasters on bulky bases with ball finials, supporting a
sinuous pediment on shaped brackets. Also notable the gatepiers, like two widely separated parts of a segmental pediment.

4. St Marnock Street, Portland Road and the south-west suburbs

ST MARNOCK STREET was laid out *c*. 1834, when the bridge
across the Marnock Water was completed, easing access
between King Street and the roads to Troon and Irvine. At its
W end it forms a cross-roads with John Finnie Street (*see* above,
p. 438), Portland Terrace and Dundonald Road. DUNDONALD
ROAD is the principal road S of the town centre and was developed with villas from the mid C19. It begins on the l. with the
return elevation of the Sheriff Court (*see* Public Buildings,
above); on the r. with the gable-end of Holy Trinity church,
Holy Trinity rectory and Winton Place E.U. Church (for all
these *see* Churches, above), and then two good High Victorian
houses: No. 3 is multi-gabled C13 Gothic of 1859–60 by *James
Ingram*, with a castellated single-storey bay and, the charming
detail which makes this building, a pretty oriel in the r. bay
with a steeply pitched faceted cap. One could imagine Rapun-
zel doing her spinning here. No. 5 is Scots Baronial, dated
1868, a feast of crowsteps, including the rather gauche l. bay,
where a canted full-height bay is corbelled out to form another

crowstepped gable just in front of the bay's gable. The return elevation faces HOWARD STREET. This attractive tree-lined street dates from *c.* 1885, with two-storey pairs of houses on both sides, mostly of grey ashlar; many of those at the W end have wall-head chimneys, while Nos. 2–4, on the N, have a porch with fish-scale slating between projecting gabled bays, and Nos. 5–7, on the S, have a channelled ground floor and a decorative frieze. Howard Street joins SEAFORD STREET, which runs N–S, from which CHARLES STREET and ELLIS STREET run W. These streets continue the late C19 residential pattern established in Howard Street, though the quotidian house is single-storey with an attic. Worthy of individual note are, in Seaford Street, No. 3, with a bracketed cornice and iron balconies, and Nos. 5–7, a wide pair with porches in the re-entrants with bracketed heads; in Charles Street, Nos. 12–14, with their curvy door lintels reminiscent of Yorkshire; and, in Ellis Street, the slightly later (*c.* 1910) terrace of red sandstone cottages with tall gables, as regular as soldiers on parade.

Dundonald Road continues beyond Howard Street. The houses here are generally two-storey, with those on the N side looking onto the Howard Park (*see* Parks, above); further out, single-storey houses with attics predominate on the N, two-storey on the S. Between the Sheriff Court and the Howard Park, a run of late C19 houses, the best No. 34, BEECHWOOD, with a full-height bow to the l.; opposite are Nos. 9–11, a Gothic pair of *c.* 1880 with corbelled-out gables; Nos. 13–15, similar, but the gables slate-hung; and No. 27, of *c.* 1860, with its tapering round-arched door frame. In the next block, No. 35 has a gabled bay to the r., but is most notable for its haunched doorway, below a stepped mould and asymmetrical stepped parapet and semicircular decorative head; the chamfered entrance reveals are corbelled out to the haunches with one short order of nailhead decoration. On the opposite side, the mostly two-storey houses are also late C19, such as the crowstepped Scots Baronial No. 52, *c.* 1870 by *James Ingram*, with an elaborate porch.

In SOUTH HAMILTON STREET, a mix of properties, including early C19 cottages such as No. 7 with its shaped doorpiece, and classical villas of *c.* 1870, such as the grey stone No. 12. MCLELLAND DRIVE introduces another compact and cohesive area of late C19 housing, mostly red sandstone: attractive curving terraces in McLelland Drive and BARBADOES ROAD, but villas and cottages in streets such as WALLACE STREET and HOWARD PARK DRIVE, e.g. Nos. 7–8 Howard Park Drive, with paired entrances under semicircular fanlights and moulded round-headed arches.

The next block of Dundonald Road contrasts mostly late C19 two-storey houses on the l. with later, often early C20, single-storey houses on the r. On the l., No. 78, WESTMONT, of 1884, is an Italianate villa with a central tower, a heavy bracketed porch on granite columns, and round-arched windows in two of the upper lights. Opposite, the mid-C19

No. 67 is painted stone, with a crowstepped porch, and chamfered and cusped entrance (*see* also Morningside, Portland
Road, below), while No. 83 is a luxuriant red sandstone house
of 1894, with a wide studded bargeboard to its gable, and a
shallow hipped dormer to the l. The chief glory of the house,
though, is the porch, with Gibbsian surround, a moulded segmental arch, and a stepped shaped head culminating in a
dainty triangular pediment. Gatepiers like a separated swan-
neck pediment, similar to those in Walker Road (*see* above, p.
446). By *Gabriel Andrew*, and a foretaste of the final glories of
Dundonald Road. At the junction with Aird Avenue and
Holmes Road, three houses of *c.* 1910, all mostly white-harled
with stone dressings. No. 90 is a substantial house, with tile-
hung panels, exposed stone porch (the stone here light brown),
window dressings and a tall battlemented bay in one re-entrant;
on the return elevation the tiled roof sweeps down between a
tiled gable and a stone-faced hipped bay to form a porch with
plain columns and a bracketed cornice. In comparison, No.
101, of 1904 by *James S. Hay*, seems subdued, despite its bow
window and very stylized catslide dormer, while the group is
completed by POINT HOUSE, also of 1904, which faces down
Dundonald Road. It has harled gables and exposed stone
dressings with slightly mannered quoins to the windows; it
succeeds because of the balance between gables and windows.

St Marnock Place continues to the w as PORTLAND ROAD.
On the r. Nos. 7–13, an appealing late C19 terrace with paired
entrances with detached cast-iron columns, and lacy barge-
boarding to cornices and gables, which also have urns; Nos.
15–21 also have the lacy woodwork. On the opposite side, a
two-storey group from the early C19, mostly plastered, with
paired entrances with bracketed heads and the occasional
shallow pilaster, is flanked by two late C19 buildings. Nos. 6–8,
of *c.* 1892, has a finialled gable and slender bargeboards, while
Nos. 28–30 is a heavy red sandstone Gothic effort of *c.* 1885,
with a bracketed porch, and a battlemented cornice, linking
the battlemented heads of the flanking canted bays. The next
stretch is marked by mostly plastered mid-C19 villas on the l.,
almost wholly now in commercial use; the best perhaps the
simple dignity of Nos. 36–38, gable-ended with windows in
lugged architraves, and paired central entrances, each with
fluted columns, and a shared entablature; and No. 40, with its
pilastered entrance and cast-iron balconies. No. 46 has at its
core a hipped two-storey pink sandstone house of *c.* 1820,
transformed *c.* 1905 by *Thomas Smellie* to form a house and
studio for himself; using red sandstone he added a single-storey
porch and bay at the front, and to the r. a prominent first-floor
glazed studio room whose w gable rises above a chimney on a
concave base. Smellie's, too, the outbuildings, the central rear
extension, with its sweeping bargeboards and gable hung with
Westmorland slate, and the boxy dormer. The house was sympathetically extended to the E *c.* 1988 when it became a nursing
home.

A pair of equally rewarding houses on Portland Road's N side. The first is No. 37, *c.* 1860, a three-bay single-storey villa with a tall central gable above a round-arched pilastered doorway which has a cornice and scrolled wreath above. Paired round-arched and pilastered windows in the outer bays, and recessed gabled wings to l. and r. with prominent finials. The other is No. 41, ETRURIA BANK, of 1861–2 by *James Ingram*, similarly of three bays and a single storey. Round-arched and pilastered entrance below a bracketed cornice, recessed between canted bays with chamfered openings. A pierced balustrade and parapet, with a central decorative crest in a circular panel, links the bays, as does the balustrade to the steps to the entrance, which returns to join the outer bays. Slightly recessed flanking hipped wings. No. 43, MORNINGSIDE, is of 1856, plastered, bargeboarded and gabled, its re-entrant porch with oddly chamfered and cusped reveals to entrance and paired windows on the E elevation. Late C19 villas beyond North Hamilton Street, the crispest the hipped grey sandstone No. 47, while Nos. 51–63 are a terrace of *c.* 1870 with canted bays, paired entrances with columns and entablatures, and French roofed towers at either end.

SPRINGHILL HOUSE is announced by its hipped and painted Greek Revival LODGE with a pediment and fluted Doric columns *in antis*. The painted ashlar classical house was built *c.* 1840 for the coalmaster Archibald Finnie; the detailing suggests *James Ingram* as the architect. It was converted by *Gabriel Steel* in 1945 into a nursing home for Kilmarnock Town Council. Two-storeys with a raised basement. The three-bay front (E) is dominated by a projecting full-height pedimented bay with Ionic columns *in antis* flanked by piers. The recessed door has a bracketed cornice and narrow flanking lights, and a window in an architrave above, also with narrow flanking windows, these with fifteen-pane glazing. The outer bays have three-light ground-floor windows with bracketed cornices, three-light windows above, and flat end pilasters. Internally, the entrance hall has a screen of fluted Corinthian columns and pilasters, decorative cornices and panelled moulded ceilings. For the grounds *Neil S. Sutherland* designed SPRINGHILL GARDENS: neat pairs of brick, harled and slated cottages, with deeply recessed corner porches, completed in 1957–66.

5. South: Titchfield Street, Glencairn Square

King Street merges seamlessly into TITCHFIELD STREET, the laying out of which was begun *c.* 1765. It runs directly S, forming a lengthy tail to the town centre, a function reflected in the varied architecture, mostly late C19, with occasional C20 intrusions. The W side begins with two early C19 blocks, Nos. 1–5, with a corbelled cornice, and the plainer Nos. 13–17, separated by a grey brick unit of *c.* 1965; beyond these two late C19 red sandstone three-storey blocks, one with smooth ashlar, the other stugged ashlar, both with corbelled oriels, the first with a central first-floor window with a bracketed swan-neck pediment. Opposite is the overwhelming Free Renaissance façade of the former KINGS THEATRE, of 1903–4 by *Alexander Cullen*. This is broadly symmetrical; the outer bays have tall hipped roofs behind pedimented gables, with Diocletian windows beneath; narrow flat-headed windows below again, and all within tall paired Corinthian pilasters. The three middle bays have round-headed windows with flat-headed windows (now blocked) above, each window with flat pilasters. The w side continues with No. 43, an impressive red sandstone block of *c.* 1890, with crowstepped gables, one rising into a corner chimneystack, upper-floor windows in projecting castellated oriels, and round-headed ground-floor windows flanking the moulded and shallowly segmentally headed entrance. Nos. 47–71, of *c.* 1880, are a long range in red sandstone, with canted oriels, except in the centre where curved oriels flank a central shaped gable with slender ball-headed finials springing from corbels. Also on this side the Galleon Centre and, opposite, the former fire station (for both *see* Public Buildings, above).

The streetscape becomes much patchier beyond these, mid-C19 vernacular jostling with the gimcrack, before Titchfield Street merges imperceptibly into HIGH GLENCAIRN STREET. This continues the pattern established in Titchfield Street. On the w side, mostly mid to late C19, usually two-storey, often harled, such as the Crown Inn, interspersed with later red sandstone blocks, such as Nos. 33–37, with a central shaped gable and canted bays to l. and r. Similarly so on the E, where the tall red sandstone tenements of *c.* 1900 dominate visually, such as No. 18, its entrance with a Gibbs surround, Nos. 20–24, dated 1903, with a tall conical tower and wide oversailing eaves, and No. 30, dated 1904, in a miniature pediment, with canted oriels and an entrance with flat pilasters. In GLENCAIRN SQUARE, the HUNTING LODGE, a pub from *c.* 1930 by *William F. Valentine*, mostly brick harled, with a stone base, half-timbered gables over big oriels, and a corner tower with a copper dome. Beyond here, LOW GLENCAIRN STREET; with interest provided only by the former ROYAL BANK OF SCOTLAND, of 1967–9, two storeys of rough concrete panels, supported on pilotis to l. and r., and Nos. 35–57, a red sandstone terrace of *c.* 1890, with six canted oriels, the central two with slated octagonal caps.

E of here is an industrial area by the River Irvine. In RIVERBANK PLACE the buildings have their main elevations to the river. At the junction with Lawson Street is a former LACE FACTORY of W. E. & F. Dobson, built *c.* 1880. Of yellow brick, with segmental-arched windows, and of four storeys. It has a tall ground floor to accommodate the lace looms. To the r., and part of the same mill, a ten-bay three-storey building also in yellow brick, and probably contemporary. Beyond this a tall yellow brick two-storey block, again with a tall ground floor, a low mid-C19 building with its gable facing the road, and a yellow brick two-storey mid-C19 factory with a ground floor of normal height and round-headed windows.

6. North: Hill Street

HILL STREET lies close to the town centre, but mentally separated from it by the railway. It is dominated by the factory of JOHN WALKER & SONS LTD on its w side. The earliest building on site is a gabled stone shed at the SE corner, close to the station, with a six-bay end elevation to Hill Street; the openings blocked, that to the r. round-headed. It appears to be late C19, though not built for Walkers. Centralization of the company's operations on the Hill Street site began in 1939, and the first building, trapezoidal in plan, was completed in 1940. Its frontispiece is a long brick four-storey block, with a canted N corner, with shallow brick pilasters, and dominated by a central clock in a lugged red and black tiled frame. Similarly detailed return elevations. To the N of this the brick barrel-vaulted former bottling hall, of 1951–6, and E of this the large square gatehouse, dominated by its grey tiled roof. S of this a brick two-storey office block of c. 1966–8, with continuous bands of glazing in brightly painted frames, and alternate bays with granite panels between the window bands. Opposite is a two-storey concrete-framed brick-skinned office block (SCOTTISH ENTERPRISE AYRSHIRE), originally for Walkers, 1967–9. S of this St Joseph (see Churches, above); to the N the hulking red sandstone presence of DERWENT HOUSE. This was Nazareth House, a children's home built in 1901–2, incorporating at the rear a classical three-bay house of c. 1802. Mostly two-storey, with a third storey in mansard roofs; the four central bays a storey higher with a central pedimented gable. The original main entrance in the l.-hand of these central bays, round-headed beneath three basket-arched windows, a triangular pediment and a first-floor niche with a marble statue of the Virgin. To the r. a harled three-bay extension, with a veranda across the first-floor return, supported on a single central column. This seems to have been added c. 1975. Converted into flats 2005–6.

RICCARTON

One of Ayrshire's original parishes, now largely subsumed into southern Kilmarnock. It may take its name from Richard Wallace, an ancestor of Sir William Wallace, and claims to be the patriot's birthplace. It began to develop industrially in the C18, with the exploitation of coal, but once Kilmarnock began to expand southwards, its separate identity was always threatened, and it was within the boundaries of the parliamentary burgh created in the 1830s. The presence of the river encouraged industrial development on both banks, though the physical evidence of this has now all but vanished; the river corridor is now a conduit for the Kilmarnock southern by-pass which barges its way through what was the historic heart of Riccarton. The church looks on in bewilderment.

RICCARTON PARISH CHURCH, New Road. Built 1822–3. A classical preaching box with a w tower and spire, all in pink ashlar, and set on a prominent hill, known as the Seat of Judgement. The raised position necessitates an attractive stone perron, with iron-railed balustrades, and a stone and railed boundary wall. The plans are signed by *John Richmond*, but it is so similar to Tarbolton (q.v., 1819–21) that the architect might have been *Robert Johnstone*, with Richmond as contractor. Three-bay w elevation, the three-stage tower and spire rising from the slightly projected wider central entrance bay. This has the church's most pronounced motif of an extraordinary incurved Baroque pediment; its form repeated over the porch and over the windows of the outer bays on this front. This gives the 'almost Chinese character' identified by Hay. Below the pediment a blind Venetian window and flanking square-headed windows. The first two stages of the tower are square with emphatic cornices; the first stage has round-headed windows with Y-tracery, the second clock faces. The octagonal third stage has round-headed bell-openings, and supports an octagonal spire with roll-moulded angles. Severely plain side elevations of four bays, the ground-floor windows with Y-tracery, the gallery windows similar but with round-headed lights also. The chancel, added by *Ingram & Brown*, 1910, is red sandstone, with a hipped roof and a Venetian E window.

Broad vestibule, with dog-legged stairs under round arches to l. and r. Open plastered and galleried interior, with a flat ceiling and broad cornice, and deeply recessed windows. Panelled gallery front, supported on cast-iron columns. Basket-arched chancel arch, of dressed and painted stone; within the arch a prominent moulding, which dies into corbelled columns on either side. Coved wooden chancel roof; round-headed organ recess to the l., with panelled pilasters. – STAINED GLASS. E window (war memorial), 1919 by *Stephen Adam Studio*. The subject is the Ascension, but the glory of the window is the evocative battlefield images in the lower panels, tanks and makeshift graves amongst the mud. The church was restored in 2000–1 by *Patience & Highmore* of Edinburgh.

N of the church, RICCARTON OLD BRIDGE, traditionally dated to 1723, but widened in 1806. Three-arched stone bridge with segmental arches, triangular cutwaters and a low parapet, renewed as part of flood prevention works in 2004. Just downstream is RICCARTON NEW BRIDGE, of 1839, but widened on the w side in the mid C20. It is also stone, and of three arches, with channelled voussoirs and semicircular cutwaters whose conical heads merge into the pilaster-strips which flank the arches.

RICCARTON NURSERY SCHOOL, Old Street. 1875, a light brown T-plan with a gable and bellcote and flat-headed windows. Hipped and parapeted bays in the angles and a steeply gabled wing across the N gable were added in 1908.

NORTH AND EAST KILMARNOCK

CHURCHES AND PUBLIC BUILDINGS

OUR LADY OF MOUNT CARMEL (R.C.), Kirkton Road. 1961–3 by *Charles W. Gray* of Edinburgh. Brick, gabled, with a shallow copper roof and an unusual baptistery to the r. of the main elevation, the whole forming a pleasing and cohesive ensemble. Projecting gabled entrance with a tall small-paned window with at its centre a flowing cast metal crucifixion. The hexagonal baptistery (no longer used as such) has concrete pilasters, a copper roof, and distant echoes of Gray's demolished Our Lady & St Barbara, Dalmellington (q.v.). Full-height paired side windows. Inside, a spacious vestibule, separated from the church by a glazed screen, with a gallery above; a 'hall' was created *c.* 1992 from the back part of the church. The church has exposed brick walls, painted in the chancel, and a canti-levered roof on free-standing pillars. The big SW window is filled with swirling blue STAINED GLASS in a concrete matrix, of 1962 by *Gabriel Loire*, the quarries behind the Crucifixion blank, in the form of a cross; its vibrant effect has been reduced by the insertion of the hall. The baptistery, among the most attractive C20 rooms in Ayrshire, has more equally masterly glass by *Loire*, the concrete matrix preponderant, the richness of the glass ensuring harmony. In the sacristy a six-panel Creation by *Mies Steegers-Murphy*, made by *The Wee Glass Works*, 1992; more figurative but with the swirling mysticism of Loire's glass.

ST JOHN'S ONTHANK PARISH CHURCH, Wardneuk Drive. 1955–6 by *Alexander Dunlop*. Simple brick hall church, with a chancel recess. Windows with reticulated glazing and shallow pediments. Simple plastered interior, originally with demount-able seating. PEWS came from a church in Tongue (Sutherland) in 1966. HALL of 1965–6, also by *Dunlop*. Brick harled, with big square windows arranged in a refreshing asymmetrical pattern.

ST KENTIGERN'S PARISH CHURCH, Dunbar Drive. 1969–72, by *James Hay & Steel*. Brick harled church with a heart-shaped plan, sweeping concave roof, harled bell-tower and halls. The design owes much to Gillespie Kidd & Coia's St Benedict, Drumchapel (Glasgow) of 1964–70 (*see* also Hay Steel & Partners' Relief Church, Bourtreehill, 1976–8). The off-centre entrance leads into a spacious vestibule with a large MOSAIC of 1997. The church is roughly trapezoidal, with an open wooden-fronted gallery along one wall; opposite, a high hori-zontal band of windows. To the l. of the gallery, a striking wooden ORGAN CASE with strong vertical elements; equally good contemporary furnishings including a simple COMMU-NION TABLE with V-plan legs. The roof is wooden, and the walls plastered, except beneath the window band, where a wall of moveable doors links the church with the big hall behind, the roof here supported on exposed steel beams.

ST MATTHEW (R.C.), Forbes Place. 1974–7 by *Sam Gilchrist*, with a MOSAIC of the Four Evangelists by *Alan Potter* of London. Simple plastered interior, with demountable walls between church and hall. Notable oily glass in the screen between church and vestibule, and in the church windows. Two unusual CRUCIFIXES. A large ceramic one above the altar, and one of metal in the vestibule: the crown of thorns, the cross and the nails, but no figure.

HILLHEAD PRIMARY SCHOOL, Kilmaurs Road. 1936–8 by *William Reid*, County Architect. Long stone-faced SE façade, its classical severity challenged only by the curvy hipped roof, central shouldered pediment and central single-storey projection below the pediment.

JAMES HAMILTON ACADEMY, MacDonald Drive. 1973–6 by *Ayr County Council Architects Dept*, completed by *Strathclyde Regional Council*, and from the same drawing board as Kilwinning Academy (*see* p. 474), having an identical central entrance block with a canted front, linked by glazed first-floor corridors to teaching blocks with long horizontal window bands. Steel-framed, with concrete panels; similar parallel blocks behind.

MOUNT CARMEL R.C. PRIMARY SCHOOL, Meiklewood Road. 1962–5 by *Ayr County Council Architects Dept.* Two mostly two-storey brick blocks set in a similar butterfly pattern to Bellfield Primary School (*see* below, p. 459).

NEW FARM LOCH COMMUNITY CENTRE, Keith Place. 1972–4. Flat-roofed single-storey hall, brick, finished in rough concrete render. Projecting wooden heads to the full-height windows; walls elsewhere cod-castellated. Not unattractive, and a good foil to St Kentigern's Parish Church (*see* above).

NORTH WEST KILMARNOCK AREA CENTRE, Western Road. 2005–7 by *Austin-Smith:Lord* for East Ayrshire Council, in the bold harl, glass and steel idiom pioneered by Drongan Area Centre (q.v.). As there it brings a variety of public services under one roof. Two blocks meet at right angles: that to the l. has a glazed front, and a shallow oversailing roof, while the r. block also has a glazed front, but a more steeply pitched roof, and curves forward to form an almost semicircular wing, the sheet steel roof of which forms the most dramatic element in the composition. This curving wing reminiscent of a motherly hand, ushering people into the centre.

ONTHANK PRIMARY SCHOOL, Meiklewood Road. 1955–8, extended 1960–2 by *Ayr County Council Architects Dept.* A large school originally intended for both junior and senior pupils. Mostly two-storey, brick, with glazed and fibreglass panels, arranged in two long parallel blocks, that to the rear of three storeys, with the central section supported on pilotis.

ST JOSEPH'S ACADEMY, Grassyards Road. 2005–8 by *SMC Parr Architects* for East Ayrshire Council. A large complex housing secondary and primary schools, and built under the same contract as Grange Campus (*see* below). A little more adventurous architecturally, with the obligatory drum tower raised on pilotis, and a conical structure rising through and above one wing.

DEAN CASTLE

With the exception of the royal castle of Dundonald, the most substantial of Ayrshire's castles and an unusual example of a large and strongly fortified keep of the late C14–early C15, reflecting the standing of the Boyds of Kilmarnock who built it. Lord Boyd was raised to the peerage by James II; Sir Alexander Boyd (his brother) was appointed instructor in chivalry to the young James III. In 1466 Lord Boyd (Robert) was made Governor of Scotland, controlling the boy king. His son, created Earl of Arran, was married to Princess Mary, the King's sister. The Palace range was built *c.* 1460 during this period of the family's national prominence. But in 1469 their power was swiftly curtailed, Lord Robert fled, Sir Alexander was beheaded for treason, the estates forfeited and the Earl of Arran escaped to Denmark. The Princess is said to have been confined in Dean Castle. The confiscated lands were returned to Princess Mary and her son James, 2nd Lord Boyd, in 1482. Pont *c.* 1690 described the castle: 'It is a staitly faire ancient building, arising in tuo grate heigh towers, and bult around courtwayes with fine low buldings.' The castle was gutted by fire in 1735. William Boyd, 4th Earl of Kilmarnock was executed in 1746 for supporting the Stewart cause and the estate was forfeit to the crown. The castle remained ruinous until 1908 when its restoration and re-creation was begun for the 8th Lord Howard de Walden, first by *Ingram & Brown*, followed by *James S. Richardson*, and completed in 1946. It was given to Kilmarnock, with its policies and collections, in 1975. In its re-created state it offers a readily understandable interpretation of the development, complexity and function of a medieval castle and deserves to be better known.

It is not an obvious site for a castle, being set down in the valley of the Fenwick Water, the land on either side formerly rising up to bleak uplands. Nearby is a raised mound, possibly a motte, associated with an earlier defensive site. The castle is entered through a GATEHOUSE near the NE angle. This was created *c.* 1937 and is an assembly of medieval and later detail not intended to deceive; it is irregular in plan, built into the walls with access to the fighting platforms. A tall pend with an iron yett flanked by drum towers in the manner of Rowallan. These towers have eyelet and horizontal gunloops and are linked by a string course which encloses the Howard de Walden arms with an inscription below, above a ribbon-moulded eaves course.

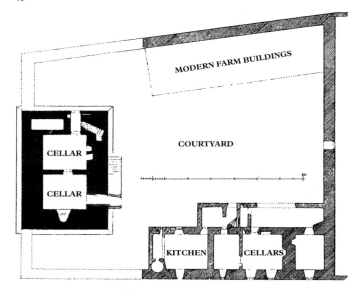

Kilmarnock, Dean Castle.
Plan

Facing the gatehouse is the rectangular KEEP, standing at
the NW corner of the courtyard. It is approximately 15.8 m. by
9.75 m., built of roughly coursed rubble on a battered plinth,
and rises four storeys to the re-created crenellated parapet and
wall-walk. There is no corbel table (cf. Craigmillar Castle,
Lothian). Tall crowstepped gables, rebuilt in the C17, and at
the SE angle a crowstepped gabled caphouse rebuilt in the C20.
There are no original openings in the vaulted ground storey,
but on the NE elevation a round-arched door has been inserted,
above this a blocked arched door, the original entrance once
serviced by timber steps or a ladder, with an arrowslit to the
r. On the main SE elevation a door has been inserted into a
former window embrasure at first-floor level accessed by a later
stone stair, one window in the floor above and diminutive slits
to light closets and the stair in the E angle. On the SW wall is
a small opening in the ground storey, possibly for cleaning the
garderobe chute, and a window which unusually is set above
the chimneypiece in the first-floor hall. Inside is a vaulted cellar
area divided into two but neither compartment with a chimney
suitable for a kitchen, which must have been in a courtyard
building. Inside the inserted door to the N cellar an awkward
mural stair leads l. to a secure mural guard chamber off the
first-floor hall, the original access from the hall floor to the
cellar. The barrel-vaulted hall, 8.2 m. high, is now entered
through an inserted door at the S. Stone seats for the original
window survive but are too high for sitting. Opposite this

Kilmarnock, Dean Castle.
Engraving by J.J. Hinchliffe, 1838

entrance, a window with inset seats, at the high end of the hall
with a chimneypiece on the SW wall, now a C20 version.
Around the hall a low stone bench. From the SE corner a door
to the guardroom at the head of stairs to the cellar, all within
the wall thickness. At the E angle is a wall passage to the
original entrance with a turnpike stair within the angle leading
to the caphouse, to the N a guardroom with a hatch to the
dungeon within the wall below. From the turnpike stair is an
entrance into a large, square window embrasure with stone
bench seating on three sides forming a minstrels gallery (cf.
Doune Castle (Stirling and Central Scotland); a similar
arrangement is illustrated by MacGibbon and Ross at Mearns
Castle, Renfrewshire) with a further private chamber off it to
the N. Above the hall the solar, lit from one window on the SE
wall, closets and a garderobe in the SE and SW walls; an additional chimneypiece was added when the chamber was divided.
Off the N chamber a vaulted oratory dedicated to St Andrew
with a damaged piscina and aumbry.

The PALACE RANGE of *c*. 1460 stands within the courtyard;
it is part of the wall of enceinte and was originally detached
from the keep (a similar arrangement is found at Huntingtower
Castle, Perth and Kinross). Masons from Roslin Abbey are
known to have worked on the construction. At the S angle is a
five-storey tower block, and extending from this towards the
earlier keep is a three-storey hall range, built to provide more
commodious accommodation. All rubble-built. The tower has
a smartly corbelled parapet and a caphouse over the turnpike
stair at the E angle; access to the SE parapet wall-walk is from
this tower. In 1642 James, 8th Lord Boyd, improved this range
with the addition of a stair-tower facing the courtyard; a worn

panel with his and Lady Boyd's monogram is visible above the first-floor window, an additional lean-to attached to its r. The outward-facing SW elevation of the hall is much reconstructed with small openings to ground floor and stone cross-windows above were enlarged in the C17. The simply corbelled parapet, small bartizan at the W angle and the gabled dormers are all part of the C20 reconstruction. The tower openings still reflect the C15 arrangement, on the SE wall two ashlar-built corbelled garderobes. Inside, the ground floor of the palace range is vaulted, with a kitchen at the W end with a large arched chimneypiece and requisite drains and ovens. At first-floor level, the hall to the r. and a private chamber to the l., each with a chimneypiece, the Boyd arms over the hall chimneypiece, clustered keeled columns to the other. The C17 three-quarter panelling and moulded plasterwork, including the deep frieze with the portrait bas relief of Alexander the Great, were introduced from Balgonie Castle (Fife) in 1935. From the S corner of the chamber, steps down to the first-floor tower room, formerly a guardroom, with a roll-moulded chimneypiece on the NE wall, plaster frieze with deep-relief chunky fruit detailing added.

The courtyard walls, still extant at the SE and NE at the end of the C19, were substantially rebuilt and additional walls created by *Richardson*, with timber and stone fighting galleries erected over the wall-walk, although it is unlikely that such constructions, interesting though they are, actually crowned these walls in the past. Also added, an oversailing gabled squat tower at the E angle.

Outside the castle beyond the tower is an asymmetrical gabled HOUSE. It probably incorporates an C18 building and was remodelled *c.* 1840 with double-height canted windows and a pyramid-roofed tower over the entrance. Formerly known as Dean Cottage, it was used by the Howard de Waldens before the palace range was made habitable.

STREETS

DEAN ROAD runs E–W past the lodge and gates of Dean Castle (*see* above). To the E of the lodge it crosses the Marnock Water by a ford, where there is an iron pedestrian SUSPENSION BRIDGE of 1905. To the W there are a number of attractive early C20 houses, mostly in red sandstone, such as the rock-faced Nos. 20–22, and Nos. 12–14, its central entrance with a big shaped gable with balustraded shoulders and ball finials; between the doors, a corbelled slender projection, flat-headed in the Mackintosh manner. More villas and bungalows of *c.* 1905–10 in INGRAM PLACE and (to the N) LANDSBOROUGH DRIVE, where No. 2 is a crisply detailed house in white harl, with an ashlar and tiled circular corner bay, tiled porch and roofs, and tall stepped harled stacks.

TURNER PLACE, S of Dean Road, is a short street of two houses only, both of *c.* 1870, in a raised position looking across the Dean Park. DEANHILL, of two storeys, is in snecked ashlar with polished dressings. The three-bay main (s) elevation has crowstepped gables, geometric ridge tiles, chamfered windows and a projecting cast-iron porch with a decorative panel above. The other house, HIGHFIELD, repeats many of these details, but its main elevation faces w; this has a central crowstepped porch and haunched entrance arch.

ASSLOSS FARM, Assloss Road. A courtyard steading of *c.* 1840 with the remains of a small C16 rectangular tower, approximately 4.5 m. square, embedded in its sw angle. Rubble-built and heavily whitewashed, it has been lowered to two storeys with a piended slate roof. A first-floor door on the N face may be the original entrance; it now is reached by a forestair. On the s wall a small window. The vaulted ground floor survives with one slit opening still visible.

SOUTH KILMARNOCK

CHURCH OF JESUS CHRIST OF LATTER DAY SAINTS, Whatriggs Road. 1963–5 by *John Easton*. Brick and harled hall, with a sharp prow at the s end, beneath a broad asymmetrically pitched slate roof. Slender octagonal brick and concrete tower.

ST MICHAEL (R.C.), Treeswoodhead Road. 1950–3 by *Reginald Fairlie & Partners*. A peculiar five-bay brick church with a gently curving metal roof which resembles an overgrown Nissen hut or Anderson shelter. The front elevation has a minimal segmental pediment above a deep flat-roofed porch. To l. and r., single-bay transepts. Simple plastered interior with flat boarded ceiling. Set back to the r., the contemporary presbytery, with a hipped roof and prominent end stacks.

ST NINIAN'S BELLFIELD, Whatriggs Road. 1958–9 by *T. Harley Haddow & Partners*, Edinburgh. Brick harled church with a shallow gable and tall projecting side windows. Central brick panel to the front (sw) gable. To the r. a slender brick campanile with a pitched cap on thin columns; r. again the contemporary hall. The three elements are linked by a broad open flat-roofed walkway with very thin columns. Airy interior with plaster walls, a panelled roof and a rear gallery.

SHORTLEES PARISH CHURCH, Central Avenue. 1949–51 by *Alexander Dunlop*. Simple brick and tiled hall church with a sw pyramidal-headed entrance tower, forming a focal point in the generously planned heart of a post-war local authority housing scheme, set back between two terraces of single-storey shops, though the original vision and the modern reality are now only distantly related. The entrance between stone pilasters under a delicate ogival copper porch. Tall steel windows under hipped dormers; internally these create breaks in the coved plastered ceiling.

BELLFIELD PRIMARY SCHOOL, Tinto Avenue. 1959–64 by *Ayr County Council Architects Dept*. Mostly two-storey, brick and flat-roofed, the larger units laid out in a butterfly manner.

SHORTLEES PRIMARY SCHOOL, Knockmarloch Drive. 2005–8
by *SMC Parr Architects* for East Ayrshire Council. A large
complex housing a primary school and community uses, and
built under the same contract as Grange Campus, to which it
is architecturally similar.

WEST AND SOUTH-WEST KILMARNOCK

GRANGE CAMPUS, Beech Avenue. 2005–8 by *SMC Parr Architects* for East Ayrshire Council. Secondary, primary and special
needs schools. The major elements of the design are an internal
courtyard, a central tall atrium – 'the street' – and a series of
round-ended blocks projecting from the central core. Panelled
exterior.

Former SOUTHHOOK POTTERIES, Western Road. The red brick
company offices of *c.* 1936, probably designed to showcase
their ceramic and brick products. Two-storey central section,
a long concrete veranda, and a semicircular concrete porch
above the central entrance, which is flanked by fluted black tile
pilasters. Also of black tile, the low walls and stumpy piers with
incised decoration which flank the entrance steps.

GRANGE TERRACE. A small cluster of mid-C19 and later villas.
The brown ashlar Grange Nursing Home (No. 4) has a canted
bay to the r. with plate-glass windows; otherwise lying-pane
glazing, and a pedimented entrance. Ornate openwork cast-
iron GATEPIERS with barrel heads and fleur-de-lis finials;
probably of *c.* 1880. No. 6. also has lying-pane glazing, and a
castellated porch, while No. 8, perhaps of *c.* 1850, has a shallow
porch with chamfered and cusped details similar to Morningside, Portland Road (*see* above, p. 449). It has a livelier rear (E)
elevation, with canted bays, enjoying its raised position. Nos.
10–12 are of *c.* 1905, red sandstone below, but above, the outer
canted bays swell into half-timbered gables beneath wide
bargeboarded eaves; the bay between also half-timbered with
a similarly gabled dormer. The setting for a Swiss horror
movie? At its N end Grange Terrace joins IRVINE ROAD; to the
r. (E), two red sandstone villas of *c.* 1905: No. 52 has a conically
headed full-height bow to the l. and a door recessed beneath
a very stilted head, while No. 54 has a canted l. bay and an
entrance with a shallow shouldered and dentilled pediment
supported on attached columns with idiosyncratic caps, like
cushions with tassels.

ANNANHILL HOUSE, 1.8 km. w. The lands of Annanhill were
acquired in 1796 by William Dunlop, whose fortune had been
made in India. The present rendered Palladian house was built
for him, and was presumably largely completed before his
death in 1801. Additions were made for his son, James, probably after his marriage in 1818. A sensitive and exemplary
conversion *c.* 1990–2 by *Nicholas Groves-Raines & Partners*
returned it to residential use. Two-storey and three-bay, with

attics and basements, and flanking single-storey pavilion wings; the central bays slightly projected and pedimented, that to the N embellished with a grand Ionic portico *c.* 1818. Bracketed cornices to the ground-floor windows, eared architraves above, and a panelled parapet and hipped roof, brought forward to form a dome-like roof above the entrance. The wings have Ionic pilasters and pediments. To the W of the house, DUNN MEWS, inventive enabling development of 1991–3 by *Nicholas Groves-Raines & Partners*: a semicircle of flats in a pared-down Neoclassical style with big Diocletian windows in the end gables, and a central pedimented feature. This is repeated in the central projection of the eight-bay block which sits between the ends of the semicircle.

STRATHLEA, Holmes Road, 1.5 km. SW. Originally the Kilmarnock Dairy School, first opened in 1889 in Holmes Farm, replaced by the existing buildings by *Allan Stevenson* in 1903–4. A pleasant brick harled building in spacious grounds, U-plan with red sandstone dressings to the shaped gables and the main entrance in the r. wing.

MOUNT HOUSE, 2.5 km. SW, off Dundonald Road. Three-bay classical house of *c.* 1810, with an advanced pedimented central bay; a portico with paired Doric columns was added in the late C19, probably contemporary with the three-storey Italianate tower to the r. This has attractive decorative carving in the dressings. The single-storey balustraded bay to the l. is also late C19, while substantial additions were made to the rear *c.* 1907, in a subdued Arts and Crafts manner. Many C20 additions, including one hipped Neo-Georgian two-storey block, reflect its use as a nursing home. Sympathetically converted to flats, 2001–2 by *Nicoll Design*.

DAMHEAD HOUSE, 2.8 km. SW, off Cunninghame Drive. 1907–8 by *J. R. Johnstone* as the factor's house for the Caprington estate. Generously scaled harled and tiled Arts and Crafts, and a precursor of Johnstone's many villas in Troon.

BLACKSYKE TOWER, 3 km. SSW on Caprington Golf Course. An early C19 colliery building, probably an engine house, but dressed in an antiquarian coat. Rectangular, with dressed quoins, a vault on the ground floor, irregularly placed windows, a corbelled parapet on two elevations and evidence of crow-stepped gables.

TREESBANK HOUSE, 2 km. SSW off Ayr Road. Large and incoherent in English Cotswold style. Built 1926–8 for Gavin Morton of Blackwood & Morton, carpet manufacturers, by *James Carrick* of J. K. Hunter's office. Roughly U-plan in mannered random rubble with polished ashlar dressings. Asymmetry the hallmark with projecting windows, large gabled bays and plenty of stone-mullioned windows. The garden front with projecting polygonal two-storey bay at r. with very deeply overhanging eaves, drawing its inspiration from American Midwestern domestic architecture. Boldly stepped chimney-breast on the side elevation. – STABLE COURT. *c.* 1770 with much later alteration. Big arched entrance with raised pediment above and possibly incorporating material from the earlier buildings on the site. Large WALLED GARDEN.

DOOCOT. Unusual octagonal plan dated 1771 in raised brickwork. Brick-zig-zagging to the rat course and cornice, a circle of flight-holes below the eaves cornice and a few additional holes above the rat course. Tiers of stone nesting boxes. Impressive bellcast slate roof.

KILMAURS

4040

The parish church stands on commanding high ground on the l. bank of the Carmel, and the original village was presumably here also, but this is now on lower ground to the N. This transposition may be related to the mid-C16 erection of the village as a Burgh of Barony for the Cunninghames of Glencairn. In the C19 Kilmaurs was predominantly a weaving and agricultural centre; the railway arrived in 1873, and the village today is a dormitory for Kilmarnock, with many of the cottages which line the sinuous main street well restored. The Carmel runs close behind the village on its S and E sides, and is crossed by three C19 stone BRIDGES linking the village with the impressively large public open space on the l. bank of the river.

CHURCHES AND PUBLIC BUILDINGS

Former GLENCAIRN (U.P.) CHURCH, Fenwick Road. 1864–5 by *Peddie & Kinnear*. Over-sized Romanesque. Gable front with a rose window and a bellcote; central round-headed entrance with shafted columns. Four-bay side elevations. Converted *c.* 1990 as a workshop for the *Stained Glass Design Partnership* (*Paul Lucky* and *Susan Bradbury*). – Many of the windows filled with their work.

KILMAURS MAXWELL AND KILMARNOCK UNITED FREE CHURCH, Crosshouse Road. 1844, rebuilt in 1881 by *Gabriel Andrew*. The original building had two gables facing the road; Andrew's rebuilding made of these one broad gable, with a pedimented pilastered doorway, round-headed windows and tall finial chimneys.

KILMAURS PARISH CHURCH, Kilmarnock Road. In a large stone-walled churchyard. Mixed Gothic of 1887–9 by *R. S. Ingram*, replacing the medieval church. It is T-plan with a four-stage entrance tower, NW, but made into a Greek cross by the retention of the burial aisle of the Earls of Glencairn of *c.* 1600 as the SE arm. The tower has a pointed entrance, with block moulding, and a large five-light Geometric window above; three-light bell-openings and a parapet with finials. Rose windows in the other gables, tall lancets elsewhere.

The GLENCAIRN AISLE is of large grey ashlar blocks, with crowstepped gables. In the E wall a blocked four-light mullioned window, and another blocked light in the gable above. Entrance in the w gable. Inside, stone-vaulted. – MONUMENT. A very striking work dated 1600, for one of the Cunninghames,

Earls of Glencairn, either William, 6th Earl who †1581 or
James, 7th Earl, who built the aisle and †c. 1614–28, WROUGHT
BE DAVID SCWGAL MASSON BURGES IN CAREL (i.e. David
Scougal of Crail, Fife). A hybrid of medieval and Renaissance
details and in its design very similar to the contemporary
Kennedy monument at Ballantrae (q.v.). A deep recess contains upright demi-figures, l. and r. of a rectangular panel, with
scrolls projecting from behind, that presumably carried the
inscription (some traces could still be made out in 1912). The
earl is in an attitude of prayer, an open book before him; his
wife, well-dressed, arms loose across her body, also with an
open book. Below, across the front of the monument, eight
smaller and well-worn figures, and beneath these a projecting
moulding supported by stone console brackets, with scrolled
ends. Framing this an entablature supported on three pairs of
columns stepping back to the wall. The inner pair are round,
with much-weathered decoration, and capitals of a crude and
typically unlearned Composite order (the abacus has the Cunninghame shakefork), the middle columns going towards the
octagonal, with egg-and-dart moulding, and the square outer
pair with simpler capitals still. Above the entablature a big coat
of arms, in a square panel, with scrolled volutes to either side,
watchful birds perched on each volute. Above the abacus of
the innermost column to the r., an odd finial with an oval and
strapwork; the corresponding finial to the l. much simpler.

In the church, a Gothic PULPIT and COMMUNION table,
probably contemporary with it. – STAINED GLASS. – NW arm,
w wall. The Good Shepherd, 1905 by *Norman M. MacDougall*
of Glasgow. – sw arm, w wall, an attractive St Luke, 1984 by
Roland Mitton, and in the E wall, The Reaper and The Sower,
1932 by *Guthrie & Wells*. – NE arm, E wall, Walk in the Light,
1971 by *Stanley M. Scott* for the *City Glass Co.* Plain but early
monument to Rev. Hugh Thomson.

KILMAURS PRIMARY SCHOOL, Crofthead Road. 1939–41 by
Ayr County Council Architects Dept. A long and featureless two-
storey block, brick harled. Hipped roof probably added later.
LIBRARY AND LOCAL OFFICE, Irvine Road. 1997–8 by *East
Ayrshire Council Dept of Architecture* (*Scott Andrews*, project
architect). Harled and slated, thoughtful, though without many
windows. Entrance slightly curved, with an overhanging porch,
and horizontal and vertical detailing in glazed brick.
MERCAT CROSS, Main Street. Dated 1830. Octagonal stone
shaft and three-step base. Heavy ball finial. The cross stands
in a D-plan enclosure, with low stone walls, which was formerly
the buttermarket of Kilmaurs.
Former PUBLIC HALL, Main Street. 1890–1 by *Robert P. McHoull*
of Kilmarnock. Red sandstone, two storeys. Projecting off-
centre gabled entrance bay with a four-centred arched doorway
beneath a bracketed balcony.
TOWN HOUSE, Main Street. Invariably known locally as THE   90
JOUGS, after the neck iron which is attached to the s face of

the building. C18, with a steeple of 1799–1800 by *Hugh & David Barclay*, masons, occupying a prominent island site in the centre of the village, where Main Street is at its widest. The earlier part is a simple harled two-storey building, with a slated roof and plain skews. The ground floor is divided into two small barrel-vaulted cells; the upper floor a single chamber with a wooden ceiling and a fireplace (now blocked). It may have been in existence by 1709, and was certainly so in 1743, when repairs were authorized. The steeple, rising in front of the s gable, is ashlar. Straight flight of granite steps to a raised entrance, with a round-arched door, a keystone and a mock fanlight; the stage above this has a lunette on the s face, and the next stage, the clock stage, has clock faces, dated 1866, in square panels on the N and s. Bell-stage with lancets, a pyramidal spire and, finally, an odd ovoid finial.

WAR MEMORIAL, Morton Park, off Kilmarnock Road. 1920–1 by *Kellock Brown*. Octagonal stone stepped plinth (with bronze panels) and column; on one face of the column a life-size bronze soldier leans wearily on his rifle.

DESCRIPTION

From the Parish Church, KILMARNOCK ROAD runs N, and soon begins to descend towards the Carmel Water. On the l., a former WOOLLEN FACTORY, of c. 1900, eight weaving sheds hiding behind a castellated brick wall. Also on the l., beyond the skewed red sandstone early C20 bridge, Nos. 46–50

Kilmaurs. General view.
Watercolour by W. Parker, 1895

TOWNEND, mid-C19 cottages, curving with the river. On the r., No. 25, a well-sited exposed rubble cottage of *c.* 1800, originally thatched, as is obvious from the deep skews. Townend snakes prettily, climbing up and away from the river crossing, and on the l. is the best run of early C19 cottages in Kilmaurs, Nos. 8–22, mostly harled and with painted dressed margins, and making full use of the slope and the curve. Townend becomes MAIN STREET, which widens noticeably at the Town House and Mercat Cross (*see* above). Beyond the Town House, and forming an attractive group with it, the crowstepped and harled WESTON TAVERN, dated 1777 on the r. skew, with dressed windows and a simple central door. Main Street continues, narrowing gradually, climbing, and curving gently round to the l., becoming TOWNHEAD, with a particularly cohesive group of cottages (Nos. 59–61 MAIN STREET and Nos. 1–5 TOWNHEAD). Adjacent, the SCOUT HALL, the former parish hall of 1939. Harled, with plentiful brick decoration.

IRVINE ROAD and Fenwick Road run w and e from the Mercat Cross. In Irvine Road one pretty classical cottage of *c.* 1840, with an Ionic doorpiece and, beyond the railway bridge, some late C19 villas mostly in Mauchline red sandstone. The best perhaps No. 46, *c.* 1900, with a deep entrance on the return elevation, and No. 52, of *c.* 1895, with a wooden porch on shafted columns. The early C20 No. 54 combines red sandstone with a tall harled central gable dominated by the big staircase window. It has earlier anvil-capped GATEPIERS. In FENWICK ROAD, No. 19 stands out. It is from 1995 by *Graeme Robertson*, with Japanese-style timber embellishments. Beyond is the former Glencairn Church (*see* Churches and Public Buildings, above) and, at right angles with the road, the harled gabled two-storey OLD MANSE, probably of *c.* 1788, possibly by *John Gebbie*. Late C19 porch.

THE HAUGHS, Mill Avenue. 1974–5 by *H. Roan Rutherford* for himself: stylish modern vernacular, harled and glazed, with a chunky chimneystack.

KIRKFAULD, 100 m. sw of the church. In the grounds, a bold crowstepped gabled DOOCOT, dated 1636 on its door lintel. Stone, with a prominent rat course; openings like gunloops above it in either gable. One carved skew; nesting boxes survive on three of the internal walls, while a window has been inserted in one gable, below the openings, probably in the early C19.

OLD MANSE, 0.3 km. sw of the Parish Church. *John Swan*'s manse of 1779–81, extended *c.* 1882 by *Gabriel Andrew*, was comprehensively recast and extended in 1925–6 by *James Hay & Steel* in a lush vernacular style, inside and out.

PLACE OF KILMAURS, 0.4 km. nw of the church, surrounded by the public open spaces of the village. A delightful small C17 mansion house said to have been built *c.* 1630 for William Cunninghame, 9th Earl of Glencairn, later Lord Chancellor of Scotland. Steeply pitched slate roof and crowstepped gables; the ragged interface between the harl and the crowsteps, especially on the e gable, reminiscent of Fenwick Parish Church of

1643 (q.v.). Present main stair in the projecting s wing, which may originally have contained the entrance, and has an empty moulded panel high on its w elevation. To its l., two bays with half-dormers, to its r. a C19 lean-to extension with a catslide dormer. Restored from 1969 onwards, retaining some interior features such as simple cornices and a stone fireplace. Attached to the w, a tower house of possibly C15 date, now much reduced and ruinous. Part of the vaulted ground floor has been converted, perhaps in the mid-C19, into an additional room.

TITWOOD FARM, 3.3 km. NW. Early C19 courtyard farm, unusually orientated so that one of the parallel wings flanks the public road. This wing contains a cartshed, while the base of the U is connected to the farmhouse, which sits at right angles to it. This is of painted stone, and appears to be an early C19 single-storey house raised to two storeys in the late C19 or early C20.

TOWERHILL FARM, 0.5 km. W. Two-storey C19 farmhouse with flanking single-storey wings; the gable apex of the byre to the r. is dated 1846. The farm itself was 'about being finished' in 1871.

TOUR HOUSE. *See* p. 652.

KILWINNING

The burgh of Kilwinning owes its existence to the Abbey, in whose shadow a small secular settlement grew up at the lowest point where the River Garnock could be forded. After the Dissolution the town grew little. Coal mining developed in the area in the late C18 and early C19, and in the mid C19 iron works were built to the s, partly as a result of the arrival of the railway in 1839. Kilwinning's industrial base declined in the late C20, and in 1976 it was included within the area of Irvine New Town: a unique challenge to its independence and character. The major impact has been substantial residential growth: one of I.D.C.'s first big housing schemes – Pennyburn – is within the burgh. But Kilwinning has retained its distinctiveness, with its pedestrianized Main Street and – at the heart of the town – the ruins of the Abbey.

KILWINNING ABBEY*

The surviving fragments of the Tironensian abbey of Kilwinning are perhaps not the most visually arresting monastic remains to

---

*The account of Kilwinning Abbey is by Richard Fawcett.

have come down to us from the Scottish Middle Ages, but they embody a number of unusual and intriguing features.

The abbey is thought to have been founded by Richard de Morville, which places its establishment between his inheritance of his father's Scottish estates in 1162 and his own death in 1189. It was probably believed that the foundation perpetuated the site of an earlier church associated with the shadowy St Winnin. The first monks were brought from Kelso, and the earliest reference to an abbot occurs as late as 1186–9, though it is possible one had been in place before then. Little is known of the later history of the house, other than that the abbot was granted the right to wear the mitre in 1409. From 1513 the abbots were replaced by commendators – royal appointees who were not themselves monks – the first being James Beaton, Archbishop of Glasgow. The abbey was attacked by the reformers in 1559 and, although materials were being gathered for repairs in that year, it was said to have been cast down in 1561; in 1592 its estates were eventually erected into a temporal lordship for the last of the commendators, William Melville.

There is some evidence that the plan first intended for the CHURCH was no more than an aisleless cross. But, as eventually built, it had a short rectangular aisleless presbytery at the E end, W of which were transepts with a two-bay chapel aisle on the E side of each. There was presumably a low tower over the crossing. The eight-bay nave was flanked by aisles with a pair of towers over the W bays. This type of plan (apart from the towers) is presumed to have been introduced to Scotland by the Cistercians, but was soon adopted by other orders, possibly on account of its relative cheapness to build. However, Kilwinning had the exceptional feature of tall arches that opened into the W towers from the central vessel and which thus created a space that was essentially a W transept.

Part of the church continued in parochial use into the C18, and it is likely that a wall across the central vessel of the nave, one bay E of the original W front, was part of the post-Reformation adaptation. The parish church of 1773–5 was built on the site of the medieval presbytery (*see* Churches, below), and a free-standing bell-tower was built in 1815 by *David Hamilton* on the site of the NW tower, albeit with a smaller footprint.

The chief surviving elements of the church are: the gable wall of the S transept, together with one bay of the arcade that opened into its E chapel aisle; the lower W wall of that transept; the outer wall of the S nave aisle; and the arch from the S nave aisle into the SW tower, with the lower part of the NE pier of that tower.

The S TRANSEPT gable and adjacent E transept arcade arch incorporate masonry work of several phases. An internal building break near the centre of the lower wall of the transept gable, together with fragmentary remains of a pilaster-buttress on the exterior, suggest that a narrower transept had been first intended. An aisleless nave was possibly part of the same proposal, since a

Kilwinning Abbey.
Engraving, 1789

doorway was initially provided into the cloister on the transept's W side rather than in the nave wall, an arrangement
that is more common in aisleless churches, since it allowed
the monks' stalls to be placed against the nave wall. However,
before work had progressed far, the ambitions – and presumably the resources – of the community appear to have
increased, and the transept was widened eastwards, with provision for an E chapel arcade. The S arcade respond has a
single keeled shaft projecting from a broad pilaster with
chamfered angles; the compressed lower roll of its base points
to a late C12 date although the surviving arcade pier may be
a little later, probably *c.* 1200. It has triplets of keeled shafts
to N and S, but – most unusually – pairs of rounded shafts
flanking a detached shaft to E and W. The moulded caps of
both respond and pier, together with the arch they support,
are probably early C13. There are tight concentrations of rolls
and deep hollows to the arch, most of the rolls being filleted,
and there is dogtooth to the middle order. Stubs of the upper
parts of the E arcade wall survive, showing that the triforium
stage was relatively tall, and that its S respond was of three
detached orders alternating with bands of dogtooth; there
was a circular quatrefoil in the spandrel. The respond of the
squat clearstorey arch was broadly chamfered. The chapel
aisle was vaulted, and in its S wall is a lancet framed by an
arch carried on detached shafts.
    The blank lower part of the transept gable wall has the door
to the spiral night stair at its W end. Above, a triplet of tall
lancets rises through both triforium and clearstorey stages,

with a wall passage at sill level. Internally, the lancets were framed by detached shafts with three levels of shaft-rings; externally there are chamfered reveals and hoodmouldings. The line of the lost dormitory roof cuts across the lower parts of the W and central lancets. The upper parts of the corner buttress have sunk shafts at their angles. In the lower part of the gable itself is an oculus, which internally is flanked on each side by a pair of small lancets; a second wall passage runs at this level. At mid height of the gable is an intake, which was presumably at the level of the roof collars, and there is a single lancet above.

W of the transept is the pointed-arched SE PROCESSIONAL DOORWAY from the nave into the cloister, which was probably inserted into the existing wall *c.* 1200. The order framing the opening is continuously moulded with a triplet of rolls and a hollow; the three outer orders were carried on detached shafts with chalice, waterleaf, crocket or figurative caps. The bases are of waterholding profile. In the arch one of the orders had deeply undercut chevron projected out over a triplet of rolls, while another has a ringed roll; the hoodmoulding is decorated with dogtooth. Along the present wall-head of the S aisle are a number of corbels that presumably supported aisle vaulting.

The W bays of the NAVE are unlikely to have been reached before the mid C13. In the second bay E of the SW tower is a doorway of around that date, provided as part of the processional route between church and cloister. It was blocked when the W claustral range was expanded eastwards (*see* below), and a simple round-arched doorway with chamfered arrises was cut in the bay to its E. The NE pier of the SW TOWER combines heavy filleted leading rolls, intermediate unfilleted rolls and angled faces, comparable to the crypt piers of Glasgow Cathedral of *c.* 1242. Although truncated, this pier clearly rose to a considerable height above the nave aisles, suggesting that the arch opening into the tower from the central vessel would have risen through a height equivalent to the three storeys of the rest of the nave. The consequent sense of these being W transepts would have been emphasized by the relatively large area covered by the towers. (Partial analogies for this arrangement can be found at other Tironensian churches: in the fully developed W transepts of Kelso Abbey (Borders); and to a lesser extent in the absence of floors in the towers at Arbroath (Dundee & Angus), which meant that the arches of the triforium and clearstorey stages there were essentially flying screens.) At Kilwinning a surviving respond of the S triforium that is adjacent to the later W wall shows that the middle storey in the nave was of more compressed proportions than that in the main transept. The W wall, which was built one bay E of the original W front at an unknown date after the Reformation, has a doorway with doubled-chamfered mouldings below a tall Y-traceried and transomed window. Views of the NW tower made before it was replaced show that its N face was braced

7

by three buttresses, and that there were pairs of pointed windows in the belfry stage. Changes were evidently made to its capping. Grose in 1790 shows a saddleback roof within crowsteps, but by 1806 it had a spire. It was shortly afterwards hit by lightning, and rebuilt by *David Hamilton* in 1815 (*John Connell*, Hamilton, builder) with a smaller footprint, and with four storeys braced by diagonal buttresses; the belfry stage has pairs of Y-tracery windows to each stage below a crenellated parapet with gabled pinnacles at the angles.

The MONASTIC BUILDINGS are now only partly comprehensible. The best-preserved medieval features are on the E side of the cloister, where it can be seen that the range was unusually narrow. Immediately adjacent to the S transept is the SLYPE or parlour, entered by a round-headed doorway; traces of its barrel vault survive at the base of the transept gable. The most intriguing feature is the CHAPTER HOUSE entrance. This is of the common type, with a central doorway flanked on each side by a two-light window, and on first sight it looks like mid-C12 Romanesque work. But that is too early for the abbey's foundation and the details suggest instead that this is a late medieval revival of earlier forms; see e.g. the massive edge-rolls to the flanking windows, which are of a form more frequently found in the early C16, while the doorway capitals are treated as simple horizontal mouldings (cf. the S doorway at Tullibardine church, of *c.* 1500 (Perth & Kinross)). Round arches were also by this time almost as frequently employed in Scotland as pointed arches. The chapter house itself was rectangular, and projected a short way E of the range.

On the S side of the cloister, the footings of the REFECTORY, together with the outer parts of the E and W ranges, were revealed through excavation in 1962–3. These showed that the cloister was very small in relation to the scale of the church. This discovery, together with evidence of a number of masonry changes in the S transept and S nave aisle wall, suggest that – like the church – the first intentions were relatively modest, but that the complex was enlarged in the course of construction. At some stage, perhaps during construction, the cloister was possibly extended a short distance to the W, since it is considerably larger E–W than N–S. The C13 W RANGE probably contained the abbot's residence. Evidence for it can be seen in the stubs of walls against the SW tower, in a cut-back wall rib in the aisle wall E of the tower, and in the blocked processional doorway already noted. This doorway was blocked on its S side by a barrel vault over the basement of an eastward expansion of the W range. The date of this expansion is uncertain, though the cutting of the new doorway into the cloister from the nave to its E indicates it was built while there was still an active monastic community. It seems likely that it was part of a campaign to provide a more commodious residence for the commendator, and it says much for its structural qualities that it evidently continued to be occupied until at least the end of the C18.

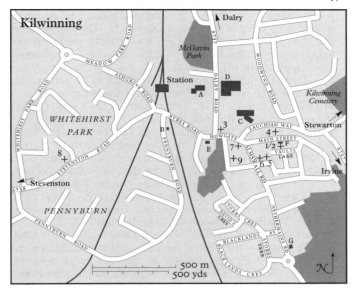

CHURCHES AND CEMETERY

ABBEY PARISH CHURCH, Main Street. Gabled T-plan preaching box of 1773–5 by *John Swan* of Kilmaurs. The mason was
John Garland of Kilwinning. Built on the site of the abbey
church's presbytery. Of finely diagonally tooled ashlar in a wide
range of colours, from white to dark red, creating a unique and
kaleidoscopic effect. Tall pointed windows on the S elevation,
in pairs flanking a tall late C19 pedimented projection. Two
tiers of windows to the gables, square-headed beneath, pointed
windows flanking a circular window above and blind pointed
panels in the gables, which are expressed as pediments with
corner finials. Lower N wing; on its E elevation a straight
forestair leading to the simple entrance to the Eglinton Loft.
To the r. of this a re-set carved coat of arms in a rectangular

panel, dated 1598. On its w elevation, a late C19 entrance, framed by a three-arched stone tabernacle. The single-storey castellated W porch to the church also late C19. Spacious and light interior. Galleries on three sides, supported on columns; those supporting the Eglinton Loft (N) and its canopy are fluted with Corinthian capitals. At the back of the loft, a wide segmental arch above the entrance to the retiring room. – PULPIT and ORGAN CASE. In the centre of the S wall. Gothic, the organ pipes naturalistically painted. – STAINED GLASS. S wall. Tall windows flanking the organ, I am the Way, the Truth and the Life (l.) and Christ the Shepherd (r.), both of 1890 by *W. & J. J. Kier*, with figures under canopy-work. In the outer window r., The Sower, of *c.* 1950 by the *Abbey Studio*. w wall, S window, a striking Annunciation by *Gordon Webster*, 1951. E wall, S window, a bright and busy window by *Sax Shaw*, 1989, to mark the 800th anniversary of the foundation of the abbey. Gallery: The Presentation in the Temple, 1903 by *J. T. & C. E. Stewart* for *William Meikle & Sons* (l.) and Suffer Little Children (r.), 1912 – the central figure must be modelled on the ten-year-old dedicatee. Finally in the circular E window, another Suffer Little Children, of 1890, and in the corresponding w window, St Paul, of 1903 by *Stephen Adam & Son* in their usual rich translucent glass.

Outside the church door, a WAR MEMORIAL of 1921 by *Peter Macgregor Chalmers*: a Celtic cross on three steps, the shaft carved with the figure of St Winnin, between chequerboard and knotwork patterns. Bronze memorial panels on a low-walled stone bench. Most of the churchyard MEMORIALS have been removed, but one of considerable interest remains, SE of the church: Quintin Craufurd †1747. Paired Corinthian columns and a swan-neck pediment with a carved coat of arms. At the base an amazingly cheerful display of skulls and bones.

ABBEY CHURCH HALL, Vaults Lane. 1911–12 by *J. & J. Armour*. Gothic, in brown stone, with finialled buttresses flanking a boldly advanced single-storey gabled T-plan porch, with three lancets above with shallower buttresses dying into the wall.

CORNERSTONE CHURCH, Howgate. *See* Description, p. 476.

ERSKINE CHURCH, Garden Square Lane. Gabled classical of 1838, with two tiers of square-headed windows, round-headed windows in the gables, and attractive corner finials. The S gable supports an impressive eyecatching aedicular bellcote of 1883 with shouldered pediment and a big floriated finial. The mason has gloried in this work, and it is in strong contrast to the severity of the original building. Low addition on the N gable, faced in dark stone composite, *c.* 1970. Compact galleried interior, with a flat plaster ceiling with cornice and central lozenge. The panelled gallery front has rounded corners and rests on strongly tapered columns. The rear side pews are placed in arched recesses. Richly gabled Gothic PULPIT. Opposite the N gable, the ERSKINE HALL, of *c.* 1970, in the same dark stone composite.

FREE CHURCH, Abbeygreen. 1825, as an Original Secession Church. Gabled preaching box, with square-headed windows in two tiers; the side elevations plastered, the gables of exposed stone.

Former FREE CHURCH, Almswall Road. Now Orange Hall. 1845–6; the mason was *James Ramsay*. Wide and gabled with flat corner buttresses and big flat-headed advanced bays either side of the gable, carried through and above the eaves, finishing level with the pineapple finial on the apex.

Former MANSEFIELD CHURCH, Howgate. Now a nursery. 1859–61 by *Boucher & Cousland*. Gothic, grey sandstone, with a prominent bellcote on the N gable. This springs from a square stage, with a corbelled advanced gabled panel with a clock on the N face; above this the tall bell-stage with foliated openings, and above this the octagonal spire, now truncated. Big Dec window in the N gable above a pointed doorway with a foliated inner panel; foliated windows elsewhere separated by buttresses.

MANSEFIELD TRINITY CHURCH, West Doura Way. 1998–2000 by *James F. Stephen Architects* of Glamis. Circular, planned with flair and conviction. Rendered brick walls beneath a three-part roof; the first, of sheet steel, and the second, slated, separated by a narrow band of windows; capped with a glazed pyramid lantern. Welcoming glazed entrance leads into a bright vestibule-cum-café; beyond this the airy, top-lit church, plastered; wooden radial ribs in the roof. Big wall recess opposite the entrance, lit from the sides, and from behind by a blue glazed cross. Simple and effective TABLE and FONT, both designed by *Stephen*.

ST WININ (R.C.), St Winning's Road. 1936–7 by *Thomas Cordiner*. Gable-ended, with a tall central nave and flanking aisles. Harled with shallow buttresses, steel-framed windows, a gabled W porch and a narrow E chancel. Interior reordered in the 1970s by *Sam Gilchrist*. The altar is now forward of the N wall, and the former chancel used as a subsidiary chapel. The eye is caught by the curved boarded ceiling with a subsidiary suspended ceiling, also curved and boarded, narrower and shorter, like a giant sounding board. – STAINED GLASS, 2005, of saints, winningly child-like; the best the Virgin Mary, Our Lady of the Sea, in the W gable. To the S the contemporary harled presbytery and to the rear (E) the gabled Church Hall, both probably by *Cordiner*.

KILWINNING CEMETERY, Bridgend Lane. 1870, designed and laid out by *Rae*, the Eglinton estate gardener. Low stone boundary walls topped with rocks, two entrances with oversized gatepiers. The more easterly entrance gives onto an avenue leading directly to the EGLINTON FAMILY VAULTS; these are understated, just a stone wall behind, railings to front and sides, and the vaults themselves with a tarred felt roof. At the time of the opening a 'handsome' chapel was intended above the vaults. Lining the avenue, MONUMENTS of the great and the good of the town, as if in homage to the earls.

The removal of the trees in 2006 has robbed the cemetery of much of its charm. At the W entrance the town's WAR MEMORIAL, a Creetown marble cenotaph of 1933 by *J. & G. Mossman*.

PUBLIC BUILDINGS

ABBEY PRIMARY SCHOOL, Claremont Crescent. 1927 by *Ayr County Council*. Long façade of grey harl, with the details (regular gables and two central gabled entrances) highlighted in red sandstone. Rear addition of 2005–6 by *North Ayrshire Council Technical Services* (*Irene Farish*, project architect); white harl over red stone, tall windows in groups, respectful while making its own statement.

ACCOUNTANT IN BANKRUPTCY OFFICES, Pennyburn Road, by the station. 2003–5 by *Austin-Smith:Lord*. Linear, on a narrow site. The roof floats above a fully glazed clearstorey.

BUCKREDDAN CARE CENTRE, Irvine Road. At the core is an early C19 two-storey house with a canted bay to the r., and a lower two-storey gabled wing set back to the l. In 1936–7 the house was converted into a maternity home by Ayr County Council. To accommodate this the County Architect *William Reid* stretched a Neo-Georgian addition transversely across the front of the W gable. Converted to its present use 1986.

CRANBERRYMOSS COMMUNITY CENTRE, Cambusdoon Place. Stone-built U-plan farmhouse of 1855 in the heart of Pennyburn, converted 1971–4 by *Irvine Development Corporation*. 'The value of retaining and adapting the existing building would be to retain some of the old character of the area in the midst of the new modern design and housing thus creating the necessary homely effect.'

JAMES WATT COLLEGE (North Ayrshire Campus), Lauchlan Way. 1998–2000 by *Boswell Mitchell & Johnston*. Three-storey main elevation of two wings, slightly angled to each other, in dark engineering brick and white sheet-metal cladding, with a prominent glazed porch below a big glazed area, and an equally generously glazed stair-tower to the l. Subtle articulation in the varying and overlapping roof pitches. Businesslike interiors; the entrance area spacious, airy and welcoming.

KILWINNING ACADEMY, Dalry Road. 1973–7, by *Ayr County Council*, similar to the contemporary James Hamilton Academy, Kilmarnock (q.v.). Big secondary school faced in brown concrete panels, broadly symmetrical about a three-storey entrance block with a canted front, slightly advanced from the flanking wings (two-storey to the l., three to the r.). These have horizontal bands of windows, and are linked to the central block by first-floor glazed corridors on pilotis.

KILWINNING STATION, Townhead. The railway reached Kilwinning in 1839; the existing single-storey station, its roofs swept down onto cast-iron verandas, is of 1862–3.

KILWINNING TOWN HALL, Byres Road. 1907 by *Hugh Thomson* of Saltcoats. Symmetrical Free Renaissance of seven bays of

Mauchline red sandstone. The central entrance bay has a seg-mental-headed doorway, wrought-iron balcony and tall finials to its raised parapet. The advanced second and sixth bays have subsidiary entrances and terminate in shaped gables. Free-standing addition of the 1950s behind, joined by a first-floor bridge.

MOTHER LODGE, Main Street. 1892–3, by *J. B. Wilson* of Glasgow, with *John Armour Jun.* as resident architect, in Free Renaissance style. Kilwinning is regarded as the birthplace of freemasonry in Scotland; its establishment and initial codifica-tion associated by popular belief with the masons of the abbey. The lodge, known as the Mother Lodge, has the honorific title of Lodge 0. A crowded façade; the unifying element the con-tinuous bracketed sill course which to the l. creates a hood for a two-light mullioned-and-transomed window and supports a five-light canted oriel; to the r. it continues as a hood for the round-headed door and carries a balustraded balcony. Above the oriel a fussily stepped gable terminating in a shield in a panel under a segmental gablet. Extended 1972–3 by *Robert Allan*, dark brick with a thick band of lighter brick and advanced concrete panels. Inside, narrow ENTRANCE HALL, divided by a heavy arch on detached marble half-columns. The TEMPLE is rectangular. Coved and panelled ceiling, with a long raised centre, with glazed sides, rising into the roof space above. The lowest band of panels decorated with masonic symbols. Tiers of wooden benches around the walls and three ritually arranged seats with raised backs. An altar encases the founda-tion stone of the previous lodge, of 1779. Simple marble war memorial.

NETHERMAINS COMMUNITY CENTRE, Nethermains Road. 1899–1900, built as an Institute for the local iron workers. Italianate, red sandstone, with a dumpy central tower; a panelled band below the big clock stage and a slated pyramid roof. Gabled hall to l., lower gable canted across the r.-hand corner.

ST WINNING'S R.C. PRIMARY SCHOOL, St Winning's Road. 1937, extended 1966–8, both by *Ayr County Council*. The hall, with full height glazing, is noteworthy.

WHITEHIRST PARK PRIMARY SCHOOL, West Doura Way. 1973–5, *Ayr County Council Architects Department*.

DESCRIPTION

The medieval lay settlement appears to have been largely N of the abbey. Here the town's heart is formed by the E–W Main Street, pedestrianized in 1968–9 to plans of *Hay Steel MacFarlane & Partners* which is squeezed between the abbey ruins and the too-close inner by-pass (LAUCHLAN WAY, 1978–9). It begins from the E end at the late C18 GARNOCK BRIDGE (widened in 1857). Two segmental arches, with central triangular cutwaters, flat pilasters above these, and a low parapet. MAIN STREET begins with the clumsy ROBERT SERVICE MEMORIAL, of

2000, with mosaic panels illustrating the poet's life and work.*
On the N side No. 14, tall, narrow, harled, with a prominent
corner, corbelled over the entrance: good *Irvine Development
Corporation* infill of 1985–6 (job architect *H. Roan Rutherford*)
that supplemented the restoration of the next two buildings:
No. 16, early C19, equally tall but wider and slightly advanced,
with string coursed and chamfered windows, and the MASONS'
HOWFF, a joyous late C18 house, harled, with simple dressings
and skews, and long-and-short quoins. The taller BUFFS
TAVERN is also harled, with a gable pediment with a circular
datestone and stone dressings. It is dated 1714, but early C19
in appearance. In front of this group, the MERCAT CROSS, an
octagonal shaft with a Late Gothic capital with carved heads,
carrying a simple wooden cross pattée of 1987 by *Ian Cooper*.
Opposite, also late C18, MORRISONS, with stone dressings and
one crowstepped gable, lower early C19 bay to the r. Otherwise
the street on both sides is mostly early and mid-C19, and
without much to offer until THE FOUNDRY (Nos. 86–90).
Late C19 commercial, with a wide centre bay, and first-floor
broken segmental pediments, THE LEMON TREE, of *c.* 1820,
with elaborate first-floor architraves and a panelled eaves
course, and MOTHER LODGE (*see* Public Buildings, above).
After this the street widens into a public space, with at the SE
corner inspired harled *I.D.C.* infill housing (*H. Roan Rutherford*, project architect) of 1995–6, a synthesis of Scottish vernacular architecture, with strongly emphasized chimneys; the
result an original piece of urban renewal. Main Street continues as HOWGATE, passing the former Mansefield Church (*see*
Churches, above), MANSFIELD COTTAGE (No. 19) of 1862
with castellated eaves and a bay to the r. with a frieze of quatrefoils in panels, and CLAREMONT, late C19, its windows in
basket-arched moulded frames. Opposite, Nos. 18–20, an
eccentric semi-detached pair of 1877 with a channelled ground
floor and quoins, porches with balustrades and urns, and urns
along the parapet; *Alexander Watt*'s Commercial Bank of 1854,
remodelled by *David Rhind* in 1877. But the most interesting
building here is the long range along the s side (now CORNER-
STONE CHURCH) built in 1982–4 by *Irvine Development Corporation* (*H. Roan Rutherford*, project architect) as a centre and
accommodation for young people. L-plan, with the entrance in
the outer angle, at the junction with Dalry Road. Along
Howgate is the residential wing, with a slate roof but fully
glazed along one side, lighting an internal passage and with
roof-lights over the doors. At the corner this evolves into a
faceted glazed hinge, with the cross wall continued upwards as
a stone stack at the peak of its roof. To the rear, the flats
become two-storey, owing to the fall in the land, and have
canted bays. Facing Dalry Road, the hall is simpler, with a

---

*Service, the 'laureate of the Yukon' and the author of *The Ballad of Dan McGrew*,
grew up in Kilwinning.

continuous band of windows below the broad eaves. Exposed timber ceilings.

EGLINTON COUNTRY PARK

The Country Park is like Hamlet without the prince: Eglinton Castle, the hub of the estate, is a fragmentary ruin, no longer the symbol of an ancient family with accumulated estates, wealth and prestige. Now a major public park for Irvine New Town, although the boundaries have been compromised by new roads, including the Irvine by-pass.

The consolidated remains of EGLINTON CASTLE stand beside a bend of the Lugton Water. From the C14 the seat of the Montgomeries, who became Earls of Eglinton in 1508. The tower house, to which additions were made by *William Adam* before 1729 for the 9th Earl, was pulled down by the 12th Earl and replaced by a powerful, castle-style mansion of 1798–1803 by *John Paterson*, the earl's architect for Montgomerie House, near Tarbolton (also dem. after a fire, in 1971). Ill-conceived investment by the Earls of Eglinton in Ardrossan Harbour and the Glasgow, Paisley & Ardrossan Canal and the 13th Earl's outrageously extravagant Eglinton Tournament, a medieval pageant to end all pageants, in 1839 hastened the estate's decline. The castle was unroofed in 1925, used for target practice by the Royal Engineers and dismantled in 1973, leaving the crenellated SW corner turret, of the original four sported by Paterson's house. It is four storeys high in pink sandstone with a battered base and corbelled top, and footings of the remainder. They show the ground plan, including the circular base of the once dominant central tower. Also surviving, the façade of the stylistically faithful two-storey W wing added in 1857–60 by *William Railton*, of Kilmarnock, who made other additions including a large porch; its footprint remains.

The park's hub is now the VISITOR CENTRE, 0.5 km. SW of the castle remains, formerly the service range and home farm. Although altered, it retains its courtyard with a single-storey, rubble-built cottage on the NW side and a small doocot inserted into a gable on the NE with rows of nesting boxes intact. NW is the tall pilastered and pedimented RACQUET COURT of 1846, built for the 13th Earl and believed to be the first covered court in the world, converted for leisure facilities. Pinkish, roughly squared rubble with ashlar dressings and a Roman Doric pedimented doorcase, the court top-lit through an open-trussed roof. SE of the Visitor Centre the BELVIDERE GATES into the park. Four square, ashlar-built gatepiers, with pineapple urn finials; nearby, a simple fluted COLUMN with no capital, a memorial to Hugh Montgomerie (†1817), grandson of the 12th Earl. W of the castle, the new TOURNAMENT BRIDGE of *c.* 1845, beautifully restored 2008–9 by *Jacobs Engineering Ltd*. It has four tall octagonal stone piers carved with cusped panels and crenellations at each end of the two arched cast-iron bridge and a balustrade of Gothic arches with

68, p. 47

Eglinton Country Park, Bridge.
Engraving, 1811

merlons and ogee finials (refurbished by the *Ballantine Bo'ness Iron Co.*). It succeeded, and reuses parts of, a similar bridge of three arches, built before 1811 and possibly designed by *David Hamilton*, which stood slightly further downstream, giving access to the tilt yard for contestants at the tournament (1839).

STABLE COURT, probably by *Paterson*. It is a large square with a pedimented centrepiece, entrance now a window, and broad outer advanced bays with crenellations. On the s side a tall Doric-columned bellcote with ogee lead roof, ball finial and weathervane. To the N the simple shallow-arched early C19 STABLE BRIDGE with square piers and diminutively corbelled caps. Further W, an extensive WALLED GARDEN with high brick-lined walls and a circular, neatly constructed ashlar GAZEBO, now roofless, all early C19. 100 m. NW is EGLINTON HOUSE, formerly the gardener's house, an early C19 Picturesque two-storey hexagon with low splayed wings all tied together by a curved Doric pilastered porch, a typical Picturesque pattern-book design. At the W entrance KILWINNING LODGE, *c.* 1800. The only remaining lodge to relate sensibly to the estate but unsympathetically extended. It has a prominent semi-octagonal centre with arched windows and low wings with segmental-headed windows set into panels. Bold *c.* 1840 cast-iron curved railings link to the piers. Much plainer MILBURN LODGE and GATEPIERS of 1807, 1.3 km. W of the castle. For the STANECASTLE GATES *see* Girdle Toll.

Of the LANDSCAPING a series of formal avenues radiate out from the late C20 Doric-colonnaded BELVIDERE. The layout is C18 but replanted in the late C20. The pleasure grounds were greatly enlarged and improved in the C19 by *John Tweedie* for Alexander, the 10th Earl, with lakes and plantations. On the s side of the park, a late C18 egg-shaped ICE HOUSE with tunnel entrance and lectern DOOCOT, formerly associated with Eglinton Mains Farm, large, late C18, with a pointed-arched entrance and blind crosses indented into the masonry. The flight-holes have been blocked and all the nesting boxes removed.

HOUSING AND VILLAS

PENNYBURN, 0.7 km. SW. Housing by *Irvine Development Corporation*, their first major building project, and constructed in three phases, the first (CRANBERRY ROAD and the streets off) begining in 1967 (job architect, *Robert Thomson*). The second phase (Muirside Road) was begun in 1969, and the final phase, which lies to the E and extends N, separated from the remainder of the estate by the railway, in 1973. The houses are mostly two-storey, harled, often with timber panelling, in short terraces. The earlier phases established the tone of much of the Corporation's subsequent housing developments, firstly through the adoption of Radburn model planning with a perimeter road (Pennyburn Road) and segregation of pedestrians and traffic, and secondly through high awareness of the importance of design detail, often boldly expressed, particularly in the choice of typefaces and colours for house numbers and street names. Primary schools (PENNYBURN, 1971–2, and ST LUKE'S, 1973–5) by *Ayr County Council Architects Dept.*

Of the I.D.C.'s other housing, PATHFOOT is two terraces of harled cottages, of *c.* 1995, their tiled roofs, exposed rafter ends and incised dressings a simplification of the Corporation's contemporary work in Irvine Harbourside (q.v.).

IRVINE ROAD. The best of the late C19 houses is LARCHFIELD (No. 9). Of cherry-cocked whin, with jolly bargeboarded gabled dormers, finials to the side gables, and wide eaves.

KYLESWELL ROAD. RED CROSS HOUSE (No. 20). Mid-C18, two-storey, rubble-built with raised quoins and margins. The flagged area in front of the house is probably C19.

DALRY ROAD. LEDCAMEROCH. Now in commercial use. White-harled Baronial by *J. J. Burnet*, of 1898–1901. Broadly T-plan, but with the entrance in the l. bay of the long single-storey wing, with a gabled pend, which forms an internal courtyard. Typically Burnetian dormers, while some original interiors survive including a big fireplace, with a cartouche supported by cherubs, in one room. Undistinguished additions.

SMITHSTONE, 1.8 km. NW. Much altered three-bay ashlar rural villa of *c.* 1830, with thin end pilasters and a central first-floor tripartite window with guttae; a canted bay to the r., and, internally, a bowed balustered stair of *c.* 1856. Extension to the l., with a conical-roofed bowed projection, of 1902 by *Frank Burnet, Boston & Carruthers*. Poor late C20 alterations.

KINGENCLEUGH HOUSE 5020
1.5 km. SE of Mauchline

A small, two-storey, asymmetrical country house, harled with a pink colourwash and grey painted margins. Mostly the result of radical remodelling in 1956–7 by *Mervyn Noad* of *Noad &*

Wallace for Sir Claud Hagart-Alexander. Claud Alexander purchased the property as part of the Ballochmyle estate in 1785.
At its centre is a modest farmhouse of *c.* 1756, three bays wide,
which has a two-storey w addition of 1777 and a single-storey
E extension that was raised in the C19. Service wing also sympathetically raised by *ARP Lorimer*, *c.* 2003. Noad introduced
a certain gravitas to the starkly plain s elevation by converting
its central entrance porch into a bold two-storey gabled bay
crowned with an elephant finial (reputedly by *Hew Lorimer*),
the symbol of the East India Company for whose Bengal troops
Claud Alexander was Paymaster General. Stone doorcase with
the family motto 'perseverancia vincis sans peur' ('by persever-
ance you will conquer without fear'), and heraldic shield above.
On the garden front Noad added a corresponding bay which
rises into a nepus gable. All the windows have been enlarged
and typically 1950s open ironwork guards added to lowered
first-floor windows. All that is visible of the C18 house inside
is the stone newel stair. Two later C18 chimneypieces are said
to come from a house in the High Street, Edinburgh. Both are
finely carved with a delicate lace-like moulding. One has an
equally delicate acorn moulding, the other rather corpulent
rams' heads.

Low detached SE range with two tiers of arched openings
forming a small dovecot in the w gable.

The house succeeded KINGENCLEUCH OLD CASTLE, now
a romantic ruin perched above the wooded glen to the s of the
house. All that remains is the roofless, four-storey jamb of an
L-plan tower house of *c.* 1600 with a crowstepped gable at SW.
Evidence of an entrance in the re-entrant angle and of corbelling for a stair-turret. Larger upper windows with glazing slots.
Built of red sandstone rubble, some traces of lime plaster
surviving.

4040   KINGSFORD

Roadside hamlet on the road between Stewarton and Glasgow.

Former KINGSFORD PRIMARY SCHOOL. *c.* 1875, altered 1904
by *Andrew & Newlands*, who added the characterful single-
storey and harled SCHOOL HOUSE.

KIRKBRIDE *see* FISHERTON

3000   KIRKBRIDE HOUSE
                          2 km. SSE of Crosshill

Begun in 1861 as a compact two-storey-and-attic villa with Baronial touches, more suburban than rural. Low-key two-storey
wing added in 1924 for Col. Houldsworth, possibly by *J. K.
Hunter*, and partly demolished and altered for him in 1965 by
J. A. Carrick, who moved the entrance to the w wing. It was

formerly on the asymmetrical N front, in the steeply gabled projecting bay. Adjoining, an E-facing gabled wing having a Bryce-like square angle turret with a step-faceted roof and finial; the wall between the original entrance and the turret has been raised in a redder sandstone and given an incongruous crenellation. A canted window pushed out from the S garden front of the original house is linked to the projecting garden entrance on the 1920s wing; the latter has wall-head gables and cross-windows with a canted window on the S gable and a big inglenook in the W gable. Extended and reordered by *ARP Lorimer & Associates* 2006.

KIRKMICHAEL

3000

Attractive parochial centre and former weaving village, broadly triangular in shape, with the Parish Church lying at the NE angle.

KIRKMICHAEL PARISH CHURCH, Patna Road. 1786–7 by *Hugh Cairncross*. One of the better late C18 churches in Ayrshire, sitting low in a 'truly romantic' (Paterson) spot beside the tree-banked Dyrock Burn. A regulation gabled T-plan preaching box with round-headed windows, a tall W porch, a bellcote on the W gable, a dog-leg gallery stair at the E gable, hugger-mugger with two stone-walled burying places, and a small minister's porch in the middle of the S wall. All heavily harled with freestone dressings. Two tall windows in the S wall, with double tiers elsewhere. Plastered and galleried interior. The Cloncaird Gallery (N) has Doric columns and a broad segmental arched head to the recess. Retiring room with a good fireplace behind. – PULPIT. Unusual and stylish stone octagon, by *James A. Morris*, 1920 as a First World War memorial. Five sides carved beautifully by *Alexander Carrick* with figurative representations of gallantry, bravery and patriotism. The panels were conceived by *Hugh R. Wallace* of Cloncaird, and developed by *W. R. Sutherland* of Edinburgh. – STAINED GLASS. W arm: He Went About Doing Good (S) by *A. Ballantine & Son*, Edinburgh, 1911, and What Must I Do To Be Saved (N), 1898, possibly by *Clayton & Bell*. Flanking the pulpit: the Resurrection (l.), again possibly by *Clayton & Bell*, and Suffer Little Children (r.), a brilliantly expressed window by *Christopher Whall*, c. 1905, the gathering children in the lower panel especially well depicted. – MONUMENTS. N wall. Two plain but elegant marble designs: Colonel Cunynghame of Cloncaird, †1817, by *David Hamilton & Sons* of Glasgow; Henry Fairlie, †1911, by *James A. Morris* with bronze portrait by *Robert Bryden*.

The CHURCHYARD is bounded on two sides by the burn, and elsewhere by a stone dyke. – LYCHGATE, SW, with a semi-circular arch, rusticated pillars and a curvilinear gable. Apparently c. 1700, but with a C20 roof, from which is suspended a bell. Nearby, the burial place of the Ritchies of Cloncaird.

Classical. Its back forms part of the boundary dyke and to the external side of this is affixed the village WAR MEMORIAL, a bronze plaque of *c.* 1919.

KIRKMICHAEL CEMETERY, Ayr Road, 1 km. W. 1922, by *George P. Greenlaw* of Maybole. Concrete walled enclosure, with all the decoration concentrated in the ornamental gates and ball-finialled gatepiers.

McCOSH CLUB, Patna Road. Former working men's club, now village hall. 1898–9 by *J. S. Baxter*. A remarkably gauche exercise in red Ballochmyle stone. Two storeys, five bays, the outer bays brought forward, that to the r. extended upwards as a Gothic-detailed clock tower, with a further flat-headed towerlet at one corner of this. Square-headed ground floor windows, round-headed above.

DESCRIPTION. PATNA ROAD runs W from the church, curving between rows of late C18 cottages, some plain, some painted, some harled, all evidence of the original kirktoun. On the S side is the narrow stone hump-backed PORTCHEEK BRIDGE, dated 177(5?), leading to PORTCHEEK (No. 3 Bolestyle Road), an C18 farmhouse, with a detached barn to the r. Off the N side of Patna Road, hiding in trees, the former MANSE (now Gemilston), gabled Tudor Gothic of 1836–8, built by *James Paton* of Ayr, and attributed to *William Burn*. Conserved and reordered by *Patrick Lorimer*, of *ARP Lorimer & Associates*, 1991. The firm also designed the new Manse, adjacent, 1988–9. After one final gentle curve the street proceeds straight into the 'new village', built from 1806 (when feus were first advertised) and called 'thriving' by 1822. Mostly single-storey, with some original two-storey houses, and forming a remarkably unified ensemble. Harl and plaster predominate, but where the stone is exposed, it is often large cherry-cocked whin (particularly fine at No. 16); steeply pitched slate roofs and occasional heavy skews.

KIRKMICHAEL HOUSE, 1 km. SW. A Kennedy property and an architectural ragbag of the late C16 or early C17 to the earlier C20, mildly Baronial in character. Early fabric now only visible in the basement: two vaulted stores and a near-contemporary addition to their E that includes the base of a small turret in the shallow angle, the turret itself (on S elevation) rebuilt in the C19. The wide entrance front has a three-bay centre, now only visible above the ground floor, plain and classical, with an uncompromisingly horizontal parapet and flat roof (formerly pitched). It has the Kennedy coat of arms in the parapet and may be early C18 (the date of two redundant but splendid rusticated gatepiers, like those at Old Dalquharran, q.v.). The flanking wings may have C18 origins but they are not symmetrical and have C19 crowstepped gables. *William Burn* (*see* below) extended the W front and formed the present central porch, extended in the 1920s by *Allan Stevenson & Cassels* when this was the Miners' Welfare Home. The pilastered loggia (E) and a small room to the W were inserted into the front court. J. C. Loudon notes in 1831 that the house is 'rebuilding in a sort of

Elizabethan style from the design of Mr Burns [*sic*]'; on the W and S elevations the two-storey canted windows have crenellated parapets and silhouette gablet heads, familiar Burn details. Stark four-storey block at the house's N end, added in 1861 with a stair-turret at the SW angle; both this and the NE turret have candle-snuffer roofs and fish-scale slating.

Much remodelled inside, the panelled interior of the loggia presumably 1920s as too the T-plan hall. Three rooms were created by Burn: the Dining Room (SE) has a featured black marble chimneypiece, with a later C19 pilastered overmantel and deeply moulded foliate cornice; the Drawing Room at the NE corner similarly detailed but with a grey veined marble chimneypiece and two French windows opening onto a re-created balcony, originally offering expansive views of the lake and gardens (it has been recently panelled); the Library opens from the Drawing Room and mirrors its decorative details. At the top of the 1860s block is a panelled Billiard Room with elaborate cornice.

Attached to the house's N end, a low and plain two-storey T-plan SCHOOL, late C19. Its upper floor has the coved-ceilinged former assembly hall.

CLONCAIRD CASTLE. *See* p. 220.

KIRKOSWALD   *2000*

Parochial centre in mid Carrick, and of considerable antiquity. Oswald, King of the Northumbrians, is said to have gained a victory here in the late C7. Robert Burns's mother, Agnes Broun, came from Kirkoswald, and he received some of his education here, while the protagonists of his epic poem *Tam o'Shanter* are modelled on villagers. Kirkoswald was largely by-passed by the late C19 and C20, and R. L. Stevenson, in 1876, found it 'Highland-looking'. It remains a small closely knit settlement, though bisected by the impossibly busy A77.

Former KIRKOSWALD FREE CHURCH. *See* below.

KIRKOSWALD PARISH CHURCH, Kirk Brae. The parish church for Culzean, built 1777, and therefore widely regarded as the work of *Robert Adam*, but perhaps more likely the work of his clerk-of-works at Culzean, *Hugh Cairncross*, whose competence as an architect in his own right, and one well versed in the Adam oeuvre, is demonstrated e.g. at Ardgowan (Renfrewshire). Should we not credit Cairncross with this attractive and unique church?

Built on an elevated site above the village, succeeding the Old Kirk (*see* below). T-plan constructed of large blocks of rough ashlar, which was originally harled, except for the prominent long-and-short quoins. The W projection has an oddly unarticulated main doorcase, a blind balustrade above it and arched windows breaking through the base of the pediment.

Crowning the pediment a chimney, and two urns surmounted by pelicans. On the sides of this arm, large square-headed sash windows in keystoned architraves above elliptical windows in moulded frames, a feature repeated on the W walls of the other arms. The N and S gables have elaborately detailed Venetian windows; a simple open bellcote, to the S an urn. To the E eleva-tion, two tall round-headed windows either side of a later narrow-waisted projection containing the organ and the vestry. It is of 1892, as are the N and S porches.

Interior restored after a fire in 1997. Plastered, with galleries to l. and r. with wooden fronts with fluted strips. The third gallery, facing the pulpit, is the Culzean Loft, its detailing Adam-inspired. Bowed panelled front, supported on fluted Doric columns, while fluted end pilasters are carried through to the curving plastered entablature above. Behind the loft, a withdrawing room. – ORGAN CASE, PULPIT and COMMUNION TABLE. Harmonious ensemble, classically detailed, of 1892. – STAINED GLASS. From Kincraig Church, Maybole. *c.* 1880. Perhaps by *W. & J. J. Kier.* GLEBE HOUSE, S, is the former manse of 1847 by *James Paton & Son* of Ayr; two-storey, of ashlar, with a projecting pilastered doorway.

OLD KIRK, Main Road. Roofless remains of a long, and sub-stantial, rectangular and gabled-ended church. Buttressed seven-bay E elevation, with a multi-ordered early C13 pointed doorway in the second bay from the S. N bellcote, post-Refor-mation, with a square window and a square-headed doorway beneath. The blind rear wall snuggles into the steeply rising churchyard. Inside, much of the N half serves as a MAUSO-LEUM for the Kennedys of Culzean. Low vaulted roof and a s doorway, mimicking that in the original E wall. Probably C19. Within the church a rugged quern-like FONT, mounted like a bird bath, said to be that in which Robert Bruce was baptized in 1274. The churchyard has pyramid-headed gatepiers and in the NE corner is the WAR MEMORIAL, a simple granite cross of 1921 by *Hugh McLachlan* of Ayr. Many carved C17 and C18 HEADSTONES. The earliest is a dramatic and deeply carved Adam and Eve, probably of mid to late C17 date. One group, close to the E door, includes an animated skeleton, which is probably of 1692, and, on another stone alongside, an angel above flames or leaf-like scrolls. This is probably early C18. Close to the N end of the church MEMORIAL to James Kennedy with two seraphic lions. Also in this area, a nicely lettered memorial to a family of Kennedys, probably done shortly after 1788. The C18 carved stone to Jean Aird or Kennedy, the inn-keeper known as 'Kirkton Jean', has two skulls, crossbones and a doll-like female figure between a book and a bundled pack of wool. There are other stones connected with associates of Burns, or those who inspired his verse, e.g. the simple lettered stone commemorating Douglas Graham, the original for Tam o' Shanter. The Broun family, Burns's mother's family, has a memorial swathed in a dull Annan red sandstone overcoat by *Hay & Henderson*, 1883.

RICHMOND HALL, Main Road. 1923–5 by *James Miller*. The benefactor was John Richmond, for whom Miller designed Blanefield (q.v.) in the same Late Arts and Crafts style. Cream sandstone. T-plan, with a tall, narrow, church-like main block, containing the hall, whose slate roofs fall steeply on both sides and are broken at eaves level by four big multi-paned windows, and much smaller wings at the rear. Narrow gabled front, unadorned above the round-headed entrance; low pavilions to l. and r., emphasizing the height of the hall.

DESCRIPTION. KIRK BRAE descends from the Parish Church, with parallel rows of early C19 stone cottages, but drops swiftly down to MAIN ROAD, which runs N, with the Old Kirk and kirkyard on its l. Unmissable at the foot of the brae is SOUTER JOHNNIE'S INN, a restoration by *John Smith* in 2007–8 of two C19 two-storey run-down village inns. They have been recast with plaster walls, toothpaste-lined to resemble stonework, and thatched roofs whose detailing owes nothing to Scottish thatching traditions, and much to chocolate boxes and jigsaws.* Further on, on the r., SOUTER JOHNNIE'S COTTAGE is a necessary reminder of the once uniform harled and thatched appearance of the village cottages, and has been maintained in that condition by the National Trust for Scotland. It was built in 1786 for John Davidson, a shoemaker ('souter'), the original for Tam o' Shanter's drinking buddy. Originally a house and workshop, each with a separate street entrance. The workshop is now arranged domestically, with fireplace in one wall, a flagged floor, plaster walls and a low beamed ceiling. Open stairs to the loft, and a door to the original house, which has built-in bed spaces. Rear extension of *c*. 1820, with a low slated workshop wing. This has an earthen floor, and one wall boarded, the others of exposed stone. In the garden to the rear a small thatched C18 cottage, in which are four life-size STATUES, of Tam, the Souter, the landlord and his wife, executed by *James Thom*, 1802 (*see* also his statues at Alloway). Adjoining Souter Johnnie's Cottage to the N is a COTTAGE of almost identical age, size and style, but with exposed stone, slated roofs and closed-up openings. On the opposite side of the road, set back behind characterful wall and railings, OLD HALL is the former Free Church of 1848–9, converted to residential use in 1976. CAIRNHILL PLACE, an attractive crescent of timber- and shingle-clad semi-detached cottages built in 1938–9 by *William Reid*, County Architect, forms a welcome visual link between the heart of the village and the Richmond Hall.

KNOCK CASTLE
3.5 km. N of Largs

A self-confident country house, and the best mid-Victorian example in Ayrshire of the stylish Tudor Gothic that was made

2060

75

---

*The main building was badly damaged by fire in April 2012.

popular in Scotland by William Burn (cf. Blairquhan, q.v.). Built
for Robert Steele, a Greenock merchant, in 1851–3 by *J. T.
Rochead*, and sympathetically extended in 1908 by *Fryers &
Penman* for F. G. MacAndrew.

The setting is dramatic, placed high above the coast road with
  spectacular panoramic views of the Firth of Clyde and against
  a backdrop of steep hills. The house is of two storeys above a
  raised and battered basement, with a weighty sill course at first
  floor and a crenellated parapet, corbelled in a variety of ways.
  Grouped diamond-plan stacks on big plinths with bold copings
  add drama to the silhouette, and subtle changes of detail add
  originality. The walls are of finely coursed creamy stugged
  sandstone ashlar with polished dressings to the square-headed
  hoodmoulded windows, most of which have Perp-style tracery.
  The main elevation, facing W, is tightly composed into four
  regular bays whose outer bays are expressed as square towers
  of unequal depth, the larger one at the S also with a big canted
  bay window. The asymmetry is further articulated by the striking three-storey entrance tower which is set back against the
  N front and has on two faces an oriel window, that to the W
  above a basket-arched doorway. Rising from its SW angle a tall
  octagonal pencil stair-turret, reaching skyward like a lighthouse to an open platform. On the S front, there is another
  canted bay, here full-height, narrowing above its battered base
  and corbelled to the top stage. Projecting E, a small service
  wing. The two-storey wing to its N, for the billiard room, is by
  Fryers & Penman. The infill between the two and below the
  stair window may also be an addition. A parapet wall encloses
  the basement-level service court.
    The elevations express the interior plan. From the rib-
  vaulted inner lobby in the entrance tower, a wide CORRIDOR
  extends across the rear of the house with the principal rooms
  to the W. All have Tudor-arched door frames and vertically
  panelled doors. Walls are lined to imitate ashlar with a stencil
  frieze above. Ribbed ceiling, decorated with delicate stencil
  patterns, spanned by very shallow four-centred arches rising
  from corbels set into the frieze. At the S end of the corridor a
  spacious inglenook, two deep pointed-arched recessed niches
  with bench seats and openings above with Gothic-detailed iron
  grilles. They flank a C17-style chimneypiece, probably a replacement by Fryers & Penman. The WELL-STAIR, opening to the
  E, has a Gothic traceried balustrade of the same design as the
  window heads and newel posts supporting rampant lions. On
  the upper floor, an arcaded, galleried landing and a corridor
  detailed as before. At the half-landing a doorway, formed from
  a light of the original window when the Edwardian E wing was
  added. Abstract coloured glass of that date.
    All the ceilings in the principal rooms are detailed as the hall
  but with some variety in the patterns. The cornices have sharply
  moulded geometric patterns. Figured marble chimneypieces

with some Gothic detailing. The former LIBRARY has smart glass-fronted cases set within Gothic arches. The DRAWING ROOM was remodelled by Fryers & Penman when the s alcove was deepened and a rather incongruous classically detailed pilastered arch introduced. It was probably at this time that the Gothic door in the E wall was blocked and the mildly French-styled moulded panels with tapestry infill were introduced. The door to the service wing is of 2008 by *ARP Lorimer*, contemporary with alterations to the wing itself. The TOWER ROOM on the second floor has the same rib-vaulting as the entrance lobby but also a basket-arched fireplace lined with tiles painted with sailing ships. Its tall outer pilasters finish with cusped decoration and flank a paired mirrored overmantel. The house was fitted out with many similar chimneypieces.

– WEST LODGE. By *Fryers & Penman*, 1904, with crow-stepped gables and angle turret for the entrance. Imposing castellated gateway in the manner of Rochead, the ornate wrought-iron GATES by *Frazer Bros* of Largs. – NORTH LODGE very similar. In the same style, also *c.* 1900, is the COACH-HOUSE at the top of the E drive, like a simple red sandstone toy fort. Modified as a motor house *c.* 1908 by *Fryers & Penman*, the inner court covered by a Belfast-trussed roof.

KNOCK OLD CASTLE, 100 m. SW and slightly below at the edge of the steep slope to the coastal plain. Remains of a Z-plan tower house of probable late C16/early C17 date (stones dated 1603 and 1604 are re-set in the barmkin wall, the latter with the initials of John Fraser and Jeane Brisbane who married in 1583). Described by Pont in 1608 as a 'pretty dwelling house', it had two rooms, aligned E–W (the walls of the larger E one now mostly ruinous) and round angle towers at the NE (also mostly destroyed) and SW here surprisingly tall and slender housing the stair with the upper stage rebuilt convincingly. Extending from the SW corner a straight section of the barmkin wall, much restored and reconstructed in 1853 with crenellated top and a corbelled tourelle at the end. Of the same date, the round-headed s door to the tower's W end (which was maintained as a dwelling). Several circular shot-holes are clearly re-set, others are C19 copies. Also C19 a diminutive doocot set into a gableted dormerhead. On the s front there are unaltered single windows at ground, first and second floor with original roll-moulded architraves, the larger ones higher up having slots for fixed glazing. The second-floor window is possibly a late C17 enlargement, and the wall-head dormer has a mid-C19 shouldered crowstepped gablet with a diminutive doocot. Plain windows in the crowstepped W gable, and at the foot of this wall there is what appears to be a drain exit. Dividing the tower house is a crowstepped gable wall with a blocked door at first floor. The details and the carved skewputt with indecipherable initials suggest it is original. Part of the N wall survives with two windows and a small opening at the NW, again possibly a drain.

KNOCKDOLIAN HOUSE
2.5 km. w of Colmonell

A picturesque site with expansive views of the Stinchar. Built for Alexander Cathcart in 1842 by *David Rhind* in a smart Neo-Jacobean style owing much to William Burn. Crisp pinkish red sandstone ashlar throughout except for the rear service area which is grey whin rubble. The elevations are asymmetrical; the w (entrance) front has a gabled porch with a corbelled chimneystack to the l. of the door over a square projecting window. Flanking the stack two monogrammed (AC and MM), gablet-headed windows. The finialled gables, steeply pointed gablets and tall, square corniced chimney flues, in banks, paired or singly, make for a lively roof-line. Consistent lying-pane glazing adds to the elegant picture. The house is laid out on a hierarchical plan with the public rooms in the prominent SE section and the gabled porch linking this to the more discreet N part. Beyond this are lower service ranges. Alterations and additions to the service quarters 1904 and 1908 by *Allan Stevenson & Thomas McGill Cassels* and again *c.* 1985 by *Patrick Lorimer* of *ARP Lorimer & Associates.*

KNOCKDOLIAN CASTLE, 125 m. s, stands high above the Stinchar on a platform. Its setting, with land rising behind it to the w, appears more for shelter than defence. Now, fronted by lawns, it remains a testimony to the antiquity of the site. It was built in the first half of the C16 as a rectangular, four-storey tower of rubble-built walls with quoins but substantially recast, probably *c.* 1650, for Fergus McCubbin and his wife Margaret Kennedy (small worn crest inserted into the N wall). It is clear that the upper storey and parapets are built onto the earlier structure, but presumably reusing existing continuous corbelling and embryo angle rounds which would be otherwise very old-fashioned for the date. On the river (SE) elevation the arrangement is different. Here the continuous corbelling has been untidily broken and replaced with individual corbels supporting a slightly projecting parapet. Could it have been created to provide a view?

The sw gable is crowstepped and set behind the parapet, but the NE gable is continuous with the wall, although here too the masonry has clearly been rebuilt. Beside this gable, the remains of a caphouse with a fragment of cornice suggesting that it too was altered in the C17. A small door at ground-floor level with a simple billet-moulded lintel; one inverted keyhole gunloop to the N (onto the newel stair) and two to the s, one somewhat smaller than the others. Inside at this level are two vaulted cells – the w one has no entrance from the outside and can only have been accessed by ladder from the first floor. The entrance at the E end leads into a chamber with a single arrow-slit opening. The newel stair, set at the N angle, rises within the 1.5-m.-thick wall immediately to the l. of the door. The large chimneystack emerging behind the NW parapet served the first-floor hall, which was lit at the SW end by windows on each long wall; the SW one appears to have been enlarged. On the floor above, a single clustered-column shaft from a smart chimneypiece of C16 or C17 date. It could have been re-set when this level was rebuilt. There is another chimney opening on the opposite wall suggesting that there were two chambers at this level.

Mounds in the grounds were part of a tranquil GARDEN. To Abercrummie in 1696 it indicated 'what art and industry can doe to render a place to which nature has not been favourable very pleasant by planting of gardens, orchards, walks and rows of trees that surprise the beholder with things so far beyond expectation in a country so wild and mountainous'.

KNOCKENTIBER

3030

Late C19 mining village, now largely mid-C20 local authority housing.

PLANN HOUSE, 0.5 km. N. Mid-C19. Plastered single-storey gabled cottage with end stacks, a central entrance with entablature and flanking oriel bows.

KYLE CASTLE

6010

7 km. E of Cumnock

Scant ruins occupying a rocky promontory at the confluence of the Guelt Water and Glenmuir Water in remote moorland. A similar site to Glengarnock Castle (q.v.), and Kyle may well have guarded a route, now forgotten, into Ayrshire from the E. There was probably an outer bailey to the W of the stone keep, of which only a fragment, to a height of about 3 m., remains. It appears to have been abandoned at an early date, and subsequently quarried for building stone.

LADY ISLE

2020

Flat rocky island lying off the coast near Troon. Of the pre-Reformation chapel dedicated to the Virgin nothing remains. Always a hazard to shipping in the Clyde, as the island's buildings suggest.

BEACON. The smaller of two erected c. 1772 by Glasgow merchants. Painted stone pillar, originally designed to hold a beacon fire. The site and materials of the other beacon were used to build the modest LIGHTHOUSE in 1902–3. By D. & C. Stevenson. Cruciform plan with external spiral stair. The lantern was automated from the outset.

3020

LADYKIRK
2.9 km. E of Monkton

(A large mansion built in 1903–6 by *J. & R. S. Ingram* for Robert Angus with no concern to costs. Muscular Tudor, asymmetrically planned, built in bull-nosed red sandstone from Skares. Central entrance in crenellated porch with dummy turrets. Two big Flemish crowstepped gables with more tiny turrets to r. and l., the latter advanced and with a prominent mansard roof, railed and with a flagstaff. Unusual window detail with two and three lights linked under flat block pediments. Similarly detailed garden front with a balustraded terrace.

Inside, panelled hall, decorative plasterwork with pendants, scale-and-platt oak stair, newel posts with heraldic beasts, columned screens at ground- and first-floor level. Elaborate plaster ceilings and marble chimneypieces with wooden overmantels. Panelled billiard room. (Described as in 1993.)

In the grounds the remains of a CHAPEL dedicated to the Virgin, possibly C15 with a later C19 top stage. A single turret of the four which originally flanked the chapel survives. Singlestorey lodge in similar style to the house, 1903.)

3050

LADYLAND HOUSE
3.3 km. NNE of Kilbirnie

A delightful classical villa by *David Hamilton*, 1817–21, resembling an overgrown dolls' house. Built for the Cochranes of Ladyland to replace a tower house. Nearly square plan, three by three bays and two storeys above a basement with broad, clasping pilasters (a Hamilton hallmark, *see* Swindridgemuir) that break through the eaves cornice as raised entablatures. Built of rubble with pale, pinkish dressings creating a stripy effect on the pilasters. Render was probably intended, and without it the house seems charmingly unsophisticated. Three-bay front elevation with a Doric porch fronting a wide arched doorway with sidelights, their curved heads continuing the arc of the fanlight. Distinctive glazing pattern to all the windows with the central panes and the crossing bar framed by tramlines. The side elevations have outer blind windows to allow for the chimney flues. Large CONSERVATORY projecting at the rear, probably introduced in the later C19 but rebuilt. Low SE WING, by *James Houston* in 1925, repeating the motifs but with rendered walls; crudely detailed NW wing.

Inside the plan is simple. A square lobby leads to the central stair compartment, with the staircase rising in an oval well, more commonly a feature of a terraced house. It has cast-iron balusters with anthemion detail. There is good Neoclassical plasterwork in the principal rooms and seen at its best in the stairwell with its oval drum and domed cupola. Greek-key mouldings abound, sometimes interrupted with paterae in lozenges, and in the dome lively husked swags and bows and Vitruvian scroll detail A window is set into the oval drum to borrow light for the landing. The two main reception rooms are entered from the tiny hall: the drawing room (SE) appears to have been two rooms, probably united in 1925 when the wing was added. An inserted and over-sized Venetian-type doorpiece cuts across the cornice.

SUNDIAL. Dated 1673 with the initials M P C, on a baluster support. Many-faceted stone lectern dial, and a good example of the genre.

The STABLES are probably of 1817–21 and are built on the site of the earlier tower house. U-plan courtyard range, incorporating some C17 fabric. Entered through a low segmentally arched pend with very broad flanking pilasters, a familiar Hamilton treatment. Now converted to domestic use.

LAGAFATER LODGE   *1070*
8 km. SE of Ballantrae

Shooting lodge built 1913 for a Liverpool businessman, Cedric Boult, father of the conductor Adrian Boult. The r. bay gabled, with a two-storey bay window; to the l. a gable-headed full-height bay window.

LAGGAN   *1080*
3.5 km. E of Ballantrae

On a picturesque site above the Water of Tig. The estate was inherited from his father in 1867 by *David MacGibbon*. He probably had a part in the design of the sprawling Baronial house, built 1886. Largely demolished, apart from the elaborate billiard room gable and a round tower linked to a wing added 1913 by *James Miller* for the Hughes-Onslows (*see* also Auchenflower and Balkissock), a discreet essay in Scottish vernacular with boat-shaped dormerheads and crowstepped gables. House added at the W *c.* 2002. – Two LODGES in the style of the first mansion with bold cast-iron railings, piers and gates.

LAINSHAW HOUSE *see* STEWARTON

LANFINE HOUSE   *5030*
1.5 km. SW of Darvel

Dramatically set in well-wooded policies looking over the River Irvine valley. Enlarged several times, on the last occasion in an unusually sensitive and subtle Arts and Crafts manner. At the centre of the N front, the original three-bay two-storey house built in 1770–2 for John Brown, the Glasgow banker, who bought Waterhaughs (*see* Darvel) soon after. The work was directed by the mason *James Armour*, today best known as the father of Robert Burns's wife. On the S front its pediment with apex urn is partly hidden by two large five-windowed bows added in 1912–13 by *James Carrick* (at that time associate-in-charge in *J. K. Hunter*'s office) for the shipping magnate, Sir Charles Cayzer, who purchased the estate for his son in 1911. Cayzer's arms were added to the pediment. The W wing, also given a bow window on its gable at this time, had been added in the mid C19 and the L-plan E wing in 1870. Both are simple vernacular. Also mid-C19, the S wing on the entrance front, but extended cleverly in 1919–21 by *J. K. Hunter* with a small chapel and pretty study above. He also added the angled porch set into the ground-floor projection, and gave the house a sense of unity by adding a parapet to all the main elevations and placing urns at strategic places. Extensive additions for bedrooms and services appear at the SE.

The interior is essentially Edwardian: oak panelling in the entrance hall and garden hall, the latter with a large egg-and-dart fireplace surround and an Ionic-columned and architraved overmantel. Billiard room again panelled but with fabric infills. Good-quality plasterwork and chimneypieces all of this period.

The house has extensive balustraded terracing to the N, again Edwardian. To the W, in less formal surroundings, a circular columned and domed TEMPLE (C21), an eyecatcher at the W end of the first terrace, and nearby a circular DOOCOT, possibly late C18 but given its deeply overhanging conical roof *c.* 1920. To the E a service court and further E a large brick-lined walled garden with internal walled divisions. – At the entrance from Darvel a single-arched BRIDGE over the river. Of 1829, set in rustic masonry with panelled pilasters, low piers and a panelled parapet. – Three single-storey LODGES, two in Burn/Bryce manner with canted columned entrances, penticed slabs as window lintels and paired octagonal stacks. At the East Lodge, handsome gatepiers and good cast-iron gates in a semicircular sweep. The West Lodge has Doric columns *in antis*.

LARGS

The expression 'out of Ayrshire and into Largs' hints at the town's relatively isolated position between the sea and the moorland hills of NW Ayrshire. The parish is recorded from the mid C12, and the name, derived from the Gaelic for a hillside, well reflects its site on the kinder slopes where the Noddsdale and curiously named Gogo Waters flow into the Firth of Clyde. The original medieval settlement seems to have been slightly inland, as evidenced by the position of the original parish church and the tight street pattern to its E, though beside the Skelmorlie Aisle, nothing survives of this period. Although licensed as a Burgh of Barony (Newton of Gogo) in 1595, and again (as Largs) in 1629, substantial growth only took place following the improvement of transport links by road, in the late C18, and by Clyde steamer, in the early C19. The present street pattern dates from this period, while the villas (many in the style of *David Hamilton*) which dot the coast N and S of the town centre date from the years immediately after the establishment of regular steamer services, and the erection of the pier (1832–4). The opening of the railway from Glasgow in 1885 gave the town a further boost,* with considerable residential growth and the erection of some of the county's best late C19 churches. It became, and remains, a popular destination for holidaymakers, enjoying a heyday in the 1930s, from which period dates its most famous building, Nardini's Café, and much of its bungalow hinterland. The economy of the modern town remains based on the tourist trade, reinforced by trading on the town's rather tenuous Viking history, and it is also popular as a local shopping and retirement centre, and now spreads to N and S, and NE up Brisbane Glen, while some of the larger seafront houses have been replaced by, generally, undemanding blocks of flats. It remains, however, a vibrant, if slightly blowsy, town with a strong sense of its vocation.

CHURCHES AND CEMETERIES

BRISBANE EVANGELICAL CHURCH, School Street. Late C19. Gabled, harled, with five wide flat-headed windows on the side elevation, and a Venetian window on the N elevation altered to form a door. The adjoining HALL of *c.* 1995 is of yellow brick, with contrasting brown bands.

CHURCH OF THE NAZARENE, Aitken Street. Late C19 mission hall with a gabled front elevation, with a round-headed window above and three linked round-headed openings below.

CLARK MEMORIAL CHURCH, Bath Street. Former U.P. Church 37 of 1890–2 by *William Kerr*, while working for *T. G. Abercrombie* of Paisley. Mixed Dec and Perp on a grand scale, paid for by John Clark with money made from the Anchor thread mills of Paisley. Before working for Abercrombie, Kerr had worked in J. J. Burnet's office, and the design is indebted to Burnet's unsuccessful entry for the Coats Memorial Church, Paisley. Of red Locharbriggs sandstone ashlar, a seven-bay gabled nave aligned W–E, with a SE tower and vestry, a SW porch and NE transept, all well-furnished with pointed windows and buttresses. A fine church, inside and out, let down by the cramped site, which has low stone boundary walls and two pairs of broad octagonal gatepiers with decorative friezes and hemispherical heads, very Burnetian. The dominant feature is the mighty 55-m. three-stage tower and spire, which is linked to, but stands apart from, the body of the church. Tall first and third stages, stepped angle buttresses, tall pointed bell-openings and faceted

---

* Though an article, first published in the *Hereford Journal*, 1868, found one of the town's charms to be that there was no railway, and hence no 'tagrag and bobtail'.

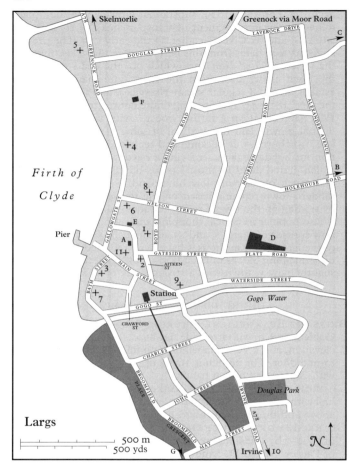

Largs

500 m
500 yds

1	Brisbane Evangelical Church	A	Former Brisbane Academy
2	Church of Nazarene	B	Brisbane Primary School
3	Clark Memorial Church	C	Inverclyde National Sports
4	Our Lady Star of the Sea (R.C.)		Training Centre
5	St Columba (Episcopal)	D	Largs Academy
6	St Columba's Parish Church	E	Police Station
7	St John's Parish Church	F	Vikingar!
8	United Free Church	G	Monument to the Battle
9	Former United Presbyterian		of Largs
	Church		
10	Largs Cemetery		
11	Largs Old Kirkyard		

spire with lucarnes. Equally powerful w front, with its five-light Geometric window, and flanking stepped buttresses with gablets and image niches with figures of Moses (l.) and St John (r.) under canopies. Big sw porch with finely chamfered arches to the entrance. Tucked between the church and tower the session room, like a chapel with buttresses, apsidal end and two-light windows with trefoils. Behind the tower the transeptal hall, with its own four-light s window, and one five-light window in the E gable. Along the flanks the gables of the buttresses break through the eaves of the roof.

The INTERIOR is amongst the finest in Ayrshire, its huge space given gravitas by the woodwork and grace by the outstanding display of stained glass; the effect obtained by scale and proportion rather than elaborate detailing. Broad and high nave, and a shallow square-ended chancel framed by a pointed stone arch on clustered shafts with subsidiary pointed arches l. and r. and a two-bay stone arcade to the NE transept. A hammerbeam roof springs from stone corbels and has carved angels at the beam-ends from which depend octagonal glazed light fittings. The windows, also stone-dressed, are placed high up in the plastered walls, so for the length of the nave there is a tall oak-panelled DADO of Perp character, with rectangular panels, recessed in broad surrounds, which in the upper tier have cusped blind tracery, usually flanking a memorial bronze plaque, and a fine coved cornice with brattishing. The panelling of the chancel is similarly treated but slightly more elaborate with the cornice as a canopy of openwork tracery, and a gilded inscription 'Seek Ye My Face – Thy Face Lord Will I Seek'. In the narrow arches l. and r. of the main arch the ORGAN CASES, again with elaborate carved Gothic frames. The w gallery rises above the tiled vestibule, with a panelled front, echoed in the gallery front across the transept arches. The stair in the transept has a pretty pitched wooden ceiling.

FITTINGS. The octagonal PULPIT, FONT, COMMUNION TABLE and CHAIRS all Gothic, contemporary with the church; the PEWS, too, understated, almost too much so. – STAINED GLASS. An unrivalled display of *fin-de-siècle* Glasgow work. E window given by Clark, a luminous five-light Crucifixion by *William Meikle & Sons*, 1892, and by the same firm also probably the E window in the s wall of Dorcas. – The vibrant five-light w window, Christ in Majesty, is *Stephen Adam & Son*, also 1892, also given by Clark. Of the same date, by the same maker, The Centurion and The Good and Virtuous Woman (both in the transept gallery) in Adam's characteristic deep colours. Also theirs, the windows of the N wall: Jesus, Mary and Martha, Ruth with Boaz, and David and Saul, all 1893, and the transept, SS Mary, Agnes and Elizabeth, by the *Stephen Adam Studio*, 1907. Also contemporary with the church, the particularly fine windows in the s wall of Noah, Samuel with Eli, Abraham and Isaac, and the Good Samaritan, by *Christopher Whall* for *Guthrie & Wells*. Arts and Crafts glass of the highest order and a significant early commission for the artist.

OUR LADY STAR OF THE SEA (R.C.), Greenock Road. 1960–2 by *A. R. Conlon* of *Reginald Fairlie & Partners*. Designed as an abstract sailing boat to reflect its seaside location. Low harled side walls with steep lightweight A-frame, Westmorland slate roof. Granite W front with a glazed centrepiece surrounding a cross. Four projecting gabled bays on either side, and a copper NE flèche. In front a tall sensuous granite Virgin & Child by *Hew Lorimer*; they stand on the prow of a ship. Inside, the roof comes down almost to floor level, sliced into by the pitched roofs of the window bays, the whole supported on wooden pillars. – Panels of darkly hued expressionistic STAINED GLASS in the W window, perhaps by *Gabriel Loire*.

ST COLUMBA (Episcopal), Aubrey Crescent. 1876–7 by *Alexander Ross*, of *Ross & MacBeth* of Inverness. Simple gabled Gothic. Four-bay nave and lower two-bay chancel, SW porch. Paired cusped lights to nave and chancel, with pilasters and angle buttresses on the S elevation. Stepped three-light E window; two two-light windows in the W gable. The porch has a pointed moulded arch supported by stumpy nook-shafts, and an applied timber gable, instead of the belfry tower originally envisaged. The interior has exposed stone walls, and pitched boarded timber roofs. Pointed chancel arch on imposts with decorative heads. Elaborate crocketed marble reredos below the E window, which has attached columns with foliated caps. – Gothic octagonal PULPIT, STALLS and ORGAN CASE, all of 1930, and COMMUNION RAIL, of 1938, all with meticulously intertwined naturalistic detail. – FONT. Brora stone on a Peterhead granite shaft. – STAINED GLASS. At the W end, SS Ninian, Columba, Kentigern and Margaret, with the Holy Dove above, 1877, by *Heaton, Butler & Bayne*. N wall, W window, David and Jonathan, 1912, by *Herbert W. Bryans*; the third pair from the l., St George and St Andrew, 1902, by *James Powell & Sons*. – In the S wall, the middle window is of 1898, also by *Powells*, the subjects St Michael and St Margaret. – E window. 1877, again by *Heaton, Butler & Bayne*, the Crucifixion, flanked by Mary and St John. Chancel S wall. 1892, with inscribed scrolls above the sedilia, the Light of the World and the Good Shepherd in the larger window. Executed by *James Powell & Sons* to designs by *G. W. Rhead*.

To the l., the former RECTORY of 1876–7, Gothic, probably also by *Ross & MacBeth*.

ST COLUMBA'S PARISH CHURCH, Gallowgate Street. 1890–3 by *Andrew Balfour* of *Steele & Balfour*, on the site of the second Largs Parish Church of *c.* 1802. A soaring exercise in First Pointed Gothic, matching in scale, materials and exuberance the contemporary Clark Memorial Church (*see* above), but beating it for its seafront site. Cruciform, with the main entrance gable facing the sea (W); there is a prominent NW tower, and a suite of halls across the E elevation. That W gable has angle buttresses and pinnacles, and three tall lights above, modelled on the W window of Dunblane Cathedral (Stirling & Central Scotland), a gabled porch with a pointed doorway and nook-shafts, and to its l. the five-stage tower. This has stepped angle buttresses, gabled pilaster-strips, octagonal pinnacled angle piers and a faceted spire. The side elevations have paired lancets, gabled buttresses and stepped clerestory windows with plate tracery, details which are largely repeated in the transept, which has a blind arcade and Geometric window. The E elevation is taken up by the halls, which run transversely and have a gabled N porch. Slate roofs; both church and hall with a decorative flèche, that to the church very tall. Equally impressive INTERIOR. Nave and aisles with tall E transepts and an organ recess in the E end; these all with semicircular heads. A shallow W gallery, and further galleries in the transepts, all with panelled wooden fronts. Pointed arcades of clustered columns with foliated caps; attached columns rise between the arches to support the barrel-vaulted roof. The S transept has been enclosed as the Mactaggart Memorial Chapel; the screen of 1983–4 by *Margaret B. Brodie* with etched glass by *Avril Gibb*.

– FITTINGS. Oak ORGAN CASE by *Steele & Balfour* (ORGAN by *Henry Willis & Sons*, and amongst the finest in Scotland). Very fine octagonal oak PULPIT, by *Miles S. Gibson*. Traceried panels with carved scenes from Christ's life and parables; both carved by *John Craig* of Pollokshields. – Variegated marble FONT, its bowl supported by four banded columns. – COMMUNION TABLE. (Mactaggart Chapel). From Woodside Church, Aberdeen. – A wealth of excellent STAINED GLASS. Six-light W window of 1893, by *Daniel Cottier & Co.*: The Woman at the Well (l.), Suffer Little Children, and Jesus with Mary and Martha (r.) – N aisle. Three two-light windows by *Gordon M. Webster*, characterized by the prevalent use of many shades of blue; from W to E: The Resurrection, 1955, Joshua, 1952, and The Three Kings, 1931. In the S aisle, by way of instructive contrast, three more variegated windows by *Douglas Strachan*; from W to E: Christ Walking on the Water, of 1919, The Miracle at Bethesda, of 1928, and Mr Valiant-for-Truth Passing Over to the Other Side, of 1924. A further *Strachan* window in the N transept: a masterly interpretation of the 23rd Psalm spread across seven lights, installed in 1925. – N gallery. By *Winfield* of Birmingham, 1893, The Ministry at Galilee. – S gallery. A richly coloured Life of Christ by the *Stephen Adam Studio*, also of 1893. – Vestibule. Two by *Gordon M. Webster*, 1977: St Columba and St Margaret. – MONUMENTS. Sir Thomas Makdougall Brisbane †1860. Marble, with the pioneering amateur astronomer shown in profile against a background of astronomical paraphernalia. – Bronze FIRST WORLD WAR MEMORIAL, E end of S aisle, designed by *Robert S. Lorimer* and executed by *Charles Henshaw*; in the corresponding position in the N aisle, the similar SECOND WORLD WAR MEMORIAL, also by *Henshaw*.

ST JOHN'S PARISH CHURCH, Bath Place. First built 1844 as a Free Church, substantially reconstructed in 1885–6 in Romanesque basilica style by *A. J. Grahame*. Rectangular, with an apsidal E end (rebuilt in 1951 by *James Drummond*), and a tall square NW tower with a recessed octagonal belfry and corbelled and faceted spire. This is linked across the front to the SW vestry by an arcaded narthex of five moulded round arches with slender columns and foliated capitals. The decorative eaves band continues into the bow-fronted vestry. N elevation of four bays, three with round-headed windows, that to the W having a similar smaller opening below and a big oculus above. Unusually open interior with a broad nave with SE transept, semicircular chancel arch and an apsidal chancel. Two-bay semicircular-headed transept arcade, the pier and responds with decorative caps. A gallery runs across each arch, with an arcaded wooden front, echoed by the main W gallery, supported by a wooden arcade of four-centred arches, with narrower, cusped arches over the passages. Under the gallery an inner vestibule with an arcaded eight-light window. – STAINED GLASS. Mostly *c.* 1885–6; all unsigned. The best glass is the vestibule windows by *Douglas Strachan*, 1911, depicting The Life of St John.

UNITED FREE CHURCH, Brisbane Road. 1932–3 by *William F. Valentine*. Harled and gabled, with two gabled bays on the side (N) elevation. Large projection to the E, with a round-headed entrance beneath a cusped balustrade, and flanked by shouldered gabled bays with paired windows and blind gunloops.

Former UNITED PRESBYTERIAN CHURCH, Waterside Street. 1826. The façade, with a wide central pedimented bay and two flanking bays with windows defining the ground-floor and gallery levels, fronts a large plain rectangular hall.

LARGS CEMETERY, Dalry Road. 1866, by *Haddin*, engineer; an attractive garden cemetery on a sloping site. Delicate Gothic LODGE with cusped lights; on the SE elevation a semicircular window projects beneath a half-conical slated roof, with a miniature trefoil light to the l. – MONUMENTS. Two of note close to the W drive: Dr Stevenson of Haylie (†1903) by *J. J. Stevenson*, 1906, Frosterley marble, with wreath and bronze plaque, under a Greek arch with Ionic columns and pilasters; the McNair family, by *Herbert J. McNair*, *c.* 1900, more like an elongated chimneypiece than a conventional monument. Sinuous Glasgow Style decoration, stretched ogee heads to the central void and flanking panels, of which that to the l. has a densely packed inscription in a script resembling that of McNair's colleague, Mackintosh. An ENCLOSURE with an arcaded screen wall marks the Burrell family burial place, including the insatiable art collector William Burrell (†1958).

LARGS OLD KIRKYARD, Manse Court (off Main Street). The kirkyard stood at the W edge of the medieval town, around the original parish church which was taken down in 1802, with the exception of the N transept, which had been built in 1636 as a burial vault by the Montgomeries of Skelmorlie, and is now the unparalleled, magnificent and beautiful SKELMORLIE AISLE.

Largs, Skelmorlie Aisle, ceiling.
Drawing, 1819

Its gabled exterior is of coursed ashlar, with a slate roof.
Slightly raised margins with strapwork decoration to the
quoins, plain skews and thistle and fleur-de-lis finials. W
entrance with roll mouldings and an ogival head; above it a
square panel with a brightly painted crested coat of arms, with
a motto above, THE LORD IS ONLY MY SUPPORT, and a dated
scroll below, ONLY TO GOD BE LAVD & GLOIR. R^{S}M 1636
M^{D}D.* Basket-arched windows l. and r., also on the E elevation, but a two-light Geometric N window; in the S gable a tall
pointed arch, now blocked.

Internally, an unexpected feast of riches. The walls and floor
of the aisle are of stone; the space is divided in half by the
monument, with the burial vault at the N end, whose floor is
correspondingly higher and reached by a dog-leg stair with a
stone balustrade. The entire space is covered by a painted
timber CEILING. It is signed and dated *J. S. Stalker*, Edin-   15
burgh, 1638, and in its Italianate character closely resembles
that at Pitcairn (Perth & Kinross). It takes the form of a barrel
vault, but with a painted framework mimicking three bays of
painted panels divided by painted ribs. In the lower tier each
of the scenes (depicting the Four Seasons but also the Sea
Beach and the Port, and the Death of St Margaret) is set over
a pair of elaborate Renaissance cartouches painted with

*Robert Montgomerie of Skelmorlie (†1651) and Margaret Douglas of Douglas
(†1624). The coat of arms impales the arms of Montgomerie and Douglas.

biblical texts, mostly from the Geneva Bible. In the spandrels above are symbols of the Zodiac; the corbels painted with the symbols of the tribes of Israel. The upper half of the vault is also divided into three, with biblical scenes surrounding the heraldic achievements of Montgomerie and Douglas in the middle, and Eglinton, Drumlanrig, Lochinvar and Sempill to the N; the S is blank. Renovation was carried out in 1899 by *Bennett Brothers* of Glasgow, and the symbols of the tribes, at least, appear to have been restored in 1932 by *John Houston.**

16　　The MONUMENT was completed in 1639 and is richly carved in freestone. The mason is unknown but it is in the style of Maximilian Colt's monument to Queen Elizabeth at Westminster Abbey (London 6: Westminster) (1605–7), and that of Elizabeth Marnix at Delft (1611) but also, perhaps tellingly, to Cornelius Cure's monument to Mary, Queen of Scots also at Westminster, of *c.* 1607–12. In the form of a triumphal arch, below which recumbent effigies were, presumably, envisaged. The outer bays of the canopy are carried on paired Corinthian uprights of one column and one decoratively panelled pillar; carrying an entablature. The central arch rises above them, Corinthian pilasters, corner obelisks and pediments, carved spandrels and coffered soffits, every surface a riot of naturalistic decoration. Further elaborate scrollwork to the crestings; angels at the corners. The chest is divided by pedestals, its face carved with cartouches; a lower course on the S side is plainer, with wooden doors in basket-arched openings giving access to the vault.

Close by is the smaller BRISBANE AISLE, built as a free-standing burial vault for the Shaws of Kelsoland in 1634 (dated heraldic panel on the E gable), and altered *c.* 1695 for the Brisbanes of Brisbane.** Very simple, of squared ashlar blocks with stepped skews and cavetto-moulded skewputts to the gables. These stand higher than the impressive late C17 roof, constructed of mighty stone slabs and mounted on the outer walls. A second carved armorial panel on the W gable.

PUBLIC BUILDINGS

Former BRISBANE ACADEMY, Lade Street. *c.* 1850; an odd Gothic confection. The main elevation has two gabled bays, and, to their r., an elaborately detailed entrance bay with a round-headed entrance beneath a cusped arcade and improbably tall gabled bellcote.

BRISBANE PRIMARY SCHOOL, Meadowbank Road. 1977–9, by *Strathclyde Regional Council DARS* and a refreshing change from the later C20 norm. White harl with grey brick banding, and many of the flat roofs hidden behind tall, notched, metal-clad parapets, painted a deep orange.

----

*For the themes of the painting, and their sources, see Teresa Grant, 'Devotional Meditation' in *Church Monuments*, v. XVII, 2002.
**Kelsoland and Brisbane are the same estate.

INVERCLYDE NATIONAL SPORTS TRAINING CENTRE, Burnside Way. Developed since 1958 around a large house of rather
peculiar character. This is especially true on the entrance (W)
front of two storeys and an attic, which has a Gothic porch
with half-timbered gable, similar timberwork in the gable of
the canted outer bay to the l., and a steep Germanic cap to
the outer bay to the r., which has a canted front and mullioned
windows. Tall chimneystack with more decorative plasterwork.
It may date from *c*. 1873–5, when the property belonged to
David Cousin of Edinburgh. Uncompromising but effective
lounge extension of *c*. 1970 to the l., glazed under a large
metalclad roof, and projecting over the understorey.

LARGS ACADEMY, Flatt Road. 1966–70 by *Ayr County Council
Architects Dept*. Large, steel-framed, mostly two-storey, with the
four-storey main range facing W across and over the town, its
central block advanced and supported on pilotis. Pavilion
blocks at either end; that to the S has a large concrete panel
with incised decoration, graphically detailed, representing the
Battle of Largs.

LARGS STATION, Main Street. Opened in 1885 by the Glasgow
& South-Western Railway, rebuilt in 1935–6 by the LMSR, but
badly damaged in a derailment, *c*. 1995. At the S end of the
platforms one parapet of a now widened cast-iron BRIDGE
across the Gogo Water, 1885 by *Arrol Bros*.

POLICE STATION, Gallowgate Lane. 1871 by *John Murdoch* of
Ayr. Red sandstone, resolutely plain, with two tall wall-head
stacks on the longer elevation. Slightly lower wing behind, with
a classical entrance, probably added by *Alexander Mair* in 1931.

Former POST OFFICE, Aitken Street. *c*. 1930 by *H. M. Office of
Works*, single-storey red ashlar classical. Three bays with
entrances (one now blocked) to l. and r. Keystoned central
window under bracketed pediment.

VIKINGAR!, Greenock Road. A Viking-themed visitor and leisure
centre, built around the former Barrfields Pavilion of 1927–30
by *William Barclay*. This is of harled brick, with a solid parapet
around a hipped slated roof; one side with tall windows
between pilasters can still be seen on the N elevation. Lying
across one end is a swimming pool, added in 1968–71 by *James
Houston & Son*, but the rest is of 1993–5 by *Cunninghame
District Council* (*Matthew Marshall*, project architect). Brick
ground floor, with a glazed veranda across the W front, harled
upper section with a broad stone eaves band with regular
raised panels. The building sits far back in its feu; the grounds
in front have an attractive harled GROUNDSMAN'S HUT of
c. 1930 by *George Arkieson*, with a neat hipped slated roof and
ridge tiles.

WAR MEMORIAL, Bath Street. *See* Description.

DOUGLAS PARK, Irvine Road. 1906, gifted to the town by
Charles Douglas of Haylie, as recorded by a pretty, almost Art
Nouveau PLAQUE of 1919 by *Archibald Hamilton* of Glasgow
on the simple single-storey SOUTH LODGE. This has turned
wood supports to its veranda, and severe stacks.

DESCRIPTION

Much more so than its rivals in the Ayrshire seaside stakes, Largs's relationship with the sea is paramount. A good place to begin description is the PIER, at the foot of Main Street. It is L-plan, of coursed rubble with a modern concrete surface, of 1832–4, designed by *John Gibb* of Aberdeen; reconstructed in 2009–10. Pier OFFICES of *c.* 1980, harled with an asymmetrical pitched roof. On the shingle shore to the N, the sketchy remains of a ramped stone PIER.

Main Street runs directly inland and SE from the present pier. Above the shore the view is of the buildings N along GALLOWGATE STREET, set back behind grass lawns and the esplanade, with the hills rising behind them. Much of what one sees is heavily altered early to mid-C19 frontages and nothing of special note other than St Columba's Parish Church (*see* Churches, above) and NARDINI'S CAFÉ, the dazzling white icon of the town. It is of 1935, by *C. Davidson & Son* of Paisley. Single-storey, flat-roofed, of plastered brick with all the classic angular Art Deco features: stepped roof-lines, exaggerated keystones, blocky fin-like buttresses with flagpoles and lots of glass. At its zenith a jazzy expression of fun. Entrance on the angled corner, another on the W front. On the long front elevation, the bays vary with function. Just N of this, in GREENOCK ROAD, set within wooded grounds, two fine houses. First, the stylish BROOKSBY HOUSE (now a hospital) is a restrained Italian Renaissance two-storey 'yachting residence' of *c.* 1837 for Matthew Perston, a Glasgow merchant, probably by *David & James Hamilton*. It was converted into a convalescent home in 1897. Polished ashlar walls. S portico on partially chamfered pillars. To its r. an elaborately detailed bay, surmounted by a shallow pediment above the cornice. The upper window is framed by pilaster-strips and has a solid balcony creating the head of the framed ground-floor window. Two chamfered consoles either side of the window frame, and a blind balustrade below. The outer bays of the symmetrical five-bay W elevation, i.e. the sea-facing front, are similar; the central trio taller and advanced, originally with a veranda. Entrance hall with a Doric screen, and main stair with an elaborate late C19 cast-iron balustrade. MOORBURN HOUSE, dated 1876, is less impressive, an asymmetrical two-storey ashlar Italianate villa, with a lower two-storey two-bay wing to the E. Porch with decorative cast-iron balustrade and gabled outer bays on the S front and an almost identical W elevation, but this with two bay windows, again with ironwork crestings. The entrance hall and stair have panelled dados and decorative plasterwork. For buildings further N *see* Villas, below. On the esplanade a sturdy whin BEACH SHELTER, with projecting wings, perhaps by *J. Sandford Kay* (*see* also 'The Pencil', below, p. 507).

From the pier, MAIN STREET begins badly, with the buildings on the pierhead and a glazed brick flat-roofed entertainment centre of 1963, before the harled prow and big chrome balconies of the NEW MOORINGS, flats of 1990–2 by *McMillan &*

Cronin, which replaced *James Houston*'s original Moorings of 1935–6. Main Street turns SE and is the commercial heart of Largs, a busy mix of shops catering for locals and day-trippers. Architecturally, largely C19, reflecting the growth of the town at that time, especially after the pier was completed and regular connections with Glasgow and Greenock began. The first item of note is on the corner with Bath Street (SW side), a classical curved frontage (called 'new' in 1856) of ashlar, with original first-floor glazing and a solid corner parapet with a central wall-head stack, scrolled end brackets and acroteria. On the other side the Northern Renaissance-style ROYAL BANK OF SCOTLAND, dated 1900, a grand red sandstone façade with fancy shaped gable. Flanking two-storey wings with canted bays at first floor, added in 1926. Excellent contemporary panelled rooms on the first floor.

Just before the Station on the SW side, Main Street widens into an informal square and has a nice little group of commercial buildings, including Nos. 72–74, the former British Linen Bank, of 1907 by *George Washington Browne* in a Cotswold Tudor manner. Paired entrances with depressed-arched heads under an entablature; the r. one with carved spandrels, a cockle-shell frieze and a square panel with floral decoration above. In the big gabled bay, mullioned windows. Also, McCABE'S, dated 1887, with a curved corner with Crawford Street, and an odd-shaped dormer in the attic storey.

Down BATH STREET the view is to the former BATH HOUSE (now BRISBANE CENTRE), built in 1816. Single storey of painted ashlar with polished dressings. Bowed s end and the entrance under a tall arch in the centre. It faces the mighty Clark Memorial Church, the finest church in Largs, to which the tower of St John's Parish Church immediately to the E can make only a modest riposte (*see* Churches, above). This is connected internally to the DUNN MEMORIAL HALL, which stands round the corner in Union Street, facing a small open green. It is a symmetrical mid-C19 two-storey house with gable and gabled dormers but now as reworked and extended in 1935–6 by *Fryers & Penman* in a Tudor style; the single-storey wing has a Deco-ish central stepped stone gable.

After that some large four-storey red sandstone tenements (SANDRINGHAM) by *William Strachan* of Greenock, 1905–8. Austere unarticulated fronts, with the occasional canted bay. They form the backdrop to the WAR MEMORIAL, of 1921, by *Kellock Brown*, a fine piece of work given extra emphasis by the well-judged setting on a curve in the esplanade. A tall, Cullaloe stone cenotaph supports a delicately realized and dynamically composed group of three figures: a kilted soldier stands, flanked by a watchful sailor crouching forward and a pensive soldier kneeling in battledress, his hat with an upraised brim of Australian type. Names and dedication on a continuous decorative bronze band; a companion added *c.* 1950.

From here, GOGO STREET runs inland and uphill, with a green sward sloping down to the Gogo Water on its s side. The houses – a largely unspoilt if conventionally styled group – face the river and are mainly mid to late C19, though the harled three-bay GOGO HOUSE (No. 17) is early C19, with a simple pilastered doorway, and the grey ashlar TIGH-AN-STRUAN (Nos. 27–29) is *c.* 1905, with shallow curved bows to l. and r. (and very bad dormers). The road s crosses the river on the charming flat-arched cast-iron BRIDGE, of *c.* 1865 by *Dorman Long* in memory of Sir Thomas Makdougall-Brisbane (†1860). The parapets are open colonnades with stumpy obelisks between; central laurel-edged roundels have portrait busts of the dedicatee, and a highly stylized view of the Battle of Largs. Towards the shore, s of the bridge, MACKERSTON PUTTING GREEN, its GREENKEEPER'S HUT of 1927–9 by *George Arkieson*, harled with pretty bargeboards and a stone plaque of crossed clubs. Also on this broad green expanse is the red and grey granite CAMPBELL MEMORIAL FOUNTAIN, of 1877–8 by *James Wright* of Aberdeen. A rocky plinth supports three tiers of basins (the lowest and largest quatrefoil), supported by banded columns, those supporting the upper basin clustered.

The shore road also provides a good hunting ground for VILLAS. About 330 m. s of the burn, facing the sea in BROOMFIELD PLACE is PRIORY LODGE of 1829–30 by *David & James Hamilton*. Tudor Gothic, almost symmetrical, with the gabled outer bays slightly advanced, and the entrance in the l. of these, beneath a charming and delicate cast-iron canopy supported on equally attractive iron legs. Tall stacks, finialled gables and basket-arched windows under dormerheads. Adjacent is the much larger ELDERSLIE, of two storeys with a basement and a battered plinth, which is in the same style, is of the same date and must surely be by the same architects. The main entrance is to John Street, in a projecting bay whose upper windows have Gothic tracery. Crenellated parapets and paired octagonal wall-head stacks. Opposite, on BROOMFIELDS CRESCENT, a little Tudor LODGE, which served Curling Hall (dem.). It has bracketed eaves, Tudor-arched windows and one prominent pair of octagonal stacks. Sensitively extended by *G. D. Lodge & Partners*, 1988. On the crescent, slightly s, LITTLERAITH is an attractive early C19 rubbly single-storey three-bay villa, with a big bowed centre to the sea, and further flanking lower pedimented bays. The gabled parallel block to the E is a mid-C19 addition. Also facing the sea, to the s, CRESCENT LODGE (Nos. 2–6 May Street), a fine, large mid-C19 two-storey painted villa, with a symmetrical sea front elevated on a basement behind a low arcaded screen wall. It has a full-height bowed centre, its upper floor recessed behind a balustrade balcony, single bays to either side, and recessed single-storey corners with urns. The E elevation much simpler, with a full-height hipped bay to the l., and a central projecting porch and parapet. Finally, in the same row, ACRE LODGE of *c.* 1885. Harled Scots Baronial. Big and broadly symmetrical about a central entrance bay with a big gable and a pretty round-arched entrance.

Corbelled dormerheads, crowstepped gables, and a dumpy battlemented NW round angle tower. Crowstepped former stable to the N, adjacent to the Italianate stable of a vanished neighbour.

VILLAS

Of individual houses in the suburbs inland from the shore road and along the shore N of the town, the following are significant:

BLACKDALES, Charles Street. Mid-C19 asymmetrical villa, greatly extended in 1876 by *Honeyman & Keppie* for the photographer John Fergus. The original house is of painted ashlar, of three broad bays, its central entrance recessed behind a Roman Doric screen and flanked to the r. by a canted bay. Mostly square-headed windows; balustraded outer bays. The addition is to the N, single-storey over a sunk basement, and culminates in a three-bay curved bow with a pierced parapet. To the rear it links with the former outbuildings, made into a studio for Fergus in 1876, with a massive new entrance in channelled bull-faced ashlar with prominent voussoirs and a projecting keystone.

CRAWFORD LEA, Brisbane Road. A classically styled house of 1903, with canted bays and gabled wall-head panels; nearby FERNESS VILLA, perhaps of *c.* 1890, with a conical tower and ogee-headed lantern, and, on its s elevation, a porch on Corinthian columns between canted bays.

DANEFIELD, No. 148 Greenock Road. Asymmetrical villa, dated *p. 506* 1883, for William Crum by *John Douglas* of Chester, who has added a dash of Scots Baronial to a simplified version of his Arts and Crafts Paddocks, Eccleston (Cheshire). Asymmetrical, in yellow ashlar with red dressings and band courses, two storeys with attic and raised basement. The busy w front has a projecting conical-roofed tower to the l., and to the r. a gabled bay, the upper floors of which are framed by corbelled engaged columns ending in ball finials. Canted corner bay to the r. of this, the upper floor boldly corbelled. Entrance on the s elevation, an elliptically arched doorway in a billet-moulded frame, beneath a pedimented gable; ball-finialled. The bay above corbelled out, with a corbelled stack and a smaller gabled bay to the r. From the porch, stairs lead to an arched and panelled hall; beamed ceilings.

HALKHILL, Waterside Street, at the very E edge of the town by the Gogo Water. The land was acquired by John Scott, a Greenock shipbuilder, in 1810, but the planned house was never built. The present house was completed *c.* 1822, possibly by David Hamilton, and reputedly conceived as the stables. Its U-plan and pedimented and bell-turreted centrepiece certainly recall grand East Lothian steadings. Panelled pilasters and round-headed recessed panels. Good interior decoration including a coffered basket arch in the hall and an elegant cast-iron cantilevered stair.

Largs, Danefield.
Engraving, 1886

HAYLIE HOUSE, No. 97 Irvine Road. Harled two-storey Italianate villa of 1885 on a prominent site, with a pyramidal-
headed tower to the l., and a projecting semicircular bay to
its r. Ground-floor openings have bracketed cornices, the
projecting eaves with paired brackets. Contemporary plain
LODGE.

NETHERHALL, Kelvin Gardens. Substantial house of 1876–92
by *Campbell Douglas & Sellars* for the great C19 physicist
William Thomson, Lord Kelvin. In coursed whin, with red
sandstone dressings, abundant drum towers and pedimented
dormers; platform roof with cast-iron brattishing. Franco-
Scots Baronial: a much-inflated three-storey-and-attic version
of a suburban Glasgow villa of the period. Now subdivided.
Most of the interest is in the two long façades. The N-facing
entrance front has four asymmetrical bays, with a square projecting pyramid-headed tower to the l., with a porch and
round-arched entrance with roll moulding. A shallower, later
porch in the centre of the elevation; to the r. of this a datestone
(1892) with Kelvin's coat of arms. The garden (s) elevation has
conical-headed drum towers at either end; five bays with
dormers between, that in the middle with a canted battlemented bay. Scots Baronial STABLES, with crowstepped gables
above the central round-arched and roll-moulded pend; the
other gables similarly finished. Much prettier is the former

GATELODGE, of 1875, whin and red ashlar with a tall hipped roof. The former pended entrance, round-arched and roll-moulded, has been infilled with glass. A plain COTTAGE in the same materials adjoins.

NORTHFIELD, in Northfield Park, off Greenock Road. Tudor Gothic of c. 1834, in the style of the Hamiltons' Priory Lodge (*see* Description, p. 504). Plastered, with many finial-headed stacks, and tall stone stacks, in pairs and triplets. The w elevation is virtually symmetrical, with advanced flanking gabled bays (one with a stack, one with a finial); pedimented and finialled porch on the s elevation. Now subdivided. Other houses in this stretch of GREENOCK ROAD, between the all-pervasive blocks of late C20 marine flats, include No. 25, of c. 1928 in a crisp harled and tiled Arts and Crafts, with a big hipped roof, heavy stacks and a triple-arched entrance porch, and HAUS SARON (No. 106), of a similar date, but in a restrained classical idiom.

WARREN PARK, No. 2 Anthony Road. A mid-C19 house which has grown considerably. Mostly two-storey, harled with polished dressings. The core is a four-bay two-storey house, with a projecting bay to the l., and a canted single-bay return to the r.; entrance porch with round-headed windows and balustrade balcony. Of the substantial additions only the bowed and glazed single-storey lounge of 1933 by *John Fairweather*, which projects to the r., deserves notice. The glories of Warren Park lie elsewhere: in the LODGE and GARDENER'S COTTAGE in Anthony Road, built c. 1892 for Otto Ernest Phillipi by *Arthur J. Fryers*.[*] These are in an unrestrained English Domestic-style, with red tiled roofs and abundant applied timbering. The cottage, which is on a cyclopean scale, has mostly applied timber gables, but one is tile-hung in a Leiperian manner. Small-pane windows, and decorative woodwork and plasterwork; the bay below the tile-hung gable especially so, with a corbelled jetty and carved brackets. The Lodge is quieter, smaller, with the same palette, but more restrained in its use of applied timbering. Also in the grounds, forming part of the w boundary wall, an irregular castle-like tufa GROTTO of c. 1830.

WARRISTON, No. 1 Anthony Road. c. 1830, Tudor Gothic, probably by *David & James Hamilton* (cf. Priory Lodge (Description, p. 504)). Harled, two-storey, L-plan (with a projecting rear wing) with basket-arched first-floor windows, and conjoined stacks, of variable number, on the gables. On the w-facing elevation a broad veranda on cast-iron stanchions.

MONUMENT TO THE BATTLE OF LARGS, 2 km. s on the coast. A handsome work, raised in 1912 by *James Sandford Kay* of Newton Stewart to commemorate the battle of 1263, when the

---

[*] Phillipi was the sales manager of J. & P. Coats Ltd, thread manufacturers of Paisley. In 1900 he became lord of the manor of Crawley in Hampshire where he provided the estate with buildings designed by *Fryers & Penman*. (*See* Buildings of England, *Hampshire: Winchester and the North*.)

defeat by the Scots of the fleet of Haakon Haakonson ended the Norse threat to the western Scottish seaboard. Its tapering form is inspired by Early Christian round towers at Abernethy (Perth & Kinross) and Brechin (Angus). Built of whinstone, and topped with a conical slate roof – earning its nickname 'The Pencil'. The raised round-headed entrance, with crucifix, figures and grotesque beasts, is copied from Brechin. Around the base a cobble walkway and shelter.

THREE SISTERS, Waterside Street. A trio of square rubble pillars, each about 3 m. tall, on a low hill E of the town, erected in 1808 by *Sir Thomas Brisbane* for his astronomical observations, and aligned with his observatory at Brisbane (q.v.). The middle one has a pediment top, the others had three uprights in a gunsight arrangement. Now in a poor state of repair, and much overgrown.

ROMAN FORTLET, Outerwards, 7.75 km. NE. Of Antonine date and the only Roman monument in Ayrshire that is still visible on the surface of the ground. It commands a fine view out over the Firth of Clyde. Appearing roughly circular on the ground, it is in fact sub-rectangular on plan, and its turf rampart is reduced to a low mound 0.3 m. high within an external ditch some 0.5 m. deep.

BRISBANE. *See* p. 208.
KNOCK CASTLE. *See* p. 485.
NODDSDALE HOUSE. *See* p. 562.
QUARTER HOUSE. *See* p. 588.

LENDALFOOT

1080

A straggling settlement squeezed between the rocky coast and the cliff-like banks of the raised beach to the E, these still showing evidence of the terracing created to grow early potatoes. At the S end is CARLETON FISHERY, development of which was initiated in 1832 by William Johnston of Girvan, encouraged by the proprietor Sir John Cathcart. The inspiration came from the fishing practices of the Moray coast and the planning is reminiscent of the contemporary fishing stations developed by the British Fisheries Society. A row of single-storey limewashed rubble cottages, with an enclosed yard in front and a free-standing two-storey house at the S built for the overseer.

To S and N along the coast road, a series of HOLIDAY HUTS built on feus let by the Hamilton estate from 1933. By 1938 twenty-five cottages were built when Mr Heneage of Killochan produced a scheme for a holiday resort, its realization prevented by the outbreak of war. The S group remain the least altered, but in the larger group (Carleton Terrace) the hand of progress has left its mark.

CARLETON CASTLE, standing high above the road on a dominant site perched between two burns, was built probably in the late C14 or early C15 by the Cathcarts of Carleton. It has a plain rectangular plan, 9.1 m. by 7.6 m. with walls 1.8 m. thick. The SE angle has been lost, but enough evidence survives to suggest that the entrance was at this angle and opened into the first-floor hall with a turnpike stair on the r. leading to the upper floors. On the l. there is also evidence of a mural stair within the walls in the SW angle leading to the cellar. There were vaults over the ground and hall floors, both of which appear to have included an entresol making this tower five storeys high despite its small footprint. A chimney survives precariously on the N gable-head. The tower was set into a courtyard on a tongue of land between the two burns (*see* also Ardstinchar) with turrets at its angles.

VARYAG MONUMENT, 0.9 km. SW. In memory of the Russian cruiser *Varyag* which sank near Lendalfoot in 1920. Bronze and cruciform, of unmistakably Russian character, 2007, by *Victor Pasenko*, architect, and *Vladimir & Danila Surovtsev*, sculptors.

LITTLE CUMBRAE   *1050*

An island in the Firth of Clyde, which like Great Cumbrae (q.v.) was part of the estates of the Earls of Glasgow and within the county of Bute until 1975. Rocky, with a central ridge; the better land is on the E side, where the present house is. The first lighthouse on the island, one of the first in Scotland, was erected in the C18.

LITTLE CUMBRAE CASTLE. On a low tidal island off the E shore. A largely entire tower house of 1534–7 bearing strong similarities to those at Law (West Kilbride) and Fairlie (q.v.). Rectangular, being the same length as Law, and slightly taller than Fairlie, and rising to the same checkered corbels and continuous cornice, with roundels at three corners. The entrance gives access to the vaulted ground floor and the newel-stair. Vaulted first floor, with a stone partition between hall and kitchen. This is small, with a fireplace, and subdivided by a stone arch. Two rooms, each with a fireplace and garderobe, on the second floor. *p. 510*

LITTLE CUMBRAE HOUSE. C18 farmhouse, enlarged *c.* 1862, and substantially extended in 1913 and 1926–9, perhaps by *C. E. Bateman* of Birmingham, to form a holiday retreat for Evelyn Parker, who had bought the island in 1900. What one sees is largely the C20 work, in a free Arts and Crafts manner, with a conspicuous parapeted tower. L-plan, with the main elevation facing E; many-gabled first floor, with the tower asymmetrically placed towards the S; the entrance beneath it and the final bay to the S. The S wing projects forward, is single-storey and most noticeably reveals the original vernacular steading. C20 interiors with carved stone mantelpieces and, in the drawing room, a decorative plaster barrel ceiling. The terraced gardens in front of the house were laid out in 1918 by

Little Cumbrae Castle, view from south-west.
Engraving

Gertrude Jekyll, but have been alternately altered and neglected subsequently.

OLD LIGHTHOUSE. 1756–7 by *James Wyatt*. A 9.1 m.-high circular stone tower, originally carrying a coal-fired beacon.

NEW LIGHTHOUSE, w shore. 1793 by *Robert Stevenson*. Cliff-top circular stone tower with a glazed lantern, linked to a mostly single-storey accommodation complex, and enclosed within a stone-walled compound. Automated in 1997.

LOANS

3030

In the C18, when the Loans of Dundonald were a sandy whin-infested desolation, and the Troon merely a rocky headland, this was the home of some of Ayrshire's most professional, audacious and unscrupulous smugglers. It just manages to maintain its identity as Troon edges closer.

The dog-leg shape of MAIN STREET reveals the form of the pre-turnpike settlement. Some simple cottages, probably of *c.* 1800, and one pair with lying-pane glazing, probably of *c.* 1830. ROBERTLOAN HOUSE (No. 32) is a large house of *c.* 1810, conventional except for its semicircular porch with the door in the l. bay. Low stone boundary wall and bell-headed gatepiers.

Large early C20 additions to the rear. Also, LOANS VILLAGE HALL, of 1926, simple harled Late Arts and Crafts. The former VILLAGE SCHOOL of 1878, part harled, has a steep front gable forming an elegant wooden porch. Opposite is ROWANTREE COTTAGE, of *c.* 1800; the least altered example in the village. Three bays, with a simple doorpiece and a lower hipped addition.

HIGHGROVE HOUSE, 0.6 km. NE. 1916, almost certainly by *J. R. Johnstone*. Large harled and tiled Arts and Crafts villa commanding wide views across the Firth of Clyde. Buttressed central gable and a prominent battered chimneystack to the l. Large sympathetic additions of 1961 (*Francis B. Dunbar*) and, for restaurant use, from 1974 by *Hay Steel MacFarlane & Partners*.

LOCH DOON CASTLE
8 km. s of Dalmellington

4090

40

An unusual castle of enceinte, probably C13 in origin. Between 1926 and 1936 the water level of Loch Doon was raised as part of the Galloway Hydro-Electric Scheme, and the island on which the castle had stood submerged. Moved to its present position in 1933, under the superintendence of *James S. Richardson* of *H. M. Office of Works*.

The castle consists of a massive, well-constructed curtain wall, of eleven sides of varying length, presumably echoing the shape of the island. The walls have a pronounced batter, and there is one entrance, with a pointed head, and sockets for a portcullis and drawbars. Originally a postern gate too. The castle resembles that at Balvenie (Moray), but offers little evidence for the manner of its internal layout. It appears to have still been occupied in the early C16, when William Craufurd and others were accused of treasonably taking the king's castle of Lochdoun and plundering the castle and its captain.

LOCHGOIN
5 km. NE of Waterside by Fenwick

5040

A good example of an unimproved mid-C19 upland farm, rebuilt in 1858, although the door lintel is inscribed with the dates 1175 1710 1810. Single-storey with one gabled and one hipped end. In the C17 it was a regular haunt of Covenanters, and an early C18 tenant, John Howie, became, through his writing, the keeper of the Covenanters' flame. It now belongs to the Fenwick and Lochgoin Covenanters Trust, with one room set aside as a museum. – w of the farm is a MONUMENT to Howie of 1896 by *Thomas Lyon* (executed by *Matthew Muir & Co.*). Creetown granite obelisk on a rocky base and square pedestal.

The C21 has brought WIND FARMS to the moors, including Whitelee Hill wind farm of 2007–8, which removes forever Lochgoin's sense of isolation.

MONUMENT, Kingswell Bridge, 0.3 km. w. To members of the Corbett family (of Rowallan (q.v.)), probably first erected for Alice Corbett †1902. Concrete cross with a curvily decorative head, and incised decorative texts in the style of *Robert S. Lorimer*. It was her death that caused the scaling-back of Lorimer's proposals for Rowallan.

LONGBAR

3050

AUCHENGREE FOUNDRY, 0.2 km. S. A wood-turning business was established here *c*. 1823 by Andrew Kerr, and expanded by his son Robert into an iron foundry, supplying the tools and machine parts required by the cabinet works in Beith and the thread and net works in Kilbirnie. The present buildings, no longer in industrial use, were erected *c*. 1878–82; closest to the road is the brick two-storey nine-bay engineering and pattern shop. Beyond is the rubble-built, single-storey foundry. A rare survival.

LOUDOUN CASTLE

5030

1.5 km. NNE of Galston

A huge castle-style mansion of 1804–11 by *Archibald & James Elliot* for Flora Countess of Loudoun and her husband the 2nd Earl of Moira (afterwards 1st Marquess of Hastings), but incorporating a C15 tower house, built by the Craufurds, and a grand C17 library range built for the 1st Earl of Loudoun. It remains an unforgettable symbol of Campbell power, despite having succumbed to fire in 1941.

The style owes much to Robert Adam's castle style but also to the evolving designs for Taymouth Castle (Perth & Kinross), where in 1806–10 the Elliots took over the remodelling from James Paterson. What they did here was to enclose the L-plan layout of the existing house within a massive rectangular shell. Built of squared and coarsed pinkish sandstone rubble with square turrets at every angle, creating a pronounced articulation and symmetrical elevations. Running round the entire façade, a bull-nosed string course and a cavetto sill course at principal and second-floor level; at the top a corbelled and crenellated parapet.

The dramatic ENTRANCE FRONT is at the head of the long w drive. A heavily battered, ramped carriageway with a pierced and panelled parapet leads to the main entrance on the principal floor in the dominating four-storey centrepiece. This is ashlar and, like Gelston Castle (Dumfries and Galloway) of 1805, has two tall, square towers framing the centre section. At each level a trio of round-arched openings. At the principal

level and in the floor above these are divided by attached octagonal colonnettes with acanthus-leaf capitals in the principal
floor. A balcony at second-floor level is supported by console
brackets which are crudely cut into the diminutive arcade
below. At this level, the colonnettes and the ogee mouldings of
the windows terminate with fleur-de-lis with an arched corbel
table above. To l. and r. of the centre, three bays of openings
in two storeys, the lower ones round-headed under hoodmoulds, square-headed above. Three-storey towers at the
angles have plain pointed-arched windows and inset blind
cross motifs below the parapet.

On the grass in front, a WELL-HEAD with Gothic detail to
the panels, angle gableted finials and a metal finial over the
ribbed crown.

On the long S FRONT, which is raised above a terrace
with a hefty crenellated retaining wall, the square turrets are
in pairs at either end with a single bay set back between them
containing windows with narrow sidelights, very tall and
arched at principal level, and, as on the W front, a balcony
above. The principal part of the façade (roughly corresponding
to the C17 wing of the earlier house) has eight simply detailed
bays between the turrets with a continuous balcony to the
second floor and a broad canted bay, with slit lights at the
centre of the lower storey providing a platform opening out
from the principal floor. The N FRONT is similar but between
the pairs of turrets the wall of the house is set well back, with
pairs of blind openings arched at principal level. Here the
Elliots had intended to build a Great Drawing Room. At the
E end remains of the very thick E wall of the C15 tower can be
seen, and the retention of this feature made the composition
of the E FRONT more complex than the others; but alas much
more has been lost than on the other elevations and it is very
overgrown. One can still see that the tower house was incorporated at the centre and raised from three to six storeys,
deliberately emphasizing the historic significance of the early
tower and its symbolism of a heroic past. The N E angle survives
with an elongated angle tourelle. At its N and S front angles,
two more of the paired turrets were added, but of these only
the N one survives to full height, and N of it is a further two-bay
section, also terminating in a square tower. The desire for symmetry was frustrated by the fact that the tower house, its
adjoining kitchen wing and the C17 range are randomly
arranged. To counter this problem a screen wall was built
across the E wall of the tower linking the inner C19 turrets, but
this has mostly vanished. The S wall of the S turret survives and
it is possible to define the chimney in the N wall of the C15/C16
kitchen range.

Projecting in front of the N and S sections of the façade are
two-storey ranges with octagonal angle turrets. These appear
from the straight joints to be slightly later in date, and in form
are closer to the romantic E GATEWAY, which was possibly the
last part of the Elliots' work to be completed. It is arranged on

an axis with the old tower and is separated from it by a bridge
over a deep ravine that acts as a moat to the castle. The gateway
displays more mock defences than the castle itself, including a
central carriage arch which was originally closed by a portcullis
that could be raised into the squat tower above. To l. and r.
remains of two guardhouses with paired arched windows, one
still retaining its tiny corbelled angle turret on the E. On the
inner side towards the castle these have octagonal angle turrets
with corbelled parapets and blind arrowslits.

PARKLAND. The castle is the theatrical set piece in a landscape devised by *Alexander Nasmyth* in 1803–6, which was
superimposed onto a more formal layout of radiating avenues.
Now it forms the centrepiece of a leisure park with new drama
in the form of spine-chilling rides filling the walled garden.

STABLE COURT. E range built in two sections and now converted to facilities for the park. Two-storey, cement-harled N
range dated 1764 on one of the keystones of the five-arched
ground storey, loft above and forestair on N gable, scrolled
skewputts. Further arches on the E elevation. Building to the
S rubble-built, two storeys with five widely spaced openings,
the central at first floor a loft entrance. Attached to its S gable
a pavilion, with a S-facing Venetian window in the ground floor
and a Diocletian window above. This range is a haphazard
interpretation of an unexecuted design in the Adam style for
a symmetrical range with pavilions at either end. Opposite,
part of the courtyard wall with a finialled pier. – WALLED
GARDEN. Stone and brick. Arched W entrance. – ESTATE
HOUSE. N of the castle. *c.* 1800, two storeys with an (earlier?)
wing returning at the E. Main block painted harl with a porch
and asymmetrical tripartite windows of *c.* 1830.

LOUDOUN OLD KIRK, 1.5 km. WSW on the N bank of the Irvine.
The church for the northern half of the upper Irvine valley
until the parish church was built in Newmilns in 1738 (q.v.).
The gabled coursed brown sandstone chancel remains entire
and is roofed in slate. The chancel arch, now blocked, is visible
in the buttressed W wall. The S doorway, with simple moulding,
dates from conversion in 1622 to a burial vault for the Campbells of Loudoun, whose arms are in a recessed panel above
the door. To its r. another panel, but Neo-Jacobean, by *R. Weir
Schultz*, recording his restoration of 1897–9 for the 3rd Marquess of Bute. Schultz also rearranged the interior for worship,
with a new ceiling and a table placed against the E wall. Of the
rest of the church all that remains is the uninformative W gable.
– Several MONUMENTS in the churchyard, including an
OBELISK to Flora, Lady Hastings, †1839, erected in 1887,
designed by *Thomas Lyon* and executed by *Matthew Muir*, both
of Kilmarnock.* SE of the church, the GRAVESTONE of John
Mair of High Waterside, †1732, with the inscription panel
framed in a chain of ellipses, topped with an angel.

---

*Her early death, following a perceived slighting by Queen Victoria, famously
blighted the first years of the queen's reign.

LUGAR

5020

Blackband ironstone was discovered locally *c.* 1840, and an iron works built, but the village was only begun effectively in 1866 when the works were acquired by the Eglinton Iron Co. Iron production ceased in 1928. Post-war development was concentrated at LOGAN (1 km. S), with a simple harled CHURCH of 1956–9 by *Robert Allan* amidst the local authority and S.S.H.A. housing.

LUGAR CHURCH. *See* below.

EAST AYRSHIRE COUNCIL OFFICES. On the site of the iron works. Long two-storey office range built in the 1950s for the National Coal Board, and extended 1963; both phases by *Egon Riss*, chief architect to the N.C.B., Scotland. Converted in 1975 for Cumnock & Doon Valley District Council by *Douglas Buchanan*, with a wooden-lined Council Chamber, heavily influenced by Mackintosh. Short boulevard outside with twin-headed concrete lampposts, perhaps also by Riss.

In the village, at the foot of Peesweep Brae, PARK TERRACE, six terraces of early C20 brick cottages, CRAIGSTON HOUSE, of *c.* 1845 for the iron works manager, and, beyond this, CRAIGSTON SQUARE, a cheerful L-plan group of stone cottages for the foremen, with lying-pane glazing. The N end of its W wing is slightly taller, with an elegant stone and timber bellcote and tall windows. This is LUGAR CHURCH, converted in 1867 from a former engine house; on the E elevation a big round-headed arch, now infilled. Its spacious plastered interior has a wide kingpost roof, a boarded rear gallery, and simple C20 Gothic fittings; the big arch expressed as a shallow recess. Within the grounds, the WAR MEMORIAL, *c.* 1922, a stone monument on two steps, with a marble and bronze dedicatory panel and the names of the returned.

BELLO MILL, 0.6 km. NE. Single-storey harled farm of 1797, though much rebuilt and now late C19 in appearance. Memorial to William Murdoch, pioneer of gas lighting, born here in 1754. Bronze panel, with a portrait bust, by *Henry S. Gamley*, 1913.

ROSEBANK VIADUCT 0.2 km. SE. Of 1872, to carry the GSWR branch line to Muirkirk. The engineer was *William Johnstone*. Seven segmental arches.

CRONBERRY, 1.5 km. NE. Former mining village built by the Eglinton Iron Co. It had a population of 997 in 1871, but all that survives is a row of two-storey brick houses, of 1924 by *Allan Stevenson* and, in splendid isolation, the large former SCHOOL and SCHOOLMASTER'S HOUSE, of 1930–1 by *William Reid*, County Architect.

LUGTON

4050

Hamlet in the valley of the Lugton Water, which in the late C19 became a busy railway junction, as indicated by the CANNY

MAN, a stone Baronial hotel of 1877, with one big widow's-cap gable.

EAST HALKET, 1.5 km. SE. A farmhouse on one of the higher points of the Halket road, which winds through some typically rocky N Ayrshire countryside. The house is of 1847, conventional with a hipped roof, but *c.* 1900 was reorientated to face S, and given a simply detailed classical front.

MIDDLETON, 2.1 km. SW. A spaciously planned courtyard farm which has at its heart an appealing two-storey farmhouse dated 1769, with the initials WC and JS. Restored in the late C20. Three bays, with the entrance to the l. The crowstepped-gabled raised wall-head stack has unusual triangular doocots. To the r., the successor farmhouse, built in the early C19 upon an earlier farm building; at the same time the main entrance was moved to the rear elevation.

MAIDENS

2000

Small Carrick shore village clustered round the broad sweep of Maidenheads Bay. Popular with C18 smugglers; the car brought it within reach of holidaymakers in the C20, and its residential growth is mostly interwar. The harbour was improved in the later C20.

CHAPEL, Kirkoswald Road. 1892, simple Gothic, with a prominent clock. Open timber roof. Cast-iron lozenge-pattern windows stamped with the mark of *James Allan Sen. & Son* of Glasgow. In the chapel a Fitzroy BAROMETER presented to 'the fishermen at the Maidens' after their prompt action following the foundering of the smack *Jane* of Girvan in 1881.

MAIDENS HARBOUR. Some rudimentary stone piers were probably in existence by the late C18, but the present irregular stone pier, mostly repaired and refaced in concrete with a low parapet, was begun in 1948 by local fishermen with material salvaged from Turnberry Airfield, and completed in 1954–8 by *Ayr County Council*. At the pierhead, a brick and cast-iron BARKING POT, probably early C20, used to boil fishing nets and lines in bark extract to preserve them: a practice which ceased with the introduction of nylon nets (*see* also the barking house at Lochranza, Arran).

DESCRIPTION. The village was largely rebuilt by the Kennedys of Ailsa in the last third of the C19. Of this date red sandstone houses; in KIRKOSWALD ROAD, No. 20, with a crisp, if fussy, wooden porch, was the schoolhouse. Also some earlier rows of simple cottages, such as DOUGALSTON guarding the entrance to Shanter Road, and others in Ardlochan Road.

1 km. E, two big houses have captured the hilltop and the views. Both were built in 1938–9 by *Alexander Mair*, in an easy Late Arts and Crafts manner. GLENRONNIE dresses its multi-gabled template in white harl and red tiles, while BLAWEARIE adopts exposed stone and grey tiles.

Former CULZEAN CONVALESCENT HOME, Ardlochan Road. Now immured amidst caravans. Built in 1886 'for working men recovering from illness who require sea air and rest', and underwritten by Lady Ailsa. A bargeboarded red sandstone villa with a biblical quotation on the main window lintel.

PORT MURRAY, off Harbour Road. The best mid-C20 house in Ayrshire, dramatically sited on the rocky shore by the old slipway for McCreadie's steamer building yard. 1961–3 by *Peter Womersley* as a holiday home for the building contractor Andrew McCracken. Built of a random rubble base, cubic and flat-roofed, timber-framed with glazed walls and originally dark-stained weatherboarding (now sheathed in white plastic reducing the impact of its de Stijl-like grid). The design is strongly similar to Womersley's Mies-inspired High Sunderland in the Borders (1956–8), and in the advantage it takes of its site to cantilever out the seaward part of the house, increasing both the drama of the position and the panorama seen from within, it is a precursor of his Bernat Klein studio near Galashiels (1972), bearing an obvious debt to Frank Lloyd Wright (e.g. Fallingwater). Z-plan, with the single-storey E wing sitting into the hillside; extended *c.* 1990 for a small flat and workshop and a new entrance (this may be more suited to year-long occupation in this exposed position but compromises the internal plan). This wing shares the same concrete slab floor as the one-and-a-half-storey cross-wing which links to a two-storey, cantilevered W wing.

The INTERIOR is clearly divided by function. The western L-plan comprising dining hall, sitting room and a discreet study is open-plan, split-level and very light. The alteration to the entrance has reduced the essentially private nature of the eastern kitchen and bedroom wing by utilizing the southern corridor with its built-in storage cupboards as an entrance passage. Originally visitors would have approached through the southern courtyard, now occupied by a swimming pool, into the dining hall and received the full impact of the interpenetrating spaces, the brilliant light and the spectacular views over the Firth of Clyde. Open steps lead from the dining hall to the sitting room, lit by large windows on three sides; the W windows are sliding doors leading onto the cantilevered balcony. This room is divided from the small study by a chimney wall containing two flues, and a square opening above the bold black marble mantelshelf which projects asymmetrically beyond the chimney-breast over the stairs leading down to the master bedroom on the lower level. The study is in effect a gallery to the dining hall. Most of the flooring is in Sicilian marble and throughout the house there are teak or spruce panels interspersed between plaster panels and much glass, the latter often fixed because of the exposed position. The eastern wing could have been designed for a liner, with a galley kitchen with glazed screens opening onto the conservatory/porch, from which steps lead down to the shore. Bedrooms and bathroom beyond the kitchen have smoothly running, glazed sliding doors and can be variously configured to provide light and privacy.

46   THOMASTON CASTLE, 3 km. NE on the edge of the Culzean estate. L-plan, three-storey, roofless rubble-built tower, one of a group in the west of Scotland that that has a recognizable stylistic motif of continuous corbelling (*see* also Cassillis House and Law Castle). Built in the early C16, probably by Thomas Corry of Kelwood who acquired a charter from James IV in 1507. His daughter married a Kennedy of Coif around the same time. Unusually large and horizontal in character, with one long range (18.3 m. by 8.5 m), aligned SW–NE, with a SE wing and stair-tower containing the entrance in the re-entrant angle. It has the unusual feature of a pend through the wing, so the entrance courtyard cannot be later than the wing. There is evidence of a substantial building having abutted its SE wall. The SE elevation of the long block has narrow loops at ground level into the four vaulted cellars, and a large window in the first floor with evidence of another beside it, now blocked, probably an C18 insertion to provide more light and taking advantage of a thinner section of outer wall, the result of a mural stair at this point. Two small nearly square windows above; similar windows light the top floor of the NW elevation with three taller first-floor windows, the W one smaller and lighting the chamber off the hall at the E. On the shorter SW wall a further window lights this chamber with a small slit to the closet contained within the wall. The NW wall has a similar random collection of openings mostly with simple moulded arrises and evidence of others now blocked. The ragged opening at the N end marks the former chimney for the hall fire; at the S end in the wing a window over the pend, and above it a panel with bold roll moulding, presumably to hold carved arms or emblems. The continuous corbelling was combined with angle rounds probably open.

Apart from the vaults, one of which probably housed the kitchen, and the newel stair, nothing remains of the internal arrangements. The disposition of windows, closets and presses indicates the hall and chamber with a further chamber in the wing on the first floor and smaller rooms on the second. The extent of the former courtyard can be guessed from the shallow mounds to the SE.

MANOR PARK

2060

1.5 km. S of Meigle

Also known as St Fillans. The core is an symmetrical A-plan villa by *David & James Hamilton*, built in 1843 for William Stewart, a Greenock merchant. It was a diminutive version of William Adam's Minto House (Borders), composed of N and E wings with the entrance in the inner angle between them. But its symmetry has been spoiled by extensions of 1905 and 1910 for T. C. Stewart, by *Fryers & Penman*.

Except for the three-storey tower, the house is two storeys over a basement, built in a pinkish sandstone ashlar, finely broached with polished ashlar for the channelled and battered basement and the margins, sill and eaves bands. On each elevation the first-floor windows are sandwiched between sill and eaves courses, foreshortening the visual impact of this storey. Deep modillion cornice throughout. In spite of the N extension of 1905 to the N wing, the NE entrance front gives the best impression of the original design. The wings, each of a single bay, are linked by an angled splay with a central shallow pediment behind which the roof slopes to a glazed dome. The restrained balance of this composition is upset, however, by the imposing Roman Doric pillared porch projecting from the centre, which has been doubled in size (probably in 1910). At first floor, a central window flanked by two blind ones, a pattern repeated elsewhere. The windows in the wings have plain architraves dropping just below the sill, embryo lugs and simple keystones. In the N face of the E wing the window is blind but the stone cut to imitate the glazing pattern of the others. Over it, three square flues linked by a cornice, a detail found also at Brooksby House, Largs (q.v.). The extension of the N wing is in the same spirit but without the panache. Three bays with a central full-height canted bay window to front and back. Of the same date, the canted bay on the E face of the E wing. On the S front of this wing is a slightly taller advanced section, also with a canted bay added. Originally it would have matched the carefully balanced window arrangement on the W front with a tripartite window in the ground floor and three single lights above and below. As on the S front the end bay of the wing was originally set back, but this has been infilled at principal-floor level with a tripartite window (probably that removed from the S front of the E wing). The tower at the SW angle has no respect for the Hamiltons' elevations, presenting an inelegant cliff-like wall to the S and ruining the symmetry of the W front with an aggressively assertive two-storey bay window and a big, circular, corbelled stair-turret to its platform roof. Raised panel in the balustraded parapet, fussily detailed. Can this really be by the same hand as the sensitive work of 1905?

The theatrical entrance hall is a geometric feast. The square-plan centre has alcoves with framing pilasters, a circular gallery with more alcoves behind recessed Corinthian columned screens, and a segmented glazed dome opening the centre to the full height of the house. At principal level the N wall has been removed to provide access to an oak stair (probably inserted 1905) and the N extension. Elaborate cornice and ceiling plasterwork at gallery level. Above the gallery a square opening set in a simply panelled frame. Within the opening shallow arches to each face and angle squinches with scrolled decoration surrounding crests (one with the unidentified initials MP). More mouldings surround the shallow drum supporting the ribbed dome. Elsewhere in the house the decoration is more modest although the principal room in the tower

has a distinctly Frenchy look with delicate ceiling plasterwork
and a Louis Quinze-style marble chimneypiece.
STABLE COURT, also by the Hamiltons with a big semicircular
entrance archway and dovecot above inserted into the piend
roof. Now domestic.

MARTNAHAM LODGE
3010
4.2 km. NE of Dalrymple

A multi-gabled and harled house with a spectacular setting overlooking Martnaham Loch. Beginning as a simple cottage and
apparently first added to in the early C19 by the Earl of Cassillis, probably as a fishing lodge, and continuously altered
thereafter. The wing to the r. of the entrance, the porch and
the wing on the l. of the garden front are in *J. K. Hunter*'s
simple Arts and Crafts-inspired manner. The penticed ingle-
nook-like projection at the curved NE angle is especially
memorable. Altered inside by *Noad & Wallace* in 1945, including a new staircase.

OLD MARTNAHAM, 0.4 km. E, on the opposite bank of the loch.
Sketchy remains of a large rectangular house, approached by
a boulder causeway. The entrance was on the S, and the ground
floor had two compartments. Courtyard to the E. C17 features,
recorded in the mid C20, now lost.

MAUCHLINE
5020

Colin McWilliam called Mauchline the brightest of red stone
towns. This is true today, even if recent residential developments
have no use for local materials. The centre is a refreshing jumble,
with an early C19 grid-plan laid over the organically grown earlier
street pattern; the interplay between these makes for exploration
and unexpected discoveries. That so much of the earlier core
survives is due to Robert Burns, who lived here in the late C18
with his wife Jean Armour, the daughter of a Mauchline master
builder, *James Armour*.

The lands of Mauchline were granted by Walter Stewart to
Melrose Abbey in 1165, and remained in its possession until the
Reformation; the town was the centre of the abbey's estates in
Ayrshire, and has long been a trading community at the heart of
a prosperous agricultural area. Weaving was an important factor
in the economy from the late C18, and in the C19 the town
became well known for the manufacture of painted wooden
boxes. The New Red Sandstone which colours the town was
extensively commercially quarried from the late C19. The town
still services the local farming community; boxes are no longer
made, though Andrew Kay & Co. continue to make curling
stones here from granite (originally from Ailsa Craig (q.v.)), as
they have done since the late C19.

CHURCHES AND PUBLIC BUILDINGS

MAUCHLINE PARISH CHURCH, Loudoun Street. Built of the
local red sandstone in 1829 by *James Dempster* of Greenock,
though based on a plan furnished by one of the heritors,
William Alexander of Southbar, and replacing a medieval
church on the same site.

Tudor Gothic three-bay NE front with square battlemented
entrance tower of three stages and angle buttresses ending in
corner pinnacles. The SE door has grotesque headstops.
Windows with four-centred heads and hoodmoulds. Four-light
SW window, and three two-light windows to the side elevations,
all within deep cavetto reveals. Tiled vestibule in the tower,
with a single curving stone gallery stair. Inside, exposed stone
walls, a vaulted and panelled plaster ceiling and a rear gallery
on quatrefoil columns. The light oak panelled gallery front is
contemporary with the reconstruction of the interior in 1956–7
by *Hay & Steel*, when other galleries were removed. Light oak
furnishings of the same date. – ORGAN. From Strathbungo
Parish Church (Glasgow), introduced in 1980. – STAINED
GLASS. SW window. Healing the Centurion's Son by *Powells*,
1903.

Crowded, roughly rectangular CHURCHYARD. The entrance
from Castle Street is protected by a simple early C19 stone and
slated WATCH HOUSE. Within the churchyard, several HEAD-
STONES to friends and acquaintances of Burns, though few are
of artistic merit. At the NE end, however, a nicely lettered
memorial erected in 1727 (renewed 1805) to a Covenanter,
James Smith. He †1684 in Mauchline prison after being
'Wounded by Captain Ingles and his Dragoons at the Burn of
Ann in Kyle'. – Close to the SW churchyard wall, monument
of *c.* 1821 to the Rev. John Walker and his family: a central
panel with fluted pilasters and lintel, and side panels with
upwardly curving heads. – Close to the NW wall a tall monument to George Julian Harvey, Chartist leader, †1897, '. . . now
only a memory. It ought, however . . . to be a sweet and grateful memory . . .'.

CHURCH HALL, Castle Street. Late Gothic. 1895 by *John B.
Wilson*. Red sandstone, with a spreading five-light window in
the main (E) gable. Stepped corner buttresses; elliptically
headed entrance to the l. in a gabled porch with a further,
smaller, stepped buttress.

MAUCHLINE CEMETERY, Barskimming Road. *c.* 1880. One
remarkable red sandstone MONUMENT, on the E boundary
wall, to the family of Marcus Bain, quarrymaster who did most
to promote Mauchline stone. Doleful angels holding an
inscribed shield, the carving seems designed to demonstrate
the qualities of the stone. Probably erected *c.* 1886; Bain
(†1910) himself has a flat stone with a bronze cross and
extravagant inscription, 'One who never turned his back,
but marched breast forward, never doubted clouds would
break . . .' etc.

FIRE STATION, Kilmarnock Road. 1962–4 by *Ian G. McGill*, of *Park & McGill*. Mostly of grey brick, with the garage flanked by a retaining wall and offices.

LIBRARY AND LOCAL OFFICE, The Cross. 1996 by *Cumnock and Doon Valley District Council*, at an important site in the heart of the town. Asymmetrical, harled and large, with the higher blocks mustered at the rear in a T-plan, whose cross-bar faces W to High Street with a single-storey forework of five bays and central round-headed pend under a stilted pediment. In front, a cast bronze STATUE of Jean Armour, one hand outstretched in supplication or greeting, by *R. Maciver* of *Beltane Studios*, 2002.

MAUCHLINE PRIMARY SCHOOL, Loan. The original building is a simple red sandstone gabled block of 1889, with gabled wings forming a U-plan, extended W in 1911 and again, on a much grander scale, in 2006–7 by *SMC Parr Architects* (*Kevin Cooper*, project architect). The C21 work has pink sandstone gables borrowing from the original, but with half-glazed gables and low half-circular nursery professing its modernity. A glazed and timber link connects old and new. In front of the school, the MARTYRS' MONUMENT to five Covenanters killed in 1685. Of 1885 by *Thomas Lyon*, sculpted by *Matthew Muir*. Red sandstone obelisk on a square base, the decoration faintly Grecian. Earlier inscribed monuments are in the school wall: 'Bloody Dumbarton, Douglas and Dundee/ Moved by the Devil and the Laird of Lee/ Dragg'd these five men to death with gun and sword . . .'

WAR MEMORIAL, Cumnock Road. 1926–7 by *A. C. Thomson* of Ayr, completed after his death by *William Meikle*. An arresting introduction on the approach to the town from the E. Red sandstone Ionic column, surmounted by an urn, on a heavy square plinth with Greek-key decoration.

MAUCHLINE CASTLE
(Abbot Hunter's Tower)

A medieval tower house at the heart of Mauchline, with an L-plan Georgian house attached. It was built by and for the abbey of Melrose, and seems to have been erected during the abbacy of Andrew Hunter, 1444–71. From here the abbey ran and controlled their estates in Ayrshire. After the Reformation it passed into the possession of the Campbells of Loudoun, but by the late C18 it had passed to Gavin Hamilton, lawyer in Mauchline and patron of Burns. The later wing of the house probably dates from his occupancy. Conserved 1976–8 by *Andrew C. Traub*.

The TOWER is square in plan, and built of the local red sandstone. The walls rise to a parapet, carried on individual corbels. Above this a crowstepped and slated roof. On the E elevation, a two-light round-headed window, now blocked, and on the N elevation a big garderobe chute. The entrance is in the SW angle, and leads into the ground floor. This has two barrel-vaulted chambers. To the l., a newel-stair leads to the first-floor hall (7.6 m. by 6 m.) which has a ribbed vault in two bays, with groined arches springing from carved corbels. The boss of the N bay of the vault has a carved armorial of Abbot Hunter. The large N window has been partially blocked, but retains its original stone seats. The newel-stair continued to a further floor behind the parapets.

Adjoining to the S is the harled L-plan house. It has sashes and painted margins, but the wings are of different dates. The earlier is of *c.* 1700, of three bays, and faces W. It has crow-stepped gables, and is connected to the tower by a single lower bay, apparently of *c.* 1800, with a pend on the ground floor, the upper floor providing access between the house and tower. On the ground floor of this wing, however, is a vaulted chamber that may be contemporary with the tower, no doubt part of the ancillary buildings with which it must have been provided. The later wing has a hipped roof and a porch supported on columns in the re-entrant angle. Of *c.* 1760, and originally single-storey, but raised to two *c.* 1800. Some panelling of *c.* 1820 survives in both wings of the house.

DESCRIPTION

The planned town was superimposed in 1819–20, when 'a new road through Mauchline' was made by *David Lamont* and *William Stevenson*. It runs roughly NW–SE, and comprises Kilmarnock Road, New Street and Earl Grey Street. Joining this axis at the staggered cross-roads of Mauchline Cross are Loudoun Street (W) and High Street (E), both of which are older streets modified to suit the Late Georgian plan. Also commencing at the Cross, and running WNW, is the setted CASTLE STREET. It conveys in its short length an authentic feeling of how the town must have been before 1820. Three properties in the street have associations with Burns and were acquired between 1915 and 1924 by Charles Cowie, who gifted them to the Glasgow & District Burns Association. Used initially as homes for old people, the necessary restoration and alterations being made by *Ninian MacWhannell.* Most of the original interiors had been lost by 1994–6 when *ARP Lorimer & Partners* undertook a thorough restoration for the Ayrshire Architectural Heritage Trust as a museum and exhibition space. First, on the l. is NANSE TINNOCK'S, early C18, of two storeys of exposed grey and brown sandstone, with simple dressings and a slate roof (originally thatched). Then on the r. are DR MACKENZIE'S HOUSE and BURNS HOUSE, both of 93 *c.* 1760. Red sandstone, with smooth dressings. Burns House has a canted corner, with a tall stone chimneystack; here Burns lived, and it retains the simply plastered family bedroom.

In LOUDOUN STREET, on the S side, firstly the neat painted stone and hipped roof of the MAUCHLINE PHARMACY, probably of *c.* 1820; then the four-bay harled Nos. 3–7, with simple openings and two small, and early, dormers either side

of a big wall-head gable, and two-attic windows below a pediment with a recessed elliptical panel, and a long two-storey
block of *c.* 1800, partly painted and partly red ashlar, with
rolled skews at either end. Then, set back, POOSIE NANSIE'S,
a pub associated with Burns. Three wide harled bays, with
small sash windows, a pilastered front and a slate roof (thatched
until the 1950s). To the l., an odd single-storey projection, of
c. 1900, which was a shop but is now incorporated into the
pub; to the r., and behind, a single-storey extension dated 1888,
with large windows. Loudoun Street continues with a terrace
of C19 two-storey properties, mostly of exposed red sandstone,
broken by the harled C18 OLD PRINTERS. The corner block,
however, is harled, of six bays, with a dressed course around
the central four bays, as though indicating the proportions of
the original house. The terrace ends at Barskimming Road,
with the former POST OFFICE, of *c.* 1900, with some of the
same quirky detailing seen at Poosie Nansie's. Interest now
switches to the N side of the street, with the GATEPIERS of
Mauchline Castle (*see* above) with pyramidal heads on ball
feet, the bracketed entrance of the mid-C19 FAIRBURN HOTEL
and the LOUDOUN SPOUT, a spring from which water has
poured since 1763. Lion-headed spigot given a red granite
surround in 2000. Beyond this, a round-arched and chunkily
stepped late C19 GATEWAY, formerly leading to Netherplace,
a Tudor Gothic house built for the Campbells in 1827, but
demolished in 1956. Its former WEST LODGE is of the same
date and style as the house.

EARL GREY STREET, SE of the Cross, begins with a good group
of *c.* 1820 or soon after, including the BLACK BULL, of four
bays, ashlar, with a round-headed pend to the l., and another
house of four bays, with a basket-headed pend, and a wall-head
dormer gable. Its big doorway in the r. bay has a floral keystone
and pediment with acroteria. The group is completed by the
ROYAL BANK OF SCOTLAND, with a pilastered doorpiece and
square skews. The interest in its S continuation, CUMNOCK
ROAD, is almost exclusively on the E side. The L-plan red
sandstone HAPLAND (No. 15) is of 1905 by *A. N. Paterson*, in
his luxuriant Art and Crafts manner. In the re-entrant a slated
porch, above which rises a tall octagonal chimney; to the l. a
ground-floor bay with leaded roof; to the r. the wing is terminated by a full-height round tower with a slated conical tower.
Rolled skews and finial-headed dormers. Nos. 19–21 are late
C19, set back, with bays to l. and r., and tall French entrance
bays to either side. VIEWFIELD (No. 27) is a villa of 1824 with
flanking hip-roofed wings, a pilastered doorpiece and wrought-
iron first-floor balconies.

NEW ROAD and KILMARNOCK ROAD running in the other
direction from the Cross are also of course mostly of 1819–20,
with the distinguished exception of the VETERINARIAN
SURGERY (No. 16), of 1963–4 by *Ian G. McGill*, then of *Park
& McGill*. Grey brick, set back and irregularly composed:
'the design of the main elevation is an abstraction of the

severe triangular gable shapes which bound it on either
side.' On the W side is the NORTH LODGE for Netherplace
(*see* above), classical, of *c.* 1820, with segmentally headed
openings.

In HIGH STREET, on the N side, No. 3 is late C18, harled, two
storeys with thin end pilasters and eaves course, central pedimented doorcase, and chamfered corner to the r. At the junction with Mansefield Road, SPRINGFIELD, a conventional late
C19 red stone house with a pilastered doorpiece and a full-
height bay to the l.; at the apex of its garden a beautiful Gothic
GAZEBO of *c.* 1820. Beneath a battlemented parapet, a central
window of three ogee-headed lancets, and flanking similar
single windows, all with fleur-de-lis heads.

Further out in SORN ROAD is ABBEY HOUSE, the former Free
Church Manse of 1844, restored, for himself, by *Ian G. McGill*,
c. 1964. In the same road, an attractive Late Arts and Crafts
house of 1924, harled, with a wide gabled bay to the l. and a
round-headed dormer to the r. The architect was *David M.
Brown* of Kilmarnock.

WOODSIDE, Station Road. Bulky Gothic villa of *c.* 1870, with
big eaves, and a castellated screen wall to the l.

BURNS NATIONAL MEMORIAL, 1 km. NW. A prominent, and
not easily forgotten, landmark conceived by the Glasgow &
District Burns Association to mark the centenary of Burns's
death. The design, for a tower and cottage homes for old
people, was won in competition by *William Fraser* of Glasgow
and erected 1896–8, all in red sandstone. The TOWER is
unscholarly Scots Baronial, four-square and of three stages,
with a NW stair-tower at the angle corbelled out into a crowstepped caphouse, a tourelle at the SE angle of the balustraded
parapet and bartizans at the other corners. Entrance with flat
pilasters and a triangular pediment with a carved tympanum
on the S elevation. On each side at the second stage, doors
behind heavily bracketed balconies with open balustrades and
ball finials. In the wider top stage, deeply recessed paired
round-headed openings with big aprons. The memorial sits in
a pleasant triangular garden, with a low stone and rail wall,
and ball-and-pyramid gatepiers.

The single-storey COTTAGE HOMES lie behind, and are
altogether more successful. They now form a canted U-plan,
though originally comprised just the single block of cottages
immediately behind the memorial tower. The side wings
fronting the Tarbolton and Kilmarnock roads were added, to
Fraser's plans, in 1909–10 and 1930–1 (with *Ninian MacWhannell* as executant architect). Articulation is given by the prominent battered ridge stacks and alternation of round-headed
and triangular-headed dormers. The final smaller blocks date
from *c.* 1938; that facing the Kilmarnock road has a prettily
carved dedication plaque. The brick L-plan JEAN ARMOUR
BURNS HOME, which fronts Tarbolton Road beyond the
cottage homes, is of 1957–9.

BALLOCHMYLE VIADUCT, 2.1 km. SE. An unforgettable sight, sweeping the railway between Kilmarnock and Cumnock 51 m. above the Ayr as it flows through Ballochmyle Gorge. 1846–8, designed by *John Miller*, engineer to the Glasgow, Paisley, Kilmarnock & Ayr Railway (opened 1850). The resident engineer was *William McCandlish*, and the contractors *Ross & Mitchell* of Falkirk. The zenith of C19 engineering in Ayrshire, and of national and international importance. Seven arches, the largest in the centre spanning 55 m. across the river; when built this was the largest masonry railway arch in the world. The other arches are narrower, 15.2 m. across, with semicircular heads of dressed stone from Millfield Quarry, Dundee, and spandrels and unimaginably tall piers of coursed rubble from Boswell Quarry at Mauchline. A simple description; it is the scale that, even today, occasions a sense of awe and wonder. The cost was estimated to be £60,000, of which £8,500 was spent on the 3,500 logs of Memel pine used to make the centring.

The viaduct is one of three bridges which cross the Ayr here. 0.6 km. E is the attractive late C18 HOWFORD BRIDGE. It has two segmental arches, and a triangular cutwater. Its mason is traditionally held to be *James Armour*, Burns's father-in-law. Its successor, towering 15.5 m. above the river, is the BALLOCHMYLE BRIDGE of 1959–62 by *W. A. Fairhurst* of *F. A. Macdonald & Partners*. A single 91.4-m. concrete deck carried on two graceful parallel arch ribs. It has not, could not have, the bravura of Miller's viaduct, but it is a worthy companion.

CUP-AND-RING-MARKED ROCK, 0.4 km. E of Ballochmyle Viaduct. A spectacular sheet of cups and multiple rings extending across a vertical pinkish sandstone rock face.

WEST MONTGARSWOOD FARM, 2.1 km. E. harled two-storey farmhouse with a central pediment, probably late C18. Open courtyard to the rear, the other wings single-storey.

HAUGH, 2.3 km. S. A cluster of buildings close to the River Ayr, including remains of a former MILL, stone with a hipped roof, a late C18 single-arch stone BRIDGE over the mill lade, and, between them, a painted stone FARMHOUSE dated 1776. This is two-storey, gabled, with simple skews, with ground-floor windows of *c*. 1930. To the W is HAUGHBANK HOUSE and a former MARGARINE FACTORY, both of 1911.* The former is vaguely Arts and Crafts, with swept eaves, a porch with a stack above, and applied timbering in the eaves. It was the manager's house for the factory. This is a complex structure, with a faintly Germanic air, due to its deep eaves and swept gambrel roof, and the prominent bellcast ventilator on the tallest range. Set at an angle is a lower range, probably of *c*. 1890, but incorporating parts of an earlier lint mill on the site. In HAUGH ROAD, to the N, a group of late C19 red sandstone cottages, with tall wall-head stacks. The fields here were the quarries; this is the epicentre of Mauchline red sandstone.

---

*Succeeded in the 1930s by the present Mauchline Creamery, 0.3 km. NW. This was designed by *Alexander Mair*, but nothing of his building remains in its original form.

Ballochmyle Viaduct, under construction.
Engraving, published 1865

SKEOCH FARM, 2.8 km. NW. Late Georgian except for the large
porch with Ionic columns, reputedly from Hamilton Palace
(Lanarkshire, dem. 1925).

KINGENCLEUGH HOUSE. *See* p. 479.

MAYBOLE

3000

Minniebole is a dirty wee hole; it sits abune a mire, as the rather
damning local ditty has it. The original settlement must indeed
have been on the low ground to the SE of the present High Street,
and was in existence by the C12. In 1193 Duncan, Earl of Carrick,
granted the lands of Maybole to the abbey of Melrose. In 1516
Maybole was made a Burgh of Barony – the first in Carrick. It
was probably in the C16 that the High Street was laid out on the
hillside above the original settlement. Maybole Castle, the town
house of the superiors, the Kennedys of Cassilis, was built at the
NE end of the High Street, and in the C17 many of Carrick's

gentry built town houses here. That of the Kennedys of Blair-quhan survives as part of Maybole Town Hall, while others are presumed to survive, hidden behind C19 façades. The late C19 brought the railway (which reached Maybole in 1856) and industry, particularly the manufacture of boots and shoes. The C20 was less kind to Maybole. The shoe industry declined while necessary redevelopment in the SE quarter has removed almost every last trace of the pre-C16 settlement. Maybole has history, and a strong sense of place. With a by-pass it could begin to rediscover and uncover the architecture that lies beneath its present appearance.

CHURCHES AND CEMETERIES

BAPTIST CHURCH, Carrick Road. Dec. 1913–14 by *Hugh Campbell* of Glasgow. Red sandstone gable front with a five-light window above a lean-to porch and entrance with cavetto reveals.

CARRICK CENTRE, Culzean Road. 2007–12 by *Raymond Angus*. Bright, functional wood-framed building which is both parish church and multi-use community facility.

MAYBOLE COLLEGIATE CHURCH, Kirk Port.* A chapel dedicated to St Mary, with initial endowments for three chaplains and a clerk, was founded in 1371 by John Kennedy of Dunure, the ancestor of the Earls of Cassillis and Marquises of Ailsa. This was said to have been within the parish churchyard, though the parish church was in fact a short way to the NE. The chapel became collegiate in 1382, when it was affirmed that the building was largely complete; it is thus the earliest surviving example in Scotland of a late medieval collegiate chapel. The chapel's collegiate functions ceased at the Reformation, but it continued in use for burials. A description by the parish minister of between 1683 and 1722 says it had been recently re-roofed as a burial place for the Earls of Cassillis and other gentlemen, and that a burial aisle for the earl's kinsman, the laird of Colaine (Culzean), had been built on the N side. Above the door of that aisle, however, is a heraldic tablet with arms that evidently relate to the 7th Earl (1668–1701) and his wife, Susan Hamilton. There is a second enclosure to the E of the sacristy. After falling into decay, in 1832 the roofless shell of the chapel was repaired and a wall constructed around it. It is now in state care.

The chapel is an oriented rectangular building of five bays, the W bay being longer than the others, with a small square sacristy towards the E end on the N side. Externally, the rubble walls with ashlar dressings rise from a broad chamfered base course. Along the W, S and E sides the bay divisions are marked by buttresses, some now heavily robbed, and there is also a buttress at the centre of the W wall; along the S flank they have a single offset and a weathered back top, but those at the E

---

* This account is by Richard Fawcett.

angles are additionally finished with gablets. There is a door on the N side of the nave with simply chamfered external reveals, which is now partly blocked by the W wall of the late C17 aisle. The imposing principal entrance is towards the W end of the S wall, where it is surmounted by a shield bearing the arms of Kennedy. The jambs and arch, which are separated by a moulded impost, are of three orders of triplets of rolls, the leading roll of each being nibbed; there is a band of dogtooth to two of the orders. The use of dogtooth and nibbed rolls offers one of the earliest cases of the revived use of earlier architectural forms, a revival that was to be a significant element in the evolution of Scottish later medieval ecclesiastical architecture. There may also have been a related form of revival in the tracery of the windows in the chapel's E parts, all of which are now blocked. In the E wall was a three-light window with reticulated tracery within reveals consisting of three orders of chamfers. In the easternmost bay on both the S and N sides was a two-light window with a single reticulation unit and double-chamfered reveals. There may also have been a similar window in the third bay from the E, which has three orders of chamfers to reveals. While the choice of reticulated tracery in 1382 is not as surprising as the use of dogtooth mouldings, it does point to either a marked conservatism or a renewed interest in past architectural forms. In the fourth bay from the E on each side is a narrow, cusped lancet (that on the N now blocked), corresponding to the internal division between choir and nave. The only other window was in the S part of the W wall, which may have been a later insertion.

Internally, the chapel shows evidence for virtually all of the liturgical arrangements that were to be characteristic of subsequent late medieval collegiate foundations; most of these will be listed under the furnishings. The presbytery and choir areas would have been relatively brightly lit by the large windows in three of the walls; by contrast, the nave must have been very dark. In the E wall, flanking the E window, is a pair of corbels; since these would have been too high to support the *mensa*, they may have been for the principal images. There is a piscina towards the E end of the S wall. In the N wall is a tomb that was presumably intended for the founder, but that perhaps also served as an Easter Sepulchre, while in the S wall is a modified rectangular recess where the sedilia may have been located. The doorway into the sacristy on the N side of the choir has continuous mouldings of a filleted roll between hollows and angled fillets. The site of the screen between choir and nave is marked by a narrow cusped lancet on each side a little to the W of the mid-point of the interior; each of those lancets has a round-headed rere-arch, and a pocket on the E side of the N window may indicate the location of the screen itself. The existence of at least one altar in front of the screen is indicated by the piscina beneath the sill of the S window. The barrel-vaulted sacristy has blocked embrasures in its E and N walls, possibly for a doorway and window respectively, though there is no evidence of these externally. Its w wall was demolished when the late C17 burial aisle to its w was extended into it.

FURNISHINGS. PISCINA to main altar, trifoliate pointed arch, the basin now hidden below the raised floor level. – PISCINA to s nave altar, trifoliate pointed arch, the basin recessed within the wall thickness. – FOUNDER'S TOMB. Pointed arch framed by hoodmoulding, the arch with four uniform orders of rolls, and with three bands of dogtooth between. – The C17 N BURIAL AISLE, on the w wide of the sacristy, is ashlar-faced with block-rusticated quoins. It is entered through a door in its w wall which has an architrave flanked by bands decorated with rosettes, and there are further rosettes and fleur-de-lis to the frieze below the dentilled cornice. Late C19 views show that the heraldic tablet above the door was framed by a lugged architrave flanked by swags. There is a window in the N wall with a lugged architrave, above which is a framed recess, presumably for a heraldic tablet. The second, rubble-built enclosure, E of the sacristy, projects a little to the E of the church's E gable; it was covered by a single-pitch roof but has no architectural features.

Former MAYBOLE PARISH CHURCH, Cassillis Road. A large rectangular hall church, of squared yellow rubble, with ashlar dressings, with a prominent, unusual and astylar tower centrally placed on the SE elevation. Built in 1807–9; *Robert MacLachlan* of Ayr was the master mason, but the architect is not known. The first stage of the tower rises through the wall-head to a blind parapet, with four square stages above in steps rising to an obelisk spire. The third stage has circular panels, while the parapet and the final stage have curious incised carving. These, coupled with its shape, give the tower an Egyptian flavour, at a time when Egyptian art was becoming known in Britain. From where did the unknown architect of this little masterpiece draw his inspiration? Flanking the tower, tall wide lancets, and in the outer bays, pairs of smaller lancets, with paired round-headed gallery windows. Corbelled eaves, and a shallow hipped roof. Similar fenestration patterns on the other elevations; on the shorter side elevations the windows flank tall hipped stair projections; these have tall round-headed two-light windows, and gunloops on the returns. The interior has been largely dismantled. – STAINED GLASS. SE windows. 1900 by *Stephen Adam & Son*.

Behind the church, the CHURCH HALL of 1882–4, a simple gabled five-bay hall with foliated windows and buttresses, and a gabled SW porch. The church stands within low stone boundary walls, with railings and two sets of gatepiers with attractive wrought-iron gates.

OUR LADY AND ST CUTHBERT (R.C.), Dailly Road. Rectangular five-bay Gothic church and presbytery on an elevated site. Built 1876–8, the architect unfortunately unknown, for the detailing is imaginative and carried out with verve. The cost was largely borne by David Hunter Blair, subsequently abbot at Fort Augustus, and it is possible that some of the artistic inspiration was his also. Yellow stugged ashlar, with polished dressings. Tall four-light Geometric window in the main gable, with a four-stage octagonal tower and spire to the r., and the entrance to the l. in a gabled porch. The entrance has a pointed head and splayed reveals. Two-light Geometric windows between buttresses on the side elevations. All the windows have hoodmoulds and portrait label stops which have been modelled from life. The interior is remarkable. Pointed vaulted plaster ceiling with stone ribs, springing from portrait corbels; the polygonal chancel also with a rib-vault on portrait corbels. Where these are not obviously religious in character, they are again based on local clergy and lay members of the community; some are quite expressive. Pointed chancel arch with marble columns and richly painted decorative capitals; smaller arches to either side springing from equally bright and florid responds. – STAINED GLASS. In the chancel: SS Christopher and Mary, contemporary with the church, and probably German.

Set back, to the l. of the church, is the former school (now used as a HALL) with a pair of pointed-headed doors in a triangular gabled porch. To the r. the church is linked to the rather gaunt asymmetrical and red sandstone Gothic PRESBYTERY with its cusped lights, tall skews and gableted skewputts.

ST OSWALD (Episcopal), Cargill Road. 1882–3 by *Miles S. Gibson* of Glasgow. E.E., but of a very domestic character in light brown ashlar with tall slated roofs over the three-bay nave and polygonal chancel. Curious splayed porch covered by conjoined bell-cast roofs. Simple but effective interior, with triglyph-like corbels supporting the nave roof. – ORGAN, 1892 by *Alfred Kirkland* of London with particularly fine Gothic case. – Bland church hall, *c.* 1968.

Former WEST PARISH CHURCH, Coral Glen. Simple Romanesque T-plan church of 1836–40 by *George Meikle Kemp*, of Scott Monument fame. Converted to residential use, 2007, *ARP Lorimer & Associates*. Rubble-built, with polished dressings. Each wing is gabled, with a round-headed door with moulded reveals beneath tall three-light round-headed windows. Tall round-headed windows elsewhere, while the rear wall is encrusted with a hall and session house. The NE gable has a bellcote added in 1859, built by *John McConnochie*. To the l. of the NE door, a Creetown granite WAR MEMORIAL, within a red sandstone frame, of 1924 by *George P. Greenlaw*. The adjoining former MANSE of 1861 is of three bays; the central entrance has a fanlight and a hoodmould which is raised above a square panel with the inscription 'Peace'. The flanking bays have steep gables, while the central window is corbelled out under a shaped gable with a ball finial.

MAYBOLE CEMETERY, Crosshill Road. 1850 by *Reid*, and later extended. Large stone-walled enclosure with a simple sexton's house and entrance, described as 'a forest of high-rise obelisks, broken pillars, shrouded urns and Celtic crosses' (Philip

Howard); shrouded urns do appear to be a particular favourite here.

OLD CHURCHYARD, St Cuthbert's Road. The site of the C12 church. The low boundary walls and narrow gabled gateway date from 1835. Within the churchyard a number of good grave-stones. Close to the w wall, a table tomb, dated 1618, but prob-ably restored in the C19. SE of this a carved headstone with a skeleton in a coffin, probably C18, and SE again, another carved stone with a child with an hourglass, and a skull, of *c.* 1747.

MAYBOLE CASTLE
High Street

The dominant building of the burgh, in several senses, particu-larly visually when seen on the NE approach to the town. It dates from the early C17, almost certainly built for John, 5th Earl of Cassillis (†1615), though it has been much altered and enlarged subsequently. It is a four-storey, grey-harled tower house and, although within an urban setting, it is clear that it was essentially defensible; its verticality anachronistic and perhaps evidence of continuing uncertainty in Carrick. It conforms to a typical L-plan with a four-storey tower and a SW stair-tower that rises slightly higher to a corbelled and ashlar caphouse, gabled and crowstepped with scroll skews, which is adorned on its W face by the castle's most famous and, follow-ing its publication by Billings, much-copied feature: the canted ORIEL WINDOW, which is stone-roofed and corbelled out in two steps, below which is a weathered teardrop-shaped ornament. The three lights have simple mouldings on three sides, and a more prominent outer framework, whose vertical mouldings finish in carved headstops, with further heads placed in the frieze between bands of billet decoration.

On the NE elevation, above the second floor are ashlar NW and NE angle turrets, each with three windows, a conical cap and a finial. Between these turrets a tall wall-head chim-neystack and, flanking this, small dormer windows with highly decorative pediments formed from three semicircles, unique Anglo-Flemish decoration which lifts Maybole beyond the ranks of typical tower houses. The windows of the upper floors are indicative of the original fenestration but at first floor are much enlarged sashed openings created in 1849–50 by *David Cousin*, who also added the low Baronial N wing during his conversion of the castle into a factor's house and office. (It had been advertised to let as early as 1834.) Cousin's wing is ashlar, with a crowstepped gable above a large oriel window. To the l. is the entrance, with simple moulding and Jacobethan strap-work, repeated in the small dormer above. The projecting two-storey SW wing was probably added after 1660 for John, 6th Earl (†1668). It is crowstepped and gabled, but unharled. On its SE face, a dormer pediment decorated like those on the NE face. The interior was largely altered during Cousin's mid-C19 changes, but originally comprised kitchens on the

Maybole Castle.
Engraving by J. Godfrey, *c.* 1852

ground floor, with a principal room on the first floor, and
further rooms above. Of this there remains only the vaulted
basements and, high in the stair-turret, the wood-panelled
Prospect Room. The castle sits within a spacious garden, with
stone walls and pyramid-headed gatepiers with banded vermiculation, said to be of *c.* 1812, contemporary with the
realignment of the road into Maybole from the N.

PUBLIC BUILDINGS

CAIRN PRIMARY SCHOOL, Cairnfield Avenue. 1889–90 by *J. K.
Hunter* of *James A. Morris & Hunter*. Austere well-massed red

sandstone U-plan, largely single-storey, with four gables to the main elevation, and spreading gables to the wings.

CARNEGIE LIBRARY, High Street. A lush and self-confident Scots Renaissance exercise by *J. K. Hunter*, 1905–6, with sculptural carving by *Holmes & Jackson* of Glasgow. On a corner site with a three-bay elevation to High Street, and a taller and wider three-bay elevation on the downward slope of St Cuthbert's Road. Pairs of mullion windows to the curved corner bay, the central upper one framed by prominent pilasters either side, rising from corbels and ending in pyramidal finials. First-floor Venetian windows on both flanking elevations. The original central entrance now a window, the flanking windows now modern full-height openings, that to the l. the entrance.

CARRICK ACADEMY, Kirkoswald Road. 1924–7 by *J. St Clair Williamson* and *William Reid*, for the Ayrshire Education Authority. Large U-plan secondary school, mostly of red brick with Ballochmyle sandstone facings. Two-storey eight-bay main elevation with the bays rendered between brick pilaster-strips. Flanking three-bay parapeted pavilions and recessed stone-faced entrances.

DYKES MEMORIAL FOUNTAIN, Ballgreen. 1882. Fountain under a gableted head, with stumpy columns, on a tall plinth and supporting a rather phallic column, all executed in grey Peterhead granite.

MAYBOLE HEALTH CENTRE AND DAY HOSPITAL, High Street. 1987–90, *Common Services Agency*. Adjoining the Castle to the SW, a respectful Neo-vernacular group in red stone and grey harl, with slated roofs and simple stone skews. A recessed pend under the tallest of the High Street buildings leads to a long harled two storey wing behind.

MAYBOLE STATION, Culzean Road. The railway arrived in Maybole in 1856, and the Glasgow & South-Western Railway rebuilt the station in 1879–80. What remains is an attractive composition in red stone rubble, very domestic in appearance, its business function almost an afterthought. Since 2004 the station has been dwarfed by an over-engineered footbridge.

POST OFFICE, High Street. Highly competent Scots Renaissance of 1912, presumably by *H. M. Office of Works*, making a fine pair with the near-contemporary Carnegie Library (*see* above), facing the Castle and creating an immediate sense of civic pride. Two storey and five bays, the upper windows in the three bays to the l. with pedimented and finialled dormerheads. Below these two square-headed windows and the door with an open segmental pediment. The r.-hand bay is wider, with a four-light window, and a crowstepped gable with two Jacobethan-headed windows. Balustraded single-storey two-bay extension of *c.* 1930 to the r., and a gabled glazed brick rear extension.

TOWN HALL, High Street. This began as the late C16 town house of the Kennedys of Blairquhan, but was acquired in 1673 by the Town Council, who used it as a Tolbooth. The Town Hall was added in 1887–8 by *R. S. Ingram* in a consciously harmonious

Scots Baronial. The principal feature is the tall, square NW stair-tower. The entrance is on its NE elevation, a late C16 doorway with a roll-moulded surround rising into two round-headed arches which meet in a central cusp; the lintel head is straight. Above, on the same elevation, a small moulded panel surround. At wall-head height, a corbel course, and then a stage with a clock recess on the NE elevation. Above this the bell-stage, with Y-tracery, and a crenellated parapet. These upper stages may date from the late C17,* but were altered in 1812, when the existing parapet replaced the 'pyramide, and a row of ballesters round it' recorded in 1696 by Abercrummie. The tall French spire with clock faces and an iron crown is part of Ingram's work. The tower retains a stone newel stair. At right angles to this is the late C16 house's main block, of coursed rubble, with dressed margins, and retaining some original small rectangular openings; now of two storeys and gutted, but Billings's view, of *c.* 1845, shows it with a further storey – a crowstepped monopitch roof set against the tower; possibly late C17 work. The main room on the ground floor is barrel-vaulted. Ingram's Town Hall adjoins to the NE, on the site of two-storey buildings depicted by Billings. Two storeys, with three asymmetrical bays to the High Street. Central entrance with a moulded round-arched doorpiece. Above this a heavily consoled and bracketed balcony, a tall mullioned-and-transomed three-light window, a crowstepped gable and little corbelled turrets. Elsewhere one-, two- and three-light windows of similar style, and a corbelled and castellated parapet. To the l. of the principal elevation a circular angle turret, corbelled out at first floor. It ends in a conical slate roof. Return elevation with crowstepped gable, a further miniature turret and a subsidiary entrance in a tall-shouldered doorpiece. Inside, on the first floor, the panelled Council Chamber.

WAR MEMORIAL, Memorial Park. 1920–4 by *J. K. Hunter.* A tall, powerful, slightly tapering monument in rough Creetown granite, with a relief of a cross-like sword above a bronze panel by *H. H. Martyn & Co.* of Cheltenham.

DESCRIPTION

HIGH STREET runs NE–SW. It is funnel-like, the views broadening appreciably at either end, and begins and ends with the town's best buildings, the Castle and the Town Hall. The rest is mixed (and the shopfronts universally dire) but earlier façades must be hidden behind the rather drab mostly C19 face that Maybole's commercial quarter shows to the world.

Description begins at the NE end with the good group of the castle, the Carnegie Library and the Post Office (for which see above) on the SE side, where KIRKWYND drops steeply down towards the Old Churchyard (*see* Churches and Cemeteries,

---

* The original BELL, of 1696, 'fovnded at Maiboll bi *Albert Danel Geli* a Frenchman', is preserved in the Council Chamber.

above); on its r. a three-bay house with half-dormers. It is probably c18, and virtually all that remains above ground of the network of streets and vennels that comprised the medieval town. On High Street itself, No. 11, crowstepped Scots Baronial by *John Murdoch*, 1875, and opposite at the junction with Castle Street (NW side), Nos. 24–26, of *c.* 1900, red sandstone with a conical roofed corner turret. Round the corner in CASTLE STREET the former Star Inn, of *c.* 1810, with an oculus in its centre pediment and, opposite, a run of mostly two-storey houses of the same period.

Further along High Street, climbing uphill, some late C20 infill, Nos. 56–62, in brick and harl, and the more successful Nos. 64–66 of 1982–4 by *John S. McMillan* for Kyle and Carrick District Council, in yellow brick with strong vertical emphases. On the other side, the BANK OF SCOTLAND, dated 1875 on the rainwater heads but clearly early C19. The two bays to the l. are more widely spaced than the three to the r., suggesting two houses were given a unified appearance for the bank in 1875. Round-headed doorpiece with a simple early C19 fanlight. The late C19 Nos. 71–73 has two shallow oriels enlivened by ball-headed finials. The central wall-head stack has a carved panel depicting a plough. At the junction with School Vennel, No. 82, a well-restored three-storey harled late C18 house with a two-bay gable to the High Street, and a three-bay return to School Vennel; polished dressings and a panelled chimneystack. In SCHOOL VENNEL, No. 2, also three bays, harled and of *c.* 1800. On the other corner with School Vennel, No. 84 High Street is a striking, if ugly, late C19 commercial block with a three-bay front façade, prominent red stone pilasters and eaves course, and an exposed stone return elevation; Nos. 92–94 are a late C19 display of Baronial red sandstone crowstepped gables. The High Street canyon ends on this side with the smart Italian palazzo of the ROYAL BANK OF SCOTLAND (No. 2 Whitehall) of 1857 by *Peddie & Kinnear*. Round-headed central moulded doorpiece with pilasters, with flanking paired round-headed windows with pilasters, and similar first-floor windows.

CASSILLIS STREET runs in the other direction from the Castle towards the former parish church (*see* Churches and Cemeteries, above), and was presumably laid out contemporaneously with the church, i.e. *c.* 1808. On the l. (NW) side, there is now an almost continuous run of two-storey stone-faced properties as far as the church, which despite insensitive alterations and neglect, provides townscape of great quality for the visitor approaching from Ayr. Nos. 16–18 are an unspoilt pair of smart Late Georgian two-storey houses, each of five bays, and linked by a basket-arched pend with a Venetian window above. Each house has a central door and fanlight, and twelve-pane glazing. The upper windows at No. 18 have miniature wrought-iron balconies.

Before Cassillis Road begins, ST CUTHBERT'S ROAD turns SE; here is ST CUTHBERT'S PLACE, dramatic housing of

1997–9 by *Wren Rutherford* for the Carrick Housing Association on the site of the St Cuthbert's Shoe Factory. The prow
– no other word seems appropriate – is sharply pointed with
big windows and a balcony, below a steeply pitched roof.
Harled, like the remainder of the development, where motifs
such as the corner windows recur. Further down, KIRKLAND
STREET crosses. This was part of the medieval route through
Maybole, though nothing remains of that period. A few late
C18 cottages, and amongst them, Nos. 8–10, painted stone
two-storey houses of *c.* 1840, with a pair of round-headed
windows on the first floor. In VICARLANDS, ten *Tarran* pre-fab
houses of 1947 and, here and in KIRKMICHAEL ROAD, early
astylar local authority houses by *J. K. Hunter*, 1919–22.

Finally, the area on the hillside above High Street and 'ahint the
station', where, in the late C19 and early C20, to have a house
was a sign of wealth, privilege and position. Although no longer
so exclusive, it still contains the best domestic architecture in
the town, much of it of a surprisingly high quality. Between
the Castle and the railway line, in BARNS TERRACE, is
LISMORE, a good harled Arts and Crafts house of *c.* 1900 with
a full-height pentagonal bay, and a semicircular bay on the side
gable. BARNS HOUSE is an earlier villa, of *c.* 1820, of three
neat, broad bays in warm brown stone, with scrolled skews and
an entrance with a cavetto reveal. In CULZEAN ROAD to the
w, on the l., WELLPARK (No. 19), of *c.* 1840, a three-bay ashlar
house in its own grounds, with a hipped roof, and a ground-
floor bay to the l. Culzean Road continues across the line and
w of the station; here the late C19 villas are built above the
railway, enjoying views across the valley. Of particular note are
KINCRAIG (No. 40), crowstepped red sandstone Baronial with
a conical entrance tower and rope moulding to the entrance;
Nos. 56–58, of *c.* 1900, rocky red sandstone, with paired round-
headed doors, and possibly by *William Cowie*; HOMELEA (No.
62), hipped, with exposed rafter ends, and ground-floor bays
to l. and r.; CARGILL VILLA (No. 64), dated 1899, gently and
asymmetrically Arts and Crafts, especially the recessed r.
entrance bay; and finally, DELCOMBE (No. 74), of 1891, with
a hipped roof, tall end stacks, and ground-floor bays l. and r.,
with tall solid parapets.

CARGILL ROAD runs e of the station above the railway, with
more good late C19 houses, including GREENLEA, with full-
height bays to l. and r., and the imposing and impressive
FAIRKNOWE NURSING HOME (No. 5). Of light brown ashlar,
with its front elevation dominated by a big bracketed balcony
over the entrance and the window to its r. The projecting l. bay
is gabled above a big semicircular two-storey balustraded bay
window. ASHGROVE lies uphill from the road, now surrounded
by later housing. It was built in 1888 for the shoe manufacturer,
James Gray, and combines Baronial and Jacobethan features.
The composition turns on the tall circular tower offset to the
r. in the asymmetrical front elevation. Above wall-head height
this breaks out into a boldly corbelled and castellated parapet,

from which rises a smaller stage with an aedicular window, a
frieze with initials and a conical roof. To the l. of the tower,
recessed entrance and tripartite window below a balustraded
balcony, to the r. a similar window and balcony. Upper-floor
windows with crowstepped gable-heads. On the l. return elevation a semicircular bay window and balustrade with a Jacobethan two-light window above. The architect is not recorded;
from 1897 the house was a children's home, the alterations for
which were designed by *Robert A. Bryden*.

To the w is GARDENROSE PATH, climbing steeply uphill. It
has two idiosyncratic but attractive white-harled early C20
houses, both built for members of the shoe manufacturing
Ramsay family. WARRISTON (No. 14) is the earlier, of *c*. 1910,
probably by *Thomas A. Jack*, and has a red ashlar bay to the l.,
and tall stacks rising from first-floor sill height culminating in
red stone heads and tall quirky caps. To the r., and set back, a
rear wing with a tall tapering stack and a small splayed oriel,
obviously influenced by Charles Rennie Mackintosh. ARD-
NA-COILE (No. 16), dated 1912, by *Thomas A. Jack*, has a
tile-hung panel on the l. bay, an entrance and two semicircular
windows under a big tile porch, and prominent stacks. These
have thin copes and clasping corner details, all in red stone.

66   ST JOHN'S COTTAGE, Kirkmichael Road. An exquisite small
villa of *c*. 1820, neatly built in ashlar. It is reproduced from a
design in Richard Elsam's *Essay on Rural Architecture* (1803),
which itself was 'a humble imitation' of Asgill House,
Richmond, London by Sir Robert Taylor (1757–8). It has a
two-storey spine with a full-height canted N end, a shallow
pitch roof, and single-storey flanks with monopitch roofs that
have pronounced eaves expressed as half-pediments butted up
to the central block. Tall ground-floor windows are set under
blind arches in the outer bays, and such arches also characterize the three-bay E front which has an umbrella-pattern
fanlight over its central recessed inner door. On the w front a
bold Nashian three-window bow. Projecting s, two diminutive
service wings around the rear court. Beyond the courtyard a
low carriage house and stable.

The interior plays games with geometry, cleverly deceiving
the eye into imagining the house is bigger than it really is. The
main rooms open from an oval inner hall, from which the
top-lit cantilevered stair, with a typical early C19 cast-iron
balustrade, rises to a horseshoe-plan landing serving the upper
rooms. There are four doors from the hall set in the curves, at
the NW into the w-facing DRAWING ROOM with the bow
window on its long wall and a simple marble chimneypiece; it
opens through a wide arch into an additional sitting room, a
later alteration. The DINING ROOM, through the hall's NE
door, has a bowed end within the canted elevation of the N
front. The chimneypiece has been moved from the wall dividing this room from the hall to the w wall. Various modest
alterations including a subtle extension into the rear court by
Ronald Alexander c. 1992.

WEST ENOCH, 1 km. W. Charming late C18 or early C19 farm-house of three bays with sashed windows in white-painted surrounds. Arched central window over the entrance. Steading to rear.

NETHER CULZEAN, 1.5 km. NE. Unusually smart *c.* 1800 U-plan, single storey farmhouse with dormers in the big piended roof, facing E. Central door with flanking tripartite windows, single windows in wide outer bays. Adjoining rear courtyard with arched entrance on the S, two cart arches to its r.. Rear W range of the court set into slope with gabled entrance at loft level on W; facing detached range with former byre and altered dwelling to W. Further detached range to S.

FORT, Kildoon Hill, 2.5 km. S. Iron Age, occupying the E end of the prominent ridge. It measures some 46 m. by 23 m. within a timber-laced wall that has been burnt and vitrified. There are also two outer ramparts with external ditches cutting across the spine of the ridge above the entrance on the WSW. Within its area, a MONUMENT to Sir Charles Fergusson of Kilkerran (†1849), erected in 1853. Tapering obelisk of channelled stone on a square plinth.

BALTERSAN CASTLE. *See* p. 180.
DRUMELLAN. *See* p. 294.

MEIGLE

2060

Barely there hamlet on the steep l. bank of the Skelmorlie Water.

Former CHAPEL. Dated 1876; made of mass concrete. Provided by the Miss Stewarts of Ashcraig (*see* below).

In the higher part of the hamlet two good later C20 houses, both maximizing the benefits of their position with their living rooms on the upper floor. One (TRAINARD) is of 1974, boarded over light brick, with asymmetrically arranged mono-pitch roofs; the other (MEIGLE HOUSE) is of *c.* 1975, by *Drew Forbes*, with an aggressively angular and overhanging boarded first floor, and a hipped roof.

ASHCRAIG, 0.4 km. S. Orderly pink stone marine villa of *c.* 1840, but with a castellated turret on the E front and a sharply real-ized ashlar N front, with bargeboards carved with scrolls and floral motifs, both of which look late C19. The N front presides over spacious formal gardens.

MANOR PARK. *See* p. 518.

MILLPORT *see* GREAT CUMBRAE

MINISHANT

3010

Small roadside hamlet, developed around a woollen waulking mill established in the late C18 by James Limond, its character partly eroded by large-scale late C20 and C21 residential development.

Former COATS MEMORIAL CHURCH, Main Road. 1877 by *D. Thomson & Turnbull* (*David Thomson*) for Sir Peter Coats of Auchendrane (q.v.) as a memorial to his wife. Bold Early French Gothic style in red sandstone. Tall bellcoted gable with a broad panel with colonettes, a big wheel window, and a gabled porch, which has a richly moulded pointed arch and flanking pairs of columns with stiff-leaf capitals, now gold-painted. Five-bay side elevations of tall lancets and buttresses. To the rear, with a prominent chimneystack, a domestic range, originally for a caretaker and a library and reading room. Church interior divided horizontally *c.* 2004.

The mill survives as the VILLAGE HALL, converted in 1925 by *James Carrick*. Two storeys and five bays, harled with dressed windows. MURE PLACE is an attractive *Ayr County Council* development begun in the late 1930s, and finished in the 1950s: mostly timber semi-detached cottages, with shingle facings. Here, too, the WAR MEMORIAL, an Aberdeen granite Celtic cross of 1920 by *Hugh McLachlan* of Ayr.

MONKWOOD BRIDGE, 1 km. N, across the Doon. Stone, with vermiculated masonry and rustic keystones to the wide single arch. Plaques on either side give the date, 1798, and builders, *John and James Rutherford*.

FINGERPOST, 2.2 km. S, at the junction of the roads to Ayr, Kirkmichael, Maybole and Dalrymple. Cast-iron, probably early C20, and among the best-preserved of the small number of these in Carrick, despite the loss of two arms.

KNOCKDON, 2 km. SW. Facing the road, a symmetrical farm-house, of five bays and two storeys. But its rubble-built ground floor shows its single-storey origins, the red ashlar upper storey added *c.* 1869 when the farm was expanded into a large indus-trial farmstead. Rendered margins and pilastered doorpiece of the same date. To its rear, the former steading probably of 1818–19 when work was carried out for the Grange (later Knockdon) estate. E of this, two courtyards, the E dated 1869, of red sandstone byres, stables, farm workers' accommodation and a low range including a Sunday School room. Granite arched cart bays under a granary with neat granite ventilation holes. To the N a grey-harled U-plan STABLE COURT, 1937 by *Allan Stevenson & Cassels*, with an octagonal bellcast-roofed doocot on the ridge of the two-storey house. Now mainly domestic.

AUCHENDRANE. *See* p. 106.
GRANGE HOUSE. *See* p. 354.
MONKWOOD. *See* p. 544.
OTTERDEN. *See* p. 567.
SAUCHRIE. *See* p. 606.

MONK CASTLE

2 km. s of Dalry

Ruins of a late C16 or early C17 T-plan laird's house, now virtually adjoining a C20 single-storey house, for which it provides a dramatic garden folly. Built on lands which formerly belonged to Kilwinning Abbey. The surrounding site suggests earlier vanished buildings. The outline plan is a mirror image of Crosbie Tower (q.v.), and may have influenced the latter. Substantially altered at various times, it is now a two-and-a-half-storey roofless shell surviving to wall-head height with crowstepped gables. Pinned rubble walls with dressed quoins; a few small rectangular windows with chamfered reveals and hooks for shutters survive at first floor. The remaining windows on the s elevation enlarged, probably in the mid C19 when the crowstepped dormerheads were added. Possibly at the same time the rear wall was radically altered to access an addition. Simple low, broad entrance in jamb with three pieces of inset C16 or C17 sculpture above, including a head and two creatures, possibly watchful dragons guarding the entrance (cf. Barholm Castle, Dumfries and Galloway). A gunloop guards the entrance. Above the door between first- and second-floor levels a square panel with moulded frame, like Blair (q.v.).

MONKCASTLE HOUSE

2.5 km. s of Dalry

The successor to Monk Castle (q.v.), erected *c.* 1810 by Alexander-William Miller who inherited the estate in 1802. A straightforward, rectangular-plan Neoclassical house with broad outer bays on the front acting like giant pilasters, and three narrower central bays. Two storeys above a raised basement, band courses at ground-floor level and ground- and first-floor sills, a modillion cornice and parapet, with a raised and fluted panel on the entrance front. The front elevation owes something to Robert Adam's unexecuted design for the centre block of Auchincruive (q.v.). Broad flying steps with decorative cast-iron railings. Paired, engaged, Roman Doric doorpiece. Three-bay return elevations and a plain five-bay rear elevation. An early C20 raised roof and three dominant dormer windows compromise this smart design. Inside there is a generous hall, leading to the staircase at the rear which rises from the basement to the first floor. The principal rooms flank the hall. Dining room with a bow end. Its plaster cornice includes an unusual Vitruvian scroll moulding with olive twigs filling the scrolls.

MONKREDDING HOUSE

3.3 km. NE of Kilwinning

The land was feued from the lay abbots of Kilwinning Priory by Thomas Nevin in 1532. The present house may contain part of a C16 tower. Now essentially a C17 laird's house with C19 and C20 additions. The initials of Nevin's grandson Thomas Nevin and the date 1602 appear in the NW gable, and those of his son Thomas with his wife Margaret Blair with the date 1638 appear in part of a dormerhead now resited high in the SW gable. They probably record the period when the house became L-plan. The long entrance front comprises two bays of this L-plan house, almost certainly originally with wall-head dormers, at the SW, distinguished from the three early C19 NW bays by smaller windows. Gabled porch by *Hugh Thomson*, 1905, when the swan-necked pediment, probably from an earlier doorcase, was moved to the NE wall of the new rear wing and the inscription 'Domine Deus Meus' ('O Lord my God') and the date added. This wing, projecting NW, makes a U-plan rear elevation with the circular stair-tower in the re-entrant angle of the C17 house. All these alterations are neatly united by white harl. The upper part of the stair-turret is much rebuilt and now has a small circular room at the top, possibly suggesting that the C17 house was a storey higher. There is a door at the foot of the stair in a simple chamfered moulding with small gunloop overlooking it, opening from the low vaulted room to its l., in the earliest part of the house. This wing has a square window set in three bands of roll moulding on the NE face, and an open pediment with the date 1602 in the gable now uncomfortably close to the skew and chimney-stack; it may have been a reused dormerhead. A late C20 addition links to a low service range.

MONKTON

The modest village, formerly at the junction of roads to Ayr, Irvine and Kilmarnock, now lies at the NE edge of Prestwick Airport. But for the noise of aircraft taking off and landing it is a scene of quiet domesticity.

MONKTON COMMUNITY CHURCH, Main Street. Built in 1845 as a Free Church School, a simple two-room cottage. Converted into a parish hall in 1890, and converted again in 2004, with a harled gabled elevation to the road. To the l. a canted corner bay and tower, while one window has a diagonal head. Bright wooden interiors. – STAINED GLASS. By *Moira Parker*, 2004: the central panel represents the place of Monkton and Scotland within the world, the flanking panels the land and the sea.

ST CUTHBERT, Main Street. Medieval. Disused since 1838 and now roofless. 14 m. by 6.1 m., with stone walls of 1.1 m. to 1.2 m., altered in 1788 by *William Andrew*, mason, who enclosed the churchyard in the same year. W window probably of this date. Gables with simple skews, and a post-Reformation E bellcote. Round-headed C13 S doorway originally with nook-shafts, of which the bell-shaped caps survive; simpler round-headed N doorway. The gabled post-Reformation (perhaps mid-C17) N wing, now a burial vault, has simple skews and square-headed windows. – Some early HEADSTONES in the churchyard, e.g. James Young of Tong, †1757, with Doric columns, a scrolled pediment and a much-worn angel at the base. Also a grand Doric MAUSOLEUM for William Weir of Adamton and Kildonan, †1913, perhaps by *James Miller* who worked for Weir elsewhere. It has recessed fluted corner columns, one surviving copper grille and lion-head masks in the entablature.

CARVICK WEBSTER MEMORIAL HALL. 1843, as a Free Church, converted 1874 and reconstructed 1928–9 by *W. R. Watson*. Gabled and harled with two lancets in the W gable and open timberwork eaves and a round-headed bellcote to the E. The S doors and the two diagonally placed square chimneystacks at the E corners are of 1874, the lower E extension, with red sandstone dressings, of 1928–9.

MONKTON PRIMARY SCHOOL, Station Road. 2007–8, by *Ryder HKS*. Large, its panelled exterior characterized by a sweeping overhang and a drum tower entrance. Typical of the schools built under the Private Finance Initiative.

WAR MEMORIAL, Main Street. 1920 by *Hugh McLachlan* of Ayr. A square Kemnay granite cenotaph.

DESCRIPTION

s of St Cuthbert's Church, in Main Street, the former MONKTON MANSE, 1820–2 by *William Gibson*, architect and mason; *John Bryden*, wright. A two-storey three-bay harled house with a central S porch which has curved splayed sides and a panelled pilastered doorcase. In the grounds, marching with the churchyard, a simple single-storey OFFICE RANGE, perhaps of 1806 by *Gibson*, with a pigeon house in the apex of its central pediment. Main Street, formerly the main road from Glasgow to Ayr, is then dramatically bisected by the main runway of Prestwick Airport (q.v.), but on the E side is the remarkable former PALACE OF ENGINEERING, originally designed by *Thomas Tait* (with *Launcelot H. Ross*, project architect) for the 1938 Empire Exhibition at Bellahouston Park, Glasgow, but moved here in 1940 for manufacture of aircraft by Scottish Aviation Ltd (*see* Prestwick Airport, p. 587). Built in three months, this was the largest of Tait's functional and temporary exhibition buildings, steel-framed with asbestos-cement sheet cladding. Six giant columns originally marked the entrance (replaced with doors in 1940). The curved pavilion to the l. has been subsumed in ancillary offices, while that to the r. survives. As the Palace was originally designed as a temporary building, the current manifestation, while being a powerful icon of the 1930s, has something of 'my grandfather's hammer' about it.

In MAIN STREET, N of the cross, on the l., the former Monkton School, refaced in 1911–12 by *J. & J. Armour*, with shouldered gables and two entrances, one with huge ball finials. Thereafter, single-storey cottages of *c.* 1800 on either side, with, on the r., No. 46, a classically detailed painted stone cottage of *c.* 1840, with a pilastered doorway and a lower wing to the l. In BAIRD ROAD, social housing by *Alistair Murdoch Partnership*, for the Carrick Housing Association, 2005–6, big monopitch blocks, their backs turned to the road, with windows placed symmetrically within each block, and prominent windows on the corners.

FAIRFIELD, 0.5 km. N. Fairfield House, *c.* 1800, was demolished *c.* 1964. A classical single-storey harled LODGE, of *c.* 1840, survives, with panelled GATEPIERS and a curved screen wall and railings.

MACRAE'S MONUMENT, 0.75 km. NE. 1748–50 by *John Swan* of Kilmaurs; restored 2000–1 by *Peter Drummond* of *ARP Lorimer Architects*. Classical monument on a square rusticated base; alcoves with shell-ornamented heads on each elevation. Corinthian corner columns, with urns above; stout obelisk. It sits on a prominent ridge, a position that emphasizes its striking quality. William Macrae, †1744, was the archetypal boy-made-good, rising from Ayrshire poverty to the Governorship of Madras. He also commissioned and paid for the statue of William of Orange in Glasgow. To the SW on the same ridge, the stump of an C18 WINDMILL, with a vaulted base and a conical slated roof.

MANOR PARK HOTEL, Kilmarnock Road, 0.5 km. NE. A grand white-harled Arts and Crafts house of *c.* 1896, with exposed brick chimneystacks, red sandstone dressings to the openings, tiled roofs and expansive timbered gables. Entrance elevation with two gables flanking a small canted bay, and the entrance in the l. gable; to the r., a big hipped bay. Panelled entrance hall.

MONKTONHEAD, 1.25 km. N. 1910–11 by *James Miller*. A large house in Miller's Shavian Old English style, with harled ground floors, tiled roofs, prominent brick chimneystacks, and one big applied timbered gable over the main entrance. Matching L-plan LODGE, now disjoined from the house by the adjacent dual carriageway. In the grounds a turreted DOOCOT, also coeval with the house.

TOWNHEAD FARM, 0.9 km. N. An early C19 three-bay two-storey farm, of coursed stone, with a pilastered central doorway. To the l., single-storey byre ranges and a circular THRESHING BARN.

MONKWOOD

1.3 km. NE of Minishant

A charming early–mid C18 small country house, one of a group of C18 houses that have picturesque settings by the Doon. Possibly built for George Hutchison of Monkwood, or his son. Rectangular in plan, of two storeys over a raised basement with a symmetrical façade, it is harled with angle margins and eaves band. Central door at the head of steps with a channelled architrave overlaid with a timber Doric pedimented doorpiece, similar timber architraves and pediments to the flanking windows intended to add grandeur. The lintels of the upper windows share the eaves band. A steep piended roof with stacks on the cross walls. Raised and fielded panelling to the window shutters.

MONTGREENAN HOUSE   3040
1.8 km. NNE of Benslie

Latterly a hotel. A classical mansion built in 1810–17 for Robert Glasgow, a successful West Indian merchant; no architect is known. Two storeys of finely droved ashlar over a channelled basement, with polished details to the moulded sill band, architraves and modillion cornice. At the three-bay centre of the entrance front, a Doric portico; the flanking bays then step back in stages to wider outer bays with broad panelled pilasters and blocking course over the eaves cornice; a detail that might suggest the hand of David Hamilton. Tall sash windows at ground floor with cornices on delicately elongated consoles. The syncopated rhythm of this front is unsettling but chiefly because two-bay early C20 additions, by *John Arthur* for Sir James Bell, have, despite the faithfulness of their details, exaggerated the horizontality. The nine-bay garden front, set proudly above terraces, is more harmonious, with its basement partly revealed by the fall of the land, and a full-height bow in the centre; the depth of the basement windows in the bow reminds one of Culzean (q.v.). The outer bays are defined by tall Doric pilasters, the whole united by a modillion eaves cornice with a balustrade above the bow and blocking course over the outer bays. Only the inserted roof dormers strike an incongruous note (mid C20). Cast-iron balustrade with anthemion detailing to the steps to the garden.

The early C19 rooms, laid out *enfilade* around the central top-lit stairwell, have particularly well-preserved woodwork and plasterwork. The ENTRANCE HALL has a shallow domed ceiling supported on arches with rosette and scrolled mouldings, fan details in the pendentives. In the STAIR HALL, the cantilevered well-stair rises to the attic with an oval top light set within a double-scroll-moulded frame with swags below the dome (*see* Ladyland House). Elegant balustrade with sinuous S-scrolled baluster interspersed with paired rods (*see* Auchincruive), balustraded galleries at first and attic level, the latter with Greek-key moulded plinth and a ramped mahogany handrail. The first-floor gallery has blind arcading. Along the garden front, the LIBRARY is lined with pilastered bookcases set under shallow arches with rosettes in the soffits, decorative cornice and large sunburst in an oval frame surrounds the ceiling rose; reeded white marble chimneypiece with rosettes, and similarly detailed brass register and grate. More crisply detailed plasterwork in the DRAWING ROOM (probably designed as the Dining Room) in the bowed centre, including a huge sunburst in a diamond panel with rosette-filled diamonds attached at each point. White marble chimneypiece, classically detailed with a central panel possibly of Diana with a dog, and elegant figures over the decorated pilasters. Finally, the SMALL DRAWING ROOM, similarly detailed. Linking the two rooms, a large Ionic-columned double doorcase probably inserted by Arthur who adopted the early C19 style in the N addition.

MONTGREENAN MAINS, E, has a segmental arch entrance with a wide pediment over and an upper storey with a pyramid roof. The former OFFICE COURT has a domed tower. LODGES. Contemporary with the house and smartly detailed with panelled pilasters at the outer ends of the elevations. Gatepiers with big anthemion caps and cast-iron spearhead railings.

MOSSIDE BRIDGE, carrying the drive to the former office court, is bizarrely decorated with stylized patterns of leaves, the voussoirs and keystone with thistles, and blank panels in the spandrels. Placed along the drives through the estate are elegantly carved C18 and C19 Ayrshire MILESTONES assembled by Sir James Bell in the early C20.

MOORPARK HOUSE *see* KILBIRNIE

MOSSBLOWN

3020

The Ayr Coal Co. began to exploit the coal on the Auchincruive and Enterkine estates in the late 1860s, and erected row housing for their colliers at Annbank (q.v.), Drumley and Mossblown. The latter two communities have coalesced into the present settlement, which consists largely of post-war *Ayr County Council* housing. Auchincruive colliery closed in 1959; its 1930s PIT-HEAD BATHS were well converted into a house in 2002–3.

ANNBANK PARISH CHURCH, Annbank Road. 1903 by *J. B. Wilson*. Simplified Gothic with lancet windows. Nave, S aisle and recessed SW entrance tower rising to a tiled pyramidal roof. Attractive cast-iron lamp bracket. Barrel-vaulted interior, with a W gallery above the vestibule, cusped details throughout, e.g. in the gallery front and the pulpit. – COMMUNION TABLE. Classical, with semi-fluted Ionic legs, brought in *c.* 1961 from elsewhere. – STAINED GLASS. E window, Truth, Justice and Mercy, by *J. T. Stewart* and *J. S. Melville* for *William Meikle & Sons*, 1903.

Former ANNBANK U.F. CHURCH, Annbank Road. 1901–2. The shouldered and buttressed gabled W front is topped by an openwork bellcote with a prominent finial.

ST ANN (R.C.), Annbank Road. 1898, extended in 1910 by *J. K. Hunter*. A resolutely harled structure, originally combining church, school and two-storey presbytery. Stone dressings to the windows, mostly single lancets. Plain plaster interiors.

ANNBANK PRIMARY SCHOOL, Annbank Road. 1902–3 by *John Eaglesham* to a conventional School Board plan; extended sympathetically in 1997–2000 by *Robert Potter & Partners* to incorporate previously free-standing additions. Symmetrical gabled front, with segregated entrances recessed to either side, and an attractive pyramidal ventilator. w-facing entrance elevation also gabled, but livelier, and this liveliness echoed in Potter's extension.

MOSSBLOWN AND DRUMLEY COMMUNITY CENTRE, Annbank Road. 1924–6 by *Allan Stevenson & Cassels*. The two-storey red sandstone façade, severely plain with a Free Style classical treatment to the pedimented entrance bay, masks a large harled and buttressed hall.

WAR MEMORIAL, Annbank Road. 1923; stylish but inconspicuously sited. A granite pillar on a stepped base and plinth. At the head, recessed panels on two sides, decorated with incised swords with bas-relief hilts.

DRUMLEY HOUSE, 0.9 km. NW. A villa begun *c.* 1800 by Captain Robert Davidson, an Ayr merchant, who purchased the estate in 1791. Symmetrical, of three bays, and two storeys above a basement, of local creamy sandstone, with a canted bay on the E front and a semicircular rear projection. Now it is extended N and S, *c.* 1900, in red sandstone. Early C20 classically detailed porch. N are grey brick and harled additions of 1971–2, when the house was a school.

AFTON LODGE, 1.5 km. NE. Smart two-storey-and-basement villa (now flats) built *c.* 1790 for Mrs Catherine Stewart, a patron of Burns. In a style derived from Robert Adam and of a type popular among the smaller Ayrshire landowners in the late C18 (*see* Drumley House, above). Unfortunately completely dwarfed by early C20 additions by *Allan Stevenson*. Full-height canted bay in the centre of the entrance front clasped by substantial chimneystacks and rising above the eaves. On the garden front it is echoed by a deeply projecting bowed bay with three windows to each floor. Big pilastered and pedimented porch, spanning the basement area, added in 1905 at the same time as the wings were lengthened. The NW wing was greatly enlarged in 1919 when the fulsome five-window canted bay was pushed out on the garden front.

MUIRKIRK

6020

Parochial centre, originally a chapel of ease to Mauchline until the 1630s, and from the late C18 to the later C20 an industrial village. The Muirkirk Iron Co. established its first furnace in 1787; tar works were opened by the Earl of Dundonald and John Loudon McAdam. By 1795 Sir William Forbes could write that 'long before I saw the place itself, it was distinctly to be markt from the immense volume of smoke rising in the air – from the iron forges.'

Former EVANGELICAL UNION CHURCH, Glasgow Road. Now
a house. Gothic, of 1893–4 by *John Murdoch*. Red sandstone s
front with a two-light window in the gable, set back within a
pointed and inscribed panel. Below this four small and narrow
lancets; uncomplicated bellcote to l.

Former FREE CHURCH, Glasgow Road. 1844–5, enlarged in
1891–2 by *William Tennant* of Glasgow with a broad grey ashlar
front (E) gable and a substantial forework consisting of a
central porch flanked by gabled pavilions with single tall
round-headed windows. Disused. To the r., the former MANSE
of 1851, also grey ashlar, with a bracketed doorpiece and
painted dressings, eaves course and thin corner pilasters.

24 MUIRKIRK PARISH CHURCH, Kirk Green. 1812–14, design by
William Stark, but completed to plans by *Thomas Smith*. A
straightforward brown ashlar Georgian preaching box similar
to Stark's church at Saline (Fife, 1808–10), but with a squat
square crenellated tower in the centre of the three-bay s front
providing a rather menacing appearance. Two-storey elevation
with buttresses continuing into a solid stone parapet on the
front. Six-bay side elevations, with flat buttresses and two tiers
of four-centred windows within deep cavetto reveals. Two
prominent cast-iron ridge ventilators, and a three-light N
window. Long narrow galleried interior, almost wholly of
1952–4 when the church was restored by *Harry S. McNair*,
after a fire. Plaster walls and shallow vaulted roof. The wide
gallery has a plain panelled wooden front and is supported on
locally made cast-iron columns, now enclosed within wooden
'pillars'. Broad pointed chancel arch, painted to resemble
stone; a simple panelled REREDOS and octagonal PULPIT. –
STAINED GLASS. Richly coloured three-light Good Shepherd,
with SS Peter and John to either side, formerly at the Mission
Church at Kames (*R. S. Ingram*, 1901–4, demolished *c.* 1955);
it looks like the work of *Stephen Adam*.

Several good early HEADSTONES in the churchyard including some well-worn flat stones from the C17 and a number
from the C18, mostly decorative with scrolls and cross-bones,
e.g. that erected in 1771 to the Covenanter John Smith (†1685),
and that of John Gibb, *c.* 1800, with well-carved urn and swags.
One unusual stone is that locally believed to commemorate a
pair of children savaged by wildcats, *c.* 1755. The crude but
effective carving shows two figures, bare legged and with what
may well be school bags; above each what may be an Ionic
capital, and between these, the face of a cat. In the SE corner
of the churchyard, an inscribed memorial to local Covenanters,
brought here from Glenbuck Church (1881–2 by *McDerment
& Murdoch* of Ayr, dem.).

ST THOMAS (R.C.), Wellwood Street. 1905–6 by *J. Montgomerie
Pearson*. Simple gabled red sandstone chapel with a gabled
porch, a three-light window on the front (s) elevation, and a
tall ridge ventilator. Shallow transept to the l., and apsidal
chancel. Equally simple INTERIOR of plastered walls and
boarded barrel-vault roofs. In the E wall a now blocked choir

loft, with openings either side of the chancel arch; a simple lancet to the chancel, an arcade in the nave, its columns painted to resemble marble. The loft is reached by an exterior spiral cast-iron stair. To the E is attached the undemonstrative PRES-BYTERY of 1882 by *R. S. Ingram*.

Its predecessor of 1856 is now the CHURCH HALL in Kirk Green. Its appearance largely due to extensions of 1882 by *R. S. Ingram*, and a dwarfing Fyfestone addition of 1975.

MUIRKIRK CEMETERY, Glasgow Road. Two monuments of particular interest. Imposing COVENANTERS' MONUMENT of 1887, a 7-m.-high obelisk of Dunmore (Stirlingshire) sandstone on a tall square plinth. By *Thomas Lyon*, executed by *Matthew Muir*. The plinth has finely carved pediments and base panels, between them granite panels with gilt inscriptions. Equally visible, s of the central path, MONUMENT to John Hunter of Glenapp (q.v.) (†1886); classical triptych of finely bedded grey ashlar, the central panel between paired Ionic columns and beneath a broken pediment, through which rises a pedimented panel with a coat of arms.

Former KAMES INSTITUTE, Furnace Road. 1902–4 by *R. S. Ingram*. Single storey of red sandstone, completely unbalanced by the colossal astylar square clock tower under a pyramidal roof with triangular finials.

WAR MEMORIAL, Smallburn Road. 1922 by *J. Montgomerie Pearson*. It forms the entrance to the public park. Classical red sandstone arch a broken pediment, lower side walls for memorials and short return walls with rhomboidal finials. Within its enclosure is the Glenbuck WAR MEMORIAL, an irregularly shaped piece of granite carved with a furled flag and appropriate inscriptions.

HERITAGE PARK, Smallburn Road/Glasgow Road. 2004 by *Kirti-Mandur*. – MONUMENT to the town's miners and a cheerful figurative sculpted bronze fence, all made by *Black Isle Bronze Ltd*, of Nairn.

AULDHOUSEBURN, 1.4 km. SE. Large farmhouse or small mansion of 1854 in a pared-down gabled Burnian idiom. Detached farm offices to the rear of the same date and style.

AIRDS MOSS, 5 km. W, is a tract of boggy and unforgiving moorland. An OBELISK of 1832 and an early C18 flat stone record the death here in 1680 of the Rev. Richard Cameron and other Covenanters, 'in an encounter with the Bloody enemies of truth and godliness'.

NEILSHILL HOUSE

4020

2.25 km. SW of Tarbolton

From a distance a conventional late C19 Italianate villa built of bull-nosed red Mauchline sandstone. On closer acquaintance it is a surprise to find that it wears Moorish dress, yet it is as far from any understanding of Moorish architecture as dried figs are from fresh ones. Who commissioned and executed this curious conceit? It is an exercise in asymmetry given unity by the keyhole windows, in a variety of sizes, used singly, paired or, in the Prospect Room of the tower in triplicate, and all with casements and fixed horseshoe-shaped glazing above. The off-centre entrance bay is the most highly decorated. A simply pilastered doorcase is set within a giant keyhole frame with a scalloped head, and the arch filled with chequered masonry. All this is in ashlar which continues into the first floor where a small window is framed by pilastered panels. The entrance range is the pivotal part of the composition, with a lower section to the N joining the plainer service court, to the S it rises up to emphasize the Dining Room and Drawing Room above, with beyond and set back the Italianate tower which at ground and first-floor levels provides a well-lit recess to each of the main rooms. The first-floor Drawing Room is further emphasized with floor-length windows and cast-iron balconies in a geometric pattern with stylized flower heads in the Aesthetic manner.

The interior is a *tour de force* of the decorator's art and is a remarkable survival (sensitively conserved and retouched in 2005 by *Robert Howie & Son*). No doubt much derives from pattern books such as Owen Jones's *The Grammar of Ornament* (1856) or is inspired by the 1870s enthusiasm for this style (e.g. Lord Leighton's Arab Hall, London, of 1877–9). The ENTRANCE HALL is dominated by tall arched doors all set in keyhole frames, and the keyhole detailing continued in the upper panels of the doors. In the centre of the star-patterned polychrome tiled floor there is a five-sided tiled pedestal with an elaborate scalloped Moorish arcade symbolizing a fountain, rather less useful in the Scottish climate than the colourfully tiled arched and scalloped chimneypiece to its r. The coloured glass in the window takes up the theme of the tiled floor. The walls to dado height are covered with a hard lincrusta-type material with a low-relief geometric pattern coloured in tones of brown, beige and blue and imitating tilework. Above the dado the walls are covered with an embossed paper. The only discordant element of the hall is the STAIR with cast-iron fretwork balusters of a type found in many late C19 houses. The decorative detailing continues on the top-lit landing.

Off the hall to the l. is the MORNING ROOM, the only one of the public rooms to break with the Moorish theme. The *trompe l'œil* painted ceiling imitating geometric ribbed plasterwork, with scallop shells and four panels representing the arts, is in a French manner. Next to it the DINING ROOM, with a boldly detailed geometric-patterned ceiling looking like a design for a tile floor. The walls have lost their original finish but the glass in the arched window heads survives with portraits of worthies set in coloured geometric-patterned glass. On the chimney wall three big Moorish-arched panels frame two doors and the suave polished black marble arched chimneypiece with an onion-like topknot; set into it, an arched grate and the tiled inset with a frieze of *de Morgan* tiles and glazed pink tiles imitating bricks. At the head of the stairs the DRAWING ROOM, a mirror image of the dining room but with a grey-veined chimneypiece and all the surfaces decorated with intricate patterns and a frieze, like frosted icing, full of symbols and picked out in gold leaf. Here the ceiling design is very delicate, reminiscent of a most elaborate fretwork pattern. Somewhat incongruously the arched window heads are filled with sporting cherubs partaking in golf, curling, archery etc.

NETHER AUCHENDRANE   3010
2 km. SE of Alloway

A complex house incorporating the remains of a C16 tower of the Blairs, which was later in the possession of the Cathcarts. Added to progressively from the C17 to the late C20, when it was a care home; the uncoordinated collision of these additions only partly concealed by unifying white harl. The present owner is attempting to regain some order.

The entrance (N) front has the C16 tower embedded behind the later parts but partly visible in the centre. The big pilastered porch and the crenellated lobby (moved forward to accommodate a lift shaft in the later C20) and the uncomfortably bulky tower to its r. were added in the 1890s. To the l. a narrow double-pile range of *c.* 1850, with paired crowstepped gables and apex stacks, but very restrained. W of the 1890s tower, aligned N–S, is a long, much altered, gabled range of *c.* 1800 which possibly incorporates earlier material. Further W much C20 building. If anything the S elevation is even less coherent. Here the tower house has been brutally altered, all that survives is the wall above its first floor and the corbelled, conical-roofed turret at the SE angle. Wings of varying date flank the tower, that on the r. of the 1870s and quite smart but marred by heightening on its S elevation in the C20.

Inside, through the prettily plastered lobby, the inner hall with a boxy dentilled cornice and pomegranate band on the ceiling leads to the big timber scale-and-platt stair (*c.* 1850); a tight circular stone cantilevered stair, possibly on the site of a stair wing to the C16 tower at its NE angle. Cottier-like glass with the Cathcart crest in a window lighting this stair.

NEW CUMNOCK   6010

Large and straggling village, set in rolling moorland close to the border with Dumfriesshire. It developed as the area became increasingly industrial during the late C19, with coal mining pre-eminent. Now only extensive opencast mining remains.

Former ARTHUR MEMORIAL U.F. CHURCH, Castlehill. Free
Gothic of 1911–13, by *W. Beddoes Rees* of Cardiff.* On a raised
site, with octagonal SE tower and shallow W transepts. The
gabled E front has a five-light window, its tracery handled in
an attractive flowing manner, with Arts and Crafts details. The
tower has narrow square-headed windows in carved cusped
heads, bell-openings separated by columns, a battlemented
parapet and a squat slated spire. Side windows with swirling
tracery. Plainer offices piled up against the W elevation, culminating in a multi-gabled, steeply canted chancel projection.

NEW CUMNOCK BAPTIST CHURCH, Lanehead Terrace. 1965–6
by *Robert B. Rankin* of Ayr. Harled and slated, with regularly
spaced windows on the rear elevation, asymmetrically placed
smaller windows to the front, with a stone-faced entrance bay
to the r., under a monopitched roof. Simple interior, with a
pitched boarded roof, and plaster walls.

Former NEW CUMNOCK PARISH CHURCH, off Castle. Built in
1657 following the granting of parochial status in 1650. Ruinous,
and largely ivy-clad, T-plan. Gothic survival. When whole, it
would have resembled Ayr Auld Kirk (q.v.). The long S elevation has four square-headed windows, with internal segmental
heads. A window in the W gable, a door and window above in
the E gable, and a cusped window in the gable of the N wing.
A two-light window in the NW wall and a single window in the
W wall of the wing. What appears to be the remains of a fireplace, presumably for a laird's loft, in the N wing, and also a
recess; another recess in the middle of the S wall. In the large
stone-walled churchyard (walls of 1801–2), some good lettered
C18 HEADSTONES, and a pedimented MEMORIAL to the
Hyslops of Blackcraig, early C19, with a well-carved urn
and swags.

NEW CUMNOCK PARISH CHURCH, Castle. Castellated Gothic
of 1831–3 by *James Ingram*; his first major work. The mason
was *David Reid*. Hipped rectangle with a polished ashlar E front
dominated by a central buttressed projecting tower with angle
pinnacles and stages separated by bold string courses. Tall
pointed-arch windows of two lights to the front, side and rear
elevations, all with Y-tracery. Clasping octagonal buttresses at
the angles with battlemented pinnacle heads. The low vestry
has one surviving battlemented pinnacle. Good decorative
glass and brass door fittings to the vestibule, all of *c.* 1900. The
galleried interior has plaster walls and a flat plaster ceiling, with
a delicate panelled wooden gallery front, curved at the angles
and bowed in the centre, supported on quatrefoil cast-iron
columns. The galleries are pulled back from the windows in
semicircular reveals (*see* also St Andrew's and St Marnock's,
Kilmarnock). – Excellent original dark oak PULPIT AND
SOUNDING-BOARD, with a curved panelled front, and two
curving stairs with wrought-iron handrails; the sounding-board

---

* The commission appears to be unrelated to the Cardiff connections of the Bute
family, the major landowners at the time.

is octagonal, surmounted by foliage and a pineapple. Original austere upright PEWS. – STAINED GLASS in the W windows, by unknown artists. Faith, Hope and Charity of *c.* 1900, with strong colours and bold images; the fourth light a naturalistic-ally portrayed war memorial of *c.* 1950.

Dull harled HALLS of 1952–6 by *Gabriel Steel* behind. – WAR MEMORIAL. Celtic cross of 1926, inscribed 'Our Heroes and Gentlemen', formerly at the Arthur Memorial Church (*see* above).

AFTON CEMETERY, Afton Road, 1 km. S. Stone-walled enclos-ure of 1901 by *Allan Stevenson*; extended in brick *c.* 1955. In a beautiful rural setting. – WAR MEMORIAL of 1919–21 by *Sir J. J. Burnet*. A stout Northumberland freestone cenotaph, with the names of the fallen carved on all sides, rising from two broad steps and a bevelled base.

NEW CUMNOCK PRIMARY SCHOOL, Castle. 1875 by *J. & R. S. Ingram*. Conventional, if large, single-storey grey sandstone Board School with three gabled bays, asymmetrically disposed. These bays have grouped pointed windows with smaller cusped windows in the panel above, all under tall pointed moulds. To the rear a big Neo-Georgian addition of 1931–4 by *William Reid*, County Architect.*

NEW CUMNOCK TOWN HALL, Castle. Scots Renaissance of 1888–9 by *Allan Stevenson* in red sandstone. Big gable with a semicircular pediment in the apex, and a tall three-light window with a broad panelled transom under a triangular pediment. Entrance under an open pediment with finial and blank motto ribbon, with a recessed bay to the l., with a shaped gable, but now with a dull extension in front. To the N side elevation, a series of stepped flying buttresses.

DESCRIPTION. The village stretches for a kilometre or so, between Pathhead (N) and Afton Bridgend (S), settlements that grew up close to the bridges over the Nith and the Afton. NITH BRIDGE is of 1863 by *James Campbell*, with three arches, low parapets and channelled voussoirs. Otherwise there is little that calls for individual comment. Midway along CASTLE, on the W side, STATUE of Burns (*Richard Price*, 2010), and at its S end, ST BLANES, of *c.* 1880, hip-roofed, with raised quoins and tall stacks on the S. On the E side, beyond the school, a house of *c.* 1860, L-plan, with stepped gables, triangular skewputts, a penticed porch and good gatepiers with triangular pediments. Opposite, OLD MILL FARM, early C19 with painted polished dressings and a round-ended single-storey steading to the l. Further E, beyond the Afton, is AFTON COURT, well-judged sheltered housing of 1981–2 by *Roy Maitland* for Cumnock & Doon Valley District Council. Neo-vernacular.

EAST POLQUHIRTER, 2 km. E. Courtyard farm of *c.* 1820, its harled two-storey farmhouse flanked by projecting gabled steadings.

*Reconstruction and extension began in 2011, for East Ayrshire Council.

AFTON RESERVOIR, 9 km. S. 1935–9 by *William Reid*, County
Architect (engineers, *Babtie, Shaw & Morton*). A large concrete
DAM fills the valley, the grassed downstream face given sculptural grace by flights of stairs that ascend crab-like. These, the
sluices, gatehouse and other buildings are all finished in a
muscular Scots Baronial that harmonizes with the Highland-
like setting. Large commemorative bronze plaque and (disused)
stone and cast-iron fountain.

NEWARK CASTLE

3010

0.8 km. SW of Alloway

An imposing castle that began as a small tower *c.* 1520, built for
the Kennedys of Bargany, with an extension in similar vein probably of late C16 date. Additions were made by *David Cousin* in
1848–9 to create a Baronial-style house for the Marquis of Ailsa,
with further sizeable enhancements, by *James Miller* in 1907–8
for Archibald Walker, respecting the verticality of the original
tower.

At the E end is the earliest tower, imposing out of all proportion
to its actual height, being raised up on a natural outcrop of
rock, protected by a moat (filled in the mid C19) and with
commanding views. It is almost square (30 m. by 25.5 m.) and
rises vertically through four storeys to a simply corbelled wall-
walk with angle rounds projected on three tiered corbels,
similar to those on the oriel at Baltersan (q.v.). A big crowstepped dormer set in the steep gabled roof on the W elevation,

Newark Castle.
Etching by J. Clerk of Eldin, 1776

a bold outlook point, has gone. The extension, late C16, mirrors the first tower, with the addition of a lower storey because of the fall in the land, but without the wall-walk and bartizans; the SW angle round from the first tower was removed at this time but leaving the corbels, from which it was re-created (1980s?). Various windows in this block have been enlarged in the C20. All this is now harled.

Cousin's self-confident addition wraps round the towers and it is likely that material from a modestly scaled C17 range is concealed within this addition. Indeed one has to wonder whether the projecting and corbelled entrance block is C17 remodelled by Cousin, because the scale bears little relationship to the new build. The door is set into a moulded architrave with a cornice, and the Ailsa arms and emblems above. This extension, built in neatly coursed masonry, provides a much needed entrance (presumably made possible by draining the moat) and includes a library, a drawing room and a dining room. The W and S elevations of the drawing room make a bold Baronial statement with all the accoutrements: crowstepped gables, candle-snuffer turrets, finialled wall-head dormers, strapwork pediments to the windows, a canted bay supported by giant console brackets, balustraded windows. To its N the dining room elevation is more restrained but has an anchoring round turret with a huge candle-snuffer roof at the NW angle. Miller's wing is bland, making up in size for what it lacks in finesse and using his characteristic mullion-and-transom windows and widely spaced balusters to the roof parapets. It continues the asymmetry of Cousin's range, the linking bay with a curved angle returning into the doorstopper end block which is corbelled out over the principal floor. A pronounced corbelled chimney-breast gives character to the end bay.

The entrance leads to a wide straight flight of steps with light oak openwork balusters all under a tunnel vault, the vault remodelled by Miller. A spine corridor providing access to the public rooms links from the old tower, where a new newel stair was installed, to Miller's inner hall, beyond which he provided a smoking room and billiard room. Within the first tower there is a newel stair rising the full height within the NW angle. A barrel-vaulted ground floor, now a dining room, and above, the hall with two rooms each in the floors above. These rooms have deep-set windows, decorative cornicing and C18, C19 and C20 details. Of the 1848–9 work the DRAWING ROOM is a *tour de force* of plaster decoration with very deep relief-work in the cornicing and elaborate Jacobean-style detailing to the ceiling, all by *John Ramage & Son*. On the N wall a wonderfully frothy Louis XV-style caramel-coloured marble chimneypiece by *Wallace & Whyte*. The more restrained DINING ROOM still has good plasterwork, although the Adamesque chimneypiece may be imported or possibly reused from a room used by the Kennedys in the C18, when to escape the building works at Culzean they retreated to Newark. Adam does appear to have been consulted on Newark. Of Miller's rooms the HALL is the most elaborate. It has a barrelled plaster ceiling using the same motifs as for the stair tunnel. It is three-quarter panelled with stained wood and a very handsome burr walnut chimneypiece.

NEWMILNS

5030

A gem of a town in a narrow valley on both banks of the River Irvine. It was made a Burgh of Barony in 1490/1 for the Campbells of Loudoun, hereditary sheriffs of the county. The parish centre had been further downstream (*see* Loudoun Old Kirk, p. 514) but this settlement grew up around the mill, and from 1738 had the new parish church. In the late C18 it became important for weaving, and the early C19 planned settlement on the S bank of the river is associated with that, but like Darvel it also developed, and retains, a machine lace industry. It is only recently that lace curtains in the town's windows have ceased to be ubiquitous. As in Beith (q.v.), its decaying townscapes were revitalized by a Townscape Heritage Initiative in the early years of this century, under the supervision of *Page & Park*. Several old buildings have been brought back into use, and new developments created to add life and character to the town.

CHURCHES AND CEMETERY

LOUDOUN PARISH CHURCH, Main Street. Classical of 1844–5 by *James Ingram* of Kilmarnock; rebuilt internally 1897–8. Square, stone-built, with a tower above the main entrance. Dressed ashlar front elevation symmetrical about a four-stage tower, with an octagonal bell-stage with round-headed openings, and an octagonal spire. Entrance in a simple aedicule, below a round-headed window, all within a round-headed overarch; the flanking bays have windows in slight round-headed recesses. Three-bay exposed rubble side elevations, and a full-height rear projection, with two tall round-headed blind windows, of 1897–8. Plastered and galleried interior, with a flat ceiling and over-sized sunburst in the centre. The panelled gallery front is supported on plain stone pillars. – Much STAINED GLASS including a Good Shepherd of *c.* 1928 by *G. Maile & Son* and, in the E gallery, two characteristic windows of 1975 and 1976 by *Gordon Webster*. – Small square stone-walled CHURCHYARD, with, in the SW corner, a neat early C19 house in tooled ashlar.
LOUDOUN PARISH CHURCH HALLS, East Strand. Dated 1934, a large complex in ochre harl with a brick base and dressings. The main elevation of three bays and two storeys.
NEWMILNS NEW CEMETERY, Dalwhatswood Road. 1885 by *Charles Reid* of Kilmarnock. Stone-walled enclosure on a high site overlooking the town.

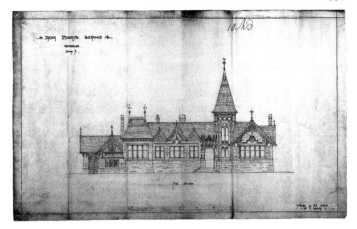

Newmilns, Lady Flora's Institute.
Original proposals by F. T. Pilkington, 1873

PUBLIC BUILDINGS

Former LADY FLORA'S INSTITUTE, Main Street. Free Gothic of 1873–7 by *F. T. Pilkington* with plenty of character but scaled back from his original propoals. Built as a school for girls, the gift of the Marquess and Marchioness of Bute.* The main elevation, of three gabled bays with fleur-de-lis heads, is set back at an angle to the street. Square-headed windows, an inscription panel with floral scroll and, to the r., an advanced entrance bay with a four-light window, with stone mullions and transoms. The porch has its own gablet, and a squat Peterhead granite column. Large but complementary extension to the rear by *Robert Potter & Partners* of Ayr, 1987–90 as part of conversion into sheltered housing. – In front, WAR MEMORIAL of 1922 by *Scott & Rae* of Glasgow. A watchful soldier, in the uniform of the county regiment, the Royal Scots Fusiliers, rests on his rifle.

LIBRARY, Craigview Road. 1931–2, by *Gabriel Steel*, of *James Hay & Steel*. Five bays and two storeys of red brick, with a central single-storey porch and stone moulded door frame with coat-of-arms keystone.

MORTON HALL, Main Street. Free Scots Renaissance of 1896–7 by *Arthur Harrison* of Birmingham, given by William Morton, a native of Newmilns who made his fortune as a shoe manu-facturer in Birmingham. Five-bay gable-ended hall, with a projecting entrance porch to the l., and a lower gabled exten-sion to r. Ballochmyle red sandstone. The entrance has two

* The Marchioness was a Campbell of Loudoun and the institute named for her relative Lady Flora Hastings (†1839) (*see* Loudoun Old Kirk, p. 514).

finial-headed pilasters and a crowstepped gable; the doorpiece
has a three-light segmental-headed fanlight and an urn-capped
decorative panel above. Two-light segmental-headed windows,
under square-headed moulding, those in the first and fourth
bays (from the l.) taller, beneath crowstepped gablets and
flanked by pyramid-headed buttresses. Slated roof, with a
central decorative copper ventilator. The main hall has a sturdy
open roof, rising from moulded stone corbels, with decorative
wooden pendants, brackets, and balusters.

NEWMILNS POST OFFICE, Brown Street. 1909 by *John Macintosh*. Red sandstone. Two-storey elevation to Brown Street,
with a pedimented entrance to r., a shell-headed dormer to far
l., and a central canted oriel.

TOWN HOUSE, Main Street. Dated 1739 on its weathervane.
Crowstepped Toytown-scaled Tolbooth of painted rubble, with
a slate roof. On the main (E) elevation a double flight of stone
steps, with railings; pilastered and pedimented first-floor
entrance flanked by round-headed windows. A rectangular
bellcote above with Doric columns and an ogival roof. The N
elevation has two square-headed windows in the upper floor,
and an off-centre doorway below.

NEWMILNS TOWER
Castle Street

47   Small, rubble-stone tower house, finished in thin lime plaster.
Probably of *c.* 1525, a property of the Campbells of Loudoun;
restored to domestic use 1992–7 by *Page & Park* for the
Strathclyde Building Preservation Trust. Round-headed
ground-floor S entrance with a rectangular recessed panel
above. Two further floors, with string courses to the S only,
each with a large window, and narrow slits to the r., lighting
the stairwell. The entrance and windows appear to be C18
enlargements. Further windows on the upper floors on the N
elevation. The parapet with three levels of continuous corbelling and open corner bartizans survives only on the E elevation.
Vaulted ground floor, and a turnpike stair in the SE corner
leading to the upper floors, with large mural cupboards on
each floor. Banded gatepiers with geometrical vermiculation.

DESCRIPTION

The C18 Town House (*see* above) marks the centre of Newmilns
at a slight widening of MAIN STREET and is nicely complemented by other buildings of comparable date, e.g. Nos. 56–66,
a range of harled vernacular two-storey houses on the S side,
and the LOUDOUN ARMS, opposite, a large harled five-bay
three-storey inn with black margins, crowstepped gables, and
dormers with alternate triangular and round-headed pediments. Also, immediately in the foreground of the Town House,
a good red sandstone premises, dated 1883, with a contemporary shopfront with consoles at either end, and at the opposite

end of this row, to the corner with Craigview Road, the former
BROWN'S INSTITUTE of 1870 by *James Stark*, converted to
flats by *Page & Park*. This was the first of the series of institutes
provided for the valley towns by Martha Brown of Lanfine (*see*
also Darvel and Galston). Two storeys of rock-faced red sandstone with wide end pilasters and dentilled cornice. Entrance
on Main Street, with pilasters, entablature and cavetto reveals,
and curved corner with three-light windows. Facing this, No.
71, dated 1826. It has a centre doorway with balcony and balustrade, a shouldered wall-head stack with an elliptical datestone, and flanking oriels. Its neighbour is classic Georgian of
c. 1800, with a central pedimented chimneystack. Restored
faithfully 2001–3 by *Page & Park*, who also added the sensitive
infill to its r. with recessed ground-floor window and square
lead-clad window above. Immediately behind this, in Castle
Street, is Newmilns Tower (*see* above) and also further housing
(JOHN LAW CLOSE) by *Page & Park*, 2001–3, of two storeys
around a courtyard, white-harled with random contrasting
blocks of ochre harl, and wooden panels between the entrances.
Theirs too is MURDOCH NISBET COURT, further along Main
Street, facing the Parish Church, which has three recessed bays
with small windows with leaded heads, columns between the
bays and a lead roof. To the rear, white-harled blocks with
windows and other features picked out in ochre, leaded
oriel windows and recessed porches. Then a former inn, built
of pink ashlar with polished red sandstone dressings, dated
1869 on its wall-head chimney. Next, the two highlights of
Morton Hall and Lady Flora's Institute (*see* Public Buildings,
above), but thereafter less of interest except a somewhat
decayed early C19 group, e.g. No. 144 which has a pend to the
l., and a pilastered entrance with a sunburst entablature. Visible
behind these frontages, crossing Newmilns public green and
the River Irvine, is the disused VIADUCT built in 1894, when
the Glasgow & South-Western Railway branch was extended
to Darvel. Twenty-six arches, slightly curved plan, in rock-
faced ashlar, with blue-grey brick arch-rings.

In the opposite direction from the Town House, Main Street has
another coherent sequence of two-storey buildings but here it
is the late C19 which plays the strongest hand, with the outstanding red sandstone showpiece of WESTGATE HOUSE, on
the N side up to the corner with High Street. This is of 1898–
1900 by *Gabriel Andrew* (of *Andrew & Newlands*) of Kilmarnock, but rebuilt in 1908–9 after a major fire, and restored as
flats (with shopfronts) in 2001–3 by *W. I. Munro* for Strathclyde
Building Preservation Trust. It is a powerful free Baroque
work, very much in the Glasgow vein, on a narrow triangular
plot, with at its apex a prominent tower that is corbelled out
to the octagon and finished by a scalloped parapet enclosing a
drum cupola with ogee leaded roof, linked to the parapet by
curved ribs. On each of the long side elevations, bays divided
by Ionic pilasters and at either end two with pedimented and
shaped gables at the wall-head. On Main Street, the entrances

in these bays also have rusticated pilasters and broken pediments, and the centre bay is expressed as a shallow bow with a big round-headed dormer.

Hereafter the road is open on the s side to the river, the scale of building modest once more as the street becomes LOUDOUN ROAD with continuous late C19 red sandstone cottages on both sides, continued by two-storey tenements, e.g. Nos. 38–40 of 1881, Nos. 51–59, of *c.* 1886, both by *John Macintosh*. Then villa-land takes over, mostly with semi-detached red sandstone pairs of *c.* 1900, but also, on the s side, the light brown stone No. 69, of 1911, which has a two-storey advanced bay to r., and an entrance with a triangular pediment and an oval window above, and two of *c.* 1885, both set back in their own grounds: Nos. 81–83, in grey ashlar, with canted bays that have bracketed eaves and a paired porch with Doric columns. GLENROSA (No. 85) is a slightly more lavish version of the same composition but in red sandstone ashlar, with an Ionic-columned entrance and a piended platform roof with conspicuous cast-iron brattishing. Further out on the N side, GLEBE HOUSE (No. 114), of *c.* 1920, in red sandstone. Symmetrical, with a central round-arched keystoned entrance. Flanking ground-floor flat-roofed bays have rounded ends and metal windows with deep stone courses above and below. Its neighbour is OLD MANSE, apparently of *c.* 1760, but added to, perhaps in 1817, when *William Crooks* prepared plans, and again in 1898 when 'the manse is now being altered to an extent that will probably efface much of the interest attaching to it'. White harl, with painted stone dressings. Original five-bay centre section, with eaves and sill courses, square windows, and entrance with architrave in third bay from l. Flanking wider identical bays at either end probably date from 1817, the projecting canted stone bays almost certainly from 1898. Finally, GILFOOT (No. 124), built *c.* 1900 for Robert Hendrie, the Loudoun estate factor. A harled two-storey L-plan villa with red sandstone dressings. It has a full-height crowstepped bay to the r., with a canted ground-floor window, a full-height bow to the l. and a crowstepped side gable.

In the areas off the main street are some other buildings of interest. In BRIDGEND, which leads s off the E end of Main Street, LAMLASH HOUSE, a crowstepped Baronial villa of 1888, dominated by a three-storey tower with tall, almost Moorish stair windows with pinched necks to the windows. It has a good wooden porch and interiors, with plaster cornices with cornucopiae and, in the stair windows, stained glass by *Stephen Adam*; poets above (Burns, Tannahill, Ramsay, Scott, Hogg) and floral panels below in broad frames of roundels.

BROWN STREET, continuing Bridgend arrow-straight SW, is a planned settlement, also known as Greenholm, based on a feuing plan drawn by the Glasgow surveyor *John Wilson* for the Browns of Lanfine. The earliest feus date from 1806 and the street retains much of its original character. Its immediate surroundings are industrial and the even row of terraces is

interrupted at Nos. 52–54 by the former GREENHOLM POWER
LOOM FACTORY of 1867 for Joseph Hood & Co. This is one
of the earliest machine-weaving factories in the country, and
an important survival. It has simple square-headed openings
with entrances in the first and fifth bays. Further SW begins
the greatest concentration of LACE MILLS, where the valley
widens and offered flat land for building. The mills have an
odd charm. Their brickwork, often gently decorative, contrasts
with the general stone appearance of Newmilns. No. 76 Brown
Street, for Haddow, Aird & Crerar Ltd, originally of 1881 by
John Macintosh, was rebuilt after a fire in 1923. Seven bays and
two storeys of red brick, with the bays separated by brick
pilasters with stone copes. Nos. 78–86, the IRVINEBANK
POWER LOOM FACTORY of 1877 for Morton, Cameron &
Co., was rebuilt after the same fire. It is a tall three-storey
six-bay block in white brick, with ground-floor windows in
low-relief segmental arches, brick pilasters, a stone cornice and
brick blocking course. The outer bays project slightly and their
upper windows have arched stone pediments, and slightly projecting brick frames. A nine-bay two-storey extension to the l.
has low-relief ground-floor segmental arches with curious vermiculated stone imposts. Further on, Nos. 88–90, the VALE
LACE WORKS, of 1886 for Johnston, Shields & Co., has a red
ashlar six-bay two-storey office building, with decorative
capped pilasters, and twelve-bay, two-storey brick weaving
sheds. No. 92 (ANNABANK FACTORY) of 1882 for Robert
Muir was the first lace mill of more than one storey, and has
a twenty-five-bay yellow brick weaving shed with characteristic
tall ground-floor windows. In STONEYGATE ROAD, No. 2, the
RIVERBANK LACE FACTORY (now Moonweave Ltd), of 1897,
for Goldie, Steel & Co., has a two-storey yellow brick office
block, of three bays by five, the bays separated by brick pilasters, and with a cut-away ground-floor corner, with stone
arches supported by a pillar. N of Brown Street, in NELSON
STREET, more mid-C19 cottages and the long ten-bay two-
storey brick façade of Hood Morton & Co.'s LACE MILL of
1930.
  Finally, N of Main Street where HIGH STREET clambers up the
valley from Westgate House (*see* above). It is spacious, quite
urban in feel and mainly with mid-C19 houses, though midway
has a nice ensemble of varied early C19 houses and cottages,
in pink ashlar (Nos. 24, 32 and 36), coursed rubble (No. 26)
and harl (No. 34). No. 30 is mid-C19, a three-bay two-storey
house with a channelled ground floor, and a wide central
doorway with fluted columns and fanlight. W along KING
STREET, No. 18, built as the Police Station in 1896–9 by *John
Murdoch*, a domestic design with a prominent doorcase with
consoles and triangular pediment. Opposite, a diminutive tenement of 1885 by *John Macintosh*, faced in white glazed brick,
with a multi-coloured brick sill course.
  From the foot of High Street, Drygate Street and Borebrae
climb the hill, leading to an enclave of houses capturing the

views. Late C19 villas in LOUDOUN CRESCENT, such as No. 1 of 1892–3 by *John Macintosh*, a red sandstone former manse, with a bow window, and paired columns to the entrance. In CLEARMOUNT AVENUE, late C20 housing, e.g. No. 22, of 1972, with a big harled monopitched main block, stone-dressed windows and a big wooden panel, and No. 5, of 1975, again a monopitch, with a deep wooden panel and an entrance at first-floor level.

Separate from the built-up area of Newmilns's E end is another enclave of villas, some erected by mill-owners, along FOULPAPPLE ROAD, set on rising ground, and commanding extensive views. The grandest of these is WESTLANDS, built in 1927 by *Gabriel Steel*. Two storeys with dormers, harled with dressed-stone base course and dressings to the mostly square-headed windows. L-plan, with the entrance in the centre of the long wing; slightly projected, with a hoodmoulded doorway beneath a single-light first-floor window and a big Dutch-gabled dormer with a central circular window. Stairwell window with stone mullions and transoms. In spacious grounds approached through pyramid-headed gatepiers.

TOWNHEAD FARM, Mill Road. A harled L-shaped farmhouse with crowstepped gables and simple skews, probably late C18. Pilastered doorway in a corner of the advanced wing; rubble stone enclosure wall to S, and unusual geometrical railings between courtyard and roadway, perhaps from the 1930s. The harled LOUDOUN'S MILL was built in the late C18 as a corn mill. A single-storey gabled barn fronts the road, with the taller, two-storey mill behind, and a later brick, now harled, addition to the l, with the inscription NO MILL, NO MEAL J.A. 1914.

NEWTON KENNEDY *see* GIRVAN

2050

NODDSDALE HOUSE
2.5 km. NE of Largs

83   Nestled into the hillside above the Noddsdale Burn and over-looking Largs with expansive views of the Firth of Clyde. The house is a delightfully idiosyncratic confection of gables, jettying and timber framing which was transformed from a simple Arts and Crafts design of 1902 for Dr Walker Downie by *James Miller*, into one of distinctly Old English manner in 1924–32 by *Fryers & Penman* for John M. Robertson, owner of the Gem Shipping Line and an amateur enthusiast for architecture.

Ashlar and rubble are employed for the walling of the more important ground-floor elevations, elsewhere white harl, half-timbering, tile-hanging and red tile roofs. Of the original w elevation only the bays to either side of the gabled centre remain, the rest extensively remodelled including the enclosure of the former veranda in the centre, the creation of the entrance in a deep moulded frame and rebuilding of the centre gable

itself with patterned brickwork infill, in the Norman Shaw
tradition, jetties and an oriel tucked under the bargeboarded
eaves. Of the contemporary enlargements, there is the irregular
N wing with more half-timbering, jettying and elaborate gable-
heads, and a prettily detailed entrance with recessed door set
into timber framing and herringbone brickwork. Suspended
from the porch lintel, a bronze ship's bell inscribed 'the Lord
of the Isles'. Crowsteps to the E bay are a Scottish vernacular
touch but its huge shafted stack comes from Shaw. The N-
facing gable, again jettied and timber-framed with herringbone
brickwork above the ground floor. The long gabled E elevation
appears to be growing out of the hillside; the S gable virtually
rises from the ground and also has big Shavian stacks. The SE
gable is part of a quirky angular extension created from former
outbuildings for a music room and guest accommodation. It
forms the E side of the S-facing court and joins an addition
made in 1914 by *T. G. Abercrombie*, of which there is now only
a glimpse in the form of an incongruous rectangular crenellated block. Strangely, it was given a flat roof to provide a very
urban clothes-drying area.

A light interior, despite much oak panelling; in the beamed
hall an inglenook chimneypiece with an overmantel. The
dining room has dado panelling, a Queen Anne-style chimneypiece and overmantel. The library is the former morning
room added in 1914. The bookcases were added *c.* 1932. The
music room in the 1920s wing is the most atmospheric, partly
panelled with a large inglenook fireplace and an arched screen
to the bay. In the room above the rafters are arranged umbrella-
like, more ecclesiastical than domestic.

Electricity is still supplied by the original small hydro-electric scheme and generators installed when the house was built.

OCHILTREE

5020

Village and parish centre in the heart of dairy country. The parish
was granted to the Melrose Abbey in the early C14, and remained
part of their Ayrshire estates until the Reformation. The barony
of Ochiltree passed into the hands of the Cunninghames of
Glencairn, who, in the late C18, planted the present village,
running steeply uphill from the original settlement close to the
crossing of the Lugar. It has a wide main street and, where the
original single-storey cottages survive, a pleasing and well-proportioned appearance, accentuated by the changes in level and
perspective. AYR ROAD is an early by-pass; the steep brae of
Main Street was found to be over-taxing for horses, and a new
turnpike was laid in 1838.

OCHILTREE PARISH CHURCH, Main Street. 1789 by *Hugh
Morton*, the foundation stone laid by James Boswell. Restored
by *J. M. Dick Peddie* in 1897. A gabled preaching box in heavy
dull grey harl, with stone corner dressings and a W bellcote.

Four tall round-headed windows in rusticated architraves on the s side, two tiers of windows elsewhere, round-headed in the gables. Porches by *William McLetchie & Son*, 1862, when the s door was blocked up. Equally unassuming interior dominated on three sides by large panel-fronted galleries and well-made artisan joiner-work stairs, all of 1854. – STAINED GLASS. Flanking the pulpit two incredibly deeply hued and imaginatively composed Resurrection scenes of 1905 by *Stephen Adam* (brought from the Free Church in 1947*). CHURCH HALL, 1908. Boarded wagon roof inside.

OCHILTREE NEW CEMETERY, Mauchline Road. 1904 by *Allan Stevenson*.

OCHILTREE OLD KIRKYARD, off Mill Street. The site of the pre-1789 parish church. Now a numinous, rather neglected graveyard, with stone boundary DYKES of 1796. The mostly C18 and C19 HEADSTONES include some nicely lettered C18 ones. That of Hugh Wallace in Killoch, †1800, near the E boundary, is particularly deeply and carefully cut.

COMMUNITY CENTRE, Main Street. 1970–2 by *Ayr County Council*. Boarded wooden hall on a brick base, with a steel exoskeleton. To its w, OCHILTREE PRIMARY SCHOOL, 1974–6, *Ayr County Council Architects Department*. Dull.

MARKET CROSS, The Cross. Of uncertain date, though probably contemporary with the planned village. A chamfered square stone pillar with a cushion head. The three Arbroath flagstone steps date from renovation in 1897.

Former OCHILTREE PRIMARY SCHOOL, Main Street. 1909 by *A. C. Thomson*. Red sandstone, broadly symmetrical about a wide central bay, with flanking set-back entrances under lintels with eared mouldings. Dainty circular open bellcote to the boys' side. Converted to residential use in 2007–8.

DESCRIPTION

The heart of the original village was close to the Old Kirkyard, at the crossing of the Lugar. From here MILL STREET runs w, climbing steadily up the side of the hill. Its r. side sets the template for the village: an admixture of single- and two-storey houses, some harled, others painted, each almost invariably slightly higher than its neighbour, some with substantial base courses. One is dated 1789 (though has been thoroughly rebuilt), and leases are known from 1785. At the Cross, the neat rounded end elevation of the two-storey Nos. 1–5 BURNOCK STREET, harled with painted dressings, and a fine example of vernacular design. Built 1807–8 for John Samson; above one door a plaster coat of arms with the Cunninghame shakefork; their motto Over Fork Over repeated on a C19 fascia. The Market Cross (*see* above) is rather lost amongst street furniture.

MAIN STREET runs w from the Cross. In places undeniably steep, but also wide, and, at first, slightly curving. Its buildings

* Of 1845–6; demolished.

are much like those of Mill Street, including some relatively unspoilt cottages, such as Nos. 58 and 60 on the r., the latter with an extensive workshop to the l., with a rough stone pavement in front. Of the others, THE HOUSE WITH THE GREEN SHUTTERS (No. 90) has a bronze TABLET of 1919 by *Robert Bryden*, commemorating the author George Douglas Brown.*

OLD MANSE, Mauchline Road, 0.2 km. N. Of 1798–1800; two-storey, three-bay, of stone, with a central porch, and considerable outbuildings to the rear.

OCHILTREE MILL, 0.3 km. N. 1859, now ruinous. Tall and gabled, of three storeys, with a lower wing at right angles. The adjoining painted stone single-storey miller's house is early C19.

LUGAR BRIDGE, 0.4 km. E. 1818. Two segmental arches, with a central splayed cutwater. Its flat-arched concrete replacement was built in 1959–62 (contractors, *Murdoch MacKenzie Ltd*).

BURNOCKHOLM, 0.3 km. SE. An unusually interesting house of *c*. 1830, said to have been built for one of the Crichton-Stuarts (of Dumfries House), and worthy of further investigation. From the front it appears to be a plastered single storey with attics, wide central hipped gable, and a bracketed hoodmould above a framed entrance door with flanking sidelights: a successful fusion of vernacular and classical elements. The rear elevation, however, is of four storeys, with the lower storeys originally used as storage and outbuildings, with a wide wagon entrance to the lower storey, and the first floor originally entered from the side. A basement passage between the house and the road gives access to cellars under the road.

Former KILLOCH COLLIERY, 3 km. SW. 1952–9, by *Egon Riss*, chief architect to the National Coal Board, Scotland. One of two new pits associated with a planned new town for the area between Ayr and Cumnock (*see* Drongan), but beset from the outset by unexpected geological problems. The buildings, now demolished, were similar to Riss's Frances Colliery (Fife), including enclosed headgear towers. Only concrete administrative blocks point to what has been.

CROSSHILL COTTAGES, 3.8 km. NW. Two rows of early C19 cottages, in parallel. Single storey, painted, with crisp dressings and a moulded eaves. A similar cottage, at right angles, was originally a school.

OLD AUCHANS CASTLE *see* DUNDONALD

OLD AUCHENFAIL HALL   *4020*
1.5 km. E of Failford

William Cooper, a Glasgow tobacco merchant, purchased the Smithston estate in 1786 and immediately commissioned a

---

*Douglas Brown's novel *The House with the Green Shutters*, a caustic rejoinder to the romanticized 'kailyard' vision of Scottish life, is set in Barbie, generally held to be Ochiltree. The house of the title is, however, two-storey, and is often said to be modelled on No. 74 Main Street.

smart if somewhat conservative mansion. Built in muted pink dressed sandstone with ashlar dressings and margins; some traces remain of limewash applied first in 1796. It is tall, of three storeys with attics, and five bays wide with a large pediment over the advanced centre, a design which looks back to Dumfries House and Auchinleck House (qq.v.). A crisply carved Cooper coat of arms and crest dominate the pediment. As at Hillhouse (q.v.). the entrance at first floor was reached by a flying stair; the door retains its delicate scalloped and arched traceried fanlight but since 1808 has opened to a balcony. This dates from alterations for Alexander Cooper by *John Paterson,* and his assistant *Mr McEwan,* who provided the Doric porch for a new front door. Above the porch was a cast-iron balustrade, made by the Catrine foundry, since replaced by a chunky stone one in C17 style. Service wings were built at the rear, but only the ground floor of the rear wing survives together with the altered carriage house.

Simply planned interior, with a spacious, stone-flagged hall leading to a plain balustraded, neat geometric stone stair rising to the second floor. Off the hall to the w the dining room, possibly designed as a parlour with a shallow elliptical bay on the long N wall and an alcove between the two windows. A frieze of fruit and ribbons and an unusual rectangular buckle-like motif set within bold mouldings on the ceiling. Could this be Paterson too? The upper hall, now library, opens off the stair; it appears to have been recast *c.* 1900, when the oak chimneypiece was inserted, possibly after a fire. The drawing room occupying the whole depth of the house on the E side has a deep alcove on the N wall and an elegant Adam-style chimneypiece, of late C18 date but not related to any other decoration in the house and probably inserted in the 1960s. The geometric patterned plaster ceiling is *c.* 1840 with later inserted decoration.

OLD DAILLY

The parish of Dailly was granted to Paisley Abbey by Duncan, Earl of Carrick, but was later transferred to Crossraguel Abbey. Today the ruinous church stands almost alone.

OLD DAILLY CHURCH. One of the biggest and most impressive of the county's ruined churches. Built in 1674–5, it replaced the previous church, but was abandoned for the new church at Dailly (q.v.) in 1696–7. Aligned roughly E–W, 28.1 m. long by 7.9 m. wide, and of coursed stone. Both gables have an open bellcote, that to the E the more decorative. A square-headed entrance and a number of irregularly spaced windows in the s wall; much less remains of the N wall. The E third of the church is now the BARGANY BURIAL AISLE, and has a low shallow flagged roof, and a broad pediment. Abutting the NE corner, the Killochan burial vault, C17, also flagged, with three deep niches on the N elevation, that in the middle originally a doorway, with a square recessed panel and ball finial to the gable. On the E gable a memorial to William Bell Scott (†1890, *see* Penkill Castle), a bronze roundel in a granite frame; his tomb, below, is by Girvan builder *Andrew Murray*.

Within the churchyard some Covenanter MEMORIALS, such as that to John Stevenson †1729, erected in 1886 (by *Thomas Lyon* and executed by *Matthew Muir*). Simple obelisk with a carved group of Bible, rifle and sword. Also a plainer early C19 monument with an artisan inscription to George Martin, schoolmaster, who 'suffered in the Grassmarket Edinburgh 22nd Feb 1684 for his adherence to the Covenant' and two others 'one of whom, according to tradition, was shot dead while herding his cow at Killoup'.

Former GEORGE TODD MEMORIAL HALL, 100 m. E. 1930–1, by *W. A. Thomson*. Pedimented central door and a large ventilator, blandly converted to domestic use, 2007.

LOVESTONE HOUSE, 1 km. NE. Former factor's house for Bargany (q.v.), built *c.* 1850. A pleasant, well-proportioned country villa with generous bay windows and low-pitched roofs in a mildly Italianate style.

PENWHAPPLE RESERVOIR, 4 km. SE. 1921–6, by *Warren & Stuart*, engineers, for Girvan Town Council. A simple earthen dam with attractive contemporary railings. The reservoir is surrounded by AEROGENERATORS, erected in 2005–6.

BARGANY. *See* p. 184.
KILLOCHAN CASTLE. *See* p. 413.
PENKILL CASTLE. *See* p. 569.
TROCHRAIGUE. *See* p. 652.

OTTERDEN
1.8 km. W of Minishant

3010

Formerly West Knockdon. A much-altered small laird's house of the later C18, but thick walls in the S gable and the cellar, where there are small openings well below ground level, indicate an earlier dwelling of *c.* 1700. Two storeys and three bays with service wings making it L-plan. Harled with ashlar dressings. The simply moulded doorpiece, the moulded stair risers, the cornices and woodwork belong to the later C18. The house was altered again in the early C19 when the full-height canted windows were added. Two rear wings: one C19, the other 1926. Below, a neat house and garage by *Thomas McGill Cassels* of *Allan Stevenson & Cassels*, 1935.

PATNA

4010

Almost nothing remains of the planned weaving village founded in 1802 by William Fullarton of Skeldon, its name borrowed from

India, where Fullarton had spent his working life. It grew in the
late C19 with the coal industry, and yet further in the late C20
with new housing for families displaced from the row villages
such as Lethamhill, Burnfoothill and Benquhat high in the hills
on the r. bank of the Doon.

PATNA WATERSIDE PARISH CHURCH, Main Street. Simple
    Gothic of 1837, extended in 1878 by *John Murdoch* and in 1899
    by *John B. Wilson* of Glasgow. Low and unassertive. The ori-
    ginal grey stone three-bay building has angle buttresses, a
    wooden bellcote, and pairs of round-headed windows, enlarged
    in 1899. The buttresses have particularly unusual decorative
    finials. Gabled rear extension of 1878 with paired foliated
    windows, and porch of 1899. Plastered interior, with a gently
    coved wooden ceiling, and a panelled gallery front of 1839, but
    otherwise of 1899. The low broad PULPIT, with steps at either
    end, ELDERS' CHAIRS, COMMUNION TABLE and corner
    COMMUNION RAILS have all come from other churches, but
    form a cohesive, if understated, whole. – High-quality STAINED
    GLASS. In the E arm, a brightly coloured and strongly narrative
    Good Samaritan of 1909, in the manner of Christopher Whall,
    formerly in the U.F. Church, installed here in 2002. – Flanking
    the pulpit, Jonathan and David (l.) and Charity and Faith (r.),
    all of 1899 by *Stephen Adam & Son*. Rich vivid colours, the
    equal of Adam's windows, for the same donor, in Pollokshields
    Parish Church (Glasgow). – Attractive wrought-iron GATES
    and GATEPIERS of 1838.
Former UNITED FREE CHURCH, Main Street. 1901–3 by *John
    B. Wilson* of Glasgow. Early Dec in red Ballochmyle stone, with
    a pedimented porch and an octagonal tower, with four tall
    paired bell-openings, and a slated octagonal roof; a proposed
    spire was never built. Unusually tall front gable with a central
    buttress which ends in a foliated niche. Two tiers of windows
    to either side of the buttress; of three lights below, taller two-
    light windows above.
PATNA OLD AND NEW CEMETERIES, off Main Street. The Old
    Cemetery, late C19, has stone walls; those of the late C20 New
    Cemetery brick or brick rendered.
PATNA PRIMARY SCHOOL, Carnshalloch Drive. 1957–9 by
    Edward A. Darley. Construction of a replacement began in
    2011.
WAR MEMORIAL. 1920 by *Hugh McLachlan* of Ayr. 4.9 m.-high
    Kemnay granite obelisk on a hilltop overlooking the village.
DESCRIPTION. MAIN STREET begins with DOON BRIDGE, a
    single-arch stone bridge of *c.* 1805–6. On the l., No. 13, the
    former Established Church manse, dated 1882, and the more
    adventurous red sandstone No. 15, the former United Free
    Church manse, of 1912, probably by *William Cowie*, its front
    consisting of two shallow full-height bows. Also on the l., No.
    41, a big harled house of 1911 in the subfusc Arts and Crafts
    manner of *J. K. Hunter*. In front of the Parish Church a granite
    plinth of a FOUNTAIN presented in 1872 by the Liverpool
    brewer A. B. Walker, who was brought up in the Doon valley.

The architect was *H. H. Vale* of Liverpool. Beyond are the early C19 stone and slate vernacular DUNASKIN DOON BAND HALL, all that survives of Fullarton's village, and, on the r., an odd COLUMN, resembling nothing so much as a tall, chamfered safety match, erected by Fullarton in 1821; it originally bore the legend NULLA SINE DEO MENS BONA EST ('No mind without God is good').

PENKILL CASTLE

1 km. SE of Old Dailly

2090

The ultimate fairytale castle, Penkill is hidden away in the steep, wooded glen of the Penwhapple Burn, with distant views from the upper floors out to sea and Ailsa Craig. Its early history is unexceptional, a tower built for the Boyds in the first half of the C16 with an addition of *c.* 1628 for Thomas Boyd and Marion Mure which was connected to the earlier house via the original stair-tower. By 1857 all of this addition had virtually vanished and the old tower house was ruinous. At this date Spencer Boyd embarked on a major restoration, with the encouragement of his sister Alice who succeeded him in 1865. Assisted by *Alexander G. Thomson*, Boyd 'set about restoring . . . with the genuine feeling of an antiquary adhering strictly to the original construction'. His artistic vision was to ensure Penkill's recognition not only as one of the most individual Victorian buildings in Ayrshire but also nationally as a shrine to the Pre-Raphaelite Brotherhood, housing important murals and paintings by the artist and poet, *William Bell Scott*, who died at Penkill. Spencer's work was financed with money inherited from his mother, a member of the Losh family, ironfounders from Northumberland. (It was Sara Losh who designed Wreay Church, Cumbria, in 1842, which drew admiration from Rossetti and Bell Scott. Could this have been the inspiration for Spencer and Alice Boyd's artistic imagination also?)

77

The old tower is to the W of the entrance, built of whin rubble and rectangular in plan, approximately 8.2 m. by 6.7 m. with diagonally opposing conical roofed bartizans with fish-scale slates, each with a rectangular opening and two small gunloops, more for show than earnest. A round entrance and stair-tower at the NE angle had collapsed by 1857 and their place is now taken by the present entrance. At this time the tower's precarious S gable was reinforced by doubling its thickness to act as a buttress. A curious side effect of this work was to cut the SE angle turret off from its angle position and leave it perched above a pentice roof. Above a vaulted lower floor with narrow ventilation slits (some doubling as gunloops) are three storeys with one room to each floor. There was some window enlargement in the C17 but a small light to the first-floor closet at the NW remained; re-cut in the 1850s, a dormer on the E face with scrolly lugs to the bottom angles and a pediment with a cross finial.

The mid-C19 additions are muscular: attached at the NE angle of the tower the entrance bay with a big door in a roll-moulded frame recessed under a deep round-headed arch corbelled out from the lower wall. Above the arch, a string course stepped up on either side of the first-floor window like ears and linked by a curved ledge at sill level. The upper walls are all in tough whin stone with red sandstone for the dressings including the staccato corbel course with a continuous roll mould over the second floor supporting the crowstepped gable. E of the entrance, the domineering stair-tower, battered at the base with a boldly corbelled midriff and an even more elaborately corbelled and crenellated crown-like parapet, is linked to the assumed S wall of the C17 range, re-created by Boyd faithful to antiquarian ideals rather than functional convenience. In 1883 *Bell Scott* himself extended the castle along lines set out in the initial plans by Thomson to provide a dining room-cum-picture gallery in the low, crowstepped gabled range to the E of the great stair-tower. This has lancets in the E gable and is reminiscent of a smart village hall. A stepped buttress to the W of the mullioned-and-transomed window supports a brooding owl.

80   Inside, the *tour de force* is the STAIR-TOWER where Bell Scott began in 1865 a great MURAL in spirit fresco, partly painted on zinc, illustrating James I's poem the 'King's Quaire'. It still dazzles with the brightness of the palette. The painting includes portraits of Spencer Boyd, Swinburne, Christina and W. M. Rossetti and Bell Scott himself as well as Alice's pet duck Quasi. Many of the walls and ceilings are covered with Scott's decorative work including the *trompe l'oeil* ceiling of a vine-covered trellis figured with dragonflies and swallows in ALICE BOYD'S ROOM in the re-created C17 wing. The LIBRARY on the first floor of the C16 tower has a large segmentally arched stone chimneypiece with a hood, a beamed ceiling, and in the window reveals painted Gothic inscriptions and arabesque panels. Bell Scott's painting of Spencer and Alice gazing out from the battlements is inserted over the nook-shafted chimneypiece in the second-floor TOWER ROOM where Scott's Twa Corbies fill the window recess. The HALL CORRIDOR has decorative woodwork designed as a setting for tapestries. The HALL, intended for the picture collection, is timber-lined, with an open timber roof and elaborate chimneypiece with granite inset. More painted decoration in the window reveals.

The GARDENS laid out by Scott are a rare survival of the Aesthetic Movement in gardening. His ironwork in the fences and gates is almost Art Nouveau.

PERCETON
Irvine

One of the ancient parishes of the county, united with Dreghorn in 1668. Like Dreghorn it was a possession of Kilwinning Abbey. The late C18 and C19 saw mineral exploitation, principally of coal and brick clay, but little physical development. This came in the late C20, when the area fell within the boundaries of Irvine Development Corporation.

Former PERCETON CHURCH. Pre-Reformation. A gabled rectangle, with a gabled N aisle, later used as a burial vault by the Mures of Perceton. Now roofless and smothered in ivy. It sits on a small natural hillock, which it shares with the former FREE CHURCH of 1843, renovated in 1895, harled and gabled, with lower aisles and a prominent finial.

PERCETON HOUSE (North Ayrshire Council). The estate was 63 acquired from the Barclays by Andrew Macredie, provost of Stranraer, in 1720. The present house was built *c.* 1764 for his grandson, William Macredie, but excitingly and attractively extended *c.* 1968–72 by *Robert Dunlop* as the Irvine Development Corporation headquarters. The house is matronly, wide and of four bays on a raised basement, harled with black-painted quoins, and a pedimented columned porch approached by a splayed flight of steps with curved rails. Projecting splayed full-height rear wing with balustraded parapet. A linking block maintains a discrete separation between the house and Dunlop's flat-roofed extension. This projects backwards and is 122 of three storeys, harled, with regular recessed window bays; these are in pairs, with the upper windows punched out, with similarly projecting heads floating above. The colours, black and white, replicate those of the house, and are designed to tone with the changing colours of the surrounding trees. Simple LODGE of *c.* 1860.

In the immediate vicinity, a number of good private houses of the late 1970s and early 1980s, especially in THE PADDOCK, where No. 6, of 1976, was built for *John Billingham*; it, and many of the other houses in this nationally noteworthy development, reflect a freer approach to the tropes of I.D.C. architecture: bright white harling, dark dressings, widely varying treatments of fenestration and roof-lines. Equal attention has been paid to the landscaping, and the whole scheme contrasts considerably with much contemporary, and subsequent, private house building

MUIRHOUSES FARM, 0.9 km. SE. Attractive mid-C19 stone farmhouse, with a gabled projecting bay to the l., and gabled dormer to the r. Shouldered gables and finials; stone outbuildings further to the l.

PERCETON ROW, 1.2 km. SE. A pleasing group of two harled rows of mid-C19 single-storey cottages, built for colliers and brickmakers, rescued by I.D.C. Nicely varied window patterns.

PINMORE   *2090*

A tiny settlement which grew up beside the railway halt on the Girvan & Portpatrick Railway (opened 1877).

KINCLAER VIADUCT, I km. S. 1874. One of the most significant engineering works at this end of the line. Tall and curved, with eleven arches, built of granite rubble, spanning the Assel valley and crossing and recrossing the A714. I km. S, crossing the Stinchar, is PINMORE BRIDGE. 1830s, built by Hugh Hamilton 'of his bounty', so reads the worn plaque. 200 m. S, by a second viaduct, is a charming small estate CHAPEL of 1878 built by *Allan Stevenson* for Hew Hamilton of Pinmore House (dem.). Above this uphill, two sets of decaying C19 LIMEKILNS.

3   MOTTE, Dinvin, 1.5 km. N, overlooking the road from Girvan. Among the most striking mottes in the country, standing over 7 m. high within two concentric ditches. The inner ditch is interrupted by a causeway on the ESE, which forms a ramp extending up on to the summit of the mound, but the outer ditch sweeps past unbroken, suggesting that the gate was equipped with some form of timber bridge.

PINWHERRY

A small hamlet established *c.* 1876 beside a station on the Girvan & Portpatrick Railway.

PRIMARY SCHOOL (former). Built *c.* 1880. Asymmetrical single storey on a steep bank. Granite with sandstone dressings. High paired windows and a big offset entrance porch. Attached w, an L-plan school house. Free-standing schoolroom of 1913 by *Allan Stevenson*. Below to the w, PINWHERRY BRIDGE of *c.* 1838, a single segmental span with granite voussoirs crossing the Stinchar.

PINWHERRY CASTLE, S of the bridge, is a small and ruinous L-plan tower probably built by the Kennedys in the late C16. Main block 9.1 m. by 7.6 m., the jamb approximately 3 m. square. It is a smaller version of Baltersan (q.v.) with a similar square stair-turret in the re-entrant angle linking the first-floor to the upper floor and attic. The main three-storey-and-attic block has crowstepped gables with simple skewputts to E and W with corbelled angle rounds at the SW and SE (the latter now gone). The jamb is a storey higher which makes for an awkward joint with the W gable of the tower; it still has remnants of a cavetto-moulded eaves course and skewputts. The entrance is in the re-entrant angle and opened to a newel stair rising to the first floor; above this level there were rooms and a cap-house. The first-floor hall fireplace was on the N wall. A door from the hall opened to the main stair and also to the small newel in the projecting turret over the main door and leading from this level to the upper floors. A further small mural stair in the SW angle of the hall provides private access to the ground floor. Toothing in the N wall suggests that there was a courtyard on this side.

PINWHERRY HOUSE, just s of the tower, is a prim villa of
c. 1860, the asymmetrical w front built in whin stone with red
sandstone quoins, the other elevations harled. A stair projection to the rear. DRUMSPILLAN, set back on the village road's
N side, is by *James Lindsay*, 1896, and in its heyday a flamboyant villa in the French Renaissance manner, alas reduced to a
single storey after a fire.

DALJARROCK HOTEL 1.2 km. N. Built at a strategic position at
the head of a fertile brae and close to the River Stinchar. Late
C17 for the Kennedys of Daljarroch, described as 'a good residence for a Heritor' in 1696. The three-storey rectangular
block has a vaulted ground floor. Several lower additions were
made in the C18 and C19; further N additions of 1928 by *Reginald Fairlie* for William Hew Coltman but these were demolished after a fire in the 1980s. The large enclosing boundary
walls have also gone. 200 m. s is DALJARROCK BRIDGE, like
the Pinwherry crossing one of a series of elegant single-span,
segmental-arched masonry bridges constructed in the early
C19 over the Stinchar. It rises up to meet the higher E bank.
MONUMENT, Almont, 1 km. NW. John Snell †1679. He was born
at Almont and founded the Snell exhibition for Glasgow stu-
dents to attend Balliol College, Oxford. Tall plinth with tiny
urn finial, of 1919 by *Robert S. Lorimer*; his commission influenced by Robert Finnie McEwen of Bardrochat (q.v.).

PITCON
1.25 km. NE of Dalry

2040

A plain but elegant simple classical house. Perhaps of 1787 when
James Robertson acquired the estate. Roughly coursed rubble
with polished ashlar dressings and rusticated quoins. The
entrance front has a shallow advanced central pedimented bay
with the door set in plain margin mouldings and two sidelights;
the window above has an apron panel. The centre of the rear
elevation has an advanced bay which breaks through the eaves
and has a very tall pointed stair window rising into the pediment. Inside, a hall leads to the curved, cantilevered stair at
the rear. A drawing room to the r. was probably two rooms,
but altered *c.* 1924 when the substantial, but remarkably subservient, SW wing was added by *James Houston*. It contains a
large dining room with a grand white marble chimneypiece in
early C19 style; central cherub-filled panel. C18 WALLED
GARDEN with various C17 stones inset.

PORTENCROSS
1040

Coastal hamlet whose seemingly randomly arranged and largely
C19 cottages convey a strong sense of the West Highlands. It is
dominated by its castle, precariously perched on the rocky shore.

Tradition affirms that royal burial parties trans-shipped here en
route for Iona.

44   The CASTLE was abandoned in the C18 and the roof removed in
        1739 but the ruins carefully conserved in 2009–10 by *Peter
        Drummond* and *Gray Marshall Associates* for the Friends of
        Portencross Castle. Portencross and its barony were conferred
        on Sir Robert Boyd of Kilmarnock in 1306 by Robert the
        Bruce. Sir Robert probably built the tower house. It is com-
        posed of a hall range and a narrower block built in line. This
        unusual arrangement the result of the site and particular
        requirements. Despite some anomalies in the masonry, which
        may indicate annual building campaigns, archaeology has
        shown that the plan is original and may be accounted for by
        the prescriptive nature of the site, which is a rocky outcrop in
        a strategic position in the Firth of Clyde. The walls are approxi-
        mately 1.8 m. thick, built in pink sandstone rubble, now very
        weathered, with some sneck harling and squared quoins of a
        white stone. The hall block is 17.7 m. by 9.4 m. and has three
        storeys. Simply corbelled parapet. Drainage shoots from the
        wall-walk. The E block is narrower but 2.4 m. taller. The only
        alteration of substance here is the raising of the S parapet wall
        which brought the wall-walk into an attic room. There are two
        entrances at ground level: one is a simple arched stone doorway
        in the E wall leading into the vault below the hall; the other,
        immediately to its l. in the E block, is later. Above this, however,
        is the original main entrance to the castle which opened into
        a lobby outside the hall. Over it is a tiny window at entresol
        level. A further window exists just below the corbelling to the
        upper floor. There are few windows and some of these have
        been enlarged, particularly those on either side of the high end
        of the hall on the N and S sides, and one in the vaulted ground
        floor.
            The internal planning is the most intriguing and curious
        feature, and may be connected with royal visits. King Robert
        II signed charters at Portencross in the late C14. Of particular
        interest is the existence of two kitchens in the wing, one above
        the other. The ground-floor entrance is into a dog-leg lobby
        from which a mural stair, which could be sealed off, rises to
        the first floor in the thickness of the wall between the hall range
        and the wing. At the foot of the stair there is an entrance to
        the vaulted stores beneath the hall and an opening to the lower
        kitchen in the E block. This has a substantial arched fireplace
        and flue. On the floor above, the mural stair opens onto the
        landing originally the passage from the first-floor entrance to
        the hall. The turnpike stair to the upper floors is off the SE
        corner of the hall, its landing provided access to the upper
        kitchen which had a servery hatch into a lobby off the passage
        to the hall. The very tall vaulted hall has a pointed arched
        fireplace on the W wall and two windows with stone seats. A
        mural chamber at the SW is entered from the window recess.
        The window in the W wall below the vault lit a room created

above the hall at a later date. The rooms above the upper kitchen have garderobes in the s wall.

AUCHENAMES HOUSE, 200 m. NE of the castle, is a marine villa which has its genesis in a straightforward early C19 two-storey house. This has been subsequently altered and extended, most noticeably by *Fryers & Penman* in 1904, when projecting gabled bays were added at either end, with a connecting veranda on the garden front.

HILLHOME, 0.8 km. E. 1937 by *J. Austen Laird*, the best *Moderne* house in Ayrshire. Harled, on a steel frame, with the elements of varying height, rising to a three-storey central block, strikingly well massed. The semicircular bay on the s elevation takes full advantage of the setting. Inside, some original bronze fittings and a stunning full-height stairwell.

PRESTWICK

3020

Known nationally (and beyond) for its airport and as one of the spiritual homes of golf. Other elements too have helped to shape Prestwick – sea bathing, coal mining, weaving, the railway – and to create the town we see today: well-to-do, largely late C19 and C20 in character. Architecturally varied, with some good churches and villas, and other surprises, though not reaching the same heights as its neighbour (and rival) Troon. An ancient parochial centre, granted to Paisley Abbey by Walter FitzAlan in 1172. Prestwick was created a Burgh of Barony in 1600, but remained little more than a village, and for parochial purposes was united with Monkton (q.v.). Salt manufacture, weaving and farming were the staple trades into the early C19. The arrival of the railway, opened through to Glasgow in 1840, altered everything. Prestwick quickly became popular with golfers, while it was also ideally situated to benefit from the increasing enthusiasm for sea bathing and romantic scenery. The late C19 saw an explosion in the population, and this has continued throughout the C20, with a proliferation of interwar bungalows.

CHURCHES AND CEMETERY

KINGCASE PARISH CHURCH, Waterloo Road. Subdued Gothic of 1911–12 by *William Cowie*; extensions of 1954–6 by *Robert Allan* and 2009–10 by *Gordon Fleming* of *ARPL*. Round-headed windows throughout. Cowie's the gabled red sandstone hall church and porch; transepts and chancel form the first extension. Original s windows reused in the w transept; one has

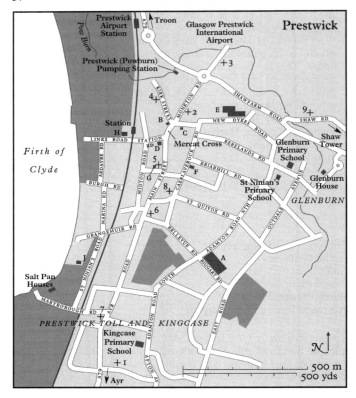

Prestwick

Firth of

Clyde

1   Kingcase Parish Church
2   Prestwick North and
     Monkton Church
3   New Life Christian Fellowship
4   Old St Nicholas Church
5   Prestwick South Parish Church
6   St Nicholas Parish Church
7   St Ninian (Episcopal)
8   St Quivox (R.C.)
9   Monkton and Prestwick Joint
     Cemetery

A   Biggart Hospital
B   Freemen's Hall
C   Kirkhall Surgery
D   Police Station
E   Prestwick Academy
F   Prestwick Community
     Centre
G   Prestwick Library
H   Old Prestwick Golf Club
J   Prestwick St Nicholas Golf
     Club

moulded decoration including one order of dogtooth, and an odd dripmould decorated with features like tiny beer barrels. Simple plastered interior with an open timber roof, and a raised area at the N end. – STAINED GLASS. In the chancel, from the *Abbey Studio* of Edinburgh: two of 1950, by *R. Douglas McLundie*, while the Children's Window of 1956 by *James A. Crombie* is a talented piece of work.

PRESTWICK NORTH AND MONKTON CHURCH, Monkton Road. Former Free Church of 1873–4 by *James Salmon & Son*,

with additions of 1895–6 by *John Keppie* of *Honeyman &
Keppie*. The original church is of three by five bays, built of
pink rubble, with a gabled front with paired lancets within a
round arch. To this Keppie added the entrance tower in grey
ashlar. This has angle buttresses, windows with Y-tracery, a tall
bell-stage with paired pointed windows, open balustrade and
corner finials. The relief of the Burning Bush in a roundel is
re-set from the original front. Soothingly austere plastered and
galleried interior, the panel-fronted gallery supported on cast-
iron columns. Recently reordered, with a large projection
screen between the windows in the E end, and an enlarged
platform. The fittings, e.g. the COMMUNION TABLE, Gothic;
so too the exquisitely and exuberantly carved SCREEN: a reas-
sembly of the panels of a pulpit from the former Parish Church
(*see* New Life Christian Fellowship, below). – STAINED GLASS.
E wall. The Crown of Victory and The Water of Life, of 1910
by *James Benson* of Glasgow: competent if unadventurous.

The HALL, set back to the l., is contemporary with the
church but also extended by *Keppie* and thoroughly remodelled
in 1932 by *Alexander Mair*; the dominant element is his arcaded
loggia with a balustrade above. Also the MANSE of 1885.

NEW LIFE CHRISTIAN FELLOWSHIP, Monkton Road. The
former Parish Church of Prestwick and Monkton, and equi-
distant between the two but now hard up against the airport.
Gothic of 1834–7 by *David Bryce* (*John Parker*, mason, and
William Alexander, contractor). A pink sandstone T-plan church
with a prominent square entrance tower, which has a dumpy
square base with buttresses, a tall bell-stage with two-light
pointed openings on each face, octagonal corner buttresses
carried up as finials, and an open foliated diamond balustrade.
Pointed-arched windows to the flanking bays and side elevations, including two broader gabled bays. Bright red sandstone
additions of 1924–6 by *J. J. Waddell* of Glasgow form a further
transept and a chancel with a five-light Dec E window. Single-
storey addition to the S, 1937 by *Alexander Mair*, with a round-
headed entrance, a heavy stepped pediment, and the SESSION
HOUSE, marked by a canted hipped bay with square-headed
windows. The plastered interior has a vaulted and groined
ceiling with prominent stone bosses, and a horseshoe gallery
with panelled wooden fronts and cast-iron column, but has
been extensively altered since 1986 to suit the needs of evangelical worship. The area below the back gallery enclosed,
and chancel raised to create a stage. Geometric-pattern decorative paper of 1961, when alterations were made by *J. &
J. A. Carrick*. – Stunning STAINED GLASS in the chancel: a
five-light Te Deum of 1925–6 by *Stephen Adam*; also by *Adam*,
and of the same date, the Suffer Little Children in the circular
window to the r. In the S wall, two windows of 1951 by *Gordon
Webster*.

OLD ST NICHOLAS CHURCH, Kirk Street. Perhaps C12, but
this brown-grey stone ivy-clad and gabled ruin yields few
clues. It stands on a prominent knoll, and is 13.4 m. by 6.1 m.

internally, with E buttresses, a pointed-headed entrance on the S, and a matching blocked entrance on the N; MacGibbon and Ross also detected the base courses of an E bellcote. Three blocked, post-Reformation, square-headed windows on the S elevation. The stone-walled CHURCHYARD is an inchoate one, with few stones of individual interest; most are Victorian, echoing the town's rapid growth in the C19. One HEADSTONE to the Hunter family with a blank panel between scroll supports, skull and bones beneath, is perhaps mid-C18.

PRESTWICK SOUTH PARISH CHURCH, Main Street. 1882–4 by *James A. Morris*, as a United Presbyterian Church. Gabled Gothic grey freestone, with entrance bay and attached four-stage tower to r. This has a tall square base with lancets and buttresses, bell-stage with paired round-headed openings, corner buttresses continued as octagonal finials, an octagonal stage with tall gableted windows and an octagonal spire. Big Dec four-light gable window. Naturalistic label stops. Side elevations of paired tall lancets. Spacious plastered interior of nave and aisles, with a barrel-vaulted roof and pointed arcades rising from silver-grey marble columns with richly decorative floriated caps. – STAINED GLASS. Most dramatic is *Catriona R. McKinnon*'s swirling Millennium window of 2000 (s wall, fourth from W). – In the W wall, a vibrant St Michael and a woman with a trident, each despatching a dragon; of 1921 by *Oscar Paterson*. – In the N wall, second from W, a mannered David (of 1972) and Suffer Little Children (of 1967), both by *G. Maile Studios*, Canterbury, and fourth from W, Christ and a Warrior, *c.* 1922 by *William Meikle & Sons*. – In the S wall, second from W, the Virtuous Woman, of 1905, unsigned. – In the NE vestibule, a bronze and marble WAR MEMORIAL of 1921, designed by *James A. Morris*, and made by *Holmes & Jackson*, and *Galbraith & Winton*.

To the rear, the original church, of 1879–80 by *John Mercer*, now used as a hall; gabled red sandstone with lancets.

ST NICHOLAS PARISH CHURCH, Main Street. Neo-Romanesque of 1904–8 by *Peter Macgregor Chalmers* in rock-faced red Ballochmyle stone. Cruciform, with a W tower under a pyramidal slated head. This contains the entrance, round-arched with simple columns and three orders of mouldings, the inner order fatter with trumpet capitals. Some nailhead also. Paired arched openings to the belfry, two levels of corbels, like billet moulding. Four-bay side elevations with flat buttresses and gabled one-bay transepts, all with simplified round-arched windows in recesses. The interior similarly sober with exposed stone walls. Open timber nave roof, the chancel with a ceiled barrel vault, panelled ceilings in the transepts. Twin arches to the transepts, and round arches to the tower, chancel and organ loft (N of the chancel). Good Neo-Romanesque decoration for the capitals of the chancel arch; one capital of the organ loft arch is a lion-headed serpent devouring its own tail. Corbelling to the chancel roof, broad zigzag decoration on the E door in the N transept. Narrow vestibule in the tower, with a high-panelled ceiling and, on the N wall, an open metal balcony for the bellringer.

PULPIT, COMMUNION TABLE AND CHOIR STALLS all part of Chalmers's designs, using Craiksland stone and Austrian oak. – STAINED GLASS. A bold C20–C21 collection. The earliest are the three E windows, 1921, by the *Abbey Studio* of Glasgow, as a war memorial. The Ascension, with Christ and the Apostles; the names of the fallen recorded in the lower panels. – Next, chronologically, the S transept S wall, 1929, again by the *Abbey Studio*: St John and St Paul. By the same firm, the three windows in the chancel side walls: Inspiration, Praise and Prayer, rather old-fashioned for their period; their St Nicholas in the W wall of the tower rather better. – In the nave S wall four from 1949–50: the central pair, with scenes from the life of Christ (war memorial) by *Gordon Webster*. The flanking windows (Jairus's Daughter and the Marriage at Cana, and The Women at the Tomb and Christ and Mary in the Garden) must be his too and he also designed the contemporary window in the N transept W wall, The Stilling of the Storm, a particularly telling design. – Nave N wall, second from l., Thanksgiving, by *James A. Crombie*, 1950, for the *Abbey Studio*. – S transept E wall, another St Paul, of 1964, again by the *Abbey Studio*; – N transept N wall, a striking blue Christ Healing the Lepers, of 1976 by *Harvey Salvin*, an Edinburgh-based American, the style described by him as 'conservative modern'. – Finally nave N wall, third from the W, a delightful St Elizabeth of Hungary of 1979 by *George Maile Studios*, the eagle, the Victoria Falls and the crest of Northern Rhodesia recalling the dedicatee's time in that country; fourth from the W, Blessed are the Meek, of 1989, and, first from the W, a Millennium window, of 2002, by *Moira Parker*, all sinuous bands of colour, the light of the world moving forward to the future.

A single-storey N range has a five-bay enclosed loggia with round-headed windows, linked to the red sandstone gabled HALL with round-headed lights and a circular W window. S of the church, the MANSE of 1908, asymmetrical in rock-faced red sandstone.

ST NINIAN (EPISCOPAL), Maryborough Road. C14 Gothic of 1925–6 by *James Scott Hay*; just two bays, for nave and chancel in one with a W apse. An E tower 'in the Sussex style' was initially envisaged. Gabled N porch with filleted moulding and one wide order with floral decoration. Four-light W window. Exposed stone walls inside, except at the E end, waggon roof, and narrow aisles with arcades. Wooden panels define the chancel. – HALL of 1999 by *Robert Potter & Partners*.

To the W, BRUCE'S WELL, the mute remains of a well which served a lazaretto here at which Robert Bruce was treated and which he subsequently generously endowed. Restored in 1912; fourteen steps down, stone walls and a brass plaque.

ST QUIVOX (R.C.), St Quivox Road. 1932–3 by *James Carrick*. Very debased Gothic, from the side more suggestive of an interwar cinema than a church. Dark red brick, with a green

Westmorland slate roof. Gabled front elevation with flanking canted lower wings with narrow windows. Side elevation of five bays, one slightly advanced, of tall round-headed windows, and a lower flat-roofed block with two bays of square-headed windows. – Polished brass STATIONS OF THE CROSS of 1984. – STAINED GLASS. One unmistakably of *c.* 1969, the other of 2000, by *Ormsby* of Scarisbrick, conservative and figurative. Harled and copper-roofed HALL, of 1998, with windows at eaves level.

MONKTON AND PRESTWICK JOINT CEMETERY, Shaw Road. 1905 by *J. & H. V. Eaglesham*, with a simple red sandstone LODGE and a low boundary WALL with attractive wrought-iron RAILINGS, naturalistic in a low-key Arts and Crafts manner.

PUBLIC BUILDINGS

BIGGART HOSPITAL, Biggart Road. 1903–5 by *R. A. Bryden* of Glasgow. Given by the Biggart family of Beith as a home for disabled children. A broad red sandstone U-plan, its main block of three gabled bays, two with fully timbered gables, the third with a rather clumsy full-height canted and balustraded bay rising to obscure the gable. Segmental-headed entrance with inscription panel above and large bow to the r. Flanking single-storey wings and single-storey gable-ended pavilions, harled but with canted balustraded red sandstone frontispieces. That to the r. has been extended, in a respectful style, probably by *J. K. Hunter*, 1909–10; other extensions are less respectful. To the r., the DAY HOSPITAL, brick with a tiled roof, with a dramatic inwardly sloping glazed porch, *c.* 1996.

FREEMEN'S HALL, The Cross. Of 1844 as a Council House and Schoolroom. Three-bay two-storey brown ashlar Gothic front elevation with a central octagonal tower and (until 2011) a spire. The flanking bays have small lancets on the ground floor and round-headed windows above. Two tiers of round-headed windows on the side elevations, the upper ones with aprons.

GLENBURN PRIMARY SCHOOL. *See* Description, below.

KINGCASE PRIMARY SCHOOL, Adamton Road South. 1970–1 by *Ayr County Council Architects Dept.* Two main blocks of harled brick. In the grounds a brick tower, with a bell originally from Old St Nicholas Church (*see* Churches, above), made by *Burgerhuys*, 1619.

KIRKHALL SURGERY, Alexandra Avenue. 1915 by *Allan Stevenson*, as church hall for the Established Church. Red sandstone, with a three-bay gabled front with tall lancets, corner buttresses with finials, an oculus in the gable and a cross apex finial.

MERCAT CROSS, The Cross. *See* Description, below.

POLICE STATION, Main Street. 1903–4 by *John Murdoch*. Three-bay red sandstone block, with the entrance beneath an inscribed panel and a shouldered semicircular pediment. To the l., a later red sandstone block, of *c.* 1925, with harled side elevation and chimneystacks. The mannered domestic style suggests *William Cowie*.

POST OFFICE, The Cross. *See* Description, below.

PRESTWICK ACADEMY, Newdykes Road. 2007–9 by *Ryder HKS*, for South Ayrshire Council. Large, panel-faced, and with the usual drum tower entrance. Playground enclosed by walls and railings, the entrance enlivened by wrought-iron SCULP-TURES, 2002, by school pupils, under the tutelage of *Elspeth Bennie*.

PRESTWICK COMMUNITY CENTRE, Caerlaverock Road. Of 1881–2 by *John Murdoch* as a school, and converted in 1979 by *Strathclyde Regional Council*. Single-storey red sandstone U-plan with a broad asymmetrical front, which has a projecting gabled bay to the l., beneath a triangular-headed bellcote, and a projecting hipped bay to the r., both with three-light windows. Trefoil-headed and square-headed windows, some of the latter with stone trefoils above. Former playground enclosed with walls and railings.

PRESTWICK LIBRARY, Kyle Street. A Billiards Hall of 1925, converted in 1947. Tall gabled and harled front, with a stone base course and a three-light window in the gable, beneath a head with a raised semicircular centre. Flanking entrances of dressed stone with similar heads.

PRESTWICK MUNICIPAL CHAMBERS, Links Road. *See* Description, below.

PRESTWICK TOWN STATION. The Ayr to Irvine section of the Glasgow, Paisley Kilmarnock & Ayr Railway was opened in 1839, though the present buildings date from *c.* 1900; the main building on the down platform a long range harled with red sandstone dressings and a rock-faced stone base. Open porch above the entrance. On the platform side, vertical wooden boarded finishes and a glazed awning.

WAR MEMORIAL, The Cross. *See* Description, below.

GOLF CLUBS

OLD PRESTWICK GOLF CLUB, Links Road. The club was founded in 1851, and a 12-hole course laid out by *Tom Morris Sen.*, on part of the common lands of Prestwick. The first Open Championship was played over the course in 1860. At the heart of the CLUBHOUSE is a three-bay two-storey sandstone villa of 1866–7, with its main elevation facing W. Central single-storey canted bay with flanking doors (originally windows?) beneath segmental pediments. In 1893–5 significant additions were made by *James A. Morris & Hunter*: this is the single-storey extension to the l. of the original building, with its main façade facing N, on to the course. Big canted bay at the corner; to the l. of this a large single-storey porch, now blocked, with a window with Roman Doric columns, and a big pedimented clock on the roof. Considerably altered inside in 1998–9 by the *Alistair Murdoch Partnership*, but the three main 1890s interiors remain intact, and retain the luxuriant relaxed feel of an

Edwardian gentleman's club: the Smoke Room, with tall
wooden panelled walls, a coved plaster ceiling, two red marble
fireplaces, doors in lugged wooden frames and, most importantly, unsurpassed views of the course; the Dining Room, with
a low boarded dado, plaster walls and ceiling, and simpler
wooden door frames; and the Card Room, also with a low
dado, but with more modern wooden display panelling above.
The wood-panelled original Entrance Hall also Morris's, with
a bronze and marble WAR MEMORIAL, of *c.* 1920. As part of
Murdoch's alterations, the upper floor of the Morris extension,
which had been small committee rooms, was opened up to
form a restaurant.

PRESTWICK ST NICHOLAS GOLF CLUB, Grangemuir Road.
CLUBHOUSE, 1892 by *John Mercer*, with substantial additions.
The original building is L-plan, with canted bays. On one wall,
facing the course, a stone semicircular headed bas relief of a
golfer at play by *W. G. Stevenson*, 1892.

DESCRIPTION

The town has two parts that merit description, the historic centre
of The Cross and streets off, and the area to the w, developed
around the attractions of the golf links and the esplanade along
the shore.

The first part can be described from THE CROSS at the N end
of the Main Street, which has the grey stone chamfered
MERCAT CROSS as its focal point. Square base, three steps,
and shaft with a moulded cornice and ball finial. Rebuilt 1777.
Behind it, the Baroque red sandstone POST OFFICE of 1927-8
by *H. M. Office of Works*, a very striking design. Two-storey,
with the entrance in the l. bay, and a pended vehicle entrance
in the recessed sixth bay. Bold Gibbsian surrounds to the
ground-floor openings and a partially balustraded cornice. To
the sw, the BANK OF SCOTLAND, a pleasant but unexceptional late C19 villa, and in front the WAR MEMORIAL of
1920-1 by *James A. Morris*, an octagonal tapering 7 m.-tall
column with diminutive Celtic cross on a plinth, with bronze
panels on four faces and deep roll-moulded panels on the
others; smaller apron panels below on all faces. *Morris* also
designed Nos. 21-37 MAIN STREET, opposite, in 1898-9 for
Prestwick Unionist Club. Five tall square-headed windows,
with shops below, flanking the prominent channelled stone
entrance, with a heavily moulded semicircular pediment. The
consoles are reminiscent of Chinese lanterns. Facing this,
BOYDFIELD GARDENS, laid out in 1935 by *Maxwell M. Hart
Ltd* on the site of Boydfield House (dem. 1933), after plans to
erect the Burgh Chambers and municipal offices here had
come to naught.* The eyecatcher is a huge SUNDIAL, of 1998

---

* The competition for this design was won 1933 by *R. Mervyn Noad*, of Glasgow,
but abandoned in 1934.

by *Elspeth Bennie* of Balfron, with pupils of Prestwick Academy. A giant bright blue wrought-iron gnomon, approached through an avenue of naturalistic wrought-iron bollards inspired by local fungi, with stone hour markers that have wrought-iron representations of local historical and architectural landmarks.

The rest of Main Street has the usual mix of periods but is surprisingly undominated by commercial buildings. The most memorable thing is Prestwick South Parish Church (*see* Churches, above) and then former Broadway Cinema (now PRESTWICK LEISURE), w side, of 1934–5 by *Alister G. MacDonald*. A bold assemblage of three big harled cubes, the centre one taller and set back with the outer bays curving inward to the entrance in streamlined fashion. At first-floor level, a painted brick band with horizontal windows. In the outer bays, original curved shopfronts. After that, very little until one reaches St Nicholas (*see* Churches, above) on the E side, 300 m. s.

The street continues as AYR ROAD, with some individual houses of interest. First, Nos. 2–4, *c.* 1909, grey stone with applied-timbered gables with canted oriels and decorative friezes and paired basket-headed entrances with mannered keystones and a single Roman Doric column between. No. 25, *c.* 1870, has a flurry of bargeboarded gables, while No. 27, of *c.* 1860, has a sinuously bargeboarded gable, and No. 29 is a brown stone and harl three-storey house of *c.* 1919 with a central entrance beneath a timber balcony and two three-light windows with stubby columns. Opposite, No. 22, a harled Gothic cottage of *c.* 1820.

In the opposite direction from Main Street, one leaves The Cross past a late C19, two-storey four-bay painted stone building with a semi-octagonal tower to the r., with a steep slated conical roof, almost Swiss in feel. Opposite, the RED LION, in two early C19 three-bay properties, both rendered with dressed stone margins. The older of the two, to the r., has a pilastered doorway. Opposite, some much altered COTTAGES of *c.* 1800 and the Freemen's Hall (*see* Public Buildings, above). KIRK STREET runs NW to the Old Church (*see* Churches, above) and was once an important thoroughfare, but now has little interest. Near the top, however, in MACINTYRE ROAD, is OLD ST CUTHBERTS. This has a bland front of 1983–4 by *J. & J. A. Carrick* but to the r. reveals its genesis as the clubhouse for St Cuthbert's Golf Club of 1908 by *J. Gibb Morton* of Glasgow: big harled porch with catenary arched entrance and stone benches, and a dumpy harled tower, with a tiled hipped roof. Also here, a PUMPING STATION, of *c.* 1980 by *Cowie Torry & Partners*. A striking explosion of harled angularity, making what could have been mundane a sculptural triumph.

SE of here, on MONKTON ROAD, THE CRESCENT, of 1901–2 by *William McGeachin*, builder, has four pairs of villas, mostly grey-harled with red sandstone margins, with central entrances and flanking canted bays. On the opposite side of the road, a mini-Pollokshields: three big red sandstone villas – perhaps the grandest in Prestwick. No. 38, REDLANDS, of *c.* 1894, has a hipped slated roof, a four-centred arched entrance flanked by big ground-floor canted bays with heavy cornices, and very tall finials and end stack. The hipped Nos. 40–42, CRAIGARD and GLENCAIRN, are of *c.* 1898, and again have canted bays, here full-height, flanking paired entrances with consoled heads, fanlights, panelled entablatures, and round-headed niches. Nos. 44–46, BALGREGAN and MONTCLAIR, of 1902–3 by *Thomas Dykes & Robertson* of Glasgow, are also hipped, and not quite symmetrical. Outer hipped bays, with projecting full-height heavily corniced bay windows rising to the white stone eaves band, with flanking entrances set back. Big rear wings, and many tall and prominent finials and chimneystacks; these of red sandstone with white freestone above.

STATION ROAD, W of The Cross, has on the S side the MATTHEW SMITH MEMORIAL FOUNTAIN, 1903, Aberdeen granite with a very good bronze portrait by *Robert Bryden*. Moved from The Cross in 1913, when it lost its horse-watering trough and gained a lamp standard. Such is fame. No. 1 is of *c.* 1896, in cream freestone, with one crowstepped gable, a corner turret and a central round-arched entrance between red granite columns. Before this on the N side, however, Nos. 2–4, a big dark brown sandstone pair of *c.* 1865 with segmental-headed entrances, flanking canted bays and, at No. 4, on the side elevation, a sweet cast-iron and lead-roofed porch. The rustic brick single-storey No. 6 is of 1968–9 by *Clunie Rowell* of *Rowell & Anderson*, for himself, with one square window projected in a stepped frame. Round the corner, in MANSEWELL ROAD, MIDLAND (No. 2), of *c.* 1890, with a round bay to the l., and decorative cast-iron railing to the upper windows, and RAVENSCRAIG (No. 8) of 1898 by *W. J. Anderson*, with a big semicircular two-storey bay, tall stacks and crowstepped gables.

s, in MIDTON ROAD, the excellent Nos. 2–4, *c.* 1912, a broad pair of crowstepped creamy freestone villas with semicircular bays flanking the square-headed entrances, which have blank panels beneath small Lorimerean boat-shaped dormers, and the harled brick PRESTWICK BOWLING CLUB, of 1927–8 by *William Cowie*, with brick dressings to the big picture windows and tile banding.

Beyond Prestwick Town Station (*see* Public Buildings, above) LINKS ROAD has Old Prestwick Golf Club (*see* above) on its N side and, on the S, a run of villas of *c.* 1880, mostly semi-detached, e.g., Nos. 9–11, with entrances with chunky consoles and finials. No. 15, now PRESTWICK MUNICIPAL CHAMBERS, is of 1877 by *Alexander Hunter* and *William Urie*, builders, of Troon, with a grey-harled extension for civic use of 1938–41 by *Francis Pritty*, Burgh Surveyor, while No. 23, KIRKMAY, has a pedimented three-light window and pilastered entrance. No. 25 is of *c.* 1898, a big brown stone house with an oriel to the r. corbelled out on a column with lotus capital in front of a pair of square-headed windows. On the N side of Links Road, MALCOLM SARGENT HOUSE occupies two former private homes, linked by a glazed corridor block. The bigger is The Homestead, Arts and Crafts of *c.* 1901 by *Sydney Mitchell & Co.*, white-harled with red sandstone dressings. Three-light window with stone mullions over modern porch, and end stacks, one with decorative crowsteps, the other with scrolled shoulders. The three-bay two-storey Golf Park is of *c.* 1865, its basket-headed doorway flanked by narrow round-headed windows, all under a scrolled entablature.

At the foot of Links Road a cast-iron colonnaded BEACH SHELTER AND KIOSK of 1921–2 by *Francis Pritty*. To the N the sanitized remains of Prestwick's BATHING LAKE of 1929–31 by *William Cowie*. Only the stone seals now raise a smile. 0.5 km. in the distance to the N is the helical stone INSPECTION CHAMBER, part of the coastal sewage pumping system, with conical slated and glazed roof, of *c.* 1980 by *Cowie Torry & Partners*, again making of a necessary evil a positive architectural statement.

The backdrop to the green sward of the ESPLANADE is mostly mid to late C19 villas. The best is STONEGARTH (No. 10 Ardayre Road*), of 1907–8 by *J. K. Hunter*. Confidently handled Cotswold pastiche, with many stone-mullioned windows. The outer bays are gabled, while the central bay has a canted window with a heavy cornice and small triangular pediment.** PARKSTONE (No. 6 Ardyare Road) is of 1870: three bays and two storeys to the sea, with a big bow to the l., and painted quoins. To the rear a big harled flat-roofed two-storey ballroom of 1959 by *Robert Allan*, with a rounded corner, and long ranges of stone-mullioned windows. GRACEFIELD (No. 21 BURGH ROAD), is of 1923–5 by *Watson, Salmond & Gray*, and all the interest here is on the entrance front, where the house is shown to be L-plan, with a moulded doorway, with a segmentally headed panel above, under a big consoled hood-mould, in a big grey stone porch in the re-entrant. Flanking wings marry grey stone and white harling with creamy dressed stone margins and metal windows.

OUTER PRESTWICK

NORTH PRESTWICK is an enclave of mostly interwar houses close to the former Parish Church (see New Life Christian Fellowship, above). Of special interest are two houses at the very edge of the airport. THE BOWER, McNee Road, of 1927 by *Alexander Mair* for himself, linking two cottages to form an H-plan. It has a central lean-to porch and deeply recessed doorway, with a chimneystack above, midway up the slope of

---

*The houses which front the Esplanade take their addresses from their rear entrances in the roads behind, such as Ardayre Road.
** In the grounds, WAR MEMORIAL to Polish servicemen, originally erected *c.* 1946 at a camp at Monkton.

the roof. The gables on the garden front have stone-framed round-headed windows. Also WESTBURN HOUSE, Shavian Domestic Revival of c. 1900, in brick and half-timbering with many gables. Its garage uses the same elements more modestly.

GLENBURN is the town's erstwhile industrial suburb, 1.25 km. E of the centre. It developed 1910–12 after William Baird & Co. sank a colliery here, and built 184 row houses. Of this period, GLENBURN PRIMARY SCHOOL, Sherwood Road, of 1913–14 by *William Cowie*, a large symmetrical design with pavilion blocks. Harl with red sandstone details, such as broken pediments. The rows were demolished in 1972; the colliery closed in 1973. Now it is dominated by companies and services dependent on the airport. PRESTWICK AIR TRAFFIC CONTROL CENTRE, in Sherwood Road, is a major extension of 2004–10 of Atlantic House (the former National Coal Board offices, originally converted to this use in 1972).

In Monument Crescent, lost amid huge industrial sheds, is the SHAW TOWER, built before 1775, a circular stone tower with a broader base, doorway and window, three small openings in the tower, and a crown spire. Its purpose is unknown; unconfirmed legend has it that it was used for falconry. Also within the industrial area is GLENBURN HOUSE, Glenburn Road, of 1894–6 by *James A. Morris* for the Rev. Edward D. Prothero. Attractive asymmetrical harled Arts and Crafts villa with polished red sandstone dressings, and a tiled roof. Wooden entrance porch with a semicircular window to the l.; round first-floor windows intermingled with small segmentally headed windows like rather startled eyebrows. Now offices, with a big extension to the l.

PRESTWICK TOLL AND KINGCASE first developed around the toll on the Ayr Road about 1.5 km. S of the centre, but is now an area of almost seamless suburban transition from Prestwick into Ayr. Much of the area of historic settlement has been redeveloped but ST MARNOCK COTTAGE (No. 128 Ayr Road) is an early C19 harled cottage with smooth painted dressings, a pilastered doorway and chamfered windows. Also, just behind, Nos. 1–3 JAMES STREET, a pair of painted stone cottages of c. 1800, with windows tending to the horizontal, and deeply recessed entrances. In the same street, No. 10, of c. 1985, a skilled aggregation of monopitch roofs and exposed timber detail. Much else was lost to rebuilding at this time, especially 1964–7; see, to the S of Pleasantfield Road, eight shops and a pub 'of Scandinavian design' by *William Loudon & Sons Ltd*, of Newmains, based on a prototype at Cumbernauld, Lanarkshire. In WATERLOO ROAD and WELLINGTON STREET, early *Prestwick Town Council* housing of 1926–8 by *Francis Pritty*, of harled brick; noteworthy are the original stencilled house numbers. OBSERVER COURT, close to Kingcase Parish Church (*see* Churches, above), is affordable housing of 2008–10 by *ARPL Architects* (*Gordon Fleming*, project architect), a mixed development given unity by the use of vertically hung roof tiles on many elevations.

SALT PAN HOUSES, Maryborough Road, overlooking the sea on the edge of St Nicholas Golf Course. Erected 1764–7 and associated with the salt pans acquired by Richard Oswald of Auchincruive in 1764. Roughly symmetrical, with dressed margins; each has an external stair to the first-floor level. The lower floors have brick vaults where the salt was stored; the upper floors were residential. The linking wall may be later. They must be the most substantial surviving structures of the Scottish salt industry.

91

PRESTWICK INTERNATIONAL AIRPORT
0.75 km. N of the town centre

The flat sandy lands between Prestwick and Monkton proved popular with the first generation of aviators, though the genesis of the present airport lies in the airfield constructed in 1935–6 by Scottish Aviation Ltd (S.A.L.). Their architect was *Alexander Mair*, who designed a hangar and an office block, both now gone, and converted Orangefield House (*c.* 1790, dem. 1966) to provide the officers' and airmen's messes.* The original grass runway was concreted and lengthened by the RAF in 1939, while S.A.L. began aircraft construction at Monkton (q.v.). A second runway, at right angles to the main runway, was built in 1954–5, and the original runway was extended seawards in 1959–60 (contractors, *Richard Costain Ltd*). In 1954 *Joseph Gleave*, then of *Keppie, Henderson & J. L. Gleave* (afterwards *J. L. Gleave & Partners*) was asked to design a new CONTROL TOWER (built 1960–2) and to provide sketch plans for a PASSENGER TERMINAL (built 1961–4). The latter is long and steel-framed, with concrete floors and curtain walling (alas, it has lost its original interiors of afrormosia hardwood, black aluminium mullions and dark glass panels but retains a large ceramic MURAL by *Robert Stewart*, 1972–3, a representational aerial view of the airport and its surroundings). Close to the road, an aluminium SCULPTURE, The Celestial Navigator, 1997 by *Carole Gray*. A conical base supports a half-moon, from which a sun and a further crescent moon are suspended. A tubular exoskeleton, resembling a flying man, is lit at night, when it becomes the dominant element in the design. PRESTWICK INTERNATIONAL AIRPORT STATION is of 1993–4 by *Holford Associates*. Form following function: the striking silhouette is created by paired red blockwork stairwells on each platform, linked by a glazed corridor, subsequently extended across the road as an umbilical link to the terminal.

---

* The estate of Monkton was acquired by James Macrae (*see* Monkton) who, wearing his politics on his sleeve, renamed it Orangefield.

PRIESTLAND

5030

Small roadside settlement strung out along the main road E of Darvel.

At the W end, INVERGOWER HOUSE, of *c.* 1900, stark white harl with red sandstone dressings and its entrance in a thin slated porch beneath a conical-headed corner turret.

CHAMBERED CAIRN, Loanfoot, 2 km. SE. A little over 100 m. in length and containing at least one chamber, and possibly four.

LOUDOUN HILL, 3 km. E. A volcanic plug which forms a prominent landmark and visual stop to the upper Irvine Valley. The low sandy watershed between the Irvine and the Avon Water forms one of the easier accesses into Ayrshire. It was the site of a 1.4-ha. Roman AUXILIARY FORT, with a later annexe surrounded by a double ditch, all now lost to gravel workings, and of several battles, most notably in 1307 when Robert Bruce defeated the English, an early success in the campaign that culminated at Bannockburn. Spirit of Scotland, a figurative steel SCULPTURE by *Richard Price* of Douglas, 2004, reflects this history.

QUARTER HOUSE

2060

3 km. NW of Largs

A straightforward classical early C19 country house of three bays and two storeys, with a pedimented centre, a simple doorpiece and thin end pilasters. Subsequent additions, including a two-storey projection to the rear, enclosing the original bowed staircase projection. Mid-C19 flanking single-storey wings with canted bays were added to the front elevation; the l. one raised to two storeys in the late C19. The house commands unparalleled views across the waters and islands, making even more inexplicable its derelict and roofless condition.

RANKINSTON

4010

Before the mid C19 Rankinston was a remote rural fastness. In 1864 ironstone was found in exploitable quantity, and development of the area began. By 1881 there were 170 row houses, and another thirty were being built. Coal mining at Littlemill Colliery extended the life of the village into the C20, and it was rebuilt by *Ayr County Council* during the 1950s, as one long street striding purposefully uphill, an easily recognizable feature in the local landscape at night.

RANKINSTON COMMUNITY CENTRE. 1956, for the Coal Industries Social Welfare Organisation. Substantial hall, originally of exposed brick, but now harled. WAR MEMORIAL. 1921 by *J. Kennedy* of Ayr, a simple Aberdeen granite obelisk.

ROBERTLAND

4040

2.2 km. NE of Stewarton

Eyecatching and well-positioned classical three-bay two-storey house of *c.* 1813 for Alexander Kerr, with an ashlar front and a Doric doorpiece in the slightly advanced pedimented central bay. Doric pilasters, set slightly in from the corners, give a sense of tautness to the façade, cutting short the base and sill courses. It is, perhaps, by *David Hamilton*, with similarities to his Ladyland (q.v.). The other elevations of painted stone, as is the substantial two-storey rear wing which contains the main stair and offices. Restrained interior with simple cornices. To the rear the offices include two C18 cottages, one immediately behind the house, single-storey and rubble; the other, at right angles, is two-storey, hipped, with wall-head stacks. The estate has a late C19 classical hipped LODGE and GATEPIERS with swept pyramidal caps, and a single-span segmentally arched BRIDGE with low parapets, said to be of 1835

Beyond this the WALLED GARDEN, which incorporates a number of sculptured fragments from ROBERTLAND CASTLE, including a panel of 1597 inscribed [VI]VIT POST FVNERA VIRTU[S] ('Virtue lies beyond the grave'). The castle lay to the SE of the present house; it was built for, and perhaps designed by, *Sir David Cunningham* of Robertland, James VI's master of works from 1602. It has been argued that the prominent fleur-de-lis on one fragment pre-dates James's claim, first made in 1603, to be King of France.

RODINGHEAD HOUSE

4030

5 km. NNE of Mauchline

A comfortable late C18 country house of two storeys with a shallow advanced central bay, pedimented with a blind oculus and ball finial, all neatly defined by bold rusticated quoins. Early C19 Greek Doric porch filled with delicate wrought-iron screening, probably inserted in the early C20, balancing single-storey outer bays of 1805 with bowed ends. Rear additions of the mid C19, 1903 and 1909–10. The main house considerably altered inside in the early C20 when the original hall was opened into an adjoining room and panelled. Stone newel stair at rear. Good delicate period plasterwork in the dining room and drawing room in the wings. Large walled garden, lodge and cast-iron gates.

ROWALLAN CASTLE

4040

3 km. NE of Kilmaurs

A courtyard house evolving over four centuries under the long tenure of the Mure family and important, as Geoffrey Stell has said, as 'an ancient lairdly residence which was transformed into a Renaissance home' rather than a truly defensible castle or tower house. The Mures of Rowallan were the epitome of the polymath culture of the C16 and C17, illustrated by the survival of the 'Rowallan Lute Book' of *c.* 1620. Serious archaeological analysis has thrown much light on the development of this site.

The site, a mound on a steep bend in the Carmel Water, has been identified as a Bronze Age burial place. The earliest building here, however, is what remains of a late C13 or early C14 tower, erected for either Gilchrist Mure or Walter Comyn. It is of small scale, comparable with Portencross or Seagate Castle (Irvine, qq.v.), suggesting that it might not have been the principal family dwelling. How its courtyard arrangement evolved is not clear but by the late C15 or early C16 there was a s w range probably built by John Mure (who died at Flodden). Mungo Mure (†1547) continued this range and created a hall and chamber inside it. It is however to John Mure (1547–91) that the present building owes its picturesque appearance; first he built the s E entrance range, in two phases, and made further embellishments including the N W wall of the court and the range returning on the N E side to join to the original tower. In the mid C17, however, this N range was largely rebuilt by William Mure IV and the s E outer courtyard re-created. Perhaps as the result of a collapse, the external w corner of the inner court was rebuilt in the early C18 and given a much greater symmetry. The interior planning and its decoration date from the mid C17 through to the early C18. From the mid C18 the house underwent a slow and gentle decline. Plans made in 1896 by *Leadbetter & Fairley* to convert and extend it for the Earl of Loudoun were unexecuted, and when A. Cameron Corbett, later Lord Rowallan, purchased the estate in 1901 he built afresh on a new site (*see* Rowallan House, below). In 1950 the castle was handed into Guardianship by the 2nd Lord Rowallan.

The approach is across a small arched bridge below the remains of the TOWER, and from the N the mound on which it was built is clearly visible along with the fragmentary rubble walls. The castle entrance is reached through an elaborately pedimented GATE, dated 1661 with the monogram of William Mure IV and his wife Elizabeth Hamilton. This led into the s E courtyard, also re-created at that time, of which nothing else remains. Set into rubble walls, this gate has an ashlar archway with mannered Jacobean detailing including a broken segmental pediment with a central bulbous pedestal. The lost doorway at Auchans of *c.* 1644 was remarkably similar. In the walls to either side small circular gunloops all part of the showy effect.

Behind is the s E RANGE of the castle, the show front created in the C16. In its first phase it was two storeys with the lower wall at the E retaining part of the mound of the earlier tower that abuts to the N but is now ruinous. Incorporated into the s end of this range is the s end of the s w range. This retains a dumb-bell gunloop of *c.* 1480 at the basement level, one of the few displays of defence. In the second phase of 1562 John Mure added the third storey containing a long gallery, apparently raising the SW range at the same time (see the wall-head chimney which served its upper rooms), and created the splendid frontispiece. Built in roughly dressed ashlar, this comprises two drum towers with conical roofs flanking a quirked triple-arched pend, reached by a substantial forestair. The design mimicks, on a domestic scale, the substantial towered entrances of the palaces at Stirling, Falkland and Holyrood. It is both a conscious reference to the Mure's distant royal connections through Elizabeth Mure, the first wife of Robert II (1371–90) and a powerful symbolic statement of the family's position. The forestair may take as its model a similar stair of 1535–6 at Holyrood (now replaced). In scale the late C16 turreted entrance at Tolquhon, Aberdeenshire, provides the closest comparison. That the towers are later than the pend and the rest of the SE range is confirmed by the remains of a window at the junction of the front with the S tower. These additions are remarkable for the complete absence of defensive features such as parapets or battlements. There are circular gunloops in the towers but these must be largely symbolic. Above the entrance level a heavy cable moulding, run as a string course, links the towers; a smaller version also frames the circular gunloops, details such as are found at Blairquhan Castle (dem.) and exuberantly at Kenmure (Dumfries and Galloway). Above the arched pend a rectangular chamfered heraldic panel bearing the royal arms and supporters with the Mure arms beneath, surrounded by cabled bosses and capped with a Moor's head, a pun on the family name. The head wears a curious turban with a crown, this head-dress is also used for the finials on the conical tower roofs and above the large window to the gallery between the towers, here raised on a token piece of parapet with flanking armorial panels bearing the Mure arms and the paternal arms of Marion Cunningham. Below this an inscription

JON MVR

M.CVGM

SPVSIS

1562

recording John Mure and his wife Marion Cunningham. The ornament is characteristic of a particular style of decoration which flourished in domestic building in the west of Scotland in the later C16. The wide FORESTAIR is a puzzle for it is not placed square to the pend and intersects with the drums unevenly, suggesting that its position, if not its present form, may have related to an earlier entrance to the inner court.

The SW AND NW ELEVATIONS of the castle are plain. As on the SE front, dumb-bell gunloops survive in the vaulted lower storey of the S end of the SW range. At principal-floor level, which contained the hall created in the early C16, windows on the external elevation have been altered, with, a little above them, a blind panel formerly housing a carved armorial. At cornice level two dropped lintels indicate former dormers. The gable at the s end was raised to accommodate the Long Gallery in the s E range and in it is a large window, like that at Auchans, which was intended for viewing the garden and wider landscape. The w end of the s w range is symmetrically glazed as a result of c18 rebuilding. Originally this end appears to have been stepped back but the rebuilding brought its s w wall flush with the retaining wall of the courtyard, reusing some original buckle quoins. There are two horizontal gunloops at the level of the courtyard. At the n corner of the courtyard are the remains of the mid-c16 block with arrises of a similar form to those on the earliest part of the s E range, and the remains of a corbelled angle round which was once mirrored further s E. This block was linked to the ruined tower and to a partially walled n E enclosure. It is probable that the Woman House, known to have been created by John Mure in the later c16, was in this building.

Inside the courtyard, can be seen the remaining rubble walls of the tower. They are 2.5 m. thick. The entrance at the w has been cut through later into a passage leading to the straight mural stair. The ground floor was once vaulted but apart from the evidence of a large fireplace with c15 mouldings in the N w wall little of the medieval work can be seen. Alterations occurred as the domestic accommodation around the court was developed. On this side, the N w block is as rebuilt in the c. 1660s: reusing the c16 N E and N w walls but with a new s w wall that encloses a horizontal gunloop in the court's N w wall, and abuts the N w wall of the earlier tower. The monogram and armorial panel of Sir William and Elizabeth Hamilton appear in the segmentally pedimented head over the entrance in its stair-turret.★

The s w range is the most complex. The lower vaulted floor, as noted outside, is probably late c15 or early c16. It has a passage to the N E, its N E wall retaining the castle mound, and was vaulted over in the early c16 when the hall and chamber range was built above, creating a level access from the court. Two doors at the N end at hall level were blocked, the architrave of the main door still visible. In the early c18 a bolection-moulded entrance was made in a window opening to the s E; further s E is a large stack serving the hall fireplace; beyond again, where there was formerly a window and filling the re-entrant angle with the s E range, is a stair-turret of c. 1560. Its stone newel provided access to the Long Gallery, the garret rooms above the hall and the best bedroom over the chamber; it replaced an earlier stair. At the N w end of the range, giving the elevation symmetry, is another newel stair, a reconstruction

★ The magnificent oak door for the entrance is in the Museum of Scotland. It has a carved fan head with arcading and serpents. Sir William, a staunch Presbyterian, added a very unusual Hebrew inscription ('The Lord is the portion of mine inheritance and of my cup').

of the early to mid C17, replacing an earlier stair which may have served a lost NW range as well as the basement area of the SW range. The turret's upper stage has buckle quoins of the kind found at the Skelmorlie Aisle, Largs (1636, q.v.).

Inside the SW range the W compartment of the vaulted lower level was probably a kitchen, enlarged in the early C18 when the windows were inserted; the well in the small chamber to its SE is part of the late C15 work; the stairs here leading to the hall have been much altered. The hall has undergone a number of alterations; it retains some full-height panelling and a c. 1700 double door in an Ionic-pilastered doorcase with a bolection frieze and modillion cornice. This was re-set in the C20 and leads to a lobby replacing in function the former screens passage. This work compares with the interior panelling of a similar date at Kelburn (q.v.), and Dame Jean Mure, who inherited Rowallan in 1700, was the second wife of the 1st Earl of Glasgow. At the SE of the hall is a door to the stair-turret. The W chamber beyond also has C18 panelling. The Great Chamber or Solar to the SE formerly had elaborate Jacobean-style late C17 panelling. Fragmentary remains of the C16 chimneypiece have allowed a rather crude reconstruction (c. 1988) indicating the scale. To its NE a closet and to the SW a window ingo with an aumbry which once had elaborately framed and panelled doors and stone window seats. Leading from this room a mural stair to the basement. The communications between floors and the various alterations here are complex and underline the value of the current stripped-out condition helping an understanding of the evolution. The downside is that it is not easily read and gives no sense of the importance or use of these ranges. Above the Solar a bedchamber with the remains of a timber-arched bed recess flanked with panelled cupboards on the NW wall. The SE range has an equally stripped-out appearance. The entrance-level floor was divided when the drum towers were added. In the former Long Gallery there is a simple fireplace on the NE wall, on the SE openings to the drums and three windows, the central one large and, like the big window in the SW gable, designed to provide views of the surroundings.

Blaeu's map shows Rowallan surrounded with PARKLAND and suggests that its design has evolved at least from the C17; prior to that there were gardens and orchards around the castle. The formal avenues of the early C18 still define the grounds, part of which have become a golf course. The WALLED GARDEN encloses a substantial area of ground NW of the castle. There is a lintel to a gate dated 1687 and another datestone, possibly 1688, on a crowstepped gable of the small cottage set into the wall at the SE. The rubble-built walls on three sides appear to be of this date, and link into the remains of various enclosures around the castle. In the NE corner is a delightful pavilion of c. 1904 by *Lorimer*, who was then at work on Rowallan House (*see* below), with an arched loggia below a garden room, the latter lit by tall balconied windows with sinuously scrolled pediment-heads, these together with the faceted bell-cast roof as lively as the garden they survey. Outside the w wall a large gabled gardener's house and to its w a new CLUBHOUSE and RESTAURANT for the golf club, a huge glass house mimicking a greenhouse *c.* 2008.

84   ROWALLAN HOUSE, NW of Rowallan Castle, dates from 1901–5. This was *Robert S. Lorimer's* first Scottish commission for an entirely new mansion, brought to him through his Glasgow connections, particularly William Burrell. The client was A. Cameron Corbett, a developer and Liberal M.P. for Tradeston (Glasgow) and his wife Alice. She died before a stone was laid and her mother substantially funded the house's completion. The first proposal was for a large house for entertaining, designed around three courtyards with the service areas segregated from the public and private quarters, but it was reduced in size after Alice Corbett's death. Even without the large E bachelor wing, it is very substantial. The materials are sandstone from the estate, with dressings from Hailes near Edinburgh. The original intention was to paint or even harl the walls, but neither treatment appealed to the clients.

The style is Lorimer's very personal interpretation of C16–C17 Scots architecture with plenty of crow- or corbie-stepped gables, a particularly playful reference to the client's name, perhaps mindful of the pun played on the Mures' name at the old castle (*see* above, p. 591). *Boyd & Forrest* of Kilmarnock were the contractors and the carved work is by many of Lorimer's usual associates, including *William Beveridge* and *William Stoddart.*

The approach is through a GATEHOUSE, modelled on that at Earlshall, Fife, a miniature T-plan tower, set into the policy walls and with the carriageway running through it under a bold arch. A rounded stair-turret to the l. is corbelled to square at cornice level. On the inner face decorative cusped dormerheads.

The long drive passes the old castle as it winds through the policies to the N FRONT, which is a dramatic grouping of interlocking blocks of varying heights, roof levels and pitches. The lowest block, to the w of the entrance, has a mansard roof, a ruse that emphasizes the height of the main blocks and was intended to accommodate a balcony extending across the entrance hall, linking to a similar block to the E. This build-up would have had even more drama if the E bachelor wing had been completed. The entrance is in a tall steep gable, somewhat ecclesiastical in appearance, with a mannered frontispiece: a pair of arched panelled doors under a moulded arch-head set on solid impost blocks, tall flanking piers, with panelled blocks instead of rustication, supported at intermediate level by diminutive consoles and rising high above the door arch, each to finish with a stylized rose in the frieze and scrolled console supporting carved fruit. The piers enclose an inverted arch in which, jauntily placed, is a shield with the family arms, framed by foliage with a crowning crow and a ribbon banner above on which is inscribed DEUS PASCIT CORVOS ('God feeds the crows'). In the gable-head an oculus in a foliate frame with two flanking scrolls, one inscribed ANNO the other 1905. The gable apex is stepped up to a consoled panel. Behind the entrance block is an asymmetrically crenellated tower housing the main stair, lit from a large mullion-and-transom window facing W into a court. The position of the planned E range is marked by toothing and a blocked arched door into the entrance hall. Set back at the E beyond the tower is a tall E–W-oriented range with rounded stair-turret in C16 style, on the N, corbelled to square just below eaves level. The low passage block to the W of the entrance has a central door with an exaggerated consoled and pedimented oval dormer growing from its lintel. Beyond, an E–W block with tall mullion-and-transom ground-floor windows linked to further extensive kitchen quarters.

The long S FRONT builds up from the low service area at the W linked to the three-storey rectangular dining-room block with its big bellcast-roofed drum at the W (the model for which is possibly Auchans), the prominent projecting range housing the Library with a crowstepped gable and an unusual curved apex stone. This block would have been mirrored at the E had the whole design been implemented with the square tower and its circular stair-turret in the re-entrant angle and the Great Hall set between, the latter now slightly enlarged to form the three-windowed drawing-room block. Now the E end is emphasized by its height and the balustraded first-floor terrace with steps descending to the garden and a loggia underneath. Large multi-pane windows, a favourite Lorimer device evoking the style of the C17 but on a C20 scale, light the Drawing Room and Library at the E end, between the Library and the Dining Room there is a playful arched recess with a curved balcony. Carved decoration is chiefly reserved for the individually shaped dormerheads, with monograms and heraldic devices, in Lorimer's idiosyncratic style; below the second-floor windows in the dining-room range decorated lead gutters direct the water from between the dormerheads to downpipes, a delightfully quirky detail. The lower asymmetrically placed gables further W are smaller in scale and the dormerheads simpler, with Lorimer's much favoured hull-shaped heads. They front a low WALLED GARDEN with tall ashlar piers linked by looped ironwork and carrying baskets of fruit or leaf-covered balls. In the garden a square column with a diagonally placed block and a crowning platform looking like an unfinished sundial.

Inside, the stone-walled ENTRANCE HALL is lit from the mullioned windows on the side walls, and on the E wall there is a blocked door which would have led to the abandoned bachelors' wing. Its character comes from the high-quality late C16 panelling from the Solar of the Old Castle partially lining the E wall. Fluted pilaster-strips divide arcaded panels with elaborate strapwork detailing and geometric designs above and below.

Opposite the door, an arched stone recess with a fireplace set
into a lugged surround with flanking shell-head niches. A large
arch to the l. frames the STAIRCASE, a straight flight of stone
steps with one break, lit by side windows and fully lined with
oak panelling under a barrel-vaulted ceiling. The effect is of a
great mural stair and precedes Lutyens's similar stair at Castle
Drogo (Devon). The panelled UPPER STAIR HALL opens
from the vestibule at the head of the stone stairs and is lit by
windows overlooking the W court. The woodwork comes from
Nathaniel Grieve, including the open-well oak stair with carved
blocks to the newel posts and splat-balusters with carved
panels, the carving probably by the *Clow* brothers. The stair
rises to a gallery, supported on a panelled arched cantilever
and with an arched opening into the upper corridor. A crisp
C17-style plaster wreath and pendant on the ceiling above the
stairwell. Further stairs lead down to the billiard, gun and
garden rooms, which have been modified.

The public rooms on the principal floor include the
DRAWING ROOM to the l. from the vestibule. It is lit by five
large sash windows and has an American oak floor. A large
white and black carved marble chimneypiece, incorporating
dolphins said to be Italian, on the E wall. The ceiling, divided
into three compartments, has a plain oval hollow in the centre
with a lusciously moulded plaster frame of vines and grapes
which sprout out onto the surrounding ceiling. This work by
Sam Wilson. Ahead at the top of the stairs the LIBRARY with a
plaster vault and lined with bookcases with a delicate frieze of
tendrils and leaves above. All the fittings are by *Scott Morton &
Co*. On the E wall a large segmentally arched chimneypiece with
an elongated keystone supporting a small curved platform
with a simple wrought-iron curved balustrade. The door to
this balcony is set into a frame with a sinuously curved head.
The balcony is reached from the bookroom in the SE re-entrant
tower which was intended to give access into the minstrels'
gallery of the planned hall. The DINING ROOM contrasts
markedly with the other public rooms, being lower with a
heavily beamed ceiling and fully panelled with dark stained oak,
some of the panels with linenfold detailing, again by Scott
Morton. Above the simply moulded stone chimneypiece an
arched centrepiece with pilasters and flanking panelled sections
taking up the theme of the C17 panelling in the Entrance Hall.
The ceiling beams, liberally wrapped in plasterwork, and
cornice are enriched with vine motifs, all the work of the *Bromsgrove Guild*. At the W end a deep recess into the drum turret.

More elaborate plasterwork, again by *Sam Wilson*, in the
BEDROOMS; the SE bedroom has a combed ceiling with a plain
central oval hollow; the curved areas outside are covered with
plaster roses growing through a trellis. On the S wall a deeply
set diminutive leaded window with tiled surrounds, presumably to light a washstand. The most striking room is the main
bedroom on the S over the Library. It is panelled in C17 style
with a stone bolection-moulded chimneypiece with flanking

panelled pilasters and a lugged frame imitating the frame of
the entrance-hall chimneypiece. The ceiling is very deeply
coved, made possible by the steep pitch of the roof, with a
central dome from which an athletic cupid lets fly his arrow.
The cove has a superimposed trellis entwined with vines, their
grapes the target of small birds.

Lorimer was also responsible for the associated buildings,
including the BARN MILL with a swept half-hipped roof and
a hull-shaped head to the doorway at the head of external steps
to the loft and the STABLE COURT, a U-plan square with a tall
L-plan range on the W anchored by a bellcast-roofed drum
tower and with an elaborate oval window over the arched
doorway. Lower garage/coachhouse buildings on its E side. To
the E a pair of single-storey COTTAGES with half-hipped roofs
and rear courts.

ST QUIVOX

3020

Small kirktoun hamlet.

ST QUIVOX PARISH CHURCH. Gabled, harled and slated early
post-Reformation church of 1595 aligned NW–SE, to which a
classically detailed church has been added on the NE in the
late C18: a busy and likeable combination. The C16 church has
square-headed windows, external stone forestairs at either
gable, a simple NW bellcote and a worn moulded inscribed
panel on the SW wall supposed to commemorate its building
by Allan, Lord Cathcart. The T-plan addition may have been
added in two stages: the cross-piece lying parallel with the
church is of red sandstone, its square-headed windows almost
domestic, but the wing is of a superior grey sandstone with a
simple Venetian window set within an arch in the gable, below
an urn finial. It is of 1767, for Richard Oswald of Auchincruive,
benefiting from his contacts with Robert Adam; did Oswald
continue work, initiated by his predecessors, but to a higher
standard? The interior is particularly attractive and largely
unaltered from its late C18 appearance, when it was recast to
form a traditional T-plan layout. The medieval church and the
cross-piece of the C18 addition now form one single plastered
space, the greater length of the medieval church creating small
wings l. and r. of the pulpit with panel-fronted galleries. The
flat two-part plastered ceiling is divided on the line of the
original wall by a load-bearing cross-beam with a bowed
tension rod (C18?) beneath, secured by turned baluster-like
members. The NE wing is the Auchincruive Aisle, at mezzanine
level (*see* also Craigie), with a coved ceiling, a panelled front
beneath a wide basket arch; the family vault below. Excellent
dark-wood-panelled late C18 PULPIT and SOUNDING-BOARD,
the tall backboard with fluted pilasters flanking a panelled
cross within a round arch. The simply styled but gently curving
PEWS may also be C18. To the r. of the pulpit, MONUMENT of

1932 to Rev. James Wilson †1906, with a bronze portrait medallion by *Robert Bryden*.

The church sits in a large, raised, approximately square
22 CHURCHYARD, with a stone wall. Textbook Doric MAUSO-
LEUM of the Campbells of Craigie, of 1822 by *W. H. Playfair*.
Some weathered carved C18 headstones, such as the skull and
cross-bones close to the N corner of the mausoleum. Elsewhere,
23 the outstanding HEADSTONE to James McCalla and family
1776–84, with Adam and Eve framed by trees laden with tempting fruit. John Forbes, Inspector General of Hospitals, has an
elaborate MONUMENT with a segmental head, and subsidiary
vertical elements at the far l. and r., their heads approximately
oval, with the moulding unfinished below, rather like forceps
or pliers. They threaten to catch the downcast torches beneath.
Also an anonymous early C19 oval TABLE TOMB, with fluted
pilasters; the quality evident despite the weathering.

At the N corner of the churchyard, a double-pile harled Tudor
Gothic cottage of *c.* 1840. To the SW of the churchyard,
COTTAR HOUSE, an L-plan group of exposed stone cottages
of *c.* 1810, well restored to form one house. To the S, the two-
storey pink ashlar KENNOCH HOUSE, the former manse of
1823, has a central entrance with plain columns and an entablature with a triglyph frieze.

MOUNT HAMILTON HOUSE, to its E, is a conventional
two-storey harled T-plan house of *c.* 1800 with a broad bowed
front to the subsidiary wing, built for the factor of the Auchincruive estate but converted, 1948–51, into staff accommodation for the HANNAH DAIRY RESEARCH INSTITUTE. This
lies to the W (now in the HANNAH RESEARCH PARK) and was
built on land donated in 1928 by John M. Hannah (*see* also
Auchincruive). The institute was established by the government for the investigation of milk, its production, its use and
its health benefits. The design is of 1929–31 by *A. G. Ingham*,
of the Dept of Agriculture for Scotland, in the Lorimerian
Scots vernacular often associated with state buildings of that
period. Broadly H-plan, on a prominent site, brick harled, on
a stone base of varying depth, with a tiled roof. Stone dressings
to the main entrance and flanking elongated hexagonal
windows. Behind the main building, the congruent REFEC-
TORY of 1958–9, by *D. S. MacPhail*. To the S of the main building, a beaten metal SCULPTURE, The Milkmaid, by *Denys
Mitchell*, 1980: a cow and calf being bucket-fed by a milkmaid
in a startlingly large hat and surprisingly long skirt.

AUCHINCRUIVE. *See* p. 107.

SALTCOATS

Saltcoats was made a Burgh of Barony in 1528. The natural
harbour on the boundary between the parishes of Ardrossan and
Stevenston formed a welcome refuge for shipping on the Clyde.

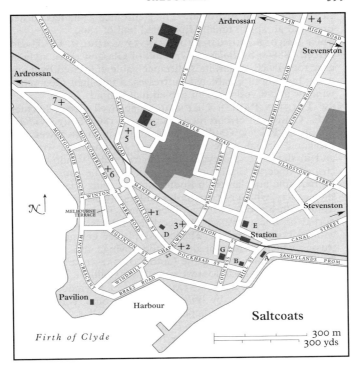

Saltcoats

1   Former E.U. Congregational Church
2   Former Landsborough & Trinity Church
3   New Trinity Parish Church
4   North Parish Church
5   St Cuthbert's Parish Church
6   St Mary (R.C.)
7   South Beach Baptist Church

A   Adelaide College
B   Bradshaw Nursery School
C   Caledonia Primary School
D   North Ayrshire Heritage Centre
E   Police Station
F   St Matthew's Academy
G   Saltcoats Town Hall

A small settlement developed and grew, especially after improvements were carried out to the harbour, beginning in the C17. It developed a strong trade in coal export, and only declined in the late C19 as it failed to compete with the ports at Troon and Ardrossan. During the same period, Saltcoats also became popular as a coastal resort.

CHURCHES

Former ARDROSSAN PARISH CHURCH. *See* North Ayrshire Heritage Centre, below.

Former EVANGELICAL UNION CONGREGATIONAL CHURCH, Hamilton Street. Simple Gothic gabled chapel of 1862–3 by

Lewis Fullarton of Ardrossan. The s entrance gable has corner
urns and an apical finial. Hip-roofed hall of 1899.

Former LANDSBOROUGH AND TRINITY CHURCH, Dockhead
Street. 1888–9 by *Baldie & Tennant* of Glasgow. E.E. style in
grey rock-faced ashlar, its s entrance gable enlivened by a yo-
yoing hoodmould, gableted buttresses, a five-light Geometric
window and a vesica. Plain gabled hall behind.

30   NEW TRINITY PARISH CHURCH, Chapelwell Street. Former
U.P. Church. Polychromed Gothic of 1864–6 by *William
Stewart* of Paisley. Gable-ended e front with a ne tower and
octagonal broach spire with lucarnes. Geometric e window,
and in the lower storeys, spherical triangular windows with
cusped tracery. Contemporary HALL with the same motifs.
Remarkable and largely unspoilt interior, with a large horseshoe gallery, which has a complex and highly distinctive gallery
front, with a series of fretwork openings, like gunloops, supported on decorative wooden corbels and cast-iron columns
with elaborate capitals. The coved plaster ceiling has roof
trusses which form triangles in the coving, also filled with
fretwork. Equally striking the Gothic ORGAN, PULPIT, COM-
MUNION TABLE AND COMMUNION RAILS; all of *c.* 1895, their
value lying in their unity. – STAINED GLASS. N windows, e and
centre. High-quality, by *William Meikle & Sons*, King David,
1929, and The Good Shepherd, 1932. s wall e, an equally
competent Sower of 1951 by *Douglas Hamilton*.

NORTH PARISH CHURCH, Dalry Road. 1963–5 by *Margaret B.
Brodie*; brick with a broad V-pitched roof, a large w window,
and the chancel projecting as an angular brick oriel. Two tiers
of windows, separated by deep wooden panels, on the gently
canted n elevation. At the nw corner the low brick porch and
the tall thin V-plan detached concrete tower, originally for a
bell of 1773. Light wedge-shaped auditorium interior, with a
rear gallery, its plaster front decorated with symbols of the
Evangelists. Its predecessor is the adjacent hall church of
1953–5 by *Black & Shapley*, built under the Post-War Extension Scheme for the new housing areas.

ST BRENDAN (R.C.), Corrie Crescent. 1962–5 by *Robert Rennie
& Watson*. A striking group of flat-roofed church, hall, campanile and priests' houses, all emphatically non-traditional. One
end of the church roof is raised into a clearstorey, lighting the
altar. The e wall has a MOSAIC PANEL of Christ in Majesty.
Dazzling white *dalle-de-verre* panels to the campanile. Bright
open interior, with narrow aisles and a rear gallery. Striking
metal CRUCIFIX behind the simple altar, the struggle and the
agony well caught. Abstract STAINED GLASS.

ST CUTHBERT'S PARISH CHURCH, Caledonia Road. 1906–8
by *Peter Macgregor Chalmers*. Romanesque Revival in white
freestone. Nave with clearstorey, choir, sanctuary and aisles of
equal height to the nave. sw entrance tower, the round-headed
entrance with three orders of decoration, including a band of
nailhead, and figurative label stops. The tower's top stage has
two-light shafted bell-openings, a round-arched balustrade and

plain gargoyles. Three tall windows in the w gable, with a gable porch to the l. Muddled N elevation, of session house, aisle and transept. The nave, chancel and sanctuary step down, each lower than the other, ending with a tall three-light E window. Exposed stone interior, with a steeply pitched timber roof and barrel-vaulted chancel and sanctuary, reminiscent of St Nicholas, Prestwick (q.v.), e.g. with round arches to the four-bay arcades, the s with gallery behind. w gallery also. – REREDOS. A depiction of the Last Supper, in white and pink alabaster, strikingly at odds with everything else. It is of 1929, and is a copy of that at St Mildred, Whippingham (Isle of Wight), designed by *A. Y. Nutt* in 1902 as part of Edward VII's memorial to his mother. – Above the NW door, a MODEL SHIP, made and given to Ardrossan Old Parish Church *c.* 1804 by *William Dunlop*. – STAINED GLASS. Chancel window, by *Percy Bacon & Brothers* of London, and contemporary with the church. It is pale and lifeless in comparison with the remarkable N and s aisle windows by *William Wilson*, 1947, with scenes in the life of Christ. They are among the best of Wilson's work anywhere. – Under the w gallery, two good windows of 1976 by *Gordon Webster*, Praise the Lord and I was in Prison.

To the s, CHURCH HALL of 1969–70 by *Andrew Watson* of *Robert Rennie & Watson*: big brick harled suite of halls, at sufficient distance to avoid too great a clash with Chalmers's cool manner.

ST MARY (R.C.), Ardrossan Road. 1855–6 by Mr *Baird* of Airdrie.* Brown sandstone gabled church with a bellcote. Circular window in the N gable, otherwise lancets. Two incongruous angular additions of 1972–3 by *Sam Gilchrist*, to the rear at the l., and in front of the front elevation, in panelled green granite; that to the front especially irredeemable and reminiscent of a freight container. Comprehensively reordered inside in 1972–3: the liturgical orientation moved through 90 degrees to focus on the w wall, resulting in the loss of an ornate High Gothic altar and other fittings of 1890 by *Pugin & Pugin* and *Hardman & Co.* The new altar is alongside the long w wall while the former chancel has been enclosed to form confessionals. Late C19 PRESBYTERY to l.

SOUTH BEACH BAPTIST CHURCH, Ardrossan Road. Gabled Gothic of 1867 by *John Honeyman*. Three-light window in the gable, within a pointed moulded arch. Beneath this a later porch, which reuses the original moulded doorway with granite columns. Side elevations have shallow buttresses and tall lancets. To the rear, a simple HALL of 1901.

PUBLIC BUILDINGS

ADELAIDE COLLEGE, Bradshaw Street. The former Mission Coast Home, established by Glasgow merchants to provide escape, especially for children, from the industrial areas of

* There are a number of candidates.

central Scotland. Begun 1868 by *Hugh Barclay* (this part now
Byers House) who extended it s in 1874, and considerably
aggrandized in 1888–9 by *H. & D. Barclay*, with the much more
confident part at the sw corner. This has a round-headed
entrance within a steeply pedimented porch with stumpy grey
granite columns and a short attached octagonal tower rising
through the eaves carved with the monograms of the founders
James Smith, William Bryden and Thomas Corbell.

BRADSHAW NURSERY SCHOOL, Bradshaw Street. 1858 by
Thomas Wallace. Single-storey H-plan in light brown sandstone.
Central entrance with porch. Flanking sharply carved Jacobethan gables give some style, and the requisite gravitas for
learning. Low stone walls and iron railings.

CALEDONIA PRIMARY SCHOOL, Argyle Road. 1901–2 by *John
Armour Jun.* Long single-storey red sandstone range, with a
central round-headed entrance, with flanking pairs of square-
headed windows. Beyond these, slightly advanced gabled bays,
with four-light windows and a circular window with curving
tracery above. A final bay, to the r., at an angle, connected with
the original school, of 1876, by *Alexander Adamson*.

DYKESMAINS PRIMARY SCHOOL, Carey Road. 1994–6 by
Strathclyde Regional Council DARS. Brick T-plan, mostly single-
storey, with decorative bands of darker brick and a curved
concrete porch supported by a single column.

MAYFIELD PRIMARY SCHOOL, Kenilworth Drive. 2003–4 by
North Ayrshire Council Technical Services (project architect, *Irene
Farish*). One of several good schools of this period in North
Ayrshire, and among the most thoughtful in Scotland. Attractive, mostly single-storey, brick-clad, with a darker brick base
course. Two-storey hall behind, with the rooms arranged in
front in a broad U. GRP roofs, oversailing to sharp points.

NORTH AYRSHIRE HERITAGE CENTRE, Kirkgate. The former
Ardrossan Parish Church of 1744, virtually rebuilt after a
storm in 1773–4 by *John Swan* of Kilmaurs; converted 1906–8
as a church hall by *J. J. Burnet* and adapted to its present use
in 1957. Rectangular, rubble-built, with gabled ends. Slight
central projection to the s side with a pediment and tall bellcote with corner columns and an ogee-headed cupola – the
pediment was built 1803–4 (*Alexander Cuningham*, wright, Kilwinning, and *William McEwen*, mason, Eglinton) and the bellcote moved from elsewhere on the church. The tall round-headed
windows flanking this are by *James Paton*, 1846. Square-headed
windows of the N front probably 1906–8. C18 E porch. W extension, probably 1957. On the E wall of the churchyard an artisan
classical MONUMENT, *c.* 1830, to the family of *Peter King*,
mason (†1847).

PAVILION, Winton Circus. 2001 by *Stuart Jamieson* of *Stuart
Duncan Partnership*, West Kilbride. Adjacent are the concrete-
walled BATHING POOLS, with terraces, laid out in 1933,
designed by the Burgh Surveyor, *George Harley*. The concrete
and castellated LOOK-OUT TOWER must also date from this
development.

POLICE STATION, Raise Street. 1998–2000 by *Holmes Partnership*. Striking stone and harl composition, with lots of glazing, and a prominent stone fin on the side elevation. The Police Station and the adjacent commercial building with its more fashion-conscious, curving roof make a positive and encouraging statement.

ST MATTHEW'S ACADEMY, Jack's Road. 2004–7 by *Keppie Design* for North Ayrshire Council. Large panel-clad structure with the ubiquitous drum hinge and expansive oversailing roofs.

SALTCOATS STATION, Vernon Street. 1894, for the Glasgow and South-Western Railway, replacing the station that served the line to Ardrossan opened in 1840. Two-storey three-bay red sandstone Renaissance station house; on the w elevation tall doors, one pedimented, a cornice, and parapet with decorative segmental panels. On the opposite platform, an eight-bay single-storey block with paired round-arched windows.

SALTCOATS TOWN HALL, Countess Street. Of two periods, *p. 604* making an odd pair and handicapped by its side street location. The first part is straightforward artisan classicism of 1825–6 by *Peter King* (*Alexander McGibb*, mason, *John Service*, joiner), just three bays wide and two storeys but with a mighty five-stage tower that has an archway at its base under a cornice with acroteria, a small oculus draped with swags and a pediment. Then three square stages, the uppermost with corner Ionic pilasters and ball finials, and finally an octagonal lantern and a faceted spire. To its l. the new Town Hall of 1891–2 by *W. H. Howie & H. D. Walton* of Glasgow (*James Millar*, mason, *Hugh Thomson* of Stevenson, joiner), more richly treated with three round-arched windows under an open pediment with acroteria and a fourth bay to the l. under a square balustraded tower. Ornate central doorcase of richly carved console brackets supporting a wrought-iron balcony.

SPRINGVALE NURSERY CENTRE, Sannox Drive. *c.* 1998 by *North Ayrshire Council*. At the heart of the school a circular tower, surrounded on most sides by single-storey lean-to blocks, while a segmental wedge extends from one face. Mostly brick, with some GRP; this school is another that makes a considerable impact, though it cries out for a more prominent site.

Former TELEPHONE EXCHANGE, Campbell Avenue. 1931, by *H.M. Office of Works*. A gaunt grey-harled two-storey T-plan house, quite deliberately historicist, and conscious of its proximity to St Cuthbert's church (*see* Churches, above). Now residential, and dwarfed by its less deferential replacement of 1964.

WAR MEMORIAL, Ardrossan Road. 1922 by *Henry Hutchison*, sculptor. A crouching fusilier, bayonet to the ready, watches warily from atop a tall square pillar of Kemnay granite.

DESCRIPTION

One should start with the HARBOUR, although it is now rather forlorn. The first improvement to the natural harbour was an

E elevation (partially reconstructed)

Saltcoats Town Hall.
Reconstructed c18 elevation

L-shaped rubble stone pier, built by Robert Cunninghame of Auchenharvie between 1686 and 1700; the main arm was extended seawards in 1805.* In 1914 a major restoration, in concrete, was made by *Babtie, Shaw & Morton*, engineers of Glasgow. On the quay a two-storey three-bay gable-ended HOUSE for the harbourmaster, of *c.* 1805, rubble-built, with stone dressings, and a castellated concrete LOOK-OUT TOWER of 1914, possibly based on a predecessor of 1805. The inner harbour has now been covered over; the SEA WALL was built in the 1920s, while the seats and walls with their features like the prows of Viking longboats date from the 1990s.

A road, pushed through in 1963–4, some stunningly unaware commercial developments and a tall bank of flats now effectively separate harbour from town, a deplorable state of affairs. In QUAY STREET, which runs N from the harbour and Harbour Street, some jolly three-storey local authority flats of *c.* 1935, harled with tubular steel balconies, intentionally nautical. Off Quay Street, in BRADSHAW STREET, the MASONIC HALL, 1910, red sandstone with an oriel window and balustrades, and, at the corner with Countess Street, two-storey late C18 houses, the best of the vernacular buildings, with crowstepped gables, but sadly disfiguring shopfronts. Opening W from here is the suggestively named DOCKHEAD STREET, the town's commercial heart, though not specially rewarding architecturally. It seems to have been laid out in and after 1765 but anything of that date is well concealed by C19 and C20 frontages and the earliest buildings are now Nos. 81–85, early C19 single-storey cottages. The most distinguished building, however, is the former National Bank (Nos. 87–89) of 1931–2 by *A. Balfour & Stewart* of Glasgow in a free Venetian. Entrances to l. and r. with moulded architraves and coats of arms; on the first floor a continuous band of nine lights, a heavy bracketed frieze and cornice. In CHAPELWELL STREET, running N from the W end of the street, the two-storey corner block dated 1765 but probably *c.* 1800. Also No. 28, *c.* 1830, a squat square single-storey cottage with a hipped roof, and a central stack.

HAMILTON STREET extends the commercial area W. It begins with, on the r., *J. & J. A. Carrick*'s boldly detailed reconstituted stone and harled former Trustee Savings Bank of 1986–7, with a corner turret to the r. and a prominent clock. Then two former cinemas: on the r., LA SCALA (now a pub), 1912–13, offering to the road a long unadorned façade, and a tower with panelled plaster decoration; on the l., the REGAL (now a night club) of 1930–2 by *John Fairweather*, the main decoration a pink and white plaster sunburst. Early C19 single-storey cottages are plentiful, e.g. Nos. 21–27, which also boast a nice 1950s shopfront, but few are unmolested. Only No. 28, with a three-light window instead of a shopfront, might indicate how the row of which it is a part must have looked when new. On

---

*There appears to be no contemporary evidence for the date of 1797 often put forward for this work.

the N side, the conservative hip-roofed brick and stone Clydes-dale Bank of 1938 by *Baird & Thomson* of Glasgow, the former E.U. Church (*see* Churches, above) and more early C19 cot-tages, at an angle to the road. No. 49, a painted stone single-storey cottage of *c.* 1820, has a very narrow bay squeezed in to the l., with a gabled oriel. On the S side, at the W end, the unspoilt interior (*c.* 1954) of the MELBOURNE CAFÉ.

The streets beyond Hamilton Street, between the sea and the railway, are mostly mid- and late C19 residential, with single-storey cottages with attics and two-storey villas, espe-cially in the streets nearer the sea, predominating. BANKSIDE (No. 11 Ardrossan Road), of *c.* 1820, is bigger, a detached three-bay two-storey house, with a painted stone front eleva-tion, an entrance with a broken pediment and consoles, and a scrolled wall-head stack. EGLINTON STREET was proposed as a new street in 1859 and feuing began in 1861. It is remarkably uniform, of single-storey cottages with dormered attic storeys. The nonconformists are worthy of note: the bloated grey-harled No. 4, Lucerne Cottage, of *c.* 1865, with a pilastered doorway and raised quoins, and Nos. 6–8, *c.* 1900, a profusion of red sandstone gables making some genuflection towards the Arts and Crafts movement. The railway makes a neat job of dissecting Saltcoats. The streets to its N, such as RAISE STREET, SPRINGVALE STREET, ARGYLE ROAD and CALEDONIA ROAD, are quieter, much more residential in character. Some good detached houses in Caledonia Road, e.g. No. 61, of *c.* 1900, in chunky rock-faced brown ashlar, with a crisp round-headed entrance, the red sandstone Arts and Crafts No. 79, also of *c.* 1900, with shaped chimneystacks and a dainty glazed porch, and No. 81, of 1888 by *Gabriel Andrew*, an exercise in Jacobean strapwork and crowstepped gables.

AUCHENHARVIE PARK, 0.75 km. E. The rubbly sandstone remains of an ENGINE HOUSE, built in 1719, to house the second Newcomen engine put into use in Scotland, used to pump water from one of Cunninghame of Auchenharvie's col-lieries. One gabled wall still reasonably entire, with three blocked square openings.

3010 # SAUCHRIE

2.5 km. W of Minishant

A multi-period house which may incorporate fabric from the C17 but which was recast in the earlier C18, again in 1783 by John McAdam who purchased the estate on his return from America, and finally in 1817–18 for Archibald Kelso. The C18 house now forms the S section of the SW elevation. It has a central door and two full-height flanking canted windows added in the early C19 (*see* also Otterden, nearby). To its NW a three-storey service range, possibly the one known to have been added by McAdam. The smart SE entrance façade added in the early C19 is in the manner of David Hamilton. Two-storey, five bays wide, with tripartite windows on the ground floor flanking a handsome tripartite porch with arched doorway. (Interior recast in 1817–18. Good plasterwork.)

On the hill above to the NE a large STEADING COURT, *c.* 1817 with an imposing arched pend set into a raised piend-roofed centrepiece.

CARWINSHOCH, 2.5 km. N on the road through the Carrick Hills, began as a mid-C19 keeper's cottage for the estate. Now it is the service wing to the spectacularly sited L-plan house of 1981–4 by *Ian McGill* of *Cowie Torry & Partners*. Porch in the re-entrant angle and two big arched windows in the E wing imitating cart openings. Full-height shallow bowed windows on the W front. Inside, various fittings, including finely carved Corinthian pilasters, from Fullarton House (q.v.). Small white-washed rubble stable opposite, earlier than the rest, and adjoining this mid-C19 kennels.

SEAMILL

A coastal settlement merging seamlessly into the S end of West Kilbride (q.v.). It owes much of its development to the opening of the railway to West Kilbride in 1878, and the establishment by John Newbigging of the SEAMILL HYDRO in Ardrossan Road in 1879. This is unmissable on the seafront but somewhat altered. The original sanatorium forms the S half: two-storey, with a central gabled bay, and a battlemented tower behind. The N extension, with a domed corner tower, appears to be *c.* 1890 (the similarly styled rear wing is dated 1894) and possibly by *Thomas Smellie*, who exhibited designs but, if so, it demonstrates none of his usual bravura. On the front lawns, a sweet two-storey GARDEN HOUSE of *c.* 1905, with big over-hanging eaves, swept up to a tall finial.

Immediately S of the Hydro, the late C18 SEA MILL itself. In four distinct sections; the two to the E are two-storey, comprising the mill (with a much decayed wooden mill-wheel) and the miller's house. S again a group of three large late C19 Baronial villas in red and grey sandstone (Tarbet and Sandylands and Annfield and Carlton), possibly all by *Gardner & Millar*. Unusual stable blocks whose hipped roofs rest on big corbel tables.

SEAMILL TRAINING CENTRE, Glenbride Road. Built in 1895–6 and extended 1901–2 by *James Davidson*, as the Co-operative Seaside Home, a convalescent home for Co-op members. Leaden Scots Baronial in grey sandstone, but with some good details such as the characterful round-headed W entrance with decorative spandrels and a blank panel within a scrolled frame. The E wing, added by Davidson in 1901–2, has the present main entrance within a conically headed SE tower. High-quality woodwork inside, and much stained glass, e.g. the staircase window with photographic images of six original benefactors

of the Seaside Home and symbols of co-operation and prosperity, the dining-room screen, and more on the floor below,
depicting birds, hills and clouds (dated June 1935). Scots
Baronial E LODGE of 1903, also by *Davidson*. In the same street
and in similar fashion, GLENBRYDE MILL, with an abundance of conical towers and THE MEADOW of *c.* 1890 by
Gardner & Millar, red sandstone with a half-timbered oriel.

In ARDROSSAN ROAD, to the N, the plastered two-storey
CLYDEVIEW, with a simple wooden pedimented porch and
modern jalousies, is probably the house called 'new-built' and
available for sea bathing in 1807. Further on, SEAMILL
COTTAGE, also early C19, its deeply recessed entrance flanked
by canted bays with lying-pane glazing.

In Fullerton Drive, WEST KILBRIDE GOLF CLUB. Clubhouse of 1904, by *Frank Southern*, greatly enlarged. On the
course, to the W, a harled and tiled C18 COTTAGE, with a
segmental-headed cart entrance. Nearby, and in SUMMERLEA
ROAD, houses dating from Seamill's interwar heyday when
there was much building along the coast below the main road.
Of particular note HEARTHSTANES, 1934–5 by *Campbell,
Hislop & Welsh*, white-harled with a flat entrance head and
shaped stone dormerheads, and ARDCHATTAN, a spreading
grey-harled and tiled Cotswold vernacular house of 1930 by
J. Austen Laird. Within its grounds a brash, bold house of
c. 2000, white-harled and tiled, with a central look-out tower.

SINCLAIRSTON

Small roadside hamlet. Late C19 lion-faced WATER PUMP from
Glenfield & Kennedy Ltd, of Kilmarnock, and a former SCHOOL
(now residential) of 1875 by *John Murdoch*, consisting of a
central hall, with ancillary accommodation behind, with additions of *c.* 1910 by *A. C. Thomson* (*see* also Ochiltree).

BONNYTON HOUSE, 1.5 km. SW. Small brown-red Burnian
Baronial mansion house of *c.* 1860, with a three-bay main
elevation of two storeys, bows in the outer gables and prominent gables. L-plan, with an earlier rear wing, perhaps late C18.

HAYHILL, 1 km. SW. Six pairs of semi-detached harled brick
single-storey cottages, of 1920 by *Allan Stevenson* for Ayr
County Council, their earliest housing scheme, intended for
agricultural labourers.

SKARES

Two rows of cottages, facing each other, form the scant remains
of a late C19 mining community.

Former GARALLAN SCHOOL, 1.5 km. E. Of 1874–6 by *J. & R. S.
Ingram*. L-plan, with hipped slated roofs and a pedimented
re-entrant porch.

GARALLAN HOUSE, 0.3 km. NE. A multi-gabled house of 1856, extended in 1874, incorporating earlier structures.

SKELDON

3010

2 km. SE of Dalrymple

An elegant Palladian mansion set in parkland on a dramatic bend of the River Doon.

The house appears to have been built *c.* 1760 for a Mr Ross of Sandwick, reputedly using stonework from Kerse Castle (Dalrymple) which was owned by Ross. It has a symmetrical plan, of five bays and two storeys over a raised basement. The walls are grey sandstone ashlar, neatly coursed with polished margins and band courses. The stonemason *James Armour*, father of Burns's wife Jean, is said to have helped build Skeldon. He worked also at Dumfries House (q.v.) to which, although smaller in scale, the house bears a resemblance, particularly in the simple detailing, the piended and platform roof and the chimneystacks on the cross walls.

The approach is along a sweeping drive onto a forecourt that slopes gradually away towards a ha-ha. The centre bay of the entrance front is slightly advanced and pedimented. The windows have corniced architraves in pinkish red sandstone but at the ground floor the centre three bays have been overlaid by a capacious curved porch with an Ionic colonnade and a semi-dome, by *James Miller*, 1908, for William Weir. In the quadrant curves in the angles l. and r. are two tiny cloakrooms (*see* also the porch at Glenapp). The wide steps to this are of the same date, possibly reusing the original flight. On the garden front, the advanced central bay has a Diocletian window below the pediment, but here the elevation is overwhelmed by Miller's huge barrel-roofed conservatory, somewhat reminiscent of his station at Weymss Bay (Renfrewshire). A perron stair leads down to the garden reusing the arch below the platt from the original perron to provide a sheltered sitooterie. On the side elevations, the masonry is different and the treatment slightly less sophisticated, although this is a house intended to be seen in the round. The substantial full-height canted bays are late C18 additions, probably after the property was acquired by Major General John Fullarton, and have a rather crude set-back at the level of the earlier C18 band course. Their crowning balconies were probably added in 1937 when the square roof dormers were inserted by *Alexander Mair*.

The hall inside was extensively remodelled by Miller. The stair, with C18 decorated S-shaped wrought-iron balusters, rises round the wall to the galleried landing (*see* Auchincruive). Very refined modillion cornice detailing in the two main rooms, which also have mid-C19 chimneypieces.

Below the house on the flat ground in the curve of the river, an enclosed GARDEN with one wall to the S and glasshouses against it.

STABLE COURT. C18. U-plan with a blind arch in the entrance gable. Additional attic storey on one wing, either by Miller or Mair. – DALRYMPLE LODGE, probably C18, a simple rectangular lodge with a bowed front and deep eaves, to which balancing bays have been sympathetically added in the C20. – CASTLE COTTAGE has the remains of Skeldon Castle built into it in a reconstruction, probably by Miller.

SKELMORLIE

A resort village on the Firth of Clyde, whose expansion for summer and weekend retreats for Glasgow businessmen followed on from the development of Wemyss Bay to its N (Renfrewshire). By 1845 it was reported that the Earl of Eglinton had 'determined on feuing his estate of Skelmorlie for marine villas'. The original settlement was on the narrow strip of land between the sea and the cliffs; later housing, boosted by the opening of the railway to Wemyss Bay in 1865, is to be found above the cliffs. *John Honeyman* was closely associated with Skelmorlie, and the village has much evidence of this association. The late C20 and first years of the C21 have seen a tendency towards subdivision, and the replacement of villas by blocks of flats, usually of minimal architectural value: a slow erosion of the village's distinctive character.

SKELMORLIE AND WEMYSS BAY PARISH CHURCH, Shore Road. 1893–5 by *John Honeyman* (of *Honeyman & Keppie*) in the local warm pink sandstone. It is the same C13 Gothic he adopted for Brechin Cathedral (Angus). Buttressed five-bay nave of paired lancets with quatrefoils, under pointed mouldings with label stops. Narrower single-bay chancel with a three-light S window and an E aisle, tucked hard against the cliffs. Square four-stage N entrance tower; the entrance has paired trefoil-headed openings, recessed between three orders of moulding with simple columns. The second stage has small lancets close to its base course, and the third has moulded paired bell-openings, a solid parapet, faceted finials and prominent water chutes, and is topped by a set-back octagonal spire with lucarnes. Gloriously crisp interior: timber-vaulted roof, plastered walls and stone dressings. The nave arcade with quatrefoil columns, and taller pointed chancel arch. Luxuriant chancel S wall, with its richly moulded three-light window. – REREDOS. Gothic, by *William Gibson Rowan*, expertly carved by *John Crawford*. Birth, Death and Resurrection of Christ, flanked by the Evangelists in niches. – COMMUNION TABLE, CHOIR STALLS and crocketed ORGAN CASE are all from the same hands. – STAINED GLASS. S window (Baptism, the Passion and the Ascension) by *William Guthrie*, who also made the small three-light window in the W wall with Scottish saints to designs by *Honeyman*. – W wall. A notable gallery. From S to N, Charity and Truth by *Stephen Adam & Son*, 1909: deeply coloured and well-drawn, with a border of cabbage-like Glasgow Style roses; next a dramatic Stilling the Storm by *Douglas Strachan*, *c.* 1920. He is Risen, by *Morris & Co.*, 1918, based on a design by *Burne-Jones*. Figures, of the Three Maries, drawn by *J. H. Dearle*, and painted by *Titcomb*. The fourth window, with Love and Faith against a background of fruit and leaves, is also by *Morris & Co.*, *c.* 1900. The final window, of *c.* 1901, is by *C. E. Kempe*, and depicts St Michael and St George. – N wall, two stunning windows in back-lit frames. Formerly at St Andrew, Greenock. Pre-Raphaelite toppling gorgeously into Arts and Crafts, with scenes from the life of Galahad and the Quest for the Holy Grail intermingled with warships, seaplanes and the arms of Greenock. Almost certainly by *Robert Anning Bell*.

Attached at the N, the previous church of 1854, now HALL. Pointed windows, a gabled porch and bellcote. *Honeyman* may have been its architect, though the 'site was chosen by Admiral Montgomerie, under whose management and direction, assisted by James Scott, Esq., of Kelly, and W. Brown of Wemyss, it has been erected'. At the main entrance, a free-standing wrought-iron LAMP STANDARD, coeval with the church and attributed to the firm's apprentice *Charles Rennie Mackintosh*. Four verticals with a band of rings and sinuous, tendril-like decoration within the rings, and breaking free of the uprights.

Former SKELMORLIE EVANGELICAL CHURCH, The Lane. 1904 by *H. E. Clifford*, as a village hall. Simple harled Arts and Crafts with distinctive battered walls; now residential.

SKELMORLIE LIBRARY AND COMMUNITY CENTRE, Skelmorlie Castle Road. 1956–9 by *Robert Hurd*. An unassuming rendered and well-slated building, extended to the rear, 1970–3 by *Margaret B. Brodie*.

DESCRIPTION

The spine of LOWER SKELMORLIE is SHORE ROAD. First from the N, on the l. a house converted from the United Free Church Hall of 1885–6 by *A. Lindsay Miller* of Glasgow.★ But all the interest is provided by the villas, though the first, topographically and chronologically, Beach House, built in 1844 for George C. Arbuthnott, was demolished in 2009. Italianate; Millar (*Castles and Mansions of Ayrshire*) saw it as the model for a modern marine villa. A run of good *c.* 1850–70 villas beyond the Parish Church, e.g., on the seaward side, REDESDALE, with its scallop-headed first-floor windows and wide eaves; WOODSLEY, with a broad piended platform roof and classical porch, and pretty additions of *c.* 1900; and INCHGOWER built in 1857 ('a neat villa, now erecting'), with broad gables, overhanging bracketed eaves, a porch with a tall pyramidal roof, and a tall conical tower on the bowed W elevation.

★ The church itself, of 1874 by *Alexander Watt*, was demolished in 1972.

ACHNACRAIG, of *c.* 1857 and extended *c.* 1866, spreads widely, with neat wooden detailing in its many gables. Among them one excellent house of 1996–7 by *Bruce D. Kennedy*: timber-framed and harled, with its gable to the road, with windows grouped in larger openings, and thoughtful use of stone panels. But the best are further S, once the cliffs relent, on the landward side. Of special note is *John Honeyman*'s OAKCRAIG of 1873, all broad overhanging eaves, and the substantial THORNDALE, of *c.* 1859, an unsettlingly busy display of fancy barge-boarding and barley-sugar chimney cans. It was built by *Thomas Lamb* and *James Rankin*, builders in Glasgow. To the S are conventional late C19 villas, and RED SAILS, flats of 1990–1 by *Canata & Seggie*, red brick with tile-hanging and big cantilevered balconies in keeping with the jaunty seaside villa aesthetic. Further S, a pair of MEASURED MILE MARKERS, tall posts on concrete bases with iron stays, provided in 1866 by shipbuilders Robert Napier & Son for ships undergoing tests and sea trials (plans devised by land surveyors *Kyle & Frew* and *Smith & Wharrie*).

UPPER SKELMORLIE developed along the cliff-like backdrop to the lower village, where the villas, mostly from *c.* 1870 and after, could take advantage of the spectacular views. The village street, SKELMORLIE CASTLE ROAD, has little of interest. The best villas are to its S, in Montgomerie Terrace, Eglinton Gardens and The Crescent, which lie parallel to the cliff, and Halketburn Road on the rising ground. THE CRESCENT is the highest of the roads, with villas set well back. Those of principal interest are Edwardian, beginning with TUDOR HOUSE (No. 9) of 1904–5 by *Watson & Salmond*; of stugged red sandstone, the style English C16 with a Tudor arch for the entrance in a battered three-storey crenellated tower, and projecting gabled bays to the r. resemble a hall; to the l. a section with half-timbering. The interior is remarkably well-preserved, with varied and rich materials: oak panelling in the dining room, Lebanese cedar in the hall, mahogany in the drawing room and Cory pine in the library; beautiful metalwork too for light fittings and inset in chimneypieces; good Morris-style stained glass in the stair window. THE BIRKENWARD (No. 11) is probably *c.* 1890, remodelled in 1904 in Arts and Crafts manner with a rambling turreted rear wing and, on the W, a veranda linking two outer bays. Interior with Art Nouveau detailing and glass. CROFTMOHR (No. 15), 1904–5 by *H. E. Clifford* in Arts and Crafts manner, uses stugged red sandstone and both harl and applied timbering above the ground floor. L-plan with semicircular, canted and square bays to the main W elevation. Door set in Tudor arch with deeply splayed reveals and a corbelled oriel above on the S elevation with an inglenook to its W. Three gables to E, the southern deeply swept, large mullioned-and-transomed stair window with stained glass. The square pyramid-roofed CROFTMOHR LODGE, 1910–11 by *Francis Robertson & Hacking*, appears to derive from Clifford's design of 1904 for a gardener's cottage.

Skelmorlie, Tudor House.
Engraving, 1904

In EGLINTON GARDENS a series of red sandstone villas of
c. 1875 such as MALLOWDALE, with interior decoration of
1911, and OAKHILL, with its faceted roofed turret, conservatory and stained glass. In MONTGOMERIE TERRACE, the
asymmetrical THE MANSE (No. 3) is by *Honeyman*, 1874 and
distinguished from its neighbours by Gothic detailing, while
the unexceptional GLENDOWER HOUSE (No. 5) of *c.* 1875 has
in its stair window stained glass of the Battle of Largs. At the
s end, ROSSVIEW, a large asymmetrical red sandstone late C19
villa, altered by *Fryers & Penman* in 1906, has a bold octagonal
porch and arcaded passage, both with open timber balustrades,
a w front with angle turret and initials CPH and FSE in pediment, and another good interior: the dining room with majol-
ica tiles with sunflowers to the chimneypiece and Aesthetic
Movement Japanese discs in the grate register – reminiscent of
William Leiper, or could it be Honeyman? Elsewhere inlaid
panelling, columned chimneypieces and stained glass including a Zodiac.

In HALKETBURN ROAD, BALVONIE, of 1903 by *H. E. Clifford*, an L-plan house in harsh red sandstone with applied
timber above the ground storey, retains fittings such as inglenooks, stained glass and built-in furnishings. The LODGE and
STABLE in similar style with Arts and Crafts ventilator. Finally,
in LONG HILL, MORLAND, a large phased villa of 1862, with
additions of 1874 (the N wing) and 1893 by *Honeyman &
Keppie*. The original villa essentially L-plan with canted bays,
pedimented window heads and additional oriels. Imposing
five-sided conical-roofed SE porch of 1893, with elaborate Jacobean detailing. Cast-iron brattishing and finials embellish the
roof-line. Now flats, but elaborate Neo-Jacobean interiors
survive with inglenooks, etc. In the grounds, two small VILLAS,

1991, faced in mechanically tooled red sandstone, but given
character with deep eaves and red-stained herringbone woodwork in projecting bays. They incorporate a former water
tower.

SKELMORLIE CASTLE
1.5 km. s

The castle stands proudly on the high raised beach that dominates the coast between Skelmorlie and Largs, occupying a platform above boldly sculptured, grassy terraces.

From the mid c15 the lands of Skelmorlie belonged to a
branch of the Montgomerie family; a marriage in 1820 linked it
to the Montgomeries of Eglinton and it remained with the earls
until after a major fire in 1959, when it was sold to Sir Clement
Wilson who had also acquired Eglinton Castle. The house has
evolved into its present L-plan form from a severely plain, but
substantial, rectangular tower house, essentially of *c.* 1502 but
probably incorporating earlier work, which was altered in the
earlier c17 and received large additions by *William Railton* of
Kilmarnock in 1856–64 before reduction and alterations by *Noad
& Wallace* after 1959. Pont desribed the site as '. . . not to be
surpassed in picturesque scenery by any prospect in Britain', and
this is not an extravagant claim, for the views out to Bute, Arran
and the Cumbraes have strongly influenced the c19 and the c20
works.

The early c16 tower stands at the N end of the house and is of
   particular interest as the largest of a local quartet, including
   Law, Fairlie and Little Cumbrae Castles (qq.v.), with which it
   has much detailing in common and in particular the unusual
   feature of a kitchen placed on the first floor behind the hall.
   Its elevations have been much altered and unified in the c20
   but on the s side the original entrance is preserved with the
   arms of Montgomerie and Douglas supported by lions with
   two saltires and Douglas emblems above, set into a red sandstone frame with roll moulding and a cyma reversa inset. As
   at Fairlie, there is a newel stair within the wall thickness to the
   r. The fenestration above the ground floor is also unaltered.
   The entrance was moved to the N front as part of the mid-c19
   works, and a large doorway inserted. This has a generous roll-
   and-hollow-moulded frame with a datestone above containing
   the coat of arms of the 13th Earl of Eglinton and various
   emblems. Above, two windows flank the very wide chimney-
   breast of the first-floor hall, and above again three smaller
   windows light two upper chambers and a former closet, the
   latter having a tiny additional light. All these are in remodelled
   plain architraves. There are also two small slit windows, one at
   the E into a small closet, one at the w lighting a mural stair
   rising from the first to the second floor. The upper storey was
   radically altered in the first quarter of the c17. The two stumpy
   angle rounds at the NE and sw angles were probably given their

conical roofs at this time, but on the NE round there is a small stump of wall showing that there was formerly a parapet and that it was probably carried on continuous corbelling. When the parapet was removed the roof was extended E over the former wall-walk and given its crowstepped gable. Behind it, the chimneystack serving the kitchen flue was enlarged to take additional flues, giving it an exceptional dimension. Two small windows in the E wall have roll-moulded frames. The upper part of the W gable was also remodelled in the C17 but is now as reconstructed after the fire, following the removal of a W wing added by Railton. Three storeys of paired sash windows in roll-moulded architraves.

The S wing built in the C17 was replaced by Railton in 1864. His is a roguish Baronial but well detailed: for example, where it joins the tower there are discreet squints set into the inner angle to allow light through to the original newel stair windows (the existence of an opening just below the eaves indicates that before the C17 the stair continued to the wall-walk). Within the wing itself, sizeable Gothic windows with etched and coloured glass light the new stair added by Railton. The W front of the wing projects slightly forward from the stair, to allow enough width for a passage on the E side. It has three bays of which the wider l. bay has a quirky roof-line with a split crowstepped gable that collides with a hefty octagonal turret, like an over-grown ornamented chimneystack. To the r. dormerheads with finials and, at the SW angle, a tourelle with narrower top stage that sports dummy cannon and a candle-snuffer roof. Unusual starburst-pattern ventilators to the basement. The rear is simpler, with a strongly modelled angle turret at the NE marking the return to the tower. A wall in front of the ground floor screens the servants' passage.

The C19 N door leads into an unusually tall vaulted hall, made wonderfully light by Noad's inserted W windows. A door to the E leads into a similarly vaulted dining room into which the curve of the C16 newel stair projects. In both these chambers, set high on the S wall at their E ends, are large framed recesses. What was their use? From the entrance hall is a door into a lobby off which, through a short defensible passage, there is the newel stair. It is wide and rises the full height of the tower. At first floor this formerly served a wide lobby now incorporated into the drawing room created from the former hall. In the N wall, an enormously wide fireplace with a strong roll-moulded surround (revealed after the fire). On its r. jamb a clear star-like mason's mark. In the reveal to the r. window an opening to a chute with a pointed head and a cusped lozenge finial. A moulded doorpiece in the NW angle leads onto a secondary newel stair to the upper floor, and at the SW is a checked opening for a press in the W wall. Through a door at the SE corner is the narrow kitchen and the space for the former large fireplace. From the SE corner of the tower a passage curves round the stair compartment. This was origin-ally created in the C17 to provide access to the S wing and now leads past the C19 stair (good barley-sugar cast-iron balusters), to the E passage of Railton's wing.

To the S of the castle, outside the former enclosure but linked by an archway, an L-plan range of 1636, forming two sides of the W courtyard, all in warm red sandstone. The original purpose is unclear. It appears rather smart for stables, with a segmental pedimented S gable, a crowstepped one to the N and the E-facing windows set in pilastered aedicules with the segment heads breaking through the wall-head. The central window was once a door, the forestair now gone. One suggestion is that it was a chapel, plausible given that it was built for Sir Robert Montgomerie who had commissioned the Skelmorlie Aisle, Largs (q.v.). The upper windows in the S-facing range also have segment dormerheads. At the SW a wonderfully generous two-storey clasping angle tower with a supply of gun-loops and damaged tiny mock cannon just above the corbelling. A weighty crenellated parapet and a conical roof set back within it. The crowstepped W gable of the S range has a small lean-to block linking it to the tower. More segment dormer-heads within the W high-walled court and large stacks on both elevations. It all seems more than a service arrangement. A further E range, possibly the addition undertaken by *John Honeyman* in 1876, is in the style of the C17 ranges and intended for carriage housing and accommodation. Anchored at the NE by a solid turret with a large bas-relief fleur-de-lis set into a pointed quatrefoil panel, and a fish-scale-slated bellcast roof, it is linked to the earlier buildings through a squint passage.

SORN

Small village and parochial centre attractively sited on the N bank of the River Ayr, with wooded hills to N and S.

SORN PARISH CHURCH. A good example of a mid to late C17 church, erected after the parish was disjoined from Mauchline in 1656. 1658 is the date generally given for it but without evidence.* Galleries were added in 1788, and in 1825–6 the walls were heightened and a new roof constructed; the plans were by *James Nimmo*, though the work was superintended by *James Paton* of Ayr. T-plan, of exposed rubbly grey-pink sandstone with polished dressings to pointed windows with intersecting tracery. Main S façade, with two windows flanking the minister's door (blocked), and smaller ones to l. and r. The wings end in gables, each with a stone forestair (their elegant iron rails are 1820s), E gable bellcote surmounted by a cross. Interiors of restful uniformity, with plastered walls, N aisle arch and coved ceilings. Panelled gallery fronts of 1788; that in the N wing is supported on two wooden columns, with wooden

---

* The parish was in the heart of Covenanting country, and no minister was ordained until 1692.

pilaster strips giving the illusion of additional support. PEWS, 1883. Simple bell-shaped heads. Names of the seat-holders (estates and farms) and the number of seats allocated to each stencilled on the bench ends. – The broad platform area was redesigned by *H. E. Clifford* in 1910, financed by T. W. McIntyre, his client at Sorn Castle. The PULPIT has an attractive openwork brass stair rail; it, the COMMUNION TABLE, and ELDERS' CHAIRS all of Austrian fumed oak, with attractive Glasgow Style carving, with teardrops in square panels. The ORGAN CASE has flat-headed corner pinnacles reminiscent of Mackintosh. – STAINED GLASS. s wall, flanking the pulpit. 1892. Coats of arms in clear glass settings (Somervell of Sorn to the l., Farquhar of Gilmilnscroft to the r.).

Iron JOUGS (or neck-irons) on the W wall and MONUMENTS along the s wall. Rev. Mungo Lindsay †1738. It has a decorative border and long, affectionate verse. Also two memorials (E wall) to a local Covenanting martyr, George Wood, shot at Tinkhorn Hill, 1688, 'by bloody John Reid truper'; one probably late C17 and much worn, the other looks early C19. – MAUSOLEUM. Archibald Buchanan of Catrinebank †1841. Castellated, with clasping and pinnacled columnar buttresses. Close to the SW gate, a pair of C18 carved HEADSTONES, now displaced; one shows a head, with a plentiful head of hair, within a ropework circlet, the other a shepherd with his crook and dog, and a skull.

SORN PRIMARY SCHOOL, Main Street. 1849–50, of cherry-cocked local pink ashlar, the only pre-1870 school in mainland Ayrshire still in use. Charming, broadly symmetrical N front with central gabled projection for the main schoolroom, with a Venetian window and a tall wooden clock tower with circular clock faces. Schoolmaster's house to the E and classroom to the W, also with a Venetian window in its gable. s wing added 1873–5 by *William Railton*, with tall square-headed windows. Some original panelling to the corridors and classrooms remains. In one corridor, malleable iron coat-hooks, numbered, and said to be original. In the porch, a simple BOOK-CASE is a rare survivor of the small libraries presented to rural schools in the late C19 by James Coats Jun. of Paisley, after he discovered that his yacht had a bigger library than the school at Kildonan, Arran.

SORN VILLAGE HALL, Main Street. 1954 by *Robert G. Lindsay*, County Architect. Substantial but sparsely detailed Neo-Georgian. Harled. Broad single-storey E wing.

DESCRIPTION. Opposite the church is the spectacular early C18 SORN OLD BRIDGE. This is of two arches, almost semicircular, with arch-rings of dressed stone and splayed cutwaters; curving abutments to the s. Incised MILESTONE at the NE corner. It is flanked by a former mill (now Church Hall). This is probably late C18, converted in 1927 by *William Niven*, the Sorn estate factor. Exposed stone with polished dressings, with a big wooden door in the former cart entrance. To its r., the mid-C19 mill cottage has gabled dormers and a rustic porch.

E of the bridge, LADESIDE COTTAGE, also mid-C19, with end
stacks and a rustic porch. E of the church the two-storey gabled
former MANSE of *c.* 1750, with flanking late C18 single-storey
wings. It was considerably remodelled *c.* 1850, with oriel
windows on the S elevation, and a projecting gabled wing and
entrance under a big bracketed pediment on the N elevation.
The village stretches leisurely E from the church.

At the E end of the village, SORN NEW BRIDGE of 1871 by
James Campbell, road surveyor. Two segmental arches, with
dressed arch-rings and rounded cutwaters. Across the river,
BEECHGROVE is an attractive mid-C19 farmhouse, of two
storeys, painted stone, and slated.

SMIDDYSHAW, 0.7 km. SW. Routine mid-C19 L-plan farmhouse
distinguished by the octagonal stone DOOCOT attached to the
rear wing. The farm was advertised to let in 1787, having been
'under improvement, in the natural possession of the proprietor', and the doocot may have been part of those improvements. Most rustic of rustic porches.

THE ROUND HOUSE, 1.25 km. W of the castle gates on the B743,
was built *c.* 1820 as a gamekeeper's cottage, and picturesquely
composed. Broadly elliptical in plan, with a steep slated roof
and over-sized stacks at either end. These have deeply channelled vermiculated rustication, like the door and window
frames. Imaginatively restored and extended *c.* 1960 by *David
Somervell*, with a simple two-storey rear wing, and a central
front dormer. The disproportionately large, but somehow
appropriate WEATHERVANE, and iron GATES, came from
Catrine Mill (q.v.). The urn-headed GATEPIERS are salvage
too. Elegant classical interiors of *c.* 1960, with the original two-
room house converted into an oval drawing room.

EAST MONTGARSWOOD, 2.2 km. NW. Relatively unspoilt early
C19 harled courtyard farm. The single-storey dwelling house
has a projecting porch and a roundel in the gable. The wing
to the r. has a cart opening, that to the l. a rear outshot
extension.

SORN CASTLE
0.5 km. W

Set high on a dramatic and defensive bluff above the River Ayr.
Although now dominated by additions in a simple but bold
Baronial style by *David Bryce* in 1864–5 for James Somervell, on
the river elevation the appearance is still medieval with an early
C15 tower house to the l. (SW) and a large C16 addition extending
to the r. along the bank. Joined to the original tower is a tall wing,
facing SW, which was built in 1793 but radically remodelled by
Bryce, who united this and all the other phases with his own
additions by creating a roof-line of a corbelled, crenellated
parapet and embryo bartizans, using the corbels of the tower for
a model. Substantially remodelled by *H.E. Clifford*.

Bryce created the asymmetrical entrance front on the NE but in its present form it is as adjusted 1908–10 by *H. E. Clifford* for Thomas Walker McIntyre. He raised the drive in order to create an entry at principal floor level and added the balustrade in front of the basement area thus created, and in doing so destroyed the verticality of Bryce's original composition. The *porte cochère* of this date is very hefty and crenellated, projecting like a gargantuan mouth from a handsome face. It shields the arched doorway which had to be re-set along with the bold rope hoodmould, obliterating the four-light window which originally lit the entrance hall. Above is a slender corbelled oriel set into the entrance bay at the point where its curved angles are neatly corbelled to square. The upper level of this elevation is emphasized by distinctive chequer-corbelling, mock cannon spouts, crenellated parapet, gabled dormers, crowstepped gables and gable-head stacks. To the r. of the door is the gable-end of the 1793 range remodelled to take a string course which steps up to frame a panel with the Somervell crest. To the l., the two-storey, basement and attic Bryce addition. Beyond this a billiard room by Clifford.

The tall late C18 range faces the garden. It was originally executed in the Castle Style of Culzean but as remodelled by Bryce has enlarged windows and a dominant projecting canted bay, corbelled over the raised ground floor. Bryce's orginal proposal of 1862 intended to retain more of its C18 character but add chunky conical-roofed bartizans. Set back from this range at the SE is the original tower, thought to have been built after the Hamiltons of Cadzow acquired the property in 1406. It is approximately 6.1 m. by 9.1 m., rectangular in plan with walls about 1.8 m. thick and built in squared red rubble. A plaque let into the wall *c.* 1909 lists the building chronology. It is possible that there was a stair-turret or jamb at the NE angle, but no traceable sign of an original stair can be seen inside now. The insignificant corbelling that clasps the angles is also just discernible on the river elevation at the point where the first tower terminated: chequer-set corbelling runs below the rebuilt parapet. The same detailing continues in the C16 extension on the river front. Apart from a gun- (or arrow) loop on the SW elevation and the odd diminutive opening on the SE, all the other openings in both medieval parts have been enlarged, probably in the C18. The oriel in the centre of the old tower's river front is by Bryce but was moved from its original position, lighting the dining room created by Bryce in the C16 part, when Clifford built the arcaded loggia with roof terrace in front of the C16 additions. This is enclosed by a balustrade with half-rounds at the angles. The NE wall of the C16 range is approx. 3 m. thick partly to act as a buttress where the site falls steeply away but mainly to house the kitchen chimney. The lower service range beyond is dated 1864.

The INTERIOR was almost totally refurbished by Clifford. The ENTRANCE HALL floor and steps to the outer hall were replaced in white-grained marble. Of 1909 too the oak-panelled walls with linenfold decoration on the pilasters and the plaster barrel ceiling with geometric designs, inset plaster panels of lions, thistles and roses and pendants, the latter possibly reused from Bryce's period. This detail continues in the wide passage to the l. leading to the MUSIC ROOM (or Smoking Room), with framed walls originally covered with hessian, and the BILLIARD ROOM in the addition. Unusually the latter had no top light, just windows to three sides. It has an open timber arched tie-beam roof and under the windows of the short wall an oak settle. The INNER HALL was created by joining the Library and Stair Hall. The wide archways linking the Outer Hall and the lobby leading to the Dining Room and new Library are of the 1860s, as is the door into the Drawing Room, although this was resited by Clifford and in its former position is an imposing neo-medieval hooded stone chimneypiece. The big imperial STAIRCASE reuses much of the woodwork of Bryce's unsatisfactory well stair (e.g. twisted balusters). At the half-landing, a stained-glass window inserted by Thomas McIntyre in a romantic gesture for his wife, depicting Edinburgh and music from a folksong. The DINING ROOM entered from the lobby off the Inner Hall occupies the hall of the C16 addition. Almost nothing of the Bryce work survives. The Ionic pilasters, bulbous frieze and Ionic screened buffet recess are all 1909, the latter formed in the thickness of the external wall. The chimneypiece is a puzzle: the register is probably Bryce but the tiles and wooden surround appear to belong to the 1930s. The LIBRARY in the hall of the first tower has a rectangular entrance recess in the thickness of the original outside wall from which a door leads onto a tight newel stair introduced, surprisingly, in 1909. The decoration also belongs to this date with oak panelling, and a Flemish Renaissance chimneypiece replacing an angle chimneypiece formerly in the opposite l. corner. Crowning the bookcases, Gothic brattishing and pinnacles, said to have come from a demolished Glasgow church. More debatable is the oak-beamed ceiling. The beams are definitely old but whether they were imported is not clear. There are some simple roll stops which have been replicated in oak and attached to other beams. The small newel stair leads down to a vaulted GUN ROOM, fitted with a neo-medieval chimneypiece. Set into the panelling, a glazed frame displaying the gunloop as though it were a porthole. The fitted drawers and cupboards all have Arts and Crafts designed handles. Two further vaulted cellars, one partly filled by the stair, reflect a particular pattern for the lower storey of C16 tower houses with vaulted cellars leading off a passage to the kitchen.

Finally, on the ground floor, the DRAWING ROOM, entered from the Outer Hall. The large bay window was introduced by Bryce but the rest of the room is Clifford in a very competent Renaissance manner owing much to his admiration for Richard Norman Shaw. Clifford introduced the excellent electric light fittings throughout the house, the best in the Drawing Room where a lobed square has been scooped out of the ceiling, creating groined segments with C17-style plaster roundels designed to carry light bulbs and shine through the crystal chandelier suspended from the centre of a fruit-enriched garland. All this is set into a geometric, Bryce-style plaster ceiling but must surely be Clifford. Upstairs in the BOUDOIR over the front door, a sumptuous Baroque marble chimney-piece probably from Bryce's drawing room. The first-floor BEDROOM over the Library was completely re-fitted in 1909 in an Arts and Crafts manner, the skilfully made beaded panel-ling concealing built-in storage and a writing desk. The C17 Scots-style plasterwork of geometric patterns has the McIntyre initials and floral sprigs inset. There are more Arts and Crafts details in the other bedrooms of the older part of the house.

COACHHOUSE. Probably the offices designed by *David Hamilton* in 1806. An imposing range overlooking the slope down to the house. An ashlar-built pedimented centrepiece supported on paired Doric pilasters and flanked by rubble-built bays with windows set into arched openings. The pilasters supporting the arch at the front and rear of the archway are slightly bowed to deflect carriage wheels. Low flanking ranges link to taller, piend-roofed bays with large arched carriage doors, now changed to windows. Through the arch, an irregular courtyard with a simple archway on the opposite wall. All now converted for domestic use by *Ronald Alexander*.

TURBINE HOUSE, SW of the house. By *Clifford*, *c.* 1910. Adjacent, a pedestrian SUSPENSION BRIDGE, of before 1857, super-ficially similar to the bridge at Gattonside (Borders).

NORTH GATE LODGE. By *Clifford*, *c.* 1910. Arched entrance and two-storey lodge all under a pitched red-tile roof and with a corbelled, crenellated parapet. Over the arch bold knotted rope hoodmouldings to both elevations, imitating the detail intro-duced for the front door of the castle by Bryce. On the road elevation a generous turret with a candle-snuffer roof behind the parapet linked to a crowstepped gabled bay. Splayed coped walls curve in to the lodge from the road.

CLEUGH COTTAGE, opposite the E entrance on the village road, is of 1917, probably by *Clifford*. Tucked, as the name implies, into a narrow defile. Scots Baronial in rock-faced red sandstone, with a conically headed entrance tower and crowstepped gable.

GILMILNSCROFT. *See* p. 335.
GLENLOGAN HOUSE. *See* p. 354.

SORNHILL *see* GALSTON

SOUTHWOOD

2.5 km. SE of Troon

3020

An exclusive enclave of houses laid out on the Duke of Portland's lands between 1890 and 1914, and made popular with merchants and businessmen because of easy access to Glasgow by rail and the best golf courses; like the contemporary developments in Lothian at North Berwick and Gullane or indeed Sunningdale in Berkshire. Each plot was substantial and screens of Corsican pine provided privacy for the houses, which are in varied Arts and Crafts styles, mining Scots and English sources. They had all the appurtenances of country mansions: lodges, gardeners' cottages and stables or, more commonly, garages with accommodation for chauffeurs. The epithet 'Millionayrshire' has its origin here.

All the plots are set back from SOUTHWOOD ROAD, running N–S, with a few more discreetly set off an unmade road in woods at the southern end. Here is the earliest villa, SAND-HILL, which unlike the rest of the development is sited for the spectacular views over Ayr Bay and Arran. It was built 1891–2 and purchased soon after by its tenant William Alexander Robertson, a Glasgow wine merchant. His crest is above the door. Atypically for Southwood, it is built of harsh red brick, with red sandstone string courses, bows and canted bays, a red tiled roof, Shavian-style stacks and, on the W, an oversailing, mock timber gable. It would fit seamlessly into suburban Birmingham. Spacious outer and inner halls, simple panelling. The sitting room chimneypiece is carved with a mouse, the motif of *Robert Thompson*, presumably installed *c*. 1956 when *Robert and John Cartwright*, his grandsons, provided fittings for St Ninian's, Troon.

Between here and Southwood Road is SOUTH PARK HOUSE, also red brick but with inset decorative flint panels, of *c*. 1909–10 by *L. D. Penman* of *Fryers & Penman*, for William Stewart, secretary of Coats Paton, the Paisley thread manufacturers. It is tall and gabled, reminiscent of North Oxford or The Park in Nottingham and with a strongly English character. The stone mullions and transoms throughout have sash windows set behind them and the upper sashes have Tudor-arched heads. A deep cast-iron balustraded balcony links the large two-storey canted windows on the SE. All the gables have decorated bargeboards. The mildly Baroque open pedimented doorcase breaks the Late Victorian Gothic spell. The tall pan-elled stacks are again of Shaw's influence but better detailed than at Sandhill. Further N down a long drive off Southwood Road is FROGNAL of 1909, substantially repaired after a fire in 1913 by *J. Scott Hay* for the Hart family. This is a large Edwardian Free Style house built from warm, squared rubble sandstone and ashlar dressings. Roughly rectangular in plan, the design picks up the popular C18 Ayrshire fashion for full-height balustraded bows. A large pilastered and balustraded porch with a bowed window above and a round-arched pediment breaking the cornice. Big outer bows, that to the r. fronting a two-bay projection. A similar arrangement to the garden front where a big stair-tower replaces the porch and dominates the elevation. Behind the solid corbelled parapet, at the rear of the tower, an octagonal caphouse with a domed roof. (Inside, much original detail survives with coffered ceilings, timber dado panelling, a stair with corniced newel posts and barley-sugar balusters. Robust C17-style plaster friezes and cornices.)

N along Southwood Road, first on the W side is DUNALTON of 1906 by *J. Scott Hay*, for Richard G. Allen. It is an enormous and rambling house exhibiting all the asymmetry of the Arts and Crafts movement but with unsympathetic starkly white harl and red sandstone dressings, emphasizing the disparate elements. Multi-gabled with much bargeboarding with a pegged detail found on other houses in Troon possibly by Hay. The largest gabled bay is approximately central with a Tudor-arched doorway set into a solid red sandstone corniced frame at the r., and to the l. a large projecting sandstone mullion-and-transom window bay and a centrally lipped parapet, mimicking the high end window of a medieval hall. Two bays to the r. of the door a jettied half-octagon tower with a faceted roof and on the lower wing at right angles a drum turret with an oversailing candle-snuffer roof. On the garden front a tower (cf. Frognal, above) with an attached stair-turret rising above the cornice and conically roofed. This tower no longer has its balustraded parapet, which upsets the balance of the composition. The LODGE picks up the theme with gables and a drum turret that has a bellcast roof.

E of Southwood Road is MONKTON HALL (formerly Glenholm) by *H. E. Clifford & Lunan*, whose designs were exhibited at the Royal Society of Arts in 1912. Strong English Arts and Crafts influence. An L-plan of two storeys and attic with plenty of swept gables. The entrance in a columned porch set diagonally into the re-entrant angle. A long garden front with tall, curved bays breaking through the wall-head and with small lips in the parapet heads. These bays are linked by a curved veranda with plain trunk-like columns. The lumpy harl detracts from the originality of the design. CROSBIE HOUSE, almost opposite the entrance to Monkton Hall, is also by *Clifford* but erected 1908 for Frederick Ness Henderson, a builder, and as modified from the published perspective without the invention or the charm of the original design. Rambling and heavily harled, with red sandstone dressings and an assembly of crow-stepped gables, square projecting bays and conical-roofed drum towers. Both the main elevations are dominated by large mullion-and-transomed stair windows; inside, the stair is the central feature. On the garden front, to the l. of the stair window a large projecting rectangular bay with five windows to each floor and a parapet, with a central lip, rising above the wall-head (a more exaggerated version of the same motif seen at Monkton Hall). Good gatepiers and lodge.

Immediately N is GREY GABLES, built in 1908–9 for William Alexander Collins, the Glasgow publisher. It is the most important of the houses yet the architect is unknown. The root of the design is the northern English Arts and Crafts

116

movement. It is composed of a long double-pile rectangular plan, a ground floor of immaculate pink sandstone, and subtly jettied upper storeys tile-hung with the same Westmorland slates that cover the roof. On each of the main façades three big gables. Rising into these gables are two generous two-storey bows on the entrance front and three similar semi-octagonal bay windows to the garden. The craftsmanship is everywhere excellent, from the main door, which is deeply recessed with joggled voussoirs and has a subtle bolection-moulded frame with a stepped lintel, to the elegant moulded stone mullions and transoms of the ground-floor windows, reminiscent of carpentry detail, the highly crafted catches of the *Crittall* windows and the bargeboards of the gables. The house was subdivided into four in 1977, and has an unusual baffle entrance with doors (originally only the l. one) at right angles to the porch. The centre of the house was dominated by a large hall with the stair at the front door end and a gallery above lit by three three-light windows with inset stained-glass roundels of historical and biblical scenes. The main rooms were on the garden front opening from the hall; to the r. on the entrance front, the billiard room, now cleverly altered to make the entrance dining room for one of the apartments. Flat and bold papier mâché decoration on the ceilings using fruit and pine cones (a nod to the surrounding pines?), and some wainscot panelling. Gatepiers with ball finials. The design of the GARDEN, with terraced lawns descending to a lily pond via steps with massive ball finials, is contemporary. U-plan former STABLES, with a bellcote and elegant roof with bellcast eaves and dormers. Carefully designed but now rather clumsily altered at ground floor.

Next along the road is SOUTHWOOD HOUSE, a smart piece of Scots Renaissance built for John McIntyre by *J. A. Campbell*, 1905–6. Set back within a courtyard, enclosed by tall harled walls and gatepiers with tall pyramidal finials of C17 type. The house too is harled, with pinkish grey sandstone dressings and big Westmorland slate roofs, bellcast to give deep eaves. Composed of a front and rear range with a narrow link (a lower service range to the N has been demolished), but the low service building backing on to the courtyard still survives. The entrance front has shallow oversailing upper floors at the N and s, and tall chimneys flanking an asymmetrical centre. The door is recessed into a large moulded sandstone panel, with an urn and floral swags, that also embraces a window tucked under the eaves between two other windows with crocketed dormers. Further dormerheads display a variety of detail here and on the garden front. An uncommon feature is a garden door on the side (s) elevation set into a modified version of the surround for the main entrance. Beside this door two windows linked by a stone panel light the stair. The only significant change to the garden front is the insertion of a curiously scaled arched window lighting the drawing room.

Back to the E side of Southwood Road for AUCHENKYLE, Queen Anne style of 1905–7, originally commissioned by

George Clark, of the Kilmarnock shoemakers, but completed
for James Anderson, a manufacturer. *Campbell*'s assistant, *Alexander D. Hislop*, was largely responsible. L-plan in red brick,
with brick quoins and steep slate roofs over a modillion cornice.
Of the principal part, the entrance front has a stone doorcase
set into a large two-storey projection, and to the r. three bays
of which the centre has a bull's-eye window at first floor, and
chimneystack breaking through the eaves. The garden front is
starkly symmetrical with full-height bays, two square and the
central canted. Main rooms along the garden front with a wide
corridor/hall behind. Much good Edwardian detail, particularly the C17-style plaster ceilings; the shallow-vaulted corridor/
hall ceiling with flat ribs of fruit and flowers, such as acorns,
pine cones, thistles and roses, is notable. To the l. of the door
a well stair within the entrance projection. It has wine-glass
balusters and a carved handrail, and is lit by the two leaded-
light cross-windows. The gate lodge in a similar style makes a
better composition on the smaller scale.

Finally, LOCHGREEN HOUSE (now a hotel) designed for
George Morton, a stockbroker, by *Gardner & Millar* in 1906,[*]
Scots-style harled with stone dressings sparingly used and red-
tile roofs punctuated by slab chimneystacks. Originally a long
rectangular plan with a lower service wing (the bulk of extensive late C20 additions tempered by matching materials), its
most successful elevation is the entrance (E) front with a bellcast-roofed drum tower anchoring the SE angle and a broad,
dramatic chimney tucked beside it, a stone set-piece entrance
with the door recessed behind a bolection-moulded frame, a
false parapet above dated 1905 with pine-cone finials and a big
plain frame above with a gablet breaking the eaves. To its r. a
crowstep-gabled cross-wing. Large mullion-and-transom hall
window to the l. of the door, more English than Scottish in its
derivation, with stained-glass armorial panels in the upper
lights. The garden front is dominated by two uncomfortably
large gabled bays each with three narrow lights at first floor, a
strange arrangement given the extensive views across the golf
course. Large extension enclosing the N side of the garden with
flat-roofed ground-floor public areas providing first-floor balconies. Inside, the Edwardian interior remains with some sensitive adaptation. Oak and grained panelling, a variety of
timber overmantels, set into inglenooks in the drawing and
dining rooms, the latter fully panelled with Ionic pilasters
framing the chimney-breast and both with marble slips and
original grates. Late C18-style plasterwork in the drawing room,
earlier C18 deep-relief laurel-wreath-type in the dining room.
At the E entrance from Monktonhill Road, a lodge in similar
white harl and red roof tiles.

MONKTONHILL ROAD has some other houses, notably SILVER-
GLADES (formerly Deasholm) N of Lochgreen House, by
T. Millar, 1912. Further s, close to the A79, is THE WHITE

---

[*] Thomas Millar appears to have modified a design submitted in 1905 by *George
Gunn*, assistant to *J. C. McKellar*.

HOUSE by *Alexander Mair* for Dr John Rowan, 1935–8, positioned for the views across Ayr Bay. U-plan in simple white
harl, and in a streamlined manner with a slate-hung gable-head
on the garden front, a canted stair projection on the N and a
canted porch in the courtyard.

SPRINGSIDE
Irvine

3030

Former mining village stretching along the main road between
Kilmarnock and Irvine, an amalgamation of three mid-C19 row
villages: Springside, Bankhead and Corsehill.

Former ESTABLISHED CHURCH MISSION HALL, Overtoun
Road. 1898–9. Slated gable roof, open wooden bellcote and
lean-to porch. Opposite is the SPRINGSIDE INSTITUTE,
1891–4 by *Robert S. Ingram*. Motherwell brick, with white
freestone dressings. The remarkably long and thin main hall
has an exposed timber roof and was probably designed to
function as a skittle alley.
PRIMARY SCHOOL, Garrier Road. 1977–80 by *Strathclyde
Regional Council*. Hall surrounded by lower, monopitched
blocks like waggons drawn round for protection.

STAIR

4020

Parochial centre beside the River Ayr. The parish was created in
1673, for the greater convenience of the Dalrymples of Stair. No
village as such, just the church, the house, a pub and a bridge
nestled together in pleasant harmony.

STAIR PARISH CHURCH. Simple Gothic of 1863–4 by *William
Alexander* of Ayr, in rectangular coursed ashlar. Five-bay S
elevation with two pointed windows flanking a gabled central
porch. Three stepped windows in the E gable, below a bellcote;
the W gable has a decorative chimney and rose window. Below
this the session room, sympathetically extended to the N in
2000. Pleasing interior, with plastered walls and four-centred
ceiling, the cornice of which lops the tops off the deep window
reveals. Plain pews either side of a central aisle, with two raised
rows across the E end, demonstrating some neat joinery. High
Gothic PULPIT and ORGAN, the latter particularly enjoyable,
with exposed pipes and crocketed finials atop the case. –
STAINED GLASS. W window, 1923, by the *Stephen Adam Studio*,
Glasgow: eight Celtic saints. – MONUMENT. Lt.-Col. William
Miller of Barskimming, 'mortally wounded at the age of 31
years in the action with the French army at les Quatre Bras,
16th June 1815', originally erected in the Protestant Cemetery
in Brussels, but re-erected here in 1886. In the SW wall of the
churchyard, a severely mannered mid-C20 monument for the
Galbraiths of Barskimming.

Stair Bridge.
Engraving by W.H. Bartlett, 1838

s of the church, the handsome STAIR BRIDGE of 1745 crosses the Ayr, tucked between a bend of the river and the cliffs which bound it. Three stepped arches with triangular cutwaters. To its E is the STAIR INN, mid-C19, now stripped of its harl.

STAIR HOUSE, 0.25 km. NNE of the church. The idyllic position of this picturesque house close to the River Ayr justifiably extracts superlatives but no serious analysis of the fabric exists. The estate of Stair-Montgomerie was acquired by marriage in 1450 by William de Dalrymple. His descendant, James Dalrymple, was made President of the Court of Session in 1671, and created Viscount Stair in 1689. The author of *Institutes of the Law of Scotland*, he died in 1695.* His son, John, was created Earl of Stair in 1703 and died in 1707.

When MacGibbon & Ross inspected the house was harled, neatly concealing straight joints, blocked windows and clear disturbance in the masonry. Without a careful inspection both outside and in, which was not possible, the following analysis can only be conjectural. The barely defensible position of the house suggests that it is no earlier than mid C16, a charter of 1531 makes no mention of a castle but a further charter of 1603 referred to the lands of Stair-Montgomerie with fortalice; from this the earliest part of the house would appear to be mid- to later C16 with the taller SW facing wing added in timeless vernacular style perhaps later C17 for Viscount Stair and subsequent additions made to its S.

---

* The Stair Society, for the study of the law, and the history of the law, in Scotland, is so named in his honour.

The L-plan entrance front is now C17 in character but the
entrance tower and block to its r., built of roughly squared
whin stone, is an altered mid-C16 tower house with the square
entrance tower, now in the re-entrant angle, and the circular
angle one diagonally opposite, originally making it Z-plan.
On the rear elevation of this range there is a straight joint at
its W end, the adjoining gabled range butts up to it, indicating
that it belongs to the first building period. Alterations in
the masonry at the top of the entrance tower and in the NW
gable-head are evidence that it was once taller. The door,
now in a much repaired C17 surround, has been moved from
the E face of the entrance tower, the latter a better position
for security. The tower at the NE is generous in scale, not dissimilar to the NE tower at Kelburn. It has simple roll-moulded
strings between storeys and a cyma recta moulded cornice
dating to the C17 when, from the evidence in the gable to its
l., it would appear to have been lowered and given a slightly
bell-cast roof. The wide two-bay wing facing NW onto the
garden is attached to the l. of the entrance tower, its SW
gable has been altered and now has straight skews but the
NE gable retains its crowsteps and has a segmentally pedimented window in the attic storey probably part of later
C17 work when windows were enlarged and inserted in the
early tower. Attached to its N angle a tall four-stage turret
with strings, a moulded cornice, a small section of cornice
surviving on the gable-end suggests that this tower may have
been raised (possibly c. 1700), perhaps to make provision for
the doocot in the top stage. Also on this slender turret two
carved hearts with shot-holes, probably always decorative. A
further circular shot-hole exists at first-storey level at the SW.
A lower wing of the c. 1700 recasting was added to the
SW gable and it also has a substantial circular tower at the
S angle.

The interior was much restored for Lord Stair by *James
Carrick* in 1930. Vaulted rooms remain on the ground floor.
The work included the simply detailed Arts and Crafts dining
room. The restoration also uncovered and preserved C17/18
panelling in two rooms. One C17 fireplace, together with several
in late C18 style survive. Further internal remodeling in the
1990s by *Ronald Alexander*.

STAIR HOME FARM, 0.25 km. NE of Stair House now partially
converted to a sizable house by *Patrick Lorimer* of *ARP Lorimer
& Associates*. Informal grouping dating from early to later C19.
Painted rubble, house with inserted gables to light attic, long
low range at right angles with arched entrance, boldly altered
but respecting scale and height of its neighbours. Adjoining
barn and further detached two-storey crowstepped barn and
hayloft.

WATER OF AYR AND TAM O' SHANTER HONE STONE WORKS,
Milton, 0.5 km. W. A remarkable complex and an important
survival. It had been known from the C18 that there were
beds of a particularly hard stone here, excellently suited to

sharpening tools. Commercial exploitation began in the late
C18. Buildings lie on both sides of the Ayr, connected by a
wooden-decked wire-cabled SUSPENSION BRIDGE of *c.* 1900.
On the s bank is a former corn mill, DALMORE MILL, dated
1821, later incorporated into the works. The buildings on the
N bank are predominantly single-storey, built of stone rubble,
with slated roofs, and are probably mostly late C19 or early C20
in date. There is also a row of late C19 single-storey COTTAGES
associated with the works.

Former STAIR MANSE, 0.75 km. s. Of 1805–7, the heritors
having agreed that it be built to the same size as the manse
at Dailly (designed by *James Rutherford*; *see* p. 269). The contractor was *John Key*. Dormers added 1818–19, a porch in
1862, and substantial additions made in 1878 by *William
Alexander*.

COMMUNITY CENTRE, Trabboch, 1.5 km. s. Former Stair
Primary School. Of various dates, hidden beneath a deadening
grey harl. School and master's house of 1811, altered and
enlarged in 1832–4, and again in 1865–6 by *William Alexander*.
Further additions to the house by *Allan Stevenson*, 1907, and
to the school in 1910. The interior retains much of the feel of
a School Board school, with wooden partitions, and a corridor
for drill practice.

TRABBOCH MAINS, 2.25 km. SE. Good late C18 farmhouse, of
two storeys and three sash-windowed bays, with a wide projecting gabled porch. In the field behind, TRABBOCH CASTLE,
very scant remains of what may once have been a tower house.
2.2 km. SW is TRABBOCH HOUSE, an L-shaped two-storey
early C19 house with sash windows and a low-pitched slated
roof.

Former SCHAW CHURCH, 3 km. s. Free Church of 1843–4. Big
T-plan church, formerly harled, and now roofless. The rustic
timber porch and belfry, added in 1882–3, ameliorate the austerity of the front gable.

STAIRAIRD *see* FAILFORD

STEVENSTON   2040

The lands were granted in 1170 to Stephen de Loccard, from
whom the town takes its name. In the C18 and C19 the town was
a weaving centre, and a centre for the coal-mining industry. The
coal was largely worked out by the late C19, when Alfred Nobel
began his development of the sand dunes at Ardeer as an extensive explosives factory (later ICI), which became one of the
largest employers in Ayrshire, bringing prosperity and population
growth to Stevenston. The town only became a Burgh in 1952,
one of the last to be created in Scotland. Since the closure of the
ICI works, Stevenston has lost its vibrancy, and the centre has
suffered from some ill-considered redevelopment. Ardeer just
about retains its separate identity.

CHURCHES AND CEMETERY

ARDEER PARISH CHURCH, Shore Road. Rock-faced red sand-stone Perp of 1894–5 by *Hippolyte J. Blanc*. Octagonal two-stage SW tower and gabled SE transept. Recessed W entrance in a four-centred-arched opening, with an ogival mould, beneath a five-light window, stepped over the entrance arch. Flanking single lights and, to the l., an angle buttress with a crocketed finial. To the r., the tower, with paired bell-openings, prominent corbelled angle shafts and a panelled parapet with corner pinnacles. Blanc's plans included a spire (unbuilt), while the tall crosses which originally surmounted the pinnacles became unsafe and were removed in the 1940s. Side elevations with geometrically headed windows. The open and uncluttered interior consists of a nave and S transept, with a panel-fronted gallery across the W end. Narrowly boarded shallow waggon roof divided into bays by corbelled hammer-beams, with delightful fretwork carving. Simple fittings; a bulbous red granite FONT. – STAINED GLASS. E window, war memorial, the central light of Christ, 1921 by *Guthrie & Wells*, flanked by Abraham and David, added 1948. W window, 1951, by the *Abbey Studio*, a busy Moses with the Good Samaritan and the Sower at his feet. In the transept, two richly coloured saints of 1945. To the rear the original grey sandstone gabled MISSION HALLS of 1883. In the smaller hall, a circular STAINED-GLASS window of the Good Shepherd, 1925. To the l. of the church, the straightforward two-storey MANSE of 1904 by *Hugh Thomson*, with a harled first floor.

HIGH KIRK, Schoolwell Street. Built 1832–3 by *Thomas Garven*, architect; *Peter King*, mason. Four by three bays, with gabled ends, pinnacles at the angles and S projecting entrance tower, with diagonal buttresses, pinnacles and crenellated parapet, topped by a plain octagonal bell-stage and spire. Sparely decorated, except on the tower which has a deeply recessed and moulded round arch for the entrance, a window above with a crocketed hoodmould and interlaced tracery, and three tall blind arches in each face of the next stage up to the parapet. Tall pointed windows along the flanks; two square-headed doorways on the W wall. Harled N extension of 1957 for vestry and hall. Open and airy galleried interior, with plastered walls and a flat ceiling with a simple cornice and big central rosette. The galleries are panel-fronted and supported on quatrefoil cast-iron columns. Simple, original, enclosed PEWS, and a railed sanctuary. Light oak panelled PULPIT and ogee-headed SOUNDING-BOARD, of 1832–3, of trefoil plan, in light oak, linked by a slender back-board with two marble columns. Behind the pulpit, WALL PAINTING by *James Wylie*, 1916, of scrolls, floral panels, and a burning bush above the pulpit. In the reveals of the two central windows, views of the church from four different angles, and at the four seasons. The effect, in the words of a contemporary report, is that 'of a rich altar-piece'. The surviving part of Wylie's larger scheme, which included eight painted panels on the ceiling. – STAINED GLASS.

E wall. By the *Abbey Studio*, 1957: to the l., the Fisher of Men, to the r., Mary. In the S wall, The Sower, and in the N wall, Stilling the Tempest, both of 1924 by *Oscar Paterson*, the latter a particularly effective window. W windows of 1877 with scrolled exhortations. – A large number of straightforward inscribed marble wall MONUMENTS, especially in the gallery. The finest, however, is on the lower E wall: James Wodrow D. D., †1810; sandstone, classical, with broken pediment, urn and fluted consoles, the inscription laid out as if it were a poem.

The church sits within a crowded CHURCHYARD, which falls away particularly steeply on the S and E sides. The headstones mostly late C18 and later. The entrance from the manse marked by an entrance with panelled piers. To the N of this entrance a MONUMENT to the David Landsboroughs, father and son, both ministers, historians and naturalists: a semicircular headed panel with a big Gibbs surround beneath a curved head with egg-and-dart decoration; erected *c.* 1899. To the r. of this, a weathered C18 MONUMENT, its head with a strong carving of The Last Trump. Two early inscribed stones close to the W wall of the church, one probably early C18, the other dated 1777, to IAMES BOYD SHOEMAKER IN STIVENSTOUN. – OBELISK. Francis Love, 1862, designed by *J. N. Smith* of Glasgow, executed by *William Blackley*. Its base is a feast of vermiculation.

To the l. of the church the harled T-plan two-storey five-bay MANSE of 1787, with painted quoins and dressings, and a pedimented porch with a ball finial. The rear wing is earlier, with a triangular stone panel dated 1700, while the addition to the r. is of 1885 by *John Burnet*. Church and manse are enclosed by a STONE WALL, which is perhaps C18 in origin; at the entrance a flat pointed ARCHWAY of 1933 and, adjacent but outwith the enclosure, a simple harled COTTAGE of *c.* 1800, with catslide dormers.

HIGH KIRK HALLS, High Road. 1907 by *Hugh Thomson*. Big brick harled church hall with a red sandstone frontispiece and its central entrance under a four-centred arch and an ogival and finialled dripmould. A canted and hipped stairwell bay to the r.

LIVINGSTONE PARISH CHURCH, New Street. E.E. of 1886–7 by *Alexander Petrie*, in grey sandstone. Nave and chancel in one, shallow transepts and a SW tower, with an octagonal spire chamfered out from a square base. Inside, a coved plastered ceiling, divided by simple wooden beams; the cornices a succession of billets. Rear gallery with panelled wooden front on cast-iron columns. Transept arcades of two pointed arches springing from a short cast-iron column. ORGAN CASE. Dark oak, with delicately cusped openwork tracery. The organ was given to Highlanders Memorial Church, Glasgow, by Sir Harry Lauder in 1918, and moved here in 1944. – STAINED GLASS. E window of 1937 with an effectively balanced palette of colours. A hip-roofed HALL to the r. In front of the church a

lone cast-iron GATEPIER, made by the *Ardeer Foundry Co.*
These are a feature of Stevenston, probably mid-C19.

ST JOHN (R.C.), Kilwinning Road. 1962–3 by *James Houston
Jun.* of Kilbirnie. A striking church, unashamedly of its period.
The roof is a spreading inverted V, with a separately roofed
clearstorey at the apex carrying a flèche, and has its trusses
exposed beyond the outer walls as buttresses. A narrow window
stretches from top to toe of the S gable. Double transeptal side
chapels, SW and SE. The highlight, however, is the excellent
STAINED GLASS, completely filling the side walls. By *Gabriel
Loire*, 1962, perhaps his best work in the county, with solid
leadwork and tortured imagery, including a malevolent serpent.
– The animal theme continues in the odd beaten bronze FONT
of 2002: a half tree-trunk with a fawn, a snail near the rim. –
Tilework STATIONS OF THE CROSS, and a well-designed
Scandinavian-style wooden ALTAR, all of 1962–3.

To the r. a conventional brick harled HALL, and to the l., the
two-storey PRESBYTERY.

HAWKHILL CEMETERY, Kilwinning Road. Of *c.* 1910, with a
stone-and-railed front wall, contemporary harled LODGE and
a jolly (perhaps inappropriately) little WAITING ROOM, of
brick, with wooden windows and a hipped tiled roof; a small
gem.

PUBLIC BUILDINGS

ARDEER COMMUNITY CENTRE, Shore Road. A tall gabled
yellow sandstone public hall of 1911, extended to the r. in
2005–6 by *North Ayrshire Council Technical Services*, bouncing
asymmetrically placed harled and wood-panelled blocks off the
side elevation.

ARDEER PRIMARY SCHOOL, Clark Crescent. 1979–82, by
Strathclyde Regional Council, DARS. Asymmetrical assemblage
of mostly harled monopitched blocks, with cut-away corners
and side recesses under oversailing roofs supported on thin
pillars.

AUCHENHARVIE ACADEMY, Saltcoats Road. 1969–71 by *Clark
Fyfe*, County Architect, with *Gilbert-Ash (Scotland) Ltd.* The
main block has presence: a long four-storey concrete-framed
structure, mostly clad in brick. The ancillary buildings are
clustered at one end, allowing the main block, which is carefully angled to the road, to make its statement. To the l.,
AUCHENHARVIE CENTRE, 1967–73 by *J. B. G. Houston*, a
public swimming pool, with a big steel roof.

POST OFFICE, Townhead Street. Crisp, single-storey, of red
sandstone with a Dutch-gabled entrance to the r., and crowstepped gables. 1938–9 by *J. Wilson Paterson* of *H.M. Office of
Works*. In a town as architecturally poor as Stevenston, its
continuing use as a Post Office is aesthetically important.

STEVENSTON LIBRARY AND HOUSING OFFICE, Main Street.
1995–6 by *Cunninghame District Council.* Brick. A central

square tower, with concrete panels, making some effort to turn the corner with dignity, and flanking wings in three colours of brick.

WAR MEMORIAL INSTITUTE, New Street. Unexceptional late C19 house, converted in 1930, when the WAR MEMORIAL was unveiled. By *Hugh Thomson & Sons*, this is a shrine of white marble, pedimented, with black marble columns framing a shell-headed niche with sword and wreath.

DESCRIPTION

Boglemart, Townhead and New Streets meet at Stevenston Cross: redevelopment and demolition have taken their toll, and the Cross lacks any real sense of focus. BOGLEMART STREET runs westward, with one run of early to mid-C19 two-storey houses, mostly harled or rendered, at the W end; otherwise on the N side the red sandstone former CO-OPERATIVE of 1907 by *Hugh Thomson*, with two canted oriels, a shaped gable and a decorative wall-head pediment with urns, and, on the S side, BONNIE LESLEY COURT, of 1980–2 by *Rennie, Watson & Starling*, a sheltered housing complex in blocky concrete with a prominent glazed lounge and tall projecting glazed entrance.

TOWNHEAD STREET runs E. Nos. 9–13 are of *c.* 1900, a red sandstone tenement with Arts and Crafts detailing in its shaped gables and a tall panelled chimneystack. SCHOOL-WELL STREET runs N towards the High Kirk (*see* Churches, above). The three-bay harled CHAMPION SHELL INN, of *c.* 1800, has raised rusticated quoins and ground-floor window surrounds, and a rear circular stairwell: a high-quality artisan house of the period, and well presented. Late C19 and early C20 housing in HIGH ROAD, the best being Nos. 6–12, a red sandstone and grey harled terrace of *c.* 1905, with Arts and Crafts details, while No. 41 is a perky, steeply hipped house from *c.* 1925, with an attached three-quarter-circle bay to the r., and No. 45 is a simple two-storey three-bay harled vernacular house of *c.* 1800, dwarfed by the later houses to either side.

NEW STREET runs S. On the l. the Library and Housing Office (*see* Public Buildings, above); at the corner a granite FOUNTAIN, with a square base and a bulbous head, of 1910 by *J. & J. Armour*, a memorial to the Warners of Ardeer. On the l., the MASONIC HALL, originally of 1898, by *John Armour Jun.*, though what dominates now is the 1950s extension, with its semicircular portico on thin columns; alongside it a wide grey sandstone former CHAPEL, with a prominent bellcote and flanking windows in projected square-headed bays which break through the gable. In STATION ROAD, No. 4, the hipped-roofed grey sandstone CALEY CENTRE, is the former POLICE STATION of 1899 by *John Murdoch*; opposite is LIZZIE'S BAR of 1906–7, by *Hugh Thomson* for the Glasgow District Public House Trust: big, with plentiful half-timbering on the upper floor.

NOBEL INDUSTRIAL ESTATE, 2 km. SE. The site of Alfred Nobel's explosives factory, opened in 1873. By 1951, in the hands of ICI, it covered over 1,750 acres (708.2 ha.) on the sandy peninsula between the sea and the Garnock, where the works had a jetty close to Irvine's harbour. The peninsula is still dotted with the small, semi-sunk, and careful segregated buildings in which the explosives were manufactured. Of the first period, the late C19 GATEHOUSE, where the workers were searched daily for matches. Three mid-C20 OFFICE BLOCKS, probably by *George B. Baird*, also speak of busier times: two-storey brick harled blocks in a canted formation, each slightly different, one with a bellcote, another with an elaborate copper ventilator. Close to these AFRICA HOUSE, a prefabricated building originally designed by *James Miller* as the South African Pavilion at the 1938 Empire Exhibition in Glasgow and brought to Ardeer *c.* 1940, to provide canteen accommodation. Roughly H-plan, in Cape Dutch style, Miller's consciously picturesque essay was an oddity amid Thomas Tait's Modernist exhibition buildings. Now neglected and unloved.

HULLERHIRST, 1.4 km. NE. The small estate was acquired by the Kelsos, *c.* 1707, and the house probably built for Patrick Kelso, who married in 1777 and succeeded in 1778. It is of three bays and two storeys, with a hipped roof and classical details, given character by a central pediment with a blind bull's-eye and attractively detailed flanking urns, but demeaned by a large 1950s porch (obscuring the original pedimented entrance).

KERELAW CASTLE, 1 km. N. The estate of Kerelaw belonged to the Cunninghames of Glencairn. The castle was in existence by the late C15, at which time it was sacked by the Montgomeries of Eglinton, and abandoned. A new mansion house was built to its NW in 1787 by Lt.-Col. Alexander Hamilton (dem.) and after the estate was acquired in 1841 by Gavin Fullerton he 'carefully preserved the ivy-mantled ruins of the old castle' to form one corner of his walled garden. The regularly spaced pointed windows with Y-tracery are of this date, but a round-headed and moulded archway and the remains of a vault pre-date Fullerton's work.

MAYVILLE, High Road, 400 m NW. A congenial small mansion built *c.* 1763–4* for Robert Baillie with money made in India. His daughter Lesley was immortalized by Burns in his poem *Saw Ye Bonie Lesley*. Three bays and two storeys, L-plan, with a single-storey rear wing, of exposed rubbly stone. The harled pedimented porch and central pediment were probably added *c.* 1800; both have highly prominent urns. The flanking ground-floor windows, of three lights, are a C20 replacement of late C19 bays. Internally, some plain cornices survive amidst the well-mannered C20 remodelling; one STAINED-GLASS window, of a piper, by the *City Glass Co.*, *c.* 1925.

---

*A bill of *John Crawford*, mason, Stevenston, of October 1764, includes hearth stones, exterior paving and stone for the outbuildings.

In the grounds a baluster-like SUNDIAL dated 1763, the STABLES, COACHHOUSE, and fine rusticated square GATE-PIERS, with fluted urn finials, also contemporary with the house. N of the house, in Glencairn Street, the BAILLIE MEMORIAL, a painted stone obelisk, with base and stepped plinth, erected by Robert Bailie, in memory of his wife and daughter, with naively but charmingly carved verses and Latin inscriptions. Further inscriptions, similarly appealing, added in 1798 and after Bailie's death in 1807. Those added after Lesley Baillie's death in 1843 are less blithe. Restored by *John & Matthew McLelland* in 1929, when it was moved to its present position.

STEWARTON

4040

At the heart of N Ayrshire dairying country and since the 1960s an overspill town for Glasgow. But from the C18 to the C20 it was a place of considerable industrial importance, principally for bonnet making; by the late C18 it could be said that 'almost the whole regimental and naval bonnets and caps are made here, as well as those worn by the people in the country at large' (*First Statistical Account*). The early C19 produced the regular pattern of the present town, which became a burgh in 1868.

CHURCHES AND CEMETERY

JOHN KNOX PARISH CHURCH, Main Street. Classical, of 1841–2, builders *Rankin & Gemmell* of Kilmarnock. Three-bay good-quality ashlar main front, the central bay slightly pro-jected, below the pediment and three-stage tower, with a tall square first stage with round-headed bell-openings, cuboid second stage and octagonal spire. Flanking bays with two tiers of square-headed windows. The other elevations simpler, with square-headed windows to the side, and two round-headed windows to the rear. The galleried interior has plastered and painted walls and a flat ceiling with an attractively painted ceiling rose and a simple cornice. The panel-fronted galleries are supported on cast-iron columns, with a curious row of roundels along the underside of the panelling. Narrow vesti-bule with attractive cast-iron balustrades to the gallery stairs. – STAINED GLASS. Naturalistic designs, of two main patterns, looking *c.* 1900, and influenced by the Glasgow School. To the rear, and wrapped around the church, a suite of late C19 halls, in brick and slate, linked by modern prefabricated addi-tions to the former beadle's house, a straightforward mid-C19 cottage.

ST COLUMBA'S PARISH CHURCH, off Lainshaw Street. Late C18, rectangular and gabled, but with two earlier wings retained on the SW elevation. One (r.) is the Corsehill Aisle and very probably of 1696. It has square-headed windows, a crow-stepped gable with simple skews and finial. On this elevation a blocked round-headed opening with what appears to have been a panel niche panel above. The window above this has been greatly reduced in size. The other is the mid-C18 (perhaps 1736) Lainshaw Aisle, also two-storey, with a simple gable with an apical chimney-head. Under the gable a single-storey classical projecting entrance of *c.* 1825, with pilasters and a block parapet, and a Venetian window above. The body of the church is unusual, with an irregular disposition of mostly square-headed windows. On the NE elevation, a slight projection, with splayed sides also, rather oddly, containing windows, and off-centre on the NW, a very peculiar bellcote, with chunky columns, an ogee roof and spirelet. It sits on what looks like a chimney-breast, but with a tall triangular window towards its base and above this a panel framing a shakefork, the Y-shaped emblem of the Cunninghames (a motif that recurs in this church). Is it all early C18? Abutting this feature, another porch of *c.* 1825.

The interior thus comes as something of a surprise, for it is very much of one period, having been recast in 1868–70 by *James Ingram*, so that 'instead of the old, dark and gloomy building, with its clay floor, cold and bare walls, rickety seats and doors to the number of the muses, giving access to as many corners, it has now assumed a light and cheerful appearance'. The aisles have panelled gallery fronts, as do the NW and SE galleries, supported on cast-iron columns. The space is dominated by the big classically detailed ORGAN CASE, a lectern-style PULPIT and chancel furniture, all late C19. – STAINED GLASS. Much of 1870 with the shakefork emblem prominently featured but also an outstanding collection of later windows. – Awkwardly placed l. and r. of the organ, in the splayed bays, St Paul and Dorcas, stunning windows of 1883 by *James Powell & Sons*: St Paul with an orange-red halo, Dorcas with a flowing yellow and gold dress. Flanking these, The Way, The Truth and The Light (l.), St John the Apostle (r., a memorial to John Gilmour, poet, †1828), both by *W. & J. J. Kier*, 1884. – SE wall, St Columba's Mission, 1996 by *Susan Bradbury*, using an outline map of western Scotland to illustrate the progression of Christianity under Columba from Iona. – Under the NW gallery, three strong windows of *c.* 1900, Love (crushing a striking green serpent), Faith and Hope. All were originally in the Cairns Church,★ the later two re-set here in 1996 and slightly enlarged, with many little delights in the new quarries, of which the shakefork under a Stewarton bonnet is perhaps the nicest conceit. – MONUMENTS. In the Lainshaw Aisle, the heterodox pamphleteer William Cuninghame of Lainshaw, †1849, 'author of many works on the chronology and fulfilment of prophecy' (*see* United Reformed Church, below). His portrait under a shroud. On the wall between the aisles, Mrs Donaldson †1786. Urn and a dark marble pyramid behind.

★ 1853–4, Gothic, by *James Brown* of Glasgow. Demolished. See Description, Hamilton Gardens.

Possibly by her son *James Donaldson* of London (*see* High Williamshaw).

In the N section of the CHURCHYARD, a matched pair of anonymous mausolea with stone torches, and immediately NW of the church, a nicely lettered memorial to the Rev. John Montgomerie †1757. Outside the churchyard wall, the dull harled CHURCH HALL of *c.* 1905.

UNITED REFORMED CHURCH, Avenue Street. 1829, a conversion of an earlier house for William Cuninghame (*see* St Columba's, above). Thickly harled, with three square windows and fancily headed dormers on the long elevation, and two tall round-headed windows on the gabled return. Galleried interior, with a coved ceiling and a decoratively panelled wooden gallery front. The unusual hanging PULPIT consists of a framed recess from which the pulpit proper, panel-fronted, projects, accessed by a balustraded stair to the l. In a niche in the W wall, the BUST of a poised and thoughtful Cuninghame, with an adulatory inscription below.

STEWARTON CEMETERY, Dalry Road. *c.* 1892 by *Robert Harvie*, with low stone walls and elaborate sandstone gatepiers with ball finials. The harled and crowstepped single-storey LODGE of 1907 by *J. & J. Armour* is given presence by the semicircular and heavily parapeted porch and the sharp triangular projection from the E gable.

PUBLIC BUILDINGS

CUNNINGHAM INSTITUTE, Avenue Square. 1810. Of three bays, the central one projected and pedimented, with a clock in the apex. Basket-headed openings on the ground floor, round-headed above. Three-storey return elevation, the windows respectively segmental-headed, square-headed and round-headed, with a pilastered and pedimented porch. Bad full-height 1950s extension to the r.

STEWARTON ACADEMY, Cairnduff Place. 1979–86, by *Strathclyde Regional Council DARS*. Large secondary school grouped around an inner courtyard. The two parallel main blocks are harled, with asymmetrically pitched slate roofs, and have wooden fascias above deeply recessed bands of windows on the taller faces, and the main entrance in one of the low elevations. Subsidiary blocks similar but brick. Although rather defensive-looking and unwelcoming, an advance on the postwar school architecture delivered by Ayr County Council.

STEWARTON AREA CENTRE, Avenue Street. 2006–8, by *East Ayrshire Council* (*Iain Barker*, head architect).

STEWARTON HEALTH CENTRE, Laughland Place. *c.* 1985–90. A pleasing asymmetrical mix of harled and tiled monopitches, the mix of shapes and colours well thought out.

THE CENTRE, Standalane. Drill Hall of 1903–4, harled front with red sandstone dressings concealing the hall.

WAR MEMORIAL, Kilwinning Road. Grey Aberdeen granite of 1920–1 by *Scott & Rae*. A square plinth and a tapering pillar.

DESCRIPTION

The main streets of the town form an elongated cross, with three
short streets at its head, extending the original kirktown in a
NE direction. They date from the late C18, possibly around
1775–80, although much of the town's architectural character
is set by early C19 two-storey harled properties with dressed
stone margins. Of about that time, in MAIN STREET, are Nos.
33–37, with a shouldered wall-head gable, the only example of
this vernacular style in the town. Then on the NW side, the
street opens into AVENUE SQUARE, a slightly gauche attempt
at a formal arrangement with buildings of presumably late C18
date but without unity and the Cunningham Institute (*see*
above) at its head. AVENUE STREET, laid out *c.* 1779–82 runs
N. The houses here are mostly early to mid-C19 and mostly of
brown stone with contrasted dressings, although Nos. 3–5 is
two-storey with an entrance under a big semicircular moulding, its flanking windows with Florentine arches. NE of the
square, Main Street becomes HIGH STREET. On the l., the
Italianate BANK OF SCOTLAND, of 1859–60 by *William Railton*
of Kilmarnock for the Union Bank. Five-bay façade, with
round-headed first-floor windows and a slightly projecting
heavily channelled entrance. Also on this side, the John Knox
Parish Church (*see* Churches, above), some early C19 cottages,
and Nos. 26–28, mid-C19, two storeys of coursed whin with
smooth dressings. Then HAMILTON GARDENS, harled infill
of 1973–5 by *BLG Design Group*, on the site of the Cairns
Church (*see* St Columba's Parish Church, above). On the
opposite side of the street the former UNIONIST CLUB, severe
Jacobethan of 1911–12 by *James S. Hay*. Nos. 57 and 59 are
two late C18 cottages which lie noticeably below the road level,
one with a nicely chamfered doorpiece. In SPRINGWELL
PLACE is the mid-C19 former ANNICKBANK WORKS, of John
Nairn & Sons Ltd, bonnet makers, now converted into flats,
and opposite, late C18 houses, the best being the detached No.
6, dated 1776, with a bracketed doorhead.

The SE arm of the cross is formed by VENNEL STREET with,
firstly, an unassuming enclave of attractive villas. On the l. the
pretty Gothick KERRSLAND, with a stepped gabled bay to the
r., and the three-bay CLERKHILL, of large blocks of coursed
stone, with a painted stone central porch and fanlight, are both
mid-C19. On the r. BRAEHEAD (Nos. 30–32) is the most attractive and complex, with two distinct faces. To the N a rendered
three-bay farmhouse of *c.* 1800, with panelled end stacks, polished surrounds, a late C19 wooden porch and, to its r., single-
storey gabled outbuildings, with a small doocot in the outmost
gable. To the S, an elegant three-bay ashlar front said to date
from 1809, with full-height pilasters and a painted stone Doric
porch. The square-headed ground-floor windows are flanked
by blind panels and sit within large elliptically headed panels.
Rigg Street and Dunlop Road form the short NW arm of the
cross, with on the r., Nos. 6–8 RIGG STREET, of *c.* 1800, of
five bays, harled, with painted dressed window surrounds, a

simple entrance and thin end pilaster-strips. In DUNLOP
ROAD two late C19 Gothic cottages, Afton Cottage (No. 2) and
Gowanbank (No. 4).

LAINSHAW STREET continuing Main Street SW has some
of the most interesting buildings of the town, in particular Nos.
7–13. They appear to be early C19, and are very special. They
are of three bays, and three storeys in height, with full-height
end pilasters with Ionic capitals and shopfronts of a most
original design, that are divided by pilasters with bases that
have incised diamond patterns, vermiculated pillars and scal-
lop-shell capitals – unusual in Scotland, and evocative of the
ammonite capitals of A. H. Wilds's work in Regency Brighton.
The upper windows have bold architraves with label blocks,
these with floral decoration in the second floor, while the first-
floor windows are linked by a channelled sill band. Scrolled
skews, like rams' horns. Nos. 15–19 replicate the window
pattern, but lack the other details. Opposite, a former CLYDES-
DALE BANK of c. 1860, raised a storey c. 1890, with channelled
end pilasters, a panelled cornice, entrances in four-centred
arches and a three-light window within a recessed square panel
with rounded corners, and the Italianate ROYAL BANK OF
SCOTLAND of 1858–60 by *Peddie & Kinnear*. After St Columba's (*see* Churches, above), the harled and brightly pink-washed
No. 70, MANSFIELD, the former parish manse, with a projecting central bay. Opposite is a neat mixed row containing one
good harled late C18 cottage with a deeply recessed door. The
view is closed by the gently curving ANNICK WATER VIADUCT
of 1868–73 for the Glasgow & South-Western Railway. It has
ten impressively tall arches, and dressed stone arch-rings. The
engineer was *George Cunninghame*, and the contractor *James
McNaughton* of Ayr.

KIRKFORD, 0.8 km. S, is almost a hamlet apart. A pleasingly
mixed row, mostly two-storey and mostly early C19. Amongst
these paragons, one painted late C18 cottage on exposed rocky
foundations, while another late C18 cottage, BRIDE'S BRIDGE
COTTAGE, sits at right angles. In LOUDOUN STREET, on the
l., the harled brick flat-roofed No. 2, of c. 1966, with a big
monopitched wedge, and, on the r., cottages of c. 1800. At the
crest of the hill, CAIRNDUFF, a rock-faced red ashlar villa of
c. 1895, and CRAGSTON, a stunning yellow sandstone villa of
1902 by *H. E. Clifford*. It is a mixture of English Domestic and
Scots Baronial, with two prominent gables on the front elevation. That to the l. is pointed and crowstepped, the other is
shaped, and two similar gables appear on the garden front. Tall
stairwell window, and an understated entrance in the r. bay.
The wing to the r., with timber panelling on the upper floor,
was added c. 1935, while the suite of garages, with a central
shaped gable, is of c. 2002.

The NETHER ROBERTLAND housing development lies at the E
edge of the town. It was planned from 1967 by the *Scottish
Special Housing Association*, with car–pedestrian separation,
achieved through a combination of main arterial roads, such

as Jubilee Drive, and short residential streets. The houses are
primarily harled, in the Neo-vernacular manner developed by
the S.S.H.A. Pre-dating this expansion, ARDGOWAN, a former
manse of 1870–2 by *Robert Baldie*, with a prominent pedimented porch with ball finials, and the well-tended development of PREFABS in Netherland Road and adjoining streets.
The LAMPPOSTS here also worthy of note, with the lights
suspended from circular heads.

OTHER HOUSES AND FARMS

CORSEHILL CASTLE, 0.7 km. N. The scant remains of the
L-plan early C17 mansion house built for the Cuninghames. An
engraving of 1791 shows the surviving mute fragment, but also
a much larger ruin, with a vaulted basement and a stepped
gable. It presumably made an ideal quarry for the growing
town.

EASTBURN, No. 9 Old Glasgow Road, 1 km. NE. The grandest
of a flush of late C19 villas. Of *c.* 1880, its two storeys of brown
stone culminating in two crowstepped dormers and a crowstepped gable to the r. Basket-headed moulded entrance, and
plentiful nailhead decoration. Good prominent GATEPIERS,
also with nailhead.

LAINSHAW HOUSE, off David Dale Avenue. The estate belonged
to the Montgomeries until 1779 when it was acquired by
William Cuninghame of Bridgehouse. GATE LODGES of
c. 1820. Small, T-plan, with crenellated tops, originally linked
by an entrance screen. These have been superseded further w
by two parodies of lodges, built in *c.* 2005 by Travis Homes,
who have carefully restored the main house and converted it
to flats. Their reconstituted stone and rendered façades introduce the materials employed for an extensive development of
variously styled, brash villas laid out on a sweeping curve
beyond the main house.

The HOUSE is large, mostly of three storeys in pinkish sandstone ashlar, but architecturally undistinguished. It has
spawned random additions, and conversion makes it impossible to see where the story begins. In the centre of the rear
(w) elevation, however, is a two-bay section whose walls are of
rubble and of a thickness associated with C16 tower houses. It
also has a simple cyma recta cornice, which may indicate a C17
or early C18 remodelling. Additions were planned in 1822 and
the *Ayr Advertiser* in 1824 reported building work as commencing. This may refer to the mildly Tudor Gothic block at the N
end of the E front. It has slender octagonal clasping angle piers
rising above the parapet to moulded caps, hoodmoulded first-
floor windows, and on the N front a shallow pediment breaking
the parapet. It is possible that there was an entrance on the N
side but if so it is concealed by the low N range, which housed
the orangery, lit by Gothic windows. N of the orangery, somewhat incongruously placed, is a crenellated squat tower guarding the entrance to the former service complex.

The S end of the house is a bulky range of *c.* 1840, set back from the 1820s block, also with hoodmoulded windows and distinctive octagonal glazing to the top lights. Its entrance on the E front has a wide recessed porch with columns *in antis* and three closely spaced windows above. A lobby and the main open-well staircase back onto the earliest surviving part of the house. The S range has its best front overlooking Annick Water, composed of three wide bays, the centre advanced, with large first-floor windows arranged 2+3+2. Simple Tudor-arched windows to the ground floor.

N of the house the stylish STABLE COURT of *c.* 1800, its W façade with a pedimented basket-arched centre and three flanking windows to each side set into blind arched panels, the rear block of similar height, two stone stacks against the low N range. To the N again, set on the brow of the hill, LAINSHAW MAINS, *c.* 1800, a steading disguised as an eyecatcher. An ashlar frontage with neat rubble side and rear walls. Three-bay two-storey house at the centre flanked by low ranges. The farmhouse has a slightly advanced, pedimented central bay with rusticated quoins, a consoled pediment above the door; rising behind the main pediment a striking two-stage octagonal tower with *œil de bœuf* in the N and S facets. It is very smart. Behind, a large well-built courtyard steading.

LOCHRIDGE HOUSE, 1 km. SW. Frenchified crowstepped Baronial of *c.* 1860, an almost total rebuilding of an earlier C17 house betrayed by a single door on the rear projection, with pediment and moulded frame. The C19 house has a narrow central bay rising to a tall tower, topped by an iron parapet with one over-sized thistle finial. To the l. of this a gabled bay; to the r. a further two bays, with the entrance in the l. of these two bays, in a porch approached by steps.

WARDHEAD HOUSE, 1.2 km. SW. A wide three-bay ashlar house of *c.* 1850 with moulded windows and a projecting central porch, and a later plainer bay to the r. Now offices of a firm of aerogenerator manufacturers; examples of their work enliven the grounds.

CLERKLAND FARM, 1.7 km. N. L-plan farm, with a detached barn. The barn and the lower wing, which is dated 1766, of painted stone, while the two-storey farmhouse is early C20, harled with red dressing, half-dormers and a circular window in the central gable, in a manner which suggests *Thomas Smellie*.

HIGH WILLIAMSHAW. *See* p. 365.
KENNOX HOUSE. *See* p. 399.

STRAITON

3000

A most attractive and unspoilt village, lying close to the Water of Girvan, where the valley narrows and the hills press in on all sides. The church and parish were initially granted in the early

CI3 by Duncan, Earl of Carrick, to Paisley Abbey, and were in the late CI4 transferred to their daughter foundation of Crossraguel, whose property it remained until the Reformation.

STRAITON PARISH CHURCH, Main Road. T-plan of 1758, incorporating as its SW wing the late medieval aisle, or chantry chapel, of the Kennedys of Blairquhan. This is perhaps *c.* 1500, with a gable of massive crowsteps that have pitched copings, and a slightly bellcast slated roof. In the gable, a big four-light window, its design markedly similar to the nave window of *c.* 1530 at Crossraguel Abbey (q.v.). Simple, minimally ogivally headed, entrance in the NW re-entrant, with a cusped niche above. Two blocked openings high on the SE elevation, while the entrance was originally by a stone stair to the NW upper floor; the two classically attired busts by the present door are supposed to have come from this stair. The church was restored 1899–1901 by *Kinross & Tarbolton* and the projecting square four-stage NE tower built at the same date by *John Murdoch*, with round-headed openings, and a crenellated and stubby slated spire. The church windows, Venetian in the SE and NW gables, and unusually tall, broad and square-headed in the flanks, are of the restoration.

Kinross & Tarbolton's hand is clearly visible internally, in the riot of richly ornamented carved yellow pine, at its most striking in the very fine collar-beam roof, with its decorative collars and cornice running the full width of the church. The opulent woodwork continues through the two galleries' panelled fronts, the tall half-octagonal oaken PULPIT and sounding-board, and the flanking rows of Elders' seats. The area around the pulpit has a decorative marble floor, and the whole swaggers exuberantly. The Kennedy Aisle has a tall pointed stone arch and pitched wooden ceiling and, inside, two niches and a stoup on the SE wall, and another stoup to the r. of the door in the NW wall. Also in the Kennedy Aisle, two POORS' BOARDS, one appears to be CI8, the other a good late CI9 copy. – STAINED GLASS. – Flanking the pulpit, two good windows, though very different in character. The Good Shepherd (l.), 1939 by *Herbert Hendrie* of Edinburgh, and The Light of the World (r.), a dramatic rendering by *Sadie McLellan* of Glasgow, 1977. – In the Kennedy Aisle, The Four Apostles, 1901 by *Powells* of London, though more than competent, suffers by comparison. – MONUMENTS. In the aisle, John Kennedy of Blairquhan †1501, and his wife. Effigies on a chest tomb, within a richly decorated segmentally headed recess, with four orders of rolled moulding, with two interstitial rows of dogtooth; decoration repeated in the flanking vertical elements. At the centre of the arch a coat of arms, quartering Kennedy of Blairquhan and McDowall of Garthland. Within the recess, traces of the original early CI6 paintwork are clearly visible. – Re-set in the NW wall, outside, an CI8 HEADSTONE with carved coat of arms (Crawford?) and naturalistic decoration: THE BURYING PLACE OF

KEIRS 1712 REP 1796. On the outer face of the tower, a much-weathered granite WAR MEMORIAL tablet, inscribed PALMAM QUI MERUIT FERAT ('Let him who deserved it take the palm'). There are a number of good C17 and C18 carved HEADSTONES, including two E of the Kennedy Aisle, each with a plough team. Also one minimalist late C18 stone, with two fluted pilasters flanking a broad space only partially filled by an hourglass and a skull. At the foot of the churchyard the white-harled OLD SCHOOL HOUSE, probably late C18. Pretty early C20 wrought-iron GATES to the churchyard.

STRAITON PRIMARY SCHOOL, Newton Stewart Road. Simple single-storey school and master's house of 1877 by *John Mercer*.

DESCRIPTION. Little more than the church and two rows of picturesque stone cottages lining Main Street. These have pronounced dressings to doors and windows, and were probably (if one lintel dated 28 June 1766 is *in situ*) built by the White-foords, the Hunter Blairs' predecessors in Blairquhan. At the W end the white-harled McCANDLISH HALL of 1912 by *Thomas A. Jack* of Maybole. Oddly colonial with a wooden veranda but curiously likeable. Shouldered gable and ball finials, and a clock in a bull's-eye surround. At the E end, the WAR MEMORIAL of 1920, by *Hugh R. Wallace* of Cloncaird (executed by *Hugh McLachlan*); an adaptation of the late medieval Inveraray Cross (Argyll) with an interlace decoration and entwined hearts. E of this in its own grounds, TRABOYACK is the former manse, mostly of 1795. Charmingly proportioned two storeys and three bays with a blind oculus in the central pediment formerly with an apex stack, and panelled end stacks. Angular porch with an arched doorway, added in the 1950s and reportedly reused from a house in Paisley. Part of the previous manse, of 1753, is incorporated at the rear but altered in the 1930s. Inside, a remarkably grand dog-leg staircase with curving winders, stone to the first floor with quarter-round moulded panels to the risers. Possibly from the mid-C18 house, as are some of the two-panelled doors in the upper floors and the proportion of the door to the dining room and the drawing room, suggesting that the house was refronted.

COLONEL HUNTER BLAIR'S MONUMENT, 1 km. SE on a hilltop. 1855–6 by *William Burn*. 18.2-m high obelisk, on a tall plinth, all built of locally quarried granite. James Hunter Blair, a Lieutenant-Colonel in the Scots Guards, was killed at Inkerman, 1854.

SHELTER, Kirkmichael Road, 2 km. NW. A memorial to Jean Galloway Hunter Blair †1953. Simple but effective, harled inside and out, with red sandstone dressings. The architect was *Ian G. Lindsay*.

LONGHILL, 3.5 km. W. Early C19, genteel farmhouse, two storeys with a large projecting bow to the front, single flanking bays, like an overgrown toll house. Central stack on bow. Low wings to either side formerly byres.

BALBEG HOUSE. *See* p. 176.
BLAIRQUHAN. *See* p. 204.
MILTON HOUSE. *See* Blairquhan.

SUNDRUM CASTLE

4020

2 km. N of Coylton

Built on a bluff above the S bank of the Water of Coyle. Duncan Wallace acquired the Barony of Sundrum in 1373 and sometime after that date he built a substantial rectangular tower comparable to the tower at Cassillis (q.v.). The property was acquired for John Hamilton of Sundrum, a minor, in 1750, and in 1792 he employed *John Paterson* to extend the tower E and replace collapsed rear additions which had been built by the Cathcarts. In 1917 Ernest Coats commissioned *J. B. S. Abercrombie* to make further extensions incorporating a C19 addition. A period of neglect in the 1980s was followed by a major restoration entailing the vertical division of the house into three units and the conversion of the service court for residential use undertaken by *R. T. L. Salmon* for Salopian Estates Ltd, begun in 1991.

Beginning with the S elevation of the main house, the W two-thirds contains the C14 TOWER built for Duncan Wallace. The subtle lime harl, while helping to unify the whole building, does not completely conceal the straight joint with Paterson's addition. This addition and the insertion of sash windows through the very thick walls of the tower (in excess of 3 m.) regularized the S elevation but could not give it complete symmetry because of the wall thickness and the height of the first-floor hall. The hall vault means that the second-floor windows in the tower section are blind. A small slit opening to the E of the first-floor windows probably marks the site of a mural stair leading from the hall to the upper floors. The tower appears to have been lowered at the time of extension in 1792, and the barely projecting corbelled and crenellated ashlar parapet embellishment and the two set-back stumpy conical-roofed angle turrets provide a feeble association with a fortified past. At ground floor is a door, inserted in the late C20 conversion, which returned the Wallace tower to a single unit. Prior to 1792, however, the tower was entered at first floor on the N side from an outside stair. Within, the vaulted Great Hall survives at first floor, and in the N wall there is a straight mural stair (*see* also Cassillis). Over the fireplace, the arms of John Hamilton and Lilias Montgomery, married 1762. On the N elevation a canted stone oriel, inserted in the C19 to take full advantage of the views over the ravine below.

Moving to the late C18 E WING, the door inserted by Paterson on the S front is now a window and the entrance is instead on the E gabled elevation through a delightful crenellated conceit, which was originally added in 1917 for a cloakroom. Its conical roof has been modified to match that on the

contemporary w extension, *see* below. The main purpose of this
E wing was to contain the elegant cantilevered stair, installed
to improve circulation within the Castle, which rises round
three walls with wide landings at each level. Cast-iron balusters
of alternately clustered column and lyre pattern support a
mahogany handrail. Paterson's delicate Adam-style ceilings did
not survive the period of dereliction.

At the w is the L-plan addition by Abercrombie (now called
the Coats House), which formerly provided a link from the
Castle to the service court. It is set back from the main elevation, taking the form of a four-storey tower with a two-storey
semi-conical roofed projecting bay on the s elevation. The
narrow four-storey range across the w gable of the tower is
completed with crenellated parapet, giving the appearance of
a wall-walk, and on the recessed western jamb there is a substantial full-height four-light canted bay.

The nature of the site resulted in the unusually designed
long SERVICE COURT (now The Mews and sensitively converted to residential use) having a particular prominence. This
may have been part of the improvement noted by Boswell in
1781. It has retained much of its random character. The long
elevation facing the drive is symmetrical and now comprises
three dwellings. At the centre the Clock Tower, a picturesque
pedimented pavilion with a birdcage bellcote at its apex built
into the southern wall of the court. Two arched windows flank
a central door with a plaque over with the inscription 'The
clock and bell above are a gift of farmers, tenants, feuers,
labourers and others to Claude and Marion Hamilton on their
marriage 10 April 1877'. In the upper storey a simple Venetian
widow with a blind central light and a clock face in the pediment. The flanking walls that mask the single-storey buildings
facing into the mews have inserted windows. Behind the main
courtyard the former Stable Master's House, a detached one-
and-a-half-storey cottage with low wings.

A considerable amount of enabling development has occurred.
The new properties to the w of the house are reasonably sympathetic but continued development along stretches of the drive
pays no respect to the character and antiquity of the estate. Of
some note, to the w of the Mews, COYLE HOUSE, 1997, a plain
Neo-Georgian detached house with an advanced simply pedimented central bay and low wings.

s of Coyle House and w of the main drive, the COURTYARD,
a development around three sides of a court in simple vernacular style and set on a slight slope designed to look like a converted steading but too polite to be genuine. CASTLE LODGE
is a rather crude and inflated re-creation of the former gate
lodge. L-plan with a conical-roofed turret.

SUNDRUM MAINS. Dated 1831. A shallow U-plan range with a
low two-storey house and steading. The house is five bays with
single-bay advanced wings, and may incorporate C18 fabric.
Five four-centred arches on the steading range with plain
upper floor, ventilation slits and a large central loft access door.

At the rear a largely intact big horsemill. All built in sandstone rubble with slate roofs.

SWINDRIDGEMUIR
3 km. NE of Dalry

65   An elegant country villa, of basement, two storeys, and attic and shallow-piended roof. Built *c.* 1815 for John Smith, a renowned agricultural improver. Probably by *David Hamilton*, it is like his Ladyland (q.v.) but more generously proportioned, and its finely coursed ashlar, which is channelled at basement level, makes it altogether more sophisticated. Broad, clasping pilaster-strips at each angle. Modillion cornice with parapet above and a raised panel at the centre and above the angles. Subtly projected centre bay on the entrance (s) front, the splayed steps with cast-iron balusters of a teardrop design (cf. Ladyland). Ionic-columned porch. Windows with panelled architraves with rosettes at the upper angles, those on the upper floor also with lugs. Battery of continuous chimney flues along the roof ridge.

Interior with curious cornice to the hall of small, stepped blocks and a central plaster ceiling rose surrounded by husked swags, again as at Ladyland. It is divided from the stair compartment by a Roman Doric screen. The stair curves up the rear wall in a shallow well reminiscent of a town-house stair, with cast-iron teardrop balusters and a domed cupola set into an elaborate plaster ceiling with swags, Vitruvian scrolls and florets. Smart plasterwork in the two main rooms with a sunburst ceiling rose in the SE drawing room and an acanthus leaf one in the dining room. Handsome classically detailed white marble chimneypiece with fluted columns and an urn in the dining room; a pilastered, wooden one in the drawing room with pretty plaster ornamentation. Good woodwork with reeded detail, characteristic of the period.

To the rear a STABLE COURT, possibly late C18, a generous three-bay house with a basket-arched carriage entrance. Two lower flanking wings. Beyond, a large WALLED GARDEN incorporating stones from an earlier building, one dated 1720, and with a charming applehouse/summerhouse built into one angle.

SWINLEES *see* DALRY

SYMINGTON

Attractive village and parish centre, named for a mid-C12 holder of the lands, Simon Loccard (Lockhart). In 1252 the parish was granted to Fail Monastery (1.75 km. NW of Tarbolton), remaining with them until the Reformation.

SYMINGTON PARISH CHURCH, Brewlands Street. Probably   8
mid-C12, but extended in 1797, and restored in 1919 by *Peter
Macgregor Chalmers*. The original church is rectangular, of
exposed stone and slated, aligned E–W; its present quasi-cross
plan dates from 1797, when a harled galleried N transept and
smaller gabled S vestry wing were added. During Macgregor
Chalmers's restoration, the Romanesque features which distinguish it were revealed beneath centuries of plaster. The interior
is as much his as of the C12, and with its simple details and
interplay between light and dark is one of the most charming
in Ayrshire. The bellcoted E elevation most clearly shows the
Romanesque origins with three narrow windows, the middle
one of 1919 (the original replaced by a door in 1797). On the
S elevation a mixture of small C12 round-headed lights and
larger windows, also round-headed, also restorations, with a
dormer-like clock high in the S roof. Two original small lights
on the N elevation, flanking the transept, and a tall round-
headed W window, above the low Neo-Romanesque porch
added by *J. & J. A. Carrick* in 1960. N porch of 1998–2004, as
part of conservation and restoration by *ARP Lorimer & Associates*. The windows on the W side of the transept were enlarged
by Macgregor Chalmers; against the E side a straight flight of
stairs with a simple iron rail.
The nave and chancel walls are of exposed stone, below a pitched,
plastered, barn-like roof with simple wooden beams. The three
E windows are the only decorative Romanesque features: they
have deep reveals, and are linked by a billet-moulded arcade
on detached columns. The other original windows are
unadorned, though that in the chancel S wall has a piscina in
the cill. The transept is plastered with a restrained dark timber-
panelled gallery front. – FITTINGS. A curious mix, some of
wood, others of light Blaxter limestone; they include the COM-
MUNION TABLE (of 1954 by *T. J. Beveridge*), FONT and two
sets of STALLS, which are of 1960. – STAINED GLASS. Almost
wholly by *Douglas Strachan*, 1919–21. E windows, Nativity,
Crucifixion and Ascension; S chancel window, an anguished
Last Supper, and in the central large S window, the Ayrshire
Yeomanry war memorial, a fine representation of Christ
preaching from a boat. W window, Christ in Glory. His final
window is Mary Washing Christ's Feet, of 1942, N wall W
window. – In the N chancel window, a 1970 Baptism of Christ
by *Gordon Webster*. – The churchyard's polished stone GATE-
PIERS, broad steps and iron gates are of 1907.
SYMINGTON COMMUNITY HALL, No. 31 Main Street. A simple
harled gabled church hall of 1908, with a gabled porch, and a
lower wing of *c.* 2006–7.
Former SYMINGTON PRIMARY SCHOOL, Symington Road
North. 1876–7 by *J. & R. S. Ingram*. Very simple symmetrical
early Board School, with a tall ventilator and fish-scale slating.
WAR MEMORIAL, Brewlands Street. 1921 by *Thomas Lyon*, executed by *Matthew Muir & Co*. A polished Peterhead granite

column, with four rusticated bands and a ball finial, on a square panelled base and rusticated steps.

DESCRIPTION. The church sits in the angle between the two streets which form the historic core of the village: Main Street and Brewlands Street. MAIN STREET runs broadly SE–NW; the buildings are mostly single-storey cottages, generally unfussy, and displaying the full range of finishes, from natural stone to render and harl. The charm of the street lies in its almost wilful slight changes of direction, coupled with the occasional widening; the cottages, too, are sometimes set close to the road, sometimes set back. SYMINGTON HOUSE was built in 1785–6 by *John Swan* of Kilmaurs as the manse, with scroll skews, curving screen walls and one pavilion. Of the others, TOWNEND COTTAGE (No. 70) has a graceful formality. It has prominent quoins and an unusual but attractive semicircular porch. This is of 1819, the house itself perhaps a generation earlier. Panelled gatepiers with bellcast caps. In BREWLANDS STREET, further C18 and C19 vernacular, brought to a visual full stop by BREWLANDS, of painted stone, which is set at right angles.

FLATFIELD HOUSE, Symington Road North. *c.* 1830. Long two-storey house with hipped ends, polished and painted dressings, canted dormers and a projecting full-height entrance bay asymmetrically placed.

HELENTON MOTE HOUSE, off Kilmarnock Road. A good house of 1960–1 by *J. R. Notman*, all exposed stone, boarding and a big irregularly ribbed glazed entrance. Pitched roof added 2008–9.

MUIREND HOUSE, Kilmarnock Road. 1935–6 by *W. F. Valentine* as the Halfway House Hotel. A broadly symmetrical harled and tiled interwar roadhouse, with prominent gables and generous applied timberwork. The gables on the front elevation project above canted oriels on concave bases.

HANSEL VILLAGE, 1.2 km. SW. Since 1963, a residential and vocational centre for people with learning disabilities, first planned by *Guy H. Copeland* of *Robert Allan & Partners*. At its heart is Murdoch House, formerly BROADMEADOWS, a very fine and well-massed English Manorial Arts and Crafts house of 1932–4 by *Mervyn Noad* for J. Percival Agnew. Broadly L-plan, the long arm plentifully gabled on its inner face; the outer face, which faces a spacious terraced garden, quieter, with a projecting bellcast semicircular bay at one end. Much striking Lorimeresque stone carving, such as the hunting scene over the door in this bay, and the hare and tortoise on one of the corbels supporting a projecting bay on the S elevation. Equally fine wood carving within, especially on the stair: twisted balusters and world-weary elves on the newels. Two LODGES, steeply hipped in the manner of Nesfield.

TOWNEND HOUSE, 1 km. W. A smart villa of *c.* 1820 dwarfed by a substantial Italianate addition of *c.* 1860 with a tower. The original house, at the r. on the entrance front, is built in squared whinstone but given a striking appearance with the use of contrasting cream sandstone for the wide central bay and broad outer giant pilasters reminiscent of David Hamilton. The central corniced window now with an apron panel was once the door. Continuous wall of chimney flues on the roof ridge (*see* Swindridgemuir). Balustraded basement area. Italianate addition to l. with three-storey entrance tower and bold paired Roman Doric columned porch. Stylish former STABLE COURT, also *c.* 1820, in whin and ashlar. Front elevation with central pedimented entrance and Venetian window over shallow-arched entrance, low links to outer two-storey piend-roof bays with carriage arches, now windows. Residential conversion, 1990s, *ARP Lorimer & Associates.*

CORRAITH, 1.7 km. NW. Corraith House (by *Bryce*, 1846) has been demolished. West Lodge of 1901, a creamy ashlar, crow-stepped L-plan building with the door in a conical-roofed drum turret in the re-entrant angle. Fine wrought-iron gates and gatepiers, the inner with cupped finials to hold lanterns, and the outer at the ends of the quadrant railings with elaborate finials. E of the old house a lectern DOOCOT, probably *c.* 1800. Nearby stables converted to housing *c.* 1965.

COODHAM. *See* p. 225.

TARBOLTON

4020

Sizeable village in the farming country of central Ayrshire. Made a Burgh of Barony for Cunninghame of Enterkine in 1671, though it never developed much beyond a village in scale or aspirations. Weaving was important in the C18 and early C19, coal mining in the early C20. One local farmer was Robert Burns, whose family briefly farmed Lochlea, NE of the village.

CHURCHES AND PUBLIC BUILDINGS

Former ERSKINE UNITED FREE CHURCH. *See* Erskine Hall.

TARBOLTON PARISH CHURCH, Cunningham Street. Classical box of 1819–21 by *Robert Johnstone* of Kilmarnock, with broad projecting centre bay in the ashlar s front. This contains the raised entrance, with torchères flanking, and a Venetian window above with recessed arch and above this a four-stage tower. The first stage has Ionic pilasters framing round-headed openings, some blind, the clock stage above also with pilasters, then the octagonal bell-stage and spire. Windows in two tiers, those of the s front with moulded surrounds; pediments to the upper ones. In the four-bay side elevations, segment-headed windows on the lower floor and round-headed windows above. Two large round-headed windows to the rear. Pilasters at the angles. Narrow vestibule inside, with dog-leg gallery stairs neatly hidden to l. and r. To either side of the main door round-headed niches, with a matching pair opposite. The church proper is bright and well proportioned, with plaster walls, flat plaster ceiling, simple dentil cornice and a panel-fronted gallery on three sides. Dominating classical ORGAN CASE, PULPIT, COMMUNION TABLE, DESK and COMMUNION RAILS, all of 1907 by *Allan Stevenson*; he presented the FONT in 1908 to mark his family's long association with the parish. – STAINED GLASS. Two windows from the Erskine U.F. Church (Erskine Hall, *see* below), installed 1995 in back-lit frames. A remarkably relaxed and pastoral Christ as the Sower (vestibule), 1920 by *William Meikle & Sons*. A radiant Good Shepherd (vestry), 1905 by *J. T. Stewart* for *William Meikle & Sons*.

The church sits in a raised position in the centre of the village, within a large irregular CHURCHYARD, whose walls were raised to 1.8 m. high in 1808, the present main gateway piers probably contemporary with the church. A number of interesting HEADSTONES, including some early carved stones. Two appear to commemorate millwrights, with depictions of cogs and wheels; one, close to the SW corner of the church, appears to bear the date 1728. Against the front wall of the church, Alexander Cooper of Failford †1832, with a draped urn, and adjacent to this a big red sandstone wall shelters monuments to other members of the Cooper family, including one, probably early C19, with a Gibbsian pediment. The monument to James Rintoul †1838, overseer at Coilsfield (Montgomerie), has acroteria and scrolls over the narrow triangular pediment (cf. the doorway of Nos. 21–23 Polwarth Street, Galston). The churchyard also boasts a late C19 *Glenfield & Kennedy* WATER PUMP.

92   BACHELORS' CLUB, Sandgate. The C18 former pub, where in 1780 Robert Burns and seven friends established their literary and debating society. Acquired by the National Trust for Scotland in 1937; restoration completed in 1951. Two-storey, limewashed and thatched, with two plain windows to each floor, and central entrance. To the rear, a later stone stair to the first-floor entrance. One room on the ground floor, with a flagged floor, flat wooden ceiling and plastered walls. Fireplace in one wall, and a bed recess at the far end; to the r. of this access to the former byre. The upper room was originally two, made into one in the late C18, and has a fireplace in either end, wooden floors, plaster walls and a slightly coved plaster ceiling.

ERSKINE HALL, Park Road. A square preaching box of 1777 as a Burgher Secession Church, with round-headed windows, a gabled porch added in 1850, and finished in thick detail-obscuring harl.

LORIMER LIBRARY, Montgomerie Street. 1879 by *Gabriel Andrew*. Symmetrical, with a projecting canted central bay that has a quasi-Romanesque three-light window.

TARBOLTON PRIMARY AND NURSERY SCHOOLS, Park Road. Facing School Avenue is the original symmetrical red sandstone Board School of 1873–6 by *John Mercer*, with two large gables with triple lancets, and three gablet-headed windows between these. Extended in harled brick at both ends in 1912–14 by *J. & H. V. Eaglesham*.

TOWN HOUSE, Burns Street. Red sandstone vernacular of 1832–6. Two-storey, three bays, with a blocked pend on the ground floor, and an external stair to the l., giving access to the former Council Chamber.

WAR MEMORIAL, Montgomerie Street. Of 1920 by *Thomas Lyon*. Granite Celtic cross on an octagonal base, with a red sandstone enclosing wall.

DESCRIPTION

The houses are predominately late C19 and later, but with a few earlier buildings. There is little cohesion and some unfortunate C20 additions. In KIRKPORT, the harled two-storey MANSE of *c.* 1986, an L-plan house in a determinedly traditional manner, but with a grey-tiled roof, no chimneys and a double garage in the wing. Beyond, its predecessor of 1836 by *James Paton* of Ayr, is very Late Georgian but assured and attractive Adamesque. It is a three-bay two-storey harled T-plan, with a slightly projected entrance bay with a round-headed arch within a taller arch. Above this a pedimented three-light window and a roundel in the gable. In CROFT STREET, the overly elaborate painted stone single-storey No. 23, THISTLE COTTAGE, of *c.* 1820, with a pilastered and pedimented projected centre bay, wide pilasters either side of the door, end pilasters, and skewputts with palmette decoration.

S of Tarbolton Cross in MONTGOMERIE STREET, DARGAI COTTAGE of 1902 by *Andrew & Newlands* of Kilmarnock, harled with red sandstone dressings, a canted bay window in the bargeboarded r. bay, and a wooden entrance porch in the re-entrant angle. After the Lorimer Library (*see* above), No. 52, a wide three-bay, two-storey harled house of *c.* 1820. On the opposite side, the MASONIC HALL (No. 67), a harled and slated three-bay house, with a big stone-arched doorway, with an inscription recording its restoration in 1924–5. Back on the E side, the 1930s PRINCES CAFÉ has a good wooden and engraved glass shopfront, and, finally, the BLACK BULL, mid-C19 with main entrance on the S front, in a simple pilastered doorway; to its r. a two-storey circular wing, perhaps of the 1930s.

The village also has a few houses of interest in JAMES STREET. DAISYBANK is a grand two-storey house of *c.* 1790, with big end stacks and prominent polished dressings including eaves, base and sill courses, and corner pilasters. The main elevation faces S, with windows in architraves and a big porch with Roman Doric columns *in antis*. ERSKINE HOUSE is the former Erskine church manse of 1862–3 by *William Ingram* of Glasgow. Red sandstone and harl, Scots Baronial, with gableted windows flanking the central N stairwell window. A Gothic porch on the main S elevation, with a shouldered pediment. Between these, NETHERCROFT, with its main elevation facing N, and hard up to the street. Another manse (U.P.) of *c.* 1820, harled with polished dressings, narrow end pilasters, a curious eaves course of little arches, panelled skewputts and end stacks. Extended, late C19, to form a T.

MONTGOMERIE (or COILSFIELD). 1804, Neoclassical, *John Paterson*. Dem. 1971. A grievous loss. Dull C19 lodge remains.

NEILSHILL HOUSE. *See* p. 549.

THOMASTON CASTLE *see* MAIDENS

TOUR HOUSE
1 km. SE of Kilmaurs

4040

Acquired 1841 by Robert Parker Adam, a Glasgow merchant with Brazilian interests. He seems to have enlarged, rather than rebuilt, a house that had already been added to in 1823. The Tudor Gothic appearance in the manner of David Hamilton (cf. Hafton House and Castle Buildings, Dunoon, Argyll) was probably established at that time. Two storeys and roughly square plan. Main front added 1841, three bays, but subtly asymmetrical around a central tower with clasping crenellated buttresses. It rises higher than the rest and at the rear of its top stage has two further turrets, linked by a stepped parapet. The corners of the outer bays also have turrets. Single-storey rear range linked to the low service court, which is entered through a muscular Tudor-arched gateway with domed bartizans, its upper storey now lost, set into a bold retaining wall. This is all 1840s but masks the earlier, rubble-built courtyard with segmental-headed openings. Late C18 urn over the garden entrance. The interior had three public rooms and six bedrooms when it was advertised in 1839 to be let for the Eglinton Tournament. Completely recast in the 1840s with a plaster-vaulted porch with stiff-leaf bosses, an inner hall, its cornice and ceiling panel with fleuron detail, opening through a Tudor-arched screen to the staircase which is also set behind a screen. The well stair has flat candelabra-like cast-iron balusters and a plaster-panelled, coved ceiling with a central octagonal roof-light, the spandrels filled with looped ribs and supported on stiff-leaf corbels. The landing has an oval light set into a heavily moulded frame with more Gothic mouldings. The plaster ceilings of the public rooms appear Edwardian.

Beyond the service range a rubble-built BARN, dated 1636, one end converted in the C19 for a doocot.

TREESBANK HOUSE *see*
KILMARNOCK WEST AND SOUTH-WEST

TROCHRAIGUE
1.8 km. NW of Old Dailly

2090

An ungainly pile of several dates, unified by ubiquitous grey harl. The estate belonged to the Boyd family from 1548 and the house appears to have begun as a rectangular-plan tower of the later C16 for James Boyd, built just after the tower at Penkill (q.v.). Of this tower something survives in the S elevation which has very thick walls and a much rebuilt bartizan at the SW angle. The tower was extended to the E in the C17 and a matching bartizan added; the continuous, intricate chequerboard detailing extending from the corbelling of the bartizans vertically to the wall-head and continuing as an eaves band is probably C17. There is also a reused carved dormerhead dated 1684 which may date the transformation of the tower to a simple unfortified house. As it stands the main S front has four plain bays and is three storeys high with angle bartizans. The scrolled dormerheads date from the remodelling in 1910–23 for George Todd by *John Burnet & Son*. Theirs is the brash, rather graceless, four-storey tower at the E end of 1910–13 (the design by *Norman Dick*) with a big *porte cochère*. At its rear a conical-roofed stair-turret rises through the parapet. Faced in grey harl for the height of the earlier building, the attic storey and tall stepped parapet are sandstone ashlar. On the entrance elevation, set above the second-floor window, a framed escutcheon with carved decoration dropping down on either side of the window. On the E elevation a tall canted window projection rises into the stone upper storey. Surviving from a remodelling undertaken for the Boyds in 1819–25 is the tiny single-storey canted and crenellated bay on the W gable of the house, a similarly detailed extension ending in an octagon, at the E of Burnet's tower, may have been the terminal to a screen wall.

The rear is undistinguished, with numerous additions that firstly transformed the house to a double-pile plan and then added wings around a light well. A curious low wing in Baronial style was added by *Clarke & Bell* in 1881–3, when this became the principal residence of John Kerr. Work was done on the interior in 1915 and 1920–3. The house was given to the Sisters of St Joseph in 1957 and is now a retreat and guesthouse. Some *c.* 1800 plasterwork inside, but much altered.

OFFICES and former STABLES. Dated 1911 but incorporating earlier work.

TROON

3030

Port, holiday resort, residential centre and golfing Mecca, but before the late C18 there was little here but whin and sand, and the rocky promontory known as the Troon (*An Tron* in Gaelic), frequently used to land smuggled goods. Change came in two forms. Firstly, the developing interest in sea bathing led the proprietor, William Fullarton of Fullarton, to offer feus here for the building of villas. Later, the Marquis of Titchfield began to seek ways to export coal to Ireland from his recently acquired Kilmarnock estates. Initially his proposals were for a new harbour at Troon, linked by canal to Kilmarnock, but revised plans substituted a horse-drawn waggon-way for the canal. The harbour was first mooted in 1806, received parliamentary consent in 1808, and was completed in 1819.*

Titchfield, who had also purchased the financially embarrassed Fullarton estate, became 4th Duke of Portland in 1809 and envisaged a planned town for Troon. In 1841 the author of the *Second Statistical Account* could report that an 'entire new town' had been erected since the *Statistical Account* of the 1790s, while the coming of the Glasgow, Paisley, Kilmarnock & Ayr Railway encouraged further growth, which continued until the duke's death in 1854. Under his successor, best known for his reclusive existence at Welbeck Abbey, Troon stagnated. He died in 1879; in 1881 the *Ayrshire Post* could report that 'the lethargy which has for nearly twenty years characterised the feuing of ground [in Troon] is now thrown aside since the advent of the accession of the young Duke of Portland. During the deadlock of his predecessor it was with the utmost difficulty as much could be obtained as would suffice for a police office and a lifeboat house.' It was as if a dam had broken: Troon experienced a renewed building boom, fuelled equally by its popularity as a residence for Glasgow commuters, served by a new station in the town from 1892, and as a superior resort for holidaymakers drawn by its sandy beaches and the quality of its golf. Its best buildings date from this prosperous era. The C20 saw a continuation of this development, and today Troon is still a vibrant yet relaxed residential centre, which retains a working harbour, remains Ayrshire's premier beach resort, and is a byword for quality golf. The modern town is the result of careful, often intuitive, balancing of the needs of these differing elements.

CHURCHES AND CEMETERY

38   OUR LADY OF THE ASSUMPTION AND ST MEDDAN (R.C.), St Meddans Street. 1909–11 by *Reginald Fairlie*; one of his earliest churches, and a scholarly and skilled design in which he displays his thorough knowledge of Scots Gothic, especially of the Church of the Holy Rood (Stirling), the influence of which is seen most clearly in the heavily buttressed apse. Light brown squared rubble walls, with polished ashlar dressings and greygreen slate roof. Nave and aisles, aligned NW–SE, with a nicely

---

* Titchfield's plans were the culmination of ideas first proposed by Fullarton, who was a noted improver and the author of the first *General View of the Agriculture of Ayrshire*.

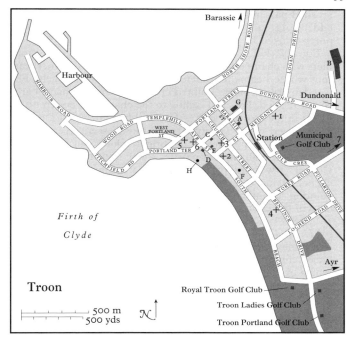

Troon

500 m
500 yds

Firth of Clyde

1   Our Lady of the Assumption (R.C.)
2   Portland Parish Church
3   St Meddan's Parish Church
4   St Ninian (Episcopal)
5   Seagate Evangelical Church
6   Troon Old Parish Church
7   Troon Cemetery

A   Barassie Street Clinic
B   Marr College
C   St Patrick's Primary School
D   Town Hall
E   Troon Library
F   Troon Portland Bowling Club
G   Troon Primary School
H   War Memorial

asymmetrical liturgical (w) front, dominated by a powerful low tower with clasping buttresses. This is of three stages, with a round-headed entrance in the first, flanked by square-headed windows, a four-light arched window above with swirling teardrop tracery, and a chamfered top stage with corbelled parapet topped by individually designed finials (some crocketed, others apostolic symbols). To its l. a slightly higher stair-tower finished with a finely and richly crocketed crown spirelet. The aisles have two-light windows (taller on the sw aisle), with varied tracery (as is the case throughout), and stepped and pinnacled buttresses. On the NW side also a crowstep-gabled transept. The higher roof at the crossing is also crowstepped. The five-sided apse has stepped buttresses, pointed-headed windows and a chequerboard base course of red and yellow stone. An arcaded passage connects the church with the PRESBYTERY, added 1911–14 by *Fairlie*. The latter is two-storey, with an offset porch flanked by projecting bays with canted oriels.

Equally skilful interior. Nave arcades of octagonal stone piers with chamfered plaster arches and a simple hammerbeam roof whose beams terminate in painted wooden angels. Flat wooden aisle ceilings. Pointed crossing arch, the chancel arch round-headed. Panelled ceiling to the chancel. Wooden ROOD BEAM in the crossing arch. – Unusual large marble REREDOS: a castellated stepped triptych with a mosaic scene in each panel below oddly cusped heads; the bright colours out of harmony with the generally muted palette. – The REREDOS of the Lady Chapel (NW transept) is Neo-Romanesque, of stone. The chapel has an elaborate Gothic SCREEN and decorative wall painting; a similar screen in the opposite transept forms the base of the choir gallery. – PULPIT with linenfold carving.

PORTLAND PARISH CHURCH, South Beach. Perp of 1912–14 by *H. E. Clifford & Lunan* in glowing brown Auchenheath limestone. Superficially the most straightforward of the town's major churches, but, especially inside, investigation is amply repaid by Clifford's close attention to detail. Nave with projecting porches, aisles and transepts. Five-light window to the gabled NW main façade, flanked by tall angle buttresses with big gableted heads, and low porches with deeply recessed doors with moulded reveals. Buttressed side elevations and transepts. An arched narthex opens into the spacious ashlar-walled interior. Hammerbeam roof, with wooden shields at the hammerbeam ends. Three-bay stone aisle arcades, with smaller arches transversely across the aisles, and individual pitched roofs to the aisle bays and transepts. Vestibule under the rear gallery, separated from the church by a SCREEN that has sinuous carved decoration and Glasgow Style insets. The chancel has a panelled pitched roof, an elaborate Gothic organ case, a wooden panelled screen in the recess to r., and a stone REREDOS. – STAINED GLASS in the chancel, a richly coloured war memorial of 1921 by *Guthrie & Wells*; three of the lower panels depict the three armed services.

Contemporary HALLS to the S; further sympathetic halls of 1964 extended in 2000.

ST MEDDAN'S PARISH CHURCH, Church Street. Dec of 1888–9 by *J. B. Wilson* in Ballochmyle red sandstone; aligned NW–SE with a tall SE tower, NW and NE transepts. Front gable with a five-light window, flanking stepped porches, flat pedimented buttresses and smaller cusped windows in square frames. Two tiers of cusped windows to the side elevations and transepts; the upper tier in the transepts, with circular lights above, are within recessed panels. The tower, a dominant feature in the townscape, rises above the porch. Tall first stage with clasping buttresses; the second stage has paired round-headed bell-openings with recessed cusped tracery above square clock panels. Broach spire. Plastered galleried nave with a panelled plastered barrel vault, the transverse ribs springing from corbels which have their own mini-corbels. Panel-fronted galleries, with a regular pattern of cusped openings, supported on cast-iron columns. Further cast-iron columns rise from the side gallery fronts, supporting arcades which are tied into the external walls by triangular cross-beams with very big cusped openwork decoration. – STAINED GLASS. – SE window. Jairus's Daughter, 1892 by *William Smith* of London, its rich colours and naturalistic imagery reminiscent of the work of Morris & Co. – NE wall. The Mothers of Salem by *Norman M. MacDougall*, *c.* 1926. Opposite, Go and Do Thou Likewise, 1977 by *John Blyth*.

ST NINIAN (Episcopal), Bentinck Drive. Arts and Crafts Gothic. Nave by *James A. Morris*, 1912–13, the chancel by him in 1920–1. The builder of the nave was *Mathew Muir & Co.* of Kilmarnock, of the chancel *Henry Adams* of Troon. Simply imagined, skilfully and thoughtfully executed. This is Morris's only major ecclesiastical work, and showcases his advocacy of craftsmen and craftsmanship. Red sandstone, the church is gabled, aligned broadly N–S, with a tiled roof, gabled NE porch with applied timberwork, and gabled SW block linking with the hall. The side elevations of the nave have groups of square-headed windows; a similar window, of six lights, in the N gable. The chancel taller than the nave, its windows with Dec cusped tracery; five-light S window and diagonal buttresses. Stepped buttress at the junction of nave and chancel.

Numinous interior, with an Arbroath flag floor, exposed stone walls and hammerbeam nave roof. The nave windows have shallow curved heads. Simple pointed chancel arch; panelled barrel vault, marble floor. To the r. PISCINA and SEDILIA with crocketed finialled heads, and arched recess for the organ, the wooden organ case supported on an octagonal half-column. – FONT. Pavonazzo marble. By *Morris*, 1917. Stone PULPIT, oak CHOIR STALLS and CHANCEL SCREEN, all 1921, again by *Morris*. BISHOP'S CHAIR of *c.* 1937, by *Robert Thompson* of Kilburn, who also made the church door. – STAINED GLASS. In the S gable, a Crucifixion of 1923 by *Charles Payne* for *Guthrie & Wells*. – In the chancel E wall, from N to S, Suffer Little Children of 1937 by *George Cooper-Abbs* in bright primary colours; Feast at Cana, 1931 by *Douglas Strachan*; and Christ in Majesty, 1920, an emotive almost monochrome war memorial by *Guthrie & Wells*, with starkly realized scenes from the trenches. – In the N wall, a well-drawn and well-executed The Seasons, St Ninian and the Signs of the Zodiac, 1953 by *William Wilson*.

At right angles to the church, the sandstone and tiled HALL, with castellated N porches, and a ribbed barrel-vaulted plaster ceiling. 1927 by *J. R. Johnstone*. The church sits within spacious grounds, entered through the tiled and wooden Gothic LYCHGATE of 1913 by *Morris*, with a collar-beam roof, arched braces and sinuous bargeboards. To the N, symmetrical harled RECTORY, *c.* 1925 by *Johnstone*, with a semicircular-headed porch and tapering diagonal buttresses.

SEAGATE EVANGELICAL CHURCH, West Portland Street. Classical of 1843, as a U.P. Church, extended in 1857. Rendered; the gabled NW front elevation has a recessed central bay with a pilastered doorpiece, flanked by tall windows with margin glazing.

TROON OLD PARISH CHURCH, Ayr Street. 1892–5 by *Hippolyte J. Blanc* succeeding the first parish church (*see* below). The commission was for a church to 'resemble as nearly as possible [his] St Matthew's Morningside' in Edinburgh (1889–90, now Cluny Parish Church). Nave, aisles and transepts, the entrance in the buttressed and pinnacled NE gable; to the l. of this the stump of an unbuilt tower.* E.E. and Dec details. The entrance is pointed-headed with nook-shafts and small flanking windows; above are a big five-light Geometric window and three small lights high in the finialled gable. Paired aisle windows, with three-light windows above, and flying buttresses. The interior markedly resembles Cluny: the NE gallery over the vestibule, arcaded aisles with diapered plaster decoration in the spandrels, and tall paired transept arches are all borrowed directly, as is the panelled barrel-vaulted roof rising from wall-shafts. Tall shafted chancel arch; panel-fronted rear and transept galleries. First-class Gothic panelling of 1906 in the chancel, with a central traceried and cusped canopy. – STAINED GLASS. Some distinguished work. – Chancel SW, a Crucifixion by *Ballantine*, 1895. – Opposite (NE), the Ascension of 1903 by *J. Henry Dearle* for *Morris & Co.*, a glorious window in their blues, pinks and grey-greens. Also by *Morris & Co.*, Faith, Hope and Charity (SE aisle), 1904: Charity by *J. Henry Dearle*, her companions earlier designs by *Burne-Jones*. – Several of the 1920s and others by *Gordon Webster* in the NW transept (1955) and NW aisle (The Water of Life, 1936, and war memorial, 1949). Low stone boundary WALL with cast-iron panels, erected in 1937.

The CHURCH HALL is the church of 1837–8,** as converted in 1933–4 by *Henry Brown*. A characteristic Late Georgian sandstone preaching box, with a projecting four-stage entrance tower, terminating in an octagonal spire. Flanking the tower tall round-headed windows, with cast-iron Y-tracery; square-headed side windows in two tiers. Brown introduced the plastered combed ceiling which descends low to the heads of the ground-floor windows; inset panels borrowing the light from the now hidden gallery windows. Some mannered plasterwork decoration in the reveals in the NE wall. Decorative plaster ceilings in the linking block, also by Brown.

TROON CEMETERY, Dundonald Road. 1862, enlarged 1913–14. Two stone-walled enclosures, separated by a broad lane. That

---

* *Blanc*'s sketch with the proposed tower and spire is preserved at the church.
** The architect is unrecorded. The galleried interior, removed in the conversion, was of 'elegant simplicity altogether becoming the *simplex mutuditiius* of a Scotch Presbyterian church that says much for the taste and sound judgment of its projectors'. (*Ayr Advertiser*, 1838)

to the s is the older and plainer; the other has square gatepiers and a gabled single-storey lodge, with ridge tiles: to its s a similarly detailed waiting room.

PUBLIC BUILDINGS

BARASSIE PRIMARY SCHOOL, Burnfoot Avenue. 2007–9, by *Ryder HKS* for South Ayrshire Council.

BARASSIE STREET CLINIC, Barassie Street. Grey-harled English Manorial quondam nurses' home of 1903–4 by *James Scott Hay* of Kilmarnock; extended 1923 by *Alexander Mair*. On the return elevation a semicircular two-storey bay and Mair's forceful single-storey addition.

MARR COLLEGE, Dundonald Road. Established by the will of Charles K. Marr (†1919) who made his fortune in shipping. An expensive and imaginatively interpreted classical design in fawn Blaxter stone and Westmorland slate by *John Arthur*, 1925, built 1928–30 but not opened until 1935, and the finishing-out done by Arthur's partner *A. G. McNaughtan*. The two-storey sw front has a massive projecting octagonal tower at its centre, topped by a balustraded parapet behind which a stone drum rises to a copper dome. The raised entrance has a bolection moulding surround with armorial keystone. The walls of the tower are of channelled masonry, so too the hip-roofed pavilions at the ends of the wings l. and r. They have to their fronts also Ionic columns *in antis* flanking a blank aedicule. Metal windows to the wings, in unmoulded openings, those at the attic storey between panelled piers. Cornice with paired brackets. The other elevations are similarly detailed. On the NE elevation a gabled central block, again with Ionic columns *in antis*. Inside, entrance hall ringed with Doric columns, with a bronze BUST of Marr by *Benno Schotz*, 1942–3, placed centrally. Steps lead into a second, wood-panelled reception area, with broad tiled corridors to either side. Assembly Hall, again panelled, with plaster proscenium arch and gently curved rear gallery; open corridors to either side of the hall.

Extension of *c.* 1982, with a tall first floor, and a shallow upper floor with long window bands, supported at one end on widely spaced pilotis. Of the same date the free-standing GAMES HALL, with more window bands, and a CLASSROOM BLOCK with staccato bursts of windows, and two glazed fins running asymmetrically across the roof, lighting the upper floor.

For his ancillary buildings *Arthur* turned to a simpler Lutyensesque palette, e.g. the wide-eaved T-plan former JANITOR'S HOUSE, and, at the end of the tree-lined drive, the square similarly detailed LODGE and four tall square GATEPIERS with raised panels, monogrammed MC, and key-pattern tops.

Former POST OFFICE, Church Street. *See* below p. 663.

ST PATRICK'S PRIMARY SCHOOL, Academy Street. 1993–5 by *Strathclyde Regional Council*. Mostly single-storey brick and tiled, with a prominent gabled main entrance and a horizontal band of windows in one roof.

TOWN HALL, South Beach. Handsome Neo-Georgian of 1930–2 by *James Miller* for municipal offices and a concert hall, largely paid for by the whisky magnate, Sir Alexander Walker. Red brick with ashlar dressings and pantiled roofs. Substantial s extension of 1973–5 by *Noad & Wallace*. Main elevation of two storeys with a low raised basement and attic dormers. Nine bays wide, round-arched windows below, square-headed above. The central three bays are advanced and separated by tall fluted pilasters supporting an entablature and balustrade. Doric porch. The eleven-bay side elevations similarly detailed, with three regularly spaced balconies and the entrance to the concert hall, with its low-key porch on spindly columns, on the NW elevation. To the rear, five full-height windows and giant pilasters, and wide recessed flanking bays. Internally, offices with wooden panelling and simple cornices; the CONCERT HALL has a gallery round three sides with a wooden front. The simple detailed extension, known as the WALKER HALL, is also of brick, with stone dressings (but without any historicism), and shallowly pitched roofs. The hall has tall metal clearstorey windows above single-storey wings and, to the rear, a smaller first-floor hall with tall picture windows, supported on pilotis.

TROON LIBRARY, South Beach. 1972–4 by *Ayr County Council*. Single-storey, brick, flat-roofed, with a wide stone fascia and prominent projecting stone window heads. To the s is the restful GORDON BROWN MEMORIAL GARDEN, of *c.* 2002, Japanese character. A bronze rugby ball commemorates '*Broon fae Troon*', †2001, a Scottish international forward.

TROON PORTLAND BOWLING CLUB, Dallas Road. The original clubhouse of *c.* 1897 has an attractive cast-iron veranda and a central gable with applied timbering.

TROON PRIMARY SCHOOL, Burnside Place. Big red sandstone Free Renaissance of 1897–1900 by *R. S. Ingram*; respectfully extended in 1907–9 by *James Miller*. Ingram's school to the l., with a broad sill course, square-headed windows with multipane upper sashes, central shaped gable to the SE and a pedimented porch to the SW. Miller's addition has three-bay gables at either end and a large porch to the far r. In the W corner of the playground, the shaped gables of Ingram's JANITOR'S HOUSE, a neat and successful synthesis of the details.

TROON STATION, St Meddans Street. 1890–2 by *James Miller*, with *William Melville*, company engineer, for the Glasgow & South-Western Railway. The Glasgow, Paisley, Kilmarnock & Ayr Railway reached Troon in 1839, with a station near Dundonald Road. The present station was erected on a short loop line, and is the most successful of the brick, harled and 'half-timbered' through-stations designed by Miller for the GSWR in Ayrshire (*see* also Prestwick, West Kilbride). Single-storey block on both platforms, that on the E being smaller, with each platform roofed by a series of shallow glazed pyramids, linked across the tracks by steel trusses.

WAR MEMORIAL, Esplanade. 1923–4, by *Walter Gilbert* of Birmingham: an imposing and well-conceived work. 2.9-m. bronze Britannia, amidst the shattered chains of bondage, with victory in one hand, the other palm outstretched to those 'resting in and beyond the seas', supported by an equally tall granite plinth, with a Vitruvian scrolled band, bronze panels naming the fallen and inscription. Granite bench, with similar details to the plinth, on the landward side.

GOLF CLUBS

The first golf club at Troon was founded in 1878, shortly before the death of the 5th Duke, by which time courses and clubs were well established elsewhere, e.g. at Prestwick. Once established, the natural advantages of Troon ensured that it soon became the pre-eminent golfing centre on the Ayrshire coast. The course at Troon (now Royal Troon) is a regular venue for the Open Championship, first played at Prestwick in 1860.

KILMARNOCK (BARASSIE) GOLF CLUB. *See* Barassie.

MUNICIPAL GOLF CLUB, Harling Drive. Harled and tiled CLUBHOUSE of 1903–5 by *James Scott Hay* of Kilmarnock; internally reconstructed in 1934–6 by *J. B. McInnes* and extended in the late C20. Scots Renaissance; to the front a tall, half-timbered gable and a round tower with a conical turret flank bays with catslide dormers. Facing the course, an impressive square tower, with battlement and tall corner pinnacle, somewhat lost in an inchoate display of gables and picture windows.

ROYAL TROON GOLF CLUB, Craigend Road. The club was founded in 1878 at the Portland Arms Hotel, and the first clubhouse was a converted railway carriage. The present CLUBHOUSE is of 1885–6 by *H. E. Clifford*, who made extensions in 1897–8 and 1905; *J. R. Johnstone* added the shallow curved entrance porch in 1926–7. Substantially enlarged and reconstructed in 2004–6 by *Hurd Rolland Partnership*, creating a new E entrance front. Pale ashlar. The N façade is dominated by the simple columns and plain parapet of Johnstone's porch. The W elevation faces the first tee and is of three gabled bays. The two to the l., with canted bay windows, a stilted screen entrance between (now blocked), and three round-headed windows in recessed semicircular panels in the gables, form the main front of 1885–6. The cast-iron balcony, too, of this date, and lengthened to the r. in 1897–8, when the clubhouse was substantially extended to provide additional accommodation and a S-facing elevation, with a central gabled bay and canted bays to either side. Details such as the semicircular panels and the balcony are echoed in the C21 additions. The interior was largely remodelled in 2004–6, but three of Clifford's rooms of 1897–8 survive, the best the DINING ROOM, which fills the centre of the S elevation. It has an open wood and plaster roof with segmental braces and neatly detailed hammerbeams. The CLUB ROOM, to the W, is simpler, with a low panelled dado, while the SMOKE ROOM, at the SW corner,

has a coved plaster roof and two classical wooden fireplaces,
each with a bronze war memorial incorporated above the mantelpiece. To the NW of the clubhouse a delightful wooden
boarded STARTER'S BOX of c. 1900, with a pyramidal felt roof.
TROON LADIES' GOLF CLUB, Crosbie Road. Simple hipped
Arts and Crafts CLUBHOUSE of 1897 by *H. E. Clifford*, with a
polished red sandstone ground floor and harled upper floor.
TROON PORTLAND GOLF CLUB, Crosbie Road. CLUBHOUSE
of 1914–15; enlarged subsequently. An amorphous structure,
harled with tiled roofs and prominent gables.

HARBOUR

Laid out from 1806 by *William Jessop*, engineer. Parliamentary
consent was granted in 1808, and work began the same year.
It was completed in 1819, at a total cost of c. £200,000. It
consists of two basins, separated by two short piers, and there
are also a W pier and a long E pier. All of red sandstone from
the quarries at Corrie (Arran). At the end of the W pier, a
circular cast-iron LIGHTHOUSE of 1904. To the NW of the
inner basin a late C19 POWER HOUSE, now used as a restaurant: a series of gabled stone bays with slate roofs; tall C20
additions at one end. GRAVING DOCKS for shipbuilding were
built to the SE of the basins in 1811–17 as part of the original
plan. One remains, as part of the AILSA SHIPBUILDING
YARD (established 1885; closed 2003), as does a larger stone-
faced GRAVING DOCK of 1897–9 by *McTaggart Cowan &
Barker* of Glasgow. Of the surviving buildings associated with
the shipyard, the most noteworthy is the red brick two-storey
gabled block of 1910–11 by *James Miller*; given character by the
asymmetrically placed bands of windows.

DESCRIPTIONS

The town is described in two parts, the centre and then the residential suburbs to the S.

1. Centre

The planned development initiated by the Duke of Portland
accounts for the town centre and the streets N and S. Its pattern
has two elements: a grid-plan centre, with principal streets
running NE inland from the shore, and a series of parallel roads
running round the gentle curve of the promontory. Troon
Cross is the junction of Ayr Street and Templehill (SE–NW)
with Portland Street and West Portland Street (SW–NE) at the
promontory's narrow neck. The town centre itself occupies
little more than a single square of the grid SE of the Cross,
defined by Ayr Street (S), Portland Street (W), Church Street
(N) and Academy Street (E).
AYR STREET has, on its SW side, a terrace of two storey blocks,
with flats above shops, of 1840–1, including Nos. 18–22, with

a wall-head gable surmounted by an unusual chimney with an octagonal base, followed by the Old Parish Church (*see* Churches, above). Opposite are red sandstone commercial buildings of the early years of the C20. Of mixed heights, the tallest the Scots Renaissance Nos. 1–15 of 1902–3 by *James Campbell McKellar*, which has canted bays with pedimented first-floor windows, and a partially harled circular corner tower flanked by corbelled chimneystacks. The corresponding corner building at Academy Street is dated 1900, by *James Scott Hay*, and more tactile than McKellar's work. The round-headed ground-floor windows have Gibbsian surrounds; in the rounded corner bay three small windows with their quoins run together. Above them, a corbelled two-storey oriel with a panelled parapet with shields. Three first-floor windows have big architraves and shaped gables, linked by a balustrade to the oriel.

PORTLAND STREET runs NE from The Cross and has little coherent character on either side. The best things again are the later C19 red sandstone interventions, e.g. Nos. 61–63 of 1890, by *Gabriel Andrew*, with two-storey corbelled oriels and roundheaded entrances, the main one with subsidiary windows, like a stretched Diocletian window. After Church Street, there is the grey sandstone former Police Station of 1867 by *John Murdoch*, with shaped gables over the second and fifth bays, and Nos. 82–86, a dramatic free Arts and Crafts tenement with a bravura suggesting the hand again of *Gabriel Andrew*. It retains its original plate-glass shopfronts with cast-iron columns and brackets. Nos. 125 and 127–131 are two adjoining harled and gabled early C19 cottages, one with a hipped wing to the r. and a pilastered doorway, the other with flanking hipped wings, gently curving dormers and a Doric portico.

CHURCH STREET is mostly forgettable but for the unshowy assurance of the red sandstone former Post Office, of 1929–32 by *J. Wilson Paterson* of *H.M. Office of Works*. At the corner with Academy Street, an attractive commercial range of 1934–5 by *Henry Brown*, mostly in red sandstone, with rendered panels to the recurring pedimented gables. Some original shopfronts remain, with tiled stall-risers and etched glass.

ACADEMY STREET has some early C19 survivors, but none of special distinction. West Portland Street and Templehill (running SW and NW respectively) lead from Troon Cross onto and around the rocky headland. It is almost impossible to imagine how the gorse wastes and the promontory rising above and beyond them appeared before the early C19. TEMPLE-HILL* is particularly rewarding. The S side, which has a broad pavement, is an almost continuous run of neat, painted early C19 two-storey properties. Opposite, however, firstly the castellated red sandstone Bank of Scotland, of *c.* 1880, the former Unionist Club of 1893–4 by *R. S. Ingram*, with a big harled

---

*So named from the classical temple or summerhouse erected on the highest part of the point *c.* 1750 by William Fullarton of Fullarton. It was 'Erected to Bacchus the giver of happiness for friends and for leisure'.

and crowstepped gable, refenestrated as part of its residential
conversion, and a long grey sandstone terrace, with pilastered
doorways and wall-head chimneys. The site was feued to the
Kilmarnock builder *James Rome* in 1888. Back on the s side,
the red sandstone Tudor Gothic Nos. 93–95 are of *c.* 1900, and
have been attributed to *George Washington Browne*. There
follows a series of early C19 classical villas, among the earliest
in Troon, mostly built by Kilmarnock merchants seeking a
family home for the sea-bathing season. Of these, the ANCHOR-
AGE HOTEL is built of doleritic whin with painted dressings
and a pilastered central doorway, and has lower hipped wings,
while BANK VILLA is of painted tooled ashlar, with a Doric
portico, ground-floor windows recessed in segmentally headed
panels, and giant pilasters, which suggest the hand of *James
Ingram*. Its r. wing has been given, perhaps *c.* 1850, a symmetrical front, with a central three-light window in a shallow segmentally headed recess, and flanking pilastered bays.

WEST PORTLAND STREET has little of interest until towards
the sea it becomes PORTLAND TERRACE, with houses of 1881,
one of the first major developments after feuing recommenced
under the 6th Duke, and 'built on the beautiful meadow, so
long the ornament of Troon and a great attraction to visitors
thither' (*Ayrshire Post*). The developer was James Dickie, who
also donated the Peterhead granite DRINKING FOUNTAIN
surmounted by a tall obelisk in 1891, by *William Muir* of
London. Then begins the long sweep of houses round the N
side of the bay as far as one can see along the sea front in both
directions.

THE ESPLANADE, built in 1912–13 by *J. & H. V. Eaglesham*, who
had first prepared plans in 1899. Low concrete walls and a
wide promenade. Several flights of access steps, each with a
central iron handrail.

2. South of the Centre

SOUTH BEACH, continuing for 2 km. along the seafront, is the
southward continuation of Ayr Street, beginning properly at
Portland Parish Church (*see* Churches, above). The houses of
its w side are almost exclusively of before 1853 and have their
back to the sea; they are mostly of exposed stone, while scale,
style and ambition vary greatly. The first group are mostly
single-storey, the earliest probably No. 36, of 1836, pleasingly
asymmetrical with Tudor details, an elaborate keyhole window
in the gable of an advanced off-centre bay, columns in its
canted corners supporting the gable-ends. Its seaward front
allows one to discern the equal importance originally given to
the back elevation of the houses.

Mostly two-storey houses with lower flanking wings follow,
many from the lean years of the 5th Duke. The first, No. 56,
of 1849, has hipped wings, a pilastered doorpiece, lying-pane
glazing, a complex bracketed gable on the seaward elevation,
and a contemporary coachhouse in the N boundary wall.

Nos. 58–60 were built by the Troon builder *William Young* for himself in 1854. Nos. 66 and 68 are cheerful Picturesque cottages of 1855, all gables, wooden porches, fish-scale slating and tiled ridges, their frothiness contrasting with the sturdier, more rooted manner of the final group on this side, typified by No. 72, of 1858, in painted stugged ashlar, with pilastered doorway, mostly lying-pane glazing and central windows in architraves.

In the resurgence in development after the 5th Duke's death in 1879, preferred feus were those on the landward (E) side of the street, with front rooms enjoying the sea views, and the rear gardens offering privacy. Other contrasts with the earlier houses are also immediately obvious. These houses are mostly in pairs, are set further back from the street, and are, most frequently, red sandstone. In the part of South Beach between Yorke Road and Lochend Road, a consistent group of villas, Nos. 89–117, of the years either side of 1900. More of the same s of Lochend Road, the best of which is the very English WINDYHAUGH (Nos. 119–121) of 1899, harled and tiled with a tile-hung first floor and prominently bolted bargeboards. Two gables face W, flanking a central bay with a tall roof and a stepped dormer; on the return elevation the entrance in a tall exposed stone projection with an arched and pilastered entrance canopy, tall stair window and an escutcheon breaking through the parapet, flanked by small carved panels. Parts of the original harled boundary wall remain, with the name of the house in a carved stone panel. Further down, Nos. 135–137 have conically roofed and finialled corner drum towers, flanking a roof supported on wooden brackets and two gabled dormers, while the entrances are in recessed crowstepped outer bays. The boundary wall has drum piers and ball finials. The grey sandstone Italianate CROSBIE TOWER is earlier, of *c.* 1883; the tower set back to the rear of the s elevation, behind the main entrance. The main façade has a canted bay to the l., and three recessed bays to the r., with a cast-iron balcony. There is a substantial later wing projecting to the s, and a contemporary boundary wall.

A number of streets connect South Beach with its landward parallel, Bentinck Drive. In DALLAS ROAD, on its N side, houses of *c.* 1880, including two pairs with stepped chimneys. Each has gabled end bays, one with studded bargeboards, the other with gables shaped like Dutchwomen's caps. To their r., No. 11, *c.* 1910, perhaps by *William Cowie*. Red sandstone, with a bracketed open pediment over the entrance, a castellated bay to the r., and an oriel on the return elevation, corbelled out and almost all stone and no window. In VICTORIA DRIVE, REDCLIFF (No. 6), a spry brown sandstone house of 1893 by *H. E. Clifford*, with a very tall hipped tiled roof, big end stacks, small-paned windows with stone mullions and transoms, a canted bay breaking the eaves line, and dormers with plastered heads. Also of *c.* 1893, No. 10, a red sandstone flurry of crow-stepped gables and catslide dormers with a spindly corner turret. In YORKE ROAD, Nos. 9–11, on the N, are of *c.* 1905, red sandstone and tiled, with a central pair of big gables. Small-pane windows and flat-headed half-dormers; stylistically similar to the work of *H. E. Clifford*. On the S, Nos. 10–12, of *c.* 1904, in a fresh free Arts and Crafts manner, perhaps by *Thomas Smellie*. The last of these cross-streets is LOCHEND ROAD. Here No. 9 (with No. 108 Bentinck Drive) is a creamily harled pair of *c.* 1911, with tiled roofs, starkly unadorned gables and dormers, tapering buttresses and polished red dressings, as on the full-height canted bay and the semicircular head to the entrance to the l.

Parallel with South Beach to the E is BENTINCK DRIVE, an extension of Church Street. It is broad, gently curving, and spaciously laid out with equally spacious Victorian and Edwardian houses. From the N end, after St Meddan's Church (*see* Churches, above) the gloriously decorative red ashlar DALLAS HOUSE (No. 2), with a corner turret, windows with stone mullions and transoms, bargeboarded gables and tall slated roofs with finials. Below the turret roof a band of panels each with a central moulded ring enclosing a boss, and moulded ribs. Round-headed entrance, with a narrow window to the l., the doors themselves boarded with round-headed fanlights in tympana. The upper turret windows have basket-arched heads; the lower one stilted segmental heads, repeated elsewhere on the ground floor. The detailing is very similar to an unidentified house by *W. H. McLachlan*, published in *Building News* in 1900. Among the red sandstone villas, Nos. 9–11, *c.* 1895 by *Thomas Smellie*, with one hipped half-dormer, the projecting curving sill of which rests on a single bracket. BRANDON HOUSE (No. 25), an L-plan of rock-faced red sandstone, is of *c.* 1905. It has a shaped gable to the r. above a castellated and corbelled oriel and two semicircular-headed ground-floor windows separated by a plain square buttress. Re-entrant porch, dominated by a powerful Flamboyant window, with a parapet with ball finials and a heavy cylindrical pinnacle. Then, on the r., the severely austere two-storey WELBECK HOUSE, 1910–12, freely managed asymmetrical Arts and Crafts, probably by *J. R. Johnstone*, added to in 1922 and 1925 by *Henry Brown*. Harled with metal-framed windows, tiled roofs, tall stacks, and horizontal window bands tight under the eaves. Tall ground-floor windows, and tapering buttresses at the ends, and to the corners of the gabled projections. Beyond St Ninian's (*see* Churches, above), noticeably bigger houses, e.g. the fussily detailed Nos. 83–85, of 1912 for the Irvine builder John Parker, with its tiled porch and castellated screen walls. Grander again are the eclectic loosely Arts and Crafts harled and tiled early C20 houses in BENTINCK CRESCENT, which curves around an irregularly shaped grassed area. The best are EBOR HOUSE, of *c.* 1925 by *J. R. Johnstone*, with a stark gabled bay to the r. and a stone-faced porch with round-headed openings and a harled balcony balustrade, THE GARTH, of *c.* 1922, with a central porch with a pronounced batter and semicircular

headed entrance, and SHANDWICK, of 1911–12, again by
Johnstone, with a prominent front gable and circular window.
CRAIGEND ROAD is the s boundary to the town and its golfing
heart, with courses on both sides. The buildings, almost wholly
of after 1890, include substantial villas, golf clubhouses and
hotels. The first of note is the Royal Troon Golf Club (*see*
above) at the junction with South Beach, but the most considerable architectural presence lies further E: this is PIERSLAND
LODGE (now Piersland House Hotel), a luxuriant English
Domestic villa-mansion of 1898–9 by *William Leiper* for the
whisky magnate, Sir Alexander Walker. One of Leiper's most
ambitious and successful villas; sympathetic additions of 1920
by *J. R. Johnstone*. Ground floor of red sandstone, upper floors
abundantly treated with applied timberwork, Westmorland
slate roofs, and slate-hanging in the gable-heads. Ground-floor
windows mullioned and transomed; small-pane casements
above. The main façade faces W, with a central timber porch
and a gabled bay with splayed bay window to the r; the garden
façade faces S, with three similar gabled bays, that to the r.
grander and projected forward, that to the l. partially hidden
behind a gargantuan stack. Beneath the gables, Johnstone has
added a triple-arched loggia with a simple wooden balcony.
From this façade a covered terrace runs around the E side of
a sunken garden, with two summerhouses with pyramidal
roofs. Sumptuous interiors include a panelled entrance hall
with a Jacobean screen, and the main bar, with a balustraded
stair and first-floor gallery, more panelling, tapestry friezes and
two fireplaces, the larger with a tall decorative wooden overmantel, the other with beaten bronze panels. In Bentinck Drive
are the former STABLES, with applied timber gables and circular tower, and the well-mannered WEST LODGE, with a big
chimney-breast, a catslide dormer and a neat oriel tucked into
its half-timbered s gable.
    The other villas in this part of Craigend Road pale by com-
parison but LANDALE, of 1908–9 by *J. B. S. Abercrombie* of
Glasgow (now flatted) is harled with small-pane casement
windows, tall slender stacks, slated roofs and slate-hanging in
the many gables.
CROSBIE ROAD is dominated by the red sandstone free Scots
Renaissance bulk of the MARINE HIGHLAND HOTEL of
1894–7 by *James Salmon Jun.* and *J. Gaff Gillespie*, of *James
Salmon & Son*, extended in 1901–2 by *Gillespie*; subsequently
enlarged and modernized internally. The nine-bay two-storey
main elevation faces W, across the links, towards the sea and
Arran, with advanced and gabled outer and central bays, and
a central entrance beneath a four-light oriel and balcony. The
outer bays have ground-floor Venetian windows, pedimented
two-light windows above. Carved crowns on skewputts and
apices. Gabled return elevations, that to the S emerging from
glazed lounges of the 1930s and 1960s and elongated to the E
by Gillespie's mannered four-storey extension of 1901. A
gabled bay to the l., with a very tall canted bay window, and

decorative finials; a tall square balustraded tower to the r., with a taller NE stair-tower and a shorter semi-octagonal turret on the SE, linked to a second-floor balcony with a Gibbsian window behind. Close by to the S, BLACKROCK COTTAGE of *c.* 1912–13, a large L-plan Arts and Crafts house, harled with roofs of small slates. Competent architecture given added frisson by its island setting within the golf course. The E side of Crosbie Road has a succession of large early C20 villas, all to a greater or lesser extent Arts and Crafts-inspired. ARDERY is of *c.* 1903 by *J. C. McKellar* for himself, Free Style, pale stone with a tiled hipped roof, and full-height canted bay to the r. terminating in a rooftop balcony. Its neighbour SUN COURT, now a nursing home and much enlarged, is of the same year by *Fryers & Penman.* It was acquired in 1905 by J. O. M. Clark of the Paisley thread manufacturers. Harled with red tiles and sandstone dressings, e.g. to the stepped stair window, and a projecting tile-hung gable. At the rear is a REAL TENNIS COURT built by *Joseph Bickley* for Clark, a leading exponent of the game. Long roof-light; the walls buttressed. Disused but intact; apart from Falkland Palace (Fife), it is the only such court in Scotland.

MUIRHEAD, 2 km. ENE of the town. Developed as a new housing area from 1937 by Troon Town Council, the design won in competition by *John A. W. Grant* of Dundee. Work on 220 houses began in 1938 but was interrupted by the Second World War, while subsequent infill and alterations have diluted the original concept. It was laid out on spacious Garden Suburb principles with a main spine (CENTRAL AVENUE), and longer and shorter cross roads. The houses are harled, with tiled roofs, in a variety of patterns, such as gabled blocks with paired front gables, or hipped with gabled dormers.

SOUTHWOOD. *See* p. 621.

2000

TURNBERRY

There has been a settlement at Turnberry for many centuries, and in 1876 the correspondent of the *London Scottish Journal* wondered that the Ailsa family had not called into existence 'a northern Brighton on the Carrick shore. There is no better sea bathing in the Empire', but it was the huge surge of interest in golf at the end of the C19 that led to its major development. The white harl and red tile roofs of the hotel complex have a jaunty holiday character of their own.

117　TURNBERRY HOTEL, Maidens Road. Self-importantly straddling the high raised beach and commanding views of the golf courses and the Firth of Clyde. Built 1904–6 and paid for by the Glasgow & South-Western Railway Co. who acquired Turnberry Golf Course (laid out 1901) and opened a station at the same time on their line between Ayr and Girvan (closed 1942). The design, by *James Miller*, assisted by *A. McInnes Gardner*, was for the most ambitious golfing hotel to date. The style is a variation of Queen Anne Revival but strongly influenced in scale and appearance by the rural resort hotels and country clubs being built in the United States.

Originally an E-plan with E courtyards and a 60-m.-long W elevation extended N and S in the 1920s to nearly 150 m. Two storeys and attic throughout with red tile roofs punctuated by square-headed dormers and tall chimneystacks. The centre of the W front is the most interesting architecturally and reflects both American and English domestic design of the later C19. To l. and r. are gables projecting over two-storey bay windows. In the centre, over the entrance, a hip-roofed columned veranda set on a red brick and stone chequered parapet. Between these projections were formerly colonnades, later reconstructed as bows. The extensions follow the same pattern. Miller advocated the brick and render construction, concluding that it would be more practical than stone, and given the size of the additions his advice must have been right. On the E side, the expansive entrance courtyard is a clear forerunner of Miller's design for Kildonan (q.v.) but the later pedimented entrance spoils the clever Free Style massing of the original entrance and stair block. Over the balustrade to the r. of the huge mullion-and-transom stair window, a tall, constrained small-paned canted window, of clear Glaswegian inspiration, rises through two storeys. Set back to the S, a taller tower with a projecting stone doorway at the ground and the two small upper windows united in a stone panel with carved decoration between floors. Above is a corbelled blind storey to house the water tanks, and a crowning parapet with widely spaced balusters. The slightly lower side elevations have prominent gabled bays, and tall stacks with red tile cans, some quite elaborate, break the skyline. With subsequent additions and alterations the elevations have a restless appearance.

The INTERIOR is decked out in a grand Edwardian Beaux Arts manner, with plenty of coffering and modillion and egg-and-dart cornicing. The columned entrance hall opens to the wide panelled stairwell with boldly swagged plasterwork in the ceiling. Opening from the hall to the front of the building, two large columned public rooms extending into the bowed bays seen on the W front. There are big classically styled chimneypieces and plenty of columns and pilasters in the restaurants. The former swimming pool has been converted to a function suite with a big conservatory. The pagoda-roofed Health Spa with a large curved terrace lies to the S, by the *Cunningham Glass Partnership*, 1990–1.

To the N of the hotel on the lower ground a range of linked, gabled COTTAGE BLOCKS originally for staff use; *c.* 1990 the number was doubled to provide self-contained guest accommodation. They are in a similar style but without stone detailing and metal balconies. Set within this group is the 1906

GARAGE BLOCK with a wide arched entrance, now infilled, a decorative gable above and flanking ball finials.

Across the road, the TURNBERRY GOLF CLUBHOUSE, 1991–3 by the *Cunningham Glass Partnership*, designed apparently with the idea of a stable court in mind but who would put stables *in front* of their house? It continues the white render and red-tiled roof idiom with a clock tower on the golf course elevation and wide columned porch with a curved head.

The white wall and red tile palette of the hotel was picked up in several golfing villas and bungalows erected after the First World War, a large number of which (mostly unidentified) were designed by *James Houston* from 1925 to 1956. Worth noting in Maidens Road are CARLYON LODGE of *c.* 1937, with big eaves over the ground floor, chimneystacks clasping the dormers and a deep swept rear roof; and PARKNAVILLA (No. 18) of 1929–30 with a huge prospect room supported on brick legs forming a porch; in Turnberry Lodge Road, CRAIG LODGE of *c.* 1910 with a red tiled roof and two big curved headed dormers. KINGSBURN on the Girvan road to the S of the junction of the A77 and the A719 is a smart pared-down Arts and Crafts villa of *c.* 1925. Two storeys and L-plan with the entrance in the re-entrant angle in the rear court. Smooth-rendered with slate roof. The W elevation has a three-arched veranda recessed into the house and a big bowed bay. Also DOLPHIN LODGE, Drumdow Road, by *J. K. Hunter*, 1912 in a similar vein.

TURNBERRY LODGE, Turnberry Lodge Road. A farmhouse of *c.* 1800 in the Culzean estate's picturesque Gothick style. Designed as an eyecatcher, with Gothic windows on the main façade, which has a central two-storey block, pedimented to the front with flanking half-pedimented bays that have angled crenellations. The southern bay was raised behind the crenellated parapet in 1861 when the interior was recast and the present staircase with heavy timber balusters inserted. Rear STEADING, sandstone with silvery grey granite blocks inserted in most of the ranges, except at the SW corner, probably the earliest part. Two-storey granary on the E range and four cart arches on the SE. A new cheese house was built in 1899 and is probably the building to the SW of the entrance. Along the whole N side is an extensive dairy, much remodelled in 1937.

TURNBERRY CASTLE, 1.5 km. NNW, also known as BRUCE'S CASTLE. Very fragmentary ruins of the C13 castle built in a strong position on a rocky promontory. Remnants of the enclosure walls and a central keep which was partly circular, with the base of an entrance, a portcullis slot and evidence of a drawbridge are still visible on the landward side. Interpretation of the various walls and ruined parts of vaults or bridges built over steep inlets to the N is difficult. To the N a large natural cavern. Built on the site is TURNBERRY LIGHTHOUSE by *D. & T. Stevenson* for the Commissioners for Northern Lights, 1871–3. A tapering tower, painted brick with long-and-short sandstone dressing to the entrance and a projecting wall-head masonry course supporting a concrete cap, cast-iron gallery and the cast-iron lattice lantern. Two flat-roofed keepers' cottages. To the E a large walled enclosure.

ROYAL FLYING CORPS MEMORIAL, 1.5 km. NNW. 1923 by *Hugh Wallace*. An elegant and lofty double cross in silvery granite on a tall plinth. In memory of men of the School of Aerial Gunnery and Fighting killed in 1917–18. Set on a hill overlooking the former AIRFIELD (the triangular pattern of runway strips still evident) which is now the Turnberry Golf Course. E of the airfield the former CONTROL TOWER, built after the site was reopened in the 1930s but converted into a house (Turnberry House) after 1945. Modernist, composed of three stacked flat-roofed blocks in diminishing stages. Metal-framed windows.

LADYBANK HOUSE, 3 km. S. Begun, as the informative lintel tells us, in 1791 by the Rev. James Cadell and completed by his widow the following year. The harled façade with stone margins and a shallow central pediment is interrupted by red sandstone canted full-height bays, added 1910. A double pile, the rear a single storey and attic on a raised basement, lit at ground level by a series of small square openings.

UNDERWOOD HOUSE
2 km. S of Symington

3020

Built for Capt. John Kennedy after 1785, and classically detailed. Two storeys over a basement, harled with stone dressings and angle margins. Three wide bays with the centre slightly advanced and pedimented. The pediment enclosing a roundel with a dolphin rampant on a bar, the motto VINCIT VIM VIRTUS ('Virtue overcomes force') and an urn on the apex. Rear elevation with full-height projecting bow with a steeply raked roof and large curved dormer. Enlarged by two bays to the SE after a fire in 1862; the roof heightened at the same time. Presumably contemporary is the enlargement of one of the stacks defining the centre bay, upsetting the symmetry. Interior recast after the fire. Sturdy cast-iron balusters to the stair with intertwined and scrolled detail. The stair rises gracefully to the attic from an oval entrance hall.

WATERSIDE
By Fenwick

4040

A carding mill, established *c.* 1784, provided the impetus for the hamlet's development.

WATERSIDE HOUSE, at the N end, of *c.* 1835, has neatly chamfered windows, lying-pane glazing and paired pilastered entrances. To its S, in the pavement, a substantial mosaic PLAQUE with the coat of arms of the burgh of Kilmarnock commemorates the completion of the burgh's waterworks in

1901.* The former WATERSIDE MILL is on the w. The existing eight-bay building with square-headed windows is early
C19; converted to residential use, 2008–9. Beyond are two
flat-roofed COTTAGES, one still with a deep porch recess, of
1943, by *Sam Bunton*: an early experiment in pre-fabrication
using Gyproc, a composite material based on woodwool.
Finally, s again, but on the E side, the simple harled two-bay
two-storey former SCHOOL of 1833. An inscription, within a
pretty rope-moulded frame, records that it was 'erected by
subscription under favour of George fourth Earl of Glasgow'.

HARESHAWMUIR LODGE. *See* p. 364.

WATERSIDE
By Patna

Scattered industrial settlement in the central Doon valley which
owes its existence to the mid-C19 development of the Dunaskin
Ironworks.

ST FRANCIS XAVIER (R.C.), Chapel Row. Brick Gothic of 1895,
probably by *William Cowie*, who added the convent in 1905.
Stepped three-light window in the E gable, below a tall cross-
topped corbelled bellcote. Plain concrete open porch by
Charles W. Gray, 1965.
Former WATERSIDE CHURCH. Red sandstone Gothic of 1894–5
by *John B. Wilson*. Gabled NE porch, simple lancets and a
cusped timber bellcote set back from the w gable, capped by
a squat pyramidal roof. Stepped cusped E window.
Former WATERSIDE INSTITUTE. Irregularly planned and nicely
composed Free Style workmen's institute of 1904, by *John B.
Wilson*, one of his most successful designs. Crisp red brick, with
the upper walls harled; Westmorland-slated roof. The prominent coolie-hatted ventilators and tall harled stacks make
telling contributions. Now residential; in the grounds the
village WAR MEMORIAL, 1921, a Peterhead granite Celtic cross
by *Matthew Muir & Co.*
Former WATERSIDE STATION. Of 1857–8, for the Ayr & Dalmellington Railway. Ashlar, two-storey, with a neatly curving external stair. The masons were *Young & Co.* of Glasgow.
Former DUNASKIN IRONWORKS. An iron-smelting complex
was established 1847–8 by the Dalmellington Iron Co. and
soon grew in size. Iron manufacture ceased in 1921 and the
site converted in 1928 as a brickworks (closed 1976). The site
lies on the NE side of the main road through the valley, tucked
into the hillside behind. Distant views are dominated by two
tall C20 brick CHIMNEYS. These rise from the foot of the
former FURNACE BANK, which runs through the site, parallel
to the road, defining the layout. This tall buttressed stone wall

---

* There are a number of RESERVOIRS in the hills NE of Waterside; these include
Craigendunton, first dammed in 1820, and enlarged in 1901, and Lochgoin, opened
in 1910.

ran behind the top-fed blast furnaces (demolished in the 1920s). Between the chimneys is the stone Italianate former BLOWING ENGINE HOUSE, a remarkable piece of industrial architecture, a potent symbol of the company's faith in its future, dated 1847, and extended to the r. in 1865.* It has large arched openings, big channelled quoins and a heavily bracketed cornice. The original section has a low hipped roof, the addition is flat-roofed. To either side are two brick mid-C20 BRICK KILNS. That to the l. is taller, buttressed, and has a barn-like corrugated-iron roof, while the other is lower, with twelve round-headed arches giving access to the kilns. The other buildings on the site include a long range of late C19 stone WORKSHOPS and offices, opposite the blowing engine house and kilns, with square-headed windows, and round-arched openings for men and machinery. To the s of the kilns, a brick-built gabled POWER STATION of 1917, built in partnership with the War Office, partly to provide electricity for an abortive aerial gunnery school at Loch Doon. At the N entrance to the complex, the single-storey ashlar former COMPANY OFFICES, with many gables with deep eaves. The style is somewhat in the manner of William Burn, and the buildings may date from the original development of the site, i.e. c. 1848–50. On the hillside above the works is ARDOON, also c. 1850, the house of the works manager, which too has gabled bays and simple Jacobethan details.

WEST KILBRIDE

A substantial village just inland from, and above, the N Ayrshire coast. It had some villas and seaside residences but grew up mostly as a result of the railway, which arrived in 1878, and again in the boom of the interwar period. Since 1998 West Kilbride has promoted itself as Scotland's Crafts Town, with the aim of reviving its commercial heart; the scheme's success best seen in the unifying simple, uncluttered shop fascias which indicate the various craft shops and studios.

CHURCHES AND CEMETERY

Former BARONY CHURCH, Main Street. 1871–3 by *Harry Blair* of Glasgow; converted for exhibition centre etc. in 2010–12 by *Archial* of Glasgow.** E.E. A gabled T-plan, the gable windows with Y-tracery. Sharply pointed entrance, flanked by cusped lights. To the l., a squat three-stage tower, with an octagonal bell-stage with pointed windows and alternate circular clock faces, and a tall set-back spire. Interiors gutted. The church

---

* The second datestone is hidden behind the cast-iron cabin which now adorns the front elevation.
** The competition for the church was originally won by *James Bogue* of Edinburgh, but the design was found to have been made by a Mr *Richardson* who was in *David Bryce*'s office. Neither man was employed, and Blair appointed instead.

sits in a small KIRKYARD, with a few C18 HEADSTONES, and square pyramid-headed GATEPIERS, linked by a thin decorative metal head.

Former BARONY CHURCH HALL, Manse Road. Of *c.* 1873, a simple gabled rectangle with square-headed windows, plain skews, and a lean-to entrance porch of *c.* 1965.

Former CHAPEL, Hunterston Road. Dated 1893. The gabled entrance front has machine-cut crowsteps, a pedimented gable finial, and a projecting entrance under a shouldered pediment.

Former OVERTON CHURCH, Ritchie Street. 1882–3 as a United Presbyterian Church, by *Hippolyte J. Blanc*, altered *c.* 1921 by *L. D. Penman*. Closed in 2012. French Gothic in pink sandstone. Nave and chancel, NW tower and SW transept. The N front has a big gable with a rose window and, offset to the l., the entrance with a moulded pointed arch under a gable. The tower, projecting to the r., has chamfered corners, with clasping pyramidal buttresses at the angles. In the bell stage, round-headed openings, in pairs on the longer sides, and a corbel table below the stumpy spire, with lucarnes. The buttressed side elevations have two-light windows with a small circular window above. Inside, a cusped panelled gallery front, over a glazed and wooden vestibule screen, and a big boarded barrel roof, with ribs springing from corbels. The chancel was lengthened by Penman. His is the panelling with cusped tracery and swooping cornice with finials and organ case with excellent naturalistic carving. – STAINED GLASS. The best is *Paul Lucky*'s window of 1989 in the N gable, lots of clear lenses in a swirling vortex of blue glass. – In the E wall, first from the N, Creation, with lively flowers, *c.* 1985, in the style of *Susan Bradbury*, and two typically restrained blue windows by *Gordon Webster*, of 1949 and *c.* 1955, the r. light of the latter incorporating a representation of the nearby Hunterston A power station. – In the W wall, an old-fashioned Love One Another, by *C. E. Stewart*, 1947. – A bright Ascension of 1907 in the transept, and, in the circular chancel window, a memorial to Rev. Watson †1918.

ST ANDREW, Main Street. 1880–1 by *James Ritchie* of Glasgow as a Free Church. A tight site, well used. Very spare Gothic, in pink Ardrossan sandstone with dressings of Ballochmyle red. Soaring tower and broach spire with corner spirelets. Big rose window over an entrance with deep panelled reveals and a pointed head. The tower has open tracery in the bell-stage with a lobed circle in the arched heads. Five-bay E elevation, one bay gabled, with a circular window in an arched recess in the gable. The other windows mostly two-light with circular tracery. A prettily detailed vestibule, with tiled floors, plastered ceilings and glazed and wooden partitions; the woodwork particularly well done, a feature throughout the church. The plastered interior has a central wagon roof, and coved sides, divided into bays by wooden ribs and wooden ties, which rest on cog-like corbels. Panel-fronted gallery above the vestibule. Transept arcade with one decoratively headed column, but no responds. The artificial stone infill beneath the N gable jars a little; organ cases to l. and r., Gothic fittings, including the octagonal biscuit barrel FONT: panelled, with angels carrying shields. LECTERN. Late C20. Bleached and naturalistically carved, as if assembled from driftwood. – STAINED-GLASS window in the w wall: a First World War memorial by *William Meikle & Sons*. In the vestibule, two brass MEMORIALS, of *c.* 1902, with relief heads, by the *Metallic Art Co.* of Glasgow.

The halls behind much altered, and linked to *Margaret B. Brodie*'s sympathetic and respectful brick HALL of 1968–70.

ST BRIDE'S (R.C.), Hunterston Road. 1907–8 by *Brenan & Hunter* of Glasgow. Simple brick harled gabled rectangle, with one gabled bay on the long side facing the road. Good wooden

West Kilbride, Simson Monument.
Original proposals by F. T. Pilkington
Engraving

STATIONS OF THE CROSS, each like a cross pâtée, with incised imagery. Of perhaps *c.* 1958. Excellent HALL extension of 1998 by *James F. Stephen Architects* of Stirling, round-ended and harled. Internally, paired wooden beams rising to the apex.

WEST KILBRIDE CEMETERY, Dalmilling Road. *c.* 1865, a simple stone-walled enclosure, dominated by *F. T. Pilkington*'s fantastic monument of 1869 to the mathematician Robert Simson, †1768. He, as the inscription relates, was 'the restorer of Grecian geometry and by his works the great promoter of its study in the schools. . . . And buried learning rose redeemed to a new morn.' Octagonal, of two stepped stages, and an ogee top with ball finial. Ecletic ornament, mostly in a faintly Byzantine manner.

p. 675

PUBLIC BUILDINGS

COMMUNITY CENTRE, Corse Terrace. Former convalescent home built for the Paisley Co-operative Society, 1885; extended in 1897 and converted 1972–5 by *Ayr County Council Architects Dept.* A very domestic design, both parts in red sandstone, with some half-timbered gables. The earlier block is to the W and is a quadrangular plan around a small court. On the S front, four bays and two-storeys, with attics in gabled outer wings. Sturdy stone balcony in the centre. The r. wing has a clumsy two-storey canted bay of *c.* 1935. The building of 1897 to the E is in a similar spirit, and with the roofs of its canted ground-floor bays nicely linked to form a porch. At its rear, a caretaker's house with its entrance in an attached conically headed tower. Between the two parts a charming single-storey link, perhaps added *c.* 1906–11 by *Whyte & Galloway*, with big arched window under a gable, and inside, a pitched timber and glass roof, springing from curved cross-beams.

LIBRARY, Halfway Street. 1995–6 by *Cunninghame District Council*; completed by *North Ayrshire Council* (*David Kirk*, project architect). A bold statement on a sloping site, with a dramatic *tour de force* on the N front of a full-height glass bow raised on a stepped base and set behind a colonnade carrying the eaves of the roof. Otherwise harled with simple details.

Former POST OFFICE, Ritchie Street. 1911 by *Fryers & Penman*. Grey sandstone, broadly symmetrical, with outer gabled bays with canted oriels on stepped cushion corbels. Central entrance with a broken semicircular pediment.

WAR MEMORIAL, Yerton Brae. 1921, by *L. D. Penman*. Slender tapering cross in Cullaloe stone, a laurel wreath looped over the upper arm.

WEST KILBRIDE INSTITUTE, Arthur Street. 1898–1900 by *A. N. Paterson*. Wonderfully tactile and well-judged Arts and Crafts in brown-grey sandstone, with slated roofs. The large hall has an elongated Venetian window with a moulded surround in its gable to Ritchie Street, but the detailing of the lower wing is superior, especially the entrance with elaborately carved head and the picturesque narrow dormer which emerges from the hip of the roof and has a dainty finial. This lights the upper hall, now an Aladdin's-cave of a museum, also lit by a roof-light.

WEST KILBRIDE PRIMARY SCHOOL, Hunterston Road. 1980–2, by *Strathclyde Regional Council*. The main block harled with a sloping metal-clad fascia. The INFANTS SCHOOL is vernacular of 1835, possibly built as a girls' industrial school, with a front wing added in 1875 by *Thomas Wallace*.

WEST KILBRIDE STATION. Rebuilt *c.* 1900 by *James Miller* and a good example of his Arts and Crafts work for the GSWR (*see* also Troon and Prestwick Town stations). Single-storey, harled, with tiled roof, and applied timbering in the gables. The platform elevation is vertically boarded, with a projecting canopy.

DESCRIPTION

MAIN STREET W of the railway station has a small group of distinguished painted and harled cottages and houses of late C18 and mid-C19 date, well restored in the 1990s by West Kilbride Amenity Society. They are set close to a deep glen spanned by a late C19 BRIDGE with a datestone: IC MAU 1623. To the W on the rising ground is St Andrew's Church (*see* Churches, above); hereafter Main Street adopts a much more enclosed, urban feel as it narrows and curves slightly SW as it descends. Though slightly down-at-heel, it is given further character by the constant rising and falling topography which ensures an ever-changing vista.

The S side begins with the KINGS ARMS, late C19 with shallow curved bays on the upper floors; beyond this is the former Barony Church (*see* Churches, above). The N side begins with a characteristic mixed group of the C19 and C20. No. 63 is a smart harled two-storey house set back from the street behind a low stone and rail boundary wall. Entrance and sidelights recessed beneath a pilastered doorpiece. Dated 1739, but this front looks *c.* 1800. Beyond it is the tall plastered three-storey KILBRIDE TAVERN, with chamfered windows, and a neat curving corner which adjoins the set-back WELLINGTON INN. This is probably late C18, but almost certainly with an older core. Three storeys with dormers; painted, with polished margins. In HUNTERSTON ROAD, opposite the return elevation of the Wellington Inn, KIRKLAND HOUSE, a douce, painted three-bay L-plan farmhouse of the late C18, with end stacks, raised long-and-short quoins, dressed margins and a plain gabled porch. Main Street continues with, on the r., Nos. 77–81, very stark late C19, of grey-brown stone, with one crowstepped gable and austere gabled dormerheads, and on the l., the ROYAL BANK OF SCOTLAND. An odd design, two-storeyed and plastered, with a canted corner, finialled gables, and finial-headed pilasters. Hardly any of its decorative motifs are alike. Beyond this a tall block of *c.* 1900, then low mid-C19 climbing uphill on both sides to the junction with

Glen Road. In Glen Road itself, a pretty PUBLIC CONVE-NIENCE of the 1930s, harled with a tiled roof.

Back in Main Street, KIRKTONHALL is the best house in West Kilbride. Its main front is to the S, facing its gardens, and is of three storeys, harled, with dormers and windows with dressed margins. It all looks consistent with a rebuilding known to have taken place in 1791. Big off-centre porch dated 1807, with columns at the angles supporting a ponderous battle-mented upper storey. Its central Venetian window has Gothick motifs. Also battlemented, the two-storey N wing of 1868 and the stark elevation to Main Street. Near the base of this eleva-tion a reused datestone, RS MW 1660. Much-altered interior; what is visible is C19 and later. Entrance hall bisected by an arcade; the stair is ahead, with a wooden top rail, and iron banisters. The mezzanine window has some simple heraldic stained glass and broad linenfold panels to either side. The room to the l. of the entrance hall has a boarded wooden ceiling, the boarding parallel with each wall, and a central feature akin to a spider's web. In the grounds an obelisk-type SUNDIAL, dated 1717, said to have been made by Robert Simson (see Cemetery, above).

RITCHIE STREET is the southward continuation of Main Street and has the eyecatching former Post Office, the West Kilbride Institute (see Public Buildings, above), and further S, on the l., the Overton Church (see Churches, above); otherwise single-storey cottages and late C19 villas dominate. In the streets S of Ritchie Street a considerable cluster of such villas, especially in YERTON BRAE, sloping downhill towards the sea (e.g. the red sandstone and heavily bracketed eaves of BERNAL, No. 2, 1893) and OVERTON DRIVE, off its N side, which has some interesting houses in pairs with good shared porches. HAZELDENE (No. 26 Overton Drive), of 1902 by *Fryers & Penman*, has a spreading rounded corner bay, a Venetian window and heavily framed entrance with finials. To the S of Yerton Brae, streets such as BOWFIELD ROAD and CALD-WELL ROAD form the main axes of the inter- and post-war village, traversing the steeply rising hillside, so that all houses have uninterrupted sea views. Seen from below, West Kilbride appears as a succession of residential terraces.

0.4 km. SE of the station, a group of wooden HUTS flank the road to Law Hill. Built in the 1930s, they are an increasingly rare example of self-built 'summer houses', a type of development once found more widely along the Ayrshire coast. In a variety of styles, with tarred, felted or corrugated iron roofs, and with an admirable advocacy of 'reuse', as, for example, the round-headed half-doors which form the gate to one hut. They were always more transient than the more substantial summer houses at, for instance, Lendalfoot (q.v.).

45   LAW CASTLE, 0.2 km. E of West Kilbride Station. A solid rect-angle, of four storeys and a garret, built by Robert Boyd (Lord Boyd, *see* Dean Castle, Kilmarnock), who was Governor of

Scotland during James III's minority, supposedly for Princess Mary, sister of James III, on her marriage to Boyd's son Thomas in 1467. Father and son were attainted for high treason in 1469; the former was beheaded, the latter died in exile. The roofless castle was brought back into occupation in the 1990s by Dr Anthony Phillips under the benign eye of *Ian Begg*. Gleaming white harl over boulder footings and rubble walls approximately 1.8 m thick. Ashlar crenellated parapet with simple water-chutes and embryo open angle rounds supported on continuous corbelling. Re-created low caphouse at SE with conical roof. Tall stacks on the gables of the rebuilt garret roof, within the wall-walk, and an additional stack on the rear wall. On the S elevation an arched door with a tiny spyhole to the r. In the ground floor also horizontal gunloops to two stone-vaulted cellars. The window sizes in the upper floors have been faithfully kept. Narrow slits light the turnpike stair to the r. of the entrance and the mural stair from the first-floor hall to the vaulted ground floor in the rear wall. The first-floor hall has large opposing windows at the high end with an additional window to the l. of the fireplace. The re-creation of the interior included remaking the turnpike stair.

The plan, as in the external appearance, follows that of the towers at Fairlie, Little Cumbrae and Skelmorlie (qq.v.). Common to all is a narrow first-floor kitchen entered from the turnpike stair. Here W wide, low, roll-moulded arch spanning the fireplace, in which was a bread oven and a drain. A low wall marks the line of a partition which formerly divided kitchen from hall. A second door, with a small recess for a candle to its l., opened from the stair to the hall. This room has a large re-created chimneypiece with a relieving arch over it on the W wall, and at the NE a closet and private stair to the cellar. The floors above have been re-created making use of garderobes and mural closets. Some windows still retain their wall seats, and several simply moulded chimneypieces have been restored.

UNDERHILL, 0.6 km. NE of the station. A complex house, formerly known as Springside, though the present name well reflects its position in the shadow of Law Hill. The earliest part is the crowstepped three-bay two-storey block to the r., which has one lintel dated 1739 (?). The entrance must have been on the inner face, which suggests that this block, and the lower one to its r., which is also crowstepped, originally formed two wings of a U-plan courtyard. This was infilled *c.* 1830 with a projecting three-bay Regency block, with first-floor wrought-iron balconies and a partially pierced parapet. Canted bay to the r., awkwardly incorporated internally, and false crow-stepped gable to the l. are probably contemporary, as are the interiors. A brick, timber and glazed porch, and steps, were added later in the C19.

SUNNYSIDE, Meadowfoot Road, 1 km. S. Substantial harled and slated Arts and Crafts house, 1898, with its pedimented entrance in a circular tower with an ogee tiled roof. Projecting decorative metal balcony and red sandstone dressings.

CUP-AND-RING-MARKED ROCK, Blackshaw Hill, 2.5 km. E. A heavily weathered rock outcrop at the foot of the SE flank of the hill is carved with numerous cup marks, together with multiple rings and spirals.

CARLUNG HOUSE. *See* p. 211.

3050
WOODSIDE
1.5 km. N of Beith

Originally a square tower house built after 1551 for Hew Ralston, which was enlarged in the mid C17 but then entirely altered by Gavin Ralston in 1759, who reduced the tower and extended N to form a symmetrical front with a 2+3+2 pattern of windows on two storeys. Handsome pedimented porch, with Gibbsian surround, and balustraded retaining wall, added for William Cochran-Patrick in 1848 at the same time as the sub-Bryce-like three-storey rear extension; the crowstepped gabled SW elevation of the addition has a five-light canted window to the principal floor and in the gable a plaque with the family coat of arms and date. The Baronial appearance of the house was introduced by *Charles S. S. Johnston* in 1890, heightening the original (but lowered) tower by two storeys, including a garret with corbelled bartizans and crowstepped gables. Roof dormers of the same date. Incorporated, perhaps as conscious antiquarianism, are datestones with initials of the C16–C19 owners.

(The entrance hall has a Roman Doric screen to the stair with an anthemion-pattern balustrade of 1848. The sitting room was probably the dining room in 1759; it has mid-C18 details including an arched buffet recess, with charming Rococo plasterwork and remarkable wall paintings of picturesque landscape and hunting scenes in illusionist frames. More may survive below later decorations. The dining room occupies the former C16 hall, its five very deep-set windows, two arched and key-blocked to either side of the chimney-breast, all with panelled window seats. The drawing room, added in 1848, has a scrolled plaster cornice, mid-C18-style chimneypiece and an C21 overmantel painting in the manner of 1759. Under the hall the vaulted stores of the tower.)

– LODGES. Two of the mid-C18 but altered: the S *c.* 1848, asymmetrical with Gothic detailing and sawtoothed skews; beside, four panelled gatepiers with fan-ornamented cast-iron gates.

NE, the later C18 former STABLES (now Woodside House), as enlarged 1848 and altered *c.* 1870 by Robert Cochran-Patrick. Neo-Tudor style with crenellated parapet over the entrance to the court and wings with sawtoothed skews and apex stacks.

ARRAN

(including Holy Isle and Pladda)

The island has a superficial land area of just over 43,000 ha. (166 square miles, 107,000 acres), and a permanent population of *c.* 5,000. Its highest point is Goat Fell, at 874 m. (2867 ft), and its mountainous profile forms a prominent feature in the view from the Ayrshire coast. It has been closely linked with Ayrshire by coastwise shipping, but is geologically linked to the Scottish highlands, and has a different socio-political history.

The N part of the island, including Goat Fell, is formed of granite, ringed by schist and other metamorphic rocks. The S part of the island is dominated by a broad plateau, formed largely of Permian, Triassic and Carboniferous sedimentary rocks, intermixed with many whin sills, such as that which forms the backbone of Holy Isle. These overlie a band of Old Red Sandstone, which was commercially quarried at Corrie and is the building stone most regularly seen on the island. Raised beaches, especially in the S, provide the best cultivated land and sites for the island's major settlements.

In the early modern period Arran became, with the Cumbraes, part of the sheriffdom and county of Bute (administered from Rothesay), though the W half of the island, particularly around Lochranza in the NW corner, retained close links with Argyll, especially Kintyre and Knapdale. There are, for instance, strong similarities between Lochranza Castle and castles, such as Castle 48
Sween, in Argyll. The island is divided into two ancient parishes: Kilmory to the W, Kilbride to the E; the ruined medieval chapel of the latter survives at Lamlash, as do the remains of a later medieval chapel at Shiskine. Partly Highland in geography, Arran was also Highland in its buildings, with a series of small nucleated townships lining the coast wherever there was cultivatable land. Most have now been abandoned or rebuilt, though scantling remains can be found, e.g. above Catacol. The best-preserved of these townships is High Corrie (Corrie), where the 96
close-knit, but irregularly placed nature is well seen, though it is smaller than other examples such as Keills (Jura, Argyll & Bute).

Arran was granted to the Boyds by James III in the mid C15, and the main residence on the island, Brodick Castle, was prob- 74
ably initially built for them, but after the Boyds fell out of royal favour, the island was granted to the Hamiltons by James IV in 1503, and they remained the largest landowners on the island

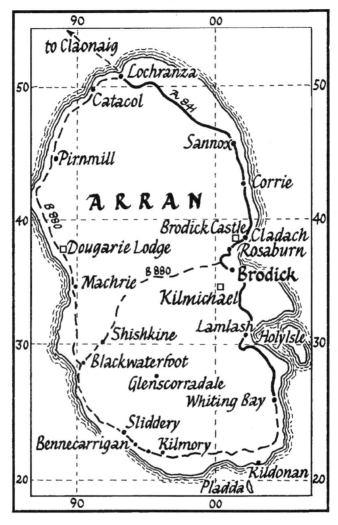

Map of Arran

into the C20. The Hamiltons initiated a comprehensive programme of improvement and clearance in the mid C18, particularly under Douglas, the 8th Duke (succ. 1766, †1799) and
Archibald, the 9th Duke (†1819). Much of the implementation
of the changes was in the hands of their chamberlains (agents)
on the island, particularly John Burrell. The Hamiltons' aims
were no different from those of other Highland landowners: a

profitable and better-managed estate. Depopulation and resettlement continued into the early C19, and a road around the island
was begun in 1810, with the section between Lamlash and
Brodick. The best-known emigration from Arran was from
Sannox to Canada in 1823, on the *Metagama*, while the most
interesting of the post-clearance houses are the mid-C19 row,
known as the Twelve Apostles, at Catacol.   101

Unlike the majority of Highland estates, Arran was close to
populated and wealthy parts of Scotland. From the late C18 it
became popular with those seeking the health-restoring nature
of the countryside and sea bathing, especially once the Romantic
Movement had altered popular perceptions of wild and mountainous places, and the introduction of regular steamer services
eased access. There was a demand for summer residences on the
island, which was occasionally met by the granting of a long lease,
e.g. at Seafield, Lamlash, but largely the Hamiltons and their
island agents, especially the notoriously inflexible John Paterson,
and his son, also John, sought to preserve the sanctity of their
estate. To partially supply demand, and to allay the concerns of
the Arranachan, who saw in the tourists a useful source of
income, the Hamiltons developed a solution by which the islanders were allowed to build 'summer houses', usually to the back
of their houses. To these they would move in the summer, while
letting the main house to summer visitors. Although many have
been converted or upgraded, some of these summer houses
remain throughout the island, though the grandest, and among
the last, manifestations of this policy is the purposely designed
row of elongated, boarded huts behind Hamilton Terrace,
Lamlash.* It is due to the paternalism, and protectionism, of the
Hamiltons, especially of the 11th Duke, that Arran retains much
of its early C19 post-clearance character, and we have been spared
the villas 'from Sannox to Largiebeg' (s of Whiting Bay) that the
Rev. Allan Macnaughton urged in 1845.

Estate buildings of the early to mid C19 have a pronounced
Burnian flavour, e.g. in the former manse and school at Whiting
Bay, or in the terraces such as Alma Terrace, built when the old
village of Brodick was cleared from the vicinity of the castle and
rebuilt on the old townships of Invercloy and Strathwhillan. The
farmhouses and other buildings, however, are usually two-storey,
with prominent gables, a familiar pattern throughout the Highlands. With the death of the younger Paterson in 1881, and the
succession of the 13th Duke in 1895, Arran entered a period of
considerable building activity. Piers had been built at Brodick
and Whiting Bay in 1872, and a new pier was completed at
Lamlash in 1885. Many of the new buildings were designed by
J. J. Burnet, such as the churches as Corrie (1887) and Shiskine   34, 36
(1886–9), which are among his earliest churches, and remain
among the best buildings on the island, with creatively thought-
out exteriors and numinous artistic interiors. Other Burnet, or

*A similar practice is known to have been operated at Braemar on Royal Deeside
(Aberdeenshire).

Burnet-inspired, buildings include the estate office at Rosaburn, Auchrannie, the former chamberlain's house at Strabane, a number of properties in Brodick, e.g. the station-like former Post Office (1886), and Hamilton Terrace, Lamlash (1892–5), a glorious example of his English Domestic Revival style. At Lochranza, the former hotel of 1893–5, also by *Burnet*, reveals a newer approach to the island's tourists.

During the C20 development on Arran has continued, though at a measured rate. It has its quota of uninspiring bungalows, and some poorly planned late C20 and early C21 developments. The string of rather angular Arts and Crafts early C20 houses at Whiting Bay are the final flowering of the late C19 reconstruction of Arran. Thereafter, although there are landmark buildings, they have to be seen as part of the wider Scottish picture, but in the Post Office and Telephone Exchange, Brodick, of 1946–7, and Whiting Bay Primary School, of 1963–7 the island can claim two of the best C20 buildings of their date.

BENNECARRIGAN

Former BENNECARRIGAN FREE CHURCH, at the junction of the Ross Road and the main coastal road. 1894. Gabled, buttressed and skilfully executed single cell with a prettily corbelled W bellcote and pointed windows. The SW porch has a shouldered door and a cast-iron finial, and the windows have wavy etched glass. Cast-iron GATES by *R. & R. Fleming & Co.*, Glasgow. Opposite, WAR MEMORIAL. *c.* 1920 by *Scott & Rae* of Glasgow. Granite, with a rocky base and an oddly shaped shaft, on which a rifle has been carved.

BENNECARRIGAN FARM, 0.3 km. N. 1817. Substantial Hamilton estate improvement farm, the house of two storeys, grey-harled, with a gabled porch, and extended to the l. in the late C19. Single-storey wings flank the rear courtyard.

BLACKWATERFOOT

Small harbour and village at the SW extremity of the island, developed in the late C19 and C20 as a holiday and residential centre, replacing Shiskine as the local commercial hub.

The HARBOUR, of *c.* 1900, is little more than a hollowing out of the mouth of the Blackwater, backed by a stone-walled jetty. Behind it the late C19 single-arch red sandstone BLACKWATERFOOT BRIDGE, with dressed voussoirs and a low parapet. Dominating the scene, though, is the ugly KINLOCH HOTEL, late C20, but with some traditional features reflecting its origin as a C19 guesthouse.

Upstream, VICTORIA LODGE, a smartly composed asymmetrical Arts and Crafts house of *c.* 1905, with its entrance beneath a flat-headed dormer abutting a chimney; a wide corbelled gabled bay to the r. and a timber pentice on the l.

elevation. In the main street, BLACKWATERFOOT LODGE, of *c.* 1850, a good example of the mid-C19 Arran palette in exposed stone, with the upper floor jettied out above canted ground-floor bays, and three gabled half-dormers with cast-iron finials. On the village's NW edge, QUEENSCLIFF, red sandstone of *c.* 1897, with a big finialled gable to the l., chamfered windows and a hipped re-entrant porch. Above the porch is a delightful round-headed dormer with a decorative head, and to the r. a carved head, which looks like a Roman emperor but is perhaps intended to portray Queen Victoria.

FORT, Drumadoon, 1.5 km. WNW. The commanding cliff-girt headland is defended on its landward side by a single rampart to form a fortified enclosure of about 4.8 ha.

ENCLOSURE, 2 km. SSE. A curiosity, standing on the crest of the hill at the edge of the forestry plantations SE of Kilpatrick. Its interior measures 16.8 m. in diameter within a stony ring-bank with low inner and outer kerbs of stones set up on edge. A slab-built entrance can be seen on the SE, beside which excavations in the early C20 uncovered a small cist containing a cremation and part of a cinerary urn. This discovery within the body of the ring-bank, and other large stones exposed on the NW, suggest that rather than a domestic structure, this enclosure is some form of Bronze Age ceremonial monument.

BRODICK

0030

The ferry terminal, and hence the best-known of Arran's villages, but its economic and commercial pre-eminence is a C20 phenomenon, caused by the concentration of mainland ferry services here, transferring trade away from the other E coast settlements. The first settlement on the 'broad bay' was on the N shore, and *p. 689* grew in the shadow of the castle. When, in the C19, the Hamiltons deemed it imprudent to have the village close to the castle, it was removed and the inhabitants resettled at Invercloy, at the N end of the bay. The steamer pier was subsequently built at Strathwhillan, at the S end of the bay, and modern Brodick developed between the two. More so than Lamlash or Whiting Bay, Brodick is predominantly late C19 and C20.

CHURCHES

BRODICK PARISH CHURCH, Glencloy Road. 1910 by *D. & J. R. McMillan* as a United Free Church, comprehensively refurbished internally in 1959. Plain red sandstone Gothic with a gabled E front and square SE tower. Pointed window in the gable with Y-tracery, above a segmental-headed entrance with flanking paired square-headed windows. To the l., the tower has raised quoins, a castellated parapet and a hipped roof; tall square-headed stair lights and three-light reductive Venetian bell-openings. The side elevations have pointed three-light windows, with a wide gabled transept on the S, and a shallower transept to the N, each with three-light stepped windows. On the W elevation a shallow canted tiled-roofed apse. Light and airy plastered interior, with a rear gallery with panelled and fretted front, supported on curved wooden brackets, and a coved boarded roof and simple beams on plain stone corbels. The S transept can be closed off by panelled folding doors, recognition (as at Kilmory and Whiting Bay) of the island's population fluctuations. – Unmistakably of 1959 is the hexagonal PULPIT, with dark wood panels within a spindly six-legged light wood framework, and steps to either side. By *William Scott* of Corrie and *Archibald Hamilton* of Brodick. – STAINED GLASS. Apse, two figurative pastels, St Bride and Follow Me, 1961, by *Guthrie & Wells Ltd* (sketched by *Douglas Hamilton*, completed after his death by *Nina Davidson*).

CHURCH HALL. The former United Free Church at Bennecarrigan, erected *c.* 1900, moved here in 1954. White and red painted corrugated iron.

FREE CHURCH, Alma Road. *c.* 1930. Small, with a disproportionately large porch.

HOLY CROSS (R.C.), off Shore Road. A mid-C19 court house. Round-headed windows, a forestair to the N entrance, and an understated cross finial above. Converted 1982–3 for Canon *Iain Gillies* of Arisaig, who designed and built the ALTAR.

PUBLIC BUILDINGS

BRODICK PRIMARY SCHOOL, Low Glencloy Road. 1854–6, for the 11th Duke of Hamilton, and a perfect example for its date. Red sandstone, with a central gabled bay, and a jolly bargeboard of fretwork rings. To the far r., a gabled porch; to the l. the single-storey hipped master's house, with a gabled porch, topped by one of the many tall stacks that grace the building. In front, a life-size bronze STATUE of the Duke 'from the studio of the late Baron *Marochetti*', erected 1868. He stands, be-kilted, with one foot on a rock, gazing thoughtfully into the distance.

BRODICK PUBLIC HALL AND LIBRARY, Shore Road. 1894–5 by *J. J. Burnet* for the Invercloy Improvement Trust. The HALL is an Arts and Crafts delight. Gabled and harled main part, with sandstone details and a tall slated roof whose eaves descend steeply to the first floor on both sides. On the S elevation, a long horizontal band of small-pane glazing; while the E elevation has a jettied, canted, tile-hung and glazed, almost Lutyenesque oriel, tucked under the gable. At the NE corner, a lower hexagonal entrance tower with a tiled roof. The gabled bays on the N elevation now face into a narrow courtyard, created by the Library. The W addition, of 1959–60 by *Alexander H. Thomson* of Airdrie, is lower, and projects slightly forward, but echoes the details of the original; it replaces, in part, a low single-storey wing which was probably the hall-keeper's house. The interior is dominated by the oddly proportioned (it is too tall for the width) plastered Hall; N balcony with a concave boarded front. Respectful Neo-vernacular LIBRARY added N by *Cunninghame District Council* in 1992.

ISLE OF ARRAN HERITAGE MUSEUM. *See* Rosaburn, p. 718.

POST OFFICE, Alma Road. 1946–7 by *H.M. Office of Works*, a rare date for the construction of public buildings, and a good example of the way in which the idioms of the 1930s persisted in the thin years before the Festival of Britain. Harled brick, with steel *Crittall* windows, a well-massed series of flat-roofed cubes, building up from the entrance to the tall TELEPHONE EXCHANGE at the rear (actually separate, but seen as part of the composition from the N).

WAR MEMORIAL, Low Glencloy Road. 1922, by *Gray & Co*. Creetown granite. The polished and inscribed base supports a mostly rough-hewn monument. The smooth front face bears a kilted soldier.

DESCRIPTION

The present FERRY TERMINAL is of 1993, brick, with a bell-shaped wooden-roofed waiting room; the pier itself is C19, but largely reconstructed in the late C20. To the S are the plain red sandstone former PIERMASTER'S HOUSE, *c.* 1896, with two gabled dormers, and the TOURIST INFORMATION CENTRE, 1979 by *Baxter, Clark & Paul*, an 'eyecatcher' in pink concrete and stained wood with asymmetrical slated roofs, pyramidal roof-lights and a conical fibreglass finial. To the r. of this the much widened STRATHWHILLAN BRIDGE, late C19, with low stone parapets and big abutments to the N.

Shore Road begins here, with the DOUGLAS HOTEL. Built as the Springbank Hotel of 1857, of which the two-storey gabled and harled main block remains to the rear, though only its own rear elevation remains relatively unspoilt, with hipped dormers and small windows with polished dressings. Dwarfing this is the late C19 Georgian Revival front in red sandstone, to which a mighty two-storey bay of *c.* 1930 has been added. There is little else at this end of Shore Road: a disappointing melange of shops, holiday flats and visitor attractions. Only at the N end (Invercloy), close to the beach, does it have the feeling of a town, with some nice commercial buildings, beginning with the red sandstone ALEXANDERS of 1896, with a finialled widow's-cap gable to the r., and the ROYAL BANK OF SCOTLAND, of 1924, also red sandstone, with a hipped manager's house to the l., and single-storey office to the r. Red sandstone again is the late C19 COOPERS, with bargeboarded gables and tumbled brickwork decoration over the window in its larger bay, but the best thing is its shopfront, with a classical frame. This is perhaps contemporary with the block to the l., WOOLEY'S BAKERY of *c.* 1902, in the island style of white-harled walls and polished red details. The red sandstone BANK

OF SCOTLAND, of 1888, is half-hipped with dormers, and a
single-storey office wing to the r., terminated by a circular
turret. Enlarged in 1926: a tall bay with three-light windows
and a scrolled bracketed pediment, reminiscent of the detail
in the loggia wing at Auchrannie (*see* below). At the junction
with Alma Road, KAMES COTTAGE, of 1820, harled, with flat
dormers and a pedimented doorhead. Opposite is BRODICK
PHARMACY, a quirky red sandstone building, originally the
village Post Office, of 1886. It presents a gabled front to the
street, with prominent bargeboards (the wooden supports to
the l. transparently not structural) and a recessed panel with a
round head, with a clock within; to the r. a hipped porch supported on a cast-iron column and beautiful dragon bracket. All
this probably of *c.* 1913, when it became, fleetingly, the Golf
Clubhouse, while the hip-roofed tea-caddy behind is probably
the original building.

ALMA ROAD runs parallel and uphill to the w; the highlight is
the red sandstone Neo-Tudor ALMA TERRACE of 1856, built
by the estate as part of the forced resettlement of the old village
at the castle (*see* also Douglas Place, below). Eight cottages,
with gabled two-storey bays book-ending the central block,
with four sharp trussed gables of its own. It has the pentices
over the doors and windows that are the characteristic motif
of all the mid-C19 estate buildings. Some original diamond-
lattice glazing, but now shorn of many of the original paired
stacks. When newly built, Alma Terrace must have been comparatively isolated, but was later joined by mostly late C19 red
sandstone villas in Alma Road. Their style suggests that
the estate office had a considerable hand in their design.
Similar groups of villas to the w in West Mayish Road and
Manse Road.

AUCHRANNIE, 0.3 km. SW. Now a hotel, spa and country club.
The original house is dated 1869; it is red sandstone with a
gabled half-dormer and a canted two-storey bay in the gable
to the l. The shaped gable to the rear, above a square two-
storey bay window, was probably added in the late C19,
perhaps at the time when the house became the home of the
Dowager Duchess of Hamilton, following the death of the
12th Duke in 1895. Certainly of her time is the first extension
to the r., also in red sandstone, with a loggia of four-centred
openings, now glazed. In the centre of this elevation, an odd
detail, like the base for a big wall-head gable, with decorative
scrolls at either end; it may have been taller, but reduced to
allow the unattractive full-length dormer behind. Fully reconstructed in 1988, with a further pink sandstone extension to
the r. in 1990–1, including a long rear wing. In front of the
house a cast-iron FOUNTAIN of three diminishing bowls, the
lower one supported on three dolphins. The large SPA RESORT
to the NW of the hotel was built in 2000–1, international
pick'n'mix resort architecture, traditionally inspired but
over-inflated.

CORRIEGILLS, 2.1 km. SE. Two former townships, North and South Corriegills, now largely given over to mid C20 development. Two early C19 COTTAGES remain, one at right angles to the road, with rendered stone walls, painted dressings and a lower wing to the l. Roofed in tin, under which the thatch may remain. A little to the SE, the other cottage, slightly later, is crisply presented, with painted stone walls, grey painted dressings and two gable-headed dormers. At the road end, CARRICK LODGE, a large crowstepped and turreted red sandstone former manse of 1894, with a wide crowstepped porch, its entrance under a semicircular tympanum panel.

DOUGLAS PLACE, 0.4 km. NW. 1856. Built to house the tenants displaced from Old Brodick (but less fancy than Alma Terrace, *see* above). Two red sandstone slated single-storey rows of cottages, of twelve and eight respectively, with simple shallow-headed openings and hipped dormers. A broad swathe of communal grass separates the cottages from their gardens. At the NE end, STRONACH, dated 1897, is a simple single-storey red sandstone house with hipped dormers and a two-light window to the r.

HOTEL ORMIDALE, 0.2 km. SE. Built *c.* 1860, red sandstone, with a gabled wing to the l. with prominent skews, chamfered windows, and pretty fretted and cusped woodwork, especially in the bargeboards and the re-entrant porch. To the rear a substantial late C19 conservatory or garden room. In the grounds the two-storey half-hipped STABLES, with lower flanking wings, one hipped, one gabled.

STRATHWHILLAN, 1.5 km. SE. A former township, now mostly mid C20 ribbon development. BRANDON FARM is a first-rate example of a small mid-C19 Arran farm but presently (2011) abandoned. Single-storey farmhouse, dated 1863, at the NE corner of the rear courtyard, which has a tall E range for the mill (r.) and cartshed (l.), a single-storey S range (stable) and W range for the byre. Simple end skews and stone finials.

Brodick Bay.
Painting by G.F. Hering, 1857

0030

BRODICK CASTLE
2 km. N of Brodick

74   The seat of the Hamiltons until the mid C20. The setting is especially impressive, built on a platform in rising ground, the naturally defensive site commanding the N side of Brodick Bay and backed up by the hills ascending to Goat Fell. Surrounded by shelter belts of trees and terraced lawns and luxuriant gardens, this is the very image of a Victorian Highland estate and little changed from its depiction in a delightful vignette of *c.* 1873. Seen from the water one is reminded of the views of Dunrobin Castle, Sutherland, from the Dornoch Firth.

The earliest surviving fabric is late C13, and it was twice sacked in the C14 by the English when it was in royal ownership (*see* also Lochranza); it was through the marriage of James, Lord Hamilton, to Mary Stewart, daughter of James II (her second marriage, *see* Dean Castle, Kilmarnock), that so much of Arran, including the castle, came to the Hamiltons. Then, in 1503, James IV created his cousin Earl of Arran; the 2nd Earl, deposed from the Regency of Scotland in 1554, returned to the island and remodelled and enlarged the castle *c.* 1558. The form it took has been obscured by later alterations but appears to have comprised a three-storey tower with its entrance on the E side, an outer courtyard, a gatehouse and a barbican protected by a rock-cut ditch. The castle was taken in 1652 by English troops and extended as barracks with a gun battery to the E of the earlier buildings.

The C19 transformation was brought about by two marriages. First, in 1809, the 10th Duke of Hamilton married William Beckford's daughter Susan Euphemia; then their son and heir, the Marquis of Douglas and Clydesdale, married Princess Marie of Baden, cousin of Napoleon III, in 1843, and Brodick was reconstructed as their home. With the proceeds of the Beckford inheritance in 1844 it became possible to instigate a major enlargement by *James Gillespie Graham.* He had produced plans for additions in 1808 which anticipated destruction of the old buildings, but when construction was initiated in 1844 it was to an entirely new design, and one sympathetic to the earlier work. This was his first foray into the Scottish Baronial style; the only other example is Ayton Castle in the Borders, which was under way from 1845 and bears the influence of the Brodick design. The principal new feature was a great entrance tower, which collapsed in the course of construction during 1845 and the contractor, *Thomas Brownlie* of Ayr and Glasgow, had to rebuild it. *Thomas Hamilton,* brought in to arbitrate on the quality of the building work, found the cause of collapse to be the slow drying qualities of Arran lime.

When work was finished in 1846, the 10th Duke was reluctant to countenance further lavish expenditure and frustrated pleas by the couple that 'unless the new and the old parts are made to harmonise, the new part that has already [been] added, becomes entirely useless.' The Princess pursued her desire for a palatial house in the years before and after the death of her husband in 1863 with a litany of grand but unexecuted schemes for house

1. Stair up from entrance hall
2. Boudoir Landing
3. Boudoir
4. Bedroom
5. Drawing Room
6. Old Library
7. Dining Room
8. Gallery
9. China Room
10. Old Kitchen
11. Bruce's Room

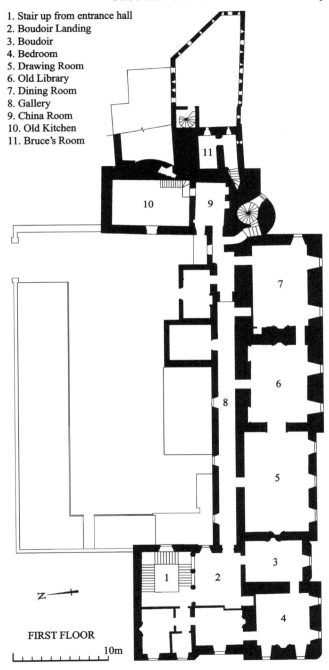

FIRST FLOOR

10m

Brodick Castle.
First Floor Plan

and garden by *W. A. Nesfield* in 1853; *William Burn* in 1860, proposing an entrance court modelled on Thirlestane Castle (Borders), and ambitious plans in 1875 by *William J. Green* to double the house around a courtyard. Lady Mary Hamilton, heir to the 12th Duke married the 6th Duke of Montrose in 1906 and they became the first family to occupy Brodick permanently, until her death in 1957. Much of the interior reflects their taste but their legacy lies mainly in the gardens; they considered and rejected additions by Reginald Blomfield in 1919. In 1958 the castle and policies were passed to the National Trust for Scotland together with 7,000 acres (2,832.8 ha.) of hill country including Goat Fell and Glen Rosa. Restoration for the Trust was carried out in the 1960s by *Watson, Salmond & Gray*.

The castle is long, roughly rectangular, and of three and four storeys and attics with wings projecting N at either end. The EXTERIOR is in native pinkish red sandstone, neatly squared and tooled for the 1840s work. There are only two show elevations, the S and W; the N elevation with its service accretions is partly concealed by the courtyard wall, and the narrow E elevation, also mainly hidden, is a confusion of additions and alterations. The long S ELEVATION starts from the E with the Cromwellian BATTERY, a strongly fortified wall fronting a vaulted chamber with shot-holes. This is linked to a three-storey block at least partly of similar date, which appears to have been built in front of the gatehouse to the medieval courtyard castle.* Before the Victorian additions the main entrance to the castle was here. Adjoining this to the W are two bays, which at ground level, at least, contain evidence of the late C13 work and were part of the gatehouse and barbican. Frequent attacks in the C14 and C15 resulted in much rebuilding but the l. block, which steps slightly forward of its neighbour, has a boldly curved lower wall that encloses a newel stair, an early example for the west of Scotland. It was corbelled to square above the ground floor, probably in the C16. Remains of a corresponding tower have been found to the N, under the old scullery, supporting the suggestion that it began as the gatehouse to the castle. The rest of the S front stands well forward of these earlier parts and continues with the tower house erected *c.* 1558 by the 2nd Earl. Its form is still easily discerned and has strongly battered walls at ground level containing horizontal gunloops. In the masonry there is evidence of altered windows, now replaced by regular C19 fenestration at first and second floor. Corbel table at eaves level with plenty of dummy guns for waterspouts set in the crenellated parapet and scarcely bowed angle bartizans. Those on the W face lost to the addition of *c.* 1652. This is also two bays and of equal height in a similarly sturdy and unostentatious style but with a simplified corbelled parapet that concludes with a square

---

* We are grateful to Tom Addyman for sharing the results of his archaeological investigation.

corbelled bartizan at the W. Here too the fenestration is altered but there is a small blocked closet vent at the second floor.

Now we come to Gillespie Graham's contribution, a self-confident composition sensitively scaled to the earlier building but with all the Baronial trappings that the former never had – corbelled turrets, crowstepping on the gables etc. – all of the type popularized by Billings's *Baronial and Ecclesiastical Antiquities of Scotland* (1845–52). His addition is L-plan, concluding the S front and forming a new entrance front to the W, with the mighty tower at the angle. This has a deep corbelled and crenellated parapet with variously detailed corbelled bartizans open to the S but with later, copper candle-snuffer roofs to the N. Under the parapet on the S and W elevations mock machicolation projections modelled on that at Lochranza Castle (q.v.). Big caphouse with crowstepped gables to all elevations. The heavily battered profile of the ground floor is a favourite device of the architect (cf. the W wing of Taymouth Castle, Perth and Kinross, 1837), with the effect that the windows in the tower are set into very deep embrasures. To the r. of the tower on the S front the new work is slightly set back from the mid-C17 part, with a marginally lower parapet mimicking the earlier detail but with a lower roof-line. The three segment-headed windows at first floor are a motif found also at Cloncaird Castle (*c.* 1810–19, q.v.), a house with which Gillespie Graham may have been associated. This part is linked by a further recessed and crowstepped gabled bay to the corner tower. On the W front, N of the tower is a wing of comparable height which contains the entrance in a projecting outer bay. Door set in segment-headed architrave swept through the battered ground-floor walling. Above the parapet, whose corbelling runs over the segmental heads of a pair of windows, is a crowstepped gable with the Hamilton coat of arms, initials and the date 1844. The N face of this wing is blind and brings the 1840s work to an abrupt ending, suggesting that the 10th Duke's reluctance to pay thwarted all of Princess Marie's schemes for further additions. Within the rear service court many accretions including the first-floor gallery/passage added by Gillespie Graham to improve the circulation. Above the service door at the E a corbelled, square turret belonging to the 1558 tower projects through the NE corner of the roof.

INTERIOR. Before the C19 the tower house was approximately Z-plan but was transformed into a U-shape with the creation of three rooms on the S, a large stair hall and the long N gallery or passage behind the principal rooms which linked to the N-projecting kitchen wing. The decorations belong to the 1840s and later. The ENTRANCE HALL lit from the large stair window is Jacobean in flavour with a geometric coffered ceiling, heavily carved Renaissance-style chimneypiece (imported in the 1920s, probably when the dining room also acquired a new chimneypiece) with a big armorial panel above. Jacobean-style interlaced balustrade to the stair which rises to the second floor, the ceiling above it with scrolled plaster decoration, pendants and a big central rose. The walls are lined with stags' heads.

At first floor, to the l., behind a stone screen of panelled pilasters with ornamented capitals and heavily moulded basket arches, is the BOUDOIR LANDING. More Jacobean-style plasterwork in the ceiling. Consoled niche on the w wall. Ahead at the top of the stairs are the PRIVATE APARTMENTS comprising BATHROOM (originally the Duke's dressing room), DRESSING ROOM, DUCHESS'S BEDROOM, in the corner tower, and the BOUDOIR, all simply detailed. The chimneypiece in the Boudoir is reminiscent of that in the Hall. This room opens onto the long RED GALLERY, with a plaster barrel-vaulted ceiling, running behind, and providing access to, the reception rooms of the s front. These rooms are, however, also arranged *enfilade* and all have 1844 geometric Jacobean-style plaster ceilings with pendants. The light and airy DRAWING ROOM at the w end is the only one to benefit from the scale of Gillespie Graham's addition and here the hand of Princess Marie is clear. The ceiling has richly ornamented ribs of squared quatrefoil patterns and roundels displaying Hamilton heraldry from the C14 to the C19. White statuary marble chimneypiece in French C18 fashion, the flanks with *Minton* tiles decorated with fleur-de-lis. Monogrammed fireback. The rich green silk hung by the Princess has been replaced by lightweight moulded plaster panels, probably in the 1920s. The LIBRARY is contained within the Cromwellian addition, indicated by the thick wall separating it from the Drawing Room, the lower height of the ceiling and the deeper-set windows. The big door to the Red Gallery is of 1844 as is the black-veined marble chimneypiece with inset *Minton* tiles bearing the motto of the Dukes of Hamilton. The DINING ROOM occupies the hall of the 1558 tower. Its ceiling is even more ornate than the Drawing Room, with dense patterns of scrollwork between the moulded ribs. The dado and doors have elaborate oak panelling with strapwork patterns, and are probably C16, brought to Brodick from Letheringham Abbey, Suffolk, when the Hamiltons' Easton Park estate was broken up in 1924. The stone chimneypiece with its Tudor arch is also of that date.

Below the rooms of the *piano nobile* are, from the w, the former SMOKING ROOM which has a good statuary marble chimneypiece brought from the Duke of Montrose's seat at Buchanan Castle, Stirlingshire. To the E of this are various vaulted chambers off the N corridor, and to the N in its own wing the KITCHEN of the 1840s. At the E end of the castle there is some evidence of the building before 1558, including the newel stair already noted and also the much-altered BRUCE'S ROOM (displayed as a dungeon) and a small closet with ribbed barrel vault, diminutive windows and a gunloop.

GARDENS. From the wide s terrace two wide flights of steps, unrelated to any entrance to the Castle, descend the steep terraced slope created in 1844. At the E end of the top terrace an octagonal SUMMER SHELTER (of 1992 by *Henry Murdo* of Corriegills but replacing an earlier shelter). Timber posts with decorative braces, herringbone timber partitions and a heather-thatch roof. To its E, wrought-iron GATES set in a welded frame, a silver wedding commemoration of 1931 for the Duke and Duchess of Montrose. Above is the NW corner of the WALLED GARDEN of 1710. Within its W wall are two square bee-bolls, and against the E wall another thatched rustic octagonal summerhouse, C19, with herringbone panelling and a scalloped timber apex cap. Through the woodland garden below is the charming BAVARIAN SUMMER HOUSE, the sole survivor of four built for Princess Marie on the rocky promontory overlooking Brodick Bay and intended to conjure up memories of her Baden home. It is twelve-sided and timber-framed with arched, Y-traceried, diamond-paned windows in alternate bays and a low basket-arched entrance to N. Intertwined faggots clad the vertical posts and crazily latticed twigs cover all the exterior walls. Inside, a low bench around the walls, the latter lined with vertical sticks below the bench, planks for half the height above and topped with elaborate fir-cone-patterned panels (restored by children from a primary school on the Isle of Wight in 1966). More sticks and cones create a fantastic star decoration on the ceiling with circles of pendant cones. Also, a late C18 ICE HOUSE, bottle-shaped with domed roof in immaculate masonry. The door has gone.

ESTATE BUILDINGS. N of Castle and facing each other are GREENHIDE COTTAGE and CASTLE COTTAGE, each of a single storey with windows stepped up the slope. Late C19 but in a simple timeless vernacular of granite rubble and sandstone dressings with slate roofs. KEEPER'S COTTAGE and KENNELS, off the W drive, are mid-C19 in the simple Tudor style found also at Alma Terrace, Brodick (*see* p. 688). Low U-plan gabled range of kennels with railed enclosures. The WALLED GARDEN, SW of the castle by the shore road near Cladach (q.v.), is probably late C18 and may have been designed as a tree nursery, but upgraded to a kitchen garden in 1850 when the walled garden (*see* above) near the castle was converted to a flower garden. Red sandstone rubble walls with saddleback copings. For the Home Farm, see Cladach.

RECEPTION CENTRE, below the castle to the E. 1990–1 by *Page & Park* for the National Trust for Scotland. An elegantly simple prefabricated portal-framed rectangle, very much in tune with its setting. Its form derives from the architects' design for the Countryside Commission Pavilion at the Glasgow Garden Festival (1988). Galvanized steel frame filled with Douglas fir and glass panels. Roof of blue-grey slates and finished inside with boards of American willow. Particularly original is the splitting of the flanges of the supporting columns and the insertion of tall slots of glass providing shafts of light. The gable at the exhibition end is fully glazed with views to the bank and the route to the Castle. Some modifications have been made on the S side.

CATACOL

Small community in the NW of the island, at the foot of Glen
Catacol, which widens out to form one of the few easily cultivated areas on the W coast. A farm here is recorded as early as
the C15 and the foundations of the pre-Clearance township can
be seen in the glen. Now it is famous for the TWELVE APOS-
TLES, an iconic row of cottages facing the sea in bright white
painted stone with slated roofs, gabled wall-head dormers and
simple shallow door canopies; the result a restful articulation.
At first sight uniform, but on closer inspection varied in the
details. The gardens are enclosed and divided by stone walls.
Possibly built 1843–4, but for whom is uncertain. It is believed
that they stood empty for some years, but claims that they
were spurned by their prospective new tenants cannot be
substantiated.

Behind the row, at the N end, COLMAR, a well-designed
house of the 1960s. Further N, the mid-C19 harled CATACOL
BAY HOTEL, a former manse, has two big gables in the familiar
Arran manner and lying-pane glazing.

Barking House, 100 m. S. C19, stone-built. More ruinous than
that at Lochranza (q.v.) but retaining its three boiling vats.

CLADACH

1.5 km. N of Brodick

Formerly Old Brodick, whose inhabitants were rehoused at
Brodick in the late C19 (*see* Alma Terrace and Douglas Place,
pp. 688, 689) to allow development of a deerpark below the
castle. The surviving buildings have been converted for shops
etc. at the entrance to the castle. They include the former inn,
now THE WINEPORT, built by the Duchess Anne in the early
C18. Two storeys, its windows evenly arranged 2 + 2 + 2 but with
nice variation in the design of the sash windows on each floor,
and the door squeezed into the centre. Harled walls, ashlar
margins and steep crowstepped gables.

E of here is the walled garden for the castle (q.v.) and, on the
shore, BRODICK OLD QUAY. It is a small harbour constructed
in the early C19 of squared rubble battered walls and paved
quays. SE entrance into the bay, angled steps at the NW. Plaque
on the estate wall opposite records 'King Edward and Queen
Alexandra after their coronation first set foot on Scottish soil
at this place 26th August 1902'.

S towards Brodick on the side of the bay, DUCHESS COURT, the
former HOME FARM for the castle. Built *c.* 1860 on an industrial scale, but now much altered for retail and manufacturing
units. A U-plan complex with a long, two-storey, red sandstone
barn range on one side. Smaller windows on the upper floor
to granary/workshops; on the S gable the loft door remains. A
wider N bay with steps to upper floor. Various additions step
down to the N.

STRABANE, 0.25 km. S of Duchess Court, is a villa of *c.* 1860
built in snecked and stugged pink sandstone rubble with ashlar
dressings. Large gabled bays at either end of the main front,
facing the sea, are finished with decorative open bargeboards,
hammer braces and openwork finials. The big E bay was added
in 1883 when the house was substantially remodelled by
George Paterson for Patrick Murray, the Duke of Hamilton's
Chamberlain. The low red sandstone addition to the N is of
1900, built as the estate office. Of the same date the rear transverse range for service rooms, all in the estate style of that time.
Inside, a white and grey marble chimneypiece brought from
the Duke of Montrose's Buchanan House, Stirlingshire, after
its sale in 1925. Much remodelling when the estate office
moved out in the C20. STABLE COURT. Dated 1887. Curvilinear gabled porch. It forms a U-plan with the outbuildings.

CORRIE   *0040*

Picture-postcard village on the E coast unmolested by recent
growth and retaining the essence of Arran villages. It is largely a
creation of the C19 and is, more so than any other island village,
industrial in origin, for the rows of cottages are squeezed between
the sea and the cliffs behind, which yielded limestone and red
sandstone that were quarried and exported. The church and
school form a compact group at the far N end.

CORRIE CHURCH. Free Gothic of 1886–7 by *J. J. Burnet* of *John
Burnet, Son & Campbell*, earlier than Burnet's church at
Shiskine (q.v.), and before he had fully evolved the model that
served him well at Shiskine and was developed further on the
Scottish mainland. Gabled nave and aisle aligned E–W, with a
heavy stepped bellcote rising from a skew just to the W of the
NE transept containing the vestry; the skew merging into pinnacled buttresses. Substantial stone and timber NW porch,
clearly antecedent to Shiskine. Minister's door in the transept,
with a shouldered arch, approached by a railed stone stair, as
the church burrows out from the hillside behind. Big stabilizing
central E buttress, with a single lancet either side. Small square-
headed windows on the N elevation; taller round-headed
windows facing S; three stepped lancets in the W gable. Delightful interior, little altered, and with a remarkable unity. The   34
nave has a boarded wooden floor, a low boarded dado,
plastered walls and an open pitched roof supported on
scissor trusses. The chancel ceiling is panelled and stencilled
(where lost replaced rather oddly with flock wallpaper);
chancel arch of polished stone, the N pier cut away to form
a niche holding the FONT and a bronze panel, the S pier
broadening to become the PULPIT. The aisle arcade of chamfered wooden pillars, the arcade and the pitched aisle roof
creating a forest of exceptionally well-crafted, prominently
pegged timber. – Dark oak ELDERS' STALLS in the chancel;

otherwise the original wooden chairs. – Original LIGHT FITTINGS. Like cartwheels. – STAINED GLASS. Chancel: in the E gable, Baptism, contemporary with the church; in the two S windows, naturalistic seascapes with red-sailed yachts, by *Richard Leclerc*, *c.* 2000.

Former CHURCH HALL. 1898, a tall and rather ungainly exercise in grey harl and red sandstone, perched high above the road, with low buttresses and applied timbering in the bargeboarded gable.

Former FREE CHURCH. Simple red sandstone Gothic of *c.* 1894. Two-light window in the buttressed E gable; on the S elevation gabled windows break through the eaves. Stone and timber S porch. The influence of Burnet is everywhere, even in the conical-headed drum gatepiers. Converted 2002–4 by *Kirsten Lees/Gavin Miller*, with an imaginatively executed long flat glazed dormer on the N elevation.

CORRIE PRIMARY SCHOOL. Of 1858, given by the Duke of Hamilton, the cost £400. It forms the S end of the present building, with a sharply gabled dormer and penticed window heads that epitomize the mid-C19 estate style. The N addition, of 1889, in a brighter stone, reprises the same details.

Between the church and church hall a run of early C19 cottages, mostly of painted stone, usually with C20 dormers, often of the canted type. Such rows of cottages are characteristic of the village, punctuating its length and often arrayed picturesquely between shore and cliff. Of this group, CLIFF COTTAGE has lying-pane glazing and thin dressings, and may be dated to *c.* 1840. Below the church hall CORRIE PORT is a delightful miniature harbour, probably mid-C19, the piers and the retaining wall of local red sandstone. This is followed by the biggest group of C19 cottages, set back behind gardens, notably KELSO COTTAGE with a pretty bargeboarded porch. More substantial is CORRIE HOUSE, the former Post Office, in the estate's Arts and Crafts style. Red sandstone, with small-paned windows, half-timbered gable and a hipped porch and bay window combined. Burnet's influence can again be seen in the gabled hall added in 1899 to the CORRIE HOTEL, a neat and well-mannered three-bay building of 1857, its dormers with skewed gables, fronted by a big, and later, gabled porch. S of the hotel, CROMLA LODGE is set in a densely wooded garden behind high walls. A sophisticated single-storey ashlar villa, on a raised basement, whose present appearance dates from enlargement in 1815 by Dr Thomas McCredie; entrance with a Roman Doric porch approached by a big straight flight of steps.*

Further S, terminating a long run of houses set well back from the road, ARNVHOR, with to its rear the crenellated LOOKOUT TOWER erected in 1847 on the occasion of Queen Victoria's visit to Arran. After this the former Free Church (*see*

---

*For many years in the C19 it was the Arran home of the Rev. David Landsborough (*see* Stevenston), who wrote widely on the natural history of Arran; the garden is his creation.

above). Set back behind the church is HEATHFIELD, late C19, all bristling finialled bargeboards, and with a hipped roof linking the ground-floor bays to form a porch. Finally QUARRY PIER, built *c.* 1882 of the local red sandstone which was shipped from here. Of the same material the house opposite the pier entrance, ALPINE, dated 1883, built for the quarry-master, James King; three straight gables over the dormers.

HIGH CORRIE, 1.5 km. SSW. Of the pre-enclosure farming   96
townships of Arran, High Corrie is the only one to have survived relatively intact. The typical appearance of the cottages, barns and byres seems haphazard but their orientation and openings were planned for the efficient execution of domestic and agricultural chores. Ten or so houses remain, though the footings of others can be discerned; mostly of stone, harled or painted, with simple openings and stacks. The earliest is probably late C18 or early C19, but others later C19; at least one is a late C20 replacement, but convincingly done. Since the late C19 the settlement, blessed with stunning sea views, has attracted artists, and the roll-call of those who have summered here, drawn by the light, the views, and the romanticized image of a pre-enclosure prelapsarian idyll, is a lengthy one.

DIPPIN LODGE *see* KILDONAN

DOUGARIE LODGE   8030
3 km. N of Machrie Bay

A large, rambling and idiosyncratic sporting lodge-cum-summer-   70
house, built *c.* 1850 for the 11th Duke of Hamilton. The principal feature, on the W front towards the sea, is a large tower with a crowstepped top stage but the rest is low, no more than one-and-a-half storeys and with a vigorous rhythm of steep, bargeboarded gables intermingled with small gablets to the attic. Gothic windows in several places. All this is Picturesque but of a strongly Germanic rather than Scots tone, and in this respect may show the influence of the Duke's wife, Princess Marie of Baden. The walls are covered in white-painted harl disguising various alterations (e.g. the addition of projecting bay windows in several places) and in the Late Victorian period were pricked all over with antlers. At the rear, a narrow open court crossed by a covered walkway to the gun rooms etc. with fish-scale slate roof. At the W end of this court is a curved stair-tower corbelled to square at first floor.

Extensive alterations and additions planned in 1894 by *J. J. Burnet* were unexecuted but there was a good deal of remodelling to the interior at about this time. The spacious entrance hall has a good cast-iron fire grate of a type found in other rooms, all with distinctive Aesthetic Movement disc designs. In the main corridor and continuing up the stairs, dado panelling with a cresting and deer-skin lining. Doors have antler handles. The light and airy drawing room at the E has an unusual chimneypiece set immediately below the E window and composed of geometric-patterned tiles framing enamelled panels with wonderfully delicate and colourful grotesque-style decoration of urns, foliage and birds. Elsewhere much pine panelling.

E of the lodge in the rising ground are TERRACED GARDENS. These are mid-C19 and very remarkable, composed of picturesquely crenellated granite rubble walls, eyecatching ruined arches, turrets etc. suggesting the remains of earlier fortified buildings, in the manner of the Culzean Viaduct (q.v.). There is also a rustic polygonal GAME LARDER, with tree-trunk columns between vertical glazing and a slated roof with a tall finial. Many hooks for hanging game. To its E is the original FARM COURT, romanticized in the same vein as the terraced garden but with more substantial towers, ruins and arches. A tall, curved rubble wall with a large Gothic archway set into a ruined turreted frame faces W down the drive to the lodge, further to its E a U-plan piece of irregular walling suggesting a ruined tower from the outside. Within the walls buildings both built and adapted for the purposes of running a sporting estate with kennels, stables, haylofts and carthouses, all rubble-built with red sandstone dressings, some of the cart openings with shallow pointed arches, some of the buildings with crow-stepped gables. At the NW angle of the court an inhabited tower (once the factor's house). It is nearly square in plan, rubble-built with red sandstone dressings. At the upper level facing W two slit openings possibly lighting a stair. A subtly corbelled parapet supports a mock angle turret at the NW with an incised cross at parapet level and a crowstepped gable at the E as though part of a caphouse.

BOATHOUSE, by the shore opposite the entrance to the house. An extremely memorable design in red sandstone, built 1884–5 and thus attributed to *J. J. Burnet* (*Thomas Weir*, civil engineer, was clerk of works). It comprises two boathouses placed parallel, each with a roof of dramatically swept profile of almost Oriental appearance (originally both with scissor trusses inside), and a central link – built in two stages, part for a smoking room that opens onto a veranda facing the sea. Inside, whitewashed walls with chalk caricatures of sporting characters and other satires, mostly of *c.* 1890 by *Liberio Prosperi*, who drew cartoons for *Vanity Fair*.

GLENSCORRADALE

Remote erstwhile farm on the ROSS ROAD, the more southerly of the two roads that traverse the island, laid out 1821–2.

The farm is now SAMYE DECHEN SHING – The Place of Inconceivable Happiness – a closed male retreat attached to the monastery on Holy Isle (q.v.). To the original single-storey painted and slated early C19 ranges, arranged about three sides of a courtyard, has been added, *c.* 2002, a harled and slated fourth (W) range. Of the same date the stone walls linking the ranges, their piers flat-capped in a Mackintoshian manner.

HOLY ISLE

0030

The steep, stern bulk of Holy Isle rises out of Lamlash Bay, sheltering the village, and providing a dramatic element in views along the E coast. 'Holy' because of its connection with St Molios, a C6–C7 Scoto-Irish monk and later abbot, through the cave which bears his name on the W side of the island, in which he spent a period as an anchorite. A chapel, C14 or C15 in origin, existed, and was used for burials, until the late C18. In 1992 the Rokpa Trust acquired the island; and it is now a Buddhist Centre for Retreat and Meditation.

CENTRE FOR WORLD PEACE AND HEALTH. Mid-C19 farmhouse, restored and extended *c.* 1998–9. The core is three bays, two-storey with small windows and a gabled porch. Flanking two-bay lower wings, with gabled wings extending to the rear of these, creating an inner courtyard, which is closed to the rear by a separate hipped and dormered block. Uncontroversial Neo-vernacular; adopted in preference to the more dramatic original proposals of *Bosch Haslett* of Amsterdam (1994).

Shipping in the Firth is protected from Holy Isle by two lights: the HOLY ISLE (INNER) LIGHTHOUSE of 1877 by *D. & T. Stevenson*, a traditional white-painted stone circular tower with a broader base, a balcony and ogee-headed lantern, and the square HOLY ISLE (OUTER) LIGHTHOUSE of 1905 by *D. & C.*, with polished stone dressings and a solid parapet. The associated houses and offices, now used as a closed female retreat, are at the former. One painted two-storey block is presumably of *c.* 1877, while another, with a first-floor entrance approached by a dog-leg stair, and extensive single-storey offices, may be of 1905. There is also a large walled garden.

KILDONAN

0020

Scattered community at the very S of the island; an agricultural area which is also popular with tourists drawn by the beaches and the views. With no discernible centre, and piecemeal development along the shore, Kildonan's architectural highlights are few.

KILDONAN CASTLE. The ivy-shrouded ruins of a rectangular tower of the late C14 or early C15, built for the Clan Macdonald, with clear views over the Sound of Pladda. Sacked 1558. The site is protected on the S by the cliffs and deep gullies on the E and W. Description is aided by William A. Railton's survey made *c.* 1880 for MacGibbon & Ross; he had the benefit of

p. 702

Kildonan Castle.
Engraving

more masonry and less ivy. The castle is built of granite rubble
and is 8.6-m. by 6.7 m. with ground-floor walls that are 1.8 m.
thick, decreasing to 1.4 m. in the first floor. There is evidence
for one floor above the first-floor hall; two surviving corbels on
the N wall above the second floor suggest a joisted ceiling at
this level. Whether there was a further storey or how the castle
was roofed is impossible to say. The entrance appears to have
been at the SE at ground level, opening onto a newel stair; only
fragments of this angle survive. Railton found evidence for a
newel at the NW leading from the hall to the upper floor. The
ground and first floors were barrel-vaulted using carefully
graded thin flat slabs. Evidence for a slightly pointed vault,
3.9 m. high, over the first-floor hall can be seen in the surviving
masonry. There is a narrow slit opening in the ground floor at
E and W. Fireplace on the W wall of the hall and a garderobe
in the SW angle with the bottom of the chute visible from the
outside. The hall appears to have been lit from the S, where
Railton found evidence for a large window. A small window is
tucked in close to the vault on the E, and in the second floor
there is a small press on the N wall.

KILDONAN HOTEL, 0.5 km. W of the castle, was described
in 1861 as 'a comfortable place but of course without any
pretension to tiptopism'. A harled and slated three-bay mid-
C19 E range with flat gabled half-dormers, much extended,

particularly *c.* 1890–1900, as suggested by the Glasgow-inspired
SE corner turret, and *c.* 2002, with a timber and glazed monopitch lounge. On the shore's edge, to the E, three late C19 or
early C20 gabled BOATSHEDS, one with a small carving of a
lighthouse above the door.

DRIMLA LODGE, 1.2 km. W of the castle. One of the island's
odder houses, built in 1896 for the Kilmarnock shoe manufacturer George Clark. His long residence in Rio de Janeiro
explains the curious style: a synthesis of Brazilian grandeur and
West of Scotland practicality. It is of brick (unusual in itself on
Arran) and of two storeys; the ground floor taller than the
upper, and with two-storey verandas in the colonial manner,
under a hipped roof. On the front, off-centre, a tower terminating in a low brick parapet with cruciform openings. The
package is finished with good brick stacks, corbelled out at the
top. Set back to the l. (W) is DRIMLA COTTAGE, a former
stable (or garage), also of brick and tile, but single-storey, with
similar stacks.

KIRK KILDONAN, 1.9 km. W of the castle. 1910 by *John Russell
Thomson*, as the Kildonan U. F. Church; reduced and converted to residential use, 1995.* Simple harled Arts and Crafts;
painted dressings to the square-headed, and mostly three-light,
windows.

DIPPIN LODGE, 2.3 km. NE on the cliff top. A sporting lodge
for the Hamilton estate, whose precise historical development
is unclear. Its main (E) front is *c.* 1870, like a suburban villa,
of painted render with a slate roof and generous canted window
in the gabled bay to the l. of its porch. Attached to this on the
S front is a stone block of two bays with dormerheads. At the
back, a further two-bay two-storey W range in neat red sandstone ashlar. Linking these elements at the centre of the plan
is the original building; to improve internal circulation it was
raised *c.* 1900 to house a new staircase, and has a shallow
corbelled first floor, a style favoured by the estate at this time.
Inside, the tiled entrance hall opens l. and r. to two public
rooms in the front range, both with taller ceiling heights in
the fashion of the day. Through a full-height archway the
semi-panelled, open-well, toplit staircase with balustraded
landings.

To the W former KENNELS and ancillary building converted
to domestic use.

KILMICHAEL

0030

1.5 km. SW of Brodick

A simple, classically detailed, house built in the mid C18 for the
Fullartons at the centre of a small estate in Glencloy, believed

---

*It originally had a SE tower and a low castellated porch below the wide pointed S
window.

to have been granted to the family by Robert II. It is the only property on the island never to have been in the possession of the Hamiltons. It is now a hotel.

Two storeys and three bays with a steep, slated piend roof and chimneystacks on the cross walls, the latter with big thacking stanes. Low wings l. and r. with shallow piend roofs. Fullarton coat of arms above the door. Minor alterations to the front, e.g. the loss of a doorpiece and addition of mid-C19 dormers. At the rear an extension of *c.* 1830 for a large room at first floor. Inside the curving stair to the first floor is probably the same date; simple cast-iron balusters, banded with open-diamond detail. Main reception rooms originally on first floor. The left one has delicate waterleaf mouldings to an arched panelled alcove. Later C19 stained-glass window at the half-landing with the Fullarton arms and motto, Lux in Tenebris ('Light in darkness'), set into subtle monochrome quarries. Some mid-C18 woodwork survives, particularly in the doors.

A single-storey service court at the rear, sensitively converted in 2000 for hotel accommodation. It incorporates a re-set datestone IF 1719 EH, probably from an earlier building on the site. – LODGE. L-plan *c.* 1870, single-storey, red sandstone set outside repositioned attractive cast-iron octagonal GATEPOSTS with finialled gates and railings.

KILMORY

One of the two ancient parishes of Arran, encompassing the island's western half from Lochranza to Dippin. The name is now restricted to the immediate vicinity of the parish church, a township also known as Torrylinn.

KILMORY PARISH CHURCH, remote from the hamlet. Of 1785, on the site of its predecessor, with a N transept of 1810. Substantially altered in Gothic style in 1881. Squared rubble walls; the W gable has a bellcote with a cast-iron finial, above a spherical triangular window enclosing six circular lights. Buttressed side elevations with two-light windows with Y-tracery; a three-light window in the transept gable. At the E end a transversely arranged addition, presumably of 1881, gabled with paired lancets. Very simple rectangular box interior, with plastered walls and an open pitched roof supported on plain stone corbels; at the W end the inner face of the vestibule presents itself as a panelled hipped lean-to like an over-sized tabernacle. The N transept is framed by a wide four-centred stone arch on simple columns, and can be curtained off when not required. PULPIT and other fittings of 1881. – MONUMENT, S wall, to Surgeon Major William Stewart †1873, by *McGlashan* of Edinburgh: the pediment with acroteria, the inscription panel with rosettes above and the edges garlanded. In the vestibule, the FIGUREHEAD of the *Bessie Arnold*, which sank off this coast in 1908.

The church sits within an attractive walled KIRKYARD, with many pleasingly carved lettered MONUMENTS from the C18 and C19. Attached to the E wall is the classical MONUMENT to Captain William McKirdy, 'suddenly cut off' in 1825, carved in a cheerfully artisan manner. To the S of the church, the TOMB-CHEST of Rev. Archibald Nicol †1876, with corner scrolls, and signed by *Douglas* of Ayr.

Adjacent to the church is the L-plan harled former MANSE. The earlier part of the house has an exposed rocky base course. It was built in 1701–3, and was initially thatched, but slated following a fire in 1710. Substantially altered in 1848, when the additional wing and the gabled re-entrant porch were added.

0.5 km. SW, in the hamlet, the former SCHOOL of 1865, converted to an outdoor pursuits centre, 1978–9, and, in TORRLINN TERRACE some deep-roofed *Bute County Council* houses of *c.* 1950. A little W, the late C20 KILMORY SCHOOL, rather like an overgrown bungalow, but not without character, and VILLAGE HALL of 1934, in the manner of an unpretentious picture house.

LAGG, to the W, where the coastal road weaves down to cross the Torrylinn Water, is a sylvan spot. The LAGG HOTEL is dated 1791, and the core may well be of that date but with daintily bargeboarded gabled dormers of 1861 and late C19 brick stacks. Inoffensive C20 extensions; well-mannered enough to hide themselves behind. The concrete BRIDGE, with low stone parapets, is by *James Mather*, the Hamilton estate civil engineer, 1899. 0.5 km. W is CLACHAIG FARM, a well-preserved early C19 courtyard farm, typical of many island estate farms of that period. Two-storey three-bay gabled stone house, with flanking single-storey ranges, and a hipped two-storey rear range. On the opposite side of the road, a hipped kiln with a piggery.

CHAMBERED CAIRN (Carn Ban), 5 km. N of Kilmory church. Excavated by Thomas Bryce at the beginning of the C20. Roughly rectangular on plan, the Neolithic cairn measures some 30 m. in length by 18 m. in breadth and 4.5 m. in height and has a deep semicircular forecourt in its NE end. Two portal stones at the centre of the façade of the forecourt mark the entrance into the chamber, though this was filled in after the excavations. Bryce recorded the plan and elevation of the chamber, which even then was the only one that remained complete. It comprised four slab-built compartments, each divided from its neighbours by what are known as septal slabs set between the sides. The overall length of the chamber was about 5.6 m., and the sides were carried up above these compartments in drystone masonry to a height of up to 2.75 m. above the floor. The upper courses oversailed and the four slabs forming the roof stepped progressively downwards towards the inner end from a lintel set immediately behind the two portal stones. Towards the SW end of the cairn there are traces of a second axial chamber. There are two other chambered cairns, less well-preserved, near Torrylin, 0.5 km. s of the Lagg Hotel, and East Bennan, 3.5 km. E.

LAMLASH

This sizeable village stretches for some 3 km. along the sandy shore of Lamlash Bay on the E side of the island. Guarded by Holy Isle (q.v.), the bay forms the best and safest natural harbour on the island; as a result Lamlash was the main port for the island and, in consequence, the main administrative centre, which it remains. The original settlement would have been close to the shore, with farm settlements at a higher level behind. In 1701 Lord Basil Hamilton visited Arran: 'The more I know Arran I like it ye more. Its vastly improveable . . . I have agreed on ye place to begin a little town at Lamlash and where the harbour should be.' The early C18 pier which may have been the result of Hamilton's initiative had been 'most imprudently demolished' by 1807. Development as a resort was steady during the C19, partly because the waters of the bay were at a tolerable temperature for sea bathing, and received a further impetus after a new pier was opened in 1885. Lamlash Bay had been from the C18 an important shelter for naval vessels, and the bay, and village, was a major base for the Royal Navy in both world wars.

Former FREE CHURCH, towards the N end of Shore Road. 1891–2 by *James Hamilton* of Glasgow. Lancet style. Nave and aisles, with a gabled SE front, and a tower to the l. with a pyramidal spire. Three tall lancets to the front, above a gabled and buttressed entrance, and a small circular window high in the gable. The tower's tall pointed bell openings have Y-tracery and steep gables over. Pinnacled buttresses to the sides, and unusual long narrow catslide ventilators in the slated roof. Disused since the 1980s, and in poor condition.

Former KILBRIDE CHURCH. The rectangular ivy-clad ruin of one of the two original parish churches on the island. It is still largely complete to the wall-head, where some cavetto moulding survives, but the openings are late C18. Subdivided, presumably after 1773 when Lamlash Church was built (*see* below), and one cell used for burials of the Fullartons of Kilmichael; three medieval grave-slabs with incised crosses have also been placed there. AUMBRY in the E wall and an odd stone with a carving of a horse's head. Another AUMBRY in the other cell. The original KIRKYARD, which has a late C19 stone and rail wall, has been extended to form Lamlash Cemetery. To the E of the cemetery is the harled three-bay former MANSE, of 1827, with a tall pilastered entrance.

LAMLASH CHURCH. A prominent landmark on the shore road. 1884–6 by *H. & D. Barclay* on the site of the church of 1773. Plans were first prepared in 1871 by *Pilkington & Bell* (*F. T. Pilkington*) and although nothing further was done some elements of the Barclays' Free Gothic design suggest it provided an influence. Nave, transepts and a NE tower in small blocks of randomly coursed red sandstone. Thoroughly restored by *ARP Lorimer & Partners*, 2002–8.

Facing the road is the gabled E front with three stepped lancets and angle buttresses; the side elevations, transepts and W end similarly treated. Set back on the r., the soaring tower, again severely plain but with a burst of decoration at the peak, where bell-openings have finialled gablets (the finials unfinished) under a frieze of small cusped openings, and a slated roof rising to an urn finial. Inside, a barrel-vaulted roof divided into bays by ribs springing from shield-like corbels, and transept arcades with polished stone bases, foliated caps, round arches and attractive responds, and columns of Peterhead granite. At the wall-head a miniature arcade of pointed arches on stubby columns runs around the nave. Big classical doorpiece in the N wall with quatrefoil decoration in the entablature. There is another in the S transept.

Contemporary High Gothic FURNISHINGS (notably the multi-seated PULPIT) and brass LIGHT FITTINGS. – STAINED GLASS. – Nave, S wall, from the E: Fishers of Men of 1981, by *Gordon Webster*; Rev. Peter Robertson †1913, by *Andrew Rigby Gray* of *William Meikle & Sons*; Good Shepherd, *c.* 1896, in memory of David Richmond, erstwhile Lord Provost of Glasgow; Blessed are the Peacemakers, a memorial to Patrick Murray †1907, the Hamiltons' chamberlain on the island.[*] Very darkly blue, this must be the window by *R. Anning Bell* called 'recent' in 1909. – S transept W, a naturalistic Earth, Sea and Heaven by *Christian Shaw*, 1993. – N transept W, another by *Gordon Webster*, the Resurrection, 1951. – Vestry, an abstract window, *c.* 1980, like a fissuring of the glass. Some beautifully carved linenfold PANELS in the vestry window reveals.

In front of the church, BRIGID'S CROSS, an enigmatic medieval stone, carved with a representation of Christ's body disappearing into a chalice, from which blood flows to a kneeling supplicant below. Brought from Holy Isle in 1860, initially to Kilbride Church, and re-erected here *c.* 1892. Behind the church is a red sandstone circular structure with a conical roof: this is the MINISTER'S PRIVY.

CHURCH HALL, W of the church, reputedly of 1880, probably also by *H. & D. Barclay*, restored by *ARP Lorimer & Partners* in 1999–2001. Red sandstone, with half-hipped slate roofs, ridge tiles and tall windows whose hipped heads just break the eaves line. The hall and entrance hall have excellently detailed linenfold dado panelling, as in the vestry, which is echoed in the plaster panel above the entrance hall fireplace. Facing the N side of the church is the very simple parish SCHOOL of 1808 (now Belhaven, with later dormers).

ARRAN OUTDOOR LEISURE CENTRE, Clauchlands Road. 2006–8 by *North Ayrshire Council Architects Dept* (*Colin*

---

[*] Murray succeeded the younger Paterson as chamberlain, and did much to restore harmony between the islanders and the estate. The choice of subject reflects this.

Templeton, project architect). Neo-vernacular, with two projecting prow-like gables, in a variety of materials, plentifully
glazed.

ARRAN HIGH SCHOOL. 2007–8 by *Keppie Design* for North
Ayrshire Council. It is broadly L-plan, steel-framed, and clad
in harl, with large areas of glazing; the N wing extends
northwards to create a further round-ended wing with asymmetrically placed windows.

ARRAN WAR MEMORIAL HOSPITAL, 1.4 km. NE. 1920–2 by
Archibald Cook of Glasgow. Unassuming English Arts and
Crafts, in coursed red sandstone, the main elevation of two
storeys; the centre with five gables, the outer ones advanced
and with applied half-timbering. In the centre a pentice-roofed
entrance loggia on slight wooden supports. Flanking lower
ward wings, and a projecting central two-storey wing to the
rear. Subsequent additions mostly of *c.* 1970, harled and tiled.

ARRANTON BRIDGE, over the Benlister Burn. Late C19 with
polished voussoirs and bell-like cutwaters.

COMMUNITY CENTRE, Park Terrace. 1914, by *Speirs & Co.* of
Glasgow, for the Admiralty as a canteen, reading rooms and
gymnasium for the Royal Navy fleets stationed at Lamlash.
Impressively large, of corrugated iron, with half-timbered
gables and flanking penticed aisles. Later used as a hospital,
and converted *c.* 1920.

NORTH AYRSHIRE COUNCIL OFFICES, Shore Road. Former
Board School of 1875–6, converted by Bute County Council
c. 1948. A brown stone single-storey H-plan with gabled wings
at either end, and square-headed windows. Porch and alterations to the r. wing date from *c.* 1990.

DESCRIPTION

WHITEHOUSE, immediately S of the parish church, was built in
the late C18 for the Hamilton estate factor (or chamberlain)
and demolished in the late C20. Its LODGE survives and is in
the Hamilton estate style of the late C19 – red sandstone with
slated roofs, decorative ridge tiles, etc.

On SHORE ROAD, N of the church and set back behind an open
space, is the best estate building on the island, HAMILTON
TERRACE, twenty-eight two-bay brick harled cottages of
1892–5 by *J. J. Burnet* in the English Domestic Revival taste
seen elsewhere on the island. The houses are paired in a continuous row with tall harled stacks with corbelled brick heads
and catslide dormers in the steep roof. Big half-timbered transverse gables at each end, but pure symmetry has been upset
by the addition of the Post Office at the S end in 1898. At the
back they have lean-to scullery wings, all more-or-less altered.
In a parallel line, across the back lane, and running back into
the hillside, is the contemporary BACK ROW, of twenty mostly
timber-boarded houses in pairs, the best example of the island's
purpose-built summer houses to which the tenants would
transfer when letting their houses to visitors for the season.

These are long and narrow, with paired gables facing the lane. Originally clad in vertically laid floorboards, and with sliding front windows. The grassy area in front of Hamilton Terrace has, besides the CLEARANCE MONUMENT of 1977, two robust circular gatepiers, similar to that at Burnet's St Molios, Shiskine (q.v.), suggesting that the area was originally enclosed.

Thereafter the best houses in Shore Road are later C19 villas, some single, others in pairs, and one or two oddities such as MADE IN ARRAN (ISLEORNSAY) of c. 1890, which has on two fronts a motif of a big half-timbered gable, sheltering an oriel.

On the seaward side of Shore Road, a gaggle of buildings around the functional SLIPWAY, close to the site of the pier erected in 1885 by *Thomas D. Weir*, engineer (demolished in the early 1950s). All that remains is the L-plan hipped red sandstone former PIER OFFICES, with a squat capped clock tower. Adjacent to the slipway itself is the LIFEBOAT HOUSE of 1997, harled on a brick base, and a striking modern HOUSE of 2006–7 by *Ian Ferguson*, the upper floor clad in sheet metal resembling weatherboarding. On the l. side of Shore Road the gentle slope allows the houses to sit well back and take advantage of the views. They include the plastered KINNEIL, of 1885, with three wide bays, a heavy porch and openwork balcony above, which extends to the flanking canted bays. Further N the former MARINE HOUSE HOTEL, with at its heart a three-bay harled house of c. 1820; the canted windows are later, their roofs extended to form a porch, its sense of enclosure deepened by projections from the lower part of the bay walls. Extended to the l. c. 1960, the upper floor almost wholly glazed. Between the Council Offices and the former Free Church (for these, *see* above) is MONAWILLINE, a mid-C19 stone cottage with a large, and later, gabled porch with stepped windows and pegged bargeboards. Hereafter a nice ensemble of other C19 houses, including, next to the church, its OLD MANSE of 1897–8. Decidedly faux-Gothic, especially the cusped detailing in the bargeboards. THE SHORE is of c. 1966, good for the date, with a harled ground floor and a big picture window in the boarded gabled upper floor. An interesting pair is MILLBURN and MILLHILL, late C19, of brown red sandstone, which present their gables to the road; the plainer, slightly smaller Millhill was the summer house. SEAFIELD is a neat and very elegant two-storey harled late C18 house, one of the first to be permitted to be built by the Hamiltons, though only on a long lease. It has a delicate mid-C19 wrought-iron porch.

In PARK TERRACE, which runs s from, and in line with, Hamilton Terrace, are two neat harled houses with red sandstone dressings, both attributed to *J. J. Burnet*. ROSE COTTAGE, dated 1900, is single-storey, with a crowstepped gabled wing to the r., while the two-storey DALGORM, dated 1899, has a steeply pitched roof and a tower-like wing with a low parapet and iron balcony. Further s in Park Terrace HOUSES of c. 1950 by *Bute County Council*, with swept-down roofs at the ends (as at Montrose Terrace, Whiting Bay, Kilmory and elsewhere, qq.v.).

CLAUCHLANDS FARM, 3 km. NE. Mid-C19; a good example of a T-plan Hamilton estate farmhouse. Stone, two-storey, with finialled and skewed gables and a canted and hipped bay on the front elevation. Elsewhere flat pedimented half-dormers, while the main entrance has a shallow flight of steps and a stilted, segmental-arched doorpiece.

9050

LOCHRANZA

Loch Ranza forms one of the few safe havens on the island's W coast, and until the early C19 the sea provided the main access, with the result that this area's links, cultural and architectural, were with Kintyre and Knapdale, rather than the rest of Arran. This can be seen in the history of its major monument, Lochranza Castle. The loch encouraged the growth of a small crofting and fishing community, which from the late C19 benefited from the growth of summer steamer traffic on the Clyde and the consequent tourism to the island, especially after the steamer pier opened in 1888; as a result the village has several attractive houses from *c.* 1900. The village sits snugly round the S side of the loch, the castle ever-present in the foreground, and tourism remains important in the economy, boosted by the late C20 restoration of the maritime links with mainland Argyll.

48 LOCHRANZA CASTLE. The centrepiece of the village, standing on a spit of land jutting out into the loch in a sheltered position protected by the rising hills on either side and looking down the water to Argyll. There is a long history of occupation on the site: the earliest castle appears to have been a two-storey hall house, which in the late C14 became, with Brodick, one of two royal castles on Arran. In 1452 the castle passed by Royal grant to Alexander, Lord Montgomery, an ancestor of the Earls of Eglinton. James V granted a charter of land to Hugh, Earl of Eglinton, in 1528, but it makes no mention of a castle. By 1565 when a charter of confirmation was granted there is reference to a tower and fortalice, and the castle's present form agrees with a mid-C16 date. How much of anything previously on the site was incorporated is, without archaeological investigation, impossible to say. In 1705 it came to the Hamilton family and was subsequently in disrepair. It is now in the care of Historic Scotland.

It is built of rubble, much of it in the thin slabs that could be quarried locally, the quoins in both grey and pink sandstone. It is L-plan, composed of a hall block and integral crosswing (19.8 m. by 10.6 m.), aligned N and S, and with a SW tower (4.7 m. by 5 m.). The castle makes its impact by bulk not height; the N cross-wing was four storeys but the central hall block had only three, while the tower is of five. The

approach is from the w and the present entrance formed in
the C16 faces it (for the original access see the E wall). Immediately inside the door to the l. a generous newel stair; the two
slit windows lighting it can be seen to the l. of the doorway.
Above the door the remains of a corbelled panel which must
have housed an armorial panel, above again a small rectangular
boxed machicolation projected on corbels and a window facing
w, for the protection of the door below. This detail became a
favourite with C19 architects and builders in Arran and further
afield (*see* e.g. Brodick Castle and Killochan Castle). Further
protection was provided in the form of the circular bartizan at
the NW angle, and another from the SW tower which is corbelled out to give a wall-walk over the w and s faces, rather
strangely dying into the N wall. All evidence of windows on the
w wall of the hall has been obliterated by later repair and
consolidation, but from inside it appears that there were two.
The tower has small windows in each face of each storey above
the ground floor except to the w on the second. On the s elevation there are narrow windows lighting the stair giving access
to the tower, and one larger at the dais end of the hall. Again
on the E wall there is a singular lack of windows, with one
narrow slit at ground- and first-floor levels. This lack of window
gives the castle a fortified appearance although actual fortifications in the walls are absent. There is a blocked door that was
the original entrance and would have been reached by an
external timber stair; because the land has built up here it
would have been further from the ground. This door entered
onto a wide landing on the mural stair within this wall. In 1897,
as a result of storm damage, there was a dramatic collapse of

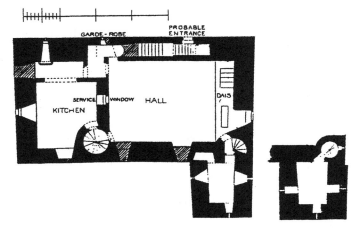

Lochranza Castle.
First Floor Plan

the NE angle of the castle; the NE square bartizan, an important vantage point to the sea, was lost.

The ground floor may always have been entered from the W but access was also available from the raised door on the E wall via the mural stair. Only the two intercommunicating compartments at the N and the lower level of the tower are barrel-vaulted; the later with a narrow door was the dungeon. Beside this entrance is a partition and a small arched chamber with a slit window, a small sink and drain, and an oblong aperture in the vault (1.8 m. by 6.1 m.) which opens to the dais floor in the hall above. There also appears to be some form of hoist. At some time this chamber has had a strong drawbar for protection but the l. slot has been lost with the later insertion of mural steps, which probably ascended to the dais. The ground-floor opening to the mural stair in the E wall is in the SE angle. At the landing level, where the former door opened, there is evidence of doors preventing access either up or down. The top of this stair was blocked at an early stage and a garderobe created; the access to this too is now blocked. Access to the SW tower is from the hall dais; at this level there is a garderobe, above three small unheated chambers. The N wall of the hall is gabled, and at hall level in the NE corner there is a blocked door originally leading, via the large kitchen hearth with a drain beside it, into the kitchen itself. Unusually this was on the first floor. The spacious newel stair in the SW corner of the kitchen continues to a private chamber above with a fireplace on the W wall and enjoying the benefit of the heat from the kitchen chimney. Above this, another chamber with a fireplace on its S wall.

Former LOCHRANZA FREE CHURCH. Free Arts and Crafts of c. 1905, in roughly coursed whin, with red sandstone dressings. Not without character: the architect deserves to be known. Gabled, with a tall transeptal projection, formerly the porch. Circular E window with four cusped circles within; three-light W window, now altered. The N elevation originally had three pointed windows, but now altered for a door, and a catslide dormer introduced above the l. window. – Original cast-iron GATEPIERS by *A. & J. Main & Co.*, of Glasgow, London and Dublin. Converted as a house c. 1990.

ST BRIDE'S CHURCH. The island's oldest church still in use. A simple harled and gabled preaching box of 1712, by *James Strong*, mason, for the Hamiltons. It replaced the medieval building, and the N and E walls are repaired medieval masonry, but those on the S and W rebuilt; a late C17 tombstone with skull and cross-bones re-set in the E wall. Further changes c. 1835, include the pedimented round-headed N windows, the gabled W addition, and the open cast-iron bellcote. The circular E window is probably contemporary. The S windows suggest that the pulpit was on this wall, but if so, the church has been reordered internally and now has an E 'chancel'; the walls and coved roof all boarded. Simple pews, said to date from 1835, and equally unassuming PULPIT. – STAINED GLASS. E window, a three-masted sailing ship with a border of knotted rope, 1931, in memory of the Rev. John Colville. – Two from the former Free Church (*see* above), hung in frames, of 1917 by *J. & W. Guthrie & Wells*, to designs of *James Gordon Guthrie*. The subject is The Parable of the Talents, though the attitudes of the grouped figures suggest that a central panel has been lost. The groups of figures include images of the donor and her husband (Archibald Kerr †1900) based on photographs. – Tidy KIRKYARD with many neatly lettered headstones from the C18 and C19. The well-constructed LYCHGATE, 1931, is also a memorial to Colville.

LOCHRANZA FIELD STUDIES CENTRE, immediately SE of St Bride's. 1975–9 by *A. D. Holmes & McDonald*, with at its core the much-altered mid-C19 village SCHOOL, of two storeys, with finialled dormers.

DESCRIPTION. The heart of the village extends for about 1.4 km. NW from St Bride's, running along the S side of the loch as far as the sheet-piled ferry pier, 2003.* Early cottages mingle with mid-C19 houses and the bigger, brasher villas of *c.* 1900. Some are individually noted below, but in Lochranza the village is more than the sum of the parts, especially when seen from across the loch, providing with the hills behind an excellent backdrop for the castle.

Across the road from St Bride's is a BARKING HOUSE, in ruinous condition. This is early C19, stone-built, with later red sandstone steps giving access to the upper storey on the S side. In it, fishing nets and bark were steeped together in vats to prevent mould forming on the nets (cf. Catacol). Further on, where the road begins to open to the loch, is LOCHRANZA YOUTH HOSTEL, formerly a hotel, set in spacious grounds, of 1893–5 by *John Burnet, Son & Campbell*, that is to say by *J. J. Burnet* (with *Alexander Wingate* as assistant), for the Duke of Hamilton, and originally intended to be larger.** Asymmetrically laid out, with slated roofs, harled white walls on a rubble base, and many small-paned windows with red sandstone dressings; this is the style which proved so influential in the design of all the estate's buildings. Beyond are the soulless LOCHRANZA AND CATACOL VILLAGE HALL, 2000–1, a row of mostly mid-C19 cottages, the former Free Church (*see* above) and, much further, on THE OLD ANCHORAGE. This is one of the earliest cottages, an unspoilt late C18 harled range of two parts, that to the r. set back and lower, possibly slightly later and used as a tenant's summer house. Mid-C19 gabled rustic porch with tree-trunk supports.

Beyond this the mostly larger houses of the late C19 and early C20, often set well back from the road in spacious grounds. BENVAREN, of 1911, is the best of these villas, harled with red dressings, with a stepped and panelled wall-head

* The original pier of 1887–8 by *D. & T. Stevenson* was of concrete and timber. It closed in 1971.
** Burnet exhibited the plans at the 1894 Royal Scottish Academy.

chimney, and its entrance set back to the r. Here the steep hillside relents a little, allowing a short second tier of buildings above the road, including the former FREE CHURCH MANSE, of *c.* 1860, its porch with columns of Aberdeen granite. The ferry pier marks the end of the village.

In NEWTON ROAD, running along the N side of the loch, THE LODGE is a neatly proportioned house of *c.* 1790, with three bays of small windows, although the upper windows are bigger, suggesting that the house was originally single-storey. Its single-storey mid-C19 wing has a canted bay window in red sandstone of *c.* 1895.

ISLE OF ARRAN DISTILLERY, 0.8 km. SE. 1996–7 by *David Hutchison & Associates* of Glasgow. Harled, with two hipped roofs rising to ventilators, an unfussy reworking of the traditional distillery form. Contemporary touches are provided by the tall windows which allow sight of the copper stills within, and the adjacent VISITOR CENTRE, also harled with an apical ventilator.

LOCHRANZA WATER TREATMENT WORKS, 0.8 km. SE. *c.* 2002, and trying hard to look like an early C19 courtyard farm. Harled, with thin slates; the major openings with exposed quoins.

SALT PANS, Cock of Arran, 0.3 km. NE. In a remote location close to the N tip of the island, the remains of C18 salt pans include the footings and lower courses of a number of rectangular houses, probably domestic in character.

MACHRIE

An amorphous settlement on the W side of the island overlooking Machrie Bay.

MACHRIE BAY HALL, overlooking the sea on the coast road, is of *c.* 1930. Built as a village hall, tearoom and golf clubhouse for the links above the beach. Harled brick with a hipped slated roof and two gabled projections on the front. DUNEDIN, 0.6 km. N, is a red sandstone house of *c.* 1895, very much in the estate office's idiom of that period, with big bargeboarded gables, the bargeboards widening to the base in the manner of the nearby boathouse at Dougarie (q.v.). Gabled porch to the r. supported by tree trunks.

MACHRIE MOOR FARM, 1.3 km. SE.* Two-storey mid-C19 Scots Baronial red sandstone L-plan farmhouse, with a crowstepped porch, crowstepped gables and little bartizans at the angles. In the re-entrant angle, a circular tower with a conical slated roof and cast-iron finial.

AUCHENCAR, 2 km. N. Pre-improvement settlement, mostly single-storey cottages. Among these, ROSEMOUNT, of *c.* 1900 in the Burnetian Arts and Crafts idiom.

---

* Distances and directions are given from the Machrie Bay Hall.

POSTBOX, 4 km. E at the junction of the String Road near Glaister Bridge (first constructed 1817 to plans of *Thomas Telford*) with the minor road to Machrie. Built *c.* 1864 by *David Wilson*, said to have been provided to expedite the movement of mail to and from Dougarie Lodge (q.v.). A dumpy stone casing enlivened by a variety of deep carvings, some based on masons' marks, some seeming to emulate mythical beasts, others wholly abstract.

DOUGARIE LODGE. *See* p. 699.

MACHRIE MOOR. A very special place in the Arran landscape, if 4 not the whole of western Scotland, a low-lying topographical bowl hemmed in on virtually every side by a distant rim of craggy mountains and lower hills, which for at least three millennia was a focus for not only burial and ritual, but also settlement and agriculture. The approach to the STONE CIRCLES is via a track from the coast road. The first encountered (known as Moss Farm) is not so much spectacular as unusual, comprising a flat-topped cairn some 19 m. in diameter and a stone kerb which includes slabs up to 1.7 m. high. None of the other monuments on the moor are quite like it, though another large cairn at Auchagallon, about 2 km. N, also incorporates a ring of relatively tall stones in its kerb, including a broad slab set between two taller pillars looking W over the sea to Kintyre that resonates with the architecture of stone circles in Aberdeenshire; the Moss Farm cairn is too disturbed to say whether it too had an equivalent feature. Passing on E, the track wends between several hut circles, a small standing stone set upright on the crest of a rise to the N, the remains of a robbed chambered tomb across the fence to the S, and, hard on the track, what is probably another shattered chamber reduced to little more than two slabs, before dropping down to another unusual circle above Moss Farm itself. Apparently two concentric circles, this is another monument with architectural features that are found much further afield (e.g. Croft Moraig, Perthshire). Rather than a free-standing circle of stones, the outer ring here is almost certainly the kerb of a platform measuring about 19 m. in overall diameter and enclosing an inner ring about 12 m. in diameter. Comprising eight rounded granite boulders, these are clearly graded in height, the taller being two pairs opposing each other along an axis lying NE and SW, though one of the two on the SW is now fallen. The matrix of the platform has been entirely robbed, but this probably formed a continuous surface across the interior of the inner ring. Excavations in 1861 uncovered a rifled stone cist at the centre.

Standing at this monument the eye is immediately drawn eastwards to the other circles on the moorland beyond the ruined farm, though the nearest is an altogether more subtle ring, now comprising four low granite boulders that are almost lost amongst the rushes. These are certainly not set out to form the corners of a square or trapeze in the way of other four-poster settings elsewhere, and it is possible that other stones have been removed from the circumference. At the centre, though nothing is visible today, a cist containing a food vessel and a bronze awl was discovered in 1861. The contrast between this ring and that lying due N could not be more complete. Originally comprising nine stones, the sole one of the latter intact is a massive slab standing no less than 4.3 m. high, but the stumps of another three can also be seen. In 1861 two cists were discovered in its centre. The clue to the fate of such massive stones is provided by the next circle, where the silhouette of the three surviving stones, the tallest over 5 m. high, has become an iconic image for Scottish stone circles. Originally comprising seven or eight, the two discarded millstones lying beside them tell their own story. Nevertheless, excavation here in 1861 revealed a cist containing a food vessel at the centre, while a second cist lay to its NE.

The last two circles, diameters measuring about 13.5 m. and up to 14.5 m. respectively, have never had the stature of these last two, indeed their stones have barely projected above the mantle of later peat. They are no less important, however, for excavation in 1985–6 revealed a dimension of the complex that would otherwise be missing: beneath both were timber predecessors. The larger and south-western of the two circles is strictly speaking an ellipse, comprising eleven stones which alternate between rounded granite boulders and slighter sandstone slabs. The symmetry of the ring is broken on the NE, facing its neighbour, where a sandstone slab seems to be missing and a pit located where it might have stood was filled with sand rather than packing. In contrast the NE ring has ten stones, all but one of which are of sandstone, the exception being a granite boulder on the NE. As with the axis of the ring above Moss Farm, these anomalies on the NE are almost certainly deliberate features of their architecture, though their significance is now lost to us. The stone circles had been erected directly above their timber precursors, so much so that they might be conceived of as straightforward replacements, but the excavation revealed that the stone-holes had been cut through a tilled soil which covered the earlier post-holes. Furthermore, a complex series of stake fence-lines and ploughmarks showed that this soil had been cultivated over an extended period. The north-eastern timber circle comprised a single ring of ten timbers, and where impressions of the posts survived they were of the order of 0.3 m. thick. The south-western was more complex, comprising two roughly concentric rings around a horseshoe-shaped arrangement of five timbers facing NW. These timbers were probably about 0.5 m. in diameter, and ramps had been dug down one side of each post-hole to facilitate their erection; this implies that they were of considerable height. The sixty-three posts that made up the inner ring enclosing them, which at 14.5 m. was almost exactly the same diameter as its stone successor, were up to 0.2 m. in diameter, while those of the outer, lying about 2.5 m. further out, were a maximum of 0.15 m. Reconstructing this monument architecturally poses several problems, but taking our cue from the stone structures, these were open enclosures in which the timbers of the inner ring were probably taller than those of the outer, while the inner setting was evidently significantly taller again and clearly the focus of the design.

CAIRN and STONE CIRCLE, Auchagallon, 0.5 km. N. This imposing mound of stones fills the interior of a circle of standing stones which includes two of the tallest standing to either side of a lower slab to form a curious setting on the W looking out across the sea towards Kintyre. The mound itself, however, is possibly no more than the result of clearance from the adjacent fields.

PIRNMILL

8040

Small community on the W of the island, which has its origins in an early C19 MILL exploiting the abundant local timber to provide 'pirns' (bobbins) for the thread mills of Paisley.

PIRNMILL CHURCH. Well-cared-for tin tabernacle of c. 1920, originally for the Free Church, but now Church of Scotland. – BELL by *John C. Wilson*, 1859, said to have come from a Glasgow church. Erected here, 2008, the frame by *Simon Horne*.

Former UNITED FREE CHURCH, now residential. 1910. Harled with red sandstone dressings and mostly square-headed openings. A four-centred window in the W gable. In the garden, a granite MONUMENT to John Kennedy (†1910), with hexagonal shaft and Celtic cross finial.

PIRNMILL PRIMARY SCHOOL. T-plan, with one exposed rubble mid-C19 arm; the remainder harled, with red dressings, and dated 1912.

MID THUNDERGUY, 2.2 km. N. Atmospheric pre-improvement settlement, with one- and two-storey cottages haphazardly juxtaposed. At the S end, WELLSIDE, an urbane house of 1929, which uses traditional Arran elements.

HAZELWOOD FARM, Imachar, 4 km. S. Coursed rubble house, late C19, with unusual fireclay dressings and octagonal glazing. The rear steading mixes locally quarried stone, field boulders, brick and other stone in a melange that reflects the economic realities of a remote rural environment.

BURIAL GROUND, Lenimore, 3 km. N. Early C19 burial ground surrounded by a decayed low stone wall. Mostly C19 memorials, including that to John Brown †1855, carved by *W. Blackley* of Saltcoats:

> HIS IDEAS WERE RICH, EDIFYING AND HEAVENLY
> AND OF LATE YEARS ESPECIALLY HIS ADDRESSES &
> PRAYERS
> GREW MORE SEARCHING AND LIVELY
> BETOKENING THAT HE WAS DRAWING NEAR HIS
> HEAVENLY HOME

0010
PLADDA

Small, low, comma-shaped island off the S coast.

PLADDA LIGHTHOUSE. 1790, by *Thomas Smith*, engineer; the first built for the Commissioners of Northern Lights in the Clyde. A 29-m.-tall circular brick tower, now painted. The light was originally a fixed light, and a lower auxiliary light, also circular and brick, was added in 1800 by *Robert Stevenson* to avoid confusion with other lighthouses. The upper light was converted to a flashing light in 1901, and automated in 1990. The single-storey keepers' houses, flat-roofed with tall stacks, were added in 1826 by *Stevenson*.

0030
ROSABURN

Not a settlement as such, but the N end of the straggle round Brodick Bay, a link between the village and the castle.

ISLE OF ARRAN HERITAGE MUSEUM. Converted 1976–83 from the buildings of Rosaburn Farm. These are late C18–mid-C19 and typify the small Arran farm; mostly single-storey buildings, of painted stone and slated. At the W end the main FARM building (now café and exhibition space) is parallel to, and set back from, the road. Probably late C18, with small dressed openings, and late C19 hipped dormers on the rear; original main elevation, with its simple gabled and finialled porch. To its N the mid-C19 gabled ROADSIDE COTTAGE projects forward. It has end stacks and one original fireplace. Between the farm and cottage is the former SMIDDY, built *c.* 1860, and SHOEING SHED, a conversion (after 1856) of a school of 1779; both have earth and cobbled floors. Adjoining is a sandstone WATER FOUNTAIN of *c.* 1875 with a granite bowl, by *Thomas Kennedy* of Kilmarnock, originally at Brodick Pier, as were the cast-iron GATES to the E, by *A. & J. Main & Co. Ltd* of Glasgow. Opposite, a two-storey late C19 former stable and cartshed, later converted as a COTTAGE, now restored to show a typical early C20 Arran domestic interior. Timber-framed walls are filled with sandstone rubble. The parlour has lath-and-plaster walls and ceiling, an open fire with a swee, and a box bed; the walls and ceilings of the kitchen are boarded; it has an open range with a small oven. On the upper floor, a bedroom with a simple plaster ceiling and papered walls. Also shown are the wash house and milk house. To the l. of the cottage is the former late C19 STABLE and COACHHOUSE (now exhibition space) retaining original details such as the wooden stalls, although the cobbled floor has been concealed. In the grounds, the remarkable wooden DUNCAN THOMSON MEMORIAL SEAT of 1964 by *David Gilbert*. It originally stood at the summit of the Brodick to Lamlash Road. Three gargantuan seat backs, irregularly shaped, carved to represent the Sun, the Cross of Christ and a Hand. Also exhibited is a brightly painted wooden BATHING HUT, one of those which were used on Brodick Beach in the mid C20, after the Brodick Improvement Trust imposed a unified design on the hut operators in 1929.

ROSA BRIDGE. 0.4 km. NW. Mid-C19 two-arch stone bridge with polished voussoirs, low parapets and triangular cutwaters. Immediately SW of the bridge a low stone WALL, dated 1898, provides a water trough for horses and a drinking fountain for their masters, with a stone bowl and head.

ARRAN ESTATE OFFICE, 0.5 km. NW. Formerly the manse for Brodick, becoming the estate office in 1932. It belongs in the late C19 Burnet-inspired tradition also seen at Whitehouse Lodge, Lamlash, and Lamlash Church Hall (qq.v.): L-plan, red sandstone, the roof rising from the outer edges of the many square-cornered bay windows, creating a wide eaves overhang between them. Decorative ridge tiles, and tall slender stone stacks. To the l. a two-storey hipped wing, also with ridge tiles; the upper floor has a large canted window, more suited to a racecourse grandstand.

GLENSHURIG CEMETERY, 0.6 km. NW. Possibly C18 in origin, with a much-reduced low stone wall, and now forming an oasis amid the surrounding woodland. Mostly C19 and C20 monuments, a riot of moss and lichen. The MONUMENT to the artist John Adams-Acton (†1910) is a tall Celtic cross with decorative carved panels on the shaft.*

GREYHOLME, 0.3 km. SE. 1938 by *William J. Gibson* of Glasgow. Unusual L-plan house, clad in roughly cut timber boards, with a shingled gabled roof, pegged bargeboards and brick stacks. The whole is raised up on brick columns, with the entrance approached by a flight of steps, a veranda at one gable, and a timber porch at another. The door flanked by panels of naturalistic blue tiles.

SANNOX

Small village on the island's NE coast, where the glen of the Sannox Burn meets the sea; little more than a few late C19 paired villas enjoying the views across one of the island's best beaches. Sannox has an industrial past, with important barytes mines in Glen Sannox that opened in 1840, but were closed *c.* 1860 by the protectionist 11th Duke of Hamilton, as they 'spoilt the solemn grandeur of the scene.' Reopened after the First World War, when the present simple stone PIER was built, but closed again by 1938.

SANNOX CONGREGATIONAL CHURCH. Built 1822, following successful evangelizing among the local crofters by James Haldane and John Campbell, itinerant preachers. Simple

---

*Adams-Acton spent his summers at Ormidale, Brodick (q.v.).

gabled harled church with polished dressings, and attached manse. It occupies a poignant place in the emotive history of the Clearances in Arran as the bulk of the congregation emigrated to Canada in 1829, building, it is said, a similar church in their new homeland. The church has an elaborate ogee-headed wooden W bellcote and a gabled porch with pointed-headed openings, including a S door tucked tight against the main gable wall. The manse occupies the E end; it has a gabled porch, flanked by square-headed windows smaller than those of the church, and big late C19 gabled dormers. The church interior is plastered, with a coved wooden ceiling and wood-lined window reveals. Simple furnishings include a Gothic PULPIT with a semicircular head, raked PEWS and a stone and bronze FONT of c. 1917. Windows with small-pane margins. Sharing the church's enclosure is DUNDARROCH COTTAGE, also early C19, harled, originally a stable, subsequently altered to provide accommodation for the minister's family. Restored, with a mansarded roof, 1977.

SANNOX CEMETERY, 0.4 km. SW. Walled enclosure, its current appearance early C20, but an ancient burial site, with the vestigial remains of St Michael's Chapel, recorded in the C14 as a daughter chapel of Kilwinning Abbey.

CORRIE GOLF CLUB. 0.3 km. NW. The club was formed in 1892; jolly wood and corrugated-iron CHANGING AND WAITING ROOM presumably of that date. It has gable finials and a veranda of wooden columns linked by gently curving braces.

SANNOX BRIDGE, 0.2 km. W. Late C19. Two arches with polished voussoirs and low curving parapets. Flat concrete carriageway. Immediately S, SONABURN, a house of 1927, faintly *Moderne* Arts and Crafts, brick harled with a big asymmetrical gable, tiled roofs and round-headed brick entrance. Substantially extended, c. 1998, in a congruous manner.

SANNOX HOUSE. Standard early C19 harled farmhouse, two storeys and three bays with a three-bay shallow bow addition to the E. Painted dressings and a simple panelled doorcase with rosettes at angles, entablature above with blocking course stepped forward at the centre. Rear gabled extensions. Adjacent to N, an enclosed FARM COURT, single-storey, painted rubble with slate roofs.

WOODSIDE COTTAGE, 0.2 km. N. Harled three-bay cottage of c. 1840, originally thatched, with painted margins, flat gabled dormers and a late C19 hipped wooden porch. Odd gable detail, as though the harl has been applied over bargeboards.

SHISKINE

The village, also called Shedog or Shedock, originally grew in the early C19, especially after the String Road was completed in 1817. It became the main centre for this corner of the island and remains sizeable, even though shops and services are now largely in Blackwaterfoot. Easily the least 'touristy' of the island villages, and with the finest church.

St Molios. At the s end of the village by the road. 1888–90 by *J. J. Burnet* of *John Burnet Son & Campbell*. Mixed Roman-esque and Late Gothic, a more successful combination of these styles than the slightly earlier and smaller Corrie Church (q.v.). Its motifs, notably the porch and tower, reappear in the suc-cession of mainland churches, such as St Geraldine's Loss-iemouth and Broomhill Trinity (Glasgow), that Burnet designed over the next twenty years. Red sandstone exterior, with a red tiled roof and plentiful woodwork. Broad gabled nave and chancel, the roof sweeping down over the s aisle, SE 'transept', and squat square w tower that has a machicolated parapet, buttresses and a low pyramidal tiled roof. Paired Romanesque bell-openings, narrow square-headed stair lights. Inserted in the SW buttress is a carved limestone SCULPTURE (claimed to be St Molios) of a priest holding a chalice and shepherd's crook. It is probably C13 or C14, and may have come originally from Saddell Abbey (Argyll), but came via Clachan (*see* below), where it had covered the saint's reputed grave. Dominating gabled SW porch, which has a stone base and a band of small-paned glazing in wooden frames. Its heavy bargeboards taper outwards gradually to the bottom, with prominent pegging. The porch interior is panelled with an open pitched roof. Tall round-headed windows on the N eleva-tion, and two more in the E gable; tiny square-headed windows to the s. Little extraneous detail: a gargoyle on the N elevation, at the angle with the tower, oddly positioned and possibly unfinished; better the beautifully carved one, with beasts fight-ing, at the angle between tower and porch.

Magnificent INTERIOR with an elaborate scissor-truss roof over the nave; a pitched and braced roof in the aisle and a boarded barrel vault in the chancel. The roofs are supported on stone corbels and wooden pillars, and the nave arcade is formed of arched braces; all the woodwork is connected by prominent pegs, a true celebration of the joiner's craft. The chancel windows Romanesque, finely worked, the capitals and arches bristling with detail; those in the E wall with four marble columns. Flank-ing these, empty niches; below, panelled REREDOS and PULPIT with a coved head. The ends of the ELDERS' BENCHES resem-ble Celtic crosses, and are done in a darker wood; they are carved with the royal arms to the l., and an image of St Molios to the r. Simple contemporary PEWS. Small-pane glass in the windows, the border quarries delicately frosted. Only the ill-chosen modern light fittings detract. The entrance to the church grounds has one very large domed sandstone GATE-PIER, similar to those at Hamilton Terrace, Lamlash (q.v.).

SHISKINE FREE CHURCH, Torbeg, 1 km. NW. *c.* 1958, replacing a church of 1847. Simple brick harled and hipped hall. Entrance wing to the l., with a half-hipped roof. The door is protected by a tapering stone buttress that terminates in a tall, angular metal finial, an attractive and unusual feature, as is the end baluster of the handrail, shaped like a shepherd's crook. Adjacent is the three-bay two-storey MANSE of *c.* 1850, with a pilastered doorway. At the road junction immediately s of the church, MONUMENT to Rev. Archibald Nicol †1876, base, plinth, obelisk and foliated cross. Carved by *Cumming* of Ardrossan. 0.3 km. s from here, SHISKINE HALL, of 1910 as Torbeg United Free Church, converted to present use *c.* 1958. Gabled, and now harled, with painted dressings.

SHISKINE PRIMARY SCHOOL, 0.2 km. NE. The original gabled school late C19, extended in 1900 (gabled with a ball finial) and *c.* 1963 (mostly white-harled and single-storey).

SHISKINE WAR MEMORIAL, 0.9 km. SW. 1922, by *David Cumming* of Ardrossan. Granite, crossed rifles carved on an irregularly shaped and roughly hewn shaft.

The village itself is mostly C20. Worthy of individual note at the N end of the village are HAMILTON HOUSE, a crisply presented early C19 three-bay stone house with painted dressings and two dormers, extended in 1888, and the grey-harled INGLEWOOD, of *c.* 1925, whose main (s) front has a large conically roofed semicircular bow to the r., while its crow-stepped return elevation features a window in an odd etiolated surround.

BALMICHAEL FARM VISITOR CENTRE, 2.3 km. NE. Converted mid-C19 farm buildings. Two-storey farmhouse, with the offices arranged around the rear courtyard. The buildings have mostly been altered, but the BYRE retains its cobbled floor, central drain and one stall, while the MILL has preserved its iron overshot wheel and other machinery.

CLACHAN CEMETERY, 1.8 km. NE. Adjacent are the rather stark remains of the CHURCH of 1805, succeeded by St Molios in 1889. The walls, with round-headed openings, survive only to wall-head height.

SLIDDERY

Small roadside settlement at the SW corner of the island. The former SCHOOL was built *c.* 1860 by the estate, and commended for both its generous specifications and the philanthropy of the Duke; single-storey school house and two-storey master's house.

DUN, Corriecravie, 1.6 km. WNW. Known as Torr a' Chaisteil. Of the Roman Iron Age. Roughly circular, measuring at least 23 m. in diameter over the footing of a wall about 4 m. in thickness. It stands eccentrically on the summit of a knoll on the coastal escarpment below the road, while a bank on the E lip of the summit is possibly the remains of an outwork protecting the easiest line of approach.

WHITING BAY

A convenient and sheltered landing place where a small community began to grow in the early C19, particularly on the lands of the North, Mid and South Kiscadale townships. Improving road connections (the shore road was laid out in 1843; the earlier road took a higher, inland, route through the townships) and timetabled steamer services from Glasgow led to slow growth in the mid and late C19, before development was accelerated by the opening of a pier in 1899 (demolished in 1964). Contemporary Whiting Bay stretches (in places, it straggles) for over 2 km. along the shore, while the gentle slopes behind have allowed development behind the shore road, up to and beyond the original road.

Former PARISH CHURCH, Shore Road. 1873, by *Thomas Wallace* of Ardrossan. Simple Gothic with an E bellcote, and corner buttresses with gabled fleur-de-lis pinnacles. Nearby is the former SCHOOL, which became the manse. Of two builds: the lower block to the r., probably originally the schoolroom, is lower and plainer, with an entrance in the N gable; the other has a central gabled dormer above a window with a pentice head. Prettily bargeboarded S porch.

ST MARGARET (Episcopal). 1963, by *Eric Shilton*, as a Free Church; it was subsequently a house, before reopening as a church *c.* 1995. Gabled and harled, domestically detailed, with an E porch. – STAINED GLASS. 1996 by *Eilidh Keith* of Glasgow, figurative.

Behind the church, the severe gabled grey sandstone former MANSE, of 1877–8, perhaps by *James Hamilton*, architect of the original Free Church (1874) on this site.

WHITING BAY AND KILDONAN PARISH CHURCH, at the N end of the village. 1910 by *John Russell Thomson*, as the Stewart Memorial U.F. Church. Arts and Crafts Gothic in partially harled red sandstone, orientated N–S, with N transepts and a SE tower added in 1920 (and restored by *ARP Lorimer & Associates*, 2008). Three-light S gable window with panel tracery, above a projecting gabled porch with a segmentally headed entrance under a moulded head. Buttressed side bays have three-light square-headed windows. Stepped lancets in the transepts. The tower has stepped corner buttresses, wide segmental bell-openings, a castellated parapet and a spirelet. Light and spacious plastered interior, with an open pitched wooden roof, divided into bays by big curving braces, supported on simple stone corbels. The seasonal fluctuation in congregation has been acknowledged: behind the paired segmental stone transept arches, folding screen doors which can close off the transepts when necessary. Prettily finialled PULPIT, contemporary with the church. – STAINED GLASS. Four Seasons by *Christian Shaw*, 1997. – MANSE, of 1920. Pared down Arts and Crafts. – Rough-hewn granite WAR MEMORIAL, *c.* 1920, its polished front face with a bas-relief rifle and laurel wreath.

123 WHITING BAY PRIMARY SCHOOL, Shore Road. 1963–7 by *Baron Bercott & Associates* of Glasgow for Bute County Council (*George Horspool*, project architect). Dramatic and eyecatching, unlike most schools of this date, and sensitively scaled. To the road, three low pitch-roofed classrooms in a row, composed into a dynamic pattern of superimposed triangles and diamond shapes. At right angles, to the l., is a larger triangle, forming the wall and roof of a play shelter. To the r. the narrow windows of the headteacher's room and school office, and the tall harled wall of the hall, its monopitch roof sloping away behind. Main entrance to the rear, leading to a corridor which runs the length of the building, giving access to all the rooms, including the staff room (on the landward side, pupils may enjoy the view, but teachers must mark), and, at the s end, a simpler extension with a further classroom and school library.

WHITING BAY VILLAGE HALL, Shore Road. 1926, renovated 1999. Surprisingly large and burrowing gently into the slope behind, with two tiers of square-headed windows on the front and sides of tall windows and full-height buttresses. Set back to the r., a single-storey wing, resembling the pavilion at a seaside pitch-and-putt course.

The village has a good many early C20 houses, strung out along Shore Road, the best in harl and red sandstone. One especially good group of villas stretches s from the Parish Church and the former parish church (*see* above), including a trio of 1904–5 that includes BURLINGTON (now a hotel), of 1905 by *D. W. Sturrock*, with harled gables, a generous porch and a delicate canted oriel below the slightly advanced l. gable. The style and materials suggest he must have been the architect for the others (INVERMAY HOTEL and TERAGRAM) which flank it to N and S.

About 0.6 km. further s is the area known as THE SQUARE, with buildings that developed close to the pier opened in 1889; its waiting room survives as a shop (Pillar Box). Of the houses, a good example is CRAIGIELEA, a harled and slated Arts and Crafts house of *c.* 1903 built for himself by *William Logan*. Long horizontal bands of windows on the upper E-facing front, which overlooks sloping gardens and the sea. Close by on the W side of the road is the Village Hall (*see* above), and THE BUNGALOW, of *c.* 1925, brown sandstone with a castellated canted porch at one angle, at the other a bowed window with a big parapet and a mannered porch set back; one canted bay with an ogival leaded roof. GRANGE HOUSE is a severe L-plan house dated 1896, displaying a pair of tall gables to the road and a canted bay in the angle to their l. Scots Baronial dormerheads and tall paired stacks adorn the other elevations. Further on, set back, COORIEDOON (now a nursing home) has two elements, both of some distinction. To the r. a mid-C19 house, all finialled and bargeboarded gables, projecting and recessing restlessly. The part to the l. is dated 1900, Arts and Crafts in the restrained manner of James A. Morris of Ayr. It has a big central gable, a tall bay with a heavy parapet to the

r., and a flat-headed bay projecting from the return gable. To
the S, EDEN LODGE, dated 1903; three gable-headed half-
dormers on the S elevation, with the roof between them swept
unusually far out. Uphill, in SOUTH KISCADALE ROAD, THE
RIGGS, a red sandstone, harled and gabled Arts and Crafts
house of *c.* 1900, has a delicate stone, timber and slated semi-
octagonal porch, while SILVERHILL is a long semi-detached
pair of *c.* 1870, harled with end turrets and finialled dormers.

Further S on Shore Road, in spacious grounds, SILVER-
BANK, a neat hipped and rendered villa of *c.* 1830, demeaned
and devalued by modern glazing and the loss of its stacks.
Contemporary service court to the S. In MONTROSE TERRACE,
Bute County Council housing of *c.* 1950, harled with big swept-
down roofs (*see* also Park Road, Lamlash, and elsewhere on
the island). Furthest out, the lively LARGIEMHOR, of *c.* 1870,
with simply bargeboarded gables, swept-down roofs between
half-dormers, and penticed verandas either side of a glazed bay.
The architect *John MacNicol* died here in 1899; is the house
by him? On the hill above, ARDMHOR, a final Arts and Crafts
house of *c.* 1900, with a round-headed dormer and tapering
stack on the N elevation, the entrance on the E elevation under
a Florentine arch.

ARNHALL, off Shore Road's N end. A large and sumptuous Scots
Renaissance villa, built *c.* 1903 for the Port Glasgow shipbuilder William Hamilton, by *Macwhannell & Rogerson* of
Glasgow. Brown sandstone, broadly rectangular, with a NW
combined porch and portico, and a SE turret. Tiled roofs, with
exposed rafter-ends. The portico has two Doric columns, the
porch three tall windows to either side, all under a flat roof
with a dentil cornice. To the l. of this the stair windows; other
original windows are sash-and-case, single-pane below, with a
margin of small panes above. Most detail in the seaward-facing
E elevation, with the turret to one side, and a two-storey canted
bay under a gable with applied timber (now painted out) to
the other; between these a filigree cast-iron balcony and brackets. LODGE, on the road side.

AUCHENCAIRN, 0.8 km. NW. One of the townships dotted at
intervals along the original inland road. ROSE COTTAGE is
one of the few remaining C18 cottages on the island. It is of
painted stone, with a plain entrance and windows with painted
dressings on the S elevation, and further small windows and a
flat-roofed outshot to the rear (N) elevation. It lurches drunk-
enly with the slope, and has recently been restored, with a turf
roof from which project stone stacks with rudimentary
thackstanes.

DUN, Kingscross Point, 2 km. N on the rocky summit of the
headland at the mouth of the S entrance into Lamlash Bay.
Roman Iron Age. Roughly circular on plan, measuring about
19 m. in diameter over a wall about 3.5 m. in thickness. The
wall still stands over 1 m. high internally where it was exposed
by excavation in the early C20. At that time an elongated

mound immediately to the SW was also dug over, revealing evidence for a Viking age cremation associated with a few iron rivets, decorated whalebone and a coin of about AD 850. Measuring about 8.5 m. in length by up to 3.5 m. transversely overall, a low bank remains to mark the outline of the mound.

GLOSSARY

Numbers and letters refer to the illustrations (by John Sambrook) on pp. 738-745

ABACUS: flat slab forming the top of a capital (3a).

ACANTHUS: classical formalized leaf ornament (3b).

ACCUMULATOR TOWER: see Hydraulic power.

ACHIEVEMENT: a complete display of armorial bearings (i.e. coat of arms, crest, supporters and motto).

ACROTERION: plinth for a statue or ornament on the apex or ends of a pediment; more usually, both the plinth and what stands on it (4a).

ADDORSED: descriptive of two figures placed back to back.

AEDICULE (*lit.* little building): architectural surround, consisting usually of two columns or pilasters supporting a pediment.

AFFRONTED: descriptive of two figures placed face to face.

AGGREGATE: see Concrete, Harling.

AISLE: subsidiary space alongside the body of a building, separated from it by columns, piers or posts. Also (Scots) projecting wing of a church, often for special use, e.g. by a guild or by a landed family whose burial place it may contain.

AMBULATORY (*lit.* walkway): aisle around the sanctuary (q.v.).

ANGLE ROLL: roll moulding in the angle between two planes (1a).

ANSE DE PANIER: see Arch.

ANTAE: simplified pilasters (4a), usually applied to the ends of the enclosing walls of a portico (q.v.) *in antis*.

ANTEFIXAE: ornaments projecting at regular intervals above a Greek cornice, originally to conceal the ends of roof tiles (4a).

ANTHEMION: classical ornament like a honeysuckle flower (4b).

APRON: panel below a window or wall monument or tablet.

APSE: semicircular or polygonal end

of an apartment, especially of a chancel or chapel. In classical architecture sometimes called an *exedra*.

ARABESQUE: non-figurative surface decoration consisting of flowing lines, foliage scrolls etc., based on geometrical patterns. Cf. Grotesque.

ARCADE: series of arches supported by piers or columns. *Blind arcade* or *arcading*: the same applied to the wall surface. *Wall arcade*: in medieval churches, a blind arcade forming a dado below windows. Also a covered shopping street.

ARCH: Shapes *see* 5c. *Basket arch* or *anse de panier* (basket handle): three-centred and depressed, or with a flat centre. *Nodding*: ogee arch curving forward from the wall face. *Parabolic*: shaped like a chain suspended from two level points, but inverted.
Special purposes. *Chancel*: dividing chancel from nave or crossing. *Crossing*: spanning piers at a crossing (q.v.). *Relieving* or *discharging*: incorporated in a wall to relieve superimposed weight (5c). *Skew*: spanning responds not diametrically opposed. *Strainer*: inserted in an opening to resist inward pressure. *Transverse*: spanning a main axis (e.g. of a vaulted space). *See also* Jack arch, Overarch, Triumphal arch.

ARCHITRAVE: formalized lintel, the lowest member of the classical entablature (3a). Also the moulded frame of a door or window (often borrowing the profile of a classical architrave). For *lugged* and *shouldered* architraves *see* 4b.

ARCUATED: dependent structurally on the arch principle. Cf. Trabeated.

ARK: chest or cupboard housing the tables of Jewish law in a synagogue.

ARRIS: sharp edge where two surfaces meet at an angle (3a).

ASHLAR: masonry of large blocks wrought to even faces and square edges (6d). *Broached ashlar* (Scots): scored with parallel lines made by a narrow-pointed chisel (broach). *Droved ashlar*: similar but with lines made by a broad chisel.

ASTRAGAL: classical moulding of semicircular section (3f). Also (Scots) glazing-bar between window panes.

ASTYLAR: with no columns or similar vertical features.

ATLANTES: *see* Caryatids.

ATRIUM (plural: atria): inner court of a Roman or C20 house; in a multi-storey building, a toplit covered court rising through all storeys. Also an open court in front of a church.

ATTACHED COLUMN: *see* Engaged column.

ATTIC: small top storey within a roof. Also the storey above the main entablature of a classical façade.

AUMBRY: recess or cupboard, especially one in a church, to hold sacred vessels used for the Mass.

BAILEY: *see* Motte-and-bailey.

BALANCE BEAM: *see* Canals.

BALDACCHINO: freestanding canopy, originally fabric, over an altar. Cf. Ciborium.

BALLFLOWER: globular flower of three petals enclosing a ball (1a). Typical of the Decorated style.

BALUSTER: pillar or pedestal of bellied form. *Balusters*: vertical supports of this or any other form, for a handrail or coping, the whole being called a *balustrade* (6c). *Blind balustrade*: the same applied to the wall surface.

BARBICAN: outwork defending the entrance to a castle.

BARGEBOARDS (corruption of 'vergeboards'): boards, often carved or fretted, fixed beneath the eaves of a gable to cover and protect the rafters.

BARMKIN (Scots): wall enclosing courtyard attached to a tower house.

BARONY: *see* Burgh.

BAROQUE: style originating in Rome

c.1600 and current in England *c*.1680–1720, characterized by dramatic massing and silhouette and the use of the giant order.

BARROW: burial mound.

BARTIZAN: corbelled turret, square or round, frequently at an angle (8a).

BASCULE: hinged part of a lifting (or bascule) bridge.

BASE: moulded foot of a column or pilaster. For *Attic* base *see* 3b. For *Elided* base *see* Elided.

BASEMENT: lowest, subordinate storey; hence the lowest part of a classical elevation, below the piano nobile (q.v.).

BASILICA: a Roman public hall; hence an aisled building with a clerestory.

BASTION: one of a series of defensive semicircular or polygonal projections from the main wall of a fortress or city.

BATTER: intentional inward inclination of a wall face.

BATTLEMENT: defensive parapet, composed of *merlons* (solid) and *crenelles* (embrasures) through which archers could shoot (8a); sometimes called *crenellation*. Also used decoratively.

BAY: division of an elevation or interior space as defined by regular vertical features such as arches, columns, windows etc.

BAY LEAF: classical ornament of overlapping bay leaves (3f).

BAY WINDOW: window of one or more storeys projecting from the face of a building. *Canted*: with a straight front and angled sides. *Bow window*: curved. *Oriel*: rests on corbels or brackets and starts above ground level; also the bay window at the dais end of a medieval great hall.

BEAD-AND-REEL: *see* Enrichments.

BEAKHEAD: Norman ornament with a row of beaked bird or beast heads usually biting into a roll moulding (1a).

BEE-BOLL: wall recess to contain a beehive.

BELFRY: chamber or stage in a tower where bells are hung. Also belltower in a general sense.

BELL CAPITAL: *see* 1b.

BELLCAST: *see* Roof.

BELLCOTE: bell-turret set on a roof or gable. *Birdcage bellcote*: framed structure, usually of stone.

BERM: level area separating a ditch from a bank on a hillfort or barrow.

BILLET: Norman ornament of small half-cylindrical or rectangular blocks (1a).

BIVALLATE: of a hillfort: defended by two concentric banks and ditches.

BLIND: *see* Arcade, Baluster, Portico.

BLOCK CAPITAL: *see* 1a.

BLOCKED: columns etc. interrupted by regular projecting blocks (*blocking*), as on a Gibbs surround (4b).

BLOCKING COURSE: course of stones, or equivalent, on top of a cornice and crowning the wall.

BÖD: *see* Bü.

BOLECTION MOULDING: covering the joint between two different planes (6b).

BOND: the pattern of long sides (*stretchers*) and short ends (*headers*) produced on the face of a wall by laying bricks in a particular way (6e).

BOSS: knob or projection, e.g. at the intersection of ribs in a vault (2c).

BOW WINDOW: *see* Bay window.

BOX FRAME: timber-framed construction in which vertical and horizontal wall members support the roof. Also concrete construction where the loads are taken on cross walls; also called *cross-wall construction.*

BRACE: subsidiary member of a structural frame, curved or straight. *Bracing* is often arranged decoratively, e.g. quatrefoil, herringbone. *See also* Roofs.

BRATTISHING: ornamental crest, usually formed of leaves, Tudor flowers or miniature battlements.

BRESSUMER (*lit.* breast-beam): big horizontal beam supporting the wall above, especially in a jettied building.

BRETASCHE (*lit.* battlement): defensive wooden gallery on a wall.

BRICK: *see* Bond, Cogging, Engineering, Gauged, Tumbling.

BRIDGE: *Bowstring*: with arches rising above the roadway which is suspended from them. *Clapper*: one long stone forms the roadway. *Roving*: *see* Canal. *Suspension*: roadway suspended from cables or chains slung between towers or pylons. *Stay-suspension* or *stay-cantilever*: supported by diagonal

stays from towers or pylons. *See also* Bascule.

BRISES-SOLEIL: projecting fins or canopies which deflect direct sunlight from windows.

BROACH: *see* Spire and 1c.

BROCH (Scots): circular tower-like structure, open in the middle, the double wall of dry-stone masonry linked by slabs forming internal galleries at varying levels; found in W and N Scotland and mostly dating from between 100 B.C. and A.D. 100.

BÜ or BÖD (Scots, esp. Shetland; *lit.* booth): combined house and store.

BUCRANIUM: ox skull used decoratively in classical friezes.

BULLSEYE WINDOW: small oval window, set horizontally (cf. Oculus). Also called *oeil de boeuf.*

BURGH: formally constituted town with trading privileges. *Royal Burghs*: monopolized foreign trade till the C17 and paid duty to the Crown. *Burghs of Barony*: founded by secular or ecclesiastical barons to whom they paid duty on their local trade. *Police Burghs*: instituted after 1850 for the administration of new centres of population and abolished in 1975. They controlled planning, building etc.

BUT-AND-BEN (Scots, *lit.* outer and inner rooms): two-room cottage.

BUTTRESS: vertical member projecting from a wall to stabilize it or to resist the lateral thrust of an arch, roof or vault (1c, 2c). A *flying buttress* transmits the thrust to a heavy abutment by means of an arch or half-arch (1c).

CABLE or ROPE MOULDING: originally Norman, like twisted strands of a rope.

CAMES: *see* Quarries.

CAMPANILE: freestanding bell-tower.

CANALS: *Flash lock*: removable weir or similar device through which boats pass on a flush of water. Predecessor of the *pound lock*: chamber with gates at each end allowing boats to float from one level to another. *Tidal gates*: single pair of lock gates allowing vessels to pass when the tide makes a level. *Balance beam*: beam projecting horizontally for opening and closing lock gates. *Roving bridge*: carrying a towing path from one bank to the other.

CANDLE-SNUFFER ROOF: conical roof of a turret (8a).

CANNON SPOUT: *see* 8a.

CANTILEVER: horizontal projection (e.g. step, canopy) supported by a downward force behind the fulcrum.

CAPHOUSE (Scots): small chamber at the head of a turnpike stair, opening onto the parapet walk (8a). Also a chamber rising from within the parapet walk.

CAPITAL: head or crowning feature of a column or pilaster; for classical types *see* 3a; for medieval types *see* 1b.

CARREL: compartment designed for individual work or study, e.g. in a library.

CARTOUCHE: classical tablet with ornate frame (4b).

CARYATIDS: female figures supporting an entablature; their male counterparts are *Atlantes* (*lit.* Atlas figures).

CASEMATE: vaulted chamber, with embrasures for defence, within a castle wall or projecting from it.

CASEMENT: side-hinged window. Also a concave Gothic moulding framing a window.

CASTELLATED: with battlements (q.v.).

CAST IRON: iron containing at least 2.2 per cent of carbon, strong in compression but brittle in tension; cast in a mould to required shape, e.g. for columns or repetitive ornaments. *Wrought iron* is a purer form of iron, with no more than 0.3 per cent of carbon, ductile and strong in tension, forged and rolled into e.g. bars, joists, boiler plates; *mild steel* is its modern equivalent, similar but stronger.

CATSLIDE: *see* 7.

CAVETTO: concave classical moulding of quarter-round section (3f).

CELURE or CEILURE: enriched area of roof above rood or altar.

CEMENT: *see* Concrete.

CENOTAPH (*lit.* empty tomb): funerary monument which is not a burying place.

CENTRING: wooden support for the building of an arch or vault, removed after completion.

CHAMBERED TOMB: Neolithic burial mound with a stone-built chamber and entrance passage covered by an earthen barrow or stone cairn.

CHAMFER (*lit.* corner-break): surface formed by cutting off a square edge or corner. For types of chamfers and *chamfer stops see* 6a. *See also* Double chamfer.

CHANCEL: E end of the church containing the sanctuary; often used to include the choir.

CHANTRY CHAPEL: often attached to or within a church, endowed for the celebration of Masses principally for the soul of the founder.

CHECK (Scots): rebate.

CHERRY-CAULKING or CHERRY-COCKING (Scots): decorative masonry technique using lines of tiny stones (*pins* or *pinning*) in the mortar joints.

CHEVET (*lit.* head): French term for chancel with ambulatory and radiating chapels.

CHEVRON: V-shape used in series or double series (later) on a Norman moulding (1a). Also (especially when on a single plane) called *zigzag*.

CHOIR: the part of a church E of the nave, intended for the stalls of choir monks, choristers and clergy.

CIBORIUM: a fixed canopy over an altar, usually vaulted and supported on four columns; cf. Baldacchino.

CINQUEFOIL: *see* Foil.

CIST: stone-lined or slab-built grave.

CLACHAN (Scots): a hamlet or small village; also, a village inn.

CLADDING: external covering or skin applied to a structure, especially a framed one.

CLEARSTOREY: uppermost storey of the nave of a church, pierced by windows. Also high-level windows in secular buildings.

CLOSE (Scots): courtyard or passage giving access to a number of buildings.

CLOSER: a brick cut to complete a bond (6e).

CLUSTER BLOCK: *see* Multi-storey.

COADE STONE: ceramic artificial stone made in Lambeth 1769–*c.*1840 by Eleanor Coade (†1821) and her associates.

COB: walling material of clay mixed with straw.

COFFERING: arrangement of sunken panels (coffers), square or polygonal, decorating a ceiling, vault or arch.

COGGING: a decorative course of bricks laid diagonally (6e). Cf. Dentilation.

COLLAR: *see* Roofs and 7.

COLLEGIATE CHURCH: endowed for the support of a college of priests, especially for the saying of masses for the soul(s) of the founder(s).

COLONNADE: range of columns supporting an entablature. Cf. Arcade.

COLONNETTE: small column or shaft.

COLOSSAL ORDER: *see* Giant order.

COLUMBARIUM: shelved, niched structure to house multiple burials.

COLUMN: a classical, upright structural member of round section with a shaft, a capital and usually a base (3a, 4a).

COLUMN FIGURE: carved figure attached to a medieval column or shaft, usually flanking a doorway.

COMMENDATOR: receives the revenues of an abbey *in commendam* ('in trust') when the position of abbot is vacant.

COMMUNION TABLE: table used in Protestant churches for the celebration of Holy Communion.

COMPOSITE: *see* Orders.

COMPOUND PIER: grouped shafts (q.v.), or a solid core surrounded by shafts.

CONCRETE: composition of *cement* (calcined lime and clay), *aggregate* (small stones or rock chippings), sand and water. It can be poured into *formwork* or *shuttering* (temporary frame of timber or metal) on site (*in-situ* concrete), or *pre-cast* as components before construction. *Reinforced*: incorporating steel rods to take the tensile force. *Prestressed*: with tensioned steel rods. Finishes include the impression of boards left by formwork (*board-marked* or *shuttered*), and texturing with steel brushes (*brushed*) or hammers (*hammer-dressed*). *See also* Shell.

CONDUCTOR (Scots): down-pipe for rainwater; *see also* Rhone.

CONSOLE: bracket of curved outline (4b).

COPING: protective course of masonry or brickwork capping a wall (6d).

COOMB or COMB CEILING (Scots):

with sloping sides corresponding to the roof pitch up to a flat centre.

CORBEL: projecting block supporting something above. *Corbel course:* continuous course of projecting stones or bricks fulfilling the same function. *Corbel table*: series of corbels to carry a parapet or a wall-plate or wall-post (7). *Corbelling*: brick or masonry courses built out beyond one another to support a chimneystack, window etc. For *continuous* and *chequer-set* corbelling see 8a.

CORINTHIAN: *see* Orders and 3d.

CORNICE: flat-topped ledge with moulded underside, projecting along the top of a building or feature, especially as the highest member of the classical entablature (3a). Also the decorative moulding in the angle between wall and ceiling.

CORPS-DE-LOGIS: the main building(s) as distinct from the wings or pavilions.

COTTAGE ORNÉ: an artfully rustic small house associated with the Picturesque movement.

COUNTERSCARP BANK: low bank on the downhill or outer side of a hillfort ditch.

COUR D'HONNEUR: formal entrance court before a house in the French manner, usually with flanking wings and a screen wall or gates.

COURSE: continuous layer of stones etc. in a wall (6e).

COVE: a broad concave moulding, e.g. to mask the eaves of a roof. *Coved ceiling*: with a pronounced cove joining the walls to a flat central panel smaller than the whole area of the ceiling.

CRADLE ROOF: *see* Wagon roof.

CREDENCE: shelved niche or table, usually beside a piscina (q.v.), for the sacramental elements and vessels.

CRENELLATION: parapet with crenelles (*see* Battlement).

CRINKLE-CRANKLE WALL: garden wall undulating in a series of serpentine curves.

CROCKETS: leafy hooks. *Crocketing* decorates the edges of Gothic features, such as pinnacles, canopies etc. *Crocket capital*: see 1b.

CROSSING: central space at the junction of the nave, chancel and transepts. *Crossing tower*: above a crossing.

CROSS-WINDOW: with one mullion and one transom (qq.v.).

CROWN-POST: *see* Roofs and 7.

CROWSTEPS: squared stones set like steps, especially on a crowstepped gable (7, 8a).

CRUCKS (*lit.* crooked): pairs of inclined timbers (*blades*), usually curved, set at bay-lengths; they support the roof timbers and, in timber buildings, also support the walls. *Base*: blades rise from ground level to a tie-or collar-beam which supports the roof timbers. *Full*: blades rise from ground level to the apex of the roof, serving as the main members of a roof truss. *Jointed:* blades formed from more than one timber; the lower member may act as a wall-post; it is usually elbowed at wall-plate level and jointed just above. *Middle*: blades rise from halfway up the walls to a tie-or collar-beam. *Raised*: blades rise from halfway up the walls to the apex. *Upper*: blades supported on a tie-beam and rising to the apex.

CRYPT: underground or half-underground area, usually below the E end of a church. *Ring crypt*: corridor crypt surrounding the apse of an early medieval church, often associated with chambers for relics. Cf. Undercroft.

CUPOLA (*lit.* dome): especially a small dome on a circular or polygonal base crowning a larger dome, roof or turret. Also (Scots) small dome or skylight as an internal feature, especially over a stairwell.

CURSUS: a long avenue defined by two parallel earthen banks with ditches outside.

CURTAIN WALL: a connecting wall between the towers of a castle. Also a non-load-bearing external wall applied to a C20 framed structure.

CUSP: *see* Tracery and 2b.

CYCLOPEAN MASONRY: large irregular polygonal stones, smooth and finely jointed.

CYMA RECTA and CYMA REVERSA: classical mouldings with double curves (3f). Cf. Ogee.

DADO: the finishing (often with panelling) of the lower part of a wall in a classical interior; in origin a formalized continuous pedestal. *Dado rail*: the moulding along the top of the dado.

DAGGER: *see* Tracery and 2b.

DEC (DECORATED): English Gothic architecture *c.* 1290 to *c.* 1350. The name is derived from the type of window tracery (q.v.) used during the period.

DEMI- or HALF-COLUMNS: engaged columns (q.v.) half of whose circumference projects from the wall.

DENTIL: small square block used in series in classical cornices (3c). *Dentilation* is produced by the projection of alternating headers along cornices or stringcourses.

DIAPER: repetitive surface decoration of lozenges or squares flat or in relief. Achieved in brickwork with bricks of two colours.

DIOCLETIAN or THERMAL WINDOW: semicircular with two mullions, as used in the Baths of Diocletian, Rome (4b).

DISTYLE: having two columns (4a).

DOGTOOTH: E.E. ornament, consisting of a series of small pyramids formed by four stylized canine teeth meeting at a point (1a).

DOOCOT (Scots): dovecot. When freestanding, usually *Lectern* (rectangular with single-pitch roof) or *Beehive* (circular, diminishing towards the top).

DORIC: *see* Orders and 3a, 3b.

DORMER: window projecting from the slope of a roof (7). *Dormer head*: gable above a dormer, often formed as a pediment (8a).

DOUBLE CHAMFER: a chamfer applied to each of two recessed arches (1a).

DOUBLE PILE: *see* Pile.

DRAGON BEAM: *see* Jetty.

DRESSINGS: the stone or brickwork worked to a finished face about an angle, opening or other feature.

DRIPSTONE: moulded stone projecting from a wall to protect the lower parts from water. Cf. Hoodmould, Weathering.

DRUM: circular or polygonal stage supporting a dome or cupola. Also one of the stones forming the shaft of a column (3a).

DRY-STONE: stone construction without mortar.

DUN (Scots): small stone-walled fort.

DUTCH or FLEMISH GABLE: *see* 7.

EASTER SEPULCHRE: tomb-chest, usually within or against the N wall of a chancel, used in Holy Week ceremonies for reservation (entombment) of the sacrament after the mass of Maundy Thursday.

EAVES: overhanging edge of a roof; hence *eaves cornice* in this position.

ECHINUS: ovolo moulding (q.v.) below the abacus of a Greek Doric capital (3a).

EDGE RAIL: *see* Railways.

EDGE-ROLL: moulding of semi-circular section or more at the edge of an opening.

E.E. (EARLY ENGLISH): English Gothic architecture *c.* 1190–1250.

EGG-AND-DART: *see* Enrichments and 3f.

ELEVATION: any face of a building or side of a room. In a drawing, the same or any part of it, represented in two dimensions.

ELIDED: used to describe a compound feature, e.g. an entablature, with some parts omitted. Also, parts of, e.g., a base or capital, combined to form a larger one.

EMBATTLED: with battlements.

EMBRASURE: splayed opening in a wall or battlement (q.v.).

ENCAUSTIC TILES: earthenware tiles fired with a pattern and glaze.

EN DELIT: stone laid against the bed.

ENFILADE: reception rooms in a formal series, usually with all doorways on axis.

ENGAGED or ATTACHED COLUMN: one that partly merges into a wall or pier.

ENGINEERING BRICKS: dense bricks, originally used mostly for railway viaducts etc.

ENRICHMENTS: the carved decoration of certain classical mouldings, e.g. the ovolo with *egg-and-dart*, the cyma reversa with *waterleaf*, the astragal with *bead-and-reel* (3f).

ENTABLATURE: in classical architecture, collective name for the three horizontal members (architrave, frieze and cornice) carried by a wall or a column (3a).

ENTASIS: very slight convex deviation from a straight line, used to prevent an optical illusion of concavity.

ENTRESOL: mezzanine floor subdividing what is constructionally a single storey, e.g. a vault.

EPITAPH: inscription on a tomb or monument.

EXEDRA: *see* Apse.

EXTRADOS: outer curved face of an arch or vault.

EYECATCHER: decorative building terminating a vista.

FASCIA: plain horizontal band, e.g. in an architrave (3c, 3d) or on a shopfront.

FENESTRATION: the arrangement of windows in a façade.

FERETORY: site of the chief shrine of a church, behind the high altar.

FESTOON: ornamental garland, suspended from both ends. Cf. Swag.

FEU (Scots): land granted, e.g. by sale, by the *feudal superior* to the *vassal* or *feuar*, on conditions that usually include the annual payment of a fixed sum of *feu duty*. Any subsequent proprietor of the land becomes the feuar and is subject to the same obligations.

FIBREGLASS (or glass-reinforced polyester (GRP)): synthetic resin reinforced with glass fibre. GRC: glass-reinforced concrete.

FIELD: *see* Panelling and 6b.

FILLET: a narrow flat band running down a medieval shaft or along a roll moulding (1a). It separates larger curved mouldings in classical cornices, fluting or bases (3c).

FLAMBOYANT: the latest phase of French Gothic architecture, with flowing tracery.

FLASH LOCK: *see* Canals.

FLATTED: divided into apartments. Also with a colloquial (Scots) meaning: 'He stays on the first flat' means that he lives on the first floor.

FLÈCHE or SPIRELET (*lit.* arrow): slender spire on the centre of a roof.

FLEURON: medieval carved flower or leaf, often rectilinear (1a).

FLUSHWORK: knapped flint used with dressed stone to form patterns.

FLUTING: series of concave grooves (flutes), their common edges sharp (arris) or blunt (fillet) (3).

FOIL (*lit.* leaf): lobe formed by the cusping of a circular or other shape in tracery (2b). *Trefoil* (three), *quatrefoil* (four), *cinquefoil* (five) and *multifoil* express the number of lobes in a shape.

FOLIATE: decorated with leaves.

FORE-BUILDING: structure protecting an entrance.

FORESTAIR: external stair, usually unenclosed.

FORMWORK: *see* Concrete.

FRAMED BUILDING: where the structure is carried by a framework - e.g. of steel, reinforced concrete, timber - instead of by load-bearing walls.

FREESTONE: stone that is cut, or can be cut, in all directions.

FRESCO: *al fresco*: painting on wet plaster. *Fresco secco*: painting on dry plaster.

FRIEZE: the middle member of the classical entablature, sometimes ornamented (3a). *Pulvinated frieze* (*lit.* cushioned): of bold convex profile (3c). Also a horizontal band of ornament.

FRONTISPIECE: in C16 and C17 buildings the central feature of doorway and windows above linked in one composition.

GABLE: peaked external wall at end of double-pitch roof. For types *see* 7. Also (Scots): whole end wall of whatever shape. *Pedimental gable*: treated like a pediment.

GADROONING: classical ribbed ornament like inverted fluting that flows into a lobed edge.

GAIT or GATE (Scots): street, usually with a prefix indicating use, direction or destination.

GALILEE: chapel or vestibule usually at the W end of a church enclosing the main portal(s).

GALLERY: a long room or passage; an upper storey above the aisle of a church, looking through arches to the nave; a balcony or mezzanine overlooking the main interior space of a building; or an external walkway.

GALLETING: small stones set in a mortar course.

GAMBREL ROOF: *see* 7.

GARDEROBE: medieval privy.

GARGOYLE: projecting water spout, often carved into human or animal shape. For cannon spout *see* 8.

GAUGED or RUBBED BRICKWORK: soft brick sawn roughly, then rubbed to a precise (gauged) surface. Mostly used for door or window openings (5c).

GAZEBO (jocular Latin, 'I shall gaze'): ornamental lookout tower or raised summer house.

GEOMETRIC: English Gothic architecture *c.* 1250–1310. *See also* Tracery. For another meaning, *see* Stairs.

GIANT or COLOSSAL ORDER: classical order (q.v.) whose height is that of two or more storeys of the building to which it is applied.

GIBBS SURROUND: C18 treatment of an opening (4b), seen particularly in the work of James Gibbs (1682–1754).

GIRDER: a large beam. *Box*: of hollow-box section. *Bowed*: with its top rising in a curve. *Plate*: of I-section, made from iron or steel plates. *Lattice*: with braced framework.

GLACIS: artificial slope extending out and downwards from the parapet of a fort.

GLAZING-BARS: wooden or sometimes metal bars separating and supporting window panes.

GLAZING GROOVE: groove in a window surround into which the glass is fitted.

GNOMON: vane or indicator casting a shadow onto a sundial.

GRAFFITI: *see* Sgraffito.

GRANGE: farm owned and run by a religious order.

GRC: *see* Fibreglass.

GRISAILLE: monochrome painting on walls or glass.

GROIN: sharp edge at the meeting of two cells of a cross-vault; *see* Vault and 2b.

GROTESQUE (*lit.* grotto-esque): wall decoration adopted from Roman examples in the Renaissance. Its foliage scrolls incorporate figurative elements. Cf. Arabesque.

GROTTO: artificial cavern.

GRP: *see* Fibreglass.

GUILLOCHE: classical ornament of interlaced bands (4b).

GUNLOOP: opening for a firearm (8a).

GUSHET (Scots): a triangular or wedge-shaped piece of land or the corner building on such a site.

GUTTAE: stylized drops (3b).

HALF-TIMBERING: archaic term for timber-framing (q.v.). Sometimes used for non-structural decorative timberwork.

HALL CHURCH: medieval church with nave and aisles of approximately equal height. Also (Scots C20) building for use as both hall and church, the double function usually intended to be temporary until a separate church is built.

HAMMERBEAM: see Roofs and 7.

HARLING (Scots, *lit.* hurling): wet dash, i.e. a form of roughcasting in which the mixture of aggregate and binding material (e.g. lime) is dashed onto a wall.

HEADER: see Bond and 6e.

HEADSTOP: stop (q.v.) carved with a head (5b).

HELM ROOF: see 1C.

HENGE: ritual earthwork with a surrounding ditch and outer bank.

HERM (*lit.* the god Hermes): male head or bust on a pedestal.

HERRINGBONE WORK: see 6e (for brick bond). Cf. Pitched masonry.

HEXASTYLE: see Portico.

HILLFORT: Iron Age earthwork enclosed by a ditch and bank system.

HIPPED ROOF: see 7.

HOODMOULD: projecting moulding above an arch or lintel to throw off water (2b, 5b). When horizontal often called a *label*. For label stop see Stop.

HORIZONTAL GLAZING: with panes of horizontal proportions.

HORSEMILL: circular or polygonal farm building with a central shaft turned by a horse to drive agricultural machinery.

HUNGRY-JOINTED: see Pointing.

HUSK GARLAND: festoon of stylized nutshells (4b).

HYDRAULIC POWER: use of water under high pressure to work machinery. *Accumulator tower*: houses a hydraulic accumulator which accommodates fluctuations in the flow through hydraulic mains.

HYPOCAUST (*lit.* underburning): Roman underfloor heating system.

IMPOST: horizontal moulding at the springing of an arch (5c).

IMPOST BLOCK: block between abacus and capital (1b).

IN ANTIS: see Antae, Portico and 4a.

INDENT: shape chiselled out of a stone to receive a brass. Also, in restoration, new stone inserted as a patch.

INDUSTRIALIZED or SYSTEM BUILDING: system of manufactured units assembled on site.

INGLENOOK (*lit.* fire-corner): recess for a hearth with provision for seating.

INGO (Scots): the reveal of a door or window opening where the stone is at right angles to the wall.

INTERCOLUMNATION: interval between columns.

INTERLACE: decoration in relief simulating woven or entwined stems or bands.

INTRADOS: see Soffit.

IONIC: see Orders and 3c.

JACK ARCH: shallow segmental vault springing from beams, used for fireproof floors, bridge decks etc.

JAMB (*lit.* leg): one of the vertical sides of an opening. Also (Scots) wing or extension adjoining one side of a rectangular plan making it into an L-, T- or Z-plan.

JETTY: the projection of an upper storey beyond the storey below. In a stone building this is achieved by corbelling. In a timber-framed building it is made by the beams and joists of the lower storey oversailing the wall; on their outer ends is placed the sill of the walling for the storey above.

JOGGLE: the joining of two stones to prevent them slipping by a notch in one and a projection in the other.

KEEL MOULDING: moulding used from the late C12, in section like the keel of a ship (1a).

KEEP: principal tower of a castle.

KENTISH CUSP: see Tracery.

KEY PATTERN: see 4b.

KEYSTONE: central stone in an arch or vault (4b, 5c).

KINGPOST: see Roofs and 7.

KNEELER: horizontal projecting stone at the base of each side of a gable to support the inclined coping stones (7).

LABEL: see Hoodmould and 5b.

LABEL STOP: see Stop and 5b.

LACED BRICKWORK: vertical strips of brickwork, often in a contrasting colour, linking openings on different floors.

LACING COURSE: horizontal reinforcement in timber or brick to walls of flint, cobble etc.

LADE (Scots): channel formed to bring water to a mill; mill-race.

LADY CHAPEL: dedicated to the Virgin Mary (Our Lady).

LAIGH or LAICH (Scots): low.

LAIR (Scots): a burial space reserved in a graveyard

LAIRD (Scots): landowner.

LANCET: slender single-light, pointed-arched window (2a).

LANTERN: circular or polygonal windowed turret crowning a roof or a dome. Also the windowed stage of a crossing tower lighting the church interior.

LANTERN CROSS: churchyard cross with lantern-shaped top.

LAVATORIUM: in a religious house, a washing place adjacent to the refectory.

LEAN-TO: see Roofs.

LESENE (lit. a mean thing): pilaster without base or capital. Also called pilaster strip.

LIERNE: see Vault and 2c.

LIGHT: compartment of a window defined by the mullions.

LINENFOLD: Tudor panelling carved with simulations of folded linen.

LINTEL: horizontal beam or stone bridging an opening.

LOFT: gallery in a church. Organ loft: in which the organ, or sometimes only the console (keyboard), is placed. Laird's loft, Trades loft etc. (Scots): reserved for an individual or special group. See also Rood (loft).

LOGGIA: gallery, usually arcaded or colonnaded along one side; sometimes freestanding.

LONG-AND-SHORT WORK: quoins consisting of stones placed with the long side alternately upright and horizontal, especially in Saxon building.

LOUVRE: roof opening, often protected by a raised timber structure, to allow the smoke from a central hearth to escape. Louvres: overlapping boards to allow ventilation but keep the rain out.

LOWSIDE WINDOW: set lower than the others in a chancel side wall, usually towards its w end.

L-PLAN: see Tower house and 8b.

LUCARNE (lit. dormer): small gabled opening in a roof or spire.

LUCKENBOOTH (Scots): lock-up booth or shop.

LUGGED ARCHITRAVE: see 4b.

LUNETTE: semicircular window or blind panel.

LYCHGATE (lit. corpse-gate): roofed gateway entrance to a churchyard for the reception of a coffin.

LYNCHET: long terraced strip of soil on the downward side of prehistoric and medieval fields, accumulated because of continual ploughing along the contours.

MACHICOLATIONS (lit. mashing devices): series of openings between the corbels that support a projecting parapet through which missiles can be dropped (8a). Used decoratively in post-medieval buildings.

MAINS (Scots): home farm on an estate.

MANOMETER or STANDPIPE TOWER: containing a column of water to regulate pressure in water mains.

MANSARD: see 7.

MANSE: house of a minister of religion, especially in Scotland.

MARGINS (Scots): dressed stones at the edges of an opening. 'Back-set margins' (RCAHMS) are actually set forward from a rubble wall to act as a stop for harling (q.v.). Also called rybats.

MARRIAGE LINTEL (Scots): door or window lintel carved with the initials of the owner and his wife and the date of building work, only coincidentally of their marriage.

MATHEMATICAL TILES: facing tiles with the appearance of brick, most often applied to timber-framed walls.

MAUSOLEUM: monumental building or chamber usually intended for the burial of members of one family.

MEGALITHIC: the use of large stones, singly or together.

MEGALITHIC TOMB: massive stonebuilt Neolithic burial chamber covered by an earth or stone mound.

MERCAT (Scots): market. The Mercat Cross of a Scottish burgh was the focus of market activity and local ceremonial. Most examples are post-Reformation with heraldic or other finials (not crosses).

MERLON: see Battlement.

MESOLITHIC: Middle Stone Age, in Britain c. 5000 to c. 3500 B.C.

METOPES: spaces between the triglyphs in a Doric frieze (3b).

MEZZANINE: low storey between two higher ones or within the height of a high one, not extending over its whole area.

MILD STEEL: see Cast iron.

MISERICORD (*lit.* mercy): shelf on a carved bracket placed on the underside of a hinged choir stall seat to support an occupant when standing.

MIXER-COURTS: forecourts to groups of houses shared by vehicles and pedestrians.

MODILLIONS: small consoles (q.v.) along the underside of a Corinthian or Composite cornice (3d). Often used along an eaves cornice.

MODULE: a predetermined standard size for co-ordinating the dimensions of components of a building.

MORT-SAFE (Scots): device to secure corpse(s): either an iron frame over a grave or a building where bodies were kept during decomposition.

MOTTE-AND-BAILEY: CII and CI2 type of castle consisting of an earthen mound (motte) topped by a wooden tower within or adjoining a bailey, an enclosure defended by a ditch and palisade, and also, sometimes, by an inner bank.

MOUCHETTE: *see* Tracery and 2b.

MOULDING: shaped ornamental strip of continuous section; *see* Cavetto, Cyma, Ovolo, Roll.

MULLION: vertical member between window lights (2b).

MULTI-STOREY: five or more storeys. Multi-storey flats may form a *cluster block*, with individual blocks of flats grouped round a service core; a *point block*, with flats fanning out from a service core; or a *slab block*, with flats approached by corridors or galleries from service cores at intervals or towers at the ends (plan also used for offices, hotels etc.). *Tower block* is a generic term for a high multi-storey building.

MULTIVALLATE: of a hillfort: defended by three or more concentric banks and ditches.

MUNTIN: *see* Panelling and 6b.

MUTULE: square block under the corona of a Doric cornice.

NAILHEAD: E.E. ornament consisting of small pyramids regularly repeated (1a).

NARTHEX: enclosed vestibule or covered porch at the main entrance to a church.

NAVE: the body of a church W of the crossing or chancel, often flanked by aisles (q.v.).

NEOLITHIC: New Stone Age in Britain, c. 3500 B.C. until the Bronze Age.

NEWEL: central or corner post of a staircase (6c). For Newel stair *see* Stairs.

NIGHT STAIR: stair by which religious entered the transept of their church from their dormitory to celebrate night offices.

NOGGING: *see* Timber-framing.

NOOK-SHAFT: shaft set in the angle of a wall or opening (1a).

NORMAN: *see* Romanesque.

NOSING: projection of the tread of a step (6c). *Bottle nosing*: half round in section.

NUTMEG: medieval ornament with a chain of tiny triangles placed obliquely.

OCULUS: circular opening.

OEIL DE BOEUF: *see* Bullseye window.

OGEE: double curve, bending first one way and then the other, as in an *ogee* or *ogival arch* (5c). Cf. Cyma recta and Cyma reversa.

OPUS SECTILE: decorative mosaic-like facing.

OPUS SIGNINUM: composition flooring of Roman origin.

ORATORY: a private chapel in a church or a house. Also a church of the Oratorian Order.

ORDER: one of a series of recessed arches and jambs forming a splayed medieval opening, e.g. a doorway or arcade arch (1a).

ORDERS: the formalized versions of the post-and-lintel system in classical architecture. The main orders are *Doric*, *Ionic* and *Corinthian*. They are Greek in origin

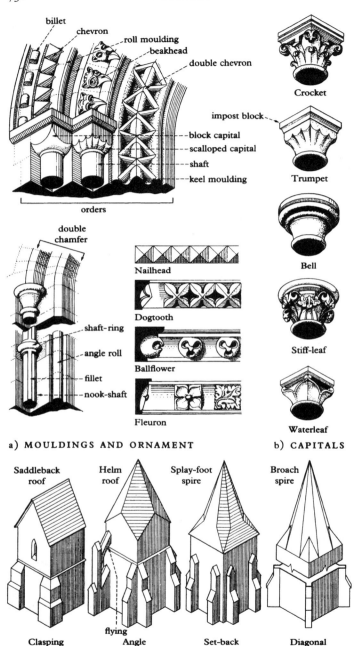

a) MOULDINGS AND ORNAMENT

b) CAPITALS

c) BUTTRESSES, ROOFS AND SPIRES

FIGURE 1: MEDIEVAL

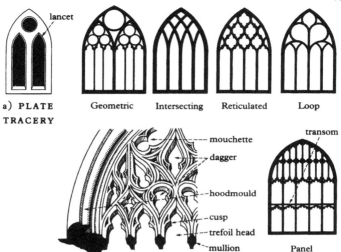

a) PLATE TRACERY

lancet

Geometric   Intersecting   Reticulated   Loop

mouchette

dagger

hoodmould

cusp

trefoil head

mullion

Curvilinear

transom

Panel

b) BAR TRACERY

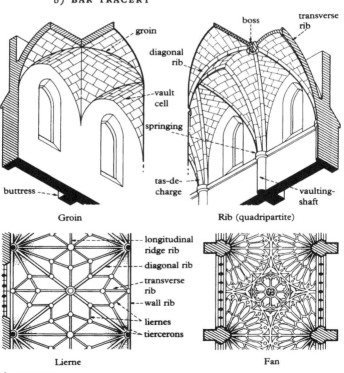

groin

diagonal rib

vault cell

springing

buttress

Groin

boss

transverse rib

tas-de-charge

vaulting-shaft

Rib (quadripartite)

longitudinal ridge rib

diagonal rib

transverse rib

wall rib

liernes

tiercerons

Lierne

Fan

c) VAULTS

FIGURE 2: MEDIEVAL

ORDERS

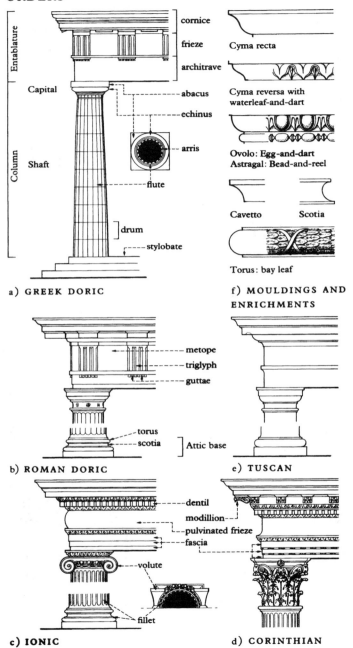

a) GREEK DORIC

f) MOULDINGS AND
ENRICHMENTS

b) ROMAN DORIC

e) TUSCAN

c) IONIC

d) CORINTHIAN

FIGURE 3: CLASSICAL

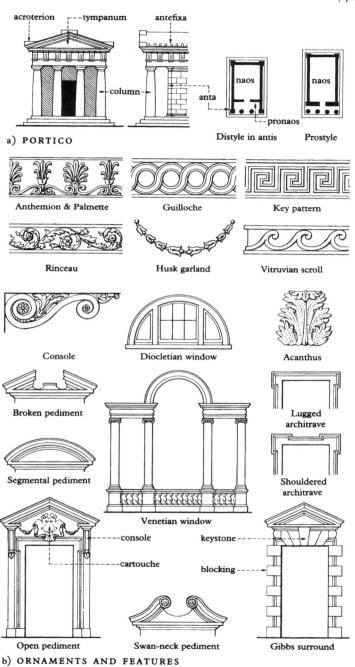

a) PORTICO

Distyle in antis   Prostyle

Anthemion & Palmette   Guilloche   Key pattern

Rinceau   Husk garland   Vitruvian scroll

Console   Diocletian window   Acanthus

Broken pediment   Lugged architrave

Segmental pediment   Shouldered architrave

Venetian window

Open pediment   Swan-neck pediment   Gibbs surround

b) ORNAMENTS AND FEATURES

FIGURE 4: CLASSICAL

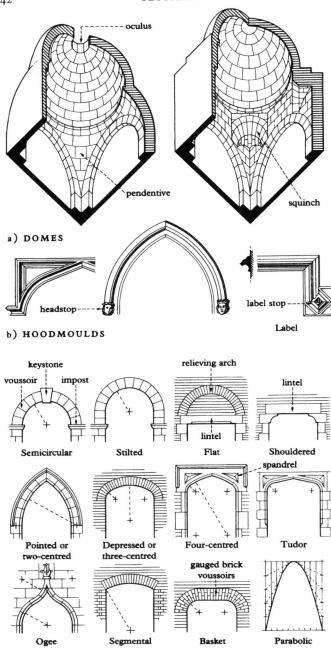

a) DOMES

b) HOODMOULDS

c) ARCHES

FIGURE 5: CONSTRUCTION

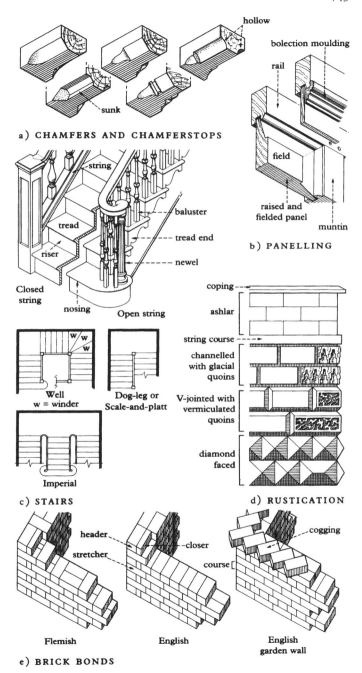

a) CHAMFERS AND CHAMFERSTOPS

b) PANELLING

c) STAIRS

d) RUSTICATION

e) BRICK BONDS

FIGURE 6: CONSTRUCTION

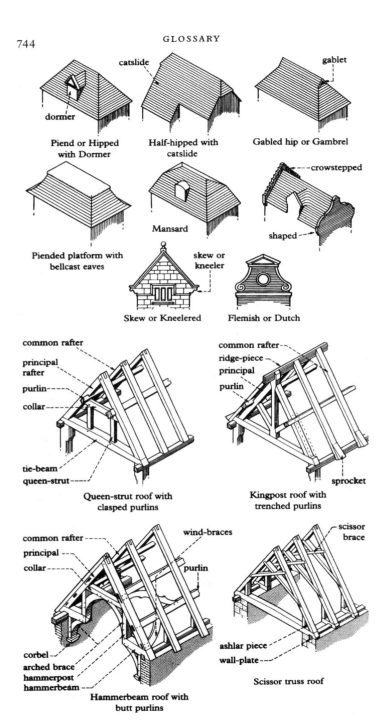

Piend or Hipped
with Dormer

dormer

catslide

Half-hipped with
catslide

gablet

Gabled hip or Gambrel

Piended platform with
bellcast eaves

Mansard

crowstepped

shaped

skew or
kneeler

Skew or Kneelered

Flemish or Dutch

common rafter
principal
rafter
purlin
collar

tie-beam
queen-strut

Queen-strut roof with
clasped purlins

common rafter
ridge-piece
principal
purlin

sprocket

Kingpost roof with
trenched purlins

common rafter
principal
collar

wind-braces

purlin

corbel
arched brace
hammerpost
hammerbeam

Hammerbeam roof with
butt purlins

scissor
brace

ashlar piece
wall-plate

Scissor truss roof

FIGURE 7: ROOFS AND GABLES

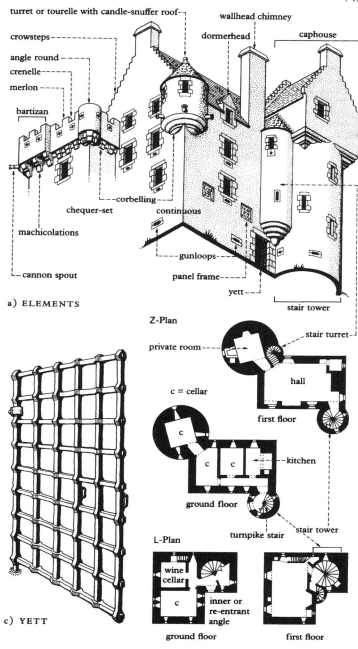

turret or tourelle with candle-snuffer roof

crowsteps

angle round

crenelle

merlon

bartizan

wallhead chimney

dormerhead

caphouse

corbelling

chequer-set

continuous

machicolations

gunloops

panel frame

cannon spout

yett

stair tower

a) ELEMENTS

Z-Plan

stair turret

private room

hall

c = cellar

first floor

kitchen

c

c

c

ground floor

stair tower

turnpike stair

c) YETT

L-Plan

wine cellar

c

inner or re-entrant angle

ground floor

first floor

b) FORMS

FIGURE 8: THE TOWER HOUSE

but occur in Roman versions. *Tuscan* is a simple version of Roman Doric. Though each order has its own conventions (3), there are many minor variations. The *Composite* capital combines Ionic volutes with Corinthian foliage. *Superimposed orders*: orders on successive levels, usually in the upward sequence of Tuscan, Doric, Ionic, Corinthian, Composite.

ORIEL: *see* Bay window.

OVERARCH: framing a wall which has an opening, e.g. a window or door.

OVERDOOR: painting or relief above an internal door. Also called a *sopraporta*.

OVERTHROW: decorative fixed arch between two gatepiers or above a wrought-iron gate.

OVOLO: wide convex moulding (3f).

PALIMPSEST: of a brass: where a metal plate has been reused by engraving on the back; of a wall painting: where one overlaps and partly obscures an earlier one.

PALLADIAN: following the examples and principles of Andrea Palladio (1508–80).

PALMETTE: classical ornament like a palm shoot (4b).

PANEL FRAME: moulded stone frame round an armorial panel, often placed over the entrance to a tower house (8a).

PANELLING: wooden lining to interior walls, made up of vertical members (*muntins*) and horizontals (*rails*) framing panels: also called *wainscot*. *Raised-and-fielded*: with the central area of the panel (*field*) raised up (6b).

PANTILE: roof tile of S section.

PARAPET: wall for protection at any sudden drop, e.g. at the wallhead of a castle where it protects the *parapet walk* or wall-walk. Also used to conceal a roof.

PARCLOSE: *see* Screen.

PARGETING (*lit.* plastering): exterior plaster decoration, either in relief or incised.

PARLOUR: in a religious house, a room where the religious could talk to visitors; in a medieval house, the semi-private living room below the solar (q.v.).

PARTERRE: level space in a garden laid out with low, formal beds.

PATERA (*lit.* plate): round or oval ornament in shallow relief.

PAVILION: ornamental building for occasional use; or projecting subdivision of a larger building, often at an angle or terminating a wing.

PEBBLEDASHING: *see* Rendering.

PEDESTAL: a tall block carrying a classical order, statue, vase etc.

PEDIMENT: a formalized gable derived from that of a classical temple; also used over doors, windows etc. For variations *see* 4b.

PEEL (*lit.* palisade): stone tower, e.g. near the Scottish-English border.

PEND (Scots): open-ended ground-level passage through a building.

PENDENTIVE: spandrel between adjacent arches, supporting a drum, dome or vault and consequently formed as part of a hemisphere (5a).

PENTHOUSE: subsidiary structure with a lean-to roof. Also a separately roofed structure on top of a C20 multi-storey block.

PEPPERPOT TURRET: bartizan with conical or pyramidal roof.

PERIPTERAL: *see* Peristyle.

PERISTYLE: a colonnade all round the exterior of a classical building, as in a temple which is then said to be *peripteral*.

PERP (PERPENDICULAR): English Gothic architecture *c.* 1335–50 to *c.* 1530. The name is derived from the upright panels then used (*see* Tracery and 2a).

PERRON: external stair to a doorway, usually of double-curved plan.

PEW: loosely, seating for the laity outside the chancel; strictly, an enclosed seat. *Box pew*: with equal high sides and a door.

PIANO NOBILE: principal floor of a classical building above a ground floor or basement and with a lesser storey overhead.

PIAZZA: formal urban open space surrounded by buildings.

PIEND AND PIENDED PLATFORM ROOF: *see* 7.

PIER: large masonry or brick support, often for an arch. *See also* Compound pier.

PILASTER: flat representation of a classical column in shallow relief. *Pilastrade*: series of pilasters, equivalent to a colonnade.

PILE: row of rooms. *Double pile*: two rows thick.

PILLAR: freestanding upright member of any section, not conforming to one of the orders (q.v.).

PILLAR PISCINA: *see* Piscina.

PILOTIS: C20 French term for pillars or stilts that support a building above an open ground floor.

PINS OR PINNINGS (Scots): *see* Cherry-caulking.

PISCINA: basin for washing Mass vessels, provided with a drain; set in or against wall to S of an altar or freestanding (*pillar piscina*).

PITCHED MASONRY: laid on the diagonal, often alternately with opposing courses (*pitched and counterpitched* or herringbone).

PIT PRISON: sunk chamber with access from above through a hatch.

PLATE RAIL: *see* Railways.

PLATEWAY: *see* Railways.

PLATT (Scots): platform, doorstep or landing. *Scale-and-platt stair*: *see* Stairs and 6c.

PLEASANCE (Scots): close or walled garden.

PLINTH: projecting courses at the foot of a wall or column, generally chamfered or moulded at the top.

PODIUM: a continuous raised platform supporting a building; or a large block of two or three storeys beneath a multi-storey block of smaller area.

POINT BLOCK: *see* Multi-storey.

POINTING: exposed mortar jointing of masonry or brickwork. Types include *flush*, *recessed* and *tuck* (with a narrow channel filled with finer, whiter mortar). *Bag-rubbed*: flush at the edges and gently recessed in the middle. *Ribbon*: joints formed with a trowel so that they stand out. *Hungry-jointed*: either with no pointing or deeply recessed to show the outline of each stone.

POPPYHEAD: carved ornament of leaves and flowers as a finial for a bench end or stall.

PORTAL FRAME: C20 frame comprising two uprights rigidly connected to a beam or pair of rafters.

PORTCULLIS: gate constructed to rise and fall in vertical gooves at the entry to a castle.

PORTE COCHÈRE: porch large enough to admit wheeled vehicles.

PORTICO: a porch with the roof and frequently a pediment supported by a row of columns (4a). A portico *in antis* has columns on the same plane as the front of the building. A *prostyle* porch has columns standing free. Porticoes are described by the number of front columns, e.g. tetrastyle (four), hexastyle (six). The space within the temple is the *naos*, that within the portico the *pronaos*. *Blind portico*: the front features of a portico applied to a wall.

PORTICUS (plural: porticūs): subsidiary cell opening from the main body of a pre-Conquest church.

POST: upright support in a structure.

POSTERN: small gateway at the back of a building or to the side of a larger entrance door or gate.

POTENCE (Scots): rotating ladder for access to doocot nesting boxes.

POUND LOCK: *see* Canals.

PREDELLA: in an altarpiece, the horizontal strip below the main representation, often used for subsidiary representations.

PRESBYTERY: the part of a church lying E of the choir where the main altar is placed. Also a priest's residence.

PRESS (Scots): cupboard.

PRINCIPAL: *see* Roofs and 7.

PRONAOS: *see* Portico and 4a.

PROSTYLE: *see* Portico and 4a.

PULPIT: raised and enclosed platform for the preaching of sermons. *Three-decker*: with reading desk below and clerk's desk below that. *Two-decker*: as above, minus the clerk's desk.

PULPITUM: stone screen in a major church dividing choir from nave.

PULVINATED: *see* Frieze and 3c.

PURLIN: *see* Roofs and 7.

PUTHOLES or PUTLOG HOLES: in wall to receive putlogs, the horizontal timbers which support scaffolding boards; not always filled after construction is complete.

PUTTO (plural: putti): small naked boy.

QUARRIES: square (or diamond) panes of glass supported by lead strips (*cames*); square floor-slabs or tiles.

QUATREFOIL: *see* Foil.

QUEEN-STRUT: *see* Roofs and 7.

QUILLONS: the arms forming the cross-guard of a sword.

QUIRK: sharp groove to one side of a convex medieval moulding.

QUOINS: dressed stones at the angles of a building (6d).

RADBURN SYSTEM: pedestrian and vehicle segregation in residential developments, based on that used at Radburn, New Jersey, U.S.A., by Wright and Stein, 1928–30.

RADIATING CHAPELS: projecting radially from an ambulatory or an apse (*see* Chevet).

RAFTER: *see* Roofs and 7.

RAGGLE: groove cut in masonry, especially to receive the edge of a roof-covering.

RAIL: *see* Panelling and 6b.

RAILWAYS: *Edge rail*: on which flanged wheels can run. *Plate rail*: L-section rail for plain unflanged wheels. *Plateway*: early railway using plate rails.

RAISED AND FIELDED: *see* Panelling and 6b.

RAKE: slope or pitch.

RAMPART: defensive outer wall of stone or earth. *Rampart walk*: path along the inner face.

RATCOURSE: projecting string-course on a doocot to deter rats from climbing to the flight holes.

REBATE: rectangular section cut out of a masonry edge to receive a shutter, door, window etc.

REBUS: a heraldic pun, e.g. a fiery cock for Cockburn.

REEDING: series of convex mouldings, the reverse of fluting (q.v.). Cf. Gadrooning.

RENDERING: the covering of outside walls with a uniform surface or skin for protection from the weather. *Lime-washing*: thin layer of lime-plaster. *Pebbledashing*: where aggregate is thrown at the wet plastered wall for a textured effect. *Roughcast*: plaster mixed with a coarse aggregate such as gravel. *Stucco*: fine lime plaster worked to a smooth surface. *Cement rendering*: a cheaper substitute for stucco, usually with a grainy texture.

REPOUSSÉ: relief designs in metalwork, formed by beating it from the back.

REREDORTER (*lit.* behind the dormitory): latrines in a medieval religious house.

REREDOS: painted and/or sculptured screen behind and above an altar. Cf. Retable.

RESPOND: half-pier or half-column bonded into a wall and carrying one end of an arch. It usually terminates an arcade.

RETABLE: painted or carved panel standing on or at the back of an altar, usually attached to it.

RETROCHOIR: in a major church, the area between the high altar and E chapel.

REVEAL: the plane of a jamb, between the wall and the frame of a door or window.

RHONE (Scots): gutter along the eaves for rainwater: *see also* Conductor.

RIB-VAULT: *see* Vault and 2c.

RIG (Scots): a strip of ploughed land raised in the middle and sloped to a furrow on each side; early cultivation method (runrig) usually surrounded by untilled grazing land.

RINCEAU: classical ornament of leafy scrolls (4b).

RISER: vertical face of a step (6c).

ROCK-FACED: masonry cleft to produce a rugged appearance.

ROCOCO: style current between c. 1720 and c. 1760, characterized by a serpentine line and playful, scrolled decoration.

ROLL MOULDING: medieval moulding of part-circular section (1a).

ROMANESQUE: style current in the C11 and C12. In England often called Norman. *See also* Saxo-Norman.

ROOD: crucifix flanked by representations of the Virgin and St John, usually over the entry into the chancel, painted on the wall, on a beam (*rood beam*) or on top of a *rood screen* or pulpitum (q.v.) which often had a walkway (*rood loft*) along the top, reached by a *rood stair* in the side wall. *Hanging rood*: cross or crucifix suspended from roof.

ROOFS: For the main external shapes (hipped, gambrel etc.) *see* 7. *Helm* and *Saddleback*: see 1c. *Lean-to*: single sloping roof built against a vertical wall; also applied to the part of the building beneath. *Bellcast*: sloping roof slightly swept out over the eaves. Construction. *See* 7. *Single-framed* roof: with no main trusses. The rafters may be fixed to the wall-plate or ridge, or longitudinal timbers may be absent altogether.

Double-framed roof: with longitudinal members, such as purlins, and usually divided into bays by principals and principal rafters. Other types are named after their main structural components, e.g. *hammerbeam*, *crown-post* (*see* Elements below and 7).

Elements. *See* 7.

Ashlar piece: a short vertical timber connecting an inner wall-plate or timber pad to a rafter.

Braces: subsidiary timbers set diagonally to strengthen the frame. *Arched braces*: curved pair forming an arch, connecting wall or post below with a tie- or collar-beam above. *Passing braces*: long straight braces passing across other members of the truss. *Scissor braces*: pair crossing diagonally between pairs of rafters or principals. *Wind-braces*: short, usually curved braces connecting side purlins with principals; sometimes decorated with cusping.

Collar or *collar-beam*: horizontal transverse timber connecting a pair of rafter or cruck blades (q.v.), set between apex and the wall-plate.

Crown-post: a vertical timber set centrally on a tie-beam and supporting a collar purlin braced to it longitudinally. In an open truss lateral braces may rise to the collar-beam; in a closed truss they may descend to the tie-beam.

Hammerbeams: horizontal brackets projecting at wall-plate level like an interrupted tie-beam; the inner ends carry *hammerposts*, vertical timbers which support a purlin and are braced to a collar-beam above.

Kingpost: vertical timber set centrally on a tie-or collar-beam, rising to the apex of the roof to support a ridge piece (cf. Strut).

Plate: longitudinal timber set square to the ground. *Wall-plate*: along the top of a wall to receive the ends of rafters; cf. Purlin.

Principals: pair of inclined lateral timbers of a truss. Usually they support side purlins and mark the main bay divisions.

Purlin: horizontal longitudinal timber. *Collar purlin* or *crown plate*: central timber which carries collar-beams and is supported by crown-posts. *Side purlins*: pairs of timbers placed some way up the slope of the roof, which carry common rafters. *Butt* or *tenoned purlins* are tenoned into either side of the principals. *Through purlins* pass through or past the principal; they include *clasped purlins*, which rest on queenposts or are carried in the angle between principals and collar, and t*renched purlins* trenched into the backs of principals.

Queen-strut: paired vertical, or near-vertical, timbers placed symmetrically on a tie-beam to support side purlins.

Rafters: inclined lateral timbers supporting the roof covering. *Common rafters*: regularly spaced uniform rafters placed along the length of a roof or between principals. *Principal rafters*: rafters which also act as principals.

Ridge, ridge piece: horizontal longitudinal timber at the apex supporting the ends of the rafters.

Sprocket: short timber placed on the back and at the foot of a rafter to form projecting eaves.

Strut: vertical or oblique timber between two members of a truss, not directly supporting longitudinal timbers.

Tie-beam: main horizontal transverse timber which carries the feet of the principals at wall level.

Truss: rigid framework of timbers at bay intervals, carrying the longitudinal roof timbers which support the common rafters. *Closed truss*: with the spaces between the timbers filled, to form an internal partition.

See also Cruck, Wagon roof.

ROPE MOULDING: *see* Cable moulding.

ROSE WINDOW: circular window with tracery radiating from the centre. Cf. Wheel window.

ROTUNDA: building or room circular in plan.

ROUGHCAST: *see* Rendering.

ROUND (Scots): bartizan, usually roofless.

ROVING BRIDGE: *see* Canals.

RUBBED BRICKWORK: *see* Gauged brickwork.

RUBBLE: masonry whose stones are wholly or partly in a rough state. *Coursed*: coursed stones with rough faces. *Random*: uncoursed stones in a random pattern. *Snecked*: with courses broken by smaller stones (snecks).

RUSTICATION: *see* 6d. Exaggerated treatment of masonry to give an effect of strength. The joints are usually recessed by V-section chamfering or square-section channelling (*channelled rustication*). *Banded rustication* has only the horizontal joints emphasized. The faces may be flat, but can be *diamond-faced*, like shallow pyramids, *vermiculated*, with a stylized texture like worm-casts, and *glacial* (frost-work), like icicles or stalactites.

RYBATS (Scots): *see* Margins.

SACRAMENT HOUSE: safe cupboard in a side wall of the chancel of a church and not directly associated with an altar, for reservation of the sacrament.

SACRISTY: room in a church for sacred vessels and vestments.

SADDLEBACK ROOF: *see* 1c.

SALTIRE CROSS: with diagonal limbs.

SANCTUARY: part of church at E end containing high altar. Cf. Presbytery.

SANGHA: residence of Buddhist monks or nuns.

SARCOPHAGUS: coffin of stone or other durable material.

SARKING (Scots): boards laid on the rafters to support the roof covering.

SAXO-NORMAN: transitional Romanesque style combining Anglo-Saxon and Norman features, current *c.* 1060–1100.

SCAGLIOLA: composition imitating marble.

SCALE-AND-PLATT (*lit.* stair and landing): *see* Stair and 6c.

SCALLOPED CAPITAL: *see* 1a.

SCARCEMENT: extra thickness of the lower part of a wall, e.g. to carry a floor.

SCARP: artificial cutting away of the ground to form a steep slope.

SCOTIA: a hollow classical moulding, especially between tori (q.v.) on a column base (3b, 3f).

SCREEN: in a medieval church, usually at the entry to the chancel; *see* Rood (screen) and Pulpitum. A *parclose screen* separates a chapel from the rest of the church.

SCREENS or SCREENS PASSAGE: screened-off entrance passage between great hall and service rooms or between the hall of a tower house and the stair.

SCRIBE (Scots): to cut and mark timber against an irregular stone or plaster surface.

SCUNTION (Scots): reveal.

SECTION: two-dimensional representation of a building, moulding etc., revealed by cutting across it.

SEDILIA (singular: sedile): seats for clergy (usually for a priest, deacon and sub-deacon) on the S side of the chancel.

SEPTUM: dwarf wall between the nave and choir.

SESSION HOUSE (Scots): a room or separate building for meetings of the minister and elders who form a kirk session. Also a shelter by the church or churchyard entrance for an elder collecting for poor relief, built at expense of kirk session.

SET-OFF: *see* Weathering.

SGRAFFITO: decoration scratched, often in plaster, to reveal a pattern in another colour beneath. *Graffiti*: scratched drawing or writing.

SHAFT: vertical member of round or polygonal section (1a, 3a). *Shaftring*: at the junction of shafts set *en délit* (q.v.) or attached to a pier or wall (1a).

SHEILA-NA-GIG: female fertility figure, usually with legs apart.

SHELL: thin, self-supporting roofing membrane of timber or concrete.

SHEUGH (Scots): a trench or open drain; a street gutter.

SHOULDERED ARCH: *see* 5a.

SHOULDERED ARCHITRAVE: *see* 4b.

SHUTTERING: *see* Concrete.

SILL: horizontal member at the bottom of a window-or door-frame; or at the base of a timber-framed wall into which posts and studs are tenoned.

SKEW (Scots): sloping or shaped stones finishing a gable upstanding from the roof. *Skewput*: bracket at the bottom end of a skew. See 7.

SLAB BLOCK: *see* Multi-storey.

SLATE-HANGING: covering of overlapping slates on a wall. *Tile-hanging* is similar.

SLYPE: covered way or passage leading E from the cloisters between transept and chapter house.

SNECKED: *see* Rubble.

SOFFIT (*lit.* ceiling): underside of an arch (also called *intrados*), lintel etc. *Soffit roll*: medieval roll moulding on a soffit.

SOLAR: private upper chamber in a medieval house, accessible from the high end of the great hall.

SOPRAPORTA: *see* Overdoor.

SOUNDING-BOARD: *see* Tester.

SOUTERRAIN: underground stone-lined passage and chamber.

SPANDRELS: roughly triangular spaces between an arch and its containing rectangle, or between adjacent arches (5c). Also non-structural panels under the windows in a curtain-walled building.

SPERE: a fixed structure screening the lower end of the great hall from the screens passage. *Spere-truss*: roof truss incorporated in the spere.

SPIRE: tall pyramidal or conical feature crowning a tower or turret. *Broach*: starting from a square base, then carried into an octagonal section by means of triangular faces; *splayed-foot*: a variation of the broach form, found principally in the south-east of England, in which the four cardinal faces are splayed out near their base, to cover the corners, while oblique (or intermediate) faces taper away to a point (1c). *Needle spire*: thin spire rising from the centre of a tower roof, well inside the parapet: when of timber and lead often called a *spike*.

SPIRELET: *see* Flèche.

SPLAY: of an opening when it is wider on one face of a wall than the other.

SPRING OR SPRINGING: level at which an arch or vault rises from its supports. *Springers*: the first stones of an arch or vaulting-rib above the spring (2c).

SQUINCH: arch or series of arches thrown across an interior angle of a square or rectangular structure to support a circular or polygonal superstructure, especially a dome or spire (5a).

SQUINT: an aperture in a wall or through a pier, usually to allow a view of an altar.

STAIRS: *see* 6c. *Dog-leg stair* or (Scots) *Scale-and-platt stair*: parallel flights rising alternately in opposite directions, without an open well. *Flying stair*: cantilevered from the walls of a stairwell, without newels; sometimes called a *geometric* stair when the inner edge describes a curve. *Turnpike* or *newel stair*: ascending round a central supporting newel (8b); also called a *spiral stair* or *vice* when in a circular shaft, a *winder* when in a rectangular compartment. (Winder also applies to the steps on the turn.) *Well stair*: with flights round a square open well framed by newel posts. *See also* Perron.

STAIR TOWER: full-height projection from a main block (especially of a tower house) containing the principal stair from the ground floor (8a).

STAIR TURRET: turret corbelled out from above ground level and containing a stair from one of the upper floors of a building, especially a tower house (8a).

STALL: fixed seat in the choir or chancel for the clergy or choir (cf. Pew). Usually with arm rests, and often framed together.

STANCHION: upright structural member, of iron, steel or reinforced concrete.

STANDPIPE TOWER: *see* Manometer.

STEADING (Scots): farm building or buildings; generally used for the principal group of buildings on a farm.

STEAM ENGINES: *Atmospheric*: worked by the vacuum created when low-pressure steam is condensed in the cylinder, as developed by Thomas Newcomen. *Beam engine*: with a large pivoted beam moved in an oscillating fashion by the piston. It may drive a flywheel or be *non-rotative*. *Watt* and *Cornish*: single-cylinder; *compound*: two cylinders; *triple expansion*: three cylinders.

STEEPLE: tower together with a spire, lantern or belfry.

STIFFLEAF: type of E.E. foliage decoration. *Stiffleaf capital*: *see* 1b.

STOP: plain or decorated terminal to mouldings or chamfers, or at the end of hoodmoulds and labels (*label stop*), or stringcourses (5b, 6a); *see also* Headstop.

STOUP: vessel for holy water, usually near a door.

STRAINER: *see* Arch.

STRAPWORK: decoration like inter-laced leather straps, late C16 and C17 in origin.

STRETCHER: *see* Bond and 6e.

STRING: *see* 6c. Sloping member holding the ends of the treads and risers of a staircase. *Closed string*: a broad string covering the ends of the treads and risers. *Open string*: cut into the shape of the treads and risers.

STRINGCOURSE: horizontal course or moulding projecting from the surface of a wall (6d).

STUCCO: decorative plasterwork. *See also* Rendering.

STUDS: subsidiary vertical timbers of a timber-framed wall or par-tition.

STUGGED (Scots): of masonry hacked or picked as a key for ren-dering; used as a surface finish in the C19.

STUPA: Buddhist shrine, circular in plan.

STYLOBATE: top of the solid plat-form on which a colonnade stands (3a).

SUSPENSION BRIDGE: *see* Bridge.

SWAG: like a festoon (q.v.), but rep-resenting cloth.

SYSTEM BUILDING: *see* Industri-alized building.

TABERNACLE: safe cupboard above an altar to contain the reserved sacrament or a relic; or architec-tural frame for an image or statue.

TABLE STONE or TABLE TOMB: memorial slab raised on free-standing legs.

TAS-DE-CHARGE: the lower courses of a vault or arch which are laid horizontally (2c).

TENEMENT: holding of land, but also applied to a purpose-built flatted block.

TERM: pedestal or pilaster tapering downward, usually with the upper part of a human figure growing out of it.

TERRACOTTA: moulded and fired clay ornament or cladding.

TERREPLEIN: in a fort the level sur-face of a rampart behind a parapet for mounting guns.

TESSELLATED PAVEMENT: mosaic flooring, particularly Roman, made of *tesserae*, i.e. cubes of glass, stone or brick.

TESTER: flat canopy over a tomb or pulpit, where it is also called a *sounding-board*.

TESTER TOMB: tomb-chest with effigies beneath a tester, either freestanding (tester with four or more columns), or attached to a wall (*half-tester*) with columns on one side only.

TETRASTYLE: *see* Portico.

THERMAL WINDOW: *see* Diocletian window.

THREE-DECKER PULPIT: *see* Pulpit.

TIDAL GATES: *see* Canals.

TIE-BEAM: *see* Roofs and 7.

TIERCERON: *see* Vault and 2c.

TIFTING (Scots): mortar bed for verge slates laid over gable skew.

TILE-HANGING: *see* Slate-hanging.

TIMBER-FRAMING: method of con-struction where the structural frame is built of interlocking timbers. The spaces are filled with non-structural material, e.g. *infill* of wattle and daub, lath and plaster, brickwork (known as *nogging*) etc., and may be covered by plaster, weatherboarding (q.v.) or tiles.

TOLBOOTH (Scots; *lit.* tax booth): burgh council building containing council chamber and prison.

TOMB-CHEST: chest-shaped tomb, usually of stone. Cf. Table tomb, Tester tomb.

TORUS (plural: tori): large convex moulding, usually used on a column base (3b, 3f).

TOUCH: soft black marble quarried near Tournai.

TOURELLE: turret corbelled out from the wall (8a).

TOWER BLOCK: *see* Multi-storey.

TOWER HOUSE (Scots): for elements and forms *see* 8a, 8b. Compact fortified house with the main hall raised above the ground and at least one more storey above it. A medieval Scots type continuing well into the C17 in its modified forms: *L-plan* with a jamb at one corner; *Z-plan* with a jamb at each diagonally opposite corner.

TRABEATED: dependent structurally on the use of the post and lintel. Cf. Arcuated.

TRACERY: openwork pattern of masonry or timber in the upper part of an opening. *Blind* tracery is tracery applied to a solid wall. *Plate tracery*, introduced *c.* 1200, is the earliest form, in which shapes are cut through solid masonry (2a).

Bar tracery was introduced into England *c.* 1250. The pattern is formed by intersecting moulded ribwork continued from the mullions. It was especially elaborate during the Decorated period (q.v.). Tracery shapes can include circles, *daggers* (elongated ogee-ended lozenges), *mouchettes* (like daggers but with curved sides) and upright rectangular *panels*. They often have *cusps*, projecting points defining lobes or *foils* (q.v.) within the main shape: *Kentish* or *split-cusps* are forked.

Types of bar tracery (*see* 2b) include *geometric(al)*: *c.* 1250–1310, chiefly circles, often foiled; *Y-tracery*: *c.* 1300, with mullions branching into a Y-shape; *intersecting*: *c.* 1300, formed by interlocking mullions; *reticulated*: early C14, net-like pattern of ogee-ended lozenges; *curvilinear*: C14, with uninterrupted flowing curves; *loop*: *c.* 1500–45, with large uncusped loop-like forms; *panel*: Perp, with straight-sided panels, often cusped at the top and bottom.

TRANSE (Scots): passage.

TRANSEPT: transverse portion of a cruciform church.

TRANSITIONAL: generally used for the phase between Romanesque and Early English (*c.* 1175–*c.* 1200).

TRANSOM: horizontal member separating window lights (2b).

TREAD: horizontal part of a step. The *tread end* may be carved on a staircase (6c).

TREFOIL: *see* Foil.

TRIFORIUM: middle storey of a church treated as an arcaded wall passage or blind arcade, its height corresponding to that of the aisle roof.

TRIGLYPHS (*lit.* three-grooved tablets): stylized beam-ends in the Doric frieze, with metopes between (3b).

TRIUMPHAL ARCH: influential type of Imperial Roman monument.

TROPHY: sculptured or painted group of arms or armour.

TRUMEAU: central stone mullion supporting the tympanum of a wide doorway. *Trumeau figure*: carved figure attached to it (cf. Column figure).

TRUMPET CAPITAL: *see* 1b.

TRUSS: braced framework, spanning between supports. *See also* Roofs.

TUMBLING or TUMBLING-IN: courses of brickwork laid at right angles to a slope, e.g. of a gable, forming triangles by tapering into horizontal courses.

TURNPIKE: *see* Stairs.

TUSCAN: *see* Orders and 3e.

TUSKING STONES (Scots): projecting end stones for bonding with an adjoining wall.

TWO-DECKER PULPIT: *see* Pulpit.

TYMPANUM: the surface between a lintel and the arch above it or within a pediment (4a).

UNDERCROFT: usually describes the vaulted room(s) beneath the main room(s) of a medieval house. Cf. Crypt.

UNIVALLATE: of a hillfort: defended by a single bank and ditch.

VAULT: arched stone roof (sometimes imitated in timber or plaster). For types *see* 2c.

Tunnel or *barrel vault*: continuous semicircular or pointed arch, often of rubble masonry.

Groin vault: tunnel vaults intersecting at right angles. *Groins* are the curved lines of the intersections.

Rib vault: masonry framework of intersecting arches (ribs) supporting *vault cells*, used in Gothic architecture. *Wall rib* or *wall arch*: between wall and vault cell. *Transverse rib*: spans between two walls to divide a vault into bays. *Quadripartite* rib vault: each bay has two pairs of diagonal ribs dividing the vault into four triangular cells. *Sexpartite* rib vault: most often used over paired bays, has an extra pair of ribs springing from between the bays. More elaborate vaults may include *ridge-ribs* along the crown of a vault or bisecting the bays; *tiercerons*: extra decorative ribs springing from the corners of a bay; and *liernes*: short decorative ribs in the crown of a vault, not linked to any springing point. A *stellar* or *star* vault has liernes in star formation.

Fan vault: form of barrel vault used in the Perp period, made up of halved concave masonry cones decorated with blind tracery.

VAULTING-SHAFT: shaft leading up to the spring or springing (q.v.) of a vault (2c).

VENETIAN or SERLIAN WINDOW: derived from Serlio (4b). The motif is used for other openings.

VERMICULATION: *see* Rustication and 6d.

VESICA: oval with pointed ends.

VICE: *see* Stair.

VILLA: originally a Roman country house or farm. The term was revived in England in the C18 under the influence of Palladio and used especially for smaller, compact country houses. In the later C19 it was debased to describe any suburban house.

VITRIFIED: bricks or tiles fired to a darkened glassy surface. *Vitrified fort*: built of timber-laced masonry, the timber having later been set on fire with consequent vitrification of the stonework.

VITRUVIAN SCROLL: classical running ornament of curly waves (4b).

VOLUTES: spiral scrolls. They occur on Ionic capitals (3c). *Angle* volute: pair of volutes, turned outwards to meet at the corner of a capital.

VOUSSOIRS: wedge-shaped stones forming an arch (5c).

WAGON ROOF: with the appearance of the inside of a wagon tilt; often ceiled. Also called *cradle roof*.

WAINSCOT: *see* Panelling.

WALLED GARDEN: in C18 and C19 Scotland, combined vegetable and flower garden, sometimes well away from the house.

WALLHEAD: straight top of a wall. *Wallhead chimney*: chimney rising from a wallhead (8a). *Wallhead gable*: gable rising from a wallhead.

WALL MONUMENT: attached to the wall and often standing on the floor. *Wall tablets* are smaller with the inscription as the major element.

WALL-PLATE: *see* Roofs and 7.

WALL-WALK: *see* Parapet.

WARMING ROOM: room in a religious house where a fire burned for comfort.

WATERHOLDING BASE: early Gothic base with upper and lower mouldings separated by a deep hollow.

WATERLEAF: *see* Enrichments and 3f.

WATERLEAF CAPITAL: Late Romanesque and Transitional type of capital (1b).

WATER WHEELS: described by the way water is fed on to the wheel. *Breastshot*: mid-height, falling and passing beneath. *Overshot*: over the top. *Pitchback*: on the top but falling backwards. *Undershot*: turned by the momentum of the water passing beneath. In a *water turbine*, water is fed under pressure through a vaned wheel within a casing.

WEALDEN HOUSE: type of medieval timber-framed house with a central open hall flanked by bays of two storeys, roofed in line; the end bays are jettied to the front, but the eaves are continuous.

WEATHERBOARDING: wall cladding of overlapping horizontal boards.

WEATHERING: or SET-OFF: inclined, projecting surface to keep water away from the wall below.

WEEPERS: figures in niches along the sides of some medieval tombs. Also called *mourners*.

WHEEL HOUSE: Late Iron Age circular stone dwelling; inside, partition walls radiating from the central hearth like wheel spokes.

WHEEL WINDOW: circular, with radiating shafts like spokes. Cf. Rose window.

WROUGHT IRON: *see* Cast iron.

WYND (Scots): subsidiary street or lane, often running into a main street or gait (q.v.).

YETT (Scots, *lit.* gate): hinged openwork gate at a main doorway, made of iron bars alternately penetrating and penetrated (8c).

Z-PLAN: *see* Tower house and 8b.

INDEX OF ARCHITECTS AND ARTISTS

INDEX OF ARCHITECTS AND ARTISTS 769

Royal Label Factory 236, 305
Russell, James 317
Rutherford, H. Roan (b. 1946) 336,
337, 385, 386, 388, 389, 391, 465,
476
Rutherford, James 54, 64, 269, 540,
629
Rutherford, John 54, 412, 540
Ryder HKS 82, 91, 173, 174, 543,
581, 659

Sage (Frederick) & Co. 84, 435
St Enoch Stained Glass Works 325
Salmon, James Jun. (1873–1924) 76,
667
Salmon (James) & Son (James
Salmon, 1805–88; William Forrest
Salmon, 1843–1911; James
Salmon Jun, q.v.; John Gaff
Gillespie, q.v.) 26, 576, 667
Salmon, R. T. L. 644
Salvin, Harvey 579
Sandeman, W. Y. (1890–1962) 342
Schotz, Benno (sculptor, 1891–
1984) 33, 83, 263, 419, 659
Schultz, Robert Weir (1860–1951)
27, 49, 261, 296–302, 329, 360,
514, Pl. 56
Scott, Sir George Gilbert (1811–78)
29, 31, 420–1, Pl. 31
Scott (Charles) & Partners 269
Scott, Joanna 363
Scott Morton & Co. (decorators
and cabinetmakers) 223, 596
Scott & Rae 177, 190, 344, 346, 557,
637, 684
Scott, Stanley M. 463
Scott, William (of Corrie) 33, 686
Scott, William Bell (artist, 1811–90)
49, 569–70, Pl. 81
Scottish Landscaping Ltd 322
Scottish Special Housing
Association 237–8, 266, 639
Scougal, David 20
SCWS Cabinet Works 99
Seifert (John) Architects 371
Sellars, James (1843–88) 133, 193n.
Service, John (joiner) 603
Shadewi, Mohammed 195
Shanks, James (sculptor) 36, 168
Shaw, Christian (glass-stainer) 124,
707, 723
Shaw, Sax 472
Shaws (faience) 141
Sheppard Robson 85
Shilton, Eric 723
Sim, Stewart 169
Simister, David 208
Simpson & Brown (James Simpson,
q.v.; Andrew Stewart Brown,
b. 1945) 85, 91, 92, 114, 122, 139
Simpson, James (b. 1944) 114

Simpson, John 334
Skirving, Alexander (1890–1958)
346
Slade, Basil 210
Small, John 311
SMC Parr Architects 82, 455, 460,
522
Smellie, Thomas (1860–1938) 28,
74, 391, 417, 419, 435, 436, 437,
445, 448, 607, 641, 666
Smiley, Jenny 208
Smirke, Sir Robert (1780–1867) 48,
225, Pl. 82
Smith Design Associates 439n., 443
Smith, J. N. 631
Smith, J. Walker 78, 404
Smith, John (of Kilmaurs, C17) 324,
Pl. 17
Smith, John (C21) 485
Smith, Lance 388
Smith & McMillan 263
Smith, Robert 195
Smith, T. H. (1859–1934) 71, 286
Smith, Thomas 283
Smith, Thomas (engineer) 55, 548,
718, Pl. 24
Smith & Wharrie 612
Smith, William (b. 1856) 657, Pl. 32
Snodgrass, John 194, 195, 407
Snodgrass, Robert (c. 1839–97) 187,
195, 400, 403
Snodgrass, Robert Sen. (1799–
1869) 23, 25, 277, 278
Somervell, David 335, 618
South Ayrshire Council 174, 304
Southern, Frank 608
Southern & Orr 361
Speirs & Co. 55, 162, 708
Spencer, James 388, Pl. 107
Spiers, Arthur (glass-stainer) 402
Stained Glass Design Partnership
34, 462
Stalker, J. S. 20, 499, Pl. 15
Stark, James 331, 559
Stark, William (1770–1813) 22, 548,
Pl. 24
Steegers-Murphy, Mies 453
Steel, Gabriel (1888–1962) 29, 32,
79, 277, 324, 328, 330n., 333,
428, 429, 431, 449, 553, 557, 562,
Pl. 17
Steele & Balfour (Henry Bell Wesley
Steele, c. 1852–1902; Andrew
Balfour, 1863–1948) 27, 29, 496,
497
Steell, John 73, 93, 385
Stellmacs 346
Stephen (James F.) Architects 33,
473, 676
Steven Bros & Co. 133
Stevens, Alexander (c. 1730–96) 53,
69, 121, 135, 137, 153n.

INDEX OF PLACES

Principal references are in **bold** type; demolished buildings are shown in *italic*.

Towns in Arran are indexed under their names. Ayr is indexed in two separate entries: 'Ayr central', which covers pp. 119–69 and includes Newton-upon-Ayr and Wallacetown, and 'Ayr outer areas', which covers the suburbs (pp. 169–75). *See* the map on p. 123.